Frommer's®
Mexico

My Mexico

by David Baird

THERE ARE MANY REASONS TO TRAVEL, BUT THE ONE THAT MOST often prompts me to leave home is a foreign culture's ability to jostle me from complacency. Mexico is good for this. It's vibrant and full of vivid sights and sensations. In the mountains, the contrast between strong sun and cool air makes me feel alive. There's a lifetime's worth of beaches to explore. But above all, I appreciate the Mexican people, who have a love of vigorous expression in just about every form of human endeavor. Witness the country's emphatically flavored food and drink, its over-the-top music and dance, its bold creations in art and architecture. After spending time in Mexico, I find other places to be dull and lackluster.

If this were all Mexico had to offer, it would be enough. But beneath the color lies a deep-seated complexity that makes the country fascinating. The national culture was born of two distinct civilizations: the Spanish and the Indian. The end result after centuries of synthesizing these contradictory forces is a rich symbolism that encapsulates multiple, often opposing, meanings. To get to know and understand Mexico in its entirety would be the work of several lifetimes. But to enjoy Mexico need take no more than an open mind and heart. These photos give you a taste of Mexico's complex allure.

Few experiences inspire as much awe as close contact with a whale in its natural habitat. Along Baja's Pacific coast, various protected bays and lagoons have become the preferred winter waters for migrating **GRAY WHALES (left)** as they journey south to mate and give birth to their calves. Naturally friendly and curious, these whales frequently come up to the sightseeing boats and stay close by. Baja's whale-watching season generally runs from January to March.

The megalithic **OLMEC HEADS (above)** are some of the most intriguing pre-Colombian artifacts. Seventeen have been discovered, and though they share a common style, the variations in their facial features suggest that they might depict something part human, part Jaguar god. Most of the heads are in south-central Mexico, around Veracruz and Tabasco.

ÉLAGUÉ

The various regional cuisines of Mexico lend great variety to eating in Mexico, especially when you choose to eat in a local **FONDA (above)**, or food stall, like this one at Libertad Market in Guadalajara. I love the guisados (stews), such as the ones this woman has prepared here.

I always enjoy visiting **MARKETS (right)** like this one, Oaxaca's Abastos Market. You see a variety of produce in most of them that would put a supermarket to shame. They also serve as a place for friends and neighbors to meet, eat, and chat about local events and the latest scandals.

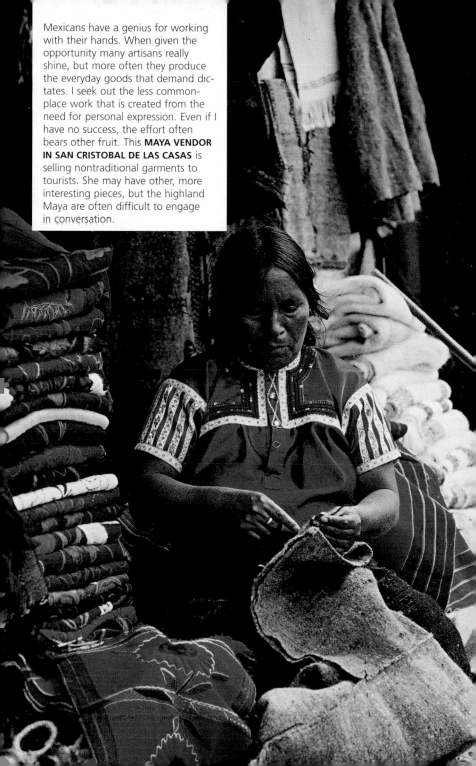

Mexicans have a genius for working with their hands. When given the opportunity many artisans really shine, but more often they produce the everyday goods that demand dictates. I seek out the less commonplace work that is created from the need for personal expression. Even if I have no success, the effort often bears other fruit. This **MAYA VENDOR IN SAN CRISTOBAL DE LAS CASAS** is selling nontraditional garments to tourists. She may have other, more interesting pieces, but the highland Maya are often difficult to engage in conversation.

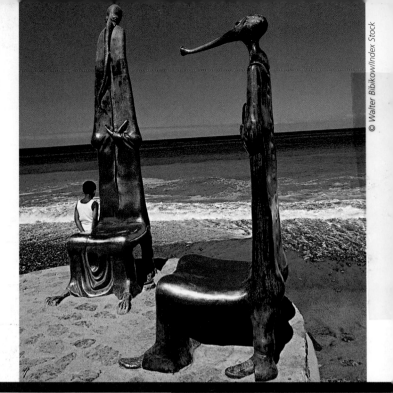

One of my favorite pastimes in Puerto Vallarta is strolling along its waterfront boardwalk, known as the malecón. Here, you'll find a collection of majestic monumental sculptures, including these, part of the *FANTASY OF THE SEA* **COLLECTION (above)** by noted Mexican artist Alejandro Colunga. Especially at sunset, or on Sunday evenings, the malecón buzzes with activity: vendors selling balloons, street musicians, and romantics of all ages holding hands.

No trip to Acapulco is complete without witnessing the dramatic performance of the **CLIFF-DIVERS (right)** at La Quebrada. For just a moment, when the diver springs from his perch, he seems suspended, weightless in the still air high above the roiling sea. It's almost impossible to tear your eyes away as he plummets more than 40m (130 ft.) toward the rocks and surf below.

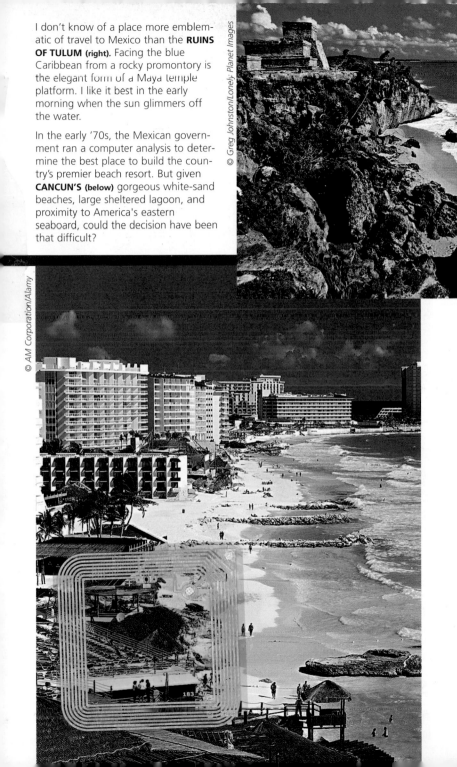

I don't know of a place more emblematic of travel to Mexico than the **RUINS OF TULUM (right).** Facing the blue Caribbean from a rocky promontory is the elegant form of a Maya temple platform. I like it best in the early morning when the sun glimmers off the water.

In the early '70s, the Mexican government ran a computer analysis to determine the best place to build the country's premier beach resort. But given **CANCUN'S (below)** gorgeous white-sand beaches, large sheltered lagoon, and proximity to America's eastern seaboard, could the decision have been that difficult?

The 17th and 18th centuries, when a European art form known as baroque arrived, was a time of great artistic achievement in Mexico, especially in architecture. This church in Oaxaca City, **SANTO DOMINGO (above)**, is one of my favorite examples. Think of it as an expression of ecstatic religious feeling that rejects limitations of structure, proportion, and balance.

Mexicans have a direct, almost personal, relationship with their Catholic saints. You need go no further than Mexico City to see this dynamic unfold. Stalls selling **RELIGIOUS ICONS (right)** line the way to the Basilica of Our Lady of Guadalupe.

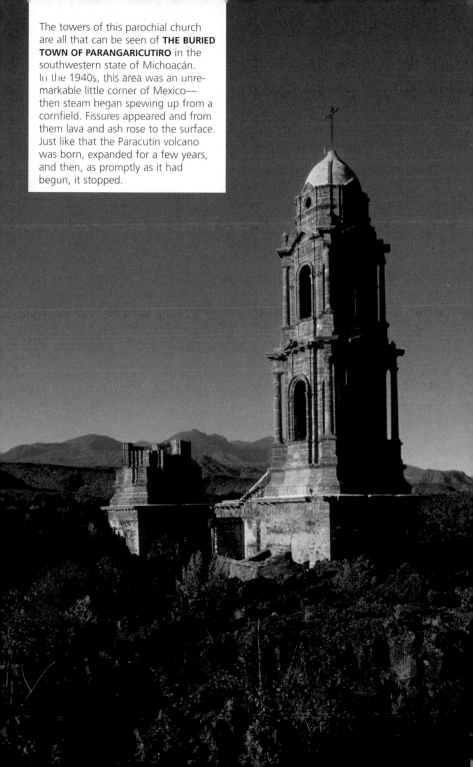

The towers of this parochial church are all that can be seen of **THE BURIED TOWN OF PARANGARICUTIRO** in the southwestern state of Michoacán. In the 1940s, this area was an unremarkable little corner of Mexico—then steam began spewing up from a cornfield. Fissures appeared and from them lava and ash rose to the surface. Just like that the Paracutín volcano was born, expanded for a few years, and then, as promptly as it had begun, it stopped.

The Yucatán Peninsula

Chichén Itzá Ruins

Snack bar and toilets

Well of Sacrifice
(Sacred Cenote)

Sacred Way *(Sacbé)*

NORTH TEMPLE

Main Ball Court

Parking

Temple of Jaguars

"NEW" CHICHÉN

Main Tourist Entrance

Temple of the Skulls
(Tzompantli)

Platform of Venus

Temple of the Warriors

Platform of the Eagles

Ball Court

Pyramid of Kukulkán
(El Castillo)

Councillor's House

Group of the Thousand Columns

Northeast Colonnade

Tomb of the High Priest
(Tumba del Gran Sacerdote)

Ball Court

Temple of the Grinding Stones

Secondary Tourist Entrance

Ball Court

Steambath 2

"OLD" CHICHÉN

Temple of the Deer

Ball Court

Cenote Xtoloc

The Market

Little Holes
(Chichan-Chob)

Hotel Mayaland

The Observatory
(El Caracol)

Steambath 1

Temple of Obscure Writing
(Akab Dzib)

Temple of the Sculptured Panels

Edifice of the Nuns
(Edificio de las Monjas)

Church

Hotel Hacienda Chichén

Villas Arqueológica Chichén Itzá

0		1/8 mi
0	125 meters	

North Group
(Grupo Norte)

↑ To Mérida

Hotel Hacienda Uxmal

0		330 feet
0	100 meters	

Northwest Group
(Grupo Noroeste)

Platform of the Stelae
(Plataforma de las Estelas)

Columns Group
(Grupo de las Columnas)

Quadrangle of the Nuns
(Cuadrángulo de las Monjas)

To Puuc Route & Campeche

Villa Arqueológica Uxmal

(i)

PARKING

Cemetery Group
(Grupo del Cementerio)

Pyramid of the Magician
(Pirámide del Advino)

House of the Doves

Ball Court
(Juego de Pelota)

House of the Turtles
(Casa de las Tortugas)

West Group
(Grupo Oeste)

Governor's Palace
(Palacio del Gobenador)

South Temple
(Templo Sur)

Great Pyramid
(Gran Pirámide)

House of the Old Woman
(Pirámide de la Vieja)

To Chimez Temple ↙

To Temple of the Phallus ↓

Uxmal Ruins

Information *(i)*

Frommer's®

Mexico

2009

by David Baird, Lynne Bairstow, Juan Cristiano & Joy Hepp

Here's what the critics say about Frommer's:

"Amazingly easy to use. Very portable, very complete."

—*Booklist*

"Detailed, accurate, and easy-to-read information for all price ranges."
—*Glamour Magazine*

"Hotel information is close to encyclopedic."

—*Des Moines Sunday Register*

"Frommer's Guides have a way of giving you a real feel for a place."
—*Knight Ridder Newspapers*

WILEY
Wiley Publishing, Inc.

Published by:

Wiley Publishing, Inc.

111 River St.
Hoboken, NJ 07030-5774

ISBN 978-0-470-28561-9

Editor: Maureen Clarke
Production Editor: Jonathan Scott
Cartographer: Elizabeth Puhl
Photo Editor: Richard Fox
Production by Wiley Indianapolis Composition Services

Front cover photo: Guanajuato State, Rancho Viejo art market, folk painting
Back cover photo: Baja California Sur, Los Cabos: Couple snorkeling

For information on our other products and services or to obtain technical support, please contact our Customer Care Department within the U.S. at 800/762-2974, outside the U.S. at 317/572-3993 or fax 317/572-4002.

Wiley also publishes its books in a variety of electronic formats. Some content that appears in print may not be available in electronic formats.

Manufactured in the United States of America

5   4   3   2   1

Contents

List of Maps   viii

What's New in Mexico   1

1   The Best of Mexico   7

by David Baird, Lynne Bairstow, Juan Cristiano & Joy Hepp

1 The Best Beach Vacations 7

2 The Best Cultural Experiences 10

3 The Best Archaeological Sites 11

4 The Best Active Vacations 12

5 The Best of Natural Mexico 13

6 The Best Places to Get Away from It All .14

7 The Best Art, Architecture & Museums 15

8 The Best Shopping 16

9 The Best Luxury Hotels 17

10 The Best Inexpensive Inns 19

11 The Best Spa Resorts 20

12 The Best Mexican Food & Drink 21

2   Mexico in Depth   23

by David Baird

1 Mexico Today 23

2 Looking Back at Mexico 24

   It's Just a Game 26

   A Sticky Habit 28

3 Eating & Drinking in Mexico 32

   Dining Service Tips 35

4 The Regions in Brief 36

5 Mexico's Art & Architecture 38

6 Mexico in Popular Culture: Books, Film & Music 40

3   Planning Your Trip to Mexico   45

by Juan Cristiano

1 Visitor Information 45

2 Entry Requirements 46

   Cut to the Front of the Airport Security Line 48

   Calendar of Events 51

3 When to Go 50

4 Getting There & Getting Around 57

5 Money & Costs 63

6 Health 65

7 Safety 68

   Smoke Free Mexico? 68

8 Specialized Travel Resources 71

9 Sustainable Tourism 75

   It's Easy Being Green 76

Frommers.com: The Complete
Travel Resource 77
10 Packages for the Independent
Traveler 78

11 Special-Interest Trips 80
12 Staying Connected 83
13 Tips on Accommodations 85

(4) Suggested Mexico Itineraries 87

by David Baird

1 Central Mexico's Pre-Columbian
Treasures in a Week 87
2 The Best of Western Mexico
in a Week 89

3 Los Cabos to Copper Canyon 90
4 La Ruta Maya in 2 Weeks 91

(5) Mexico City 94

by Juan Cristiano

1 Orientation 96
*Taxi Safety Precautions
in Mexico City* 99
The Neighborhoods in Brief 102
2 Getting Around 105
Fast Facts: Mexico City 110
3 Where to Stay 113
4 Where to Dine 120

¡Café, Por Favor! 126
5 Exploring Mexico City 126
6 Organized Tours 146
7 Shopping 147
8 Mexico City After Dark 149
9 A Side Trip to the Pyramids
of San Juan Teotihuacán 154

(6) Silver, Spas & Spiritual Centers: From Taxco to Tepoztlán 159

by Juan Cristiano

1 Taxco: Cobblestones & Silver 159
*Spanish Lessons & Art Classes
in Taxco* 164
2 Ixtapan de la Sal: A Thermal
Spa Town 170
3 Valle de Bravo & Avándaro:
Mexico's Switzerland 172

4 Cuernavaca: Land
of Eternal Spring 175
Fast Facts: Cuernavaca 178
5 Tepoztlán 185

7   San Miguel de Allende & the Colonial Silver Cities   190

by David Baird

1 San Miguel de Allende 192

*Fast Facts: San Miguel
de Allende* 195

*Learning at the Source: Going
to School in San Miguel* 197

2 Guanajuato 206

Fast Facts: Guanajuato 209

Ranch Museum 214

The Redolent Mexican Cantina 220

3 Santiago de Querétaro 221

Fast Facts: Querétaro 224

All Things Querétaro 225

Shopping for Opals 227

Hot Tamales 229

4 Zacatecas 231

Fast Facts: Zacatecas 234

5 San Luis Potosí 241

Fast Facts: San Luis Potosí 242

8   Michoacán   248

by David Baird

1 Morelia 249

Fast Facts: Morelia 250

Free-Market Forces 253

A Brief Pause for the Food Cause ...254

Michoacán's Monarch Migration ...259

2 Pátzcuaro 260

Fast Facts: Pátzcuaro 262

3 Uruapan: Handicrafts &
Volcanoes 270

9   Guadalajara   273

by David Baird

1 Orientation 273

The Neighborhoods in Brief 274

2 Getting Around 275

Fast Facts: Guadalajara 276

3 Where to Stay 277

4 Where to Dine 281

5 Exploring Guadalajara 284

Guadalajara Bus Tours 286

6 Shopping 289

7 Guadalajara After Dark 292

Tequila: The Name Says It All 293

10   Puerto Vallarta & the Central Pacific Coast   294

by Lynne Bairstow

1 Puerto Vallarta 294

Fast Facts: Puerto Vallarta 300

A Huichol Art Primer 314

2 Mazatlán 343

Fast Facts: Mazatlán 347

*Mazatlán's Carnaval:
A Weeklong Party* 351

3 Costa Alegre: Puerto Vallarta
to Barra de Navidad 359

4 Manzanillo 369

Fast Facts: Manzanillo 372

11 Acapulco & the Southern Pacific Coast   379

by Juan Cristiano

1 Acapulco 380

Fast Facts: Acapulco 385

2 Northward to Zihuatanejo &
Ixtapa 403

Fast Facts: Zihuatanejo & Ixtapa ... 407

3 Puerto Escondido 420

Fast Facts: Puerto Escondido 424

*Ecotours & Other Adventurous
Explorations* 426

4 Bahías de Huatulco 434

Fast Facts: Bahías de Huatulco 437

12 The Southernmost States: Oaxaca & Chiapas   443

by David Baird

1 Oaxaca City 444

Peace & Poverty in Oaxaca 446

Fast Facts: Oaxaca 449

Oaxacan Street Food 460

2 Villahermosa 470

3 Palenque 473

4 San Cristóbal de las Casas 481

*The Zapatista Movement &
Chiapas* 484

*Fast Facts: San Cristóbal
de las Casas* 485

13 Eastward from Mexico City: Puebla & Veracruz   496

by David Baird

1 Puebla & Cholula 496

Fast Facts: Puebla 499

*Cinco de Mayo & the Battle
of Puebla* 500

2 Tlaxcala 508

3 Xalapa 511

4 Veracruz City 515

Fast Facts: Veracruz 517

5 El Tajín & the Town of Papantla ... 523

14 Cancún   527

by Juan Cristiano

1 Orientation 528

The Best Websites for Cancún ... 530

Fast Facts: Cancún 532

2 Where to Stay 534

3 Where to Dine 542

4 Beaches, Watersports &
Boat Tours 547

5 Outdoor Activities & Attractions ... 551

6 Shopping 552

7 Cancún After Dark 554

15 Isla Mujeres & Cozumel   556

by David Baird

1 Isla Mujeres 556

The Best Websites for Isla Mujeres
& Cozumel 558

Fast Facts: Isla Mujeres 560

2 Cozumel 569

An All-Inclusive Vacation
in Cozumel 572

Fast Facts: Cozumel 574

16 The Caribbean Coast: The Riviera Maya, Including Playa del Carmen & the Costa Maya   587

by David Baird

1 Puerto Morelos & Vicinity 590

2 Playa del Carmen 595

Fast Facts: Playa del Carmen 598

Choosing an All-Inclusive
in the Riviera Maya 602

3 South of Playa del Carmen 604

4 Tulum, Punta Allen & Sian Ka'an . . .611

The Sian Ka'an Biosphere
Reserve 615

5 Cobá Ruins 615

6 Majahual, Xcalak & the Chinchorro
Reef 618

7 Lago Bacalar 620

8 Chetumal .621

9 Side Trips to Maya Ruins
from Chetumal 623

17 Mérida, Chichén Itzá & the Maya Interior   625

by David Baird

The Best Websites for Mérida,
Chichén Itzá & the Maya Interior . . .626

1 Mérida: Gateway to the
Maya Heartland 627

Daily Festivals & Special Events
in Mérida .630

Fast Facts: Mérida 631

Of Haciendas & Hotels 642

2 The Ruins of Uxmal 653

3 Campeche 659

Fast Facts: Campeche 661

4 The Ruins of Chichén Itzá 665

5 Valladolid .672

18 The Copper Canyon   677

by David Baird

1 The Copper Canyon Train & Stops
Along the Way 678

Choosing a Package or Tour
Operator .681

2 Los Mochis: The Western
Terminus .689

3 Chihuahua: The Eastern
Terminus .691

Fast Facts: Chihuahua 692

19 Los Cabos & Baja California   698

by Joy Hepp

1 Los Cabos: Resorts, Watersports
& Golf 701

Fast Facts: San José del Cabo 704

Fast Facts: Cabo San Lucas 718

Surf & Sleep 723

2 Todos Santos: A Creative Oasis 730

3 La Paz: Peaceful Port Town 732

Fast Facts: La Paz 735

4 Mid Baja: Loreto, Mulegé &
Santa Rosalía 742

Whale-Watching in Baja 748

5 Tijuana & Rosarito Beach 749

*First Crush: The Annual
Harvest Festival* 753

A Northern Baja Spa Sanctuary 755

Surfing, Northern Baja Style 758

6 Ensenada: Port of Call 759

Appendix A: Mexico Fast Facts   761

Appendix B: Survival Spanish   766

Index   771

List of Maps

Mexico   8

Central Mexico's Pre-Columbian
Treasures   88

The Best of Western Mexico   90

Los Cabos to Copper Canyon   91

La Ruta Maya   92

Mexico City & Environs   95

Downtown Mexico City   106

Polanco/Chapultepec Area   115

Historic Downtown (Centro
Histórico)   127

Chapultepec Park   129

Coyoacán   131

San Angel   133

Alameda Park Area   135

Teotihuacán   155

Side Trips from Mexico City   160

Taxco   163

Ixtapan de la Sal   171

Valle de Bravo & Avándaro   173

Cuernavaca   177

The Colonial Silver Cities   191

Where to Stay in San Miguel de
    Allende   193

Guanajuato   207

Santiago de Querétaro   223

Zacatecas   233

San Luis Potosí   243

Morelia   251

Pátzcuaro   261

Uruapan   271

Downtown Guadalajara   285

Puerto Vallarta: Hotel Zone &
    Beaches   295

Downtown Puerto Vallarta   311

Mazatlán Area   345

Costa Alegre & Central Pacific
    Coast   361

Barra de Navidad Bay Area   365

Manzanillo Area   371

Acapulco Bay Area   382

Zihuatanejo & Ixtapa Area   405

Downtown Zihuatanejo   411

Puerto Escondido   421

Oaxaca Area   445

Downtown Oaxaca   447

Monte Albán   465

Palenque Archaeological Site   475

Where to Stay &
    Dine in Palenque   477

San Cristóbal de las Casas   483

Puebla   497

Tlaxcala   509

Xalapa Orientation   513

Downtown Veracruz   516

Downtown Cancún   529

Isla Cancún (Zona Hotelera)   535

Isla Mujeres   557

Cozumel   571

San Miguel de Cozumel   575

The Yucatán's Upper Caribbean
    Coast   591

Playa del Carmen   597

The Yucatán's Lower Caribbean
    Coast   619

Where to Stay & Dine in Mérida   639

The Copper Canyon   679

Chihuahua   693

The Baja Peninsula   699

San José del Cabo   703

The Two Cabos & the Corridor   714

Cabo San Lucas   717

The Lower Baja Peninsula   743

Tijuana   751

The Upper Baja Peninsula   757

An Invitation to the Reader

In researching this book, we discovered many wonderful places—hotels, restaurants, shops, and more. We're sure you'll find others. Please tell us about them, so we can share the information with your fellow travelers in upcoming editions. If you were disappointed with a recommendation, we'd love to know that, too. Please write to:

Frommer's Mexico 2009
Wiley Publishing, Inc. • 111 River St. • Hoboken, NJ 07030-5774

An Additional Note

Please be advised that travel information is subject to change at any time—and this is especially true of prices. We therefore suggest that you write or call ahead for confirmation when making your travel plans. The authors, editors, and publisher cannot be held responsible for the experiences of readers while traveling. Your safety is important to us, however, so we encourage you to stay alert and be aware of your surroundings. Keep a close eye on cameras, purses, and wallets, all favorite targets of thieves and pickpockets.

About the Authors

A writer, editor, and translator, **David Baird** has lived several years in different parts of Mexico. Now based in Austin, Texas, he spends as much time in Mexico as possible. A former resident of Mexico City, Los Angeles native **Juan Cristiano** has written extensively about destinations in Mexico and Latin America, the United States, and Western Europe. **Lynne Bairstow** has lived in Puerto Vallarta for most of the past 17 years. Her travel articles on Mexico have appeared in numerous publications, including *The New York Times* and *Los Angeles Times*. A native of Los Angeles, **Joy Hepp** writes for several print and online publications including her own blog, AlegriaTapatia.Blogspot.com.

Other Great Guides for Your Trip:

Frommer's Spanish PhraseFinder & Dictionary
Frommer's Cancún & the Yucatán Day by Day
Frommer's Cancún, Cozumel & the Yucatán 2009
MTV Best of Mexico
Mexico's Beach Resorts For Dummies

Frommer's Star Ratings, Icons & Abbreviations

Every hotel, restaurant, and attraction listing in this guide has been ranked for quality, value, service, amenities, and special features using a **star-rating system.** In country, state, and regional guides, we also rate towns and regions to help you narrow down your choices and budget your time accordingly. Hotels and restaurants are rated on a scale of zero (recommended) to three stars (exceptional). Attractions, shopping, nightlife, towns, and regions are rated according to the following scale: zero stars (recommended), one star (highly recommended), two stars (very highly recommended), and three stars (must-see).

In addition to the star-rating system, we also use **eight feature icons** that point you to the great deals, in-the-know advice, and unique experiences that separate travelers from tourists. Throughout the book, look for:

Finds	Special finds—those places only insiders know about
Fun Fact	Fun facts—details that make travelers more informed and their trips more fun
Kids	Best bets for kids and advice for the whole family
Moments	Special moments—those experiences that memories are made of
Overrated	Places or experiences not worth your time or money
Tips	Insider tips—great ways to save time and money
Value	Great values—where to get the best deals
Warning	Warning—traveler's advisories are usually in effect.

The following **abbreviations** are used for credit cards:

AE	American Express	DISC	Discover	V	Visa
DC	Diners Club	MC	MasterCard		

Frommers.com

Now that you have this guidebook to help you plan a great trip, visit our website at **www.frommers.com** for additional travel information on more than 4,000 destinations. We update features regularly to give you instant access to the most current trip-planning information available. At Frommers.com, you'll find scoops on the best airfares, lodging rates, and car rental bargains. You can even book your travel online through our reliable travel booking partners. Other popular features include:

- Online updates of our most popular guidebooks
- Vacation sweepstakes and contest giveaways
- Newsletters highlighting the hottest travel trends
- Podcasts, interactive maps, and up-to-the-minute events listings
- Opinionated blog entries by Arthur Frommer himself
- Online travel message boards with featured travel discussions

What's New in Mexico

The news out of Mexico is mostly sunny. The economy is chugging along at a decent clip, inflation remains at historic lows, and the government continues to invest substantial amounts in the nation's infrastructure. For the American traveler, Mexico remains a budget destination, as the dollar continues steady against the peso at press time, even while it falls against other currencies. For Brits and Canadians, Mexico is an outright bargain.

Public safety remains a challenge, with the government locked in combat against four strong drug syndicates. It seems to be making advances and improving its intelligence. Most of the conflict is well removed from the popular tourist destinations, except for some areas along the U.S. border. For most Mexicans, the drug war is something they read about in the papers, not something they are living through. The same is true for tourists who steer clear of drug dealers.

Though it isn't making headlines anymore, Mexico's tortilla crisis continues in force, mostly in the northern and eastern parts of the country, less so in the south and west, and more so in cities than in small towns. For visitors, it means occasionally being served tough, dark tortillas instead of pliant, white ones. It occurs more often in budget restaurants or places where the owners aren't sweating the details (a sign, perhaps, that you should try eating elsewhere) or where the crisis is so widespread that bad tortillas are unavoidable.

PLANNING YOUR TRIP TO MEXICO As of January 23, 2007, citizens of the United States, Canada, Mexico, and Bermuda are required to present a passport or other accepted document that establishes the bearer's identity and nationality to enter the United States when arriving by air from any part of the Western Hemisphere. This change in travel document requirements is the result of recommendations made by the 9/11 Commission, which the U.S. Congress subsequently passed into law in the Intelligence Reform and Terrorism Prevention Act of 2004. A separate proposed rule addressing land and sea travel will be published at a later date, proposing specific requirements for travelers entering the United States through land and sea border crossings. As early as January 1, 2008, U.S. citizens traveling between the United States and Canada, Mexico, Central and South America, the Caribbean, and Bermuda by land or sea could be required to present a valid U.S. passport or other documents as determined by the U.S. Department of Homeland Security.

Travelers to Mexico are now able to make tax-free purchases while vacationing, thanks to a law passed by Mexico's Congress. The law grants international visitors a full refund of the tax added to purchases if the buyer adheres to certain criteria. The merchandise must be purchased in Mexico and verified by airport or seaport Customs, and be verified with a receipt presented at time of departure to be worth at least 1,200 Mexican pesos

($110/£55 at current exchange rates). Reimbursement to tourists is contingent upon any added costs a possible return may generate.

Here are highlights on new flight services to and within Mexico:

- **Alaska Airlines** (www.alaskaair.com) now serves Cancún, Los Cabos, and Puerto Vallarta from Seattle and Portland.
- **Aviacsa Airlines** (www.aviacsa.com) flies to destinations throughout Mexico from Los Angeles, Las Vegas, and Houston.
- **Click Mexicana** (www.clickmx.com), a low-cost subsidiary of Mexicana Airlines, has continued to expand its domestic routes, with connections to international destinations via Mexico City on Mexicana.
- **Delta Airlines** (www.delta.com) now offers nonstop flights from LAX to Mexico City.
- **Frontier Airlines** (www.frontierair lines.com) has expanded service to include Acapulco, Cabo San Lucas, Cancún, Cozumel, Ixtapa/Zihuatanejo, Mazatlán, and Puerto Vallarta.
- **InterJet** (www.interjet.com.mx) runs low-cost flights connecting Toluca (near Mexico City) with most Mexican resort destinations.
- **Volaris** (volaris.com.mx) also offers low-cost flights connecting Toluca (near Mexico City) with Cabo San Lucas, Cancún, Puerto Vallarta, and other Mexican destinations.

MEXICO CITY For complete information, see chapter 5.

Benito Juárez International Airport opened a new international terminal and continues to upgrade the infrastructure in and around the airport. International flights depart from the new Terminal 2 and from the international section of Terminal 1; domestic flights are accommodated by the rest of Terminal 1.

Embassy Suites (© 800/362-2779; www.embassysuites1.hilton.com) opened its first hotel in Mexico, an impressive glass high-rise on Paseo de la Reforma. The hotel features the capital's most modern suites. Guests receive complimentary evening cocktails and breakfast cooked to order.

SILVER CITIES For complete information, see chapter 7.

San Miguel de Allende This last year, San Miguel moved it's *pamplonada* (running of the bulls) to the town of Irapuato. They were having too many problems with public disturbances. It appears that this move will be permanent, which means that you no longer need to avoid San Miguel on that weekend in September. At press time, the Museo Casa de Allende remains closed for remodeling. It should open in late 2008.

Guanajuato The Museo Diego Rivera is expanding its exposition space and hopes to attract a few traveling exhibits, especially those that explore early postrevolutionary painting.

The new **Hotel Camino Real** (www.caminoreal.com) has opened on the site of the former Hacienda San Javier (where the old Parador San Javier was). It's downtown, a few blocks above the Alhóndiga. The hotel's layout is basically the same as with the old Parador San Javier, but with a total makeover of the ruins and an upgrade in services and amenities.

If you're in the market for the distinctive pottery of Capelo or of La Cruz, you no longer have to go way up above La Valenciana to visit their stores. There are two downtown outlets—one in Plaza San Roque, the other at Positos 69—both of which display pieces from the two workshops.

Querétaro There is now direct bus service from Querétaro to Puebla, eliminating the need to change buses in Mexico City. This service is being offered by Futura/Chihuahuenses. The schedule wasn't really settled when I was checking into it, but at the time there were four departures per day. The trip takes about 4 hours.

Zacatecas Cabs here are all getting meters in an effort to make the costs more uniform. The change in fare structure is slated to begin in 2008.

Museo Virreinal in Guadalupe is undergoing an extensive remodeling. You should check with Zacatecas tourism office before you decide to take a cab out there just to make sure it is open. On my last visit, it was open, but you never know.

San Luis Potosí I've given up on when the Museo Nacional de Máscaras will reopen. It has been more than two years since it closed, which means something's up.

MICHOACAN For more details, see chapter 8.

Bus service between the coastal resort Ixtapa/Zihuatanejo and either Morelia or Uruapan is convenient and quick. The regional bus company, Parihikuni, has improved its buses and makes use of the new super highway to the coast. It runs six buses per day.

GUADALAJARA For complete information, see chapter 9.

New ticket counters are going up in all the terminals of Guadalajara's main bus station, in an effort to establish more order and trust between the public and the taxi drivers.

The Canadian consulate has moved to its new location in the Rinconada del Bosque neighborhood.

Admission to the Instituto Cultural Cabañas has shot up to $10 for foreign tourists. It's still worth the price of admission to see Orozco's murals.

PUERTO VALLARTA & THE CENTRAL PACIFIC COAST For complete information, see chapter 10.

The **St. Regis Resort Punta Mita** (www.starwoodhotels.com) has scheduled its grand opening for October 2008, and is already taking reservations. The resort will include 100 guest rooms—each with private outdoor shower—as well as 65 luxury villas, a spa and fitness center, two restaurants, and the second Jack Nicklaus Signature Golf Course in Punta Mita. Just outside the gates of this resort development, the **Café des Artistes del Mar** (www.cafedesartistes.com) opened early in 2008, a sister-restaurant to the famed venue in Vallarta. The restaurant is within the oceanfront boutique hotel **Hotel des Artistes** (© 866/628-2693 U.S. toll free; 329/291-5005; www.hoteldesartistesdelmar.com), which features fully equipped condos with two or three bedrooms. Rates are $325 to $795 (£163–£398) nightly.

In the recent past, you couldn't score a decent glass of wine in Vallarta. Not only has that changed, but now there is a place dedicated to the enologists. **Cava Cinco** (www.cavacinco.com, © 322/223-2808; Paseo Diaz Ordaz 920, Small Vallarta Local 1D) combines a wine market with wine bar—so you can bring home what you enjoyed. The market—with an offering of over 350 vintages, wine accessories, and even cigars—is open 10am to 2am, while the Wine Bar is open from 5:30pm to 4am. The bar has an ultra-cool lounge-style atmosphere and DJ-spun tunes. No worries if wines or champagne aren't your thing—beer and drinks are also served.

Vallarta's club scene continues to expand. The newest addition is the Pan-Asian-themed **Mandala** (© 322/223-0966), welcoming revelers from 11am to 6am—now that's a *party!*

The storied sport of **Americas' Cup Sailing** has comes to the waters of Banderas Bay, courtesy of **Vallarta Adventures**

(© **888/303-2653** in the U.S., or 322/ 297-1212, www.vallarta-adventures.com). Once the venue of only the world's finest sailors, now even rank novices can experience the thrill of participating in a professional race. You'll first learn the basics, and then sail aboard either the Team Australia AUS 29 or 31 authentic competitor vessels, vying for victory with the rival team of people just like you. It's an unparalleled experience. The 3-hour adventure is $99 (£50) per adult.

On the dining front, **deSantos** (© **322/ 223-3052;** www.desantos.com.mx) has seriously upgraded its culinary team, and now offers exceptional catering services as well. If you're planning to throw a party while in town, theirs is the number to call.

ACAPULCO & SOUTHERN PACIFIC COAST

The **Fairmont Acapulco Princess** (© **800/441-1414;** www.fairmont.com/acapulco) has completed a thorough renovation, restoring its place as the grande dame of Acapulco. Its expansive beach and multiple pool areas are the best in the area.

OAXACA & CHIAPAS

For complete information, see chapter 12.

Oaxaca The city remains peaceful and much less visited. This year would most likely be a good time to visit, as you are probably not going to have to deal with crowds. The city is getting a large influx of Mexican visitors, but most of these come during the July/August vacations or during national holidays. There are no elections this year that could spark conflict; only the annual teacher's strike in May and June.

Villahermosa This low-lying capital city of the state of Tabasco, situated on the Gulf coast between Oaxaca and Chiapas had horrendous flooding in 2007 and as of the time of this writing, hasn't yet fully recovered. The Museo Regional de Antropología will most likely be closed until early 2009, but the Parque Museo

La Venta—the one with the megalithic Olmec sculptures—has reopened.

PUEBLA & VERACRUZ

For complete information, see chapter 13.

Puebla and Tlaxcala One of the murals in Cacaxtla was damaged in after some bad storms. The site is closed right now for repairs. You should check with the local tourism office of Tlaxcala if you're planning a trip to see the ruins.

Veracruz The Hotel Emporio was completely gutted when I was last in town. I could not get a date for when it would reopen, so check the website (www.hotelesemporio.com).

CANCUN

Cancún has fully recovered from the 2005 wreckage of Hurricane Wilma, and some would say it's emerged better than before. Many hotels, restaurants, and shopping centers used the hurricane's aftermath as an opportunity to upgrade their facilities and services.

Cancún's International Airport has expanded to three terminals and offers greatly improved facilities and services when compared with just a few years ago.

Accommodations Reopened at the end of 2007 after having been destroyed by Hurricane Wilma, **Aqua** (© **800/343-7821;** www.siente-aqua.com) once again reigns as one of Cancún's most enticing resorts. The hotel includes spacious oceanview rooms, eight oceanfront pools, an invigorating spa, and world-class cuisine. The high-tech rooms feature flatscreen TVs with DVD/CD players, large bathrooms with Molton Brown goods, and aromatherapy kits for private spa treatments.

ME (© **866/436-3542;** www.meby melia.com) brings to Cancún a new level of minimalist chic by the Spanish Meliá hotel group. This hotel includes trendy bars, sensual artwork, and chill-out music in the public spaces; guest rooms have distinctive contemporary furnishings and modern amenities such as plasma TVs.

The stylish Yhi Spa overlooks the ocean and offers every type of facial and body treatment. Opened in 2007, the **Royal** (© **800/ 760-0944;** www.realresorts.com.mx) is an over-the-top, all-inclusive, adults-only resort. Luxury abounds, from the stunning infinity pools and gorgeous beach to the gourmet restaurants and sophisticated spa. The elegant marble lobby overlooks the Caribbean on one side and the lagoon on the other. The guest suites offer every conceivable amenity, including two-person Jacuzzis. Guests in the top-category suites have access to BMW Mini Coopers. The all-inclusive package includes gourmet meals, premium drinks, and evening entertainment.

ISLA MUJERES & COZUMEL For complete information, see chapter 15.

Isla Mujeres This small island remains a laid-back resort of small hotels, despite the recent construction of multistory condo towers on the north side of town. Also, Palace Resorts has opened up a small all-inclusive on the island, on the landward side about in the middle of the island. I wasn't able to visit because it hadn't opened yet, but I'm not sure it's sound reason to put an all-inclusive on this island. The hotels and restaurants in town are inexpensive, they have easy beach access, and there isn't a lot of traffic in town. All of this makes an all-inclusive less desirable.

Cozumel The town of San Miguel is busy at work on urban beautification projects, and so a couple of streets were closed when I was last there. Word is that the town will continue this work off and on during low seasons, repaving streets and adding trees and shrubs in the areas that see the most visitors.

The Reef Club all-inclusive resort is going to be converted into a Wyndham property, though the ownership will remain local.

THE RIVIERA MAYA For complete information, see chapter 16.

Playa del Carmen I'm sorry to say that the continued growth of condos in town has meant the demise of a few more hotels. One of my favorites, the Shangri-la Caribe, has closed, and so has the budget hotel Treetops. Playa has had trouble controlling growth and preserving the feel of an alternative resort.

Mayakoba (www.mayakoba.com), the new golf course resort development between Playa and Puerto Morelos, has continued to grow. The developers attracted a stellar lineup of resorts including The Fairmount, Rosewood, and Banyan Tree—all have spas and border a grand golf course designed by Greg Norman. The Fairmount has been open for a while. The Rosewood opened in 2008. And the other resorts are set to open later in the year.

Tulum Land ownership problems continue to plague the coast along Tulum. All the hotels I have listed in the book have secure titles, but some hotels operating on this coast do not and might be closed in the future.

MERIDA, CHICHEN ITZA & THE MAYA INTERIOR For complete information on this region, see chapter 17.

Chichén Itzá Villas Arqueológicas— the small chain of hotels that was run by Club Med, with properties at Chichén Itzá, Uxmal, and Cobá—was sold to a Mexican chain of resorts called Islander Collection. Some of the contact information changed. Check the website, **www. islandercollection.com.**

LOS CABOS & BAJA CALIFORNIA For more details on this region, see chapter 19.

Fed up with shady merchants and hawkers creating a negative image of Tijuana's Avenida Revolucion, a group of business owners called CeturMex worked in concert with the Baja Secretary of Tourism to create the **Outstanding Host** program. Businesses that pass a certification process are given a logo to display in their window and are listed online at **www.ceturmex.com.mx**.

Many of the businesses, such as the embroidery shop **Hand Art,** have been around for more than 40 years, and each pledges to provide honesty, quality, and service. If you're one of the scores of people planning to visit Tijuana just for the shopping, it's worth a visit to the website to narrow down your hunt. For more information about **Outstanding Host,** call © **664/685-2642.**

Casa Dahlia (© **624/142-2120;** www.casadahlia.com) is a charming new addition to San José del Cabo's gallery district. The contemporary art gallery and cafe is co-owned by Leah Porter, daughter of famed local artist Dennis Wentworth, a talented artist in her own right. Locals and tourists frequent art shows or just stop by for a cup of tea, some tapas or to smoke a hookah pipe in the evening. There's a great view of the back of the cathedral from the outside patio.

Accommodations Pacific Monarch Resorts adds it's unique contribution to San José del Cabo's hotel zone with **Cabo Azul Resort and Spa** (© **877/216-2226;** www.caboazul.com). The resort is made up of villas that are decorated by famed L.A. interior designer Dodd Mitchell. He apparently believed that guests should never leave their rooms. Each villa features an indoor whirlpool and a fully functional kitchen with everything from champagne glasses to sauté pans. Guests can opt to shop for food at the onsite market—which has prices comparable with the nearby Mega supermarket—or request a personal chef to come cook for them.

Attractions Just when you thought you were running out of places to park your megayacht, the Grupo Questro officially opens the $50-million **Marina at Puerto Los Cabos** (www.marinapuertoloscabos).

The marina is the centerpiece of the master-planned Puerto Los Cabos community east of downtown San José de Los Cabos and is predicted to bring tourist traffic to rival that of the bustling marina in Cabo San Lucas.

Expect to see new restaurants, tour activities, a new museum, and even a ferry to Cabo San Lucas as the area continues to develop.

Cabo Adventures (© **888/303-2653** in the U.S. or 624/173-9500; www.caboadventures.com) unfurled its own version of the America's Cup Challenge. In the last 10 years, Los Cabos has earned a reputation as a place where everyday Joes can get the chance to party and play like millionaires, and this new activity will only enhance its status.

The day starts off at the Cabo Dolphins Center in Marina San Lucas, where teams are formed and racers are given a brief history of the America's Cup yachting regatta. The teams then board one of two former New Zealand racing test yachts, where they are briefed on all things nautical before they jib and grind their way around Lover's Arch. The 3-hour race ends with a victory party back on the dock, where winners and losers alike are presented with personalized certificates.

The Best of Mexico

by David Baird, Lynne Bairstow, Juan Cristiano & Joy Hepp

Across Mexico, in villages and cities, in mountains, tropical coasts, and jungle settings, enchanting surprises await travelers. These might take the form of a fantastic small-town festival, delightful dining in a memorable restaurant, or even a stretch of road through heavenly countryside. Below is a starter list of our favorites, to which you'll have the pleasure of adding your own discoveries.

1 The Best Beach Vacations

- **Puerto Vallarta:** Spectacularly wide Banderas Bay is graced by 42km (26 miles) of sandy beach. Some, such as Playa Los Muertos—the popular public beach in town—abound with *palapa* restaurants, volleyball players, and parasailers. The beaches of Punta Mita, the exclusive development north of Vallarta, have white-sand, crystalline waters, and coral reefs just offshore. Others around the bay nestle in coves, accessible only by boat. Puerto Vallarta is the only beach town in Mexico with an authentic colonial feel as well as first-rate resort amenities. See "Puerto Vallarta," in chapter 10.
- **Puerto Escondido:** The best overall beach value in Mexico is principally known for its world-class surfing beach, Playa Zicatela. The surrounding beaches all have their own appeal; colorful fishing *pangas* dot the central town beach, parked under the shade of palms leaning over so far they almost touch the ground. Puerto Escondido offers unique accommodations at excellent prices, with exceptional budget dining and

nightlife. See "Puerto Escondido," in chapter 11.
- **Ixtapa/Zihuatanejo:** These side-by-side resorts afford beach-goers the best of both worlds: serene simplicity and resort comforts. For travelers seeking to get back to basics, the best and most beautiful beach is Playa La Ropa, close to Zihuatanejo. The wide beach at Playa Las Gatas, with its restaurants and snorkeling sites, is also a great place to play. The high-rise hotels in Ixtapa, on the next bay over from Zihuatanejo, front Playa Palmar, a fine, wide swath of beach. See "Northward to Zihuatanejo & Ixtapa," in chapter 11.
- **Cancún:** Cancún and the coastline of the Yucatán state of Quintana Roo are home to Mexico's most enticingly beautiful beaches, with powdery white-sand and water the color of a Technicolor dream. Cancún also has the widest assortment of luxury beachfront hotels, plus more restaurants, nightlife, and activities than any other resort destination in Mexico. See chapter 14.

Mexico

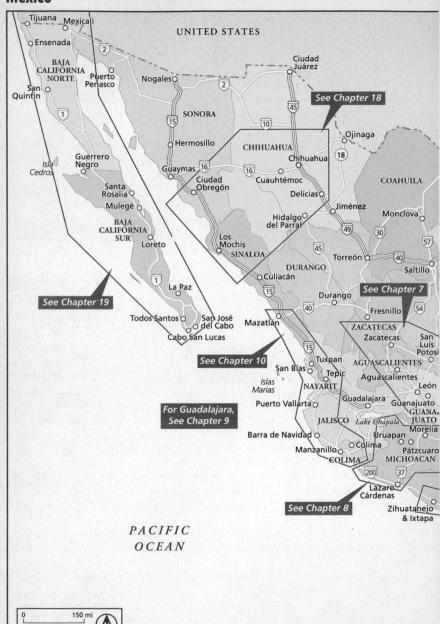

UNITED STATES

Tijuana
Mexicali
Ensenada
2
BAJA
CALIFORNIA
NORTE
Puerto
Peñasco
San
Quintín
1
Nogales
2
Ciudad
Juárez
See Chapter 18
45
SONORA
15
10
Hermosillo
CHIHUAHUA
Ojinaga
Isla
Cedros
Guerrero
Negro
Chihuahua
18
Guaymas
16
16
Chihuahua
COAHUILA
Santa
Rosalía
Ciudad
Obregón
Cuauhtémoc
Mulegé
Delicias
Jiménez
Monclova
BAJA
CALIFORNIA
SUR
Loreto
Hidalgo
del Parral
49
30
Los
Mochis
SINALOA
45
Torreón
40
57
1
La Paz
DURANGO
Culiacán
Saltillo
See Chapter 19
15
Durango
See Chapter 7
40
Todos Santos
San José
del Cabo
Mazatlán
Fresnillo
54
Cabo San Lucas
ZACATECAS
Zacatecas
San
Luis
Potosí
See Chapter 10
15
Tuxpan
AGUASCALIENTES
San Blas
Tepic
Aguascalientes
León
Islas
Marías
NAYARIT
Puerto Vallarta
Guadalajara
Guanajuato
GUANA-
JUATO
*For Guadalajara,
See Chapter 9*
JALISCO
Lake Chapala
Morelia
Barra de Navidad
Uruapan
Manzanillo
Colima
Pátzcuaro
COLIMA
MICHOACAN
200
37
Lázaro
Cárdenas
See Chapter 8
Zihuatanejo
& Ixtapa

*PACIFIC
OCEAN*

0   150 mi
0   150 km
N

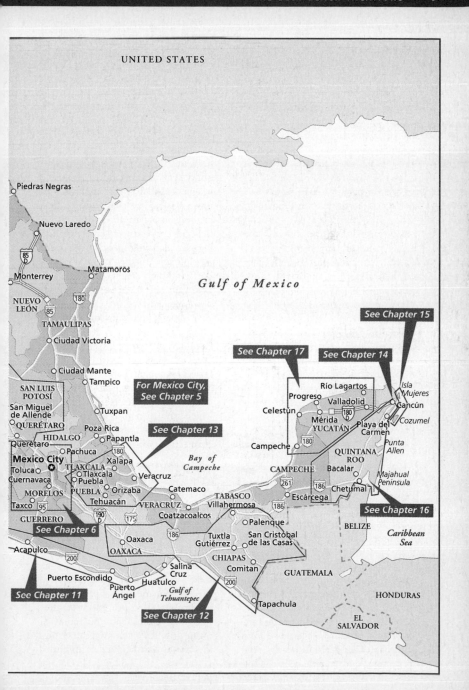

UNITED STATES

Piedras Negras

Nuevo Laredo

85

Monterrey

Matamoros

NUEVO
LEÓN   180   Gulf of Mexico

85

TAMAULIPAS

Ciudad Victoria

Ciudad Mante

SAN LUIS   Tampico
POTOSÍ   See Chapter 15

San Miguel   Río Lagartos   Isla
de Allende   Tuxpan   For Mexico City,   Progreso   Mujeres
QUERÉTARO   See Chapter 5   Celestún   Valladolid   Cancún
                     Poza Rica   180
Querétaro   Papantla   See Chapter 13   Mérida   Playa del   Cozumel
HIDALGO   YUCATÁN   Carmen
          Pachuca   180   180   Punta
Mexico City   Xalapa   Bay of   Campeche   QUINTANA   Allen
Toluca   TLAXCALA   Campeche   CAMPECHE   ROO   Bacalar
Cuernavaca   Tlaxcala   Veracruz   Majahual
MORELOS   Puebla   261   186   Peninsula
Taxco   PUEBLA   Orizaba   Catemaco   TABASCO   Escárcega   Chetumal
          Tehuacán   VERACRUZ   Villahermosa   186
GUERRERO   190   175   Coatzacoalcos   See Chapter 16
          See Chapter 6   186   Palenque   BELIZE   Caribbean
Acapulco   Oaxaca   Tuxtla   San Cristóbal   Sea
          200   OAXACA   Gutiérrez   de las Casas   GUATEMALA   HONDURAS
          Puerto Escondido   CHIAPAS   Comitán
          Puerto   Salina   200
See Chapter 11   Ángel   Cruz   Gulf of   EL
          Huatulco   Tehuantepec   Tapachula   SALVADOR
          See Chapter 12

See Chapter 17   See Chapter 14

- **Isla Mujeres:** There's only one main beach here—Playa Norte—but it's superb. From this island, you can dive El Garrafón reef, snorkel off-shore, and take a boat excursion to the Isla Contoy national wildlife reserve, which features great birding and a fabulous, uninhabited beach. See "Isla Mujeres," in chapter 15.
- **Tulum:** Fronting some of Mexico's best Caribbean beaches, Tulum's small *palapa* hotels afford guests a lit-tle slice of paradise far from crowds and megaresorts. The bustling town lies inland; the coast is quiet and should remain so, because all the hotels there are small and have to generate their own electricity. If you can pull yourself away from the surf, you'll find nearby ruins to explore and a vast nature preserve as well. See chapter 16.
- **Playa del Carmen:** "Playa" is Mex-ico's hip beach destination with a pronounced *mañana* attitude. Above all, it's easy and low key. You walk to the beach, you walk back to the hotel, you walk to one of the many good restaurants. Next day, you repeat. The sand is white; the water is clear blue and ideal for swimming. If you

want more variety, you'll find that ancient Mayan ruins, Cozumel, and the megaresort of Cancún are near enough to round out your beach vacation. See "Playa del Carmen," in chapter 16.
- **La Paz:** This state capital borders a lovely beach, dotted with colorful playgrounds and lively open-air restaurants. Take a cue from the local residents, though, and pass on swim-ming here in favor of the exquisite beaches just minutes from down-town. La Paz's beaches and the islets just offshore have transformed this tranquil town into a center for div-ing, sea kayaking, and other adven-ture pursuits. See "La Paz: Peaceful Port Town," in chapter 19.
- **Los Cabos:** Dramatic rock forma-tions and crashing waves join forces with wide stretches of soft sand and rolling surf breaks. Start at Playa Palmilla and work your way down the Tourist Corridor to the famed Lovers' Beach at Land's End. Some beaches are more appropriate for con-templation than for swimming, which isn't all bad. See "Los Cabos: Resorts, Watersports & Golf," in chapter 19.

2 The Best Cultural Experiences

- **Passing Time in the Plazas & Parks:** All the world may be a stage, but some stages have richer backdrops than others. Town plazas are the place to sit and watch daily Mexican life unfold before your eyes. Alive with people, these open spaces are no mod-ern product of urban planners, but are rooted in the traditional Mexican view of society. Several plazas are standouts: **Veracruz**'s famous *zócalo* (see chapter 13) features nearly non-stop music and tropical gaiety. One look tells you how important

Oaxaca's *zócalo* (see chapter 12) is to the local citizenry; the plaza is remark-ably beautiful, grand, and intimate all at once. **Mexico City**'s Alameda (see chapter 5) has a dark, dramatic his-tory—heretics were burned at the stake here during the colonial period—but today it's a people's park where lovers sit, cotton-candy vendors spin their treats, and the sound of organ grinders drifts over the chang-ing crowd. **San Miguel de Allende**'s Jardín (see chapter 7) is the focal point for meeting, sitting, painting, and sketching. During festivals, it fills with dancers, parades, and elaborate fireworks. **Guanajuato** and **Querétaro** (see chapter 7) have the coziest plazas, and **Mérida's** El Centro (see chapter 17), can't be beat on Sundays.

- *Música Popular:* Nothing reveals the soul of a people like music, and Mexico has given rise to various styles, which you can hear in many different settings. You can hear brassy **mariachi** music in the famous Plaza de Garibaldi in Mexico City (see chapter 5), under the arches of El Parián in Tlaquepaque, and in other parts of Guadalajara (see chapter 9). Or perhaps you want to hear romantic **boleros** sung to the strumming of a Spanish guitar, or what Mexicans call *música tropical* and related *cumbias,* mambos, and cha-cha-chas (see chapter 14).

- **Regional Folk Dancing:** From the Ballet Folklórico in Mexico City to the Ballet Folclórico in Guadalajara (see chapters 5 and 9) or the almost-nightly park dances in Mérida (see chapter 17), Mexican folk dance events are diverse and colorful expressions of Mexican traditions.

- **Fireworks:** Mexicans share such a passion for fireworks and such a cavalier attitude toward them that it's a good thing the buildings are stone and cement, or the whole country would have burned down long ago. Many local traditions surround fireworks, and every festival includes a display. The most lavish are the large constructions called *castillos,* and the wildest are the *toros* that men carry over their shoulders while running through the streets, causing festival-goers to dive for cover.

- **Strolling** *El Malecón:* Wherever there's a seafront road, you'll find *el malecón* bordering it. This is generally a wide sidewalk for strolling, complete with vendors selling pinwheels and cotton candy. In some places, it has supplanted the plaza as a centerpiece of town life. The best examples are in **Puerto Vallarta, Mazatlán** (see chapter 10), **La Paz** (see chapter 19), **Cozumel** (see chapter 15), and **Veracruz** (see chapter 13).

- **Regional Fairs:** Almost every city and town has its regional fair *(feria regional).* They showcase the best products of the region—tequila or fruit liquors, livestock, carved silver, or clay handicrafts. One of the most notable regional fairs is La Feria del Caballo in Texcoco, which takes place in late March or early April.

3 The Best Archaeological Sites

- *** Teotihuacán:** It's so close to Mexico City, yet centuries away. You can sense the majesty of the past in a stroll down the pyramid-lined Avenue of the Dead, from the Pyramid of the Sun to the Pyramid of the Moon. Imagine what a fabulous place this must have been when the walls were stuccoed and painted brilliant colors. See "A Side Trip to the Pyramids of San Juan Teotihuacán," in chapter 5.

- **Monte Albán:** A grand ceremonial city built on a mountaintop overlooking the valley of Oaxaca, Monte Albán affords visitors panoramic vistas; a fascinating view of a society in transition, reflected in the contrasting methods of pyramid construction; and intriguing details in ornamentation. See "Oaxaca City," in chapter 12.

- **Palenque:** Like the pharaohs of Egypt, the rulers of Palenque built tombs deep within their pyramids.

Imagine the magnificent ceremony in A.D. 683 when King Pacal was entombed in his magnificent burial chamber, which lay unspoiled until its discovery in 1952. See "Palenque," in chapter 12.

- **Ek Balam:** Archaeologists at this site have made the most astonishing discoveries of the decade. Ek Balam's main pyramid is taller than Chichén Itzá's, and it holds a sacred doorway bordered with elaborate stucco figures of priests and kings and rich iconography. See "Ek Balam: Dark Jaguar," in chapter 17.
- **Uxmal:** No matter how many times you see Uxmal, the splendor of its stone carvings is awe-inspiring. A stone rattlesnake undulates across the facade of the Nunnery complex, and 103 masks of the rain god Chaac project out from the Governor's Palace. See "The Ruins of Uxmal," in chapter 17.
- **Chichén Itzá:** Stand beside the giant serpent head at the foot of El Castillo pyramid and marvel at the architects and astronomers who positioned the building so precisely that shadow and sunlight form a serpent's body slithering from the peak to the earth at each equinox (Mar 21 and Sept 21). See "The Ruins of Chichén Itzá," in chapter 17.

4 The Best Active Vacations

- **Scuba Diving in Cozumel & along the Yucatán's Caribbean Coast:** The coral reefs off Cozumel, Mexico's premier diving destination, are among the top five dive spots in the world. See chapter 15. The Yucatán's coastal reef is part of the second-largest reef system in the world and affords excellent diving. Especially beautiful is the Chinchorro Reef, 32km (20 miles) offshore from Majahual or Xcalak. You can also dive in the clear, cool water of the many caverns and *cenotes* (sinkholes, or natural wells) that dot the interior. See chapter 16. Other excellent dive sites are in and around **Puerto Vallarta** and off **Los Cabos.** See chapters 10 and 19.
- **Fly-Fishing off the Punta Allen Peninsula:** Serious anglers will enjoy the challenge of fly-fishing the saltwater flats and lagoons of Ascension Bay, near Punta Allen. See "Tulum, Punta Allen & Sian Ka'an," in chapter 16.
- **Hiking & Horseback Riding in the Copper Canyon:** Miles and miles of beautiful, remote, challenging canyon lands are paradise for the serious hiker or rider. **Canyon Travel** (© **800/843-1060** in the U.S.; www.canyontravel.com) can set hikers up with a Tarahumara Indian guide, who can take you deep into the canyons to places rarely viewed by tourists. Doug Rhodes of **Paraíso del Oso** (© **800/884-3107** in the U.S.) leads tours of experienced horseback riders on a 12-day ride that tests a rider's skill in mountainous terrain. It has to be the most challenging ride in North America. See "The Copper Canyon Train & Stops along the Way," in chapter 18.
- **Golf in Los Cabos & Puerto Vallarta:** Puerto Vallarta, with its seven championship courses, is *the* new destination for golfers to watch—and an eighth course will open in fall of 2008 with the addition of Punta Mita's second Jack Nicklaus Signature course. Added to the appeal of golf here are courses within easy driving distance along the Pacific Coast at El Tamarindo, Isla Navidad, and Manzanillo. See chapter 10. The Corridor between San José del Cabo and Cabo

San Lucas is one of the world's premier golf destinations, with seven championship courses and a total of 207 holes slated for the area. See chapter 19.

- **Surfing Zicatela Beach in Puerto Escondido:** This world-class break is a lure for surfers from around the globe. It challenges the best in the sport each September and October, when the waves peak and the annual surf competitions take place. See chapter 11. Other noted surf breaks in Mexico include Sayulita, Punta Mita, and Las Islitas Beach near **San Blas** (all north of Puerto Vallarta); Playa Costa Azul, on the outskirts of **San José del Cabo;** and "Killers" at Todos Santos Island in northern Baja. See chapters 10 and 19.

- **Sportfishing in La Paz:** Billfishing for magnificent marlin and sailfish is popular in southern Baja, and La Paz pulls in the most consistent share. See chapter 19. Fishing is excellent in Los Cabos, Mazatlán, Manzanillo, and Zihuatanejo too. See chapters 10, 11, and 19.

- **Sea Kayaking in the Sea of Cortez:** From Cabo San Lucas to La Paz, and continuing north, the Sea of Cortez is a sea kayaker's dream. It has dozens of tiny coves and impressive inlets to pull into and explore, under the watchful gaze of sea lions and dolphins. Professional outfitters provide gear, guides, and instruction for novices. See chapter 19.

5 The Best of Natural Mexico

- **Michoacán's Million Monarch March:** Mexico is an exotic land, and no place drives this home more forcefully than a mountain forest where you stand surrounded by the fluttering wings of millions of monarch butterflies—it's like being in a fairy tale. The setting is the rugged highlands of Michoacán, from mid- to late November through March. See "Morelia," in chapter 8.

- **Whale-Watching:** Each winter, between December and April, magnificent humpback and gray whales return to breed and instruct their young in the waters of Banderas Bay, fronting **Puerto Vallarta,** and in **Los Cabos.** See "Puerto Vallarta" in chapter 10, and "Los Cabos: Resorts, Watersports & Golf," in chapter 19.

- **Sea Turtle Nesting Beaches:** Between June and November, sea turtles return to the beaches of their birth to lay their eggs in nests on the sand. With poaching and natural predators threatening these species, communities along Mexico's Pacific coast have established protected nesting areas. Many are open for public viewing and participation in the egg collection and baby-turtle release processes. Turtles are found along the Yucatán coast, in Baja Sur, on the Oaxaca coast, in Puerto Vallarta, and on Costa Alegre. See chapters 10, 16, and 19.

- **Lago Bacalar** (Yucatán Peninsula): The waters of this crystal-clear, spring-fed lake—Mexico's second largest—are noted for their vibrant color variations, from pale blue to deep blue-green and turquoise. The area surrounding the lake is known for birding, with over 130 species identified. See "Lago Bacalar" in chapter 16.

- **The Rugged Copper Canyon:** The canyons, known collectively as the Copper Canyon, are beautiful, remote, and unspoiled. The entire network is larger than the Grand

Canyon; it incorporates high water-falls, vertical canyon walls, mountain forests in the canyon-rim country, and semiarid desert inside the canyons. This is the land of the Tarahumara Indians, who gained their legendary endurance from adapting to this wilderness. See chapter 18.

- **Desert Landscapes in Baja Sur:** The painted-desert colors and unique plant life are a natural curiosity in **Los Cabos,** where horseback, hiking, and ATV trips explore the area. The arid desert contrasts sharply with the intense blue of the strong sea surrounding the peninsula. See "Los Cabos: Resorts, Watersports & Golf," in chapter 19.

6 The Best Places to Get Away from It All

- **Costa Alegre:** Between Puerto Vallarta and Manzanillo, a number of ultra-exclusive hotels cater to those with both excessive time and money. These resorts, such as Hotelito Desconocido, Las Alamandas, Hotel Careyes, and El Tamarindo are miles from civilization on private beaches. See "Costa Alegre: Puerto Vallarta to Barra de Navidad," in chapter 10.
- **San Sebastián:** A 15-minute flight from Puerto Vallarta takes you a century back in time. The colonial mountain town of San Sebastián used to be the center of Mexico's mining operations; today, it's simply a place of delicious seclusion in a magical mountain setting. See "Puerto Vallarta," in chapter 10.
- **Punta Mita:** Its ancient inhabitants considered the northern tip of the Bay of Banderas sacred ground. Today, the point where the Sea of Cortez, the Pacific Ocean, and Banderas Bay meet has evolved into Mexico's most exclusive residential resort development. The beaches are white and the waters crystalline. See "Puerto Vallarta," in chapter 10.
- **Riviera Maya & Punta Allen Peninsula:** Away from the popular resort of Cancún, the Riviera Maya's heavenly quiet getaways offer tranquillity at low prices on beautiful palm-lined beaches. South of the Tulum ruins,

Punta Allen's beachside budget inns are among the most peaceful getaways in the country. See chapter 16.
- **Lago Bacalar:** The spring-fed waters of Lake Bacalar make an ideal place to unwind. South of Cancún, near Chetumal, there's nothing around for miles. If you want adventure, you can paddle a kayak on the lake, follow a birding trail, or venture to Belize or nearby Maya ruins. See "Lago Bacalar," in chapter 16.
- **Cerocahui:** Up in the high Sierra Tarahumara, far from where the large tours stop, you'll find a peaceful little town surrounding a former mission. Nearby are two small hotels that are even more peaceful—no phones, no crowds, no traffic, just beautiful mountains and canyons clothed in pine forest. See "The Copper Canyon Train & Stops along the Way," in chapter 18.
- **Cabo Pulmo:** It's only a 60-mile drive from the Los Cabos airport to Cabo Pulmo, yet if the mounded Sierra de La Laguna peaks weren't a dead giveaway for Baja, you could be in the South Pacific. Swaying in the shade of a *palapa*-roofed bungalow at Cabo Pulmo Beach Resort, you won't care where you are—you just won't want to leave. The Sea of Cortez breaks on a coral reef, allowing only the finest bits of sand and smooth

pebbles to pad the coast. The coral itself is a sight to behold, but the real attraction is the sea life in this protected marine park. Extensive

hiking/mountain biking trails loop through the mountains for those who prefer the peace of the desert. See chapter 19.

7 The Best Art, Architecture & Museums

- **Museo Nacional de Antropología:** Among the world's most outstanding museums, the Museum of Anthropology in Mexico City contains riches representing 3,000 years of the country's past. Also on view are fabulous artifacts of still-thriving indigenous cultures. The award-winning building, designed by architect Pedro Ramírez Vázquez, is stunning. See p. 130.

- **Palacio Nacional:** Mexico's national center of government overlooks one of the three biggest public squares in the world (the *zócalo*) and was originally built in 1692 on the site of Moctezuma's "new" palace, to be the home of Hernán Cortez. The top floor, added in the late 1920s, holds a series of stunning Diego Rivera murals depicting the history of Mexico. See p. 132.

- **Palacio de Bellas Artes in Mexico City:** The country's premier venue for the performing arts, this fabulous building is the combined work of several masters. The exterior is early-20th-century Art Nouveau covered in marble; the interior is 1930s Art Deco. See p. 134.

- **The Templo Mayor's Aztec Splendor:** The Templo Mayor and Museo del Templo Mayor constitute an archaeological excavation and museum with 6,000 objects on display. They showcase the variety and splendor of the Aztec Empire as it existed in the historic center of what is now Mexico City. See p. 132.

- **Catedral Metropolitana:** This towering cathedral, begun in 1567 and finished in 1788, blends baroque,

neoclassical, and Mexican *churrigueresque* architecture, and was constructed primarily from the stones of destroyed Aztec temples. See p. 136.

- **Santa Prisca y San Sebastián Church:** One of Mexico's most impressive baroque churches, completed in 1758, this church in Taxco has an intricately carved facade, an interior decorated with gold-leafed saints and angels, and paintings by Miguel Cabrera, one of Mexico's most famous colonial-era artists. See p. 166.

- **La Parroquia in San Miguel de Allende:** Inspired by European gothic, but lighter and more cheerful; this fanciful church is like a fiesta captured in stone—especially at night when it's illuminated. See p. 196.

- **Murals of José Clemente Orozco in Guadalajara:** Of the great Mexican muralists of the Revolutionary period, Orozco is perhaps the most technical and the most expressive of his generation's concerns. To see his image of Hidalgo bearing down on you from the ceiling of the grand staircase of the Palacio de Gobierno is to understand almost instantly what he and his *compañeros* were striving to accomplish. See p. 274.

- **Museo Virreinal de Guadalupe:** Six kilometers (4 miles) southeast of Zacatecas in the small town of Guadalupe, this Franciscan convent and art museum holds a striking collection of 17th- and 18th-century paintings by such masters as Miguel Cabrera and Cristóbal de Villalpando. The expressive, dramatic works will fascinate art lovers. See p. 238.

- **Morelia's Cathedral:** Sober lines, balanced proportions, a deft blending of architectural styles, and monumental height—Morelia's cathedral is the most beautiful in the country. It's built of brownish-pink stone that turns fiery rose in the late-afternoon sun. See p. 252.
- **Museo Pantaleón Panduro in Tlaquepaque:** The peoples of Mexico have always placed a high value on pottery as a field of artistic achievement. It's a cultural continuity that spans from pre-Columbian times to the present. And this museum is perhaps the greatest single expression of this love for pottery. Its collection holds prized pieces from the yearly national ceramics competition. See p. 289.

- **Museo Antropología de Xalapa:** Along with the finest examples of Olmec and Totonac sculpture and ceramics, this museum includes the best collection of the Olmec megalithic heads. See p. 513.
- **Puebla's Capilla del Rosario:** In the church of Santo Domingo, this chapel is a tour de force of baroque expression, executed in molded plaster, carved wood, Talavera tile, and gold leaf. The overall aim is to overpower the senses. See p. 500.
- **Puebla's Museo Amparo:** This museum contains a magnificent collection of pre-Columbian and colonial art, which is beautifully displayed. See p. 502.

8 The Best Shopping

- **Bazar del Sábado in San Angel:** This festive Saturday market in and around Plaza San Jacinto in colonial San Angel, one of Mexico City's more exclusive southern neighborhoods, offers exceptional crafts of a more sophisticated nature than you'll see in most *mercados*. Furnishings, antiques, and collectibles are also easy to find in surrounding shops and street plazas. See p. 148.
- **Polanco, Mexico City:** This fashionable neighborhood is noted for its designer boutiques, formal dress shops, fine jewelers, and leather-goods offerings. Avenida Presidente Masaryk is Mexico City's equivalent of Rodeo Drive. See "Shopping," in chapter 5.
- **Contemporary Art:** Latin American art is surging in popularity. Galleries in Mexico City feature Mexico's masters and emerging stars. Oaxaca, Puerto Vallarta, and San Miguel de Allende galleries also have excellent selections. See chapters 5, 7, 10, and 12.

- **Taxco Silver:** Mexico's silver capital, Taxco, has hundreds of stores featuring fine jewelry and decorative objects. See "Taxco: Cobblestones & Silver," in chapter 6.
- **Talavera Pottery in Puebla & Dolores Hidalgo:** An inheritor of the Moorish legacy of ceramics, Puebla produces some of the most sought-after dinnerware in the world. And the tiles produced there adorn building facades and church domes throughout the area. See chapter 13. Dolores Hidalgo, 40km (25 miles) northwest of San Miguel de Allende, produces attractive, inexpensive Talavera of less traditional design. See "San Miguel de Allende," in chapter 7.
- **San Miguel de Allende's Diverse Crafts:** Perhaps it's the influence of the Instituto Allende art school, but something has given storekeepers here savvy about choosing their merchandise. The stores have fewer typical articles of Mexican handicrafts and more interesting and eye-catching

works than you'll find in other towns. See "San Miguel de Allende," in chapter 7.

- **Pátzcuaro's Fine Crafts:** Michoacán is known for its crafts, and Pátzcuaro is at the center of it all. You can find beautiful cotton textiles, woodcarvings, pottery, lacquerware, woven straw pieces, and copper items in the market, or you can track the object to its source in one of the nearby villages. See "Pátzcuaro," in chapter 8.

- **Decorative Arts in Tlaquepaque & Tonalá:** These two neighborhoods of Guadalajara offer perhaps the most enjoyable shopping in Mexico. Tlaquepaque has attracted sophisticated and wide-ranging shops that sell a wide variety of decorative art. In Tonalá, more than 400 artisans have workshops, and you can visit many of them; on market days, wander through blocks and blocks of market stalls to find that one perfect piece. See "Shopping," in chapter 9.

- **Huichol Art in Puerto Vallarta:** One of the last indigenous cultures to remain faithful to their customs, language, and traditions, the Huichol Indians come down from the Sierra Madre to sell their unusual art to Puerto Vallarta galleries. Inspired by visions received during spiritual ceremonies, the Huichol create their art with colorful yarn or beads pressed into wax. See "Shopping," in chapter 10.

- **Oaxacan Textiles:** The valley of Oaxaca produces the best weavings and naturally dyed textiles in Mexico; it's also famous for its pottery, and colorful, imaginative woodcarvings. See "Oaxaca City," in chapter 12.

- **The Markets of San Cristóbal de las Casas:** This city, deep in the heart of the Maya highlands, has shops, open plazas, and markets that sell distinctive waist-loomed wool and cotton textiles, leather shoes, local pottery, genre dolls, and Guatemalan textiles. See "San Cristóbal de las Casas," in chapter 12.

9 The Best Luxury Hotels

- **Condesa*df*** (Mexico City; © 55/ 5241-2600): The city's trendiest hotel sits in the hip urban neighborhood of Condesa. In an early 20th-century French building, it combines Art Nouveau with contemporary designs, and features one of the city's hottest restaurants and rooftop bars. See p. 119.

- **Hotel Four Seasons** (Mexico City; © 800/332-3442 in the U.S.): The standard of excellence in Mexico, and the most classically luxurious option in Mexico City, this hotel captures serenity and elegance in a palace-style building that surrounds a picturesque courtyard. Bonuses include the gracious staff and unique cultural tours on offer. See p. 116.

- **W Mexico City** (Mexico City; © 877/946-8357 in the U.S.): Stylish and high-tech, this W is where the young and cool come to stay. With its super-*caliente* red hues and lively bar, the W Mexico City has infused the country's capital with a dose of minimalist urban chic. Luxury extras include expansive bathrooms with circular tubs. See p. 114.

- **Villa Montaña** (Morelia; © 800/ 223-6510 in the U.S., or 800/448-8355 in Canada): The Villa Montaña defines perfection. From the layout of the grounds to the decoration of the rooms, every detail has been skillfully handled. The hotel perches on a ridge that overlooks Morelia; from its terraces, guests can survey the city below. The restaurant is one of the city's best. See p. 256.

- **Four Seasons Resort Punta Mita** (north of Puerto Vallarta; © 800/ 332-3442 in the U.S.): This luxury resort offers an unrivaled location (on a remote, pristine stretch of beach) and the stellar service characteristic of the Four Seasons chain. Also on-site are an expansive spa and a private Jack Nicklaus Signature golf course. See p. 340.

- **El Tamarindo** (between Manzanillo and Puerto Vallarta; © 315/351- 5032): The most exclusive remote resort in Mexico, this stylish place combines large private casitas facing the Pacific with a stunning private oceanfront golf course. Guests are likely to be Hollywood celebrities and rich folk from around the world. It's about 1 hour north of Manzanillo along Costa Alegre. See p. 362.

- **La Casa Que Canta** (Zihuatanejo; © 888/523-5050 in the U.S.): This is one of Mexico's most romantic spots, an unforgettable boutique hotel where music plays throughout the open-air corridors. *Palapa*-style guest rooms have their own furnished outdoor terraces, many with private plunge pools overlooking the sea. The food, service, and amenities here are as good as it gets. See p. 414.

- **The Tides** (Zihuatanejo; © 888/ 389-2645 in the U.S.): This stunning hotel sits on one of Mexico's calmest and most beautiful beaches. Modern rooms and suites overlook the bay or a man-made lagoon, and many have private plunge pools. It's a luxurious retreat you won't want to leave. See p. 414.

- **Ritz-Carlton Cancún** (Cancún; © 800/241-3333 in the U.S.): Thick carpets, sparkling glass and brass, and rich mahogany surround guests at this hotel, for years the standard-bearer of luxury in Cancún. The

service is impeccable, leaving guests with an overall sense of pampered relaxation. And, post–Hurricane Wilma, the Ritz received a significant makeover. See p. 538.

- **Le Méridien Cancún Resort & Spa** (Cancún; © 800/543-4300 in the U.S.): This is the most intimate of the luxury hotels in Cancún, with an understated sense of highly personalized service. Most notable is its 4,570 sq. m (49,190-sq.-ft.) Spa del Mar. See p. 537.

- **JW Marriott** (Cancún; © 800/223- 6388 in the U.S.): This extraordinary resort offers sophistication without pretense. Its free-form infinity pool is one of the most impressive anywhere, and the spa is one of Cancún's best. Service is outstanding. See p. 537.

- **Presidente InterContinental Cozumel** (Cozumel; © 800/327-0200 in the U.S., or 987/872-9500; www. cozumel.intercontinental.com): Redesigned after the hurricane, this second edition of the hotel includes some impressive upgrades, including redesigned rooms, a large second pool, and more services. And, as before, it has all that coastline where you can stretch out on some sand and forget about life back home for a while. See p. 582.

- **Maroma** (north of Playa del Carmen; © 866/454-9351 in the U.S.): You can't ask for a better setting for a resort than this beautiful stretch of Caribbean coast with palm trees and manicured gardens. You'll start to relax before you even take the first sip of your welcome cocktail. Service is very attentive, and the rooms are luxurious. See p. 592.

- **Hacienda Xcanatún** (outskirts of Mérida; © 888/883-3633 in the U.S.): Large, boldly designed suites built with extravagance in mind, extensive grounds, private spa, excellent restaurant, and ample staff—this hotel does the difficult trick of being small in size but large in offerings. See "Of Haciendas & Hotels," on p. 642.

- **Las Ventanas al Paraíso** (Los Cabos; ℂ 888/767-3966 in the U.S.): Stunning in its relaxed elegance, Las Ventanas has a deluxe European spa, excellent gourmet restaurant, and elegantly appointed rooms and suites. From fireplaces and telescopes to private pools and rooftop terraces, each suite offers a slice of heaven. See p. 713.

- **Esperanza** (Los Cabos; ℂ 866/311-2226 in the U.S.): This Auberge resort pampers guests in a desert-chic setting, on a bluff overlooking twin coves below. Spacious, sumptuous rooms are enhanced by ample terraces, and the resort's spa and dining services make a stay here even more memorable. See p. 713.

- **One&Only Palmilla** (Los Cabos; ℂ 800/637-2226 in the U.S.): A popular Mexican resort with the Hollywood crowd, the completely renovated Palmilla has reclaimed its rank as the most deluxe hotel in this seaside playground known for sumptuous quarters and great golf. The exceptional spa, fitness center, and yoga garden, as well as a restaurant under the direction of renowned chef Charlie Trotter, are added bonuses. See p. 714.

10 The Best Inexpensive Inns

- **Best Western Hotel Majestic** (Mexico City; ℂ 800/528-1234 in the U.S.): This historic building and former home of Augustinian friars offers exceptionally clean, comfortable, value-priced lodgings. It's on La Alameda park, near the Palace of Fine Arts and the Franz Mayer Museum. See p. 118.

- **Holiday Inn Zócalo** (Mexico City; ℂ 888/465-4329 in the U.S.): This unique Holiday Inn is one of the city's most charming hotels. Located next to the capital's historic central square, it's decorated in a colonial Mexican style with colorful art, antiques, and handicrafts. See p. 119.

- **Hotel San Francisco Plaza** (Guadalajara; ℂ 33/3613-8954): This two-story colonial-style hotel is a more agreeable place to stay than lodgings that cost twice the price, and it's every bit as comfortable. It's in the downtown area, near the main plaza and several good restaurants and nightspots. See p. 280.

- **Hotel Los Flamingos** (Acapulco; ℂ 744/482-0690): Once a private club for Hollywood's elite, this hotel will enchant you with its pervasive midcentury charm, funky profusion of hot pink, and breathtaking clifftop views. See p. 396.

- **Paraíso Escondido** (Puerto Escondido; ℂ 954/582-0444): This eclectic inn is a great bargain, especially for the originality of the decor and the excellent service. It's a short walk to the beach and the action along Puerto's main drag. See p. 428.

- **Misión de los Arcos** (Huatulco; ℂ 958/587-0165): Just 1 block from the central plaza, this hotel has a similar style to the elegant Quinta Real, at a fraction of the cost. An all-white facade and intriguing decorative touches give it an inviting feel. There's shuttle service to the Huatulco beaches. See p. 441.

- **Las Golondrinas** (Oaxaca; ℂ 951/514-3298): We receive more favorable letters about this hotel than about any other in the country. It's small, simple, and colorful, with homey touches of folk art and pathways lined with abundant foliage. See p. 459.

- **Casa Na-Bolom** (San Cristóbal; ℰ **967/678-1418**): This beautiful colonial house was once the home and office of Frans and Trudy Blom and a gathering place for anthropologists interested in the region's various ethnic groups. It is now a museum and library full of materials about the region and its indigenous peoples. Rooms have fireplaces and are decorated in local fashion. See p. 486.
- **Rey del Caribe Hotel** (Cancún; ℰ **998/884-2028**): An ecological oasis in downtown Cancún, this hotel has considered every detail to achieve an organic and environmentally friendly setting. Amid a tropical garden, it's a welcome respite from the party-hearty crowd, with sunny rooms, warm service, yoga and meditation classes, and healthful dining. See p. 541.
- **Cabo Inn** (Cabo San Lucas; ℰ **619/819-2727** in the U.S. or 624/143-0819): This former bordello is the area's best budget inn. Rooms are small but extra clean and invitingly decorated, amenities are generous, and the owner-managers are friendly and helpful. Ideally located, close to town and near the marina, the inn caters to sportfishers. See p. 726.

11 The Best Spa Resorts

- **El Santuario Resort Spa** (Valle de Bravo; ℰ **726/262-9100**): The suites at this spa resort, built into the foot of a quartz mountain, overlook a vast lake. A 1,858-sq.-m (20,000-sq.-ft.) spa offers a wealth of therapies, plus yoga, Pilates, Tai Chi, and meditation classes. See p. 174.
- **Misión Del Sol Resort & Spa** (Cuernavaca; ℰ **777/321-0999** in the U.S.): Mexico's finest spa resort, with every architectural and functional detail designed to soothe body and soul—from meditation rooms to reflexology showers to magnets under your mattress. The sumptuous, full-service spa and fitness center and delicious vegetarian cuisine make this a heavenly base for personal renewal. See p. 182.
- **Paradise Village** (Nuevo Vallarta; ℰ **800/995-5714**): Excellent fitness facilities combined with pampering-yet-affordable spa services make this one of the best all-around spas in Mexico. It actively promotes the beneficial properties of indigenous Mexican spa therapies and natural treatments. See p. 337.
- **Hotel Ixtapan Spa and Golf Resort** (Ixtapan; ℰ **800/638-7950** in the U.S.): In operation since 1939, this resort is a classic, traditional spa with consistently upgraded amenities and services. It's also close to the region's renowned thermal baths. See p. 172.
- **Le Méridien Cancún Resort & Spa** (Cancún; ℰ **800/543-4300** in the U.S.): The Spa del Mar is a state-of-the-art, 1,400 sq. m (15,069-sq.-ft.) facility bordering the brilliant Caribbean. It boasts the most complete spa in the area, with inhalation rooms, saunas, steam, Jacuzzis, cold plunges, Swiss showers, a cascading waterfall whirlpool, and 14 treatment rooms. See p. 537.
- **ME** (Cancún; ℰ **866/436-3542** in the U.S.): The ultrachic Yhi Spa of Cancún's new ME hotel overlooks the ocean and offers body glows and exfoliations, aromatherapy massages, body masks, and wraps—this is a place to indulge yourself until you're convinced that you've landed in heaven. See p. 540.
- **Casa de los Sueños Resort & Spa Zenter** (Isla Mujeres; ℰ **998/877-0651**). This luxury B&B has a small

but well-appointed spa and "Zenter," which is also accessible to nonguests. Highlights include yoga classes, massages, and holistic spa treatments, which take place either indoors or out, in one of the most tranquil places you'll find. See p. 564.

- **The Tides Riviera Maya** (© 800/578-0281 in the U.S. and Canada); **Maroma** (© 866/454-9351 in the U.S.); and **Paraíso de la Bonita** (© 866/751-9175 in the U.S.): The area north of Playa del Carmen, around Puerto Morelos, is a hotbed of spa-resort luxury. These three establishments, in lovely settings, offer guests an impressive range of pampering treatments. See p. 593, 592, and 593, respectively.

- **One&Only Palmilla** (Los Cabos; © 800/637-2226 in the U.S.):

Home to Mexico's most extravagant spa, 13 private treatment rooms set amid gardens offer the most pampering array of services, complemented by a yoga garden, fitness center, and classes designed to put you in touch with—or indulge—your inner self. See "The Best Luxury Hotels" above, and p. 714.

- **Rancho La Puerta** (Baja Norte; © 800/443-7565 in the U.S.): One of Mexico's best-known spas, Rancho La Puerta is a spa-vacation pioneer, having opened its doors (at the time, tent flaps) in 1940. A steady stream of guests returns to this pristine countryside for the constantly expanding facilities, spa services, and outdoor opportunities. See p. 755.

12 The Best Mexican Food & Drink

- **Aguila y Sol** (Mexico City; © 55/5281-8354): One of the world's best Mexican restaurants, the recently expanded Aguila y Sol serves haute Mexican cuisine incorporating indigenous and pre-Hispanic ingredients. Acclaimed chef-owner Martha Ortiz has written many cookbooks, and her magical dishes brim with imagination. See p. 121.

- **La Opera** (Mexico City; © 55/5512-8959): This legendary cantina, in the style of an opulent European cafe, has attracted the capital's most illustrious personalities for decades—Pancho Villa shot a still-visible hole through the roof. In the historic center, it doubles as a restaurant, but it's best as a late afternoon watering hole. See p. 125.

- **El Sacromonte** (Guadalajara; © 33/3825-5447): Various dishes delight the senses with novel tastes and textures and skillful presentation. The

menu describes each dish in Spanish couplets. See p. 282.

- **Adobe Fonda** (Tlaquepaque; © 33/3657-2792): Delicious Mexican food is served inside one of those gorgeous decorative arts stores that line Tlaquepaque's Calle Independencia. The point of departure for the food is with some uncommon Mexican recipes, which are then given sparkling Italian and Argentine accents. See p. 281.

- **El Arrayán** (Puerto Vallarta; © 322/222-7195): The colorful atmosphere may be casual, funky, and fun, but the food is seriously and authentically Mexican. The owner, Carmen, has taken her prime beef filet tacos off the menu—wanting guests to try more traditional Mexican fare—but you can still ask for them. Or, take her cue and order the duck confit, shrimp *pozole,* or homemade ice creams from indigenous fruits. Don't miss her martini made from *raicilla*, Mexico's version of moonshine. See p. 327.

- **El Mirador** (Acapulco, in the Hotel Plaza Las Glorias; ✆ **744/483-1221** in the U.S.): You can enjoy a great margarita at many places in Mexico, but this is the only one that serves them with a view of the spectacular La Quebrada cliff divers. See p. 389.

- **Zibu** (Acapulco; ✆ **744/433-3058**): This chic open-air restaurant combines Mexican and Thai architectural and culinary styles to create one of the nation's best dining experiences, including a breathtaking view of the sea. See p. 398.

- **Los Flamingos** (Acapulco; ✆ **744/ 482-0690**): If you're in Acapulco on a Thursday, you can enjoy a bowl of *pozole,* a traditional hominy and meat stew. Although you'll find it served at lunchtime throughout town, the best place to savor it is at Los Flamingos' cliff-top restaurant. Order a Coco Loco to accompany it, and you're in for a real treat. See p. 396.

- **La Habichuela** (Cancún City; ✆ **998/884-3158**): In Cancún's original downtown, this gourmet seafood restaurant is a romantic retreat off the beaten path. An expert waitstaff attends to the diners seated in the restaurant's lovely garden patio. See p. 546.

- **Mariscos Villa Rica Mocambo** (Veracruz; ✆ **229/922-2113**): Nobody else does seafood the way Veracruz does seafood, and this restaurant is the showcase for the region's cuisine. See p. 522.

- **La Pigua** (Campeche; ✆ **981/811-3365**): Campeche's regional specialty is seafood, and nowhere else will you find seafood like this. Mexican caviar, coconut-battered shrimp, and chilies stuffed with shark are just a few of the specialties. Thinking about La Pigua's *pompano* in a fine green herb sauce makes me want to start checking flight schedules. See p. 665.

- **Don Emiliano** (downtown San José del Cabo; ✆ **624/142-0266**): Don Emiliano wields farm-fresh ingredients laced with Mexican tradition and emerges from the kitchen with modern delights such as stepped-up *chile en nogada* for Día de Independencia and *lemon atole* with candied pumpkin for Day of the Dead. Apart from holiday menus, don't miss the regular menu, which combines the likes of locally made cheeses with roasted tomatillos and dried hibiscus flowers with beef tenderloin. See p. 710.

Mexico in Depth

by David Baird

Despite the long and porous border Mexico shares with the United States, it's a world apart from its northern neighbor. Flying into Mexico City, you'll see what I mean when you catch your first glimpse of the snowcapped volcanoes below and hear their majestic but strange-sounding names—Popocatépetl and Ixtaccihuatl. They're emblematic of this nation's exotic landscape, with its pyramids and cenotes, mountains and jungles, where ancient civilizations have left behind a wealth of ruins, place names that twist the tongue, and more.

Millions of native Mexicans still speak their pre-Columbian languages—such as Náhuatl (Aztec), Maya, Zapotec, and nearly 60 others—and their customs and beliefs have shaped a national culture distinct from any other in the Spanish-speaking world. The past is inescapable even in sprawling cities such as the capital, which buzzes with 21st-century innovation and technology, and supports a sophisticated and vibrant film, music, and visual arts culture that remains uniquely Mexican, even as it absorbs influences from around the globe.

1 Mexico Today

Mexico stretches nearly 3,200km (1,984 miles) from east to west and more than 1,600km (1,000 miles) north to south. Only one-fifth the size of the United States, it has more coastline, and it encompasses trackless deserts in the north, dense jungles in the south, the mountain ranges that crisscross the central highlands, and lush seacoast and beaches along the Pacific Ocean and the Caribbean Sea.

Mexico has more than 104 million inhabitants, and 19 million of them live in greater Mexico City. Mexico's economy is the 14th largest on earth, and it has been growing over the last 5 years from between 2.6% to 3%.

By most measures, the gap between rich and poor has widened in the last 30 years. Cycles of boom-and-bust weighed more heavily on the poor than the rich.

The middle class has also had a rough ride, especially during the monetary crisis and recession of the mid-1990s. Wages for the working class have not kept pace with inflation.

In the face of economic inequality, Mexican society remains amazingly resilient and cohesive—due in no small part to the way Mexicans live. They place a high value on family and friends, social gatherings, and living in the present. In Mexico, there is always time to meet with friends for a drink or a cup of coffee or to attend a family get-together. The many spirited public celebrations that Mexico is famous for are simply another manifestation of this attitude.

WHAT'S YOUR HURRY?

American and English travelers have often observed that Mexicans have a

Did You Know?

Mexico is the largest Spanish-speaking country in the world. In addition to Spanish, 62 different native languages are actively spoken.

different concept of time, and that life in Mexico moves at a slower pace. This is true, and an imperfect appreciation of this difference can lead to misunderstandings.

For instance, on several occasions, Mexican acquaintances have asked me why Americans grin all the time. At first, I wasn't sure what to make of the question, and only gradually came to appreciate what was at issue. As the pace of life for Americans, Canadians, and others has quickened, they have come to skip some of the niceties of social interaction. When walking into a store, many Americans simply smile at a clerk and launch right into a question or request. The smile, in effect, replaces the greeting. In Mexico, it doesn't work that way, and this American manner of greeting is misinterpreted. After all, a smile out of context can be ambiguous; it can convey amusement, smugness, or superiority. A Mexican must

at least say *"¡Buenos días!"* or its equivalent to show proper respect. And when an individual meets with a group, he will greet each person separately, which can take quite a while. For us, the polite thing would be to minimize our interruption and extend a general greeting to all.

Mexicans, like most people, will consciously or subconsciously make quick judgments about individuals they meet. Most divide the world into the *bien educado* (well raised and cultured) and the *mal educado* (poorly raised). Unfortunately, many visitors are reluctant to try out their Spanish, preferring to keep exchanges to a minimum. Don't do this. To be categorized as a foreigner isn't a big deal. What's important in Mexico is to be categorized as one of the cultured foreigners. This makes it easier to get the attention of waiters, hotel desk clerks, and even people on the street.

2 Looking Back at Mexico

PRE-HISPANIC MEXICANS

The earliest "Mexicans" were Stone Age hunter-gatherers from the north, descendants of a race that probably crossed the Bering Strait and reached North America around 12,000 B.C. They arrived in what is now Mexico by 10,000 B.C. Sometime between 5200 and 1500 B.C., in what is known as the **Archaic period,** they began practicing agriculture and domesticating animals.

THE OLMECS & MAYA (THE PRE-CLASSIC PERIOD 1500 B.C.–A.D. 300)

Eventually, agriculture improved and could support large communities and free some of the population from agricultural

work. A civilization emerged that we call the **Olmec**—an enigmatic people who settled the lower Gulf Coast in what is now Tabasco and Veracruz. Anthropologists regard them as the mother culture of Mesoamerica, because they established a cultural pattern for later civilizations.

The Olmec are best known for the colossal stone heads they carved. These sculptures were immense projects: The basalt stone from which they came was mined miles inland and transported to the Olmec cities on the coast, probably by river rafts. The heads share a rounded, baby-faced look, marked by the peculiar "jaguar mouth"—a high-arched lip that's common in Olmec sculpture. If you're visiting Villahermosa, Tabasco, or Xalapa, Veracruz, you can see several examples of these sculptures.

After the Olmec cities began declining, other civilizations rose to the south and north of the Olmec heartland. The **Maya** civilization developed around 500 B.C., in the late pre-Classic period. North of the Valley of Mexico, a city we know as **Teotihuacán** also began its long life. In the valley of Oaxaca, the construction of the city of **Monte Albán** began. These cultures would shape the next age of Mesoamerica.

TEOTIHUACAN, MONTE ALBAN & PALENQUE: THE CLASSIC PERIOD (A.D. 300–900)

The rise and fall of these three centers of civilization defines this period—the heyday of pre-Columbian Mesoamerican culture and art. These include the pyramids and palaces in Teotihuacán; the ceremonial center of Monte Albán; and the temple complexes and pyramids of Palenque and Calakmul.

The inhabitants of **Teotihuacán** (100 B.C.–A.D. 700), near present-day Mexico City, built a city that is thought to have had 200,000 inhabitants or more. It was well-organized, covering 30 sq. km (12 sq. miles), and built on a grid with streams channeled to follow the city's plan.

Farther south, the **Zapotec,** influenced by the Olmec, raised an impressive civilization in the Oaxaca region. Their principal cities were **Monte Albán,** inhabited by an elite class of merchants and artisans, and **Mitla,** reserved for the high priests.

TOLTECS & AZTEC INVASIONS: THE POST-CLASSIC PERIOD (A.D. 900–1521)

War raged during this period. Social development was impressive but lacked the extensive trade networks and cultural exchanges of the earlier age. In central Mexico, the **Toltec** established their capital at Tula in the 10th century. They revered a god known as **Tezcatlipoca,** or "smoking mirror," who later became an Aztec god. The Toltec maintained a large military class divided into orders symbolized by animals. At its height, Tula may have had 40,000 people, and its influence spread across Mesoamerica. By the 13th century, however, the Toltec had exhausted themselves, probably in civil wars and in battles with northern invaders.

The **Aztec** were the most warlike of those invaders. They first served as mercenaries for established cities in the valley of Mexico, and so acquired an unwanted, marshy piece of land in the middle of Lake Texcoco for their settlement. It eventually grew into the island city of Tenochtitlán. Through aggressive diplomacy and military action, the Aztec soon conquered central Mexico and extended their rule east to the Gulf Coast and south to the valley of Oaxaca.

During this later period, the Maya civilization flourished in northern Yucatán,

Yeah, but What About Thirty Days Hath September?

The Olmec developed the basic calendar used throughout the region and established the predominance of a 52-year cycle, which they used to schedule the construction and enlargement of pyramids. They also established principles of urban layout and architecture and originated the cult of the jaguar and the sacredness of jade. They may have invented the sacred ritual of "the ball game" as well—a universal element of Mesoamerican culture.

It's Just a Game

The ancient Maya played a game with a solid rubber ball that held great importance for them. Go to any Maya city and you can view the ball courts where it was played (Bonampak being a rare exception). These are readily identifiable by their I-shaped layout with sloping walls in the center. The Maya weren't the only ones to play this game—ball courts have been found as far south as Nicaragua and as far north as Arizona.

We know little about the details of the game or its rules. What we do know comes from ancient depictions of the game, early accounts by the Spanish, and from the Maya epic, the Popol Vuh. We know that the ball was heavy and could inflict injury. The players wore thick cloth padding and protective gear. They played in teams of between 2 and 10 members, and the object was to get the ball to pass through a stone ring or other goal using mainly the hips.

We also know that the game was part sport and part religious ritual that, at times, involved human sacrifice, but we're not sure who was sacrificed—the winners, the losers, or perhaps prisoners of war who were allowed to play the game one last time before losing their heads. We know that the game was symbolically the affirmation of a cosmological belief system. In the Popol Vuh, the hero twins, Hunahpu and Xbalanque, challenge the lords of the underworld to a game, part of which they play with the head of one of the twins. Eventually the twins win the game and are allowed to return to the world of the living. Playing the game might have been one of the ways to cheat the underworld.

especially in cities such as Chichén Itzá and Uxmal.

CORTEZ, MOCTEZUMA & THE SPANISH CONQUEST

In 1517, the first Spaniards arrived in what is today known as Mexico and skirmished with Maya Indians off the coast of the Yucatán Peninsula. One of the fledgling expeditions ended in shipwreck, stranding several Spaniards as prisoners of the Maya. The Spanish sent out another expedition, under the command of **Hernán Cortez,** which landed on Cozumel in February 1519. Cortez inquired about the interior's gold and riches, and the coastal Maya were happy to describe the wealthy splendor of the Aztec empire in central Mexico. Cortez promptly disobeyed his superior, the

governor of Cuba, and sailed into the Gulf of Mexico, landing at what is now Veracruz.

Cortez arrived when the Aztec empire was at the height of its wealth and power. **Moctezuma II** ruled over the central and southern highlands and extracted tribute from lowland peoples. His greatest temples were plated with gold and encrusted with the blood of sacrificial captives. Moctezuma was a fool, a mystic, and a coward of sorts. Despite his wealth and military power, he dithered in Tenochtitlán, sending messengers with gifts and suggestions that Cortez leave. Meanwhile, Cortez blustered and negotiated his way into the highlands, cloaking his intentions. Moctezuma, terrified by the Spaniard's military tactics and technology, convinced himself that Cortez was the god Quetzalcoatl making his long-awaited return. By the time the Spaniards arrived in the Aztec capital, Cortez had gained some ascendancy over the lesser Indian states that were resentful tributaries to the Aztec. In November 1519, Cortez confronted Moctezuma and took him hostage in an effort to leverage control of the empire.

In the middle of Cortez's dangerous game of manipulation, another Spanish expedition arrived with orders to end Cortez's authority over the mission. Cortez hastened to meet the rival's force and persuade them to join his own. In the meantime, the Aztec chased the garrison out of Tenochtitlán, and either they or the Spaniards killed Moctezuma. For the next year and a half, Cortez laid siege to Tenochtitlán, with the help of rival Indians and smallpox, to which the Indians had no resistance. When the Aztec capital finally fell, all of central Mexico lay at the feet of the conquistadors.

The Conquest started as a pirate expedition by Cortez and his men, unauthorized by the Spanish crown or its governor in Cuba. The Spanish king legitimized Cortez, following his victory over the Aztec, and ordered this new colony (to be called New Spain), to convert to Christianity. Guatemala and Honduras were explored and conquered, and by 1540, the territory of New Spain included possessions from Vancouver to Panama. In the 2 centuries that followed, Franciscan and Augustinian friars converted millions of Indians to Christianity, and the Spanish lords built huge feudal estates on which the Indian farmers were little more than serfs. The silver and gold that Cortez looted made Spain the richest country in Europe.

THE RISE OF MEXICO CITY & SPANISH COLONIALISM

Hernán Cortez set about building a new city upon the ruins of the old Aztec capital. To accomplish this, he collected from the Indians the tributes they once paid to the Aztec emperor, often in the form of manual labor. This exploitative arrangement became the basis for the construction of the new colony, but it backfired over the next century, as the workforce perished from diseases imported by the Spaniards.

Cortez soon returned to Spain and was replaced by a governing council, and, later, the office of viceroy. Over the 3 centuries of the colonial period, 61 viceroys governed Mexico. Spain became rich from New World gold and silver, chiseled out by Indian labor. The colonial elite built lavish homes in Mexico City and in the countryside. They filled their homes with ornate furniture, had many servants, and adorned themselves in imported velvets, satins, and jewels.

A new class system emerged. Those born in Spain (*peninsulares*) considered themselves superior to the Spanish born in Mexico (*criollos*). And, below the latter, were the other races and the *castas* (mixtures of Spanish, Indian, and African).

Discontent with Spain simmered over social and political issues: taxes, royal monopolies, the bureaucracy, the superior position of *peninsulares* over *criollos,* and restrictions on commerce with Spain and other countries. In 1808, Napoleon invaded Spain and crowned his brother, Joseph, king in place of Charles IV. To many in Mexico, allegiance to France was out of the question; discontent escalated into revolt.

HIDALGO, JUAREZ & MEXICO'S INDEPENDENCE

The rebellion began in 1810, when **Father Miguel Hidalgo** gave the *grito,* a cry for independence, from his church in the town of Dolores, Guanajuato. The uprising soon became a full-fledged revolution, as Hidalgo and Ignacio Allende gathered an "army" of citizens and threatened Mexico City. Although Hidalgo ultimately failed and was executed, he is honored as "the Father of Mexican Independence." Another priest, José María Morelos, kept the revolt alive with several successful campaigns through 1815, when he, too, was captured and executed.

After the death of Morelos, prospects for independence were rather dim until the Spanish king who replaced Joseph Bonaparte decided to make social reforms in the colonies. This convinced the conservative powers in Mexico that they didn't need Spain after all. With their tacit approval, Agustín de Iturbide, then commander of royalist forces, changed sides and declared Mexico independent and himself emperor. Before long, however, internal dissension brought about the fall of the emperor, and Mexico was proclaimed a republic.

Political instability engulfed the young republic and Mexico waged a disastrous war with the U.S., losing half its territory. A central figure was **Antonio López de Santa Anna,** who assumed the leadership of his country no fewer than 11 times and was flexible enough in those volatile days to portray himself variously as a liberal, a conservative, a federalist, and a centralist. But, by 1855, he was finally left without a political comeback and ended his days in Venezuela.

Political instability persisted, and the conservative forces, with some encouragement from Napoleon III, hit upon the idea of inviting in a Habsburg to regain control (as if that strategy had ever worked for Spain). They found a willing volunteer in Archduke Maximilian of Austria, who accepted the position of Mexican emperor with the support of French troops. The ragtag Mexican forces defeated the French force—a modern, well-equipped army—in a battle near Puebla (now celebrated annually as **Cinco de Mayo**). A second attempt was more successful, and Ferdinand Maximilian Joseph of Habsburg became emperor. After 3 years of civil war, the French were finally induced to abandon the emperor's cause; Maximilian was captured and executed by a firing squad near Querétaro in 1867. His adversary and successor (as president of Mexico) was **Benito Juárez,** a Zapotec Indian lawyer and one of the

A Sticky Habit

Cigar smoking and gum chewing are two pleasures that we have the Maya to thank for, and, of the two, the latter is the more innocuous. Gum comes from the sap of a species of zapote tree that grows in the Yucatán and Guatemala. Chewing causes it to release natural sugars and a mild, agreeable taste. From the Maya, the habit of chewing gum spread to other cultures and eventually to the non-Indian population. In the second half of the 19th century, a Mexican (said to have been General Santa Ana) introduced gum to the American Thomas Adams, who realized that it could be sweetened further and given other flavors. He brought the idea to the U.S. and marketed chewing gum with great success. Chemists have since figured out how to synthesize the gum, but the sap is still collected in parts of the Yucatán and Guatemala for making natural chewing gum. *Chicle* is the Spanish word originally from the Nahuatl (Aztec) *tzictli,* and those who live in the forest and collect the sap are called *chicleros.* Because the tree takes so long to produce more sap, there is no way to cultivate the tree commercially, so it is still collected in the wild.

great heroes of Mexican history. Juárez did his best to unify and strengthen his country before dying of a heart attack in 1872; his impact on Mexico's future was profound, and his plans and visions bore fruit for decades.

ZAPATA, PANCHO VILLA & THE MEXICAN REVOLUTION

A few years after Juárez's death, one of his generals, **Porfirio Díaz,** assumed power in a coup. He ruled Mexico from 1877 to 1911, a period now called the "Porfiriato." He stayed in power by imposing repressive measures and courting the favor of powerful nations. Generous in his dealings with foreign investors, Díaz became the archetypal *entreguista* (one who sells out his country for private gain). With foreign investment came the concentration of great wealth in few hands, and social conditions worsened.

In 1910, Francisco Madero called for armed rebellion, which became the **Mexican Revolution** (La Revolución in Mexico; the revolution against Spain is the Guerra de Independencia). Díaz was sent into exile; while in London, he became a celebrity at the age of 81, when he jumped into the Thames to save a drowning boy. He is buried in Paris. Madero became president but was promptly betrayed and executed by **Victoriano Huerta.** Those who had answered Madero's call responded again—to the great peasant hero **Emiliano Zapata** in the south, and to the seemingly invincible **Pancho Villa** in the central north, flanked by Alvaro Obregón and Venustiano Carranza. They eventually expelled Huerta and began hashing out a new constitution.

For the next few years, the revolutionaries Carranza, Obregón, and Villa fought among themselves; Zapata stayed out of the feuds and did not seek national power, though he fought hard for land for the peasants. Then president Carranza betrayed and assassinated Zapata.

Obregón finally consolidated power and likely had Carranza assassinated. He, in turn, was assassinated, when he tried to break a tenet of the Revolution—no reelection. His successor, Plutarco Elias Calles, learned this lesson well, installing one puppet president after another, until **Lázaro Cárdenas** exiled him.

Until Cárdenas's election in 1934, the outcome of the revolution remained in doubt. There had been some land redistribution, but other measures took a back seat to political expediency. Cárdenas changed that. He implemented massive redistribution of land and nationalized the oil industry. He instituted many reforms and gave shape to the ruling political party (now the **Partido Revolucionario Institucional,** or PRI) by bringing a broad representation of Mexican society under its banner and establishing mechanisms for consensus building. Most Mexicans practically canonize Cárdenas.

MODERN MEXICO

The presidents who followed were noted more for graft than for leadership. The party's base narrowed as the reform-minded were marginalized. Economic progress, largely in the form of big development projects, became the PRI's main basis for legitimacy. In 1968, the government violently repressed a **student protest** in the Tlatelolco section of Mexico City and killed an unknown number of citizens. Though the PRI maintained its grip on power, it lost all semblance of being a progressive party.

In 1985, a devastating **earthquake in Mexico City** brought down many of the government's new, supposedly earthquake-proof buildings, exposing shoddy construction and the widespread government corruption that fostered it. The government's handling of the relief efforts also drew heavy criticism.

In 1994, a political and military **uprising in Chiapas** and the occupation of

¡Hola!

The most important advice I can offer travelers is this: Offer a proper greeting when addressing Mexicans. Don't try to abbreviate social intercourse. Mexican culture places a higher value on proper social form than on saving time.

San Cristobal de las Casas focused world attention on Mexico's great social problems. A new political force, the Ejército Zapatista de Liberación Nacional, or EZLN (Zapatista National Liberation Army), skillfully publicized the plight of the peasant.

In the years that followed, opposition political parties grew in power and legitimacy. Facing pressure and scrutiny from national and international organizations, and widespread public discontent, the PRI began to concede defeat in state and congressional elections throughout the '90s. Party reformers were able to make changes over the objections of many hard-liners. They instituted a partial system of primary elections to give greater voice to the rank and file. This made for successful campaigns in several states, but in other states the old-style party leaders held on to their right to appoint the official party candidate. Internal strife reached a climax with the assassination of the party's presidential candidate, Luis Donaldo Colosio. A quick compromise between different party factions resulted in the nomination of **Ernesto Zedillo** for president. Once in power, Zedillo proved to be a reformer. Over his 6-year term, he steadily led the country toward open and fair elections by strengthening the electoral process, gaining the public's confidence, and getting his own party to accept the possibility of losing power.

VICENTE FOX

In the presidential elections of 2000, **Vicente Fox,** candidate for the Partido Acción Nacional (National Action Party, or PAN), won by a landslide. It couldn't have been otherwise. For many voters, this election was an experiment to see if their votes would really count. They voted for the most prominent opposition candidate to see if, in fact, he would be allowed to assume the presidency. For Mexicans, a government under the PRI was all that they had ever known.

During Fox's presidency, the three main political parties had to adjust to the new realty of power sharing. The old government party, the PRI, still had a large infrastructure for getting out the vote and still controlled the local governments of several states. Fox's center-right PAN had control of the presidency and the most seats in the legislature, while the center-left PRD (Partido de la Revolución Democrática, or Democratic Revolution Party) controlled the city government of Mexico City as well as a few southern states. Many observers anticipated gridlock. But the three parties, to their credit, handled the transition better than expected.

But by the end of Fox's term, the situation turned ugly, and Mexico's experiment with pluralistic democracy faced a crisis. The Fox administration showed no finesse in dealing with the legislature and failed to pass most of its initiatives. In the off-year elections of 2004, PAN lost many seats in the legislature and several governorships.

The main beneficiary was the PRI, which looked to be in an excellent position for the presidential election of 2006, but not for long. In 2005, the party's leader, Roberto Madrazo, sought to become the party's nominee without going through primary elections. His power plays worked to make him the nominee but splintered the party badly and reminded voters of the old days when their votes didn't count for anything.

MAYOR LOPEZ OBRADOR

Meanwhile, the PRD's choice of nominee seemed inevitable. Mexico City mayor **Andrés Manuel López Obrador** (AMLO for short) was, without question, the most important figure in the party. He was tremendously popular for creating programs such as a pension for the city's elderly. And his popularity soared when he became the target of political dirty tricks to make him ineligible to run for president. He was genuinely interested in helping the poor, but there was something unsettling about the way he would take political opposition personally. He dismissed a large demonstration in Mexico City against kidnapping and other crimes as the work of his political enemies, rather than local citizens expressing the need to feel safe in their own city.

FELIPE CALDERON

The PAN ended up having the only meaningful primary elections, which resulted in an underdog candidate, **Felipe Calderón,** becoming the party nominee. He is a social conservative and a devout Catholic who believes in privatization and market forces.

A bitter campaign between AMLO and Calderón, followed by an incredibly close election in the summer of 2006, made for a serious crisis. So close was the election that it took over a month for the elections tribunal to declare Calderón the winner. AMLO refused to recognize the verdict and launched a protest that lasted another month. Supporters in his party even tried to physically prevent Calderón from taking office by occupying the legislative chambers. All of this diminished AMLO's popularity.

The crisis shows that Mexico must continue to strengthen its political institutions. PAN now has the most seats in the legislature, but not a majority. To pass legislation it will need to compromise with the other parties. The PRD has the second highest number of seats. It must put AMLO behind it if it doesn't want to be marginalized. And the PRI must learn from its mistakes and move towards democracy and transparency. But at the moment, its legislators enjoy the role of powerbrokers between the government and a powerful opposition party. It will be the key player in deciding what gets accomplished in the next few years.

DRUGS & OTHER BORDER ISSUES

Crime in Mexico has been on the rise. Powerful drug cartels, waging war on each other and on local law enforcement, killed over 2,500 people last year. In shoot-outs with local police, they have demonstrated superior firepower, and it's no secret where the weaponry is coming from. Calderón's first act as president was to send troops to the state of Michoacán. Shortly after that, he sent the army into

Ancient Mexican Treats
Where would we be without peanuts, tomatoes, and chocolate? These and the following products came to the New World from Mexico.

chocolate	vanilla
tomatoes	tobacco (and cigars)
peanuts	avocado
corn	chili peppers
chewing gum	papaya

five other areas, mostly border states. This was a last option for the government because soldiers aren't police and don't tread lightly around the public. It appears that some of these efforts are working. The government's intelligence has improved, as it has been able to identify many officials who have been tipping off the cartels. There have been some major operations and arrests, but victory is still somewhere in the distant future.

Most of the conflict is confined to particular areas of the country, border towns and remote rural areas. It plays itself out unseen by most Mexicans except for news reports and headlines. Travelers, too, will not see signs of the struggle except in places where the flows of tourists and drugs intersect—mostly along the border, especially in Tijuana and the border towns around Nuevo Laredo and Matamoros. Places in the interior of the country are less likely to experience drug violence than are cities in the U.S., and beach resorts, too, are unlikely scenes for shoot-outs between the army and the cartels. See p. 68 in chapter 3 for safety-related information.

Mexico's political classes view emigration to the U.S. as a pressure valve for social tension. They are insistent that the U.S. sit down and negotiate a common border policy. Whatever the U.S. does, it will need to address the other border issues: the flow of drugs northward into the U.S. and the flow of weapons southward into Mexico.

Another issue that riles people up on both sides of the border is the North American Free Trade Agreement (NAFTA). I am one critic. As a traveler, I don't look favorably on globalization in general, but the specific problems I see in this agreement are mainly the way it favors large companies at the expense of smaller ones. I've witnessed the demise of several small manufacturing and agricultural producers on both sides of the border. They were either eaten up by large corporations wanting a beachhead in the new market, or they were driven out of business by unfair pricing. This has led to a broad and general impoverishment of both societies, which affects both economics and quality of life issues.

3 Eating & Drinking in Mexico

Mexican food differs quite dramatically from what is frequently served under that name in the United States. Thus for many travelers, Mexico will be new and exciting culinary territory. Even grizzled veterans will be pleasantly surprised by the wide variation in specialties and traditions from region to region.

Despite regional differences, some generalizations can be made. Mexican food usually isn't spicy-hot or piquant when it arrives at the table (though many dishes

The Red & the Black

An invisible "bean line" divides Mexico: It starts at the Gulf Coast in the southern part of the state of Tamaulipas and moves inland through the eastern quarter of San Luis Potosí and most of the state of Hidalgo, then straight through Mexico City and Morelos and into Guerrero, where it curves slightly westward to the Pacific. To the north and west of this line, the red or pink bean known as the *flor de mayo* is the staple food; to the south and east, the standard is the black bean.

Tequila Sun Rising

In the past 15 years, both the quality and the popularity of tequila have sky-rocketed. The makers of tequila are still, with one exception, based in the state of Jalisco. They have formed an association to establish standards for labeling and denomination. The best tequilas are invariably 100% agave, which means that they were made with a set minimum of sugar to prime the fermentation process. These tequilas come in three categories based on how they were stored: *blanco, reposado,* and *añejo. Blanco* is white Tequila aged very little, usually in steel vats. *Reposado* (reposed) is aged in wooden casks for between 2 months and a year. And *añejo* (aged) has been stored in oak barrels for at least a year.

must have a certain amount of piquancy, and some home cooking can be very spicy, depending on a family's or chef's tastes). The *picante* flavor is added with chiles and salsas after the food is served; you'll never see a table in Mexico without one or both of these condiments. Mexicans don't drown their cooking in cheese and sour cream, a la Tex-Mex, and they use a greater variety of ingredients than most people expect. But the basis of Mexican food is simple—tortillas, beans, chiles, squash, and tomatoes—the same as it was centuries ago before the arrival of the Europeans.

For additional food terms, see Appendix B: Survival Spanish.

THE STAPLES

TORTILLAS Traditional tortillas are made from corn that's been cooked in water and lime, then ground into *masa* (a grainy dough), patted and pressed into thin cakes, and cooked on a hot griddle known as a *comal.* In many households, the tortilla takes the place of fork and spoon; Mexicans merely tear them into wedge-shaped pieces, which they use to scoop up their food. Restaurants often serve bread rather than tortillas because it's easier, but you can always ask for tortillas. A more recent invention from northern Mexico is the flour tortilla.

ENCHILADAS The tortilla is the basis of several Mexican dishes, but the

most famous of these is the enchilada. The original name for this dish would have been *tortilla enchilada,* which means a tortilla dipped in very hot oil and then a chile sauce. In like manner, there's the *entomatada* (tortilla dipped in a tomato sauce) and the *enfrijolada* (in a bean sauce). The enchilada began as a very simple dish: A tortilla is dipped in chile sauce (usually with ancho chile) and then into very hot oil, then quickly folded or rolled on a plate and sprinkled with chopped onions and a little *queso cotija* (crumbly white cheese) and served with a little fried potatoes and carrots. You can get this basic enchilada in food stands across the country. I love them, and if you come across them in your travels, try them. In restaurants you get the more elaborate enchilada, with different fillings of cheese, chicken, pork, or even seafood, and sometimes prepared as a casserole.

TACOS For Mexicans, the taco is the quintessential fast food, and the taco stand *(taquería)* is a ubiquitous sight. A taco is anything folded or rolled into a tortilla, and sometimes a double tortilla. The tortilla can be served either soft or fried. *Flautas* and quesadillas (except in Mexico City, where they are something quite different) are species of tacos.

FRIJOLES In private households, pink or black beans are served at least once a day, and among the working class and

Food Hygiene

Many travelers to Mexico ask about the safety of beverages with ice. The truth is that most restaurants and bars buy ice made from purified water. This ice is made by the same kind of machinery all across Mexico. It produces ice cubes that have a rough cylindrical shape with a hollow center. They're easy to spot in your glass and are a sign that the ice is hygienic. Plain block ice carries no such guarantee. Likewise, almost all restaurants that cater to middle-class Mexicans use filtered water and disinfect vegetables, but street vendors and market stalls may not. I do eat in the market and in the street, but I'm careful to find places and pick foods that are relatively safe.

peasantry, with every meal if the family can afford it. Mexicans almost always prepare beans with a minimum of condiments, usually just a little onion and garlic and a pinch of herbs. Beans are to be a contrast to the heavily spiced foods in a meal. Sometimes they are served at the end of a meal with a little Mexican-style sour cream.

Mexicans often fry leftover beans and serve them on the side as *frijoles refritos*. *Refritos* is often translated as "refried," but this is a misnomer—the beans are fried only once. The prefix *re* means "well" (as in "thoroughly"), so a proper translation would be "well-fried beans."

TAMALES You make a *tamal* by mixing corn masa with a little lard, beating the batter, adding one of several fillings—meats flavored with chiles—then wrapping it in a corn husk or in the leaf of a banana or other plant, and steaming it. Every region in Mexico has its own traditional way of making tamales. In some places, a single tamal can be big enough to feed a family; while in others, they are barely three inches long and only about an inch thick.

CHILES There are many kinds of hot peppers, and Mexicans call each of them by one name when they're fresh and another when they're dried. Some are blazing hot with little flavor; some are mild but have a rich, complex flavor. They can be pickled, smoked, stuffed, or stewed.

DRINKS

All over Mexico, you'll find shops selling *licuados*—excellent and refreshing juices and smoothies made from several kinds of tropical fruit. You'll also come across *aguas frescas*—water flavored with hibiscus, melon, tamarind, or lime. Soft drinks come in more flavors than in any other country I know. Pepsi and Coca-Cola taste the way they did in the United States years ago, before the makers started adding corn syrup.

The coffee is generally good, and **hot chocolate** is a traditional drink, as is *atole*—a hot, corn-based beverage that can be sweet or bitter.

Of course, Mexico has a proud and lucrative **beer**-brewing tradition. A lesser-known brewed beverage is *pulque,* a pre-Hispanic drink made of the fermented juice of a few species of maguey or agave. Mostly you find it for sale in *pulquerías* in central Mexico. It is an acquired taste, and not every gringo acquires it. **Mezcal** and **tequila** also come from the agave. Tequila is a variety of mezcal produced from the *a. tequilana* species of agave in and around the area of Tequila, in the state of Jalisco. Mezcal comes from various parts of Mexico and from different varieties of agave. The distilling process is usually much less sophisticated than that of tequila, and, with its stronger smell and taste, mezcal is much more easily detected on the drinker's breath. In some places, such as Oaxaca, it comes with a worm in the bottle; you are supposed to eat the worm after polishing off the mezcal. But for those teetotalers out there who are interested in just the worm, I have good news—you can find these worms for sale in Mexican markets when in season. ¡Salud!

MARKET & RESTAURANT TYPES

I feel compelled to debunk the prevailing myth that the cheapest place to eat in Mexico is in the market. Actually, this is rarely the case. You can usually find food at a better price without going more than 2 blocks out of your way. Why? Food stalls in the marketplace pay high rents; they have a near-captive clientele of market vendors and truckers; and they get a lot of business from many Mexicans for whom eating in the market is a traditional way of affirming their culture.

On the other side of the spectrum, avoid eating at those inviting sidewalk restaurants that you see beneath the stone archways that border the main plazas. These places usually cater to tourists and don't need to count on getting any return business. But they are great for getting a coffee or beer and watching the world turn.

In most nonresort towns, there are always one or two restaurants (sometimes it's a coffee shop) that are social centers for a large group of established patrons. These establishments over time become virtual institutions, and change comes very slowly to them. The food is usually good standard fare, cooked as it was 20 years ago, and the decor is simple. The patrons have known each other and the staff for years, and the *charla* (banter), gestures, and greetings are friendly, open, and unaffected. If you're curious about Mexican culture, these are fun places to eat in and observe the goings-on.

During your trip you're going to see many *taquerías* (**taco joints**). These are generally small places with a counter or a few tables set around the cooking area; you get to see exactly how they make their tacos before deciding whether to order. Most tacos come with a little chopped onion and cilantro, but not with tomato and lettuce. Find one that seems popular with the locals and where the cook performs with brio (a good sign of

---

Dining Service Tips

- For the main meal of the day, many restaurants offer a multicourse blue-plate special called *comida corrida* or *menú del día*. This is the most inexpensive way to get a full dinner.
- In Mexico you need to **ask for your check**; it is considered inhospitable to present a check to someone who hasn't requested it. If you're in a hurry, ask for the check when your food arrives.
- Tips are about the same as in the U.S. You'll sometimes find a 15% value-added tax on restaurant meals, which shows up on the bill as "IVA." This is effectively the tip—a boon to arithmetically challenged tippers.
- To **summon the waiter**, wave or raise your hand, but don't motion with your index finger, which is a demeaning gesture that may even cause the waiter to ignore you. Or if it's the check you want, you can motion to the waiter from across the room using the universal pretend-like-you're-writing gesture.

pride in the product). Sometimes, there will be a woman making the tortillas right there (or working the masa into *gorditas* or *sopes* if these are also served). You will never see men doing this—this is perhaps the strictest gender division in Mexican society. Men do all other cooking and kitchen tasks, and work with already-made tortillas, but will never be found working *masa.*

4 The Regions in Brief

BAJA CALIFORNIA

A peninsula longer than Italy, Baja stretches 1,402km (869 miles) from its border with California, at Mexico's northernmost city of **Tijuana,** to **Cabo San Lucas** at its southern tip. On one side is the Pacific Ocean; on the other, the **Sea of Cortez.** Volcanic uplifting created the craggy desertscape you see today. Culturally and geographically, Baja sits apart from mainland Mexico, and it remained isolated for centuries. The southern tip of Baja has evolved into a vacation haven, availing golf, fishing, diving, and whale-watching opportunities in beautiful settings and at posh resorts. Mid-Baja is known more for its ecological excursions.

THE COPPER CANYON

The Copper Canyon is the common name for a region of roughly 16,800 sq. km (6,487 sq. miles) in the northern state of Chihuahua, midway between the state's capital city and the Pacific coast. Here you'll find a network of canyons deeply etched into the volcanic rock of the **Sierra Tarahumara.** The dramatic canyon area is one of those rare places where one can sense the earth's creation. To get there, you ride the famous Chihuahua al Pacífico railroad. It starts at the seaport of Topolobampo, outside **Los Mochis,** and runs 624km (387 miles) to **Chihuahua City,** climbing to 2,425m (7,954 ft.) above sea level. The train skirts the edge of more than 20 canyons. Tours can accommodate any kind of traveler, from primitive camper to modern hotel patron.

THE PACIFIC COAST

The Pacific coast has virtually every kind of beach and landscape imaginable. You can stay in modern resorts that offer inexhaustible arrays of amenities and activities, from sailing to scuba diving to golf, capped off by exuberant nightlife. Or you can stay in a sleepy coastal town where the scenery abounds with rustic charm, life is slower, and the beaches are quieter. By **Mazatlán,** the northern desert disappears, replaced by tropical vegetation and plantations of coconut and other fruit. At **Puerto Vallarta,** mountains covered in tropical forests meet the sea. For many, this is the most appealing place on the coast. From here, it's a 5-hour car ride inland to **Guadalajara,** the most Mexican of cities and a superb place to shop. Tropical forests interspersed with banana, mango, and coconut palm plantations cover the coast from Puerto Vallarta to **Manzanillo.** Well south of Manzanillo, in the state of Guerrero, are the beach towns **Zihuatanejo** and **Ixtapa.** Tree-covered mountains remain around **Acapulco,** though hillside development has marred them. From Acapulco, a road leads inland to **Taxco,** a mountainside colonial city famed for its hundreds of silver shops. Farther south along the coast are the beach villages of **Puerto Escondido** and

Map Pointer

To locate these regions, see p. 8 for the map of Mexico.

Portals to the Underworld

The Yucatán Peninsula is a flat slab of limestone that millions of years ago absorbed the force of the giant meteor thought to have extinguished the dinosaurs. The impact sent shock waves through the brittle limestone, fracturing it throughout, creating an immense network of fissures that drain rainwater away from the surface. When driving through northern and central Yucatán, you'll notice no bridges, rivers, or watercourses. The vast subterranean basin, which stretches for miles across the peninsula, is invisible but for the area's many cenotes—sinkholes or natural wells that don't exist outside the peninsula. Many are perfectly round vertical shafts that look like nothing else in nature; others are in caverns that retain a partial roof, often perforated by tree roots. To the Maya, they were passageways to the underworld. Indeed, they look sacred: Quiet, dark, and cool, they are the opposite of the warm, bright world outside.

Puerto Angel, and beyond them, the nine gorgeous bays of **Huatulco.**

THE NORTH-CENTRAL REGION

This funnel-shaped region stretches from the northern border with Texas and New Mexico to **Mexico City** and includes the beautiful colonial **silver cities.** Most of this territory lies in the vast Chihuahua/Coahuila desert of the north between the two great **Sierra Madre ranges,** which meet in the south to form the central valley of Mexico. The colonial cities nestle in the mountains not far north and west of Mexico City.

THE GULF COAST

This region is probably Mexico's least known, yet the entire coast, which includes the long, skinny state of Veracruz, holds marvelous pockets of scenery and culture. Highway 180 leads from **Matamoros** at the Texas border and offers a few glimpses of the Gulf of Mexico. Highlights of this region are the ruins of **El Tajín,** near the mountain village of Papantla; the mountain town of **Xalapa,** Veracruz's capital and home of the magnificent Museo de Antropología; and the lively, colorful port of **Veracruz.** This is a good region to visit if you're longing for the Mexico of yesteryear.

WESTERN HIGHLANDS

This region, in the state of Michoacán, presents two distinct visions of colonial architecture: **Pátzcuaro,** a town of tile roofs and adobe walls painted traditional white with dark-red borders; and **Morelia,** a stately city of stone mansions, broad plazas, and a monumental cathedral. The eastern part of the state consists of high mountains with large tracts of pine and fir forests. Every year, millions of **monarch butterflies** make the long journey to congregate in a small part of the forest here. The central part of the state, a land of lakes, is the homeland of the Purépecha or Tarascan Indians. The villages throughout this area specialize in crafts for which the region is well known. Farther west lie the hot lands and the coast. Tourists largely neglect Michoacán, except during the Days of the Dead.

OAXACA & CHIAPAS

This is the southern land of the Zapotec, Mixtec, and Maya cultures. Most people fly around this region, but a toll highway from near Puebla to **Oaxaca City** makes the area more accessible by car. The valley of Oaxaca is one of the grandest places in Mexico, with fascinating Indian villages, beautiful ruins, and a wonderful colonial city. **San Cristóbal de las Casas,** in Chiapas, is harder to reach but worth the effort. Approaching San Cristóbal from any direction, you see small plots of corn tended by colorfully clad Maya. Oaxaca and Chiapas are rich in craftspeople, from woodcarvers to potters to weavers.

THE YUCATAN PENINSULA

Travelers to the peninsula have an opportunity to see pre-Hispanic ruins—such as **Chichén Itzá, Uxmal,** and **Tulum**—and the living descendants of the cultures that built them, as well as the ultimate in resort Mexico: **Cancún.** The peninsula borders the dull aquamarine Gulf of Mexico on the west and north, and the clear blue Caribbean on the east. It covers almost 217,560 sq. km (84,000 sq. miles), with nearly 1,600km (1,000 miles) of shoreline.

5 Mexico's Art & Architecture

ANCIENT ART & ARCHITECTURE

Art in Mexico begins with one piece, called the **Tequixquiac bone.** It isn't very big, having been made from the sacrum (hip bone) of an extinct form of camelid that existed in the upper Paleolithic. From this sacrum, some artist sculpted the head of a coyote. The bone was discovered in 1870 in the area of Tequixquiac, north of Mexico City. It's impossible to establish with certainty when the bone was worked by human hand, but, given where and how deep it was buried, it might be as old as 12,000 B.C. A striking piece, it merits special attention should you visit the National Anthropology Museum in Mexico City, where it's on display.

Aside from a few other artifacts, the record of artistic achievement in Mexico must await the arrival of the pre-Classic age and the great Olmec and earliest Maya cities. These date from the third millennium before Christ, roughly the same time as cities were growing in Mesopotamia, Egypt, and Peru. Fortunately for us, the inhabitants left behind a wealth of objects in pottery and stone, with intriguing images and a clear artistic style, whose component elements vary from site to site. These can be viewed in the National Anthropology Museum or in the museums of Puebla, Xalapa, or Villahermosa.

The Classic and post-Classic periods have left us with much more artwork and better preserved architecture. Visiting cities such as Teotihuacán, Palenque, or Monte Albán allows us to see the clear-cut geometry of these spaces and comprehend something of what the builders were envisioning. To understand the artistic achievement of these civilizations, you must witness the large sculptures that they left behind, such as the massive Aztec calendar stone or the many stelae (large stone monuments) and murals of the Maya. These contain thickly textured imagery, meshed into complex allegorical structures—difficult to understand but visually striking.

AFTER THE CONQUEST

After the Conquest, everything takes an abrupt turn. The Spanish wish to instill

---

Impressions

"Any contact with the Mexican people, no matter how fleeting, will show that beneath Western forms lie ancient beliefs and customs. These remnants, alive even now, are a testament to the vitality of Mexico's pre-Hispanic cultures."

_—Octavio Paz, *The Labyrinth of Solitude.*

in their new subjects an entirely alien belief system, and the Indians, inheritors of a highly complex system of their own, must make sense of things by using what they know. The result of this clash of beliefs is a fluid artistic tradition that is not discomforted by dialectical symbols embodying contradictory principles. But this synthesis takes more than a century. A stroke of good fortune is the arrival from Europe of the Baroque style. This is the perfect form and idea for the situation. Its breadth of scope and possibility and its lack of emphasis on overarching structure and consistency allow it to accommodate both symbol systems. Furthermore, its parallels with pre-Columbian art resonate with Mexican artists, who began producing with a vigor and brilliance that marks the pinnacle of artistic achievement in the colonial era. Much of this work has not survived to modern times, but much has. Good examples include the Capilla del Rosario in Puebla, the altar pieces of Santa Rosa de Viterbo and Santa Clara in Querétaro, the church of Santo Domingo in Oaxaca, and the Sagrario Metropolitano in Mexico City's cathedral, to name a few.

POST-REVOLUTIONARY ART & ARCHITECTURE

National independence brought near-constant social and economic upheaval until a measure of stability was reached under the long regime of dictator Porfirio Díaz, which began in 1876 and ended in 1911 with the Mexican Revolution. During these years, known as the *Porfiriato,* the ruling ideas and art forms came from Europe. The country experienced a surge in the construction of public buildings—most of which took inspiration from French architecture, especially Beaux Arts, examples of which include many of the municipal theaters and opera houses throughout the country, such as Bellas Artes in Mexico City, and several government palaces.

La Revolución did as much to give Mexico its own voice as it did to establish the nation's present governing institutions. The great Mexican muralists, Diego Rivera, Clemente Orozco, and David Alfaro Siqueiros, were a product of these times as were painters Frida Kahlo and Rufino Tamayo. All expressed through their personal styles a quintessentially Mexican sensibility that was artistically revolutionary. The same is true of architects Luis Barragán and Juan O'Gorman, especially the former, who absorbed the ideas of modernist architecture (which, at its heart is internationalist) and wedded them to warm Mexican colors and an Indian stoicism to create architecture with a strong sense of place.

CONTEMPORARY ART & BUILDING

What began during *La Revolución* continues to this day, with a strong Mexican voice that persists in the plastic arts, as contemporary artists and architects find new ways to express the ever-changing nature of national identity.

Luis Barragán never built anything outside of Mexico, and much of what he built was residential and thus unavailable for public viewing. Yet this didn't hinder the growth of his reputation. In 1980, he was awarded the Pritzker Prize; he died in 1988.

Two architects who have followed in his footsteps, Ricardo Legorreta and Teodoro González de León, have constructed many public buildings both in Mexico and abroad. Both construct modernist buildings with flair. Legorreta's use of forceful colors and bold lines sets apart his works, including the Public Library of San Antonio (Texas), the Tech Museum of San Jose (California), and the Hotel Camino Real in Mexico City.

González León's work is more futuristic and includes skyscrapers in Mexico City, the Mexican embassy in Berlin, and museums and cultural centers in the U.S.

6 Mexico in Popular Culture: Books, Film & Music

BOOKS

Studying up on Mexico can be one of the most fun bits of "research" you'll ever do. If you'd like to learn more about this fascinating country before you go—which I encourage—these books are an enjoyable way to do it.

LITERATURE

My favorite writer remains Jorge Ibargüengoitia. Although he died in 1983, he remains popular in Mexico. You can occasionally find his works in translation. His novel *Estas Ruinas que Ves (These Ruins You See)* gently pokes fun at Mexico's provincial life. His *The Dead Girls* is a fictionalized telling of a famous crime that happened in Mexico in the '70s. He has several personal narratives, too. His works display a deft touch at characterization and an insightful and ironic view of Mexican life.

Novelist Carlos Fuentes is Mexico's preeminent living writer. His earlier novels, such as *The Death of Artemio Cruz* are easier to read than his most recent works, which are heavily post-structural and demand a great deal of effort from the reader. More of a page-turner, Angeles Mastretta's *Arráncame la Vida (Tear Up My Life)* covers the same subject— Mexican society after the Revolution and its values, contradictions, and pleasures. Fuentes has an ironic touch and dips into the surreal on occasion. Mastretta's book is a well-written, straightforward narrative about life in Puebla; brimming with political gossip, it's a delightful read.

Another good novel covering roughly the same period, but with fewer social observations and more magical realism is *Like Water for Chocolate* by Laura Esquivel. This book and the movie of the same title did much to popularize Mexican food abroad.

Hasta No Verte by Elena Poniatowska is worth a read, as is anything by Luis Alberto Urrea, the master of heart-wrenching works about third-world realities.

Mexico has attracted writers from other parts of Latin America, including Gabriel García Márquez, who has lived in Mexico City for many years.

HISTORY & NONFICTION

For contemporary culture, start with *The Labyrinth of Solitude,* by the Mexican Nobel laureate poet and essayist Octavio Paz. It still generates controversy among Mexicans.

The Life and Times of Mexico by Earl Shorris offers a decidedly in-depth analysis of Mexican history. It's really the only text you'll ever need if you're seeking to learn the history of the country, from the rituals of Aztecs to the 70-year-rule of the PRI.

For an overview of pre-Hispanic cultures, pick up a copy of Michael D. Coe's *Mexico: From the Olmecs to the Aztecs,* or Nigel Davies's *Ancient Kingdoms of Mexico.* Richard Townsend's *The Aztecs* is a thorough, well-researched examination of the Aztec and the Spanish conquest. For the Maya, Michael Coe's *The Maya* is probably the best general account. For a survey of Mexican history through modern times, *A Short History of Mexico* by J. Patrick McHenry provides a complete, yet concise account.

John L. Stephens's travel classics, *Incidents of Travel in the Yucatán, Vol. I and II,* are considered among the great books of archaeological discovery. The two volumes chart the course of Stephens's discoveries of the Yucatán, beginning in 1841. Before his expeditions, little was known of the region, and the Mayan culture had not been discovered.

Lesley Byrd Simpson's *Many Mexicos* provides a comprehensive account of Mexican history within a cultural context. A classic on understanding the culture of this country is *Distant Neighbors,* by Alan Riding.

If you want to learn about Mexican *corridas*, or ballads, check out *True Stories from Another Mexico* by *Los Angeles Times* award-winning journalist Sam Quiones. The chapter on Chalino is enlightening, and the Mazatlán drag queen chapter is a must-read before traveling to that city.

NATURE

A Naturalist's Mexico, by Roland H. Wauer, is a fabulous guide to birding. *A Hiker's Guide to Mexico's Natural History,* by Jim Conrad, covers flora and fauna and tells how to find even the out-of-the-way spots he describes. *Peterson Field Guides: Mexican Birds,* by Roger Tory Peterson and Edward L. Chalif, is an excellent guide.

MEXICAN CINEMA
GOLDEN AGE & CLASSICS

Mexico's "Golden Age of Cinema" refers to a period in the 1940s when the country's film studios dropped their attempts at mimicking Hollywood and started producing black and white films that were Mexican to the core. The stars of the day are now icons of Mexican culture. **Mario Moreno,** aka Cantinflas, was the comedic genius that personalized the cultural archetype of *el pelado*—a poor, picaresque, slightly naughty character looking to get ahead by his wits alone, which, in fact, don't get him very far. His speech is a torrent of free association and digressions and innuendo that gives the comedy a madcap quality. **Dolores del Río** was the Mexican beauty who was later shipped off to Hollywood to fill the

role of steamy Latin babe. **Pedro Infante** expressed the ideal of Mexican manhood, and was also Mexico's singing cowboy.

For Hollywood's vision of Mexico, check out Elia Kazan's 1952 classic, *Viva Zapata!,* written by John Steinbeck and starring Marlon Brando as the Mexican revolutionary Emiliano Zapata. Then there's Orson Welles's *Touch of Evil,* about drugs and corruption in Tijuana (preposterously starring Charlton Heston as a Mexican). Or rent the HBO flick *And Starring Pancho Villa as Himself* with Antonio Banderas, a true story about how revolutionaries allowed a Hollywood film company to tape Pancho Villa in actual battle.

Luis Buñuel's dark 1950 film *Los Olvidados* explores the lives of young hoodlums living in the slums of Mexico City. It was filmed partially in the Plaza de La Romita, a charming, somewhat hidden section of Colonia Roma.

Directed brilliantly by John Huston, the Academy Award–winning classic *Night of the Iguana* is a must-watch if you're visiting Puerto Vallarta or Acapulco. Starring Ava Gardner as a down-on-her-luck hotel owner in the '50s, the film fired fantasies for many a gringa pursuing the good life, beach boys and all, south of the border.

THE NEW CINEMA

After the 1940s, Mexico's film industry entered a long period of unoriginal endeavors, until a new generation of filmmakers came along who've had success both in Mexico and abroad. This new age

---

Mexico's Oscar Nominees

Several Mexican filmmakers were nominated for Academy Awards in 2007, including Alejandro Gonzaléz Iñárritu for *Babel;* Guillermo del Toro for *Pan's Labyrinth;* and Alfonso Cuarón for *Children of Men,* starring Clive Owen. Keep an eye on all three of these directors and let's hope they film more pictures about their native country soon.

is being dubbed *El Nuevo Cine Mexicano* (The New Cinema).

The first film to become a big hit outside Mexico was *Like Water for Chocolate* (1992), which was directed by Alfonso Arau, author Laura Esquivel's husband at the time. He continues to make films, mainly in Mexico.

But a year earlier, filmmaker Alfonso Cuarón had scored a critical and commercial success in Mexico with his debut film *Sólo con tu pareja* (1991), a mordant social satire that any film buff interested in Mexico should see. His *Y Tu Mamá También* (2001) follows a pair of teenage boys who end up on an impromptu road trip to a fictional beach with a sexy older woman they meet at a wedding. The film touches on the hypocrisy of the country's governing classes, and issues of social inequality, all with an ironic slant. Its main focus is the picaresque, improvisational character of the Mexican male adolescent.

In search of larger budgets, Cuarón has since directed major international productions, including *Harry Potter and the Prisoner of Azkaban* and the science fiction thriller *Children of Men*.

In *Amores Perros* (2000), the director of *21 Grams* and *Babel*, Alejandro González Iñárritu, presents three different narratives, set in Mexico City, that become intertwined at the site of a car accident. Taken together, the stories offer a keen glimpse into contemporary Mexican society. González Iñárritu's Academy Award–nominated *Babel* is another tour de force; its Mexican border scene is realistic, exhilarating, and frightening all at once.

Guillermo del Toro has also had parallel success. His debut film, *Cronos* (1993), was a dark, atmospheric piece that garnered critical acclaim in Mexico. From there, he moved on to the international scene and has directed several films with similar moods, including *Hellboy* and *Pan's Labyrinth*.

Julie Taymor's *Frida* (2002), produced and acted by Mexican national Salma Hayek, is a wonderful biopic about Frida Kahlo. Watch it and you'll learn everything you need to know about Kahlo's life and work, from her devastating accident to her relationships with Diego Rivera and Leon Trotsky. The exquisite cinematography captures Mexico's inherent spirit of magic realism, evinced in Kahlo's work.

Director Robert Rodriguez's breakout film, *El Mariachi* (1992) is set in a small central Mexican town. Made on a shoestring budget, this somewhat cheesy action flick is at least highly entertaining. His *Once Upon a Time in Mexico* (2003) isn't as great but it's fun to see scenes of San Miguel Allende, where it was filmed. Ditto for Brad Pitt and Julia Roberts' *The Mexican* (2001).

Man on Fire (2004) stars Denzel Washington and Dakota Fanning, as a bodyguard in Mexico City and the little girl he is hired to protect. There are some great scenes shot around the city, even though the plot is pretty depressing.

Sexo, Pudor y Lágrimas (1999), by Antonio Serrano, is a gritty, unflinching look at the battle of the sexes in Mexico City in the '90s. It was the second film to emerge from the new era of Mexican cinema, after *Like Water for Chocolate*.

Tijuana Makes Me Happy (2005), directed by Dylan Verrechia with music by Pepe Mogt from Nortec Collective, shows a thankfully bright and realistic picture of Tijuana. The film's goal is "to break down the preconceived notion of Tijuana as a city of sin by showing the humanity of its people: their struggle, the strength of character, and the love of life that flourishes within." Something must be working—the film has won Latin film awards and was screened in 2007 at the Slamdance festival.

If you want more info on what's happening now in border towns, rent

Stephen Soderberg's Academy Award–winning *Traffic* (2000), starring Benicio del Toro. It includes some powerful scenes focusing on the drug war at the Tijuana border. Or get a hold of the documentary *Tijuana Remix* (2002), which celebrates that city's cultural idiosyncracies. You can also get a great "tourist guide" online via a short film called *Tijuana es Addiccion* made by local Jacinto Astiazaran.

MEXICAN FILM STARS

Gael García Bernal's work in *Amores Perros* and *Y Tu Mamá También* landed him leading roles in international films such as *The Motorcycle Diaries* and *Bad Education*. Another actor who has found work in Hollywood is **Diego Luna,** García Bernal's costar in *Y Tu Mamá También.* Before acting in film both had worked in Mexican soap operas. The brightest career launched by Mexican soaps has been the aforementioned actor, producer, and model **Salma Hayek.**

MUSIC
MARIMBA & SON

Marimba music can be heard in many parts of southern and central Mexico, but it is considered a traditional music in only two places: the state of Chiapas, and the port city of Veracruz. From here, many bands travel to such places as Oaxaca and Mexico City, where they play in clubs and restaurants.

Son is a native art form from many parts of Mexico. It is played with a variety of string instruments. One of the most famous forms is *Son Jarocho,* which often is fast paced and has a lot of strumming and fancy string picking. Dancing to this form of music requires a lot of fast rhythmic pounding with the heels of the feet *(zapateado).* It comes from the southern part of the state of Veracruz. One of its traditional songs, "La Bamba," was popularized by Ritchie Valens in the '50s.

DANZÓN & BOLERO

Both of these musical forms came from Cuba in the late 19th century and gained great popularity here. *Danzón* is orchestra music, which combines a Latin flavor with a stateliness absent from later Latin music. Its popularity is greatest in Veracruz and Mexico City. *Bolero* (or *trova*) is the music mainly of guitar trios such as Los Panchos. It's soft, romantic, and often a touch melancholy.

MARIACHI & RANCHERA

Mariachi is the music most readily identified with Mexico, and *mariachis,* with their distinctive costume—big sombreros, waist-length jackets, and tight pants—easily standout. The music originated from a style of *son* played in the state of Jalisco. It was rearranged to be played with guitars, violins, a string bass, and trumpets. Now you hear it across Mexico and much of the American southwest, but Jalisco and its capital, Guadalajara, are still considered the best place to hear mariachis.

Ranchera music is closely associated with mariachi music and is performed with the same instruments. It's defined by its expression of national pride, strong individualism, and lots of sentiment; hence its favored status as drinking music. The most famous composer is José Alfredo Jiménez, whose songs many Mexicans know by heart.

NORTEÑA, GRUPERA & BANDA

Norteña owes its origins to *tejano* music, coming out of Texas. Mexicans in south central Texas came in contact with musicians from the immigrant Czech and German communities of the Texas Hill Country and picked up a taste for polkas and the accordion. Gradually the music became popular farther south. *Norteña* music tweaked the polka for many of its popular songs and later borrowed from the *cumbia,* slowing the tempo a bit and adding a strong down beat. It also incorporated a native form of song known as the *corrido,* which is a type of ballad that was popularized during the Mexican revolution (1910–17). *Norteña* became hugely popular in rural northern Mexico though the 1970s and later generated spin-offs, which are known as *grupera* or *banda,* a style of *norteña* from the area of Sinaloa, which replaces the accordion with electric keyboards. *Grupera/banda* is now heard nationwide. The most famous norteña band is undoubtedly **Los Tigres del Norte,** with their catchy melodies backed by a hopped-up accordion and a pounding bass guitar.

ROCK EN ESPAÑOL

Mexican rock gained its identity in the 1980s and exploded in popularity during the 1990s with bands such as Los Jaguares, Maná, and Molotov. Named for the old (1920s) cafe in the capital's Centro Histórico, **Café Tacuba** has been together since 1989. Their music is influenced by indigenous Mexican music as much as folk, punk, bolero and hip-hop.

3

Planning Your Trip to Mexico

by Juan Cristiano

Planning your trip to Mexico is the first step in what promises to be a fascinating journey. Mexico's geographic and cultural diversity make this country among the world's most interesting to visit. Climate, food, dress, dialect, and social norms often differ markedly from one region to the next: You may be surprised to see how much a trip to Baja California or the Pacific Coast will differ from an excursion to the Caribbean; how distinctive the Mexican culture is on the U.S. border, compared to the Central American border; and how liberal Mexico City seems in the context of the conservative colonial cities surrounding it.

A little planning can make the difference between a bum trip and a great journey. When should you go? What's the best way to get there? How much should you plan to spend? What festivals or special events will occur during your visit? What safety or health precautions should you take? This chapter answers these and other questions.

In addition to these basics, I highly recommend taking a little time to learn about the culture and traditions of Mexico. It will help enrich even the simplest seaside getaway. See chapter 1, "Mexico in Depth," for more details.

1 Visitor Information

MEXICO TOURISM BOARD OFFICES

The **Mexico Tourism Board** (© **800/446-3942;** www.visitmexico.com) is an excellent source for general information; you can request brochures and get answers to the most common questions from the exceptionally well-trained, knowledgeable staff.

More information (15,000 pages worth) about Mexico is available on the official site of Mexico's Tourism Board, **www.visitmexico.com**. The **U.S. Department of State** (© **888/407-4747** or 202/501-4444; fax 202/647-1488; www.travel.state.gov) consistently updates its **Consular Information Sheet** on Mexico. It's loaded with safety, medical, driving, and general travel information, gleaned from reports by the Mexico offices. The **Centers for Disease Control and Prevention Hot Line** (© **800/311-3435** or 404/639-3534; www.cdc.gov) is a reliable source of medical information for travelers to Mexico and elsewhere. For travelers to Mexico and Central America, the number (with recorded messages) is © **877/394-8747.** Information is also available at **www.cdc.gov/travel**. The U.S. Department of State's website (see above) also offers medical information for Americans traveling abroad and a list of air ambulance services.

The **Mexican Government Tourist Board's** main office is in Mexico City (© **55/5278-4200**). There are satellite offices in the U.S., Canada, and the UK. In the **United States:** Chicago (© **312/228-0517**), Houston (© **713/772-2581**), Los Angeles (© **310/282-9112**),

Miami (© **786/621-2909**), and New York (© **212/308-2110**).

In **Canada:** Toronto (© **416/925-0704**). In the **United Kingdom:** London (© **020/7488-9392**).

MEXICAN EMBASSIES

The **Mexican Embassy** in the **United States** is at 1911 Pennsylvania Ave. NW, Washington, DC 20006 (© **202/728-1750** or -1600).

The **Mexican Embassy** in **Canada** is at 055 Rue Peel, Suite 1000, Montreal,

QUE, H3A 1V4 (© **514/288-2502**); Commerce Court West, 199 Bay St., Suite 4440, Toronto, ON, M5L 1E9 (© **416/925-0704**); 710 West Hastings St., Suite 1177, Vancouver, BC V6E 2K3 (© **604/684-1859**); 1500-45 O'Connor St., Ottawa, ON, K1P 1A4 (© **613/233-8988;** fax 613/235-9123).

The **Mexican Embassy** (Consular Section) in the **United Kingdom** is at 8 Halkin St., London SW1X7DW (© **020/7235-6393**).

2 Entry Requirements

PASSPORTS

All travelers to Mexico are required to present **photo identification** and **proof of citizenship,** such as a valid passport, naturalization papers, or an original birth certificate with a raised seal, along with a driver's license or official ID, such as a state or military-issued ID. Driver's licenses and permits, voter registration cards, affidavits, and similar documents are not sufficient to prove citizenship for readmission into the United States. If the last name on the birth certificate is different from your current name, bring a photo identification card *and* legal proof of the name change, such as the original marriage license or certificate. *Note:* Photocopies are *not* acceptable.

New regulations issued by the Department of Homeland Security now require virtually every air traveler **entering the U.S.** to show a passport. As of January 23, 2007, all U.S. and Canadian citizens traveling by **air** to Mexico are required to present a valid passport or other valid travel document to enter or reenter the United States. Other valid travel documents (known as WHTI-compliant documents; visit www.travel.state.gov for more information) include the new **Passport Card** and SENTRI, NEXUS, FAST, and the U.S. Coast Guard Mariner

Document. Members of the U.S. Armed Forces on active duty traveling on orders are exempt from the passport requirement. U.S. citizens may begin applying in advance for the new, limited-use, wallet-size **Passport Card** beginning February 1, 2008. Cards should be available and mailed to applicants in spring 2008. When available, it will be valid only for land and sea travel between the U.S. and Canada, Mexico, the Caribbean region, and Bermuda.

Effective January 31, 2008, U.S. and Canadian citizens traveling between the United States and Mexico by **land** or **sea** will need to present either a WHTI-compliant document (see above), or a government-issued photo ID, such as a driver's license, plus proof of citizenship such as a birth certificate. The Department of Homeland Security (DHS) also proposes to begin alternative procedures for U.S. and Canadian children at that time.

From our perspective, it's easiest just to travel with a valid passport. Safeguard your passport in an inconspicuous, inaccessible place, like a money belt, and keep a copy of the critical pages with your passport number in a separate place. If you lose your passport, visit the nearest consulate of your native country as soon as possible for a replacement.

For information on how to get a passport, see p. 764 ("Passports," in "Appendix A: Mexico Fast Facts"). The websites listed provide downloadable passport applications and current fees for processing passport applications. The "Foreign Entry Requirements" brochure no longer exists. For information on entry requirements for Mexico, see the Entry/Exit Requirements section in the Country Specific Information for Mexico at **http://travel.state.gov/travel/cis_pa_tw/cis/cis_970.html**. You may also contact the U.S. embassy or consulate of Mexico for further information.

VISAS

For detailed information regarding visas to Mexico, visit the Mexican Ministry of External Relations (SRE) at **www.sre.gob.mx/english/services/visasforeigners.htm**.

U.S. citizens do not require a visa or a tourist card for stays of 72 hours or less within "the border zone," defined as an area from 20 to 30km (12–19 miles) of the U.S. border, depending on the location. A visa is required, however, if you are going to stay in Mexico more than 72 hours and venture beyond the border tourist zone.

U.S. citizens traveling as tourists beyond the border zone or entering Mexico by air must pay a fee to obtain a **tourist card (FM-T),** available from Mexican consulates, Mexican border crossing points, Mexican tourism offices, airports within the border zone, and most airlines serving Mexico. The fee for the tourist card is generally included in the price of a plane ticket for travelers arriving by air. For visitors arriving by other means, it's about $21. Airlines generally provide the necessary forms aboard your flight to Mexico. The FMT is more important than a passport, so guard it carefully. If you lose it, you may not be allowed to leave until you replace it—a bureaucratic hassle that can take anywhere from a few hours to a week.

The FMT can be issued for up to 180 days. Sometimes officials don't ask but just stamp a time limit, so be sure to tell them you're going to stay 6 months, or at least twice as long as you intend to stay. If you decide to extend your stay, you may request that additional time be added to your FMT by an official immigration office in Mexico.

In **Baja California,** immigration laws have changed; they allow FMTs for a maximum of 180 days per year, with a maximum of 30 days per visit. This is to encourage regular visitors, or those who spend longer periods in Mexico, to obtain documents that denote partial residency.

For travelers entering Mexico by car at the border of Baja California, note that FMTs are issued only in Tijuana, Tecate, and Mexicali, as well as in Ensenada and Guerrero Negro. If you travel anywhere beyond the frontier zone without the FMT, you will be fined $40 (£20). Permits for driving a foreign-plated car in Mexico are available only in Tijuana, Ensenada, Tecate, Mexicali, and La Paz.

Note on travel of minors: Mexican law requires that any non-Mexican citizen under the age of 18 departing Mexico without both parents must carry notarized written permission from the parent or guardian who is not traveling with the child to or from Mexico. This permission must include the name of the parent, the name of the child, the name of anyone traveling with the child, and the notarized signature(s) of the absent parent(s). The U.S. Department of State recommends that permission include travel dates, destinations, airlines, and a summary of the circumstances surrounding the travel. The child must be carrying the original letter (not a facsimile or scanned

Cut to the Front of the Airport Security Line

In 2003, the **Transportation Security Administration (TSA;** www.tsa.gov) approved a pilot program to help ease the wait time for airport security screenings. In exchange for information and a fee, persons can be pre-screened as **registered travelers,** granting them a spot at the front of the line when they fly. The program is run through private firms—the largest and most well-known is Steven Brill's **Clear** (www.flyclear.com), and it works like this: Travelers complete an online application providing specific points of personal information including name, addresses for the previous 5 years, birth date, social security number, driver's license number, and a valid credit card (you're not charged the **$99 fee** until your application is approved). Print out the completed form and bring it with you, along with proper ID, to an "enrollment station" (found in more than 20 participating airports and in a growing number of American Express offices around the country). At this point, the process gets a little sci-fi: At the enrollment station, a Clear representative will record your biometrics, necessary for clearance, and digitally record your fingerprints and irises.

Once your application has been screened against no-fly lists, outstanding warrants, and other security measures, you'll be issued a clear plastic card that holds a chip containing your information. Each time you fly through participating airports (and the numbers are steadily growing), go to the Clear Pass station located next to the standard TSA screening line. Here you'll insert your card into a slot and place your finger on a scanner to read your print—when the information matches up, you're cleared to cut to the front of the security line. You'll still have to follow all the procedures of the day— such as removing your shoes and walking through the X-ray machine—but Clear promises to cut 30 minutes off your wait time at the airport.

On a personal note: Each time I've used my Clear Pass, my travel companions are still waiting to go through security while I'm already sitting down, reading the paper and sipping my overpriced smoothie. Granted, registered traveler programs are not for the infrequent traveler, but for those of us who fly on a regular basis, it's a perk worth paying for.—David A. Lytle

copy), and proof of the parent/child relationship (usually a birth certificate or court document) and an original custody decree, if applicable. Travelers should contact the Mexican Embassy or closest Mexican Consulate for current information.

MEDICAL REQUIREMENTS

No special vaccinations are required for entry into Mexico. For other medical requirements and health-related recommendations, see "Health," p. 65.

CUSTOMS

Mexican Customs inspection has been streamlined. At most points of entry, tourists are requested to press a button in front of what looks like a traffic signal, which alternates on touch between red and green. Green light and you go through without inspection; red light and your luggage or car may be inspected. If you have an unusual amount of luggage or an oversized piece, you may be subject to inspection anyway.

WHAT YOU CAN BRING INTO MEXICO

When you enter Mexico, Customs officials will be tolerant if you are not carrying illegal drugs or firearms. Tourists are allowed to bring in their personal effects duty-free. A laptop computer, camera equipment, and sports equipment that could feasibly be used during your stay are also allowed. The underlying guideline is: Don't bring anything that looks as if it's meant to be resold in Mexico. **U.S. citizens** entering Mexico by the land border can bring in gifts worth up to $50 duty-free, except for alcohol and tobacco products. Those entering Mexico by air or sea can bring in gifts worth a value of up to $300 duty-free. The website for Mexican Customs ("Aduanas") is **www.aduanas.sat.gob.mx/web adunet/body.htm**.

WHAT YOU CAN TAKE HOME FROM MEXICO

U.S. Citizens: Returning U.S. citizens who have been away for at least 48 hours are allowed to bring back, once every 30 days, $800 worth of merchandise duty-free. You'll pay a flat rate of duty on the next $1,000 worth of purchases. Any dollar amount beyond that is subject to duties at whatever rates apply. On mailed gifts, the duty-free limit is $200. Be sure to keep your receipts for purchases accessible to expedite the declaration process. *Note:* If you owe duty, you are required to pay on your arrival in the United States—either by cash, personal check, government or traveler's check, or money order (and, in some locations, a Visa or MasterCard).

To avoid paying duty on foreign-made personal items you owned before your trip, bring along a bill of sale, insurance policy, jeweler's appraisal, or receipts of purchase. Or before you leave, you can register with Customs items that can be readily identified by a permanently affixed serial number or marking—think laptop computers, cameras, and CD players. Take the items to the nearest Customs office or register them with Customs at the airport from which you're departing. You'll receive, at no cost, a Certificate of Registration, which allows duty-free entry for the life of the item.

For specifics on what you can bring back and the corresponding fees, download the invaluable free pamphlet "Know Before You Go!" online at **www.cbp.gov** (click on "Travel," and then click on "'Know Before You Go!' Online Brochure"). Or contact the **U.S. Customs & Border Protection (CBP),** 1300 Pennsylvania Ave. NW, Washington, DC 20229 (℃ **877/287-8667**) and request the pamphlet.

Canadian Citizens: For a clear summary of Canadian rules, write for the booklet "I Declare," issued by the **Canada Border Services Agency** (℃ **800/461-9999** in Canada, or 204/983-3500; www.cbsa-asfc.gc.ca).

U.K. Citizens: For information, contact **HM Revenue & Customs** at ℃ **0845/010-9000** (from outside the U.K., 020/8929-0152), or consult their website at www.hmrc.gov.uk.

Australian Citizens: A helpful brochure available from Australian consulates or Customs offices is "Know Before You Go." For more information, call the **Australian Customs Service** at ℃ **1300/363-263,** or log on to **www.customs.gov.au**.

New Zealand Citizens: Most questions are answered in a free pamphlet available at New Zealand consulates and Customs offices: "New Zealand Customs Guide for Travellers, Notice no. 4." For more information, contact **New Zealand Customs Service,** The Customhouse, 17–21 Whitmore St., Box 2218, Wellington (℃ **04/473-6099** or 0800/428-786; www.customs.govt.nz).

3 When to Go

Mexico has two principal travel seasons. **High season** begins around December 20 and continues to Easter (the end of *Semana Santa*); in some places it begins as early as mid-November. **Low season** is from the day after Easter to mid-December; during low season, prices may drop 20% to 50%. In beach destinations popular with Mexican travelers, such as Veracruz and Acapulco, prices will revert to high season during July and August, the traditional national summer vacation period. Prices in inland cities seldom fluctuate from high to low season, but may rise dramatically during the weeks of **Easter** and **Christmas.** Taxco and Pátzcuaro raise prices during their popular Easter-week celebrations. In Isla Mujeres and Playa del Carmen, on the Yucatán Peninsula, high season starts earlier than in the rest of the country and includes the month of August, when many European visitors and Mexican families arrive.

Mexico has two main climate seasons: **rainy** (May to mid-Oct) and **dry** (mid-Oct to Apr). The rainy season can be of little consequence in the dry, northern regions of the country. Southern regions typically receive tropical showers, which begin around 4 or 5pm and last a few hours. Though these rains can come on suddenly and be quite strong, they usually end just as quickly and cool off the air for the evening. **Hurricane season** particularly affects the Yucatán Peninsula and the southern Pacific coast, especially from June through October. If no hurricanes strike, however, the light, cooling winds, especially from September through November, can make it a perfect time to tackle the pre-Hispanic ruins that dot the interior of the peninsula.

Norte **(northern) season** runs from late November to mid-January, when the jet stream dips far south and creates northerly winds and showers in many resort areas. These showers usually last only for a couple of days.

June, July, and August are unrelentingly hot on the Yucatán Peninsula and in most coastal areas, though temperatures rise only into the mid-80s to 90°F (mid-20s to 32°C). Most of coastal Mexico experiences temperatures in the 80s°F (20s°C) in the hottest months. The northern states that border the U.S. endure very high summer temperatures.

Elevation is another important factor. High-elevation cities, such as Mexico City and San Cristóbal de las Casas, can be very cold. Temperatures can drop near freezing at night in winter, even in San Miguel de Allende and Guanajuato, which are at lower elevations.

Mexican beaches are very hot in summer, and most foreign visitors prefer the Caribbean and Pacific Coasts after the hurricane and rainy seasons end in October. Although the weather is ideal, the craziest time to visit Cancún is during the American spring-break period in March and April, so avoid this time if you're looking for rest and relaxation. The north of Mexico is unspeakably hot in summer, so it's probably best to avoid extensive travel there during this season. Mexico City is temperate year-round, and the only important difference is whether it's the rainy season or not. The chapters that follow mention all of these exceptions and others.

Mexico City's Average Temperatures

	Jan	Feb	Mar	Apr	May	June	July	Aug	Sept	Oct	Nov	Dec
Avg. High (°F)	70	72	76	78	79	76	74	74	73	73	72	70
Avg. High (°C)	21	22	24	25	26	24	23	23	22	22	22	21
Avg. Low (°F)	45	46	50	53	55	57	56	56	55	52	48	45
Avg. Low (°C)	7	7	10	11	12	13	13	13	12	11	8	7

Cancun's Average Temperatures

	Jan	Feb	Mar	Apr	May	June	July	Aug	Sept	Oct	Nov	Dec
Avg. High (°F)	81	82	84	85	88	89	90	90	89	87	84	82
Avg. High (°C)	27	27	28	29	31	31	32	32	31	30	28	27
Avg. Low (°F)	67	68	71	73	77	78	78	77	76	74	72	69
Avg. Low (°C)	19	20	21	22	25	25	25	25	24	23	22	20

Acapulco's Average Temperatures

	Jan	Feb	Mar	Apr	May	June	July	Aug	Sept	Oct	Nov	Dec
Avg. High (°F)	87	87	87	87	89	89	89	89	89	89	89	88
Avg. High (°C)	30	30	30	30	31	31	31	31	31	31	31	31
Avg. Low (°F)	72	72	72	73	76	77	77	77	77	77	75	73
Avg. Low (°C)	22	22	22	22	24	25	25	25	25	25	23	22

CALENDAR OF EVENTS

For an exhaustive list of events beyond those listed here, see http://events.frommers.com, where you'll find a searchable, up-to-the-minute roster of what's happening in cities all over the world.

January

Año Nuevo (New Year's Day), nationwide. This national holiday is perhaps the quietest day in Mexico. Most people stay home or attend church. All businesses are closed. In traditional indigenous communities, new tribal leaders are inaugurated with colorful ceremonies rooted in the pre-Hispanic past. January 1.

Día de los Reyes (Three Kings' Day), nationwide. This day commemorates the Three Kings' presenting gifts to the Christ Child. Children receive presents, much like they do at Christmas in the United States. Friends and families gather to share the Rosca de Reyes, a special cake. Inside the cake is a small doll representing the Christ Child; whoever receives the doll must host a tamales-and-*atole* (a warm drink made of corn dough) party on February 2. January 6.

Regional Fair, León, Guanajuato. One of Mexico's largest fairs celebrates the founding of this shoemaking and leather-craft city. The fair features parades, theater, craft exhibits, music, and dance. Month of January.

Feast of San Antonio Abad, Mexico City. This feast is celebrated through the Blessing of the Animals at the Santiago Tlatelolco Church on the Plaza of Three Cultures, at San Juan Bautista Church in Coyoacán, and at the Church of San Fernando, 2 blocks north of the Juárez-Reforma intersection. January 17.

February

Día de la Candelaria (Candlemas), nationwide. Music, dances, processions, food, and other festivities lead up to a blessing of seed and candles in a ceremony that mixes pre-Hispanic and European traditions marking the end of winter. Those who attended the Three Kings celebration reunite to share *atole* and tamales at a party hosted by the recipient of the doll found in the Rosca. Celebrations are especially festive in Tlacotalpan, Veracruz. February 2.

Día de la Constitución (Constitution Day), nationwide. This national holiday is in honor of the current Mexican constitution, signed in 1917 as a result of the revolutionary war of 1910. It's celebrated through small parades.

February 5.

Carnaval, nationwide. Carnaval takes place the 3 days preceding Ash Wednesday and the beginning of Lent. The cities of Tepoztlán, Huejotzingo, Chamula, Veracruz, Cozumel, and Mazatlán celebrate with special gusto. In some places, such as Veracruz, Mazatlán, and Cozumel, the celebration resembles New Orleans's Mardi Gras, with a festive atmosphere and parades. In Chamula, the event harks back to pre-Hispanic times, with ritualistic running on flaming branches. On Shrove Tuesday, in Tepoztlán and Huejotzingo, brilliantly clad *chinelos* (masked dancers) fill the streets. Transportation and hotels are packed, so it's best to make reservations 6 months in advance and arrive a couple of days ahead of the beginning of celebrations.

Ash Wednesday, nationwide. The start of Lent and time of abstinence, this is a day of reverence nationwide; some towns honor it with folk dancing and fairs.

March

Annual Witches Conference, Lake Catemaco, Veracruz. Shamans, white witches, black witches, and practitioners of Caribbean, Afro, and Antillean ritualistic practices gather on the shores of the lake. Taking place the first Friday night of March every year, the annual gathering is a spectacle of witches, healers, magicians, and wizards.

Benito Juárez's Birthday, nationwide. This national holiday celebrating one of Mexico's most beloved leaders is observed through small hometown celebrations, especially in Juárez's birthplace, Guelatao, Oaxaca. March 21.

Spring Equinox, Chichén Itzá. On the first day of spring, the Temple of Kukulkán—Chichén Itzá's main pyramid—aligns with the sun, and the shadow of the plumed serpent moves slowly from the top of the building down. When the shadow reaches the bottom, the body joins the carved stone snake's head at the base of the pyramid. According to ancient legend, at the moment that the serpent is whole, the earth is fertilized. Visitors come from around the world to marvel at this sight, so advance arrangements are advisable. Elsewhere, equinox festivals and celebrations welcome spring, in the custom of the ancient Mexicans, with dances and prayers to the elements and the four cardinal points. It's customary to wear white with a red ribbon. March 21 (the shadow appears Mar 19–23).

April

Semana Santa (Holy Week), nationwide. Mexico celebrates the last week in the life of Christ, from Palm Sunday to Easter Sunday, with somber religious processions, spoofing of Judas, and reenactments of biblical events, plus food and craft fairs. Among the Tarahumara Indians in the Copper Canyon, celebrations have pre-Hispanic overtones. Pátzcuaro, Taxco, and Malinalco hold special celebrations. Businesses close during this traditional week of Mexican national vacations.

If you plan to travel to or around Mexico during Holy Week, make your reservations early. Seats on flights into and out of the country will be reserved months in advance. Buses to these towns and to almost anywhere else in Mexico will be full, so try arriving on the Wednesday or Thursday before Good Friday. Easter Sunday is quiet, and the week following is a traditional vacation period. Early April.

Festival de México en el Centro Histórico (Annual Mexico City Festival), Mexico City. Regarded as one of Latin America's most vibrant celebrations of art and culture, this 2-week festival features diverse events including opera, concerts, theater, art exhibits, dance productions, and gourmet fare. Proceeds go toward the rescue and restoration of the art and architecture of Mexico City's historic downtown area. For a detailed schedule and more information, visit **www.fchmexico. com**. Mid-March to early April, depending on Easter.

San Marcos National Fair, Aguascalientes. Mexico's largest fair, first held in 1604, lasts 22 days. About a million visitors come for bullfights and rodeos as well as *ranchera* music and mariachis. There are craft and industrial exhibits, markets, fireworks, and folk dancing. April 12 to May 4.

May

Labor Day, nationwide. Workers' parades countrywide; everything closes. May 1.

Cinco de Mayo, Puebla and nationwide. This national holiday celebrates the defeat of the French at the Battle of Puebla. May 5.

Feast of San Isidro, nationwide. A blessing of seeds and work animals honors the patron saint of farmers. May 15.

International Gay Festival. This 5-day event in Cancún kicks off with a welcome fiesta of food, drinks and mariachi music. Additional festivities include a tequila party, tour of Cancún, sunset Caribbean cruise, bar and beach parties, and a final champagne breakfast. For schedule information, check www.cancun.eventguide.com.

June

Día de la Marina (Navy Day), various towns. All coastal towns celebrate the holiday, with naval parades and fireworks. June 1.

Corpus Christi, nationwide. This day, celebrated nationwide, honors the Body of Christ (the Eucharist) with

processions, Masses, and food. Festivities include performances of *voladores* (flying pole dancers) beside the church and at the ruins of El Tajín, Veracruz. In Mexico City, children dressed as Indians and carrying decorated baskets of fruit for the priest's blessing gather with their parents before the National Cathedral. *Mulitas* (mules), handmade from dried cornhusks and painted, are traditionally sold outside all churches on that day to represent a prayer for fertility. Dates vary, but celebrations take place on the Thursday following "Holy Trinity" Sunday.

National Ceramics Fair and Fiesta, Tlaquepaque, Jalisco. This pottery center on the outskirts of Guadalajara offers craft demonstrations and competitions as well as mariachis, dancers, and colorful parades. June 14 to July 14.

Día de San Pedro y San Pablo (St. Peter and St. Paul Day), nationwide. This feast day is celebrated wherever St. Peter is the patron saint; it also honors anyone named Pedro or Peter. It's especially festive at San Pedro Tlaquepaque, near Guadalajara, with mariachi bands, folk dancers, and parades with floats. June 29.

July

Guelaguetza Dance Festival, Oaxaca. This is one of Mexico's most popular events. Villagers from the seven regions around Oaxaca gather in the city's amphitheater. They dress in traditional costumes, and many wear colorful "dancing" masks. The celebration dates from pre-Hispanic times. Make advance reservations—this festival attracts visitors from around the world. Call © **800/446-3942** for more details. Late July.

August

International Chamber Music Festival, San Miguel de Allende. Held since 1982 in this beautiful town, the festival features international award-winning classical music ensembles. August 1 to August 15.

Fall of Tenochtitlán, Mexico City. The last battle of the Spanish Conquest took place at Tlatelolco, ruins that are now part of the Plaza of Three Cultures. Wreath-laying ceremonies there and at the Cuauhtémoc monument on Reforma commemorate the surrender of Cuauhtémoc, the last Aztec king, to Cortez, and the loss of thousands of lives. August 13.

Assumption of the Virgin Mary, nationwide. This day is celebrated throughout the country with special Masses, and in some places with processions. In Huamantla, flower petals and colored sawdust carpet the streets. At midnight on August 15, a statue of the Virgin is carried through the streets; on August 16 is the running of the bulls. On August 15 in Santa Clara del Cobre, near Pátzcuaro, Our Lady of Santa Clara de Asis and the Virgen de la Sagrado Patrona are honored with a parade of floats, dancers on the main square, and an exposition of regional crafts. Buses to Huamantla from Puebla and Mexico City will be full, and there are few hotels in Huamantla. Plan to stay in Puebla and commute to the festivities. August 15 to August 17.

Fiestas de la Vendimia (Wine Harvest Festival), Ensenada, Baja California. This food and wine festival celebrates the annual harvest, with blessings, seminars, parties, and wine tastings. Call ✆ **800/446-3942** for more details. Mid- to late August.

September

International Mariachi Festival, Guadalajara, Jalisco. These public concerts of mariachi music include visiting mariachi groups from around the world (even Japan!). Workshops and lectures focus on the history, culture,

and music of the mariachi in Mexico. Call ✆ **800/446-3942** (www.mariachijalisco.com.mx) to confirm dates and the performance schedule. August 30 to September 9.

Reto al Tepozteco (Tepozteco Challenge), Tepoztlan, Morelos. This celebration of King Tepoztecatl's conversion to the Catholic religion includes a performance depicting the event. A procession leads toward the Tepozteco Pyramid, where people offer food and beverages. This event includes hypnotic *chinelo* dances, fireworks, and a food festival. September 7 and 8.

Independence Day, nationwide. Celebrates Mexico's independence from Spain with parades, picnics, and family reunions. At 11pm on September 15, the president gives the famous independence *grito* (shout) from the National Palace in Mexico City. At least half a million people crowd into the *zócalo* (main plaza), and the rest of the country watches on TV or participates in local celebrations. Tall buildings downtown are draped in the national colors (red, green, and white), and the *zócalo* is ablaze with lights. Many people drive downtown at night to see the lights. Querétaro and San Miguel de Allende, where Independence conspirators lived and met, also celebrate elaborately; the schedule of events is exactly the same in every village, town, and city across Mexico. September 15 and 16.

Fall Equinox, Chichén Itzá. The same shadow play that occurs during the spring equinox is repeated. September 21 and 22.

October

Fiestas de Octubre (October Festivals), Guadalajara. This "most Mexican of cities" celebrates for a month with its trademark mariachi music. It's a bountiful display of popular culture and fine arts, and a spectacular spread of traditional food, Mexican beer, and wine. All month.

Festival Cervantino, Guanajuato. This festival began in the 1970s as a cultural event, bringing performing artists from all over the world to this picturesque village northeast of Mexico City. Now the artists travel all over the republic after appearing in Guanajuato. Call © **800/446-3942,** or see **www.festivalcervantino.gob.mx** for details. Mid- to late October.

Dia de la Raza ("Ethnicity Day," or Columbus Day), nationwide. This day commemorates the fusion of the Spanish and Mexican peoples. October 12.

Feria Nacional del Mole, Mexico City. Just south of Mexico City, thousands of varieties of *mole* will be prepared for sampling and competition. This spicy sauce is a Mexican staple, made of unsweetened chocolate, peppers, and spices, often served with meat or poultry. Between October 1 and 15.

November

Day of the Dead, nationwide. This holiday (Nov 1) actually lasts for 2 days: All Saints' Day—honoring saints and deceased children—and All Souls' Day, honoring deceased adults. Relatives gather at cemeteries countrywide, carrying candles and food, and often spend the night beside graves of loved ones. Weeks before, bakers begin producing bread in the shape of mummies or round loaves decorated with bread "bones." Sugar skulls emblazoned with glittery names are sold everywhere. Many days ahead, homes and churches erect altars laden with bread, fruit, flowers, candles, favorite foods, and photographs of saints and of the deceased. On both nights, costumed children walk through the streets,

often carrying mock coffins and pumpkin lanterns, into which they expect money to be dropped.

The most famous celebration—which has become almost too well known—is on Janitzio, an island on Lake Pátzcuaro, Michoacán, west of Mexico City. Mixquic, a mountain village south of Mexico City, hosts an elaborate street fair. At around 11pm on both nights, solemn processions lead to the cemetery in the center of town. Cemeteries around Oaxaca are well known for their solemn vigils, and some for their Carnaval-like atmosphere. November 1 and 2.

Fiestas de Noviembre (November Festivals), Puerto Escondido, Oaxaca. The month's events include the annual Pipeline of Mexico, Zicatela Beach's International Surfing Tournament, the International Sailfish Tournament, and the Coastal Dance Festival. Check local calendars or call © **800/446-3942** for details. All month.

Gourmet Festival, Puerto Vallarta, Jalisco. In this culinary capital of Mexico, chefs from around the world join with local restaurateurs to create special menus and host wine and tequila tastings, cooking classes, a gourmet food expo, and other special events. For detailed information, see **www. festivalgourmet.com**. Dates vary, but the festival generally runs from November 13 to November 23.

Revolution Day, nationwide. This holiday commemorates the start of the Mexican Revolution in 1910 with parades, speeches, rodeos, and patriotic events. November 20.

Sixth Annual Yucatán Bird Festival, Mérida, Yucatán. Bird-watching sessions, workshops, and exhibits are the highlights of this festival designed to illustrate the special role birds play in our environment and in the Yucatán.

Call ✆ **800/446-3942,** or visit **www. yucatanbirds.org.mx** for details. Late November to early December.

National Silver Fair, Taxco. This competition pits Mexico's best silversmiths against some of the world's finest artisans. There are exhibits, concerts, dances, and fireworks. Check local calendars or call ✆ **800/446-3942** for details. Late November to early December.

December

Annual Hot Air Balloon Festival, León, Guanajuato. This is the largest festival in Latin America, with more than 60 balloons and pilots from all over the globe participating. Call ✆ **800/446-3942,** or visit **www. festivaldelglobo.com.mx** for details. Early December.

Feast of the Virgin of Guadalupe, nationwide. Religious processions, street fairs, dancing, fireworks, and Masses honor the patroness of Mexico. It is one of the country's most moving and beautiful displays of traditional culture. The Virgin of Guadalupe appeared to a young man, Juan Diego, in December 1531 on a hill near Mexico City. It's customary for children to dress up as Juan Diego, wearing mustaches and red bandanas. One of the most famous and elaborate celebrations takes place at the Basílica of Guadalupe, north of Mexico City, where the Virgin appeared. But every village celebrates this day, often with processions of children carrying banners, and with *charreadas* (rodeos), bicycle races, dancing, and fireworks. In Puerto Vallarta, the celebration begins on December 1 and extends through December 12, with traditional processions to the church for a brief Mass and blessing. In the final days, the processions and festivities take place around the clock. There's a major

fireworks exhibition on the feast day at 11pm. December 12.

Festival of San Cristóbal de las Casas, San Cristóbal de las Casas, Chiapas. This 10-day festival in Chiapas includes a procession by the Tzotzil and Tzetzal Indians, *marimba* music, and a parade of horses. December 12 to December 21.

Christmas Posadas, nationwide. On each of the 9 nights before Christmas, it's customary to reenact the Holy Family's search for an inn. Door-to-door candlelit processions pass through cities and villages nationwide, especially Querétaro and Taxco. Hosted by churches, businesses, and community organizations, these take the place of the northern tradition of a Christmas party. December 15 to December 24.

Fiesta de los Rábanos (Festival of the Radishes), Oaxaca, Oaxaca. Local artisans and sculptors set up stalls around the main square to display their elaborate pieces of art—made entirely from radishes! The local crop is used for creating nativity scenes and famous Mexican figures. Balloons and birds crafted from local flowers add even more color. December 23.

Christmas, nationwide. Mexicans often extend this national holiday and take vacations for up to 2 weeks before Christmas, returning after New Year's. Many businesses close, and resorts and hotels fill. Significant celebrations take place on December 23 (see above). Querétaro has a huge parade. On the evening of December 24 in Oaxaca, processions culminate on the central plaza. On the same night, Santiago Tuxtla in Veracruz celebrates by dancing the *huapango* and with *jarocho* bands in the beautiful town square. December 24 and 25.

What's on When?

For an exhaustive list of events beyond those listed here, check **http://events. frommers.com**, with its searchable, up-to-the-minute roster of events in cities all over the world.

New Year's Eve, nationwide. Like the rest of the world, Mexico celebrates New Year's Eve with parties, fireworks, and plenty of noise. New Year's Eve in Mexico is typically spent with family.

Special festivities take place at Santa Clara del Cobre, near Pátzcuaro, with a candlelit procession of Christ, and at Tlacolula, near Oaxaca, with commemorative mock battles. December 31.

4 Getting There & Getting Around

GETTING TO MEXICO
BY PLANE

Mexico has dozens of international and domestic airports throughout the country. Among the major airports and their online airport codes are Mexico City (MEX), Cancún (CUN), Acapulco (ACA), Guadalajara (GDL), Puerto Vallarta (PVR), Ixtapa/Zihuatanejo (ZIH), and Los Cabos (SJD).

THE MAJOR INTERNATIONAL AIRLINES The main airlines operating direct or nonstop flights from the United States to Mexico include **AeroMéxico** (© 800/237-6639; www. aeromexico.com), **Air France** (© 800/ 237-2747; www.airfrance.com), **Alaska Airlines** (© 800/252-7522; www.alaska air.com), **American Airlines** (© 800/ 433-7300; www.aa.com), **Continental** (© 800/525-0280; www.continental. com), **Frontier Airlines** (© 800/432-1359; www.frontierairlines.com), **Mexicana** ((© 800/531-7921; www.mexicana. com), **Northwest/KLM** (© 800/225-2525; www.nwa.com), **Taca** (© 800/ 400-8222; www.taca.com), **United** (© 800/241-6522; www.united.com), and **US Airways** (© 800/428-4322; www.usairways.com). **Southwest Airlines** (© 800/435-9792; www.southwest. com) serves the U.S. border.

The main departure points in North America for international airlines are Atlanta, Chicago, Dallas/Fort Worth, Denver, Houston, Las Vegas, Los Angeles, Miami, New York, Orlando, Philadelphia, Phoenix, Raleigh/Durham, San Antonio, San Francisco, Seattle, Toronto, and Washington, D.C.

Arriving at the Airport

IMMIGRATION & CUSTOMS CLEARANCE Immigration and customs clearance at Mexican airports is efficient. Expect longer lines during peak season, but you can usually clear immigration and customs within an hour.

BY CAR

Driving is not the cheapest way to get to Mexico, but it is a convenient way to see the country. Even so, you may think twice about taking your own car south of the border once you've pondered the bureaucracy involved. One option is to rent a car once you arrive and tour around a specific region. Rental cars in Mexico generally are clean and well-maintained, although they are often smaller than rentals in the U.S., may have manual rather than automatic transmission, and are comparatively expensive due to pricey mandatory insurance. Discounts are often available for rentals of a week or longer, especially when you make arrangements in advance online or from the United States. Be careful about estimated online rates, which often fail to

> ## ⌐Tips Carrying Car Documents
>
> You must carry your temporary car-importation permit, tourist permit (see "Entry Requirements," earlier in this chapter), and, if you purchased it, your proof of Mexican car insurance (see below) in the car at all times. The temporary car-importation permit papers are valid for 6 months to a year, while the tourist permit is usually issued for 30 days. It's a good idea to overestimate the time you'll spend in Mexico so if you have to (or want to) stay longer, you'll avoid the hassle of getting your papers extended. Whatever you do, don't overstay either permit. Doing so invites heavy fines, confiscation of your vehicle (which will not be returned), or both. Also remember that 6 months does not necessarily equal 180 days—be sure that you return before the earlier expiration date.

include the price of the mandatory insurance. (See "Car Rentals," later in this chapter, for more details.)

If, after reading the section that follows, you have additional questions or you want to confirm the current rules, call your nearest Mexican consulate or the Mexican Government Tourist Office. Although travel insurance companies generally are helpful, they may not have the most accurate information. To check on road conditions or to get help with any travel emergency while in Mexico, call © **01-800/482-9832,** or 55/5089-7500 in Mexico City. English-speaking operators staff both numbers.

In addition, check with the **U.S. Department of State** (see "Visitor Information," earlier in this chapter) for warnings about dangerous driving areas.

Car Documents

To drive your car into Mexico, you'll need a **temporary car-importation permit,** which is granted after you provide a required list of documents (see below). The permit can be obtained through Banco del Ejército (Banjercito) officials at the *aduana* (Mexican Customs) building after you cross the border into Mexico.

The following requirements for border crossing were accurate at press time:

- **A valid driver's license,** issued outside of Mexico.

- **Current, original car registration and a copy of the original car title.** If the registration or title is in more than one name and not all the named people are traveling with you, a notarized letter from the absent person(s) authorizing use of the vehicle for the trip is required; have it ready. The registration and your credit card (see below) must be in the same name.
- **Original immigration documentation.** This is either your tourist permit (FMT) or the original immigration booklet, FM2 or FM3, if you hold more permanent status.
- **Processing fee and posting of a bond.** With a credit card, you are required to pay a $27 (£14) car-importation fee. The credit card must be in the same name as the car registration. Mexican law also requires the posting of a bond at a Banjercito office to guarantee the export of the car from Mexico within a time period determined at the time of the application. For this purpose, American Express, Visa or MasterCard credit card holders will be asked to provide credit card information; others will need to make a cash deposit of $200 to $400 (£100–£200), depending on the make/model/year of the vehicle. In order to recover this bond or avoid

credit card charges, travelers must go to any Mexican Customs office immediately before leaving Mexico.

If you receive your documentation at the border, Mexican officials will make two copies of everything and charge you for the copies. For up-to-the-minute information, a great source is the Customs office in Nuevo Laredo, or *Módulo de Importación Temporal de Automóviles, Aduana Nuevo Laredo* (© 867/712-2071).

Important reminder: Someone else may drive, but the person (or relative of the person) whose name appears on the car-importation permit must *always* be in the car. (If stopped by police, a nonregistered family member driving without the registered driver must be prepared to prove familial relationship to the registered driver—no joke.) Violation of this rule subjects the car to impoundment and the driver to imprisonment, a fine, or both. You can drive a car with foreign license plates only if you have a foreign (non-Mexican) driver's license.

Mexican Auto Insurance (Seguros de Auto)

Liability auto insurance is legally required in Mexico. U.S. insurance is invalid; to be insured in Mexico, you must purchase Mexican insurance. Any party involved in an accident who has no insurance may be sent to jail and have his or her car impounded until all claims are settled. This is true even if you just drive across the border to spend the day. U.S. companies that broker Mexican insurance are commonly found at the border crossing, and several quote daily rates.

You can also buy car insurance through **Sanborn's Mexico Insurance,** P.O. Box 52840, 2009 S. 10th, McAllen, TX (© 800/222-0158; fax 800/222-0158 or 956/686-0732; www.sanbornsinsurance. com). The company has offices at all U.S. border crossings. Its policies cost the same as the competition's do, but you get legal coverage (attorney and bail bonds if needed) and a detailed mile-by-mile guide for your proposed route. Most of the Sanborn's border offices are open Monday through Friday; a few are staffed on Saturday and Sunday. **AAA** auto club (www.aaa.com) also sells insurance.

Returning to the U.S. with Your Car

You *must* return the car documents you obtained when you entered Mexico when you cross back with your car, or within 180 days of your return. (You can cross as many times as you wish within the 180 days.) If the documents aren't returned, heavy fines are imposed ($250 for each 15 days you're late), your car may be impounded and confiscated, or you may be jailed if you return to Mexico. You can only return the car documents to a Banjercito official on duty at the Mexican *aduana* building *before* you cross back into the United States. Some border cities have Banjercito officials on duty 24 hours a day, but others do not; some do not have Sunday hours.

BY SHIP

Numerous cruise lines serve Mexico. Some (such as Carnival and Royal Caribbean) cruise from California to the Baja Peninsula and ports of call on the Pacific coast, or from Houston or Miami to the Caribbean (which often includes stops in Cancún, Playa del Carmen, and Cozumel). Several cruise-tour specialists sometimes offer last-minute discounts on unsold cabins. One such company is **CruisesOnly** (© 800/278-4373; www. cruisesonly.com).

BY BUS

Greyhound-Trailways (or its affiliates) offers service from around the United States to the Mexican border, where passengers disembark, cross the border, and buy a ticket for travel into Mexico. Many border crossings have scheduled buses from the U.S. bus station to the Mexican bus station.

GETTING AROUND
BY PLANE

Mexico has two large private national carriers: **Mexicana** (© **800/531-7921;** www.mexicana.com) and **AeroMéxico** (© **800/237-6639;** www.aeromexico. com), in addition to several up-and-coming low-cost carriers. Mexicana and AeroMéxico offer extensive connections to the United States as well as within Mexico.

Up-and-coming low-cost carriers include **Aviacsa** (www.aviacsa.com), **Avolar** (www.avolar.com.mx), **Click Mexicana** (www.click.com.mx), **InterJet** (www.interjet.com.mx), and **Volaris** (www.volaris.com.mx). Regional carriers include **Aerovega** (www.oaxaca-mio. com/aerovega.htm), **Aero Tucán** (www. aero-tucan.com), and **AeroMéxico Connect** (www.amconnect.com). The regional carriers can be expensive, but they go to difficult-to-reach places. In each applicable section of this book, we've mentioned regional carriers with all pertinent telephone numbers.

Because major airlines may book some regional carriers, check your ticket to see if your connecting flight is on one of these smaller carriers—they may use a different airport or a different counter.

AIRPORT TAXES Mexico charges an airport tax on all departures. Passengers leaving the country on international flights pay about $24 (£12)—in dollars or the peso equivalent. It has become a common practice to include this departure tax in your ticket price, but double-check to make sure so you're not caught by surprise at the airport. Taxes on each domestic departure within Mexico are around $17 (£8.50), unless you're on a connecting flight and have already paid at the start of the flight.

Mexico charges an $18 (£9) "tourism tax," the proceeds of which go into a tourism promotional fund. Your ticket price may not include it, so be sure to have enough money to pay it at the airport upon departure.

RECONFIRMING FLIGHTS Although Mexican airlines say it's not necessary to reconfirm a flight, it's still a good idea. To avoid getting bumped on popular, possibly overbooked flights, check in for an international flight 1½ hours in advance of travel.

BY CAR

Most Mexican roads are not up to U.S. standards of smoothness, hardness, width of curve, grade of hill, or safety markings. Driving at night is dangerous—the roads are rarely lit; trucks, carts, pedestrians, and bicycles usually have no lights; and you can hit potholes, animals, rocks, dead ends, or uncrossable bridges without warning.

The spirited style of Mexican driving sometimes requires keen vision and reflexes. Be prepared for new customs, as when a truck driver flips on his left turn signal when there's not a crossroad for miles. He's probably telling you the road's clear ahead for you to pass. Another custom that's very important to respect is turning left. Never turn left by stopping in the middle of a highway with your left-turn signal on. Instead, pull onto the right shoulder, wait for traffic to clear, and then proceed across the road.

GASOLINE There's one government-owned brand of gas and one gasoline station name throughout the country—**Pemex** (Petroleras Mexicanas). There are two types of gas in Mexico: *magna*, 87-octane unleaded gas, and *premio* 93 octane. In Mexico, fuel and oil are sold by the liter, which is slightly more than a quart (1 gal. equals about 3.8L). Many franchise Pemex stations have bathroom facilities and convenience stores—a great improvement over the old ones. Gas stations accept both credit and debit cards for gas purchases.

TOLL ROADS Mexico charges some of the highest tolls in the world for its network of new toll roads, so they are rarely used. Generally, though, using toll roads cuts travel time. Older toll-free roads are generally in good condition, but travel times tend to be longer.

BREAKDOWNS If your car breaks down on the road, help might already be on the way. Radio-equipped green repair trucks, run by uniformed English-speaking officers, patrol major highways during daylight hours. These **"Green Angels"** perform minor repairs and adjustments free, but you pay for parts and materials.

Your best guide to repair shops is the Yellow Pages. For repairs, look under *Automóviles y Camiones: Talleres de Reparación y Servicio;* auto-parts stores are under *Refacciones y Accesorios para Automóviles.* To find a mechanic on the road, look for the sign TALLER MECÁNICO.

Places called *vulcanizadora* or *llantera* repair flat tires, and it is common to find them open 24 hours a day on the most traveled highways.

MINOR ACCIDENTS When possible, many Mexicans drive away from minor accidents, or try to make an immediate settlement, to avoid involving the police. If the police arrive while the involved persons are still at the scene, everyone may be locked in jail until blame is assessed. In any case, you have to settle up immediately, which may take days. Foreigners who don't speak fluent Spanish are at a distinct disadvantage when trying to explain their version of the event. Three steps may help the foreigner who doesn't wish to do as the Mexicans do: If you were in your own car, notify your Mexican insurance company, whose job it is to intervene on your behalf. If you were in a rental car, notify the rental company immediately and ask how to contact the nearest adjuster. (You did buy insurance with the rental, right?)

Finally, if all else fails, ask to contact the nearest Green Angel, who may be able to explain to officials that you are covered by insurance. See also "Mexican Auto Insurance," in "Getting There," earlier in this chapter.

CAR RENTALS You'll get the best price if you reserve a car at least a week in advance in the United States. U.S. car-rental firms include **Advantage** (© 800/777-5500 in the U.S. and Canada; www.arac.com), **Avis** (© 800/331-1212 in the U.S., 800/879-2847 in Canada; www.avis.com), **Budget** (© 800/527-0700 in the U.S. and Canada; www.budget.com), **Hertz** (© 800/654-3131 in the U.S. and Canada; www.hertz.com), **National** (© 800/227-7368 in the U.S. and Canada; www.nationalcar.com), and **Thrifty** (© 800/847-4389 in the U.S. and Canada; www.thrifty.com), which often offers discounts for rentals in Mexico. For European travelers, **Kemwel Holiday Auto** (© 800/678-0678; www.kemwel.com) and **Auto Europe** (© 800/223-5555; www.autoeurope.com) can arrange Mexican rentals, sometimes through other agencies. These and some local firms have offices in Mexico City and most other large Mexican cities. You'll find rental desks at airports, all major hotels, and many travel agencies.

Cars are easy to rent if you are 25 or older and have a major credit card, valid driver's license, and passport with you. Without a credit card, you must leave a cash deposit, usually a big one. One-way rentals are usually simple to arrange, but they are more costly.

Car-rental costs are high in Mexico because cars are more expensive. The condition of rental cars has improved greatly over the years, and clean new cars are the norm. You will pay the least for a manual car without air-conditioning. Prices may be considerably higher if you rent around a major holiday. Also double-check charges for insurance—some companies

(Warning **Bus Hijackings**

The U.S. Department of State notes that bandits target long-distance buses traveling at night, but daylight robberies have occurred as well. First-class buses on toll (*cuota*) roads sustain a markedly lower crime rate than second-class and third-class buses that travel the less secure "free" (*libre*) highways.

will increase the insurance rate after several days. Always ask for detailed information about all charges you will be responsible for.

Car-rental companies usually write credit card charges in U.S. dollars.

Deductibles Be careful—these vary greatly; some are as high as $2,500 (£1,250) which comes out of your pocket immediately in case of damage. On a compact car, Hertz's deductible is roughly $1,000 (£500) and Avis's is $500 (£250).

Insurance Insurance is offered in two parts: **Collision and damage** insurance covers your car and others if the accident is your fault, and **personal accident** insurance covers you and anyone in your car. Read the fine print on the back of your rental agreement and note that insurance may be invalid if you have an accident while driving on an unpaved road.

Damage Inspect your car carefully and note every damaged or missing item, no matter how minute, on your rental agreement, or you may be charged.

BY TAXI

Taxis are the preferred way to get around almost all of Mexico's resort areas, and around Mexico City. Fares for short trips within towns are generally preset by zone, and are quite reasonable compared with U.S. rates. (Los Cabos is one exception; another is taxi service to the north side of the bay from Puerto Vallarta. Travelers are better off renting a car than paying these exorbitant taxi fares—about $100/£50 for a one-way trip to Punta Mita.) For longer trips or excursions to nearby cities,

taxis can generally be hired for around $15 to $20 (£7.50-£10) per hour, or for a negotiated daily rate. A negotiated one-way price is usually much less than the cost of a rental car for a day, and a taxi travels much faster than a bus. For anyone who is uncomfortable driving in Mexico, this is a convenient, comfortable alternative. A bonus is that you have a Spanish-speaking person with you in case you run into trouble. Many taxi drivers speak at least some English. Your hotel can assist you with the arrangements.

BY BUS

Except for the Baja peninsula, where bus service is not well developed, Mexican buses run frequently, are readily accessible, and can transport you almost anywhere you want to go. Taking the bus is much more common in Mexico than in the U.S., and the executive and first-class coaches can be as comfortable as business class on an airline. Buses are often the only way to get from large cities to other nearby cities and small villages. Don't hesitate to ask questions if you're confused about anything, but note that little English is spoken in bus stations.

Dozens of Mexican companies operate large, air-conditioned, Greyhound-type buses between most cities. Classes are *segunda* (second), *primera* (first), and *ejecutiva* (deluxe), which goes by a variety of names. Deluxe buses often have fewer seats than regular buses, show video movies, are air-conditioned, and make few stops. Many run express from point to point. They are well worth the few dollars more. In rural areas, buses are often of the school-bus variety, with lots of local color.

Whenever possible, it's best to buy your reserved-seat ticket, often using a computerized system, a day in advance on long-distance routes and especially before holidays.

5 Money & Costs

Overall, Mexico is considerably cheaper than most U.S. and European destinations, although prices vary significantly depending on the specific location. The most expensive destinations are those with the largest number of foreign visitors, such as Cancún and Los Cabos. The least expensive are those off the beaten path and in small rural villages. In the major cities, such as the capital, prices vary greatly depending on the neighborhood. As you might imagine, tourist zones tend to be much more expensive than local areas.

The currency in Mexico is the **peso.** Paper currency comes in denominations of 20, 50, 100, 200, and 500 pesos. Coins come in denominations of 1, 2, 5, 10, and 20 pesos, and 20 and 50 **centavos** (100 centavos = 1 peso). The current exchange rate for the U.S. dollar, and the one used in this book, is 11 pesos; at that rate, an item that costs 11 pesos would be equivalent to US$1 (50p). The exchange rate for the British pound is 22 pesos.

Getting **change** is a problem. Small-denomination bills and coins are hard to come by, so start collecting them early in your trip. Shopkeepers and taxi drivers everywhere always seem to be out of change and small bills; that's doubly true in markets. There seems to be an expectation that the customer should provide appropriate change, rather than the other way around.

Many establishments that deal with tourists, especially in coastal resort areas, quote prices in dollars. To avoid confusion, they use the abbreviations "Dlls." for dollars and "M.N." (*moneda nacional,* or national currency) for pesos.

Don't forget to have enough pesos to carry you over a weekend or Mexican holiday, when banks are closed. In general, avoid carrying the U.S. $100 bill, the bill most commonly counterfeited in Mexico and therefore the most difficult to exchange, especially in smaller towns. Because small bills and coins in pesos are hard to come by in Mexico, the $1 bill is very useful for tipping. *Note:* A tip of U.S. coins, which cannot be exchanged into Mexican currency, is of no value to the service provider.

The bottom line on exchanging money: Ask first, and shop around. Banks generally pay the top rates.

Casas de cambio (exchange houses) are generally more convenient than banks because they have more locations and longer hours; the rate of exchange may be the same as at a bank or slightly lower. Before leaving a bank or exchange-house window, count your change in front of the teller before the next client steps up.

Large airports have currency-exchange counters that often stay open whenever flights are operating. Though convenient, they generally do not offer the most favorable rates.

A hotel's exchange desk commonly pays less favorable rates than banks; however, when the currency is in a state of flux, higher-priced hotels are known to

Money Matters

The **universal currency sign ($)** is used to indicate pesos in Mexico. The use of this symbol in this book, however, denotes U.S. currency.

Tips A Few Words about Prices

Prices in this book have been converted to U.S. dollars and British pounds at 11 pesos to the dollar and 22 pesos to the pound. Most hotels in Mexico—except places that receive little foreign tourism—quote prices in U.S. dollars. Thus, currency fluctuations are unlikely to affect the prices most hotels charge.

Mexico has a **value-added tax** of 15% (*Impuesto de Valor Agregado*, or IVA; pronounced "ee-bah") on most everything, including restaurant meals, bus tickets, and souvenirs. (Exceptions are Cancún, Cozumel, and Los Cabos, where the IVA is 10%; as ports of entry, they receive a break on taxes.) Hotels charge the usual 15% IVA, plus a locally administered bed tax of 2% (in most areas), for a total of 17%. In Cancún, Los Cabos, and Cozumel, hotels charge the 10% IVA plus 2% room tax. The prices quoted by hotels and restaurants do not necessarily include IVA. You may find that upper-end properties (three or more stars) quote prices without IVA included, while lower-priced hotels include IVA. Ask to see a printed price sheet and ask if the tax is included.

pay higher rates than banks, in an effort to attract dollars. *Note:* In almost all cases, you receive a better rate by changing money first, then paying.

You'll avoid lines at airport ATMs (automated teller machines) by exchanging at least some money—just enough to cover airport incidentals and transportation to your hotel—before you leave home (though don't expect the exchange rate to be ideal). You can exchange money at your local American Express or Thomas Cook office or at your bank. American Express also dispenses traveler's checks and foreign currency via **www.americanexpress.com** or © **800/673-3782,** but they'll charge a $15 (£7.50) order fee and additional shipping and handling costs.

Banks in Mexico are rapidly expanding and improving services. They tend to be open weekdays from 9am until 5pm, and often for at least a half day on Saturday. In larger resorts and cities, they can generally accommodate the exchange of dollars (which used to stop at noon) anytime during business hours. Some, but not all, banks charge a 1% fee to exchange traveler's checks. But you can pay for most purchases directly with traveler's checks at the establishment's stated exchange rate. Don't even bother with personal checks drawn on a U.S. bank—the bank will wait for your check to clear, which can take weeks, before giving you your money.

Travelers to Mexico can easily withdraw money from **ATMs** in most major cities and resort areas. The U.S. Department of State recommends caution when you're using ATMs in Mexico, stating that they should only be used during business hours and in large protected facilities, but this pertains primarily to Mexico City, where crime remains a significant problem. In most resorts in Mexico, the use of ATMs is perfectly safe—just use the same precautions you would at any ATM. Universal bank cards (such as the Cirrus and PLUS systems) can be used. This is a convenient way to withdraw money and avoid carrying too much with you at any time. The exchange rate is generally more favorable than at *casas de cambio*. Most machines offer Spanish/English menus and dispense pesos, but some offer the option of withdrawing dollars.

HEALTH 65

The **Cirrus** (© 800/424-7787; www. mastercard.com) and **PLUS** (© 800/ 843-7587; www.visa.com) networks span the globe. Go to your bank card's website to find ATM locations at your destination. Be sure you know your daily withdrawal limit before you depart. *Note:* Many banks impose a fee every time you use a card at another bank's ATM, and that fee can be higher for international transactions (although seldom more than $2 in Mexico) than for domestic ones. The bank from which you withdraw cash may also charge a fee. For international withdrawal fees, ask your bank.

Credit cards are another safe way to carry money. They also provide a convenient record of all your expenses, and they generally offer relatively good exchange rates. You can withdraw cash advances from your credit cards at banks or ATMs, but high fees make credit-card cash advances a pricey way to get cash. Keep in mind that you'll pay interest from the moment of your withdrawal, even if you pay your monthly bills on time. Also, note that many banks now assess a 1% to 3% "transaction fee" on **all** charges you incur abroad (whether you're using the local currency or your native currency).

In Mexico, Visa, MasterCard, and American Express are the most accepted cards. You'll be able to charge most hotel, restaurant, and store purchases, as well as almost all airline tickets, on your credit card. Pemex gas stations have begun to accept credit card purchases for gasoline, though this option may not be available everywhere and often not at night—check before you pump. You can get cash advances of several hundred dollars on your card, but there may be a wait of 20 minutes to 2 hours. Charges will be made in pesos, then converted into dollars by the bank issuing the credit card. Generally you receive the favorable bank rate when paying by credit card. However, be aware that some establishments in Mexico add a 5% to 7% surcharge when you pay with a credit card. This is especially true when using American Express. Many times, advertised discounts will not apply if you pay with a credit card.

For tips and telephone numbers to call if your wallet is stolen or lost, go to "Lost & Found," in the "Fast Facts" section of this chapter.

6 Health

GENERAL AVAILABILITY OF HEALTH CARE

In most of Mexico's resort destinations, you can usually find health care that meets U.S. standards. The U.S. Department of State notes that excellent health facilities are available in Mexico City, but training and availability of emergency responders may be below U.S. standards. Care in more remote areas is limited. Standards of medical training, patient care, and business practices vary greatly among medical facilities in beach resorts throughout Mexico. In recent years, some U.S. citizens have complained that certain health-care facilities in beach resorts have taken advantage of them by overcharging or providing unnecessary medical care.

Prescription medicine is broadly available at Mexico pharmacies; however, be aware that you may need a copy of your prescription or to obtain a prescription from a local doctor. This is especially true in the border towns, such as in Tijuana, where many Americans have been crossing into Mexico specifically for the purpose of purchasing lower-priced prescription medicines.

Contact the **International Association for Medical Assistance to Travellers (IAMAT;** © 716/754-4883 or, in

Canada, 416/652-0137; www.iamat.org) for tips on travel and health concerns in the countries you're visiting and for lists of local, English-speaking doctors. The United States **Centers for Disease Control and Prevention** (✆ **800/311-3435;** www.cdc.gov) provides up-to-date information on health hazards by region or country, and offers tips on food safety. **Travel Health Online** (www.tripprep. com), sponsored by a consortium of travel medicine practitioners, may also offer helpful advice on traveling abroad. You can find listings of reliable medical clinics overseas at the **International Society of Travel Medicine** (www.istm.org).

COMMON AILMENTS

SUN EXPOSURE Mexico is synonymous with sunshine; most of the country is bathed in intense sunshine most of the year. Avoid excessive exposure, especially in the tropics where UV rays are more dangerous. The hottest months in Mexico are April and May in the south, and July through September along the Pacific Coast, including Baja California. The deserts of northern Mexico are extremely hot in summer.

DIETARY RED FLAGS Travelers' diarrhea (locally known as *turista,* the Spanish word for "tourist")—persistent diarrhea, often accompanied by fever, nausea, and vomiting—used to attack many travelers to Mexico. (Some in the U.S. call this "Montezuma's revenge," but you won't hear it called that in Mexico.) Widespread improvements in infrastructure, sanitation, and education have greatly diminished this ailment, especially in well-developed resort areas. Most travelers make a habit of drinking only bottled water, which also helps to protect against unfamiliar bacteria. In resort areas, and generally throughout Mexico, only purified ice is used. If you do come down with this ailment, nothing beats Pepto Bismol, readily available in Mexico.

Imodium is also available in Mexico and is used by many travelers for a quick fix. A good high-potency (or "therapeutic") vitamin supplement and even extra vitamin C can help; yogurt is good for healthy digestion.

Since dehydration can quickly become life-threatening, the Public Health Service advises that you be careful to replace fluids and electrolytes (potassium, sodium, and the like) during a bout of diarrhea. Drink Pedialyte, a rehydration solution available at most Mexican pharmacies, or natural fruit juice, such as guava or apple (stay away from orange juice, which has laxative properties), with a pinch of salt added.

The U.S. Public Health Service recommends the following measures for preventing travelers' diarrhea: **Drink only purified water** (boiled water, canned or bottled beverages, beer, or wine). **Choose food carefully.** In general, avoid salads (except in first-class restaurants), uncooked vegetables, undercooked protein, and unpasteurized milk or milk products, including cheese. Choose food that is freshly cooked and still hot. Avoid eating food prepared by street vendors. In addition, something as simple as **clean hands** can go a long way toward preventing *turista.*

HIGH-ALTITUDE HAZARDS Travelers to certain regions of Mexico occasionally experience **elevation sickness,** which results from the relative lack of oxygen and the decrease in barometric pressure that characterizes high elevations (more than 1,500m/5,000 ft.). Symptoms include shortness of breath, fatigue, headache, insomnia, and even nausea. Mexico City is at 2,100m (6,720 ft.) above sea level, as are a number of other central and southern cities, such as San Cristóbal de las Casas (even higher than Mexico City). At high elevations, it takes about 10 days to acquire the extra red blood corpuscles you need to adjust to

Tips Over-the-Counter Drugs in Mexico

Antibiotics and other drugs that you'd need a prescription to buy in the States are often available over the counter in Mexican pharmacies. Mexican pharmacies also carry a limited selection of common over-the-counter cold, sinus, and allergy remedies.

---

the scarcity of oxygen. To help your body acclimate, drink plenty of fluids, avoid alcohol, and don't overexert yourself during the first few days. If you have heart or lung trouble, consult your doctor before flying above 2,400m (7,872 ft.).

BUGS, BITES & OTHER WILDLIFE CONCERNS Mosquitoes and **gnats** are prevalent along the coast and in the Yucatán lowlands. *Repelente contra insectos* (insect repellent) is a must, and it's not always available in Mexico. If you'll be in these areas and are prone to bites, bring along a repellent that contains the active ingredient DEET. Avon's Skin So Soft also works extremely well. Another good remedy to keep the mosquitoes away is to mix citronella essential oil with basil, clove, and lavender essential oils. If you're sensitive to bites, pick up some antihistamine cream from a drugstore at home.

Most readers won't ever see an *alacrán* (scorpion). But if one stings you, go immediately to a doctor. The one lethal scorpion found in some parts of Mexico is the *Centruroides,* part of the Buthidae family, characterized by a thin body, thick tail, and triangular-shaped sternum. Most deaths from these scorpions result within 24 hours of the sting as a result of respiratory or cardiovascular failure, with children and elderly people most at risk. Scorpions are not aggressive (they don't hunt for prey), but they may sting if touched, especially in their hiding places. In Mexico, you can buy scorpion toxin antidote at any drugstore. It is an injection, and it costs around $25 (£13). This is a good idea if you plan to camp in a remote area, where medical assistance can be several hours away.

TROPICAL ILLNESSES You shouldn't be overly concerned about tropical diseases if you stay on the normal tourist routes and don't eat street food. However, both dengue fever and cholera have appeared in Mexico in recent years. Talk to your doctor or to a medical specialist in tropical diseases about precautions you should take. You can also get medical bulletins from the U.S. Department of State and the Centers for Disease Control and Prevention (see "General Availability of Health Care," earlier in this chapter). You can protect yourself by taking some simple precautions: Watch what you eat and drink; don't swim in stagnant water (ponds, slow-moving rivers, or wells); and avoid mosquito bites by covering up, using repellent, and sleeping under netting. The most dangerous areas seem to be on Mexico's west coast, away from the big resorts.

WHAT TO DO IF YOU GET SICK AWAY FROM HOME

Any English-speaking embassy or consulate staff in Mexico can provide a list of area doctors who speak English. The U.S. Embassy's consular section, for example, keeps a list of reliable English-speaking doctors. If you get sick in Mexico, consider asking your hotel concierge to recommend a local doctor—even his or her own. You can also try the emergency room at a local hospital or urgent care facility. Many hospitals also have walk-in clinics for emergency cases that are not

Tips Smoke Free Mexico?

In early 2008, the Mexican president signed into law a nationwide smoking ban in workplaces and public buildings, and on public transportation. Under this ground-breaking law, private businesses are only permitted to allow public smoking in enclosed ventilated areas. Hotels may maintain up to 25% of guest rooms for smokers. Violators will face stiff fines, and smokers refusing to comply could receive up to 36-hour jail sentences. Businesses have until October 3, 2008, to create the ventilated smoking areas. It is too early to know how strictly authorities will enforce the law, and its application is likely to be uneven across the country. Despite some uncertainty over how thoroughly the legislation will be followed and enforced, they place Mexico—where a significant percentage of the population smokes—at the forefront of efforts to curb smoking and improve public health in Latin America. So before you light up, be sure to ask about the application of local laws in Mexican public places and businesses you visit.

life-threatening; you may not get immediate attention, but you won't pay emergency room prices.

For travel to Mexico, you may have to pay all medical costs upfront and be reimbursed later. Medicare and Medicaid do not provide coverage for medical costs outside the U.S. (that means neither Medicare nor Medicaid reimburses for emergency health care in Mexico, either). Before leaving home, find out what medical services your health insurance covers. To protect yourself, consider buying medical travel insurance (see "Medical Insurance," under "Travel Insurance," above).

Very few health insurance plans pay for medical evacuation back to the U.S. (which can cost $10,000 and more). A number of companies offer global medical evacuation services. If you're ever

hospitalized more than 150 miles from home, **MedjetAssist** (© **800/527-7478;** www.medjetassist.com) will pick you up and fly you to the hospital of your choice, virtually anywhere, in a medically equipped and staffed aircraft—24 hours day, 7 days a week. Annual memberships are $225 (£113) individual, $350 (£175) family; you can also purchase short-term memberships.

It is generally less expensive and more reliable to contract a U.S.-based company for a medical evacuation from Mexico to the U.S. than to contract a Mexican-based company. Contact the consular affairs section of the U.S. Embassy in Mexico City or nearest consulate for suggestions.

We list **additional emergency numbers** in the "Fast Facts" appendix, p. 762.

7 Safety

Although the vast majority of visitors to Mexico return home unharmed, it should be noted that taxi robberies, kidnappings, highway carjackings, and other crimes have beset tourists as well as locals in recent years. And in border regions—

including tourist cities such as Tijuana and Ciudad Chihuahua—drug-related violence and organized crime have escalated.

Throughout Mexico, precautions are necessary, but travelers should be realistic. You can generally trust a person whom you approach for help or directions, but be wary of anyone who approaches you offering the same. The more insistent the person is, the more cautious you should be.

Exercise caution when you're in unfamiliar areas, and be aware of your surroundings at all times. Leave valuables and irreplaceable items in a safe place, or don't bring them at all. A significant number of pickpocket incidents, purse snatchings, and hotel-room thefts do occur. Use hotel safes when available. And remember that public transportation is a popular place for wallet thefts and purse snatchings.

Before you travel to any notable hot spots in Mexico (see below), consult **www.travel.state.gov** for the U.S. Department of State's country specific information and travel alerts.

U.S.-MEXICO BORDER VIOLENCE

On April 14, 2008, the U.S. Department of State heightened its Travel Alert regarding crime along the U.S.–Mexico border. Most violence has afflicted drug gang members and their patrons, Mexican police and judges, or journalists. In 2007 in Tijuana, however, dozens of U.S. citizens were kidnapped or killed in crimes apparently unrelated to drugs. Daylight gun brawls have taken place in shopping centers, and armed robberies and carjackings are on the rise. Criminals have been known to wear police or military uniforms and travel in vehicles that resemble police cars. Some travelers along the border and in Tijuana have been followed and harassed while in their vehicles.

MEXICO CITY

Violent crime is also serious in the capital. Do not wear fine jewelry, expensive watches, or display any other obvious signs of wealth. Muggings are common by day and by night. Theft is even common at the Benito Juárez International Airport, where items such as briefcases,

cameras, or laptops are common targets. To avoid theft upon arrival, incoming passengers in need of pesos should use the exchange counters or ATMs in the arrival/departure gate area, where access is restricted, rather than changing money after passing through Customs.

Avoid the use of the **green Volkswagen** and **libre taxis** taken off the street, many of which have been involved in "pirate" robberies, muggings, and kidnappings. These taxis are also common in incidents where passengers are "hijacked" and released only after they are forced to withdraw the limit on their ATM bank cards. Always use official airport or radio taxis (called *sitios*), instead.

CRIME IN RESORT TOWNS

A significant number of rapes have been reported in Cancún and other resort areas, usually at night or in the early morning. Drug-related violence, including shooting and kidnapping, has increased in Acapulco recently. Although this violence is not targeted at foreign residents or tourists, visitors in these areas should be vigilant in their personal safety. Armed street crime is a serious problem in all the major cities. Some bars and nightclubs, especially in resort cities such as Cancún, Cabo San Lucas, Mazatlán, Acapulco, and Tijuana, can be havens for drug dealers and petty criminals.

CRIME NATIONWIDE
KIDNAPPINGS

Kidnapping—including the kidnapping of non-Mexicans—continues at alarming rates. The U.S. Department of State Travel Alert for Mexico states the following: "In recent years, dozens of U.S. citizens have been kidnapped in Mexico and many cases remain unresolved. Moreover, new cases of disappearances and kidnap-for-ransom continue to be reported. No one can be considered immune from kidnapping on the basis of occupation, nationality, or other factors. Criminals have been known to follow and harass U.S. citizens traveling in their vehicles, particularly in border areas including Nuevo Laredo, Matamoros, and Tijuana. U.S. citizens who believe they are being followed should notify Mexican officials as soon as possible."

So-called "express kidnappings"—an attempt to get quick cash in exchange for the release of an individual—have occurred in almost all the large cities in Mexico and appear to target not only the wealthy, but the middle class. Car theft and carjackings are also a common occurrence. More specific precautions appear in chapter 5. (See also "Emergencies" in "Appendix A: Fast Facts in Mexico.")

HIGHWAY SAFETY

Travelers should exercise caution while traveling Mexican highways, avoiding travel at night, and using toll (cuota) roads rather than the less secure free (libre) roads whenever possible. It is also advised that you should not hike alone in backcountry areas nor walk alone on less-frequented beaches, ruins, or trails.

U.S. citizens are advised to cooperate with official checkpoints when traveling on Mexican highways.

Bus travel should take place during daylight hours on first-class conveyances. Although bus hijackings and robberies have occurred on toll roads, buses on toll roads have a markedly lower rate of incidents than second-class and third-class buses that travel the less secure "free" highways. The Embassy advises caution when traveling by bus from Acapulco toward Ixtapa or Huatulco. Although the police have made some progress in bringing this problem under control, armed robberies of entire busloads of passengers still occur.

BRIBES & SCAMS

As is the case around the world, there are the occasional bribes and scams in Mexico, targeted at people believed to be naive, such as telltale tourists. For years, Mexico was known as a place where bribes—called *mordidas* (bites)—were expected; however, the country is rapidly changing. Frequently, offering a bribe today, especially to a police officer, is considered an insult, and it can land you in deeper trouble.

If you believe someone is soliciting a **bribe** from you, don't utter a word of Spanish to Mexican officials, even if you're fluent. That way you'll appear innocent, all the while understanding every word.

When you are crossing the border, should the person who inspects your car ask for a tip, you can ignore this request—but understand that the official may suddenly decide that a complete search of your belongings is in order. If you sense you're being asked for a *propina* (literally, "tip"; colloquially, "bribe"), how much should you offer? Usually $3 to $5 (£1.50-£2.50) or the equivalent in pesos will do the trick.

Many tourists have the impression that everything works better in Mexico if you "tip"; however, in reality, this only perpetuates the *mordida* tradition. If you are pleased with a service, feel free to tip. But you shouldn't tip simply to attempt to get away with something illegal or inappropriate—whether it is evading a ticket that's deserved or a car inspection as you're crossing the border.

Whatever you do, **avoid impoliteness;** you won't do yourself any favors if you insult a Mexican official. Extreme politeness, even in the face of adversity, rules Mexico. In Mexico, *gringos* have a reputation for being loud and demanding. By adopting the local custom of excessive courtesy, you'll have greater success in negotiations of any kind. Stand your ground, but do it politely.

As you travel in Mexico, you may encounter several types of **scams,** which are typical throughout the world. One involves some kind of a **distraction** or feigned commotion. While your attention is diverted, for example, a pickpocket makes a grab for your wallet. In another common scam, an **unaccompanied child** pretends to be lost and frightened and takes your hand for safety. Meanwhile the child or an accomplice plunders your pockets. A third involves **confusing currency.** A shoeshine boy, street musician, guide, or other individual might offer you a service for a price that seems reasonable—in pesos. When it comes time to pay, he or she tells you the price is in dollars, not pesos. Be very clear on the price and currency when services are involved.

8 Specialized Travel Resources

TRAVELERS WITH DISABILITIES

Mexico may seem like one giant obstacle course to travelers in wheelchairs or on crutches. At airports, you may encounter steep stairs before finding a well-hidden elevator or escalator—if one exists. Airlines will often arrange wheelchair assistance to the baggage area. Porters are generally available to help with luggage at airports and large bus stations, once you've cleared baggage claim.

Mexican airports are upgrading their services, but it is not uncommon to board from a remote position, meaning you either descend stairs to a bus that ferries you to the plane, which you board by climbing stairs, or you walk across the tarmac to your plane and ascend the stairs. Deplaning presents the same problem in reverse.

Escalators (and there aren't many in the country) are often out of order. Stairs without handrails abound. Few restrooms are equipped for travelers with disabilities; when one is available, access to it may be through a narrow passage that won't accommodate a wheelchair or a person on crutches. Many deluxe hotels (the most expensive) now have rooms with bathrooms designed for people with disabilities. Those traveling on a budget should stick with one-story hotels or hotels with elevators. Even so, there will probably still be obstacles somewhere. Generally speaking, no matter where you are, someone will lend a hand, although you may have to ask for it.

One exception is Puerto Vallarta, which has renovated the majority of its downtown sidewalks and plazas with ramps that accommodate wheelchairs (as well as baby strollers). Even the airport has ramps adjacent to all stairways, and special wheelchair lifts. A local citizen with disabilities deserves the credit for this impressive task—hopefully setting the stage for greater accessibility in other towns and resorts.

Most disabilities shouldn't stop anyone from traveling. There are more options and resources out there than ever before.

Organizations that offer a vast range of resources and assistance to travelers with disabilities include **MossRehab** (© 800/CALL-MOSS;** www.mossresourcenet. org); the **American Foundation for the Blind (AFB;** © 800/232-5463; www. afb.org); and **SATH (Society for Accessible Travel & Hospitality;** © 212/447-7284; www.sath.org). **AirAmbulance Card.com** is now partnered with SATH and allows you to pre-select top-notch hospitals in case of an emergency.

Access-Able Travel Source (www. access-able.com) offers a comprehensive database on travel agents from around the world with experience in accessible travel; destination-specific access information; and links to such resources as service animals, equipment rentals, and access guides.

Many travel agencies offer customized tours and itineraries for travelers with disabilities. Among them are **Flying Wheels**

Travel (© 507/451-5005; www.flying
wheelstravel.com) and **Accessible Jour-
neys** (© 800/846-4537 or 610/521-
0339; www.disabilitytravel.com).
Flying with Disability (www.flying-
with-disability.org) is a comprehensive
information source on airplane travel.
Avis Rent a Car (© 888/879-4273) has
an "Avis Access" program that offers services for customers with special travel
needs. These include specially outfitted
vehicles with swivel seats, spinner knobs,
and hand controls; mobility scooter
rentals; and accessible bus service. Be sure
to reserve well in advance.

Also check out the quarterly magazine
Emerging Horizons (www.emerging
horizons.com), available by subscription
($16.95/£8.50 year in the U.S.; $21.95/
£11 outside the U.S.).

The "Accessible Travel" link at **Mobil-
ity-Advisor.com** (www.mobility-advisor.
com) offers a variety of travel resources to
people with disabilities.

British travelers should contact **Holiday Care** (© 0845-124-9971 in the
U.K. only; www.holidaycare.org.uk) to
access a wide range of travel information
and resources for people with disabilities
and elderly people.

For more on organizations that offer
resources to travelers with disabilities, go
to **www.frommers.com/planning**.

GAY & LESBIAN TRAVELERS

Mexico is a conservative country, with
deeply rooted Catholic religious traditions. Public displays of same-sex affection are rare and still considered shocking
for men, especially outside of urban or
resort areas. Women in Mexico frequently walk hand in hand, but anything
more would cross the boundary of
acceptability. However, gay and lesbian
travelers are generally treated with respect
and should not experience harassment,
assuming they give the appropriate regard
to local customs.

In Mexico City, the **Zona Rosa** is a
gay-friendly neighborhood with numerous bars and cafes dedicated to gay and
lesbian patrons. Puerto Vallarta is perhaps
the most welcoming and accepting destination in Mexico. Susan Weisman's travel
service, **Bayside Properties** (© 322/
223-4424; www.baysidepropertiespv.
com), rents gay-friendly condos, villas,
and hotels for individuals and large
groups. Her services are customized to
individual needs, and she can offer airport pickups and in-villa cooks.

**The International Gay and Lesbian
Travel Association** (IGLTA; © 800/
448-8550 or 954/776-2626; www.iglta.
org) is the trade association for the gay and
lesbian travel industry, and offers an online
directory of gay- and lesbian-friendly
travel businesses and tour operators.

Many agencies offer tours and travel
itineraries specifically for gay and lesbian
travelers. Among them are **Above and
Beyond Tours** (© 800/397-2681; www.
abovebeyondtours.com); **Now, Voyager**
(© 800/255-6951; www.nowvoyager.
com); and **Olivia Cruises & Resorts**
(© 800/631-6277; www.olivia.com).

Gay.com Travel (© 415/834-6500;
www.gay.com/travel or www.outand
about.com) is an excellent online successor to the popular *Out & About* print
magazine. It provides regularly updated
information about gay-owned, gay-ori-
ented, and gay-friendly lodging, dining,
sightseeing, nightlife, and shopping
establishments in every important destination worldwide. British travelers
should click on the "Travel" link at **www.
uk.gay.com** for advice and gay-friendly
trip ideas.

The Canadian website **GayTraveler**
(www.gaytraveler.ca) offers ideas and
advice for gay travel all over the world.

The following travel guides are available at many bookstores, or you can order
them from any online bookseller: *Spar-
tacus International Gay Guide, 35th*

Edition (Bruno Gmünder Verlag; www. spartacusworld.com/gayguide), and the *Damron* guides (www.damron.com), with separate, annual books for gay men and lesbians.

For more gay and lesbian travel resources, see **www.frommers.com/ planning**.

SENIOR TRAVEL

Mexico is a popular country for retirees. For decades, North Americans have been living indefinitely in Mexico by returning to the border and recrossing with a new tourist permit every 6 months. Mexican immigration officials have caught on, and now limit the maximum time in the country to 6 months within any year. This is to encourage even partial residents to acquire proper documentation.

Some of the most popular places for long-term stays are Guadalajara, Lake Chapala, Ajijic, and Puerto Vallarta, all in the state of Jalisco; San Miguel de Allende and Guanajuato in Guanajuato state; Cuernavaca in Morelos; Alamos in Sinaloa; and increasingly destinations in Baja California.

AIM-Adventures in Mexico, Apartado Postal 31–70, 45050 Guadalajara, Jalisco, is a well-written, informative newsletter for prospective retirees. Issues have evaluated retirement in Aguascalientes, Puebla, San Cristóbal de las Casas, Puerto Angel, Puerto Escondido and Huatulco, Oaxaca, Taxco, Tepic, Manzanillo, Melaque, and Barra de Navidad. Subscriptions are $29 (£15) to the United States.

Sanborn Tours, 2015 S. 10th St., P.O. Drawer 519, McAllen, TX 78505-0519 (© **800/395-8482;** www.sanborns.com), offers a "Retire in Mexico" orientation tour.

Mention the fact that you're a senior citizen when you make your travel reservations. Although all the major U.S. airlines have canceled their senior discount and coupon book programs, many hotels still offer lower rates for seniors. In most cities, people older than 60 qualify for reduced admission to theaters, museums, and other attractions, and discounted fares on public transportation.

Members of **AARP,** 601 E St. NW, Washington, DC 20049 (© **888/687-2277;** www.aarp.org), get discounts on hotels, airfares, and car rentals. AARP offers members a wide range of benefits, including *AARP: The Magazine* (www. aarpmagazine.org) and a monthly newsletter. Anyone over 50 can join.

Many reliable agencies and organizations target the 50-plus market. **Elderhostel** (© **800/454-5768;** www.elder hostel.org) arranges study programs for those ages 55 and older. **ElderTreks** (© **800/741-7956;** www.eldertreks.com) offers small-group tours to off-the-beaten-path or adventure-travel locations, restricted to travelers 50 and older.

Recommended publications offering travel resources and discounts for seniors include: the quarterly magazine *Travel 50 & Beyond* (www.travel50andbeyond. com) and the bestselling paperback *Unbelievably Good Deals and Great Adventures That You Absolutely Can't Get Unless You're Over 50 2005–2006, 16th Edition* (McGraw-Hill), by Joann Rattner Heilman.

For more information and resources on travel for seniors, see **www.frommers. com/planning**.

FAMILY TRAVEL

If you have trouble getting your kids out of the house in the morning, dragging them thousands of miles away may seem like an insurmountable challenge. But family travel can be immensely rewarding, giving you new ways of seeing the world through the eyes of children.

Children are considered the national treasure of Mexico, and Mexicans will warmly welcome and cater to your children. Many parents were reluctant to

Tips Advice for Female Travelers

Mexicans in general, and men in particular, are nosy about single travelers, especially women. If a taxi driver or anyone else with whom you don't want to become friendly asks about your marital status, family, and so forth, my advice is to make up a set of answers (regardless of the truth): "I'm married, traveling with friends, and I have three children." Saying you are single and traveling alone may send the wrong message. U.S. television—widely viewed now in Mexico—has given many Mexican men the image of American single women as being sexually promiscuous. Check out the award-winning website **Journeywoman** (www.journeywoman.com), a "real-life" women's travel information network where you can sign up for a free e-mail newsletter and get advice on everything from etiquette and dress to safety; or the travel guide *Safety and Security for Women Who Travel,* by Sheila Swan and Peter Laufer (Travelers' Tales, Inc.), offering common-sense tips on safe travel. In Mexico City, consider riding the women-only bus (see. p. 108).

bring young children into Mexico in the past, primarily due to health concerns, but I can't think of a better place to introduce children to the exciting adventure of exploring a different culture. Some of the best destinations include Puerto Vallarta, Cancún, and La Paz. Hotels can often arrange for a babysitter.

Before leaving, ask your doctor which medications to take along. Disposable diapers cost about the same in Mexico but are of poorer quality. You can get Huggies Supreme and Pampers identical to the ones sold in the United States, but at a higher price. Many stores sell Gerber's baby foods. Dry cereals, powdered formulas, baby bottles, and purified water are easily available in midsize and large cities or resorts.

Cribs may present a problem; only the largest and most luxurious hotels provide them. However, rollaway beds are often available. Child seats or high chairs at restaurants are common.

Consider bringing your own car seat; they are not readily available for rent in Mexico.

Every country's regulations differ, but in general children traveling abroad should

have plenty of documentation on hand, particularly if they're traveling with someone other than their own parents (in which case a notarized form letter from a parent is often required). For details on entry requirements for children traveling abroad, go to the U.S. Department of State website (www.travel.state.gov); click on "International Travel," "Travel Brochures," and "Foreign Entry Requirements."

To locate accommodations, restaurants, and attractions that are particularly kid-friendly, refer to the "Kids" icon throughout this guide.

Recommended family travel websites include **Family Travel Forum** (www.familytravelforum.com), a comprehensive site that offers customized trip planning; **Family Travel Network** (www.familytravelnetwork.com), an online magazine providing travel tips; and **Travel WithYourKids.com** (www.travelwithyourkids.com), a comprehensive site written by parents for parents, offering sound advice for long-distance and international travel with children.

For a list of more family-friendly travel resources, visit **www.frommers.com/planning**.

STUDENT TRAVEL

Because Mexicans consider higher education a luxury rather than a birthright, there is no formal network of student discounts and programs. Most Mexican students travel with their families rather than with other students, so student discount cards are not commonly recognized.

However, more hostels have entered the student travel scene. **Hostelling International México** (℗ **55/5518-1726;** www.hostellingmexico.com) offers a list of hostels that meet international standards in Guadalajara, Guanajuato, Merida, Mexico City, Oaxaca, and Puebla. **Hostels.com** offers a list of hostels in Acapulco, Cancún, Guadalajara, Mexico City, Oaxaca, Playa del Carmen, Puerto Escondido, Puebla, and Zacatecas.

9 Sustainable Tourism

Sustainable tourism is conscientious travel. It means being careful with the environments you explore and respecting the communities you visit. Two overlapping components of sustainable travel are **ecotourism** and **ethical tourism. The International Ecotourism Society (TIES)** defines ecotourism as responsible travel to natural areas that conserves the environment and improves the well-being of local people. TIES suggests that ecotourists follow these principles:

- Minimize environmental impact.
- Build environmental and cultural awareness and respect.
- Provide positive experiences for both visitors and hosts.
- Provide direct financial benefits for conservation and for local people.
- Raise sensitivity to host countries' political, environmental, and social climates.
- Support international human rights and labor agreements.

You can find some eco-friendly travel tips and statistics, as well as touring companies and associations—listed by destination under "Travel Choice"—at the **TIES** website, **www.ecotourism.org.** Also check out **Ecotravel.com,** which lets you search for sustainable touring companies in several categories (water-based, land-based, spiritually oriented, and so on).

While much of the focus of ecotourism is about reducing impacts on the natural environment, ethical tourism concentrates on ways to preserve and enhance local economies and communities, regardless of location. You can embrace ethical tourism by staying at a locally owned hotel or shopping at a store that employs local workers and sells locally produced goods.

Responsible Travel (www.responsible travel.com) is a great source of sustainable travel ideas; the site is run by a spokesperson for ethical tourism in the travel industry. **Sustainable Travel International** (www.sustainabletravelinternational.org) promotes ethical tourism practices, and manages an extensive directory of sustainable properties and tour operators around the world.

In the U.K., **Tourism Concern** (www.tourismconcern.org.uk) works to reduce social and environmental problems connected to tourism. The **Association of Independent Tour Operators** (**AITO;** www.aito.co.uk) is a group of specialist operators leading the field in making holidays sustainable.

Volunteer travel has become increasingly popular among those who want to venture beyond the standard group-tour experience to learn languages, interact with locals, and make a positive difference while on vacation. Volunteer travel usually doesn't require special skills—just a willingness to work hard—and programs vary in length from a few days to a

Tips It's Easy Being Green

Here are a few ways you can help conserve fuel and energy when you travel:

- Each time you take a flight or drive a car, greenhouse gases release into the atmosphere. You can help neutralize this danger to the planet through "carbon offsetting"—paying someone to invest your money in programs that reduce your greenhouse gas emissions by the same amount you've added. Before buying carbon offset credits, just make sure that you're using a reputable company, one with a proven program that invests in renewable energy. Reliable carbon offset companies include **Carbonfund** (www.carbonfund.org), **TerraPass** (www.terrapass.org), and **Carbon Neutral** (www.carbonneutral.org).

- Whenever possible, choose nonstop flights; they generally require less fuel than indirect flights that stop and take off again. Try to fly during the day—some scientists estimate that nighttime flights are twice as harmful to the environment. And pack light—each 15 pounds of luggage on a 5,000-mile flight adds up to 50 pounds of carbon dioxide emitted.

- Where you stay during your travels can have a major environmental impact. To determine the green credentials of a property, ask about trash disposal and recycling, water conservation, and energy use; also question if sustainable materials were used in the construction of the property. The website **www.greenhotels.com** recommends green-rated member hotels around the world that fulfill the company's stringent environmental requirements. Also consult **www.environmentallyfriendlyhotels.com** for more green accommodation ratings.

- At hotels, request that your sheets and towels not be changed daily. (Many hotels already have programs like this in place.) Turn off the lights and air-conditioner (or heater) when you leave your room.

- Use public transport where possible—trains, buses, and even taxis are more energy-efficient forms of transport than driving. Even better is to walk or cycle; you'll produce zero emissions and stay fit and healthy on your travels.

- If renting a car is necessary, ask the rental agent for a hybrid, or rent the most fuel-efficient car available. You'll use less gas and save money at the tank.

- Eat at locally owned and operated restaurants that use produce grown in the area. This contributes to the local economy and cuts down on greenhouse gas emissions by supporting restaurants where the food is not flown or trucked in across long distances.

- For sustainable travel information about Mexico, visit the **Global Journal of Practical Ecotourism** (www.planeta.com), **GloCal Mexico** (www.glocaltravel.net), or **Go Nomad** (www.gonomad.com).

number of weeks. Some programs provide free housing and food, but many require volunteers to pay for travel expenses, which can add up fast.

For general information on volunteer travel, visit **www.volunteerabroad.org** and **www.idealist.org**. Specific volunteer options in Mexico are listed under "Special Interest Trips," later in this chapter.

Before you commit to a volunteer program, it's important to make sure any money you're giving is truly going back to the local community, and that the work you'll be doing will be a good fit for you. **Volunteer International** (www.volunteer international.org) has a helpful list of questions to ask to determine the intentions and the nature of a volunteer program.

ANIMAL-RIGHTS ISSUES
BULLFIGHTS

Bullfighting is considered an important part of Latin culture, but before you attend a correo, you should know that, in all likelihood, the bull will undergo torture, shed lots of blood, and die before a team of horses drags its carcass unceremoniously out of the ring. That said, a bullfight is a portal into understanding Mexico's Spanish colonial past, and traditional machismo is on full display. Bullfights take place in towns as different as Tijuana and Puerto Vallarta, and they afford a colorful spectacle like no other, with a brass band playing; the costumed matador's macho stare; men shaking their heads at less-than-perfect swipes of the cape; and overly made-up, bloodthirsty women chanting *"ole,"* waving their white hankies, and throwing roses, jackets, and hats at the matador's feet. There is also the extremely miniscule chance that, if the bull puts up a good enough fight or pierces his horn through the matador's leg, he will be spared for breeding purposes. It does happen, if only rarely. To read more about the implications of attending a bullfight, visit **www.peta.org**, the website of People for the Ethical Treatment of Animals (PETA).

Frommers.com: The Complete Travel Resource

Planning a trip or just returned? Head to **Frommers.com,** voted Best Travel Site by *PC Magazine*. We think you'll find our site indispensable before, during, and after your travels—with expert advice and tips; independent reviews of hotels, restaurants, attractions, and preferred shopping and nightlife venues; vacation giveaways; and an online booking tool. We publish the complete contents of over 135 travel guides in our **Destinations** section, covering over 4,000 places worldwide. Each weekday, we publish original articles that report on **Deals and News** via our free **Frommers.com Newsletters.** What's more, **Arthur Frommer** himself blogs 5 days a week, with cutting opinions about the state of travel in the modern world. We're betting you'll find our **Events** listings an invaluable resource; it's an up-to-the-minute roster of what's happening in cities everywhere—including concerts, festivals, lectures, and more. We've also added weekly **podcasts, interactive maps,** and hundreds of new images across the site. Finally, don't forget to visit our **Message Boards,** where you can join in conversations with thousands of fellow Frommer's travelers and post your trip report once you return.

SWIMMING WITH DOLPHINS

Many resort cities advertise opportunities to swim with dolphins, but organizations such as Greenpeace and the Humane Society are questioning the ethics of the activity. Often, the dolphins in question are cooped up in unhealthy, overcrowded conditions, and many of the organizations that offer dolphin swims don't adhere to international regulations for the treatment of animals. For more information, see the websites of the **Whale and Dolphin Conservation Society** (www.wdcs.org) and **Tread Lightly** (www.treadlightly.org).

10 Packages for the Independent Traveler

Package tours are simply a way to buy the airfare, accommodations, and other elements of your trip (such as car rentals, airport transfers, and sometimes even activities) at the same time and often at discounted prices.

One good source of package deals is the airlines themselves. Most major airlines offer air/land packages, including **American Airlines Vacations** (© 800/321-2121; www.aavacations.com), **Delta Vacations** (© 800/654-6559; www.delta vacations.com), **Continental Airlines Vacations** (© 800/301-3800; www.co vacations.com), and **United Vacations** (© 888/854-3899; www.unitedvacations. com). Several big online travel agencies— **Expedia, Travelocity, Orbitz, Site59,** and **Lastminute.com**—also do a brisk business in packages.

Travel packages are also listed in the travel section of your local Sunday newspaper. Or check ads in the national travel magazines such as *Arthur Frommer's Budget Travel Magazine, Travel + Leisure, National Geographic Traveler,* and *Condé Nast Traveller.*

RECOMMENDED PACKAGERS

- **AeroMéxico Vacations** (© 800/245-8585; www.aeromexico.com) offers year-round packages to almost every destination it serves, including Acapulco, Cancún, Cozumel, Ixtapa/Zihuatanejo, Los Cabos, and Puerto Vallarta. AeroMéxico has a large selection (more than 100) of resorts in these destinations and more, in a variety of price ranges. The best deals are from Houston, Dallas, San Diego, Los Angeles, Miami, and New York, in that order.

- **Alaska Airlines Vacations** (© 800/468-2248; www.alaskaair.com/vaca tions) sells packages to Ixtapa/Zihuatanejo, Loreto, Los Cabos, Manzanillo/Costa Alegre, Mazatlán, and Puerto Vallarta. Alaska flies direct from Los Angeles, San Diego, San Jose, San Francisco, Seattle, Vancouver, Anchorage, and Fairbanks. The website offers unpublished discounts that are not available through the phone operators.

- **American Airlines Vacations** (© 800/321-2121; www.aavacations. com) has year-round deals to Acapulco, Cancún, the Riviera Maya, Guadalajara, Los Cabos, Mexico City, and Puerto Vallarta. You don't have to fly with American if you can get a better deal on another airline; land-only packages include hotel, hotel tax, and airport transfers. American's hubs to Mexico are Dallas/Fort Worth, Chicago, and Miami. The website offers unpublished discounts that are not available through the operators.

- **US Airways Vacations** (© 800/235-9298; www.usairwaysvacations.com) has deals to Acapulco, Cancun, Cozumel, Guadalajara, Ixtapa, Los Cabos, Manzanillo, Mexico City, and Puerto Vallarta. Many packages to Los Cabos include car rentals. The website offers discounted featured specials that are not available through the operators. You can also book hotels without air by calling the toll-free number.

- **Apple Vacations** (© 800/365-2775; www.applevacations.com) offers inclusive packages to all the beach resorts, and has the largest choice of hotels in Acapulco, Cancún, Cozumel, Huatulco, Ixtapa, Loreto, Los Cabos, Manzanillo, Mazatlán, Puerto Vallarta, and the Riviera Maya. Scheduled carriers for the air portion include American, United, Mexicana, Delta, US Airways, Reno Air, Alaska Airlines, and AeroMéxico. Apple perks include baggage handling and the services of a company representative at major hotels.

- **Classic Vacations** (© 800/635-1333; www.classicvacations.com) specializes in package vacations to Mexico's finest luxury resorts. It combines discounted first-class and economy airfare on American, Continental, Mexicana, Alaska, America West, and Delta with stays at the most exclusive hotels in Cancún, the Riviera Maya, Mérida, Oaxaca, Guadalajara, Mexico City, Puerto Vallarta, Mazatlán, Costa Alegre, Manzanillo, Ixtapa/Zihuatanejo, Acapulco, Huatulco, and Los Cabos. The prices are not for bargain hunters but for those who seek luxury, nicely packaged.

- **Continental Vacations** (© 800/301-3800; www.covacations.com) has year-round packages to Acapulco, Cancún, Cozumel, Guadalajara, Huatulco, Ixtapa, Los Cabos, Mazatlán, Mexico City, and Puerto Vallarta. The best deals are from Houston; Newark, NJ; and Cleveland. You must fly Continental. The Internet deals offer savings not available elsewhere.

- **Delta Vacations** (© 800/654-6559; www.deltavacations.com) has year-round packages to Acapulco, Cancún,

Cozumel, Guadalajara, Ixtapa/Zihuatanejo, Los Cabos, Mazatlán, Mérida, and Puerto Vallarta. Atlanta is the hub, so expect the best prices from there.

- **Funjet Vacations** (© 888/558-6654; www.funjet.com) is one of the largest vacation packagers in the United States. Funjet has packages to Acapulco, Cancún, Cozumel, the Riviera Maya, Los Cabos, Mazatlán, Ixtapa, and Puerto Vallarta. You can choose a charter or fly on American, Continental, Delta, AeroMéxico, US Airways, Alaska Air, or United.

- **GOGO Worldwide Vacations** (© 888/636-3942; www.gogowwv.com) has trips to all the major beach resorts, including Acapulco, Cancún, Mazatlán, Puerto Vallarta, and Los Cabos. It offers several exclusive deals from higher-end hotels. Book through any travel agent.

- **Mexicana Vacations,** or MexSeaSun Vacations (© 800/531-7921; www.mexicana.com) offers getaways to all the resorts. Mexicana operates daily direct flights from Los Angeles to Los Cabos, Mazatlán, Cancún, Puerto Vallarta, Manzanillo, and Ixtapa/Zihuatanejo.

- **Mexico Travel Net** (© 800/511-4848 or 619/474-0100; www.mexicotravelnet.com) offers most of the well-known travel packages to Mexico beach resorts, plus last-minute specials.

- **Pleasant Holidays** (© 800/742-9244; www.pleasantholidays.com) is one of the largest vacation packagers in the United States, with hotels in Acapulco, Cancún, Cozumel, Huatulco, Ixtapa/Zihuatanejo, Los Cabos, Mazatlán, Mérida, Mexico City, Oaxaca, and Puerto Vallarta.

REGIONAL PACKAGERS
From the East Coast: Liberty Travel (© 888/271-1584; www.libertytravel.com), one of the biggest packagers in the

Finds Boutique Lodgings

Mexico lends itself beautifully to the concept of small, private hotels in idyllic settings. They vary in style from grandiose estate to palm-thatched bungalow. **Mexico Boutique Hotels** (www.mexicoboutiquehotels.com) specializes in smaller places to stay with a high level of personal attention and service. Most options have less than 50 rooms, and the accommodations consist of entire villas, *casitas*, bungalows, or a combination. The Yucatán is especially notable for the luxury haciendas throughout the peninsula.

Northeast, often runs a full-page ad in the Sunday papers, with frequent Mexico specials. You won't get much in the way of service, but you will get a good deal.

From the West: SunTrips (© **800/ 514-5194** for departures within 14 days; www.suntrips.com) is one of the largest West Coast packagers for Mexico, with departures from San Francisco and Denver; regular charters to Cancún, Cozumel, Los Cabos, and Puerto Vallarta; and a large selection of hotels.

From the Southwest: Town and Country (book through travel agents) packages regular deals to Los Cabos, Mazatlán, Puerto Vallarta, Ixtapa, Manzanillo, Cancún, Cozumel, and Acapulco with America West from the airline's Phoenix and Las Vegas gateways.

For more information on Package Tours and for tips on booking your trip, see **www.frommers.com**.

11 Special-Interest Trips

ACADEMIC TRIPS & LANGUAGE CLASSES

For Spanish-language instruction, **IMAC** (© **866/306-5040;** www.spanishschool. com.mx) offers programs in Guadalajara and Playa del Carmen. The **Spanish Institute** (© **800/539-9710;** www. spanishtoday.com) is affiliated with intensive Spanish language schools in Puebla and Merida.

To explore your inner Frida or Diego while in Mexico, look into **Mexico Art Tours,** 1233 E. Baker Dr., Tempe, AZ 85282 (© **888/783-1331** or 480/ 730-1764; www.mexicanarttours.com). Typically led by Jean Grimm, a specialist in the arts and cultures of Mexico, these unique tours feature compelling speakers who are themselves respected scholars and artists. Itineraries include visits to Chiapas, Guadalajara, Guanajuato, Puebla, Puerto Vallarta, Mexico City, San Miguel

de Allende, and Veracruz. Special tours involve archaeology, architecture, interior design, and culture—such as a Day of the Dead tour.

The **Archaeological Conservancy,** 5301 Central Ave. NE, Suite 402, Albuquerque, NM 87108 (© **505/266-1540;** www.americanarchaeology.com), presents various trips each year, led by an expert, usually an archaeologist. The trips change from year to year and space is limited; make reservations early.

ATC Tours and Travel, Av. 16 de Septiembre 16, 29200 San Cristóbal de las Casas, Chis. (© **967/678-2550** or -2557; fax 967/678-3145; www.atctours.com), a Mexico-based tour operator with an excellent reputation, offers specialist-led trips, primarily in southern Mexico. In addition to trips to the ruins of Palenque and Yaxchilán (extending into Belize and Guatemala by river, plane, and bus if desired), ATC runs horseback tours to Chamula or Zinacantán, and day trips to the ruins of Toniná around San Cristóbal de las Casas; birding in the rainforests of Chiapas and Guatemala (including in the El Triunfo Reserve of Chiapas); hikes to the shops and homes of textile artists of the Chiapas highlands; and walks from the Lagos de Montebello in the Montes Azules Biosphere Reserve, with camping and canoeing. The company can also prepare custom itineraries.

ADVENTURE & WELLNESS TRIPS

AMTAVE (Asociación Mexicana de Turismo de Aventura y Ecoturismo, A.C.) is an active association of ecotourism and adventure tour operators. It publishes an annual catalog of participating firms and their offerings, all of which must meet certain criteria for security, quality, and training of the guides, as well as for sustainability of natural and cultural environments. For more information, contact **AMTAVE** (© **55/5688-3883;** www.amtave.org).

Baja Expeditions, 2625 Garnet Ave., San Diego, CA 92109 (© **800/843-6967**

or 858/581-3311; fax 858/581-6542; www.bajacx.com), offers natural-history cruises, whale-watching, sea kayaking, camping, scuba diving, and resort and day trips from Loreto, Baja California. Small groups and special itineraries are Baja Expeditions' specialty.

The California Native, 6701 W. 87th Place, Los Angeles, CA 90045 (© **800/ 926-1140** or 310/642-1140; www.cal native.com), offers small-group deluxe 7-, 8-, 9-, 11-, and 14-day escorted tours through the Copper Canyon. Many trips visit the towns of Batopilas, Urique, and Tejeban as well as the customary destinations of Creel, El Fuerte, Divisadero, Chihuahua, and Cerocahui. The guides are known throughout the area for their work with the Tarahumara Indians. They also cover Chiapas, the Yucatán, and Baja California.

Canyon Travel, 900 Rich Creek Lane, Bulverde, TX 78163-2872 (© **800/843- 1060** in the U.S. and Canada, or 830/ 885-2000; fax 830/885-2010; www. canyontravel.com), specializes in the Copper Canyon and has a variety of adventures, from easy to challenging. It designs trips for special-interest groups of

---

Tips The Mexican Sports Scene

Mexico has more than 120 **golf courses,** concentrated in the resort areas, with excellent options in Mexico City and Guadalajara. Los Cabos, in Baja Sur, has become the country's preeminent golf destination; the Puerto Vallarta area enjoys a growing reputation. For details on courses and events, see chapters 10 and 19. Visitors to Mexico can also enjoy **tennis, racquetball, squash, water-skiing, surfing, bicycling,** and **horseback riding. Scuba diving** is excellent, not only off the Yucatán's Caribbean coast (especially Cozumel), but also on the Pacific coast at Puerto Vallarta and Manzanillo, and off Baja in the Sea of Cortez. **Mountain and volcano climbing** is a rugged sport that allows you to meet like-minded adventurers from around the world. The top peaks are just 80km (50 miles) south of Mexico City—the snowcapped volcanoes Ixtaccihuatl (5,255m/ 17,236 ft.) and Popocatépetl (5,420m/17,778 ft.). Popocatépetl was not accepting visitors at press time, due to recent volcanic activity. For information on visiting and climbing the volcanoes, contact the **Club de Exploraciones de México A.C.** in Mexico City (© **55/5740-8032;** www.cemac.org.mx).

agriculturists, geologists, rock hounds, and birders, and custom trips to the Copper Canyon. The owner works with the Tarahumara Indians.

Far Flung Adventures, P.O. Box 377, Terlingua, TX 79852 (☎ **800/359-2627;** www.farflung.com), organizes specialist-led river trips to the Antigua, Actopan, and Filobobos rivers, in Veracruz.

Mexico Travel Link Ltd., 300-3665 Kingsway, Vancouver, BC V5R 5W2 Canada (☎ **604/454-9044;** fax 604/454-9088; www.mexicotravel.net), runs adventure, cultural, and sports tours to Mexico City and surrounding areas, Baja, Veracruz, the Copper Canyon, the Mayan Route, and other destinations.

Mountain Travel Sobek, 6420 Fairmount Ave., El Cerrito, CA 94530 (☎ **888/687-6235** or 510/594-6000; www.mtsobek.com), takes groups kayaking in the Sea of Cortez and hiking in Copper Canyon. Sobek is one of the world's leading ecotour outfitters.

Natural Habitat Adventures, 2945 Center Green Court, Suite H, Boulder, CO 80301 (☎ **800/543-8917** or 303/449-3711; www.nathab.com), offers naturalist-led natural history and adventure tours. Expeditions focus on monarch butterfly-watching in Michoacán and gray whale-watching in Baja.

NatureQuest, 30872 South Coast Hwy., Suite PMB, Laguna Beach, CA 92651 (☎ **800/369-3033** or 949/499-9561; www.naturequesttours.com), specializes in the natural history, culture, and wildlife of the Copper Canyon and the remote lagoons and waterways off Baja California. A 10-day hiking trip ventures into rugged areas of the canyon; a less strenuous trip goes to Creel and Batopilas, in the same area. Baja trips get close to nature, with special permits for venturing via two-person kayak into sanctuaries for whales and birds.

Sea Kayak Adventures, P.O. Box 3862, Coeur d'Alene, ID 83816 (☎ **800/616-1943** or 208/765-3116; fax 208/

765-5254; www.seakayakadventures.com), features kayak trips in both the Sea of Cortez Loreto Bay National Marine Park and Magdalena Bay, with a focus on whale-watching. This company has the exclusive permit to paddle Magdalena Bay's remote northern waters, and they guarantee gray whale sightings. Trips combine paddling of 4 to 5 hours per day, with hiking across dunes and beaches, while nights are spent camping.

Sea Trek Ocean Kayaking Center, P.O. Box 1987, Sausalito, CA 94966 (☎ **415/488-1000;** fax 415/332-8790; www.seatrekkayak.com), has been alternating sea-kayaking trips between Alaska and Baja for 20 years, which has provided them an intimate knowledge of the peninsula's coastline. Eight-day trips depart from and return to Loreto. An optional day excursion to Bahía Magdalena for gray whale–watching is available. Full boat support is provided, and no previous paddling experience is necessary.

Tour Baja, P.O. Box 827, Calistoga, CA 94515 (☎ **800/398-6200** or 707/942-4550; fax 707/942-8017; www.tour baja.com), offers sea-kayaking, mountain bike, and mule pack tours in the Loreto area. Owner Trudi Angell has guided these trips for more than 20 years. She and her guides offer firsthand knowledge of the area. Kayaking, mountain biking, pack trips, and sailing charters combine these elements with outdoor adventures.

Trek America, P.O. Box 189, Rockaway, NJ 07866 (☎ **800/873-5872;** www.trekamerica.com), organizes lengthy, active trips that combine trekking, hiking, van transportation, and camping in the Yucatán, Chiapas, Oaxaca, the Copper Canyon, and Mexico's Pacific coast, and a trip that covers Mexico City, Teotihuacán, Taxco, Guadalajara, Puerto Vallarta, and Acapulco.

Veraventuras, Santos Degollado 81-8, 91000 Xalapa, Ver. (☎ **228/818-9579,** or 01-800/712-6572 in Mexico; fax

228/818-9680; www.veraventuras.xalapa. net), uses specially trained leaders on well organized and -outfitted adventures into the state of Veracruz, including hiking, mountain climbing, repelling, extreme sports, and rafting the rapids of the Antigua, Actopan, Barranca, and Filobobos rivers.

FOOD & WINE TRIPS

If you're looking to eat your way through Mexico, sign up with **Culinary Adventures,** 6023 Reid Dr. NW, Gig Harbor, WA 98335 (© **253/851-7676;** fax 253/851-9532; www.marilyntausend.com). It runs a short but select list of cooking tours in Mexico. Culinary Adventures features well-known cooks, with travel to regions known for excellent cuisine. The owner, Marilyn Tausend, is the author of *Cocinas de la Familia* (Family Kitchens), *Savoring Mexico,* and *Mexican,* and co-author of *Mexico the Beautiful Cookbook.*

VOLUNTEER & WORKING TRIPS

For numerous links to volunteer and internship programs throughout Mexico involving teaching, caring for children, providing health care, feeding the homeless, and doing other community and public service, visit **www.volunteer abroad.com.**

If you're interested in teaching English to Mexican university students in the colonial town of Dolores Hidalgo or Queretaro, **Global Volunteers,** 375 E. Little Canada Rd., St. Paul, MN 55117 (© **80/487-1074;** fax 651/482-0915; www.globalvolunteers.org) arranges 2-week programs for a fee.

ProWorld Service Corps, 1215 Taylor Ave., Bellingham, WA (© **877/429-6753;** fax 406/252-3973; www.mypro world.org) organizes health care projects in Oaxaca such as working in local health clinics, vaccinating children, and assisting in health outreach to rural areas. Programs last 5 days and longer, and require basic medical knowledge (such as first aid) and intermediate Spanish.

12 Staying Connected

TELEPHONES

Mexico's telephone system is slowly but surely catching up with modern times. Most telephone numbers have 10 digits. Every city and town that has telephone access has a two-digit (Mexico City, Monterrey, and Guadalajara) or three-digit (everywhere else) area code. In Mexico City, Monterrey, and Guadalajara, local numbers have eight digits; elsewhere, local numbers have seven digits. To place a local call, you do not need to dial the area code. Many fax numbers are also regular phone numbers; ask whoever answers for the fax tone (*"me da tono de fax, por favor"*).

The **country code** for Mexico is **52.**

To call Mexico: If you're calling Mexico from the United States:

1. Dial the international access code: 011 from the U.S.; 00 from the U.K., Ireland, or New Zealand; or 0011 from Australia.
2. Dial the country code: 52.
3. Dial the two- or three-digit area code, then the eight- or seven-digit number. For example, if you wanted to call the U.S. consulate in Acapulco, the entire number would be 011-52-744-469-0556. If you wanted to dial the U.S. embassy in Mexico City, the entire number would be 011-52-55-5209-9100.

To make international calls: To make international calls from Mexico, dial 00, then the country code (U.S. or Canada 1, U.K. 44, Ireland 353, Australia 61, New Zealand 64). Next, dial the area code and number. For example, to call the British Embassy in Washington, you would dial 00-1-202-588-7800.

For directory assistance: Dial ⓒ **040** if you're looking for a number inside Mexico. *Note:* Listings usually appear under the owner's name, not the name of the business, and your chances to find an English-speaking operator are slim.

For operator assistance: If you need operator assistance in making a call, dial ⓒ **090** to make an international call, and ⓒ **020** to call a number in Mexico.

Toll-free numbers: Numbers beginning with 800 within Mexico are toll-free, but calling a U.S. toll-free number from Mexico costs the same as an overseas call. To call an 800 number in the U.S., dial 001-880 and the last seven digits of the toll-free number. To call an 888 number in the U.S., dial 001-881 and the last seven digits of the toll-free number. For a number with an 887 prefix, dial 882; for 866, dial 883.

CELLPHONES

Telcel is Mexico's expensive, primary cellphone provider. It has upgraded its systems to GSM and offers good coverage in much of the country, including the major cities and resorts. Most Mexicans buy their cellphones without a specific coverage plan and then pay as they go or purchase pre-paid cards with set amounts of air-time credit. These cellphone cards with scratch-off pin numbers can be purchased in Telcel stores as well as many newspaper stands and convenience stores.

Many U.S. and European cellphone companies offer networks with roaming coverage in Mexico. Rates can be very high, so check with your provider before committing to making calls this way. An increasing number of Mexicans, particularly among the younger generation, prefer the less expensive rates of **Nextel** (www.nextel.com.mx), which features push-to-talk service. **Cellular Abroad** (www.cellularabroad.com) offers cellphone rentals and purchases as well as SIM cards for travel abroad. Whether you rent or purchase the cellphone, you need to purchase a SIM card that is specific for Mexico.

To call a Mexican cellular number in the same area code, dial 044 and then the number. To dial the cellular phone from anywhere else in Mexico, first dial 01, and then the three-digit area code and the seven-digit number. To dial it from the U.S., dial 011-52, plus the three-digit area code and the seven-digit number.

VOICE-OVER INTERNET PROTOCOL (VOIP)

If you have Web access while traveling, consider a broadband-based telephone service (in technical terms, **Voice over Internet Protocol,** or **VoIP**) such as Skype (www.skype.com) or Vonage (www.vonage.com), which allow you to make free international calls from your laptop or in a cybercafe. Neither service requires the people you're calling to have that service (though fees apply if they do not). Check the websites for details.

INTERNET & E-MAIL
WITH YOUR OWN COMPUTER

Wireless Internet access is increasingly common in Mexico's major cities and resorts. Mexico's largest airports offer Wi-Fi access provided for a fee by Telcel's Prodigy Internet service. Most five-star hotels now offer Wi-Fi in the guest rooms, although you will need to check in advance whether this service is free or for a fee. Hotel lobbies often have Wi-Fi, as well. To find public Wi-Fi hotspots in Mexico, go to **www.jiwire.com**; its Hotspot Finder holds the world's largest directory of public wireless hotspots.

WITHOUT YOUR OWN COMPUTER:

Many large Mexican airports have **Internet kiosks,** and quality Mexican hotels usually have business centers with Internet access. You can also check out such copy stores as **Kinko's** or **OfficeMax,** which offer computer stations with fully loaded software (as well as Wi-Fi).

13 Tips on Accommodations

MEXICO'S HOTEL RATING SYSTEM

The hotel rating system in Mexico is called "Stars and Diamonds." Hotels may qualify to earn one to five stars or diamonds. Many hotels that have excellent standards are not certified, but all rated hotels adhere to strict standards. The guidelines relate to service, facilities, and hygiene more than to prices.

Five-diamond hotels meet the highest requirements for rating: The beds are comfortable, bathrooms are in excellent working order, all facilities are renovated regularly, infrastructure is top-tier, and services and hygiene meet the highest international standards.

Five-star hotels usually offer similar quality, but with lower levels of service and detail in the rooms. For example, a five-star hotel may have less luxurious linens or, perhaps, room service during limited hours rather than 24 hours.

Four-star hotels are less expensive and more basic, but they still guarantee cleanliness and basic services such as hot water and purified drinking water. Three, two-, and one-star hotels are at least working to adhere to certain standards: Bathrooms are cleaned and linens are washed daily, and you can expect a minimum standard of service. Two- and one-star hotels generally provide bottled water rather than purified water.

The nonprofit organization Calidad Mexicana Certificada, A.C., known as Calmecac (www.calmecac.com.mx), is responsible for hotel ratings; visit their website for additional details about the rating system.

HOTEL CHAINS

In addition to the major international chains, you'll run across a number of less-familiar brands as you plan your trip to Mexico. They include:

- **Brisas Hotels & Resorts** (www. brisas.com.mx). These were the hotels that originally attracted jet-set travelers to Mexico. Spectacular in a retro way, these properties offer the laid-back luxury that makes a Mexican vacation so unique.
- **Fiesta Americana** and **Fiesta Inn** (www.posadas.com). Part of the Mexican-owned Grupo Posadas company, these hotels set the country's midrange standard for facilities and services. They generally offer comfortable, spacious rooms and traditional Mexican hospitality. Fiesta Americana hotels offer excellent beach-resort packages. Fiesta Inn hotels are usually more business oriented. Grupo Posadas also owns the more luxurious Caesar Park hotels and the eco-oriented Explorean hotels.
- **Hoteles Camino Real** (www.camino real.com). Once known as the premier Mexican hotel chain, Camino Real still maintains a high standard of service at its properties, although the

company was sold in 2005, and many of the hotels that once formed a part of it have been sold off or have become independent. Its beach hotels are traditionally located on the best beaches in the area. This chain also focuses on the business market. The hotels are famous for their vivid and contrasting colors.

- **NH Hoteles** (www.nh-hotels.com). The NH hotels are noted for their family-friendly facilities and quality standards. The beach properties' signature feature is a pool, framed by columns, overlooking the sea.

- **Quinta Real Grand Class Hotels and Resorts** (www.quintareal.com). These hotels, owned by Summit Hotels and Resorts, are noted for architectural and cultural details that reflect their individual regions. At these luxury properties, attention to detail and excellent service are the rule. Quinta Real is the top line Mexican hotel brand.

HOUSE RENTALS & SWAPS

House and villa rentals and swaps are becoming more common in Mexico, but no single recognized agency or business provides this service exclusively for Mexico. In the chapters that follow, we have provided information on independent services that we have found to be reputable.

You'll find the most extensive inventory of homes at **Vacation Rentals by Owner** (**VRBO;** www.vrbo.com). They have more than 33,000 homes and condominiums worldwide, including a large selection in Mexico. Another good option is **VacationSpot** (© **888/903-7768;** www.vacationspot.com), owned by Expedia and a part of its sister company Hotels.com. It has fewer choices, but the company's criteria for adding inventory is much more selective and often includes on-site inspections. They also offer toll-free phone support.

For tips on surfing for hotel deals online, visit **www.frommers.com**.

Suggested Mexico Itineraries

by David Baird

Mexico is a land of contrasts, which makes it the perfect destination for those seeking a little variety in their travels. Several of the suggested itineraries described below will take you through changing landscapes and both big-city and small-town Mexico. A few itineraries conclude at a beach resort so that you can relax a little at the end of your trip. But there's another reason for this: I wanted to make use of Mexico's major points of entry—the big international airports—and many of these happen to serve resorts. When I visit Mexico, I seldom book a round-trip ticket. I enter through one airport and leave through another, and usually I don't have to pay extra to do this. Times have changed, and round-trip fares aren't what they used to be.

Once inside Mexico, most travel is by bus, rental car, or a hired car and driver. There is only one true passenger train still operating. This train runs along the Copper Canyon to Chihuahua City and works well for the surf-to-sierra approach that I like (see "Los Cabos to Copper Canyon," below). I've tried to keep travel time to a minimum for obvious reasons, and so none of these itineraries can be called exhaustive explorations of Mexico. If you want to see all of Mexico's most famous sites, however, you can link the central archaeological tour with the Ruta Maya, which would take about 3 weeks.

Renting a car works really well for the Yucatán and a few other parts of the country. In other areas, it can be confusing, as road signs are not always posted. Hiring a car and driver or taking the bus for certain legs of the trip are reasonable options. Mexico has good buses with various categories of service. Once you're inside a town or city, it's usually best to use taxis, which are, for the most part, cheap and plentiful.

1 Central Mexico's Pre-Columbian Treasures in a Week

Most of Mexico's great archaeological sites, aside from those left by the Maya, are in the country's center, from Mexico City to the east. This trip takes you to the best of these and to the three most impressive archaeological museums in Mexico. The area in which all of this is located is relatively compact. It doesn't require a lot of travel time to cover, unless you add on a side trip to Oaxaca for the ruins of Monte Albán and Mitla.

Days ❶, ❷ & ❸: Mexico City

If you arrive at an early hour, go straight to the very heart of the nation: Mexico's City's *zócalo,* or main square (p. 144). There, poetically situated between the nation's preeminent cathedral and its National Palace, are the ruins of the Aztec's **Templo Mayor** (p. 132), left buried and forgotten until 1978. Explore the ruins and the museum. Dedicate your

Central Mexico's Pre-Columbian Treasures

first full day of activity to the **Museo Nacional de Antropología** (p. 130). By the third day, you should have adapted to the altitude and will be ready for a day trip to **Teotihuacán** (p. 154), "City of the Gods," where you can explore palaces and pyramids and climb to the summit of the **Pyramid of the Sun** (p. 157).

Day ④: Tlaxcala

Drive or take a bus to colonial Tlaxcala to view the vivid murals of **Cacaxtla** and the hilltop stronghold of **Xochitécatl** (p. 511). The murals are painted in an intriguing Maya style, with rich symbolism that invites speculation. Stay the night here and enjoy the slow rhythms and street life of the town. Though it is a state capital (in the smallest state in Mexico), Tlaxcala is small and off the beaten path. It still retains an unhurried, graceful air. Stroll over to the **Government Palace** (p. 509) to view the modern murals of artist Desiderio Hernández Xochitiotzin, which chronicle the history of the Tlax-caltecans, ancient rivals of the Aztecs. See p. 508.

Day ⑤: Puebla 🕭🕭 & Cholula

From Tlaxcala, it's a quick car or bus ride to colonial **Puebla** (p. 496) and its satellite town, Cholula, which was the ancient religious center of central Mexico. In the afternoon, visit the **Museo Amparo** (p. 502) to see its stunning collection of pre-Hispanic art, then head over to **Cholula** (p. 507) the next day to view the ruins of Mexico's largest pyramid, with the beautiful volcano "El Popo" as a backdrop. Visit the local churches of **Tonantz-intla** (p. 508) and **San Francisco Acatepec** (p. 508) for their beautiful Indian baroque design.

Day ⑥: Xalapa

From Puebla, it's on to bustling **Xalapa** (p. 511), a 3-hour drive from the dry central plateau to the misty slopes of the Sierra Madre Oriental. Visit the city's wonderful **Museo de Antropología** (p. 513), with a collection of megalithic Olmec heads and expressive Totonac art.

Day ⑦: Veracruz City 🕭

Next travel down to the old port city of **Veracruz** (p. 515). Enjoy a relaxing day in this lively town, with its coffee shops, tropical music, and dance. From here, you can fly out directly or via Mexico City. To extend your trip, you can head north to see the ruins of **El Tajín** (p. 523) or south to **Oaxaca** (p. 463) to see Monte Albán and Mitla.

2 The Best of Western Mexico in a Week

On this route, you enter Mexico through the León/Guanajuato International airport and leave from Ixtapa/Zihuatanejo. In between, you're treated to a variety of places and scenes—from the maze of streets and alleyways of the old mining town of Guanajuato, to the stately colonial city of Morelia, to the Indian town of Pátzcuaro, to the modern resort hotels of Ixtapa and Zihuatanejo. From November to March you can add a day trip from Morelia to a magical place in the mountain forests east of the city where millions of monarch butterflies congregate in a yearly ritual that is one of the most intriguing of nature's mysteries.

Day ❶: Guanajuato ❀❀❀

Take it easy until you get used to the altitude. Contract a taxi to give you a tour of the city by taking you along the panoramic highway that circles the narrow valley where the old city is nestled. Stop to take in the **view** from the statue of **El Pípila** (p. 210) before descending to the subterranean highway to see the houses cantilevered out over the road. Once you're ready for a stroll, try navigating through the jumble of streets surrounding the city's main plaza, taking time to visit a couple of the downtown **museums.** See p. 211.

Days ❷ & ❸: Morelia ❀

Take a taxi or bus for the 2½-hour drive to **Morelia** (p. 249). Build in some time to enjoy the **cathedral** from the vantage point of one of the many cafes and restaurants that front Avenida Madero. This is best done in late afternoon/early evening, when it appears to the casual visitor that no one in Morelia is at the office. Take a tour of the city the next day and enjoy coffee, a drink, or dinner on the terrace of the **Villa Montaña Hotel** (p. 256). In winter you can take a day trip to see the

monarch butterflies (p. 259). Another option is a day trip to the dormant volcano **El Paricutín** (p. 271).

Days ❹ & ❺: Pátzcuaro ❀❀❀ & the Lakeside Villages of the Purépecha

From Morelia, it's only an hour's drive to the picturesque town of **Pátzcuaro** (p. 260) and the heart of the Purépecha homeland. This is the Indian version of colonial Mexico. Enjoy a stroll around the two principal plazas of the town and pay a visit to the **House of Eleven Patios** (p. 264) and the **Museo de Artes e Industrias Populares** (p. 263) for a fascinating examination of all the different art forms practiced in the region. On your next day, hire a car or guide to take a tour of the lakeside villages and perhaps take a taxi to the town of **Santa Clara** (p. 269) to watch the coppersmiths at work.

Days ❻ & ❼: Ixtapa ❀ & Zihuatanejo

The new toll highway connecting the central highlands to these resorts will get you there in 4 to 5 hours. Relax for a couple of days and then catch a flight back home. See p. 403.

The Best of Western Mexico

3 Los Cabos to Copper Canyon

This itinerary offers a great deal of contrast and starts in the resort area of Los Cabos. After enjoying any number of seaside activities, take a short tour of southern Baja that includes bohemian Todos Santos before crossing the Sea of Cortez and boarding a train that climbs up through rugged Sierra Tarahumara, hugging the sides of the Copper Canyon. Stop here to enjoy the peace and the beauty, and then reboard the train heading to the historical city of Chihuahua, which was home to Pancho Villa. This tour has been made easier by improvements to the ferry service between La Paz and Topolobampo.

Days ❶, ❷ & ❸: Cabo San Lucas, San José del Cabo & Todos Santos 𝒜𝒜

Take your time partaking of the area's beauty and the many activities this large resort offers. Rent a car to drive along the coast and perhaps visit the town of **Todos Santos** (p. 730) to get a feel for the character of the region. See p. 698.

Day ❹: La Paz 𝒜𝒜 to Los Mochis

Take a bus or *colectivo* to **La Paz** and, from there, to the ferry dock. After a 5-hour voyage, you'll arrive at **Topolobampo** (p. 690), the port area of Los Mochis.

Days ❺ & ❻: Bahuichivo & Cerocahui 𝒜𝒜𝒜

The train departs early in the morning and, by late morning, is snaking its way through some of the most beautiful canyon land on the trip. By midday, you reach **Bahuichivo,** where you can get

transportation to the town and mission of **Cerocahui.** This is a good place for hiking, horseback riding, and driving tours to the overlook of **Cerro Gallego.** See p. 683.

Days ❼ & ❽: Creel 𝒜

Continue by train on to **Creel,** where you can get a car to take you to the nearby **Copper Canyon Sierra Lodge** (p. 686). Here you can enjoy the peace and quiet of the sierra, visit an old mission, hike to a nearby waterfall, and meet Tarahumara Indian women, who come to sell their pine-needle baskets and other handicrafts. See p. 684.

Days ❾ & ❿: Chihuahua 𝒜

You'll arrive at night. Use part of the next day to enjoy the historic downtown area and visit **Pancho Villa's house** (p. 694) before flying back home. See p. 691.

Los Cabos to Copper Canyon

4 La Ruta Maya in 2 Weeks

This route connects all the major Maya sites in Mexico. You could cover it quickly in 2 weeks or more slowly in a month; you could also break it up into two trips. (If you choose the 2-week route, you run the slight risk of overdosing on ruins by seeing too many in too short a time.) The best mode of travel is a rental car: The highways are not terribly busy and are, for the most part, in good shape.

Day ❶: Arrive in Cancún
After you arrive, enjoy the remainder of the day with a swim in the Caribbean or a relaxing afternoon poolside. See p. 527.

Day ❷: Ek Balam ৯৯৯ & Chichén Itzá ৯৯৯
Get on the modern toll highway that heads toward Mérida and take the exit for Valladolid. Head north, away from the town, to visit the ruins of **Ek Balam** (p. 675). Highlights include a sacred doorway richly decorated with vivid figures of gods and men. Then backtrack to Valladolid for lunch before driving the short distance to **Chichén Itzá** (p. 665) on the old federal highway. Just outside of town, stop to see the **cenotes of Dzitnup** and **Sammulá** (p. 674). Farther on is the **cave of Balankanché** (p. 672). When you get to Chichén, check into your hotel, and then go to the **ruins** later in the evening for the **sound-and-light show.** See p. 667.

Day ❸: Continuing to Uxmal ৯৯৯
Spend more time at the **ruins of Chichén Itzá** in the morning, then continue west on the toll highway toward Mérida, and turn off at Ticopó. Head south toward the town of **Acanceh** (p. 651) and Highway 18. Stop to see the small but interesting ruins in the middle of town, then proceed down Highway 18 to the ruins of **Mayapán** (p. 652). Afterward, continue through Ticul to Santa Elena and Uxmal. Experience the sound-and-light show. See p. 654.

Day ❹: Edzná
Visit **Uxmal** (p. 653) in the morning, then drive back toward Santa Elena and take Highway 261 south to Hopelchén and on to the impressive ruins of **Edzná** (p. 659). Nearby is a fancy hacienda turned hotel called **Uayamón** (p. 643) or drive into the town of Campeche and stay at more modest digs.

La Ruta Maya

Days ⑤ & ⑥: Palenque 🐾🐾, Bonampak & Yaxchilán

Stay on Highway 261 to Escárcega, then head west on Highway 186 toward Villahermosa, then south on Highway 199 to the town of **Palenque** (p. 473) with its magnificent ruins. The next day, go to the **ruins of Bonampak and Yaxchilán** (p. 480) using one of the local tour operators.

Days ⑦ & ⑧: San Cristóbal de las Casas 🐾🐾

Keep south on Highway 199 toward **San Cristóbal** (p. 481). On the way, take a swimming break at **Misol Ha** (p. 480),

and visit the ruins of **Toniná** outside of the town of Ocosingo. From San Cristóbal, go with one of the local guides to see the present-day Maya communities of **Chamula** and **Zinacantan** (p. 488). Spend some time enjoying the town.

Day ⑨: En Route to Calakmul 🐾🐾🐾

Retrace your steps to Escárcega and continue east on Highway 186. If there's time, visit the fascinating sculptures of **Balamkú** (p. 624). Spend the night at one of the hotels in the vicinity of the turnoff for Calakmul, one of the prime city-states of the classic age of the Maya, and not often visited.

Day ⑩: Calakmul & Becán ★★★

Get to **Calakmul** (p. 624) early. Keep your eyes open for wildlife as you drive along a narrow jungle road. All the area surrounding the city is a **wildlife preserve.** For most of the city's history, Calakmul was the main rival to the city of Tikal, which is present day Guatemala. It eventually defeated Tikal and subjugated it for a hundred years. Calakmul's **Structure 2** is the highest Maya pyramid in Mexico. Afterward, continue east on Highway 186 to see the ruins of **Becán,** a large ceremonial center with tall temples. Also in the vicinity are **Xpujil** and **Chicanná.** Spend the night on the shores of **Lake Bacalar,** where you can cool off in its blue waters. See p. 624.

Days ⑪ & ⑫: Tulum

Drive north on Highway 307 to **Tulum** and settle into one of the small beach hotels there. In the morning, walk through the ruins and enjoy the lovely view of the coast. See p. 611.

Day ⑬: Back to Cancún

Drive back to Cancún. Depending on your schedule, you can enjoy some more beach time or simply head to the airport (25 min. south of Cancún) and depart. See p. 527.

5

Mexico City

by Juan Cristiano

Mexico City is a passionate, cosmopolitan, sprawling metropolis—and one of the largest cities in the world. In recent years, travelers dismissed Mexico's capital because of its problems with crime, pollution, and unbridled growth. Now that these unsavory trends have begun to reverse, the culturally curious are rediscovering what originally led so many to this magnificent place. I love Mexico City, with all of its urban energy and historic and cultural treasures. Although many compare it to the great cities of Europe, I find it a singular experience. Along with urban sophistication, you'll find enduring traditions that date back to pre-Hispanic civilizations and a strong sense of Latin culture shaped by Spanish influence; it's an endearing mix of the majestically ancient with the irresistibly new.

Standing 2,239m (7,347 ft.) high, on an enormous dry lakebed in a highland valley surrounded by mountains, this was the power center of pre-Hispanic America, and it remains one of the most dynamic, fascinating, and charismatic cities in the world today.

For me, Mexico City is the only place where you can find clear insight into this captivating country—veiled in mysticism, infused with an appreciation of the moment, and proud of its heritage. Founded in 1325 A.D. as the ancient city of Tenochtitlán, it was the capital of the Aztec Empire and most important city in Mesoamerica by 1428 A.D. Today, Mexico City and its immediate surroundings

hold more than 25 million inhabitants—making it the most populated city in the Western Hemisphere (only Tokyo, in Asia, is larger).

You need only to stand in the center of the *zócalo*—the central plaza—to visually comprehend the undisputed significance of the Mexican capital. Here, the remains of an Aztec pyramid, a colonial church, and a towering modern office building face one another, a testament to the city's prominence in ancient and contemporary history. The Teotihuacán, Toltec, Aztec, and European conquistadors all contributed to the city's fascinating evolution, art, and heritage. Although residents refer to their city as simply México (*meh-hee-koh*), its multitude of ancient ruins, colonial masterpieces, and modern architecture has prompted others to call it "The City of Palaces."

The central downtown area resembles a European city, dominated by ornate French and Spanish-style buildings and broad boulevards, and interspersed with public art, parks, and gardens. This sprawling city is thoroughly modern and, in places, unsightly and chaotic, but it never strays far from its historical roots. In the center are the partially excavated ruins of the main Aztec temple; pyramids rise just beyond the city.

The sheer number of residents trying to exist here—amid economic malaise, high unemployment, and government corruption—has created an environment where petty crime (principally robberies) is common. Several years ago, Mexico

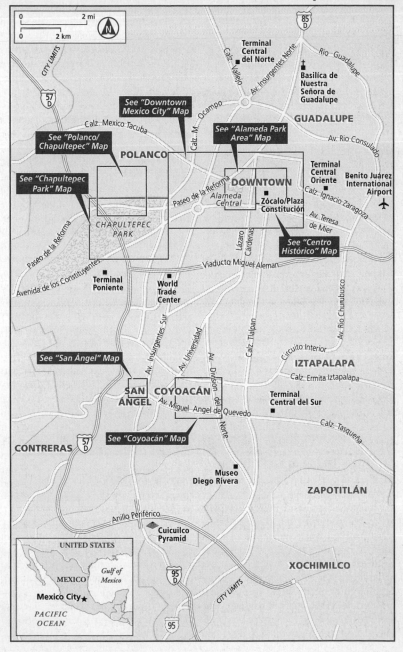

0   2 mi

0   2 km

CITY LIMITS

Terminal Central del Norte

Río Guadalupe

Av. Insurgentes Norte

Calz. Vallejo

Basilíca de Nuestra Señora de Guadalupe

GUADALUPE

Av. Río Consulado

Calz. Mexico Tacuba

Calz. M. Ocampo

See "Downtown Mexico City" Map

See "Alameda Park Area" Map

See "Polanco/ Chapultepec" Map

POLANCO

See "Chapultepec Park" Map

DOWNTOWN

Terminal Central Oriente

Benito Juárez International Airport

Paseo de la Reforma

Alameda Central

Zócalo/Plaza Constitución

Calz. Ignacio Zaragoza

Av. Teresa de Mier

CHAPULTEPEC PARK

Paseo de la Reforma

Lázaro Cárdenas

See "Centro Histórico" Map

Viaducto Miguel Aleman

Av. Río Churubusco

Avenida de los Constituyentes

Terminal Poniente

World Trade Center

Av. Insurgentes Sur

Av. Universidad

Av. División del Norte

Calz. Tlalpan

Circuito Interior

IZTAPALAPA

Calz. Ermita Iztapalapa

See "San Ángel" Map

SAN ÁNGEL

COYOACÁN

Av. Miguel Angel de Quevedo

Terminal Central del Sur

Calz. Tasqueña

CONTRERAS

See "Coyoacán" Map

ZAPOTITLÁN

Museo Diego Rivera

Anillo Periférico

Cuicuilco Pyramid

XOCHIMILCO

UNITED STATES

Gulf of Mexico

MEXICO

Mexico City ★

PACIFIC OCEAN

CITY LIMITS

City's notoriety came from its rising crime rate, a trend that is fortunately in reverse. Over the past several years, the city has achieved admirable progress in making visitors feel more secure, with special safety programs, faster response to reports of crime, a vastly increased police presence, and programs that are effectively combating corruption. By 2006, Mexico City had reduced crime rates by almost 40% from 1994's historic highs, with only .02% related to visitors to the city.

Violent crime in Mexico is largely concentrated among drug traffickers and politicians, but kidnappings and murders of businesspeople, both Mexican and foreign, are numerous. Mexico City has many treasures, but safety concerns demand that you dress and behave conservatively as you explore the city.

Technically, Mexico City is a federal district (similar to Washington, D.C.), called the Distrito Federal, or D.F. One finds here a microcosm of all that is happening in the rest of the country. It's not just the seat of government; in every way, it's the dominant center of Mexican life.

You've undoubtedly heard about Mexico City's pollution. Major steps to improve the air quality (restricted driving, factory closings, emission-controlled buses and taxis) have worked wonders, but the problem persists. On some days you won't notice it (especially during the summer rainy season); on other days it can make your nose run, your eyes water, and your throat rasp. If you have respiratory problems, be very careful; the city's elevation makes matters even worse. Minimize your exposure to the fumes and refrain from walking busy streets during rush hour. Sunday—when many factories are closed and many cars escape the city—should be your prime outdoor day. One positive note: In the evenings, the air is often deliciously cool and relatively clean. (See "Pollution," in "Fast Facts," later in this chapter.)

Mexico City is a feast of urban energy, culture, dining, and shopping. The city has sidewalk cafes and cantinas; bazaars and boutiques; pyramids, monuments, and museums; and a multitude of entertainment options. And when you've had your fill of the city, it's easy to explore memorable towns and historic national landmarks only a couple of hours away in any direction.

1 Orientation

GETTING THERE & DEPARTING

BY PLANE   For information on carriers serving Mexico City from the United States, see chapter 3.

Mexico City's **Benito Juárez International Airport** is something of a small city, where you can grab a bite, have an espresso (including Starbucks!), or buy duty free goods, clothes, books, gifts, and insurance, as well as exchange money or stay in a hotel. It was recently expanded—filled with marble floors, upscale shops, and improved services—and overall has become a much more welcoming airport. International flights depart from the new Terminal 2 and from the international section of Terminal 1; domestic flights are accommodated by the rest of Terminal 1.

Near Gate A is a guarded **baggage-storage area** (another is near Gate F). The key-operated metal lockers measure about .5×.5×.5m (2×2×1½ ft.) and cost $8 (£4) daily. Larger items are stored in a warehouse, which costs $9 to $12 (£4.50–£6) for each 24 hours, depending on the size. You may leave your items for up to a month.

The Mexico City Hotel and Motel Association offers a **hotel-reservation service** for its member hotels. Look for its booths before you leave the baggage-claim area, or near Gate A on the concourse. Representatives will make the call according to your specifications for location and price. If they book the hotel, they require 1 night's advance payment and will give you a voucher, which you must present at the hotel. Ask about hotels with special deals. **Telephones** (operated by Telmex using prepaid Ladatel cards) are all along the public concourse; for instructions on how to use them, see chapter 3.

When you're getting ready to leave Mexico City and need local information on flights, times, and prices, contact the airlines directly (most airlines in Mexico City have English-speaking personnel). Although airline numbers change frequently, the following may be useful:

- **Air Canada** (© 55/9138-0280; www.aircanada.ca) serves Toronto (direct flight), Montreal, Vancouver, Frankfurt, Munich, London, Paris, Rome, Beijing, Hong Kong, Shanghai, Taipei, and Tokyo from inside Mexico.
- **AeroMéxico** (© 55/5133-4000; www.aeromexico.com.mx) serves Guadalajara, Monterrey, Tijuana, Chihuahua, Ciudad Juárez, La Paz, Los Cabos, Loreto, Mazatlán, Manzanillo, León, Aguascalientes, Ixtapa/Zihuatanejo, Puerto Vallarta, Veracruz, Acapulco, Huatulco, Oaxaca, Tapachula, Campeche, Mérida, Cancún, Tuxtla Gutiérrez, New York, Chicago, Houston, Los Angeles, San Diego, Paris, Madrid, São Paulo, Santiago de Chile, and Lima.
- **American Airlines** (© 55/5209-1400; www.aa.com) has direct flights from inside Mexico to Chicago, Dallas, Los Angeles, and Miami, and connecting flights to all over the world.
- **Aviacsa** (© 55/5716-9005; www.aviacsa.com.mx) serves Acapulco, Cancún, Chetumal, León, Guadalajara, Mérida, Mexicali, Monterrey, Morelia, Oaxaca, Puerto Vallarta, Tapachula, Tijuana, Tuxtla Gutierrez, Veracruz, Villa Hermosa, and operates flights from Houston, Los Angeles, and Las Vegas.
- **Continental** (© 55/5283-5500; www.continental.com) serves Houston, New York, and other U.S., Canadian, and European destinations.
- **Delta** (© 55/5279-0909; www.delta.com) serves Atlanta, Chicago, Los Angeles, Miami, and New York.
- **Mexicana** (© 55/5448-0990; www.mexicana.com) has flights to Acapulco, Guadalajara, Puerto Vallarta, Monterrey, Ixtapa/Zihuatanejo, Mexicali, Tijuana, Hermosillo, Loreto, Los Cabos, Nuevo Laredo, Monterrey, Mazatlán, Zacatecas, Saltillo, Tampico, León, Morelia, Poza Rica, Manzanillo, Colima, Veracruz, Xalapa, Oaxaca, Puerto Escondido, Huatulco, Minatitlán, Villa Hermosa, Tuxtla Gutiérrez, San Cristóbal de las Casas, Tapachula, Ciudad del Carmen, Mérida, Cancún, Cozumel, Santiago de Chile, Buenos Aires, São Paulo, Rio de Janeiro, Bogotá, Caracas, Panamá, San José (Costa Rica), Santo Domingo, San Salvador, Guatemala City, Havana, Miami, Orlando, San Antonio, Los Angeles, San Jose (California), Oakland, Las Vegas, Washington, D.C., Chicago, New York, Montreal, Toronto, and Frankfurt.
- **United** (© 55/5627-0222; www.united.com) has flights to Chicago, Los Angeles, San Francisco, and Washington, D.C.

Be sure to allow at least 45 to 60 minutes' travel time from the Zona Rosa or the *zócalo* (plaza) area to the airport—add about 30 minutes more if you're traveling during rush hour or bad weather. Check in 3 hours before international flights and 2 hours before domestic flights. Note: Mexican airlines will usually not let you check in for a domestic flight if it's less than an hour before departure time.

Getting to Town   Ignore those who approach you in the arrivals hall offering taxis; they are usually unlicensed and unauthorized. **Authorized airport taxis,** however, provide good, fast service. After exiting the baggage-claim area and before entering the public concourse (as well as near the far end of the terminal near Gate A), you'll see a booth marked TAXI. Staff members at these authorized taxi booths wear bright-yellow jackets or bibs emblazoned with TAXI AUTORIZADO (authorized taxi). Tell the ticket-seller your hotel or destination; the price is based on a zone system. Expect to pay around $18 (£9) for a *boleto* (ticket) to Polanco. Present your ticket outside to the driver. Taxi "assistants" who lift your luggage into the waiting taxi naturally expect a tip for their trouble. Putting your luggage in the taxi is the driver's job. (See also "Important Taxi Safety Precautions in Mexico City," below.)

The **Metro,** Mexico City's modern subway system, is cheap and faster than a taxi, but it seems to be gaining popularity among thieves who target tourists. If you try it, be forewarned: As a new arrival, you'll stand out. If you are carrying anything much larger than a briefcase, including a suitcase, don't even bother going to the station—they won't let you on with it. For Metro information, see "Getting Around," later in this chapter.

Here's how to find the Metro at the airport: As you come from your plane into the arrivals hall, turn left toward Gate A and walk all the way through the long terminal, out the doors, and along a covered sidewalk. Soon, you'll see the distinctive Metro logo that identifies the Terminal Aérea station, down a flight of stairs. The station is on Metro Line 5. Follow the signs for trains to Pantitlán. At Pantitlán, change for Line 1 ("Observatorio"), which takes you to stations that are just a few blocks south of the *zócalo* and La Alameda park: Pino Suárez, Isabel la Católica, Salto del Agua, and Balderas.

BY CAR   Driving in Mexico City is as much a challenge and an adventure as driving in any major metropolis. Here are a few tips. First, ask the rental company whether your license-plate number permits you to drive in the city that day (break the rule and the fine can be well over $1,000 (£500). Traffic runs the course of the usual rush hours—to avoid getting tangled in traffic, plan to travel before dawn. Park the car in a guarded lot whenever possible.

Here are the chief thoroughfares for getting out of the city: Insurgentes Sur becomes Highway 95 to Taxco and Cuernavaca. Insurgentes Norte leads to Teotihuacán and Pachuca. Highway 57, the Periférico (loop around the city), is also known as Bulevar Manuel Avila Camacho, to denote street addresses; it goes north and leads out of the city to Tula and Querétaro. Constituyentes leads west out of the city past Chapultepec Park and connects with Highway 15 to Toluca, Morelia, and Pátzcuaro. (Reforma also connects with Hwy. 15.) Zaragoza leads east to Highway 150 to Puebla and Veracruz.

BY BUS   Mexico City has a bus terminal for each of the four points of the compass: north, east, south, and west. You can't necessarily tell which terminal serves which area of the country by looking at a map, however.

Some buses leave directly from the **Mexico City airport.** Departures are from a booth located outside **Sala D (Gate D),** and buses also park there. Tickets to Cuernavaca and Puebla each run about $20 (£10), with departures every 45 minutes. Other destinations include Querétaro, Pátzcuaro, and Toluca.

Warning Taxi Safety Precautions in Mexico City

There has been a marked increase in violent crime against both residents and tourists using taxis for transportation in Mexico City, concentrated among users of Volkswagen Beetle and *libre* (those hailed off the street) taxis. Robberies of taxi passengers are sometimes violent, with beatings and even murders reported. Victims have included U.S. citizens. Many times the robberies involve taking passengers to an ATM, where they are forced to withdraw whatever limit their card or cards will allow.

If you plan to use a **taxi from the airport or bus stations,** use only an authorized airport cab with all the familiar markings: yellow car, white taxi light on the roof, and TRANSPORTACIÓN TERRESTRE painted on the doors. Buy your ticket from the clearly marked taxi booth inside the terminal—nowhere else. After purchasing your ticket, go outside to the line of taxis, where an official taxi chief will direct you to the next taxi in line. Don't follow anyone else.

In Mexico City, *do not hail a passing taxi on the street.* Most hotels have official taxi drivers who are recognized and regulated by the terminal and city; they are considered safe taxis to use. These are known as **authorized** or *sitio* **taxis.** Hotels and restaurants can call the radio-dispatched taxis. **Official Radio Taxis** (© **55/5590-3325,** or 5698-5192) are also considered safe. You can hire one of these taxis from your hotel; the driver will frequently act as your personal driver and escort you through your travels in the city. This is a particularly advisable option at night.

All official taxis, except the expensive "turismo" cars, are painted predominantly yellow, orange, or green, have white plastic roof signs bearing the word TAXI, have TAXI or SITIO painted on the doors, and are equipped with meters. Look for all these indications, not just one or two of them. Even then, be cautious. The safest cars to use are sedan taxis (luxury cars without markings) dispatched from four- and five-star hotels. They are the most expensive, but worth it(taxi crime in Mexico City is very real.

Do not use VW Beetle taxis, which are frequently involved in robberies of tourists. Even though they are the least expensive taxis, you could be taking your life into your hands should you opt to use one. In any case, never get In a taxi that does not display a large 5×7-inch laminated **license card** with a picture of the driver on it; it's usually hanging from the door chain or glove box, or stuck behind the sun visor. *If there is no license, or if the photo doesn't match the driver, don't get in.* It's illegal for a taxi to operate without the license in view. No matter what vehicle you use for transportation, lock the doors as soon as you get in. Do not carry credit cards, your passport, or large sums of cash, or wear expensive jewelry when taking taxis.

If you're in doubt about which station serves your destination, ask any taxi driver—they know the stations and the routes they serve. All stations have restaurants, money-exchange booths or banks, post offices, luggage storage, and long-distance telephone booths where you can also send a fax.

Taxis from bus stations: Each station has a taxi system based on fixed-price tickets to various zones within the city, operated from a booth or kiosk in or near the entry foyer of the terminal. Locate your destination on a zone map or tell the seller where you want to go, and buy a *boleto.* See also the "Important Taxi Safety Precautions in Mexico City" box, above.

Terminal Central de Autobuses del Norte   Called "Terminal Norte," or "Central Norte" (② **55/5133-2444** or 5587-1552), Avenida de los Cien (100) Metros, is Mexico's largest bus station. It handles most buses coming from the U.S.–Mexico border. It also handles service to and from the Pacific Coast as far south as Puerto Vallarta and Manzanillo; the Gulf Coast as far south as Tampico and Veracruz; and such cities as Guadalajara, San Luis Potosí, Durango, Zacatecas, Morelia, and Colima. You can also get to the pyramids of San Juan Teotihuacán and Tula from here. By calling the above number, you can purchase tickets over the phone, charging them to a credit card. The operators can also provide exact information about prices and schedules, but few speak English.

To get downtown from the Terminal Norte, you have a choice: The **Metro** has a station (Terminal de Autobuses del Norte, or TAN) right here, so it's easy to hop a train and connect to all points. Walk to the center of the terminal, go out the front door and down the steps, and go to the Metro station. This is Línea 5. Follow the signs that say DIRECCION PANTITLÁN. For downtown, you can change trains at La Raza or Consulado (see the Mexico City Metro map on the inside back cover). Be aware that if you change at La Raza, you'll have to walk for 10 to 15 minutes and will encounter stairs. The walk is through a marble-lined underground corridor, but it's a long way with heavy luggage. If you have heavy luggage, you most likely won't be allowed into the Metro in the first place.

Another way to get downtown is by **trolleybus.** The stop is on Avenida de los Cien Metros, in front of the terminal. The trolleybus runs down Avenida Lázaro Cárdenas, the "Eje Central" (Central Artery). Or try the Central Camionera Del Norte–Villa Olimpica buses, which go down Avenida Insurgentes, past the university. Just like the Metro, the trolley will not let you board if you are carrying anything larger than a small carry-on suitcase. Backpacks seem to be an exception, but not large ones with frames.

Terminal de Autobuses de Pasajeros de Oriente (② **55/5786-9341**)   The terminal is known as **TAPO.** Buses going east (Puebla, Amecameca, the Yucatán Peninsula, Veracruz, Xalapa, San Cristóbal de las Casas, and others) and Oaxaca buses, which pass through Puebla, arrive and depart from here.

To get to TAPO, take a Hipodromo–Pantitlán bus east along Alvarado, Hidalgo, or Donceles; if you take the Metro, go to the San Lázaro station on the eastern portion of Line 1 (DIRECCION PANTITLÁN).

Terminal Central de Autobuses del Sur (Taxqueña; ② **55/5689-9745)**   Mexico City's southern bus terminal is at Av. Taxqueña 1320, right next to the Taxqueña Metro stop, the last stop on Line 2. The Central del Sur handles buses to and from Acapulco, Cuernavaca, Guadalajara, Huatulco, Puebla, Puerto Escondido, Taxco, Tepoztlán, Zihuatanejo, and intermediate points. The easiest way to get to or from the Central del Sur is on the Metro. To get downtown from the Taxqueña Metro station, look for signs that say DIRECCION CUATRO CAMINOS, or take a trolleybus on Avenida Lázaro Cárdenas.

Terminal Poniente de Autobuses (© 55/5271-4519) The western bus terminal is conveniently located right next to the Observatorio Metro station, at Sur 122 and Tacubaya.

This is the smallest terminal; it mainly serves the route between Mexico City and Toluca. It also handles buses to and from Ixtapan de la Sal, Valle de Bravo, Morelia, Uruapan, Querétaro, Colima, Ixtapa/Zihuatanejo, Acapulco, and Guadalajara. In general, if the Terminal Norte also serves your destination, you'd be better off going there. It has more buses and better bus lines.

VISITOR INFORMATION

The Federal District Department provides several information services for visitors. The **Centro Integral de Atención al Turista (CIAT);** (© 888/401-3880 from the U.S., or toll-free inside Mexico 01-800/987-8224 or simply 078) offers information in English and Spanish, including maps, a wide selection of brochures, and access to information from the Mexico Secretary of Tourism (SECTUR) website. The office sits in Polanco at Av. President Masaryk 172 (© 55/3002-6300), at the corner of Hegel. It's open Monday to Friday from 8am to 6pm and Saturday from 10am to 3pm.

SECTUR, Mexico's Secretary of Tourism, developed a website to address safety concerns about travel to this city and other areas in Mexico. The website **www. sectur.gob.mx** offers perhaps not-so-objective assessments of destinations, as well as travel safety tips and help with lodging reservations throughout Mexico.

There are branches of the **Mexico City Tourist Office** in the Zona Rosa at Paseo de la Reforma and Florencia (across from the Angel de la Independencia; © 55/5208-1030), at the TAPO bus terminal (©) 55/5784-3077), and at the airport (© 55/5786-9002). They're generally open daily from 9am to 6pm. **The Mexico City Secretary of Tourism** also has a website, **www.mexicocity.gob.mx**, which includes details on things to do, special events, safety precautions, and tourist services.

The **Mexico City Chamber of Commerce** (© 55/5592-2665) maintains an information office with a very friendly, helpful staff that can sell you detailed maps of the city or country and answer questions. It's conveniently located at Reforma 42—look for the Cámara Nacional de Comercio de la Ciudad de México. It's open Monday through Thursday from 9am to 2pm and 3 to 6pm; Friday from 9am to 2pm and 3 to 5:30pm.

Day and night diversions are listed in the Spanish-language magazine *Tiempo Libre,* which is published each Thursday, and is available at hotels and newsstands. It also has a website, **www.tiempolibre.com.mx.** Excellent English-language sources of visitor information are the **Mexico File** (www.mexicofile.com) and **Solutions Abroad** (www.solutionsabroad.com). Current event information and visitor tips are offered on the excellent site **www.mexicocity.gob.mx.**

CITY LAYOUT

FINDING AN ADDRESS Despite its size, Mexico City is not hard to get a feel for. The city is divided into 350 *colonias,* or neighborhoods. Taxi drivers are sometimes not aware of the major tourist sights and popular restaurants. Before getting into a taxi, always give a street address, *colonia,* and cross streets as a reference, and show the driver your destination on a map that you carry with you. Some of the most important *colonias* are Colonia Centro (historic city center); Zona Rosa (Colonia Juárez); Polanco (Colonia Polanco), a fashionable neighborhood immediately north of

Chapultepec Park; colonias Condesa and Roma, south of the Zona Rosa, where there are many restaurants in quiet neighborhoods; all the Lomas—including Lomas de Chapultepec and Lomas Tecamachalco—which are exclusive neighborhoods west of Chapultepec Park; and San Angel and Coyoacán, the artsy neighborhoods toward the south of Mexico City. In addresses, the word is abbreviated *Col.*, and the full *colonia* name is vital in addressing correspondence.

STREET MAPS   Should you want more detailed maps of Mexico City than the ones included in this guide, you can get them easily. The **CIAT** office (see "Visitor Information," above) generally has several free maps available. Bookstores carry several local map/guides, with greater detail. The best detailed map is the *Guía Roji* (www.guiaroji.com.mx), available at bookstores in Mexico City. It features all the streets in Mexico City and is updated annually.

THE NEIGHBORHOODS IN BRIEF

Colonia Centro   The heart of Mexico City, this business, banking, and historic center includes the areas in and around La Alameda and the *zócalo*, the capital's historic central square. The Spaniards built their new capital city on top of the destroyed capital of the conquered Aztec, and today, it is home to over 1,500 buildings. In the Centro Histórico—the concentrated historical center within Colonia Centro—you'll find the most historic landmarks, the most important public buildings, the partially unearthed Aztec ruins of the Great Temple, and numerous museums. There are restaurants, shops, and hotels in this area as well. In the past few years, public improvements have spurred the development of a few new hotels here, as well as a surge in nightlife and dining options, with some exquisite bars and clubs located in historic buildings.

A $300-million (£150-million) facelift was completed in 2003 in honor of the city's 675th anniversary. Mexican telecommunications magnate Carlos Slim Helú, now widely considered the richest person in the world, has also put a lot of money into renovating the area. In addition to a beautification program for the *zócalo*—including the addition of a grassy knoll—other elements of the program included the restoration and conversion of more than 80 18th- and 19th-century buildings.

A special corps of police on horseback outfitted in traditional *charro* attire (along with many female police on foot) now patrols the Centro Histórico and Alameda Park. Many speak English, and they have been specially trained in the history and culture of the area they patrol.

Chapultepec Park & Polanco   A large residential area west of the city center and Zona Rosa, it centers on Chapultepec Park. The largest green area in Mexico City, it was dedicated as a park in the 15th century by the Aztec ruler Netzahualcóyotl. Together with the neighboring *colonia* of Polanco (north of the park), this is Mexico City's most exclusive address. With its zoo, many notable museums, antiques shops, stylish shopping, fine dining and nightlife, and upscale hotels, it's an ideal place for discovering contemporary Mexican culture. **Avenida Presidente Masaryk** is the main artery—think of it as the Rodeo Drive or Madison Avenue of Mexico City. Some of the city's best high-rise hotels are located along **Campos Eliseos,** Polanco's version of the Champs Elysees.

Condesa & Roma These side-by-side bohemian neighborhoods, located just south of the Zona Rosa, are home to some of the city's hippest cafes, restaurants, and bars, from cutting-edge restaurants to offbeat shops, art galleries, and nightclubs. The neighborhoods are also known for their parks and restored Art Deco buildings.

Coyoacán Eight kilometers (5 miles) from the city center, east of San Angel and north of the Ciudad Universitaria, Coyoacán (koh-yoh-ah-*kahn*) is an attractive, colonial-era suburb noted for its beautiful town square, cobblestone streets, fine old mansions, and several of the city's most interesting museums. This was the home of Frida Kahlo and Diego Rivera, and of Leon Trotsky after his exile from Stalin's USSR. With something of a hippy feel, it's a wonderful place to spend the day, but overnight accommodations are almost nonexistent. Attractions in Coyoacán are listed in the section "Southern Neighborhoods," later in this chapter. A fun hippy market takes place here on Sundays.

From downtown, Metro Line 3 can take you to the Coyoacán or Viveros station, within walking distance of Coyoacán's museums. Iztacala–Coyoacán buses run from the center to this suburb. If you're coming from San Angel, the quickest and easiest way is to take a cab for the 15-minute ride to the Plaza Hidalgo. Francisco Sosa, a beautiful cobblestone street surrounded by old aristocratic homes, is the main artery into Coyoacán from San Angel, which you can also walk. Or you can catch the Alcantarilla–Col. Agrarista bus heading east along the Camino al Desierto de los Leónes or Avenida Altavista, near the San Angel Inn. Get off when the bus reaches the corner of Avenida México and Xicoténcatl in Coyoacán.

San Angel Eight kilometers (5 miles) south of the city center, San Angel (sahn *ahn*-hehl) was once a weekend retreat for Spanish nobles but has long since been absorbed by the city. It's a stunningly beautiful neighborhood of cobblestone streets and colonial-era homes, with several worthwhile museums. This is where the renowned Bazar del Sábado (Saturday Bazaar) is held at Plaza San Jacinto. It's full of artistic and antique treasures and surrounded by excellent restaurants and cantinas— a wonderful place to spend a day. Other attractions in San Angel include a magnificent baroque fountain made of broken pieces of porcelain at the Centro Cultural Isidro Fabela, better known as the Casa del Risco (Plaza San Jacinto 15), and the ethereal Iglesia San Jacinto, a 16th-century church with an exquisite baroque altar, bordering the Plaza San Jacinto.

The nearest Metro station is M.A. de Quevedo (Line 3). From downtown, take a *colectivo* (minibus) marked SAN ANGEL, or bus marked INDIOS VERDES–TLALPAN or CENTRAL NORTE–VILLA OLIMPICA, south along Insurgentes near the Zona Rosa. Ask to get off at La Paz. To the east is a pretty park, the Plaza del Carmen, and to the west is a Sanborn's (a well-known department store chain in Mexico), on the eastern side of Insurgentes.

Santa Fe Eight kilometers (5 miles) west of the town center, this is Mexico City's newest and most modern neighborhood. It includes high-tech and multinational companies, banks, Iberro Americana University, and a large shopping complex. Santa Fe looks more like a modern American neighborhood than anywhere else in Mexico City.

Many of the capital's well-off young professional have moved to this area, which has developed a booming restaurant and nightlife scene. To reach Santa Fe, take Reforma Avenue west to the Toluca highway and follow the signs to Santa Fe.

Xochimilco Twenty-four kilometers (15 miles) south of the town center, Xochimilco (soh-chee-*meel*-coh) is noted for its famed canals and Floating Gardens, which have existed here since the time of the Aztec. Although the best-known attractions are the more than 80km (50 miles) of canals (see "Parks & Gardens," later in this chapter, for details), Xochimilco itself is a colonial-era gem: It seems small, with its brick streets, but they can become heavy with traffic—it has a population of 300,000. Restaurants are at the edge of the canal and shopping area, and historically significant churches are within easy walking distance of the main square. In the town of Xochimilco, you'll find a busy market, specializing in rugs, ethnic clothing, and brightly decorated pottery.

Xochimilco hosts an amazing 422 festivals annually, the most famous of which celebrate the **Niñopa,** a figure of the Christ Child that is believed to possess miraculous powers. The figure is venerated on January 6 (Three Kings' Day), February 2 (annual changing of the Niñopa's custodian), April 30 (Day of the Child), and from December 16 to December 24 (*posadas* for the Niñopa). Caring for the Niñopa is a coveted privilege, and the schedule of approved caretakers is filled through 2031. The week before Easter is the Feria de la Flor Más Bella del Ejido, a flower fair when the most beautiful girl with Indian features and costume is selected. For more information and exact dates, contact the

Xochimilco Tourist Office (Subdirección de Turismo), Pino 36, Barrio San Juan (© **55/5676-8879;** fax 55/5676-0810), next to VIPS, 2 blocks from the main square. It's open weekdays from 9am to 8pm, and weekends from 10am to 7pm. Attractions in Xochimilco are listed in the section "Southern Neighborhoods," later in this chapter.

To reach Xochimilco, take the Metro to Taxqueña, then the *tren ligero* (light train), which stops at the main plaza of Xochimilco. From there, take a taxi to the main plaza of the town of Xochimilco. Buses run all the way across the city from north to south to end up at Xochimilco, but they take longer than the Metro. Of the buses coming from the center, the most convenient is La Villa–Xochimilco, which you catch going south on Correo Mayor and Pino Suárez near the *zócalo,* or near Chapultepec on Avenida Vasconcelos, Avenida Nuevo León, and Avenida División del Norte. Since Xochimilco is located in the far south of the city, it can take a long time to reach in traffic during the workweek. Consider visiting it on the weekend.

Zona Rosa West of the Centro, the "Pink Zone" was once the city's most exclusive residential neighborhood. It has given way to just about every segment of society, and offers an array of moderate hotels, antique and silver shops, casual restaurants, gay bars, and kitsch nightlife venues. Although the Zona Rosa has become increasingly tacky with time, many of the streets here are pedestrian-only, and you will find inviting cafes, ice cream shops, and shopping plazas along the way. It's a good place to shop or grab a bite, but there are few real historic or cultural attractions within the area. It's not safe to walk in this area at night.

2 Getting Around

Mexico City has a highly developed and remarkably cheap public transportation system. It is a shame that the sharp increase in crime and resulting safety concerns have made these less comfortable options for travelers. The Metro, first- and second-class buses, *colectivos,* and yellow or green VW Beetle taxis or Nissan Tsuru *libre* taxis will take you anywhere you want to go for very little money—but the recent visitor warnings about the use of public transportation should be respected. Because *sitio* taxis (official taxis registered to a specific locale or hotel) are relatively inexpensive and the safest way to travel within the city, you are best off using them.

BY TAXI Taxis operate under several distinct sets of rules. *Warning:* Read the cautionary box "Important Taxi Safety Precautions in Mexico City," earlier in this chapter, before using any taxi.

"Turismo" and Sitio Taxis These are by far the safest way to travel within Mexico City. Turismo taxis are unmarked cabs, usually well-kept luxury cars assigned to specific hotels that have special license plates. Although more expensive than the VW and *libre* taxis (usually Nissan Tsurus), "turismo" taxis, along with radio-dispatched *sitio* taxis, are the safest ones to use. The drivers negotiate rates with individual passengers for sightseeing, but rates to and from the airport are established. Ask the bell captain what the airport fare should be, and establish it before taking off. These drivers are often licensed English-speaking guides and can provide exceptional service. In general, expect to pay around $15 (£7.50) per hour for guided service, and about 15% more than metered rates for normal transportation. Often, these drivers will wait for you while you shop or dine to take you back to the hotel, or they can be called to come back and pick you up.

Metered Taxis Yellow or green VW Beetle and *libre* cabs provide low-cost service, but *you should not use them for safety reasons.* Some *sitio* taxis (radio taxis, which are safe) use meters, while others have set rates. Although you may encounter a gouging driver or one who advances the meter or drives farther than necessary to run up the tab, most service is quick and adequate.

BY METRO The subway system in Mexico City offers a smooth ride for one of the lowest fares anywhere in the world (20¢/10p per ride). Twelve lines crisscross the sprawling city. Each train usually has nine cars.

Tips The Subway Skinny

The Metro system runs workdays from 5am to 12:30am, Saturday from 6am to 1:30am, and Sunday and holidays from 7am to 12:30am. Baggage larger than a small carry-on is not allowed on the trains. In practice, this means that bulky suitcases or backpacks will make you persona non grata. On an average day, Mexico City's Metro handles more than five million riders—leaving little room for bags! But in effect, if no one stops you as you enter, you're in.

Watch your bags and your pockets. Metro pickpockets prey on the unwary (especially foreigners) and are very crafty—on a crowded train, they've been known to empty a fanny pack from the front. Be careful, and carry valuables inside your clothing. Women should avoid traveling alone.

Downtown Mexico City

ACCOMMODATIONS ■

Best Western Hotel Majestic **29**
Condesa*df* **1**
Embassy Suites **10**
Hilton Airport Hotel **35**
Holiday Inn Zócalo **28**

Hotel Catedral **25**
Hotel Four Seasons **3**
Hotel María Cristina **9**
Hotel Sheraton María Isabel **8**
La Casona Hotel-Relais **2**
Sheraton Centro Histórico **13**

DINING ◆

Cafe Tacuba **22**
Casa Bell **4**
Fonda el Refugio **5**
La Casa de las Sirenas **26**
Restaurante Danubio **17**

ATTRACTIONS

Alameda Park **14**

Casa de los Azulejos **18**

Catedral Metropolitana **27**

Lagunilla Market **21**

La Torre Latinoamericana **16**

Mercado de la Merced **34**

Mercado Insurgentes **6**

Monumento a la Revolución/
Plaza de la República **11**

Monumento a los Héroes
de la Independencia **7**

Museo de la Ciudad
de México **33**

Museo Nacional de Arte **19**

Museo Nacional
de San Carlos **12**

Palacio de Bellas Artes **15**

Palacio Nacional/
Diego Rigera Murals **31**

Plaza de Garibaldi **20**

Plaza de Santo Domingo **23**

Secretaría de Educación
Pública **24**

Suprema Corte de Justicia **32**

Templo Mayor **30**

Women-Only Buses

In January 2008, Mexico City designated a number of city buses for women only, distinguished by conspicuous pink placards. The popular program was designed to prevent men from groping female passengers—a fairly common problem in the capital's crowded public transportation system. Bus drivers are charged with keeping men off of these buses, and their female passengers are delighted. During peak hours, Mexico City's subway system also designates the first three cars for women and children.

As you enter the station, buy a *boleto* at the glass *taquilla* (ticket booth). Insert your ticket into the slot at the turnstile and pass through; inside, you'll see two large signs showing the line's destination (for example, for Line 1, it's OBSERVATORIO and PANTITLÁN). Follow the signs in the direction you want and *know where you're going;* there is usually only one map of the routes, at the entrance to the station. You'll see two signs everywhere: SALIDA (exit) and ANDENES (platforms). Once inside the train, you'll see above each door a map of the station stops for that line, with symbols and names.

CORRESPONDENCIAS indicates transfer points. The ride is smooth, fast, and efficient (although hot and crowded during rush hours). The beautifully designed stations are clean and have the added attraction of displaying archaeological ruins unearthed during construction. A subterranean passage goes between the Pino Suárez and Zócalo stations, so you can avoid the crowds and rain along Pino Suárez. The Zócalo station features dioramas and large photographs of the different periods in the history of the Valley of Mexico. At Pino Suárez you'll find the foundation of a pyramid from the Aztec Empire.

The Metro is crowded during daylight hours on weekdays and consequently pretty hot and muggy in summer. In fact, you may find it virtually unusable downtown between 4 and 7pm on weekdays, because of sardine-can conditions. At some stations, there are even separate lanes roped off for women and children; the press of the crowd is so great that someone might get molested. Buses, *colectivos,* and taxis are all heavily used during these hours, less so during off hours (such as 10:30am–noon). Avoid the crowds by traveling during off-peak hours, or simply wait a few minutes for the next train.

BY BUS   Moving millions of people through this sprawling urban mass is a gargantuan task, but the city officials do a pretty good job of it. Bus stops on the major tourist streets usually have a map posted with the full route description.

The large buses that used to run on the major tourist routes (**Reforma** and **Insurgentes**) tended to become overpacked and have been phased out in favor of smaller, more frequent buses. Crowding is common during peak hours. The cost in pesos is the U.S. equivalent of 25¢ to 50¢ (15p–30p). Although the driver usually has change, try to have exact fare or at least a few coins when you board.

One of the most important bus routes runs between the *zócalo* and the Auditorio (National Auditorium in Chapultepec Park) or the Observatorio Metro station. The route is Avenida Madero or Cinco de Mayo, Avenida Juárez, and Paseo de la Reforma. Buses marked ZÓCALO run this route.

Another important route is **Indios Verdes–Tlalpan,** which runs along Avenida Insurgentes, connecting the northern bus terminal (Terminal Norte), Buenavista railroad station, Reforma, the Zona Rosa, and, far to the south, San Angel and University City.

BY COLECTIVO   Also called *peseros* or *microbuses,* these are sedans or minibuses, usually green and gray, that run along major arteries. They pick up and discharge passengers along the route, charge established fares, and provide slightly more comfort and speed than the bus. Cards in the windshield display routes; often a Metro station is the destination. One of the most useful routes for tourists runs from the *zócalo* along **Avenida Juárez,** along **Reforma** to **Chapultepec,** and back again. Board a *colectivo* with a sign saying ZOCALO, not VILLA. (The Villa route goes to the Basílica de Guadalupe.) Some of the minibuses on this route have automatic sliding doors—you don't have to shut them.

As the driver approaches a stop, he may put his hand out the window and hold up one or more fingers. This is the number of passengers he's willing to take on (vacant seats are difficult to see if you're outside the car).

BY TOURIST BUS   A convenient and popular way to see the city is on one of the red double-decker **Turibuses** (© **55/5133-2488;** www.turibus.com.mx), which offers separate circuits in the north and south of the city. Each of the double-decker buses seats 75 and offers audio information in five languages, plus street maps. The buses operate from 9am to 9pm, with unlimited hop-on, hop-off privileges after paying $10 (£5) for a day pass ($11/£5.50 weekends). Along the Chapultepec-Centro Histórico Route there are 25 stops at major monuments, museums, neighborhoods, and landmarks along the 35km (22-mile) route, which runs from the National Auditorium to the city center (including the *zócalo*) and from there to La Plaza de las Tres Culturas (Square of the Three Cultures), returning via Reforma Avenue towards the posh neighborhood of Polanco and finally to Museo del Niño (Children's Museum). The full circuit takes a little under 3 hours. Another Turibus circuit runs in the city south, taking passengers from La Roma neighborhood south along Insurgentes Avenue to San Angel, Coyoacán, and Tlalpan. Stops include the World Trade Center, Plaza de Torros bull ring, Carillo Gil museum, Perisur shopping center, UNAM university, and Frida Kahlo museum, among others.

BY RENTAL CAR   If you plan to travel to Puebla (see chapter 13) or a surrounding area, a rental car might come in handy. Due to high rates of auto theft, I don't recommend renting a car. Taxis and the Metro also eliminate the risk of getting lost in an unsavory area.

Finds Free Sunday Concerts

Every Sunday, concerts organized by Mexico City's Cultural Institute take place at the *zócalo,* generally around 6pm. They feature a changing array of traditional and classical Mexican talent—and can draw crowds of 5,000 or more to the historic central plaza. For more information, and listings of upcoming events, visit the Mexico City website **www.mexicocity.gob.mx**. Listings also appear in *Tiempo Libre* magazine.

> ## *Tips* Festival de México en el Centro Histórico
>
> In March of every year, a series of concerts, cultural events, art exhibits, and public performances takes place in—and in honor of—Mexico City's historic downtown district. For more information or a calendar of events, check the Festival de México website (www.festival.org.mx).

If you must rent, be aware that that the least-expensive rental car is a manual-shift without air-conditioning. The price jump is considerable for automatics with air-conditioning. (See also "Getting around Mexico," in chapter 3.) The safest option is to leave the driving to someone else—**Avis** offers chauffeur-driven rental cars at its nine locations in the Mexican capital. The chauffeur is on an 8-hour shift, but the car is available to the customer for 24 hours. For prices and reservations, call Avis (℃ **800/ 352-7900** in the U.S.).

FAST FACTS: Mexico City

American Express The Mexico City office is at Reforma 234 (℃ **55/5207-7282**), in the Zona Rosa. It's open for banking, the pickup of American Express clients' mail, and travel advice Monday through Friday from 9am to 6pm and Saturday from 9am to 1pm.

Banks Banks are usually open Monday through Friday from 9am to 4pm (some later); many now offer Saturday business hours, typically from 8am to 3pm. Bank branches at the airport are open whenever the airport is busy, including weekends. They usually offer ATMs and decent rates of exchange. Banks and money-exchange offices line Avenida Reforma. The Centro Histórico downtown also has banks and money-exchange booths on almost every block, as does the Zona Rosa.

Bookstores In Mexico City, **Sanborn's** always has a great selection of books in English, as well as magazines and newspapers.

   About the most convenient foreign- and Spanish-language bookstore in Mexico City, with a good selection of guidebooks and texts on Mexico, is **Librería Gandhi,** Av. Juárez 4, near Avenida Lázaro Cárdenas (℃ **55/2625-0606;** www.gandhi.com.mx), right across from the Bellas Artes. It's open Monday to Saturday from 10am to 9pm, Sunday from 11am to 8pm. The **New Option,** Rosas Moreno 152 (℃ **55/5705-3332** or -0585), is open Monday through Friday from 9am to 6pm and weekends from 10am to 4pm. The **Museo Nacional de Antropología,** in Chapultepec Park (℃ **55/5553-1902** or 5211-0754; www.mna. inah.gob.mx), also has a fair selection of books on Mexico, particularly special-interest guides. It's open Tuesday through Sunday from 9am to 7pm. Also in Chapultepec, the bookstore **Otro Lugar de la Mancha,** Esopo 11 Chapultepec (℃ **55/5280-4826**), offers a small but outstanding collection of books, music, and art, plus an upstairs cafe in a historic home. It's open Monday through Friday from 8am to 10pm, Saturday and Sunday from 9am to 10pm.

Currency Exchange The alternative to a bank is a currency-exchange booth, or *casa de cambio*. These often offer extended hours, with greater convenience to hotels and shopping areas, and rates similar to bank exchange rates. Usually, their rates are much better than those offered by most hotels. Use caution when exiting banks and currency exchanges, which are popular targets for muggings.

Drugstores The drug departments at Sanborn's stay open late. Check the phone directory for the location nearest you. After hours, check with your hotel staff, which can usually contact a 24-hour drugstore.

Elevation Remember, you are now at an elevation of 2,239m (7,344 ft.)—over a mile in the sky. There's a lot less oxygen in the air than you're used to. If you run for a bus and feel dizzy when you sit down, it's the elevation. If you think you're in shape but huff and puff getting up Chapultepec Hill, it's the elevation. If you have trouble sleeping, it may be the elevation. If your food isn't digesting, again, it's the elevation. It takes about 3 days or so to adjust to the scarcity of oxygen. Go easy on food and alcohol the first few days in the city.

Emergencies The Mexico City government has an emergency number for visitors—dial © **060** for assistance 24 hours a day. The number is hard to reach, so have a local or Spanish speaker help you. **SECTUR (Secretaría de Turismo;** © **078;** www.sectur.gob.mx) staffs telephones 24 hours daily to help tourists in difficulty. In case of theft, you can contact **Quejas de Turistas Contra Robos** (© **55/5592-2677**). A government-operated service, **Locatel** (© **55/5658-1111**), is most often associated with finding missing persons anywhere in the country. With a good description of a car and its occupants, they'll search for motorists who have an emergency back home.

Hospitals The **American–British Cowdray (ABC) Hospital** is at Calle Sur 136, at the corner of Avenida Observatorio, Col. las Américas (tel] **55/5230-8000;** www.abchospital.com).

Hot Lines If you think you've been ripped off on a purchase, call the **consumer protection office (Procuraduría Nacional del Consumidor;** © **55/5568-8722** or 01-800/468-8722; www.profeco.gob.mx). SECTUR also sponsors **CIAT,** a 24-hour tourist-assistance line (© **078**).

Internet Access Surprisingly enough, it is easier to find cybercafes in some resort areas than in Mexico City. However, most hotels that cater to business travelers offer Internet connections in their business centers. The **Internet Café,** Rep. de Guatemala 4, connected to the international youth hostel in the Centro Histórico (© **55/5618-1726**), is open daily from 7:30am to 11pm. The price per hour of access is $1.50 (75p).

Pollution The rainy season, usually lasting from May to October, has less pollution than the dry season. Mid- to late November, December, and January are noted for heavy pollution. During January, schools may even close because of it, and restrictions on driving that are usually imposed only on weekdays may apply on weekends; be sure to check before driving into or around the city. (See "Rental Cars" under "Getting Around," above.) Be careful if you have respiratory problems. Just before your visit, call the Mexican Government Tourist

Board office nearest you (see "Visitor Information" in chapter 2 for the address) and ask for the latest information on pollution in the capital. Minimize your exposure to fumes by refraining from walking busy streets during rush hour. Make Sunday, when many factories are closed and many cars escape the city, your prime outdoor sightseeing day.

Post Office The city's main post office, the **Correo Mayor,** is a block north of the Palacio de Bellas Artes on Avenida Lázaro Cárdenas, at the corner of Tacuba. For general postal information, call **FonoPost** (© **55/5385-0960**); the staff is very helpful, and a few operators speak English.

If you need to mail a package in Mexico City, take it to the post office called Correos Internacional 2, Calle Dr. Andrade and Río de la Loza (Metro: Balderas or Salto del Agua). It's open Monday through Friday from 8am to noon. Don't wrap your package securely until an inspector examines it. Although postal service is improving, your package may take weeks, or even months, to arrive at its destination.

Restrooms There are few public restrooms. Use those in the larger hotels and in cafes, restaurants, and museums. Seasoned travelers frequently carry their own toilet paper and hand soap. Many public restrooms at museums and parks have an attendant who dispenses toilet paper for a "tip" of 5 pesos (50¢), in lieu of a usage charge.

Safety Read the "Safety" section in chapter 3 and the "Important Taxi Safety Precautions in Mexico City" box earlier in this chapter. In response to rising crime, Mexico City has added hundreds of new foot and mounted police officers, and there's a strong military presence. But they can't be everywhere. Watch out for pickpockets. Crowded subway cars and buses provide the perfect workplace for petty thieves, as do major museums (inside and out), crowded outdoor markets and bullfights, and indoor theaters. The "touch" can range from light-fingered wallet lifting or purse opening to a fairly rough shove by two or three petty thieves. Be extra careful anywhere that attracts a lot of tourists: on the Metro, in Reforma buses, in crowded hotel elevators and lobbies, at the Ballet Folklórico, and at the Museo de Antropología.

Robberies may occur in broad daylight on crowded streets in "good" parts of town, outside major tourist sights, and in front of posh hotels. The best way to avoid being mugged is to not wear any jewelry of value, especially expensive watches. If you find yourself up against a handful of these guys, the best thing to do is relinquish the demanded possession, flee, and then notify the police. (You'll need the police report to file an insurance claim.) If you're in a crowded place, you could try raising a fuss—whether you do it in Spanish or English doesn't matter. A few shouts of *"¡Ladrón!"* ("Thief!") might put them off, but that could also be risky. Overall, it's wise to leave valuables in the hotel safe and to take only the cash you'll need for the day, and no credit cards. Conceal a camera in a shoulder bag draped across your body and hanging in front of you, not on the side.

Taxes Posted prices generally include Mexico's 15% sales tax; however, it may be added. If in doubt, ask *"¿Mas IVA?"* ("Plus tax?") or *"¿Con IVA?"* ("With tax?"). There are also airport taxes for domestic and international flights, but the price of your ticket usually includes them. (See "Getting around Mexico," in chapter 3.)

Telephones Telephone numbers within Mexico City are eight digits; the first digit of the local phone number is always 5. Generally speaking, Mexico City's telephone system is rapidly improving (with new digital lines replacing old ones), offering clear, efficient service. Some of this improvement is resulting in numbers changing. As elsewhere in the country, the telephone company changes numbers without informing the telephone owners or the information operators. Business telephone numbers may be registered in the name of the corporation, which may be different than the name of a hotel or restaurant owned by the corporation. Unless the corporation pays for a separate listing, the operator uses the corporate name to find the number. The local number for **information** is © **040**, and you are allowed to request three numbers with each information call.

Coin-operated phones are prone to vandalism; **prepaid Ladatel card-only Telmex phones** have replaced most of them. Ladatel cards are usually available at pharmacies and newsstands near public phones. They come in denominations of 30, 50, and 100 pesos. **Long-distance calls** within Mexico and to foreign points can be surprisingly expensive. See "Appendix A: Fast Facts in Mexico," for information on using phones.

Weather & Clothing Mexico City's high altitude means you'll need a warm jacket and sweater in winter. The southern parts of the city, such as the university area and Xochimilco, are much colder than the central part. In summer, it gets warm during the day and cool (but not cold) at night. From May to October is the rainy season (this is common all over Mexico)—take a raincoat or rain poncho. People tend to dress somewhat conservatively in Mexico City, and neither shorts nor short skirts are common.

3 Where to Stay

Not only is Mexico City one of the most exciting cities in the world, it can also be one of the most affordable when it comes to accommodations. For around $50 (£25), you can find a double room in a fairly central hotel, including a bathroom and often air-conditioning and TV. Many hotels have their own garages where guests can park free.

The best hotel values concentrate in the downtown **Centro Histórico (historic district),** which has recently undergone a dining and nightlife renaissance. Luxury hotels are mostly in the two most popular areas for mainstream tourism: The Financial District, running alongside Reforma Avenue and near the **Zona Rosa,** attracts predominantly those in the city for business or shopping, whereas **Chapultepec Park** and the **Polanco** neighborhood are ideally located near museums and other cultural attractions. This area is where you'll find trendy places to sleep, including the **W Mexico City** and the acclaimed **Hotel Habita,** as well as more classic hotels such as the **JW Marriott** and **Presidente InterContinental** (see below).

Hotels in these zones not only offer more deluxe accommodations and amenities, but also generally have their own fleets of taxis (see "By Taxi," under "Getting Around," earlier in this chapter) and secured entrances for guests. The crime rate, though on the decline, is still quite high; given this unfortunate reality, visitors should consider staying in the most secure accommodations they can afford.

The ultrahip and happening **Condesa** neighborhood boasts the 40-room **Condesa*df*** (p. 119), which opened in 2005 to rave reviews.

CHAPULTEPEC PARK & POLANCO
VERY EXPENSIVE

Casa Vieja 🌟🌟🌟 *Finds* Pure Mexican style and service are the hallmarks of this luxury boutique hotel, a true gem known more to locals than tourists. Once a private residence, Casa Vieja is decorated with bold colors, unique handicrafts, exquisite antiques, and original furnishings. Each individually decorated suite is named after a Mexican artist, such as Frida Kahlo or Diego Rivera, and includes a living and kitchen area, 36-inch TV, spacious bedroom, and large bathroom with Jacuzzi tub. Notwithstanding the lovely decor, the real attraction is the highly personalized, gracious service. Guests receive a welcome drink and fruit basket upon arrival. An intimate rooftop restaurant and lounge serves made-to-order breakfast, lunch, and dinner (not included in the room rate). The only drawback is that in some rooms, you may overhear conversations in the halls and common areas.

Eugenio Sue 45 (a half-block from Av. Presidente Masaryk), Col. Polanco, 11560 Mexico D.F. © 55/5282-0067 or 5281-4468. Fax 55/5281-3780. www.casavieja.com. 10 suites. $300 (£150) junior suite; $430 (£215) master suite; $950 (£475) presidential suite. Rates include continental breakfast. AE, MC, V. Limited free parking. Metro: Polanco. **Amenities:** Bar and cafe w/light meal service; concierge; room service; laundry service; dry cleaning. *In room:* A/C, TV/DVD, free Wi-Fi, kitchenette, minibar, hair dryer, safe.

JW Marriott 🌟🌟 The JW Marriott is one of the city's most luxurious and expensive hotels, and a number of the city's most important visitors stay here. The refined marble lobby leads past world-class artwork and gorgeous flower displays to a dark wood library and a piano lounge. The hotel is home to the Club Industriales business center, as well as La Griglia, a beautiful Mediterranean-Italian restaurant. Spacious, state-of-the-art guest rooms have panoramic city and park views, plush furnishings, and separate showers and tubs with spray jets. The full-service spa includes body and facial treatments, massages, a well-equipped fitness center, and a lovely outdoor pool and Jacuzzi. Executive-level rooms afford premium wines, gourmet food presentations, complimentary pressing and shoe shine, and free Wi-Fi. Impeccable service complements the elegant surroundings, within easy walking distance of Chapultepec Park and Avenida Presidente Masaryk. It's a short drive to the financial center.

Andrés Bello 29 (at Campos Eliseos), Col. Polanco, 11560 Mexico, D.F. © 800/228-9290 in the U.S., or 55/5999-0000. Fax 55/5999-0001. www.marriott.com. 312 units. $379 (£180) and up double; $489 (£245) junior suite. AE, DC, MC, V. Parking $10 (£5) per day. Metro: Polanco. **Amenities:** 2 restaurants; piano lounge; outdoor pool; health club with spa services and fitness center; Jacuzzi; concierge; full-service business center; room service; laundry service; dry cleaning; executive level rooms. *In room:* A/C, TV, Wi-Fi, minibar, hair dryer, safe.

W Mexico City 🌟🌟🌟 This dramatic 26-story business hotel is a sophisticated mixture of style, comfort, and technology. The entry encompasses a series of stepped lounge areas with koi ponds; the trendy four-section Whiskey Bar also features a heated outdoor terrace. Rooms are striking, with cherry-red walls, white featherbeds, terrazzo floors, plasma TVs, and a spacious and comfortable work area. Stylish bathrooms have walk-in showers and a hanging hammock; some rooms have a large circular tub. Eight high-ceiling "loft" suites afford views of Chapultepec Park, green-glass showers, and plasma TVs on the ceiling above the beds. Business traveler amenities include nine high-tech conference rooms that seat up to 400, a complete business center, and "cyber rooms" with printers, scanners, and fax. The hotel's full-service spa and health club are excellent. Solea, a fashionable seafood restaurant blending Mexican and Asian flavors, offers terrace dining for breakfast or lunch.

Campos Eliseos 252 (corner of Andrés Bello), Col. Polanco, 11560 Mexico, D.F. (C) **888/625-5144** in the U.S., or 55/9138-1800. Fax 55/9138-1899. www.starwood.com/whotels. 237 units. $379 (£180) double; $569 (£285) and up suite. AE, MC, V. Valet parking $9 (£4.50). Metro: Polanco. **Amenities:** Restaurant; 4 bars; full-service spa; concierge; tour services; business center; room service; laundry service; dry cleaning; CD and DVD library. *In room:* A/C, plasma TV, Wi-Fi, minibar, hair dryer, safe.

EXPENSIVE

Hotel Camino Real 🌟🌟   Although it is aging, the Camino Real remains one of the capital's top spots for business and social entertaining, and frequently sells out. Set amid Mexico's finest museums, it's a work of art in itself. Designed by renowned architect Ricardo Legorreta, the building is a classic example of contemporary Mexican architecture; more than 400 works of art by Mexican masters and other celebrated contemporary artists complement the design. Spacious rooms are brightly colored with a sitting and desk area and armoires that conceal the TV and minibar. Some could use a renovation. Executive Club rooms come with bathrobes; rates here include continental breakfast, evening cocktail hour, and daily newspaper. The hotel houses a branch of **China Grill,** the 24-hour **Bice Bistro,** and the first **Le Cirque** restaurant outside of the U.S. The lobby's **Blue Lounge**—with waterfall and seating on an acrylic floor over a pool—occasionally features live music.

Mariano Escobedo 700, Col. Anzúrez, 11590 Mexico, D.F. ℂ **800/722-2646** in the U.S. and Canada, or 55/5263-8888. Fax 55/5263-8889. www.caminoreal.com/mexico. 712 units. $198 (£99) double; $234 (£117) executive club; $335 (£168) junior suite. AE, DC, MC, V. Parking $8.50 (£4.25). Metro: Chapultepec. **Amenities:** 6 restaurants; popular bar w/live entertainment; outdoor pool; gym; sauna; steam room; concierge; travel agency; car rental; full-service business center; salon; 24-hr. room service; massage; laundry service; dry cleaning. *In room:* A/C, TV, Wi-Fi, minibar, hair dryer, safe.

Hotel Habita ☆ Habita deserves credit for helping to modernize the Mexico City hotel scene, even if it's now less trendy than it was a few years ago. A boutique hotel of chic minimalist design, Habita quickly became a preferred hotel in the city's most stylish neighborhood. The white-and-steel room decor is understated, with flatscreen TVs and elegant gray Mexican marble lining the bathrooms from floor to ceiling. Beds are super comfortable, with down comforters and pillows. Located on the rooftop terrace, the hotel's AREA bar remains among the city's chic nightspots, despite newer arrivals. The lower level of the terrace features AREA's VIP section, along with a lap pool and small fitness center for guests. Adjacent to the lobby is a designer restaurant and lounge serving fusion cuisine and exotic martinis.

Av. Presidente Masaryk 201, Col. Polanco, 11560 Mexico, D.F. ℂ **55/5282-3100.** Fax 55/5282-3101. www.hotel habita.com. 36 units. $275 (£138) double. AE, MC, V. Free parking. Metro: Polanco. **Amenities:** Restaurant; 2 bars; rooftop heated pool and solarium; small gym; Jacuzzi; sauna; steam room; concierge; tour services; business center; room service; massage; laundry service; dry cleaning. *In room:* A/C, TV, Wi-Fi, minibar, hair dryer, safe.

Presidente InterContinental ☆☆ The buzzing Presidente is a leading destination for business executives and international visitors, a self-contained hotel city in a sleek 42-story building. Situated in the fashionable Polanco neighborhood, the Presidente is a short walk to some of the city's trendiest restaurants and nightlife and to Mexico City's world-class museums housed in Chapultepec Park. The hotel's excellent restaurants, including the **Palm, Au Pied de Cochon,** and **Zhen,** are fed by the Presidente's wine cellar, the largest in Latin America. Contemporary Mexican designs decorate public areas and guest rooms, which are spacious and well-appointed with flatscreen TVs and city or park views. Executive club rooms include private check-in service, breakfast, and evening hors d'oeuvres and cocktails; there's also a floor dedicated to rooms with special amenities just for women. The hotel's numerous event salons make this as much of a business as a social center, and the large staff is known for its friendly, professional service. The knowledgeable concierges will help familiarize you with the area and point you in the direction you wish to travel.

Campos Eliseos 218, Col. Polanco, 11560 Mexico, D.F. ℂ **800/424-6835** in the U.S., or 55/5327-7700. Fax 55/5327-7730. www.ichotelsgroup.com. 661 units. $239–$299 (£120–£150) double; $450 (£225) junior suite. AE, MC, V. Parking $10 (£5) per day. Metro: Auditorio. **Amenities:** 5 restaurants; lobby bar w/live entertainment; fitness center; concierge; travel agency; car rental; full-service business center; 24-hr. room service; babysitting; laundry service; dry cleaning; executive level rooms. *In room:* A/C, TV, Wi-Fi, minibar, hair dryer, safe.

REFORMA AVENUE
VERY EXPENSIVE
Hotel Four Seasons ☆☆☆ One of the finest hotels in Mexico, the Four Seasons sets the standard for service with a staff noted for gracious manners. In the style of a

> ### *Tips* Weekend Deals
>
> Traveling business professionals make up most of the clientele of the top hotels, which often offer substantially lower rates Friday through Sunday.

colonial-era palace, it offers sumptuous guest rooms surrounding a beautiful central courtyard. The restaurant and bar offer seating under the colonnaded walkways around the courtyard. The luxurious guest rooms have high ceilings, plush bedspreads, Talavera lamps, Indonesian tapestries, and dark-wood furnishings, including a desk. Bathrooms have dual sinks and illuminated makeup mirrors. Most face the courtyard; two deluxe suites have courtyard-facing patios, and most executive suites overlook Reforma Avenue. The hotel offers expert-led private tours to many of the city's historic sites and museums; weekend guests have the option of joining a cultural tour. You won't be able to walk to any tourist attractions from here, but you are within easy driving distance to many of them.

Paseo de la Reforma 500, Col. Juárez, 06600 Mexico, D.F. © **800/332-3442** in the U.S., 800/268-6282 in Canada, or 55/5230-1818. Fax 55/5230-1808. www.fourseasons.com. 240 units. $370 (£185) and up. Special weekend packages generally available. AE, DC, MC, V. Valet parking $10 (£5). Metro: Sevilla. **Amenities:** Restaurant; bar; heated rooftop swimming pool; gym; spa; whirlpool; sauna; business center; room service; massage; laundry service; dry cleaning; 1-hr. pressing service; 2 rooms for travelers w/disabilities. *In room:* A/C, TV, minibar, hair dryer, iron, safe.

EXPENSIVE

Embassy Suites ★★   One of Mexico City's newest and most modern hotels, the Embassy Suites is a welcome addition to what are mostly older hotels on this busy strip of Reforma, part of the capital's financial district. The first Embassy Suites in Mexico, the striking glass high-rise offers two-room suites with living areas including sleeper sofas, dining nooks, and flatscreen TVs; bar areas with microwaves and coffeemakers; marble bathrooms with deep soak tubs; and bedrooms with luxury bedding. The corner and premier rooms are slightly larger than the standards. This is an outstanding value for families and travelers looking for extra space. Guests also enjoy a complimentary cocktail reception and cooked-to-order breakfast. This Embassy Suites houses a small but inviting indoor pool and gym, Starbuck's, and an Argentine restaurant and bar. Concierge and nightly turndown service (uncommon at Embassy Suites elsewhere) are available.

Paseo de la Reforma 69 (Ignacio Ramirez), 06030 Mexico, D.F. © **800/362-2779** in the U.S., or 55/5061-3000. Fax 55/5061-3001. www.embassysuites1.hilton.com. 162 units. $159 (£80) and up suite. Parking $8 (£4). Metro: Hidalgo. **Amenities:** Restaurant; 2 bars; Starbuck's; indoor pool; gym; business center; concierge; babysitting; laundry service; dry cleaning. *In room:* A/C, TV, Wi-Fi, minibar, hair dryer, safe.

Hotel Sheraton María Isabel   The Sheraton María Isabel's location in front of the Monumento de la Independencia is ideal: It's next to the U.S. Embassy and across Reforma from the heart of the Zona Rosa. A favorite for business travelers, the updated 1950s-era hotel offers premium amenities in all its rooms. Tower suites, the most deluxe, occupy the 14th through 17th floors and offer private check-in, butler service, and continental breakfast and evening canapés. Some have views of the beautiful Angel of Independence monument in front, and rooms on the 15th floor are specially designed for women travelers. The excellent health club includes two tennis courts, massage services, a fitness center, and small rooftop pool. The **Jorongo Bar,** a

Mexico City institution, offers some of the best live Mexican music nightly from 7pm to 1am. (See "Mexico City After Dark," later in this chapter.). A Starbuck's and Manhattan deli are adjacent to the lobby.

Paseo de la Reforma 325 (at Río Tiber), 06500 Mexico, D.F. ⓒ 800/325-3535 in the U.S., or 55/5242-5555. Fax 55/5207-0684. www.sheraton.com. 755 units. $195 (£98) and up double; $250 (£125) and up tower. AE, MC, V. Covered parking $12 (£6). Metro: Insurgentes (6 blocks away). **Amenities:** 2 restaurants; 2 bars; outdoor pool; privileges at nearby golf course; 2 tennis courts; full-service fitness center; concierge; business center; salon; room service; laundry service; dry cleaning. *In room:* A/C, TV, Wi-Fi, minibar, hair dryer, safe

INEXPENSIVE

Hotel María Cristina   This classic choice for budget travelers is conveniently located just a 10-minute walk from the Zona Rosa. Resembling an aged Andalusian palace, the hotel is decorated with wrought-iron chandeliers, mahogany furnishings, and colonial patios and corridors. Standard rooms have one king or two double beds, ample closets, and modern bathrooms; the larger deluxe rooms include minibars and air-conditioning. The large lobby with overstuffed couches and a fireplace makes for a comfortable meeting place. A grassy courtyard offers lounge chairs for reading or relaxing. The hotel lies at Río Neva, on the north side of Reforma.

Río Lerma 31, Col. Cuauhtémoc, 06500 Mexico, D.F. ⓒ 55/5703-1212 or 5566-9688. Fax 55/5566-9194. www.hotel mariacristina.com.mx. 150 units. $80 (£40) standard double; $100 (£50) deluxe double. AE, MC, V. Free guarded parking. **Amenities:** Restaurant; bar; travel agency; salon; private garden. *In room:* A/C (deluxe rooms only), TV, Wi-Fi in most rooms, safe.

CENTRO HISTORICO & SURROUNDING AREAS
EXPENSIVE

Sheraton Centro Histórico Hotel & Convention Center ⓡⓡ   Across from the Alameda Central park, this is the most luxurious option in the Historic Center. The striking marble-filled lobby leads to three outstanding restaurants, including the power lunch spot **El Cardenal,** and a wine bar. Spacious, modern guest rooms have separate marble showers and tubs, flatscreen TVs, and ample work spaces; corner rooms are even larger and suites include kitchenettes and Jacuzzis. Eastern rooms overlook the Alameda and adjacent Palace of Fine Arts; western rooms have city views. The Sports City gym features one of the best fitness centers of any hotel in the city, as well as an indoor pool, sun deck, and limited spa services. Despite the hotel's role as a convention center, the five-star service remains attentive and personalized. You can easily walk from here to the Palace of Fine Arts, and the major destinations in the Historic Center. *Note:* This Sheraton is scheduled to become a Hilton in 2008, but it should remain open during the transition.

Av. Juárez 70 (at Balderas), 06010 Mexico, D.F. ⓒ 800/325-3535 in the U.S. and Canada, or 55/5130-5300. Fax 55/5130-5255. www.sheraton.com/centrohistorico. 457 units. $178–$425 (£89–£213) double; $620 (£310) suite. AE, MC, V. Covered guarded parking $10 (£5). Metro: Hidalgo. **Amenities:** 4 restaurants; wine bar; heated indoor swimming pool; fully equipped fitness center; limited spa services; Jacuzzi; concierge; full-service business center; room service; laundry service; dry cleaning. *In room:* A/C, TV, Wi-Fi, minibar, coffeemaker, hair dryer, safe.

MODERATE

Best Western Hotel Majestic ⓡ   A Mexico City institution that visitors should experience at least once, this classic hotel has a prime location facing the *zócalo*—reason enough to stay here. The lobby's glass ceiling is the floor of a sitting area surrounded by guest rooms. Rooms that don't overlook the *zócalo* overlook Avenida Madero or the hotel's inner court. The lobby and courtyard are decorated with stone arches, beautiful tiles, and stone fountains. Room furnishings are dated, and renovation plans continually stall. In lower-floor rooms facing Avenida Madero, street noise may be a problem. Guests in rooms that face the *zócalo* will suffer the periodic early-morning flag-raising ceremony, complete with marching feet, drums, and bugle. Quieter rooms overlook the courtyard, with its own aviary. The popular Terraza rooftop cafe/restaurant serves three meals. You can save considerably by booking directly with the hotel and by asking for promotional rates or discounts.

Av. Madero 73, Col. Centro, 06000 Mexico, D.F. © 55/5521-8600. Fax 55/5512-6262. www.majestic.com.mx. 85 units. $113 (£57) and up double. AE, MC, V. Nearby parking $10 (£5). Metro: Zócalo. **Amenities:** Restaurant/bar; travel agency; room service; business services; babysitting; laundry services. *In room:* TV, coffeemaker.

Holiday Inn Zócalo *Finds* Located next to the city's historic central square, this unique Holiday Inn is decorated in colonial Mexican style with colorful art, antiques, handicrafts, and other charming touches. In fact, it's one of the most inviting Holiday Inns I've seen anywhere. Photos of old Mexico City hang in the guest rooms, which have high ceilings, hardwood floors, marble bathrooms, robes, and modern conveniences such as wireless Internet access. Nonsmoking rooms are available. The rooftop terrace overlooks the *zócalo,* and the hotel also features a small restaurant, gym, concierge, and travel services. The multilingual staff caters to an international clientele that includes mostly Europeans and Americans.

Av. Cinco de Mayo 61, 06000 Mexico, D.F. © 55/5130-5130. Fax 55/5521-2122. www.hotelescortes.com. 105 units. $130 (£65) double; $160 (£80) suite. AE, MC, V. Free parking. Metro: Zócalo. **Amenities:** Restaurant; bar; gym; concierge; travel desk; room service; laundry service; nonsmoking rooms. *In room:* A/C, TV, Wi-Fi.

INEXPENSIVE

Hotel Catedral *Value* This bargain hotel enjoys a stellar location 1 block north of Calle Tacuba on tree-shaded Calle Donceles, half a block from the Templo Mayor, and a block from the Museo San Ildefonso. Guest rooms have purified drinking water from a special tap, over-bed reading lights, and TVs with U.S. cable channels. Some have tub/shower combinations, and others have whirlpool tubs. The furnishings are dated, however. Rooms on the upper floors afford views of the cathedral. On the seventh floor, a terrace with small tables and chairs offers great views. Because of heavily trafficked streets surround the hotel, add 45 minutes to your departure time if you leave for the airport from here. In front of the big, marble-embellished lobby lies the bustling restaurant. The cozy bar beyond the reception desk also serves food. Ask for a top-floor room with a view. Breakfast costs $10 (£5) extra for a double room.

Calle Donceles 95 (between Brasil and Argentina), 06020 Mexico, D.F. © 55/5518-5232. Fax 55/5512-4344. www.hotelcatedral.com. 116 units. $66 (£33) double; $73 (£37) junior suite. AE, MC, V. Free parking. Metro: Zócalo. **Amenities:** Restaurant; bar; travel agency; room service; laundry service. *In room:* TV, Wi-Fi, hair dryer, safe.

CONDESA/ROMA
EXPENSIVE

Condesa*df* Developed by the same group that brought Hotel Habita to Polanco, Condesa*df* became the city's hottest place to stay after opening in 2005. Housed in a 1928 triangular Beaux Arts building, it features several rooms and bars that open onto a plant-filled interior courtyard. These spaces tend to be popular for small VIP parties and special events, which makes it a perfect place to check in on the local who's who. Interiors were fashioned by the French designer India Mahdavi, described as "Mexican with a twist"—stone floors, alpaca carpets, and a heavy dose of turquoise accents offset by cream leather sofas. Guest rooms feature high ceilings, balconies or terraces overlooking Parque España, hand-woven rugs, rocking chairs, flatscreen TVs, DVD players, and iPods. The rooftop sushi lounge is generally packed with the city's beautiful people, and a basement "cinema" screening room transforms into a sizzling nightclub Thursday through Saturday nights.

Av. Veracruz 102, Col. Condesa, 06700 Mexico, D.F. © 800/337-4685 in the U.S., or 55/5241-2600. www. condesadf.com. 40 units. $195–$425 (£98–£213) doubles and suites. AE, MC, V. Free parking. Metro: Insurgentes. **Amenities:** 2 restaurants; bar; club; Jacuzzi; concierge; tour services; room service; massage; laundry service; dry cleaning. Inquire about pets. *In room:* A/C, plasma TV/DVD, iPod, Wi-Fi, minibar, hair dryer, safe.

La Casona Hotel-Relais *(★★ (Finds* Reminiscent of a small European luxury hotel, this exquisite establishment opened in 1996 in a formerly dilapidated 1923 building. Mexico's National Institute of Fine Arts has since designated it an artistic monument. Modern conveniences such as flatscreen TVs are juxtaposed with antique furniture in the individually decorated guest rooms. Tall interior shutter doors on guest-room windows keep out sound and light at night, and thick glass mutes street noise by day. Oriental-style rugs warm the hardwood floors and black-and-white marble throughout the common areas, decorated with prints of classical composers and fox hunts. A small French-inspired restaurant next to the lobby is a popular gathering spot. The hotel lies 3 blocks south of the Diana Circle on Reforma, and 4 longish blocks west of the western edge of the Zona Rosa. More important than decor or location is the excellent service here—truly capable of pampering you.

Durango 280 (corner of Cozumel), Col. Roma, 06700 Mexico, D.F. © 800/223-5652 in the U.S., or 55/5286-3001. Fax 55/5211-0871. www.hotellacasona.com.mx. 29 units. $200 (£99) double. Rates include American breakfast. AE, MC, V. Gated parking $5 (£2.50). Metro: Sevilla (4 blocks away). **Amenities:** Restaurant; bar; small gym w/steam room; concierge; business center; room service; laundry service; safe; currency exchange. *In room:* A/C, TV, Wi-Fi.

NEAR THE AIRPORT
MODERATE
Hilton Airport Hotel *(★* The Hilton is located inside the expansive Mexico City airport. The lobby bar is a popular gathering place, and if the international restaurant happens to be closed, there's 24-hour room service. The staff is attentive and the rooms nicely furnished, though small. Each has an entertainment system with satellite TV, pay-movies, and video games, work desk with an ergonomic executive chair, and bath amenities by Crabtree & Evelyn. It can't be beat for convenience and a guarantee of making an early morning plane. The Hilton is located on the third level of gate F1, International Arrivals.

International Mexico City Airport (Sala F1, 3rd floor), 15620 Mexico, D.F. © 800/228-9290 in the U.S., or 55/5133-0505. Fax 55/5133-0500. www.hilton.com. 129 units. $195 (£98) double; $225 (£113) executive room. AE, DC, MC, V. Parking $23 (£12). **Amenities:** Restaurant; lobby bar; small health club; concierge; business center; room service; laundry and pressing service; executive floor. *In room:* A/C, TV w/pay movies and games, Wi-Fi, minibar, coffeemaker, hair dryer, iron, safe.

4 Where to Dine

As in most of the world's major cities, dining in Mexico City is sophisticated, with cuisine that spans the globe. From high chic to the Mexican standard of *comida corrida* (food on the go), the capital offers something for every taste and budget. The **Polanco** area in particular has become a place of exquisite dining options, with new restaurants rediscovering and modernizing classic Mexican dishes. The **Centro Histórico** led a resurgence of popular restaurants and bars open for late-night dining and nightlife, which has spread to the **Condesa** and **Roma** neighborhoods—now known as the SoHo of Mexico City. Cantinas, until not so very long ago the privilege of men only, offer some of the best food and colorful local atmosphere. **San Angel** houses some of Mexico City's finest traditional restaurants.

Everybody eats out in Mexico City, regardless of social class. Consequently, you can find restaurants of every type, size, and price range scattered across the city. Mexicans take their food and dining seriously, so if you see a full house, that's generally recommendation enough. But those same places may be entirely empty if you arrive early—remember, here, lunch is generally eaten at 3pm, with dinner not seriously considered before 9pm. Many establishments add a "cover" charge of $2 to $4 (£1–£2) per person to the bill.

CHAPULTEPEC PARK & POLANCO
VERY EXPENSIVE

Aguila y Sol ✿✿✿ MEXICAN HAUTE CUISINE   This sophisticated and acclaimed establishment is without question my favorite Mexican restaurant. Serving the best Mexican cuisine you will find anywhere in the world, chef-owner Martha Ortiz blends indigenous and pre-Hispanic ingredients with contemporary creations, and the results attain the level of art. (Ortiz has designed a number of excellent cookbooks, for sale at the restaurant). Among the delectable selections are duck mole, salmon in a maize crust, pork loin with gingered mango, and seared tuna with smoked chile. An outstanding wine list accompanies the exotic menu. Dishes are carefully presented but not overly big. The beautiful space reflects soft Mexican colors and is casually elegant but not stuffy, and the clientele includes some of the city's best-known personalities.

Emilio Castelar 229, 3rd floor (above Louis Vuitton shop at Av. Presidente Masaryk), Col. Polanco. © 55/5281-8354. Reservations recommended. Main courses $20–$35 (£10–£18). AE, MC, V. Mon–Sat 1:30–11:30pm; Sun 1:30–5:30pm. Metro: Polanco.

Hacienda de los Morales ✿✿ *Moments* MEXICAN HAUTE CUISINE   A 16th-century oasis amid the world's most populous city, the Hacienda de los Morales is an enchanted place for special occasions. The Spanish colonial decor includes dark wood furnishings, stone columns, and domed brick ceilings, with some tables looking out to garden fountains. The entrance patio doubles as an elegant bar, where you will find precious artwork and the original chapel where Spanish aristocrats once prayed. While the Hacienda is a bustling power lunch spot by day, it transforms into a romantic retreat at night. Expertly prepared food includes the best of Mexican dishes, with an excellent selection of meat, fish, and seafood, as well as pastas, crepes, and other selections. A constant stream of weddings and special events takes place in private salons surrounding the gardens. Jacket and tie are suggested.

Vázquez de Mella 525 (at Av. Horacio), Col. Polanco. © 55/5096-3054. www.haciendadelosmorales.com. Reservations recommended. Main courses $20–$40 (£10–£20). AE, MC, V. Daily 1pm–1am. Metro: Polanco.

Izote ✿✿✿ MEXICAN HAUTE CUISINE   Still at the top of the city's superb dining scene, this signature venue of celebrated chef Patricia Quintana pays homage to the best of classic Mexican cooking. There are only 19 tables, and the atmosphere is simple, but what's on your plate will more than compensate. Located on Mexico's version of Rodeo Drive, it remains one of the capital's most popular restaurants, so reservations are essential, even at lunch. The menu is a compilation of modern versions of pre-Hispanic dishes and draws heavily on indigenous ingredients such as yucca flower, cactus, and *masa* (corn flour). Each dish is a delight. Try traditional Oaxacan *mole,* or lamb barbecued in a banana leaf. Endings are especially sweet here—save room for Tarta Zaachila, a chocolate pastry filled with nuts, accompanied by the traditional café de olla, coffee flavored with cinnamon and brown sugar. If you're curious, *izote* is the beautiful white flower that adorns the yucca plant.

Av. Presidente Masaryk 513 (between calles Sócrates and Platón), Col. Polanco. Ⓒ 55/5280-1265. Reservations essential. Main courses $20–$50 (£10–£25). AE, MC, V. Mon–Sat 1pm–midnight; Sun 1–6pm. Metro: Polanco.

Zhen 𝄢𝄢 HAUTE CHINESE   This Shanghai-based restaurant is a recent addition to Mexico City's dining scene and one of the capital's top choices for gourmet Chinese cuisine. The contemporary dining room has round tables with revolving centerpieces for sharing, exquisite place settings, and elegant leather chairs. Soft Oriental music plays in the background as the expert servers attentively wait on the tables. Start with dim sum selections such as steamed shrimp dumplings or spring rolls with chicken and vegetables. The shark fin hot-and-sour soup is another specialty. For a main course, I recommend the braised spare-ribs with aged vinegar, stir-fried snapper with celery, or the crispy and delicious Peking duck. Dishes are beautifully presented and full of flavor.

Campos Eliseos 218, in the Presidente InterContinental, Col. Chapultepec. Ⓒ 55/5327-7700. Reservations recommended. Main courses $15–$52 (£7.50–£26). AE, MC, V. Mon–Sat 1pm–midnight; Sun 1–6pm. Metro: Auditorio.

EXPENSIVE

Au Pied de Cochon 𝄢 FRENCH/BISTRO   The *capitalaños* seem to be having a love affair with French bistros these days, and this is a perennial hotspot. A direct import from Paris, this bistro always packs in the city's jet set and fashion forward for classic cafe fare. Open 24 hours, it's the best late-night dining option in the city. The main dining room is a spirited scene of activity and conversation, in multiple languages. Two service bars offer singles places to dine without feeling "solo," and other tables are packed in together. Pâtés, cheese plates, and exquisite salads are standard starters. The French onion soup and the *foie gras* are particularly delicious. For the main course, perennial favorites are the steak frites, steamed mussels, and the specialty *pied de cochon* (pigs' feet). There's also a raw bar, an excellent selection of French wines, and an ample choice of tequilas. Desserts are classically French and rich.

Campos Eliseos 218, in the Presidente InterContinental, Col. Chapultepec. Ⓒ 55/5327-7756. Reservations recommended. Main courses $18–$56 (£9–£28). AE, MC, V. Daily 24 hr. Metro: Auditorio.

NAOS 𝄢𝄢 MEXICAN/SEAFOOD   A glass-paneled open kitchen and raw bar serve as the centerpiece of acclaimed chef Monica Patiño's NAOS restaurant, located in the fashionable Palmas neighborhood. Waiters in black ties and vests provide crisp, attentive service to the food-loving crowd. The contemporary dining room combines glass, marble, and hardwood floors with fascinating if slightly spooky wall sketches of *katrinas* (humorous skeleton representations celebrating death). Although the menu spans the gamut, seafood remains the specialty. Consider starting with a tuna carpaccio dressed up with fried capers and a citrus vinaigrette, followed by the mild sea bass prepared with three chilies. Fresh oysters and stone crabs from Baja California are offered, along with numerous creatively prepared fish and seafood dishes.

Palmas 425, Col. Lomas de Chapultepec. Ⓒ 55/5520-5702. Reservations recommended. Main courses $25–$50 (£13–£25). AE, DC, MC, V. Mon–Wed 1:30–11pm; Thurs–Sat 1:30pm–midnight; Sun 1:30–6pm. Metro: Auditorio.

MODERATE

L'Olivier *&* COUNTRY FRENCH/BISTRO This bright, bustling bistro would be reminiscent of an authentic French cafe were it not for the fact that its patrons tend to be business moguls and sophisticated socialites rather than bohemians. The restaurant is particularly buzzing at lunch, and more subdued at night. Although the menu changes seasonally, a regular starter is foie gras with black beans. Main courses range from pâté to soufflé. The lamb chops with mint jelly are delectable, as are the seafood linguini and the lamb couscous. For dessert, leave enough room (and time) for the chocolate soufflé. Service is attentive and efficient.

Masaryk 49-C (at Torcuato Tasso), Col. Polanco. (€) 55/5545-3133. Reservations recommended. Main courses $12–$30 (£6–£15). AE, MC, V. Mon–Sat 1:30–11pm; Sun 1:30–5pm. Metro: Polanco.

Villa Maria *&& Kids* TRADITIONAL MEXICAN This festive Mexican restaurant sits on a residential street of Polanco. A fun crowd comes to drink giant flavored margaritas, listen to mariachi music, and eat delicious Mexican food. The inviting dining room has two floors and is peppered with silly bar sayings such as, "I just joined alcoholics anonymous," and "I'm still drinking, but under a nickname." There are as many locals as expatriates here, and Villa Maria is every bit as much a refined celebration of Mexican food as of the culture. Typical tacos are available in every variety (I love the fish tacos with red adobe sauce), as are enchiladas and *mole* dishes. Other excellent suggestions include the red snapper cooked in a tamarind sauce and wrapped in a banana leaf, and the center beef cut served with a creamy tequila sauce. Whatever you order will be delicious, and you're bound to have a great time here. A kids' menu is available.

Homero 704 (at Galileo), Col. Polanco. (€) 55/5203-0306. www.villamaria.com.mx. Reservations recommended. Main courses $9–$20 (£4.50–£10). AE, DC, MC, V. Mon–Sat 1:30pm–midnight; Sun 1:30pm–8pm. Metro: Polanco.

ZONA ROSA & SURROUNDING AREAS

If you're up for a culinary adventure, dine at the student-staffed **Cordon Bleu Casa de Francia,** Havre 15, Zona Rosa (€ **55/5208-0660;** www.lcbmexico.com/restaurante. cfm), a training ground for Mexico's up-and-coming chefs. The restaurant occupies two lovely dining rooms inside the Casa de Francia, a French cultural center. The menu varies; it's a great way to sample imaginative variations on classics and local cuisine. Wines by the glass are available. It's open Monday to Wednesday from 8:30am to 6pm, Thursday to Friday from 8:30am to 11pm, and Saturday 8:30am to 6pm.

EXPENSIVE

Casa Bell *&* INTERNATIONAL MEXICAN A longtime favorite of Mexico City's political and business elite, Casa Bell is probably the capital's key power-lunch venue. Expect to find it filled everyday by 3pm, which is peak lunch hour, with political and business leaders. The lovely terrace begins to fill up around 2pm, as birds chirp from strategically placed cages around the patio. Exceptionally well-trained waiters move attentively around the tables as lunch unfolds, and they are likely to recommend dishes such as the duck tacos, *filete Chemite* (filet mignon), or *robalo* (sea bass) prepared any way you like. Diners typically come dressed in suits and tend to linger over their meals and perhaps a few margaritas. Finish off with a delectable pastry from the dessert cart.

Praga 14 (off Paseo de la Reforma), Zona Rosa. (€) 55/5208-3967. Reservations recommended. Main courses $20–$30 (£10–£15). AE, MC, V. Daily 1–6pm. Metro: Insurgentes.

MODERATE

Fonda El Refugio *★★* MEXICAN   More than 40 years of tradition have shaped the service, food, and atmosphere here, making this a special place for authentic Mexican dining. It's small and unusually congenial, with a large fireplace decorated with gleaming copper pots and pans. The restaurant manages the almost impossible task of being both refined and informal. The menu runs the gamut of Mexican cuisine, from *arroz con plátanos* (rice with fried bananas) to *enchiladas con mole poblano,* topped with the rich, thick, spicy chocolate sauce of Puebla. For a main course, I recommend the *huachinango a la veracruzana* (Veracruz-style red snapper with tomatoes and olives). Or if you're in a spicy mood, the *chiles poblanos* stuffed with ground beef or cheese. For dessert, opt for the coconut candy or the mouth-watering flan. The tortillas are handmade, and the margaritas are potently delicious. Fonda El Refugio is very popular, especially on Saturday night, so get here early.

Liverpool 166 (between calles Florencia and Amberes), Col. Juárez Zona Rosa. © **55/5207-2732** or 5525-8128. Main courses $13–$20 (£6.50–£10). AE, MC, V. Mon–Sun 1–11pm. Metro: Insurgentes.

CENTRO HISTORICO & SURROUNDING AREAS
MODERATE

Café Tacuba *★★* MEXICAN   One of the city's most famous restaurants, Café Tacuba dates from 1912 and boasts a handsome colonial-era atmosphere. Guests are welcomed into one of two long dining rooms, with brass lamps, dark oil paintings, and a large mural of nuns working in a kitchen. The menu is authentic Mexican with traditional dishes, including tamales, enchiladas, chiles rellenos, *mole,* and *pozole.* Wednesday through Sunday from 2 until 10pm, a wonderful group of medieval-costumed singers entertain; their sound is like the melodious *estudiantina* groups of Guanajuato accompanied by mandolins and guitars. A trio or quartet plays romantic boleros on Mondays and Tuesdays from 8 to 10pm.

Tacuba 28 (between República de Chile and Bolívar), Col. Centro. © **55/5512-8482** or 5518-4950. Breakfast $4–$18 (£2–£9); main courses $7–$17 (£3.50–£8.50); *comida corrida* $18 (£9). AE, MC, V. Daily 8am–11:30pm. Metro: Allende.

La Casa de las Sirenas *★* TRADITIONAL MEXICAN   The "house of mermaids," a 16th-century building constructed with rocks from a pyramid, is one of the loveliest restaurants in the historic center. It sits above the famous cantina with the same name (below), and has a wonderful rooftop terrace with a view to the back of the Cathedral and *Templo Mayor.* The food is as novel as the setting. Start with classic Mexican noodle soup with chicken liver, or perhaps the stuffed crepes with chicken, squash flower, and mushrooms. The best main dishes are beef medallions in a mustard seed sauce, sea bass generously stuffed with shrimp and mushrooms, and Cornish hen served with a mango *mole* sauce. Live music is offered on weekends.

República de Guatemala 32 (behind the Cathedral), Col. Centro. © **55/5704-3273**. www.lacasadelassirenas. mx. Main courses $17–$19 (£8.50–£9.50). AE, MC, V. Mon–Sat 11am–11pm; Sun 11am–7pm. Metro: Zócalo.

Restaurant Danubio *★★* SPANISH   Danubio has been a Mexico City tradition since 1936, and it remains an excellent choice for dining in the Historic Center. Photos of celebrity diners line the walls of the classically European-style room. The Basque-inspired menu offers a range of selections emphasizing seafood, and the house specialty is *langostinos* (baby crayfish). A tasting menu with five small dishes (not including wine) is available for only $15 (£7.50). Much of the food is prepared on an old coal and firewood stove. Danubio, which lies south of La Alameda, is also noted for its excellent wine cellar.

República de Uruguay 3 (near Bolívar), Alameda. ℂ 55/5521-0976. www.danubio.com. Main courses $10–$33 (£5–£17). AE, DC, MC, V. Daily 1–10pm. Metro: Bellas Artes or Salto del Agua.

CANTINAS

Cantina La Guadalupana ★★ *Finds* MEXICAN   Opened in 1928, this cantina lies in Coyoacán, the southern neighborhood that was once the home of artists Diego Rivera and Frida Kahlo and the revolutionary Leon Trotsky. From the entrance—off a narrow cobblestone colonial street—to the antiquated bar, a sense of nostalgia permeates the comfortable, jovial cantina. The operation is as traditional as the menu. For those who are only drinking, waiters bring the customary small plates of complimentary snacks (called *botanas*) that range from crisp jicama slices with lime and chile to pigs' feet in a red sauce. It's easy to imagine the communist conversations that must have bounced off the walls here in Frida and Diego's day.

Higuera 2 and Caballo Calco (1 block from the central plaza), Coyoacán. ℂ 55/5554-6253. Main courses $5–$8 (£2.50–£4); mixed drinks $2.50–$8 (£1.25–£4), more for premium tequilas. AE, MC, V. Mon–Sat 1:30pm–1am. Metro: Coyoacán.

La México ★ *Finds* MEXICAN   The "queen of cantinas" as it is known, La México boasts three floors of nonstop tequila drinking, beer guzzling, music playing fun. A favorite among locals from all social classes, this authentic cantina offers live music Wednesday through Saturday nights, including salsa and traditional Mexican. For $14 (£7), you get one drink and 12 small appetizers (*botanas*). Following their meals, or perhaps in the midst of them, patrons often take to dancing between tables. Simple Mexican fare is offered. La México is located in San Jerónimo, toward the south end of the city.

Eje 10 Sur 75 (near Revolución), San Jerónimo. ℂ 55/5550-2072. Main courses $4–$10 (£2–£5); mixed drinks $2–$7 (£1–£3.50), more for premium tequilas. No credit cards. Mon–Tues 1pm–12:30am; Wed 1pm–2am; Thurs–Fri 1pm–3am; Sat noon–2am.

La Opera ★★ *Moments* INTERNATIONAL   La Opera Bar, 3 blocks east of La Alameda, is the most opulent of the city's cantinas. Slide into a dark wood booth below gilded baroque ceilings, patches of beveled mirror, and exquisite small oil paintings. Or opt for a linen-covered table with a basket of fresh bread. La Opera is the Mexican equivalent of a London gentlemen's club, although it has become so popular for dining that fewer and fewer men play dominoes. In fact, you see people enjoying romantic interludes in cavernous booths—but tables of any kind are hard to find. Service is best if you arrive for lunch when it opens or go after 5pm when the throngs have diminished; the jacketed waiters cater to regulars at the expense of unknown diners. The menu is unimpressive, but the atmosphere and drinks are excellent. Try a margarita or a classic tequila. Specialties include Spanish tapas, Caesar salad, and Veracruz-style red snapper with olives and tomatoes. While you wait for your meal, look to the ceiling for the bullet hole that legend says Pancho Villa left when he galloped in on a horse. It's half a block toward the *zócalo* from Sanborn's House of Tiles.

Cinco de Mayo 10, Col. Centro. ℂ 55/5512-8959. Reservations recommended at lunch. Main courses $5–$21 (£2.50–£11); mixed drinks $4–$6 (£2–£3), more for premium tequilas. AE, MC, V. Mon–Sat 1pm–midnight; Sun 1–6pm. Metro: Bellas Artes.

Moments ¡Café, Por Favor!

In Mexico, the preparation and consumption of espresso have been considered an art form for generations. You can find the best coffee in small cafes with a crowd of regulars who congregate to catch up on the local *chisme* (gossip).

Café La Habana, downtown at Bucareli and Morelos, is one of the most famous, a longstanding cafe with a rich history—and a reputation for strong coffees, all roasted and ground in-house. Ask the waiter and he'll tell you how Fidel Castro and Ché Guevara planned the Cuban revolution while sipping an espresso *cortao*. Strangely, it's Mexican and not Cuban food served here. The cafe is open Monday through Thursday from 7am to 11:30pm, Friday and Saturday from 7am to 1am, and Sunday from 8am to 10pm.

In the Centro Histórico near the Zócalo, **Mumedi,** Francisco I. Madero 74, is a hip designer cafe popular with artists, architects, and graphic designers. Attached to the cafe is a bookstore and gallery featuring contemporary art objects and changing exhibitions. It's open Tuesday through Sunday from 8am to 9pm and Monday from 11:30am to 9pm.

European-style coffeehouses are in the Zona Rosa, frequented by businesspeople and trendy urban residents. Some of the most popular are **Salón de Té Auseba** and **Duca d'Este,** both on Hamburgo near Florencia. They serve excellent coffee and scrumptious cakes, as well as a variety of herbal teas. The sidewalk cafe **Konditori,** Genova 61, is another good option, on a pedestrian-only street. It's open daily 7am to midnight.

The Condesa neighborhood, east of Chapultepec Park, is another top cafe zone. **El Péndulo,** Nuevo León 115, close to Insurgentes, is a favorite. It combines its cafe setting with a book and music store and tends to draw intellectuals, writers, and students. It frequently hosts live music and poetry readings. It's open Monday through Friday from 8am to 11pm and weekends from 10am to 11pm. There's another branch in the Zona Rosa at Hamburgo 126.

5 Exploring Mexico City

The diversity of Mexico City's attractions springs from its complex layers of history. From simple bustling *mercados* to museums filled with treasures of artistic and historic significance, Mexico City has layers and layers of cultural richness to explore.

Mexico City was built on the ruins of the ancient city of Tenochtitlán. A downtown portion of the city, comprising almost 700 blocks and 1,500 buildings, is designated the Centro Histórico (Historic Center). The area has surged in popularity, and once-neglected buildings are being converted into fashionable shops and restaurants, recalling its former colonial charm.

Remember that this is a major Latin city; dress is more professional and formal here than in other parts of the country. The altitude keeps the temperature mild, which is often a surprise for travelers with preconceptions of Mexico as perpetually hot. In

Historic Downtown (Centro Histórico)

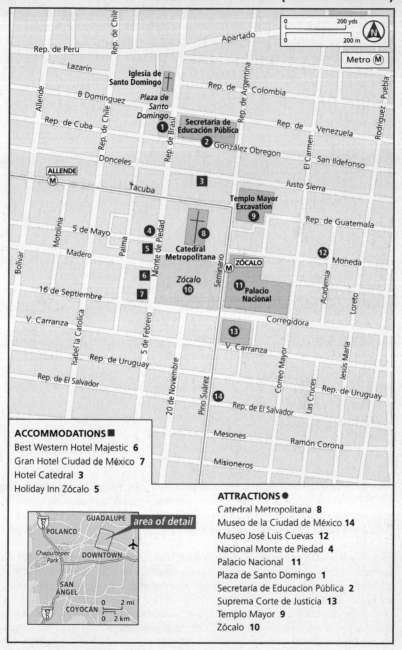

ACCOMMODATIONS ■
Best Western Hotel Majestic **6**
Gran Hotel Ciudad de México **7**
Hotel Catedral **3**
Holiday Inn Zócalo **5**

ATTRACTIONS ●
Catedral Metropolitana **8**
Museo de la Ciudad de México **14**
Museo José Luis Cuevas **12**
Nacional Monte de Piedad **4**
Palacio Nacional **11**
Plaza de Santo Domingo **1**
Secretaría de Educacíon Pública **2**
Suprema Corte de Justicia **13**
Templo Mayor **9**
Zócalo **10**

summer, always be prepared for rain, which falls for an hour or two almost daily. In winter, carry a jacket or sweater—stone museums are chilly inside, and when the sun goes down, the outside air gets quite cold.

THE TOP ATTRACTIONS

Basílica de Santa María de Guadalupe ✦✦   Within the northern city limits is the famous Basílica of Guadalupe—not just another church, but the central place of worship for Mexico's patron saint and the home of the image responsible for uniting pre-Hispanic Indian mysticism with Catholic beliefs. It is virtually impossible to understand Mexico and its culture without appreciating the national devotion to Our Lady of Guadalupe. The blue-mantled Virgin of Guadalupe is the most revered image in the country, and you will see her countenance wherever you travel. This is also one of the most important religious sites for Catholics.

The Basílica occupies the site where, on December 9, 1531, a poor Indian named Juan Diego reputedly saw a vision of a beautiful lady in a blue mantle. The local bishop, Zumarraga, was reluctant to confirm that Juan Diego had indeed seen the Virgin Mary, so he asked the peasant for evidence. Juan Diego saw the vision a second time, on December 12, and when he asked the Virgin for proof, she instructed him to collect the roses that began blooming in the rocky soil at his feet. He gathered the flowers in his cloak and returned to the bishop. When he unfurled his cloak, the flowers dropped to the ground and the image of the Virgin was miraculously emblazoned on the rough-hewn cloth. The bishop immediately ordered the building of a church on the spot, and upon its completion, the cloth with the Virgin's image was hung in a place of honor, framed in gold. Since that time, millions of the devout and the curious have come to view the miraculous image that experts, it is said, are at a loss to explain. So heavy was the flow of visitors—many approached for hundreds of yards on their knees—that the old church, already fragile, was insufficient to handle them. An audacious new Basílica, designed by Pedro Ramírez Vazquez, the same architect who designed the breathtaking Museo Nacional de Antropología, opened in 1987.

The miracle cloak hangs behind bulletproof glass above the altar of the new Basílica. Moving walkways going in two directions transport the crowds a distance below the cloak. If you want to see it again, take the people-mover going in the opposite direction; you can do it as many times as you want.

In 2002, the pope declared Juan Diego a saint, a very big deal in this predominantly Catholic country; he was the first Mexican to achieve sainthood. The achievement was not, however, without controversy—Juan Diego's images have increasingly taken on a "European" appearance, and native Mexicans insist that Juan Diego be portrayed as the dark-skinned indigenous peasant he was.

To the right of the modern basilica is the Old Basílica, which used to house the cloak. To the back of it lies the entrance to the Basílica Museum, with a very good display of religious art in restored rooms. One of the side chapels, with a silver altar, is adjacent to the museum. Nearby are several gift shops specializing in religious objects and other folk art.

Outside the museum lies a garden commemorating the moment Juan Diego showed the cloak to the archbishop. Numerous photographers with colorful backdrops gather there to capture your visit on film. At the top of the hill, behind a third basilica built in 1950, is the **Panteón del Tepeyac,** a cemetery where big names such as Santa Anna, Velasco, and Orozco are buried. The steps up this hill are lined with

Chapultepec Park

Castillo de Chapultepec/
Museo Nacional
de Historia **4**
La Feria Amusement Park **6**
Museo de Antropología **1**
Museo de Arte Moderno **3**
Museo de Historia Natural **8**
Museo Rufino Tamayo **2**
Papalote, Museo del Niño **7**
Parque Zoológico
de Chapultepec **5**
Rotonda de los
Hombres Ilustres **9**

Metro Ⓜ

1/4 mi
0.25 km

Hotel
Camino Real

Avenida Melchor
Ocampo

Calzada Mariano Escobedo

Niños
Héroes

Ⓜ CHAPULTEPEC

Calzada José Vasconcelos

Calzada M. Gandhi

Avenida Heroico Militar

Ⓜ JUANACATLAN

Paseo de la Reforma

Lago
Chapultepec

Avenida

Gran

Avenida de los Constituyentes

Ⓜ CONSTITUYENTES

Chivatito

Ⓜ AUDITORIO

Los Pinos

Ⓜ

Molino del Rey

Auditorio
Nacional

Anillo Periférico

Lago Mayor

Lago Menor

Avenida de los Constituyentes

Ave. prado Sur

DOLORES
CEMETERY

Paseo de
la Reforma

Metro Ⓜ

GUADALUPE

DOWNTOWN

POLANCO

Chapultepec
Park

SAN
ÁNGEL

COYOACÁN

XOCHIMILCO

area of detail

0   2 mi
0   2 km

129

flowers, shrubs, and waterfalls, and the climb, though potentially tiring, is worthwhile for the view from the top.

If you visit Mexico City on **December 12,** you will witness the grand festival in honor of the **Virgin of Guadalupe.** The square in front of the basilica fills with the pious and the party-minded as prayers, dances, and a carnival atmosphere attract thousands of the devout. Many visitors combine a trip to the basilica with one to the **ruins of Teotihuacán,** as both are out of the city center in the same direction.

Plaza de las Américas 1, Villa de Guadalupe. ⓒ 55/5577-6022. www.virgendeguadalupe.org.mx. Free admission; museum 50¢ (25p). Daily 6am–8pm. Free guided tours (in Spanish) Fri–Sat noon. Metro: Basílica or La Villa. Signs lead the way along the 15 minute walk to the entrance of the Basílica. No shorts, food, or drinks are allowed inside.

Museo Frida Kahlo ★★★

Although, during her lifetime, Frida Kahlo was known principally as the wife of muralist Diego Rivera, today her art surpasses his in popularity. Certainly the 2002 Salma Hayek movie *Frida* did much to bring this Mexican icon to the attention and appreciation of millions more. Kahlo dedicated her life to both her painting and her passionate, tortured love for her husband. Her emotional and physical pain—her spine was pierced during a serious streetcar accident in her youth—were the primary subjects of her canvases, many of which are self-portraits. Her paintings are now acknowledged as exceptional works of Latin American art, and some of the purest artistic representations of female strength and struggle ever created. As her paintings have surged in renown and price, so has interest in the life of this courageous, provocative, and revolutionary woman.

Kahlo was born in this house on July 7, 1910, and lived here with Rivera from 1929 to 1954. During the 1930s and 1940s it was a popular gathering place for intellectuals. As you wander through the rooms of the cornflower-blue house, you'll get a glimpse of the life they led. Most of the rooms remain in their original state, with mementos everywhere. Tiny clay pots hang about; the names Diego and Frida are painted on the walls of the kitchen. In the studio upstairs, a wheelchair sits next to the easel with a partially completed painting surrounded by brushes, palettes, books, photographs, and other intimate details of the couple's art-centered lives. Much of the movie *Frida* was filmed in this house.

Frida and Diego collected pre-Columbian art, and many of the rooms contain jewelry and terra cotta figurines from Teotihuacán and Tlatelolco. Kahlo even had a mock-up of a temple built in the garden to exhibit her numerous pots and statues. On the back side of the temple are several skulls from Chichén Itzá. A cafe on the first floor serves light snacks, and the adjacent bookstore offers a full range of Kahlo and Rivera books and other commercialized memorabilia.

Londres 247, Coyoacán. ⓒ 55/5554-5999. Admission $4.50 (£2.25). No cameras allowed. Tues–Sun 10am–5:45pm. Metro: Coyoacán.

Museo Nacional de Antropología ★★★

Occupying approximately 4,100 sq. m (44,132 sq. ft.), Mexico City's anthropology museum is regarded as one of the top museums in the world. It offers the single best introduction to the culture of Mexico.

Inside the museum is an open courtyard (containing the Chávez Morado fountain) with beautifully designed rooms running around three sides on two levels. The **ground-floor rooms** are devoted to history—from prehistoric days to the most recently explored archaeological sites—and are the most popular among studious visitors. These rooms include dioramas of Mexico City when the Spaniards arrived, and reproductions of part of a pyramid at Teotihuacán. The Aztec calendar stone "wheel" occupies a proud place.

Save some time and energy for the livelier and more readily comprehensible **ethnographic rooms** upstairs. This section is devoted to the way people throughout Mexico live today, complete with straw-covered huts, recordings of songs and dances, crafts, clothing, and lifelike models of village activities. This floor, a living museum, strikes me as vital to the understanding of contemporary Mexico because of the importance of pre-Hispanic customs in Mexican village life.

A sweeping restoration took place during 2000 and 2001. The $13-million (£6.5-million) refurbishment project was the first since the museum opened in 1964. Over 2,000 new artifacts and information garnered from some 200 recent digs were incorporated throughout the 23 rooms. In addition, new computerized touch-screen technology with video images and sound depicting rituals and customs are on display, providing visitors with a richer, more interactive experience. Exhibit signs now display English as well as Spanish explanations.

The museum has a lovely, moderately priced restaurant with cheerful patio tables. *Note:* Most of the museum is wheelchair accessible; however, assistance will be needed in places.

Paseo de la Reforma y Calzada Gandhi s/n, Chapultepec Polanco. © **55/5553-6266**. www.mna.inah.gob.mx. Admission $4.50 (£2.25); free Sun for residents of Mexico. Still camera $3 (£1.50), amateur video camera $4.50 (£2.25); no tripods or flash permitted. Tues–Sun 9am–7pm. Metro: Auditorio.

Palacio Nacional and the Diego Rivera Murals ⊘★★
This complex of countless rooms, wide stone stairways, and numerous courtyards adorned with carved brass balconies was once where the president of Mexico worked, and it remains an important site for presidential meetings and events. But it's better known for the fabulous second-floor Diego Rivera murals depicting the history of Mexico. Begun in 1692 on the site of Moctezuma II's "new" palace, this building became the site of Hernán Cortez's home and the residence of colonial viceroys. It has changed much in 300 years, taking on its present form in the late 1920s when the top floor was added. Just 30 minutes here with an English-speaking guide provides essential background for an understanding of Mexican history. The cost of a guide is negotiable: $12 (£6) or less, depending on your bargaining ability.

Enter by the central door, over which hangs the bell rung by Padre Miguel Hidalgo when he proclaimed Mexico's independence from Spain in 1810—the famous *grito*. Each September 15, Mexican Independence Day, the president of Mexico stands on the balcony above the door to echo Hidalgo's cry to the thousands of spectators who fill the *zócalo*. Take the stairs to the Rivera murals, which were painted over a 25-year period. The *Legend of Quetzalcoatl* depicts the famous tale of the feathered serpent bringing a blond-bearded white man to the country. When Cortez arrived, many Aztecs, recalling this legend, believed him to be Quetzalcoatl. Another mural tells of the American Intervention, when American invaders marched into Mexico City during the War of 1847. It was on this occasion that the military cadets of Chapultepec Castle (then a military school) fought bravely to the last man. The most notable of Rivera's murals is the *Great City of Tenochtitlán*, a study of the original settlement in the Valley of Mexico. It showcases an Aztec market scene with the budding city in the background and includes a beautiful representation of Xochiquetzal, goddess of love, with her crown of flowers and tattooed legs.

Diego Rivera, one of Mexico's legendary muralists, left an indelible stamp on Mexico City, his painted political themes affecting the way millions view Mexican history. Additional examples of Rivera's stunning and provocative interpretations are found at the Bellas Artes, the National Preparatory School, the Department of Public Education, the National School of Agriculture at Chapingo, the National Institute of Cardiology, and the Museo Mural Diego Rivera (which houses the mural formerly located in the now-razed Hotel del Prado).

Palacio Nacional, Av. Pino Suárez, facing the *zócalo*. © **55/9158-1259**. Free admission, but visitor tags required; be prepared to show a form of photo identification. Daily 9am–4:30pm. Metro: Zócalo.

Templo Mayor and Museo del Templo Mayor ⊘★★★
In 1978, workmen digging on the east side of the Metropolitan Cathedral, next to the Palacio Nacional, unearthed an exquisite Aztec stone of the moon goddess Coyolxauhqui. Major excavations by Mexican archaeologists followed, and they uncovered interior remains of the Pyramid of Huitzilopochtli, also called the Templo Mayor (Great Temple)—the most important religious structure in the Aztec capital. What you see are the remains

of pyramids that were covered by the great pyramid the Spaniards saw upon their arrival in the 16th century.

At the time of the 1521 Conquest, the site was the center of religious life for the city of 300,000. No other museum illustrates the variety and splendor of the Aztec Empire the way this one does. All 6,000 pieces came from the relatively small plot of excavated ruins just in front of the museum. Strolling along the walkways built over the site, visitors pass a water-collection conduit constructed during the presidency of Porfirio Díaz (1877–1911), as well as far earlier constructions. Shelters cover the ruins to protect traces of original paint and carving. Note especially the Tzompantli, or Altar of Skulls, a common Aztec and Maya design. Explanatory plaques with building dates are in Spanish.

The Museo del Templo Mayor (Museum of the Great Temple) opened in 1987. To enter it, take the walkway to the large building in the back portion of the site, which contains fabulous artifacts from on-site excavations. Inside the door, a model of Tenochtitlán gives a good idea of the scale of the vast city of the Aztecs. The rooms and exhibits, organized by subject, occupy many levels around a central open space. You'll see some marvelous displays of masks, figurines, tools, jewelry, and other artifacts, including the huge stone wheel of the moon goddess Coyolxauhqui ("she with bells painted upon her face") on the second floor. The goddess ruled the night, the

Aztec believed, but died at the dawning of every day, slain and dismembered by her brother, Huitzilopochtli, the sun god.

Seminario 8, off the *zócalo*. (€) 55/5542-4943. Fax 55/5542-1717. www.templomayor.inah.gob.mx. Admission to museum and ruins $4.50 (£2.25); free Sun. Video camera permit $3.50 (£1.75); no flash photos. Tues–Sun 9am–5pm. Metro: Zócalo.

ARCHITECTURAL HIGHLIGHTS

Casa de los Azulejos   This "House of Tiles" is one of Mexico City's most precious colonial gems and popular meeting places. Covered in gorgeous blue-and-white tiles, it dates from the end of the 1500s, when it was built for the count of the Valley of Orizaba. According to the oft-told story, during the count's defiant youth his father proclaimed: "You will never build a house of tiles." A tiled house was a sign of success, and the father was sure his son would amount to nothing. So when success came, the young count covered his house in tiles, a fine example of Puebla craftsmanship. The tiled murals in the covered courtyard, where the restaurant is located, were restored a few years back. Tile craftsmen from Saudi Arabia were brought in to ensure that the technique was true to the original 16th-century work. You can stroll through to admire the interior. Pause to see the Orozco mural, *Omniscience,* on the landing leading to the second floor (where the restrooms are). There's a casual but beautiful Sanborn's Mexican restaurant located in the covered patio of the building.

Madero 4, Centro Histórico. (€) 55/5512-9820. Daily 7am–1am. Metro: Bellas Artes.

Gran Hotel Ciudad de México   Originally a department store, the Gran Hotel boasts one of the most splendid interiors of any downtown building. Step inside to see the lavish lobby, with gilded open elevators on both sides, topped with a breathtaking 1908 stained-glass canopy by Jacques Graber.

On the fourth floor, overlooking the *zócalo,* El Mirador restaurant makes a great stop for a coffee or drink with a view.

Av. 16 de Septiembre 82 at 5 de Febrero. (€) 55/1083-7700. Free admission to view the lobby, except on Sundays when the hotel is not open to nonguests. Metro: Zócalo.

Museo del Palacio de Bellas Artes ⟨⟨   Opulent and dramatic, the Bellas Artes is the masterpiece of theaters in this architecturally rich city. The exterior is early-20th-century Art Nouveau, built during the Porfiriato and covered in Italian Carrara marble. Inside, it's completely 1930s Art Deco. Since construction began in 1904, the theater (which opened in 1934) has sunk some 4m (13 ft.) into the soft belly of Lake Texcoco. The Palacio is the work of several masters: Italian architect Adamo Boari, who made the original plans; Antonio Muñoz and Federico Mariscal, who modified his plans considerably; and Mexican painter Gerardo Murillo ("Doctor Atl"), who designed the fabulous Art Nouveau glass curtain that was constructed by Louis Comfort Tiffany in the Tiffany Studios of New York. Made from nearly a million iridescent pieces of colored glass, the curtain portrays the Valley of Mexico with its two great volcanoes. You can see the curtain before important performances at the theater and on Sunday mornings.

In addition to being a concert hall, the theater houses permanent and traveling art shows. On the third level are famous murals by Rivera, Orozco, and Siqueiros. The controversial Rivera mural *Man in Control of His Universe* was commissioned in 1933 for Rockefeller Center in New York City. He completed the work there just as you see it: A giant vacuum sucks up the riches of the earth to feed the factories of callous, card-playing, hard-drinking white capitalist thugs—John D. Rockefeller himself among

ACCOMMODATIONS ■
Embassy Suites **1**
Holiday Inn Zócalo **16**
Sheraton Centro Histórico **5**

ATTRACTIONS ●
Casa de los Azulejos **14**
Correo (Post Office) **11**
FONART **3**
Juárez Monument **7**
La Torre Latinoamericana **15**

Mercado de la Ciudadela **6**
Museo Franz Mayer **8**
Museo Mural Diego Rivera **2**
Museo Nacional de Arte **12**
Museo Nacional de la Estampa **9**
Palacio de Bellas Artes **10**
Palacio de Minería **13**
Plaza de la Solidaridad **4**

them—while all races of noble workers of the earth rally behind the red flag of socialism and its standard-bearer, Lenin. Needless to say, the Rockefellers weren't so keen on the new purchase. Much to their discredit, they had it painted over and destroyed. Rivera duplicated the mural here as *Man at the Crossing of the Ways* to preserve it. For information on tickets to performances of the **Ballet Folklórico,** see "Mexico City After Dark," later in this chapter.

Warning: Avoid taxis parked in front of the Bellas Artes Theater and call for a radio taxi, instead.

Calle López Peralta, east end of La Alameda, Centro Histórico. © 55/5512-2593, ext. 152. www.museobellasartes. artte.com. Free admission to view building when performances are not in progress; museum $3.50 (£1.75). Tues–Sun 10am–5pm. Metro: Bellas Artes.

Palacio de Minería   Built in the 1800s, this "mining palace" is one of architect Manuel Tolsá's finest works—considered a masterpiece of Latin American neoclassicism—and one of the capital's handsomest buildings. Formerly the school of mining, it's occasionally used today for concerts and cultural events (and in those cases, the patio is often locked off). When it's open, step inside for a look at the patios and fabulous stonework. Guided tours are available.

Tacuba 5, Centro Histórico. © 55/5623-2981. www.palaciomineria.unam.mx. Free admission. Wed–Sun 10am–6pm. Metro: Bellas Artes.

CEMETERIES
Rotonda de los Hombres Ilustres   The din of traffic recedes in the serene resting place where Mexico's military, political, and artistic elite are buried. It's more like an outdoor monument museum than a cemetery; the stone markers stand in a double circle around an eternal flame. A stroll here is a trip through who's who in Mexican history. Among the famous buried here are the artists Diego Rivera, David Alfaro Siqueiros, José Clemente Orozco, and Gerardo Murillo; presidents Sebastian Lerdo de Tejada, Valentín Gómez Farías, and Plutarco Calles; musicians Jaime Nunó (author of the Mexican national anthem), Juventino Rosas, and Agustín Lara; and outstanding citizens such as the philanthropist and writer Carlos Pellicer. Stop in the building at the entrance and the guard will give you a map with a list (in Spanish and English) of those buried here, which includes biographical information.

Constituyentes and Av. Civil Dolores, Dolores Cemetery, Chapultepec Park. Free admission. Daily 6am–6pm. Metro: Constituyentes.

CHURCHES
Catedral Metropolitana 🕮🕮🕮   The impressive, towering cathedral, begun in 1567 and finished in 1788, blends baroque, neoclassical, and Mexican churrigueresque architecture. As you look around the cathedral and the Sagrario (chapel) next to it, note how the building has sunk into the soft lake bottom beneath. The base of the facade is far from level and straight, and when one considers the weight of the immense towers—127,000 tons—it's no surprise. Scaffolding has become almost a part of the structure, in place to stabilize the building. However, much to the credit of Mexico City and its preservation efforts, the Catedral Metropolitana came off the World Monuments Fund's list of 100 Most Endangered Sites in 2000, as a result of an extensive reconstruction of the building's foundation.

In Mexico, the sacred ground of one religion often becomes the sacred ground of its successor. Cortez and his Spanish missionaries converted the Aztec, tore down their temples, and used much of the stone to construct a church on the spots of the temples that preceded it. The church they built was pulled down in 1628 while the present Metropolitan Cathedral was under construction. The building today has five naves and 14 chapels. As you wander past the small chapels, you may hear guides describing some of the cathedral's outstanding features: the tomb of Agustín Iturbide, placed here in 1838; a painting attributed to the Spanish artist Bartolomé Esteban Murillo; and the fact that the stone holy-water fonts ring like metal when tapped with a coin. Like many huge churches, it has catacombs underneath. The much older-looking church next to the cathedral is the chapel known as the Sagrario, another tour de force of Mexican baroque architecture built in the mid-1700s.

The Metropolitan Cathedral contains many prized works of art from the colonial era, in a variety of artistic styles. Jerónimo de Balbas built and carved the Altar de los Reyes (Altar of Kings) and the Altar del Perdón (Altar of Forgiveness) in 1737. For a small donation, a tour of the towers is available (sign up inside the cathedral near the entrance).

As you walk around the outside of the cathedral, you will notice a reminder of medieval trade life. The west side is the gathering place of carpenters, plasterers, plumbers, painters, and electricians who have no shops. Craftspeople display the tools of their trades, sometimes along with pictures of their work. In front of the cathedral, you can buy crystals, gemstones, and herbs, believed to provide special qualities of protection and cure from various afflictions. Visitors are asked not to tour the cathedral when masses are taking place.

The *zócalo*, on Cinco de Mayo, Centro Histórico. Free admission. Daily 8am–7pm. Metro: Zócalo.

Convent of San Bernardino de Siena   This 16th-century building is noted for its flower petals carved in stone—a signature of the Indians who did most of the work—on 16th-century *retablos* (painted boards) including one of three such altarpieces in the country that were created by pre-Hispanic Indians and that has miraculously been preserved for more than 400 years; most were destroyed by the Spaniards during the conquest and conversion to Christianity. The last Indian governor of Xochimilco, Apoxquiyohuatzin, is buried here. Inside and to the right, the skull over the font is from a pre-Hispanic skull rack signifying an Indian-Christian mixture of the concept of life and death. Eight lateral *retablos* date from the 16th to the 18th centuries. The fabulous gilt main altar, also from the 16th century, is like an open book with sculpture and religious paintings. A profusion of cherubic angels decorates columns and borders. Some of the altar paintings are attributed to Baltasar Echave Orio the Elder. Over the altar, above the figure of Christ, is San Bernardino with the *caciques* (local authorities) dressed in clothing with Indian elements, and without shoes.

Pino and Hidalgo (facing the main square), Xochimilco. Free admission. Daily 8am–8pm. *Tren ligero* (light train): Xochimilco.

HISTORIC BUILDINGS & MONUMENTS
CHAPULTEPEC PARK & POLANCO
Castillo de Chapultepec/Museo Nacional de Historia   This site had been occupied by a fortress since the days of the Aztec, although the present palace wasn't built until 1784. When open, the castle offered a beautiful view of Mexico City. During the French occupation of the 1860s, Empress Carlota (who designed the lovely garden surrounding the palace) could sit up in bed and watch her husband, Maximilian, proceeding down Reforma on his way to work. Later, this was the official home

of Mexico's president until 1939. In 2004, archaeologists discovered an ancient Teotihuacán settlement behind the landmark. They are currently working on excavations, which are expected to demonstrate that the Teotihuacán culture spread and influenced the area around Mexico City earlier than previously thought, sometime between A.D. 300 and 600.

Chapultepec Park and Polanco. ℂ 55/5061-9211. www.castillodechapultepec.inah.gob.mx. Admission $4.50 (£2.25), free Sun. Tues–Sun 9am–5pm. Metro: Chapultepec.

ZONA ROSA & SURROUNDING AREAS

Monumento a los Héroes de la Independencia 🟐 Without a doubt, the Monument to the Heroes of Independence is the most noted of Mexico City's exceptional public sculptures and monuments. The "Angel" is both a landmark and homage to those who lost their lives fighting for independence. It's also a central stage—along with the *zócalo*—for many of Mexico City's celebrations and mass demonstrations. Set upon a tall marble shaft, the golden angel is an important and easily discerned guidepost for travelers. A creation of Antonio Rivas Mercado, the 7m-high (23-ft.), gold-plated bronze angel, cast in Florence, Italy, was completed in 1906 at a cost of $2.5 (£1.75) million. With its base of marble and Italian granite, the monument's total height is 45m (148 ft.). It was renovated in 2006.

Intersection of Paseo de la Reforma, Florencia, and Río Tiber, Reforma/Zona Rosa. Metro: Sevilla.

CENTRO HISTORICO & SURROUNDING AREAS

Monumento a la Revolución and Museo Nacional de la Revolución The Art Deco Monument to the Revolution, in the large **Plaza de la República,** has a curious history. The government of Porfirio Díaz, who was perennially "reelected" president of Mexico, began construction of what was intended to be a new legislative chamber. However, only the dome was raised by the time the Mexican Revolution (1910) put an end to his plans, not to mention his dictatorship. In the 1930s, after the revolutionary turmoil had died down, the dome was finished as a monument. The remains of two revolutionary presidents, Francisco Madero and Venustiano Carranza, were entombed in two of its pillars, and it was dedicated to the Revolution. Later, presidents Plutarco Elías Calles and Lázaro Cárdenas were also buried there. (*Note:* At the time of his death, Calles was buried at La Rotonda de los Hombres Ilustres. His body was then moved to the Monumento a la Revolución by an order of President Díaz Ordaz in 1969. A plaque honoring him still remains at the Rotunda, but his actual body is at the Monumento.)

Beneath the Monument to the Revolution is the **Museo Nacional de la Revolución** (enter directly across from the Frontón). It chronicles the tumultuous years from 1867 to 1917—when the present constitution was signed—in excellent exhibits of documents, newspaper stories, photographs, drawings, clothing, costumes, uniforms, weapons, and furnishings.

Av. Juárez and La Fragua, Plaza de la República s/n, Col. Tabacalera beneath the Monumento a la Revolución. ℂ 55/ 5536-2115 or 5566-1902. Admission $1.40 (70p); free Sun. Sat–Sun 9am–6pm, Mon–Fri 9am–5pm. From the Colón Monument on Reforma, walk 2 blocks north on I. Ramírez; the monument looms ahead. Metro: Revolución.

Secretaría de Educación Pública Originally built in 1922 as a convent, this building became the home of the Secretary of Public Education in 1922 and was decorated with a great series of more than 200 Diego Rivera murals, dating from 1923 and 1928, that cover over 1,500 sq. m (16,146 sq. ft.) of wall space. Other artists did a panel here and there, but the Rivera murals are the most outstanding.

República de Argentina 28, near República de Brasil. ℂ **55/5328-1097.** www.sep.gob.mx. Free admission. Mon–Fri 9am–5pm. Metro: Allende.

Suprema Corte de Justicia   The Supreme Court of Justice, built between 1935 and 1941, is the highest court in the country. Inside, on the main staircase and its landings, are Orozco murals depicting a theme of justice.

Pino Suárez and Corregidora, Centro Histórico. No phone. Free admission. Mon–Fri 9am–5:30pm. Metro: Zócalo.

OTHER MUSEUMS & GALLERIES
CHAPULTEPEC PARK & POLANCO

Museo de Arte Moderno ✦   The Museum of Modern Art is known for having the best permanent exhibition of painters and sculptors from the modern Mexican art movement. It also features some of the most important temporary exhibitions of national and international modern art in the world. Representing the Mexican muralist movement are significant works by the three greats: Diego Rivera, José Clemente Orozco, and David Alfaro Siqueiros. The main building is a round, two-story structure with a central staircase. Two of the museum's four spaces showcase the permanent collection, which also contains works by Mexico's other modern masters—Tamayo, José Luis Cuevas, Alejandro Colunga, Francisco Toledo, and Vladamir Cora. The remaining two spaces house visiting exhibitions. The museum's surrounding gardens exhibit large-scale public sculptures.

Chapultepec Park. ℂ **55/5553-6233.** www.conaculta.gob.mx/mam. Admission $2 (£1); discounts for students and teachers w/ID; free Sun. Tues–Sun 10am–5pm. Metro: Chapultepec.

Museo de Historia Natural de la Ciudad de Mexico *Kids*   The 10 interconnecting domes that form the Museum of Natural History contain stuffed and preserved animals and birds; tableaux of different natural environments with the appropriate wildlife; exhibits on geology, astronomy, biology, and the origin of life; and more. It's a fascinating place for anyone with the slightest curiosity about nature, and it's totally absorbing for youngsters.

Chapultepec Park, Section 2. ℂ **55/5516-2848.** Admission $2 (£1); free Tues. Tues–Sun 10am–5pm. Metro: Constituyentes.

Museo Rufino Tamayo ✦   Oaxaca-born painter Rufino Tamayo not only contributed a great deal to modern Mexican painting, but also collected pre-Hispanic, Mexican, and foreign works, including pieces by Willem de Kooning, Andy Warhol, Salvador Dalí, and René Magritte. Tamayo's pre-Hispanic collection is in Oaxaca, but here you can see a number of his works and the remainder of his collection (unless a special exhibit has temporarily displaced them). A special *noche de jazz* (jazz evening), with a private tour of the museum followed by a small jazz concert, is offered one Wednesday each month; check the website for scheduling.

Paseo de la Reforma s/n (corner of Gandhi), Chapultepec Park. ℂ **55/5286-6519.** www.museotamayo.org. Admission $1.50 (75p); free Sun. Tues–Sun 10am–6pm. Metro: Chapultepec or Auditorio.

Papalote, Museo del Niño *Kids*   The Building of the Pyramids at this interactive children's museum holds most of the more than 350 exhibits, while two films alternate (10 shows daily) in the IMAX building. There's virtually nothing here that children can't touch; once they discover this, they'll want to stay a long time. As they say, adults must be accompanied by children, except on Thursday, when the museum is open until 11pm to give "big kids" a chance to enjoy it themselves. It's probably been a while since you had a chance to play "hide and seek," run around "musical chairs," crawl through a narrow pitch-black tunnel, or draw animal representations of your friends, but this return to the past is a lot of fun. The patio restaurant offers live jazz during the Thursday adults' night.

Av. de los Constituyentes 268, Chapultepec Park, Section 2. ℂ 55/5237-1700 or 5237-1773. www.papalote.org. mx. Admission to museum $8.50 (£4.25) adults, $8 (£4) children; admission to museum and IMAX show $11 (£5.50) adults, $10 (£5) children. Mon–Fri 9am–6pm; Thurs 9am–11pm; Sat–Sun and holidays 10am–7pm. Metro: Constituyentes.

CENTRO HISTORICO & SURROUNDING AREAS

Museo de la Ciudad de México   Before you enter the Museum of Mexico City, go to the corner of República del Salvador and look at the enormous stone serpent head, a corner support at the building's base. The stone was once part of an Aztec pyramid. At the entrance, a stone doorway opens to the courtyard of this mansion, built in 1778 as the House of the Counts of Santiago de Calimaya. This classic building became the Museum of the City of Mexico in 1964; it's a must for anyone interested in the country's past. Dealing solely with the Mexico Valley, where the first people arrived around 8000 B.C., the museum contains some fine maps, pictographic presentations of the initial settlements, outlines of the social organization as it developed, and models of several famous buildings. Upstairs is the studio of Mexican Impressionist Joaquín Clausell (1866–1935). There's a good bookstore to the left after you enter.

Pino Suárez 30, Centro Histórico. ℂ 55/5542-0487. www.cultura.df.gob.mx. Admission $2 (£1). Tues–Sun 10am–5pm. Metro: Zócalo.

Museo Franz Mayer   One of the capital's foremost museums, the Franz Mayer Museum opened in 1986 in a beautifully restored 16th-century building on Plaza de la Santa Veracruz on the north side of La Alameda. The extraordinary 10,000-piece collection of antiques, mostly Mexican objects from the 16th through 19th centuries, was amassed by one man: Franz Mayer. A German immigrant, he adopted Mexico as his home in 1905 and grew rich here. Before his death in 1975, Mayer bequeathed the collection to the country and arranged for its permanent display through a trust with the Banco Nacional. The pieces, mostly utilitarian objects (as opposed to pure art objects), include inlaid and richly carved furniture; an enormous collection of Talavera pottery; gold and silver religious pieces; sculptures; tapestries; rare watches and clocks (the oldest is a 1680 lantern clock); wrought iron; old-master paintings from Europe and Mexico; and 770 *Don Quixote* volumes, many of which are rare editions or typographically unique. There's so much here that it may take two visits to absorb it all. In the central courtyard, a pleasant cafe serves coffee and light snacks.

Av. Hidalgo 45, next to Plaza Santa Veracruz, Col. Guerrero. ℂ 55/5518-2265. www.franzmayer.org.mx. Admission $3.40 (£1.70); free Tues. Tues–Sun 10am–5pm (Wed until 7pm). Guided tours by appointment Mon–Sat 10:30am, 11:30am, and 12:30pm. Metro: Hidalgo or Bellas Artes.

Museo José Luis Cuevas   José Luis Cuevas is one of Mexico's leading contemporary artists, though early in his career, he was considered the "enfant terrible" of Mexican plastic arts. To this day, he can arouse controversy, and is known to draw throngs of women wherever he appears. The center that bears his name opened in 1992 and is filled with about 1,000 paintings, drawings, and sculptures donated by Cuevas, including many of his own. Don't miss the Erotic Room, a permanent exhibit of his erotic paintings, photographs, and erotic objects from the artist's personal collection. Housed in the 16th-century Convento de Santa Inés, the museum includes many works by other contemporary Latin American artists, as well as a large collection of Picassos.

Calle Academia 13, 2 blocks northeast of the Palacio Nacional and across from the Academia de San Carlos, Centro Histórico. ℭ 55/5542-6198. www.museojoseluiscuevas.com.mx. Admission $2 (£1). Tues–Sun 10am–5:30pm. Metro: Zócalo.

Museo Mural Diego Rivera   This museum houses Diego Rivera's famous mural *Dream of a Sunday Afternoon in Alameda Park,* which was painted on a wall of the Hotel Prado in 1947. The hotel was demolished after the 1985 earthquake, but the precious mural, perhaps the best known of Rivera's works, was saved and transferred to its new location in 1986. The huge picture, 15m long and 4m high (49×13 ft.), chronicles the history of the park from the time of Cortez onward. Portrayed in the mural are numerous historical figures. More or less from left to right, but not in chronological order, they include: Cortez; a heretic suffering under the Spanish Inquisition; Sor Juana Inés de la Cruz, a brilliant, progressive woman who became a nun to continue her scholarly pursuits; Benito Juárez, seen putting forth the laws of Mexico's great Reforma; the conservative Gen. Antonio López de Santa Anna, handing the keys to Mexico to the invading American Gen. Winfield Scott; Emperor Maximilian and Empress Carlota; José Martí, the Cuban revolutionary; Death, with the plumed serpent (Quetzalcoatl) entwined about his neck; Gen. Porfirio Díaz, great with age and medals, asleep; a police officer keeping La Alameda free of "riffraff" by ordering a poor family out of the elitists' park; and Francisco Madero, the martyred democratic president who caused the downfall of Díaz, and whose betrayal and alleged murder by Gen. Victoriano Huerta (pictured on the right) resulted in years of civil turmoil.

Plaza de la Solidaridad (at Balderas and Colón), Centro Histórico–Alameda. ℭ 55/5512-0754. Admission $1.50 (75p); free Sun. Tues–Sun 10am–6pm. Metro: Hidalgo.

Museo Nacional de Arte (Munal)   The National Art Museum's palacelike building, designed by Italian architect Silvio Contri and completed in 1911—a legacy of Europe-loving Porfirio Díaz's era—was built to house the government's offices of Communications and Public Works. Díaz occupied the opulent second-floor salon, where he welcomed visiting dignitaries. The National Museum of Art took over the building in 1982. Wander through the immense rooms with polished wooden floors as you view the wealth of paintings showing Mexico's art development, primarily covering the period from 1810 to 1950. There's a nice cafe on the second floor.

Tacuba 8, Centro Histórico. ℭ 55/5130-3400 or -3410. Fax 55/5130-3401. www.munal.com.mx. Admission $3 (£1.50); free Sun. Tues–Sun 10:30am–5:30pm. Metro: Allende.

Museo Nacional de la Estampa   *Estampa* means "engraving" or "printing," and this museum is devoted to understanding and preserving the graphic arts. The beautifully restored 16th-century building holds both permanent and changing exhibits. Displays include those from pre-Hispanic times, when clay seals were used for designs on fabrics, ceramics, and other surfaces. But the most famous works here are probably those of José Guadalupe Posada, Mexico's famous printmaker, who poked fun at death and politicians through his skeleton figure drawings. If your interest in this subject is deep, ask to see the video programs on graphic techniques—woodcuts, lithography, etchings, and the like.

Av. Hidalgo 39 (next door to the Museo Franz Mayer), Centro Histórico–Alameda. ℭ 55/5521-2244. Admission $1 (50p); free Sun. Tues–Sun 10am–5:30pm. Metro: Bellas Artes.

Museo Nacional de San Carlos   The San Carlos Museum exhibits 15th- to 19th-century European paintings. The museum was once the Academy of San Carlos, an art school that some of the country's great painters—Rivera and Orozco among them—attended. Architect Manuel Tolsá built the beautiful mansion in the early 1800s; it was later the home of the Marqués de Buenavista. The rooms on the first and second floors hold some of Mexico's best paintings, by both Mexican and European artists. Another gallery holds prints and engravings. In the mansion's elliptical court are displays of 19th-century Mexican statuary and busts by Manuel Vilar and his pupils, and off to one side is a pretty garden court shaded by rubber trees.

Puente de Alvarado 50 (at Arizpe). Ⓒ 55/5566-8085. Fax 55/5535-1256. Admission $2.50 (£1.25); free Sun. Wed–Mon 10am–6pm. Walk 5½ blocks west of La Alameda (2½ blocks west of San Fernando Plaza). Metro: Revolución.

SOUTHERN NEIGHBORHOODS

Museo Arqueológico de Xochimilco   The building dates from 1904, when it was the pump house for the springs. It houses artifacts from the area, many of them found when residents built their homes. These include 10,000-year-old mammoth bones; figures dating from the Teotihuacán period, including representations of Tlaloc (god of water and life), Ehecatl (god of the wind), Xipe Totec (god of renewal and of plants), and Huehueteotl (god of fire); polychrome pottery; carved abalone; and tombs showing funerary practices. One unique piece is a clay figure of a child holding a bouquet of flowers.

Av. Tenochtitlán and Calle La Planta, Santa Cruz Acalpixcan. Ⓒ/fax 55/2157-1757. Free admission. Tues–Sun 10am–4:30pm. From Xochimilco (see "Mexico City Neighborhoods in Brief," earlier in this chapter), take a cab or microbus to Tulyehualco. The museum is at Tenochtitlán and La Planta, on the left.

Museo Diego Rivera Anahuacalli 🗲   Not to be confused with the Museo Estudio Diego Rivera near the San Angel Inn (see below), this is probably the most unusual museum in the city. Designed by Rivera before his death in 1957, it's devoted to his works as well as his extensive collection of pre-Columbian art. With over 52,000 pieces, it is the largest private collection displayed in Mexico. Constructed of *pedregal* (the lava rock in which the area abounds), it resembles Maya and Aztec architecture. Anahuacalli means "House of Mexico"; *Anahuac* was the old name for the ancient Valley of Mexico.

In front of the museum is a reproduction of a Toltec ball court, and the entrance to the museum is a coffin-shaped door. Twenty-three display rooms are arranged in chronological order, with thousands of pieces stashed on the shelves, tucked away in corners, and peeking out of glass cases.

Upstairs, in a replica of Rivera's studio, you'll find the original sketches for some of his murals and two in-progress canvases. There's a photo of his first sketch (of a train), done at the age of 3, plus a color photograph of him at work later in life. Rivera (1886–1957) studied in Europe for 15 years and spent much of his life as a devoted Marxist. Yet he came through political scrapes and personal tragedies with no apparent diminution of creative energy. A plaque in the museum proclaims him "a man of genius who is among the greatest painters of all time." This is one of the most popular places in Mexico to come for Day of the Dead on November 2.

Calle del Museo 150, Col. San Pablo Tepetlapa. Ⓒ 55/5617-3797. www.diegorivera.com. Admission $4.50 (£2.25). Tues–Sun 10am–5pm. Metro: Taxqueña; then *tren ligero* (light train) to Xotepingo; go west on Xotepingo (Museo) 3 short blocks; cross División del Norte and go another 6 blocks.

Museo de Arte Carrillo Gil (MACG) Sometimes called the Museo de la Esquina (Corner Museum)—it's at a major intersection on Avenida de la Revolución—this modern gallery features a collection that includes rooms dedicated to the works of José Clemente Orozco (1883–1949), Diego Rivera (1886–1957), David Alfaro Siqueiros (1896–1974), and other Mexican painters. The museum is not accessible by Metro.

Revolución 1608 (at Desierto de los Leónes), Col. San Angel. 🕿 55/5550-6260. www.macg.inba.gob.mx. Admission $1.50 (75p); free Sun. Tues–Sun 10am–6pm.

Museo Dolores Olmedo Patiño 🕿 Art collector and philanthropist Olmedo left her former home, the grand Hacienda La Noria, as a museum featuring the works of her friend Diego Rivera. At least 137 of his works are displayed here, including his portrait of Olmedo, 25 paintings of Frida Kahlo, and 37 creations of Angelina Beloff (Rivera's first wife), many of them drawings and engravings. Among the notable Kahlo works here is her famed *The Broken Column*, which is considered the artistic embodiment of her physical suffering, the result of a trolley accident that pierced her spine when she was young. Besides the paintings, there are fine pre-Hispanic pieces on display, colonial furniture and other hacienda artifacts, and a collection of folk art. An excellent gift shop and a cafeteria are on the premises. Olmedo was the executor of both the Rivera and Kahlo estates, a close friend and former lover of Diego's, and a rival to Frida. Olmedo died in 2002, recognized as one of the most astute collectors of contemporary Mexican art.

Av. México 5843, Col. La Noria, Xochimilco. 🕿 55/5555-1016 or -0891. www.museodoloresolmedo.org. Admission $3.50 (£1.75), free on Tues. Tues–Sun 10am–6pm. Metro: Taxqueña; then *tren ligero* (light train) to Xochimilco. Get off at the La Noria station.

Museo Estudio Diego Rivera Here, in the studio designed and built by Juan O'Gorman in 1928, Rivera drew sketches for his wonderful murals and painted smaller works. He died here in 1957. Now a museum, the Rivera studio holds some of the artist's personal effects and mementos, as well as changing exhibits relating to his life and work. (Don't confuse Rivera's studio with his museum, the Anahuacalli; see above.) The museum is not accessible by Metro.

Calle Diego Rivera and Av. Altavista (across from San Angel Inn), Col. San Angel. 🕿 55/5616-0996. Admission $1 (50p); free Sun. Tues–Sun 10am–6pm. By taxi, go up Insurgentes Sur to Altavista and make a left.

Museo León Trotsky During Lenin's last days, Stalin and Trotsky fought a silent battle for leadership of the Communist Party in the Soviet Union. Trotsky stuck to ideology, while Stalin took control of the party mechanism. Stalin won, and Trotsky was exiled to continue his ideological struggle elsewhere. Invited by Diego Rivera, an ardent admirer of his work, he settled here on the outskirts of Mexico City to continue his writings on political topics and Communist ideology.

His ideas clashed with those of Stalin in many respects, and Stalin, wanting no opposition or dissension in the world Communist ranks, set out to have Trotsky assassinated. A first attempt failed, but it served as a warning to Trotsky, his wife, Natalia, and their household. The house became a veritable fortress, with watchtowers, thick steel doors, and round-the-clock guards, several of whom were Americans who sympathized with Trotsky's philosophies. Finally, a man thought to have been paid, cajoled, or blackmailed by Stalin, directly or indirectly, was able to gain admittance to the house by posing as a friend of Trotsky's and a believer of his political views. On August 20, 1940, he put an ice pick into the philosopher's head. The assailant was caught, and Trotsky died of his wounds shortly afterward. Because Trotsky and Rivera had previously had a falling out—Trotsky was having an affair with Rivera's wife, Frida Kahlo—Rivera was a suspect for a short time.

You can visit Natalia's study, the communal dining room, and Trotsky's study—with worksheets, newspaper clippings, books, and cylindrical wax dictating records still spread around—as well as the fortresslike bedroom. Some of the walls bear the bullet holes left from the first attempt on his life. Trotsky's tomb, designed by Juan O'Gorman, is in the garden. You can recognize this house by the brick riflemen's watchtowers on top of the high stone walls.

Av. Río Churubusco 410 (between Gómez Farías and Morelos), Col. Del Carmen Coyoacán. ℂ 55/5658-8732 or 5554-0687. Admission $3 (£1.50). Tues–Sun 10am–5pm. Metro: Coyoacán. From Plaza Hidalgo, go east on Hidalgo 3 blocks to Morelos, then north 8 blocks to Churubusco; house is on the left.

OUTDOOR ART/PLAZAS

Plaza de las Tres Culturas   Three cultures converge here: Aztec, Spanish, and contemporary Mexican. Surrounded by modern office and apartment buildings are large remains of the **Aztec city of Tlatelolco,** site of the last battle of the conquest of Mexico. Off to one side is the **Church of Santiago.** During the Aztec Empire, Tlatelolco was on the edge of Lake Texcoco, linked to the Aztec capital by a causeway. Bernal Díaz de Castillo, in his *True Story of the Conquest of New Spain,* described the roar from the dazzling market there, and the incredible scene after the last battle of the conquest in Tlatelolco on August 13, 1521—the dead bodies were piled so deep that walking there was impossible. That night determined the fate of the country and completed the Spanish takeover of Mexico. It was also here, in October 1968, that government troops fired on thousands of protesters who filled the square, killing hundreds.

View the pyramidal remains from raised walkways over the site. The church, off to one side, was built in the 16th century entirely of volcanic stone. The interior has been tastefully restored, preserving little patches of fresco in stark-white plaster walls, with a few deep-blue stained-glass windows and an unadorned stone altar. Sunday is a good day to combine a visit here with one to the Lagunilla street market (see "Shopping," below), which is within walking distance, south across Reforma.

Lázaro Cárdenas and Flores Magón, Centro Histórico. Metro: Tlatelolco.

Plaza de Santo Domingo   This fascinating plaza—a wonderful slice of Mexican life—has arcades on one side, a Dominican church on another. A statue of the Corregidora of Querétaro, Josefa Ortiz de Domínguez, dominates the plaza. The plaza is best known for the scribes who compose and type letters for clients unable to do so. Years ago, it was full of professional writers clacking away on typewriters, and a few still ply their trade on ancient electric typewriters among a proliferation of small print shops and presses. Emperor Cuauhtémoc's palace once occupied this land, before Dominicans built their monastery here.

Bordered by República de Venezuela, República de Brasil, República de Cuba, and Palma, Centro Histórico. Metro: Tacuba.

Zócalo 𝕲𝕲   Every Spanish colonial city in North America was laid out according to a textbook plan, with a plaza at the center surrounded by a church, government buildings, and military headquarters. Because Mexico City was the capital of New Spain, its *zócalo* is one of the grandest, graced on all sides by stately 17th-century buildings. The Plaza de la Constitución, as this square is officially called, is also one of the three biggest public squares in the world.

Zócalo actually means "pedestal" or "plinth." A grand monument to Mexico's independence was planned and the pedestal built, but the project was never completed. Nevertheless, the pedestal became a landmark for visitors, and soon everyone was calling the square the *zócalo,* even after the pedestal was removed. It covers almost 4 hectares (10 acres) and is bounded on the north by Cinco de Mayo, on the east by Pino Suárez, on the south by 16 de Septiembre, and on the west by Nacional Monte de Piedad. The downtown district—especially north of the Templo Mayor, one of the oldest archaeological sites in the city—is currently undergoing an important restoration project that is renewing much of its colonial charm. Occupying the entire east side of the *zócalo* is the majestic red *tezontle*-stone Palacio National, seat of the Mexican national government, and on the northern border is the Catedral Metropolitana.

Juárez and 20 de Noviembre, Centro Histórico. Metro: Zócalo.

PARKS & GARDENS

Alameda Park   Today the lovely tree-filled Alameda Park attracts pedestrians, cotton-candy vendors, strollers, lovers, and organ grinders. Long ago, the site was an Aztec marketplace. When the conquistadors took over in the mid-1500s, heretics were burned at the stake here under the Spanish Inquisition. In 1592, the governor of New Spain, Viceroy Luis de Velasco, converted it to a public park. Within the park, known as La Alameda, is the **Juárez Monument,** sometimes called the **Hemiciclo** (hemicycle, or half-circle), facing Avenida Juárez. Enthroned as the hero he was, Juárez assumes his proper place here in the pantheon of Mexican patriots. European (particularly French) sculptors created most of the other statuary in the park in the late 19th and early 20th centuries.

Av. Juárez and Lázaro Cárdenas. Free admission. Metro: Bellas Artes.

Chapultepec Park   One of the biggest city parks in the world, 220-hectare (543-acre) Chapultepec Park is more than a playground; it's virtually the centerpiece of the city. Besides accommodating picnickers on worn-away grass under centuries-old trees, it has canoes on the lake; jogging and bridle paths; vendors selling balloons, souvenirs, and food; a miniature train; and **Los Pinos,** home of Mexico's president. The park is also home to the **City Zoo** and **La Feria** amusement park. Most important for tourists, it contains a number of interesting museums, including the Museo Nacional de Antropología.

Between Paseo de la Reforma, Circuito Interior, and Av. Constituyentes. Free admission. Daily 5am–5pm. Metro: Chapultepec.

Floating Gardens of Xochimilco ✦   In the southern neighborhood of Xochimilco are more than 80km (50 miles) of canals known as the Floating Gardens. They consist of two main parts. The first is the tourism-oriented area in the Historic Center of town, where colorful boats called *trajineras* take loads of tourists through a portion of the canals. Lively music, some of it provided by mariachi musicians for hire who board the gondolas, is a staple. Historic buildings, restaurants, souvenir stands, curio sellers, and boat vendors border this area. The other section, north of the center of town, is the ecology-oriented area, or Parque Natural Xochimilco. On Sunday, Xochimilco is jammed; on weekdays, it's nearly deserted. As you enter Xochimilco proper, you will see many places to board boats. Should you miss them, turn along Madero and follow signs that say LOS EMBARCADEROS (the piers).

Southern neighborhood of Xochimilco. ✆ 55/5673-7890. Admission to area $2 (£1); boat rides $14–$16 (£7–£8) per boat per hour, which up to 14–18 people may share. Daily 9am–6pm.

BEST VIEW

La Torre Latinoamericana   From the observation deck on the 44th floor of this soaring skyscraper, the Latin American Tower, you can take in fabulous views of the entire city. Buy a ticket for the deck at the booth as you approach the elevators. Tokens for the telescope are on sale here, too. You then take an elevator to the 42nd floor, cross the hall, and take another elevator to the 44th floor. An employee will ask for your ticket as you get off.

Eje Central 2 (at Madero and Lázaro Cárdenas), Centro Histórico. ℂ 55/5518-7423. www.torrelatino.com. Admission $5 (£2.50) adults, $4 (£2) children. Mon–Fri 9am–11pm; Sat–Sun 9am–10pm. Metro: Bellas Artes.

6 Organized Tours

Mexico City is a great place to explore on your own, and in general this is the easiest and least expensive way to see what you like. But if your time is limited, you may want to acclimate yourself quickly by taking a tour or two.

Among the noncommercial offerings are **free guided tours** sponsored by the **Mexico City Historical Center** (ℂ 55/5345-8000, ext. 1499), in the 18th-century home of Don Manuel de Heras y Soto, at Donceles and República de Chile. Groups meet each Sunday at 10:45am at a central gathering place for that day's tour, which varies from week to week. These tours might explore a historic downtown street, cafes and theaters, cemeteries, or the colonial churches of Xochimilco. Most tours, which last about 2 hours, are in Spanish; as many as 300 people may be divided among 10 guides. Visitors can ask a day in advance for a guide who speaks their language. The center's phone is almost always busy, so you may opt to visit the office, in the far back of the building, on the right and up a spiral staircase, to get a list of upcoming tours and gathering locations. Office hours are Monday through Friday from 9am to 3pm and 6 to 9pm.

The many commercial tours include a 4-hour city tour of such sites as the **Metropolitan Cathedral,** the **National Palace,** and **Chapultepec Park and Castle;** a longer tour to the **Shrine of Guadalupe** and nearby pyramids at **Teotihuacán;** and the Sunday tour that begins with the **Ballet Folklórico,** moves on to the **Floating Gardens of Xochimilco,** and may or may not include lunch and the afternoon bullfights. Almost as popular are 1-day and overnight tours to Puebla, Cuernavaca, Taxco, and Acapulco. There are also several nightclub tours. Book through your hotel concierge or tour desk.

⌠Tips Tours: The Downside

Many readers have written to say they were unhappy with the sightseeing tours of this or that company. The reasons are myriad: The tour was too rushed; the guide knew nothing and made up stories about the sights; the tour group spent most of its time in a handicrafts shop (chosen by the tour company) rather than seeing the sights. Do tour companies get a kickback from souvenir shops? Of course! If you meet someone who has recently taken a guided tour and liked it, go with the same company. Otherwise, you might do well to see the sights on your own, following the detailed information in this book. Your hotel can arrange a private car by the hour or day—generally with a driver who is also an English-speaking guide. This can cost less or only slightly more than an organized tour, with greater flexibility and personalized service.

7 Shopping

From handicrafts to the finest in designer apparel, Mexico City, like any major metropolitan area, is a marvelous place for shopping. From malls to *mercados,* numerous places display fascinating native products and sophisticated goods.

The two best districts for browsing are on and off **Avenida Presidente Masaryk,** in Polanco, and the **Zona Rosa.** Polanco's shops include Burberrys of London, Christian Dior, Versace, Gucci, Hermès, Luis Vuitton, Giorgio Armani, Tiffany's, and Cartier. Think New York's Madison Avenue, Beverly Hills's Rodeo Drive, or Chicago's Magnificent Mile, and you'll get the picture. The 12 square blocks at the heart of the Zona Rosa are home to antiques shops, boutiques, art galleries, silver shops, and fine jewelers. A few unique shops deserve particular mention.

Several government-run shops and a few excellent private shops have exceptionally good collections of Mexico's arts and crafts. Here's the rundown on the best places to shop, from small crafts shops to vast general markets.

SHOPPING A TO Z
ART
Arvil. Galería de Arte y Libros de Arte   Collectible works of art—auction-quality pieces—by Mexican and Latin American masters. It's open Monday through Friday from 10am to 2:30pm and 4 to 7pm, and Saturday from 10am to 3pm. Cerrada de Hamburgo 7 and 9, Reforma/Zona Rosa. (✆ 55/5207-2647. www.arvil.com.mx. Metro: Insurgentes.

Exposición Nacional de Arte Popular (FONART)   This store is usually loaded with crafts: papier-mâché figurines, textiles, earthenware, colorful candelabras, hand-carved wooden masks, straw goods, beads, bangles, and glass. The Fonda Nacional para el Fomento de las Artes (FONART), a government organization that helps village craftspeople, operates the store. It's open Monday to Friday from 10am to 7pm, Saturday from 10am to 6pm, and Sunday from 10am to 4pm. Juárez 89, Centro Histórico. (✆ 55/5521-0171. www.fonart.gob.mx. Metro: Hidalgo or Juárez.

López Quiroga Gallery   Auction-quality works of art by contemporary Latin American masters, including Toledo, Tamayo, and Siqueiros. The gallery is not accessible by Metro; take a cab. It's open Monday to Friday from 9am to 7pm and Saturday from 9am to 2pm. Aristóteles 169, Polanco. (✆ 55/5280-1247. Fax 55/5280-3960. www. arte-mexico.com.

O.M.R. Gallery   This gallery has earned a reputation for discovering and introducing emerging talents and new artists from Latin America. It's open Monday through Friday from 10am to 3pm and 4 to 7pm, Saturday from 10am to 2pm. Plaza Río de Janeiro 54, Col. Roma. (✆ 55/5511-1179. www.galeriaomr.com. Metro: Insurgentes.

Pineda Covalin   This boutique shop created by two Mexican designers integrates Mexican culture and traditions into its fashionable designs. The beautiful pieces filled with vibrant colors include silk ties and scarves, handbags, shoes, and jewelry. The store's open Monday to Saturday from 10am to 8pm and Sunday from 10am to 2pm. Campos Eliseos 215 (at Galileo), Polanco. (✆ 55/5280-2179. www.pinedacovalin.com. Metro: Auditorio.

Puro Corazón   This high-quality store next to the Zócalo sells fine arts, crafts, and jewelry from across Mexico. The prices are a good bit higher than they would be where the products were made, but here you get a fabulous selection in one lovely shop. There's also a bookstore, gallery, and traditional Mexican restaurant onsite. The store's open Monday and Tuesday from 8am to 5pm and Wednesday through Sunday from 8am to 8pm. Monte de Piedad 11, Centro Histórico. © 55/5518-0300. Metro: Zócalo.

JEWELRY

Besides the shops mentioned below, dozens of jewelry stores and optical shops are on Madero from Motolinia to the *zócalo*, in the portals facing the National Palace. **Nacional Monte de Piedad (National Pawn Shop)**, also opposite the National Palace, has an enormous jewelry selection. The first Latin American branch of **Tiffany's** is on Avenida Presidente Masaryk in Polanco.

Bazar del Centro   Located between La Alameda and the *zócalo*, this colonial-era building was the palace of the Counts of Miravalle. Now it houses shops selling jewelry, precious stones, and silver. It's open Monday through Friday from 10am to 7pm and Saturday from 10am to 3pm. Isabel la Católica 30, Centro Histórico. No phone. Metro: Zócalo.

Tane   Tucked in the lobby of the hotel Presidente InterContinental, this is one of the branches of one of Mexico's top silver designers, with other locations found only in the best hotels and shopping centers. The quantity of high-quality silver work is enormous. You'll see jewelry, platters, pitchers, plates, cutlery, frames, candlesticks, and even the signature china, by Limoges. There are also branches in the Polanco and San Angel neighborhoods, and at the airport. It's open Monday through Friday from 10am to 7pm and Saturday from 11am to 3pm. Campos Eliseos 218 (at corner of Andrés Bello), Col. Polanco. © 55/5281-0820. www.tane.com.mx. Metro: Auditorio.

MARKETS

Bazar del Sábado *(Moments*   Located in San Angel, the charming colonial-era neighborhood in the southern part of the city, the "Saturday Market" is my top recommendation for passing a weekend afternoon in Mexico City. The market takes place outside on the Plaza San Jacinto and inside a bazaar building (part of a two-story mansion) next to it. High quality handicrafts, antiques, art, and Mexican food are all offered here.

In the center of the actual bazaar building is a wonderful Mexican cafe where waiters hustle to serve authentic tacos and frosty margaritas, plus *antojitos* (finger foods) and traditional dishes such as enchiladas. Marimba music plays in the background. Dozens of small rooms surrounding the courtyard serve as permanent stalls featuring original decorative art pieces. You'll find blown glass, fine jewelry, papier-mâché figures, masks, and embroidered clothing. The prices are on the high side, but the quality is equally high, and the designs are sophisticated. On adjacent plazas, hundreds of easel artists display their paintings, and surrounding homes abound with antiques, fine rugs, and hand-carved furniture for sale. Members of indigenous groups from Puebla and elsewhere bring their folk art—baskets, masks, pottery, textiles, and so on—to display in the parks. Plan to spend Saturday touring the attractions on the southern outskirts of the city. (See also "San Angel" under "Mexico City Neighborhoods in Brief," earlier in this chapter.) It's open Saturday from 9am to 6pm. Plaza de San Jacinto, San Angel. Metro: Miguel Angel de Quevado.

Centro Artesanal (Mercado de Curiosidades)   This rather modern building set back off a plaza consists of a number of stalls on two levels, selling everything from leather to tiles. They have some lovely silver jewelry and, as in most non-fixed-price stores, the asking price is high but the bargained result is often very reasonable. It's open Monday through Saturday from 10am to 5:30pm. Corner of Ayuntamiento and Dolores, Reforma North. Metro: Guerrero.

Lagunilla Market   This is one of the most interesting and unusual markets in Mexico—but watch out for pickpockets. It's open only on Sundays, when the Lagunilla becomes a colorful outdoor market filling the streets for blocks. Arrive around 9am. Vendors sell everything from axes to antiques. The two enclosed sections, on either side of a short street, Calle Juan Salvages, are open all week. They have different specialties: The one to the north is noted for clothes, *rebozos* (shawls), and blankets; the one to the south for tools, pottery, and household goods, such as attractive hanging copper lamps. This is also where to find old and rare books, many at a ridiculously low cost, if you're willing to hunt and bargain. It's open daily from 10am to 7pm, but tourists will feel safer leaving by sundown. 3 blocks east of Plaza de Garibaldi, at the corner of Francisco Bocanegra. Metro: Allende.

Mercado de la Ciudadela   An excellent place to get authentic arts and crafts, this market has hundreds of stalls with arts and crafts from all over Mexico. It's across from the Escuela Nacional de Artes. A few places take credit cards. It's open daily from 9am to 8pm. Balderas, between Reforma and Chapultepec. Metro: Balderas.

Mercado de la Merced   This is the city's biggest market and among the most fascinating in the country; the intense activity and energy level are akin to those at Oaxaca's Abastos Market (see chapter 12). Officially it's housed in several modern buildings, but shops line the tidy, crowded streets all the way to the *zócalo*.

The first building is mainly for fruits and vegetables; the others contain about what you'd find if a department store joined forces with a discount warehouse—especially housewares, such as hand-held citrus juicers of all sizes, tinware, colorful spoons, and decorative oilcloth. The main market, east of the *zócalo* on Circunvalación between General Anaya and Adolfo Gurrión, is the place to stock up on Mexican spices. The easy 13-block walk from the *zócalo* zigzags past many shops. Or take the Metro; the stop is right outside the market. It's open daily from 7am to 6pm. Circunvalación between General Anaya and Adolfo Gurrión. Metro: Merced.

Mercado Insurgentes   Mercado Insurgentes is a full-fledged crafts market tucked into the Zona Rosa. Because of its address, you might expect exorbitant prices, but vendors in the maze of stalls are eager to bargain, and good buys aren't hard to come by. It's open Monday through Saturday from 9am to 5:30pm. Londres between Florencia and Amberes, Zona Rosa. Metro: Insurgentes.

Nacional Monte de Piedad (National Pawn Shop)   This building used to be a pawn shop for all sorts of items, but now is reserved for the more profitable and saleable jewelry, with a couple of small rooms set aside for art and antiques. Pedro Romero de Terreros, the Count of Regla, an 18th-century silver magnate from Pachuca, donated the present building so that Mexican people could get low-interest loans. It's open Monday through Friday from 8:30am to 6pm, Saturday from 8:30am to 3pm. Corner of Monte de Piedad and Cinco de Mayo, Centro Histórico. http://dns.montepiedad.com.mx. Metro: Zócalo.

8 Mexico City After Dark

From mariachi, reggae, and opera to folkloric dance, classical ballet, and dinner shows, the choice of nighttime entertainment in Mexico City is enormous and sophisticated. It costs much less than comparable entertainment in most of the world's major cities. If you're willing to let *la vida mexicana* put on its own fascinating show for you, the bill will be even lower. People-watching, cafe-sitting, music, and even a dozen

> **Warning Crime at Night**
>
> Make sure to leave valuables—especially watches and jewelry—at your hotel, and bring only the cash you will need. While I list Metro stops, these should probably be used only for orientation; take only authorized *sitio* taxis (see the advisory "Important Taxi Safety Precautions in Mexico City," at the beginning of this chapter) or hire a private taxi by the hour and have an escort wait for you as you sample the festivities of the city. Your hotel can help with these arrangements.

mariachi bands all playing at once can be yours for next to nothing. For those looking for the hottest spots in dance clubs, head straight for the **Condesa** and **Roma** neighborhoods.

THE ENTERTAINMENT SCENE

Mexico City boasts a world-class nightlife scene, with hot venues for downing tequila and dancing to music ranging from salsa to house. In recent years, the **Centro Histórico** downtown has earned a reputation for having a number of hip and edgy bars and clubs concentrated within walking distance. The posh **Polanco** neighborhood is known for its perennially hot dining and bar scene, and in recent years many of the trendiest nightspots have opened in the **Condesa** and **Roma** neighborhoods (reputedly the SoHo of Mexico City, though the nightlife scene is more akin to New York's East Village). Some of the city's most exclusive nightclubs lie in the **Lomas** area. In the south of the city, **San Angel** remains highly popular, although it's a bit of a drive if you're not already staying in that area. Most bars don't even begin to get going until around 10 or 11pm and usually stay open until at least 3am; nightclubs get started after midnight and continue into the wee hours. Many clubs operate only Thursday through Saturday.

Fiesta nights give visitors a chance to dine on typical Mexican food and see wonderful regional dancing, which seems always to be a treat no matter how many times you've seen it.

For lower-key nightlife and people-watching, outdoor cafes remain a popular option. Those in the neighborhoods of **Polanco** and **Condesa** are among the liveliest. Another tradition is **Garibaldi Square,** where mariachis tune up and wait to be hired, but *be especially careful*—it's now known as much for chronic street crime as for music.

Hotel lobby bars tend to have live entertainment of the low-key type in the late afternoon and into the evening.

THE PERFORMING ARTS

Mexico City's performing arts scene is among the finest and most comprehensive in the world. It includes opera, theater, ballet, and dance, along with concerts of symphonic, rock, and popular music.

For current information on cultural offerings, *Donde Ir, Tiempo Libre,* and *Concierge,* free magazines found in hotels, are good sources for locating the newest places, though they don't have complete listings of changing entertainment or current exhibits. **Ticketmaster** (© **55/5325-9000**) usually handles ticket sales for major performances.

The **Ballet Folklórico de México (Folkloric Ballet of Mexico),** with its stunning presentation of regional dance, is perhaps the city's most renowned entertainment for visitors.

Note: The majority of the theatrical performances at the Palacio de Bellas Artes and in other theaters around the city are presented in Spanish.

FOLKLORIC BALLET

Palacio de Bellas Artes   Although various groups perform around the city, the finest offering is at the Palacio de Bellas Artes, where the famed **Ballet Folklórico de México** performs twice a week. The Ballet Folklórico is a celebration of pre- and post-Hispanic dancing. A typical program includes Aztec ritual dances, agricultural dances from Jalisco, a fiesta in Veracruz, a wedding celebration—all linked with mariachis, marimba players, singers, and dancers.

Because the Bellas Artes books many other events—visits by foreign opera companies, for instance—the Ballet Folklórico occasionally moves. In that case, it usually appears in the **National Auditorium** in Chapultepec Park. Check at the Bellas Artes box office. The show is popular and tickets sell rapidly (especially to tour agencies at twice the cost). The box office is on the ground floor of the Bellas Artes, main entrance. Ballet Folklórico performances are on Sunday at 9:30am and 8:30pm and Wednesday at 8:30pm.

The Fine Arts theater not only offers the finest in performing arts, but is also architecturally worth a visit (see "Exploring Mexico City," earlier in this chapter). It's open Monday through Saturday 11am to 7pm, and Sunday 8:30am to 7pm. Eje Central and Av. Juárez, Centro Histórico–Alameda. (C) 55/5325-9000. www.balletamalia.com.mx. Tickets $36–$60 (£18–£30). Metro: Bellas Artes.

THE CLUB & MUSIC SCENE

This warning can't be reiterated enough: **Take an authorized *sitio* taxi or hire a car for transportation to all nightspots.** Metro stops are given merely as a point of reference.

MARIACHIS

Mariachis play the music of Mexico. Although the songs they play may be familiar—ranging from traditional boleros to ranchera—their style and presentation are unique to Mexico. Known for their distinctive dress, strolling presentation, and mix of brass and guitars, they epitomize the romance and tradition of the country. They look a little like Mexican cowboys dressed up for a special occasion—tight trousers studded with silver buttons down the outside of the legs, elaborate cropped jackets, embroidered shirts with big bow ties, and grandiose sombrero hats. The dress dates to the French occupation of Mexico in the mid–19th century, as does the name. *Mariachi* is

---

Warning A Note of Caution in Garibaldi Square

Plaza de Garibaldi, *especially at night,* is known for thieves looking to separate tourists from their valuables. Although the police presence has increased, it's still best to visit by private taxi. If you go, don't take credit cards or excess money with you. Go with a crowd of friends rather than alone, or take a tour that Includes Garibaldi.

believed to be an adaptation of the French word for marriage; this was the type of music commonly played at weddings in the 15th and 16th centuries. The music is a derivative of *fandango*, which was the most popular dance music of the elite classes in 16th-century Spain. In Mexico, fandango became the peasant's song and dance. Among the most famous mariachi songs are *Mexico Lindo, El Rey, Guadalajara, Cielito Lindo,* and *La Cucaracha.*

In Mexico City, the mariachis make their headquarters around the **Plaza de Garibaldi,** 5 blocks north of the Palacio de Bellas Artes—up Avenida Lázaro Cárdenas, at Avenida República de Honduras. The plaza is liveliest at night, when at every corner guitars are stacked together like rifles in an army camp. Young musicians strut proudly in their outfits, on the lookout for *señoritas* to impress. They play when they feel like it, when there's a good chance to gather some tips, or when someone orders a song—the going rate is $7 (£3.50) per song, or $150 (£75) per hour, which is negotiable. The most famous cantina on the plaza is **Salón Tenampa,** at Plaza Garabaldi 12 (© **55/5526-6176**), which serves traditional Mexican food as well as every type of tequila amid spirited surroundings. It's open daily from 1pm to 3am, and often later on the weekend.

Should you be seeking mariachi music in a more refined setting, I recommend:

Jorongo Bar   Some of city's best mariachi and traditional Mexican music is found in this popular bar, located off the lobby of the Sheraton María Isabel. This bar has enjoyed a reputation for outstanding traditional music for decades—it's an institution, with many local regulars. Monday through Saturday from 7pm to 2am (closed Sunday), you can enjoy the smooth and joyous sounds for the price of a drink ($6–$10/£3–£5) plus cover. Hotel María Isabel Sheraton, Reforma 325, Zona Rosa. © **55/5242-5555**. Cover $14 (£7). Metro: Insurgentes.

CLUBS & MUSIC BARS

AREA Bar and Terrace at Hotel Habita *(Finds)*   The rooftop bar of this boutique Polanco hotel is among Mexico City's enduring hotspots. Umbrellas top tables, but otherwise, you're under the stars—and, likely, surrounded by a few—among a trendy crowd sipping tequila cocktails and Cosmopolitans. Decor is minimalist, of course, with a few white couches. Barstools set along the railing look out over the city. If you can make it past the bouncer and down the circular stairway to the lower terrace and pool area, you've really arrived—that's the glitzy VIP section, not unlike what you'd find in a rooftop L.A. bar. Music is mainly lounge. It's open Monday to Thursday from 7pm to midnight, and Friday to Saturday until 2am. Hotel Habita, Av. Presidente Masaryk 201, Polanco. © **55/5282-3100**. Metro: Polanco.

Bar Fly *(Finds)*   The talented house band—direct from Cuba—makes this small but stylish bar sizzle. By midnight, the tiny dance floor shakes with hot salsa moves inspired by the passionate consumption of *mojitos*. Bar Fly sits on the first floor of an upscale shopping center and is open Wednesday through Saturday from 9pm to 3am. Live music starts around 11pm. Av. Presidente Masaryk 393, Polanco. © **55/5282-2906**. Cover varies. Metro: Polanco.

Bengala   Expats, world travelers, and internationally minded Mexicans have made Bengala one of the city's hottest bars, featuring a diverse selection of music and dancing between tables. The 30-somethings crowd comes for live jazz on Tuesday and Thursday nights and a rocking DJ the rest of the week. If you like sweet cocktails, the red-apple martini is the drink of choice. Open Tuesday to Saturday from 8pm to 3am. Sonora 34 (at corner of Puebla), Col. Roma. © **55/5553-9219**. Metro: Insurgentes.

Cafeina The ultrastylish Cafeina attracts a beautiful crowd of models and young socialites, featuring a celeb DJ serving up house, jazz, bossa nova, reggaeton, and—on Monday nights—the best Brazilian party in town with live music and samba dancers. First-rate Mediterranean cuisine and potent *caipirinhas* (the traditional Brazilian cocktail made with *cachaça*, lime, and sugar) are available, along with specialty blue vodka kiwi martinis. It's open Monday to Saturday from 7pm to 4am and Sunday from 6 to 10pm. Nuevo León 73 (at corner of Juan Escutia), Col. Condesa. © 55/5212-0090. Metro: Insurgentes.

Karisma This hot Polanco cantina bar, located across the street from the Presidente InterContinental, packs nightly with a trendy local and international crowd. Beer and tequila flow steadily throughout the night, and the drinks are definitely better than the food. A number of visiting rock stars have made this a regular stop on their Mexico City tours. Customers tend to dress up here more than at other cantinas. It's open daily from noon to 2am. Campos Eliseos 219 (at Aristoteles), Col. Polanco. © 55/5280-1872. Metro: Auditorio.

Living Mexico City's most glamorous gay club is also a hotspot for open-minded heterosexuals, and its huge dance floor kicks off each weekend night with an exotic theme show. There's a second, smaller section with different music, including electronic, house, and trance. Living is open weekends from 10pm until 4am. Paseo de la Reforma 483, Col Cuauhtémoc. © 55/5286-0066. www.living.com.mx. During special shows or events, cover charge of up to $20 (£10) may apply. Metro: Insurgentes.

Rexo Credited with changing Mexico City's nightlife scene by leading people to Condesa, this Mediterranean restaurant and lounge still rules as one of the city's sexiest spots. A cube walled in by glass, Rexo consists of three contemporary floors, which integrate the restaurant and two stylish bars. The patrons are largely 30-somethings, mostly single, and very fashionable. The club is not easily accessible by Metro. It's open daily from 1pm to 2am. Saltillo 1 (corner of Nuevo León), Col. Condesa. © 55/5553-5337.

Zinco Possibly the coolest jazz club south of the U.S. border, Zinco sits in an old basement vault in the Historic Center. Top performers play in the center of the intimate club, which attracts a crowd that's both cutting edge and unaffected. A full menu is available for those who wish to dine. It's open Wednesday to Saturday from 9pm to 3am. Motolinía 20 (corner of 5 de mayo), Centro Histórico. © 55/5512-3369. Cover $20 (£10) and up. Metro: Zócalo.

BARS

La Casa de las Sirenas This old-school bar serves over 200 types of tequila—one of the widest selections available anywhere (the best of the best are part of the *selección suprema*). It's well known for its friendly bar crowd and ambience, and there's live piano music on weekends. Housed in a 17th-century colonial building, the "House of Mermaids" features a courtyard filled with flowering plants and trees, and lies almost in front of the Templo Mayor in the Centro Histórico. There's also a charming restaurant (with the same name) on the floors above. The bar's open Monday through Saturday from 1 to 11pm, Sunday from 1pm to 6pm. República de Guatemala 32, Centro Histórico, behind the cathedral. © 55/5704-3345 or -3273. Metro: Zócalo.

Tierra de Vinos Only drinks made with grapes are served in this lively wine bar and restaurant, which offers delicious tapas and other Spanish delights to accompany your wine tasting. The stylish bar has a terrific vibe and one of the city's most impressive wine cellars, with distinct cellars housing bottles from key wine regions around the world. It's open Sunday to Tuesday from 1 to 6pm and Wednesday to Saturday from 1pm to 1am. There's a second location in the Santa Fe neighborhood, at Juan Salvador Agráz 60 (℃ **55/5292-3431**), which is slightly more subdued. Durango 197 (at corner of Oaxaca), Col. Roma. ℃ **55/5208-5133**. Metro: Insurgentes.

Whiskey Bar 𝒜𝒜   The W hotel's multisection bar remains one of the city's most fashionable. It includes the Red Lounge, with its neon tube lamps visible through the lobby windows; the Living Room, with innovative leather booths; the upstairs Cocoa Bar, designated for VIPs; and the outdoor Terrace, which offers blankets for ladies. The waitstaff, dressed in jet-black attire, serves the sexy, if somewhat elitist, local and international crowd. A DJ spins lounge beats, while customers sip flavored martinis and exotic cocktails. Open until 2am Sunday through Wednesday, until 3am Thursday through Saturday. At the W Mexico City hotel, Campos Eliseos 252, at Andrés Bello. ℃ **55/ 9138-1800**. Metro: Polanco.

9 A Side Trip to the Pyramids of San Juan Teotihuacán 𝒜𝒜𝒜

50km (31 miles) NE of Mexico City

The ruins of Teotihuacán are among the most remarkable in Mexico—indeed, they are among the most important ruins in the world. Mystery envelops this former city of 200,000; although it was the epicenter of culture and commerce for ancient Mesoamerica, its inhabitants vanished without a trace. *Teotihuacán* (pronounced "teh-oh-tee-wa-*khan*") means "place where gods were born," reflecting the Aztec belief that the gods created the universe here.

Occupation of the area began around 500 B.C., but it wasn't until after 100 B.C. that construction of the enormous Pyramid of the Sun commenced. Teotihuacán's rise coincided with the classical Romans' building of their great monuments, and with the beginning of cultures in Mexico's Yucatán Peninsula, Oaxaca, and Puebla.

Teotihuacán's magnificent pyramids and palaces covered about 30 sq. km (12 sq. miles). At its zenith, around A.D. 500, the city counted more inhabitants than in contemporary Rome. Through trade and other contact, Teotihuacán's influence was known in other parts of Mexico and as far south as the Yucatán and Guatemala. Still, little information about the city's inhabitants survives: what language they spoke, where they came from, why they abandoned the place around A.D. 700. It is known, however, that at the beginning of the 1st century A.D., the Xitle volcano erupted near Cuicuilco (south of Mexico City) and decimated that city, which was the most prominent of the time. Those inhabitants migrated to Teotihuacán. Scholars believe that Teotihuacán's decline, probably caused by overpopulation and depletion of natural resources, was gradual, perhaps occurring over a 250-year period. In the last years, it appears that the people were poorly nourished and that the city was deliberately burned.

Ongoing excavations have revealed something of the culture. According to archaeoastronomer John B. Carlson, the cult of the planet Venus that determined wars and human sacrifices elsewhere in Mesoamerica was prominent at Teotihuacán as well. (Archaeoastronomy is the study of the position of stars and planets in relation to archaeology.) Ceremonial rituals were timed with the appearance of Venus as the morning and evening star. The symbol of Venus at Teotihuacán (as at Cacaxtla, 80km/50 miles away, near Tlaxcala) appears as a star or half-star with a full or half-circle. Carlson also suggests the possibility that people from Cacaxtla conquered Teotihuacán, as name glyphs of conquered peoples at Cacaxtla show Teotihuacán-like pyramids.

SAN MARTÍN

Entrance
Peripheral Highway
5 4 2
Parking
3
1
Parking
To San Juan
Teotihuacán
Parking
6
La Cueva
7 Parking
8
Entrance
9
Terraced Road
17
16
14 15
Río San Juan
11
Parking
10
To Mexico City
12
13 Entrance
Parking
Villas
Arqueológicas
Avenue of the Dead
Peripheral Highway
Roadside
Food Stands

0   0.25 mi
0   0.25 km

1 Tepantitla
2 Pyramid of the Moon
3 Palace of
   Quetzalpapálotl
4 Palace of the Jaguars
5 El Corso
6 Pyramid of the Sun
7 The High Priest's Home
8 New Museum Location
9 The Viking Group
10 The Temple of
   Quetzalcoatl
11 La Ciudadela
12 Old Museum Building
13 La Ventilla
14 Atetelco
15 Tetitla
16 Zacuala
17 Yayahuala

HIDALGO
area of detail   SAN MARTÍN
MÉXICO
ECATEPEC
DE MORELOS
MEXICO CITY

Numerous tombs with human remains (many of them either sacrificial inhabitants of the city or perhaps war captives) and objects of jewelry, pottery, and daily life have been uncovered along the foundations of buildings. It appears that the primary deity at Teotihuacán was a female, called "Great Goddess" for lack of any known name.

Today, what remains are the rough stone structures of the three pyramids and sacrificial altars, and some of the grand houses, all of which were once covered in stucco and painted with brilliant frescoes (mainly in red). The Toltec, who rose in power after the city's decline, were fascinated with Teotihuacán and incorporated its symbols into their own cultural motifs. The Aztec, who followed the Toltec, were fascinated with the Toltec and with the ruins of Teotihuacán; they likewise adopted many of their symbols and motifs. For more information on Teotihuacán and its influence in Mesoamerica, see Appendix A.

ESSENTIALS

GETTING THERE & DEPARTING   By Car   Driving to San Juan Teotihuacán on the toll Highway 85D or the free Highway 132D takes about an hour. Head north on Insurgentes to leave the city. Highway 132D passes through picturesque villages but can be slow due to the surfeit of trucks and buses. Highway 85D, the toll road, is less attractive but faster.

By Private Sedan or Taxi   If you prefer to explore solo or want more or less time than an organized tour allows, consider hiring a private car and driver for the trip. They can easily be arranged through your hotel or at the Secretary of Tourism (SEC-TUR) information module in the Zona Rosa; they cost about $15 to $20 (£7.50–£10) an hour. The higher price is generally for a sedan with an English-speaking driver who doubles as a tour guide. Rates can also be negotiated for the entire day.

By Bus   Buses leave daily every half hour (5am–10pm) from the Terminal Central de Autobuses del Norte; the trip takes 1 hour. When you reach the Terminal Norte, look for the AUTOBUSES SAHAGUN sign at the far northwest end, all the way down to the sign 8 ESPERA. Be sure to ask the driver where you should wait for returning buses, how frequently buses run, and especially the time of the last bus back. **Circuito Pirámides** (© 5141-1360, ext. 2000 and 2602; www.circuitopiramides.com.mx) offers guided air-conditioned coach tours to the ruins for $45 (£23) for adults and $39 (£20) for children, including transportation, entrance, and lunch buffet. Buses depart from the Auditorio Nacional at 9am; Angel de la Independencia at 9:15am; and Zócalo at 9:45am.

ORIENTATION   The ruins of Teotihuacán (© 59/4956-0276 or 59/4956-0052) are open daily from 7am to 5pm. Admission is $4.80 (£2.40). Using a video camera costs $3.50 (£1.75).

A small trolley-train that takes visitors from the entry booths to various stops within the site, including the Teotihuacán museum and cultural center, runs only on weekends and costs $1 (50p) per person.

Keep in mind that you're likely to be doing a great deal of walking, and perhaps some climbing, at an altitude of more than 2,120m (7,000 ft.). Take it slow, bring sun block and drinking water, and, during the summer, be prepared for almost daily afternoon showers.

A good place to start is at the **Museo Teotihuacán** *⊛*. This excellent state-of-the-art museum holds interactive exhibits and, in one part, a glass floor on which visitors walk above mock-ups of the pyramids. On display are findings of recent digs, including several tombs, with skeletons wearing necklaces of human and simulated jaw-bones, and newly discovered sculptures.

The Layout   The grand buildings of Teotihuacán were laid out in accordance with celestial movements. The front wall of the **Pyramid of the Sun** is exactly perpendicular to the point on the horizon where the sun sets at the equinoxes (twice annually). The rest of the ceremonial buildings were laid out at right angles to the Pyramid of the Sun.

The main thoroughfare, which archaeologists call the **Calzada de los Muertos (Avenue of the Dead)**, runs roughly north to south. The **Pyramid of the Moon** is at the northern end, and the **Ciudadela (Citadel)** is on the southern part. The great street was several kilometers long in its prime, but only a kilometer or two has been uncovered and restored.

EXPLORING THE TEOTIHUACAN ARCHAEOLOGICAL SITE

LA CIUDADELA   The Spaniards named the Ciudadela. This immense sunken square was not a fortress at all, although the impressive walls make it look like one. It was the grand setting for the Feathered Serpent Pyramid and the Temple of Quetzal-coatl. Scholars aren't certain that the Teotihuacán culture embraced the Quetzalcoatl deity so well known in the Toltec, Aztec, and Maya cultures. The feathered serpent is featured in the Ciudadela, but whether it was worshipped as Quetzalcoatl or a similar god isn't known. Proceed down the steps into the massive court and head for the ruined temple in the middle.

The Temple of Quetzalcoatl was covered over by an even larger structure, a pyramid. As you walk toward the center of the Ciudadela's court, you'll approach the Feathered Serpent Pyramid. To the right, you'll see the reconstructed temple close behind the pyramid, with a narrow passage between the two structures.

Early temples in Mexico and Central America were often covered by later ones. The Pyramid of the Sun may have been built up in this way. Archaeologists have tunneled deep inside the Feathered Serpent Pyramid and found several ceremonially buried human remains, interred with precise detail and position, but as yet no royal personages. Drawings of how the building once looked show that every level was covered with faces of a feathered serpent. At the Temple of Quetzalcoatl, you'll notice at once the fine, large carved serpents' heads jutting out from collars of feathers carved in the stone walls. Other feathered serpents are carved in relief low on the walls.

AVENUE OF THE DEAD   The Avenue of the Dead got its strange and forbidding name from the Aztec, who mistook the little temples that line both sides of the avenue for tombs of kings or priests.

As you stroll north along the Avenue of the Dead toward the Pyramid of the Moon, look on the right for a bit of wall sheltered by a modern corrugated roof. Beneath the shelter, the wall still bears a painting of a jaguar. From this fragment, you might be able to reconstruct the breathtaking spectacle that must have been visible when all the paintings along the avenue were intact.

PYRAMID OF THE SUN   The Pyramid of the Sun, on the east side of the Avenue of the Dead, is the third-largest pyramid in the world. The first and second are the Great Pyramid of Cholula, near Puebla, and the Pyramid of Cheops on the outskirts of Cairo, Egypt. Teotihuacán's Pyramid of the Sun is 220m (722 ft.) per side at its base—almost as large as Cheops. But at 65m (213 ft.) high, the Sun pyramid is only about half as high as its Egyptian rival. No matter—it's still the biggest restored pyramid in the Western Hemisphere, and an awesome sight. Although the Pyramid of the Sun was not built as a great king's tomb, it is built on top of a series of sacred caves, which aren't open to the public.

The first structure of the pyramid was probably built a century before Christ, and the temple that used to crown the pyramid was completed about 400 years later (A.D. 300). By the time the pyramid was discovered and restoration was begun (early in the 20th c.), the temple had disappeared, and the pyramid was just a mass of rubble covered with bushes and trees.

It's a worthwhile 248-step climb to the top. The view is extraordinary and the sensation exhilarating.

PYRAMID OF THE MOON   The Pyramid of the Moon faces a plaza at the northern end of the avenue. The plaza is surrounded by little temples and by the Palace of Quetzalpapalotl or Quetzal-Mariposa (Quetzal-Butterfly) on the left (west) side. You have about the same range of view from the top of the Pyramid of the Moon as you do from its larger neighbor, because the moon pyramid is built on higher ground. The perspective straight down the Avenue of the Dead is magnificent.

PALACE OF QUETZALPAPALOTL   The Palace of Quetzalpapalotl lay in ruins until the 1960s, when restoration work began. Today, it reverberates with its former glory, as figures of Quetzal-Mariposa (a mythical, exotic bird-butterfly) appear painted on walls or carved in the pillars of the inner court. Behind the Palace of Quetzalpapalotl is the Palace of the Jaguars, complete with murals showing jaguars.

WHERE TO DINE

Vendors at the ruins sell drinks and snacks, but many visitors choose to carry a box lunch—almost any hotel or restaurant in the city can prepare one for you. A picnic in the shadow of this impressive ancient city allows extended time and perspective to take it all in. There is a restaurant called **Las Pirámides** in the new Museo Teotihuacán, which is the most convenient place for a snack or a meal.

Silver, Spas & Spiritual Centers: From Taxco to Tepoztlán

by Juan Cristiano

It may seem as though the small towns in this region are trying to capitalize on recent trends in travel toward spas and self-exploration, but in reality, they've helped define them. From the restorative properties of thermal waters and earth-based spa treatments to the mystical and spiritual properties of gemstones and herbs, the treasures and knowledge in these towns have existed for years—and, in some cases, for centuries.

This is only a sampling of towns south and west of Mexico City. They are fascinating in their diversity, history, and mystery, and make for a unique travel experience, either on their own or combined. They vary in character from mystical villages to sophisticated spa towns, with archaeological and colonial-era attractions in the mix. And with their proximity to Mexico City, all are within easy reach by private car or taxi—or by inexpensive bus—in under a few hours.

The legendary silver city of **Taxco,** on the road between Acapulco and Mexico City, is renowned for its museums, picturesque hillside colonial-era charm, and, of course, its silver shops. North of Taxco and southwest of Mexico City, over the mountains, are the venerable thermal spas at **Ixtapan de la Sal,** as well as their more modern counterparts in **Valle de Bravo.** Verdant **Cuernavaca,** known as the land of eternal spring, has gained a reputation for its exceptional spa facilities and its wealth of cultural and historic attractions. Finally, **Tepoztlán,** with its enigmatic charms and legendary pyramid, captivates the few travelers who find their way there.

1 Taxco: Cobblestones & Silver ★★

178km (110 miles) SW of Mexico City; 80km (50 miles) SW of Cuernavaca; 296km (184 miles) NE of Acapulco

In Mexico and around the world, the town of Taxco de Alarcón—most commonly known simply as Taxco (*tahs*-koh)—is synonymous with silver. The town's geography and architecture are equally precious: Taxco sits at nearly 1,515m (4,969 ft.) on a hill among hills, and almost any point in the city offers fantastic views.

Hernán Cortez discovered Taxco as he combed the area for treasure, but its rich caches of silver weren't fully exploited for another 2 centuries. In 1751, the French prospector Joseph de la Borda—who came to be known locally as José—commissioned the baroque Santa Prisca Church that dominates Taxco's *zócalo* (Plaza Borda) as a way of giving something back to the town. In the mid-1700s, Borda was considered the richest man in New Spain.

Side Trips from Mexico City

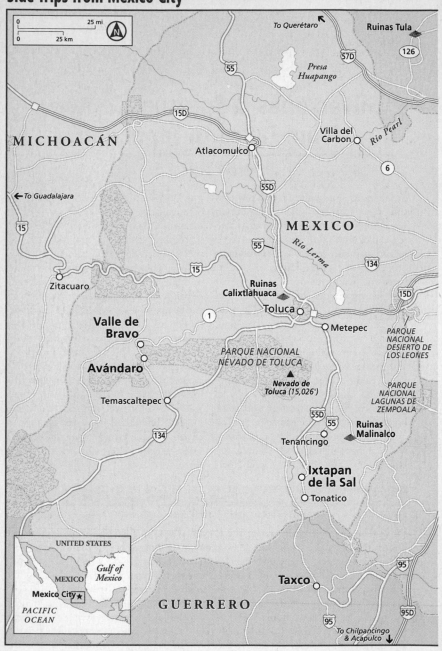

0   25 mi
0   25 km

To Querétaro

Ruinas Tula

126

57D

55

Presa Huapango

MICHOACÁN

15D

Villa del Carbon

Rio Pearl

Atlacomulco

6

← To Guadalajara

55D

MEXICO

15

55

Rio Lerma

134

15

15D

Zitacuaro

Ruinas Calixtlahuaca

Toluca

PARQUE NACIONAL DESIERTO DE LOS LEONES

1

Metepec

Valle de Bravo

PARQUE NACIONAL NEVADO DE TOLUCA

Avándaro

▲ Nevado de Toluca (15,026')

PARQUE NACIONAL LAGUNAS DE ZEMPOALA

Temascaltepec

55D

55

Ruinas Malinalco

134

Tenancingo

Ixtapan de la Sal

Tonatico

UNITED STATES

Gulf of Mexico

MEXICO

Mexico City ★

PACIFIC OCEAN

GUERRERO

95

Taxco

95D

95

To Chilpancingo & Acapulco ↓

160

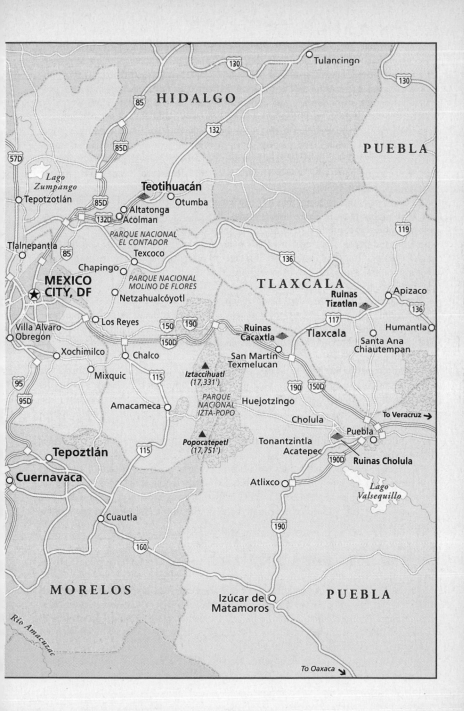

The fact that Taxco has become Mexico's most renowned center for silver design, even though it now mines only a small amount of silver, is the work of an American, William Spratling. Spratling arrived in the late 1920s with the intention of writing a book. He soon noticed the skill of the local craftsmen and opened a workshop to produce handmade silver jewelry and tableware based on pre-Hispanic art, which he exported to the U.S. in bulk. The workshops flourished, and Taxco's reputation grew.

Today, most of the residents of this town are involved in the silver industry in some way. Taxco is home to hundreds (some say up to 900) of silver shops and outlets, ranging from sleek galleries to small stands in front of stucco homes. You'll find silver in all of its forms here—the jewelry basics, tea sets, silverware, candelabras, picture frames, and napkin holders.

The tiny one-man factories that line the winding cobbled streets all the way up into the hills supply most of Taxco's silverwork. "Bargains" are relative, but nowhere else will you find this combination of diversity, quality, and rock-bottom prices. Generally speaking, the larger shops that most obviously cater to the tourist trade will have the highest prices—but they may be the only ones to offer "that special something" you're looking for. For classic designs in jewelry or other silver items, shop around, and wander the back streets and smaller venues.

You can get an idea of what Taxco is like by spending an afternoon, but there's much more to this picturesque town than just the Plaza Borda and the shops surrounding it. Stay overnight, wander its steep cobblestone streets, and you'll discover little plazas, fine churches, and, of course, an abundance of silversmiths' shops.

The main part of town is relatively flat. It stretches up the hillside from the highway, and it's a steep but brief walk up. White VW minibuses, called *combis,* make the circuit through and around town, picking up and dropping off passengers along the route, from about 7am until 9pm. These taxis are inexpensive (about 50¢/30p), and you should use them even if you arrive by car, because parking is practically impossible. Also, the streets are so narrow and steep that most visitors find them nerve-racking. Find a secured parking lot for your car, or leave it at your hotel and forget about it until you leave.

Warning: Self-appointed guides will likely approach you in the *zócalo* (Plaza Borda) and offer their services—they get a cut of all you buy in the shops they take you to. Before hiring a guide, ask to see his SECTUR (Tourism Secretary) credentials. The Department of Tourism office on the highway at the north end of town can recommend a licensed guide.

ESSENTIALS

GETTING THERE & DEPARTING   By Car   From Mexico City, take Paseo de la Reforma to Chapultepec Park and merge with the Periférico, which will take you to Highway 95D on the south end of town. From the Periférico, take the Insurgentes exit and merge until you come to the sign for CUERNAVACA/TLALPAN. Choose either *cuernavaca cuota* (toll) or *cuernavaca libre* (free). Continue south around Cuernavaca to the Amacuzac interchange, and proceed straight ahead for Taxco. The drive from Mexico City takes about 3½ hours.

From Acapulco you have two options: Highway 95D is the toll road through Iguala to Taxco, or you can take the old two-lane road (Hwy. 95) that winds more slowly through villages; it's in good condition.

Taxco

ATTRACTIONS ●

Casa de la Cultura de Taxco
(Casa Borda) **2**

Humboldt House/
Museo Virreinal de Taxco **5**

Mercado Municipal **8**

Museo Arqueológico
Guillermo Spratling **6**

Santa Prisca y San Sebastián
Church **7**

Wholesale Silver Market **8**

Workshops: Los Castillo
& Spratling **11**

ACCOMMODATIONS ■

Best Western Hotel
Taxco **10**

Hotel Los Arcos **4**

Hotel Posada
Emilia Castillo **3**

Hotel Santa Prisca **9**

Monte Taxco **1**

To
Tourism Office,
Mexico City,
Cuernavaca,
Ixtapan de la Sal
& Toluca

Av. de los Plateros

Escobar

Benito Juárez

PUENTE
RAMONET

Chavarrieta

Chavarrieta

Reforma

2a. Sierra Alta

Cjon. del Altillo

Huixteco

Guadalupe

Mezquite

1a. Sierra Alta

opuopaa

Benito Juárez

Ex-Convento de
San Bernardino
de Siena

Estacas

Guadalupe

2a. de la Palma

Altos de Redonda

Plazuela
de Bernal

Ex-Rastro

Estacas

Av. de los Plateros

Guadalupe

4 **5**

Callejón
de la Luz

Estacadas

2 **3**

■ Silver Museum

Juan Ruiz de Alarcón

**Plaza
Borda**

7 **6** C. de la Veracruz

Santa
Veracruz

Ojeda

Raful
Krayem

C. del Arco

Becerra y Tanco

Cuauhtémoc

Pajaritos

Fresno

Teitlán

Plazuela de
San Juan

Mercado
de **8**
Artesanías

Luis Montes de Oca

Callejón Miguel
Hidalgo

Estrella Blanca
Bus Station

Carlos J. Nibbi

10

9

Cena Obscuras

Miguel Hidalgo

Pilita

Zacatillo

Santísima
Trinidad

Parque
Guerrero

San Nicolás
Tolentino

Cena Obscuras

Constitución de 1857

Av. de los Plateros

José María Morelos

Av. de los Plateros

Estrella de Oro
Bus Station

11

To Acapulco

0   200 mi
0   200 km

JALISCO

MICHOACAN

Mexico
City
★
●Taxco

GUERRERO

VERACRUZ

OAXACA

Acapulco●

San Miguel

0   100 yds
0   100 m

N

163

Spanish Lessons & Art Classes in Taxco

The Taxco campus of the **Universidad Nacional Autónoma de México** (**UNAM;** © 762/622-3410; www.cepetaxco.unam.mx) houses the Center of Instruction for Foreign Students on the grounds of the Hacienda del Chorrillo, formerly part of the Cortez land grant. Here, students learn silversmithing, Spanish, drawing, composition, and history under the supervision of UNAM instructors. Classes are small, and courses generally last 3 months. The school provides a list of accommodations that consist primarily of hotels. More reasonable accommodations for a lengthy stay are available, but best arranged once you're there. At many locations all over town, you'll find notices of furnished apartments or rooms for rent. For information about the school, contact either the Dirección de Turismo (tourist office) in Taxco (see "Visitor Information," above), or write the school directly at Hacienda del Chorrillo, 40200 Taxco, Gro.

By Bus   From Mexico City, buses depart from the Central de Autobuses del Sur station (Metro: Taxqueña) and take 2 to 3 hours, with frequent departures.

Taxco has two bus stations. Estrella de Oro buses arrive at their own station on the southern edge of town. Estrella Blanca service, including Futura executive-class buses, and Flecha Roja buses arrive at the station on the northeastern edge of town on Avenida Los Plateros ("Avenue of the Silversmiths," formerly Av. Kennedy). Taxis to the *zócalo* cost around $2 (£1).

VISITOR INFORMATION   The **State of Guerrero Dirección de Turismo** (©/fax 762/622-2274) has offices at the arches on the main highway at the north end of town (Av. de los Plateros 1), which is useful if you're driving into town. The office is open Monday through Saturday from 9am to 8pm, and Sunday from 9am to 6pm. To get there from the Plaza Borda, take a ZOCALO-ARCOS *combi* and get off at the arch over the highway. As you face the arches, the tourism office is on your right.

CITY LAYOUT   The center of town is the tiny **Plaza Borda,** shaded by perfectly manicured Indian laurel trees. On one side is the imposing twin-towered, pink-stone **Santa Prisca Church;** whitewashed, red-tile buildings housing the famous silver shops and a restaurant or two line the other sides. Beside the church, deep in a crevice of the mountain, is the **wholesale silver market**—the best place to begin your silver shopping, to get an idea of prices for more standard designs. It's open daily from 9am to 7pm. You'll be amazed at the low prices. Buying just one piece is perfectly acceptable, and buying in bulk can lower the per-piece price. One of the beauties of Taxco is that its brick and cobblestone streets are completely asymmetrical, zigzagging up and down the hillsides. The plaza buzzes with vendors of everything from hammocks and cotton candy to bark paintings and balloons.

FAST FACTS   The telephone area code is **762.** The main post office, Benito Juárez 6, at the City Hall building (© 762/622-8596), is open Monday through Saturday from 8:30am to 3:30pm. The older branch of the post office (© 762/622-0501), open Monday through Friday from 8:30am to 2:30pm, is on the outskirts, on the highway to Acapulco. It's in a row of shops with a black-and-white CORREO sign.

EXPLORING TAXCO

Shopping for jewelry and other items is the major pastime for tourists. Prices for silver jewelry at Taxco's shops are about the best in the world, and everything is available, from $1 (50p) trinkets to artistic pieces that cost hundreds of dollars.

In addition, Taxco is the home of some of Mexico's finest stone sculptors and is a good place to buy masks. However, beware of so-called "antiques"—there are virtually no real ones for sale.

SPECIAL EVENTS & FESTIVALS   January 18 marks the annual celebration in honor of Santa Prisca, with public festivities and fireworks displays. **Holy Week** in Taxco is one of the most poignant in the country, beginning the Friday a week before Easter with processions daily and nightly. The most riveting, on Thursday evening, lasts almost 4 hours. Villagers from the surrounding area carrying statues of saints, followed by hooded members of a society of self-flagellating penitents, chained at the ankles and carrying huge wooden crosses and bundles of thorny branches. On Saturday morning, the Plaza Borda fills for the **Procession of Three Falls,** reenacting the three times Christ stumbled and fell while carrying the cross.

Taxco's **Silver Fair** starts the last week in November and continues through the first week in December. It includes a competition for silver works and sculptures among the top silversmiths. In late April to early May, **Jornadas Alarconlanas** features plays and literary events in honor of Juan Ruiz de Alarcón (1572–1639), a world-famous dramatist who was born in Taxco—and for whom Taxco de Alarcón is named. Art exhibits, street fairs, and other festivities are part of the dual celebration.

SIGHTS IN TOWN

Casa de la Cultura de Taxco (Casa Borda)   Diagonally across from the Santa Prisca Church and facing Plaza Borda is the home José de la Borda built for his son around 1759. Now the Guerrero State Cultural Center, it houses a bookstore, library, classrooms, and exhibit halls where period clothing, engravings, paintings, and crafts are on display. The center also books traveling art exhibits, theatrical performances, music concerts, and dance events.

Plaza Borda 1. ⓒ 762/622-6617. Fax 762/662-6634. Free admission. Tues–Sun 10am–5pm.

Humboldt House/Museo Virreinal de Taxco   Stroll along Ruiz de Alarcón (the street behind the Casa Borda) and look for the richly decorated facade of the Humboldt House, where the renowned German scientist and explorer Baron Alexander von Humboldt (1769–1859) spent a night in 1803. The museum houses 18th-century memorabilia pertinent to Taxco, most of which came from a secret room discovered during a recent restoration of the Santa Prisca Church. Signs with detailed information are in Spanish and English. As you enter, to the right are very rare *túmulos funerios* (painted funerary altars). The bottom two were painted for Charles III of Spain; the top one, with a carved phoenix, was reputedly painted for the funeral of José de la Borda.

Another section presents historical information about Don Miguel Cabrera, Mexico's foremost 18th-century artist. Fine examples of clerical garments decorated with gold and silver thread hang in glass cases, and on the bottom level there's an impressive 17th-century carved wood altar of Dolores. Next to it, a small room is devoted to Humboldt and his sojourns through South America and Mexico.

Calle Juan Ruiz de Alarcón 12. ⓒ 762/622-5501. Admission $2 (£1) adults, $1.50 (75p) students and teachers w/ID. Tues–Sat 10am–6pm; Sun 10am–4pm.

Mercado Municipal   Located to the right of the Santa Prisca Church, behind and below Berta's, Taxco's central market meanders deep inside the mountain. Take the stairs off the street. In addition to a collection of wholesale silver shops, you'll find numerous food stands, always the best place for a cheap meal.

Plaza Borda. Shops daily 10am–8pm; food stands daily 7am–6pm.

Museo Arqueológico Guillermo Spratling   A plaque in Spanish explains that most of the collection of pre-Columbian art displayed here, as well as the funds for the museum, came from William Spratling (1900–1967). You'd expect this to be a silver museum, but it's not—for Spratling silver, go to the Spratling Ranch Workshop (see "Nearby Attractions," below). The entrance floor and the one above display a good collection of pre-Columbian statues and implements in clay, stone, and jade. The upper floor holds changing exhibits.

Calle Porfirio A. Delgado 1. © 762/622-1660. Admission $2.50 (£1.75) adults, free for children younger than 13; free to all Sun. Tues–Sat 9am–5pm; Sun 9am–3pm. Leaving Santa Prisca Church, turn right and right again at the corner; continue down the street, veer right, then immediately left. The museum will be facing you.

Museo de la Platería   The silver museum holds a small collection of exquisite silver pieces, the most interesting of which is *La Conquista de Anahuac,* in which copper Aztec warriors and silver Spanish conquistadors face off on a chess board made with black wood and oyster shell. The owner, Antonio Pineda, declined a $1-million offer to sell it. This museum represents his private collection and includes silver pieces from throughout the last century, such as coins, sculptures, jewelry, and crowns. A mural created by a local artist represents the history of Mexico's silver industry.

Plaza Borda 1. © 762/622-0658. Admission $1 (50p). Daily 10am–6pm. The museum is located downstairs in the Patio de las Artesanias.

Santa Prisca y San Sebastián Church 🜲🜲   This is Taxco's centerpiece parish church; it faces the pleasant Plaza Borda. José de la Borda, a French miner who struck it rich in Taxco's silver mines, funded the construction. Completed in 1758, it's one of Mexico's most impressive baroque churches. The ultracarved facade is eclipsed by the interior, with breathtakingly intricate gold-leafed saints and cherubic angels. The paintings by Miguel Cabrera, one of Mexico's most famous colonial-era artists, are the pride of Taxco. The sacristy (behind the high altar) contains more Cabrera paintings.

Guides, both children and adults, will approach you outside the church offering to give a tour. Make sure the guide's English is passable, and establish whether the price is per person or per tour. Note that flash photos are not allowed.

Plaza Borda. © 762/622-0184. Free admission. Daily 6:30am–8pm.

NEARBY ATTRACTIONS

The impressive **Grutas de Cacahuamilpa** 🜲, known as the Cacahuamilpa Caves or Grottoes, lie less than a half-hour north of Taxco. Hourly guided tours run daily at the caverns, which house fascinating stalactite and stalagmite formations. To see them, you can join a tour from Taxco (see "Exploring Taxco," above) or take a *combi* from the Flecha Roja terminal in Taxco; one-way is $5 (£2.50), and admission to the caves is $5 (£2.50). For more information, see "Sights near Tepoztlán," later in this chapter.

Los Castillo   Don Antonio Castillo was one of hundreds of young men to whom William Spratling taught silversmithing in the 1930s. He was also one of the first to branch out with his own shops and line of designs, which over the years have earned him a fine reputation. Castillo has shops in several Mexican cities. Now, his daughter

Emilia creates her own noteworthy designs, including decorative pieces with silver fused onto porcelain. Emilia's work is for sale on the ground floor of the Posada de los Castillo, just below the Plazuela Bernal.

8km (5 miles) south of town on the Acapulco Hwy. Also at Plazuela Bernal, Taxco. © 762/622-6717. Free admission. Workshop Mon–Sat 10am–3pm and 4–7pm; open to groups at other hours by appointment only.

Spratling Ranch Workshop   William Spratling's hacienda-style home and workshop on the outskirts of Taxco still bustles with busy hands reproducing unique designs. A trip here will show you what distinctive Spratling work was all about, for the designs crafted today show the same fine work. Although the prices are higher than at other outlets, the designs are unusual and considered collectible. There's no store in Taxco, and most of the display cases hold only samples. With the exception of a few jewelry pieces, most items are by order only. Ask about U.S. outlets.

10km (6¼ miles) south of town on the Acapulco Hwy. 762/622-0026. Free admission. Call in advance for hours, which vary. The *combi* to Iguala stops at the ranch; fare is $1.80 (90p).

WHERE TO STAY
MODERATE
Best Western Hotel Taxco 🖈🖈   This is the newest and most modern hotel in the town center, with professional service and an international clientele. Rooms are small but very comfortable, with white tiles and bedspreads and Mexican architectural touches. Some have windows (interior rooms do not), and the junior suite has a terrace with views of the surrounding hills. Near the Santa Prisca church, this hotel has a quality Mexican restaurant and access to a nearby pool. The friendly staff will arrange in-room massages upon request. They offer a 10% discount on cash payments.

Carlos J. Nibbi 2, Plazuela de San Juan, 40200 Taxco, Gro. © 762/627-6194. Fax 762/622-3416. www.bestwestern taxco.com. 23 units. $110 (£55) double; $150 (£75) junior suite. AE, MC, V. Free parking. **Amenities:** Restaurant; access to outdoor pool and massage services; business center; laundry service. *In room:* AC, TV, Wi-Fi.

Monte Taxco *Overrated*   This resort and country club sits atop a hill near the entrance to Taxco coming from Mexico City. A longtime landmark of the city, it offers golf and tennis, spa services, and access to the mountain's cable car, which operates daily from 8am to 7pm. Colonial-style rooms are a bit dated but comfortable. Open weekends for dinner only, Toni's boasts the best city views of any restaurant in Taxco, and you can finish the night at the flashy dance club next door. You'll need to drive or take a taxi to reach the city center.

Fracc. Lomas de Taxco s/n, 40210 Taxco, Gro. © 762/622-1300. Fax 762/622-1428. www.montetaxco.com.mx. 156 units. $135 and up (£68) double. AE, MC, V. Free parking. **Amenities:** 2 restaurants (one w/spectacular city view; see "Where to Dine," below); bar; dance club; heated outdoor pool; 9-hole golf course; 3 tennis courts; gym; spa services; room service; laundry service; travel desk; jewelry store. *In room:* A/C, TV.

INEXPENSIVE
Hotel Emilia Castillo *Value*   Each room in this delightful small hotel is simply but handsomely appointed with carved doors and furniture; the small tile bathrooms have showers only. Ask for an interior room, which are much quieter than those facing the street. A high-quality silver shop lies next to the colorful lobby. The hotel does not have parking but contracts with a local parking garage.

Juan Ruiz de Alarcón 7, 40200 Taxco, Gro. ©/fax 762/622-1396. www.hotelemiliacastillo.com. 14 units. $45 (£23) double; $50 (£25) triple with TV. MC, V. From the Plaza Borda, go downhill a short block to the Plazuela Bernal and make an immediate right; the hotel is a block farther on the right, opposite the Hotel los Arcos (see above). **Amenities:** Internet. *In room:* TV.

Hotel los Arcos ⭐   Los Arcos occupies a converted 1620 monastery. The handsome inner patio is bedecked with Puebla pottery and rustic furnishings surrounding a central fountain. Guest rooms are nicely but sparsely appointed, with natural tile floors and colonial-style furniture; the spacious junior suite has two levels. You'll feel immersed in colonial charm and blissful quiet. To find the hotel from the Plaza Borda, follow the hill down (with Hotel Agua Escondida on your left) and make an immediate right at the Plazuela Bernal; the hotel is a block down on the left, opposite the Hotel Posada (see below).

Juan Ruiz de Alarcón 4, 40200 Taxco, Gro. 🕐 762/622-1836. Fax 762/622-7982. www.hotellosarcos.net. 21 units. $47 (£24) double; $55 (£28) triple; $67 (£34) junior suite. No credit cards. **Amenities:** Internet. *In room:* TV, fan.

Hotel Santa Prisca (*Value*   The Santa Prisca, 1 block from the Plaza Borda on the Plazuela San Juan, is one of the older and best located hotels in town. Rooms are small but comfortable ("superior doubles" are slightly larger), with standard bathrooms (showers only), tile floors, wood beams, and a colonial atmosphere. For longer stays, ask for a room in the adjacent new addition, where the rooms are sunnier, quieter, and more spacious. There is a reading area in an upstairs salon overlooking Taxco, as well as a garden patio with fountains.

Cenaobscuras 1, 40200 Taxco, Gro. 🕐 762/622-0080 or -0980. Fax 762/622-2938. 34 units. $50 (£25) double; $65 (£33) superior double; $70 (£35) junior suite. AE, MC, V. Limited free parking. **Amenities:** Breakfast cafe and bar; room service; laundry service; safe. *In room:* No phone.

WHERE TO DINE
Taxco gets a lot of day-trippers, most of whom choose to dine close to the Plaza Borda. Prices in this area are high for what you get. Just a few streets back, you'll find some excellent, simple *fondas* (taverns) or restaurants.

VERY EXPENSIVE
Toni's ⭐ STEAKS/SEAFOOD   High on a mountaintop, Toni's is an intimate, classic restaurant enclosed in a huge, cone-shaped *palapa* with a panoramic view of the city. Eleven candlelit tables sparkle with crystal and crisp linen, and piano music accompanies dinner. The menu, mainly shrimp or beef, is limited, but the food is quite good. Try tender, juicy prime roast beef carved at your table, which comes with creamed spinach and baked potato. To reach Toni's, it's best to take a taxi. Note that it's open for dinner on weekends only.

In the Hotel Monte Taxco. 🕐 762/622-1300. Reservations recommended. Main courses $9–$26 (£4.50–£13). AE, MC, V. Fri–Sun 7pm–1am.

MODERATE
Cafe Sasha ⭐⭐ INTERNATIONAL/VEGETARIAN   One of the cutest places to dine in town, Cafe Sasha is very popular with locals, and offers a great array of vegetarian options—such as falafel with tabouleh and vegetarian crepes, as well as Mexican and international classics. Try their Thai chicken curry or a hearty burrito. Open for breakfast, lunch, and dinner, it's also a great place for a cappuccino and pastry, or an evening cocktail. The music is hip, and the atmosphere is inviting and chic. Local artists often exhibit here, and there's live music on Sundays.

Calle Juan Ruiz de Alarcón 1, just down from Plazuela de Berna. No phone. www.cafesasha.com. Breakfast $2–$5 (£1–£2.50); main courses $5–$8 (£2.50–£4). No credit cards. Daily 8am–midnight.

El Adobe ⭐ MEXICAN   This charming restaurant is an eclectic Mexican mix of adobe, brick, and wood with decor that includes regional art, old black-and-white photos of Mexican and American entertainers, and some kitsch memorabilia. There are a number of romantic balcony tables lit with candles and lamps after dark. The hearty fare includes *cecina taxqueña* (thin strip steak served with guacamole), *pollo Guerrero* (chicken cooked with paprika, onion, small potatoes, and guacamole), and enchiladas prepared anyway you want. A guitar player/singer performs weekend nights, and brunch is offered on Sundays.

Plazuela de San Juan 13. ℃ 762/622-1416. Breakfast $3–$5 (£1.50–£2.50); main courses $5.50–$14 (£2.75–£7). MC, V. Daily 8:30am–11pm.

El Rincon del Toril LATIN   This festive restaurant combines Mexican, Spanish, Italian, and Argentine cuisines. Delicious steaks are served sizzling hot on the skillet at your table. For a meat-eating extravaganza, order the *parrillada El Toril* for two, which includes *arrachera* beef, ribs, chorizo, and an American steak. Apart from the steaks, the menu offers an enticing selection of fish, chicken, and pasta dishes. The casual and often crowded dining room is brightly decorated with mementos from Mexican bullfights. It leads to an outdoor terrace next to the Plaza Borda. Traditional Mexican music plays cheerfully in the background.

Plaza Borda 3. ℃ 762/627-6207. Main courses $7–$18 (£3.50–£9). MC, V. Daily 7am–11pm.

La Terraza Café-Bar INTERNATIONAL   One of two restaurants at the Hotel Agua Escondida (on the *zócalo*), the rooftop La Terraza is a scenic spot for a meal or a drink, with tasty food and a great view of the church, town, and surrounding mountains. The diverse menu includes dishes such as breaded veal, grilled pork chops, chicken fajitas, and mole enchiladas. Even if you're normally not into desserts, you should seriously think about ordering a delicious crepe or flan here. Frosty margaritas and rich cappuccinos are also on order. During the day, cafe umbrellas shade the sun, and you can stargaze here at night.

Plaza Borda 4. ℃ 762/622-1166. Main courses $4–$10 (£2–£5). MC, V. Daily noon–10pm.

Sotavento Restaurant Bar Galería 🍴🍴 ITALIAN/INTERNATIONAL Vibrant Mexican paintings decorate the walls of this stylish restaurant, which offers tables inside, on the balcony, or in the garden patio. The extensive menu features Italian and Mexican dishes—for starters, try the delicious fresh spinach salad with goat cheese and bacon, followed by a large pepper steak. For vegetarians, I recommend the Spaghetti Barbara with poblano peppers, onions, avocado, and cream. Savory crepes are also available.

Benito Juárez 12, next to City Hall. ℃ 762/627-1217. Main courses $4.50–$15 (£2.25–£7.50). MC, V. Tues–Sun 8am–midnight. From the Plaza Borda, walk downhill beside the Hotel Agua Escondida, then follow the street as it bears left on Agustin de Tulsa (don't go right on Juan Ruiz de Alarcón) about 1 block; the restaurant is on the left just after the street bends left.

INEXPENSIVE

Restaurante Ethel MEXICAN   This no-nonsense family-run eatery lies opposite the Hotel Santa Prisca, 1 block from the Plaza Borda. It has colorful cloths on the tables and a tidy, homey atmosphere. The hearty *comida corrida* (food on the go) consists of soup or pasta, meat (perhaps a small steak or roast chicken), dessert, and good coffee. Full breakfasts, typical Mexican dishes, and rich *pozole* (a thick Mexican soup) are offered, too.

Plazuela San Juan 14. ℃ 762/622-0788. Breakfast $5.50–$6 (£2.75–£3); main courses $5.50–$8.50 (£2.75–£4.25); *comida corrida* (served 1–5pm) $6.80 (£3.40). MC, V. Mon–Sat 9am–9pm; Sun 9am–7pm.

TAXCO AFTER DARK

Acerto (© 762/622-0064), located upstairs at Plaza Borda 12, is an enticing all-purpose hangout overlooking the square. It serves as an Internet cafe, sports bar, and restaurant. Taxco's popular, modern dance club, **Windows,** sits high up the mountain in the **Hotel Monte Taxco** (© 762/622-1300). The entire city is on view, and music runs the gamut from Latin pop to '80s hits. For a $5 (£2.50) cover, you can dance away Friday or Saturday night from 9pm to 3am. The club seldom gets crowded.

Completely different in tone is **Bar Berta's** (© 762/622-0172), next to the Santa Prisca Church at Plaza Borda 9. Opened in 1930 by a lady named Berta, who made her fame on a drink of the same name (tequila, soda, lime, and honey), it's the traditional gathering place of the local gentry and more than a few tourists. Spurs and old swords decorate the walls. Grab a seat on the balcony overlooking the plaza and church. A Berta (the drink, of course) costs about $5 (£2.50); rum, the same. It's open daily from 11am to 8pm.

La Concha Nostra (© 762/622-7944), has a local, edgy feel and features live rock music Saturday nights for a $2.50 (£1.25) cover. It's located upstairs inside the Hotel Casa Grande at Plazuela de San Juan 7, and is open nightly until 1am. The gay-friendly **Aztec Disco** (© 762/627-3833) features drag shows and dancing. It's located on Av. de los Plateros 184, and is open from 10pm until late.

2 Ixtapan de la Sal: A Thermal Spa Town

120km (74 miles) SW of Mexico City

The whitewashed town of Ixtapan de la Sal (not to be confused with Ixtapa, on the Pacific coast) is known for its thermal mud baths—this is an original spa town, with generations of healing traditions.

Hotels in Ixtapan (pronounced "*eeks*-tah-pahn") de la Sal tend to fill up on weekends and Mexican holidays, as the town is a popular retreat from Mexico City. Cuernavaca, Taxco, and Toluca are all easy side trips. The **Marriott Ixtapan de la Sal Hotel & Spa** *ᏒᏒ*, José Maria Morelos s/n, Fracc. Bugambilias (© 721/143-2010; www.marriott.com/hotels/travel/mexix-ixtapan-de-la-sal-marriott-hotel-and-spa), is a 189-room hotel at the town entrance with a full-service spa and more modern amenities than the better known Hotel Spa Ixtapan (below). Doubles range from $220 to $260 (£110–£230) per night.

ESSENTIALS

GETTING THERE & DEPARTING By Car From Mexico City, take Highway 15 to Toluca. In Toluca, Highway 15 becomes Paseo Tollocan. Follow Tollocan south until you see signs pointing left to Ixtapan de la Sal. After the turn, continue straight for around 15km (9⅓ miles). Just before the town of Tenango del Valle, you have a choice of the free road to Ixtapan de la Sal or the toll road. The free road winds through the mountains and takes 1½ hours. The inexpensive two-lane toll road has fewer mountain curves and takes around an hour—it's worth taking. The toll road stops about 15km (9⅓ miles) before Ixtapan; the rest of the trip is on a curvy mountainous drive.

By Bus From Mexico City's Terminal Poniente, buses leave for Ixtapan de la Sal every few minutes. Request a bus that's taking the toll road, which cuts the travel time by 30 to 60 minutes, to about 2½ hours. To return, take a bus marked MEXICO DIRECTO, which leaves every 10 minutes and usually stops in Toluca. Buses from here also go to Cuernavaca and Taxco every 40 minutes.

A PUBLIC SPA

The **Balneario Ixtapan** (© **721/143-0331**), next to the Hotel Spa Ixtapan, is the town's original public spa and bathhouse. It's not a modern, pampering spa, but a spa in the traditional manner—think Turkish baths. Over the years, the *balneario* has melded its traditional thermal waters with some features that make it more of an aquatic park. In addition to the large pools of varying temperatures, it offers modern features such as water slides, a slow-moving river, and other attractions. Entrance is $16 (£8) for adults, $8 (£4) for children between .9m and 1.2m (3–4 ft.) tall; children under .9m (3 ft.) tall enter free. The *balneario* has restaurants, so you can spend the day. The entrance fee gives you access to all of the pools and rides. Lockers are about 50¢ (30p). It's open weekdays from 8am to 7pm and weekends from 7am to 7pm. The traditional spa amenities and services are next door, where you can choose among private thermal water baths, massages, facials, hair treatments, paraffin wraps, pedicures, and manicures. Prices range from $18 to $72 (£9–£36). When you purchase a spa treatment you can include access to the *balneario* for $7 (£3.50). The spa is open daily from 8am to 8pm during holiday periods; at other times, Monday through Friday from 8am to 8pm, Saturday and Sunday from 7am to 8pm.

WHERE TO STAY & DINE

Hotel Spa Ixtapan *(Value* The town's famous spa resort sits on 14 manicured and flower-filled hectares (35 acres). In operation since 1939, it feels aged, but unrenovated areas afford guests the nostalgic feel of the original hotel and spa. The resort offers golf, tennis, swimming, and miles of trails for walking, jogging, or biking. It also has freshwater and thermal mineral swimming pools, an outdoor whirlpool, and a host of spa services such as Thai massages and Balinese hot clay treatments. Guests who opt out of the spa program can use the facilities on a per-treatment basis, and there's no daily admission charge. Rooms in the main building are slightly better furnished and more expensive than the so-called "villa" rooms, but all are fairly basic. There are two restaurants: One is vegetarian-focused, and the other serves a more traditional international menu. Many North Americans visit as part of a weight loss program. The hotel shows classic movies each night. Round-trip taxi transportation from the Mexico City airport can be arranged at the time of reservation for around $320 (£160), which can be shared by up to four people. Rates for the different packages include full American plan (three meals daily).

Bulevar San Román s/n, Ixtapan de la Sal, 51900 Edo. de México. ℂ **800/638-7950** in the U.S., or 721/143-2440. Fax 721/143-0856. www.hotelixtapan.com. 220 units, including 45 villas. $190 (£95) villa; $210 (£105) double in main building. 4-day spa package $604 (£302) per person double; 7-day spa package $1,075 (£538) per person double; 21-day spa package $2,700 (£1,350) per person double; 28-day spa package $3,600 (£1,800) per person double. Rates include meals. AE, MC, V. **Amenities:** 2 restaurants; bar; piano lounge; 2 outdoor pools; private 18-hole golf course; 2 tennis courts; gym; aerobics room and classes; full-service spa; 2 indoor and 1 outdoor whirlpool; sauna; steam room; mountain bikes; tour desk; Internet; room service; laundry service; solarium; hiking trails. *In room:* TV.

3 Valle de Bravo & Avándaro: Mexico's Switzerland

152km (94 miles) SW of Mexico City

Valle de Bravo has been called the "Switzerland of Mexico." Ringed by pine-forested mountains and set beside a beautiful lake, Valle de Bravo is a 16th-century village with cobblestone streets and colonial structures built around a town plaza. Like San Miguel de Allende, Taxco, and Puerto Vallarta, Valle de Bravo is a National Heritage village; new construction must conform to the colonial style of the original village.

The village's cobbled streets, small restaurants, hotels, spas, and shops are full on weekends—this is a very popular retreat from Mexico City. Some shops and restaurants may be closed weekdays. The crafts market, 3 blocks from the main square, is open daily from 10am to 5pm, and colorfully dressed Mazahua Indians sell their handmade tapestries daily around the town plaza.

Sailing, windsurfing, bass fishing, and water-skiing are popular on the lake. Boats of varying speeds can be rented (along with a driver and water ski equipment) at the dock for between $20 and $40 (£10–£20) per hour; look for the sign that says "Yate Cristal y Lanchas." Excursions from Valle de Bravo include a trip to the nesting grounds of the monarch butterfly between November and February. It can be very rainy and chilly September through December, in addition to the summer rainy season.

The neighboring town of Avándaro, 6km (3¾ miles) away, is a popular place for weekend homes for well-to-do residents of Mexico City.

ESSENTIALS

GETTING THERE & DEPARTING   By Car   From Mexico City, the quickest route is Highway 15 to Toluca. In Toluca, Highway 15 becomes Paseo Tollocan. Follow Tollocan south until you see signs pointing left to Highway 134 and Valle de

Valle de Bravo & Avándaro

ACCOMMODATIONS

Avándaro Golf & Spa Resort **4**
El Santuario Resort & Spa **1**
Hotel Batucada **3**
Hotel Los Arcos **2**

Post Office ✉

Bravo, Francisco de los Ranchos, and Temascaltepec. After the turn, continue on Highway 142 until Francisco de los Ranchos, where you bear right and follow signs to Valle de Bravo. The drive from this point takes about 1½ to 2 hours.

By Bus   From Mexico City's Terminal Poniente, buses leave every 20 minutes for the 3-hour journey. First-class buses depart hourly.

WHERE TO STAY & DINE

Avándaro Golf and Spa Resort 🍴   On 118 hectares (291 acres) amid large estates, lushly forested mountains, and a gorgeous, rolling 18-hole golf course, this resort occupies one of the loveliest settings in Mexico. Rooms come in two categories: large deluxe suites, and smaller, less luxurious cabañas. Rooms have fireplaces and terraces or balconies overlooking the grounds. The extensive spa includes hot and cold whirlpools, sauna and steam rooms, and a full range of body and facial treatments. The hotel has two drawbacks: Some of the rooms need upgrading, and large tour groups often stay here. Transportation from Mexico City can be arranged.

Fracc. Vega del Río s/n. Avándaro, 51200 Valle de Bravo. ℭ 726/266-1651; reservations 55/5280-1532, 5282-0954, 5280-5532, or 5282-0578 in Mexico City. www.hotelavandaro.com.mx. 82 units. $200 (£100) double cabaña; $260 (£130) deluxe suite. 7-day spa or golf package available. AE, MC, V. **Amenities:** 2 restaurants; 25m (82-ft.) junior Olympic-size pool; 18-hole golf course; 7 tennis courts; fitness center; spa w/well-trained staff and full range of services; hot and cold whirlpools; sauna; steam rooms; room service. *In room:* TV, hair dryer, safe.

Da Ciro 🍴🍴 ITALIAN   Amid flowering gardens and trickling fountains, this wonderful Italian restaurant is just a short walk from the town's central square. If you come for lunch, ask for a table on the idyllic outdoor terrace. At night, the dining room with brick walls, wood beam ceilings, Tiffany lamps, and floor to ceiling windows transforms into a romantic hideaway (be careful walking on the tile floors, which can be slippery). Start with a Caprese salad followed by a mouthwatering homemade pizza. The house specialty is pasta, including an incredibly delicious spaghetti Parmesan prepared tableside. Also excellent are risotto with shrimp, osso bucco, and sea bass stuffed with shrimp in cognac. Like many places in Valle de Bravo, Da Ciro is open only on weekends.

Virgel 201. ℭ 726/262-0122. Reservations recommended. Main courses $11–$18 (£5.50–£9). AE, MC, V. Fri–Sat 1pm–midnight; Sun 1–8pm.

El Santuario Resort Spa 🍴🍴🍴   Set on the shores of Valle de Bravo's lake, and at the foot of an "energy-conducting" quartz mountain, this resort combines soothing natural surroundings with modern amenities, recreational activities, and spa services. Natural elements such as slate, quartz, river stones, bamboo, and shells are used in the decor details. The design includes magnificent use of water, such as infinity pools that seem to fall from the sides of the resort into the lake. The guest suites are built into the mountainside, with panoramic views of the water. Each also comes with a private plunge pool and sitting area. The 1,860 sq. m (20,020-sq.-ft.) spa offers over 60 therapies in a variety of treatment rooms, including a flotation suite, as well as a cafe, oxygen bar, gym, salon, and studio for yoga, Pilates, meditation, and other mind-body activities. The signature therapy is the Yenecamú—2½ hours of treatments, which, upon request, can be performed on a pontoon boat in the middle of the lake. If you grow tired of being pampered, there's also golf, hiking, water sports on the lake, and other eco-oriented activities to while away the time.

ExHacienda San Gaspar Carretera a Colorines, Km 4.5, 51200 Valle de Bravo. ℭ 726/262-9100. www.elsantuario. com. 64 suites. $300 (£150) double on weekdays; $420 (£210) double on weekends. Spa packages start at $320

(£160) extra per person, double occupancy for 2 nights, including all meals and selected spa services. Other packages are also available. AE, MC, V. **Amenities:** Restaurant/bar; outdoor pool with whirlpools; 9-hole golf course; spa; concierge; salon; boutique; laundry service; marina. *In room:* TV, hair dryer, safe.

Hotel Batucada   If you'd like to stay right in the charming town center, this is an historic option just 2 blocks from the central square. The handful of guest rooms fill the 300-year old home and surround a flower-filled courtyard with a trickling fountain and background jazz music. The individually decorated rooms present a warm, colonial feel, with high wood-beam ceilings, rustic wood furnishings, and views of the surrounding mountains. Guests who stay 2 nights or more receive a welcome drink, fruit basket, and free continental breakfast.

Francisco González Bocanegra 207, 51200 Valle de Bravo. © 726/262-0480. Fax 726/262-0586. 9 units. $160 (£80) double. AE, MC, V. **Amenities:** Restaurant; bar; free parking; limited room service. *In room:* TV.

Hotel los Arcos *(Kids)*   The Hotel los Arcos, close to the main square, affords views of the lake and village. Two stories of rooms on one side and three stories on the other surround a swimming pool. Nineteen rooms have fireplaces, an important feature in winter here. Some rooms have balconies, and most have glass walls with views. This hotel is popular with families.

Francisco González Bocanegra 310, 51200 Valle de Bravo. ©/fax 726/262-0042, -0531, or -0168. 24 units. Mon–Thurs $85 (£43) double; Fri–Sun $110 (£65) double. AE, MC, V. **Amenities:** Outdoor pool. *In room:* TV.

4 Cuernavaca: Land of Eternal Spring *(★(★(★*

102km (63 miles) S of Mexico City; 80km (50 miles) N of Taxco

Often called the "land of eternal spring," Cuernavaca is known these days as much for its rejuvenating spas and spiritual sites as for its perfect climate and flowering landscapes. Spa services are easy to find. More importantly, Cuernavaca exudes a deep sense of connection with its historical and spiritual heritage. Its palaces, walled villas, and elaborate haciendas are home to museums, spas, and extraordinary guesthouses.

Wander the traditional markets and you'll see crystals, quartz, onyx, and tiger's eye amid the trinkets. These stones come from the Tepozteco Mountains—for centuries considered an energy source—which cradle Cuernavaca to the north and east. Mexico begins to narrow here, and several mountain ranges converge. East and southeast of Cuernavaca are two volcanoes, also potent symbols of earth energy: **Ixtaccihuatl** (the Sleeping Woman) and the recently active **Popocatépetl** (the Smoking Mountain).

Cuernavaca, capital of the state of Morelos, is also a cultural treasure, with a past that closely follows the history of Mexico. So divine are the landscape and climate that both the Aztec ruler Moctezuma II and French Emperor Maximilian built private retreats here. Today, Cuernavaca remains the most popular weekend getaway for moneyed residents of Mexico City. As a result, the roads between the capital and Cuernavaca are jammed almost every weekend, but you can avoid some of the crowds by traveling early in the morning. Cuernavaca even has a large American colony, plus many students attending the numerous language and cultural institutes.

Emperor Charles V gave Cuernavaca to Hernán Cortez as a fief, and in 1532 the conquistador built a palace (now the Museo de Cuauhnáhuac), where he lived on and off for half a dozen years before returning to Spain. Cortez introduced sugar cane cultivation to the area, and African slaves were brought in to work in the cane fields, by way of Spain's Caribbean colonies. His sugar hacienda at the edge of town is now the impressive Hotel de Cortez.

After Mexico gained independence from Spain, powerful landowners from Mexico City gradually dispossessed the remaining small landholders, imposing virtual serfdom on them. This condition led to the rise of Emiliano Zapata, the great champion of agrarian reform, who battled the forces of wealth and power, defending the small farmer with the cry of *"¡Tierra y libertad!"* (Land and liberty!) during the Mexican Revolution of 1910.

Today, Cuernavaca's popularity has brought an influx of wealthy foreigners and industrial capital. With this commercial growth, the city has also acquired the less desirable by-products of increased traffic, noise, and air pollution—although still far, far less than nearby Mexico City, which you may be escaping.

ESSENTIALS

GETTING THERE & DEPARTING   By Car   From Mexico City, take Insurgentes or Periférico south, which will take you to Highway 95D, the toll road on the far south of town that goes to Cuernavaca. From the Periférico, take the Insurgentes exit and continue until you come to signs for Cuernavaca/Tlalpan. Choose either the *cuernavaca cuota* (toll) or *cuernavaca libre* (free) road on the right. The free road is slower and very windy, but more scenic. The toll road costs about $9 (£4.50).

By Bus   *Important note:* Buses to Cuernavaca depart directly from the Mexico City airport. (See "Getting There," in chapter 3, for details.) The trip takes an hour. The Mexico City Central de Autobuses del Sur exists primarily to serve the Mexico City–Cuernavaca–Taxco–Acapulco–Zihuatanejo route. Pullman de Morelos has two stations in Cuernavaca: downtown, at the corner of Abasolo and Netzahualcóyotl (© 777/318-0907 or 312-6063), 4 blocks south of the center of town; and Casino de la Selva (© 777/312-9473), less conveniently located at Plan de Ayala 14, near the railroad station.

Autobuses Estrella Blanca (© 777/312-2626; www.estrellablanca.com.mx), depart from the Central del Sur with 4 buses daily from Mexico City. They arrive in Cuernavaca at Av. Morelos Sur 329, between Arista and Victoria, 6 blocks north of the town center. Here, you'll find frequent buses to Toluca, Chalma, Ixtapan de la Sal, Taxco, Acapulco, the Cacahuamilpa Caves, Querétaro, and Nuevo Laredo.

Estrella de Oro (© 777/312-3055; www.estrelladeoro.com.mx), Morelos 900, serves Iguala, Chilpancingo, Acapulco, and Taxco.

Estrella Roja (© 777/318-5934; www.estrellaroja.com.mx), a second-class station at Galeana and Cuauhtemotzin in Cuernavaca, about 8 blocks south of the town center, serves Cuautla, Yautepec, Oaxtepec, and Izúcar de Matamoros.

VISITOR INFORMATION   Cuernavaca's **Municipal Tourist Office** is at Calle Hidalgo 5, next to the Jardin Morelos (Morelos Garden; © 777/314-3920; www.cuernavaca.gob.mx). It's open daily from 9am to 6pm. The **Morelos State Tourism Office** is located on Av. Morelos Sur 187 (© 777/314-3881; www.morelostravel.com). It's open Monday through Friday from 9am to 5pm. There's also a **City Tourism kiosk** (© 777/329-4404) at Morelos Sur 278, beside the El Calvario Church, open daily from 9am to 5pm.

CITY LAYOUT   In the center of the city are two contiguous plazas. The smaller and more formal, across from the post office, has a Victorian gazebo (designed by Gustave Eiffel, of Eiffel Tower fame) at its center. This is the **Alameda**. The larger, rectangular plaza with trees, shrubs, and benches is the **Plaza de Armas**. These two plazas are known collectively as the *zócalo* and form the hub for strolling vendors selling balloons,

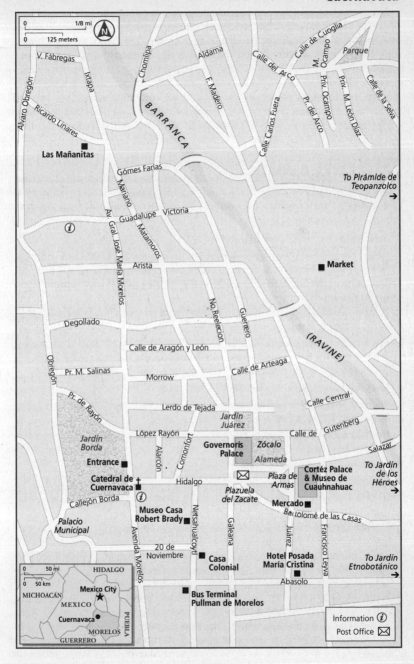

Cuernavaca

0 — 1/8 mi
0 — 125 meters

V. Fábregas
Alvaro Obregón
Ricardo Linares
Ixtapa
Chomilpa
Aldama
F. Madero
Calle del Arco
Calle de Cuoglia
Calle de Cuoglia
M. Ocampo
Priv. Ocampo
Pr. del Arco
Priv. M. León Díaz
Calle de Selva
Parque

BARRANCA

Las Mañanitas

Gómes Farias

Mariano Guadalupe Victoria
Av. Gral. José María Morelos
Matamoros

To Pirámide de
Teopanzolco
→

Arista

Market

Degollado

Obregón

No. Reelección
Guerrero

(RAVINE)

Pr. M. Salinas
Calle de Aragón y León
Calle de Arteaga
Morrow

Pr. de Rayón

Lerdo de Tejada

Calle Central

Jardín
Borda

López Rayón
Alarcón
Comonfort

Jardín
Juárez

Calle de Gutenberg

Governor's
Palace

Zócalo
Alameda

Calle de

Salazar

Entrance

Cortéz Palace
& Museo de
Cuauhnahuac

To Jardín
de los
Héroes
→

Catedral de
Cuernavaca

Hidalgo

Plaza de
Armas

Callejón Borda

Plazuela
del Zacate

Mercado

Museo Casa
Robert Brady

Bartolomé de las Casas

Palacio
Municipal

Avenida Morelos
Netzahualcóyotl
Galeana
Juárez
Francisco Leyva

20 de
Noviembre

Casa
Colonial

Hotel Posada
María Cristina

To Jardín
Etnobotánico
→

Abasolo

0 — 50 mi
0 — 50 km

HIDALGO
MICHOACÁN
MEXICO
Mexico City ★
Cuernavaca ●
MORELOS
GUERRERO
PUEBLA

Bus Terminal
Pullman de Morelos

Information ⓘ
Post Office ✉

baskets, bracelets, and other crafts from surrounding villages. It's all easy-going, and one of the great pleasures of the town is hanging out at a park bench or table in a nearby restaurant. On Sunday afternoons, orchestras play in the gazebo. At the eastern end of the Alameda is the **Cortez Palace,** the conquistador's residence, now the Museo de Cuauhnáhuac.

Note: The city's street-numbering system is extremely confusing. It appears that the city fathers, during the past century or so, imposed a new numbering system every 10 or 20 years. An address given as "no. 5" may be in a building that bears the number "506," or perhaps *"Antes no. 5"* (former no. 5).

FAST FACTS: Cuernavaca

American Express The local representative is **Viajes Marín,** Pericón 116 (© 777/ 318-9901 or 372-1000). It's open Monday to Friday from 9am to 7pm and Saturday from 10am to 2pm.

Area Code The telephone area code is **777.**

Banks Bank tellers (9am–4pm, depending on the bank), ATMs, and *casas de cambio* change money. The closest bank to the *zócalo* is **Bancomer,** Matamoros and Lerdo de Tejada, cater-cornered to Jardín Juárez (across López Rayón from the Alameda).

Drugstore **Farmacias del Ahorro** (© 777/322-2277) offers hotel delivery service, but you must ask the front desk of your hotel to place the order, because the pharmacy requires the name of a hotel employee. It has 12 locations around the city, but the individual pharmacies have no phone. Some are open 24 hours a day, while others are open daily from 7am to 10pm.

Elevation Cuernavaca sits at 1,533m (5,028 ft.).

Hospital **Hospital Inovamed** is located at Calle Cuauhtémoc 305, Col. Lomas de la Selva (© 777/311-2482, -2483, or -2484).

Internet Access **GAP,** Hidalgo 7 (© 777/318-2288), offers high-speed access for less than a dollar per hour.

Population Cuernavaca has 400,000 residents.

Post Office The *correo* (© 777/312-4379) is on the Plaza de Armas, next door to Café los Arcos. It's open Monday through Friday from 8am to 6pm, Saturday from 10am to 2pm.

Spanish Lessons Cuernavaca is known for its Spanish-language schools. Generally, the schools will help students find lodging with a family or provide a list of places to stay. Rather than make a long-term commitment in a family living situation, try it for a week, then decide. Contact the **Universidad Internacional,** San Jerónimo 304 (Apdo. Postal 1520), 62000 Cuernavaca, Morelos (© 800/574-1583 in the U.S. or 777/317-1087; www.spanish.com.mx); **Instituto de Idioma y Cultura en Cuernavaca** (© 777/317-8947; fax 777/317-0455); or **Universal Center for Language and Social Communication: Innovative Spanish,** J. H. Preciado 171 (Apdo. Postal 1-826, 62000 Cuernavaca, Morelos; © 777/318-2904 or 312-4902; www. universal-spanish.com). Note that the entire experience, from classes to lodging, can be quite expensive; the school may accept credit cards for the class portion.

EXPLORING CUERNAVACA

On weekends, the whole city (including roads, hotels, and restaurants) fills with people from Mexico City. This makes weekends more hectic, but also more fun. You can spend 1 or 2 days sightseeing pleasantly enough. If you've come on a day trip, you may not have time to make all the excursions listed below, but you'll have enough time to see the sights in town. The traditional *mercado* (**public market**) adjacent to the Cortez Palace is open daily from 10am to 10pm. The colorful rows of stands are a lively place to test your bargaining skills as you purchase pottery, silver jewelry, crystals, and other trinkets. Note that the Cuauhnáhuac museum is closed on Monday.

Catedral de Cuernavaca ✸ *Moments*   As you enter the church precincts and pass down the walk, try to imagine what life in Mexico was like in the old days. Construction on the church, also known as the *Catedral de Asunción de María,* began in 1529, a mere 8 years after Cortez conquered Tenochtitlán (Mexico City) from the Aztec, and was completed in 1552. The churchmen could hardly trust their safety to the tenuous allegiance of their new converts, so they built a fortress as a church. The skull and crossbones above the main door are a symbol of the Franciscan order, which had its monastery here. The monastery is open to the public, on the northwest corner of the church property. Also visible on the exterior walls of the main church are inlaid rocks, placed there in memory of the men who lost their lives during its construction.

Once inside, wander through the sanctuaries and the courtyard, and pay special attention to the impressive frescoes painted on the walls, in various states of restoration. The frescoes date from the 1500s and have a distinct Asian style.

The main sanctuary is stark, even severe, with an incongruous modern feeling (it was refurbished in the 1960s). Frescoes on these walls, discovered during the refurbishing, depict the persecution and martyrdom of St. Felipe de Jesús and his companions in Japan. No one is certain who painted them. In the churchyard, you'll see gravestones marking the tombs of the most devout (or wealthiest) parishioners. Being buried on the church grounds was believed to be the most direct route to heaven.

At the corner of Hidalgo and Morelos (3 blocks southwest of the Plaza de Armas). ✆ 777/318-4590. Free admission. Daily 8am–2pm and 4–7pm.

Jardín Borda   Across Morelos Street from the cathedral lies the Jardín Borda (Borda Gardens). José de la Borda, the Taxco silver magnate, ordered a sumptuous vacation house built here in the late 1700s. When he died in 1778, his son Manuel inherited the land and transformed it into a botanical garden. The large enclosed garden next to the house was a huge private park, laid out in Andalusian style, with kiosks and an artificial pond. Maximilian took it over as his private summer house in 1865. He and Empress Carlota entertained lavishly in the gardens and held concerts by the lake.

The gardens were completely restored and reopened in 1987 as the Jardín Borda Centro de Artes. In the gateway buildings, several galleries hold changing exhibits and large paintings showing scenes from the life of Maximilian and from the history of the Borda Gardens. One portrays the initial meeting between Maximilian and La India Bonita, a local maiden who became his lover.

On your stroll through the gardens, you'll see the little man-made lake on which Austrian, French, and Mexican nobility rowed small boats in the moonlight. Ducks have taken the place of dukes, however. There are rowboats for rent. The lake is now artfully adapted as an outdoor theater (see website for performance information), with seats for the audience on one side and the stage on the other. Music concerts are often held on Sunday evenings. A cafe serves refreshments and light meals, and a weekend market inside the *jardín* sells arts and crafts.

Av. Morelos Sur 271, at Hidalgo. © 777/318-1044. www.arte-cultura-morelos.gob.mx. Admission $3 (£1.50) adult, $1.50 (75p) children; free Sun. Tues–Sun 10am–5:30pm.

Jardín Etnobotánico y Museo de Medicina Tradicional y Herbolaria 🎬🎬

This serene museum of traditional herbal medicine, in the south Cuernavaca suburb of Acapantzingo, occupies a former resort residence built by Maximilian, the Casa del Olvido. During his brief reign, the Austrian-born emperor came here for trysts with La India Bonita, his Cuernavacan lover. The building was restored in 1960, and the house and gardens now preserve the local wisdom of folk medicine. The shady gardens are lovely to wander through, and you shouldn't miss the hundreds of orchids growing near the rear of the property.

Matamoros 14, Acapantzingo. © 777/312-5955, 312-3108, or 314-4046. www.inah.gob.mx. Free admission. Daily 9am–4:30pm. Take a taxi, or catch *combi* no. 6 at the mercado on Degollado. Ask to be dropped off at Matamoros near the museum; turn right on Matamoros and walk 1½ blocks; the museum will be on your right.

Museo Casa Robert Brady 🎬🎬

This private home and garden turned museum houses an eclectic collection of religious, folk, and ethnic art, including pre-Hispanic and colonial pieces; oil paintings by Frida Kahlo and Rufino Tamayo; popular Mexican art; and handicrafts from America, Africa, Asia, and India. Robert Brady, an Iowa native with a degree in fine arts from the Art Institute of Chicago, assembled the collections. The brightly decorated house (tiled with hand-painted Talavera throughout) is a work of art in its own right. Brady lived in Venice for 5 years before settling in Cuernavaca in 1960. The wildly colorful rooms remain exactly as Brady left them when he died here in 1986. Admission includes a guide in Spanish; English and French guides are available if requested in advance. A small cafe in the main patio serves refreshments.

Calle Netzahualcóyotl 4 (between Hidalgo and Abasolo). © 777/318-8554. www.bradymuseum.org. Admission $3 (£1.50). Tues–Sun 10am–6pm.

Museo Regional Cuauhnáhuac 🎬

The Palacio Cortez, once home to Mexico's most famous conquistador, is now the Museo de Cuauhnahuac, devoted to the history of Morelos state. It's also home to a stunning Diego Rivera mural *The History of Cuernavaca & Morelos*, an unflinching illustrated history of the brutality and treachery of the Spanish Conquest. In one panel, a Spanish soldier holds a hot poker, poised to brand an Aztec prisoner on the neck; behind him, men in armor pour gold pieces into a large trunk while a priest blesses the transaction. True to Rivera's Communist faith in the power of the Mexican people, the largest images in the gallery are full-length portraits of Emiliano Zapata, the revolutionary who fought for agrarian reform with the cry, "*¡Tierra y libertad!*" (Land and liberty!), and Father José Maria Morelos, a hero of the War of Independence.

On the lower level, the excellent bookstore is open daily from 11am to 8pm. Tour guides in front of the palace offer their services in the museum, and for other sights in Cuernavaca, for about $10 (£5) per hour. Make sure you see official SECTUR (Tourism Secretary) credentials before hiring one of these guides. This is also a central point for taxis in the downtown area.

In the Cortez Palace, Leyva 100. © 777/312-8171. www.morelostravel.com. Admission $3.70 (£1.85); free Sun. Tues–Sun 10am–5pm.

ACTIVITIES & EXCURSIONS

GOLF   With its perpetually springlike climate, Cuernavaca is an ideal place for golf. The **Tabachines Golf Club and Restaurant,** Km 93.5 Carr. Mexico-Acapulco (© 777/314-3999), the city's most popular course, is open for public play. Percy Clifford designed this 18-hole course, surrounded by beautifully manicured gardens blooming with bougainvillea, gardenias, and other flowers. The elegant restaurant is a popular place for breakfast, lunch, and especially Sunday brunch. Greens fees are $75 (£38) during the week and $200 (£100) on weekends, with fees reduced by half after 1:30pm. American Express, Visa, and MasterCard are accepted. It's open Tuesday through Sunday from 7am to 6pm; tee times are available from 7am to 2pm.

Also in Cuernavaca is the **Club de Golf Hacienda San Gaspar,** Avenida Emiliano Zapata, Col. Cliserio Alanis (© 777/319-4424; www.sangaspar.com), an 18-hole golf course designed by Joe Finger. It's surrounded by more than 3,000 trees and has two artificial lagoons, plus beautiful panoramic views of Cuernavaca, the Popocatépetl and Ixtaccihuatl volcanoes, and the Tepozteco Mountains. Greens fees are $80 (£40) on weekdays, $135 (£68) on weekends (discounted after 2pm); carts cost an additional $45 (£23) for 18 holes, and a caddy is $20 (£10) plus tip. American Express, Visa, and MasterCard are accepted. Additional facilities include a gym with whirlpool and sauna, pool, four tennis courts, and a restaurant and snack bar. It's open Wednesday through Monday from 7am to 7pm.

LAS ESTACAS   Either a side trip from Cuernavaca or a destination on its own, Las Estacas, Km 6.5 Carretera Tlaltizapán–Cuautla, Morelos (© 777/312-4412 or -7610 in Cuernavaca, or 734/345-0350; www.lasestacas.com) is a natural water park. Its clear spring waters reputedly have healing properties. In addition to the crystal-clear rivers with aquatic ropes, water swings, diving platforms, and hanging bridges, Las Estacas has two pools, wading pools for children, horseback riding, an 18-hole mini-golf course, and a diving school. Several restaurants serve such simple food as quesadillas, fruit with yogurt, sandwiches, and *tortas.* Admission is $21 (£11) for adults, $13 (£6.50) for children under 1.2m (4 ft.) tall. A small, basic hotel charges $120 to $150 (£60–£75) for a double room; rates include the entrance fee to the *balneario* and breakfast. Cheaper lodging options include a trailer and camping park; you can rent an adobe or straw hut with two bunk beds for $33 (£17). Visit the website for more information. MasterCard and Visa are accepted. On weekends, the place fills with families. Las Estacas is 36km (22 miles) east of Cuernavaca. To get there, take Highway 138 to Yautepec, then turn right at the first exit past Yautepec.

PYRAMIDS OF XOCHICALCO ❧   This pre-Columbian ceremonial center provides clues to the history of the whole region. Artifacts and inscriptions link the site to the mysterious cultures that built Teotihuacán and Tula, and some of the objects found here would indicate that residents were also in contact with the Mixtec, Aztec, Maya, and Zapotec. The most impressive building in Xochicalco is the Pirámide de la Serpiente Emplumada (Pyramid of the Plumed Serpent), with its magnificent reliefs of plumed serpents twisting around seated priests. Underneath the pyramid is a series of tunnels and chambers with murals on the walls. At the observatory, from April 30 to August 15, you can follow the sun's trajectory as it shines through a hexagonal opening. The pyramids (© 777/314-3920 for information) are 36km (22 miles) southwest of Cuernavaca, open daily from 9am to 6pm. Admission is $4.50 (£2.25).

WHERE TO STAY
EXPENSIVE
Camino Real Sumiya 🏮🏮   About 11km (7 miles) south of Cuernavaca, this unusual resort, whose name means "the place of peace, tranquillity, and longevity," was once the home of Woolworth heiress Barbara Hutton. Using materials and craftsmen from Japan, she constructed the estate in 1959 for $3.2 million (£1.8 million) on 12 wooded hectares (30 acres). The main house, a series of large connected rooms and decks, overlooks the grounds and contains restaurants and the lobby. Sumiya's charm rests in its relaxing atmosphere, which is best midweek (escapees from Mexico City tend to fill it on weekends). Guest rooms cluster in three-story buildings bordering manicured lawns. They're simple compared to the main house's striking Japanese architecture. Rooms have subtle Japanese accents, with austere but comfortable furnishings and scrolled wood doors. Hutton built a Kabuki-style theater and exquisite Zen meditation garden, which are now used only for special events. The theater contains vividly colored silk curtains and gold-plated temple paintings protected by folding cedar and mahogany screens. Strategically placed rocks in the garden represent the chakras, or energy points of the human body. Some regulars, who have been coming to the hotel for years, have complained that service has become less personalized under new management.

Interior Fracc. Sumiya s/n, Col. José Parres, 62550 Jiutepec, Mor. ⓒ 01-800/901-2300 in Mexico, or 777/329-9888. Fax 777/329-9889. www.caminoreal.com/sumiya. 163 units. $180 (£90) double; $385 (£193) suite. Low-season packages and discounts available. AE, DC, MC, V. Free parking. From the freeway, take the Atlacomulco exit and follow signs to Sumiya. Ask directions in Cuernavaca if you're coming from there, as the route is complicated. **Amenities:** 2 restaurants; lobby bar; poolside snack bar; outdoor pool; golf privileges nearby; tennis club; business center; concierge; room service; convention facilities w/simultaneous translation capabilities. *In room:* A/C, TV, Wi-Fi, minibar, hair dryer, iron, safe, ceiling fan.

Las Mañanitas   This hotel and garden has been Cuernavaca's most renowned luxury lodging for years. It's also a popular weekend dining spot for affluent visitors from Mexico City. Guest rooms are formal in style, with gleaming polished molding and brass accents, large bathrooms, and rich fabrics. Rooms in the original mansion, called terrace suites, overlook the restaurant and inner lawn; the large rooms in the patio section each have a secluded patio; and those in the luxurious, expensive garden section each have a patio overlooking the pool and emerald lawns. Sixteen rooms have fireplaces, and the hotel also has a heated pool in the private garden of exotic birds, flowers, and trees. Las Mañanitas is one of the only in Mexico associated with the prestigious Relais & Châteaux chain. The restaurant overlooking the peacock-filled gardens is one of the country's premier dining places (see "Where to Dine," below). It's open to nonguests for all meals.

Ricardo Linares 107 (5½ long blocks north of the Jardín Borda), 62000 Cuernavaca, Mor. ⓒ 777/362-0000. Fax 777/318-3672. www.lasmananitas.com.mx. 32 units. Weekday $215–$325 (£108–£163) double; weekend $250–$350 (£125–£175) double. Rates include breakfast. AE, MC, V. Free valet parking. **Amenities:** Restaurant; outdoor pool; massage; concierge; babysitting; airport transfer (fee); room service; laundry service. *In room:* TV, hair dryer.

Misión Del Sol Resort & Spa 🏮🏮🏮 *Finds*   This adults-only hotel and spa is an exceptional value, offering an experience that rivals any in North America or Europe. You feel a sense of peace from the moment you enter the resort, which draws on the mystical wisdom of the ancient cultures of Mexico, Tibet, Egypt, and Asia. Guests and visitors are encouraged to wear light-hued clothes to contribute to the harmonious flow of energy.

Architecturally stunning adobe buildings that meld with the natural environment house the guest rooms, villas, and common areas. Streams border the extensive gardens. Group activities, such as reading discussions, a chess club, and painting workshops, take place in the salon, where films are shown on weekend evenings. Spacious rooms are designed according to Feng Shui principles; each looks onto its own garden or stream and has three channels of ambient music. Some have air-conditioning. Bathrooms are large, with sunken tubs, and the dual-headed showers have river rocks set into the floor, as a type of reflexology treatment. Beds contain magnets for restoring proper energy flow. Villas feature two separate bedrooms, plus a living/dining area and a meditation room. Spa services include facials, body treatments, and massages, with an emphasis on water-based treatments. Elegant relaxation areas are interspersed among the treatment rooms and whirlpool.

Av. General Diego Díaz González 31, Col. Parres, 62550 Cuernavaca, Mor. ℭ **01-800/999-9100** toll-free inside Mexico, or 777/321-0999. Fax 777/320-7981. www.misiondelsol.com. 42 units, plus 12 villas. $260 (£130) deluxe double; $540 (£270) 2-bedroom villa (up to 4 persons); $595 (£298) 3-bedroom villa (up to 6 persons). Special spa and meal packages available. AE, MC, V. Free parking. Children younger than 13 not accepted. **Amenities:** Restaurant; 2 tennis courts; well-equipped gym; extensive spa services; basketball; volleyball; daily meditation, yoga, and Tai Chi classes. *In room:* Safe.

MODERATE

Casa Colonial 𝔊𝔊 *Finds*   This splendid inn consists of only 18 guest rooms, individually decorated in a warm colonial style with dark wood antique furnishings. The rooms surround an idyllic courtyard filled with palms, bamboo, and ficus plants as well as a shimmering pool. An inviting breakfast patio looks upon the courtyard, which is an intimate setting for weddings and other special events. During the day, the sound of classical music fills the air. The grounds were originally part of the cathedral property, which took up much of the neighborhood. Casa Colonial lies 1 block from the central square and within easy walking distance of all sights in the historic center.

Nezahualcóyotl 37 (at Abasolo), Col. Centro, 62000 Cuernavaca, Mor. ℭ 777/312-7033. Fax 777/310-0395. www. casacolonial.com. 18 units. $100 and up (£50) double. AE, MC, V. Limited free parking. **Amenities:** Restaurant; bar; outdoor pool. *In room:* TV, minibar, ceiling fan.

Hotel Posada María Cristina 𝔊𝔊   The María Cristina's high walls conceal many delights: a small swimming pool, lush gardens with fountains, a good restaurant, and patios. Guest rooms vary in size; all are exceptionally clean and comfortable, with firm beds and colonial-style furnishings. Bathrooms have inlaid Talavera tiles and skylights. Suites are only slightly larger than normal rooms; junior suites have Jacuzzis. La Calandria, the handsome little restaurant, overlooks the gardens and serves excellent meals based on Mexican and international recipes. Even if you don't stay here, consider having a meal. The popular Sunday brunch ($16/£8 per person) features live classical music. The hotel is a half-block from the Palacio de Cortez.

Bulevar Juárez 300 (at Abasolo), Col. Centro (Apdo. Postal 203), 62000 Cuernavaca, Mor. ℭ 777/318-2981. Fax 777/312-9126 or 777/318-2981. www.maria-cristina.com.mx. 20 units. $100 (£50) and up double. AE, MC, V. Free parking. **Amenities:** Restaurant; bar; outdoor pool. *In room:* TV, minibar, hair dryer, ceiling fan.

WHERE TO DINE
VERY EXPENSIVE

Restaurant Las Mañanitas MEXICAN/INTERNATIONAL   Las Mañanitas has set the standard for sumptuous, leisurely dining in Cuernavaca, filling with wealthy families from Mexico City on weekends and holidays. The setting of this hotel garden and restaurant is exquisite, the service superb, and the food is better than average.

Tables stand on a shaded terrace with a view of gardens, strolling peacocks, and softly playing violinists or a trio playing romantic boleros. Diners have the option of ordering drinks and making their menu selections from chairs in the garden, waiting to take their seats at their tables when their meals are served. The Mexican cuisine with an international flair draws on seasonal produce. They also serve a full selection of fresh seafood, certified Angus beef, lamb chops, baby back ribs, and free range chicken, in standard preparations. Try the zucchini flower soup, filet of red snapper in curry sauce, and black-bottom pie, the house specialty. A tasting menu is also available.

In Las Mañanitas hotel, Ricardo Linares 107 (5½ long blocks north of the Jardín Borda). © 777/362-0000, ext. 240. www.lasmananitas.com.mx. Reservations recommended. Main courses $19–$40 (£9.50–£20). AE, MC, V. Daily 8–noon, 1–6pm, and 6–11pm.

MODERATE

Casa Hidalgo ★★ GOURMET MEXICAN/INTERNATIONAL Casa Hidalgo lies in a beautifully restored colonial building across from the Palacio de Cortez. The food is more sophisticated and innovative than that at most places in town. Specialties include chilled mango and tequila soup, smoked rainbow trout, and the exquisite Spanish-inspired filet Hidalgo—breaded and stuffed with serrano ham and *manchego* cheese. There are always daily specials, and bread is baked on the premises. Tables on the balcony afford a view of the action in the plaza below. The restaurant is accessible by wheelchair.

Jardin de los Héroes 6. © 777/312-2749. www.casahidalgo.com. Reservations recommended on weekends. Main courses $14–$20 (£7–£10). AE, MC, V. Mon–Thurs 1:30–11pm; Fri–Sat 1:30pm–midnight; Sun 1:30–10pm.

Restaurant La India Bonita ★★ MEXICAN Cuernavaca's oldest restaurant is housed among the interior patios and portals of the restored home—known as Casa Mañana—of former U.S. Ambassador Dwight Morrow. The beautiful setting features patio tables amid trickling fountains, palms, and flowers. Specialties include *mole poblano* (chicken with a sauce of bitter chocolate and fiery chiles) and the signature *La India Bonita* plate with steak, enchiladas, rice, and beans. There are also several daily specials. A breakfast mainstay is *desayuno Maximiliano,* a gigantic platter of chicken enchiladas with an assortment of sauces. A Mexican folkloric dance show fills the restaurant with colorful energy on Saturday nights from 8 to 9pm.

Morrow 15 (between Morelos and Matamoros), Col. Centro, 2 blocks north of the Jardín Juárez. © 777/312-5021. Breakfast $4–$9 (£2–£4.50); main courses $7–$16 (£3.50–£8). AE, MC, V. Tues–Thurs 8am–10pm; Fri 8am–10:30pm; Sat 9am–11pm; Sun–Mon 9am–5pm.

INEXPENSIVE

La Universal ★★ *Value* MEXICAN/PASTRIES This is a busy place, partly because of its great location (overlooking both the Alameda and Plaza de Armas), partly because of its traditional Mexican specialties, and partly because of its reasonable prices. It's open to the street and has many outdoor tables, usually filled with older men discussing the day's events or playing chess. These tables are perfect for watching the parade of street vendors and park life. The specialty is a Mexican grilled sampler plate, including *carne asada,* enchilada, pork cutlet, green onions, beans, and tortillas, for $12 (£6). A full breakfast special ($11/£5.50) for two is served Monday through Friday from 9:30am to 12:30pm. Live music is played weekdays from 3 to 5pm and again from 8 to 10pm.

Guerrero 2. © 777/318-6732. Breakfast $5–$8 (£2.50–£4); main courses $9–$14 (£4.50–£7); *comida corrida* $8.90 (£4.45). MC, V. Daily 9:30am–12:30am.

CUERNAVACA AFTER DARK

Cuernavaca has a number of cafes right off the Jardín Juárez where people gather to sip coffee or drinks till the wee hours—check out La Universal (see "Where to Dine," above). Band concerts are held in the Jardín Juárez on Thursday and Sunday evenings. **La Plazuela,** a pedestrian-only stretch across from the Cortez Palace, features cafes, kitsch stores, and live-music bars. It's geared toward a 20-something, university crowd.

5 Tepoztlán ★★

72km (45 miles) S of Mexico City; 45km (28 miles) NE of Cuernavaca

Tepoztlán is one of the strangest and most beautiful towns in Mexico. Largely undiscovered by foreign tourists, it occupies the floor of a broad, lush valley whose walls were formed by bizarrely shaped mountains that look like the work of some abstract expressionist giant. The mountains are visible from almost everywhere in town; even the municipal parking lot boasts a spectacular view.

Tepoztlán remains small and steeped in legend and mystery—it lies adjacent to the alleged birthplace of Quetzalcoatl, the Aztec serpent god—and comes about as close as you're going to get to an unspoiled, magical mountain hideaway. Eight chapels, each with its own cultural festival, dot this traditional Mexican village. Though the town stays tranquil during the week, escapees from Mexico City descend in droves on the weekends, especially Sunday. Most Tepoztlán residents, whether foreigners or Mexicans, tend to be mystically or artistically oriented—although some also appear to be just plain disoriented. The village wears its New Age heart on its sleeve—homeopathic pharmacies and health-food stores coexist happily alongside Internet cafes, tortilla stands, and satellite-dish companies.

The town is famous throughout Mexico as a symbol of fierce civic pride and independence. In 1994, a multinational firm secretly negotiated a deal to build a Jack Nicklaus golf course and residential development on communally held lands; part of the plan involved construction of a heliport and a funicular to the top of Tepozteco pyramid. When the project came to light, townspeople joined forces, ran the city government out of town (hanging them in effigy), and occupied the *Ayuntamiento* (town hall), sealing off the city limits and repelling state military forces until the developers backed out of the project.

Aside from soaking up the ambience, two things you must do are climb up to the Tepozteco pyramid and hit the weekend folkloric market. In addition, Tepoztlán offers a variety of treatments, cures, diets, massages, and sweat lodges. Some of these are available at hotels; for some, you have to ask around. Many locals swear that the valley possesses mystical curative powers.

If you have a car, Tepoztlán provides a great starting point for traveling this region of Mexico. Within 90 minutes are Las Estacas, Taxco, las Grutas de Cacahuamilpa, and Xochicalco (some of the prettiest ruins in Mexico). Tepoztlán lies 20 minutes from Cuernavaca and only an hour south of Mexico City (that is, an hour once you're able to get out of Mexico City), which—given its lost-in-time feel—seems hard to believe.

ESSENTIALS

GETTING THERE & DEPARTING   By Car   From Mexico City, the quickest route is Highway 95 (the toll road) to Cuernavaca; just before the Cuernavaca city limits, you'll see the clearly marked turnoff to Tepoztlán on 95D and Highway 115. The slower, free federal Highway 95D, direct from Mexico City, is also an option, and

Cooking Classes in Tepoztlán

An engaging cooking school called **Cocinar Mexicano** offers weeklong programs in Mexican cuisine. The founder, Magda Bogin, conducts class from her large, sunny outdoor kitchen, tiled in blue-and-white Talavera. Participants study recipes typical of the festival that coincides with their visit. During the Day of the Dead workshop, for example, students learn to make tamales, the traditional dish that families bring to the gravesites of deceased love ones. For other festivals, the focus is *mole*, a typical fiesta food often made with chocolate and chiles that's arguably the most complex dish in Mexican cuisine. All the programs include a range of contemporary dishes, and participants spend a day of fine dining in Mexico City, where they meet with the country's top chefs. Prices range from $2,495 to $2,895 (£1,248–£1,448) depending on the duration of the workshop, which includes round-trip transportation from Mexico City and most meals but not airfare or accommodations. Frommer's readers receive a $100 (£50) discount. For more information, visit **www.cocinarmexicano.com**.

may be preferable if you're departing from the western part of the city. Take 95D south to Km 71, where the exit to Tepoztlán on Highway 115 is clearly indicated.

By Bus   From Mexico City, buses to Tepoztlán run regularly from the Terminal de Sur and the Terminal Poniente. The trip takes an hour.

You can book round-trip transportation to the Mexico City airport through **Marquez Sightseeing Tours** (© 777/315-5875; www.tourbymexico.com/marqueztours) and some hotels. The round-trip is about $200 (£100).

EXPLORING TEPOZTLAN

Tepoztlán's **weekend folkloric market** is one of the best in central Mexico. More crafts are available on Saturdays and Sundays, but the market also opens on Wednesdays. Vendors sell all kinds of ceramics, from simple fired-clay works resembling those made with pre-Hispanic techniques, to the more commercial versions of majolica and pseudo-Talavera. There are also puppets, carved-wood figures, and some textiles, especially thick wool Mexican sweaters and jackets made out of *jerga* (a coarse cloth). Very popular currently is the "hippie"-style jewelry that earned Tepoztlán its fame in the '60s and '70s. The market is also remarkable for its variety of food stands selling fruits and vegetables, spices, fresh tortillas, and indigenous Mexican delicacies.

The other primary activity is hiking up to **Tepozteco pyramid.** The climb is steep and fairly strenuous, although perfectly doable in a few hours and not dangerous. In fact, you'll see folks across three generations doing the hike. Dense vegetation shades the trail (actually a long natural staircase), which is beautiful from bottom to top. Once you arrive at the pyramid you are treated to remarkable views and, if you are lucky, a great show by a family of *coatis* (tropical raccoons), who visit the pyramid most mornings to beg for food; they especially love bananas. The pyramid is a Tlahuica construction that predates the Náhuatl (Aztec) domination of the area. It was the site of important celebrations in the 12th and 13th centuries. The main street in Tepoztlán, Avenida 5 de Mayo, takes you to the path that leads you to the top of the Tepozteco. The 2km winding rock trail begins where the name of Avenida 5 de Mayo changes to Camino del Tepozteco. The hike takes about an hour each way, but if you stop and take in the scenery and really enjoy the trail, it can take up to 2 hours each way. Water and drinks are available at the top. The trail is open daily from 9am to 5:30pm and, while the hike is free, the pyramid costs $3 (£1.50) to enter.

Also worth visiting is the **former convent Dominico de la Navidad**. The entrance to the Dominican convent lies through the religious-themed "Gate of Tepoztlán," constructed with beads and seeds, just east of the main plaza. Built between 1560 and 1588, the convent is now a museum, open Tuesday through Sunday from 10am to 6pm; it $1 (50p) to enter.

SIGHTS NEAR TEPOZTLAN

Many nearby places are easily accessible by car. One good tour service is **Marquez Sightseeing Tours,** located in Cuernavaca (✆ 777/315-5875; www.tourbymexico. com/marqueztours). Marquez has four- and seven-passenger vehicles, very reasonable prices, and a large variety of set tours. The dependable owner, Arturo Marquez Diaz, speaks better-than-passable English and will allow you to design your own tour, including to archeological sites and museums. He also offers transportation to and from Mexico City airport for approximately $200 (£100).

Two tiny, charming villages, **Santo Domingo Xocotitlán** and **Amatlán**, are only a 20-minute drive from Tepoztlán and can be reached by minibuses, which depart regularly from the center of town. There is nothing much to do in these places except wander around absorbing the marvelous views of the Tepozteco Mountains and drinking in the magical ambience.

Las Grutas de Cacahuamilpa ✯, the Cacahuamilpa Caves or Grottoes, are an unforgettable system of caverns with a wooden illuminated walkway for easy access. As you pass from chamber to chamber you'll see spectacular illuminated rock formations, including stalactites, stalagmites, and twisted rock formations with names like Dante's head, the champagne bottle, the tortillas, and Madonna with child. Admission for 2 hours is $5 (£2.50); a guide for groups, which can be assembled on the hour, costs about $10 (£5). The caverns are open daily from 10am to 7pm (last tickets sold at 5pm), and lie 90 minutes from Tepoztlán and 30 minutes from Taxco.

About 50 minutes southeast of Tepoztlán is **Las Estacas,** an ecological resort with a cold-water spring that is said to have curative powers (p. 181). The ruins of **Xochicalco** (see "Cuernavaca," earlier in this chapter) and the colonial town of **Taxco** (earlier in this chapter) are easily accessible from Tepoztlán.

WHERE TO STAY

The town gets very busy on the weekends, so if your stay will include Friday or Saturday night, make reservations well in advance. In addition to the choices noted below, consider two other excellent options just outside of town. **Casa Bugambilia** ✯✯✯, Callejón de Tepopula 007, Valle de Atongo (✆ 739/395-0158; www.casabugambilia. com), is a nine-room hotel property 3km (2 miles) outside Tepoztlán. Don't confuse this hotel with Posada Bugambilia, a modest hotel in town. The spacious rooms are elegantly furnished with high-end, carved Mexican furniture, and every room has a fireplace. Doubles average $250 (£125) including breakfast. **Las Golondrinas** ✯✯✯, Callejón de Términas 4 (✆ 739/395-0649; http://homepage.mac.com/marisolfernandez/LasGolondrinas), is a three-bedroom B&B in the area behind Ixcatepec church; it's so far off the beaten track that even cab drivers have trouble finding the place. But owner Marisol Fernández has imbued the house with her tranquil, down-to-earth charm; the guest rooms open onto a wraparound terrace that overlooks the garden, a small pool, and the Tepozteco Mountains beyond. Doubles cost $135 (£68), including breakfast.

Moments **Tepoznieves: A Taste of Heaven**

Don't leave town without a stop at **Tepoznieves,** Av. 5 de Mayo 21 (© **739/395-3813;** www.tepoznieves.com.mx), the sublime local ice-cream shop. The store's slogan, *"nieve de dioses"* (ice cream of the gods), doesn't exaggerate. Almost 200 types of ice cream and sorbet, made only with natural ingredients, come in flavors familiar (vanilla, bubble gum), exotic (tamarind, rose petal, mango studded with *chile piquin*), and off-the-wall (beet, lettuce, corn). It's open daily 8am to 9pm.

Hotel Nilayam   Formerly Hotel Tepoztlán, this holistic-oriented retreat lies in a colonial building, but the decor has been brightened up considerably. Stays here encourage self-exploration: The gracious, helpful staff offers complete detox programs and a full array of services, including body and facial treatments, reflexology, hot stone and shiatsu massages, and yoga, Tai Chi, and meditation. The hotel has a great view of the mountain, and the restaurant features a creative menu of vegetarian cuisine. Spa packages are available.

Industrias 6, 62520 Tepoztlán, Mor. © **739/395-0522.** Fax 739/395-0522. www.nilayam.net. 34 units. $120 (£60) double. AE, MC, V. Free parking. **Amenities:** Restaurant; outdoor pool; spa services; private *temazcal* (pre-Hispanic sweat lodge). *In room:* TV.

Posada del Tepozteco ✿✿   This inviting inn has magnificent views overlooking the town and down the length of the spectacular valley. Rooms are tastefully furnished in colonial style. All but the least expensive feature terraces with superb views, and the suites have small whirlpool tubs. The intimate restaurant focuses on healthy and vegetarian dishes. The grounds are exquisitely landscaped, and the atmosphere is intimate and romantic. The hotel reception will arrange in-room massages, and the hotel has a traditional *temazcal* with herbal healing properties. Most rates include breakfast.

Paraíso 3 (2 blocks straight up the hill from the town center), 62520 Tepoztlán, Mor. © **739/395-0010.** Fax 739/395-0323. www.posadadeltepozteco.com. 22 units. $180–$210 (£90–£105) double; $260–$370 (£130–£185) suite. MC, V. Free parking. **Amenities:** Restaurant w/stunning view; small outdoor pool. *In room:* Hair dryer, safe, no phone.

WHERE TO DINE

In addition to the two choices listed below, El Chalchi restaurant at the **Hotel Nilayam** (see above) offers some of the best vegetarian fare in the area. It's 3 blocks from the main square, with main courses priced around $6 (£3).

El Ciruelo Restaurant Bar ✿✿✿ GOURMET MEXICAN   This longstanding favorite boasts beautiful flowering gardens set amid the striking backdrop of the Tepoztlán mountains. The large courtyard is filled with lush potted foliage and topped by a soaring band shell meant to keep patrons dry without obscuring the fantastic view. The service is positively charming, and the regional food is divine. The fish tacos *Ensenada*-style are the best I've ever tasted. House specialties include cilantro soup with almonds, *chalupas* of goat cheese, chicken with *huitlacoche*, and a regional treat: milk-based gelatin with brown sugar. Try to get a seat on the outdoor patio, where a trio often serenades the crowd.

Zaragoza 17, Barrio de la Santísima, in front of the church. © **739/395-1203.** Dinner $6–$20 (£3–£10). AE. Sun 1–7pm; Mon–Thurs 1–6pm; Fri–Sat 1–11pm.

Restaurant Axitla ★★ *Finds* GOURMET MEXICAN/INTERNATIONAL
Axitla is not only the best restaurant in Tepoztlán, but it's also one of the finest in
Mexico for showcasing the country's cuisine. Gourmet Mexican delicacies are made
from scratch using the freshest local ingredients. Specialties include chicken breast
stuffed with wild mushrooms in a chipotle chile sauce, *chiles en nogada,* pepper steak,
grilled octopus, *chile Jarral* (stuffed chili with meat in an avocado sauce), and exceptional *mole.* There are also excellent steaks and fresh seafood. And, if the food isn't
enough—and believe me, it is—the enchanted setting will make your meal even more
memorable. The restaurant lies at the base of the Tepozteco Pyramid (about a 10-
minute walk from the town center), surrounded by 1.2 hectares (about 3 acres) of junglelike gardens that encompass a creek and lily ponds. The views of the Tepozteco
Mountains are magnificent. Memo and Laura, the gracious owners, speak excellent
English and are marvelous sources of information about the area.

Av. del Tepozteco, at the foot of the trail to the pyramid. ✆ **739/395-0519.** Lunch and dinner $8–$15 (£4–£7.50).
MC, V. Wed–Sun 10am–7pm.

7

San Miguel de Allende & the Colonial Silver Cities

by David Baird

Mexico's colonial silver-mining cities— San Miguel, Querétaro, San Luis Potosí, Guanajuato, and Zacatecas—lie northwest of Mexico City in the rugged mountains of the Sierra Madre Occidental. These cities have colonial settings with backdrops of rugged mountains, an ideal climate, local handicrafts, good food, and many memorable vistas.

San Miguel de Allende is the smallest of the cities. Its cobblestone streets and fanciful church set it apart from the rest, as do its numerous restaurants and interesting shops. For many years it has supported a resident population of artists, writers, and expatriates. **Guanajuato** and **Zacatecas,** with their winding streets and alleys and their small, oddly shaped plazas, seem more like medieval towns than products of the Renaissance. In contrast, **Querétaro** and **San Luis Potosí** have stately colonial centers with broad plazas and monumental civil and religious architecture.

Travel through these parts is easy and relaxing; there is little crime, and the inhabitants are gracious. The region is a good introduction to Mexico's interior and is well suited for a family vacation. All Mexicans, but especially those in this region, are family-oriented and warm up quickly when they see a family traveling together.

The colonial silver cities are close to the Mexican capital by modern standards, but at the time of their founding, this land was the frontier. In pre-Columbian times, the great civilizations of central Mexico never established more than a tenuous sway here. Mountainous and arid, this was the land of the Chichimeca, a large nation of nomadic tribes that occasionally banded together for raids upon their civilized neighbors to the south. After the Spanish conquest of the Aztec empire in 1521, the conquistadors turned their attention to this region in search of precious metals. The Chichimecans resisted the encroachers, but epidemic diseases brought from Europe soon decimated the native population. The Spanish established mining cities in quick succession, stretching from Querétaro (established in 1531) north all the way to Zacatecas (1548) and beyond. They found quantities of gold, but silver proved so plentiful that it made Mexico world famous as a land of riches.

For 3 centuries of colonial rule, much of the mines' great wealth went to build urban centers of impressive, enduring architecture. It's wonderful to stroll through these cities and view them, not one building at a time, but in broad views of colonial cityscapes. Of the five cities, three (Guanajuato, Querétaro, and

Zacatecas) have been designated World Heritage Sites by UNESCO.

Life remains civilized here; it is savored and enjoyed at a relaxed pace. Many people have ancestors who lived here at least a century ago. They maintain a broad network of kinfolk, friends, and acquaintances. I've walked down streets with locals who would greet every third or fourth person we passed. Often, I've had conversations in which I mention someone from a completely different context, only to hear something like, "Oh, he's married to my cousin." This is the kind of intimate and close-knit world you enter when visiting these cities.

EXPLORING THE SILVER CITIES

There are two common ways to get here: Fly into Mexico City and take the bus that goes directly from the airport to Querétaro, or fly into the León/Guanajuato airport.

Zacatecas, San Luis Potosí, and Querétaro also have international airports that receive a few flights from the U.S. You can also get to this region by car or bus on one of the superhighways that run from the U.S. border. From Texas, the first of the silver cities you reach will be San Luis Potosí (which, by the way, bills itself to the rest of Mexico as the "Gateway to the United States").

Once in the region, you'll find the roads are good, but not great, and the smaller ones are poorly marked. Driving within these towns can be maddening due to convoluted, narrow streets and bizarre traffic routing (especially in Guanajuato and Zacatecas). If you ever have difficulty navigating into the center of town, simply hail a cab to lead the way. Parking can also be a problem; we have included, when possible, good motels where you can park and leave your car for the length of your visit. If you prefer to travel by bus, you'll find frequent, inexpensive first-class buses connecting all these cities, which are only a few hours apart from each other.

The region has a short rainy season from June through September, which is a good time to come. I also like late fall, winter, and early spring. The hottest month is May (and sometimes early June before the rains arrive). May can also be smoky because it's when many farmers burn the stubble in their corn fields before the next planting. As to how and where to spend your time, much depends on your interests. If your chief goal is to relax and enjoy the good life, spend more time in San Miguel. If it is to be active and do some exploring, spend more time in Guanajuato and Zacatecas. If you're already comfortable running around Mexico and are looking for cultural immersion, I would point you to Querétaro and San Luis Potosí. But whichever cities you elect to visit, I recommend a stay of at least 3 days per destination—a good part of their charm will go unappreciated if you're pressing too much to see everything.

1 San Miguel de Allende ✶✶✶

288km (179 miles) NW of Mexico City; 120km (74 miles) E of Guanajuato; 64km (40 miles) NW of Querétaro

San Miguel de Allende mixes the best aspects of small-town life with the cosmopolitan pleasures of a big city. It is the smallest of the cities covered here and perhaps the most relaxed; its wide variety of restaurants, shops, and galleries makes urbanites feel quite at home. Most of the buildings in the central part of the town date from the Colonial Era or the 19th century; the law requires newer buildings to conform to existing architecture, and the town has gone to some lengths to retain its cobblestone streets.

Living in San Miguel is a large community of Americans: some retired, some attending art or language school, and some who have come here to live simply and follow their creative muses—painting, writing, and sculpting. The center of this community is the public library in the former convent of Santa Ana. It is a good place to find information on San Miguel or just to sit in the patio and read.

A notable aspect of San Migueleña society is the number of festivals it celebrates. In a country that needs only the barest of excuses to hold a fiesta, it is known far and wide for them. Most of these celebrations are of a religious character and are meant to combine social activity with religious expression. People practice Catholicism with great fervor—going on religious pilgrimages, attending all-night vigils, ringing church bells at the oddest times throughout the night (something that some visitors admittedly might not find so amusing). See "Special Events & Festivals," below.

Where to Stay in San Miguel de Allende

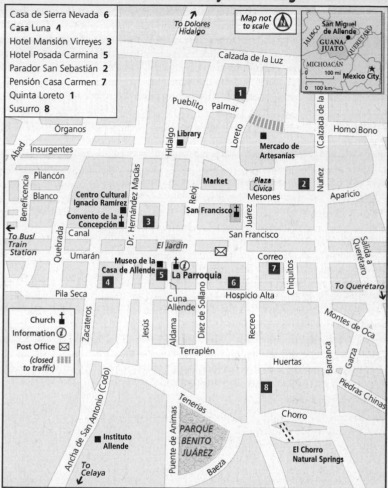

Casa de Sierra Nevada **6**
Casa Luna **4**
Hotel Mansión Virreyes **3**
Hotel Posada Carmina **5**
Parador San Sebastián **2**
Pensión Casa Carmen **7**
Quinta Loreto **1**
Susurro **8**

Map not to scale

San Miguel de Allende
JALISCO
GUANAJUATO
QUERÉTARO
MICHOACÁN
0   100 mi   Mexico City ★
0   100 km

To Dolores Hidalgo

Calzada de la Luz

Órganos
Abad
Insurgentes
Pilancón
Beneficencia
Blanco
Centro Cultural Ignacio Ramírez
Convento de la Concepción
To Bus/ Train Station
Canal
Quebrada
Umarán
Pila Seca
Zacateros
Jesús
Aldama
Pueblito Palmar
Hidalgo
Library
Loreto
Dr. Hernández Macías
Reloj
Juárez
Market
San Francisco
El Jardin
Museo de la Casa de Allende
La Parroquia
Cuna Allende
Diez de Sollano
Terraplén
Mercado de Artesanías
Plaza Cívica
Mesones
San Francisco
Correo
Hospicio Alta
Homo Bono
Nuñez
Aparicio
Chiquitos
Recreo
Huertas
Barranca
Garza
Montes de Oca
Piedras Chinas
To Querétaro
Salida a Querétaro
(Calzada de la

Church †
Information ⓘ
Post Office ✉
(closed to traffic)

Ancha de San Antonio (Codo)
Instituto Allende
To Celaya
Puente de Animas
Tenerias
PARQUE BENITO JUÁREZ
Baeza
Chorro
El Chorro Natural Springs

ESSENTIALS

GETTING THERE & DEPARTING   By Plane   The two major airports are the Mexico City airport, 3½ hours away (and has direct bus transportation to nearby Querétaro); and the León/Guanajuato airport, 1½ hours away.

By Car   You have a choice of two routes for the 3½-hour trip from Mexico City—a Querétaro bypass or via Celaya. The former is shorter—take Highway 57, a four-lane freeway, north toward Querétaro. Past the Tequisquiapan turnoff is an exit on the right marked A SAN MIGUEL. This toll road bypasses Querétaro and crosses Highway 57 again north of town. Here it narrows to two lanes and becomes Highway 111. Some 30km (20 miles) farther is San Miguel.

From Guanajuato, the quick route is to go south from the city a short distance on Highway 110, then east on a secondary, paved road passing near the village of Joconoxtle. For the long but scenic route, which passes through Dolores Hidalgo, go northeast on Highway 110 through Dolores, then south on Highway 51. If you drive this route, take a break and experience a slice of rural Mexican life near the small community of Santa Rosa, where a few restaurants serve the local *mezcal de la sierra*, a locally distilled firewater that makes tequila taste positively smooth.

By Bus   From Mexico City airport: AeroPlus buses (© **55/5786-9357**) leave directly from the airport for Querétaro about every half-hour and cost $23 (£12). They leave from outside Gate E-2. Getting there is a little confusing, and the signs don't help much. When you get to the E-2 area take the ramp or elevator up one floor and walk down a concourse that crosses over the passenger pickup area. At the end of the concourse are the ticketing booths for the different buses. Buy your ticket there, then take the elevator down to the ground floor.

From Mexico City's Central del Norte: First-class buses take 4 hours (with one stop in Querétaro). The company ETN has the best service, with wide seats that recline far back (four buses per day). Primera Plus has two buses per day. Regular service is handled by Flecha Amarilla with buses leaving every 40 minutes. Another option is to take a bus to Querétaro and change buses.

From Querétaro: Local buses run to San Miguel every 20 minutes (Flecha Amarilla and Herradura de Plata have alternating departures). If you arrive in Querétaro by first-class bus, you'll be in Terminal A. Go out the door, turn right, and walk to Terminal B.

From Guanajuato: ETN has three nonstop superdeluxe buses per day. Primera Plus/Servicios Coordinados has four nonstop buses per day.

To/from Laredo and Nuevo Laredo: Four companies offer an overnight first-class bus to/from Laredo or Nuevo Laredo: **Autobuses Americanos** (© **415/154-8233** or www.autobusesamericanos.com.mx) crosses the border to Laredo, Texas; **Futura** (© **415/152-2237**), **Primera Plus** (© **01-800/375-7587** in Mexico), and **Omnibus de México** (© **01-800/765-6636** in Mexico or www.odm.com.mx) go to Nuevo Laredo. The trip takes 12 hours and costs around $65 (£33). From San Miguel there is one departure per day per company. The four buses leave San Miguel between 6 and 7pm. Departure times from Laredo and Nuevo Laredo are also around 6 or 7pm.

The **bus station** in San Miguel is 2km (1½ miles) west of town on the westward extension of Calle Canal. Taxis to town are cheap ($3/£1.50) and available at all hours.

VISITOR INFORMATION   The city's tourist information office is in the *ayuntamiento* (city hall) facing El Jardín. The address is Plaza Principal 8, and the phone is © **415/152-0900.** Office hours are Monday through Friday from 8:30am to 8pm, Saturday from 10am to 8pm, and Sunday from 10am to 5:30pm.

CITY LAYOUT   Carefully pruned Indian laurel trees shade San Miguel's central square, **El Jardín.** The center of city life, El Jardín is the point of reference for all places in the middle of town and is bounded by Correo (Post Office St.), San Francisco, Hidalgo, and Reloj.

GETTING AROUND   Most places in San Miguel are within walking distance, so a car isn't necessary. Buses to outlying villages (La Taboada thermal pool, for example) leave from the little plaza by the *mercado*. Taxis to places inside town should not cost more than $3 (£1.50), unless ordered from a hotel.

FAST FACTS: San Miguel de Allende

American Express The local representative is **Viajes Vértiz,** Hidalgo 1 (ⓒ 415/152-1856; fax 415/152-0499), open Monday through Friday from 9am to 2pm and 5pm, Saturday from 10am to 2pm.

Area Code The telephone area code is **415.**

Climate San Miguel can be warm in summer and cold enough for wool clothing in winter, especially at night or during the occasional cold spell.

Communication & Shipping Services Several services offer packing and shipping, mail boxes, telephone messages, long distance, and the like. One is **Border Crossings,** Mesones 57, Loc. 6 (ⓒ **415/152-2497;** fax 415/152-3672); and **Pack 'n' Mail** is at Calle Canal 42 (ⓒ/fax **415/152-3191**). Both keep standard office hours: weekdays from 9 or 10am to 6pm, Saturday from 10am to 2pm.

Consular Office It's located at Hernández Macías 72, Int. 111. (ⓒ **415/152-2357**). Hours are Monday to Friday from 9am to 1pm.

Currency Exchange **Intercam** has three locations: Juárez 27, San Francisco 4, and Correo 15. Business hours are Monday through Friday from 9am to 6pm, Saturday from 9am to 2pm. **Dicambio** has three locations: Correo 3, Juárez 1, and Puente Umarán 16. Hours are Monday through Friday from 9am to 4pm, Saturday from 9am to 2pm, and Sunday from 10am to 2pm. Several banks have cash machines, including one on the corner of the Jardín in the Casa del Conde, and a few on Calle San Francisco.

Drugstore Try the **Farmacia Agundis** (ⓒ **415/152-1198**), Canal 24 at Macías. It's open daily from 10am to 1am.

Elevation San Miguel sits at 1,862m (6,107 ft.).

Internet Access Several places offer Internet access around town. These businesses come and go so fast it's not worth listing them. Ask at your hotel for the nearest cybercafe.

Library The **Biblioteca Pública (Public Library),** Insurgentes 25 (ⓒ **415/152-0293**), is a social institution for the American community. It has a good selection of books in Spanish and English. Hours are Monday through Friday from 10am to 2pm and 4 to 7pm, and Saturday from 10am to 2pm.

Newspaper An English-language paper, **Atención,** carries local news as well as full listings of what to see and do.

Parking San Miguel is congested, and street parking is scarce. A white pole or sign at the end of a street marks the stopping point for parking (so that other cars can make a turn). Police are vigilant about parking and ticket with glee.

Population San Miguel has 130,000 residents.

Post Office The *correo,* Calle Correo 16, is open Monday through Friday from 9am to 2pm for all services (and sells stamps until 5pm), Saturday from 9am to 1pm.

Seasons Because of the fast freeway access from Mexico City, San Miguel is popular with weekenders from the capital. Arrive early on Friday or make a reservation ahead of time for weekends, especially long weekends. There's also a squeeze on rooms around the Christmas and Easter holidays and around the feast of San Miguel's patron saint, on September 29.

SPECIAL EVENTS & FESTIVALS

San Miguel celebrates 30 to 40 festivals a year. These are just the standouts: January 17 is the **Blessing of the Animals.** In the morning, locals bring their decorated pets and farm animals to the town's churches to be doused with holy water. The first Friday in March celebrates **Our Lord of the Conquest,** and the day before is filled with music, fireworks, and decorated teams of oxen. After a celebratory Mass, there is dancing by the *concheros* (traditional Aztec dancers). Two weeks before Holy Week is the procession of **Our Lord of the Column.** Between then and Easter Sunday there are more processions, and altars are set up in honor of **La Virgen Dolorosa.** In May is the **Festival of the Holy Cross.** In June, around Saint Anthony's Day, is the **Fiesta de los Locos (Festival of the Madmen)** 𝕲𝕲, when many dress up in carnavalesque costumes and go cavorting about the center of town. August begins the preparatory festivals for September 29, the festival of San Miguel's **patron saint.** Parades, fireworks, and band concerts continue throughout September. Traditionally a *pamplonada* (running of the bulls) was held as part of the festivities, but last year it was moved to Irapuato because it was attracting too rough a crowd. At the beginning of November is the **Day of the Dead,** followed by the **Christmas fiestas.** In addition to all of this, you have the **Chamber Music Festival** in summer, **Jazz Music Festival** in the fall, and a couple of arts fairs that occur on varying dates.

EXPLORING SAN MIGUEL

It's hard to be bored in San Miguel. The shopping is excellent, and you'll run out of time before you can try all the restaurants. The town is well situated for side trips to Dolores Hidalgo, Querétaro, and Guanajuato. It's popular for Spanish and art classes.

The colonial architecture tends more toward domestic than monumental and offers much to see—fine courtyards, beautiful interiors, and rich architectural details. Of particular note are the town's lovely streetscapes with narrow cobblestone lanes that invite aimless strolling and make it advisable to wear walking shoes with thick soles.

THE TOP ATTRACTIONS

Centro Cultural Ignacio Ramírez (Bellas Artes/El Nigromante)   Housed in the former Convento de la Concepción (1755), 2 blocks west of El Jardín, the Centro is a branch of the Palacio de Bellas Artes of Mexico City. The two-story cloister, surrounding an enormous courtyard with large trees and a gurgling fountain, houses art exhibits and classrooms for drawing, painting, sculpture, lithography, textiles, ceramics, dramatic arts, ballet, regional dance, piano, and guitar. A mural by David Alfaro Siqueiros and some of his memorabilia are worth seeing. A bulletin board lists concerts and lectures at this institute and elsewhere in the city. You can also dine in these pleasant surroundings at the restaurant **Las Musas,** which serves pasta dishes, salads, sandwiches, and desserts. Before you leave, take a look at the magnificent dome behind the convent. It belongs to the Iglesia de la Concepción and was designed by the same unschooled architect who designed the Parroquia (see below).

Hernández Macías 75 (between Canal and Insurgentes). ℂ 415/152-0289. Free admission. Mon–Fri 10am–5:30pm; Sat 10am–2pm.

La Parroquia 𝕲𝕲𝕲   Looking nothing like any other church in Mexico, La Parroquia has become the emblem of San Miguel. It is an object of great pride for the

Learning at the Source: Going to School in San Miguel

San Miguel has several schools for learning Spanish. If you're wishing to take classes, shop around before you travel to San Miguel to find one that's a good fit for you. These schools cater to travelers and often can provide a list of apartments for long-term stays.

Instituto Allende, Calle Ancha de San Antonio 20, 37700 San Miguel de Allende, Gto. (© **415/152-0190;** www.instituto-allende.edu.mx), began in 1950 as a fine arts school and later added Spanish courses. The main focus is still on the arts, with different classes and workshops offered throughout the year. Spanish students have the option of group and individual classes, short- and long-term. The school's credits are transferable to many colleges and universities in the United States and Canada; noncredit students are also welcome.

LanguagePoint, 20 de Enero Sur 42, 37750 San Miguel de Allende, Gto. (© **415/152-4115;** www.languagepoint.org), offers instruction and immersion at all levels of competency. With a maximum of three students per instructor, students get a lot of individual attention, and the teaching method leans heavily toward conversation. Emphasis at the basic level is on gaining a working knowledge of everyday Spanish as a basis for further development of language skills.

Warren Hardy Spanish, San Rafael 6, 37700 San Miguel de Allende, Gto. (© **415/154-4017;** www.warrenhardy.com), is a popular school for those who know little Spanish. Emphasis is on the spoken language, with special focus on the use of verbs. Mr. Hardy has taught Spanish for many years and has designed his own methodology for teaching it, which involves partnering students and using a lot of flash cards. It's best to contact the school through its website. Mr. Hardy's wife, Tuli, answers questions and handles registration.

Academia Hispano Americana, Mesones 4 (Apdo. Postal 150), 37700 San Miguel de Allende, Gto. (© **415/152-0349;** www.ahaspeakspanish.com), has a reputation for offering an intensive language course with an emphasis on grammar as well as conversation. Classes are limited to 12 people and are much smaller than that on average. The school has a continuous program of study of 12 4-week sessions for 35 hours a week. Less intensive courses and private lessons are also available. It's a member of the International Association of Language Centers.

Habla Hispana, Calzada de la Luz 25, 37700 San Miguel de Allende, Gto. (© **451/152-1535;** www.mexicospanish.com), is a small school with four experienced and dedicated instructors, all locals. Classes are arranged in four-week courses. Class size is limited to 10 students. The school likes to combine a personal touch with a clearly structured teaching program.

citizenry and a source of discomfort for architectural purists. Originally built in the colonial style, the church was remade in the late 19th century by a local builder named Zeferino Gutiérrez, who reconstructed the towers and facade. Gutiérrez was supposedly unlettered but had seen pictures of Europe's Gothic churches and worked from these alone. I find the finished product fascinating—a very personal vision of the Gothic style that owes more to the builder's imagination and fancy than to the European churches that were its inspiration. The inside is not nearly so much fun as the outside; the church was looted on several occasions during times of social upheaval, and this kind of art criticism puts a damper on commissioning more paintings and decoration. Still, there are things to see. My favorite, and one often missed, is the crypt beneath the altar. You get to it through a door on the right side. You'll have to seek out the caretaker, who can unlock the door (for a small tip).

South side of El Jardín. No phone. Free admission. Daily 8am–2pm and 5–9pm.

Museo Casa de Allende   The house of San Miguel's most famous son and namesake, the independence leader Ignacio Allende, is a museum. It is of the genre known as *museos regionales* that you will find across Mexico. The objective of these museums is to present a view of the local area from prehistoric times to recent history; to explain what roles the region played in the context of national development; and to give some idea of how the great historical movements that swept across Mexico ran their courses at the local level. Featured is a small biographical exhibit on Allende as one of the initiators of the independence movement, which began in nearby Dolores Hidalgo, and on what national independence meant for San Miguel and the local area. Explanations are in Spanish only, but the artifacts—including fossils, pre-Hispanic pottery, Colonial-Era furnishings, and articles of daily life—and the beauty of the house are worth the price. On my last visit, the museum was closed for renovation but should be open by late 2008.

Southwest corner of El Jardín. No phone. Admission $3.50. Tues–Sun 9am–5pm.

MORE ATTRACTIONS

The **House and Garden Tour** 🌟🌟, sponsored by the Biblioteca Pública, is universally enjoyed. The tour opens the doors of some of the city's most interesting colonial and contemporary houses. Tours leave Sunday at 11:30am from the library, Insurgentes 25 (© **415/152-0293**), and last about 2 hours. A $15 (£7.50) donation goes to support various library projects benefiting the youth of San Miguel.

Bill Levasseur of Casa de la Cuesta Bed and Breakfast has recently opened a mask museum called **La Otra Cara de México (The Other Face of Mexico)** 🌟🌟. It's a thoughtfully arranged exhibition of masks that provides a lot of cultural context. Masks have played an important role in many of Mexico's native cultures, usually as part of a dance or ritual. Over the years Bill has collected some great pieces and has filmed dances and performances in which the masks were used. This museum is a treat for serious collectors and casual travelers. Visits are by appointment (© **415/154-4324**).

A couple of the most enjoyable walks in town are to the lookout point **El Mirador,** especially at sunset, which colors the entire town and the lake beyond, and to **Parque Juárez,** a large and shady park.

NEARBY ATTRACTIONS

Just outside of San Miguel are several hot mineral springs that have been made into bathing spots. They're all just off the road leading to Dolores Hidalgo. **La Taboada,**

La Gruta, and Escondido lie close to one another, just 8km to 10km (5–6 miles) outside San Miguel. La Gruta is perhaps the nicest, but La Taboada has a quiet, old hotel reminiscent of an earlier Mexico and makes for a relaxing stay.

Near these hot springs is the sanctuary of Atotonilco el Grande, a complex of chapels, dormitories, dining rooms, and a church. World Monuments Watch ranks the church among the most important buildings meriting preservation. Father Luis Felipe Neri Alfaro, an austere mystic, founded the church in 1740. He thought the area in dire need of a religious presence, as many people would gather at the thermal springs to bathe publicly and, in his eyes, licentiously. He commissioned a local artist, Martínez Pocasangre, to paint murals illustrating the instructive verses that Alfaro wrote with much emphasis on the dangers lying in wait for the human soul. The murals and verses cover the church's ceiling and walls. They add brightness and color to an otherwise dark and severe structure.

Father Alfaro built his sanctuary on the spot where he was granted an ecstatic vision of Christ. The location proved providential: 70 years later, when the Spanish authorities uncovered a plot to liberate Mexico that implicated Father Miguel Hidalgo, he was in the town of Dolores. Warned of the danger, he hastily declared independence and marched his impromptu army toward San Miguel. En route, he stopped at Atotonilco where he took the church's image of the Virgin of Guadalupe as his banner, declaring her the protector of the new nation—the first time that she was officially recognized as such.

The church and adjoining buildings still function throughout the year as a religious retreat for people who come from all over the country for a week of prayer, penance, and mortification. These spiritual exercises are conducted in private, with no public display. You can get to Atotonilco by cab or via the bus marked EL SANTUARIO, at the market. It passes every hour on the hour, and goes through Taboada on its way to Atotonilco.

SHOPPING

San Miguel is a town of artists; you'll find art for sale not only in galleries but also in restaurants, offices, and just about anywhere there's space in a public area. San Miguel is also a town of artisans working mainly with clay, iron, brass, tin, blown glass, and papier-mâché. And San Miguel is a town of shopkeepers who sell locally produced items as well as folk art and decorative objects from across Mexico. There are so many stores, and they are so different from each other, that a list would not be helpful. The best advice I can give is to explore the streets around the main square. If you're looking for something in particular, ask around. One place that's easily walkable but a bit outside the downtown area is Fábrica La Aurora, an old textile mill that's been converted into galleries and shops selling art, furnishings, and antiques. The old factory is an attractive space, with lots of open areas, and includes a restaurant and a cafe. It's a bit north of downtown on Calzada de La Aurora, just past the bridge.

Stores are usually open Monday through Saturday from 9am to 2pm and 4 to 7 or 8pm. Most stores close on Sunday. If you're interested in Talavera pottery, consider going to nearby Dolores Hidalgo (see "A Side Trip to Dolores Hidalgo: Fine Pottery & Shrimp Ice Cream," later in this chapter). Also, you can find some handicrafts and fun knickknacks at the Mercado de Artesanías (handicrafts market), but it will require hunting through lots of goods that are either too tacky or not tacky enough. The *mercado* occupies a walkway 3 blocks long that descends from the municipal market past the Hotel Quinta Loreto.

WHERE TO STAY

For longer stays, you might check with the language schools (see "Learning at the Source: Going to School in San Miguel," above) and other bulletin boards around town for lists of apartments or rooms to rent, or check websites such as **www. internetsanmiguel.com** or **www.infosma.com**. Most apartments have kitchens and bedding; some come with maid service. San Miguel is a popular weekend getaway for residents of the capital, and several hotels raise rates on weekends. Secured parking is at a premium; if your hotel doesn't provide it, you'll pay around $12 to $16 (£6–£8) daily in a guarded lot. Most places can arrange airport transportation. The rates listed below already include taxes, which are 17%.

VERY EXPENSIVE

Casa de Sierra Nevada *ƘƘ* The hotel consists of several 16th-century town houses on a couple of streets just above El Jardín and a second grouping bordering Parque Juárez. With picturesque terraces and courtyards bedecked in flowers and plants, some affording charming views and considerable privacy, this place feels like a true getaway from the modern world. The owner, Orient Express, continues doing major remodeling to some of the townhouses in the main part of the hotel. I'm told that these improvements will include climate control. Rooms and suites vary in shape and design; most are very large and have private patios or secluded entrances and working fireplaces. The hotel is 2 blocks southeast of El Jardín. Transportation from either airport is available.

Hospicio 35 (between Diez de Sollano and Recreo), 37700 San Miguel de Allende, Gto. ℂ 800/701-1561 in the U.S. and Canada, or 415/152-7040. Fax 415/154-9703. www.casadesierranevada.com. 33 units. $375 (£188) deluxe; $435 (£218) junior suite; $450 and up (£225 and up) suite. AE, MC, V. Free valet parking. Children younger than 16 not accepted. **Amenities:** 2 restaurants; 2 bars; large outdoor heated pool; spa; concierge; tour and activities desk; room service; laundry service; dry cleaning. *In room:* TV, hair dryer, safe.

La Puertecita Boutique Hotel *ƘƘ* *(Kids)* Those who can't find the charm in church bells and firecrackers going off at all hours of the night will appreciate this hotel, as will those who are traveling with children. Set on the side of a narrow canyon, the hotel is above and a little removed from the central part of town. A fence surrounds the grounds, with terraced gardens and the ruined remains of an aqueduct for a touch of local character. Rooms, especially deluxe units and suites, are large; many have vaulted brick ceilings, small terraces, and beautifully tiled large bathrooms. They are decorated in modern Mexican style. The junior and one-bedroom suites have living areas and, in some cases, a dining area for four. Six suites have kitchenettes. The two-bedroom suites are the equivalent of a one-bedroom suite with a deluxe room attached.

Santo Domingo 75, 37740 San Miguel de Allende, Gto. ℂ 415/152-5011. Fax 415/152-5505. www.lapuertecita. com. 32 units. $266–$293 (£133–£147) deluxe and junior suite; $324 (£162) 1-bdrm suite; $585 (£293) and up for 2- and 3-bedroom suites. AE, MC, V. Free guarded parking. **Amenities:** Restaurant; bar; 2 small outdoor pools (1 heated); golf and tennis at local club; exercise equipment; outdoor whirlpool; game room; concierge; tour desk; courtesy car; room service; in-room massage; babysitting; laundry service; dry cleaning; nonsmoking rooms. *In room:* TV, hair dryer, safe.

EXPENSIVE

Casa de la Cuesta *ƘƘƘ* In an upper *barrio* (neighborhood) stands this magnificent house, an example of how colonial architecture can be rethought in modern terms. The combined effect of architecture and location is dramatic. The entrance to the house is through a passage that opens up to the first of two courtyards. On three sides are structures of different heights, which make use, wherever possible, of rooftop terraces. In one of these structures is a studio and gallery, which the owners (who are art dealers) use for shows or workspace. Guest rooms encircle the arcaded rear courtyard, with a lot of terraces and common space, much of which has a fine view of the central part of town. Rooms are large and comfortable, with king-size beds, lots of color and detail, and a mix of modern and colonial furnishings. The house is about a 10-minute walk to the center of town, and the return is uphill. Breakfasts are great, and the hosts, Heidi and Bill Levasseur, are helpful and entertaining.

Cuesta de San José 32, 37700 San Miguel de Allende, Gto. (C)/fax **415/154-4324.** www.casadelacuesta.com. 6 units. $140–$160 (£70–£80) double. Rates include full breakfast. MC, V (for deposits). Limited street parking. **Amenities:** In-room massage; laundry service; nonsmoking rooms. *In room:* No phone.

Casa Luna Pila Seca/Casa Luna Quebrada ★★★
Casa Luna Pila Seca and Casa Luna Quebrada are both striking to look at and fun to stay in. Both are just a few blocks below the main square. The house on Calle Quebrada is a large property, enjoys lots of open space, and is designed in the hacienda style. The original house on Pila Seca is more playful and has lovely nooks and crannies and riotous vegetation. Guest rooms in both houses are roughly the same in size and amenities. They are great fun—lots of color, lots of detail. Most have some Mexican theme but not exclusively. The owner, Dianne Kushner, has a real talent for bringing together disparate design elements and making them look like they naturally belong together. Most rooms are large and come with a king bed or two twins, down comforters, gas fireplaces, and large bathrooms with shower/tub combinations. Most have private patios. The common areas are lovely and relaxing and get you right into that *mañana* attitude. Breakfasts are delicious, and cooking classes are sometimes offered.

Pila Seca 11, 37700 San Miguel de Allende, Gto. (C) **210/200-8758** or 415/152-1117. www.casaluna.com. 25 units. $135–$165 (£68–£83) double. Rates include full breakfast. MC, V (for deposits). Children younger than 16 not accepted. Limited street parking. **Amenities:** Bar; outdoor pool at Quebrada house; Jacuzzi; tour information; massage; nonsmoking rooms; Wi-Fi. *In room:* Hair dryer, safe, no phone.

Susurro ★★★ (Finds)
Spend any amount of time in places like San Miguel or Cuernavaca, and you realize that the domestic architecture is all about the creation of serene, private spaces. Susurro (which in Spanish describes the sound made by whispering wind and trickling water) has elegant interior spaces, and with only four guest rooms, you'll find plenty of time to enjoy these all to yourself. The soft sounds of flowing water can be heard all around the house. Three of the rooms are large and come with separate terraces. The fourth, the garden room, has now been enlarged and has a lovely patio area in the rear garden. All rooms are beautifully decorated, with either a queen or a king bed. The house is a few blocks from the main square. Robert Waters, the owner, is an easy-going, agreeable man who makes an excellent host.

Recreo 78, 37700 San Miguel de Allende, Gto. (C) **310/943-7163** or 415/152-1065. www.susurro.com.mx. 4 units. $155–$190 (£78–£95) double. Rates include full breakfast. AE, MC, V for deposits only. Children younger than 13 not accepted. Limited street parking. **Amenities:** Plunge pool; in-room massage; laundry service; nonsmoking rooms; computer access; Wi-Fi in half the property. *In room:* TV, hair dryer, no phone.

MODERATE
Hotel Mansión Virreyes
Soon after the Mexican Revolution ended, this became the first hotel in San Miguel. The rooms are simply furnished, but comfortable. Almost all face the interior courtyard. Half are carpeted, half are tiled. Bathrooms are small to medium. On the top floor are three suites, which are quite large and come with kitchenettes. These are usually rented out from January to March.

Canal 19, 37700 San Miguel de Allende, Gto. © 415/152-3355, -0851. Fax 415/152-3865. mansionvirreyes@ prodigy.net.mx. 23 units. Fri–Sun $105 (£53) double, $176 (£88) suite; Mon–Thurs $95 (£48) double; $165 (£83) suite. Rates include full breakfast. AE, MC, V. Free secure parking 4 blocks away. **Amenities:** Restaurant; bar; room service. *In room:* TV, hair dryer.

Hotel Posada Carmina ✹ This centrally located hotel is comfortable, beautiful, and well-managed. It's a half-block south of the plaza, next to the Parroquia, in a large colonial mansion made from the same stone as the church. The two floors of rooms surround a stately courtyard with orange trees growing around a stone fountain, and bougainvillea and *llamarada* creeping up the walls. Rooms are ample and well furnished. Most of the bathrooms are comfortably sized but simple, with small mirrors (and, in some, little counter space) and plenty of hot water. Light sleepers will find that the bells of the Parroquia prove a nuisance in the front rooms. The new section in back is quieter. Rooms there are midsize with well-lit bathrooms and firm mattresses.

Cuna de Allende 7, 37700 San Miguel de Allende, Gto. © 415/152-0458. Fax 415/152-1036. www.posadacarmina.com. 24 units. $130–$140 (£65–£70) double. Rates include full breakfast. MC, V. Limited street parking. **Amenities:** Restaurant; room service. *In room:* TV.

Pensión Casa Carmen ✹ Every B&B has its own feel, and this one feels like a friendly Mexican household. A pretty little Mexican patio with orange trees and a fountain; large rooms that are comfortably but simply furnished; and a gracious, helpful landlady who speaks English—all help set you at ease. All rooms have gas heaters and come with either two twins or one queen-size bed. Of these, the penthouse is perhaps the most comfortable, but the ones in the first courtyard have the most character. Bathrooms vary in size. Breakfast (daily) and the afternoon meal (Mon–Sat) are served in a pleasant dining room; the cooking is good. You can reserve rooms by the day, week, or month, with discounts for extended stays. The location is central, just 2 blocks east of the Jardín.

Correo 31, near Recreo (Apdo. Postal 152), 37700 San Miguel de Allende, Gto. ©/fax 415/152-0844. www.casa carmensma.com. 11 units. $95 (£48) double. Rates include breakfast and lunch (breakfast only Sun). No credit cards. Children younger than 14 not accepted. Limited street parking. *In room:* No phone.

INEXPENSIVE

Parador San Sebastián *Value* The San Sebastián is another colonial house turned hotel with a central location and comfortable rooms for the price. Standard rooms are simple and quiet. They vary in size and choice of beds. Pricing is based on bed choices. The lower price is for a double bed or two twins; the higher price is for two doubles. Bathrooms are mostly medium size. Apartments come with a double or two twin beds, a kitchen, and a living/dining area. Guests can lounge in the chairs on the courtyard and the rooftop terrace. This hotel takes only walk-ins and won't accept reservations.

Mesones 7 (between Colegio and Núñez), 37700 San Miguel de Allende, Gto. © 415/152-7084. 30 units. $35–$58 (£18–£29) double; $55 (£28) apt. No credit cards. Free parking. *In room:* No phone.

Quinta Loreto *Value* This motel is a good place to stay whether you're traveling by car or not. It has good rooms for the price, a lovely garden, and a friendly atmosphere. Rooms come with ceiling fans and heaters. The cheaper rooms, without phones or televisions, are smaller than the others. Most rooms contain one double and one twin bed. The food is good and the laundry service a bargain. Make reservations—the Loreto is popular and often books up weeks in advance. Nonguests can come for inexpensive breakfasts and lunches. Quinta Loreto is below the crafts market off Calle Loreto, about 7 blocks from the main square.

Calle Loreto 15, 37700 San Miguel de Allende, Gto. Ⓒ **415/152-0042.** Fax 415/152-3616. hqloreto@cybermatsa. com.mx. 36 units. $55–$60 (£28–£30) double. Weekly and monthly discounts available. AF, MC, V. Free parking. **Amenities:** Restaurant; small outdoor pool; tour desk; laundry service. *In room:* Some w/TV and phone; some w/ neither.

WHERE TO DINE

In San Miguel, vegetarians will have no problem—most restaurants have legitimate meat-free main courses. For the best baked goods (pastries, French bread, croissants, and cakes), try **El Petit Four,** Calle Mesones 99-1, down the street from the Angela Peralta Theater. It's open Tuesday through Saturday from 10am to 9pm, Sunday from 10am to 6pm. There's a small seating area, or you can take your baked goods with you. The shop also sells coffee.

To sample some of the people's food, you might try **Cenaduría La Alborada** at Sollano 11 (Ⓒ **415/513-0577**) by the main square. It's a traditional sort of supper place where you can get a nourishing bowl of *pozole* or a plate of enchiladas. It's open Monday to Saturday from 2pm to 1am. For tacos, try **Los Faroles** at Ancha de San Antonio 28-C (Ⓒ **451/152-1849**). The owners sell a variety of *tacos de parrilla* (tacos with grilled meats) and *volcanes* (a toasted tortilla topped with meat and cheese).

Finally, there's another dining option that's a 10-minute ride east of town. An Italian chef has taken over a small part of the former **Hacienda de Landeta** and has a "country-kitchen" thing going on there—outdoor dining, chalkboard menu, unhurried personal service. Local residents love it. Amid crumbling walls and ancient trees, the setting has a gracious Old World feel to it. The menu always includes fresh pasta dishes, usually a fish dish and three or four Italian specialties. Chef Andreas personally attends his customers from Thursday to Sunday starting around 2pm. He has only a few tables, so make reservations (Ⓒ **415/120-3481**).

MODERATE

Bella Italia 𝕽𝕽 ITALIAN   The chef, Anselmo, does wonders with just about anything. If you have time, order the risotto, which takes a little while but is worth it; it comes with asparagus, boletus mushrooms, or shrimp, depending on what's available. The chef's specials are good bets—duck breast with blueberry sauce or crabmeat pasta are both excellent choices. Pastas include fresh spinach ravioli. The restaurant occupies a large courtyard with arches draped in bougainvillea. It's lit softly at night and has live music from Wednesday to Saturday starting at 8pm.

Canal 21. Ⓒ **415/152-4989.** Reservations required Wed–Sat. Main courses $12–$28 (£6–£14). AE, MC, V. Daily 1–10:30pm.

Planta Baja 𝕽𝕽 FUSION/MEDITERRANEAN   This place has the most inventive cooking in San Miguel. The cook throws many Mexican and Asian ingredients into the mix and concocts dishes with a definite *nouvelle* character. A case in point was the delightful caramelized swordfish served on a bed of several mildly flavored components, including a bit of avocado and jalapeño. It was offered both as an appetizer and main course. The menu changes often, but there's always something for carnivores, such as a beautifully cooked rib-eye or tenderloin. All the appetizers I had on my last trip were spot on. The dining room is not large and quite comfortable.

Canal 28. Ⓒ **415/154-6555.** Reservations recommended. Main courses $12–$17 (£6–£8.50). MC, V. Daily 1pm–midnight.

Restaurant/Bar Bugambilia 𝕽𝕽𝕽 MEXICAN   One can ask little more of a restaurant—delicious and attractive dishes, a large menu, good service, well-spaced tables, and a choice between dining in an elegant plant-filled courtyard and a large dining room, which in cool weather holds a roaring fire. Señora Arteaga offers a delicious variation on *chiles en nogada* (stuffed poblano chile with walnut cream sauce)—she marinates the pepper and serves it cold, not fried in batter. The *chiles en nogada* have been the object of many innovations, but most fail because they don't preserve the essence of this baroque dish, which balances opposites like the point and counterpoint of a fugue. Too spicy or too sweet, too strong a taste of meat or onions, and the magic is lost. Something simpler, perhaps? Start with the *caldo Xochitl* (the perfect soup for an irritable stomach), followed by traditional *enchiladas del portal* cooked in *chile ancho* sauce.

Hidalgo 42 (between Insurgentes and Calzada de la Luz). © 415/152-0127. Reservations recommended on weekends. Main courses $10–$17 (£5.50–£9.35). MC, V. Daily noon–11pm.

Romanos ✦ ITALIAN   This beautiful old house offers indoor and outdoor settings that are charming and comfortable. The food is delicious and includes pizza baked in a wood-burning oven, old-style lasagna, and daily specials (try the award-winning Texas chili). The ingredients are fresh and often organic, and all but one of the pastas are made on the premises. They host live acoustic music on Wednesday, Thursday, and Saturday nights.

Hernández Macías 93. © 415/152-7454. Reservations recommended. Main courses $12–$24 (£6–£12); pizzas $9 (£4.50). No credit cards. Tues–Sat 5–11pm.

INEXPENSIVE

Cha-Cha-Cha *Finds* MEXICAN   An apt name for a fun place to eat home-style Mexican cooking. The house and dining area are informal and relaxing (made more so by being a bit distant from the hustle and bustle of downtown), and the friendly service makes you want to linger here well after the meal is over, perhaps to sample the excellent margaritas. Menu items include *albóndigas* (Mexican meat balls flavored with chipotle), chicken in a *huazontle* sauce (a vegetable vaguely similar to broccoli, but much milder), and *quesadillas* with a variety of fillings including beef in *chile pasilla* sauce. Leave room for the coffee-flavored flan.

28 de Abril Norte 37. © 415/152-6586. Main courses $5–$6 (£2.50–£3). No credit cards. Tues–Sun 1–7pm.

El Correo ✦ MEXICAN   This is a small place right across from the post office. I really like the owner's selection of menu items, offering in a small package quite a varied sampling of Mexican standards: *sopes* (little fried masa cakes topped with savory meats and veggies); *caldo tlalpeño* (chicken, rice, and vegetable soup; my preference over the tortilla soup, which is what most people come for); and *enchiladas del portal,* which are made in the classic western Mexican style. Other offerings include *mole* and *arrachera a la tampiqueña* (steak with an array of side dishes such as enchiladas, guacamole, or rice and beans).

Correo 23. © 415/152-4951. Reservations accepted. Breakfast $5–$6 (£2.50–£3); main courses $7–$12 (£3.50–£6). MC, V. Wed–Mon 8am–11pm.

El Pegaso Restaurant & Bar INTERNATIONAL   Decorated in a cheerful, colorful style, and with a friendly, helpful staff, this restaurant is popular with expatriates and visitors. It's good for breakfast and light meals of sandwiches, soups, or salads. The restaurant is 1 block east of the Jardín.

Corregidora 6 (at Correo). © 415/152-1351. Breakfast $4–$8 (£2–£4); soups, salads, sandwiches $5–$7 (£2.50–£3.50); main courses $7–$15 (£3.50–£7.50). MC, V. Mon–Sat 8:30am–10pm.

> **Tips** **Recommended Day-Trip Tours**
>
> **Dolores Hidalgo** is the most popular destination for day-trippers from San Miguel (see "A Side Trip to Dolores Hidalgo: Fine Pottery & Shrimp Ice Cream," below). Some people make a day trip of Guanajuato or Querétaro (see "Guanajuato," and "Santiago de Querétaro," both later in this chapter). It's a hurried way of seeing them, but it can be done. Several tour guides and companies in San Miguel make trips to all of these places. **Leandro Delgado** (© **415/152-0155**; leandrotours@hotmail.com) is an independent tour guide who is well informed and conscientious. He speaks English, is a good driver, and is familiar with the artisans of Dolores Hidalgo and Guanajuato. Sr. Delgado and other guides offer trips to see the **monarch butterflies, 5** hours away in the state of Michoacán (see chapter 8). This is an exhausting trip; do it in 2 days, staying overnight in the town of Angangueo, if you can. The season runs from mid- to late November to March.

Olé Olé MEXICAN   Festive and friendly, this small restaurant is a riot of red and yellow streamers and bullfight memorabilia. The small menu specializes in grilled main courses—beef or chicken fajitas, shrimp brochettes, and *arrachera* (steak).

Loreto 66 (between Insurgentes and Calzada de la Luz). © **415/152-0896.** Main courses $7–$12 (£3.50–£6). No credit cards. Daily 1–9pm.

SAN MIGUEL AFTER DARK

To see a calendar of events, find a copy of the local paper, *Atención,* or one of the free monthly periodicals for visitors. Bellas Artes and the Angela Peralta Theater also post announcements of performances around town. Local regulations favor restaurant/bars over simple bars, so live-music acts often perform in restaurants. Clubs and dance clubs tend to spring up and then die off quickly. One club that has persisted is **La Cava de la Princesa,** Recreo 3 (© **415/152-1403**). It books a lot of live acts playing different kinds of music, as well as impersonators of Mexican pop stars. The cover charge is $4 to $8 (£2–£4). A couple of restaurants are popular nightspots: **Tío Lucas** (© **415/512-4996**) is a fun place to hear jazz, have a few drinks and perhaps a bite of dinner. It's located at Mesones 105 across from the Teatro Peralta. **Mama Mía,** Umarán 8, between Jesús and Hernández Macías (© **415/152-2063**), has a bar area where salsa and jazz bands play on the weekends. There is a $4 (£2) cover. In the summer you can enjoy the late afternoon and early evening from its rooftop terrace. If you don't feel like hearing music, how about a drink and a movie? The **Cine Bar** at the Hotel Jacaranda (© **415/152-1015**), Calle Aldama 53, shows recently released American movies on a large screen and includes popcorn and a drink with the $7.50 (£3.75) price of admission. Waiters come to your table with drinks and will bring the dinner menu as well. The main show starts at 7:30pm (they just started screening a discount matinee at 5pm). A couple of bars near El Jardín are good places if you just want to enjoy a drink with friends. One is **La Fragua,** next to Allende's house.

A SIDE TRIP TO DOLORES HIDALGO: FINE POTTERY & SHRIMP ICE CREAM

Dolores Hidalgo lies 40km (25 miles) northwest of San Miguel on Highway 35. Most people go there to shop at the Talavera pottery companies, but the town itself merits a visit. It remains a quiet, provincial place with a lovely main square and parish church; on the church steps, Father Hidalgo proclaimed the independence of Mexico. The church has a charming facade that, if pressed, I would label late Mexican baroque, but that doesn't do it justice. The interior of the church was plundered at various times but retains a couple of altarpieces that are worth a peek.

The main square has a quaint, small-town feel to it. Vendors sell ice cream in exotic flavors—tequila, shrimp, and pulque (a fermented beverage made from agave) are just a few enticing examples—as well as mango, *guanábana,* and other more familiar standbys. It all started 30 years ago on a dare, and then caught on for the notoriety it gave the vendors. Ask for some impossibly bad flavor—such as cilantro-*mescal*-chocolate chip or chicken *mole* swirl—and, without batting an eye, they'll tell you they're fresh out and to come back tomorrow. Most of these ice creams are known as *nieves* and are low in fat; for a richer ice cream ask for a *mantecado.* If you're hungry, there is a restaurant, El Patio, on the east side of the square.

Dolores has two small museums. The **Casa de Hidalgo** (admission $2/£1) is filled with letters and historical artifacts having to do with Father Hidalgo, and will be of most interest to history buffs. The **Museo de la Independencia** (admission 50¢/25p), a more dramatic approach to the theme of independence, also has a small collection of memorabilia of José Alfredo Jiménez, the king of *ranchera* music.

SHOPPING FOR TALAVERA

The **Talavera** pottery produced in Dolores is quite handsome and colorful, if less traditional than Talavera produced in Puebla. It's also inexpensive and plentiful. You can find all kinds of objects, from sink basins to napkin rings to hand-painted tiles. The pieces are formed with molds and then painted freehand. Prices here are considerably lower than those in San Miguel. Workshops are usually open from 10am to 6pm, but may or may not close for the afternoon meal. Almost all are closed on Sunday.

The first couple of Talavera workshops you'll encounter aren't even in town, but are on the highway just before you get there. **Talavera San Gabriel** (© 418/185-5037) has a warehouse full of large and small decorative objects, including picture frames, candlesticks, and ginger jars. And **Talavera Mora** (© 418/185-9002) has more dinnerware, including the popular blue-and-yellow fish pattern.

Once you get into town, you're best off just asking directions for different stores and factories. There are a lot of shops and each seems to have a different specialty. At the entrance to the town, on the left side of the first roundabout is **Hacienda Style** (© 418/182-2064 or 602/288-9122 in the U.S.). It produces tiles and sink basins and other objects in traditional and contemporary patterns. The factory has a store in San Miguel at Zacateros 83-A (© 415/154-7962). Another that specializes in decorative objects is **Talavera Cortés** (© 418/182-0900), at the corner of Distrito Federal and Tabasco streets. **Azulejos Talavera Vázquez** (© 418/182-0630) has a large store at the corner of Puebla and Tamaulipas streets. It has a bit of everything, and at that same intersection are a couple of other stores with lots of dinnerware.

2 Guanajuato ⭒⭒⭒

354km (219 miles) NW of Mexico City; 56km (35 miles) SE of León; 93km (58 miles) W of San Miguel de Allende; 208km (129 miles) SW of San Luis Potosí; 163km (101 miles) N of Morelia; 280km (174 miles) SE of Zacatecas

If you're going to Mexico to lose yourself, you'll have no problem doing so on the streets of Guanajuato (gwah-nah-*whah*-toh). They seem designed for just that purpose

Guanajuato

ATTRACTIONS ●

Basílica **14**
Church of San Diego **16**
El Pípila **21**
Museo de Los Momias **2**
Museo Diego Rivera **9**
Museo del Pueblo de Guanajuato **11**
Museo Iconográfico del Quijote **18**
Museo Regional La Alhóndiga de Granaditas **7**
Teatro Juárez **17**

Church ✝
Information ⓘ
Post Office ⊠

ACCOMMODATIONS ■

Alma del Sol **13**
Camino Real **5**
Casa de Espíritus Alegres B&B **1**
Casa Estrella de la Valenciana **4**
Hotel Antiguo Vapor **8**
Hotel El Minero **6**
Hotel Embajadoras **20**
Hotel Posada Santa Fe **15**
La Casa Azul **12**
Mansion del Cantador **3**
Meson de los Poetas **10**
Quinta Las Acadias **19**

as they curl this way and that, becoming alleys or stairways, and intersecting each other at different angles. At times it can seem like the Twilight Zone; I've heard of people hurriedly passing by a curious-looking shop intending to return later, and then never being able to locate it again. To make matters worse, the streets are filled with things that can draw your attention away from the business of getting from one place to another. The town is so photogenic; everywhere you look is postcard material. Most buildings, like the streets, are irregular in shape, creating a jumble of walls, balconies, and rooftops meeting at anything but a right angle. The churches are the exception, having regular floor plans, but even they show asymmetry—despite the best efforts of their builders, none has two matching towers, which only adds to their charm.

Founded in 1559, Guanajuato soon became fabulously rich, with world-famous mines (such as La Valenciana, Mineral de Cata, and Mineral de Rayas) that earned their owners titles of nobility. Along with Zacatecas and San Luis Potosí, Guanajuato was one of Mexico's most important mining cities. From the 16th through the 18th centuries, the mines in these towns produced a third of all the silver in the world, and Guanajuato bloomed with elaborate churches and mansions. Floods plagued the city until it finally diverted the river and turned the old river bed into a road that winds into the old downtown, with cantilevered houses jutting out high above the cars. The city has also opened an impressive network of tunnels (it is, after all, a mining town).

Still, on the surface, Guanajuato seems like an old Spanish city dumped into a Mexican highland valley. It's one of Mexico's great colonial cities. Picturesque and laden with atmosphere, Guanajuato should be high on your list of places to visit.

ESSENTIALS

GETTING THERE & DEPARTING   By Plane   Air access is good, with frequent flights in and out of the León/Guanajuato (also known as León/Bajío) airport, 27km (17 miles) from downtown Guanajuato. The taxi ride costs about $35 (£18). The airport has an ATM, pharmacy, and gift store. It also has car-rental counters: **Avis** (© 477/713-3003), **Budget** (© 477/713-1404), **Hertz** (© 477/771-5050), **National** (© 477/771-3371), and **Thrifty** (© 477/713-8522).

American Airlines' number in Mexico is © 01-800/904-6000; **Continental's** is © 01-800/900-5000; **Delta's** is © 01-800/902-2100. **AeroMéxico** (© 01-800/ 021-4000) and its affiliate, **Aerolitoral,** fly to and from Los Angeles, Tijuana, Mexico City, Puerto Vallarta, Monterrey, and Ciudad Juárez. **Mexicana** (© 01-800/502-2000) flies to and from Chicago, Oakland, Los Angeles, Denver, San Jose, Guadalajara, Mexico City, and Tijuana. *Note:* For more information, including these airlines' toll-free phone numbers, please see chapter 3.

There are airline ticket offices in León and at the airport. In Guanajuato, travel agencies can arrange flight reservations.

By Car   From Mexico City take Highway 57 north and northwest to Highway 45D at Querétaro, west through Salamanca to Irapuato, where you follow Highway 45 north to Silao and then take Highway 110 east. The route is a four-lane road almost all the way and takes 4½ hours. From San Luis Potosí, the quickest way to Guanajuato is through Dolores Hidalgo (3 hr.).

By Bus   The bus station in Guanajuato is 6km (3½ miles) southwest of town. From **Mexico City's Terminal Norte,** you'll have no trouble finding a *directo* (nonstop bus) to Guanajuato. **Servicios Coordinados/Primera Plus** (© **55/5567-4388**) and **Estrella Blanca** (© **55/5729-4388**) run express buses (5 hr.). You shouldn't have to wait more than a half-hour. Try to catch one of **ETN**'s (© **55/5785-1576**) super-deluxe buses with extra-wide seats that recline far back (10 per day). They're worth the extra money.

From **San Miguel de Allende,** ETN has three nonstop buses, Primera Plus/Servicios Coordinados has nine. These go *vía la Presa* (the short route—1¼ hr.). Don't take buses that go via Dolores Hidalgo. There is also service to Guadalajara (4 hr.), Morelia (usually via Irapuato, 2½ hr.), and elsewhere.

ORIENTATION   Arriving by Plane   The only transportation from the León/Guanajuato airport, 27km (17 miles) from downtown, is a **private taxi.** You pay for the cab ($35) inside the airport. There is no shuttle service.

Arriving by Car   Try not to lose your sanity while finding a place to park. Such a winding, hilly town defies good verbal or written directions. Be alert for one-way streets. Consider parking your car until you leave town, because the frustration of driving in the city could spoil your visit.

Arriving by Bus   The bus station is about 6km (3¾ miles) southwest of town, on the road to Celaya. Cabs cost about $3 (£1.50). At night there can sometimes be a scarcity of cabs. Try to schedule your trip to arrive during the day.

VISITOR INFORMATION   The state **tourism information office** is at Plaza de la Paz 14, across from the basilica (© **473/732-1574,** ext. 1437). It's open Monday through Friday from 9am to 7pm.

CITY LAYOUT   Guanajuato is a town of narrow streets, alleys, and stairs, and small, picturesque plazas. The hilly terrain and tangle of streets are difficult to represent on a map. You'll soon learn that maps aren't drawn to scale, nor do they show every street and stairway. The best way to get oriented is to visit the overlook at El Pípila (see "The Top Attractions," below) and one by one make out the major landmarks.

The small plaza at the center of the city, **Jardín Unión** (known as the cheese wedge, for its shape)—is where students, locals, and visitors gather. Facing the Jardín from the direction of El Pípila are both the **Teatro Juárez** and **Templo de San Diego.** From this plaza, you are within walking distance of many of the major sights.

GETTING AROUND   Walking is the only way to get to know the historic district of this labyrinthine town. For longer stretches, taxis are reasonably priced and abundant, except between 2 and 4pm when office workers are trying to get home for the midafternoon meal. As usual, you should establish the price before setting out.

FAST FACTS: Guanajuato

Area Code   The telephone area code is 473.

Climate   The city has temperatures that are mild in summer, cool in winter, with the occasional freeze at night.

Drugstores   **Farmacia Embajadoras** is located at Paseo Madero 10 (© **473/732-0996**), and **Farmacia La Perla** is at Juárez 146 (© **473/732-1175**).

Elevation   Guanajuato sits at 2,008m (6,586 ft.).

Emergency & Police   Call © **473/732-0266** for the police.

Hospital **Centro Médico La Presa** is located at Paseo de la Presa 85 (© 473/ 731-1074).

Internet Access There are several Internet cafes in the downtown area, with a lot of turnover. Just keep your eyes peeled for any sign that says INTERNET or CYBERCAFE.

Language School There are five language schools in Guanajuato. The best known is **Academia Falcón,** Paseo de la Presa 80 (© 473/731-0745; www.academiafalcon.com; mailing address: Callejón de la Mora 158, 36000 Guanajuato, Gto.). The institute provides skilled and dedicated tutors for those at all levels, and gets high marks from students. It can also arrange boarding with local families.

Population Guanajuato has 160,000 residents.

Post Office The *correo,* on the corner of Ayuntamiento and Carcamanes, near the Templo de la Compañía, is open Monday through Friday from 9am to 3pm.

Seasons The rainy season is June through September. Occasionally the rain is hard, but mostly it's afternoon showers and presents no problems for travelers. The coldest part of the year is December and January; the hottest is April, May, and some of June, before the rains come.

SPECIAL EVENTS & FESTIVALS

Every year in October, the state of Guanajuato sponsors the **Festival** Internacional **Cervantino (International Cervantes Festival)** ☆☆, 3 weeks of performing arts from all over the world. In recent years, the festival has featured marionettes from the Czech Republic, the Eliot Feld Ballet from New York, the Kiev Ballet, and a host of Mexican artists. The shows are held in open plazas and theaters all over town. Book rooms well in advance during the festival; if Guanajuato is full, consider staying in San Miguel de Allende.

For ticket information and a schedule, contact Festival Cervantino, Plaza San Francisquito 1, 36000 Guanajuato, Gto. (© 473/731-1221; www.festivalcervantino.gob. mx). Once you know the schedule, you can order tickets through **Ticketmaster** in Mexico City (© 55/5325-9000). Keep your confirmation number; you'll need it to pick up your tickets in Guanajuato. The best time to be at the festival is during the week; on weekends it's absolute madness.

EXPLORING GUANAJUATO
THE TOP ATTRACTIONS

El Pípila   This is the best vantage point in Guanajuato for photographs—the entire city unfolds below you, with great views in every direction. A funicular railway runs up the hill from behind the church of San Diego. You can also climb the hill on foot, up a rugged winding pathway. Just look for signs that read AL PÍPILA (to El Pípila).

The statue is the city's monument to José de los Reyes Martínez, better known as El Pípila. According to the story, El Pípila (if he really existed) was a brave young miner in Father Hidalgo's ragtag army of peasants and workers fighting for Mexican independence. Guanajuato was the first real battle of the war. The royalist forces took up their position inside the Alhóndiga de Granaditas. It seemed impregnable to Hidalgo's army, which lacked artillery. But El Pípila managed to breach the Spanish

defenses by tying a flagstone to his back as protection, crawling to the fortress doors, and setting them ablaze. Today, El Pípila's statue raises a torch high over the city in everlasting vigilance; the inscription at his feet proclaims AUN HAY OTRAS ALHÓNDIGAS POR INCENDIAR (There still remain other *alhóndigas* to burn).
Free admission. Daily 24 hr.

Museo del Pueblo de Guanajuato 𝕽𝕽   Just north of the Plaza de la Paz is this 17th-century mansion that once belonged to the Marqués San Juan de Rayas. The first and third floors display traveling exhibits; the second holds a fascinating collection of Colonial-Era civil and religious pieces gathered by distinguished local muralist José Chávez Morado. As a collector, Chávez Morado had an eye for the macabre, acquiring death portraits, some even eerier portraits of the living, and religious paintings on the subject of mortality. Also in the collection are some paintings by the gifted Hermenegildo Bustos, a portrait artist of the 19th century. There is a small collection of pre-Hispanic artifacts and several folk-art testimonials dedicated to the miraculous powers of various saints. The museum contains a couple of Chávez's murals; other works by Bustos and Chávez can be found at La Alhóndiga, down the street.
Calle Positos 7. ⟁ 473/732-2990. Admission $2 (£1). Tues–Sat 10am–6:30pm; Sun 10am–2:30pm.

Museo Diego Rivera 𝕽𝕽   From the Museo del Pueblo, walk 1½ blocks farther down the street, and you'll find the house where the artist Diego Rivera was born on December 8, 1886. It has been restored and converted into a museum. The first floor is furnished as it might have been in the era of Rivera's birth. Upstairs there's a pretty good collection of his early works. He began painting when he was 10 years old and eventually moved to Paris, where he became a Marxist during World War I. The house contains a few sketches of some of the earlier murals that made his reputation, and paintings from 1902 to 1956. The fourth floor holds a small auditorium for lectures and conferences, and there you'll find a large representation of one of Rivera's most famous murals, *Un Sueño Dominical en la Alameda*.
Calle Positos 47. ⟁ 473/732-1197. Admission $2 (£1). Tues–Sat 10am–6:30pm; Sun 10am–2:30pm.

Museo Iconográfico del Quijote 𝕽 *(Finds*   There are only a few truly universal characters in the world of literature: Hamlet, Faust, Don Juan, and Don Quixote come to mind. Writers far and wide have taken up these characters and reworked their stories, but Don Quixote much more than the others has become a favorite subject of artists. The list includes Dalí, Picasso, Miró, Raul Angiano, José Guadalupe Posada, Daumier, José Moreno Carbonero, and Pedro Coronel. This museum, a long block southeast of the Jardín Unión, holds a fascinating collection of art based upon Don Quixote—all Quixote, all the time! Particularly forceful are the sculptures and murals, but the sheer variety of forms and thematic treatment is what makes a stroll through this museum so entertaining.
Manuel Doblado 1. ⟁ 473/732-6721. Free admission. Tues–Sat 10am–6:30pm; Sun 10am–2:30pm.

Museo Regional La Alhóndiga de Granaditas 𝕽𝕽   On the same street as the Rivera Museum, 2 blocks farther down, is La Alhóndiga de Granaditas, which was built between 1798 and 1809 as the town granary—hard to believe, because it is such a beautiful building. The Spanish took refuge here in 1810 when El Pípila (see above) and company captured Guanajuato. A slaughter ensued that Father Hidalgo was unable to stop. This convinced many people who had been leaning toward independence to remain loyal to Spain, although when the Spanish forces under Félix Calleja retook Guanajuato, they exacted a horrible revenge on the locals suspected of collusion. (The exhibits tell the story.) By the next year, the royalist forces triumphed, and the heads of the insurrectionists Hidalgo, Allende, Aldama, and Jiménez adorned the four corners of the building, where they remained until 1821 as a dissuasive reminder.

The old granary now houses a regional museum. The interior courtyard is large and beautiful. Two floors of rooms hold exhibits of pre-Columbian artifacts, displays on colonial history, and regional crafts. Adorning the two stairways to the second floor are the vivid murals of José Chávez Morado, who donated his pre-Hispanic art collection to the museum (and whose Colonial-Era collection is in the Museo del Pueblo de Guanajuato). The exhibits take you through the region's colonial era and its role in the struggle for independence, all the way up to the Mexican Revolution. Explanatory text is in Spanish only, but the artifacts are interesting and well displayed. Down the hill from the Alhóndiga is the Mercado Hidalgo (see "Shopping," below).

Mendizábal 6. ✆ 473/732-1112. Admission $3.50 (£1.75), free for students w/ID. Video camera $3 (£1.50). Tues–Sat 10am–2pm and 4–6pm; Sun 10am–3pm.

Teatro Juárez   Built in 1903 during the opulent era of the Porfiriato, this theater is now the venue for many productions, especially during the Festival Cervantino. The exterior is at odds with its surroundings—Greco-Roman portico adorned with *fin-de-siècle* bronze lions and lanterns. The interior is especially eye-catching. Box seats rise up four stories along the walls of the theater, and there's not a bad seat in the house.

Jardín de la Unión. ✆ 473/732-0183. Admission $1.50 (75p). Still camera $1 (50p), video camera $2 (£1). Tues–Sun 9am–1:45pm and 5–7:45pm.

MORE ATTRACTIONS

The **Church of San Diego,** on the Jardín Unión, stands almost as it did in 1633, when it was built under the direction of Franciscan missionaries. A flood in 1760 nearly destroyed it. The reconstruction was completed in 1786, largely at the expense of the Count of La Valenciana. The pink cantera-stone facade is a fine example of the Mexican baroque.

The **Plazuela del Baratillo,** just behind the Jardín Unión, has a beautiful fountain (a gift from Emperor Maximilian) at its center. You'll always find people sitting around it peacefully, some in the shade and others in the sun. Its name derives from its former role as a weekly *tianguis* (market); vendors would yell *";Barato!"* ("Cheap!").

Just west of Baratillo is the **Church of the Compañía.** Built in 1747 by the Jesuit order, it was the biggest of their churches. The churrigueresque decoration lightens it somewhat, but the interior, which was restored in the 19th century, is neoclassical. This church was built as part of a Jesuit university, which was founded in 1732 on orders of Philip V. It's the last of 23 universities the Jesuit order built in Mexico. The main building of the **university** is on the same block as the church. Its entrance was rebuilt in 1945 in imposing neoclassical style.

Farther west, between the main street, Juárez, and Calle Positos are three connected plazas worth seeing: **Plaza San Roque, Jardín de la Reforma,** and **Plaza San Fernando,** where you can sit at one of the outdoor tables and enjoy coffee in a perfectly charming setting. This plaza is an increasingly popular hangout.

NEARBY ATTRACTIONS

The following attractions are all a short distance above the city, and the best way to get to them is by taxi. You can hire one for $11 (£5.50) per hour. I would recommend taking the panoramic highway around the city, which allows you to pass by La

Valenciana, La Cata, and La Raya; each has a mine and a church. The highway circles around to El Pípila. The drive is enjoyable and lasts about an hour, with a couple of stops and a quick drive along the submerged highway to view the houses that are perched precariously above the road.

La Valenciana 🦌🦌🦌 The area around La Valenciana mine holds several attractions, shopping destinations, and a good restaurant. You might want to allot a couple of hours for a visit, but keep in mind that everything closes by 6pm. The star attraction is the magnificent **church of San Cayetano,** built toward the end of the colonial period in an opulent display of Mexican baroque. The interior is dazzling, with gilded carvings and *retablos* (altarpieces). The best time to see it is midafternoon, when sunlight pours through the windows, illuminating the golden carvings.

In the church plaza is an outstanding folk-art store called **Ojo de Venado** (see "Shopping," below) and a rock-and-mineral shop. Guides offer (in Spanish only) a short, so-so **tour of the mine** ($2/£1) and explain something of its operation. (Zacatecas has a more interesting mine tour.) Look for a sign that says BOCAMINA–LA VALENCIANA. Across the road from the church is the house of the Count of La Valenciana, which now holds a restaurant, **La Casa del Conde de la Valenciana** (see "Where to Dine," later in this chapter).

La Valenciana silver mine has recently ceased operations. The principle mine opening is a couple of hundred yards west of the house. It's an eight-sided vertical shaft (500m/1,640 ft. deep) surrounded by a tall stone wall in the shape of a crown with large wooden doors and a miner's chapel at the entrance.

If you keep climbing on the road that runs alongside La Valenciana, you will shortly see the driveway up to Casa de Capelo (see "Shopping," below) and to Cerámica La Cruz. Continue a few miles, and you come to the small town of Santa Rosa, where you can see yet more beautiful ceramics at Mayólica Santa Rosa (see "Shopping," below).

Templo de la Valenciana, Valenciana. Free admission. Daily 9am–6pm.

Museo de Los Momias (Mummy Museum)

First-time visitors find this museum grotesque or fascinating, or both: Mummified remains of the dead, some of whom wear tattered clothing from centuries past, are on display. Dryness and the earth's gases and minerals in this particular *panteón* (cemetery) have halted decomposition. Because graveyards have limited space, bodies are eventually exhumed in Mexico to make room for newcomers. Those on display were exhumed between 1865 and 1985. The mummies stand or recline in glass cases, grinning, choking, or staring, while tour guides tell crowds of visitors macabre stories in Spanish of the fates of some of the deceased. Are they true? *¿Quién sabe?* But it's impossible to resist the temptation to go up and look at them, and this is the only graveyard I've seen with souvenir stands. They mostly sell sugar skulls and effigies of the mummies. Next to the mummy museum is a small exhibit called "El Culto a la Muerte" (Worship of the Dead) which is a bad mix of morbid and hokey.

Esplanada del Panteón. ✆ 473/732-0639. Admission $6 (£3). Still camera $1 (50p), video camera $2 (£1). Daily 9am–6pm. At the northwest end of town, the steep Esplanada del Panteón leads up to the municipal cemetery.

Templo de Cata

Up above the city, perched on the mountain to the north, is this small, elaborate "miners' church." Cata is also the name of the mine nearby and the *barrio* (neighborhood) that surrounds the church. A lovely baroque facade, with just one tower standing, decorates the outside. Until a few of years ago, this church held

Ranch Museum

Surrounding Guanajuato were more than 150 haciendas of wealthy colonial mine owners. Most are now either in ruins or restored and privately owned, but one has been made into the **Museo Exhacienda San Gabriel de Barrera** 𝄞. About 3km (2 miles) from town on the road to Marfil, it's a lovely place noted for its elaborate gardens in different styles (Moorish, English, and Spanish, for example). The hacienda house presents a good picture of 18th-century life in the grand style. The hacienda still has its requisite chapel (baroque, of course), with a key identifying the various figures depicted in the *retablo*. There is also a state-run shop displaying all the handicrafts produced in the state. The grounds are open daily from 9am to 6pm; admission is $3 (£1.50), plus $1 (50p) for a still camera or $1.50 (75p) for a video camera. The store's hours are Wednesday through Sunday from 10am to 5pm.

an enormous number of personal testimonials that covered the walls from floor to ceiling. Most of these took the traditional form of small square sheets of tin painted with scenes (in a primitive folk style) and explanatory text describing the miracles performed by the church's Señor de Villaseca. "El Trigueñito" (roughly translated as "the olive-skinned one"), as he is affectionately called, is a popular figure in Guanajuato, especially with miners and truck and taxi drivers. The testimonials were a touching display of the highly personal relationship these people have with El Trigueñito. What has become of all these testimonials is now the question. At first, their removal was supposed to be temporary, but they haven't returned. *¡Quién sabe?!*

Carretera Panorámica. Free admission. Daily 9am–5pm.

SHOPPING

Stores in Guanajuato keep the usual hours—Monday through Saturday from 10am to 2pm and 4 to 8pm. The **Mercado Hidalgo,** or municipal market, is one of the most orderly in Mexico. You can browse on the main floor or watch the action from the raised walkway that encircles it. Aside from food and vegetable stalls, there is a lot of pottery and ceramic ware.

Artesanías Vázquez   Outlet for a factory in Dolores Hidalgo, this place is small but loaded with the colorful Talavera-style pottery for which Dolores is famous. You'll see plates, ginger jars, frames, cups and saucers, serving bowls, and the like. Open Monday to Saturday from 9am to 9pm. Cantarranas 8. 🕿 **473/732-5231.**

Casa de Capelo   Famous ceramist Javier de Jesús Hernández, known simply as "Capelo," has his workshop high above Guanajuato, past La Valenciana church. Capelo and Cerámica La Cruz have opened galleries downtown in Plaza San Roque (no phone) and at Positos 69 (🕿 **473/732-0612**). Store hours for both locations are Monday through Saturday 10am to 3pm and 5 to 8pm. If you still want to go the workshop store, take the highway to Santa Rosa/Dolores Hidalgo and, after la Valenciana, look for a sign on the left pointing to a dirt road that climbs steeply. It's open Monday through Friday from 10am to 6pm. Carretera a Dolores Hidalgo s/n. 🕿 **473/732-8964.**

Cerámica La Cruz   The new downtown galleries are listed above. The original store is in the area of La Valenciana, just below Capelo's place. The output is a bit different from Capelo's work. The potters here play a lot with glazes producing crackleware, among other things. Hours are Monday through Friday from 10am to 6pm. Carretera a Dolores Hidalgo s/n. Ⓒ 473/732-9037.

The Gorky González Workshop   This prize-winning ceramist has dedicated himself to bringing back the traditional Talavera of Guanajuato. Gorky's son, whose *nom de guerre* is GoGo, is making his own style of ceramics, which is finding favor with some collectors. The workshop is a short cab ride from the historic center. The showroom is open Monday through Friday from 10am to 2pm and 4 to 6pm, Saturday from 10am to 1pm. Call first. Calle Pastita (by the baseball field). Ⓒ 473/731-0389.

Mayólica Santa Rosa   This factory store is in the small town of Santa Rosa, on the way to Dolores Hidalgo. It carries high-quality *mayólica* for less money than in Guanajuato. It's open Monday through Friday from 8am to 5pm. On the highway. Ⓒ 473/739-0572.

Ojo de Venado   A knowledgeable dealer of folk art, Randy Walz, sells a variety of pieces from Michoacán and other areas near Guanajuato. He's good at finding unique, highly expressive works. The store is open daily from 10am to 6pm. Below the church of San Cayetano. Ⓒ 473/734-1435.

Rincón Artesanal   Objects in carved wood, wax, papier-mâché, pewter, and ceramic, produced in different workshops throughout the state of Guanajuato, stock this store. It also carries items from farther afield, including beautiful *catrina calaveras* (skeleton statues in fancy dress) from the state of Michoacán. The woman who owns the place is very helpful. It's open daily from 10am to 9pm. Sopeña 5 (1 block east of Jardín Unión). Ⓒ 473/732-8632.

WHERE TO STAY

Hotels have high-season rates for Christmas, Easter, and the Festival Cervantino. High season at moderate and inexpensive hotels also includes July and August, when schools are out and families vacation and any holiday weekend. During the Festival Cervantino, in October, rooms are virtually impossible to find without a reservation, and even then it's good to claim your room early in the day. Some visitors have to stay as far away as León or San Miguel de Allende. Rates quoted here include the 17% tax.

VERY EXPENSIVE

Camino Real Guanajuato 𝄞𝄞 *Kids*   Occupying the former hacienda that was the former hotel Parador San Javier, the new Camino Real is nicely located on the hill above La Alhónidga. A lot of investment went toward quality infrastructure. The rooms were completely refurnished, and there's a higher level of service and housekeeping. But the character of the property has remained the same. You can still see the old outlines of the original grounds of the hacienda, and the walled enclosure makes it easier to keep an eye on the kids (so long as someone is watching the pool). Rooms are decorated in an understated, modern style that goes well with the bare stone walls and arcades. The sixth floor Camino Club rooms have domed ceilings and views of the city. Most rooms are quiet, owing to the large grounds of the hotel (except perhaps for the rooms in the very back, which are closest to the streets).

Alhóndiga 100, Col. San Javier, Guanajuato, Gto. (C) **800/722-6466** in the U.S. and Canada, or 473/102-1500. Fax 473/102-1508. www.caminoreal.com.mx. 105 units. **$222 (£111) deluxe; $268 (£134) club; $316 (£158) junior suite; $444 (£222) master suite.** Discounts Mon–Thurs. AE, MC, V. Valet parking $6. **Amenities:** Restaurant; bar; heated outdoor pool; fitness room; children's programs; tour desk; car rental; business center; 24-hr. room service; babysitting; laundry; dry cleaning; nonsmoking rooms; club-level rooms. *In room:* A/C, TV, Wi-Fi, high-speed Internet access; minibar; fridge; coffeemaker; hair dryer, iron, safe.

Casa Estrella de la Valenciana 🌟🌟🌟

This beautiful modern house, on the mountainside above La Valenciana church, affords a panoramic view of the city and surrounding valley. The owners—two American women, one of whom lives on the premises—have created comfortable, spacious interiors meticulously appointed with regional tiles, pottery, and arts. All guest rooms have a balcony or terrace; two are handicap accessible. The two most expensive are large and have special amenities such as a private Jacuzzi (La Valenciana) or a steam locker (La Sirena). Each comes with a king bed. Another oversize room, the San Bernabé, comes with two queens and has a tub and a shower. The others have either a queen or a king bed. La Cata and Guadalupe are the smallest and most economical, but still of a good size. Common areas include a living room, an upstairs terrace, and a poolside patio. The hotel is nonsmoking.

Callejón Jalisco 10, Col. La Valenciana 36240 Guanajuato, Gto. (C) **866/983-8844** in the U.S., or 473/732-1784. Fax 562/430-0648 in the U.S. www.mexicaninns.com. 8 units. **$216–$240 (£108–£120) standard; $246–$275 (£123–£137) deluxe; $275–$310 (£137–£155) superior; $497–$550 (£249–£275) 2-bedroom casita.** Rates include full breakfast and beverages. AE, MC, V. Free parking. In the *colonia* above La Valenciana church. **Amenities:** Heated outdoor pool; Jacuzzi; in-room massage; babysitting; overnight laundry; nonsmoking rooms. *In room:* TV, DVD/VCR, high-speed Internet access, hair dryer, iron, safe, no phone.

Quinta Las Acacias 🌟🌟🌟

The main house dates from the late 19th century, when architecture and design in Mexico were borrowing heavily from Victorian and French *(afrancesado)* styles. It has been painstakingly remodeled. The rooms are decorated and furnished with period furniture, wallpaper, and wainscoting. There are six period rooms in the house, and in back of the property are larger modern suites, some of which have Jacuzzis. Several of these rooms surround a large cactus garden (it feels more like a cactus forest because these ancient cacti have grown so tall) and afford views of the nearby mountains. Rooms contain one king or two queen beds and have spacious, well-equipped bathrooms. Breakfast can be served in the dining room, on the terrace, or in the guest's room. The cocktail area serves drinks until 10pm.

Paseo de la Presa 168, 36000 Guanajuato, Gto. (C) **888/497-4129** in the U.S., or 473/731-1517. Fax 473/731-1862. www.quintalasacacias.com.mx. 17 units. **$218 (£109) 3rd-floor rooms; $238 (£119) 2nd-floor; $308 (£154) suite with Jacuzzi; $328 (£164) master suite.** Rates include breakfast. AE, MC, V. Free limited parking. Children younger than 12 not accepted. **Amenities:** Restaurant; bar; large outdoor Jacuzzi; concierge; tour desk; room service; laundry service; dry cleaning. *In room:* A/C, TV, Wi-Fi, hair dryer, safe.

EXPENSIVE

Hotel Antiguo Vapor 🌟🌟   Rooms at this small hotel have all the Mexican character you could wish for, from clay tile floors to beamed ceilings to Talavera tile bathrooms. They range in size from medium to large. All are colorful, and most have windows or balconies looking out over the city. For being downtown, the rooms are fairly quiet; there are some interior rooms that would be quite the thing for light sleepers. Room rates vary according to the choice of beds—the most economical have one queen, the most expensive have two doubles, rooms with king beds are in between. Bathrooms are very nicely finished and some are quite large. The location is good, close by the Diego Rivera Museum.

Galarza 5, 36000 Guanajuato, Gto. (C) **473/732-3211.** www.hotelavapor.com. 10 units. $140–$180 (£70–£90) double. Rates are higher for Cervantino and holidays. MC, V. Free guarded parking. **Amenities:** Restaurant; tour info; nonsmoking rooms. In room: TV, hair dryer.

La Casa de Espíritus Alegres B&B and Alma del Sol ★★★ *Moments*   Folk art and atmosphere abound in the idiosyncratic "house of happy spirits," a 16th-century colonial hacienda. Rooms are decorated and furnished in a vivacious and attractive style. Each fulfills the promise of "a skeleton in every closet" (festive *papier maché* Day of the Dead bones hang everywhere), and each has its own fireplace. The grounds are so lovely you won't want to leave. Breakfast, served overlooking the garden, features Californian and Mexican food, with heapings of fresh fruit. Check out the hand-painted chairs (decorated by artist friends of the owners). Guests have use of the folk art–decorated living room, and may borrow history, travel, and art books as well as paperback novels. The B&B is 3km (2 miles) from downtown (10 min. by taxi).

A smaller, downtown property is called **Alma del Sol** for its location on Sol street across from the grand church of La Compañía. It's partly a museum/gallery of folk textiles and has only four units (two of which are two-bedroom suites) and an open rooftop terrace with a broad vista.

La Exhacienda la Trinidad 1, 36250 Marfil, Gto. (C)/fax **473/733-1013.** www.casaspirit.com. 12 units. $146–$166 (£73–£83) double. Rates include breakfast. MC, V. Free guarded parking. **Amenities:** Tour info; massage; laundry service; nonsmoking rooms. In room: Wi-Fi, hair dryer, no phone.

MODERATE

El Mesón de los Poetas   I love hotels that are unselfconscious expressions of their city, and this is just such a place. Set against a hillside, it makes the most of its space by clever positioning of rooms in an irregular jumble. Following the stairs and walk-ways that led to my room, I thought for a moment I was trapped in an M. C. Escher drawing. Standard rooms are decorated in Mexican style. They vary in size, and a few come with kitchenettes. The largest hold two double beds or a king. Others come with only one double or a double and a twin. The lighting in all the rooms is good. The bathrooms are adequate. Suites have king-size beds, but I prefer the two-bedroom suites, which have a spacious, attractive living room with dining table and chairs, a sitting area, and a kitchenette. (Kitchenettes come with little in the way of cooking implements, but ask for some and you may get them.) The hotel is right downtown by the Diego Rivera museum.

Positos 35, 36000 Guanajuato, Gto. (C)/fax **473/732-6657,** -0705. www.elmesondelospoetas.com.mx. 31 units. $100–$118 (£50–£58) double; $160 (£80) 2-bedroom suite; $150–$170 (£75–£85) suite. MC, V. Limited off-site parking. **Amenities:** Tour info; laundry service. In room: TV, coffeemaker (on request).

Hotel Embajadoras   This is a quiet motel in the historic center, on Parque Emba-jadoras, a tree-lined square that's a 10-minute walk east of the main square (not much climbing). The rooms are plain and rather dark and in need of some refreshing. They come with carpeted floors and midsize bathrooms. A reasonably priced restaurant with a pleasant outdoor dining area takes care of meals.

Parque Embajadoras, 36000 Guanajuato, Gto. (C) **473/731-0105.** Fax 473/731-0063. hotelembajadoras@ hotmail.com. 27 units. $70–$80 (£35–£40) double. MC, V. Free parking. **Amenities:** Restaurant; travel agency; room service. In room: TV.

Hotel Posada Santa Fé ★   Right on the Jardín Unión, this hotel is for those who want to be in the thick of things from the moment they step out the door. It dates from the 1860s, having survived both the reform wars and the revolution, and the old lobby is a great place to have a drink. The hotel underwent extensive remodeling, and the wiring and plumbing in most of the building was replaced, which was money well spent. But the size of the rooms was one thing that couldn't be changed. They're small, except for the suites and some of the rooms with exterior views. They are, however, attractive, well kept, and comfortable. Standard rooms hold either one double or two twin beds. Exterior-view rooms and suites have larger bathrooms and fancier furniture; most have king-size beds.

Jardín Unión 12, 36000 Guanajuato, Gto. ℭ 473/732-0084. Fax 473/732-4653. www.posadasantafe.com. 47 units. $95–$135 (£48–£68) double; $150–$170 (£75–£85) suite and exterior views. Rates include full breakfast during low season. AE, DC, MC, V. Free limited valet parking. **Amenities:** Restaurant; 2 bars; whirlpool; room service; laundry service. *In room:* TV.

INEXPENSIVE

Hotel El Minero (*Value*)   Only 3 blocks above the Museo Alhóndiga, this four-story hotel (no elevator) has a rare commodity: cheap rooms that aren't ugly or small. New tile floors, attractive paint jobs, ceiling fans, and cleanliness are the high points. The location is good, and the back rooms are quiet, but the lighting is just okay; the bathrooms are small, and the TVs don't add much to the experience of staying here. Most rooms have a double and a single bed.

Alhóndiga 12-A, 36000 Guanajuato, Gto. ℭ 473/732-5251. Fax 473/732-4739. 20 units. $35–$46 (£18–£23) double. MC, V. Limited street parking. **Amenities:** Restaurant. *In room:* TV.

La Casa Azul   This house is in an upper barrio above the Plazuela del Baratillo, which could be good or bad, depending on how you look at it. Staying here would give you an idea how the locals live, always going up or down through a network of alleys (good?). But, staying here means you, too, will be always going up and down (bad?). You decide. It's a good steep climb from the plaza to the hotel, but you get to stay in an interesting part of town for not a lot of money. The rooms have lots of character and are well maintained. They are small to medium in size and come with either a double or a king bed. One room is larger and has two doubles and a twin. There's a rooftop terrace, too. *Note:* Don't stay here if you have a car; the alleys are too narrow.

Carcamanes 57, 36000 Guanajuato, Gto. ℭ 473/731-2288. www.lacasaazul.com.mx. 5 units. $50–$70 (£25–£35) double. No credit cards. No parking. **Amenities:** Bar. *In room:* TV, no phone.

Mansión del Cantador   For a no-frills hotel, this isn't too bad. It offers large, cheerful rooms on the Jardín del Cantador for a good price. Being on this square cuts down on noise, and yet it's still close to the market and the Alhóndiga. Most rooms come with two double beds. In cold weather ask at the desk for extra blankets. The bathrooms are small but in good repair.

Cantador 19, 36000 Guanajuato, Gto. ℭ 473/732-6888. hmcr84@hotmail.com. 42 units. $50–$60 (£25–£30) double. Rates include full breakfast. MC, V. Limited street parking. **Amenities:** Restaurant; bar. *In room:* no phone.

WHERE TO DINE

Restaurants in the downtown area are improving. In addition to the ones I list below, try an outdoor table at the restaurant of the **Hotel Posada Santa Fé** (see above), which affords a way to enjoy the Jardín de la Unión. The Jardín has a closed, intimate feel; if you want something more open with longer vistas, try the **Plaza de la Paz,** a block away. Here you can sit, have a drink, and perhaps nibble on an appetizer at one of the outdoor cafes in front of Guanajuato's cathedral. If you're in search of coffee, the best in town is at **Café Tal** (© **473/732-6212**). It's just off Sangre de Cristo, which runs between Jardín Unión and Plaza Embajadoras, on both sides of Calle Temezcuitate.

EXPENSIVE

La Casa del Conde de la Valenciana ✦ MEXICAN/INTERNATIONAL   Dine in the former home of the count of La Valenciana, across the street from his other creation, La Valenciana church. You can eat on the patio or in one of the dining rooms. The menu combines old standards and original recipes. For an appetizer, try a fresh salad or refreshing gazpacho served in a vessel encased in ice. For a main course, you can choose one of Mexico's traditional dishes, such as chicken *mole* or *enmoladas* (chicken-filled tortillas rolled in *mole*), or perhaps chicken breast *a la flor de calabaza* (in a mild, satisfying cream sauce of blended squash flowers and poblano chile). The shady patio is so relaxing and the chairs so comfortable that many linger here over coffee and dessert.

Carretera Guanajuato-Dolores Km 5, opposite La Valenciana church. ©/fax **473/732-2550**. Reservations accepted. Main courses $10–$18 (£5–£9). MC, V. Mon–Wed noon–6pm; Thurs–Sat noon–10pm.

MODERATE

El Abue ✦✦ MEXICAN/ITALIAN   At this comfortable little downtown restaurant, you can enjoy some good cooking in a simple, understated dining room. The *sopa azteca* was well made with a nice bite to it, and the *tostadas yucatecas* with *cochinita pibil* were good and tangy. The kitchen also produces *chiles en nogada* (if you want something rich and elaborate), and you can request fettuccine in poblano cream sauce, though it's not on the menu. They serve a few standard Italian dishes, too.

San José 14 (at the top of the Plazuela del Baratillo). © **473/732-6242**. Reservations recommended on weekends. Main courses $7–$14 (£3.50–£7); breakfast $3–$6 (£1.50–£3). MC, V. Daily 8:30am–11pm.

El Claustro MEXICAN   Many locals like this downtown hole-in-the-wall. Tables are outside on the square or inside in what was once the bodega of the building now occupied by the restaurant. My favorite things to eat here are the enchiladas (especially the *rojas* because they are made with *chile ancho*) and the *enmoladas,* which make good use of a locally made *mole*. The *pollo con mole* offers another way to enjoy it. Other dishes include various *antojitos* and main dishes. The restaurant is within 50 paces of Avenida Juárez, almost across from the market.

Jardín de la Reforma 13-B. No phone. Main courses $5–$11 (£2.75–£6.05). No credit cards. Daily 8am–10pm.

México Lindo y Sabroso ✦✦ MEXICAN   This is a fun place to go for a quiet meal in the Colonia Paseo de la Presa, not far from downtown. The menu has lots of the dishes that Mexico is known for. These are cooked with care. The surroundings are attractive, and the service is great. For all these reasons, this restaurant is popular with the locals. The best time to avoid crowds is after 5pm. You can dine outside on the front veranda, in an attractive interior patio, or inside in one of the dining rooms. I tried several things and liked them all. The tostadas, the green *pozole,* and the flautas were all great. On the menu are some Yucatecan specialties, such as *cochinita pibil* and *panuchos*—these were delicious, too. You can take a cab there and then grab any bus to take you back to downtown.

Paseo de la Presa 154. © **473/731-0529**. Reservations accepted. Main courses $4–$11 (£2–£5.50). MC, V. Daily 9am–10:30pm.

INEXPENSIVE

El Midi ✦ SALADS/MEDITERRANEAN   At this small place on the Plazuela San Fernando, you can serve yourself only as much food as you want, and you can dine outside at a table on the plaza, which is an oasis of tranquillity for the downtown area. What's more, the food is delicious and healthful. The offerings change daily—different salad fixings, different quiches, different vegetables, different desserts. On Thursday and Friday evenings, you can get a cheese and cold cuts plate, which goes well with the house bread and table wine. The owner, Véronique Marconnet, is a sweet woman from southern France who has been living in Guanajuato for a few years. She bakes a lot of cakes, pies, and other sweets. The food is always fresh, and it tends to run out late in the day, so don't show up too late. She has plans to open for breakfast.

Plazuela San Fernando 41. No phone. Salad, quiche, desserts sold by weight. No credit cards. Sun–Wed 1–6pm; Thurs–Fri 1–11pm.

Truco 7 (Value MEXICAN   With its economical prices and warm atmosphere, this place is a solid choice for any meal. The three dining rooms are small and a bit crowded, furnished with leather *equipal* (a rustic Mexican style of furniture). The restaurant occupies an 18th-century structure originally built for members of the Valenciana silver family. Calle Truco, a short street south of the basilica, runs between the Jardín Unión and the Plaza de la Paz.

Truco 7. ☎ 473/732-8374. Reservations not accepted. Breakfast $2–$4 (£1.10–£2.20); *comida corrida* (2–4pm only) $3 (£1.65); main courses $5–$8 (£2.75–£4.40). No credit cards. Daily 8:30am–11:30pm.

GUANAJUATO AFTER DARK

If city planners had known the **Jardín Unión** would be so popular, they might have made it larger. This tiny plaza, shaded by Indian laurel trees, is the heart of the city and the best hangout. No other spot in town rivals its benches and sidewalk restaurants.

(Moments   The Redolent Mexican Cantina

If you're curious about Mexican cantinas, swinging saloon doors and all, Guanajuato is a good place to do your fieldwork. You should know, however, that most of these are *men-only* drinking dives.

The town's favorite son is José Alfredo Jiménez, the undisputed master of *ranchera* music. This is the quintessential drinking music (long laments punctuated by classic Mexican yelps) that drives most non-Mexicans screaming from the building. But after downing a few *copitas,* you may warm up to it, and after asking about Jiménez, you'll probably get a few more drinks on the house. Around the Jardín Unión a couple of cantinas aren't bad; I enjoyed a few shots at one called **El Incendio (The Fire),** Cantarranas 15. Unlike most cantinas, this place welcomes women. El Incendio opens at 10am and closes at 4am.

You may be surprised to see an open urinal at the end of the bar. While this is a standard feature in cantinas and part of the, er, authentic flavor, you still may wish to opt for a seat at the opposite end.

You can catch some worthwhile free **theater** in Plazuela de San Roque at 8pm on Sunday when the university is in session. Students perform short theatrical pieces known as *entremeses* (interludes). These are usually costumed period pieces that rely more on action than dialogue, so you don't need to understand too much Spanish to get the point. The costumes are great and look curiously appropriate in this *plazuela*.

If you're looking for a place just to have a drink, try **La Clave Azul** (© 473-732-1561) at Cantaritos 31. It's a small bar tucked away off Plaza San Fernando, and it's very much a product of its environment. A couple of small, irregularly shaped rooms with rock walls and rustic furniture are connected to each other by narrow stairways. It's a popular spot with the city's bohemians, especially Thursdays and Fridays. Hours are 1pm to 9 or 10pm daily (open later on weekends).

More conventional nightspots—such as dance clubs—aren't difficult to find; ask at your hotel. A different kind of place is **La Dama de las Camelias,** Sopeña 32 (no phone), an unpretentious second-floor bar that doesn't get going until late in the evening. The music is all classic recordings of *danzón,* mambo, *son cubano,* and salsa. It opens at 8pm, starts getting busy around midnight, and closes at 4am. **Bar Ocho** (no phone), another salsa bar, is behind the San Diego church at the foot of the hill where El Pípila stands.

3 Santiago de Querétaro (★(★(★

213km (132 miles) NW of Mexico City; 96km (60 miles) SE of San Miguel Allende; 200km (124 miles) S of San Luis Potosí

Querétaro is the most historic city in the region. During the Colonial Era, it played a central role in all the expeditions headed north. Later, it was at the center of events in the three wars that forged the Mexican nation: La Independencia, La Reforma, and La Revolución. Downtown Querétaro is lively, pedestrian-friendly, and filled with eye-opening colonial architecture. The local government has spruced up the city, keeps it neat with round-the-clock cleaning crews, and provides street vendors with attractive stands, regulating them so that they don't obstruct public streets and walkways. In the evenings, the downtown area fills with people who stroll about the plazas and *andadores* (pedestrian walkways) and eat at one of the restaurants, outdoor cafes, or food stands. Since the city is only an hour by bus from San Miguel, it makes an easy day trip. But once you come, you'll be tempted to stay longer and get better acquainted with this lovely city.

The Spanish founded Querétaro in 1531 during their first large-scale expedition into the northern stretches of their new territory. During a skirmish with the Chichimeca, Santiago (St. James) appeared in the clouds. Santiago is the patron saint of Spain and of La Reconquista, the 7-century struggle to recapture all of Spain from the Moors, which had ended barely 40 years earlier. It is no wonder that the Spanish hoped he would again lend a hand in this new struggle for territory. For his appearance, Santiago also became the patron saint of Querétaro. (When you visit the Jardín Zenea at the center of town, look up at the facade of the church of San Francisco, and you will see a depiction of Santiago in battle, lopping off the turbaned head of a Moor.) In time, the city became the base of operations for all expeditions headed north.

While the conquistadors were setting out to conquer lands for the crown, the religious orders were setting out to win souls for Christ. The Franciscans established a large community in Querétaro and eventually a college for the propagation of the faith, the first such institution in the New World. From here, the missionaries set out (always on foot, as the Franciscan Rule forbade riding on horseback or in carriages) to evangelize and establish missions as far away as Texas and California. Some of their histories are nothing short of astounding. Among them was Junípero Sierra, who went all the way to California establishing missions there.

Centuries later, Mexican independence began in Querétaro with the conspiracy of 1810 (of which Father Hidalgo was a member). A little more than 50 years after that, Querétaro was again in the thick of things when Emperor Maximilian made his last stand here, and was captured and executed. Another 50 years passed, and the city became the site of the laborious constitutional convention during the Mexican Revolution. The document that it produced, the Constitution of 1917, remains the law of the land.

ESSENTIALS

GETTING THERE & DEPARTING   By Plane   Most visitors still fly to Mexico City and then take the bus that leaves directly from the airport's main terminal to Querétaro. Look about for an escalator in the E-2 area. Take it up to an elevated concourse, which leads to the bus ticket counters. A one-way ticket is $23 (£12). Departures are about every half-hour, and the trip takes 3 hours.

Querétaro's new airport has limited international service and is a half-hour from downtown. **Continental ExpressJet** (© **800/231-0856** in the U.S., or 01-800/900-5000 in Mexico) flies to/from Houston. **Delta Airlines** (© **800/241-4141** in the U.S. or 01-800/902-2100) flies to/from Atlanta. In the future, some of Mexico's newborn discount carriers might be introducing international service. There are also connecting flights from nearby Mexico City.

By Car   From Mexico City, take the super toll road 57D (2½ hr.). From San Miguel, take Highway 111 to 57D, then turn right (1 hr.). From San Luis Potosí, take 57D south (2½ hr.).

By Bus   For directions from the Mexico City airport, see "By Plane," above. From Mexico City's northern bus terminal (Central del Norte), buses leave every 15 minutes. Make sure you get a *directo* (nonstop). From San Miguel, second-class buses leave every 20 minutes. The bus station is south of town. Look for a booth in the terminal that sells cab tickets. A cab ride downtown costs $4 (£2).

VISITOR INFORMATION   There is a good **tourism information office** at Pasteur Norte 4, just off the Plaza de la Independencia on the north side. It's open daily from 9am to 8pm. The phone numbers are © **888/811-6130** in the U.S. or **442/238-5067;** or visit **www.venaqueretaro.com**. The office was running 1-hour tours of the city by trolley-style bus. These tours are now operated by private companies who have a concession from tourism and also staff the information kiosks in some of the plazas. You can get info from the staff at these kiosks, but you'll also get a pitch to take a bus tour. These concessions are, thus far, on a trial basis. Tourism still offers a self-guided audio walking tour of the *centro histórico*. At the information office, you can rent a digital player for $5 (£2.50) per day, using a credit card voucher for a deposit.

Santiago de Querétaro

Rail Station ■

57

Carretera Constitución

To San Luis Potosí
& San Miguel

Libramiento a San Luis Potosí

Camino a San Gregorio

Invierno

Corregidora

Cerro de
las Campanas ■

Av. Universidad

Av. Mariano Escobedo

Av. 15 de Mayo

Rio Querétaro

Av. Francisco I. Madero

Av. 16 de
Septiembre

Independencia

Juan Caballero y Osio

Rio Querétaro

Av. General Arteaga

Calz. Ignacio Zaragoza

Av. Ejército Republicano

Calz. de los Arcos

Av. Constituyentes

Corregidora

Luis Pasteur

Calz. de los Arquitos

To Celaya ←

Autopista

**45
D**

**45
D**

To Celaya (no toll) ←

M. Solano

Luis Pasteur

To
Mexico City →

**57
D**

Autopista

"Zona Centro" see map below

JALISCO

GUANA-
JUATO

Querétaro

MICHOACÁN

QUERÉTARO

QUERÉTARO

0   100 mi

0   100 km

Mexico City ★

0   1 mi

0   1 km

Zona Centro

Av. Mariano Escobedo

Av. José Ma. Morelos

Ignacio Allende

Luis Pasteur

Av. 15 de Mayo

Prospero C. Vega

Ignacio M. Altamirano

Septiembre

Manuel Gutiérrez Nájera

Damián Carmona

Cerro de las
Campanas ←

Av. Hidalgo

Jardín de la
Corregidora

Av. 16 de

Río de la Loza

Felipe Luna

Balvarena

Palacio
Municipal ■

Templo de
Santa Clara

Jardín
Zenea

Casa de
Ecala ■

Casa de la
Corregidora ■

Av. 5 de Mayo

V. Carranza

Museo Regional ■

Av. Francisco I. Madero

Melchor Ocampo

Vicente Guerrero

Casa de la
Marquesa ■

Casa Querétana
de Artesanía

Mesón de
Santa Rosa ■

Av. Pino Suárez

Museo
de Arte

Av. Independencia

Plaza de la
Independencia

Av. Independencia

Convento de la ■
Santa Cruz

Ezequiel Montes

Av. General Arteaga

Casa de la
Zacatecana

Reforma

Aqueduct

Av. Juárez

Corregidora

Vergara

Luis Pasteur

Av. 20 de Noviembre

■ Templo
de Santa Rosa
de Viterbo

Calzada Ignacio Zaragoza

Calzada Ignacio Zaragoza

Av. Luis Pasteur

Av. 21 de Marzo

Av. Industria

Bus 🚌

Information ⓘ

Post Office ✉

Train 🚆

Andadores
(road closed
to traffic)

Fernando de Tapia

Jalpan

ALAMEDA
HIDALGO

Av. Constituyentes

0   1/4 mi

0   0.25 km

CITY LAYOUT   The heart of downtown is the Jardín Zenea, at the intersection of the main north–south and east–west streets, Corregidora and Madero. Just east is the Plaza de Armas, and farther east are the Convento de la Cruz and the famous aqueduct. West of Jardín Zenea are several plazas, churches, convents, and museums.

FAST FACTS: Querétaro

American Express The local representative is **Agencia Turismo Beverly**, Av. Tecnológico 118, Col. San Angel (℃ **442/216-1500**), open Monday through Friday from 9am to 2pm and 4 to 6pm, Saturday from 9am to noon.

Area Code The telephone area code is **442**.

Climate The average temperature in summer is 75°F (24°C), in winter 56°F (13°C).

Elevation Querétaro sits at 1,818m (5,963 ft.).

Emergency The central emergency number (similar to 911) is ℃ **066**.

Hospital The local hospital is the **Hospital Angeles** (℃ **442/215-5901** or 442/216-2751) at Bernardo del Razo 21, Colonia Ensueño.

Internet Access Cybercafes and Internet access providers are everywhere in the central historic district.

Parking To find parking in the downtown area, look for white square signs with the capital letter E in light blue. There are a couple of places at Pino Suárez 45 and 17. Rates run about $1 (50p) for the first hour, and a little less thereafter.

Population Querétaro has 920,000 residents.

Post Office The *correo*, Arteaga 5, is open Monday through Saturday from 9am to 2:30pm.

A STROLL AROUND THE HISTORIC CENTER

In the center of Querétaro, you'll notice right away how many plazas, churches, and convents there are. If you're really observant, you'll notice that the plazas are frequently next to the churches. In fact, most of these plazas were formed at the cost of the convents, which lost much of their real estate to the government during la Reforma. This is true of the town's most important plaza, **Jardín Zenea,** where we will begin. This plaza was part of the atrium of San Francisco Church and Convent, which you see facing the park across Corregidora Street. This park is popular every night, but especially on Sunday, when the municipal band plays dance music of the '40s, '50s, and '60s. Great fun! The old bandstand dates from 1900.

Turn toward **San Francisco Church** and you will see on the facade the depiction of St. James, mentioned earlier. From the beginning, this church was the most important in town; it remains so today, the more recent cathedral notwithstanding. It and the attached cloister are all that remain of a large complex that included several chapels and an orchard that extended a few blocks east and south. Inside the church, you will see a few interesting remains of baroque decoration. The main altar is a rather uninteresting piece of neoclassicism that replaced what reputedly was a masterpiece of baroque design. This is a common story with churches in Querétaro. Many of the baroque *retablos* escaped the plunderers, only to fall prey to the "improvers," as was the case here.

All Things Querétaro

Walking up Andador Libertad, you will see a pergola of bougainvillea. Just past it, on the right hand side is the state-run store for arts and crafts, **Casa Queretana de Artesanía**, Andador Libertad 52 (© **442/224-3456**). Even though Querétaro is a small state, it has a wide variety of craft traditions. You can see a sampling of these in the three rooms in this part of the store, and in another three rooms that are farther up the walkway. Everything in this store was made in the state. Hours are Tuesday and Wednesday 11am to 2pm and 4 to 7pm; Thursday and Friday 11am to 2pm and 4 to 8pm; Saturday 11am to 8pm; and Sunday 11am to 4pm.

Next door to the church is the cloister, which is now the **Museo Regional** ✿. It's open Tuesday through Sunday from 10am to 7pm. Admission is $3.50 (£1.75). Exhibits include artifacts from pre-Hispanic, colonial, and republican times. The architecture shows common traits of Franciscan design in the simplicity of its lines and decoration, which you can contrast with the rich decoration (caryatids and all) of the former Augustinian convent, now a museum of colonial art (see below). Leaving the museum, turn left and then left again and you'll be on the pedestrians-only Andador Libertad. This leads to the small Plaza de Independencia or Plaza de Armas, with its carefully pruned Indian laurel trees, outdoor restaurants, and colonial mansions.

At the Plaza de Independencia are a few things to take note of. First is **Galería Libertad,** on your right just as you get to the plaza. It's free, and, in past visits, I've come upon some entertaining exhibits. At the far end of the plaza is the **Casa de la Corregidora.** As you walk toward it, you will pass on your left the **Casa de Ecala,** a baronial mansion with magnificent balconies and wrought iron, which dates from the 18th century.

La Corregidora was the wife of the mayor *(corregidor)* at the beginning of the struggle for independence. Her full name was Doña Josefa Ortiz de Domínguez. She was a member of the conspiracy to liberate Mexico from Spain. As the wife of Querétaro's mayor, she was in a useful position for gathering information. When the conspiracy was discovered, she was put under house arrest but still managed to get a warning to Father Hidalgo. He eluded capture and rushed to Dolores, where he gave his famous *grito* (the cry for independence). For her actions, La Corregidora was imprisoned several times between 1810 and 1817. She died impoverished and forgotten, but was later remembered when she became the first woman to appear on a Mexican coin.

The fountain in the middle of the plaza honors Querétaro's greatest benefactor, a Spanish grandee named Don Juan Antonio de Urrutia y Arana, who built a large aqueduct to bring water to the city. This colonial aqueduct is the most famous landmark in the city. To view it, continue east on Andador Libertad. It ends in one block, so you must dogleg to the next eastbound street, either Independencia or Carranza. The street gently climbs towards the church and convent of **La Santa Cruz** ✿✿, where missionaries were trained to evangelize the heathens as far away as California and Nicaragua. The church has one bell tower with an attractive tile dome. It and the convent are Franciscan. The convent continues in operation. You can take a short tour, usually led by an elderly monk, Fray Jesús Guzmán de León, who speaks English. He will show you how the water from the aqueduct arrived here and how it fed a system of fountains known as *cajas de agua* that provided water throughout the old city. From these, the citizens of Querétaro would fill their buckets. He will also show you a thorn tree said to have grown from the walking stick of Friar Antonio Margil de Jesús, a famous missionary who covered vast territories on foot. This thorn tree is considered miraculous because its thorns grow in the shape of the cross. The tour is free, but you will be given an opportunity to make a contribution to the preservation of the convent and church.

Behind the church is a small plaza from which you can view the aqueduct. Follow the rough stone wall partially covered by the branches of mesquite trees, and you can't miss it. The aqueduct extends across an expanse of bottomland from the hill in front. This feat of engineering required the construction of 74 arches. Work began in 1726 and finished in 1738.

From here, make your way back to the Jardín Zenea. If you go by way of Calle Independencia, you can pop into **La Casa de la Zacatecana** (look for a banner), Independencia 59 (© **442/224-0758**). It presents a vision of what many colonial mansions were like in Querétaro, with period furnishings and decor. Hours are from Tuesday to Sunday 10am to 6pm in winter (11am-7pm in summer). Entrance is $2 (£1). Associated with this house (as with a couple of others in town) is a tale of illicit love, murder, and retribution. Colonial Mexico is a fertile land for gothic tales.

Back at Jardín Zenea, head west on Calle Madero. At the first corner, just before the street becomes an *andador,* is **La Casa de la Marquesa** ⋆⋆⋆, an opulent colonial residence–turned–hotel. Walk in and check out the courtyard lobby, which has elaborate *mudéjar*-style (a Spanish architectural style with Moorish influences) arches and patterned walls.

Cater-corner from this hotel is the **church and former Convent of Santa Clara** ⋆⋆⋆. The church is a must-see; inside are six astonishing baroque *retablos* and a choir loft, all gilded and each a self-contained composition. In prominent positions are sculptures and paintings of saints; here and there, the faces of angels appear out of the enveloping, thickly textured ornament. Gazing upon these is like gazing upon a mandala. The juxtaposition of straight lines and multiple facets with overflowing curves that move inward and outward make the *retablos* appear fluid and rigid at the same time. The key to enjoying these *retablos* is not to look for proportion, balance, or an underlying structure, but to look at them as the expression of an ecstatic religious sentiment that rejects these very notions.

For a greater acquaintance with the colonial religious mind, walk south 1 block on Allende. On your right will be the **Museo de Arte** ⋆⋆⋆ (© **442/212-3523**), in the former **convent of San Agustín.** Admission is $2 (£1.10); it's free on Tuesday. The museum is open Tuesday through Sunday from 10am to 6pm. It contains one of the great collections of Mexican colonial art, but the architecture of the former convent alone is worth the price of admission. Highly stylized human forms, complex geometric lines, and vegetal motifs are everywhere. The art is organized by style of painting. The collection has works by Europeans, but its focus is on painters in New Spain, including the most famous of the land.

If you're still in the mood for colonial splendor, walk west 2 blocks on Pino Suárez. After you cross Melchor Ocampo, turn left down a narrow street graced with bougainvillea and you'll come to the **church and former convent of Santa Rosa de Viterbo** ⋆⋆⋆. Like Santa Clara, it is a masterpiece of baroque architecture. On the

Tips **Shopping for Opals**

The small state of Querétaro is one of the two principal places in the world that mine opals commercially (the other is southern Australia). The opal is a soft stone noted for its iridescent color. Prices vary depending on size, color, shape, and transparency. A few stores in Querétaro, usually called *lapidarias,* sell locally mined opals and other semiprecious stones. One is the **Lapidaria de Querétaro,** Corregidora Norte 149-A, a few blocks north of Jardín Zenea (© 442/212-0030), open Monday through Friday from 10am to 2pm and 5 to 8pm and Saturday 10am to 3pm. Or stop by **El Artesano,** a shop at Corregidora Norte 42, near the Jardín Zenea. Owner Alfredo Vázquez, who carves miniatures out of opals and other semiprecious stones, speaks mostly Spanish, and is a font of information on opals and the trade. He keeps interesting store hours: 1 to 9pm Monday through Saturday. Also try **Lapidaria Ramírez,** Pino Suárez 98.

outside, notice the scroll-shaped flying buttresses (a style that as far as I know is unique to Querétaro) and the imaginative tower. Inside, the church is much like Santa Clara, with magnificent gilt *retablos* occupying all available wall space. Also like Santa Clara, the main altar failed to escape the "improvers."

Farther west (a bit too far to walk) is the **Cerro de las Campanas (Hill of Bells),** where Maximilian was executed. You'll find a large, ugly statue of Juárez installed there by the Mexican government to counter a small and sad memorial chapel for Maximilian erected by his brother, Emperor Franz Josef of Austria. Immediately south of downtown is a park called Alameda Hidalgo, which is a lovely setting for a walk.

WHERE TO STAY

Rates below include the 17% tax. Most of the downtown hotels have high and low season. High season is Easter, July, August, December, and any long weekend. The city is a favorite weekend getaway from Mexico City; it's much easier to find a room during the week.

VERY EXPENSIVE

La Casa de la Marquesa ᏘᏘᏘ   Few hotels in Mexico can match this one for sheer colonial opulence. Even if you don't stay here, make a point of walking into the courtyard lobby. Built for the wife of the Marqués de Urrutia, the house, with Moorish-inspired arches, tiles, and painted walls, has an Andalusian feel. Rooms are large, have all the amenities, and are furnished with period pieces and Persian rugs. Bed choices include one queen-size, two queen-size, or one king-size. The least expensive rooms (deluxe) are across the street in another colonial house, La Casa Azul. The hotel, a member of the Small Luxury Hotels of the World, prides itself on the attention it gives its guests. The location is excellent.

Madero 41, 76000 Querétaro, Qro. © **442/212-0092.** Fax 442/212-0098. www.lacasadelamarquesa.com. 25 units. $212 (£106) deluxe; $248 (£124) royal suite; $412 (£206) imperial suite. AE, MC, V. Valet parking $5.50 (£2.75). **Amenities:** Restaurant; bar; concierge; travel agency; room service; in-room massage; laundry service; dry cleaning; nonsmoking rooms. *In room:* A/C, TV (with DVD in most rooms), coffeemaker (in some rooms), hair dryer.

EXPENSIVE

Gran Hotel 𝒌𝒌𝒌   After being boarded up for many years, the old Gran Hotel finally reopened in mid-2006 and looks grand, indeed. As is often the case with old hotels, there is a lavish use of space that is decidedly uneconomical (and attention-grabbing for precisely that reason). A grand stairway and cavernous galleries with vaulted ceilings lead the way to your room. The rooms have high ceilings and carpeted floors and are large and comfortable with independently controlled air-conditioning and beautifully finished bathrooms. The hotel is set between two plazas, and most rooms have a view of one plaza or the other (with double-glazed windows and French doors). Noise is not a problem, but for the very light sleeper, the hotel has a few interior rooms *(ejecutivos)*, which are oversize and come with a few extra amenities for virtually the same price as standard rooms. All units are nonsmoking.

Juárez Sur 5 (between Jardín Zenea and Plaza Constitución), 76000 Querétaro, Qro. ℂ **442/251-8050.** www.granhoteldequeretaro.com.mx. 42 units. $186 (£93) superior; $192 (£96) executive; $260 (£130) corner suite. AE, MC, V. Valet parking $5 (£2.75). **Amenities:** Bar; fitness room; tour desk; car rental; membership in local spa; laundry service; dry cleaning, nonsmoking rooms. *In room:* A/C, TV, Wi-Fi and high-speed Internet access, hair dryer, safe.

Hotel Mesón del Alfarero 𝒌𝒌   This place will please those who like their hotels small and with a modern aesthetic. Modern, yes, but definitely Mexican, in that it has a distinctive look that contemporary architects in Mexico have developed and made their own. Rooms are large and uncluttered. There's a lot of white and cream-colored stucco with sharp accents. The mattresses are comfortable, and the furniture has character. Bathrooms are medium to large and attractive, with Talavera tiles, and two-person tubs in the master suites. The outdoor spaces are serene. An open-air restaurant occupies a small area by the entrance.

Hidalgo 71 (between Ezequiel Montes and Melchor Ocampo), 76000 Querétaro, Qro. ℂ **442/212-7053.** Fax 442/214-0552. www.mesondelalfarero.com.mx. 12 units. $160 (£80) standard; $188 (£94) junior suite; $215 (£108) master suite. Rates include continental breakfast. AE, MC, V. Free secure parking 1/2-block away. **Amenities:** Restaurant; bar; concierge; tour info; airport transportation; car rental; room service; laundry service; dry cleaning. *In room:* A/C, TV, Wi-Fi, minibar, hair dryer, safe.

Hotel Mesón de Santa Rosa 𝒌𝒌   With its large open courtyards, clean lines, and simple stone and iron work, this hotel presents a colonial architecture that contrasts sharply with La Casa de la Marquesa (see above). There are three elegant courtyards variously holding a pool, a fountain, and a stone trough for watering your horses (a vestige of the original tavern, which served wagon and mule drivers). Rooms are quiet, large, and comfortable, with high ceilings, carpeted floors, and boring furniture and decoration. Standard rooms come with either two doubles or a king-size bed; superior rooms are much larger. Higher rates are for remodeled rooms with air-conditioning. The location, at the southwest corner of the Plaza de Armas, is ideal.

Pasteur 17 Sur (on Plaza de Armas, access from 5 de Mayo), 76000 Querétaro, Qro. ℂ **442/441-5000.** Fax 442/212-5522. www.mesonsantarosa.com. 21 units. $140–$150 (£70–£75) standard double; $196–$210 (£88–£105) superior double. AE, DC, MC, V. Valet parking $5 (£2.50). **Amenities:** Restaurant; bar; midsize heated outdoor pool; tour desk; car rental; room service; babysitting; laundry service; dry cleaning. *In room:* A/C (in 7 rooms), TV, Wi-Fi, minibar, coffeemaker, hair dryer, safe.

INEXPENSIVE

Hotel Posada Acueducto *(Value*   You get a good room for the money at this hotel. The rooms are on two floors running along one side of the narrow property. Almost all face a thin strip of patio. Most are in back, in the new section (slightly preferable).

Finds **Hot Tamales**

I love tamales—a Mexican comfort food that doesn't taste at all the same outside Mexico. Restaurants don't offer tamales, and when they do, the tamales are disappointing. Of course, tamales vary a great deal from region to region, but I have a special fondness for those of central Mexico. There are three vendors on the same block of Arteaga street between Allende and Guerrero. My favorite is at 37-A Arteaga, but all are good. These places offer two styles: I think the traditional ones are better than the Oaxacan style because the masa is lighter and has better texture. They come in three flavors: green, red, and cheese with slices of poblano chile *(rajas con queso).* All are good. They are a just a bit spicy. Two make for a nice breakfast or supper and would run you $1.60 (80p). These places are open in the mornings and evenings. They also serve flavored *atole*—a hot corn-based beverage.

They are mostly medium size with ample bathrooms. The one upstairs in the very back (Rm. 111) has a king-size bed and a little porch. The lower price listed is for a room with one double bed; the higher price is for a room with two double beds; somewhere in between is the price for a room with a king bed.

Tip: Ask the staff about their new hotel. When I was last there, it was still unfinished and didn't have a name, but it looked attractive and comfortable, with large rooms, a pool, and a fitness room. The rates might end up being between $120 and $150 (£60–£75) range.

Juárez 64 Sur (between Arteaga and Zaragoza), 76000 Querétaro, Qro. © **442/224-1289.** 15 units. $38–$54 (£19–£27) double. No credit cards. Street parking. **Amenities:** *In room:* A/C, TV, no phone.

Hotel Señorial   This is a simple hotel with plainly furnished, medium size rooms. By and large they are a little more attractive than the rooms at Posada Acueducto (see above). The carpeting has been replaced with Pergo flooring (bathrooms still have tile.) The beds (usually two twins or two doubles) are comfortable. The important thing is to reserve an even-numbered room. Odd-numbered rooms are in the south wing, which has plumbing so noisy you think it will bring down the building.

Guerrero Norte 10-A (corner of Hidalgo), 76000 Querétaro, Qro. ©/fax 442/214-3700. www.senorial-hotel.com. 54 units. $50–$64 (£25–£32) double. MC, V. Free secure parking. **Amenities:** Restaurant; room service. *In room:* A/C (in 13 rooms), TV, Wi-Fi.

Mesón del Obispado   For better or worse, this colonial hotel is in the middle of the most popular part of downtown. For better, it's on a pedestrian *andador* and is close to everything. For worse, it's by the Plaza de la Corregidora, which doesn't settle down on weekends until well after midnight. The rooms in front have balconies overlooking the *andador* and are popular with the vacationing crowd that isn't going to bed early anyway. I had a room in back that looked out toward the courtyard of the hotel, and it was perfectly quiet. The rooms are medium to large in size, usually with two double beds or a king. The furniture is plain. The best thing about the bathrooms is that there's plenty of hot water and good water pressure.

Andador 16 de Septiembre 13, 76000 Querétaro, Qro. © 442/224-2464. mesondelobispado@hotmail.com.mx.
16 units. $57–$64 (£39–£32) double. AE, DC, MC V. Limited street parking. **Amenities:** Restaurant; tour info; room
service. *In room:* TV.

WHERE TO DINE

In addition to the restaurants listed below, you might want to try the restaurant at the
Mesón de Santa Rosa on the Plaza de Armas. One local dish I can't recommend is the
enchiladas queretanas. The problem is that the enchiladas typically come buried in a
mountain of salty fresh cheese that completely overpowers the mild sauce. For fancy
baked goods try **Panadería El Globo** (© 442/212-8883) at Corregidora Sur 41.
Tip: Late breakfasts are popular on weekends. If you're not eating breakfast at your
hotel, you can beat the crowds by showing up at a restaurant by 9am.

EXPENSIVE

El Caserío 🞷🞷 SPANISH   The favorite dining spot for Querétaro's well-heeled
denizens, El Caserío owes its popularity in part to the stylish, comfortable, no-nonsense dining areas, in part to the cooking and the service, which are both good, and,
I suspect, in part to its ample off-street parking (not that common in this city). The
menu is broad enough to please a variety of tastes—with steaks cut to order, classic
Mexican soups, and pleasing salads—but Spanish food is the main attraction. Specialties include *lechón segoviano* (roast suckling pig), *pescado a la sal* (fish cooked under a
layer of rock salt, allow extra time), and paella. I had the *crema de tres quesos* (three-
cheese soup) and the *pescado a la sidra seca (fish cooked in a seafood broth with apple
cider).* Both were good. It's a long walk from the Jardín Zenea; take a cab.

Constituyentes Poniente 101 (near intersection with Ezequiel Montes). © 442/216-1777. Reservations recommended for dinner. Main courses $13–$20 (£6.50–£10). AE, MC, V. Mon–Sat 2pm–midnight; Sun 2–6pm.

San Miguelito 🞷🞷 MEXICAN   The least you should do is go for a drink and a
view of the surroundings. The restaurant occupies the restored Casa de los Cinco
Patios, a landmark colonial house that had been closed to the public for years. The
first patio (which is the main dining area) impresses with the height of its arches and
the fine wrought-iron work. It's beautifully lit at night, too. For appetizers, try the
infladitas (small puffy tostadas topped with Yucatecan-style pork). Most of the main
courses are steaks prepared with a variety of sauces. (*Tip:* In order to request your steak
cooked to taste, see p. 769, "Dining Terminology," in Appendix B: Survival Spanish.)
On one side of the main entrance is the bar **La Viejoteca,** with live music on the
weekends. On the other side is **La Antojería,** which serves traditional supper foods—
tacos, and such The decor is folksy and nostalgic for Mexicans. It's a fun place to have
a bite.

Andador 5 de Mayo 39 (between Corregidora and Vergara). © 442/224-2760. Reservations recommended on
weekends. Main courses $10–$16 (£5–£8). AE, MC, V. Tues–Sat 1–11pm; Sun 1–5pm.

MODERATE

Apolonia 🞷🞷 NUEVA COCINA   At this restaurant not far from the Plaza de
Armas you can dine on some inventive dishes that are well prepared, and enjoy them
in attractive surroundings. There's a good selection of soups and salads, including a
savory strawberry soup served hot, and a green salad with mango and cashews. The
main courses include a chicken breast in a pool of apple/corn/poblano sauce or shrimp
with tequila and roasted cactus leaves. Servings aren't overly large, and the desserts are
mostly light dishes.

Andador Libertad 46. (C) **442/212-0389.** Reservations recommended. Main courses $8–$15 (£4–£7.50). MC, V. Wed–Mon 1:30pm–midnight.

Parrilla Leonesa *Finds* TACOS   This place inside the Hotel Flamingo serves the best tacos in the city. Choose from a variety of grilled meats. The popular *parrillada leonesa* grilled combo includes chicken, beef, and pork served on a small brazier on a bed of grilled onions and chile slices, with *queso fundido* on the side. Tortillas are handmade. Salsas are fresh. I suggest taking a cab here. *Note:* This place specializes in *tacos de parrilla* (grill). To try another variety of taco—the *tacos de guisos* or *de cazuela* (both casserole tacos)—consider **Tacos del 57** ((C) **442/224-2211**) at Calle del 57 #21. It's 1 block west of Ezequiel Montes, right before you get to the first traffic light (there's no sign). It serves fare such as eggs cooked in a *chile pasilla* sauce, pork rinds cooked in a red sauce, and delicious and safe fresh-fruit drinks.

Constituyentes Poniente 138 (at Av. Technológico). (C) **442/216-2123.** Taco plates $2.50 (£1.25); *parrilladas* $12–$16 (£6–£8). AE, MC, V. Mon–Sat 8am–midnight; Sun 8am–10pm.

Restaurante Bar 1810 MEXICAN/INTERNATIONAL   This is one of the restaurants on the Plaza de Armas across from the house of La Corregidora. With a large and varied menu, it's the perfect place to enjoy an afternoon or evening meal. Your best bet is to stick with traditional Mexican specialties, which are well prepared; the soups are wonderful. Sunday brunch is especially popular.

Andador Libertad 62 (on the Plaza de Armas). (C) **442/214-3324.** Reservations recommended on weekends and holidays. Main courses $8–$16 (£4–£8). AE, MC, V. Mon–Sat 8am–midnight; Sun 8am–10pm.

INEXPENSIVE

Cafetería Bisquets *Value* MEXICAN   This modest restaurant serves inexpensive *comida casera* (home cooking) on a little patio and in adjoining dining rooms. One of the specialties is paper-thin *milanesa* served with green enchiladas on the side. Breakfasts are popular. Avoid the *bisquet*—something like an American biscuit, but larger and heavier—and try the *chilaquiles con pollo y crema* or any of the egg dishes and the *café con leche*. The *menú del día* is a bargain.

Pino Suárez 7 (between Juárez and Allende). (C) **442/214-1481.** Main courses $4.50–$8 (£2.25–£4); *menú del día* $4–$6 (£2–£3). No credit cards. Daily 7:30am–11pm.

Cafetería La Mariposa MEXICAN   This coffee shop, sweet shop, and restaurant is a popular hangout with locals. The full breakfasts are probably better at Bisquets, but this place makes its own breads and yogurt and is a nice spot for a light breakfast. The old-time dining room is comfortable (less cramped than at Bisquets). For lunch or dinner you can count on most of the Mexican standards on the menu.

Angela Peralta 7 (just off Corregidora). (C) **442/212-1166.** Main courses $5–$8 (£2.50–£4). No credit cards. Daily 8am–9:30pm. From the Jardín Zenea, walk north 2 blocks on Corregidora and turn left.

4 Zacatecas ⊛⊛⊛

627km (389 miles) NW of Mexico City; 198km (123 miles) NW of San Luis Potosí; 322km (200 miles) NE of Guadalajara; 298km (185 miles) SE of Durango

Zacatecas, like Guanajuato, owes its beauty to the wealth of silver extracted from its mines. The farthest flung of the silver cities, it still feels like an outpost of civilization. High above the center of town looms a rocky hill with a distinctive crest, which is accessible by cable car. From the summit, you have a panoramic view of the wild and desolate terrain that surrounds the city. The scene makes you realize what a frontier town Zacatecas must have been, and after you have been in town for a few days, you appreciate its present sophistication all the more. You will find surprisingly good museums, beautiful architecture, and good restaurants. The city has gone to the enormous trouble of burying all of its power and telephone cables, which adds greatly to the beauty of the town and makes strolling along the streets a pleasure.

ESSENTIALS

GETTING THERE & DEPARTING   **By Plane**   Mexicana (© 800/531-7921 in the U.S., 01-800/502-2000 in Mexico, or 492/922-7429; www.mexicana.com) flies nonstop to and from Los Angeles. So does **American Airlines** (© 800/223-5436 in the U.S., or © 01-800/904-6000 in Mexico). Seats are hard to come by around Christmas, when native Zacatecans fly home in large numbers. Several domestic carriers link Zacatecas to other points in the country.

Transportation from the airport, 29km (18 miles) north of Zacatecas, is $15 by taxi.

By Car   From the south, you can take Highway 45D, a toll road, from Querétaro through Irapuato, León, and Aguascalientes (a 6-hr. drive). It's expensive (about $30/£17) but fast. Highway 54 heads northeast to Saltillo and Monterrey (a 5- to 6-hr. drive) and southeast to Guadalajara (a 4½-hr. drive). Highway 49 leads north to Torreón (4 hr.) and southeast to San Luis Potosí (3 hr.). Highway 45 heads to Durango (4 hr.).

By Bus   Omnibus de México, Estrella Blanca, and their many affiliates handle first-class bus travel to and from Zacatecas. Together, they operate 20 buses a day to/from Guadalajara; 20 to/from León (where you would change buses for Guanajuato); 30 buses that go to/from Mexico City, stopping in Querétaro; and 12 per day to/from San Luis Potosí. The **Central Camionera** (bus station) is on a hilltop a bit out of town. The taxi ride costs about $4 (£2). You can check schedules and buy tickets from several travel agencies in town. Ask at your hotel.

VISITOR INFORMATION   The downtown office is at Hidalgo 401 at Callejón de la Caja (© **492/924-4047** or 492/925-1277); it's open daily from 9am to 9pm. Sometimes there's an information desk outside on Hidalgo.

CITY LAYOUT   Understanding traffic circulation in the middle of town requires an advanced degree in chaos theory. I either walk or let the cab driver handle it. The city's main axis is Hidalgo. From the **Plaza de Armas (main square),** it goes 8 blocks southwest to the Enrique Estrada Park and Hotel Quinta Real (changing names as it goes); in the opposite direction it reaches another 8 blocks to the Rafael Coronel Museum (again making a name change). The historical center of town extends several blocks on either side of this 1.5km (1-mile) stretch of Hidalgo.

GETTING AROUND   I enjoy walking around Zacatecas, but the terrain is hilly and the air is thin. Cabs are inexpensive and readily available. Their availability declines somewhat between 2 and 4pm, when office workers snag them to get home for the midafternoon meal.

Zacatecas

Church ✝
Information ⓘ

0 — 1/8 mi
0 — 125 meters

ACCOMMODATIONS ■
Hotel Condesa **16**
Hotel Emporio Zacatecas **7**
Hotel Quinta Real **19**
Mesón de Jobito **15**
Motel Zacatecas Courts **20**

ATTRACTIONS ●
Catedral **11**
Church of San Agustín **14**
Church of Santo Domingo **6**
La Mina "El Edén"
  (front entrance) **1**
  (back entrance) **2**
Mercado González Ortega **13**
Museo F. Goitia **18**
Museo Pedro Coronel **5**

Museo Rafael Coronel **4**
Palacio del Gobierno **9**
Palacio de la Mala Noche **10**
Plaza de Armas **8**
Teatro Calderón **12**
Teleférico Station
  (Cable Car Station) **3**
Viajes Mazzoco **17**

FAST FACTS: Zacatecas

American Express Visit travel agent **Viajes Mazzocco,** Enlace 115 (© 492/922-0859, -5159; fax 492/924-0277). Hours are Monday through Friday from 9am to 6pm, Saturday from 9am to 2pm.

Area Code The telephone area code is **492.**

Climate It can get very cold in winter here. At other times it can be chilly in the evenings. The weather has been changing and is getting warmer in the summer, to the extent that some up-market hotels have installed air-conditioning.

Elevation The city is at a lofty 2,485m (8,151 ft.). The air is crisp and cool, but a tad thin for some people.

Emergency & Police The emergency number is © **066.**

Hospital The two hospitals in town are **Clínica Santa Elena,** Av. Guerrero 143 (© **492/922-6861**), and **Hospital San José,** Cuevas Cancino 208, near the clinic (© **492/922-3892**).

Internet Access Internet cafes are cheap and very popular with the young crowd. To find one all you have to do is ask at your hotel or get directions from any young person you meet on the street.

Population Zacatecas has 265,000 residents.

Post Office The *correo,* at Allende 111, a half-block from Avenida Hidalgo, is open Monday through Friday from 9am to 3pm, Saturday from 10am to 2pm.

SPECIAL EVENTS & FESTIVALS

During Semana Santa (Holy Week), Zacatecas hosts an **international cultural festival** that the town hopes will eventually rival the Festival Cervantino in Guanajuato. Painters, poets, dancers, musicians, actors, and other artists converge on the town.

The annual **Feria de Zacatecas,** which celebrates the founding of the city, begins sometime during the first week of September and lasts for 2 weeks, incorporating the national Fiestas Patrias (independence celebration). Cockfights, bullfights, sporting events, band concerts, and general hoopla prevail. Famous bullfighters appear, and the cheap bullfight tickets go for around $8 (£4).

EXPLORING ZACATECAS
SIGHTS

In town you can visit museums and churches, tour an **abandoned silver mine,** ride a cable car up to the **Cerro de la Bufa,** perhaps take in a concert, and partake of an old tradition called *callejoneadas.* On Saturday nights, people go strolling and singing with tambourines, drums, and a burro laden with mezcal through the winding streets and *callejones* (alleyways) of the city. Zacatecas remains largely neglected by foreign tourists, though it is popular with Mexicans. Consequently, the various sights provide little descriptive material in English. If you don't speak Spanish, you might want to hire a bilingual tour guide. Try contacting **Viajes Mazzocco** (see "American Express," in "Fast Facts," above). It offers several tours that you can choose from for a fixed price. Some take you around the city; others take you to **nearby ruins** or to some of the old towns near Zacatecas, such as **Jerez** or **Fresnillo.**

SHOPPING

Zacatecan handicrafts include stone-carving, leatherwork, and silver jewelry. Examples can be found in shops inside the old **Mercado González Ortega** on Hidalgo, next to the cathedral. There are a lot of silver jewelry shops in the center of town. A few other stores on Hidalgo and Tacuba sell crafts and antiques. Huichol Indians occasionally sell their crafts around the Plaza Independencia. Zacatecas is well known for its stone carvings. Many architects and builders from the United States come to Zacatecas when they need fancy stonework.

A STROLL AROUND TOWN

The **Plaza de Armas,** the town's main square on Avenida Hidalgo, is where you'll find the **cathedral** ⟨⟨⟨, with its famous facade. Nowhere else in Mexico is there anything like this; the depth of relief in the carving and wealth of detail create the impression that the images are formed not in stone but in some softer material, such as cake icing. The cathedral took 23 years to build (1729–52), and the final tower wasn't completed until 1904.

To the left of the cathedral, on the Plaza de Armas, is the 18th-century **Palacio de Gobierno,** where governors lived in colonial times. By the time of Mexico's revolt against Spain in 1810, Don Miguel de Rivera (Count of Santiago de la Laguna), owned it. Since 1834, it's been a government building. Inside is a modern **mural** (1970) by Antonio Pintor Rodríguez showing the history of Zacatecas. It is a straightforward chronological presentation of history from left to right, except for the center panel, which represents prominent Zacatecans. Below it is a stone frieze depicting the economic underpinning that supports society and drives historical events. It flows into the mural's central panel, tying society's leaders to the soil of their motherland.

To the left of the Palacio de Gobierno is the **Residencia de Gobernadores,** with its multicolor stonework. This building is newer than the Palacio and served as the governor's house until 1950. Across the street from the plaza are the **Palacio de la Mala Noche (Palace of the Bad Night)** and the Hotel Emporio. The palace's name comes from the mine that brought great wealth to its original owner, Manuel de Rétegui, a philanthropic Spaniard. In case you're thinking that such fine stonework is becoming a lost art, look at the hotel's facade, which was done within the last 40 years.

Climb the small street next to the Palacio de la Mala Noche, and you'll face the massive walls of the **church of Santo Domingo,** which fronts an open space that it shares with the Museo Pedro Coronel (see "Museums," below). This church and the building that houses the museum belonged to the Jesuits, until their expulsion in 1767. Afterward, the Dominicans occupied the church and convent. Inside are some lovely baroque gilt *retablos.*

Two blocks south of Santo Domingo, on Calle Dr. Hierro (the mostly level street that parallels Hidalgo), is another grand church, **San Agustín.** This one is in partial ruins. During the Reform Wars, Zacatecas's liberal leaders kicked out the Augustinian friars, converted the church and convent into a brothel and casino, and destroyed the reportedly beautiful gilt altarpieces. The bishop of Zacatecas promptly excommunicated these Philistines. Twenty years later, a Presbyterian missionary society bought the property and dismantled the ultrabaroque facade that decorated the east door. Again, excommunication for all who aided the missionaries. Now the government has begun restoration of the church and has converted the inside into exhibition space.

Turn and go downhill, and you'll be back on Avenida Hidalgo. Walk back toward the cathedral (left), and you'll pass on your left the **Teatro Calderón** (inaugurated first in 1836 and again in 1891 after a fire). A stately building with lovely stained-glass windows, it is also a favorite spot for people to sit and watch passersby. The opera star Angela Peralta sang here several times in the 1800s. Zacatecas has a flourishing music school, and occasionally it offers performances here. A little farther down Hidalgo, a block before the cathedral on the same side of the street, is the 19th-century **Mercado Jesús González Ortega,** which used to be the town's main market. A pleasant, old-fashioned market, it now holds small stores selling handicrafts and some of the region's wines.

Backtrack along Hidalgo, and over the next few blocks you will pass by some lovely buildings and climb up to **Enrique Estrada Park** (the street changes names and becomes Av. General Jesús González Ortega). The **equestrian statue** (1898) portrays none other than the general himself, hero of the Battle of Calpulalpan. Behind it are a gazebo with marvelous acoustics and a pleasant, shady park that is a romantic spot for young couples at night. Beginning at Estrada Park and extending southward are the lovely arches of the **Aqueduct of Zacatecas.** Two of these arches frame the doorway to the Quinta Real Hotel, which you can enter to see the town's old bullring, a lovely sight. Go to the hotel bar and order a margarita—another lovely sight.

A RIDE UP CERRO DE LA BUFA ✶✶✶

To get to the cable car station from the Plaza de Armas, you must climb one of the streets or alleys that lead up the hill that faces the cathedral. But first, glance up to see if the cars are running; if it's windy, they won't be. The first cross street will be Villalpando or Hierro; go right, and make a left when you get to the Callejón (alley) de García Roja. If you're unaccustomed to the thin air, this is quite a climb. An easier way to get there is to catch bus no. 7, which you can pick up along Juárez, or take a cab. The cable car (© 492/922-5694) is a great ride up to the Cerro de la Bufa. The view from the top is best in the late afternoon and early evening, when the sun is low in the sky; if you intend to ride the cable car down, you can't stay too late. It operates only from 10am to 6pm, but the walk down isn't too bad should you want to stay later. A one-way ticket is $2.50 (£1.25).

On Cerro de la Bufa is the **Museo de la Toma de Zacatecas,** which will be of most interest to Spanish-speaking history buffs. It displays artifacts and enlarged newspaper articles about the capture of Zacatecas by Pancho Villa. This was a decisive battle of La Revolución, and one of Villa's greatest victories. The museum is in need of investment; admission is $2 (£1). Beside the museum is the beautiful church **La Capilla de la Virgen del Patrocinio,** patroness of Zacatecas. Around the far side of the *cerro* (hill) is the **Mausoleo de los Hombres Ilustres de Zacatecas,** where many of the city's heroes are entombed.

MUSEUMS

La Mina "El Edén" ✶   This mine is a giant gash carved diagonally through the core of a mountain following the trail of a silver vein deeper and deeper underground. To see this gash and think that all the stone and ore that once occupied this space was mined and extracted by hand provokes a sense of wonder. The mine opened in 1586, using forced Indian labor. Accidents, tuberculosis, and silicosis caused the workers' early deaths. The mine was extremely rich, yielding gold, copper, zinc, iron, and lead in addition to silver, but it eventually closed when an attempt to use explosives resulted in an inundation of water in the lower levels. Unfortunately, there are no English-speaking guides here, although the tour is eye-opening even for those who don't speak Spanish. Mannequins illustrate some of the mining process. A visit also includes a short, unremarkable train ride.

The mine's back entrance is a block from the cable-car terminal. I prefer this entrance because most people start at the main entrance, so you can avoid the crowds. When you get to the ticket office, buy your ticket right then. According to the rules, a tour must begin within 15 minutes after the first ticket is purchased. On my last two visits, I've had the guide all to myself (a tip is appreciated). After the tour is over, you can exit by the front entrance, which puts you on Juárez, a few blocks above Hidalgo.

For directions on getting to the front entrance, see "La Mina Club," below, under "Zacatecas After Dark."

Cerro Grillo. ⓒ 492/922-3002. Admission $6 (£3; includes train and tour). Daily 10am–6pm.

Museo F. Goitia 𝕽𝕽

Because my credentials as a critic are nil, I'll be brief. I was surprised by this small museum and the work of Goitia and his Zacatecan comrades, Julio Ruelas, Manuel Felguérez, and José Kuri Breña. I walked in half expecting a display of regional chauvinism, but instead I found moving, serious, and meaningful work. Francisco Goitia (1882–1960) is famous in Mexico, but the others were impressive, too.

Enrique Estrada 102, Col. Sierra de Alica. ⓒ 492/922-0211. Admission $2 (£1). Tues–Sun 10am–5pm.

Museo Pedro Coronel 𝕽𝕽

Pedro Coronel, in addition to being an artist, was a collector of inspired tastes. He acquired works from all over the world, but the strongest parts of the collection are the works of European modern masters (Dalí, Picasso, Miró, Kandinsky, Braque, Rouault), pre-Columbian Mesoamerica, and West Africa. All but a few of the pieces of modern art are illuminating. Many date from early in the artist's career, and some display a seminal character that points in the direction of later works. This collection is not large; after a while you drift into the Mesoamerican room—beautiful stuff, and seeing it so quickly after the modern art gets your mind working out strange and improbable connections. There is no filler here; all of the pieces are outstanding. The same can be said of the African material, but in this case the connections with modern art are tangible.

Plaza de Santo Domingo. ⓒ 492/922-8021. Admission $2 (£1). Fri–Wed 10am–5pm.

Museo Rafael Coronel 𝕽𝕽𝕽

First stroll through the tranquil gardens and ruins of the former Franciscan convent, filled with trailing blossoms and framed by crumbling arches and the open sky. A small wing contains Coronel's drawings on paper. Once you step inside the mask museum, you'll be dazzled by the sheer number of fantastic masks. There are 4,500 of them from all over Mexico, and they're so exotic and dissimilar that you would think that they came from all over the world. One wing of the museum is dedicated to puppets. There are dioramas showing a bullfight, battling armies, and even a vision of hell. The puppets are some of the hundreds created during the last century by the famous Rosete-Aranda family of Huamantla, Tlaxcala, where there is also a puppet museum. Also in the museum, to the left after you enter, is the Ruth Rivera room, where some of Diego Rivera's drawings are on display. Ruth Rivera is the daughter of Diego Rivera and the wife of Rafael Coronel.

Calle Chevano (between Abasolo and Matamoros). ⓒ 492/922-8116. Admission $2 (£1.10). Thurs–Tues 10am–4:30pm.

A SIDE TRIP TO NEARBY GUADALUPE

In the nearby town of Guadalupe, now almost a suburb of Zacatecas, is a large Franciscan convent and evangelical college founded by a famous member of the evangelical college of Querétaro, Fray Antonio Margil de Jesús. It remains an active monastery, but a large part of the convent houses a wonderful museum of colonial art, which will impress anyone interested in art and painting of any kind. Some people might skip this one because they suppose colonial art to be staid, scholastic, and full of arcane symbolism. Not true. The paintings, mostly from the 1700s, are by some of the greatest painters of New Spain—Cabrera, Villalpando, Correa, and others. They are detailed, expressive, dramatic, and eye-catching for their use of anachronisms and fantastical themes.

A taxi to Guadalupe runs about $5 (£2.50). Transportes de Guadalupe buses go to Guadalupe from the Central Camionera in Zacatecas. If you're driving, take López Mateos east, and follow the signs. The convent's church has a lovely facade and holds the famous 19th-century Capilla de Nápoles, a chapel in the shape of a cross with lots of gilding and decoration. You cannot enter, but you can see it from the ground floor of the church or from the organ loft, which is accessible from the museum.

Convento de Guadalupe/Museo Virreinal de Guadalupe ✸✸✸   To a dedicated museumgoer, seeing these paintings exhibited in galleries with open-air circulation and no climate control is a little unsettling. The museum has about 350 works. On the first floor are over 20 portraits depicting scenes of St. Francis's life. The stairway to the second floor has some large, striking paintings, including Cabrera's *Virgin of the Apocalypse* and Arnáez's *The Triumph of the Sweet Name of Jesus,* which is an amusing propagandistic work showing the victory of Rome over the pagans and the Reformation. Highlights on the second floor include the organ loft, 14 oval paintings by Cabrera, four by Villalpando, and the surprising work of a local artist named Gabriel José de Ovalle, who distorts space and deforms human features in a style that seems much more modern than the 1700s. Guides are available for a tour of the museum and to view the Capilla de Nápoles (if the monks aren't celebrating Mass). For 2008–09, the museum is making some changes and restoring the buildings. The entrance will change, and there will be more exhibition space for art. The collection of antique cars that used to be in the building next door has been removed.

Jardín Juárez, Oriente, Guadalupe. ✆ 492/923-2089 or -2386. Admission $4 (£2.20). Daily 9am–6pm.

WHERE TO STAY

Zacatecas has a great selection of hotels. Each of the expensive hotels that I've selected has something that sets it apart from the rest. The Quinta Real has the classic old bullring. The Emporio is on the square, and its front rooms have a great view of the Cerro de la Bufa. El Jobito captures the air of an old *vecindad.* In the fall and winter, heat can come in handy. Of the hotels listed here, all but the Condesa have heaters in the rooms, but many hotels in Zacatecas do not. And in the summer, air-conditioning would be nice, but very few hotels have it. Prices quoted here include the 17% tax. Highest rates are for Easter and Christmas holidays and August through September.

VERY EXPENSIVE

Hotel Quinta Real ✸✸✸   Mexico is littered with hotels occupying former mansions, convents, and haciendas, but how many have risen from bullrings? And yet, it's the beauty, not the novelty, that makes this hotel so great. It has won several design awards, undoubtedly because the architects knew enough to leave the beautiful old bullring intact and keep the hotel small enough to be unobtrusive. A few of the arches that remain from the town's colonial aqueduct frame the entrance. From the lobby, you can survey the entire arena. The rooms were built along the outside of the bull-ring, and their windows open onto a small courtyard. Rooms are large, with spacious, well-equipped bathrooms, a writing desk, and a couch. Master suites are one room with a king or two double beds; *gran clase* suites are a good bit larger and have a sitting area and a whirlpool tub.

Av. Rayón 434, 98000 Zacatecas, Zac. ☏ **800/445-4565** in the U.S. and Canada, or 492/922-9105. Fax 492/ 922-8440. www.quintareal.com. 49 suites. $320 (£160) master suite; $344 (£172) *gran clase* suite. Discounts and Internet specials for low season. AE, DC, MC, V. Free secure parking. **Amenities:** Restaurant; bar; golf and health club privileges at local club; fitness center; concierge; tour desk; business center; room service; in-room massage; babysitting; laundry service; dry cleaning; nonsmoking rooms. *In room:* A/C, TV, high-speed Internet access, minibar, hair dryer, iron.

EXPENSIVE

Hotel Emporio Zacatecas 𝕲𝕲 A comfortable hotel across from the Plaza de Armas, it is a popular choice with Mexican tourists and businesspeople. The spacious rooms on its six floors are carpeted and well furnished. Rooms in the back are quiet. The rooms in front, mostly junior suites, are sunny and have balconies with good views of the cathedral and Cerro de la Bufa. The ones I like most are those on the fourth floor, which have terraces. These are set back a little and offer more shielding from street noise. The rooms in back face a small interior patio, complete with gur-gling fountain. They contain one king or two double beds. Bathrooms are midsize, with a decent amount of counter space.

Av. Hidalgo 703, Col. Centro, 98000 Zacatecas, Zac. ☏ **492/925-6500.** Fax 492/922-6245. www.hotelesemporio. com. 113 units. $195 (£98) double; $212 (£106) junior suite. AE, MC, V. Sheltered parking $2. **Amenities:** Restaurant; bar; fitness center; sauna; tour desk; car rental; business center; room service; babysitting; laundry service; dry clean-ing; nonsmoking rooms. *In room:* TV, Wi-Fi, coffeemaker, hair dryer, iron, safe.

Mesón de Jobito 𝕲𝕲 This two-story hotel occupies a traditional *vecindad*, which was a common form of housing for the lower classes in olden days. The buildings ram-ble back from the entrance, forming private alleys decorated with ornamental plants and flowers and painted in traditional Mexican colors. The hotel feels intimate. Rooms are large, carpeted, and nicely furnished, with queen- or king-size beds and large bathrooms. A couple of junior suites are large and stylish. Rates vary seasonally and are highest from September to December and during festival times. The hotel is 5 blocks from the cathedral and a block above Hidalgo.

Jardín Juárez 143, 98000 Zacatecas, Zac. ☏/fax **492/924-1722,** or 01-800/021-0040 in Mexico. www.mesonde jobito.com. 53 units. $168 (£84) double; $178–$184 (£74–£84) suite. AE, MC, V. Free valet parking. **Amenities:** 2 restaurants; bar; tour desk; rental car; room service; babysitting; laundry service; dry cleaning. *In room:* A/C, TV, dataport, coffeemaker, hair dryer, iron, safe (in most rooms).

INEXPENSIVE

Hotel Condesa *Value* The good location, well-kept rooms, and economical price are the main attractions here. Many rooms, especially on the lower floors, have been remodeled and have modern furniture, cheerful paint, and new bathroom tile. These rooms have interior views. Rooms on the third floor have new bathrooms. Those fac-ing east overlook Cerro de la Bufa and the market below the hotel. Rooms are small to medium. Most come with one or two double beds.

Av. Juárez 102, 98000 Zacatecas, Zac. ©/fax 492/922-1160. www.hotelcondesa.com.mx. 52 units. $50–$53 (£25–£27) double; $75–$85 (£38–£43) minisuite. AE, MC, V. No parking. **Amenities:** Restaurant; cafe/bar; tour desk; room service; laundry service. *In room:* TV.

Motel Zacatecas Courts   Rooms have carpeting and comfortable beds. It is a 10-minute walk from the main square. Be sure to get a room in the back, away from the street. Also, you must ask to have the heat turned on in the room and for extra blankets in winter.

López Velarde 602, 98000 Zacatecas, Zac. © 492/922-0328. Fax 492/922-1225. 92 units. $50 (£25) double. MC, V. Free secure parking. **Amenities:** Restaurant; tour info; room service. *In room:* TV.

WHERE TO DINE

The dining in Zacatecas is good. Besides the establishments listed below, I've eaten well at the Quinta Real and Mesón del Jobito. The *gordita,* a thick tortilla that is split open and stuffed with any of several cooked fillings, might be considered the state food of Zacatecas, and the most popular *gordita* place is **Gorditas Doña Julia,** which operates three or four locations. The best coffee in town is at **Café San Patrizio** in the courtyard at 403 Hidalgo. It's open from 10am until 10pm.

Café Nevería Acrópolis MEXICAN   This restaurant and coffee shop with a soda fountain is a popular spot for breakfast, afternoon coffee, or dessert. I like it for breakfast, but I would go elsewhere for other meals.

Av. Hidalgo and Rinconada de Catedral. © 492/922-1284. Breakfast $4–$7 (£2–£3.50); main courses $6–$10 (£3–£5). AE, MC, V. Daily 8am–10pm.

La Cantera Musical Restaurant Bar ☞ MEXICAN/REGIONAL   This restaurant is best known for its regional cooking, especially typical dishes such as *asado de bodas* (a pork dish made with cinnamon and *ancho* and *guajillo* chiles) and *mole zacatecano* (a sweet and spicy chicken dish). You can also get a number of Mexican standards. The dining room is attractive. The restaurant is below the Mercado González Ortega, by the cathedral.

Tacuba 2, Centro Comercial El Mercado. © 492/922-8828. Main courses $6–$12 (£3–£6). AE, MC, V. Mon–Sat 1–11pm; Sun 2–10pm.

La Cuija ☞☞ INTERNATIONAL/REGIONAL   Set beneath the Centro Comercial, La Cuija's dining room has tables spaced between thick stone columns supporting close arches. The room is attractive and the seating is comfortable and well separated. The restaurant has its own vineyards (though the wine I tried was not good). The menu offers a selection of mostly Mexican dishes, such as a good *sopa azteca* and an *ancho chile* stuffed with *huitlacoche* (corn fungus) in a sauce of ground corn, cream, and a bit of *chile mestizo* (dried chile).

Tacuba T-5, Centro Comercial El Mercado. © 492/922-8275. Reservations not accepted during Semana Santa. Main courses $8–$18 (£4–£9). AE, MC, V. Daily 1:30pm–midnight.

Los Dorados de Villa ☞☞ MEXICAN   If your grandmother were Mexican, this is how you would want her to cook. The green *pozole* is excellent and safe to eat, even though it comes with shredded lettuce. The enchiladas, which come in many varieties (I prefer the *valentinas* and the *rojas*) are delicious, too. Other menu items include tostadas, tacos, soups, and guacamole. What's for dessert? *Buñuelos,* of course. The name of the place refers to "the golden ones"—Pancho Villa's honor guard of fearless soldiers. The owner is a collector of memorabilia. Artifacts and reproductions from La

Revolución cover the walls of the small dining room. Decorative paper cutouts hang from the ceiling, making the room feel even smaller, but festive, too. Los Dorados is close by the Rafael Coronel Museum; from the cathedral, walk north several blocks on Hidalgo, staying to the left each time the street forks. Diners need to ring the doorbell to enter. This place has been getting popular, so it's a good idea to call ahead to see how busy they are.

Plazuela de García 1314. © 492/922-5722. Reservations not accepted during the evenings. Main courses $4–$6 (£2.20–£3.30). No credit cards. Mon–Sat 3pm–1am; Sun 3–11pm.

ZACATECAS AFTER DARK
La Mina Club   Disco music in a mine deep inside the earth—does "Disco Inferno" ring a bell? Whose life could be considered complete without having made the scene here? The entrance is at the end of Calle Dovali. From Hidalgo, walk up Juárez, which turns into Torreón. Just past the Seguro Social building on Avenida Torreón, you'll find Dovali; turn right. Take a cab if you don't want to be so bushed that you can't boogie. The club is open Thursday through Sunday from 9:30pm to 2am. Mina El Edén, Calle Dovali. © 492/922-3727. Cover $16 (£8).

5 San Luis Potosí

418km (259 miles) N of Mexico City; 346km (215 miles) NE of Guadalajara; 202km (125 miles) N of Querétaro; 189km (117 miles) E of Zacatecas

San Luis Potosí, a mile high in central Mexico's high-plains region, was among the country's most prosperous mining cities. It's now the largest and most industrial silver city, with almost a million inhabitants, but you would never know it if you stayed in the historic central district. It has rich colonial architecture and is known for its great plazas. Capital of the state of the same name, San Luis Potosí was named for Louis IX, sainted king of France. *Potosí* is a reference to the rich Bolivian Potosí mines.

ESSENTIALS
GETTING THERE & DEPARTING   By Plane   Continental ExpressJet (© 800/231-0856 in the U.S., or 01-800/900-5000 in Mexico; www.continental.com) and **American Eagle** (© 800/433-7300 in the U.S., or 01-800/904-6000 in Mexico) fly to and from Houston and Dallas. Several domestic carriers have flights to Mexico City and other destinations within the country.

The **airport** is about 11km (7 miles) from downtown. A taxi to the city center is $20 (£10). A *colectivo* van is more economical, but don't tarry in the terminal, because they leave quickly.

By Car   From Mexico City, take Highway 57D; from Guadalajara, take Highway 80. If you're coming from the north, it takes 6 to 7 hours to drive the 536km (332 miles) from Monterrey.

By Bus   The large Central Camionera is 3km (2 miles) east of downtown on Guadalupe Torres at Diagonal Sur. Taxis cost about $5 (£2.50). Most of the bus travel is through Estrella Blanca and its many affiliates, which occupy the counters to the left as you enter. You can buy a ticket for any of the affiliates from any counter. To the right as you enter are three other first-class bus companies: ETN (mostly to Mexico City and Guadalajara), Primera Plus (to Mexico City and Querétaro), and Omnibus de Mexico (to Mexico City, Guadalajara, and Querétaro).

VISITOR INFORMATION   The **State Tourism Office** (© 444/812-9939, -9943) is at Manuel Jose Othon 130, to one side of the cathedral. The information office has a helpful staff, a good map of the city and historic district, and lots of brochures. It's open Monday through Friday from 8am to 9pm, Saturday from 9am to 2pm.

CITY LAYOUT   The **Plaza de Armas** is the center of the historic district. All the streets bordering it are pedestrian only. The principal pedestrian street runs north–south in front of the plaza; the southern part (called **Zaragoza**) extends 8 blocks to the Jardín Colón, and the northern part (called **Hidalgo**) runs 5 blocks to the main market. The city also has many plazas and a large downtown park called **La Alameda. Avenida Carranza** heads east from the Plaza de Armas, passes by the Plaza de Fundadores, and extends to the prosperous residential section of the city. Fronting this street are many banks, clubs, and restaurants.

FAST FACTS: San Luis Potosí

American Express The local representative is **Grandes Viajes,** Av. Carranza 1077 (© **444/817-6084;** fax 444/811-1166). Hours are Monday through Friday from 9am to 2pm and 4 to 7pm, Saturday from 10am to 1pm.

Area Code The telephone area code is **444.**

Climate San Luis is on the high plateau more than a mile above sea level, but the weather can get hot during May, June, and sometimes July. In winter it occasionally drops to freezing at night. Rain is rare, with an average total of 14 inches per year; it falls between May and November, mostly in August.

Currency Exchange Four *casas de cambios* near the main post office offer better rates and better service than the banks. Two are in the arcade on Julián de los Reyes, and two are on Mariano Escobedo. This is just a few blocks northeast of the Plaza de Armas. All are open Saturday. The historic district has many ATMs.

Emergency San Luis's central emergency number is © **060.**

Hospital The **Hospital Centro Médico,** Antonio Aguilar 155 (© **444/813-3797**), is one of the best in the country.

Population San Luis Potosí has 970,000 residents.

Post Office The *correo,* Morelos 235, 4 blocks north-northeast of the Plaza de Armas, is open Monday through Friday from 8am to 3pm, Saturday 9am to 1pm. Look for a narrow one-story building made of gray stone.

EXPLORING SAN LUIS POTOSI
A STROLL AROUND THE HISTORIC CENTER

San Luis has more streets dedicated solely for the use of pedestrians than any of the other silver cities. The center of town is the **Plaza de Armas,** dating from the mid-1700s and shaded by magnolia and *flamboyán* trees. The **bandstand** in the center of the plaza was built in 1947 (in colonial style), using pink volcanic stone. Free band concerts usually begin on Thursday and Sunday at around 7:30 or 8pm. On the west side of the plaza is the **Palacio de Gobierno.** It has been much repaired, restored, and

San Luis Potosí

To Monterrey and Saltillo →

Azteca

Old Train Station

To Ciudad Valles and Tampico →

Plaza España

Av. 20 de Noviembre

New Train Station

Negrete

Xochitl

Othón

ALAMEDA PARK

Universidad

Templo de San José

Lanzagorta

Insurgentes

Parrodi

Constitución

Arriaga

Juan Sarabia

11

10

9

Villerias

Moctezuma

Plaza San Juan de Dios

8

Escobedo

Plaza del Carmen

Mercado Hidalgo

Plaza Arriaga

Los Bravo

Morelos

7

Reforma

Hidalgo

5

i

Zaragoza

JARDÍN COLÓN

Juárez

Allende

Calle Bocanegra

Plaza de Armas

Iturbide

Guerrero

6

Galeana

5 de Mayo

4

Mier y Terán

J. de Los Reyes

Aldama

Plaza de San Francisco

Vallejo

Carmona

Plaza de los Fundadores

Carranza

J. de León

3

Madero

Universidad

1

Calle Abasolo

Calle Comonfort

Independencia

Arista

Obregón

Bolívar

Ocampo

F. Nieto

Zapata

Reforma

2

1/4 mi

0.25 km

Church

Information

Post Office

Train

ATTRACTIONS ●

Cathedral 5

FONART store 7

Museo Nacional de la Máscara 8

Palacio de Gobierno 4

Teatro de la Paz 9

Templo de San Francisco 1

Templo del Carmen 10

ACCOMMODATIONS ■

Hotel Filher 6

Hotel María Cristina 11

Hotel Panorama 3

Hotel Real Plaza 2

ZACATECAS

SAN LUIS POTOSÍ

San Luis Potosí

GUANAJUATO

TAMAULIPAS

HIDALGO

VERACRUZ

Gulf of Mexico

JALISCO

MICHOACÁN

★ Mexico City

100 mi

100 km

added to through the centuries—the back and the south facade were redone as recently as 1973. The front of the building retains much of the original 18th-century decoration, at least on the lower floors. On the second floor, you'll find the rooms that Juárez occupied when he established his temporary capital here. It's worth a peek.

Across the plaza from the Government Palace is the **cathedral.** The original building had only a single bell tower; the one on the left was built in 1910 to match, although today the newer tower looks older. The Count of Monterrey built the **Palacio Municipal,** on the north side of the cathedral, in 1850. He filled it with paintings and sculptures, few of which survived the city's stormy history. When the count died in 1890, the palace was taken over by the bishop and, in 1921, by the city government. Since then, it has been San Luis's city hall. On January 1, 1986, it was firebombed in a moment of social unrest. It was restored and functions again.

East of the plaza is one of the city's most famous squares, **Plazuela del Carmen,** named for the **Templo del Carmen** 𝔾𝔾 church. From the *jardín,* walk east along Madero-Othón to Escobedo and the *plazuela.* The entire area you see was once part of the extensive grounds of the 18th-century Carmelite monastery. The church has a beautiful and complex facade, in which appear Elijah and Elisha, two prophets in the Old Testament who lived on Mount Carmel and are considered by the Carmelite order as spiritual founders. The other two large figures are St. Theresa of Avila and St. John of the Cross, mystics who, in the 16th century, reformed the order in Spain and founded the congregation of the discalced (unshod) Carmelites. Inside the church are some beautiful baroque altarpieces.

The **Teatro de la Paz** and the **Museo Nacional de la Máscara** also face the plaza. The museum is scheduled to reopen in mid-2008 after a thorough remodeling. Attached to the Teatro de la Paz (enter to the right of the theater's main entrance) is the **Sala German Gedovius** (© **444/812-2698**), with four art galleries. It's open Tuesday through Sunday from 10am to 2pm and 4 to 6pm. Admission is free.

One block east of the Plaza del Carmen is a large urban green area known as **La Alameda.** Vendors sell handicrafts, fruits, and all manner of snacks. Facing the park on Negrete is the **Templo de San José,** with lots of ornate gold decorations, huge religious paintings, and *El Señor de los Trabajos,* a miracle-working statue with many *retablos* testifying to the wonders it has performed.

PLAZAS

San Luis Potosí has more plazas than any other colonial city in Mexico. In addition to those mentioned above, the **Plaza de San Francisco** is south of the Plaza de Armas along Aldama, between Guerrero and Galeana. This shady square takes its name from the Franciscan monastery on the south side of the plaza and the church on the west side. The church holds some beautiful stained glass, many Colonial-Era statues and paintings, and a crystal chandelier shaped like a sailing ship.

Another square is **Plaza de los Fundadores (Founders' Square),** at the intersection of Obregón and Aldama, northwest of the Plaza de Armas. Facing it is the **Loreto Chapel,** with its exquisite baroque facade. The neighboring church of **El Sagrario** belonged to the Jesuits before the order was expelled from Mexico.

SHOPPING

The best one-stop shopping in San Luis is at the government-operated **FONART** crafts store (© **444/814-3868**) at Morelos 1055, behind the church of San Agustín. It's open Monday through Friday from 9am to 2pm and 4 to 7pm, Saturday 10am to

5pm. Another place to try is the state-run store **La Casa del Artesano** (© 444/814-8990) at Jardín Colón 23. The store carries examples of every kind of craft made in the state. It's open Monday through Friday from 10am to 8pm. It closes at 5pm on Saturday.

Several blocks along the pedestrian Calle Hidalgo north of Jardín Hidalgo, you'll find the city's **Mercado Hidalgo,** a large building devoted mostly to food, but also offering, among other things, baskets, *rebozos* (shawls), and straw furniture. The walk along Hidalgo is an introduction to the city's commercial life. Hardware stores, crafts shops, shoe stores, groceries, and taverns crowd the street. Past the Mercado Hidalgo is another big market, the Mercado República.

A well-loved local candy factory is **Constanzo,** which has several outlets throughout the city, including three on Carranza. Most outlets are open Monday through Saturday from 10am to 1:30pm and 4 to 8:30pm.

WHERE TO STAY

There are no luxury hotels in the historic center. Most of them (the María Dolores, Real de Minas, and Holiday Inn) are to the east, where the highway from Mexico City enters the town. The Westin and the Camino Real are to the west, along the highway to Guadalajara. All rates listed below include the 17% tax. Expect higher rates for Easter, Christmas, and, in some hotels, August.

VERY EXPENSIVE

Westin San Luis Potosí ★★ Perhaps the loveliest hotel in San Luis, the Westin offers comfort and service in surroundings that exemplify how contemporary Mexican architects have worked the elements of colonial architecture to achieve an aesthetic that is new, without being divorced from its past. The rooms are along a three-story stone arcade that surrounds a broad courtyard. All are large, carpeted, and decorated with flair. They come with either two full- or one king-size bed, a writing table, and a small dining table. Bathrooms are large, with marble tiles, countertops, and shower/tub combinations. Suites are even larger and offer a stereo with a CD player, a large whirlpool tub, a safe, and bathrobes. I prefer the rooms that have an interior view of the courtyard. The center of town is 15 to 20 minutes away by car.

Real de Lomas 1000, 78210 San Luis Potosí, S.L.P. © 800/228-3000 in the U.S., or 444/825-0125. Fax 444/825-0200. www.westin.com. 123 units. $176–$208 (£88–£104) double; $194–$226 (£97–£113) suite. Rates include airport transfers. Children younger than 12 stay free in parents' room. AE, MC, V. Free valet parking. **Amenities:** Restaurant; bar; small heated outdoor pool; access to nearby health club w/tennis and racquetball; fitness center; concierge; tour desk; car rental; airport transportation; business center; executive business services; 24-hour room service; babysitting; laundry service; dry cleaning; nonsmoking rooms. *In room:* A/C, TV, Wi-Fi, minibar, hair dryer, iron.

MODERATE

Hotel Panorama Aptly named, this hotel is in a 10-story glass building near the Plaza Fundadores. Many years ago, it was *the* hotel in San Luis, but newer, fancier competitors and a certain amount of decay changed that. Rooms vary in size from medium to large; none feel cramped. Bathrooms are a little small. Most rooms come with two full-size beds. All have an exterior view. Five floors of guest rooms have been completely remodeled. The difference in the remodeled rooms is substantial; they have air-conditioning, high-speed Internet access, hair dryers, marble bathrooms with plenty of counter space, modern mahogany-stained furniture, and much better lighting,

Av. Carranza 315, 78000 San Luis Potosí, S.L.P. ☏ 444/812-1777. Fax 444/812-4591. www.hotelpanorama.com.mx. 126 units. $76 (£38) standard double; $85 (£43) *piso ejecutivo* (remodeled). AE, MC, V. Free secure parking. **Amenities:** Restaurant; cafe; bar; dance club; midsize heated outdoor pool; tour desk; car rental; room service; babysitting; laundry service; dry cleaning; executive-level rooms. *In room:* TV, A/C (in remodeled rooms), high-speed Internet access (in remodeled rooms), hair dryer (in remodeled rooms).

Hotel Real Plaza *Value*   A modern nine-story hotel 8 blocks from the Plaza de Armas, the Real Plaza offers comfort and quiet at a good price. The midsize rooms are carpeted and well lit. They are preferable to the unremodeled rooms at the Panorama (see above). Bathrooms are a little larger than at the Panorama, but some rooms have no view. Try to get a corner room.

Av. Carranza 890, 78250 San Luis Potosí, S.L.P. ☏ 444/814-6969. Fax 444/814-6639. www.realplaza.com.mx. 268 units. $68 (£34) double. AE, MC, V. Free secure parking. **Amenities:** Restaurant; bar; outdoor pool; fitness center; tour desk; business center; room service; laundry service. *In room:* A/C, TV, high-speed Internet access.

INEXPENSIVE

Hotel Filher *Value*   Good location and medium to large rooms painted in cheerful colors are the high points of this economical three-story hotel. If you want quiet, request a room on the third floor; if you want a window and a firm mattress, book a room on the second. Rates are higher for second-floor rooms. Of these, I like the ones facing the pedestrian-only Zaragoza. They have balconies with a good view, and though there may be street noise, you don't get the noise that reverberates through the rather loud lobby. This hotel is a good choice in warm weather because the rooms are airy and have tile floors rather than carpeting. They also have ceiling fans. Hot water can take as long as 5 minutes to get to the rooms.

Av. Universidad 375 (at Zaragoza), 78000 San Luis Potosí, S.L.P. ☏ 444/812-1562. Fax 444/812-1564. 50 units. $48 (£24) double. MC, V. Free parking 3 blocks away. **Amenities:** Restaurant; bar; room service. *In room:* TV.

Hotel María Cristina   The María Cristina is in a narrow nine-story building around the corner from the Plaza del Carmen. It's next door to (and often confused with) the Hotel Nápoles. All rooms are small and have a ceiling fan, and most don't offer much of a view. The bathrooms are small, with little counter space. Rooms are quiet, carpeted, and warmer in the winter than the rooms at the Filher (see above). They come with either one full or two twin beds.

Juan Sarabia 110, 78000 San Luis Potosí, S.L.P. ☏ 444/812-9408. www.mariacristina.com.mx. 74 units. $60 (£30) double. MC, V. Free guarded parking. **Amenities:** 2 restaurants; bar; tour info; room service. *In room:* TV.

WHERE TO DINE

Downtown San Luis has a number of restaurants offering standard local fare. Try the **Posada del Virrey** on the Plaza de Armas; the 24-hour **Café Pacífico** at Los Bravos and Constitución, off the Plaza del Carmen; or **La Parroquia** on the Plaza Fundadores. For something a little more special, try one of the following establishments.

MODERATE

El Callejón de San Francisco ✿ MEXICAN   If the night air is comfortable, there's no lovelier place for dinner than this restaurant's rooftop terrace, with San Francisco's cupola and bell towers for a backdrop. Even if it's a tad too chilly, you can still enjoy yourself; just ask the waiter for a *jorongo* (hoh-*rohn*-goh), a traditional woolen wrap for the shoulders. There's also a dining room downstairs. The menu has a number of Mexican standards at reasonable prices. The restaurant is on a pedestrian street beside San Francisco church.

Callejón de Lozada 1. © **444/812-4508**. Reservations recommended on weekends. Main courses $8–$12 (£4–£6). AE, MC, V. Mon–Fri 6pm–midnight; Sat 2pm–midnight.

La Corriente Restaurant Bar ✦ MEXICAN   The menu has several Mexican dishes, using mostly beef. I liked the *chamorro pibil* (pork cooked in a Huastecan *mole*), the *puntas al chipotle* (beef in a spicy chipotle sauce), and the *costillitas en chile ancho* (pork ribs in *chile ancho* sauce). It also offers a large selection of blended fruit and vegetable drinks with surprising combinations. These are filling; don't make the mistake of ordering one and a main course or a full breakfast; instead, try an appetizer such as the *quesadillas de huitlacoche*. The restaurant is in a large old house. The main dining room is a roofed patio with hanging plants, lots of photos, and tile wainscoting. Off to the sides are other dining rooms.

Carranza 700. © **444/812-9304**. Main courses $5–$10 (£2.50–£5); blended juices $3 (£1.50). MC, V. Mon–Sat 8am–midnight; Sun 8am–6pm.

La Virreina ✦✦ REGIONAL/MEXICAN   Opened in 1959, this restaurant has for years been one of the places Potosinos go to dine when there's something to celebrate. It has been under the same ownership all this time, and service and food preparation are given attention. Of all the places I've tried here, this one had the best *enchiladas potosinas* (ask for them with strips of poblano chile instead of just cheese). Or order the *carne asada a la virreina* and you'll get a couple on the side. This dish is a steak topped with a little cheese and a sauce flavored with Mexican sausage (it sounds excessive now, but it didn't taste that way at the time). A more moderate option is the pepper steak or the baked fish with bleu cheese and bread crumbs. The large dining room was once an open courtyard. It is comfortable and attractive, with plenty of space between tables.

Av. Carranza 830. © **444/812-3750**. Reservations recommended. Main courses $8–$15 (£4.40–£8.25). AE, MC, V. Mon–Sat 1pm–midnight; Sun 1–7pm.

Restaurant Orizatlán ✦✦ HUASTECAN   This colorful restaurant specializes in the traditional Huastecan cooking of eastern San Luis Potosí. If you are hungry, try the *parrillada a la Huasteca* for two. A large sampling of typical dishes, it includes portions of the *zacahuil*, Mexico's largest tamal. The waiters will keep the Huastecan enchiladas coming until you beg them to stop. Less ambitious eaters can order a la carte. After dinner, the restaurant serves complimentary home-style cordials made from several fruits, and puts on a mini Huastecan fandango, with music and dance.

Pascual M. Hernández 240. © **444/814-6786**. Breakfast $4 (£2); main courses $5–$10 (£2.50–£5). AE, MC, V. Mon–Thurs 8am–10pm; Fri–Sat 8am–11pm; Sun 8am–7pm. 8 blocks south of Plaza de Armas on Zaragoza, turn left at Jardín Colón; restaurant is about 30m (98 ft.) down.

SAN LUIS AFTER DARK

The most popular clubs in town are those where you can sit down to a late supper or drinks and hear guitarists and vocalists. Most of the music is romantic—*trovas*, or ballads. In the downtown area, a number of bars offer this kind of entertainment, usually on Thursday, Friday, and Saturday nights. They include **La Compañía,** Mariano Arista 350 (© **444/812-9693**); **Viejo San Luis,** Carranza 485-A (© **444/814-0801**); and **Restaurant Bar 1913,** Galeana 205 (© **444/812-8352**). **Play,** Carranza 423 (© **444/814-7034**), is a popular dance club for 20-somethings.

8

Michoacán

by David Baird

West of Mexico City and southeast of Guadalajara lies the state of Michoacán (mee-choh-ah-*kahn*), the homeland of more than 200,000 Tarascan Indians, properly known as the Purépecha. The land is mountainous in the east, north, and center. In the south and west, it drops to a broad lowland plain that meets the Pacific Ocean. The state gets more rain and thus is greener than its neighbors Jalisco and Guanajuato, and many Mexicans consider it the most beautiful state in their country. And yet, it remains relatively unvisited by foreigners.

High in the mountains, in the northeastern part of the state, a miraculous ritual occurs every year. Millions of monarch butterflies congregate in an isolated highland forest. They are the final link in a migratory chain stretching from Mexico to as far away as Canada and back. During peak season (Dec–Mar), the tree limbs bend under their cumulative weight, and the undulation of so many wings creates a dazzling spectacle. (See "Michoacán's Monarch Migration," later in this chapter.) In central Michoacán, highland lakes and colorful Indian towns evoke the Mexico of old. These towns are known for their handicrafts and all-night celebrations on the Day of the Dead. Farther west and south is the famous volcano Paricutín, the only major volcano born in modern times (1943).

The two most important cities in Michoacán, **Morelia** and **Pátzcuaro,** offer the visitor contrasting visions of the colonial past. Morelia is a city built of chiseled stone, planned with architectural considerations and possessed of a clearcut geometry. Pátzcuaro is all about undulating adobe walls, crooked red-tile roofs, and narrow meandering streets. The former is proud of its Spanish heritage; the latter remains rooted in its Indian origins.

The native Purépecha are an intriguing people. Where they came from and how they got here we don't know. Their language is unlike any other in Mexico; the closest linguistic connection is with native peoples in Ecuador. Their civilization developed contemporaneously with that of the Aztec, and they successfully defeated Aztec expansionism—the only highland civilization to do so.

Since they were not vassals of the Aztec, they didn't simply submit to Spanish rule after the collapse of the Aztec empire. In the history of the conquest and conversion of the Purépecha, two men represent the extremes of Spanish attitudes toward the Indians. One was the conquistador Nuño de Guzmán, a man whose rapaciousness and cruelty made him infamous even among fellow conquistadors, and eventually earned him a prison cell in Spain. The other was Vasco de Quiroga, a humanist who believed in the ideas of Erasmus and Sir Thomas More. He joined the church late in life and came to Michoacán as the first bishop of the Purépecha, establishing his see in Pátzcuaro. Here, he strove to build a utopian society of cooperative communities, organizing and instructing each village in the practice of a specific craft. To this day, his organization of crafts among the different villages is largely followed.

EXPLORING MICHOACAN

Travel between the major cities of Michoacán takes only an hour or two at most, and public transportation is frequent. You should plan 3 days in **Morelia** (more if you intend to see the butterflies) and a minimum of 3 days in **Pátzcuaro,** but more like a week if you're interested in taking day trips to the lakes and the villages in the region and want to look into the local handicrafts. **Uruapan,** another important town, is an easy day trip from either city, although you may want to stay longer to visit the **Paricutín volcano.** During Easter week or Day of the Dead observances (Nov 1–2), the Plazas Grandes in Pátzcuaro and Uruapan overflow with regional crafts. Reserve rooms well in advance for these holidays. With the new highway from Ixtapa, it's possible to plan a vacation that combines the lovely colonial cities of Michoacán with quality beach time.

1 Morelia ⊘

312km (193 miles) NW of Mexico City; 365km (226 miles) SE of Guadalajara

The first viceroy of Mexico ordered the founding of the city in 1541 under the name Valladolid. The name was later changed to Morelia to honor the revolutionary hero José María Morelos, who was born here.

Morelia was intended as a bastion of Spanish culture for the region's large population of Indians. The adjective people most frequently use to describe Morelia is "aristocratic." Indeed, the city's greatest appeal lies in its grand colonial architecture.

ESSENTIALS
GETTING THERE & DEPARTING
BY PLANE   Continental (© **800/231-0856** in the U.S., or 01-800/900-5000 in Mexico; www.continental.com) has direct flights from Houston. **Mexicana** (© **800/ 531-7921** in the U.S., or 443/324-3808; www.mexicana.com) has flights to and from several California destinations and Chicago. Several domestic carriers connect Morelia to other cities in Mexico.

Morelia's airport is **Aeropuerto Francisco J. Mújica,** a 45-minute drive from the city center on Km 27 of the Carretera Morelia-Zinapécuaro. Taxis meet each flight. **Budget** has a car-rental office there (© **800/527-0700** in the U.S. and Canada, or 443/313-3399).

BY CAR   The slow route from either Mexico City or Guadalajara is Highway 15—a winding and narrow road with beautiful vistas, which can be appreciated at leisure because you inevitably get stuck behind an old truck that can barely climb the mountains as it makes its way through a series of blind curves. The fast way is the modern **toll highway** that connects Mexico City and Guadalajara. Exit when the road crosses **Highway 43.** It's clearly marked. To Morelia from either city is about 4 hours and $20 (£10). From Guanajuato (2½ hr.), take this same Highway 43. From Morelia to Pátzcuaro (1 hr.), there is **Highway 120,** a four-lane road. The new toll road from the Ixtapa beach resort connects to this highway. From Ixtapa to Morelia now takes about 4 hours and $15 (£7.50).

BY BUS   Buses to Morelia from Mexico City depart from the Observatorio station. ETN, Pegasso, Primera Plus/Servicios Coordinados, and Autovías all go to Morelia.

Make sure to request a *directo* or *via autopista*. The trip takes 4 hours, and there are usually three or four departures every hour. ETN offers the best service. You will arrive at the new **Central Camionera** in the far northwest side of town, near the soccer stadium. First-class and deluxe bus service to and from Morelia use Terminal A, and regional service to and from Pátzcuaro uses Terminal B. Service from Guadalajara is also frequent. From Guanajuato, your best bet is Primera Plus and Servicios Coordinados, usually changing buses in Irapuato. From Ixtapa, Parhikuni has six buses per day.

In downtown Morelia several travel agencies sell bus tickets. At the corner of 20 de Noviembre and Obregón is one called **GAP** (© **443/317-2828**), and it sells tickets for ETN and Primera Plus.

ORIENTATION
VISITOR INFORMATION   The city government, in association with local guides, has a tourist information kiosk on the Plaza de Armas (main square). It's open from 9am until 8pm Monday to Saturday. The city operates a website (www.visitmorelia. com) and prints a free quarterly magazine with a calendar of events *(La Guía de Morelia)*, which is handy.

CITY LAYOUT   The heart of the city is the **cathedral,** with the Plaza de Armas on its left (west side) and the Plaza Melchor Ocampo on its right (east side). The wide street passing in front of the cathedral is **Avenida Madero,** the city's main street. It meets the lovely colonial aqueduct .8km (a half-mile) east of the cathedral. This segment of Madero, along with several blocks to either side, is the old part of town (see "Other Attractions," below.) From the fountain, the **aqueduct** heads southeast toward what has become the fashionable part of town.

GETTING AROUND   Taxis are a bargain here. Still, you should settle the fare before you enter the cab.

FAST FACTS: Morelia

American Express   The local representative is **Gran Turismo Viajes,** Av. Camelinas 3233, Int. 102–103, Fracc. Las Américas (© **443/324-0484;** fax 443/324-0495), open Monday through Saturday from 9am to 2pm and 4 to 6pm.

Area Code   The telephone area code is **443.**

Climate   Morelia can be a bit chilly in the morning and evening, especially from November through February.

Elevation   Morelia sits at 1,950m (6,396 ft.).

Emergencies   The local number for emergencies is © **066.**

Hospital   The best in town is the **Sanatorio de la Luz,** Calle Bravo 50, in the Chapultepec Norte neighborhood (© **443/314-4568** or -4464, or 315-2966).

Internet Access   You can find Internet service without much effort in the Centro Histórico (Historic District). The usual cost is about $2 (£1) per hour.

Population   Morelia has 600,000 residents.

Post Office & Telegraph Office   Both are in the Palacio Federal, on the corner of Madero and Serapio Rendón, 5 blocks east of the cathedral.

Morelia

ATTRACTIONS ●

Casa de las Artesanías **14**
Casa Museo de Morelos **13**
Catedral **10**
College of San Nicolás
de Hidalgo **3**
Conservatorio de las Rosas **1**
Instituto Michoacano
de Cultura **8**
Museo de Arte Colonial **7**
Museo del Estado **2**
Museo Regional Michoacano **11**

ACCOMMODATIONS ■

Best Western Hotel Casino **5**
Hotel D'Atilanos **12**
Hotel de la Soledad **6**
Hotel Virrey de Mendoza **4**

Palacio del Gobierno **9**

Map legend:
Bus ■
Church ✝
Information ⓘ
Post Office ⊠

SPECIAL EVENTS & FESTIVALS

In April, the **International Guitar Festival** (www.figmorelia.com) attracts performers from Latin America and Europe. In May, the city holds the **International Organ Festival** (linked to the variable feast day of Corpus Christi). The cathedral has a very large pipe organ that sounds wonderful. Every year, four organists are invited to give concerts there. In October, the city holds its increasingly popular film festival, **Festival Internacional de Cine de Morelia** (www.moreliafilmfest.com). The **International Festival of Music** is held in November, with a series of concerts performed over 2 weeks. Performers come from all over.

The largest civic celebrations are in September, the month of the *fiestas patrias*. **Independence Day** is celebrated on September 15 and 16. Then, on September 29 and 30, Morelia celebrates the **birthday of its favorite son, José María Morelos,** a patriot and revolutionary hero. The second celebration is actually bigger than the first, but both include parades, street parties, and large fireworks displays.

EXPLORING MORELIA
A STROLL THROUGH THE COLONIAL CENTER

Downtown Morelia is a good town for walking. One comes across interesting details on just about any street, and street crime is infrequent. The walk outlined below could take an entire day. The museums open at 9am; you'll find a lot of places closed on Mondays, holidays, and between 2 and 4pm. For a guided tour of the city, contact the guide mentioned in the section on the monarch butterfly migration ("Michoacán's Monarch Migration," p. 259). He can give a lot of local color and provide details about the city's history and architecture.

The **cathedral** ✦✦✦ is the place to begin. Built with the pink volcanic stone (*cantera* in Spanish) that Morelia is famous for, it's the most beautiful cathedral in Mexico. Notice how Avenida Madero widens as it passes in front of the cathedral, and how a cross street lines up with its facade. Morelia's planners sought to lend prominence to the city's churches by the placement of plazas and the alignment of streets to allow good views. This cathedral took the place of an earlier one; construction began in 1640 and ended in 1745. The new cathedral incorporated the styles of religious architecture already in the city, including plateresque, mannerist, and a reserved style of baroque. The cathedral's impressive size and monumental proportions were necessary to place it at the top of the hierarchy of the city's temples, and to make obvious Morelia's superiority to rival Pátzcuaro. The Italian architect who designed it worked closely with the authorities of Morelia's sizable religious community, and he did a masterful job balancing the architectural elements in the facade and shaping the proportions of the towers. The inside is stately, but much of the cathedral's most valuable possessions were plundered. Things to look for include the beautiful **organ** ✦ with 4,600 pipes (see "Special Events & Festivals," above); the silver baptismal font where Mexico's first emperor, Agustín de Iturbide, was baptized; and the elegant choir with carved wooden stalls. *Tip:* If you're in Morelia on a Saturday, make sure to be around the cathedral when the lights are turned on. This is accompanied by a fireworks display.

Across Avenida Madero from the cathedral is a two-story stone building crowned with finials and fanciful decorations on the corners: the **Palacio del Gobierno,** built in 1732 as a seminary. It now holds sweeping murals depicting the history of Michoacán and Mexico. Some are the work of a well-known local artist, Alfredo Zalce.

Free-Market Forces

Morelia's **city market** is 5 blocks south of San Francisco in a plain, warehouse-like structure. If you're a veteran market shopper, you'll like this one. It's especially rich in regional manufactures, such as sombreros and huaraches, and has a good produce section where you can stock up on different kinds of dried chiles if you like cooking Mexican food.

To get to the market, go downhill from San Francisco Plaza along Calle Vasco de Quiroga. Just before you get there you will see a little plaza and the **Templo de las Capuchinas**. It's a precious little baroque church with a gilt *retablo* (altarpiece) inside. Unfortunately, it is often closed; the best time to try is from 8 to 9am and from 5 to 6pm, when the priest opens the church for Mass. Behind the church is the market.

As you leave the *palacio,* turn left and walk down Madero for 2 blocks. Turn right at a small church on your right with a tall wrought-iron fence. The name of the street is Vasco de Quiroga. Walk 1 block, and to your left you'll see a broad plaza and the **church and convent of San Francisco** ✦✦. This is one of the two oldest religious buildings in Morelia. It draws on the Spanish Renaissance architectural style known as plateresque (already antiquated by the time of construction) because the builders wanted to accentuate their Spanish heritage. The convent is quite striking; it has elegant, Moorish windows on the second floor, borrowed from Spanish Mudéjar architecture. The interior courtyard, unlike any other in Morelia, has a medieval feel. Instead of being broad and open with light arches, it is closed and narrow, with heavy columns set closely together and thick buttressing. The former convent now houses a local **handicrafts museum** and the best shopping in Morelia (see "Shopping," below).

From San Francisco (if you're not going to the market), take the street that lines up with the facade of the church and walk 2 blocks west to Calle Morelos Sur (you'll see Plaza Melchor Ocampo). Turn left. One block down, on the left-hand side, is the **Casa Museo de Morelos,** Morelos Sur 323 (✆ 443/313-2651). This is where José María Morelos lived as an adult (there's another Morelos museum in the house where he was born, but it has little of interest). A grand house, with furniture and personal effects that belonged to the independence leader, as well as a period kitchen, this museum is worth a visit. For history buffs, there is an exhibition on his four campaigns against royalist forces. The museum is open daily from 9am to 7pm; admission is $3 (£1.50).

The next place to see is the **Museo Regional Michoacano** ✦, at the intersection of Allende and Abasolo (✆ 443/312-0407). To get there, walk uphill the way you came, and then make a left when you get back to Plaza Melchor Ocampo. Walk through the stone arcades behind the cathedral (For a treat, see the next sidebar.)

Continue west to the end of the arcades. Across the street, cater-corner to the Plaza de Armas, is the museum. It provides a colorful view of the state from prehistoric times to Mexico's Cardenist period of the 1930s. Isidor Huarte, father of Ana Huarte, Emperor Iturbide's wife, originally owned the building, which was finished in 1775. The museum is open Tuesday through Saturday from 9am to 7pm, Sunday from 9am to 4pm. Admission is $3 (£1.50).

A Brief Pause for the Food Cause

Behind the cathedral are two local food vendors that are institutions in the city. One is an ice cream stand called **Nieves del Correo.** It's called that because for the first 30 years of its existence, it occupied a bit of sidewalk on Avenida Madero in front of the post office. Now it's in the last doorway under the arches before you get to the pedestrian-only Cerrada de San Agustín. You can't miss it. The specialty is fruit flavors such as mango and mamey. The other option is to enjoy a fruit cocktail known locally as a *gazpacho* (nothing like a gazpacho in Spain). Turn left on the Cerrada and you'll come to **Gazpachos La Cerrada.** Order one and you'll get chopped fruit (mango, pineapple, and jicama) swimming in orange and lime juice with a touch of powdered chile.

To take a break, sit at one of the outdoor cafes under the stone arches along Avenida Madero. (No need really to over-exert one's self. Besides, sitting at a table having a little coffee or beer and watching the passersby is a favorite activity of the locals. In anthropology, you would be doing what is called "participant observation.")

After having your fill of participant observation (or beer or coffee), head west on Madero for a block and you'll come to calle Nigromante. On the right, you'll see the **College of San Nicolás de Hidalgo,** a beautiful colonial building that claims to house the oldest university in the New World. Founded in Pátzcuaro in 1540 by Vasco de Quiroga, the university moved to Morelia in 1580 and became the University of Michoacán in 1917. On the other corner is another of Morelia's oldest religious structures, the **Iglesia de la Compañía de Jesús,** built by the Jesuits. It's now a picturesque library. Through a doorway to the right of the church is the state's **tourist information office.** Attached to the church is the former convent, now called the **Palacio Clavijero.** To see the graceful arches and rose-colored stone of its broad interior courtyard (the most photographed in Morelia), turn down Nigromante and follow it to the main entrance. The former convent now houses government offices. Once you've seen the *palacio,* continue down the street to the little park. Facing the park is the **Conservatorio de las Rosas,** a former Dominican convent. It became a music school in 1785 and is now the home of the internationally acclaimed **Morelia Boys Choir.** The choir practices on weekday afternoons. If you would like to attend a concert, ask for information inside.

Cater-cornered from the conservatory, at the junction of Santiago Tapia and Guillermo Prieto, is the **Museo del Estado** (© 443/313-0629). Exhibits include a display on the archaeology and history of the area and a 19th-century apothecary shop. The museum is open Monday through Friday from 9am to 2pm and 4 to 8pm, Saturday and Sunday from 9am to 2pm and 4 to 7pm. Admission is free. Look for, or ask about, concerts and other goings-on.

To visit another interesting museum, continue east on Santiago Tapia 2 blocks to Benito Juárez and turn north (left). The **Museo de Arte Colonial** ✶, Av. Benito Juárez 240 (© 443/313-9260), is a colonial mansion that houses a large collection of religious art from the 16th to the 18th centuries. One section displays Christ figures made from the paste of corn stalks. This was a pre-Columbian artistic technique among the Purépecha, and the missionaries soon had their Indian converts using it to create the Christ figures and saints that adorn many churches in Mexico. The museum is open Tuesday through Sunday from 10am to 2pm and 5 to 8pm. Admission is free. Just around the corner from this museum (turn right as you exit) is the **Plaza del Carmen.** Across the plaza, behind a heavy wrought-iron fence, is the church and former convent of **El Carmen.** The entrance to the convent is on the opposite side of the block from the church, on Morelos Norte. The building is home to the state's **Instituto Michoacano de Cultura (***©* **443/313-1320),** which has made this a comfortable and utilitarian destination; you can examine the calendars posted at the entrance to see whether a concert, film, or exhibition is happening during your stay. You can also view the large stone courtyard built in the style often used by the Carmelites. Around the courtyard are a museum of native masks, a large bookstore, and a gallery. Entrance is free. The institute is open daily from 10am to 8pm.

OTHER ATTRACTIONS

On another day you might enjoy exploring Avenida Madero, east from the cathedral. After a couple of blocks, you'll reach the **Templo de las Monjas (Nuns' Temple),** a lovely old church with a unique twin facade and B-shaped floor plan. Beside it is the massive **Palacio Federal,** which houses, among many other official bureaus, the post and telegraph offices. Continue on and you'll reach the colonial **aqueduct.** The graceful arches of the aqueduct stretch from here about a kilometer (less than a mile) eastward. A stone walkway, lined with trees and long stone benches, starts from one of the arches in front of the fountain. This is **La Calzada Fray Antonio de San Miguel** ☆☆. In the 1940s, this walkway was used to shoot some scenes for a Hollywood movie, with Tyrone Power, called *Captains from Castile.* The Calzada leads to the **church of San Diego** ☆☆, the most ornate church in Morelia, San Diego is also known as **El Santuario de Guadalupe.** It has a colorful interior done in neobaroque, the product of a remodeling job done a century ago. In early December, food stands fill the entire plaza in front of the church, and a festival is held to celebrate the feast day of the Virgin of Guadalupe (Dec 12).

The distance from the cathedral to San Diego is about 1.6km (1 mile). You can take a taxi back or, if you still feel like walking, return by crossing the large plaza with the statue of Morelos on horseback. Go under the aqueduct, and enter Morelia's equivalent of Central Park, known as **El Bosque (The Woods).** Continue west and work your way back to the center of town. If you get turned around here, note that if you're walking on level ground, you're parallel to or heading toward Madero; if you're walking downhill, you're heading away from it.

SHOPPING

Casa de las Artesanías ☆☆   This place is both a museum and one of the best crafts shops in Mexico. In the showroom on the right, you'll find an array of objects produced in the Indian villages of Michoacán's central highlands, including carved-wood furniture from Cuanajo, pottery from Tzintzuntzan, wood masks from Tócuaro, lacquerware from Pátzcuaro and Uruapan, cross-stitch embroidery from Tarecuato, copperware from Santa Clara, guitars from Paracho, and close-woven hats from Jarácuaro. Straight ahead in the interior courtyard are showcases laden with the best regional crafts. Upstairs, individual villages have sales outlets. Sometimes artisans demonstrate their craft. The shop and museum are open daily from 9am to 2pm and 5 to 8pm. Exconvento de San Francisco, Plaza Valladolid. *©* **443/312-1248.**

Mercado de Dulces   Along the back of the former Jesuit convent is the sweets market—a collection of stalls selling the typical sweets that Morelia is famous for, such as *ates* (a thick fruit paste), candied fruit wedges, pralines, toasted coconut, and milk candies. The *mercado* is open daily from 7am to 10pm. Behind the Palacio Clavijero, along Valentín Gómez Farías. No phone. From the cathedral, head west on Madero and turn right on Gómez Farías; entrance is a half-block down on the right.

WHERE TO STAY

Rates listed here include the 17% tax. Rates at the inexpensive and moderately priced hotels can go up during Christmas, Easter, Day of the Dead, holiday weekends, and the month of August.

VERY EXPENSIVE

Hotel Virrey de Mendoza 🏅🏅   This is one of the old-style grand hotels one occasionally finds in Mexico's colonial cities. Unlike others, this one was not allowed to decay; it's beautifully kept and most impressive. It's also right on the Plaza de Armas. Furnishings vary, but all rooms are comfortable. They have lots of character—wood floors with area rugs, period furniture, old-fashioned tile bathrooms with tub/shower combinations. Bed choices include two twins, one full, two queen-size, or one king-size. Standard rooms are midsize; of the eight exterior rooms, two have balconies. Suites are large, and master suites have separate sitting rooms. The *suite virreinal* (viceroy suite) is really grand, with a large third-floor terrace that looks out over the Plaza de Armas to the cathedral. Rooms have double-glazed windows, but traffic noises still leak in.

Av. Madero Poniente 310, 58000 Morelia, Mich. ✆ 866/299-7492 in the U.S.; ✆ 877/889-2161 in Canada; or 443/312-0633. Fax 443/312-6719. www.hotelvirrey.com. 55 units. $210 (£105) double; $250–$410 (£125–£205) suite. Internet packages sometimes available. AE, MC, V. Free valet parking. **Amenities:** Restaurant; lobby bar; tour desk; car rental; business center; room service; in-room massage; babysitting; laundry service; dry cleaning; nonsmoking rooms. *In room:* A/C (in 11 rooms), TV, hair dryer.

Villa Montaña Hotel and Spa 🏅🏅🏅   High above the city on the Santa María Ridge, this hotel offers beauty and tranquility. Rooms are in a small complex of buildings on a hillside, separated by gardens and connected by footpaths. The buildings are at different levels; this, as well as the placement of the entrances, allows for privacy. Villa Montaña, a member of the Small Luxury Hotels of the World, has no rough edges. Rooms are large, impressively furnished, and have working fireplaces. Most come with two doubles or a king-size bed. Bathrooms are large, with tub/shower combinations and lots of counter space. Most of the junior suites have a separate living area and a small terrace with table and chairs. Master suites have a lot of architectural details. The restaurant does a great job with local dishes, and having a drink on the terrace overlooking the city is one of the delights of staying here. Service is attentive.

Patzimba 201, Col. Vista Bella 58090 Morelia, Mich. ✆ 443/314-0231 or -0179. Fax 443/315-1423. www.villa montana.com.mx. 36 units. $234 (£117) double; $322–$392 (£161–£196) suite; $510 (£255) 2-bedroom suite. Prices do not include 7.5% service charge. Internet specials sometimes available. Weekday discounts available. AE, MC, V. Free secure parking. **Amenities:** Restaurant; terrace bar; heated outdoor pool; golf at local country club; lighted tennis court; fitness room; spa; concierge; tour desk; business center; executive business services; room service; in-room massage; babysitting; laundry service; dry cleaning. *In room:* TV, hair dryer, safe.

MODERATE

Best Western Hotel Casino *(Value)*   A colonial hotel that's not as striking as the Hotel de la Soledad, the Best Western should still be considered for its location—across the street from the cathedral—comfort, and price. The owners continue to invest money in improvements and upgrades. They've opened three new rooms on the top floor that are large, sunny, and quite comfortable. Most rooms are midsize and carpeted. They are, for the most part, more comfortable than the rooms at the Soledad. Some second-floor rooms in front have a balcony and view of the cathedral, but they can be noisy. Many rooms have two double beds or one double and one twin.

Portal Hidalgo 229, 58000 Morelia, Mich. ⓒ 800/528-1234 in the U.S., or 443/313-1328. Fax 443/312-1252. www.bestwestern.com. 43 units. $96–$105 (£48–£53) double. AE, MC, V. Free valet parking. **Amenities:** Restaurant; bar; fitness room, tour desk; car rental; business center; room service; laundry service and courtesy washer and dryer; dry cleaning; nonsmoking rooms. In room: TV, Wi-Fi, coffeemaker, hair dryer, iron.

Hotel de la Soledad ⓖ   Past the massive wooden doors of this colonial hotel is a large, beautiful courtyard with antique carriages parked beneath stone arches. Some rooms have fireplaces and balconies. Standard rooms vary quite a bit and come with two twin beds, one double, or one king-size. The price depends on whether the room faces the more elegant front courtyard (these rooms are generally bigger) or the rear courtyard. Rooms have rugs or carpeting, Spanish-style furniture, and high ceilings. Double-glazed windows were installed recently and seemed to work well at reducing the noise and the drafts. Bathrooms vary in size and quality; most are ample, and many contain tub/shower combinations. The location is great—1 block north of the cathedral.

Ignacio Zaragoza 90, 58000 Morelia, Mich. ⓒ 800/423-4106 in the U.S. and Canada or ⓒ 443/312-1888 or -1889. Fax 443/312-2111. www.hsoledad.com. 58 units. $100–$125 (£50–£63) double; $120–$140 (£60–£70) suite. Internet specials available. AE, MC, V. Free valet parking. **Amenities:** Restaurant; bar; tour desk; 24-hr. room service; laundry service; dry cleaning. In room: TV, hair dryer (on request), safe.

INEXPENSIVE

Hotel D'Atilanos   This is the only decent inexpensive hotel in the downtown area. Two floors of rooms surround a simple patio. The rooms are simply furnished, with one or two double beds, two twins, or one king bed (king rooms are more expensive). Most rooms are midsize, but bathrooms are small. I prefer the downstairs rooms, which have high ceilings. Lighting is poor.

Corregidora 465, 58000 Morelia, Mich. ⓒ 443/313-3309 or 312-0121. 27 units. $40–$50 (£20–£25) double. No credit cards. Limited street parking. In room: TV.

WHERE TO DINE

Michoacán is known for a dish of slow-cooked pork called *carnitas*, which is sold only in joints that specialize in the dish. Who serves the best *carnitas* is a never-ending discussion in Morelia. Many locals like **Los Tabachines,** in Colonia Ventura Puente. The address is Laguna de la Magdalena 430. You can eat the *carnitas* there or buy them to go. On my last trip, I had a splendid meal at **Carnitas don Raúl** at Carpinteros de Paracho 1007, Colonia Vasco de Quiroga. It's best to go around noon.

Cenaduría Lupita ⓖ ANTOJITOS   Translated literally, *antojitos* means "little cravings." This is the traditional supper food of most Mexicans, but they usually eat it at home or in greasy-spoon joints whose cleanliness is dubious. A good-looking, comfortable restaurant that specializes in *antojitos* is a rarity; rarer still is one that does such a good job. Take your pick of *tacos dorados,* tostadas, tamales, *huchepos* (like tamales, but made with fresh corn), and *pozole* prepared Michoacán style. The restaurant is a half-block off Avenida Lázaro Cárdenas; take a cab.

Sánchez de Tagle 1004. ⓒ 443/312-1340. Antojitos $4–$6 (£2–£3). MC, V. Wed–Mon 7–11pm; Sun 7–10pm.

El Anzuelo ✹✹ SEAFOOD/STEAKS   This simple outdoor restaurant in the modern part of town serves the best seafood in Morelia. It makes the perfect Mexican seafood cocktail and wonderful ceviche. After either of those, you might order *huachinango adobado* (red snapper in a chile-based marinade) or coconut shrimp. If you don't feel like fish, there's filet mignon. The owners are meticulous about food preparation. El Anzuelo is open only in the afternoon. On Sunday, it offers paella, and the restaurant gets very crowded. Take a taxi and keep the address handy.

Av. Camelinas 3180. ✆ 443/314-8339 or 324-3237. Reservations recommended on weekends. Main courses $9–$18 (£4.50–£9). AE, MC, V. Daily noon–6pm.

La Casa del Portal REGIONAL/INTERNATIONAL   This upstairs restaurant is in a beautiful stone mansion facing the Plaza de Armas. The floors, walls, and ceilings of the old house have remained intact, including the antique wallpaper and other details. It's good to have so much to observe as service can be slow. There are several dining rooms, and on occasion the rooftop terrace is open for dining. Most of the furniture comes from the owner's workshop. The restaurant doubles as a sort of factory outlet, and all the furniture is for sale. What's for dinner? The menu includes several regional standards, such *sopa tarasca* and *enchiladas del portal*. Other dishes include the *arrachera valladolid*, a skirt steak accompanied by a few Mexican sides.

Guillermo Prieto 30 (cater-cornered from Virrey de Mendoza; entrance is on the side street). ✆ 443/313-4899. Main courses $8–$17 (£4–£8.50). AE, MC, V. Daily 8:30am–11pm.

Las Trojes STEAKS/REGIONAL   A *troje* is the traditional dwelling of the highland Purépecha Indians, constructed of rough-cut wood planks. This restaurant is made of seven connected *trojes*, with windows added for light. For starters, try *sopa tarasca*. Main courses include *cecina*, a good steak *a la tampiqueña* (marinated and grilled); rib-eye; *chistorra* (Spanish-style sausage); and chicken stuffed with cheese en brochette. Take a cab and keep the address handy.

Juan Sebastián Bach 51, Col. La Loma. ✆ 443/314-7344. Main courses $10–$16 (£5–£8). AE, MC, V. Mon–Sat 1pm–midnight; Sun 1–6pm.

Los Mirasoles ✹ REGIONAL   Los Mirasoles serves regional fare including fish tacos, *jahuácatas* or *corundas* (a kind of tamal in the form of a triangle without a filling and served in a chile sauce with bits of pork). They also serve pork ribs marinated in a dark chile sauce. There's a large selection of beer and wine to accompany your meal. Service can be slow. The dining rooms are attractive, especially at night.

Av. Madero Poniente 549 (4 blocks west of Plaza de Armas, at León Guzmán). ✆ 443/317-5775. Reservations recommended on weekends. Main courses $5–$10 (£2.50–£5); seafood/steaks $10–$25 (£5–£13). AE, MC, V. Daily 1–11pm.

San Miguelito ✹✹ *(Finds)* MEXICAN   Perhaps the most popular restaurant in town, San Miguelito offers an inventive menu, attentive service, and a setting loaded with icons of Mexican culture. One part of the main dining room is the Rincón de las Solteronas (the bachelorette corner), where many images of Saint Anthony hang upside down—the custom in Mexico when a girl is petitioning him for a boyfriend or husband. Guests are welcome to make a petition; the staff will be happy to show you how. I especially enjoy the appetizers here: tacos, *chicharrón de queso* (fried crispy cheese), and other finger foods. The *sopa tarasca* is among the best I've had in restaurants. There are several steak dishes, including one in tequila, *guajillo* chile, and orange

Moments   Michoacán's Monarch Migration

A visit to the winter nesting grounds of the monarch butterfly, high in the mountains of northeast Michoacán, is a stirring experience. It might be the highlight of your trip. The season lasts from mid- to late November to March. Tour operators in Morelia offer a day trip to see the butterflies for $50 to $60 (£25–£30) per person. The tour takes 10 to 12 hours and involves hiking up a mountain at a high altitude. You shouldn't consider doing this if you're not in decent physical condition.

The best time to see the butterflies is on a sunny day, when they flutter through the air in a blizzard of orange and black. At the center of the group, the branches of the tall fir trees bow under their burden of butterflies, whose wings undulate softly as the wind blows through the forest; it's quite a spectacle.

From Morelia, you'll have no difficulty finding a tour; most hotels and all travel agencies can put you in contact with one. I particularly recommend **Luis Miguel López Alanís** (© 443/340-4632). He speaks English, is federally licensed, and belongs to a small cooperative of guides called **Mex Mich Guías** (www.mmg.com.mx). The easiest way to contact him is through the website. Most tours provide transportation, guide, soft drinks, and usually lunch. A good guide is important, if only to answer all the questions that these butterflies and their strange migration provoke.

A few butterfly sanctuaries are open to the public. (The monarchs congregate at nine sites, but five are closed to visitors.) The sites with the best access are **El Rosario** (admission $4/£2; daily 10am–5 or 6pm) and the newer **Chincua** (same admission and hours as El Rosario). It is less of a drive, but usually more of a walk to the nucleus of the butterfly group—but not always. Throughout the season, the groups shift, moving up and down the mountains and making for a longer or shorter climb. A good guide will be aware of which is the shorter walk.

If you're driving, take the *autopista* to Mexico City, exit at Maravatío, and go right. Keep right after going through Maravatío and take the narrow two-lane road toward Angangueo. When you get to a T-junction, go right, toward San Felipe. Enter the town of Ocampo and look for a small sign pointing left to get to Rosario, where you will find a parking lot near the trail head. If you want to make this a leisurely trip, spend the night in the nearby town of Angangueo at **Hotel Don Bruno** (© 715/156-0026; $60/£30 double). It's a pretty hotel but a little overpriced, so you should ask to see the room before you accept it.

Travel agencies from **San Miguel de Allende** also book monarch tours, which take 1 or 2 days. See chapter 7 for details.

---

sauce. For dessert there's a delicious version of cherries jubilee. Take a cab and keep the address handy.

Av. Camelinas (at Ventura Puente). © 443/324-2300. Reservations recommended. Main courses $12–$19 (£6–£9.50). AE, MC, V. Mon–Wed 2–11pm; Thurs–Sat 2pm–midnight; Sun 2–5pm.

MORELIA AFTER DARK

For nighttime entertainment, be sure to check the calendar of events at the **Instituto Michoacano de Cultura** (see "A Stroll Through the Colonial Center," above). In addition, you can sit at one of the cafes under the stone arches across from the Plaza de Armas to do some people-watching (a very Moreliano thing to do). Aside from the dance clubs that are mostly on the fashionable east side, there are few nightlife options. The following are my favorites. For dancing, go to **La Casa de la Salsa** (© 443/313-9362), a large dance hall facing Plaza Morelos at the end of the Calzada Fray Antonio de San Miguel. It's open Tuesday through Saturday from 9pm to 3am. It books live music on Friday and Saturday ($4/£2 cover). You can call ahead to reserve a table; the band plays a lot of salsa, merengue, and mambo.

If you want to hear live Latin American folk music, have a drink, and eat something, try **Peña Colibrí** (© 443/312-2261), Galeana 36, behind the Virrey de Mendoza. It opens daily at 8pm and closes around midnight. There is another nearby *peña* (bar where folk music is played) at Allende 3, **Bohemia V** (no phone). The food isn't good, but the music is great.

2 Pátzcuaro ⭑⭑⭑

370km (229 miles) NW of Mexico City; 285km (177 miles) SE of Guadalajara; 69km (43 miles) SW of Morelia

Pátzcuaro is perhaps the loveliest town in Mexico. Crooked cobblestone streets, smooth stucco walls painted white with dark red borders, blackened tile roofs that join to form ramshackle rooflines—it is a town meant to be photographed and painted. During the rainy season, when low clouds roll in and curl through the trees, and water drips from the low-slung overhangs, a sweet melancholy descends upon the town.

Pátzcuaro is in the heart of the Purépecha homeland. Beside it is Lake Pátzcuaro (one of the world's highest at 2,200m/7,216 ft.), whose shores border dozens of Indian villages. In these villages and in town, visitors frequently hear the soft sounds of the Purépechan language in the background as they take in the sights. Although distinct regional costumes are seldom seen today, Indian women still braid their hair with ribbons and wear the blue *rebozos* (long woolen wraps).

ESSENTIALS
GETTING THERE & DEPARTING

BY CAR   See "Getting There & Departing" under "Morelia," earlier in this chapter, for information from Mexico City, Guadalajara, and San Miguel de Allende. From Morelia there are two routes to Pátzcuaro; the faster is the new four-lane **Highway 120,** which passes near Tiripetío and Tupátaro/Cuanajo (see "Side Trips from Pátzcuaro," later in this chapter). The longer route, **Highway 15,** takes a little more than an hour and passes near the pottery-making village of Capula and then through Quiroga, where you follow signs to Pátzcuaro (see "Side Trips from Pátzcuaro," later in this chapter).

BY BUS   The bus station is on the outskirts of Pátzcuaro, 5 minutes away by taxi ($2/£1). If you're going anywhere outside of Michoacán, it's best to go to Morelia first. If you're going straight to Mexico City, the Pegaso bus company offers nonstop service. Buses between Morelia and Pátzcuaro run every 10 minutes. To visit any of the lakeside villages or nearby towns, public transportation is an option, but taxis are not that expensive. From the Pátzcuaro bus station, there are buses to Tócuaro and Erongarícuaro every

Pátzcuaro

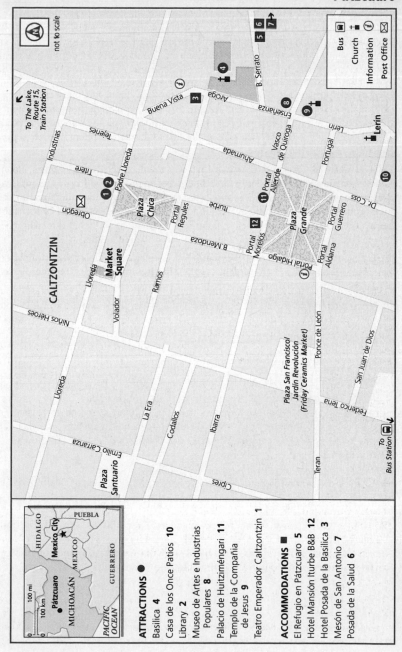

not to scale

To The Lake,
Route 15,
Train Station

CALTZONTZIN

Market Square

Plaza Chica

Plaza Grande

Plaza Santuario

Plaza San Francisco/
Jardín Revolución
(Friday Ceramics Market)

To Bus Station

Buena Vista

B. Serrato

Enseñanza

Lerín

Vasco de Quiroga

Ahumada

Portal Allende

Portal Morelos

Portal Hidalgo

Portal Aldama

Portal Guerrero

B. Mendoza

Iturbe

Portal Regules

Padre Lloreda

Tejerés

Títere

Industrias

Obregón

Lloreda

Volador

Ramos

Niños Héroes

Lloreda

La Era

Codallos

Ibarra

Cipres

Emilio Carranza

Ponce de León

San Juan de Dios

Federico Tena

Teran

Portugal

León

Dr. Coss

Arciga

Bus
Church
Information
Post Office

PUEBLA
HIDALGO
Mexico City
MICHOACÁN
MEXICO
GUERRERO
Pátzcuaro
PACIFIC OCEAN

100 mi
100 km

ATTRACTIONS ●
Basílica **4**
Casa de los Once Patios **10**
Library **2**
Museo de Artes e Industrias
Populares **8**
Palacio de Huitziméngari **11**
Templo de la Compañía
de Jesús **9**
Teatro Emperador Caltzontzin **1**

ACCOMMODATIONS ■
El Refugio en Pátzcuaro **5**
Hotel Mansión Iturbe B&B **12**
Hotel Posada de la Basílica **3**
Mesón de San Antonio **7**
Posada de la Salud **6**

20 minutes; to Tupátaro and Cuanajo every hour; to Tzintzuntzan and Quiroga every 40 minutes; and to Santa Clara del Cobre every hour. For Ihuatzio, you can pick up a minivan or a bus from the Plaza Chica.

ORIENTATION

VISITOR INFORMATION The **Tourism Office,** Cuesta Buenavista 7 (© **434/ 342-1214**), near the basilica, is open Monday through Saturday from 9am to 3pm and 4 to 7pm, and Sunday from 9am to 2pm. Although you might not find someone who speaks English, the staff can give you maps and point you in the right direction. There's also an office on the west side of the Plaza Grande (no phone). It keeps the same hours as the main office.

CITY LAYOUT In a way, Pátzcuaro has two town centers, both plazas a block apart. **Plaza Grande,** also called Plaza Principal or Plaza Don Vasco de Quiroga, is picturesque and tranquil, with a fountain and a statue of Vasco de Quiroga. Hotels, shops, and restaurants in Colonial-Era buildings flank this plaza. **Plaza Chica,** also known as Plaza Gertrudis Bocanegra, flows into the market, and around it swirls the commercial life of Pátzcuaro. Plaza Chica is north of Plaza Grande.

GETTING AROUND With the exception of Lake Pátzcuaro, the lookout, the bus station, and hotels on Lázaro Cárdenas, everything is within walking distance. Taxis are cheap. The lake is about a kilometer (less than a mile) from town; buses make the run every 15 minutes from both the Plaza Grande and the Plaza Chica, going all the way to the *embarcadero* or *muelle* (pier).

FAST FACTS: Pátzcuaro

Area Code The telephone area code is **434.**

Climate The climate is delightful most of the year, but occasional blustery days bring swirls of chilled air from across the lake, causing everyone to retreat indoors. October through April, it's cold enough for a heavy sweater, especially in the morning and evening. Few hotels have fireplaces or any source of heat in the rooms.

Elevation Pátzcuaro sits at an altitude of 2,200m (7,216 ft.).

Emergency Dial © **434/349-0209** for emergency assistance.

Hospital The **Hospital Civil Dr. Gabriel García** is at Calle Romero 18 (© **434/342-0285**).

Population Pátzcuaro has 70,000 residents.

Post Office The *correo,* located a half-block north of Plaza Chica, on the right side of the street, is open Monday through Friday from 10am to 2pm and 4 to 8pm.

SPECIAL EVENTS

The island of **Janitzio** has achieved international celebrity for the candlelight vigil that local residents hold at the cemetery during the nights of November 1 and 2, the Days of the Dead. **Tzintzuntzan,** a village about 15km (9⅓ miles) away, also hosts popular festivities, including folkloric dances in the main plaza and in the nearby *yácatas* (pre-Hispanic ruins), concerts in the church, and decorations in the cemetery. If you

> **Tips Festival Hotel Crunch**
>
> Make hotel reservations months in advance for Holy Week or Days of the Dead. Most hotels require a 3-night minimum stay during these events. There are some other, less popular festivals in Pátzcuaro and surrounding towns; check with the tourist office to see if any will occur during your visit.

want to avoid the crowds, skip Janitzio and Tzintzuntzan and go to one of the smaller **lakeside villages or other islands** on the lake that also have extraordinary rituals. The tourism office (see "Visitor Information," above) has a schedule of events for the entire area and publishes an explanatory booklet, *Días de los Muertos*.

During the week surrounding **Days of the Dead,** artisans and vendors from all over Michoacán fill the Plaza Grande in Pátzcuaro with regional crafts. **Easter week,** beginning the Friday before Palm Sunday, is special, too. Most activity centers on the basilica. There are processions involving the surrounding villages almost nightly, and in Tzintzuntzan, there's a reenactment of the betrayal of Christ and a ceremonial washing of the feet.

EXPLORING PATZCUARO: A STROLL AROUND TOWN

The **Plaza Grande** is in the middle of town, surrounded by colonial buildings. A **stone fountain** in the center of the plaza holds a large figure of the beloved Vasco de Quiroga, "Tata Vasco," depicted in a benevolent posture. On the north side of the plaza is the **Palacio de Huitziméngari,** built by the Spaniards for the Tarascan emperor. Local Indian artisans now occupy the slowly deteriorating building.

One long block north is the **Plaza Chica,** crisscrossed by walkways and adorned with the statue of Gertrudis Bocanegra, a heroine of Mexican independence. This is the commercial center of town. On the west side of the plaza are **market** stalls selling pottery, copper, *rebozos, serapes* (a small woolen blanket that is sometimes carried over the shoulder), and food. On some days, the stalls extend a couple of blocks up the street. What was once San Agustín church is on the north side of the plaza. The cloister was remodeled in the 20th century and converted into the **Teatro Emperador Caltzontzin,** the municipal theater. The old church is now the public library; inside, all the way to the back, you'll find an early work of Juan O'Gorman—a large mural stretching the width and height of the nave.

Don Vasco built the **basilica,** on a hill just east of the Plaza Chica, although he died before it was inaugurated in 1554. It was designated a basilica by papal decree in 1907. Now reconstructed, it has survived many catastrophes, human and natural—from earthquakes to the civil war of the mid-19th century. Be sure to visit the main altar to see the **Virgen de la Salud.** She is a sacred figure to the Indians of this region, who come from the villages to pay homage to her and petition her healing power on the eighth day of each month.

Two blocks south of the basilica is the **Museo de Artes Industrias Populares** ★★ (© **434/342-1029**). It occupies yet another beautiful colonial building (1540), originally Don Vasco's College of San Nicolás. The rooms, filled with fine examples of regional popular art such as crafts and costumes, open to a central courtyard. The museum guides are well informed. The museum is open Tuesday through Saturday from 9am to 7pm, Sunday from 9am to 4:30pm. Admission is $3.50 (£1.75). Behind the museum are some recent excavations of Purépechan ruins.

Of the many old churches in Pátzcuaro, one of the most interesting is the **Templo de la Compañía de Jesús,** just south of the museum. This church was Don Vasco's cathedral before the basilica; afterward, it was given to the Jesuits. The buildings across the street from the church were once part of the complex, containing the hospital, soup kitchen, and living quarters for religious scholars.

The **Casa de los Once Patios (House of Eleven Patios)** ⓡ, between José María Cos and Enseñanza, is another achievement of the colonial period. Formerly a convent belonging to the Catherine nuns, today it houses the **Casa de las Artesanías de Michoacán,** with every type of local artistry for sale (see "Shopping," below).

SHOPPING

Pátzcuaro is one of Mexico's best shopping towns: It has terrific textiles, copper, woodcarvings, lacquerwork, and straw weavings made in the region. Most shops are on the **Plaza Grande** and the streets leading from it to the **Plaza Chica,** the place of choice for copper vendors. There are also a couple of shops on the street facing the basilica. If you're interested in investigating a particular craft, you can find out which village or villages specialize in it, and if the villages have shops or a market. Tzintzuntzan, Ihuatzio, Cuanajo, Tupátaro, and Santa Clara del Cobre all have shops (see "Side Trips from Pátzcuaro," below).

Casa de las Artesanías de Michoacán/Casa de los Once Patios   This is the best one-stop shopping in the village. Small shops sell textile arts, pottery, and ceramic dishes, lacquerwork, paintings, woodcarvings, jewelry, copper work, and musical instruments (including the famous Paracho guitars). Much of the merchandise was produced in the region. Most shops are open daily from 9am to 2pm and 4 to 6pm. Calle Madrigal de las Altas Torres, between Dr. Coss and Lerín. No phone.

Diseño Artesano   Owner Esperanza Sepúlveda designs one-of-a-kind clothing using locally made fabrics. Her shop, on the west side of the Plaza Grande, is open daily from 10am to 8pm. Dr. Coss 1. No phone.

Friday Pottery Market *Finds*   Early each Friday morning this plaza, 1 block west of the Plaza Grande, fills with vendors of various styles of regionally made pottery, most of it not for sale in Pátzcuaro on other days. This is a market for locals; few tourists seem to hear about it. Prices are *cheap.* Plaza San Francisco, Ponce de León at Federico Teña. No phone.

Galería del Arcángel   Across from the Museo Regional, this store ("the Archangel's Gallery") offers a fine collection of quality regional pottery and handcarved furniture, plus some of the best crafts from other parts of Mexico. It's open daily from 9am to 7pm. Arciga 30. ⓒ/fax **434/342-1774.**

Galería Iturbe   Most of the artwork here is by local painters, mask makers, and other artists. You might also find a typical Day of the Dead altar. There's a small selection of books on Mexican art and culture. Enter through the Hotel Iturbe (go all the way to the back) or from Calle Iturbe, off the Plaza Grande. It's open daily from 10am to 8pm. Portal Morelos 59. ⓒ **434/342-0368.**

Mantas Típicas *Value*   A factory outlet for the company's textile mill, this is one of several textile outlets on the Plaza Grande. Colorful foot-loomed tablecloths, napkins, bedspreads, and bolts of fabric cover the shelves. It's open daily from 9am to 7pm. Dr. Coss 5. ⓒ **434/342-1324.**

Market Plaza   The House of Eleven Patios (see above) should be your first stop, and this your second. The entire plaza fronting the food market holds covered stalls selling crafts, clothing, rugs, *rebozos*, and more. Locally knitted sweaters are a good buy. Streets surrounding the plaza churn with exuberant sellers of fresh vegetables and caged birds. West of Plaza Chica. No phone.

Palacio Huitziméngari   On the north side of the Plaza Grande, in a colonial house, are a few shops run by folk from neighboring towns. Most of the merchandise is pottery and woodcarvings. Open daily from 8am to 10pm. Plaza Grande. No phone.

WHERE TO STAY

There are several good, comfortable hotels in Pátzcuaro. In choosing properties, I generally went with those that best reflected in some way the character of the town. Most of these are small properties; a good choice among the large hotels is **La Parroquia** (Plaza Bocanegra 24; ℭ **434/342-2515**). Another option would be to stay in Casa Santiago, a small B&B in Ihuatzio, one of the lakeside villages (see below). Rates include 17% tax.

EXPENSIVE

Hacienda Mariposas 𝒦𝒦𝒦 *Kids*   This hotel is a retreat into the Mexican countryside, just outside Pátzcuaro. Located on 12 acres of forested land above town, the hotel consists of separate or semidetached bungalows. The rooms are big and the bathrooms are spacious and well-equipped. Master suites come with Jacuzzi tubs. Emphasis is on personal attention and ecological practices. The hotel has plenty of educational activities for kids such as egg collecting and other farm activities, hiking, and pony riding. The entire hotel is nonsmoking. Breakfasts feature healthy versions of regional specialties, and there is a separate dining area with a low-fat menu. This is the first hotel in Mexico to be certified as ecological by the Mexican government. Service is attentive, and the spa is a big plus.

Carretera Pátzcuaro–Santa Clara Km 3, 61600 Pátzcuaro, Mich. ℭ 434/342-4728. www.haciendamariposas.com. 25 units. $118 (£59) junior suite; $176 (£88) master suite; $234 (£117) 2-bedroom master suite. Rates include full breakfast, horseback rides, spa, and afternoon *antojitos*. AE, MC, V. Free secure parking. **Amenities:** Restaurant; bar; spa; Jacuzzi; steam room; children's activities; tours; business center; room service; babysitting; laundry service; nonsmoking rooms. *In room:* CD player and music library, minibar w/organic snacks, hair dryer, safe.

Hotel Mansión Iturbe Bed and Breakfast 𝒦𝒦   Located on the north side of the Plaza Grande, this 17th-century mansion has kept more of its original character than any of the other colonial buildings–turned–hotels. The owners have worked hard to keep the old local touches, such as raised thresholds. Rooms are on the second floor and have the original plank flooring, along with heavy, dark, Spanish-style wooden furniture and fresh-cut flowers. Exterior rooms have double-glazed windows to keep the noise down. Most bathrooms are large. All rooms are nonsmoking. Purified ice, instant coffee, and hot water are available. The free cocktail hour every night allows guests to make acquaintances and share experiences. Guests have the use of a solarium, a library, and a study.

Portal Morelos 59, 61600 Pátzcuaro, Mich. ℭ 434/342-0368 or -3628. Fax (for reservations only) 443/313-4593. www.mexonline.com/iturbe.htm. 14 units. $90–$130 (£45–£65) double. Rates include full breakfast. Fourth night free (some restrictions apply). Ask about special promotions. AE, MC, V. Free secure parking. **Amenities:** 2 restaurants; 2 bars; complimentary bikes; tour desk; same-day laundry service. *In room:* TV, hair dryer (on request).

Tips If Pátzcuaro's Packed Solid . . .

During Easter week and Days of the Dead, Pátzcuaro's hotels fill up; visitors should be aware of three inexpensive hotels in the nearby town of Santa Clara. The **Hotel Oasis**, Portal Allende 144 (© **434/343-0040**), is the better of the two on the town's main plaza; **Hotel Real del Cobre**, Portal Hidalgo 19 (© **434/343-0205**), has a restaurant. The third hotel, **Camino Real** (© **434/343-0281**), is a few blocks away and is comparable to the Oasis.

Hotel Posada la Basílica ⚜ This colonial-style hotel in a great location across from the basilica has a lovely patio. The rooms, which border the patio on three sides, have tile floors and fireplaces. Seven have small balconies overlooking the street. The restaurant has a fabulous view of the mountains, the tile rooftops, and the lake. Rooms come with one or two double beds.

Arciga 6 (at La Paz), 61600 Pátzcuaro, Mich. © **434/342-1108.** Fax 434/342-0659. www.posadalabasilica.com. 12 units. $135 (£68) double; $180 (£90) suites. AE, MC, V. Free secure parking. **Amenities:** Restaurant; bar; tour info; room service; babysitting; laundry service; dry cleaning. *In room:* TV, hair dryer.

MODERATE

El Refugio en Pátzcuaro ⚜ *(Value)* This house captures so well the feel of Pátzcuaro—its local flavor, its serenity. The courtyard is perfectly what a courtyard of a provincial house should be. The rooms, with their clay tile or wood floors and beamed ceilings, their artwork, and their furniture, suggest the owner's affection for those simpler times. There is comfort, too. The rooms are spacious and well furnished. Each comes with a heater; beds come with heated mattress pads. The bathrooms are medium size and attractively finished in tile. Deborah, a young woman from Minnesota, manages the property. She manages a couple of other properties for the owner, and they are all centrally located and full of character.

Serrato 11, 61600 Pátzcuaro, Mich. ©/fax **434/342-5237.** www.elrefugioenpatzcuaro.com.mx. 6 units. $75–$100 (£38–£50) double; $110–$120 (£55–£60) suites. 2-night minimum stay. No walk-ins. Rates include full breakfast. No credit cards. Free limited covered parking. **Amenities:** Tours; limited room service; in-room massage; babysitting; laundry service; nonsmoking rooms. *In room:* TV, Wi-Fi in some rooms, hair dryer on request.

Mesón de San Antonio ⚜ Retired agronomist, Alfredo del Rio Mora, runs this small B&B, which retains the feel of a country house, in its informality and simple adornment. Nothing cutesy or clichéd is to be found here. The rooms are large and comfortable and have lots of character. The bathrooms are large, too, and well finished.

Serrato 33, 61600 Pátzcuaro, Mich. ©/fax **434/342-2501.** www.mesondesanantonio.com. 7 units. $70–$80 (£35–£40) double. Rates include continental breakfast. No credit cards. Off-site parking $4 £2. **Amenities:** Tour info; laundry service; nonsmoking rooms. *In room:* TV, Wi-Fi in some rooms.

INEXPENSIVE

Posada de la Salud *(Value)* This *posada* (inn) offers two floors of quiet, basic rooms built around an attractive courtyard. Rooms are clean and have simple wooden furniture. Two units have fireplaces. Rooms have one double bed, two double beds, two twins, or one twin and one double (the higher price listed below is for two doubles). The location is great—near the basilica, to the right, a half-block down.

Serrato 9, 61600 Pátzcuaro, Mich. © **434/342-0058.** www.posadadelasalud.com. 12 units. $35–$40 (£18–£20) double. No credit cards. Limited street parking. *In room:* No phone.

WHERE TO DINE

Restaurants here are okay but not great. I usually try to get by on simple local fare. In the evenings at the Plaza Chica, you can get a meal of chicken with simple enchiladas and heaps of fried potatoes and carrots. Look for a stand called **Don Emilio**. You can also get *buñuelos,* giant corn flakes that drip with cane syrup.

Tip: In the same market area you can sometimes find good tamales. But if you want tamales in a relaxing setting, have them for breakfast at the **restaurant of the Gran Hotel** (Plaza Bocanegra 6-B; ℂ **434/345-0659**), under the arches on the south side of the Plaza Chica. As a rule in Mexico, you don't find fresh tamales in restaurants. But this place is the exception. The other breakfast items, mostly *antojitos,* are good, too.

Another place to eat well and for little money is at a little *fonda* called **Mama Lupe** (no phone). It occupies a little patio off Calle Benigno Mendoza. Look for a doorway opposite the Bancomer bank offices. It opens around 9am and closes around 8pm. In the early afternoon it offers a good *comida corrida* with three courses and a drink for around $5 (£2.50).

Cha Cha Cha 𝕲 MEXICAN/INTERNATIONAL This is just the place to have a leisurely meal. You want to linger here in the relaxing and casual feel of the place. The service is friendly, and the food is good. The menu offers a variety of dishes, some traditional, some original. I tried the cream soup with *chile poblano,* the cabbage and sausage tostadas, and the pork loin with pecan stuffing in a pineapple and mango sauce. They are all worth recommending.

Buenavista 7. ℂ **434/342-1627**. Reservations accepted. Main courses $8–$16 (£4–8). MC, V. Thurs–Tues 8:30am–9:30pm.

El Patio MEXICAN/REGIONAL High ceilings, good lighting, and paintings of local scenes make this a pleasant place to dine. Specialties include *sopa tarasca, trucha salmonada al vino blanco* (farm-raised trout that are fed *achiote* to give the flesh a salmon color). Standard Mexican dishes include enchiladas and more. El Patio is on the south side of Plaza Grande. Service can be slow.

Plaza Grande 19. ℂ **434/342-0484**. Breakfast $4–$6 (£2–£3); main courses $7–$12 (£3.50–£6). MC, V. Daily 8am–10pm.

El Primer Piso MEXICAN/INTERNATIONAL El Primer Piso, which means "the first floor" (second floor in American usage), offers a bit of everything but focuses mostly on dishes of its own creation: *pechuga enogada* (chicken breast in walnut cream sauce) with cashews, for instance, and *pescado en salsa negra* (fish in a three-chile vinaigrette). These are good, as are the appetizers. The soups are more conventional—Tarascan, French onion, and Provençal. The restaurant is on the same block as El Patio. Service can be slow.

Vasco de Quiroga 29. ℂ **434/342-0122**. Main courses $8–$13 (£4–£6.50). AE, MC, V. Mon and Wed–Sat 1–10pm; Sun 1–8pm.

Restaurant Doña Paca 𝕲 MICHOACAN This is one of the best places to try regional Michoacán cuisine. It serves fish in several ways, including in cilantro sauce, *al mojo de ajo* (this is the most popular way of eating fish in Mexico—it's griddled with tiny toasted bits of garlic), or cooked in herbs. The restaurant also serves a fixed-price menu, which includes a glass of wine. For dessert, try a *buñuelo* topped with ice cream. The dining room is in the colonial Hotel Mansión Iturbe and is comfortable and welcoming. In the afternoon you can order at the tables outside under the archway.

Hotel Mansión Iturbe, Portal Morelos 59. © **434/342-3628.** Breakfast $6–$10 (£3–£5); main courses $9–$14 (£4.50–£7). AE, MC, V. Daily 8:30–11:30am, 2–5pm, and 6–9pm. Closed Sun night during low season.

PATZCUARO AFTER DARK

Generally speaking, Pátzcuaro closes down before 10pm, so bring a good book or plan to rest up. Late-night music lovers can go to **Viejo Gaucho** to hear Latin American folk music. The small restaurant serves salads and hamburgers. It's in the Hotel Mansión Iturbe (© **434/342-3627;** p. 265); enter from Calle Iturbe. It's open Wednesday through Saturday from 6pm to midnight. Music starts between 8:30 and 9pm. After the music starts, there's a $2.50 (£1.25) cover charge.

SIDE TRIPS FROM PATZCUARO

EL ESTRIBO: A SCENIC OVERLOOK   For a good view of the town and the lake, head for the lookout at El Estribo, on the hill 3km (2 miles) west of town. Driving from the main square on Calle Ponce de León and following the signs takes 10 to 15 minutes on an unpaved road. Walking up the steep hill will take about 45 minutes. Once you reach the gazebo, you can climb more than 400 steps to the summit of the hill. The gazebo area is great for a picnic; there are barbecue pits and sometimes a couple selling soft drinks and beer.

JANITZIO   No visit to Pátzcuaro would be complete without a trip on the lake to one or more of the islands. A hilltop statue of José María Morelos dominates the island of **Janitzio** 🏵🏵. The village church is famous for the annual **Day of the Dead** ceremony, held at midnight on November 1. Villagers climb to the churchyard carrying lit candles in memory of their dead relatives, then spend the night in graveside vigil. The long day begins October 30 and lasts through November 2.

The cheapest way to get to Janitzio is by *colectivo* launch, which makes the trip when enough people have gathered to go, about every 20 to 30 minutes from about 7:30am to 6pm. It's best to go during the week when fewer travelers are around. Round-trip fare is $4 (£2); children younger than 5 ride free. A private boat costs around $60 (£30) for a trip to Janitzio for 1 hour and then a cruise by the other three islands. Sometimes the cooperative has launches available that are significantly cheaper. The **ticket office** on the pier, or *embarcadero* (© **434/342-0681**), is open daily from 8am to 6pm. The pier is less than a kilometer (about a half-mile) from the main square, and the 5-minute taxi ride costs $3 (£1.50).

At the ticket office, a map of the lake posted on the wall details boat trips to various islands and lakeshore towns. Launches will take you wherever you want to go. Up to 20 people can split the cost.

TZINTZUNTZAN: RUINS & HANDICRAFTS   Tzintzuntzan (tzeen-*tzoon*-tzahn) is an ancient village 15km (9⅓ miles) from Pátzcuaro on the road to Quiroga (see "By Bus," under "Getting There & Departing," earlier in this chapter). In earlier centuries, Tzintzuntzan was the capital of the Purépechan kingdom (a confederation of more than 100 towns and villages). On a hill on the right before you enter town, pyramids, called *yácatas,* remind visitors of the town's past. There is also an interesting church and monastery from the time of Don Vasco. Today, the village is known for its pottery and woven goods. Several open-air **woodcarving workshops,** full of life-size wooden saints and other figures, are across from the basket market.

LAKESIDE VILLAGES: A PORTRAIT OF INDIAN LIFE   For a close-up view of the Purépecha, contact Kevin Quigley and Arminda Flores, who live in Ihuatzio (see below for contact info). Arminda is Purépecha and can explain much of what you'll see and hear when visiting the villages in the area. Another good guide is Miguel Angel Nuñez (© **434/344-0108;** casadetierra@hotmail.com). He's a Mexican anthropologist who has lived in the area for years.

SANTA CLARA DEL COBRE: COPPER SMITHERY   About 30 minutes away by car (an $11/£5.50 taxi ride), **Santa Clara del Cobre**✪ is a good side trip if you want to purchase copper items or see how copper is worked. Although the copper mines of pre-Conquest times have disappeared, local artisans still make copper vessels using the age-old method of hammering pieces out by hand. They don't work on Sunday and are strict observers of "San Lunes"—taking Monday off to recover from the weekend. On other days, the sound of hammering fills the air. If you want to see someone practicing the craft, go to one of the larger stores and ask if you can visit the *taller* (studio). You can also visit the **Museo del Cobre (Copper Museum)**, a half-block from the main plaza at Morelos and Pino Suárez. The museum section of the building displays copper pieces that date to pre-Columbian times. A sales showroom to the left of the entrance features the work of local craftsmen. Admission is 50¢ (25p); the museum is open Tuesday through Sunday from 10:30am to 3pm and 5 to 7pm.

The **National Copper Fair** is held here each August. It coincides with the **Festival de Nuestra Señora de Santa Clara de Asis** (second week in Aug), with folk dancing and parades. For information, call the tourism office in Morelia.

Buses for Santa Clara leave every few minutes from the Pátzcuaro bus station. If you want to spend the night in town, see "If Pátzcuaro's Packed Solid . . ." on p. 266.

TUPATARO & CUANAJO: A HISTORIC CHURCH & HAND-CARVED FURNITURE   Just off Highway 120 between Morelia and Pátzcuaro is the village of **Tupátaro** (pop. 600), which in Tarascan means "place of reeds."

The village church is the **Templo del Señor Santiago Tupátaro.** It was built in 1775. Indian artists painted the entire wood-plank ceiling with scenes of the life and death of Christ and the Virgin Mary. The gilt *retablo* (altarpiece) is adorned with Solomonic columns and paintings. Santiago (St. James) is in the center of the *retablo,* and the face of the Eternal Father is above him. The symbol of the dove crowns the *retablo.* The church and its ceiling were restored in 1994 by the National Institute of Anthropology and History, which oversees its maintenance. There's no admission charge, and photography is not permitted. The church is open daily from 8am to 5pm. Days of religious significance include the Tuesday of Carnaval week and July 25, which honors Santiago. From Tupátaro you can get back on Highway 120 or take a small road that leads to Cuanajo 8km (5 miles) away. From Cuanajo a small road leads directly to Pátzcuaro. It's not designated yet by any number.

Cuanajo (pop. 8,000) is a village of wood carvers who make brightly painted pine furniture. On the road as you enter, and around the pleasant, tree-shaded main plaza, you'll see storefronts with **colorful furniture** inside and on the street. Parrots, plants, the sun, the moon, and faces are carved on the furniture. Furniture is also sold at a **cooperative** on the main plaza. Here you'll also find soft-spoken women who weave tapestries and thin belts on waist looms. Everything is for sale. It's open daily from 9am to 6pm. Festival days in Cuanajo include March 8 and September 8, both of which honor their patron saint La Virgen María de la Natividad.

IHUATZIO: TULE FIGURES & PRE-HISPANIC ARCHITECTURE This little lakeside village is renowned for its **weavers of tule figures**—fanciful animals such as elephants, pigs, and bulls, made from a reed that grows on the edge of the lake—and for some ruins widespread through the area. Kevin Quigley, an American from San Francisco, and Arminda Flores, a Purépechan, live just outside the village (© 434/344-0880; www.casasantiagomex.com). They rent comfortable rooms to guests at economical rates. Both Kevin and Arminda take people around the area, explaining the local culture, the society, and the local crafts. The turnoff to Ihuatzio is a paved road a short distance from the outskirts of Pátzcuaro on the road to Tzintzuntzan.

3 Uruapan: Handicrafts & Volcanoes

61km (38 miles) W of Pátzcuaro

Uruapan has long been a commercial center for western Michoacán. It's a larger, busier town than Pátzcuaro; it's not very pretty, but it's set in some beautiful country. This is a rich agricultural area—the avocado capital of Mexico. Coffee and pistachios are also popular cash crops. Uruapan is useful as a base for some interesting side trips, the most famous of which is to the **Paricutín volcano** and the lava-covered church and village near **Angahuan.** See "Angahuan, Paricutín Volcano," below.

ESSENTIALS

The **tourist office** (© 452/524-0667) is at Emilio Carranza 20. It's open Monday through Saturday from 9am to 2pm and 4 to 7pm.

The main plaza, **Jardín Morelos/Plaza de los Mártires,** is a long, narrow rectangle running east to west, with the churches and La Huatápera Museum on the north side and a few hotels on the south.

WHERE TO STAY & DINE

The best hotel in town is the **Hotel Cupatitzio** (© 452/523-2022), next to the national park. It has plenty of amenities, including a large pool and garden. A room for two people costs $96 (£48). On the main square, the best option is **Hotel Plaza Uruapan** (© 452/523-3599; www.hotelplazauruapan.com.mx) Two inexpensive options are the **Hotel Villa de Flores,** Emiliano Carranza 15 (© 452/524-2800), and the slightly less desirable but slightly cheaper **Hotel Nuevo Alameda,** Av. 5 de Febrero 11 (© 452/523-3635). Rooms go for $48 (£24) in the former and about $10 (£5) less in the latter.

The restaurant at the Hotel Plaza is good. Another popular place to eat is **Café Tradicional** (© 452/523-5680), just off the plaza, at Carranza 5-B.

EXPLORING URUAPAN & BEYOND

Uruapan's main plaza fills with artisans and craft sellers from around the state before and during **Easter week.** Vendors sell an unbelievable array of wares.

La Huatápera ✸, attached to the church on the main square, is a good museum of regional crafts. It occupies a former hospital built in 1533 by Fray Juan de San Miguel, a Franciscan. It's open daily from 10am to 2pm and 4 to 6pm. Free admission.

For the finest in foot-loomed, brilliantly colored tablecloths, bedspreads, and other **textiles,** pay a visit to **Telares Uruapan** ✸✸✸ (© 452/524-0677 or -6135), in the **Antigua Fábrica San Pedro,** Calle Miguel Treviño s/n. The old factory makes for an interesting visit, and the colorful fabrics are quite popular. The owners, Bundy and

Walter Illsley, came to Mexico in the early '50s, and started up a number of rural development projects before deciding to go into the weaving business. In my travels, I come across their distinctive fabrics a lot. Hours are Monday to Saturday 10am to 7pm.

When you enter the **Parque Nacional Eduardo Ruiz,** a botanical garden 8 blocks west of the main plaza, you'll feel as if you're deep in the Tropics. This semitropical paradise contains jungle paths, deep ravines, rushing water, and clear waterfalls. The garden is open daily from 8am to 6pm, and there is a small admission fee.

A WATERFALL OUTSIDE OF URUAPAN

Eight kilometers (5 miles) outside of town is the **Tzaráracua** waterfall. The falls are pretty but not spectacular, and sometimes they smell bad. The real reason to come here is for the walk—a descent that takes you from cool pine forest to warm subtropical vegetation in no time. The return ascent takes 40 minutes, and the trail is good, with handrails in the steeper areas. You can catch a bus from Uruapan's bus station or take a cab, which costs only $6 (£3). Either one will drop you off at the trail head.

ANGAHUAN, PARICUTIN VOLCANO 🎯🎯

About 34km (21 miles) from Uruapan is **Angahuan,** a village serving as the point of departure for trips to **Paricutín volcano.** The volcano was born in 1943 and grew quickly, eventually enveloping portions of a village in lava. A taxi costs less than $20 (£10). There's also a bus.

THE ERUPTION STORY   In the afternoon of February 20, 1943, a local man was plowing his cornfield in the valley when the ground began to boil and fissures opened up, emitting steam. At first he tried to plug it up; when that proved impossible, he fled. By that evening, the earth was spitting fire and smoke. Some villagers fled that night; others, days later. The volcano remained active, continually spewing, until March 6, 1952, when it ceased as suddenly as it had begun.

USING A GUIDE   Angahuan has a little tourist center that rents cabins and runs a small cafeteria (© **452/520-8786**). It affords a good view of the volcano and the tower of the **Church of San Juan Parangaricutiro** (try saying that quickly five times), which is half-buried in lava. It takes 2½ hours to get to the volcano, because you have to take a roundabout path to get there. The best way to go is with a horse and a guide. A horse costs $20 (£10) for the day. A guide costs the same. All the guides are villagers of Angahuan. Some speak Spanish; some don't. But it doesn't make much of a difference; they're mostly there to lead the way, which is circuitous. Many visitors elect to go only as far as the church; it takes 45 minutes one way, and you don't need a horse.

CLIMBING THE VOLCANO   Allow at least 7 hours from Angahuan. The route to the foot of the volcano makes a big loop around a lava field, before approaching the cone along a "sandy" wash (the texture only seems sandy; it's actually black volcanic cinder). The approach is mostly flat, with some rises toward the end. The only way to climb the crater is on foot; the trek is exhilarating but exhausting, because of the footing. It's like climbing a giant pile of loose rock; for every step up, you slide back down a few inches. On the way to the top you pass by a fumarole. The day I was there, it rained briefly as we were approaching the volcano, which is common (all guides carry rain ponchos for their customers). By the time we got to the fumarole, steam was rising from all the crevasses in the rock. The scene, so barren and vaporous, looked either primeval or apocalyptic, depending on the point of view. At the top of the cone, the view of the surrounding mountains is splendid, and you can clearly make out the lines of the lava flows on the floor of the valley.

Guadalajara

by David Baird

As the homeland of mariachi music, the *jarabe tapatío* (the Mexican hat dance), and tequila, Guadalajara is widely considered the most Mexican of cities. Despite the fact that it's the nation's second-largest metropolis (with 3.5 million inhabitants, it's a very distant second to Mexico City), it isn't hard to navigate, and residents are friendly and helpful. Visitors can enjoy big-city pleasures without the big-city hassles that would beset them in the capital.

While in Guadalajara, you will undoubtedly come across the word *tapatío* (or *tapatía*). In the early days, people from the area were known to trade in threes, called *tapatíos*. The locals came to be called Tapatíos as well, and now the word *tapatío* has come to mean any person, thing, or even style that comes from Guadalajara.

1 Orientation

GETTING THERE & DEPARTING

BY PLANE   Guadalajara's airport (GDL) is a half-hour ride from the city. Taxi tickets, priced by zone, are for sale in front of the airport ($19/£9.50 to downtown).

Major Airlines   See chapter 3 for a list of toll-free numbers for international airlines serving Mexico. Numbers in Guadalajara are: **AeroMar** (© 33/3615-8509), **AeroMéxico** (© 01-800/021-4010), **American** (© 01-800/904-6000), **Click** (© 01-800/1225425), **Continental** (© 01-800/900-5000), **Delta** (© 33/3630-3530), **Mexicana** (© 01-800/502-2000), and **United** (© 33/3616-9489).

Of the smaller airlines, **Aviacsa** (© 33/3123-1751) connects to Los Angeles, Las Vegas, Houston, and Chicago. **Azteca** (© 33/3630-4615) offers service to and from Mexico City, and from there to several cities in Mexico. **Allegro** (© 33/3647-7799) operates flights to and from Oakland and Las Vegas via Tijuana. **Alaska Airlines** (© 01-800/426-0333) flies to Los Angeles and Reno.

BY CAR   Guadalajara is at the hub of several four-lane toll roads (called *cuotas* or *autopistas*), which cut travel time considerably but are expensive. From Nogales on the **U.S. border,** follow Highway 15 south (21 hr.). From **Tepic,** a quicker route is toll road 15D (5 hr.; $31/£16). From **Puerto Vallarta,** go north on Highway 200 to Compostela; toll road 68D heads east to join the Tepic toll road. Total time is 5½ hours, and the tolls add up to $29 (£15). From **Barra de Navidad,** on the coast southeast of Puerto Vallarta, take Highway 80 northeast (4½ hr.). From **Manzanillo,** you might also take this road, but toll road 54D through Colima to Guadalajara (3½ hr.; $26/£13) is faster. From **Mexico City,** take toll road 15D (7 hr.; $55/£28).

BY BUS   Two bus stations serve Guadalajara. The old one, south of downtown, is for buses to Tequila and other nearby towns; the new one, 10km (6¼ miles) southeast of downtown, is for longer trips.

The Old Bus Station   For destinations within 100km (62 miles) of town, including the Lake Chapala area, go to the old bus terminal, on Niños Héroes off Calzada Independencia Sur. For Lake Chapala, take **Transportes Guadalajara-Chapala,** which runs frequent buses and *combis* (minivans).

The New Bus Station   The **Central Camionera** is 15 to 30 minutes from downtown. The station has seven terminals connected by a covered walkway. Each terminal houses bus lines, offering first- and second-class service for different destinations. Buy bus tickets ahead of time from a travel agency in Guadalajara. Ask at your hotel for the closest to you. There are several major bus lines. The best service (big seats and lots of room) is provided by **ETN.**

VISITOR INFORMATION

The **State of Jalisco Tourist Information Office** is at Calle Morelos 102 (© **33/3668-1600** or -1601; http://visita.jalisco.gob.mx) in the Plaza Tapatía, at Paseo Degollado and Paraje del Rincón del Diablo. It's open Monday through Friday from 9am to 8pm, and Saturday, Sunday, and festival days 10am to 2pm. You can get maps, a monthly calendar of cultural events, and good information. Of the **city tourist information booths,** one is in Plaza Liberación (directly behind the cathedral), another in Plaza Guadalajara (directly in front of the cathedral). These are open daily from 9am to 1pm and 3 to 7pm. Ask at either of these about free weekend walking tours.

CITY LAYOUT

The **Centro Histórico (city center),** with all its plazas, churches, and museums, will obviously be of interest to the visitor. The **west side** is Guadalajara's modern, cosmopolitan district. In the northwest corner is **Zapopan,** home of Guadalajara's patron saint. On the opposite side of the city from Zapopan, in the southeast corner, are the craft centers of **Tlaquepaque** and **Tonalá.**

The main artery for traffic from downtown to the west side is **Avenida Vallarta.** It starts downtown as **Juárez.** The main arteries for returning to downtown are **México** and **Hidalgo,** both north of Vallarta. Vallarta heads due west, where it intersects another major artery, **Avenida Adolfo López Mateos,** at **Fuente Minerva** (or simply La Minerva, or Minerva Circle). Minerva Circle, a 15-minute drive from downtown, is the central point of reference for the west side. To go to Zapopan from downtown, take **Avenida Avila Camacho,** which you can pick up on Alcalde; it takes 20 minutes by car. To Tlaquepaque and Tonalá, take **Calzada Revolución.** Tlaquepaque is 8km (5 miles) from downtown and takes 15 to 20 minutes by car; Tonalá is 5 minutes farther. Another major viaduct, **Calzada Lázaro Cárdenas,** connects the west side to Tlaquepaque and Tonalá, bypassing downtown.

THE NEIGHBORHOODS IN BRIEF

Centro Histórico   The heart of the city encompasses many plazas, the cathedral, and several historic buildings and museums. Here, too, are the striking murals of José Clemente Orozco, one of the great Mexican muralists. Theaters, restaurants, shops, and clubs dot the area, and an enormous market rounds out the attractions. All of this is in a space roughly 12 blocks by 12 blocks—an easy area to explore on foot, with several plazas and pedestrian-only areas. To the south is a large green space called Parque Agua Azul.

West Side This is the swanky part of town, with the fine restaurants, luxury hotels, boutiques, and galleries, as well as the American, British, and Canadian consulates. It's a large area best navigated by taxi.

Zapopan Founded in 1542, Zapopan is a suburb of Guadalajara. In its center is the 18th-century basilica, the home of Guadalajara's patron saint, the Virgin of Zapopan. The most interesting part of Zapopan is clustered around the temple and can be explored on foot. It has a growing arts and nightlife scene.

Tlaquepaque This was a village of artisans (especially potters) that grew into a market center. In the last 30 years, it has attracted designers from all over Mexico. Every major form of art and craft is for sale here: furniture, pottery, glass, jewelry, woodcarvings, leather goods, sculptures, and paintings. The shops are sophisticated, yet Tlaquepaque's center retains a small-town feel that makes door-to-door browsing enjoyable and relaxing.

Tonalá This has remained a town of artisans. Plenty of stores sell mostly local products from the town's more than 400 workshops. You'll see wrought iron, ceramics, blown glass, and papier-mâché. A busy street market operates each Thursday and Sunday.

2 Getting Around

BY TAXI Taxis are the easiest way to get around town. Most have meters, and, though some drivers are reluctant to use them, you can insist that they do. There are three rates: for day, night, and suburbia. On my last visit, typical fares were: downtown to the west side, $6 to $8 (£3–£4); downtown or west side to Tlaquepaque, $7 to $9 (£3.50–£4.50); to the new bus station, $8 (£4); to the airport, $16 to $20 (£8–£10).

BY CAR Familiarize yourself with the main traffic arteries (see "City Layout," above) before you get behind the wheel. Several important freeway-style thoroughfares crisscross the city. **Dr. R. Michel** leads south from the town center towards Tlaquepaque. Use **González Gallo** for the return direction. **Avenida Vallarta** starts out downtown as **Juárez** and heads west past La Minerva and eventually feeds onto **Highway 15,** bound for Tequila and Puerto Vallarta.

BY BUS For the visitor, the handiest route is the TUR **706,** which runs from the Centro Histórico southeast to Tlaquepaque ($1/50p), the Central Camionera (the new bus station), and Tonalá. You can catch this bus on Avenida 16 de Septiembre. The same bus runs in the reverse direction back to the downtown area.

The **electric bus** is handy for travel between downtown and the Minerva area (50¢/25p). It bears the sign PAR VIAL and runs east along Hidalgo and west along the next street to the north, Calle Independencia (not Calzada Independencia). Hidalgo passes along the north side of the cathedral. The Par Vial goes as far east as Mercado Libertad and as far west as Minerva Circle. The city also has a light rail system, **Tren Ligero,** but it doesn't serve areas that are of interest to visitors.

FAST FACTS: Guadalajara

American Express The local office is at Av. Vallarta 2440, Plaza los Arcos, Local A-1 (© 33/3818-2323); it's open Monday through Friday from 9am to 6pm, Saturday from 9am to noon.

Area Code The telephone area code is **33**.

Books, Newspapers & Magazines **Gonvil,** a popular bookstore chain, has a branch across from Plaza de los Hombres Ilustres on Avenida Hidalgo, and another a few blocks south at Av. 16 de Septiembre 118 (Alcalde becomes 16 de Septiembre south of the cathedral). It carries few English selections. **Sanborn's,** at the corner of Juárez and 16 de Septiembre, does a good job of keeping English-language periodicals in stock, but most are specialty magazines. Many newsstands sell the two English local papers, the *Guadalajara Reporter* and the *Guadalajara Weekly.* For the widest selection of English-language books, try **Sandi Bookstore,** Av. Tepeyac 718 (© 33/3121-0863), in the Chapalita neighborhood on the west side.

Business Hours Store hours are Monday through Saturday from 10am to 2pm and 4 to 8pm.

Climate & Dress Guadalajara's weather is mostly mild. From November through March, you'll need a sweater in the evening. The warmest months, April and May, are hot and dry. From June through September, the city gets afternoon and evening showers that keep the temperature a bit cooler, but it seems as though the local climate is getting warmer. Dress in Guadalajara is conservative; attention-getting sportswear (short shorts, halters, and the like) is out of place.

Consulates The **American consular offices** are at Progreso 175 (© 33/3268-2200 or -2100). Other consulates include the **Canadian consulate** (which moved recently), Mariano Otero 1249, Col. Rinconada del Bosque (© 33/3671-4740); the **British consulate,** Calle Jesús Rojas 20, Col. Los Pinos (© 33/3343-2296); and the **Australian consulate,** López Cotilla 2018, Col. Arcos Vallarta (© 33/3615-7418). These offices all keep roughly the same hours: Monday through Friday from 8am to 1pm.

Currency Exchange Three blocks south of the cathedral, on López Cotilla, between Corona and Degollado, are more than 20 *casas de cambio.* Almost all post their rates, which are usually better than bank rates, minus the long lines.

Elevation Guadalajara sits at 1,700m (5,576 ft.).

Emergencies The emergency phone number is © **060**.

Hospitals For medical emergencies, visit the **Hospital México-Americano,** Cólomos 2110 (© **33/3642-7152** or 33/3641-3141).

Internet Access Most of the big hotels have business centers that you can use. There are many Internet cafes in the Centro Histórico; the easiest way to find one is to ask a young person.

Language Classes Foreigners can study Spanish at the **Foreign Student Study Center,** University of Guadalajara, Calle Tomás V. Gómez 125, 44100 Guadalajara,

Jal. (© **33/3616-4399**). IMAC is a private Spanish school at Donato Guerra 180, in the Centro Histórico (© **33/3613-1080**).

Police Tourists should first try to contact the Jalisco tourist information office in Plaza Tapatía (© **33/3668-1600**). If you can't reach the office, call the municipal police at © **33/3668-7983**.

Post Office The *correo* is at the corner of Carranza and Calle Independencia, about 4 blocks northeast of the cathedral. Standing in the plaza behind the cathedral, facing the Degollado Theater, walk to the left, and then turn left on Carranza; walk past the Hotel Mendoza, cross Calle Independencia, and look for the post office on the left. It's open Monday through Thursday from 9am to 5pm, Saturday from 10am to 2pm.

Safety Guadalajara doesn't have as much crime as Mexico City. Rarely do you hear of muggings. Crimes against tourists and foreign students are infrequent and most often take the form of purse snatching. Criminals usually work in teams and target travelers in busy places, such as outdoor restaurants. Keep jewelry out of sight. Should anyone spill something on you, be alert to your surroundings and step away—accidental spills are a common method for distracting the victim.

3 Where to Stay

Rates shown are the standard rack rates and include the 17% tax. In slow periods, look for discounts; the big hotels often give business discounts. In some of the cheaper hotels, air-conditioning is a relative concept.

Most of the luxury hotels in Guadalajara are on the west side, which has the majority of the shopping malls, boutiques, fashionable restaurants, and clubs. The Centro Histórico is also a good option because there's a lot to do, all in walking distance. And Tlaquepaque is a comfortable place to stay—it's relaxing in that it doesn't have the feel of a big city and is perfect for shoppers; the only drawback is that almost everything shuts down by 7 or 8pm.

Chain hotels not included below are Hilton, Marriott, Camino Real, Howard Johnson, Crowne Plaza, and Best Western.

VERY EXPENSIVE

Hotel Presidente InterContinental ★★★   This hotel offers the most comprehensive list of services and amenities in Guadalajara. The health club here is a standout among other hotels. The rooms are comfortable and quiet, with modern furnishings. Club rooms have discreet check-in, are on limited-access hallways, and come with extras. The extra privacy and services are good for Mexican soap opera stars or repeat guests who like having their preferences known in advance. If you're neither of these, opt for one of the other rooms. The lobby bar is popular; during the season, bullfighters relax here after *la corrida*. Standard rooms come as "superior" or "deluxe." Differences and price aren't that pronounced. The rooms are about the same size and come with attractive midsize bathrooms. Deluxe rooms have a few more amenities. Suites are large and come with large, attractive bathrooms.

Av. López Mateos Sur and Moctezuma (west side), 45050 Guadalajara, Jal. © **800/327-0200** in the U.S. and Canada, or 33/3678-1234. Fax 33/3678-1222. www.interconti.com. 409 units. $276–$290 (£138–£145) double; $317 (£159) club; $414 (£207) and up for suite. Internet promotional rates available. AE, DC, MC, V. Valet parking $5 (£2.50). **Amenities:** 2 restaurants; bar; outdoor heated pool; golf at nearby clubs; health club w/saunas, steam rooms, and whirlpools; concierge; tour desk; car rental; large business center; executive business services; salon; room service; in-room massage; babysitting; laundry service; dry cleaning; nonsmoking rooms; executive-level rooms. In room: A/C, TV w/pay movies, Wi-Fi, minibar, coffeemaker, hair dryer, iron, safe.

Quinta Real ⭐⭐⭐   This chain specializes in properties that are suggestive of Mexico's heritage. No glass skyscraper here—two five-story buildings made of stone, wood, plaster, and tile capture the feel of Mexican colonial architecture. Suites vary quite a bit: Eight have brick cupolas, and some have balconies. All are large, with a split-level layout and antique decorative touches. And all come with large, great bathrooms with tub/shower combinations. The "grand-class" suites have even bigger bathrooms with Jacuzzi tubs. They are also a bit larger and come with a few extras, such as a stereo. You can choose between two doubles or one king-size bed. The hotel is 2 blocks from Minerva Circle in western Guadalajara. Ask for a room that doesn't face López Mateos.

Av. México 2727 (at López Mateos, west side), 44690 Guadalajara, Jal. © **866/621-9288** in the U.S. and Canada, or 33/3669-0600. Fax 33/3669-0601. www.quintareal.com. 76 suites. $418 (£209) master suite; $439 (£219) grand-class suite. AE, DC, MC, V. Free secure parking. **Amenities:** Restaurant; bar; small outdoor heated pool; golf at local club; fitness room; discounts at local day spa; concierge; tour desk; car rental; business center; executive business services; room service; in-room massage; babysitting; laundry service; dry cleaning; nonsmoking rooms. In room: A/C, TV, high-speed Internet access, minibar, hair dryer, iron, safe.

Villa Ganz ⭐⭐⭐   This small, all-suite hotel is on the near west side of the city, near Avenida Chapultepec. It's one of the most comfortable places to stay in Guadalajara. Rooms are big, well furnished, and decorated with flair. Each holds a basket of fruit and a small bottle of wine on check-in. Bathrooms are large and well lit—some have tubs, others just showers. Bed choices include a king, a queen, or two twins. Beds come with down comforters (hypoallergenic option available). Rooms facing the garden are the quietest, but those facing the street are set back from the traffic and have double-glazed windows. The common rooms and rear garden are agreeable places to relax. Service is personal and helpful. Guests can contract with a guide or driver at the hotel. In-room dining can be arranged with one of three nearby restaurants, or arrangements can be made to bring in a chef.

López Cotilla 1739 (between Bolivar and San Martín, west side), 44140 Guadalajara, Jal. © **800/728-9098** in the U.S. and Canada, or 33/3120-1416. www.villaganz.com. 10 suites. $234 (£117) junior suite; $269 (£135) master suite; $304 (£152) grand master suite. Rates include continental breakfast. Internet specials often available. AE, MC, V. Free secure parking. Children younger than 12 not accepted. **Amenities:** Golf and tennis at local club; concierge; tour desk; room service; in-room massage; laundry service; dry cleaning. In room: A/C, TV, Wi-Fi, hair dryer, safe.

EXPENSIVE
Holiday Inn Hotel and Suites Centro Histórico ⭐⭐
This six-story downtown property has comfortable guest rooms and a handy downtown location—just a few blocks from the main square. All rooms were remodeled in 2007, with updated amenities, plush mattresses, and good light. The size is good, and the furniture is comfortable; bathrooms in standard rooms are midsize and well equipped, with ample counter space. The suites are larger with a few more amenities. Room rates include transportation to (but not from) the airport.

Av. Juárez 211, Centro Histórico, 44100 Guadalajara. Jal. © **800/465-4329** in the U.S. and Canada, 01-800/009-9900 in Mexico, or 33/3560-1200. www.holiday-inn.com. 90 units. $110–$138 (£55–£69) double; $148–$180

(£74–£90) suite; $172–$204 (£86–£102) suite with Jacuzzi. Ask about promotional rates. AE, MC, V. Free secure parking. **Amenities:** Restaurant; bar; fitness room; business center; room service; laundry service; dry cleaning; nonsmoking rooms. *In room:* A/C, TV, Wi-Fi, minibar, coffeemaker, hair dryer, iron, safe.

Hotel de Mendoza   On a quiet street next to the Degollado Theater and Plaza Tapatía, 2 blocks from the cathedral, the Mendoza has perhaps the best location of any downtown hotel. The decor would best be described as a stab at old Spanish, with wood paneling and old-world accents. Standard rooms are midsize. Bed choices are one queen, two full, or two queens. Bathrooms are midsize, with so-so lighting. Suites have an additional sitting area and larger bathrooms with the recent addition of Jacuzzi tubs. Rooms face the street, an interior courtyard, or the pool. *Note:* The bath towels are the narrowest I've ever seen—obviously the brainchild of a demented cost-cutting expert. If the hotel hasn't changed these, ask for a couple extra after you check in.

Carranza 16, Centro Histórico, 44100 Guadalajara, Jal. © **33/3492-5151.** Fax 33/3613-7310. www.demendoza. com.mx. 104 units. $114 (£57) double; $132 (£66) suite. Discounts sometimes available. AE, MC, V. Secure parking $4 (£2). **Amenities:** Restaurant; bar; small outdoor pool; fitness room; Jacuzzi; tour desk; business center; room service; laundry service; dry cleaning; nonsmoking rooms. *In room:* A/C, TV, Wi-Fi, hair dryer, safe.

MODERATE

Hotel Morales 🏠🏠   A historical hotel that's attractive and comfortable, the Morales is a good choice for anyone wishing to stay downtown. The standard rooms are called either *suite sencilla* (one queen bed) or *suite doble* (two double beds). The beds are firm. The rooms are medium or large and come with Pergo floors. The bathrooms are quite attractive, with ceramic tile floors and good looking countertops. The showers are strong. The rooms that face the street have balconies with double-glazed windows that do a good job at screening the noise. The imperial suites offer a lot for the money, with super-large bathrooms equipped with a two-person Jacuzzi tub and a separate shower. All rooms are set around an arcaded lobby holding an attractive bar area. There's live music on Thursday and Friday evenings.

Av. Corona 243 (corner of Prisciliano Sánchez) Centro Histórico, 44100 Guadalajara, Jal. © **33/3658-5232.** Fax 33/ 3658-5239. www.hotelmorales.com.mx. 64 units. $105 (£53) double; $135 (£63) junior suite; $165 (£83) imperial suite. AE, MC, V. Free sheltered parking. **Amenities:** Restaurant; bar; fitness room; tour info; business center; room service; babysitting; laundry service; dry cleaning; nonsmoking rooms. *In room:* A/C, TV, high-speed Internet access, coffeemaker, hair dryer, iron, safe.

La Villa del Ensueño 🏠🏠   This B&B in central Tlaquepaque is a lovely alternative to big-city hotels. A modern interpretation of traditional Mexican architecture, it contains small courtyards and well-tended grounds bordered by old stucco walls, with an occasional wrought-iron balcony or stone staircase. The rooms have more character than most hotel lodgings. Doubles have either two twin or two double beds. The hotel is about 8 blocks from the main plaza.

Florida 305, 45500 Tlaquepaque, Jal. © **800/220-8689** in the U.S., or 33/3635-8792. Fax 818/597-0637. www.villa delensueno.com. 20 units. $100 (£50) double; $112 (£56) deluxe double; $129 (£65) junior suite. Rates include full breakfast and light laundry service. AE, MC, V. Free valet parking. **Amenities:** Bar; indoor and outdoor pool; laundry service. *In room:* A/C, TV, Wi-Fi, hair dryer.

Old Guadalajara 🏠🏠   This downtown bed and breakfast recommends itself in many ways. In a colonial house, it's well located, quiet, and beautiful. The rooms reflect the local scene; they speak of Mexico without shouting it. They are large and airy with high ceilings, tile floors, and comfortable bathrooms. The colonial architecture makes it possible to live without A/C in the warm months, and every room is equipped with a ceiling fan. The central courtyard is cool and shaded by tall bamboo. The common rooms are open to the courtyard and are stocked with material for readers curious about the city. Paul Callahan prepares filling breakfasts for his guests using only natural ingredients.

Belén 236, Centro Histórico, 44100 Guadalajara, Jal. ©/fax **33/3613-9958.** www.oldguadalajara.com. 5 units. $125 double (£63). Rates include full breakfast. AE, MC, V for deposit; no credit cards at B&B. No children younger than 18. **Amenities:** Tour info; nonsmoking rooms. In room: Hair dryer, no phone.

Quinta Don José *★★* *(Value*   Good value, great location, friendly English-speaking owners—there are a lot of reasons to like this small establishment just 2 blocks from Tlaquepaque's main square. Rooms run the gauntlet from midsize to extra large. They are comfortable, attractive, and quiet, with some nice local touches. Most of the standard and deluxe doubles have a king or two double beds and an attractive, midsize bathroom. A couple of them have small private outdoor spaces. Some of the suites in back come with a full kitchen and lots of space—more than twice the size of the usual suite, with one king and one double bed. The breakfasts are good, and recently the owners have installed a full restaurant open for dinner. Some lodgings just have a good feel to them, and this is one of them.

Reforma 139, 45500 Tlaquepaque, Jal. © **866/629-3753** in the U.S. and Canada, or 33/3635-7522. www.quintadon jose.com. 15 units. $94 (£46) standard; $105 (£53) deluxe; $128–$164 (£64–£82) suite. Rates include full breakfast. AE, MC, V. Free secure parking. **Amenities:** Restaurant; bar; heated outdoor pool; tour info; in-room massage; babysitting; laundry service; nonsmoking rooms. In room: A/C, TV, Wi-Fi, hair dryer, iron.

INEXPENSIVE

Hotel Cervantes *★* *(Value*   This six-story downtown hotel offers modern amenities at a good price. The rooms are attractive and midsize. They have wall-to-wall carpeting and tile bathrooms with ample sink areas and shower/tub combinations. The air-conditioning is more in theory than in practice. The lower price is for one double bed; the higher price, for a king or two doubles. This is not a noisy hotel; but, if you require absolute quiet, request an interior room. The Cervantes is 6 blocks south and 3 blocks west of the cathedral.

Prisciliano Sánchez 442 (corner of Donato Guerra), Centro Histórico, 44100 Guadalajara, Jal. ©/fax **33/3613-6686.** www.hotelcervantes.com.mx. 100 units. $72–$80 (£36–£40) double; $105 (£53) suite. AE, MC, V. Free secure parking. **Amenities:** Restaurant; lobby bar; small outdoor heated pool; tour desk; room service; babysitting; laundry service; dry cleaning. In room: A/C, TV.

Hotel San Francisco Plaza *(Value*   This colonial-style downtown hotel is both pleasant and a bargain. Most rooms are medium to large and comfortable, with attractive furnishings. All have rugs or carpeting, and most have tall ceilings. The hotel is built in colonial style around four courtyards, which contain fountains and potted plants. Rooms along the Sánchez Street side are much quieter now that the management has installed double windows. Some units along the back wall of the rear patio have small bathrooms. The San Francisco Plaza is 6 blocks south and 2 blocks east of the cathedral. The air-conditioning is being upgraded.

Degollado 267, Centro Histórico, 44100 Guadalajara, Jal. © **33/3613-8954** or -8971. Fax 33/3613-3257. www.san franciscohotel.com.mx. 76 units. $52 (£26) double. AE, MC, V. Free sheltered parking. **Amenities:** Restaurant; room service; laundry service; dry cleaning; ironing service. In room: A/C, TV.

Plaza Los Reyes *(Value*   Okay, so the rooms in this 10-story downtown hotel aren't anything special, but they do have good, individually controlled A/C and strong showers, a rarity for budget hotels. The location is downtown near the market. It's central, but it's a bit decayed. For entertainment, there's a fancy new multiplex cinema across the street that shows first-run Hollywood movies. Guest rooms are midsize and come with either two doubles or a king-size bed. Those on the mezzanine level are larger and often cost the same. Ask for a room facing away from the busy Calzada Independencia. Midsize bathrooms are clean, with good water pressure and plenty of hot water.

Calzada Independencia Sur 168, 44100 Guadalajara, Jal. ℂ 33/3613-9770 or -9775. 189 units. $54 (£27) double. AE, MC, V. Free valet parking. **Amenities:** Restaurant; outdoor heated pool; tour info; room service; laundry service; nonsmoking rooms. *In room:* A/C, TV, Wi-Fi.

4 Where to Dine

Guadalajara has many excellent restaurants either for fine dining or for typical local fare. Most of the fine-dining spots are on the west side. Tlaquepaque has some good choices, but most close by 8pm. Good local fare can be had in the Centro Histórico, but for fine dining, head to western Guadalajara or, if it's early in the day, to Tlaquepaque. For a quick bite, there are several **Sanborn's** in the city. This is a popular national chain of restaurants known for their *enchiladas suizas* (enchiladas in cream sauce). If you're downtown and looking for baked goods and coffee, go to **El Globo** (ℂ 33/3613-9926), an upscale bakery at the corner of Pedro Moreno and Degollado. This is also a chain with a couple more locations around Guadalajara. *Tip:* When taking a taxi, keep the address of the restaurant handy; taxi drivers cannot be relied upon to know where even the most popular restaurants are.

Local dishes include *birria* (goat or lamb covered in maguey leaves and roasted). It comes in a tomato broth or with the broth on the side. Another favorite is the *torta ahogada,* a sandwich with pork bathed in a tomato sauce. I'm not particularly fond of them. The most popular drink here is the *paloma,* which combines tequila, lots of lime juice, and grapefruit soda on ice. I am fond of these.

EXPENSIVE

Adobe Fonda 𝄐𝄐𝄐 NOUVELLE MEXICAN   This restaurant shares space with a large store on pedestrian-only Independencia. The dining area is open and airy. Homemade bread and tostadas come to the table with an olive oil-based chile sauce, pico de gallo, and *requezón de epazote* (ricottalike cheese with a Mexican herb). Among the soups are *crema de cilantro* and an interesting mushroom soup with a dark-beer broth. The main courses present some difficult decisions, with intriguing combinations of Mexican, Italian, and Argentine ingredients. Shrimp quesadillas accompanied by *chimichurri* with *nopal* cactus, filet in creamy *chile ancho* sauce, and the crab salad tower were all excellent. Sample the margaritas, too.

Francisco de Miranda 27 (corner of Independencia, Tlaquepaque). ℂ 33/3657-2792. Reservations recommended on weekends. Main courses $14–$20 (£7–£10). AE, MC, V. Daily 12:30–6:30pm.

Chez Nené 𝄐𝄐𝄐 FRENCH   In a small and pleasant open-air dining room, you can enjoy a quiet and leisurely meal of delicious French food. After doing just this, I had to meet the owner to see who was behind such work. He turned out to be a French expatriate (whose Mexican wife, Nené, is the restaurant's namesake) with strong ideas about food and dining. Shorn of fads and pretense, his cooking aims at the essential in a dish. Freshness and quality of ingredients are what matter most, and everything (except stews and such) is cooked to order. The daily menu is on a chalkboard and depends on what the owner finds that morning at the market. There are always at least a dozen main courses. The waiter answered every question I put to him and gave excellent service.

Juan Palomar y Arias 426 (continuación Rafael Sanzio, west side). ℂ 33/3673-4564. Reservations recommended on weekends. Main courses $10–$20 (£5–£10). AE, MC, V. Tues 4–11pm; Wed–Sat 1–5:30pm and 7:30–11:30pm; Sun 1–6pm.

El Sacromonte ⭐⭐⭐ MEXICAN HAUTE CUISINE   The food is so exquisite that I try to dine here every time I'm in Guadalajara. El Sacromonte emphasizes artful presentation and design: Order "Queen Isabel's Crown," and you'll be served a dish of shrimp woven together in the shape of a crown and covered in divine lobster-and-orange sauce. Or try quesadillas with rose petals in a deep-colored strawberry sauce. For soup, consider *el viejo progreso* for its unlikely combination of flavors (blue cheese and chipotle chile). The menu features amusing descriptions in verse. The main dining area is a shaded, open-air patio. The restaurant isn't far from the downtown area, on the near west side.

In the building next door, the owners have opened an updated version of the classic Mexican bar where one drinks while snacking on complimentary *botanas*. You can also order from a limited menu. The place is called **El Duende.**

Pedro Moreno 1398 (corner of Calle Colonias, west side). ℂ 33/3825-5447 or 3827-0663. Reservations recommended. Main courses $12–$20 (£6–£10). MC, V. Mon–Sat 1:30pm–midnight; Sun 1:30–6pm.

La Tequila ⭐⭐ MEXICAN   In its new location, about a block from where it used to be, this restaurant churns out Mexican standards such as *chalupas poblanas,* as well as versions of trendy contemporary Mexican cooking, including pasta stuffed with shrimp and *huitlacoche,* grilled-vegetable salad, and *molcajetes de arrachera* (fajitas with slices of chiles and onions that are cooked and served in a three-legged stone vessel). The cooking is great, the place is lively (the locals love it), and the decorative touches, such as trimmed agaves, give the dining areas a regional point of reference. Indoor/outdoor dining areas and a popular upstairs bar make up the majority of the restaurant. *Tip:* If this place is too crowded, or you're simply looking for quieter dining, go to the original site 1 block away (Av. Mexico 2916), where you'll find a new restaurant called **La Divina Tentación** (ℂ 33/3642-7242). The menu is similar, tending slightly more toward the style of cooking in Mexico City.

Av. México 2830 (at Napoleón, west side). ℂ 33/3640-3440 or 33/3640-3110. Reservations recommended. Main courses $10–$18 (£5–£9). AE, MC, V. Mon–Sat 1pm–midnight; Sun 1–6pm.

MODERATE

Hostería del Angel ⭐⭐ TAPAS/SPANISH DELI/WINE BAR   Sip wine and munch on a few tapas in this comfortable patio restaurant and wine bar just a few blocks from the basilica in Zapopan. The chef-owner cooked for years in Spain, where he became fascinated with the making of cheeses and deli meats such as Spanish *jamón serrano.* He serves a variety of tapas, and his baguette sandwiches are popular with the locals. The menu doesn't do a good job of explaining the dishes, so don't hesitate to ask the waitstaff for explanations. Most of the tapas are under the heading "Por la noche," which also includes sandwiches and the *rotolata*—vegetables and cold cuts surrounded by a thin layer of crispy cheese, which is a house specialty. Acoustic music plays from 9 to 11pm Monday through Saturday. The restaurant is a half-block off the pedestrian-only *calzada,* which leads to the plaza in front of the basilica. For breakfast you can get the traditional *molletes.*

5 de Mayo 260, Zapopan (west side). ℂ/fax 33/3656-9516. Reservations recommended. Tapas $4–$9 (£2–£4.50); main courses $10–$15 (£5–£7.50). MC, V. Mon–Sat 9am–midnight; Sun 9am–8pm.

I Latina FUSION   Warehouse chic with a porcine motif (the owner tells me that the pig is a symbol of abundance in Thailand) is the look here. The menu is absurdly small but is supplemented with lots of daily specials. On my last visit, I sampled a steak with a coffee crust with shoestring sweet potato fries and tossed greens scattered about the plate (quite good), a chicken in peanut sauce that was okay, and a stuffed filet of snapper that was quite tasty. This is a good place for people-watching—you get to see a portion of Guadalajara's hip, intellectual crowd, who enjoy the antiestablishment surroundings, including the metal and plastic tables and chairs. My main problem is the noise, which at times gets to be too much. If you're looking for quiet dining, go elsewhere. Cabs have a hard time finding this place despite the fact that it's almost right off of Minerva Circle. It's not that difficult—Inglaterra faces the railroad tracks.

Av. Inglaterra (west side). (℃ **33/3647-7774.** Reservations recommended. Main courses $9–$16 (£4.50–£8). MC, V. Wed–Sat 7:30pm–1am; Sun 2–6pm.

La Fonda de San Miguel *Moments* MEXICAN   My favorite way to enjoy a good meal in Mexico is to have it in an elegant colonial courtyard. I love the contrast between the bright, noisy street and the cool, shaded patio. This restaurant is in the former convent of Santa Teresa de Jesús. While you enjoy the stone arches and gurgling fountain, little crisp tacos and homemade bread appear at the table. For main courses, try the shrimp *al tequila*, or perhaps the *chiles en nogada* if it's the season. Traditional *mole poblano* is also on the menu. Thursday to Saturday musicians perform from 3 to 5pm and 9 to 11pm.

Donato Guerra 25 (and Pedro Moreno, downtown). (℃ **33/3613-0809.** Reservations recommended on weekends. Breakfast $4–$8 (£2–£4); main courses $9–$16 (£4.50–£8). AE, MC, V. Mon 8:30am–9pm; Tues–Sat 8:30am–midnight.

La Trattoria Pomodoro Ristorante *⊀* ITALIAN   Good food, good service, and moderate prices make this restaurant perennially popular. The price of pastas and main courses includes a visit to the well-stocked salad bar. Recommendable menu items include the combination pasta plate (lasagna, fettuccini Alfredo, and spaghetti), shrimp linguine, and chicken parmigiana. The Italian owner likes to stock lots of wines from the motherland. The dining room is attractive and casual, with comfortable furniture and separate seating for smokers and nonsmokers.

Niños Héroes 3051 (west side). (℃ **33/3122-1817.** Reservations recommended, but not accepted during holidays. Pasta $7–$9 (£3.50–£4.50); main courses $8–$10 (£4–£5). AE, MC, V. Daily 1pm–midnight.

Mariscos Progreso SEAFOOD   On a large, open patio shaded by trees and tile roofs, waiters navigate among the tables carrying large platters of delicious seafood. Mexicans do a wonderful job with seafood, and this popular restaurant does the tradition proud. Grilling over wood is the specialty here, but the kitchen's repertoire includes all the Mexican standards. For a sampling of grilled favorites, try the *parrillada* for two. Sometimes there's quite a bit of ambience, with mariachis adding to the commotion. At other times, the crowd thins and one can rest peacefully from the exertions of shopping with a cold drink. It's a half-block from the Parián.

Progreso 80, Tlaquepaque. (℃ **33/3657-4995.** Reservations not accepted. Main courses $8–$14 (£4–£7). AE, MC, V. Daily 11am–7pm.

INEXPENSIVE

Café Madrid MEXICAN   This little coffee shop is like many coffee shops used to be—a social institution where people come in, greet each other and the staff by name, and chat over breakfast or coffee and cigarettes. Change comes slowly here. For example, despite the fact that it's an informal place, the waiters wear white jackets with black bow ties, as they did 20 years ago. The coffee and Mexican breakfasts are good, as is the standard Mexican fare served in the afternoon. The front room opens to the street, with a small lunch counter and another room in the back.

Juárez 264 (between Corona and 16 de Septiembre, downtown). © 33/3614-9504. Breakfast $2–$4 (£1–£2); main courses $5–$8 (£2.50–£4). No credit cards. Daily 7:30am–10:30pm.

La Chata Restaurant REGIONAL/MEXICAN   If you're staying downtown, don't let this place slip off your radar. It does a good job with all the Mexican classics and some regional specialties as well. Unlike most restaurants, this one has the kitchen in front and the dining area in back. For a reasonable sum you can get a filling bowl of *pozole*. They also offer *flautas, sopes, quesadillas,* and guacamole. There's also traditional *mole* and a couple of combination plates. The chairs are comfortable, and you hang out with lots of locals.

Corona 126 (between Juárez and López Cotilla, downtown). © 33/3613-0588. Reservations not accepted. Breakfast $4–$6 (£2–£3); main courses $6–$9 (£3–£4.50). AE, DC, MC, V. Daily 8am–midnight.

La Fonda de la Noche *Finds* MEXICAN   For a host of reasons, this is my favorite place in the city for a simple supper. The limited menu is excellent, the surroundings are comfortable and inviting, the lighting is perfect, and there's a touch of nostalgia for the Mexico of the '40s, '50s, and '60s. It's not far from downtown or the west side; take a cab to the intersection of Jesús and Reforma, and, when you get there, look for a door behind a small hedge. There's no sign. It's a house with five fun dining rooms. Only Spanish is spoken, but the menu is simple. To try a little of everything, order the *plato combinado,* a combination plate that comes with an *enchilada de medio mole,* an *empanada* called a *media luna,* a *tostada,* and a *sope.* The owner is Carlos Ibarra, an artist from the state of Durango. He has decorated the place with traditional Mexican pine furniture and cotton tablecloths and his personal collection of paintings, mostly the works of close friends. On weekends, La Fonda offers *chiles en nogada.*

Jesús 251 (corner with Reforma, Col. El Refugio). © 33/3827-0917. Reservations not accepted. Main courses $6–$8 (£3–£4). MC, V. Tues–Sun 7:30pm–midnight.

Los Itacates Restaurant *Value* MEXICAN   The Mexican equivalent of downhome cooking at reasonable prices. Office workers pack the place between 2 and 4pm weekdays, and there's a good crowd on weekend nights, but at other times you'll have no problem finding a table. You can dine outdoors in a shaded sidewalk area or in one of the three dining rooms. The atmosphere is bright and colorful. Specialties include *lomo adobado* and chiles rellenos. *Pollo Itacates* is a quarter of a chicken, two cheese enchiladas, potatoes, and rice. Los Itacates is 5 blocks north of Avenida Vallarta. In the evenings, they serve tacos and other *antojitos.*

Chapultepec Norte 110 (west side). © 33/3825-1106 or -9551. Reservations accepted on weekends and holidays. Breakfast buffet $6 (£3); tacos $1 (50p); main courses $5–$7 (£2.50–£3.50). MC, V. Mon–Sat 8am–11pm; Sun 8am–7pm.

5 Exploring Guadalajara

SPECIAL EVENTS

There's always something going on from September to December. In September, when Mexicans celebrate independence from Spain, Guadalajara goes all out, with a full month of festivities. The celebrations kick off with the **Encuentro Internacional**

Downtown Guadalajara

Cathedral **3**
Church of Santa María de Gracia **7**
Instituto Cultural Cabañas **12**
Mercado Libertad **11**
Museo Regional de Guadalajara **5**
Palacio del Gobierno **2**
Plaza de Armas **1**

Plaza Guadalajara **4**
Quetzalcoatl Fountain **10**
Rotonda de los Hombres Ilustres **4**
Teatro Degollado **8**
Universidad de Guadalajara Facultad de Música & Iglesia de San Agustín **9**

del Mariachi (www.mariachi-jalisco.com.mx), in which mariachi bands from around the world play before knowledgeable audiences and hold sessions with other mariachis. Bands come from as far as Japan and Russia, and the event takes on a curious postmodern hue. Concerts are held in several venues. In the Degollado Theater, you can hear orchestral arrangements of classic mariachi songs with solos by famous mariachis. You might be acquainted with many of the classics without even knowing it. The culmination is a parade of thousands of mariachis and *charros* (Mexican cowboys) through downtown. It starts the first week of September.

On **September 15,** a massive crowd assembles in front of the Governor's Palace to await the traditional *grito* (shout for independence) at 11pm. The *grito* commemorates Father Miguel Hidalgo de Costilla's cry for independence in 1810. The celebration features live music on a street stage, spontaneous dancing, fireworks, and shouts of "¡Viva México!" and "¡Viva Hidalgo!" The next day is the official Independence Day, with a traditional parade; the plazas downtown resemble a country fair and market, with booths, games of chance, stuffed-animal prizes, cotton candy, and candied apples. Live entertainment stretches well into the night.

On **October 12,** a **procession** 🌟🌟 honoring Our Lady of Zapopan celebrates the feast day of the Virgin of Zapopan. Around dawn, her small, dark figure begins the

Guadalajara Bus Tours

Two companies are now offering bus tours of the city. One is a local company, **Tranvías Turísticos** (no phone), which offers two tours on small buses that look like trolley cars. Get info and buy tickets from the kiosk in Plaza Guadalajara (in front of the cathedral) from 10am until 7pm. There are two routes. One is a circuit through downtown and surrounding neighborhoods. It lasts 1 hour and 10 minutes. The second is a slightly longer tour, going to Tlaquepaque. It lasts 1½ hours. Both cost $8 (£4). The other company, **Tapatío Tours** (© 33/3613-0887; www.tapatiotour.com), has modern, bright red double-decker buses. Its tour goes from downtown to western Guadalajara to Tlaquepaque. The tour costs $9 (£4.50) on weekdays, $11 (£5.50) on weekends. It goes farther out, into western Guadalajara. There are 10 stops; you can get off at any one and catch the next bus when it passes by, which is every 35 minutes. Catch the bus in the plaza on the north side of the cathedral after 10am.

5-hour ride from the Cathedral of Guadalajara to the suburban Basilica of Zapopan (see "Other Attractions," below). The original icon dates from the mid-1500s; the procession began 200 years later. Today, crowds spend the night along the route and vie for position as the Virgin approaches. She travels in a gleaming new car (virginal in that it must never have had the ignition turned on), which her caretakers pull through the streets. During the months leading up to the feast day, the figure visits churches all over the city. You will likely see neighborhoods decorated with paper streamers and banners honoring the Virgin's visit to the local church.

The celebration has grown into a month-long event, **Fiestas de Octubre,** which kicks off with an enormous parade, usually on the first Sunday or Saturday of the month. Festivities include performing arts, *charreadas* (rodeos), bullfights, art exhibits, regional dancing, a food fair, and a Day of Nations incorporating all the consulates in Guadalajara. By the time this is over, you enter the **holiday season of November and December,** with Revolution Day (Nov 20), the Virgin of Guadalupe's feast day (Dec 12), and several other celebrations.

DOWNTOWN GUADALAJARA

The most easily recognized building in the city is the **cathedral** ⟨ℛ, around which four open plazas form the shape of a Latin cross. Later, a long swath of land was cleared to extend the open area from Plaza Liberación east to the Instituto Cultural Cabañas, creating **Plaza Tapatía.**

Construction on the cathedral started in 1561 and continued into the 18th century. Over such a long time, it was inevitable that remodeling would take place before the building was ever completed. The result is an unusual facade—an amalgam of several styles, including baroque, neoclassical, and Gothic. An 1818 earthquake destroyed the original large towers; their replacements were built in the 1850s, inspired by designs on the bishop's dinner china. Blue and yellow are Guadalajara's colors. The nave is airy and majestic. Items of interest include a painting in the sacristy ascribed to the 17th-century Spanish artist Bartolomé Esteban Murillo (1617–82).

On the cathedral's south side is the **Plaza de Armas,** the oldest and loveliest of the plazas. A cast-iron Art Nouveau bandstand is its dominant feature. Made in France, it was a gift to the city from the dictator Porfirio Díaz in the 1890s. The female figures on the bandstand exhibited too little clothing for conservative Guadalajarans, who clothed them. The dictator, recognizing when it's best to let the people have their way, said nothing.

Facing the plaza is the **Palacio del Gobierno** ⚔⚔, a broad, low structure built in 1774. The facade blends Spanish and Moorish elements and holds several eye-catching details. Inside the central courtyard, above the staircase to the right, is a spectacular mural of Hidalgo by the modern Mexican master José Clemente Orozco. The Father of Independence appears high overhead, bearing directly down on the viewer and looking as implacable as a force of nature. On one of the adjacent walls, Orozco painted *The Carnival of Ideologies,* a dark satire on the prevailing fanaticisms of his day. Another of his murals is inside the second-floor chamber of representatives, depicting Hidalgo again, this time in a more conventional posture, writing the proclamation to end slavery in Mexico. The *palacio* is open daily from 10am to 8pm.

In the plaza on the opposite side of the cathedral from the Plaza de Armas is the **Rotonda de los Hombres Ilustres.** Sixteen white columns, each supporting a bronze statue, stand as monuments to Guadalajara's and Jalisco's distinguished sons. Across the street from the plaza, in front of the Museo Regional, you will see a line of horse-drawn buggies. A carriage ride around the Centro Histórico lasts about an hour and costs $20 (£10) for one to four people.

Facing the east side of the rotunda is the **Museo Regional de Guadalajara,** Liceo 60 (© **33/3613-2703**). Originally a convent, it was built in 1701 in the *churrigueresque* (Mexican baroque) style and contains some of the region's important archaeological finds, fossils, historic objects, and art. Among the highlights are a giant reconstructed mammoth's skeleton and a meteorite weighing 772 kilograms (1,715 lb.), discovered in Zacatecas in 1792. On the first floor, there's a fascinating exhibit of pre-Hispanic pottery, and some exquisite pottery and clay figures recently unearthed near Tequila during the construction of the toll road. On the second floor is a small ethnography exhibit of the contemporary dress of the state's indigenous peoples, including the Coras, Huicholes, Mexicaneros, Nahuas, and Tepehuanes. It's open Tuesday through Saturday from 9am to 5:30pm and Sunday from 9am to 4:30pm. Admission is $4 (£2).

Behind the Cathedral is the Plaza Liberación, with the **Teatro Degollado** (deh-goh-*yah*-doh) on the opposite side. This neoclassical 19th-century opera house was named for Santos Degollado, a local patriot who fought with Juárez against Maximilian and the French. Apollo and the nine muses decorate the theater's pediment, and the interior is famous for both the acoustics and the rich decoration. It hosts a variety of performances during the year, including the Ballet Folclórico on Sunday at 10am. It's open Monday through Friday from 10am to 2pm and during performances.

To the right of the theater, across the street, is the sweet little **church of Santa María de Gracia,** built in 1573 as part of a convent for Dominican nuns. On the opposite side of the Teatro Degollado is the **church of San Agustín.** The former convent is now the **University of Guadalajara School of Music.**

Behind the Teatro Degollado begins the Plaza Tapatía, which leads to the Instituto Cabañas. It passes between a couple of low, modern office buildings. The **Tourism Information Office** is in a building on the right-hand side.

Beyond these office buildings, the plaza opens into a large expanse, now framed by department stores and offices and dominated by the abstract modern **Quetzalcoatl Fountain.** This fluid steel structure represents the mythical plumed serpent Quetzalcoatl, who figured so prominently in pre-Hispanic religion and culture, and exerts a presence even today.

At the far end of the plaza is the Hospicio Cabañas, formerly an orphanage and known today as the **Instituto Cultural Cabañas** ⊛⊛, Cabañas 8 (© **33/3818-2000, ext. 31009**). Admission is $10 (£5). This vast structure is impressive for both its size (more than 23 courtyards) and its grandiose architecture, especially the cupola. Created by the famous Mexican architect Manuel Tolsá, it housed homeless children from 1829 to 1980. Today, it's a thriving cultural center offering art shows and classes. The interior walls and ceiling of the main building display murals painted by Orozco in 1937. His *Man of Fire,* in the dome, is said to represent the spirit of humanity projecting itself toward the infinite. Other rooms hold additional Orozco works, as well as excellent contemporary art and temporary exhibits.

Just south of the Hospicio Cabañas (to the left as you exit) is the **Mercado Libertad** ⊛, Guadalajara's gigantic covered central market, the largest in Latin America. This site has been a market plaza since the 1500s; the present buildings date from the early 1950s (see "Shopping," below).

OTHER ATTRACTIONS

At **Parque Agua Azul (Blue Water Park),** plants, trees, shrubbery, statues, and fountains create an idyllic refuge from the bustling city. Many people come here to exercise early in the morning. The park is open daily from 7am to 6pm. Admission is $1 (50p) for adults, 50¢ (25p) for children.

Across Independencia from the park, cater-cornered from a small flower market, is the **Museo de Arqueología del Occidente de México,** Calzada Independencia at Avenida del Campesino. It houses a fine collection of pre-Hispanic pottery from Jalisco, Nayarit, and Colima. The museum is open Tuesday through Sunday from 10am to 2pm and 4 to 7pm. There's a small admission charge.

The state-run **Casa de las Artesanías** (© 33/3619-4664) is at the Instituto de la Artesanía Jalisciense, just past the park entrance at Calzada Independencia and González Gallo (for details, see "Shopping," below).

Also near the park is Guadalajara's rodeo arena, **Lienzo Charro de Jalisco** (© 33/3619-0315). Mexican cowboys, known as *charros,* are famous for their riding and lasso work, and the arena in Guadalajara is considered the big time. There are shows and competitions every Sunday at noon. The arena is at Av. Dr. R. Michel 577, between González Gallo and Las Palomas.

Basílica de la Virgen de Zapopan ⊛   A wide promenade several blocks long leads to a large, open plaza and the basilica. This is the religious center of Guadalajara. On the Virgin's feast day (see "Special Events," above), the plaza fills with thousands of *tapatíos.* The 18th-century church is a combination of baroque and *plateresque* styles. The cult of the Virgin of Zapopan practically began with the foundation of Guadalajara itself. She is much revered and the object of many pilgrimages. In front of the church are several stands selling religious figures and paraphernalia. On one side of the church is a museum and store dedicated to the betterment of the Huichol Indians. It is worth a visit. Admission is 50¢ (25p).

Main Plaza, Zapopan (10km/6¼ miles northwest of downtown). No phone. Free admission. Daily 7am–7pm. Museum Mon–Sat 9:30am–6pm; Sun 10am–2pm.

Museo de la Ciudad This museum opened in 1992 in a former convent. It chronicles Guadalajara's past. The eight rooms, beginning on the right and proceeding in chronological order, cover the period from just before the city's founding to the present. Unusual artifacts, including rare Spanish armaments and equestrian paraphernalia, give a sense of what day-to-day life was like through the centuries. Descriptive text is in Spanish only.

Independencia 684 (at M. Bárcenas). © 33/3658-2531. 50¢ (25p). Tues–Sun 10am–5pm.

Museo de las Artes de la Universidad de Guadalajara Inside the main lecture hall of this building are some more murals by Orozco. On the wall behind the stage is a bitter denunciation of corruption called *The People and Their False Leaders*. In the cupola is a more optimistic work—*The Five-fold Man*, who works to create a better society and better self. There is also a small permanent collection of modern art, which will look all too familiar because the works seem so derivative of many of the modern masters.

Juárez 975 (enter on López Cotilla). © 33/3134-2222. 50¢ (25p). Tues–Sun 10am–8pm.

Museo Pantaleón Panduro 𝒜𝒜𝒜 This museum houses a magnificent collection of ceramic works. Collectors and connoisseurs of pottery will love it, but so will casual students of Mexican popular culture and the arts. This could be one of the great museums of Mexico, but I would change a few things to make it perfect. Every year a national competition is held in Tlaquepaque among ceramists from across Mexico. Prizes are awarded in seven categories and a best of show among these. (*Tip:* The competition is held every June, which is a good time for visiting Tlaquepaque.) The president of Mexico even comes to town to present the awards. After the competition, many of the winning pieces become part the museum's collection. The virtuosity manifested in some of them will take your breath away. It would be wonderful if they were organized by category, with better explanatory text. But for now, the best thing you can do is cajole someone into showing you around and explaining the pieces on display. The staff is actually quite knowledgeable, and at least one member speaks English. The museum occupies a third of a large complex that in colonial times was a large religious community. It's now called **Centro Cultural El Refugio,** and it's worth ambling through after you've seen the museum's collection.

P. Sánchez 191 (at Calle Florida, Tlaquepaque). © 33/3639-5656. Free. Tues–Sun 10am–6pm.

6 Shopping

Many visitors to Guadalajara come specifically for the shopping in Tlaquepaque and Tonalá (see below). If you have little free time, try the government-run **Instituto de la Artesanía Jalisciense** 𝒜, González Gallo 20 at Calzada Independencia (© 33/3619-4664), in Parque Agua Azul, just south of downtown. This place is perfect for one-stop shopping, with two floors of pottery, silver jewelry, dance masks, glassware, leather goods, and regional clothing from around the state and the country. As you enter, on the right are museum displays showing crafts and regional costumes from the state of Jalisco. The craft store is open Monday through Friday from 10am to 6pm, Saturday from 10am to 5pm, Sunday from 10am to 3pm.

Guadalajara is known for its shoe industry; if you're in the market for a pair, try the **Galería del Calzado,** a shopping center made up exclusively of shoe stores. It's on the west side, about 6 blocks from Minerva Circle, at avenidas México and Yaquis.

Mariachis and *charros* come to Guadalajara from all over Mexico to buy highly worked belts and boots, wide-brimmed sombreros, and embroidered shirts. Several tailor shops and stores specialize in these outfits. One is **El Charro,** which has a store in the Plaza del Sol shopping center, across the street from the Hotel Presidente Inter-Continental, and one downtown on Juárez.

To view a good slice of what constitutes the material world for most Mexicans, try the mammoth **Mercado Libertad** ✪ downtown. Besides food and produce, you'll see crafts, household goods, clothing, magic potions, and more. Although it opens at 7am, the market isn't in full swing until around 10am. Come prepared to haggle.

SHOPPING IN TLAQUEPAQUE & TONALA

Almost everyone who comes to Guadalajara for the shopping has Tlaquepaque (tlah-keh-*pah*-keh) and Tonalá in mind. These two suburbs are traditional handicraft centers that produce and sell a wide variety of *artesanía* (crafts).

TLAQUEPAQUE

Located about 20 minutes from downtown, **Tlaquepaque** ✪✪✪ has the best shopping for handicrafts and decorative arts in all of Mexico. Over the years, it has become a fashionable place, attracting talented designers in a variety of fields. Even though it's a suburb of a large city, it has a cozy, small-town feel; it's a pleasure simply to stroll through the central streets from shop to shop. No one hassles you; no one does the hard sell. There are some excellent places to eat (see "Where to Dine," earlier in this chapter), or you can grab some simple fare at **El Parián,** a building in the middle of town that houses a number of small eateries.

A taxi from downtown Guadalajara costs $6 (£3), or you can take one of the TUR 706 buses that make a fairly quick run from downtown to Tlaquepaque and Tonalá (see "Getting Around," earlier in this chapter).

The **Tlaquepaque Tourism Office** (℃ **33/3562-7050,** ext. 2320; turismo tlaquepaque@yahoo.com.mx) has an information booth in the town's main square by El Parián. It's staffed from 10am to 8pm daily.

If you are interested in pottery and ceramics, make sure to see the Pantaleón Panduro Museum, listed above. Another is the **Regional Ceramics Museum,** Independencia 237 (℃ **33/3635-5404**), which displays several aspects of traditional Jalisco pottery as produced in Tlaquepaque and Tonalá. The examples date back several generations and are grouped according to the technique used to produce them. Note the crosshatch design known as *petatillo* on some of the pieces; it's one of the region's oldest traditional motifs and is, like so many other motifs, a real pain to produce. Look for the wonderful old kitchen and dining room, complete with pots, utensils, and dishes. The museum is open Tuesday through Saturday from 10am to 6pm, Sunday from 10am to 3pm; admission is free.

The following list of Tlaquepaque shops will give you an idea of what to expect. This is just a small fraction of what you'll find; the best approach might be to just follow your nose. The main shopping is along **Independencia,** a pedestrian-only street

> **(Tips** **Packing It In**
>
> If you need your purchases packed safely so that you can check them as extra baggage, or if you want them shipped, talk to **Margaret del Río.** She is an American who runs a large packing and shipping company at Juárez 347, Tlaquepaque (© **33/3657-5652**). Paying the excess baggage fee usually is cheaper than shipping, but it's less convenient.

that starts at El Parián. It was recently resurfaced in stone and looks pretty sharp. You can go door-to-door visiting the shops until the street ends, then work your way back on **Calle Juárez,** the next street over, south of Independencia.

Agustín Parra   So you bought an old hacienda and are trying to restore its chapel— where do you go to find traditional baroque sculpture, religious art, gold-leafed objects, and even entire *retablos* (altarpieces)? Parra is famous for exactly this kind of work, and the store is lovely. It's open Monday through Saturday from 10am to 7pm. Independencia 158. © **33/3657-8530.**

Bazar Hecht   One of the village's longtime favorites. Here you'll find wood objects, handmade furniture, and a few antiques. It's open Monday through Saturday from 10am to 2:30pm and 3:30 to 7pm. Juárez 162. © **33/3657-0316.**

Sergio Bustamante   Sergio Bustamante's imaginative, original bronze, ceramic, and papier-mâché sculptures are among the most sought-after in Mexico—as well as the most copied. He also designs silver jewelry. This exquisite gallery showcases his work. It's open Monday through Saturday from 10am to 7pm, Sunday from noon to 4pm. Independencia 238 at Cruz Verde. © **33/3639-5519.**

Teté Arte y Diseño   Architectural decorative objects—especially hand–wrought iron hardware for the "Old Mexico" look—are the specialty here. The store also has a large collection of wrought iron chandeliers. It's open Monday through Saturday from 10am to 7:30pm. Juárez 173. © **33/3635-7347.**

TONALA: A TRADITION OF POTTERY MAKING

Tonalá 🕯🕯 is a pleasant town 5 minutes from Tlaquepaque. The streets were paved only recently, and there aren't fancy shops here. The village has been a center of pottery making since pre-Hispanic times; half of the more than 400 workshops produce a wide variety of high- and low-temperature pottery. Other local artists work with forged iron, cantera stone, brass and copper, marble, miniatures, papier-mâché, textiles, blown glass, and gesso. This is a good place to look for custom work in any of these materials; you can locate a large pool of craftspeople by asking around a little.

Market days are Thursday and Sunday. Expect large crowds, and blocks and blocks of stalls displaying locally made pottery and glassware, as well as cheap manufactured goods, food, and all kinds of bric-a-brac. "Herb men" sell a rainbow selection of dried medicinal herbs from wheelbarrows; magicians entertain crowds with sleight-of-hand; and craftspeople spread their colorful wares on the plaza's sidewalks. I prefer to visit Tonalá on non–market days, when it's much easier to get around and see the stores and workshops. This is the place for buying sets of margarita glasses, the widely seen blue-rimmed hand-blown glassware, finely painted *petatillo* ware, and the pottery typically associated with Mexico.

The **Tonalá Tourism Office** (© 33/3284-3092) is in the Artesanos building, set back from the road at Atonaltecas 140 Sur (the main street leading into Tonalá) at Matamoros. There is an information booth in front. Hours are Monday through Friday from 9am to 3pm, Saturday from 9am to 1pm. The office offers **free walking tours** on Monday, Tuesday, Wednesday, and Friday at 9am and 2pm, Saturday at 9am and 1pm. They include visits to artisans' workshops (where you'll see ceramics, stoneware, blown glass, papier-mâché, and the like). Tours last 3 to 4 hours and require a minimum of five people. Visitors can request an English-speaking guide. Also in Tonalá, cater-cornered from the church, you'll see a small tourism information kiosk that's staffed on market days and provides maps and useful information.

Tonalá is also the home of the **Museo Nacional de Cerámica,** Constitución 104, between Hidalgo and Morelos (© 33/3284-3000, ext. 1194). The museum occupies a two-story mansion and displays work from Jalisco and all over the country. There's a large shop in the front on the right as you enter. The museum is open Tuesday through Friday from 10am to 5pm, Saturday and Sunday from 10am to 2pm. Admission is free; the fee for using a video or still camera is $8.50 (£4.25) per camera.

7 Guadalajara After Dark

MARIACHIS

You can't go far in Guadalajara without coming across some mariachis, but seeing really talented performers takes some effort. Try **Casa Bariachi,** Av. Vallarta 2221 (© 33/ 3615-0029). In Tlaquepaque, go to **El Parián,** the building on the town square where mariachis serenade diners under the archways.

THE CLUB & MUSIC SCENE

Guadalajara, as you might expect, has a lot of variety in entertainment. For the most extensive listing of clubs and performances, get your hands on a copy of *Ocio,* the weekly insert of *Público.* You'll find listings in the back, categorized by type of music. For good mariachis, you should go to Casa Bariachi, mentioned above. Across the street from that club is another called **La Bodeguita del Medio** (© 33/3630-1620) at Av. Vallarta 2320. It offers live old-school Cuban son. The groups come from Cuba and rotate every few months. The last night I visited the place, a small combo was playing in a little corner partly mixing in with the crowd. The place is small, but people were making room to dance. Another thing to do is track down a Cuban diva, named **Rosalia,** who lives in Guadalajara. She's a great talent and always has a tight band playing with her as she belts out salsa and merengue tunes. The last time I was in Guadalajara she was singing weekends at the bar at the Hotel Presidente Inter-Continental.

Tequila: The Name Says It All

Tequila is an entertaining (and intoxicating) town, well worth a day trip from Guadalajara. Several taxi drivers charge about $55 (£28) to drive you to the town, get you into a tour of a distillery, take you to a restaurant, and haul you back to Guadalajara. A few of them speak English. One recommended driver is José Gabriel Gómez (© 33/3649-0791; jgabriel-taxi@ hotmail.com); he has a new car and drives carefully. Call him in the evening. Tour companies also arrange bus trips to Tequila; ask at the ticket kiosk of Tranvías Turísticos, mentioned above. That company has started a weekend tour to Tequila, taking people to the Cofradía distillery.

Tequila has many distilleries, including the famous brands **Sauza** and **José Cuervo**. All the distilleries—the big, modern ones and the small, more traditional ones—offer tours. If you're on your own, a good place to hook up with a tour is at the little booth outside the city hall on the main square; two young English-speaking women run tours to any of the local factories. Tours cost only $5 (£2.50) and last about 2 hours. All tours show how tequila is made, what traditions the process follows, and what differences exist between tequilas; they end, of course, with a tasting. Avenida Vallarta runs straight to the highway to Tequila, which is about an hour outside of Guadalajara.

Another approach is to take the **Tequila Express** to the town of Amatitán, home of the Herradura distillery. This excursion is more about having a good time and enjoying some of the things this area is known for than it is about sampling tequila. Serious tequila enthusiasts will be disappointed. There's a nice tour of the distillery, but most of the time is spent watching mariachis and Mexican cowboys perform. The tequila tastings are limited. Everyone has a good time and drinks a fair share, but a trip to the town proper is more informative and offers a greater opportunity for trying different tequilas.

The Tequila Express leaves from the train station on Friday and Saturday, and sometimes on Sunday during vacation and holiday season. It's well organized. You need to be there by 10am. The Guadalajara Chamber of Commerce (Cámara de Comercio), at Vallarta and Niño Obrero (© 33/3880-9099), organizes this trip. Buy tickets ahead of time at the main office; at the small office in the Centro Histórico at Morelos 395; at Calle Colón (no phone); or through Ticketmaster (© 33/3818-3800). Office hours are Monday through Friday from 9am to 2pm and 4 to 6pm. Tickets cost $85 (£43) for adults, $48 (£24) for children 6 to 12. The tour includes food and drink. It returns to Guadalajara at about 8pm. Travel time is 1¾ hours each way. For more information, see **www.tequilaexpress.com.mx**.

10

Puerto Vallarta & the Central Pacific Coast

by Lynne Bairstow

Known as the Mexican Riviera, Mexico's Pacific coastline—with its palm-studded jungles sweeping into the deep blue of the ocean—is a spectacular backdrop for some of the country's favored resort cities. From Mazatlán through Puerto Vallarta and curving down to Manzanillo, modern hotels, easy air access, and a growing array of activities and adventure tourism attractions have transformed this region into a premier resort area. And for those seeking an experience off the beaten track, the villages that border this stretch of coastline remain largely undiscovered.

Puerto Vallarta, with its traditional Mexican architecture and gold-sand beaches bordered by jungle-covered mountains, is the second-most-visited resort in Mexico (trailing only Cancún). The original town center of Vallarta maintains a small-town charm despite its sophisticated hotels, great restaurants, thriving arts community, active nightlife, and wide variety of ecotourism attractions. **Mazatlán** may be the greatest resort value in Mexico, luring visitors with exceptional fishing, a historic downtown, and the

recent addition of championship golf facilities and new residential developments. **Manzanillo** is surprisingly relaxed; even though it's one of Mexico's most active commercial ports, it also offers great fishing, diving, and golf. And along **Costa Alegre,** between Puerto Vallarta and Manzanillo, pristine coves are home to unique luxury and value-priced resorts that cater to travelers seeking seclusion and privacy. Just north of Puerto Vallarta, bordering Banderas Bay, are the increasingly popular coastal towns of **Nuevo Vallarta, Bucerías,** and, at the northern tip, **Punta Mita,** home of the first Four Seasons resort in Latin America, two Jack Nicklaus golf courses, and a newly unveiled St. Regis resort. It is rapidly gaining fame as Mexico's most exclusive luxury address.

Villages such as **Rincón de Guayabitos, Barra de Navidad,** and **Melaque** are laid-back and almost undiscovered. Starkly different from the spirited resort towns, they offer travelers a glimpse into local culture. Excursions to these smaller villages make easy day trips or extended stays.

1 Puerto Vallarta ★★★

885km (549 miles) NW of Mexico City; 339km (210 miles) W of Guadalajara; 285km (177 miles) NW of Manzanillo; 447km (277 miles) SE of Mazatlán; 239km (148 miles) SW of Tepic

No matter how extensively I travel in Mexico, Puerto Vallarta remains my favorite part of this colorful country, for its unrivaled combination of simple pleasures and sophistication. Beyond the cobblestone streets, graceful cathedral, and welcoming atmosphere, Puerto Vallarta offers a wealth of natural beauty and man-made pleasures,

Puerto Vallarta: Hotel Zone & Beaches

Marina Vallarta Accommodations & Dining

To Bucerias, Punta Mita, Sayulita & San Pancho

Playa el Salado

MARINA VALLARTA

To Vista Vallarta Golf Course & San Sebastián

Puerto Vallarta
JALISCO
PACIFIC OCEAN
MICHOACÁN
Mexico City

0 200 mi
0 200 km

Playa de Oro

Terminal Marítima (Cruise Pier)

Plaza Peninsula

Río El Pitillal

Ave. Francisco M. Ascencio

see Marina Vallarta inset

Airport

Albatros

Gaviotas

Plaza La Marina

Av. Francisco

Flamingos

Marina Vallarta Club de Golf

Plaza Neptuno

Playa Los Tules

HOTEL ZONE

Bocanegra

Pelicanos

Paseo de la Marina Norte

Paseo de la Marina

Proa

Popa

Nastil

Timon

M. Ascencio

Vallarta Adventures

Playa Las Glorias

Ancla

Paseo de la Marina Sur

Vela

Bullring

Bahía de Banderas

Playa el Salado

Galerias Vallarta

Playa Camarones

Avenida de México

Bahía de Banderas

0   0.5 mi
0   0.5 km

N

Terminal Marítima (Cruise Pier)

Playa de Oro

EL CENTRO

See "Downtown Puerto Vallarta" map

Río Cuale

Insurgentes

Vallarta

Playa Olas Altas

Playa Los Muertos

ACCOMMODATIONS ■

Casa Tres Vidas **10**
Casa Velas **2**
Dreams **12**
Fiesta Americana **6**
Hacienda San Angel **8**
Hotel Playa Los Arcos **9**
Quinta Maria Cortez **11**
Velas Vallarta Resort **1**
Villa Premier **7**
Westin Resort & Spa **5**

DINING ◆

Benitto's **4**
Porto Bello **3**

PACIFIC OCEAN

Playa Conchas Chinas

200

Airport ✈
Beach ↖
Golf ⛳

To Yelapa, Tomatlán, Playa Punta Negra, Playa Garza Blanca, Playa Gemelas, Playa Mismaloya, Los Arcos, Manzanillo, & El Eden Chino's

0   0.5 mi
0   0.5 km

N

including hotels of all classes and prices, more than 250 restaurants, a sizzling nightlife, and enough shops and galleries to tempt even jaded consumers.

Ecotourism activities flourish—from canopy tours to whale-watching, ocean kayaking, and diving with giant mantas in Banderas Bay. Forty-two kilometers (26 miles) of beaches, many in pristine coves accessible only by boat, extend around the bay. High in the Sierra Madre, the mystical Huichol Indians still live in relative isolation in an effort to protect their centuries-old culture from outside influences.

Vallarta (as locals refer to it) was never a "sleepy little fishing village" as is often claimed. It began as a port for processing silver brought down from mines in the Sierra Madre—then was forever transformed by a movie director and two star-crossed lovers. In 1963, John Huston brought stars Ava Gardner and Richard Burton here to film the Tennessee Williams play *Night of the Iguana*. Burton's new love, Elizabeth Taylor, came along to ensure the romance remained in full bloom—even though both were married to others at the time. Titillated, the international paparazzi arrived, and when they weren't photographing the famous couple—or of Gardner water-skiing back from the set, surrounded by a bevy of beach boys—they shot the beauty of Puerto Vallarta.

Luxury hotels and shopping centers have sprung up north and south of the original town, allowing Vallarta to grow into a city of 400,000 without sacrificing its small-town charms. With the services and infrastructure—and, unfortunately now the traffic—of a modern city, it still retains the authenticity of a colonial Mexican village.

Cool breezes flow down from the mountains along the Río Cuale, which runs through the center of town. Fanciful public sculptures grace the *malecón* (boardwalk), which is bordered by lively restaurants, shops, and nightclubs. The *malecón* is a magnet for both residents and visitors, who stroll the main walkway to take in an ocean breeze, a multihued sunset, or a moonlit, perfect wave.

If I sound partial, it's not just because Puerto Vallarta is my favorite sunny Mexican resort; it has been my home for the past 17 years. I live here in good company, among a sizeable colony of American, Canadian, and European residents. Perhaps they feel as I do: that the surrounding mountains offer the equivalent of a continual, comforting embrace, enhancing that sense of welcome that so many visitors feel as well.

ESSENTIALS
GETTING THERE & DEPARTING
BY PLANE   For a list of international carriers serving Mexico, see chapter 3. Local numbers of some international carriers serving Puerto Vallarta are **Alaska Airlines** (© 322/221-1350 or -1353), **American Airlines** (© 322/221-1799 or -1927), **US Airways** (© 322/221-2936, or 01-800/428-4322 inside Mexico), **Continental** (© 322/221-1025 or -2212), **Frontier** (© 800/432-1359), and **Ted** (United's lower-cost carrier offers direct service from San Francisco and Denver; © 800/225-5833 in the U.S.).

AeroMéxico (© 322/221-1204 or -1030) flies from Los Angeles, San Diego, Aguascalientes, Guadalajara, La Paz, León, Mexico City, Morelia, and Tijuana. **Mexicana** (© 322/224-8900 or 221-1266) has direct or nonstop flights from Chicago, Los Angeles, Guadalajara, Mazatlán, and Mexico City.

Major car rental agencies have counters at the airport, including **Budget** (© 800/472-3325 in the U.S., or 322/221-1730), **Hertz** (© 322/221-1473 or -1399), **National** (© 322/221-1226), and **Alamo** (© 322/221-1228), open during flight arrivals; they generally can also deliver a car to your hotel. Daily rates run $60 to $80

(£30–£40). You need a car only if you plan to explore surrounding cities or are staying either along the southern coast, or north of Nuevo Vallarta.

BY CAR   The coastal Highway 200 is the only choice from Mazatlán (6 hr. north) or Manzanillo (3½–4 hr. south). Highway 15 from Guadalajara to Tepic takes 6 hours; to save as much as 2 hours, take Highway 15A from Chapalilla to Compostela, bypassing Tepic, then continue south on Highway 200 to Puerto Vallarta.

BY BUS   The bus station, **Central Camionera de Puerto Vallarta,** is just north of the airport, approximately 11km (7 miles) from downtown. It offers overnight guarded parking and baggage storage. Most major first-class bus lines operate from here, with transportation to points throughout Mexico, including Mazatlán, Tepic, Manzanillo, Guadalajara, and Mexico City. Taxis into town cost approximately $10 (£5) and are readily available; public buses operate from 7am to 11pm and regularly stop in front of the arrivals hall.

ORIENTATION

ARRIVING BY PLANE   The airport is close to the north end of town near the Marina Vallarta, about 10km (6¼ miles) from downtown. **Transportes Terrestres** minivans and **Aeromovil** taxis make the trip. They use a zone pricing system, with fares clearly posted at the ticket booths. Fares start at $10 (£5) for a ride to Marina Vallarta and go up to $35 (£18) for the south shore hotels. Federally licensed airport taxis exclusively provide transportation from the airport, and their fares are more than three times as high as city (yellow) taxi fares. A trip to downtown Puerto Vallarta costs $25 (£13), whereas a return trip using a city taxi costs only $10 (£5). Only airport cabs may pick up passengers leaving the airport. However, if you don't have too much baggage, you can cross the highway using the overpass, and there you'll find yellow cabs lined up. Note that when you arrive at the International Arrivals gate, after you collect your baggage, you enter into an enclosed area with colorful wall displays and an aggressive group of seemingly helpful greeters; beware—these are timeshare hustlers, and their goal, often in the guise of offering you free or discounted transportation, is to get you to attend a timeshare presentation. Keep walking—just outside this booth are the bona fide taxi and transportation alternatives.

VISITOR INFORMATION   Prior to arrival, a great source of general information is the **Puerto Vallarta Tourism Board** (© 888/384-6822 in the U.S.; www.visitpuerto vallarta.com). If you have questions after you arrive, visit the **Municipal Tourism Office** at Juárez and Independencia (© 322/223-2500, ext. 230) in a corner of the white Presidencia Municipal building (city hall) on the northwest end of the main square. In addition to offering a listing of current events and promotional brochures for local activities and services, the employees can also assist with specific questions—there's usually an English speaker on staff. This is also the office of the tourist police. It's open Monday through Friday from 8am to 9pm. During low season it may close for lunch between 2 and 4pm.

The **State Tourism Office,** Plaza Marina L 144, second floor (© 322/221-2676, -2677, or -2678; fax 322/221-2680), also offers brochures and can assist with specific questions about Puerto Vallarta and other points in the state of Jalisco, including Guadalajara, Costa Alegre, the town of Tequila, and the program that promotes stays in authentic rural haciendas. It's open Monday through Friday from 9am to 5pm.

CITY LAYOUT   The seaside promenade, the *malecón,* is a common reference point for giving directions. It's next to **Paseo Díaz Ordaz** and runs north–south through the central downtown area. From the waterfront, the town stretches back into the hills a half-dozen blocks. The areas bordering the **Río Cuale** are the oldest parts of town— the original Puerto Vallarta. The area immediately south of the river, called **Olas Altas** after its main street (and sometimes Los Muertos after the beach of the same name), is home to a growing selection of sidewalk cafes, fine restaurants, espresso bars, and hip nightclubs. In the center of town, nearly everything is within walking distance both north and south of the river. **Bridges** on Insurgentes (northbound traffic) and Ignacio Vallarta (southbound traffic) link the two sections of downtown.

AREA LAYOUT   Beyond downtown, Puerto Vallarta has grown along the beach to the north and south. Linking downtown to the airport is **Avenida Francisco Medina Ascencio,** home of many high-rise hotels (in an area called the **Zona Hotelera,** or Hotel Zone), plus several shopping centers with a variety of dining options.

   Marina Vallarta, a resort city within a city, is at the northern edge of the Hotel Zone not far from the airport. It boasts modern luxury hotels, condominiums, and homes; a huge marina with 450 yacht slips; a golf course; restaurants and bars; and several shopping plazas. Because it was originally a swamp, the beaches are the least desirable in the area, with darker sand and seasonal inflows of cobblestones. The Marina Vallarta peninsula faces the bay and looks south to the town of Puerto Vallarta.

   Nuevo Vallarta is a booming planned resort north of the airport, across the Ameca River in the state of Nayarit (about 13km/8 miles north of downtown). It also has hotels, condominiums, and a yacht marina, with a growing selection of restaurants and shopping, including the new Paradise Plaza mall. Most hotels there are all-inclusive, with some of the finest beaches in the bay, but guests usually travel into Puerto Vallarta (about $15/£7.50 a cab ride) for anything other than poolside or beach action. Regularly scheduled public bus service costs about $1.50 (75p) and runs until 10pm.

   Bucerías, a small beachside village of cobblestone streets, villas, and small hotels, is farther north along Banderas Bay, 30km (19 miles) beyond the airport. Past Bucerías, following the curved coastline of Banderas Bay, you'll find **La Cruz de Huanaxcle,** a new megamarina project currently under construction, but still an authentic, colorful seaside town. Continue to the end of the road and you'll reach **Punta Mita.** Once a rustic fishing village, it has been artfully developed as a luxury destination. In the works are a total of four exclusive luxury boutique resorts, private villas, and two golf courses. The site of an ancient celestial observatory, it is an exquisite setting, with white-sand beaches and clear waters. The northern shore of Banderas Bay is emerging as the area's most exclusive address for luxury villas and accommodations.

   In the other direction from downtown is the southern coastal highway, home to more luxury hotels. Immediately south of town lies the exclusive residential and rental district of **Conchas Chinas.** Ten kilometers (6 miles) south, on **Playa Mismaloya**

Tips **Steer Clear of the Rambo Bus!**

Buses in Vallarta tend to be rather aggressive, and some even sport names— including "Terminator," "Rambo," and "Tornado." Don't tempt fate by assuming these buses will stop for pedestrians. Although Vallarta has an extremely low crime rate, bus accidents are frequent—and frequently fatal.

Tips Don't Let Taxi Drivers Steer You Wrong

Beware of restaurant recommendations from taxi drivers—many receive a commission from restaurants where they discharge passengers. Be especially wary if a driver tries to talk you out of a restaurant you've already selected.

(where *Night of the Iguana* was filmed), lies the Barceló La Jolla de Mismaloya resort. There's no road on the southern shoreline of Banderas Bay, but three small coastal villages are popular attractions for visitors to Puerto Vallarta: **Las Animas, Quimixto,** and **Yelapa,** all accessible only by boat. The tiny, pristine cove of **Caletas,** site of John Huston's former home, is a popular day- or nighttime excursion (see "Boat Tours," later in this chapter).

GETTING AROUND   By Taxi   Taxis are plentiful and relatively inexpensive. Most trips from downtown to the northern Hotel Zone and Marina Vallarta cost $5.50 to $10 (£2.25–£5); to or from Marina Vallarta to Mismaloya Beach (to the south) costs $13 to $17 (£6.50–£8.50). Rates are charged by zone and are generally posted in the lobbies of hotels. Taxis can also be hired by the hour or day for longer trips. Rates run $18 to $22 (£9–£11) per hour, with discounts available for full-day rates—consider this an alternative to renting a car.

By Car   Rental cars are readily available at the airport, through travel agencies, and through the most popular U.S. car rental services, but unless you're planning a distant side trip, don't bother. Car rentals are expensive, averaging $69 (£35) per day, and parking around town is very challenging, unless you opt for one of the two new parking garages constructed on either end of the *malecón* zone (at Park Hidalgo to the north, and adjacent to the northern border of the Cuale River to the south). If you see a sign for a $10 (£5) Jeep rental or $20 (£10) car rental, be aware that these are lures to get people to attend timeshare presentations. Unless you are interested in a timeshare, stopping to inquire will be a waste of your time.

By Bus   City buses, easy to navigate and inexpensive, will serve just about all your transportation needs. They run from the airport through the Hotel Zone along Morelos Street (1 block inland from the *malecón*), across the Río Cuale, and inland on Vallarta, looping back through the downtown hotel and restaurant districts on Insurgentes and several other downtown streets. To get to the northern hotel strip from old Puerto Vallarta, take the ZONA HOTELES, IXTAPA, or LAS JUNTAS bus. These buses may also post the names of hotels they pass, such as Krystal, Sheraton, and others. Buses marked MARINA VALLARTA travel inside this area, stopping at the major hotels there.

Other buses operate every 10 to 15 minutes south to either Mismaloya Beach or Boca de Tomatlán (a sign in the front window indicates the destination) from Constitución and Basilio Badillo, a few blocks south of the river.

Buses run generally from 6am to 11pm, and it's rare to wait more than a few minutes for one. The fare is about 50¢ (25p). You do not have to have exact change; the driver will make change.

By Boat   The *muelle* (cruise-ship pier), also called Terminal Marítima, is where **excursion boats** to Yelapa, Las Animas, Quimixto, and the Marietas Islands depart. It's north of town near the airport, an inexpensive taxi or bus ride from town. Just take any bus marked IXTAPA, LAS JUNTAS, PITILLAL, or AURORA and tell the driver to let you off at the Terminal Marítima. *Note:* Oddly enough, you must pay a $1.50 (75p) federal tax to gain access to the pier—and your departing excursion boat.

Water taxis to Yelapa, Las Animas, and Quimixto leave at 10:30 and 11am from the pier at Los Muertos Beach (south of downtown), on Rodolfo Rodríguez next to the Hotel Marsol. Another water taxi departs at 11am from the beachside pier at the northern edge of the *malecón.* A round-trip ticket to Yelapa (the farthest point) costs $25 (£13). Return trips usually depart between 3 and 4pm, but confirm the pickup time with your water taxi captain. Other water taxis depart from Boca de Tomatlán, about 30 minutes south of town by public bus. These water taxis are the better option if you want more flexible departure and return times from the southern beaches. Generally, they leave on the hour for the southern shore destinations, or more frequently if there is traffic. Prices run about $15 (£7.50) round-trip, with rates clearly posted on a sign on the beach. A private water taxi costs $60 to $120 (£30–£60), depending on your destination, and allows you to choose your own return time. They'll take up to eight people for that price, so often people band together at the beach to hire one.

FAST FACTS: Puerto Vallarta

American Express The local office is at Morelos 660, at the corner of Abasolo (© 01-800/504-0400 and 01-800/333-3211 in Mexico, or 322/223-2955). It's open Monday through Friday from 9am to 6pm, Saturday from 9am to 1pm. It offers excellent, efficient travel agency services in addition to money exchange and traveler's checks.

Area Code The telephone area code is **322.**

Climate It's warm all year, with tropical temperatures; however, evenings and early mornings in the winter can turn quite cool. Summers are sunny, with an increase in humidity during the rainy season, between May and October. Rains come almost every afternoon in June and July, and are usually brief but strong—just enough to cool off the air for evening activities. In September, heat and humidity are least comfortable and rains heaviest.

Consumer Assistance Tourists with complaints about taxis, stores, abusive timeshare presentations, or other matters should contact **PROFECO,** the consumer protection office (© 322/225-0000; fax 322/225-0018). The office is open Monday through Friday from 8:30am to 3:30pm and may not have fluent English-speaking staff.

Currency Exchange Banks are found throughout downtown and in the other prime shopping areas. Most banks are open Monday through Friday from 9am to 5pm, with shorter hours on Saturday. ATMs are common throughout Vallarta, including the central plaza downtown. They are becoming the most favorable way to exchange currency, with bank rates plus 24-hour convenience. *Casas de cambio* (money exchange houses), located throughout town, offer longer hours than the banks with only slightly lower exchange rates.

Drugstores **CMQ Farmacia,** Basilio Badillo 365 (© **22/222-1330**), is open 24 hours and makes free deliveries to hotels between 11am and 10pm with a minimum purchase of $20 (£10). **Farmacias Guadalajara,** Emiliano Zapata 232 (© **322/224-1811**), is also open 24 hours.

Embassies & Consulates The **U.S. Consular Agency** office (© **322/222-0069;** fax 322/223-0074; 24 hr. a day for emergencies) is located in Nuevo Vallarta, in the Paradise Plaza, Local L-7, on the second floor. It's open Monday through Friday from 8:30am to 12:30pm. The **Canadian Consulate** (© **322/293-0099** or -0098; 24-hr. emergency line 01-800/706-2900 in Mexico) is located in Plaza Las Glorias, 1951 Blvd. Francisco Medina Ascencio, Edificio Obelisco, Loc. 108 (you'll see the Canadian flag hanging from the balcony). It's open Monday through Friday from 9am to 3pm.

Emergencies **Police** emergency, © **060;** local police, © **322/290-0513** or -0512; intensive care **ambulance,** © **322/225-0386** (*Note:* English-speaking assistance is not always available at this number); **Cruz Roja (Red Cross),** © **322/222-1533; Global Life Ambulance Service** (provides both ground and air ambulance service), © **322/226-1010,** ext. 304.

Hospitals The following offer U.S.-standards service and are available 24 hours: **Ameri-Med Urgent Care,** Avenida Francisco Medina Ascencio at Plaza Neptuno, Loc. D-1, Marina Vallarta (© **322/221-0023;** fax 322/221-0026; www.amerimed-hospitals.com); **San Javier Marina Hospital,** Av. Francisco Medina Ascencio 2760, Zona Hotelera (© **322/226-1010**), and **Cornerstone Hospital,** Av. los Tules 136 (behind Plaza Caracol; © **322/224-9400**).

Internet Access Puerto Vallarta is probably Mexico's most wired destination. **Café.com** (© **322/222-0092**), Olas Altas 250, at the corner of Basilio Badillo, charges $2 (£1) for 30 minutes. It offers complete computer services, a full bar, and food service. It's open daily from 8am to 2am. Some hotels have lobby e-mail kiosks, but they're more expensive than the Net cafes.

Newspapers & Magazines ***Vallarta Today,*** a daily English-language newspaper (© **322/225-3323** or 224-2829), is a good source for local information and upcoming events. The bilingual quarterly city magazine ***Vallarta Lifestyles*** (© **322/221-0106**) is also very popular. Both are for sale at area newsstands and hotel gift shops. The weekly English-language *P.V. Tribune* (© **322/223-0585**) is distributed free throughout town and offers an objective local viewpoint.

Post Office The *correo* is at Colombia Street, behind Hidalgo park, and is open Monday through Friday from 9am to 6pm, Saturday from 9am to 1pm.

Safety Puerto Vallarta enjoys a very low crime rate. Public transportation is safe to use, and Tourist Police (dressed in white safari uniforms with white hats) are available to answer questions, give directions, and offer assistance. Most encounters with the police are linked to using or purchasing drugs—so don't (see chapter 3). *Note:* The tourist police conduct random personal searches for drugs. Although there is some question about their right to do this, the best course of action if they want to frisk you is to comply—objecting will likely result in a free tour of the local jail. However, you are within your rights to request the name of the officer. Report any unusual incidents to the local consular office.

BEACHES, ACTIVITIES & EXCURSIONS

Travel agencies can provide information on what to see and do in Puerto Vallarta and can arrange tours, fishing trips, and other activities. Most hotels have a tour desk on-site. Of the many travel agencies in town, I highly recommend **Tukari Servicios Turísticos,** Av. España 316 ((*C*) **322/224-7177;** fax 322/224-2350; www.tukari.com), which specializes in ecological and cultural tours. Another source is **Xplora Adventours** ((*C*) **322/223-0661**), in the Huichol Collection shop on the *malecón.* It has listings of all locally available tours, with photos, explanations, and costs; however, be aware that a timeshare resort owns the company, so part of the information you receive will be an invitation to a presentation, which you may decline. **American Express Travel Services,** Morelos 660 ((*C*) **322/223-2955**), also has a varied selection of high-quality, popular tours. One of the tour companies with the largest—and best quality—selection of boat cruises and land tours is **Vallarta Adventures** *&&&* ((*C*) **888/303-2653** in the U.S., or 322/297-1212, ext. 3; www.vallarta-adventures. com). I can highly recommend any of their offerings. Book with them directly and get a 10% discount when you mention Frommer's.

THE BEACHES

For years, beaches were Puerto Vallarta's main attraction. Although visitors today are exploring more of the surrounding geography, the sands are still a powerful draw. Over 42km (26 miles) of beaches extend around the broad Bay of Banderas, ranging from action-packed party spots to secluded coves accessible only by boat.

IN TOWN   The easiest to reach is **Playa Los Muertos** (also known as Playa Olas Altas or Playa del Sol), just off Calle Olas Altas, south of the Río Cuale. The water can be rough, but the wide beach is home to a diverse array of *palapa* restaurants that offer food, beverage, and beach-chair service. The most popular are the adjacent El Dorado and La Palapa, at the end of Pulpito Street. On the southern end of this beach is a section known as "Blue Chairs"—the most popular gay beach. Vendors stroll Los Muertos, and beach volleyball, parasailing, and jet-skiing are all popular pastimes. The **Hotel Zone** is also known for its broad, smooth beaches, accessible primarily through the hotel lobbies.

SOUTH OF TOWN   **Playa Mismaloya** is in a beautiful sheltered cove about 10km (6 miles) south of town along Highway 200. The water is clear and beautiful, ideal for snorkeling off the beach. Entrance to the public beach is just to the left of the **Barceló La Jolla de Mismaloya** ((*C*) **322/226-0600**). The movie *Night of the Iguana* was filmed at Mismaloya, and the resort has a restaurant on the restored film set—**La Noche de la Iguana Set Restaurant,** open daily from noon to 11pm. The movie runs continuously in a room below the restaurant, and still photos from the filming hang in the restaurant. The restaurant is accessible by land on the point framing the south side of the cove. Just below the restaurant is **John Huston's Bar & Grill,** serving drinks and light snacks daily from 11am to 6pm.

The beach at **Boca de Tomatlán,** just down the road, has numerous *palapa* restaurants where you can relax for the day—you buy drinks, snacks, or lunch, and you can use their chairs and *palapa* shade.

The two beaches are accessible by public buses, which depart from the corner of Basilio Badillo and Insurgentes every 15 minutes from 5:30am to 10pm and cost just 50¢ (25p).

Las Animas, Quimixto, and **Yelapa** beaches are the most secluded, accessible only by boat (see "Getting Around," above, for information about water-taxi service). They are larger than Mismaloya, offer intriguing hikes to jungle waterfalls, and are similarly set up, with restaurants fronting a wide beach. Overnight stays are available at Yelapa (see "Side Trips from Puerto Vallarta," later in this chapter).

NORTH OF TOWN   The beaches at **Marina Vallarta** are the least desirable in the area, with darker sand and seasonal inflows of stones.

The entire northern coastline from Bucerías to Punta Mita is a succession of sandy coves alternating with rocky inlets. For years the beaches to the north, with their long, clean breaks, have been the favored locale for surfers. The broad, sandy stretches at **Playa Anclote, Playa Piedras Blancas,** and **Playa Destiladeras,** which all have *palapa* restaurants, have made them favorites with local residents looking for a quick getaway—but come soon, because this area is slated for luxury development, easy access to these shores is likely to be limited in the coming years. At Playa Anclote, you'll find a broad, sandy beach with protected swimming areas and a few great *palapa* restaurants. Of the restaurants, El Anclote and El Dorado have been the long-standing favorites, but **Café des Artistes del Mar** (© **329/291-5414**), which opened in early 2008, has brought Vallarta's most renowned chef and his award-winning restaurant to these northern shores. It's open Tuesday to Sunday from 1pm to 10pm; in summer from 1 to 9pm. It's located on Ave. Anclote, in the Punta de Mita Beach Club. Choose dining on Chef Thierry Blouet's specialties either on an outdoor, beachfront terrace, or in a tranquil indoor, all-white setting.

You can also hire a *panga* (small motorized boat) at Playa Anclote from the fisherman's cooperative on the beach. Ask the captain to take you to the **Marietas Islands** 🏝🏝🏝 just offshore. These uninhabited islands are a great place for bird-watching, diving, snorkeling, or just exploring. Blue-footed booby birds (found only here and in the Galapagos) dawdle along the islands' rocky coast, and giant mantas, sea turtles, and colorful tropical fish swim among the coral cliffs. The islands are honeycombed with caves and hidden beaches—including the stunning Playa de Amor (Beach of Love) that only appears at low tide. You enter a shallow passageway to access this semicircular stretch of sand. A cave 12m (40 ft.) below the surface has an air pocket in which divers can remove their regulators and have an underwater conversation. Humpback whales congregate around these islands during the winter months, and *pangas* can be rented for a do-it-yourself whale-watching excursion. Trips cost about $35 (£18) per hour. You can also visit these islands aboard one of the numerous day cruises that depart from the cruise-ship terminal in Puerto Vallarta.

The stellar white-sand beaches of **Punta Mita,** home of the Four Seasons and St. Regis resorts, are closed to road access, except for owners in and guests of this residential resort development.

ORGANIZED TOURS
BOAT TOURS   Puerto Vallarta offers a number of boat trips, including sunset cruises and snorkeling, swimming, and diving excursions. They generally travel one of two routes: to the **Marietas Islands,** a 30- to 45-minute boat ride off the northern shore of Banderas Bay, or to **Yelapa, Las Animas,** or **Quimixto** along the southern shore. The trips to the southern beaches make a stop at **Los Arcos,** an island rock formation south of Puerto Vallarta, for snorkeling. Don't base your opinion of underwater Puerto Vallarta on this, though—dozens of tour boats dump quantities of

snorkelers overboard at the same time each day, exactly when the fish know *not* to be there. It is, however, an excellent site for night diving. When comparing boat cruises, note that some include lunch, while most provide music and an open bar on board. Most leave around 9:30am, stop for 45 minutes of snorkeling, and arrive at the beach destination around noon for a 2½-hour stay before returning around 3pm. At Quimixto and Yelapa, visitors can take a half-hour hike to a jungle waterfall or rent a horse for the ride. Prices range from $45 (£23) for a sunset cruise or a trip to one of the beaches with open bar, to $85 (£43) for an all-day outing with open bar and meals.

One boat, the *Marigalante* (✆ **322/223-0309;** www.marigalante.com.mx), is an exact replica of Columbus's ship the *Santa María,* built in honor of the 500th anniversary of his voyage to the Americas. It features a daytime "Pirate Land" Morning Cruise daily from 8am until 3:30pm ($85/£43 per person), complete with breakfast, picnic barbecue and treasure hunt, as well as a sunset dinner (adult oriented) cruise from 6 to 10pm ($85/£43 per person) with fireworks and dance party. Children 3 to 11 are half-price (children younger than 2 are free).

One of the best outings is a day trip to **Caletas** ✯✯, the cove where John Huston made his home for years. **Vallarta Adventures** (✆ **888/303-2653** in the U.S., or 322/297-1212, ext. 3; www.vallarta-adventures.com) holds the exclusive lease on the private cove and has done an excellent job of restoring Huston's former home, adding exceptional day-spa facilities, and landscaping the beach, which is wonderful for snorkeling. They also have a colony of sea lions that play with the visiting divers. You'll have a hard time deciding whether to kayak, take a yoga class, hike through surrounding trails, or simply relax in the hammocks strung between palms on the beach. The facilities and relative privacy have made this excursion ($85/£43 per person; $60/£30 for children 4 to 11) one of the most popular. The evening cruise includes dinner and a spectacular contemporary dance show, "Rhythms of the Night" (see "Puerto Vallarta after Dark," later in this chapter).

Travel agencies sell tickets and distribute information on all cruises. If you prefer to spend more time at Yelapa or Las Animas without snorkeling and cruise entertainment, see the information about water taxis earlier in this chapter, under "Getting Around."

Whale-watching tours become more popular each year. Viewing humpback whales is almost a certainty from mid- to late November to March. The majestic whales have migrated to this bay for centuries (in the 17th c. it was called "Humpback Bay") to bear their calves. The noted local authority is **Open Air Expeditions,** Guerrero 339 (✆/fax **322/222-3310;** www.vallartawhales.com). It offers ecologically oriented, oceanologist-guided 4-hour tours on the soft boat *Prince of Whales,* the only boat in Vallarta specifically designed for whale-watching. Cost is $85 (£43) for adults, $50 (£25) for children 5 to 10, and travel is in a group of up to 12. Twice-daily departures (8:30am and 1:30pm) include a healthful snack. **Vallarta Adventures** (see above) offers a variety of whale-watching excursions that may combine time for snorkeling, or simply focus on photographing these exquisite mammals. Prices range from $75 to $85 (£38–£43), and offer a choice of boats—from small boats (to bring you closest for photos) to graceful sailboats. All trips include a predeparture briefing on whale behavior. They also have a "scouting plane" flying the bay to site the whales from the air, and then they direct their boats to the location.

LAND TOURS **Tukari Servicios Turísticos** (see "Beaches, Activities & Excursions," above) can arrange trips to the fertile birding grounds near **San Blas,** 3 to 4 hours north of Puerto Vallarta in the state of Nayarit, and shopping trips to **Tlaquepaque** and

Tonalá (6 hr. inland, near Guadalajara). A day trip to **Rancho Altamira,** a 20-hectare (50-acre) working ranch, includes a barbecue lunch and horseback riding, then a stroll through **El Tuito,** a small nearby Colonial-Era village. The company can also arrange an unforgettable morning at **Terra Noble Art & Healing Center** 🌟🌟 (© 322/223-3530 or 222-5400; www.terranoble.com), a mountaintop day spa and center for the arts where participants can get a massage, *temazcal* (ancient, indigenous sweat lodge), or treatment; work in clay and paint; and have lunch in a heavenly setting overlooking the bay. Call ahead for reservations, and make sure to advise if you want to have lunch there.

Hotel travel desks and travel agencies, including Tukari and American Express, can also book the popular **Tropical Tour** or **Jungle Tour** ($40/£20), a basic orientation to the area. These excursions are expanded city tours that include a drive through the workers' village of Pitillal, the affluent neighborhood of Conchas Chinas, the cathedral, the market, the Taylor-Burton houses, and lunch at a jungle restaurant. Any stop for shopping usually means the driver picks up a commission for what you buy.

The **Sierra Madre Expedition** is another excellent tour offered by **Vallarta Adventures** (see "Boat Tours," above). The daily excursion travels in Mercedes all-terrain vehicles north of Puerto Vallarta through jungle trails, stops at a small town, ventures into a forest for a brief nature walk, and winds up on a pristine secluded beach for lunch and swimming. The $80 (£40) outing is worthwhile because it takes tourists on exclusive trails into scenery that would otherwise be off-limits.

AIR TOURS You can explore some of the most remote and undiscovered reaches of the Sierra Madre mountains in Vallarta Adventures' **San Sebastián Air Expedition** (© 888/303-2653 in the U.S., or 322/297-1212, ext. 3; www.vallarta-adventures. com). A 15-minute flight aboard a 14-seat turbo-prop Cessna Caravan takes you into the heart of the Sierra Madre. The plane is equipped with raised wings, which allow you to admire—and photograph—the mountain scenery. The plane arrives on a gravel landing strip in the beautiful town of San Sebastián, which dates from 1603. One of the oldest mining towns in Mexico, it reached its prosperous peak in the 1800s, with over 30,000 inhabitants. Today, San Sebastián remains an outstanding example of how people lived and worked in a remote Mexican mountain town—it's a living museum. The half-day adventure costs $155 (£78), which covers the flight, a walking tour of the town (including a stop at the old Hacienda Jalisco, a favored getaway of John Huston, Liz and Dick, and their friends), and brunch in town. Other excursions include overnight stays and return trips by bike or horseback. If you prefer more leisurely travel, they offer a similar tour that takes you by land in air-conditioned minivans for the 90-minute drive up the mountains, for $75 (£38) per person. Another **bus tour** to San Sebastián, which costs $75 (£38) per person and includes a guide, departs at 9am and returns at 5pm. Call **Pacific Travel** (© 322/225-2270) to make reservations.

Vallarta Adventures (see "Boat Tours," above) also offers a similar, yet different, air tour to the mountain villages of **Mascota** and **Talpa de Allende** 🌟🌟, where you'll learn about the religious significance of these traditional towns. In Mascota, stroll the cobblestone streets lined with adobe houses and colonial haciendas, stopping at the majestic town church, dedicated to the Virgen de los Dolores (Virgin of Sorrows), which was completed in 1880 and took more than 100 years to construct. You'll stop for lunch and tour a local *raicilla* distillery to sample this locally popular beverage before traveling on to Talpa. Talpa is known for being home to one of Mexico's most revered icons, the Virgen Rosario de Talpa, believed to grant miracles with her healing powers. Ask for one yourself, as you visit the Gothic church that bears her name, or simply wander around this pastoral village, set in a valley that is surrounded by pine-covered mountains. The 6-hour adventure includes airfare and lunch, for $175 (£88) per person. Departures are Mondays and Wednesdays at 10:30am, from the Aerotron private airport (adjacent to the Puerto Vallarta International Airport).

Vallarta Adventures also offers air tours to remote mountain villages where the **Huichol Indians** live (Fri departures, $210/£105 per person), as well as to the **Copper Canyon,** and the mystical village of **Mexcaltitan** (Mon departures, $255/£128 per person), all departing from Puerto Vallarta. Details and online booking options are available at **www.vallarta-adventures.com**.

TOURS IN TOWN   Every Tuesday, Wednesday, and Thursday in high season (late Nov–Easter), the **International Friendship Club** (ⓒ 322/222-5466) offers a **private home tour** of four villas in town. It costs $35 (£18) per person, with proceeds donated to local charities. Arrive early, because this tour sells out quickly. It starts at the Hotel Posada Río Cuale, adjacent to the southbound bridge over the Río Cuale. Get there at 10am, and you can buy breakfast while you wait for the group to gather. The tour departs at 10:30am and lasts approximately 3½ hours. Also ask them about a new tour of the exquisite villas on the north shore.

Galería Pacífico owner Gary Thompson hosts a tour of the **Public Sculptures** of the *malecón,* each Tuesday at 9:30am, from December through April. For a couple of hours, you'll stroll the *malecón* learning about the artists who created Vallarta's most visible art, and their inspirations. Frequently, Gary is joined by one or more of the artists on this tour. For more details, contact the gallery at ⓒ 322/221-1982.

STAYING ACTIVE

DIVING & SNORKELING   Underwater enthusiasts, from beginner to expert, can arrange scuba diving or snorkeling through **Vallarta Adventures** (ⓒ 888/303-2653 in the U.S., or 322/297-1212, ext. 3; www.vallarta-adventures.com), a five-star PADI dive center. You may snorkel or dive at Los Arcos, a company-owned site at Caletas Cove (where you'll dive in the company of sea lions), Quimixto Coves, the Marietas Islands, or the offshore La Corbeteña, Morro, and Chimo reefs. The company runs a full range of certification courses (up to Instructor). **Chico's Dive Shop,** Díaz Ordaz 772–5, near Carlos O'Brian's (ⓒ 322/222-1895; www.chicos-diveshop.com), offers similar diving and snorkeling trips and is also a PADI five-star dive center. Chico's is open daily from 8am to 10pm, with branches at the Marriott, Las Palmas, Holiday Inn, Fiesta Americana, Krystal, San Marino, Villa del Palmar, Paradise Village, and Playa Los Arcos. You can also snorkel off the beaches at Mismaloya and Boca de Tomatlán; elsewhere, there's not much to see besides a sandy bottom.

ECOTOURS & ACTIVITIES   Open Air Expeditions (ⓒ/fax 322/222-3310; www.vallartawhales.com) offers nature-oriented trips, including birding and ocean kayaking in Punta Mita. **Ecotours de México,** Ignacio L. Vallarta 243 (ⓒ/fax 322/222-6606), has eco-oriented tours, including seasonal (Aug–Dec) trips to a turtle preservation camp where you can witness hatching baby Olive Ridley turtles.

A popular Vallarta adventure activity is **canopy tours.** You glide from treetop to treetop, getting an up-close-and-personal look at a tropical rainforest canopy and the trails far below. Expert guides assist you to the special platforms, and you move from one to another using pulleys on horizontal traverse cables, while the guides explain the tropical flora surrounding you. They also offer assistance—and moral support—as you rappel back down to the forest floor. Tours depart from the **Vallarta Adventures** (see "Diving & Snorkeling," above) offices in both Marina Vallarta and Nuevo Vallarta at 8am, returning at 2pm. The price ($79/£40 for adults, $69/£35 for children 8–12) includes the tour, unlimited nonalcoholic beverages, and light snacks. Their **Outdoor Adventure** combines a ride on the canopy line with a day of adventure activities. You'll learn wilderness survival techniques while hiking through the Sierra Madre foothills, splashing through streams, rappelling down waterfalls, then taking a 300m (984-ft.) zip line over jungle landscape. The 6½ hour tour costs $95 (£48), for those who are physically fit, ages 12 and older.

A second option is available in the southern jungles of Vallarta, over the Orquidias River, through **Canopy Tours de Los Veranos** (© 322/223-6060; www.canopytours-vallarta.com). This tour will pick you up at the Canopy office, near the south side Pemex station, to transport you to their facilities upriver from Mismaloya. Departures are on the hour, from 9am to 2pm. In addition to the 13 cables—the longest being a full 350m (1,148 ft.)—it also offers climbing walls, waterslides, and horseback riding. The guides here are noted for helping even the faintest of heart propel through the treetops. Price is $79 (£40) for adults, or $58 (£29) for children ages 6 and older. Use of the natural-granite climbing wall (helmets and climbing-shoe use included) is $18 (£9); the 1½-hour jungle horseback riding tour costs $35 (£18).

FISHING   Arrange fishing trips through travel agencies or through the **Cooperativa de Pescadores (Fishing Cooperative),** on the *malecón* north of the Río Cuale, next door to the Rosita Hotel (© 322/222-1202). Fishing charters cost $120 (£60) per person, for one to eight people; or select from other options where the price varies with the size of the boat; a boat can be rented for 8 hours for $450 (£225). Although the posted price at the fishing cooperative is the same as you'll find through travel agencies, you may be able to negotiate a lower price at the cooperative, which does not accept credit cards. It's open Monday through Sunday from 7am to 10pm, but make arrangements a day ahead. You can also arrange fishing trips at the Marina Vallarta docks, or by calling **Fishing with Carolina** (© 322/224-7250; cell 044-322/292-2953; fishingwithcarolina@hotmail.com), which uses a 9m (30-ft.) Uniflite sportsfisher, fully equipped with an English-speaking crew. Fishing trips cost $350 (£175) for up to four people for 4 hours and include equipment and bait, but drinks, snacks, and lunch are optional, at $15 (£7.50) per person. If you mention Frommer's when you make your reservation, they'll offer a free lunch with your booking. All boats have brand new engines.

GOLF   Puerto Vallarta is an increasingly popular golf destination; six courses have opened in the past 7 years, bringing the total in the region to nine. The Joe Finger–designed private course at the **Marina Vallarta Golf Club** (© 322/221-0073) is an 18-hole, par-74 course that winds through the Marina Vallarta peninsula and affords ocean views. It's for members only, but most luxury hotels in Puerto Vallarta have memberships for their guests. Greens fees are $98 to $136 (£49–£68) in high season, $115 (£58) in low season. Fees include golf cart, range balls, and tax. A caddy costs $12 (£6). Club rentals, lessons, and special packages are available.

North of town in the state of Nayarit, about 15km (9⅓ miles) beyond Puerto Vallarta, is the 18-hole, par-72 **Los Flamingos Club de Golf** (© 329/296-5006; www.flamingosgolf.com.mx). It features beautiful jungle vegetation; the course underwent a renovation and upgrade in 2005. It's open from 7am to 7pm daily, with a snack bar (no restaurant) and full pro shop. The daylight greens fee is $140 (£70), which drops to $90 (£45) after 2:30pm. It includes the use of a golf cart; hiring a caddy costs $20 (£10) plus tip, and club rental is $30 to $44 (£15–£22). A free shuttle runs from downtown Puerto Vallarta; call for pickup times and locations.

There are now two breathtaking Jack Nicklaus Signature courses at the **Punta Mita Golf Club** ✦✦✦ (© **329/291-6000;** fax 329/291-6060), with the newest addition opening in October 2008. The original "Pacifico" course features 8 oceanfront holes and an ocean view from every hole. Its hallmark is the 3rd hole, the "Tail of the Whale," with a long drive to a green on a natural island—the only natural-island green in the Americas. It requires an amphibious cart to take you over when the tide is high, and there's an alternate hole for when the ocean or tides are not accommodating. The second Jack Nicklaus Signature course, "Bahia," intertwines with the original course, and also affords stunning seaside holes; its finishing hole is adjacent to the new St. Regis Resort. The courses are open only to members or guests staying in the Punta Mita resorts, or to other golf club members with a letter of introduction from their pro. Greens fees are $244 (£122) for 18 holes and $156 (£78) for 9 holes, including cart, with (Calloway) club rentals for $63 (£32). Lessons are also available.

Another Jack Nicklaus course is located at the **Vista Vallarta Golf Club** (© **322/290-0030;** www.vistavallartagolf.com), along with one designed by Tom Weiskopf. These courses were the site of the 2002 PGA World Cup Golf Championships. The club is the foothills of the Sierra Madre, behind the bullring in Puerto Vallarta. A round costs $174 (£87) per person. Cart fee is an extra $46 (£23), with club rentals available for $49 (£25) per set/per round.

The Robert von Hagge–designed **El Tigre** course at Paradise Village (© **866/843-5951** in the U.S., or **322/297-0773;** www.paradisevillage.com; www.eltigregolf.com), in Nuevo Vallarta, opened in March 2002. The 7,239-yard course is on a relatively flat piece of land, but the design incorporates challenging bunkers, undulating fairways, and water features on several holes. The favored course of local pros, El Tigre offers lessons and has an expansive clubhouse. Greens fees are $145 (£73) a round, or $90 (£45) if you play after 2pm. Club rentals are $45 (£23).

HORSEBACK-RIDING TOURS   Travel agents and local ranches can arrange guided horseback rides. **Rancho Palma Real,** Carretera Vallarta, Tepic 4766 (© **322/222-0501**), has an office 5 minutes north of the airport; the ranch is in Las Palmas, 40 minutes northeast of Vallarta. It is by far the nicest horseback riding tour in the area. The horses are in excellent condition, and you enjoy a tour of local farms on your way to the ranch. The price ($60/£30; AE or cash only) includes breakfast and lunch.

Another excellent option is **Rancho El Charro,** Av. Francisco Villa 895 (© **322/224-0114;** cell 044-322/294-1689; www.ranchoelcharro.com), which has beautiful, well-cared for horses, and a variety of rides for all levels, departing from their ranch at the base of the Sierra Madre Mountains. Rides range in length from 3 to 8 hours, and in price from $56 to $100 (£28–£50). There's even the $69 (£35) Wild Ride, where you gallop along a ridge to a jungle waterfall—too often, riders are disappointed with only trotting along well-marked trails on these excursions, and this ride allows experienced riders much more freedom. Rancho El Charro also has multiple-day rides— check their website for details. **Rancho Ojo de Agua,** Cerrada de Cardenal 227, Fracc. Las Aralias (©/fax **322/224-0607;** www.mexonline.com), also offers high-quality tours, from its ranch located 10 minutes by taxi north of downtown toward the Sierra Madre foothills. The rides last 3 hours (10am, 3 and 4pm departures) and take you up into the mountains overlooking the ocean and town. The cost is $59 (£30). Both of the ranches listed above have other tours available as well as their own comfortable base camp for serious riders who want to stay out overnight.

PARASAILING   Parasailing and other watersports are available at many beaches along the Bay of Banderas. The most popular spot is at Los Muertos Beach. WaveRunners, banana boats, and parasailing are available by the hour, half-day, or full day. Be forewarned, however, that the swiftly shifting winds in Banderas Bay can make this a dangerous proposition. Fly at your own risk.

SAILING   I personally believe that a trip to the Vallarta area is not complete without a journey out on the water—there's no better way to see the entirety of the area, the beauty of the surrounding mountains, and get a sense of the area than from the perspective of a sailboat. Banderas Bay is increasingly being used at the site of national and international regatta competitions.

Coming About ★★ (© 322/222-4119; www.coming-about.com) is a women-only sailing school that provides hands-on sailing instruction for day-sailing excursions, as well as weeklong sailing classes at a variety of skill levels. Owned and operated by Pat Henry, who spent 8 years sailing around the globe, then wrote about it in her book *By the Grace of the Sea: A Woman's Solo Odyssey Around the World.* The classes are challenging, inspiring, and entertaining, as Pat shares her adventures with participants. Dubbed "any woman's sailing school," the goal is to take away the fear and mystery, and make the skill of sailing accessible to everyone. Courses range from a 1-day introductory course to a 9-day bareboat charter captain course. Fees for the 1-day course are $475 (£238) for four people; $2,900 to $3,600 (£1,450–£1,800) per person, based on double occupancy, for the 9-day course, including hotel.

SWIMMING WITH DOLPHINS   Dolphin Adventure ★★★ (© 888/303-2653 in the U.S., or 322/297-1212, ext. 3; www.vallarta-adventures.com) operates an interactive dolphin-research facility—considered the finest in Latin America—that allows limited numbers of people to swim with dolphins Monday through Saturday at scheduled times. Cost for the swim is $142 (£71). Reservations are required, and they generally sell out at least a week in advance. **Dolphin Encounter** ($76/£38) allows you to touch and learn about the dolphins in smaller pools, so you're ensured up-close-and-personal time with them. You can even be a **Trainer for a Day,** a special 7-hour program of working alongside the more experienced trainers and the dolphins, for a cost of $250 (£125). The **Dolphin Kids** program, for children ages 4 to 8, is a gentle introduction to dolphins, featuring the Dolphin Adventure baby dolphins and their mothers interacting with the children participants ($60/£30). I give this my highest recommendation. Not only does the experience leave you with an indescribable sensation, but it's also a joy to see these dolphins—they are well cared for, happy, and spirited. The program is about education and interaction, not entertainment or amusement, and is especially popular with children ages 10 and older.

Tips A Spectator Sport

Bullfights are held December through April beginning at 5pm on Wednesday at the La Paloma bullring, across the highway from the town pier. Travel agencies can arrange tickets, which cost around $25 (£13).

Moments **A Spectacular Sight**

Performances of the **Voladores de Papantla (Papantla Flyers)** take place daily at 10 and 11am; and in the evenings, Friday to Wednesday at 7:30, 8:30, and 9:30pm on the *malecón*, adjacent to the "Boy on a Seahorse" statue. In this pre-Columbian religious ritual, four men are suspended from the top of a tall pole, circling it as though in flight, while another beats a drum and plays a flute while balancing himself at the top. It signifies the four cardinal points, and the mystic "center" of the self, a sacred direction for ancient Mexican cultures.

TENNIS   Many hotels in Puerto Vallarta offer excellent tennis facilities; they often have clay courts. The full-service **Canto del Sol Tennis Club** (*©* **322/224-0123** and 322/226-0123; www.cantodelsol.com) is at the Canto del Sol hotel in the Hotel Zone. It offers indoor and outdoor courts (including a clay court), full pro shop, lessons, clinics, and partner matches.

A STROLL THROUGH TOWN

Puerto Vallarta's cobblestone streets are a pleasure to explore; they're full of tiny shops, rows of windows edged with curling wrought iron, and vistas of red-tile roofs and the sea. Start with a walk up and down the *malecón*.

Among the sights you shouldn't miss is the **municipal building** on the main square (next to the tourism office), which has a large Manuel Lepe mural inside in its stairwell. Nearby, right up Independencia, sits the picturesque **Parish of Nuestra Señora de Guadalupe church,** Hidalgo 370 (*©* **322/222-1326**), topped with a curious crown held in place by angels—a replica of the one worn by Empress Carlota during her brief time in Mexico as Emperor Maximilian's wife. On its steps, women sell religious mementos; across the narrow street, stalls sell native herbs for curing common ailments. Services in English are held each Saturday at 5pm, and Sunday at 10am. Regular hours are Monday through Saturday from 7:30am to 8:30pm, Sunday from 6:30am to 8:30pm. Note that entrance is restricted to those properly attired—no shorts or sleeveless shirts allowed. Three blocks south of the church, head east on Libertad, lined with small shops and pretty upper windows, to the **municipal market** by the river. (It's the Río Cuale Mercado, but I once overheard a tourist ask for the "real quality" market.) After exploring the market, cross the bridge to the island in the river; sometimes a painter is at work on its banks. Walk down the center of the island toward the sea, and you'll come to the tiny **Museo Río Cuale** (no phone; Mon–Sat 10am–5pm; free admission), which has a small but impressive permanent exhibit of pre-Columbian figurines.

Retrace your steps to the market and Libertad, and follow Calle Miramar to the brightly colored steps up to Zaragoza. Up Zaragoza to the right 1 block is the famous **pink arched bridge** that once connected Richard Burton's and Elizabeth Taylor's houses. In this area, known as **"Gringo Gulch,"** many Americans have houses.

SHOPPING

For years, shopping in Puerto Vallarta was concentrated in small, eclectic, independent shops rather than impersonal malls. In the past 2 years, however, this has changed, with the addition of large, modern shopping centers between the Marina and hotel

Downtown Puerto Vallarta

PACIFIC OCEAN
Puerto Vallarta
JALISCO
Barra de Navidad
MICHOACÁN
Mexico City ★

0   200 mi
0   200 km

Bahía de Banderas

Rep. de Chile
Venezuela
Argentina
Parque Hidalgo
J. Langarica
31 de Octubre
Allende
Pipila
L. Vicario
J.O. Domínguez
Morelos
Juárez
Abasolo
Corona
Aldama
Hidalgo
Galeana
Mina
Miramar
E. Carranza
Morelos
Iturbide
Matamoros
Zócalo
Zaragoza
Libertad
Guerrero
A. Rodríguez
Encino
Cuauhtémoc
Río Cuale
Isla del Río Cuale
Aquiles Serdán
Lucero
Invierno
Lázaro Cárdenas
Aguacate
V. Carranza
Napanjo
Constitución
Insurgentes
Pino Suárez
Olas Altas
Vallarta
Basilio Badillo
Manuel M. Dieguez
Francisco Rodríguez
Rodolfo Gómez
Jacarandas
Pulpito
Libramiento

Playa Los Muertos Pier (water taxi)
R. Gómez
Pulpito
Pilitas
Amapas

Paseo Díaz Ordaz / El Malecón
G. Sánchez
Matamoros

0   1/8 mi
0   125 meters
N

zone areas. I'd recommended sticking with the former—the small shops tucked along cobblestone streets in Vallarta's central downtown areas, for a more memorable experience, and more unique goods. Here you can find excellent **folk art,** original **clothing** designs, fine jewelry, and creative home accessories at great prices. Vallarta is known for having the most diverse and impressive selection of **contemporary Mexican fine art** outside Mexico City. It also has an abundance of tacky T-shirts and the ubiquitous **silver jewelry.**

THE SHOPPING SCENE

The key shopping areas are central downtown, the Marina Vallarta *malecón,* the popular *mercados,* and the beach—where the merchandise comes to you. Some of the more attractive shops are 1 to 2 blocks in **back of the *malecón.*** Start at the intersection of Corona and Morelos streets—interesting shops spread out in all directions from here. **Marina Vallarta** has two shopping plazas, Plaza Marina and Neptuno Plaza, on the main highway from the airport into town, which offer a limited selection of shops, with Plaza Neptuno primarily featuring home decor shops. Although still home to a few interesting shops, the *marina malecón* (marina boardwalk) is dominated by real estate companies, timeshare vendors, restaurants, and boating services. A recent (Sept 2006) addition to Vallarta's shopping and dining scene is the modern **Plaza Peninsula** (located on Av. Francisco Medina Ascencio 2485, just south of the cruise ship terminal and north of the Ameca River bridge; no phone number or website), in front of a large waterfront condominium development of the same name. It's home to more than 30 businesses including Vallarta's first **Starbuck's,** as well as art galleries, boutiques, and a varied selection of restaurants. There is underground parking, plus public sculptures and comfy outdoor seating. It has quickly emerged as Vallarta's current hotspot for hanging out in the evenings, especially with teens. The newest retail addition, as of November 2007, is the **Centro Comerical Galerias Vallarta** (on Av. Francisco Medina Ascencio 2920, adjacent to Wal-Mart and directly across from the cruise ship terminal; © **322/209-1520**), a large shopping and entertainment mall anchored by the high-end Mexican department store Liverpool. It also has a variety of boutiques including Lacoste, Levis, Hugo Boss, and Bennetton. Among the selections for dining are Applebee's, Chili's, and Sirloin Stokade. For entertainment, there's a 10-screen movie theatre. The mall is open daily from 8am to 2am; most stores are open from 11am to 9pm. There is ample underground parking.

Puerto Vallarta's **municipal market** is just north of the Río Cuale, where Libertad and A. Rodríguez meet. The *mercado* sells clothes, jewelry, serapes, shawls, leather accessories and suitcases, papier-mâché parrots, stuffed frogs and armadillos, and, of course, T-shirts. Be sure to comparison-shop, and definitely bargain before buying. The market is open daily from 9am to 7pm. Upstairs, a **food market** serves inexpensive Mexican meals—for more adventurous diners, it's probably the best value and most authentic dining experience in Vallarta. An **outdoor market** is along Río Cuale Island, between the two bridges. Stalls sell crafts, gifts, folk art, and clothing. New to downtown is the **Small Vallarta** (© **322/222-7530**) on Paseo Díaz Ordaz 928, on the eastern side, just before the start of the *malecón.* It is a "small mall" featuring tourist-friendly shops and dining options, including Carl's Jr.'s burgers, Häagen-Dazs ice cream, Swatch watch shop, El Mundo de Tequila, and a Diamonds International jewelry store.

In most of the better shops and galleries, shipping, packing, and delivery to Puerto Vallarta hotels are available. Some will also ship to your home address. Note that while

Tips Beware the Silver Scam

Much of the silver sold on the beach is actually alpaca, a lower-quality silver metal (even though many pieces are stamped with the designation ".925," supposedly indicating true silver). Prices for silver on the beach are much lower, as is the quality. If you're looking for a more lasting piece of jewelry, you're better off in a silver shop.

bargaining is expected in the *mercados* and with beach vendors, stores generally charge fixed—and fair—prices for their wares.

THE LOWDOWN ON HUICHOL INDIAN ART

Puerto Vallarta offers the best selection of Huichol art in Mexico. Descendants of the Aztec, the Huichol are one of the last remaining indigenous cultures in the world that has remained true to its ancient traditions, customs, language, and habitat. The Huichol live in adobe structures in the high Sierras (at an elevation of 1,400m/4,592 ft.) north and east of Puerto Vallarta. Due to the decreasing fertility (and therefore productivity) of the land surrounding their villages, they have come to depend more on the sale of their artwork for sustenance.

Huichol art has always been cloaked in a veil of mysticism—probably one of the reasons serious collectors seek out this form of *artesanía.* Colorful, symbolic yarn "paintings," inspired by visions experienced during spiritual ceremonies, characterize Huichol art. In the ceremonies, artists ingest peyote, a hallucinogenic cactus, which induces brightly colored visions; these are considered messages from their ancestors. The visions' symbolic and mythological imagery influences the art, which encompasses not only yarn paintings but also fascinating masks and bowls decorated with tiny colored beads.

The Huichol might be geographically isolated, but they are learning the importance of good business and have adapted their art to meet consumer demand. Original Huichol art, therefore, is not necessarily traditional. Iguanas, jaguars, sea turtles, frogs, eclipses, and eggs appear in response to consumer demand. For more traditional works, look for pieces that depict deer, scorpions, wolves, or snakes.

The Huichol have also had to modify their techniques to create more pieces in less time and meet increased demand. Patterned fill-work, which is faster to produce, sometimes replaces the detailed designs that are used to fill the pieces. The same principle applies to yarn paintings. While some are beautiful depictions of landscapes and even abstract pieces, they are not traditional themes.

You may see Huichol Indians on the streets of Vallarta—they are easy to spot, dressed in white clothing embroidered with colorful designs. A number of fine Huichol galleries are in downtown Puerto Vallarta (see individual listings under "Crafts & Gifts" and "Decorative & Folk Art," below).

One place to learn more about the Huichol is **Huichol Collection,** Morelos 490, across from the sea-horse statue on the *malecón* (© 322/223-2141). Not only does this shop offer an extensive selection of Huichol art in all price ranges, but it also has a replica of a Huichol adobe hut, informational displays explaining more about their fascinating way of life and beliefs, and usually a Huichol artist at work. However, note that this is a timeshare sales location, so don't be surprised if you're hit with a pitch for

Fun Fact **A Huichol Art Primer**

Huichol art falls into two main categories: yarn paintings and beaded pieces. All other items you might find in Huichol art galleries are either ceremonial objects or items used in everyday life.

Yarn paintings are made on a wood base covered with wax and meticulously overlaid with colored yarn. Designs represent the magical vision of the underworld, and each symbol gives meaning to the piece. Paintings made with wool yarn are more authentic than those made with acrylic; however, acrylic yarn paintings are usually brighter and more detailed because the threads are thinner. It is normal to find empty spaces where the wax base shows. Usually the artist starts with a central motif and works around it, but it's common to have several independent motifs that, when combined, take on a different meaning. A painting with many small designs tells a more complicated story than one with only one design and fill-work on the background. Look for the story of the piece on the back of the painting. Most Huichol artists write in pencil in Huichol and Spanish.

Beaded pieces are made on carved wooden shapes depicting different animals, wooden eggs, or small bowls made from gourds. The pieces are covered with wax and tiny *chaquira* beads are applied one by one to form designs. Usually the beaded designs represent animals; plants; the elements of fire, water, or air; and certain symbols that give a special meaning to the whole. Deer, snakes, wolves, and scorpions are traditional elements; other figures, such as iguanas, frogs, and any animals not indigenous to Huichol territory, are incorporated by popular demand. Beadwork with many small designs that do not exactly fit into one another is more time-consuming and has a more complex symbolic meaning. This kind of work has empty spaces where the wax shows.

a "free" breakfast and property tour. **Peyote People,** Juarez 222 (© **322/222-2302** or -6268; www.peyotepeople.com), is a more authentic shop specializing in Huichol yarn paintings and bead art from San Andres Cohamiata, one of the main villages of this indigenous group, up in the high Sierra. The shop is open Monday through Friday from 10am until 9pm and Saturday and Sunday 10am to 6pm.

CLOTHING

Vallarta's locally owned department store, **LANS,** has branches at Juárez 867 (© **322/226-9100;** www.lans.com.mx), and in Plaza Caracol, next door to the supermarket Gigante, in the Hotel Zone (© **322/226-0204**). Both offer a wide selection of name-brand clothing, accessories, footwear, cosmetics, and home furnishings. Along with the nationally popular **LOB, Carlos 'n' Charlie's,** and **Bye-Bye** brands, Vallarta offers a few distinctive shops.

Laura López Labra Designs   The most comfortable clothing you'll ever enjoy. LLL is renowned for her trademark all-white (or natural) designs in 100% cotton or lace. Laura's fine gauze fabrics float in her designs of seductive skirts, romantic dresses, blouses, beachwear, and baby dolls. Men's offerings include cotton drawstring pants and lightweight shirts. Other designs include a line of precious children's clothing and some pieces with elaborate embroidery based on Huichol Indian designs. Personalized wedding dresses are also available. Open Monday through Saturday from 10am to 3:30pm and from 5 to 9pm. Basilio Badillo 329-A. © 322/113-0102.

Mar de Sueños 🐟🐟 This small shop carries stunning swimsuits and exquisite lingerie. Without a doubt, the finest women's beachwear, intimate apparel, and evening wear in Vallarta for those special occasions—or just to make you feel extra special. The shop also stocks a selection of fine linen clothing—and it's one of the few places in Mexico that carries the renowned Italian line La Perla. Other name brands include Gottex, D&G, and DKNY. Open daily from 10am to 10pm. Basilio Badillo 277-B. © 322/222-7362.

CONTEMPORARY ART

Known for sustaining one of the stronger art communities in Latin America, Puerto Vallarta has an impressive selection of fine galleries featuring quality original works. Several dozen galleries get together to offer art walks every Wednesday from 5 to 10pm between November and April. Most of the participating galleries serve complimentary cocktails during the art walks. It's a very popular weekly event among the local expat residents.

Corsica Among the best of Vallarta's galleries, Corsica features an exquisite collection of sculptures, installations, and paintings, from world-renown contemporary artists from Mexico. They offer professional packing and worldwide shipping with purchases. There are three locations—at Guadalupe Sanchez 735, Leona Vicario 230, and Plaza Península. Open Monday through Saturday 11am to 9pm. © 322/223-1821. www.galeriacorsica.com.

Galería AL (Arte Latinoamericano) This gallery showcases contemporary works created by young, primarily Latin American artists, as well as Vallarta favorite Marta Gilbert. Feature exhibitions take place every 2 weeks during high season. The historic building (one of Vallarta's original structures) has exposed brick walls; small rooms of exhibition spaces on the second and third floors surround an open courtyard. It's also rumored to have a friendly resident ghost, who partner Susan Burger says has been quite welcoming. Open Monday through Saturday from 10am to 9pm. Josefa Ortiz Domínguez 155. © 322/222-4406. www.galeriaal.com.

Galería des Artistes This stunning gallery features contemporary painters and sculptors from throughout Mexico, including the renowned original "magiscopes" of Feliciano Bejar. Paintings by a Vallarta favorite Evelyn Boren, as well as a small selection of works by Mexican masters, including Orozco, can be found here, among the exposed brick walls and stylish interior spaces. It's open Monday to Saturday 11am to 10pm Just across the street, affiliate **Galería Omar Alonso** (© 322/222-5587; www.galeriaomaralonso.com) exhibits photography by internationally renowned artists. Open Monday through Saturday 11am to 11pm. Leona Vicario 248. © 322/223-0006.

Galería Pacífico Since opening in 1987, Galería Pacífico has been considered one of the finest in Mexico. On display is a wide selection of sculptures and paintings in various media by midrange masters and up-and-comers alike. The gallery is 1½ blocks inland from the fantasy sculptures on the *malecón*. Among the artists whose careers Galería Pacífico has influenced are rising talent Brewster Brockman, internationally renowned sculptor Ramiz Barquet, and Patrick Denoun. Open Monday through

Saturday from 10am to 8pm; Sunday by appointment. Between May and October, check for reduced hours or vacation closings. Aldama 174, 2nd floor, above La Casa del Habano cigar store. (©) **322/222-1982**. galeriapacifico@prodigy.net.mx.

Galería Uno One of Vallarta's first galleries, the Galería Uno features an excellent selection of contemporary paintings by Latin American artists, plus a variety of posters and prints. During the high season, featured exhibitions change every 2 weeks. In a classic adobe building with open courtyard, it's also a casual, salon-style gathering place for friends of owner Jan Lavender. Open Monday through Saturday from 10am to 10pm. Morelos 561 (at Corona). (©) **322/222-0908**.

Galleria Dante This gallery-in-a-villa showcases contemporary art as well as sculptures and classical reproductions of Italian, Greek, and Art Deco bronzes—against a backdrop of gardens and fountains. Works by more than 50 Mexican and international artists are represented, including the acclaimed local talent Rogelio Diaz, as well as Alejandro Colunga and Tellosa. Located on the "Calle de los Cafés," the gallery is open during the winter Monday through Saturday from 10am to 5pm, and by appointment. Basilio Badillo 269. (©) **322/222-2477**. www.galleriadante.com.

Studio Cathy Von Rohr This lovely studio showcases the work of Cathy Von Rohr, one of the most respected artists in the area. For years, Cathy lived in the secluded cove of Majahuitas, on the bay's southern shore, and much of her work reflects the tranquillity and deep connection with the natural world that resulted. Paintings, prints, and sculptures are featured. It's open by appointment and does not accept credit cards. Manuel M. Diéguez 321. (©) **866/256-2739** in the U.S., or 322/222-5875. www.cathyvonrohr.com.

CRAFTS & GIFTS

Alfarería Tlaquepaque Opened in 1953, this is Vallarta's original source for Mexican ceramics and decorative crafts, all at excellent prices. Talavera pottery and dishware, colored glassware, birdcages, baskets, and wood furniture are just a few of the many items in this warehouse-style store. Open Monday through Saturday, 9am to 9pm, and Sundays from 9am to 3pm. Av. México 1100. (©) **322/223-2121**.

La Casa del Feng Shui I am enchanted by this shop's selection of crystals, candles, talismans, fountains, and wind chimes—along with many more items designed to keep the good energy flowing in your home, office, or personal space. Why not take home something to add more harmony to your life? Open Monday through Saturday from 9am to 8pm. Corona 165, around the corner from Morelos. (©) **322/222-3300**.

Safari Accents Flickering candles glowing in colored-glass holders welcome you to this highly original shop overflowing with creative gifts, one-of-a-kind furnishings, and reproductions of paintings by Frida Kahlo and Botero. Open daily from 10am to 10pm. Olas Altas 224, Loc. 4. (©) **322/223-2660**.

DECORATIVE & FOLK ART

Banderas Bay Trading Company ℛ This shop features fine antiques and one-of-a-kind decorative objects for the home, including contemporary furniture, antique wooden doors, religious-themed items, original art, hand-loomed textiles, glassware, and pewter. This unique selection is handpicked by one of the area's most noteworthy interior designers, Peter Bowman. Open Monday to Saturday 9am to 9pm. Lázaro Cárdenas 263 (near Ignacio L. Vallarta). (©) **322/223-4352** There's also a *bodega* (warehouse) annex of the shop located at Constitución 319 (©) **322/223-9817**.

Lucy's CuCu Cabaña *(Finds* Owners Lucy and Gil Givens have assembled an exceptionally entertaining and eclectic collection of Mexican folk art—about 70% of which is animal-themed. Each summer they travel Mexico and personally select the handmade works created by over 100 indigenous artists and artisans. Items include metal sculptures, Oaxacan wooden animals, *retablos* (altars), and fine Talavera ceramics. Open Monday through Saturday from 10am to 8pm. The store is closed from May 15 to October 15. Basilio Badillo 295. ℂ 322/222-4839.

Olinala This shop contains two floors of fine indigenous Mexican crafts and folk art, including an impressive collection of museum-quality masks and original contemporary art by gallery owner Brewster Brockman. Open Monday through Friday from 10am to 2pm and 5 to 8pm, Saturday from 10am to 2pm. Lázaro Cárdenas 274. ℂ 322/222-4995.

Puerco Azul Set in a space that actually has a former pig-roasting oven, Puerco Azul features a whimsical and eclectic selection of art and home accessories, much of it created by owner and artist Lee Chapman (aka Lencho). You'll find many animal-themed works in bright colors, including his signature *puercos azules* (blue pigs). Open Monday to Saturday from 10am to 8pm, closed on Sunday. Constitución 325, just off Basilio Badillo's "restaurant row." ℂ 322/222-8647.

Querubines *(Finds* This is my personal favorite for the finest-quality artisanal works from throughout Mexico. Owner Marcella García travels across the country to select the items, which include exceptional artistic silver jewelry, embroidered and handwoven clothing, bolts of loomed fabrics, tin mirrors and lamps, glassware, pewter frames and trays, high-quality wool rugs, straw bags, and Panama hats. Open Monday through Saturday from 9am to 9pm. Under the same ownership and open the same hours, **Serafina**, Basilio Badillo 260 (ℂ 322/223-4594), features a more extensive selection of cotton clothing and handmade jewelry. Juárez 501A (corner of Galeana). ℂ 322/223-1727.

TEQUILA & CIGARS

La Casa del Habano This fine tobacco shop has certified quality cigars from Cuba, along with humidors, cutters, elegant lighters, and other smoking accessories. It's also a local cigar club, with a walk-in humidor for regular clients. In the back, you'll find comfy leather couches, TV sports, and full bar service—in other words, a manly place to take a break from shopping. Open Monday through Saturday from noon to 9pm. Aldama 170. ℂ 322/223-2758.

La Casa del Tequila ✪ Here you'll find an extensive selection of premium tequilas, plus information and tastings. Also available are books, tequila glassware, and other tequila-drinking accessories. The shop has recently (2005) been downsized to accommodate the **Agave Grill** (see "Where to Dine," later in this chapter) in the back, but now you can enjoy tasty Mexican fare and margaritas while you shop. Open Monday through Saturday from noon to 11pm. Morelos 589. ℂ 322/222-2000.

WHERE TO STAY

Beyond a varied selection of hotels and resorts, Puerto Vallarta offers many alternative accommodations. Oceanfront or marina-view condominiums and elegant private villas can offer families and small groups a better value and more ample space than a hotel. For short-term rentals, check out **www.costavallartaboutiquevillas.com**, ℂ **800/728-9098** in the U.S. and Canada, or 322/221-2277. Office hours are

Monday through Friday 8am to 7pm, Saturday 9am to 2pm. Prices start at $99 (£50) a night for nonbeachside condos and go to $3,000 (£1,500) for penthouse condos or private villas. Susan Weisman's **Bayside Properties,** Francisco Rodríguez 160, corner of Olas Altas (© **322/223-4424** and 222-8148; www.baysidepropertiespv.com), rents condos, villas, and hotels for individuals and large groups, including gay-friendly accommodations. She can arrange airport pickup and in-villa cooks. Another reputable full-service travel agency is **Holland's** (© **415/841-1194** or 888/8672723; www.puertovallartavillas.com). For the ultimate, indulge in a Punta Mita Villa rental within this exclusive resort. Contact **Mita Residential** (© **877/561-2893** in the U.S., or 329/291-5300; www.mitaresidential.com).

This section lists hotels from the airport south along Banderas Bay.

MARINA VALLARTA

Marina Vallarta is the most modern and deluxe area of hotel development in Puerto Vallarta. Located immediately south of the airport and just north of the cruise ship terminal, it's a planned development whose centerpiece is a 450-slip modern marina.

The hotels reviewed below are on the beachfront of the peninsula. The beaches here are much less attractive than beaches in other parts of the bay; the sand is darker, firmly packed, and, during certain times of the year, quite rocky. These hotels compensate with oversize pool areas and exotic landscaping. This area suits families and those looking for lots of centralized activity. Marina Vallarta is also home to an 18-hole **golf course** designed by Joe Finger.

In addition to the hotels reviewed below, an excellent choice is **Casa Velas,** on the golf course at Pelícanos 311 (© **866/612-1097** in the U.S., or 322/226-6688; www. hotelcasavelas.com). The elegant, boutique-style hotel has extra large rooms, an on-site spa, and a lovely pool. Although it is not located on the beach, it has a stunning beach club with food and beverage service, a pool, and sun chairs, with shuttle service for guests. High-season rates average $650 (£325), all inclusive.

Due to traffic, a taxi from the Marina to downtown takes 20 to 30 minutes.

Velas Vallarta Grand Suite Resort *(Kids)*   The beachside Velas Vallarta is an excellent choice for families. Each suite offers a full-size, fully equipped kitchen, ample living and dining areas, separate bedroom or bedrooms, and a large balcony with seating. Suites—many of which were updated in 2007—are decorated in a sophisticated, modern design featuring jewel-tone colors, Huichol art, Mexican textiles, feather beds with goose-down comforters, 27-inch flatscreen TVs, modern kitchen appliances, and teak-wood furniture on balconies and terraces. Special extras include a pillow menu and luxury bathroom amenities. This property is part hotel, part full-ownership condominiums, which means each suite is the size of a residential unit. The suites all have partial ocean views; they face a central area where three freeform swimming pools, complete with bridges and waterfalls, meander through tropical gardens. A full range of services means you'd never need to leave the place if you don't want to. The Marina Vallarta Golf Club is across the street, and special packages are available for Velas guests. Guests may pay an extra fee for the Gold Crown All-Inclusive option, which is one of the most premium all-inclusive programs in Mexico.

Paseo de la Marina 485, Marina Vallarta, 48354 Puerto Vallarta, Jal. © 800/VELAS-PV (835-2778) in the U.S. and Canada, or 322/221-0091. Fax 322/221-0755. www.velasvallarta.com. 361 units. $340 (£170) double; $740–$1,110 (£370–£555) suite. All inclusive prices. AE, DC, MC, V. Free indoor parking. **Amenities:** 2 restaurants; deli; poolside snack bar; lobby bar; 3 outdoor pools; golf privileges at Marina Vallarta Golf Club; 3 lighted tennis courts; fitness center w/spa and massage; beach w/watersports equipment; complimentary bikes; activities program for children and adults; concierge; travel agency; car rental; minimarket; salon; room service; laundry service. *In room:* A/C, TV, kitchen, coffeemaker, hair dryer, iron, safe.

Westin Resort & Spa Puerto Vallarta ⚜⚜ Stunning architecture and vibrant colors are the hallmark of this award-winning property, considered Puerto Vallarta's finest. Although the grounds are large—over 8 hectares (20 acres) with 260m (853 ft.) of beachfront—the warm service and gracious hospitality create the feeling of an intimate resort. Hundreds of tall palms surround the spectacular central freeform pool. Hammocks are strung between the palms closest to the beach, where there are also private beach cabañas. Rooms are contemporary in style, with oversize wood furnishings, tile floors, original art, and tub/shower combinations. Rooms on the fifth to tenth floors were redecorated in 2007. Balconies have panoramic views. Eight junior suites and some double rooms have Jacuzzis, and the five grand suites and presidential suite are two-level, with ample living areas. Two floors of rooms make up the Royal Beach Club, with VIP services, including private concierge. The fitness center is modern and well-equipped, with regularly scheduled spinning and yoga classes. **Nikki Beach** (www.nikkibeach.com), a renowned haven for the hip, is on-site, with a beachfront restaurant and club with big, white bed-size lounges for sunbathing or enjoying libations, from noon until early morning. Their Sunday champagne brunch is especially popular.

Paseo de la Marina Sur 205, Marina Vallarta, 48354 Puerto Vallarta, Jal. ⓒ **800/228-3000** in the U.S., or 322/226-1100. Fax 322/226-1144. www.starwoodhotels.com/westin. 280 units. High season $265–$500 (£133–£250) double, $555–$799 (£278–£400) suite; low season $130–$389 (£65–£195) double, $440–$700 (£220–£350) suite. AE, DC, MC, V. Free parking. **Amenities:** 2 restaurants; Nikki Beach Club; 2 poolside bars; lobby bar; oceanside pool; golf privileges at Marina Vallarta Golf Club; 3 lighted grass tennis courts; state-of-the-art health club w/treadmills, StairMasters, resistance equipment, sauna, steam room, solarium, whirlpool, massage, and salon; Kids' Club; travel agency; car rental; shopping arcade; room service; laundry service. *In room:* A/C, TV, minibar, coffeemaker, hair dryer, iron, safe.

THE HOTEL ZONE

The main street running between the airport and town is Avenida Francisco Medina Ascencio. The hotels here offer excellent, wide beachfronts with generally tranquil waters for swimming. From here it's a quick taxi or bus ride to downtown.

Fiesta Americana Puerto Vallarta ⚜ The Fiesta Americana's towering, three-story, thatched *palapa* lobby is a landmark in the Hotel Zone, and the hotel is known for its excellent beach and friendly service. An abundance of plants, splashing fountains, constant breezes, and comfortable seating areas in the lobby create a casual South Seas ambience. The nine-story terra-cotta building embraces a large plaza with a pool facing the beach. Marble-trimmed rooms in neutral tones with pastel accents contain carved headboards and comfortable rattan and wicker furniture. All have private balconies with ocean and pool views.

Av. Francisco Medina Ascencio Km 2.5, 48300 Puerto Vallarta, Jal. ⓒ **322/226-2100.** Fax 322/224-2108. www.fiesta americana.com. 291 units. High season $264–$400 (£132–£200) double; low season $145–$250 (£73–£125) double; year-round $750–$950 (£375–£475) suite. AE, DC, MC, V. Limited free parking. **Amenities:** 3 restaurants; lobby bar w/live music nightly; large pool w/activities and children's activities in high season; travel agency; salon; room service; laundry service. *In room:* A/C, TV, minibar, hair dryer, safe.

Villa Premiere Puerto Vallarta Hotel & Spa ⚜⚜ You couldn't ask for a better location to be close to all that Vallarta's vibrant *centro* has to offer. Located on a wide swathe of golden sand beach—and just a few blocks north of the start of the *malecón*—the Premiere is easy walking distance or a quick taxi ride to the downtown restaurants, shops, galleries, and clubs. One of the newer hotels in Vallarta (opened

1999), the architecture is contemporary, but its size gives it an intimate feel. With a first-rate spa and a policy that restricts guests to ages 16 and older, it's a place that caters to relaxation. Four types of rooms are available, but all are decorated in warm colors with tile floors and light wood furnishings. Deluxe rooms have ocean views, a respectable seating area with comfortable chairs, plus a sizable private balcony—request one of several that has an outdoor whirlpool. There are also seven suites that have a separate living room plus a dining area with private bar, and a spacious terrace. These rooms also have a double whirlpool tub, and separate glass-enclosed shower. The top-of-the-line master suites have all that the above suites offer, plus an outdoor whirlpool on the spacious balcony. The stunning bi-level spa is the real attraction of this hotel—scented with aromatherapy and glowing with candlelight, it uses top-notch, 100% natural products, most based on Mexico's natural treasures like coconut, aloe, and papaya. If you're not tempted by the nearby and accessible dining choices in downtown Vallarta, the Premiere also offers an all-inclusive option, with all meals and drinks included.

San Salvador 117, behind the Buenaventura Hotel, Col. 5 de Diciembre, 48350 Puerto Vallarta, Jal. © 877/886-9176 in the U.S., or 322/226-7001 and 322/226-7040. Fax 322/226-7043. www.premiereonline.com.mx. 83 units. Room only: high season $135–$430 (£74–£237) double; low season $135–$370 (£74–£204) double. All-inclusive: high season $295–$545 (£162–£300) per person, based on double occupancy; low season $185–$360 (£102–£198) per person, double. AE, MC, V. Limited street parking. No children younger than 16 accepted. **Amenities:** 3 restaurants; 2 outdoor pools; fitness center; full spa; travel agency; salon; room service; laundry service. *In room:* A/C, TV, minibar, coffeemaker, hair dryer, safe.

DOWNTOWN TO LOS MUERTOS BEACH

This part of town has recently undergone a renaissance; economical hotels and good-value guesthouses dominate. Several blocks off the beach, you can find numerous budget inns offering clean, simply furnished rooms; most offer discounts for long-term stays. Much of Vallarta's nightlife activity now centers in the areas south of the Río Cuale and along Olas Altas.

Hacienda San Angel ✷✷✷ *Finds*　This enchanting boutique hotel is my top choice for a luxury stay in Puerto Vallarta—even though it's not on the beach. You'll hardly miss the surf, you'll be so pampered in the stunning suites, or satisfied by the view from the rooftop heated pool or Jacuzzi and sun deck. Once the home of Richard Burton, it's just behind Puerto Vallarta's famed church, within easy walking distance to downtown. The Hacienda consists of five villas; the first two are joined to the third villa by a path that winds through a lovely terraced tropical garden with statuary and a fountain. The Las Campañas private one-bedroom villa is on the garden's northern border. The newest villa has four suites with sweeping views. A large, heated pool and deck afford panoramic views of the city and Bay of Banderas. A second sun deck with Jacuzzi overlooks the church and water beyond. All suites have exquisite antiques, original art, and fine bed linens with goose-down pillows. Each morning, continental breakfast is served outside your suite at the hour you request. Vallarta-style casual sophistication make this place Mexico's top "find" for discriminating travelers. Hacienda is open for dinner to nonguests (see "Where to Dine," below).

Miramar 336, Col. Centro, 48300 Puerto Vallarta, Jal. © 415/738-8220 or 322/222-2692. www.haciendasanangel. com. 10 units. High season $290-$625 (£145–£313) double; low season $260–$560 (£130–£280) double. All rates include daily continental breakfast. Rates for the entire Hacienda or separate villas consisting of 3 suites each are also available. MC, V. Very limited street parking available. **Amenities:** Full menu of ensuite breakfast, lunch, and dinner, or private chef available; restaurant; 2 outdoor pools; rooftop sun deck w/Jacuzzi; concierge; tour services; complimentary Internet access. *In room:* A/C, TV/DVD, hair dryer, safe, CD player.

Hotel Playa Los Arcos *RR* This is one of Vallarta's perennially popular hotels and a favorite of mine, with a stellar location in the heart of Los Muertos Beach, central to the Olas Altas sidewalk-cafe action and close to downtown. The four-story structure is U-shaped, facing the ocean, with a small swimming pool in the courtyard. Rooms with private balconies overlook the pool. The 10 suites have ocean views; five of these have kitchenettes. The standard rooms are small but pleasantly decorated and immaculate, with carved wooden furniture painted pale pink. On the premises are a *palapa* beachside bar with occasional live entertainment, a gourmet coffee shop, and the popular Kaiser Maximilian's gourmet restaurant. It's 7 blocks south of the river.

Olas Altas 380, 48380 Puerto Vallarta, Jal. *C* **800/648-2403** in the U.S., or 322/222-1583 and 322/226-7100. Fax 322/226-7104. www.playalosarcos.com. 171 units. High season $132–$149 (£66–£75) double, $165–$185 (£83–£93) suite; low season $100–$140 (£50–£70) double, $145–$165 (£73–£83) suite. AE, MC, V. Limited street parking. **Amenities:** 2 restaurants; lobby bar; outdoor pool; tour desk; car-rental desk; babysitting; laundry; safe. *In room:* A/C, TV.

SOUTH TO MISMALOYA

Casa Tres Vidas *RR* *(Value* Terraced down a hillside to Conchas Chinas Beach, Casa Tres Vidas is three individual villas that make great, affordable lodgings for families or groups of friends. Set on a stunning private cove, Tres Vidas gives you the experience of your own private villa, complete with service staff. It offers outstanding value for the location—close to town, with panoramic views from every room—as well as for the excellent service. Each villa has at least two levels and over 460 sq. m (nearly 5,000 sq. ft.) of mostly open living areas, plus a private swimming pool, heated whirlpool, and air-conditioned bedrooms. The Vida Alta penthouse villa has three bedrooms, plus a rooftop deck with pool and bar. Vida Sol villa's three bedrooms sleep 10 (two rooms have two king-size beds each). Directly on the ocean, Vida Mar is a four-bedroom villa, accommodating eight. The staff prepares gourmet meals in your villa twice a day—you choose the menu and pay only for the food. If you're planning a wedding, Tres Vidas and its adjacent sister property, Quinta María Cortez, do a stunning job.

Sagitario 132, Playa Conchas Chinas, 48300 Puerto Vallarta, Jal. *C* **888/640-8100** or 801/531-8100 in the U.S., or 322/221-5317. Fax 322/221-53-27. www.casatresvidas.com. 3 villas. High season $750 (£375) villa; low season $500 (£250) villa. Rates include services such as housekeeping and meal preparation. Special summer 1- or 2-bedroom rates available; minimum 3 nights. AE, MC, V. Very limited street parking. **Amenities:** 2 prepared daily meals; private outdoor pool; concierge; tour desk; car rental. *In room:* A/C (in bedrooms), safe.

Dreams Puerto Vallarta Resort & Spa *RR* Formerly the Camino Real, the premium all-inclusive Dreams Resort has the nicest beach of any Vallarta hotel, with soft white sand in a private cove. Set apart from other properties, with a lush mountain backdrop, it retains the exclusivity that has always made it popular—yet it's only a 5- to 10-minute ride to town. The hotel consists of two buildings: the 250-room main hotel, which curves gently with the shape of the Playa Las Estacas, and the newer 11-story Club Tower, also facing the beach and ocean. An ample pool fronts the main building, facing the beach. Standard rooms in the main building are large; some have sliding doors opening onto the beach, and others have balconies. Club Tower rooms (from the sixth floor up) have balconies with whirlpool tubs. The top floor consists of six two-bedroom suites, each with a private swimming pool and special concierge services. All rooms feature ocean views, vibrant colors, marble floors, and artwork by local artist Manuel Lepe. The grounds include two swimming pools (including an adults-only tranquillity pool), a wedding gazebo, and upgraded health club and spa.

Carretera Barra de Navidad Km 3.5, Playa Las Estacas, 48300 Puerto Vallarta, Jal. © 866/237-3267 in the U.S. and Canada, or 322/226-5000. Fax 322/221-6000. www.dreamsresorts.com. 337 units. All-inclusive rates are per-person, and include all meals, premium drinks, activities, airport transfers, tips, and taxes. $360 (£180) double; $440 (£220) junior suite; $520 (£260) suite. AE, DC, MC, V. Free secured parking. **Amenities:** 5 restaurants; lobby bar; pool bar; 3 outdoor pools; 2 lighted grass tennis courts; fully equipped health club; spa; children's program (Easter and Christmas vacations only); travel agency; car rental; convenience store; room service; laundry service. *In room:* A/C, TV, mini-bar, hair dryer, iron, safe.

Quinta María Cortez ☆☆☆ *Finds*　A sophisticated, imaginative B&B on the beach, this is Puerto Vallarta's most original place to stay—and one of Mexico's most memorable inns. Most of the seven large suites, uniquely decorated with antiques, whimsical curios, and original art, have a kitchenette and balcony. Sunny terraces, a small pool, and a central gathering area with fireplace and *palapa*-topped dining area (where an excellent full breakfast is served) occupy different levels of the seven-story house. A rooftop terrace offers another sunbathing alternative—and is among the best sunset-watching spots in town. The quinta is on a beautiful cove on Conchas Chinas beach. A terrace fronting the beach accommodates chairs for taking in the sunset.

The Quinta María wins my highest recommendation (in fact, I enjoyed living here for a few years when it still accepted long-term stays), but admittedly it's not for everyone. Air-conditioned areas are limited, due to the open nature of the suites and common areas. Those who love it return year after year, charmed by this remarkable place and by the consistently gracious service.

A new and very popular specialty of QMC and its adjacent sister property Casa Tres Vidas (see above) is planning and hosting weddings.

Sagitario 126, Playa Conchas Chinas, 48300 Puerto Vallarta, Jal. © 888/640-8100 or 801/536-5850 in the U.S., or 322/221-5317. Fax 322/221-53-27. www.quinta-maria.com. 7 units. High season $120–$240 (£60–£120) double; low season $105–$190 (£53–£95) double. Rates include breakfast. AE, MC, V. Very limited street parking. Children younger than 18 not accepted. **Amenities:** Small outdoor pool; concierge. *In room:* Fridge, coffeemaker, hair dryer, safe.

YELAPA

Verana ☆☆☆ *Moments*　The magical Verana is among my favorite places to stay in Mexico. It has an unparalleled ability to inspire immediate relaxation and a deep connection with the natural beauty of the spectacular coast. Although Yelapa is 30 minutes by water taxi from town, even those unfamiliar with the village should consider it. Verana has nine rustic yet sophisticated suites located among eight bungalows, set into a hillside with sweeping views of the mountains and ocean. Each is a work of art, hand-crafted with care and creativity by owners Heinz Leger, a former film production designer, and prop stylist Veronique Lieve. Each has a private terrace and two beds—but you won't find TVs, telephones, or other distractions. My favorite suite is the Studio; it's the most contemporary, with a wall of floor-to-ceiling windows that perfectly frame the spectacular view. The European-trained chef prepares scrumptious creations—global cuisine with a touch of Mexico. Verana also has a magically crafted spa, and a yoga hut where daily classes take place. Compare this to the prices of the other rustic-chic resorts along Mexico's Pacific coast, and you'll find it's a true value. Adventurous travelers should not miss a stay at this unique place.

Domicilio Conocido, 48300 Yelapa, Jal. © 800/530-7176 or 310/360-0155 in the U.S., or 322/222-2360. www.verana.com. 9 villas. Winter/high season $320–$480 (£160–£240) villa per night with 5-night minimum; $750 (£375) 3-bed-room Casa Grande per night; extra person $70 (£35) per night. Mandatory daily breakfast and dinner charge $80 (£40) per person; lunch and beverages extra. Shorter stays based on availability. Closed during summer months. AE, MC, V. Management helps arrange transportation from Puerto Vallarta to Boca, where a private boat runs to Yelapa;

from there, Verana is a gentle hike or mule ride. **Amenities:** Restaurant/bar; 2 prepared daily meals; outdoor pool; morning yoga classes; spa w/massage services; tours and excursions; library. *In room:* No phone.

WHERE TO DINE

Puerto Vallarta has the most exceptional dining scene of any resort town in Mexico. Over 250 restaurants serve cuisines from around the world, in addition to fresh seafood and regional dishes. Chefs from France, Switzerland, Germany, Italy, and Argentina have come for visits and stayed to open restaurants. In celebration of this diversity, Vallarta's culinary community hosts a 2-week-long gourmet dining festival each November (see box titled "Special Events in Puerto Vallarta," earlier in this chapter).

Dining is not limited to high-end options—there are plenty of small, family-owned restaurants, local Mexican kitchens, and vegetarian cafes. Vallarta also has branches of the Hard Rock Cafe, Outback Steakhouse, and even Hooters. I won't bother to review these restaurants, where the quality and decor are so familiar.

Of the inexpensive local spots, one favorite is **El Planeta Vegetariano,** Iturbide 270, just down from the main church (© 322/222-3073), serving an inexpensive, bountiful, and delicious vegetarian buffet, which changes for breakfast and lunch/dinner. It's open daily. Breakfast ($4.50/£2.25) is served from 8am till noon; the lunch and dinner buffets ($6.50/£3.25) are served from noon to 10pm; no credit cards are accepted.

MARINA VALLARTA

Contrary to conventional travel wisdom, most of the best restaurants in the Marina are in hotels. Especially notable are **Andrea** (fine Italian cuisine), at Velas Vallarta, and **Nikki Beach** (fusion), on the beachfront of the Westin Resort & Spa. (See "Where to Stay," earlier in this chapter, for more information.) Other choices are along the boardwalk bordering the marina yacht harbor.

Benitto's ⭐ CAFE   Wow, what a sandwich! Benitto's food would be reason enough to come to this tiny, terrific cafe inside the Plaza Neptuno—but added to that are the original array of sauces and the very personable service. This place is popular with locals for light breakfasts, filling lunches, and fondue and wine in the evenings. It's the best place in town to find pastrami, corned beef, or other traditional (gringo) sandwich fare, all served on your choice of gourmet bread. Draft beer and wine are available, as are the cafe's specialty infused waters.

Inside Plaza Neptuno. © 322/209-0287. benittoscafe@prodigy.net.mx. Breakfast $3–$6 (£1.50–£3); main courses $5–$7 (£2.50–£3.50). No credit cards. Mon–Sat 8:30am–9:30pm.

Porto Bello ⭐⭐ ITALIAN   One of the first restaurants in the marina, Porto Bello remains a favorite for its authentically flavorful Italian dishes and exceptional service. For starters, fried calamari is delicately seasoned, and grilled vegetable antipasto could easily serve as a full meal. Signature dishes include fusilli prepared with artichokes, black olives, lemon juice, basil, olive oil, and Parmesan cheese, and sautéed fish filet with shrimp and clams in saffron tomato sauce. The elegant indoor dining room is air-conditioned, and there's also marinafront seating. The restaurant occasionally schedules live music in the evening.

Marina Sol, Loc. 7 (Marina Vallarta *malecón*). © 322/221-0003. Reservations recommended for dinner. Main courses $10–$26 (£5–£13). AE, MC, V. Daily noon–11pm.

DOWNTOWN

Expensive

Café des Artistes/Thierry Blouet Cocina del Autor *Ᏻ* FRENCH/INTER-
NATIONAL   This sophisticated restaurant is known as the place in town for that
very special evening. Creative in its menu and innovative in design, the dinner-only
restaurant rivals those in any major metropolitan city for its culinary sophistication.
The award-winning chef and owner, Thierry Blouet, is both a member of the French
Academie Culinaire and a Maitre Cuisinier de France. The dining experience of the
Café has evolved over the years into a trio of special places, including the upscale Bar
Constantini lounge, and separate, but connected Thierry Blouet Cocina del Autor
dining area. All are located in a restored house that resembles a castle. The interior of
the original Café des Artistes combines murals, lush fabrics, and an array of original
works of art, with both an interior dining area as well as a lushly landscaped terraced
garden area. The menu of this section is a changing delight of French gourmet bistro
fare, which draws heavily on Chef Blouet's French training, yet uses regional specialty
ingredients. Noteworthy entrees include sea bass filet served with a lentil, bacon, and
coriander stew; and the renowned roasted duck glazed with honey, soy, ginger, and
lime sauce, and served with a pumpkin risotto. At the Cocina de Autor, the atmosphere is sleek and stylish, and the fixed-priced tasting menu (prices depend on the
number of plates you select, from three to six) offers you a choice of the chef's most
creative and sumptuous creations, with each dish creatively combining ingredients to
present one memorable "flavor"—choose any combination of starters, entrees, or
desserts. After dining, you're invited to the cognac and cigar room, an exquisite blend
of old adobe walls, flickering candles, and elegant leather chairs. Or, move on to the
adjacent Bar Constantini, with its live jazz music and plush sofas, for a fitting close to
a memorable meal. It is, without a doubt, worth the splurge.

Chef Thierry also oversees the kitchen at **Thierry's Prime Steakhouse** in the Plaza
Peninsula mall (Blvd. Francisco Medina Ascencio 2485, Loc. Ancla Sub. A; © **322/
331-1212;** www.thierrysprime.com). It features aged prime steaks, plus a limited
selection of fish and chicken dishes. It's open for lunch and dinner daily.

Guadalupe Sánchez 740. © **322/222-3228,** -3229, or -3230. www.cafedesartistes.com. Reservations recommended. Main courses $9–$31 (£4.50–£16). Cocina de Autor tasting menu $25–$68 (£13–£34). AE, MC, V. Daily
6–11:30pm (lounge until 2am).

Moderate

Daiquiri Dick's *Ᏻ* MODERN AMERICAN   A Vallarta dining institution,
Daiquiri Dick's has been around for over 23 years, evolving its winning combination of
decor, service, and scrumptious cuisine. The menu is among Vallarta's most sophisticated, and the genuinely warm staff and open-air location fronting Los Muertos Beach
add to the feeling of casual comfort. As lovely as the restaurant is, though, and as notorious as the fresh-fruit daiquiris are, the food is the main attraction. It incorporates
touches of Tuscan, Thai, and Mexican. Start with grilled asparagus wrapped in prosciutto and topped with shaved Asiago cheese, then try an entree such as sesame-crusted
tuna, grilled rare and served with wild greens; pistachio chicken served with polenta; or
my favorite, simple yet indulgent lobster tacos. Chocolate banana-bread pudding makes
a perfect finish. Daiquiri Dick's is a great place for groups as well as for a romantic dinner. It's one of the few places that is equally enjoyable for breakfast, lunch, or dinner.

Olas Altas 314. © **322/222-0566.** www.ddpv.com. Main courses $6.50–$25 (£3.25–£13). AE, MC, V. Daily
9am–10:30pm. Closed Sept.

de Santos ☆ MEDITERRANEAN   After it opened a few years ago, de Santos quickly became the hot spot in town for late-night dining and bar action. Most people come here for the atmosphere and music, and you should consider it "the" place to go, if scene is as important to you in a dining experience as substance. The menu is Mediterranean-inspired; best bets include lightly breaded calamari, paella Valenciana, and thin-crust pizza. The cool, refined interior feels more urban than resort-oriented, and the sound system is the most sophisticated in town (a DJ spins to match the mood of the crowd). It probably helps that one of the partners is also a member of the wildly popular Latin group Maná. Guests can dine on the open-air terrace in the back. Prices are extremely reasonable for the quality and overall experience of an evening here. Be sure to stay and check out the adjacent club, which is still among the hottest nightspots in town (see "Puerto Vallarta after Dark," later).

Morelos 771, Centro. ℂ 322/223-3052. www.desantos.com.mx. Reservations recommended during high season. Main courses $5–$20 (£2.50–£10). AE, MC, V. Daily 5pm–1am; bar closes at 4am on weekends.

Hacienda San Angel ☆☆ MEXICAN   Meals at Hacienda San Angel were so popular with its guests, the owner decided to share the experience with other visitors to Puerto Vallarta as well. In addition to experiencing the exquisite beauty of the Hacienda itself, diners are treated to one of the most stunning views of town, overlooking the night lights of the city to the bay beyond. The very limited seating each night—by prior reservation only—is on the upper terrace of the Hacienda, near its main rooftop pool. Tables are elegantly set with linens and antique silverware. The menu changes periodically, but features classic Mexican fare, along with international favorites. Starters include crispy fried calamari with a selection of sauces, grilled seasonal vegetables in a tomato, olive oil, and basil balsamic vinaigrette, or a seafood soup flavored with mescal and thyme. The house specialty is the grilled *Cabreria,* a tender bone-in steak, served with black beans, garlic-stuffed portobello mushroom, and a three-chile sauce. Other standouts include their chicken *mole,* and the herb-crusted rack of lamb in a green-pepper sauce. They offer full bar service, and an ample selection of wines to accompany your meal. Service is understated and attentive. Start the evening by arriving at 6pm for a cocktail hour with live music—you may also enjoy strolling the grounds of the Hacienda.

Miramar 336, Centro. ℂ 322/222-2692. www.haciendasanangel.com. Reservations required. Main courses $17–$30 (£8.50–£15), with 20% gratuity added to all checks. MC, V. Mon–Sat 7pm–last guest (guests may arrive at 6pm for cocktail hour, but no later than 9pm to be served).

Las Palomas ☆ MEXICAN   One of Puerto Vallarta's first restaurants, this is the power-breakfast place of choice—and a popular hangout for everyone else throughout the day. Authentic in atmosphere and menu, it's one of Puerto Vallarta's few genuine Mexican restaurants. Breakfast is the best value. The staff pours mugs of steaming coffee spiced with cinnamon as soon as you're seated. Try classic *huevos rancheros* or *chilaquiles* (tortilla strips, fried and topped with red or green spicy sauce, cream, cheese, and fried eggs). Lunch and dinner offer traditional Mexican specialties, plus a selection of stuffed crepes. The best places for checking out the *malecón* and watching the sunset while sipping an icy margarita are the spacious bar and the upstairs terrace.

Paseo Díaz Ordaz 610. ℂ 322/222-3675. www.laspalomaspvr.com. Breakfast $3.50–$10 (£1.75–£5); lunch $8.50–$20 (£4.25–£10); main courses $8.50–$22 (£4.25–£11). AE, MC, V. Daily 8am–11pm.

Trio ☆☆☆ *Finds* INTERNATIONAL   Trio is the darling of Vallarta restaurants, with local diners beating a path to the modest but stylish cafe where chef-owners Bernhard

Tapas, Anyone?

Certainly much of modern Mexico's culture draws on the important influence of Spain, so it only makes sense that Spanish culinary traditions would be evident as well. Within the last several years, dining on tapas has soared in popularity here. Of the many options, these are my favorites: the long-standing **Barcelona Tapas,** Matamoros and 31 de Octubre streets (✆ **322/222-0510**), a large and lovely restaurant on a terrace built high on a hillside, with sweeping views of the bay. They serve tapas and a selection of Spanish entrees, including paella, from 5pm to midnight. **La Esquina de los Caprichos,** Miramar 402, corner of Iturbide (✆ **322/222-0911**) is a tiny place, known as having the most reasonably priced ($2.50–$6/£1.25–£3) tapas in town, and perhaps the tastiest. Hours are Monday to Saturday from 1 to 10pm. It closes from mid-July to the end of August.

Güth and Ulf Henricksson's undeniable passion for food imbues each dish. Trío is noted for its perfected melding of Mexican and Mediterranean flavors; memorable entrees include San Blas shrimp in a fennel-tomato vinaigrette served over broiled *nopal* cactus, herb risotto with toasted sunflower seeds and quail, and pan-roasted sea bass with glazed grapes, mashed potatoes, and sauerkraut in a white-pepper sauce. These dishes may not be on the menu when you arrive, though—it's a constantly changing work of art. The atmosphere is always comfortable and welcoming. The rooftop bar area allows for a more comfortable wait for a table or for after-dinner coffee. A real treat.

Guerrero 264. ✆ 322/222-2196. www.triopv.com. Reservations recommended. Main courses $14–$26 (£7–£13). AE, MC, V. Year-round daily 6pm–midnight; high season Mon–Fri noon–3:30pm.

Xitomates ๕๕ MEXICAN   In the heart of downtown, this creative Mexican restaurant changed locations in 2007, adding raves for the creative, intimate atmosphere to the accolades already earned by chef/owner Luis Fitch's exceptionally creative versions of the country's culinary treasures. It's named for one of Mexico's contributions to gastronomy—the tomato (*xitomatl,* in the ancient Aztec language of Náhuatl). The menu mixes Mexican with Caribbean, Asian, and Mediterranean influences, and the presentation is as creative as the preparation. Starters include their signature coconut shrimp in a tangy tamarind sauce, thinly sliced scallops with cucumber and jicama julienne, or mushrooms stuffed with shrimp or *huitlacoche* (a mushroom that grows on corn stalks). There's a new menu of creative *ceviche*—seafood "cooked" in lime juice and served cold. Main courses range from grilled salmon filet in a poblano chile sauce, to a tender rib-eye steak with mushrooms, delicately flavored with the Mexican herb, *epazote.* The house specialty dessert is a Toluca ice-cream cake. The warmly dining room is accented with tin star lamps and flickering candles. An excellent wine list and full bar complement the exquisite dining.

Morelos 601, corner with Aldama. ✆ 322/222-9434. www.losxitomates.com. Main courses $8–$30 (£4–£15). AE, MC, V. Daily 6pm–midnight.

Inexpensive

Agave Grill ๕ MEXICAN   Since opening its doors in late 2004, Agave Grill has gradually taken over the space at the Casa de Tequila in central downtown. Now it's clearly the main attraction—and after one meal here, and it's easy to see why. The location is lovely—in a beautiful garden setting, within a classic hacienda-style building—but the food is the star here. Serving modern takes on classical Mexican cuisine, it's an ideal spot to take a break from shopping for a snack or a margarita, but plan a dinner here if you want to learn how authentic Mexican fare should taste. They'll start you out with fresh salsa made at your table (spiced to your preference); and I'd suggest you follow this with an order of the *pulpa* (octopus) sautéed to tenderness in a delectable sauce. My favorite main courses include *chichilo negro,* a bone-in filet of beef with Oaxacan smoked *mole,* or the duck tacos in a *pipián* chile sauce. For a sweet finish, don't miss their *buñelelos* (deep-fried sweet batter) filled with cream cheese and dried fruit, and served with a lemon ice. All tortillas and savory salsas are handmade. An elegant bar at the entry serves Vallarta's most original selection of fine tequilas, many from small distilleries. In addition to the tequilas, Agave Grill also serves fresh fruit margaritas and a selection of fine Mexican wines.

Morelos 589. © 322/222-2000. Main courses $6–$21 (£3–£11). MC, V. Mon–Sat noon–11pm.

El Arrayán ✮✮✮ *(Finds* MEXICAN   The traditional but original Arrayán is the pot of gold at the end of the rainbow for anyone in search of authentic Mexican cuisine. Owner Carmen Porras enlisted Mexico City chef Carmen Titita (praised by James Beard) to assist in the design of the kitchen and creation of the restaurant's concise menu, which features genuine regional dishes. The open-air dining area surrounds a cozy courtyard, while its exposed brick walls and funky-chic decor showcase a modern view of Mexican classics—tin tubs serve as sinks in the bathrooms, while colorful plastic tablecloths and primitive art enliven the dining room. Start with an order of sumptuous plantain fritters filled with black beans, or an unusual salad of diced *nopal* cactus paddles with fresh cheese. Favorite main courses include their tacos filled with prime beef filet, or Mexican duck *carnitas,* served in an *arrayán*-orange sauce. (*Arrayán,* the namesake of the place, is a small bittersweet fruit native to the region.) Homemade, fresh-fruit ice creams are an especially tasty finish to your meal. The full bar offers an extensive selection of tequilas, regional liquors, and nonalcoholic *aguas frescas,* a blended drink of fresh fruit and water. Sample their signature *raicilla* martini—made with the potent local spirit *raicilla* and infused with herbs for a unique flavor. Excellent service rounds out this requisite dining experience—you can't miss the pink facade with the large bell at the entry.

Allende 344, just past Matamoros, on the corner with Miramar. © 322/222-7195. www.elarrayan.com.mx. Main courses $15–$24 (£7.50–£12). Reservations recommended. AE, MC, V. Wed–Mon 6–11pm. Closed Aug.

Vitea ✮✮✮ *(Finds* INTERNATIONAL   This beachfront bistro was opened in late 2004 by the chef/owners of Trío, and their recipe for success took hold from day one—the place is bustling at any hour, and has become a favorite among locals. Due to strategically placed mirrors on the back wall, every seat has a view of the ocean, while the eclectic interior is cheerful and inviting. Seating is at small bistro-style tables, along a banquette that runs the length of the back wall, or at umbrella-topped tables on the wide promenade fronting the restaurant. The long, narrow bistro faces the waterfront between the central plaza and river. But enough about looks—what counts here is the exceptional fare, which is both classic and original. Starters include a tomato and Roquefort salad with pecans, foie gras with Spanish plum sauce, and an exquisite bistro salad with bacon. Quiche is always on the menu, with changing selections, and main courses include chickpea ravioli with portobello mushrooms, Wiener schnitzel with salad, or a traditional steak frites. Lunch offers lighter fare, including heavenly deli sandwiches. You won't be disappointed here, no matter what you order. There's a full bar with an excellent selection of wines, and the service is exceptional.

Malecón no. 2, at Libertad. (322/222-8703 or -8695. Reservations recommended during peak dining hours. Main courses $7–$26 (£3.50–£13). MC, V. Daily noon–midnight.

SOUTH OF THE RIO CUALE TO OLAS ALTAS

South of the river is the densest restaurant area, where you'll find Basilio Badillo, the street nicknamed "Restaurant Row." A second main dining drag has emerged along Calle Olas Altas, with a variety of cuisines and price categories. Cafes and espresso bars, generally open from 7am to midnight, line its wide sidewalks.

Expensive

Café Kaiser Maximilian *ℛℛ* INTERNATIONAL   This bistro-style cafe has a casually elegant atmosphere with a genuine European feel. It's the prime place to go if you want to combine exceptional food with great people-watching. Austrian-born owner Andreas Rupprechter is always on hand to ensure that the service is as impeccable as the food is delicious. Indoor, air-conditioned dining is at cozy tables; sidewalk tables are larger and great for groups of friends. The cuisine merges old-world European preparations with regional fresh ingredients. My favorite is filet of trout with spinach, tomato, and almond ragout; but also notable is their mustard chicken with mashed potatoes; and the rack of lamb with polenta, endives, and lima beans is simply divine. Desserts are especially tempting, as are gourmet coffees—Maximilian has an Austrian cafe and pastry shop next door.

Olas Altas 380-B (at Basilio Badillo, in front of the Hotel Playa Los Arcos), Zona Romántica. (322/223-0760. Reservations recommended in high season. Main courses $18–$30 (£9–£15). AE, MC, V. Mon–Sat 6–11pm.

Le Bistro *Value* MEXICAN/INTERNATIONAL   Breakfast here is one of Vallarta's best values. I would pass on this longstanding favorite, however, for dinner. Elegant decor, great recorded jazz music, and an open-air setting on the island in the midst of the Río Cuale creating a singular experience—at once local and sophisticated. The specialty is crepes, which come in a variety of flavors for breakfast, lunch, or dinner. The lunch and dinner menu also features a selection of Mexican cuisine, including duck in Oaxacan black *mole* and rock Cornish hen stuffed with herbed rice, dried tropical fruits, and nuts, finished in mango cilantro sauce. The vegetarian offerings are more creative than most. An extensive wine list and ample selection of specialty coffees complement the menu.

Isla Río Cuale 16-A (just east of northbound bridge). (322/222-0283. www.lebistro.com.mx. Reservations recommended for dinner in high season. Breakfast $6–$10 (£3–£5); main courses $19–$32 (£9.50–£16). AE, MC, V. Mon–Sat 9am–midnight.

Moderate

Archie's Wok *ℛℛℛ* *Finds* ASIAN/SEAFOOD   Since 1986, Archie's has been legendary in Puerto Vallarta for serving original cuisine influenced by the intriguing flavors of Thailand, China, and the Philippines. Archie was Hollywood director John Huston's private chef during the years he spent in the area. Today his wife Cindy upholds his legacy at this tranquil retreat. The Thai mai tai and other tropical drinks, made from only fresh fruit and juices, are a good way to kick off a meal, as are the consistently crispy and delicious Filipino spring rolls. The popular Singapore fish filet features lightly battered filet strips in sweet-and-sour sauce; Thai garlic shrimp are prepared with fresh garlic, ginger, cilantro, and black pepper. Vegetarians have plenty of options, including broccoli, tofu, mushroom, and cashew stir-fry in black-bean-and-sherry sauce. Thursday through Saturday from 8 to 11pm, there's live classical harp and flute in Archie's Oriental garden.

Francisca Rodríguez 130 (a half block from the Los Muertos pier). © 322/222-0411. Main courses $7–$21 (£3.50–£11). MC, V. Mon–Sat 2–11pm. Closed Sept–Oct.

Espresso ✦✦ ITALIAN This popular eatery is Vallarta's best late-night dining option. The two-level restaurant is on one of the town's busiest streets—across from El Torito's sports bar, and cater-cornered from the lively Señor Frog's—meaning that traffic noise is a factor, though not a deterrent. The food is superb, the service attentive, and the prices more than reasonable. Owned by a partnership of lively Italians, it serves food that is authentic in preparation and flavor, from thin-crust, brick-oven pizza to savory homemade pasta. My favorite pizza is the Quattro Stagioni, topped with artichokes, black olives, ham, and mushrooms. Excellent calzones and panini (sandwiches) are also options. I prefer the rooftop garden area for dining, but many patrons gravitate to the pool table in the air-conditioned downstairs, which features major sports and entertainment events on satellite TV. Espresso also has full bar service and draft beer. Espresso is especially popular with *vallartenses* (locals).

Ignacio L. Vallarta 279. © 322/222-3272. Entrees $7–$19 (£3.50–£9.50). MC, V. Daily 9am–2am.

La Palapa ✦✦ SEAFOOD/MEXICAN This colorful, open-air, *palapa*-roofed restaurant on the beach is a decades-old local favorite, and with each recent visit, I have found the quality of the food and the service keeps improving. It's an exceptional dining experience, day or night. Enjoy a tropical breakfast by the sea, lunch on the beach, cocktails at sunset, or a romantic dinner (on a cloth-covered table in the sand). For lunch and dinner, seafood is the specialty; featured dishes include macadamia-and-coconut-crusted prawns, and poached red snapper with fresh cilantro sauce. Its location, in the heart of Los Muertos Beach, makes it an excellent place to start or end the day; I favor it for breakfast or, even better, a late-night sweet temptation and specialty coffee, while watching the moon over the bay. A particular draw is the all-you-can-eat Sunday brunch, which entitles you to a spot on popular Los Muertos beach for the day. You can enjoy the extra-comfortable beach chairs for postbrunch sunbathing. A classy bar area features acoustic guitars and vocals nightly from 8 to 11pm, generally performed by the owner, Alberto.

Pulpito 103. © 322/222-5225. www.lapalapapv.com. Reservations recommended for dinner in high season. Breakfast $4–$12 (£2–£6); main courses $8–$28 (£4–£14); salad or sandwiches $5–$12 (£2.50–£6). AE, MC, V. Daily 9am–11pm.

Inexpensive

Café San Angel *Moments* CAFE This comfortable, classic sidewalk cafe is a local gathering place from sunrise to sunset. For breakfast, choose a burrito stuffed with eggs and chorizo sausage, a three-egg Western omelet, crepes filled with mushrooms, such Mexican classics as *huevos rancheros* and *chilaquiles,* or a tropical fruit plate. Deli sandwiches, crepes, and pastries round out the small but ample menu. The cafe also serves exceptional fruit smoothies and perfectly made espresso drinks. Although the service is occasionally slow, keep in mind that this place affords the best people-watching in the area. Bar service and Internet access are available.

Olas Altas 449 (at Francisco Rodríguez). © 322/223-1273. Breakfast $3.50–$7 (£1.75–£3.50); main courses $3.50 (£1.95). No credit cards. Daily 8am–1am.

Jungle Restaurants

One of the unique attractions of Puerto Vallarta is its "jungle restaurants," south of town toward Mismaloya. They offer open-air dining in a tropical setting by the sea or beside a mountain river. The many varieties of "jungle" and "tropical" tours (see "Organized Tours," earlier in this chapter) include a stop for swimming and lunch. If you travel on your own, a taxi is the best transportation—the restaurants are quite a distance from the main highway. Taxis are usually waiting for return patrons.

The most recommendable of the jungle restaurants is the ecologically sensitive **El Nogalito** (☎/fax **322/221-5225**). Located beside a clear jungle stream, the exceptionally clean, beautifully landscaped ranch serves lunch, beverages, and snacks on a shady, relaxing terrace. Several hiking routes depart from the grounds, and the restaurant provides a guide (whom you tip) to point out the native plants, birds, and wildlife. It's much closer to town than the other jungle restaurants: To find it, travel to Punta Negra, about 8km (5 miles) south of downtown Puerto Vallarta. A well-marked sign points up Calzada del Cedro, a dirt road, to the ranch. It's open daily from noon to 5:30pm. No credit cards are accepted.

Just past Boca de Tomatlán, at Highway 200 Km 20, is **Chico's Paradise** (☎ **322/223-6005**). It offers spectacular views of massive rocks—some marked with petroglyphs—and the surrounding jungle and mountains. There are natural pools and waterfalls for swimming, plus a small market selling pricey trinkets. The menu features excellent seafood as well as Mexican dishes. The quality is quite good, and the portions are generous, although prices are higher than in town—remember, you're paying for the setting. It's open daily from 10am to 6pm. No credit cards are accepted.

Fajita Republic ⚜ MEXICAN/SEAFOOD/STEAKS   Fajita Republic is consistently popular—and deservedly so. It has hit on a winning recipe: delicious food, ample portions, welcoming atmosphere, and low prices. The specialty is, of course, fajitas, grilled to perfection in every variety: steak, chicken, shrimp, combo, and vegetarian. All come with a generous tray of salsas and toppings. This "tropical grill" also serves sumptuous barbecued ribs, Mexican *molcajetes* with incredibly tender strips of marinated beef filet, and grilled shrimp. Starters include fresh guacamole served in a giant spoon and the ever-popular Mayan cheese sticks (breaded and deep-fried). Try an oversize mug or pitcher of Fajita Rita Mango Margaritas—or another spirited temptation. This is a casual, fun, festive place in a garden of mango and palm trees. A second location in Nuevo Vallarta, across from the Grand Velas Resort, is drawing equal raves with the same menu and prices.

Pino Suárez 321 (at Basilio Badillo), 1 block north of Olas Altas. ☎ 322/222-3131. Main courses $9–$18 (£4.50–£9). MC, V. Daily 5pm–midnight.

Red Cabbage Café (El Repollo Rojo) ⚜⚜ *Finds* MEXICAN   The tiny, hard-to-find cafe is worth the effort—a visit here will reward you with exceptional traditional Mexican cuisine and a whimsical crash course in contemporary culture. The small room is covered wall-to-wall and table-to-table with photographs, paintings, movie posters, and news clippings about the cultural icons of Mexico. Frida Kahlo figures prominently in the decor, and a special menu duplicates dishes she and husband Diego Rivera prepared for guests.

Specialties from all over Mexico include divine *chiles en nogada* (poblanos stuffed with ground beef, pine nuts, and raisins, topped with sweet cream sauce and served cold), intricate chicken *mole* from Puebla, and hearty *carne en su jugo* (steak in its juice). In addition, the vegetarian menu is probably the most diverse and tasty in town. This is not the place for an intimate conversation, however—the poor acoustics cause everyone's conversations to blend together, although generally what you're hearing from adjacent tables are raves about the food. Also, this is a nonsmoking restaurant—the only one I'm aware of in town.

Calle Rivera del Río 204A (across from Río Cuale). © 322/223-0411. Main courses $9–$20 (£4.50–£10). No credit cards. Daily 5–10:30pm.

PUERTO VALLARTA AFTER DARK
Puerto Vallarta's spirited nightlife reflects the town's dual nature—part resort, part colonial town. In the past, Vallarta was known for its live music scene, but in recent years the nocturnal action has shifted to DJ clubs with array of eclectic, contemporary music. A concentration of nightspots lies along Calle Ignacio L. Vallarta (the extension of the main southbound road) after it crosses the Río Cuale. Along a 3-block stretch, you'll find a live blues club, sports bar, live mariachi music, a gay dance club, and the obligatory **Señor Frog's.** Walk from place to place and take in a bit of it all.

The *malecón*, which used to be lined with restaurants, is now known more for hip dance clubs and a few more relaxed options, all of which look out over the ocean. You can first stroll the broad walkway by the water's edge and check out the action at the various clubs, which extend from **Bodeguita del Medio** on the north end to **Hooters** just off the central plaza.

Marina Vallarta's clubs offer a more upscale, indoor, air-conditioned atmosphere. South of the Río Cuale, the **Olas Altas** zone's small cafes and martini bars buzz with action. In this zone, there's also an active gay and lesbian club scene.

PERFORMING ARTS & CULTURAL EVENTS
Truth be told, cultural nightlife beyond the **Mexican Fiesta** is limited. Culture centers on the visual arts; the opening of an exhibition has great social and artistic significance. Puerto Vallarta's gallery community comes together in the central downtown area to present weekly **art walks,** where new exhibits are presented, featured artists attend, and complimentary cocktails are served. Check listings in the daily English-language newspaper, *Vallarta Today,* or the events section of **www.virtualvallarta. com**, to see what's on the schedule during your stay. Also of note are the free musical performances in the downtown plaza's gazebo—check with the municipal tourism office for the current schedule.

FIESTA NIGHTS
Major hotels in Puerto Vallarta feature frequent fiestas for tourists—extravaganzas with open bars, Mexican buffet dinners, and live entertainment. Some are fairly authentic and make a good introduction for first-time travelers to Mexico; others can be a bit cheesy. Shows are usually held outdoors but move indoors when necessary. Reservations are recommended.

Rhythms of the Night (Cruise to Caletas) ✸✸✸ *(Moments* This is an unforgettable evening under the stars at John Huston's former home at the pristine cove called

Las Caletas. The smooth, fast Vallarta Adventures catamaran travels here, entertaining guests along the way. Tiki torches and drummers dressed in native costumes greet you at the dock. There's no electricity—you dine by the light of candles, the stars, and the moon. The buffet dinner is delicious—steak, seafood, and generous vegetarian options. Everything is first class. The entertainment showcases indigenous dances in contemporary style. The cruise departs at 6pm and returns by 11pm. Departs from Terminal Marítima. (C) 888/303-2653 in the U.S., or 322/297-1212, ext 3. www.vallarta-adventures.com. Cost $85 (£43; includes cruise, dinner, open bar, and entertainment).

THE CLUB & MUSIC SCENE
Restaurant & Bars
Azul 96   Among the newer clubs to open (late 2006), Azul 96 is known more for its sand-floored, rooftop Sky Bar than its sleek ground-floor restaurant, which specializes in traditional gourmet fare. The architecture is stunning, but most people pass by as they climb the stairs or take the elevator to the bar upstairs, with its panoramic views of the city. A long glass bar borders one side and serves sushi along with cocktails. In the "sandy beach" area, partiers settle into high tables or banquettes to enjoy the energizing dance music. The Sky Bar is open daily from 8pm to 4am. Morelos 696, Col. Centro. (C) 322/222-1022. www.azul96.com.

Bar Constantini *&&*   The most sophisticated lounge in Vallarta is set in the elegant eatery, Café des Artistes. It's become a popular option for those looking for a lively yet sophisticated setting for after-dinner drinks. The plush sofas are welcoming, and the list of champagnes by the glass, signature martinis, and specialty drinks is suitably tempting. Live jazz and blues in an intimate atmosphere are drawing crowds, as are regular wine tastings. An ample appetizer and dessert menu make it appropriate for late-night dining and drinks. Open daily from 6pm to 1am. Guadalupe Sánchez 740. (C) 322/222-3229.

Carlos O'Brian's   Vallarta's original nightspot was once the only place for an evening of revelry. Although the competition is stiffer nowadays, COB's still packs them in—especially the 20-something set. The late-night scene resembles a college party. Open daily from noon to 2am; happy hour is from noon to 8pm. Paseo Díaz Ordaz (malecón) 786, at Pípila. (C) 322/226-8850. Weekend cover $11 (£5.50; includes 2 drinks).

La Bodeguita del Medio   This authentic Cuban restaurant and bar is known for its casual energy, terrific live Cuban music, and mojitos. It is a branch of the original Bodeguita in Havana (reputedly Hemingway's favorite restaurant there), which opened in 1942. If you can't get to that one, the Vallarta version has successfully imported the essence—and has a small souvenir shop that sells Cuban cigars, rum, and other items. The downstairs has large wooden windows that open to the *malecón* street action, while the upstairs offers terrific views of the bay. Walls throughout are decorated with old photographs and patrons' signatures—if you can, find a spot and add yours. The food is less memorable here than the music and atmosphere, so I recommend drinks and dancing, nothing more. Open daily from 11:30am to 2am. Paseo Díaz Ordaz 858 *(malecón)*, at Allende. (C) 322/223-1585.

Z'Tai *&*   Opened in 2007, Z'Tai is a stunning array of spaces that span an entire city block. Enter from the *malecón,* and you'll discover ZBar, an upstairs lounge with chill-out music, bay views, and comfy banquettes to relax on. Venture farther into this club and you'll find an expansive open air garden area that serves cocktails as well as an array of Asian-inspired dining and snacking options, accompanied by electronic music at a level still appropriate for conversation. Seating is casual and spans several elevations, overlooking Zen gardens and flowing ponds. At the opposite end (Calle Morelos entrance), there's an air-conditioned dining area. They boast a 1,000-bottle wine menu, but the favorite drink here is their signature cucumber martini. Open daily for food service from 6pm to 2am, with bar service until 4am. They also offer valet service or shuttle service to wherever you parked your car. Morelos 737, Col. Centro. (C) 322/222-0306.

Rock, Jazz & Blues

El Faro Lighthouse Bar (★) A circular cocktail lounge at the top of the Marina lighthouse, El Faro is one of Vallarta's most romantic nightspots. Live or recorded jazz plays, and conversation is manageable. Drop by at twilight for the magnificent panoramic views, but don't expect anything other than a drink and, if you get lucky, some popcorn. Open daily from 5:30pm to 1:30am. Royal Pacific Yacht Club, Marina Vallarta. (C) 322/221-0541 or -0542.

Mariachi Loco This lively mariachi club features singers belting out boleros and ranchero classics. The mariachi show begins at 11:30pm—the mariachis stroll and play as guests join in impromptu singing—and by midnight it gets going. After 2am the mariachis play for pay, which is around $10 (£5) for each song played at your table. There's Mexican food from 8 to 10:30pm. Open daily from 8pm to 6am. Cárdenas 254 (at Ignacio Vallarta). (C) 322/223-2205. Cover is generally $7 (£3.50), but varies depending on guest performances.

Route 66 Route 66's popular house band plays a hot mix of reggae, blues, rock, and anything by Santana. Live music jams between 10pm and 2am Monday through Sunday nights. It's open daily from 6pm to 2am. Ignacio L. Vallarta 217 (between Madero and Cárdenas, south of the river). No phone.

Night Clubs & Dancing

A few of Vallarta's clubs charge admission, but generally you pay just for drinks: $6 (£3) for a margarita, $4.50 (£2.25) for a beer, more for whiskey and mixed drinks. Keep an eye out for discount passes frequently available in hotels, restaurants, and other tourist spots. Most clubs are open from 10pm to 4am.

Christine This dazzling club draws a crowd with an opening laser-light show, pumped-in dry ice, flashing lights, and a dozen large-screen video panels. Once a disco—in the true sense of the word—it received a needed face-lift in 2003, and is now a more modern dance club, with techno, house, and hip-hop the primary tunes played. The sound system is truly amazing, and the mix of music can get almost anyone dancing. Dress code: No tennis shoes or flip-flops, no shorts for men. Open daily from 10pm to 4am; the light show begins at 11pm. In the Krystal Vallarta hotel, north of downtown off Av. Francisco Medina Ascencio. (C) 322/224-0202. Cover ladies $10 (£5), men $20 (£10).

Collage Club A multilevel monster of nighttime entertainment, Collage includes a pool salon, video arcade, bowling alley, and the always-packed Disco Bar, with frequent live entertainment. It's just past the entrance to Marina Vallarta, air-conditioned, and very popular with a young, mainly local crowd. Open daily from 10am to 6am. Calle Proa s/n, Marina Vallarta. (C) 322/221-0505. Cover $5.50–$40 (£2.25–£20), which varies by theme party being offered that night.

de Santos (★★★) Vallarta's chic dining spot is known more for the urban, hip crowd the bar draws—it is *the* hot spot for locals. The adjacent club has become known as the place for the superchic to party, although competition opened in late 2006 to lure some regulars away. The lower level holds an air-conditioned bar and dance floor (after midnight, when dining tables have been cleared away), where a DJ spins the hottest of house and techno. Upstairs, there's an open-air rooftop bar with chill-out music and acid jazz. Enjoy the tunes and the fresh air while lounging around on one of the several oversize beds. One partner, a member of the superhot Latin rock group Maná, uses Vallarta as a home base for writing songs. The crowd, which varies in age from 20s on up, shares a common denominator of cool style. The restaurant bar is open daily from 5pm to 1am; the club is open Wednesday through Saturday from 10pm to 6am. Morelos 771. © 322/223-3052 or -3053. Cover ladies $20 (£10), men $25 (£13).

Hilo   You'll recognize Hilo by the giant sculptures that practically reach out the front entrance and pull you into this high-energy club, which has become a favorite with the 20-something set. Music ranges from house and electronic to rock. It seems the later the hour, the more crowded the place becomes. Open daily from 4pm to 6am. Malecón, between Aldama and Abasolo sts. © 322/223-5361. Cover $10 (£5) weekends and holidays. No cover weekdays.

J & B Salsa Club   This is the locally popular place to go for dancing to Latin music—from salsa to samba, the dancing is hot. On Fridays, Saturdays, and holidays the air-conditioned club hosts live bands. Open daily from 10pm to 6am. Av. Francisco Medina Ascencio Km 2.5 (Hotel Zone). © 322/224-4616. Cover $10 (£5).

Mandala   As of late 2007, the newest addition to Vallarta's sizzling nightlife scene is this sister-club to Hilo, geared toward a slightly more sophisticated crowd. The two-level bar and dance club has oversized windows overlooking the *malecón*, with giant Buddha sculptures situated throughout the Pan-Asian–inspired club—but there will be little meditating here, amid the din of house and Latin pop. Currently the hottest place in town, it attracts a sleek and suntanned crowd. It's open daily from 11am to 6am. There's basic bar service from opening until 8pm, when a DJ spins into action. Paseo Díaz Ordaz *(malecón)* 600 at Abasolo. © 322/223 0966. Cover (nighttime) $10–$20 (£5–£10) depending on the promotion of the evening.

Nikki Beach   This haven of the hip hails from South Beach, Miami, and St. Tropez, and has brought its ultracool vibe to Vallarta. White-draped bed-size lounges scatter the outdoor lounge area, under a canopy of tall palms and umbrellas. Indoor dining and lounge areas are also available. The music is the latest in electronic, house, and chill, with visiting DJs often playing on weekend nights. Sundays feature their signature beach brunch, and Thursday evenings feature "Beautiful People" night. It's a great choice for catching rays during the day, but its real appeal is the nocturnal action. Open Sunday to Wednesday from 11am to 1am (food service stops at 11pm); Thursday to Saturday from 11am to 3am (food service stops at 1am). On the beach at the Westin Regina Resort, Marina Vallarta. © 322/221-0252 or 226-1150. www.nikkibeach.com. No cover, unless for a special event, which will vary.

Rio Latino   For those seeking steamy salsa dancing, this new, classy locale has been a welcome addition in town since it opened in 2007. Although the dance floor is rather small for all that action, the excellent music—ranging from regional Mexican to Cuban salsa—is drawing strong crowds of mostly local residents. It's on the upper level of Plaza Peninsula, open Thursday to Sunday from 10pm to 6am. Francisco M. Ascencio #2485. Local C2 y C3. © 322/209-2042. Cover $15 (£7.50).

Zoo   Your chance to be an animal and get wild in the night. The Zoo even has cages to dance in if you're feeling unleashed. This popular club has a terrific sound system and a great variety of dance music, including techno, reggae, and rap. Every hour's happy hour, with two-for-one drinks. It opens daily at noon and closes in the wee hours. Paseo Díaz Ordaz *(malecón)* 630. © 322/222-4945. www.zoobardance.com. Cover $11 (£5.50; includes 2 drinks).

A SPORTS BAR

No Name Bar&Grill   With a multitude of TVs and enough sports memorabilia to start a minimuseum, the No Name is a great venue for catching your favorite game. It shows all NBA, NHL, NFL, and MLB broadcast events, plus pay-per-view. No Name also serves great barbecued ribs and USDA imported steaks. It's open daily from 9am to midnight. Morelos 460 *(malecón)*, at Mina. © 322/223-2508.

GAY & LESBIAN CLUBS

Vallarta has a vibrant gay community with a wide variety of clubs and nightlife options, including special bay cruises and evening excursions to nearby ranches. The free *Gay Guide Vallarta* (www.gayguidevallarta.com) specializes in gay-friendly listings, including weekly specials and happy hours.

Disco Club Paco Paco   This combination dance club, cantina, and rooftop bar stages a spectacular "Trasvesty" transvestite show every Thursday, Friday, Saturday, and Sunday night at 1:30am. It's open daily from 1pm to 6am and is air-conditioned. Ignacio L. Vallarta 278. © 322/222-7667. www.club-pacopaco.com. Cover $6 (£3; includes 1 drink) 9pm to 6am.

Garbo   This small, cozy club is gay friendly, but not exclusively gay, and features great recorded music and occasional live music on weekends. It's open daily from 6pm to 2am and is air-conditioned. Pulpito 142. © 322/223-5753. www.bargarbo.com.

La Noche   A casual, intimate "neighborhood bar" catering to a gay clientele, with great prices on drinks, and a menu of tequila cocktails. Beers are always two-for-one. Open daily from 6pm to 2am. Lazaro Cardenas 257 (2 doors from Ignacio Vallarta). © 322/222-3364.

Ranch Disco Bar   This place is known for the "Ranch Hand's Show," Wednesday through Sunday at 11:15pm and 1am. The club also has a dance floor. Open daily from 9pm to 6am. Venustiano Carranza 239 (around the corner from Paco Paco; can also be accessed directly from Paco Paco). © 322/223-0537. Cover $6 (£3; includes 1 drink).

SIDE TRIPS FROM PUERTO VALLARTA

YELAPA: ROBINSON CRUSOE MEETS JACK KEROUAC ☆

It's a cove straight out of a tropical fantasy, and only a 45-minute trip by boat from Puerto Vallarta. Yelapa has no cars and one paved (pedestrian-only) road, and got electricity 6 years ago. It's accessible only by boat. Its tranquillity, natural beauty, and seclusion make it a popular home for hippies, hipsters, artists, writers, and a few expats (looking to escape the stress of the world, or perhaps the law). A seemingly strange mix, but you're unlikely to ever meet a stranger—Yelapa remains casual and friendly.

To get there, travel by excursion boat or inexpensive water taxi (see "Getting Around," earlier in this chapter). You can spend an enjoyable day, but I recommend a longer stay—it provides a completely different perspective.

Once you're in Yelapa, you can lie in the sun, swim, snorkel, eat fresh grilled seafood at a beachside restaurant, or sample the local moonshine, *raicilla*. The beach vendors specialize in the most amazing pies you've ever tasted (coconut, lemon, or chocolate). Equally amazing is how the pie ladies balance the pie plates on their heads as they walk the beach; they sell crocheted swimsuits, too. You can tour this tiny town or hike up a river to see one of two waterfalls; the closest to town is about a 30-minute walk from the beach. *Note:* If you use a local guide, agree on a price before you start out. Horseback riding, guided birding, fishing trips, and paragliding are also available.

For overnight accommodations, local residents frequently rent rooms, and there's also the rustic **Hotel Lagunita** ☞ (© **322/209-5056** or -5055; www.hotel-lagunita. com). Its 32 cabañas have private bathrooms, and the hotel has electricity, a saltwater pool, primitive spa with massage, an amiable restaurant and bar, as well as the Barracuda Beach lounge and brick-oven pizza cafe, plus a gourmet coffee shop. Though the prices are high for what you get, it is the most accommodating place for most visitors. Double rates run $110 (£55) during the season and $80 (£40) in the off season. Special rooms are available now for honeymooners, for $125 (£63; MasterCard and Visa are accepted). Lagunita has become a popular spot for yoga retreats, and regularly features yoga classes.

A stylish alternative is the fashionable **Verana** ☞☞☞ (© **800/530-7176** or 322/222-2360; www.verana.com). See "Where to Stay," earlier, for details.

If you stay over on a Wednesday or Saturday during the winter, don't miss the regular dance at the **Yelapa Yacht Club** ☞ (no phone). Typically tongue-in-cheek for Yelapa, the "yacht club" consists of a cement dance floor and a disco ball, but the DJ spins a great range of tunes, from Glenn Miller to Kanye West, attracting all ages and types. Dinner ($5–$12/£2.50–£6) is a bonus—the food may be the best anywhere in the bay. The menu changes depending on what's fresh. Ask for directions; it's in the main village, on the beach.

NUEVO VALLARTA & NORTH OF VALLARTA: ALL-INCLUSIVES

Many people assume Nuevo Vallarta is a suburb of Puerto Vallarta, but it's a standalone destination over the state border in Nayarit. It was designed as a megaresort development, complete with marina, golf course, and luxury hotels. Although it got off to a slow start, it is finally come together, with a collection of mostly all-inclusive hotels on one of the widest, most attractive beaches in the bay. The biggest resort, Paradise Village, has a full marina and an 18-hole golf course inland from the beachside strip of hotels, plus a growing selection of condos and homes for sale. The Mayan Palace also has an 18-hole course here. The Paradise Plaza shopping center, next to Paradise Village, amplifies the area's shopping, dining, and services. It's open daily from 10am to 10pm. To get to the beach, you travel down a lengthy entrance road from the highway, passing by a few remaining fields (which used to be great for birding) but mostly real estate under construction.

Also worthwhile is a day spent at the **Etc. Beach Club,** Paseo de los Cocoteros 38, Nuevo Vallarta (© **322/297-0174**). This beach club has a volleyball net, showers, restroom facilities, and food and drink service on the beach, both day and night. To get there, take the second entrance to Nuevo Vallarta coming from Puerto Vallarta and turn right on Paseo de los Cocoteros; it is past the Vista Bahía hotel. It's open daily from 11am to 7pm. Drinks cost $2.50 to $7 (£1.25–£3.50); entrees are $4.50 to $17 (£2.25–£8.50); and they take cash only.

A trip into downtown Puerto Vallarta takes about 30 minutes by taxi, costs about $20 to $25 (£10–£13), and is available 24 hours a day. The ride is slightly longer by public bus, which costs $1.50 (75p) and operates from 7am to 11pm.

Marival Grand & Club Suites This all-inclusive hotel sits almost by itself at the northernmost end of Nuevo Vallarta. Done in Mediterranean style, it offers a complete vacation experience, from its beautiful beach to the adjacent dance club. There are a large variety of room types, ranging from standard units with no balconies to large master suites with whirlpools. The master suites have minibars and hair dryers. The broad white-sand beach is one of the real assets here—it stretches over 450m (1,476 ft.). There is also an extensive activities program, including fun for children.

Paseo de los Cocoteros and Bulevar Nuevo Vallarta s/n, 63735 Nuevo Vallarta, Nay. (C) 450/686-0226 in Canada, and 322/297-0100 or 226-8200. Fax 322/297-0262. www.gomarival.com. 495 units. High season $409 (£205) double, low season $296 (£148) double; upgrade to junior suite $90 (£45) per day, to master suite with whirlpool $345 (£173) per day. Rates are all-inclusive. Ask for seasonal specials. AE, MC, V. From the Puerto Vallarta airport, enter Nuevo Vallarta from the 2nd entrance; Club Marival is the 1st resort to your right on Paseo de los Cocoteros. Free parking. **Amenities:** 6 restaurants; 8 bars; 3 outdoor pools and an adults-only whirlpool; 2 outdoor pools and a children's water park; 4 lighted tennis courts; spa; business center; salon. *In room:* A/C, TV, safe.

Paradise Village 🏵🏵

Truly a village, this self-contained resort on an exquisite stretch of beach offers a full array of services, from an on-site dance club to a full-service European spa and health club. The collection of pyramid-shaped buildings, designed in Maya-influenced style, houses well-designed all-suite accommodations in studio, one-, two-, and three-bedroom configurations. All have sitting areas and kitchenettes, making the resort ideal for families or groups of friends. The Maya theme extends to both oceanfront pools, with mythical creatures forming water slides and waterfalls. The exceptional spa is reason enough to book a vacation here, with treatments, hydrotherapy, massage (including massage on the beach), and fitness and yoga classes. Special spa packages are always available. A compelling attraction is their El Tigre golf course (details earlier in this chapter, under "Golf"); their on-site marina continues to draw a growing number of boats and yachts.

Paseo de los Cocoteros 001, 63731 Nuevo Vallarta, Nay. (C) 800/995-5714 in the U.S., or 322/226-6770. Fax 322/226-6713. www.paradisevillage.com. 490 units. High season $197–$296 (£99–£148) junior or 1-bedroom suite, $400 (£200) 2-bedroom suite, $572 (£286) 3-bedroom suite; low season $165–$258 (£83–£129) junior or 1-bedroom suite, $378 (£189) 2-bedroom suite, $520 (£260) 3-bedroom suite. All-inclusive rates available for $89 (£45) additional per person. AE, DC, MC, V. Free covered parking. **Amenities:** 2 restaurants; 2 beachside snack bars; nightclub; 2 beachside pools; lap pool; championship golf club w/18-hole course; 4 tennis courts; complete fitness center; European spa; watersports center; marina; kids' club; travel desk; guests-only rental-car fleet; basketball court; beach volleyball; petting zoo. *In room:* A/C, TV, minibar, coffeemaker, hair dryer, iron, safe.

BUCERIAS: A COASTAL VILLAGE 🏵

Only 18km (11 miles) north of the Puerto Vallarta airport, Bucerías ("boo-seh-*ree*-ahs," meaning "place of the divers") is a small coastal fishing village of 10,000 people in Nayarit state on Banderas Bay. It's caught on as an alternative to Puerto Vallarta for those who find the pace of life there too invasive. Bucerías offers a seemingly contradictory mix of accommodations—trailer-park spaces and exclusive villa rentals tend to dominate, although there's a small selection of hotels as well.

To reach the town center by car, take the exit road from the highway out of Vallarta and drive down the shaded, divided street that leads to the beach. Turn left when you see a line of minivans and taxis (which serve Bucerías and Vallarta). Go straight ahead 1 block to the main plaza. The beach, with a lineup of restaurants, is a half-block farther. You'll see cobblestone streets leading from the highway to the beach, and hints of villas and town homes behind high walls. Second-home owners and about 1,500 transplanted Americans have already sought out this peaceful getaway; tourists have discovered its relaxed pace as well.

If you take the bus to Bucerías, exit when you see the minivans and taxis to and from Bucerías on the street that leads to the beach. To use public transportation from Puerto Vallarta, take a minivan or bus marked BUCERIAS (they run 6am–9pm). The last minivan stop is Bucerías's town square. There's also 24-hour taxi service.

Exploring Bucerías   Come here for a day trip from Puerto Vallarta just to enjoy the long, wide, uncrowded beach, along with the fresh seafood served at the beachside restaurants or at one of the cafes listed below. On Saturdays and Sundays, many of the streets surrounding the plaza are closed to traffic for a *mercado* (street market)—where you can buy anything from tortillas to neon-colored cowboy hats. If you are inclined to stay a few days, you can relax inexpensively and explore more of Bucerías.

The **Coral Reef Surf Shop**, Heroe de Nacozari 114-F (℃ **329/298-0261**), sells a great selection of surfboards and gear, and offers surfboard and boogie board rentals, surf lessons, and ATV and other adventure tours to surrounding areas.

Where to Stay   Unfortunately, I cannot recommend any of the hotels in Bucerías; they're run-down, and most people who choose to stay here opt for a private home rental. Check out the villa rental bulletin board at **www.sunworx.com**. **Las Palmas,** in Bucerías (℃ **329/298-0060;** fax 329/298-0061), will book accommodations, including villas, houses, and condos. Call ahead, or ask for directions to the office when you get to Bucerías. It's open Monday through Friday from 9am to 2pm and 4 to 6pm, Saturday from 9am to 2pm.

Where to Dine   Besides those mentioned below, there are many seafood restaurants fronting the beach. The local specialty is *pescado zarandeado,* a whole fish smothered in tasty sauce and slow-grilled.

Karen's Place ✸ INTERNATIONAL/MEXICAN   This casual oceanside restaurant offers classic cuisine, plus Mexican favorites in a style that appeals to North American appetites. Known for Sunday champagne brunch (9am–3pm), it is a perfect place to enjoy a light beach lunch, or a romantic dinner. The best-selling entrees are barbeque ribs and coconut shrimp. The casual, comfortable restaurant features live music on Tuesday and Friday at 7pm. It also has a decked terrace dining area with spectacular views, as well as a sushi menu.

On the beach at the Costa Dorada, Calle Lázaro Cárdenas. ℃ **322/133-2186** or 329/298-0832. www.all.at/karens. Breakfast $5–$6 (£2.50–£3); Sun brunch (9am–3pm) $16 (£8); main courses $5.50–$13 (£2.75–£6.50). MC, V. Mon–Sat 9am–9pm, Sun 9am–3pm.

Le Fort ✸✸✸ *Moments* FRENCH   What an unforgettable dining experience. The evening consists of watching as Chef Gilles Le Fort prepares your gourmet meal and teaches you how to re-create it. The U-shaped bar in the intimate kitchen accommodates diners, who sip fine wines and nibble on pâté while the master works. Chef Le Fort is the winner of numerous culinary awards, and his warm conviviality is the real secret ingredient of this unusual experience. Once dinner is served, the chef and his wife, Margarita, will join the table, entertaining with stories of their experiences in Mexico. The first group of six to book for the evening chooses the menu; the maximum class size is 16, so groups often blend together. Le Fort has probably the most extensive wine cellar in the bay—some 4,000 bottles. Hand-rolled Cuban cigars, homemade sausages, pâtés, and more delicacies are available in the adjoining shop.

Calle Lázaro Cárdenas 71, 1 block from the Hotel Royal Decameron. ℃ **329/298-1532.** www.lefort.com.mx. Reservations required. 3-course dinner, wines, and recipes $54 (£27) per person. No credit cards. Daily 8–10:30pm; cooking classes available 10am–1:30pm.

Mark's ✸✸ *Finds* ITALIAN/STEAK/SEAFOOD   It's worth a special trip to Bucerías just to eat at this covered-patio restaurant. The most popular American hangout in town, Mark's offers a great assortment of thin-crust pizza and flatbread, baked in its brick oven and seasoned with fresh herbs grown in the garden. Everything has exquisite flavorings—some favorites include lobster-stuffed chile relleno, macadamia-crusted red snapper filet, ahi tuna served rare, and filet mignon with blue-cheese ravioli. Multitalented chef Jan Marie (Mark's charming wife and partner) runs an adjacent boutique, featuring elegant home accessories and unique gift items. The bar televises all major sporting events.

Calle Lázaro Cárdenas 56 (a half block from the beach). © **329/298-0303.** Pasta $8.70–$19 (£4.80–£10); main courses $13–$32 (£6.50–£16). MC, V. Daily 5–10:30pm. From the highway, turn left just after bridge, where there's a small sign for Mark's; double back left at next street (immediately after you turn left) and turn right at next corner; Mark's is on the right.

Mezzogiorno 🌊🌊 ITALIAN   The owners of this elegantly casual oceanfront *trattoria* built a reputation with their Mezzaluna restaurant in Vallarta, then moved the business to their former home in Bucerías when the traffic became too much to deal with a commute. And diners on the north shore are so very grateful. It's the most attractive dining option north of Vallarta, in a sleekly restored home overlooking the bay. Choose to dine indoors or under the stars, beneath a canopy of trees on a ocean-view deck or on the sand itself. But as stunning as the minimalist decor of the restaurant is, it takes second place to the savory dishes served. Salads are ample in size, and varied in combination of ingredients. My favorite combines grilled chicken with mixed greens, sun-dried tomatoes, goat cheese, and a currant-balsamic vinaigrette. For main dishes, pasta is the specialty, with best-sellers that include their calamari and saffron ravioli in a creamy sauce. Also delightful are the shrimp, clams, and fish served over black fettuccine, with black olives, capers, and a spicy tomato sauce. There is an ample wine list, full bar service, and attentive service.

Av. del Pacífico 33. © **329/298-0350.** www.mezzogiorno.com.mx. Main courses $7.50–$19 (£3.75–£9.50). MC, V. Daily 6–11pm.

PUNTA MITA: EXCLUSIVE SECLUSION 🌊🌊🌊

At the northern tip of the bay is an arrowhead-shaped, 600-hectare (1,482-acre) peninsula bordered on three sides by the ocean, called Punta Mita. Considered a sacred place by the Indians, this is the point where Banderas Bay, the Pacific Ocean, and the Sea of Cortez come together. It's magnificent, with white-sand beaches and coral reefs just offshore. Stately rocks jut out along the shoreline, and the water is a dreamy translucent blue. Punta Mita is evolving into one of Mexico's most exclusive developments. The master plan calls for four luxury hotels, several high-end residential communities, and up to three championship golf courses. It is the first luxury residential development in Mexico intended for the foreign market. Today, what you'll find is the elegant Four Seasons Resort, its Jack Nicklaus Signature golf course, and a selection of rental luxury villas and condos. By fall of 2008, a new 120-room St. Regis Resort will open, along with Punta Mita's second Jack Nicklaus Signature golf course.

Casa de Mita 🌊🌊 *Finds*   Previously known as Casa Las Brisas, this hotel isn't technically in Punta Mita, but it's near enough to convey a sense of the area's relaxed seclusion. It's located on the back road that runs from Punta Mita to Sayulita, on the small, pristine Careyeros Bay. The six rooms and two suites are set in a villa, overlooking the exquisite beach. The villa itself is a work of white stucco walls, tile floors and patios, thatch and tile roofs, and guayaba-wood balcony detailing. Patios and intimate indoor-outdoor seating areas on varying levels are ideal for an afternoon read or an evening cocktail. Interiors of the guest rooms are simple and elegant, with touches such as carved armoires, headboards, and doors from Michoacán. The colorful bathrooms feature large showers lined with hand-painted tiles. Private balconies with ocean views surround the pool, which features submerged sunning chairs and a small fountain. There are no TVs in the rooms (only in the suites) or telephones, but a cellphone in the lobby is available for guests. A big plus here is the delicious dining, included in the price of your stay.

Playa Careyeros, 63734 Punta de Mita, Nay. ℂ 866/740-7999 in the U.S., 329/298-4114, or 322/225-4364. www. brisasdemita.com. 8 rooms and suites. High season $445–$615 (£223–£308) suite; low season $385–$545 (£193–£273) suite. Rates include all meals and drinks. Minimum 3-night stay required. AE, DC, MC, V. Limited street parking. **Amenities:** Restaurant; small outdoor pool; universal gym station; spa; tour services; entertainment room w/TV, DVD, and VCR. *In room:* A/C, minibar, safe, no phone.

Four Seasons Resort Punta Mita 🏖️🏖️🏖️   The Four Seasons Resort has brought a new standard of luxury to Mexico's Pacific Coast. The boutique hotel offers seclusion, pampering service, and comfort. Accommodations are in three-story *casitas* surrounding the main building, which houses the lobby, cultural center, restaurants, shopping arcade, and oceanfront pool. Every guestroom offers breathtaking views of the ocean from a large terrace or balcony. Most suites have a private plunge pool, a sitting room, a bar, and a powder room. Rooms are plush and spacious, with a king or two double beds, a seating area, and an oversize bathroom with a deep soaking tub, separate glass-enclosed shower, and dual vanity sink. Service is unerringly warm and unobtrusive. At least 45 minutes from Puerto Vallarta's activities, it's an ideal getaway, with a full-service spa, tennis center, and private championship golf course. In 2006, Four Seasons unveiled an adults-only tranquillity pool, with champagne and caviar bar, surrounded by cabañas available for daily rent. In 2007, they expanded their popular Kids for All Seasons club and added a building for family travelers. The resort now offers private four- and five-bedroom villas as well, with private butler services.

63734 Bahía de Banderas, Nay. ℂ 800/332-3442 in the U.S., or 329/291-6000. Fax 329/291-6060. www.fourseasons. com. 165 units. High season $545–$1,175 (£273–£588) double, $1,685–$15,000 (£843–£7,500) suite; low season $375–$925 (£188–£463) double, $1,025–$8,750 (£513–£4,375) suite. AE, DC, MC, V. Free valet parking. **Amenities:** 3 restaurants; lobby bar; beachfront bar; oceanfront pool; adults-only pool surrounded by private cabañas; tennis center w/4 courts of various surfaces; full-service fitness center; European-style spa; watersports equipment including sea kayaks, sailboards, surfboards, and sunfish sailboats; children's programs; game room, 24-hr. concierge; tour desk; room service; cultural center w/lectures and activities; complimentary video library. *In room:* A/C, TV/VCR, high-speed Internet, minibar, coffeemaker, hair dryer, iron, safe.

SAYULITA: MEXICO'S CURRENT HOT SPOT

Sayulita is only 40km (25 miles) northwest of Puerto Vallarta, on Highway 200 to Tepic, yet it feels like a world apart. It captures the simplicity and tranquillity of beach life that has long since left Vallarta—but hurry, because it's exploding in popularity. For years, Sayulita has been principally a surfers' destination—the main beach in town is known for its consistent break and long, rideable waves. Recently, visitors and locals who find Vallarta to be too cosmopolitan have started to flock here. The major travel press noticed this trend, and popularized the place to a tipping point in 2007. You'll now find more real estate offices than surf shops, and more fine jewelry stores than juice bars, but Sayulita is still gently holding on to her charms.

An easygoing attitude still prevails in this beach town, despite the niceties popping up amid the basic accommodations, inexpensive Mexican food stands, and handmade, hippie-style-bauble vendors. It's quickly becoming gentrified with new cafes, sleek shops, aromatherapy-infused spas, and elegant villas for rent.

Sayulita is most popular for surfing. Any day, you'll witness an army of surfers seeking perfect-swells offshore from the main beach. You may just as easily encounter a Huichol Indian family that has come down from the Sierra to sell their wares.

To get to Sayulita, you can rent a car, or take a taxi from the airport or downtown Vallarta. The rate is about $60 (£30) to get to the town plaza. You can also take a taxi back to Vallarta. The stand is on the main square, or you can call for pickup at your hotel. The trip to the airport from Sayulita costs $50 (£25). Guides also lead tours to Puerto Vallarta, Punta Mita, and other surrounding areas, including a Huichol Indian community.

Where to Stay

Sayulita has several private homes for rent. One local expert on Sayulita rentals is **Upi Viteri** (upiviteri@prodigy.net.mx), who has access to some of the nicest properties.

Villa Amor   Villa Amor is a collection of inviting, airy, functionally appointed guest rooms—think of it as your private villa by the sea. Owner Rod Ingram and his design team have carefully crafted each space and individual suite. The exterior walls curve invitingly and open to breathtaking views all around. The one- and two-bedroom "villa" suites have fully equipped kitchenettes, plus open-air seating or dining areas (or both); some have plunge pools or air-conditioning. TVs are available on request.

Camino Playa Los Muertos s/n, 63732 Sayulita, Nay. © 619/819-5407 from the U.S.; 329/291-3010. Fax 329/291-3018. www.villaamor.com. 33 units. $90–$260 (£45–£130) 1-bedroom villa, $350–$550 (£175–£225) 2-bedroom villa; $650–$750 (£325–£375) 3-bedroom villa; rates include continental breakfast. MC, V. **Amenities:** Restaurant; kayaks; boogie boards; surfboards; bicycles; concierge; tour desk; room service; massage. *In room:* Fan.

Where to Dine

If you are in Sayulita, chances are you heard about it because of **Don Pedro's,** the most popular restaurant in town, in the heart of the main beach. More popular than fine dining in Sayulita, however, are the pervasive stands hawking cheap fish tacos and other street fare—which are the best way to dine.

Don Pedro's INTERNATIONAL   Many say it's Don Pedro's that has brought so much attention to Sayulita in recent years. Vallarta area visitors came for the food, then booked their next vacation in this funky town. Choose between a two-level indoor dining area or shaded tables on the beach for breakfast, lunch, or dinner. Starters include crispy calamari, spring rolls, and fresh salads. Main courses include thin-crust pizza, fresh fish artfully prepared, and a changing selection of savory pasta and chicken dishes, such as chicken Provençal—a whole chicken marinated in garlic and herbs, served with sautéed spinach, roasted tomatoes, and white beans. Grilled ahi tuna with mashed potatoes is also a favorite. In the bar area, TVs broadcast sporting events of any relevance, from college football to Mexican *futból* (soccer). I enjoy a relaxing lunch here, then stay for the beach action. Full bar service is also available.

Marlin 2, on the beachfront. © 329/291-3090. Main courses $8–$25 (£4–£13). MC, V. Daily 8am–11pm.

Rollie's ௸௸ *Finds* BREAKFAST   Breakfast heaven. This family restaurant emanates a happy aura that puts its patrons in a good mood. The menu reflects the tone of the place, with options such as Rollie's Delight (blended fresh orange and banana), Adriana's Rainbow (an omelet with cheese, tomatoes, green peppers, and onions), and my personal favorite, Indian Pipe Pancakes. All dishes come with Rollie's famous lightly seasoned, pan-fried new potatoes. Rollie's recently expanded their offerings to dinner as well, served from 5:30 to 9pm. Specialties include paella. There's also an upstairs espresso bar.

Av. Revolución, 2 blocks west of the main square. © 329/291-3567 or -3075. Breakfast $5–$8 (£2.50–£4); dinner $6–$15 (£3–£7.50). No credit cards. Daily Nov–Apr 8am–noon and 5:30–9pm. Closed May–Oct.

SURFING   There are two main surf spots in Sayulita—the most popular is the break fronting the main beach in the village, which is a right longboard break. A faster, left break is found just north of the river mouth, in front of the campground. Surf instruction and board rentals are available at **Lunazul Surf School** (© 329/291-2009; www.lunazulsurf.com) located at Marlin #4, where this street ends at the beachfront. The 90-minute surf lessons cost $40 (£$20) for individual instruction, or $30 (£$15) for group instruction. They also offer 2-day weekend clinics for $80 (£$40) or weeklong clinics for $200 (£$100). Included in all lessons is the use of a surfboard and rashguard. Board rentals through Lunazul are $20 (£10) for the day, or $150 (£75) for the week. Lunazul also has a surf shop, where you can purchase surf gear ranging from wax to boards.

Among the growing number of surfer-chic shops, the standout is **Pachamama** (© 329/291-3468; Defines #6B, www.lesgazelles.com), which sells Tahitian black pearl jewelry, generally strung on leather cords in exquisite yet casual designs, as well as a tightly edited selection of clothing and home design items. The boutique—owned and operated by a group of free-spirited, lovely French girls with a passion for surfing and sunshine—is an enchanting visit, whether you end up with a purchase or not.

NIGHTLIFE   Nightlife in Sayulita is as laid back by night as by day, but options are plentiful—ranging from rowdier bars to live music venues. The locals seem to gravitate to a different locale each night, so when you arrive ask around to see where the evening's hot spot will be. One dependable option is the **Buddha Bar** (no phone), located at Calle Marlin #8, on the second floor just next to Don Pedros (you can't miss the neon pink sign). It's no relation to the famed Paris or New York venues with the same name, but it likewise serves Pan-Asian cuisine and luscious libations, served amid Buddha statues, pillowed banquettes, and lounge music. On weekends, there is often live music from 10pm until 1am, which tends to draw a dancing crowd. It's open each evening from 6:30pm until about 2am, or when the crowd abates.

SAN SEBASTIAN: MOUNTAIN HIDEAWAY ＲＲＲ

If you haven't heard about San Sebastián yet, it probably won't be long—its remote location and historic appeal have made it the Mexican media's new darling destination. Originally discovered in the late 1500s and settled in 1603, the town peaked as a center of mining operations, swelling to a population of over 30,000 by the mid-1800s. Today, with roughly 600 year-round residents, San Sebastián retains all the charm of a village locked in time, with an old church, a coffee plantation, an underground tunnel system—and wholly without a T-shirt shop.

Getting There   By car, it's a 2½-hour drive up the Sierra Madre from Puerto Vallarta on an improved road, but it can be difficult during the summer rainy season, when the road washes out frequently. **Vallarta Adventures** (© 888/303-2653 in the U.S., or 322/297-1212, ext. 3; www.vallarta-adventures.com) runs a daily plane service for half-day tours and can occasionally accommodate overnight visitors. The small private airport can arrange flights. **Aerotron** (© 322/221-1921; www.aerotron.com.mx) charges about $140 (£70) round-trip, **Aéro Taxis de la Bahía** (© 322/221-1990 and 222-2049) about $100 (£50) round-trip, depending on the type of plane and number of passengers. For more information on air tours and horseback-riding excursions, see the "Organized Tours" section, earlier in this chapter.

Where to Stay   There are two places to stay in San Sebastián. The first is the very basic **El Pabellón de San Sebastián,** which faces the town square. Its nine simply furnished rooms surround a central patio. Don't expect extras here; rates run $50 (£25) per double. The town's central phone lines handle reservations—you call (© **322/297-0200**) and leave a message or send a fax, and hopefully the hotel will receive it. Except on holidays, there is generally room at this inn. No credit cards.

A more enjoyable option, the stately **Hacienda Jalisco** (© **322/222-9638;** www.haciendajalisco.com), built in 1850, was once the center of mining operations in town. The beautifully landscaped, rambling old hacienda is near the airstrip, a 15-minute walk from town. Proprietor Bud Acord has welcomed John Huston, Liz Taylor, Richard Burton, Peter O'Toole, and a cast of local characters over the years.

The five extra-clean rooms have wood floors, rustic furnishings and antiques, and working fireplaces; some are decorated with pre-Columbian reproductions. The ample bathrooms are beautifully tiled and have skylights. Hammocks grace the upstairs terrace, while a sort-of museum on the lower level attests to the celebrity guests and importance the hacienda has enjoyed over the years. Because of its remote location, all meals are included. Rates are $80 (£40) per person per night, and includes full breakfast and dinner; alcoholic beverages are extra. Reserve through e-mail (pmt15@ hotmail.com or info@haciendajalisco.com), through the town telephone (© **322/ 297-0200**), or on their website. Group rates and discounts for longer stays are available. No credit cards are accepted. Guided horseback, walking, or mine tours can be arranged through the Hacienda.

2 Mazatlán ✶

1,078km (668 miles) NW of Mexico City; 502km (311 miles) NW of Guadalajara; 1,561km (968 miles) SE of Mexicali

Mazatlán is comfortable, casual, value-packed Mexico at its best. More than any other beach resort in the country, it represents the golden beaches, fresh seafood, and inexpensive accommodations that typified Mexico's appeal to travelers in the first place. The developments that are edging Mazatlán into the golf-playing, manicured resort that typifies most of Mexico today have quickened pace in the past year. Mazatlán seems to be going there grudgingly—most of it remains refreshingly simple.

Mazatlán's lures continue to be its expansive beaches and renowned sportfishing. The evolving golf scene, luxury-yacht harbor, and growing selection of accommodations have yet to catch the attention of enough tourists to drive prices to the levels of other Mexican resorts, and that's good news for travelers looking for economy in a beach resort.

A city with a population of nearly 500,000, Mazatlán is the largest port between Los Angeles and the Panama Canal. Elegant reminders of its history, 27km (17 miles) of sandy beaches, and a geographically diverse environment are all added attractions in Mazatlán's efforts to become a premier beach resort.

Limited flights deter Mazatlán's growth. Charter operators have picked up some of the slack and are the predominant means of arrival here.

Once known as a spring break haven and party town, Mazatlán now attracts more families, mature travelers, and other tourists with an eye for value. It enjoys strong repeat business and positive word of mouth as an exceptional vacation value.

ESSENTIALS
GETTING THERE & DEPARTING
BY PLANE   A number of airlines operate direct or nonstop flights to Mazatlán, though charters predominate. From the United States, **AeroMéxico** (© **800/237-6639**

in the U.S., or 01-800/021-4000 in Mexico) flies from Los Angeles, Atlanta, Phoenix, and Tucson, via Mexico City. **Mexicana** (② 800/531-7921 in the U.S.) has direct service from Denver, Chicago, Los Angeles, Miami, and San Antonio, most connecting through Mexico City. **Alaska Airlines** (② 800/252-7522 in the U.S., or 669/985-2730) serves Vancouver, Seattle, Portland, San Francisco, and Los Angeles. In Mexico, **AeroMexico** (② 669/914-1111) has flights from Hermosillo, Durango, Monterrey, Puerto Vallarta, Tijuana, and León, all via Guadalajara or Mexico City. **Mexicana** (② 669/982-5666) offers service from Mexico City and Los Cabos. **Aero Calafia** (② 669/985-4300; www.aereocalafia.com.mx) offers direct service from Puerto Vallarta and Los Cabos. Check with a travel agent for the latest **charter flights.**

BY BUS   First-class and deluxe buses connect Mazatlán to Guadalajara (7 hr.; $37 first class one-way) and Mexico City (16 hr.; $85/£47 first class one-way) almost hourly, and less often to other points within Mexico. The bus terminal is located on Highway 200 N. Km 1203; ② 669/982-1949.

BY CAR   To reach Mazatlán from the United States, take **International Highway 15** from Nogales, Arizona, to Culiacán. At Culiacán, change to the four-lane **tollway**—it costs about $40 (£20) but is the only road considered safe and in drivable condition. On the tollway, total trip time from the United States to Mazatlán is about 10 hours. Consider an overnight stop, because driving at night in Mexico can be dangerous. **From Puerto Vallarta,** the 560km (347-mile) drive is not easy—the road winds through the mountains, but is in generally good condition. Take **Highway 200** north to Las Varas. There it becomes four-lane **Highway 68;** follow that until you see a detour for **Highway 15.** Take 15 north to Mazatlán.

ORIENTATION

ARRIVING   The Rafael Buelna International Airport (airport code: MZT) is 27km (17 miles) southeast of the hotel-and-resort area of town. The following rental-car companies have counters in the airport, open during flight arrivals and departures: **Hertz** (② 800/654-3030 in the U.S., or 669/985-0845), **Budget** (② 800/472-3325 in the U.S., or 669/913-2000), and **National** (② 800/227-3876 in the U.S., or 669/982-4000). Daily rates run $65 to $145 (£33–£73). A car is desirable if you want to explore the coast and nearby villages, but it is not essential in Mazatlán.

Taxis and *colectivo* minivans run from the airport to hotels; the expensive airport-chartered taxis cost $40 to $50 (£20–£25), about twice as much as the *colectivo*, which runs $20 to $28 (£10–£14), depending on the location of your hotel. Only taxis make the return trip to the airport, which costs $20 to $30 (£10–£15). The **Central de Autobuses** (main bus terminal) is at Río Tamazula and Chachalacas. To get there from Avenida del Mar, walk 3 blocks inland on Río Tamazula; the station is on your right. Taxis line up in front of the bus station.

VISITOR INFORMATION   The extremely helpful and professional **City and State Tourism Office** is on Calle Carnaval 1317, corner of Mariano Escobedo, at the Plaza Machado (② 669/981-8886 or -8887; fax 669/981-8884; www.sinaloa-travel.com). The office is open Monday through Friday from 9am to 5pm; the staff speaks English. To preview what's going on in Mazatlán before you arrive, check the website of the local English-language newspaper (www.pacificpearl.com), or pick up a copy of their very helpful publication upon arrival for a complete schedule of current activities. Three other very helpful guides in English are the **Welcome Digest** (② 669/913-3628; www.welcomedigest.com), **Viejo Mazatlán** (② 669/985-3781;

Mazatlán Area

UNITED STATES

Mazatlán
MEXICO
Gulf of
Mexico

PACIFIC
OCEAN
Mexico
City

0   500 mi
0   500 km

K Beach
🔆 Lighthouse
🚌 Bus
🚂 Train
✝ Church
✉ Post office

Isla de Pájaros
(Bird Island)

Isla de Venados
(Deer Island)

Isla de Lobos
(Wolf Island)

Centro Histórico

Cerro de
Nevería

5 de Mayo
Ocampo
Valle
Mercado
Dominguez
Canizales
Serdán
21 de Marzo
Zócalo ✉
Angel Flores
Pedregoso
Escobedo
Constitución
Deer
statue
Hotel
La Siesta
Niños Heroes
Carnaval
Juárez
Av. Olas Altas
Venus
Frías
Osuna
Rojo

0   200 yds
0   200 m

Marina
Mazatlán
El Rancho Hotel
& Beach Resort
Hotel Faro
Mazatlán

Playa
Sábalo
Pueblo
Bonito

El Cid
Mega Resort

Av. Sábalo Cerritos
Estero del Sábalo

Gaviotas
Avenida Camarón Sábalo
R.T. Loaiza
**ZONA DORADO
(GOLD ZONE)**

Hotel
Playa
Mazatlán
Garzas
Sábalo
Traffic Circle
Playa Las
Gaviotas
Avenida Rafael Buelna
Internacional

Howard Johnson
Don Pelayo
Reforma
Revolución
Carretera

Avenida del Mar
Av. Insurgentes
Playa
Norte
Bus
Station
Train Station

To Airport
(10 miles)

Bahía del
Puerto Viejo

Gutiérrez Najera
Paseo Claussen
Belisario Domínguez
G. Nelson
Juan Carrasco
A. Serdán
Melchor Ocampo
Benito Juárez
Zaragoza
Angel Flores
T. Azueta
Rosales
Avenida G. Leyva
Avenida del Puerto

Cerro de la
Nevería

Playa
Olas Altas
Olas Altas
5 de Mayo
Avenida Alemán

Launches to
■ Stone Island

Cerro
del
Vigía
Avenida Barragán

See inset map

Cruise Ship and
Ferry Docks

Isla de la Piedra
(Stone Island)

Ferry Dock

■ Sport Fishing
Fleets

Acuario Mazatlán
(Aquarium) **5**

Cathedral of the
Immaculate Conception **6**

Centro de Idiomas **11**

El Faro (lighthouse) **14**

El Mirador Lookout Point **13**

Mazatlán Arts and Crafts
Center **1**

Museo Arqueológico
de Mazatlán **12**

Plaza de Toros (bullring) **3**

Plaza Principal **7**

Plazuela Machado **10**

Sea Shell City **2**

Teatro Ángela Peralta **9**

Tourism Office **8**

Valentino's/Punta Camarón **4**

www.viejo-mazatlan.com), and **Mazatlán Interactivo** (© 669/981-8435; www.
mazatlaninteractivo.com.mx).

CITY LAYOUT   Mazatlán extends north from the peninsula port area along
Avenida Gabriel Leyva and Avenida Barragan, where the cruise ships, sportfishing
boats, and ferries dock. Downtown begins with the historic area of **Viejo Mazatlán
(Old Mazatlán)** and **Playa Olas Altas** to the south. A curving seaside boulevard, or
malecón, runs 27km (17 miles) along the waterfront, all the way from Playa Olas
Altas to **Playa Norte,** changing names often along the way. Traveling north, it begins
as Paseo Olas Altas and becomes Paseo Claussen parallel to the commercial downtown
area. The name changes to Avenida del Mar at the beginning of the Playa Norte area.

About 6km (4 miles) north of downtown lies the Sábalo traffic circle in the **Zona
Dorada (Golden Zone)** near the **Punta Camarón,** a rocky outcropping over the water.
The Zona Dorada begins where Avenida del Mar intersects Avenida Rafael Buelna and
becomes **Avenida Camarón Sábalo,** which leads north through the abundant hotels
and fast-food restaurants of the tourist zone. From here, the resort hotels, including the
huge El Cid Resort complex, spread northward along and beyond **Playa Sábalo.** The
Marina Mazatlán development has changed the landscape north of the Zona Dorada
considerably; hotels, condo complexes, and private residences rise around the new
marina. Although completion of the extensive project—to comprise the marina, condominiums, and commercial centers—is still years away, the new marina will be the largest
on the western seaboard between Los Angeles and Panama, and one of the largest in all
of Latin America. This area north of the Marina El Cid is increasingly known as Nuevo
Mazatlán. North of here is **Los Cerritos (Little Hills),** the northern limit of Mazatlán.

GETTING AROUND
The downtown transportation center for buses, taxis, and *pulmonías* (see below) is on
the central Plaza Principal, facing the cathedral.

BY TAXI   Eco Taxis are green-and-white cabs with posted set fares, but generally are
about $3 or $5 (£1.50–£2.50) per trip. Taxis are easy to flag around town and can also
be rented by the day or by the hour. Agree on a price in advance. Fares between the
Zona Dorada and Old Mazatlán average $4.50 to $6.50 (£2.25–£3.25); within the
Zona Dorada, you should pay about $3.50 to $5 (£1.75–£2.50). To request a taxi, call
© 669/986-1111 or 985-2828.

BY PULMONIA   These open-air vehicles resembling overgrown golf carts carry up
to three passengers. *Pulmonías* (literally "pneumonias") have surreylike tops and open
sides. As a rule, they're slightly more expensive than taxis at about $5 (£2.50) per start-
ing fare, but they're part of the Mazatlán experience.

BY BUS   Buses, some with air-conditioning, cover most of the city and are relatively
easy to use, although knowing some Spanish is helpful. The fare is 80¢ (40p) for local
routes. The SABALO CENTRO line runs from the Zona Dorada along the waterfront to
downtown near the market and the central plaza; at Avenida Miguel Alemán, the
buses turn and head south to Olas Altas. The CERRITOS-JUAREZ line starts near the
train station, cuts across town to the *malecón* beside the Zona Dorada, and heads
north to Los Cerritos and back. The SABALO COCOS line runs through the Zona
Dorada, heads inland to the bus station, and goes on to downtown (also stopping at
the market) by a back route. The PLAYA SUR line goes to the area where the sportfishing and tour boats depart. Buses run daily from 6am to 10:30pm. Fares are about 75¢
(38p) for air-conditioned green buses or 35¢ (18p) for the yellow buses.

FAST FACTS: Mazatlán

American Express The office is on Avenida Camarón Sábalo in the Centro Comercial Balboa shopping center, Loc. 15 and 16 (© **669/913-0600;** fax 669/916-5908), between the traffic circle and the El Cid Resort. It's open Monday through Friday from 9am to 6pm, Saturday from 9am to 1pm.

Area Code The telephone area code for Mazatlán is **669.**

Banks Most banks are generally open Monday through Friday from 9am to 6pm, and some have limited hours on Saturday.

Climate As the northernmost major beach resort on the mainland, Mazatlán can be cooler in summer than the resorts farther south. The wettest month is September.

Drugstore **Farmacias Hidalgo,** German Evers and Hidalgo s/n (© **669/985-4545** or -4646), is open 24 hours and delivers to hotels.

Emergencies Dial © **066.** For medical emergencies, contact the **Sharp Hospital,** Rafael Buelna and Las Cruces (© **669/986-5676** or -5678). The **Traffic Police** can be reached at © **669/983-2616.**

Internet Access Numerous places offer access, with one long-standing business being **Internet Café Netscape** (Av. Camarón Sábalo 222, between Farmacia Benavides and Taco Loco); it's open daily, including holidays, from 8am to 11pm. Access costs $3 (£1.50) per hour; $1.50 (75p) for 30 minutes (© **669/913-1444**).

Language Classes Spanish-language classes begin every Monday at the **Centro de Idiomas** (© **669/985-5606;** fax 669/982-2053; www.spanishlink.org), 3 blocks west of the cathedral near 21 de Marzo and Canizales. In addition to small-group (maximum 10 students) and individual instruction, the language center offers a home-stay program and a person-to-person program that matches students with local people. On Friday at 7pm, the center holds free Spanish and English conversation groups open to both visitors and locals. For more information, call or write Dixie Davis, Belisario Domínguez 1908, Mazatlán, Sin.

Post Office The *correo* is downtown on Benito Juárez just off Angel Flores, on the east side of the main plaza (© **669/981-2121**). Hours are Monday through Friday from 8am to 5pm, Saturday from 9am to noon.

ACTIVITIES ON & OFF THE BEACH

To orient yourself, walk up and enjoy the panoramic view from **El Faro,** the famous lighthouse on the point at the south end of town. It's the second-highest lighthouse in the world (only Gibraltar's is higher), towering 135m (443 ft.) over the harbor. Begin at the end of Paseo Centenario, near the sportfishing docks. There's a refreshment stand at the foot of the hill. Allow about 45 minutes for the climb. The view is nearly as spectacular from the top of **Cerro del Vigía (Lookout Hill),** which is accessible by car from Paseo Olas Altas.

BEACHES   At the western edge of downtown is rocky **Playa Olas Altas,** a lovely stretch of pounding surf not suitable for swimming. Around a rocky promontory north of Olas Altas is **Playa Norte,** which offers several kilometers of good sand beach.

At the Sábalo traffic circle, Punta Camarón juts into the water, and on either side of the point is **Playa Las Gaviotas.** Farther north, **Playa Sábalo** is perhaps the best beach in Mazatlán. The next point jutting into the water is Punta Sábalo, beyond which you'll find a bridge over a channel that flows in and out of a lagoon. Beyond the marina, more beaches stretch all the way to Los Cerritos. Remember that all beaches in Mexico are public property, so you have the right to enjoy the beach of your choice.

Mazatlán is one of only a few resorts in Mexico where surfing is common on central town beaches. The waves are best at **Los Pinos,** north of the fort—known in surfing circles as "the Cannon"—and at Playa Los Gaviotas and Playa Sábalo. Waves are most notable and consistent from May to September. Other notable surf breaks are found at Olas Altos, Cerritos, Isla de la Piedra, and El Camarón, at Playa Norte. For surf gear, board rentals, lessons, and surf reports, visit the **Mazatlán Surf Center** (© **669/913-1821;** www.mazatlansurfcenter.com) in the Zona Dorada, at Camarón Sábalo, 500-4, next to the Dairy Queen. Boogie boards are widely available for rent, on the beaches in front of the Zona Dorada, for about $25 (£13) per day.

A good beach that makes a great day trip is on the ocean side of **Isla de la Piedra (Stone Island).** From the center of town, board a Circunvalación or Playa Sur bus from the north side of the Plaza Principal for the ride to the boat landing, Embarcadero–Isla de la Piedra. Small motorboats make the 5-minute trip to the island every 15 minutes or so, from 7am to 6pm, for a modest price. When you arrive on the island, walk through the rustic little village to the ocean side, where the pale-sand beaches, bordered by coconut groves, stretch for miles. On Sunday afternoons, the *palapa* restaurants on the shore have music and dancing, attracting mainly Mexican families; on other days the beach is almost empty. **Carmelita's** has delicious fish, called *lisamacho;* it's grilled over an open fire and served slightly blackened with fresh, hot corn tortillas and salsa. It's open daily from 10am to 6pm and doesn't accept credit cards.

The local gay beach is on **Isla de las Chivas.** Transportation to the island is by launches, which you can catch at the Muelle Puntilla, located next to the docks where the ferry to La Paz departs.

CRUISES & BOAT RENTALS   The **Kolonahe Sailing Adventure** departs for Isla de Venados (Deer Island) Tuesday through Sunday from Marina El Cid. Reserve through any travel agent or through El Cid (see below). This excursion sails aboard a 15m (50-ft.) trimaran to the island, where guests enjoy a picnic lunch and beverages, plus the use of snorkel equipment, boogie boards, kayaks, and canoes, for a cost of $35 (£18) per person. Departure is at 9:15am, with the boat returning at 3:30pm.

Anfibios, amphibious vehicles that operate on land and in the water, head for Isla de Venados, one of three big islands off the coast. Trips last 2 to 2½ hours; they leave from the beaches of the **El Cid Resort** (© **669/913-3333,** ext. 3341; www.elcid.com) daily at 10am, noon, and 2pm. Round-trip tickets cost $10 (£5), plus $10 (£5) for snorkeling gear.

DEEP-SEA FISHING   Mazatlán claims to be the billfish and shrimp capital of the world, and whether or not it's a valid claim, deep-sea fishing in Mazatlán is generally less expensive than in other parts of Mexico. If you request it (please do), your captain will practice "catch and release." Rates are around $250 (£125) per day for a 7m (23-ft.) *lancha* for up to three persons and $430 (£215) per day for an 11m (36-ft.) cruiser for up to four passengers; rates do not include fishing licenses, drinks, or gratuities. Try the **Aries Fleet** located at the Marina El Cid harbormaster's office (© **669/916-3468**). Locals suggest making fishing reservations for October through January at least a month in advance; at the very least, do it the minute you arrive in town. You may also choose to rent a *panga* (a small, uncovered, fiberglass boat with an outboard motor) at a rate of $50 (£25) per hour, with a minimum of 4 hours—it's the way the locals fish.

OTHER WATERSPORTS Among the best places to rent watersports equipment, from snorkeling gear to kayaks, are the Aqua Sport Center at the **El Cid Resort** (© **669/913-3333;** www.mazatlan-aquasports.com) and the Ocean Sport Center at the **Hotel Faro Mazatlán** (© **669/913-1111;** www.faromazatlan.com.mx).

SPECIAL EVENTS IN NEARBY VILLAGES The weekend of the first Sunday in October, **Rosario,** a small town 45 minutes south on Highway 15, holds a **festival honoring Our Lady of the Rosary,** with games, music, dances, processions, and festive foods. From May 1 to May 10, Rosario holds its **Spring Festival.**

In mid-October, the village of **Escuinapa,** south of Rosario on Highway 15, holds a **Mango Festival.** For information, call the **State Tourism Office** at © **669/981-8886.**

SPECTATOR SPORTS There's a bullring (Plaza de Toros) on Rafael Buelna about 1.5km (1 mile) from the Zona Dorada. From December to early April, **bullfights** take place every Sunday and on holidays at 4pm; locals recommend arriving by 2pm. Tickets range from $15 (£7.50) for general admission (ask for the shady side—*la sombra*) to $30 (£15) for the front of the shaded section; most travel agencies and tour desks sell advance tickets.

Rodeos, or *charreadas,* take place at the Lienzo Charro (bullring) of the Asociación de Charros de Mazatlán (© **669/986-3510**) on Saturday or Sunday beginning at 4pm. Tickets (around $4.50/£2.25) are available through local travel agents and hotel concierge desks, which will have the current schedule.

At Playa Olas Altas, daring **cliff divers** take to the rock ledges of **El Mirador** and plunge into the shallow, pounding surf below, a la Acapulco. The divers perform sporadically during the day as tour buses arrive near their perch, sometimes diving with torches at 7pm. After the dive, they collect donations from spectators. Follow the *malecón* to the esplanade and look for the mermaid statue to find El Mirador.

TENNIS, GOLF & OTHER OUTDOOR SPORTS Mazatlán has more than 100 tennis courts. Try the **El Cid Resort,** on Camarón Sábalo (© **669/913-3333;** hotel guests have priority), or the **Racquet Club Gaviotas, Ibis,** and **Río Bravo** in the Zona Dorada (© **669/913-5939**). Many larger hotels in Mazatlán also have courts.

Mazatlán is probably the best **golf** value in Mexico. Try the 27-hole course at the **El Cid Resort** (© **669/913-3333**). Nine holes designed by Lee Trevino complement the 18 holes designed by Robert Trent Jones, Jr. It's open to the public, with preference given to hotel guests. Tee times book up quickly. Greens fees for nonguests are $60 (£30) for 18 holes, plus $17 (£8.50) for the caddy. El Cid guests pay $42 (£21), plus $17 (£8.50) for the caddy. El Cid's facilities include a John Jacobs golf school, the only one in Mexico. It's open daily, from 7am to 5:30pm.

The 9-hole course at the **Club Campestre Mazatlán** (© **669/980-1570**) is open to the public. Greens fees are $25 (£13) for 9 holes, $35 (£18) for 18 holes; a caddy costs an extra $10 to $15 (£5–£7.50), a cart is $15 to $20 (£7.50–£10), respectively. It's on Highway 15 on the outskirts of downtown.

Mazatlán's newest course is at the **Estrella del Mar Golf Club** (© **669/982-3300;** www.estrelladelmar.com). The 18-hole, 7,004-yard course, also designed by Robert

Trent Jones, Jr., stretches along 3km (2 miles) of coastline on Isla de la Piedra, a peninsula just south of downtown Mazatlán. There's a PGA pro on staff, and daily clinics. Greens fees run $110 (£55), $69 (£35) after 1pm; fees include cart, but no caddies are available. It's open daily from 7:30am to sunset. Also on-site are a golf shop, restaurant, and bar. Clubs are available for rent for $35 (£18) plus tax.

You can go **horseback riding** on Isla de la Piedra for $6 (£3) per hour. Ask your hotel's travel agent to arrange a **kayaking excursion** on El Verde Camacho Ecological Lagoon, or take a trip to Teacapán for **birding** in one of Mexico's largest estuaries (see "Road Trips from Mazatlán," later in this chapter).

Bird-watching tours are also being offered by Sendero Mexico (© **669/940-8687;** www.senderomexico.com), an outfitter who has been offering a popular area kayaking tour. The birding tours can be arranged in conjunction with a kayak tour, or as a separate trip to either the foothills of the Sierra Madres or to the Palmito reserve (located just past Copala on the highway), home to the tufted-jay. The state of Sinaloa has 400 species of endemic birds—a bonanza for birders. The town of El Palmito, situated within 10,000 acres of wildlife preserve, is part of a government tourism program to promote sustainable and eco-friendly tourism to rural and isolated areas, which is supported in part by Cornell University. As a trip to El Palmito is a bit too far for a day trip, there are three small "safari tents," and two two-bedroom cabins available for overnight guests. Although the trip is possible to make on your own, it's best and highly recommend to notify Sendero Mexico of plans to visit, or simply set up a visit through them. Sendero Mexico has been approached by the national government to spearhead efforts to duplicate their success at El Palmito in other regions nationwide.

Kelly's Bicycle Shop, Av. Camarón Sábalo 204, Loc. 16 (© **669/914-1187;** www. kellys-bikes.com), in the Zona Dorada, arranges mountain-bike tours and rents aluminum-frame bikes with full suspension. A half-day guided tour costs $28 (£14); rentals are $8 (£4) per half-day, $15 (£7.50) per full day. Bike rentals include water bottle, snack, map, and general route information.

EXPLORING MAZATLAN

Mazatlán may be best known for its wide, sandy beaches and sporting activities, but visitors who neglect to sample the city's cultural events and attractions are missing out on a multidimensional destination.

MUSEUMS

Acuario Mazatlán *(Kids*   Children and adults interested in the sea will love the Mazatlán Aquarium. With over 200 species of fish, including sharks, eels, and sea horses, it is one of the largest and best in Mexico. Next to the aquarium are a playground and botanical garden, with an aviary and a small crocodile exhibit. Staff feed the sea lions, birds, and fish at shows held almost hourly.

Av. de los Deportes 111 (a half block off Av. del Mar). © **669/981-7815** or -7817. Admission $7 (£3.50) adults, $4.50 (£2.25) children 3–11. Daily 9:30am–5:30pm.

Museo Arqueológico de Mazatlán   This small, attractive archaeological museum displays pre-Hispanic artifacts and a permanent contemporary art exhibit. From Olas Altas, walk inland on Sixto Osuna 1½ blocks; the museum is on the right. Art exhibits sometimes take place in the Casa de la Cultura across from the museum.

Sixto Osuna 76 (1½ blocks from Paseo Olas Altas). © **669/981-1455.** Free admission. Tues–Sun 10am–7pm.

Moments   **Mazatlán's Carnaval: A Weeklong Party**

The week before Lent (usually in Feb) is Mazatlán's famous Carnaval, or Mardi Gras. People come from all over the country and abroad for this flamboyant celebration, topped in size and revelry only by those in Río de Janeiro and New Orleans. Highlights of the event include parades, special shows, the coronation of the Carnaval queen, outdoor concerts, more than 150 food and beverage vendors, all-night parties, and extravaganzas all over town. For event information, check with the major hotels or the tourism office, or look for posters around town. Every night during Carnaval week, all along the Olas Altas oceanfront drive in the southern part of town, the streets fill with music from roving mariachi groups, local traditional *bandas sinaloenses* (sporting lots of brass instruments), and electrified bands under tarpaulin shades. The crowd increases each day until the last night, Shrove Tuesday, when musicians, dancers, and people out for a good time pack the *malecón*. The following day, Ash Wednesday, the party is over. People receive crosses of ashes on their foreheads at church, and Lent begins.

ARCHITECTURAL HIGHLIGHTS

Two blocks south of the central plaza stands the lovely **Teatro Angela Peralta,** Carnaval 1024, Centro (© **669/982-4444**), a national historic monument. Built between 1869 and 1874, it most recently underwent renovation in 1998. The 841-seat Italian-style theater has three levels of balconies, two facades, and, in true tropical style, a lobby with no roof. The theater was named for one of the world's great divas, who, along with the director and 30 members of the opera, died in Mazatlán of cholera in an 1863 epidemic. Some city tours stop here; if you're visiting on your own, the theater is open daily from 9am to 6pm. The fee for touring the building is $1 (50p). It regularly schedules folkloric ballets, along with periodic performances of classical ballet, contemporary dance, symphony concerts, opera, and jazz. For information, call or check at the theater box office. This theater is the home of Delfos, one of the most important contemporary dance companies in Mexico.

The 20-block historic area near the theater, including the small square **Plazuela Machado** (bordered by Frías, Constitución, Carnaval, and Sixto Osuna), abounds with beautiful old buildings and colorful town houses trimmed with wrought iron and carved stone. The Plaza hosts local artists and vendors on Saturday afternoons, and offers arts and crafts activities and storytelling for children. Two new art galleries and art shops opened near the plaza on Sixto Osuna: the Elena Chauvet Gallery and Casa Ethnica. Check out the **town houses** on Libertad between Domínguez and Carnaval and the two **mansions** on Ocampo at Domínguez and at Carnaval. For a break, try the **Café Pacífico** (decorated with historic pictures of Mazatlán) on the Plazuela Machado.

The **Plaza Principal,** also called Plaza Revolución, is the heart of the city, filled with vendors, shoeshine stands, and people of all ages out for a stroll. At its center is a Victorian-style, wrought iron bandstand with a diner-type restaurant underneath. Be sure to take in the **Cathedral of the Immaculate Conception,** built in the 1800s, with its unusual yellow-tiled twin steeples and partially tiled facade. It's on the corner of Calle 21 de Marzo and Nelson.

ORGANIZED TOURS

In addition to 3-hour **city tours** ($20/£10), tour operators offer excursions to many colorful and interesting villages nearby, such as Concordia and Copala (see below). Some towns date from the 16th-century Spanish Conquest; others are modest farming or fishing villages. Information and reservations are available at any travel agency or major hotel, and all accept American Express, MasterCard, and Visa. The premier provider of these and other tours is **Pronatours** (© 669/916-7720 or -3333, ext. 3490; www.elcid.com.mx), yet another part of the El Cid megacomplex of activities. In addition to the city tour, they offer a 5-hour Tequila Tour, visiting a distillery ($35/ £18), a 5-hour sailing excursion to Isla de Venados ($42/£21), and a seasonal tour to visit protected turtle hatcheries ($42/£21). Two other recommended tour agencies are the very helpful **Marlin Tours** (© 669/985-4875) and **Olé Tours** (© 669/916-6288;** fax 669/916-5134; www.ole-tours.com).

COPALA-CONCORDIA   This popular countryside tour stops at several mountain villages where artisans craft furniture and other items. Copala is a historic mining village with a Spanish-colonial church. The tour ($48/£24), also known as the Mountain Tour or Country Tour, includes lunch and soft drinks. For more about Copala, see "Road Trips from Mazatlán," later.

MAZATLAN JUNGLE TOUR   Some might say that David Pérez's (King David's) **Jungle Tour** (© 669/914-1444; fax 669/914-0451) is misnamed, but it's still worthwhile. It consists of a 1½-hour boat ride past a Mexican navy base, Mazatlán's shrimp fleet and packing plants, and into the mangrove swamps to Isla de la Piedra (Stone Island). There's a 3-hour stop at a pristine beach that has what could be the world's largest sand dollars (though fewer and fewer are left). Horseback rides on the beach are $6 (£3) for a half-hour. After the beach stop, feast on *pescado zarandeado* (fish cooked over coconut husks, green mangrove, and charcoal). Tours run from 9am to 3pm and cost $45 (£23) per person. Days vary, so call for dates and reservations. MasterCard and Visa are accepted.

WHERE TO STAY

The hotels in downtown Mazatlán are generally older and less expensive than those along the beachfront heading north. As a rule, room rates rise the farther north you go from downtown. The major areas to stay are the Zona Dorada, the Playa Norte (North Beach), and Olas Altas and downtown.

THE ZONA DORADA & NORTH

The Zona Dorada is an elegant arc of gold sand linked by a palm-lined boulevard and bordered by the most deluxe hotels and elaborate beach houses. A bonus is the sunset view. Many hotels along this beach cut their prices from May through September.

El Cid Resort ⓡⓡⓡ   El Cid Resort is as much a destination as it is a hotel. Although it is large, bordering on imposing, El Cid offers every service and convenience you can think of, from deluxe rooms to ecotours. Both a hotel and a residential development, El Cid has three beachside buildings, private villas, and a 27-hole golf course on 360 hectares (889 acres). The main 17-story beachside tower, Castilla, was renovated in

1999; there's also the 28-story, all-suite El Moro Tower and the lower-rise, lower-priced Granada, near the golf course. Although room layouts vary, most are heavily detailed in marble and feature private balconies and contemporary, upscale furnishings. There are tons of extra services at El Cid as well, such as a program called Active Learning Vacations, encouraging more involved vacations and priced as special packages. There are opportunities to improve your golf, tennis, or sailing skills or indulge in a Fit for Life program through the on-site spa. Small boats are available, with departures every 10 minutes, to take guests to nearby beaches. All-inclusive options are also available; ask for special deals. This resort has something for every type of traveler and is especially ideal when size matters.

Av. Camarón Sábalo s/n (between Av. Rodolfo T. Loaiza and Circuito Campeador), 82110 Mazatlán, Sin. © 800/716-9800 in the U.S., or 669/913-3333. Fax 669/914-131. www.elcid.com. 1,320 units. High season $150–$294 (£75–£147) double, $315 (£158) junior suite, $420–$536 (£210–£268) suite; low season $95–$244 (£48–£122) double, $244 (£122) junior suite, $343–$465 (£172–£233) suite. All-inclusive program $200 (£100) double occupancy, children 3–11 $35 (£18). AE, MC, V. Free guarded parking. **Amenities:** 11 restaurants; 8 bars; glitzy dance club; 8 outdoor swimming pools (including 1 saltwater pool); 9 tennis courts; tennis academy; fitness center; spa; watersports equipment; marina; sailing school; children's programs; concierge; tour desk; car-rental desk; business center; shopping arcade; salon; room service; babysitting; laundry service; dry cleaning. *In room:* A/C, TV, hair dryer, iron, safe.

El Rancho Hotel & Beach Resort 𝒦𝒦 (Kids) Book a room at El Rancho, and you'll book yourself an apartment suite, complete with kitchen, making it a top choice for families. An intimate group of villas, the resort is located on a beautiful stretch of soft-sand beach, immediately to the north of the Zona Dorada. All units feature the same traditional Mexican-style decor, with colorful fabric accents, and are very well maintained. The difference in price depends on your view—garden, pool, or ocean. Each features two levels, with two spacious bedrooms (one with a king-size bed, the other with two queen-size beds) as well as two bathrooms, a fully equipped kitchen, and a living/dining area. The gardens are lovely, and the on-site restaurant is one level up, making it an ideal spot for watching sunsets. Note that this is also a timeshare resort, so be prepared for a sales pitch if you stay here.

Av. Sábalo-Cerritos 3000, 82110 Mazatlán, Sin. © 888/596-5760 in the U.S., or 01-800/717-1991 in Mexico. www.elrancho.com.mx. 28 units. High season $135–$200 (£68–£100) 2-bedroom suite (sleeps up to 6); low season $110–$170 (£55–£85) 2-bedroom suite (sleeps up to 6). Rates include free airport pickup and daily continental breakfast. AE, MC, V. Free parking. **Amenities:** 1 restaurant; outdoor pool; Jacuzzi; tour desk; laundry service. *In room:* A/C, TV.

Hotel Faro Mazatlán 𝒦𝒦 Formerly known as the Camino Real, this grande dame of Mazatlán hotels changed management in 2004, and underwent a much-needed renovation. Considered the most sophisticated place to stay in town, it's the best choice for those seeking seclusion. It has the best location in Mazatlán, on a rocky cliff overlooking the sea, and the beach edges a small cove that's perfect for swimming. Marble-floored hallways lead to rooms decorated in light, neutral colors, each with bathtubs and showers, large closets, and vanity tables. Junior suites have king-size beds and couches. The hotel is about a 10-minute drive from the heart of the Zona Dorada. Higher rates are for rooms with an ocean view; other rooms have a marina view.

Punta de Sábalo s/n, 82100 Mazatlán, Sin. © 800/716-9757 in the U.S., or 669/913-1111. Fax 669/914-0311 www.faromazatlan.com.mx. 165 units. High season $110–$195 (£55–£98) double, $220 (£110) junior suite; low-season discounts and special packages available. All-inclusive package $110 (£55) per person, with discounts available for families. AE, MC, V. Free guarded parking. **Amenities:** 2 restaurants; lobby bar; small heated outdoor pool; 2 tennis courts; gym; travel agency; business center; room service. *In room:* A/C, TV, minibar.

Pueblo Bonito *Kids* The all-suite Pueblo Bonito continues to be a favored place to stay in Mazatlán. The kitchenettes and ample seating areas, along with architectural touches that include curved ceilings, arched windows, and tiled floors, make you feel more at home than traditional hotels do. The extra space means it's a good choice for families or friends traveling together. The grounds are gorgeous—peacocks and flamingos stroll lush lawns, a waterfall cascades into a large pool, and a row of *palapas* lines the beachfront.

Av. Camarón Sábalo 2121 (Apdo. Postal 6), 82110 Mazatlán, Sin. © 800/699-9000 in the U.S. or 01-800/990-8250 in Mexico, or 669/989-8900. Fax 669/914-1723. www.pueblobonito.com. 250 units. $240 (£120) junior suite; $290 (£145) 2-bedroom suite (up to 2 adults and 2 children). AE, MC, V. Free guarded parking; valet parking. **Amenities:** 3 restaurants; 2 large outdoor pools; gym; whirlpool; sauna; concierge; tour desk; car-rental desk; room service; massage; babysitting; laundry service. *In room:* A/C, TV.

PLAYA NORTE

The waterfront between downtown and the Zona Dorada is Mazatlán's original tourist hotel zone. Moderately priced hotels and motels line the street across from the beach. Señor Frog's, Mazatlán's most famous restaurant, is in this neighborhood, as is the bus station. From May to September, many hotels cut their prices.

Hotel Playa Mazatlán *Kids* The most happening place on this stretch of the Zona Dorada, the Hotel Playa Mazatlán is enduringly popular with families, tour groups, and regulars who return annually for winter vacations or spring break. The quietest rooms are in the three-story section surrounding the well-tended interior gardens; those by the terrace restaurant and beach can be noisy. All rooms are decorated in bright colors, with dark-wood furnishings and colonial accents. The beach is one of the liveliest in town. The hotel hosts popular Mexican fiestas on Tuesday, Thursday, and Saturday, and a fireworks display on Sunday.

Av. Playa Gaviotas 202 Zona Dorada, 82110 Mazatlán, Sin. © 800/762-5816 in the U.S., or 669/989-0555. Fax 669/914-0366. www.playamazatlan.com.mx. 423 units. $135 (£68) gardenview double; $160 (£80) oceanview double. AE, MC, V. Free guarded parking. **Amenities:** 2 restaurants; bar; 3 outdoor pools; gym; 2 outdoor whirlpools; watersports rental equipment; tour desk; room service; laundry service. *In room:* A/C, TV, coffeemaker, hair dryer, iron.

DOWNTOWN SEAFRONT/PLAYA OLAS ALTAS

The old section of Mazatlán spreads around a picturesque beach a short walk from downtown. Movie stars of the 1950s and 1960s came here for sun and surf, and the hotels where they stayed are still here. There are a few seafront restaurants here, making it easy to dine near your hotel.

Hotel La Siesta *Kids* The historic La Siesta occupies a well-maintained building surrounded by the old mansions of Mazatlán. Inside, three levels encircle a central courtyard; rooms facing the ocean have balconies opening to sea breezes and pounding waves. Guest rooms at the back of the hotel are quieter but less charming; all have two beds, a small table and chair, good lighting, and dependably hot water. For such functional accommodations, there's a surprising array of guest services. A bonus is the popular **El Shrimp Bucket** restaurant, in the courtyard, where live marimbas and recorded music play until 11pm. This is one of the most popular hotels in Old Mazatlán and fills up quickly. Reservations are strongly advised.

Av. Olas Altas 11 Sur, 82000 Mazatlán, Sin. © 669/981-2640 or -2334. Fax 669/982-2633. www.lasiesta.com.mx. 57 units. $85 (£43) interior double; $100 (£50) oceanview double. AE, MC, V. Street parking. From the deer statue on Olas Altas, go right 1 block. **Amenities:** Restaurant; bar; concierge; room service; in-room massage; laundry service; currency exchange; safe. *In room:* A/C, TV.

WHERE TO DINE

Mazatlán boasts one of the largest shrimp fleets in the world, so it's no surprise that shrimp and seafood are the specialties. Most restaurants are very casual and moderately priced, offering good value. A cheap-eats treat is to stop in one of the many *loncherías* (small establishments that are only for lunch, kind of like a home-cooking place, but not a counter) scattered throughout the downtown area. Here you can get a *torta* (a sandwich on a small French roll) stuffed with a variety of meats, cheeses, tomatoes, onions, and chiles for around $2 (£1). Also recommendable is the **Deli 28 Centro,** Belisario Domínguez 1503, Historic Downtown (✆ 669/981-1577), serving gourmet baguettes, focaccia, brioche, quality deli meats and cheeses, as well as pizzas.

THE ZONA DORADA
Expensive

Angelo's ✵ ITALIAN/SEAFOOD   Even locals consider this hotel restaurant one of the best in town, as much for its ambience as for its food. Beveled glass doors reveal a dining room gleaming with brass, polished wood, and crystal chandeliers. A pianist plays in the background as formally dressed waiters present menus featuring homemade pastas; shrimp dishes, including superb scampi; and a large selection of imported wines. The dress code forbids beachwear, jeans, tennis shoes, and flip-flops.

In the Pueblo Bonito hotel, Av. Camarón Sábalo 2121. ✆ **669/989-8900,** ext. 8608. www.pueblobonito-mazatlan. com. Reservations required. Main courses $13–$47 (£6.50–£24). AE, MC, V. Daily 6–11:30pm.

Papagayo Restaurant ✵ INTERNATIONAL   Nestled on the beach, diners at Papagayo enjoy the natural beauty of the sea, with a choice of beach or open-air patio seating, and a view across the water to Las Tres Islas, the three imposing islands just offshore. The food is consistent and elegantly presented, with an extensive menu of international fare; favorites are shrimp CocoLoco, and tournedos Rossini in wild mushroom sauce.

The Inn at Mazatlán, Av. Camarón Sábalo 6291. ✆ **669/913-4151.** www.innatmazatlan.com.mx. Main courses $12–$40 (£6–£20). AE, MC, V. Daily 7am–11pm.

Señor Pepper's ✵✵ INTERNATIONAL   Managing to be both elegant and comfortable, this restaurant is known for serving the best steaks in Mazatlán. Potted plants, candlelight, and lots of polished crystal, silver, and brass give the dining room a romantic feeling, and some nights it seems as if all the diners are old friends. The enormous Sonoran beef steaks are grilled over mesquite; lobster and shrimp are also big hits. The nightly special includes appetizer, steak or seafood, vegetables, and soup or salad; those having only drinks at the bar receive a complimentary appetizer.

Av. Camarón Sábalo s/n, across from the Hotel Faro Mazatlán. ✆ **669/914-0101.** Reservations recommended. Main courses $25–$48 (£13–£24). MC, V. Daily 5–11pm; bar daily 5pm–2am.

Moderate

Terraza Playa MEXICAN/INTERNATIONAL   During the day, diners enjoy a view of the beach and Isla de Venados. After sundown, the stars overhead (in the open terrace) and the sound of the surging waves are a backdrop to live music and dancing from 7pm to midnight. The menu is standard international fare, well prepared, with excellent, friendly service. Especially popular is the breakfast buffet.

In the Hotel Playa Mazatlán, Av. Rodolfo T. Loaiza 202. ✆ **669/989-0555.** Breakfast $4–$8 (£2–£4); Mexican plates $5–$10 (£2.50–£5); seafood and meat $8.50–$17 (£4.25–£8.50). AE, MC, V. Daily 6am–midnight.

Inexpensive

Jungle Juice *(Finds)* MEXICAN/STEAKS/SEAFOOD   This comfortable patio and upstairs bar has a definite Mexican flair that gives the partially open-air restaurant a festive touch. Grilled meats and lobster are the specialties at this juice-and-smoothie joint, which has evolved into a full-fledged grill and bar. Smoothies and juices are still the specialties, as are vegetarian plates and meat dishes grilled over mesquite on the patio. This casual spot also serves good breakfasts and makes a nice stop after shopping in the Zona Dorada. Look for daily specials on the blackboard.

Las Garzas 101. (℃) 669/913-3315. Main courses $6–$22 (£3–£11). MC, V. Daily 8am–10pm; bar daily 6pm–2am. From Pastelería Panamá, take Sábalo and turn right on Las Garzas; it's 1 block down on your right. Heading north on Loaiza, Las Garzas and the Pastelería Panamá are on the right after the Sábalo traffic circle, before the Mazatlán Arts and Crafts Center.

Pura Vida I *(Moments)* VEGETARIAN/HEALTH FOOD   Nearly hidden behind thick plants, Pura Vida has several small seating sections with wood picnic tables and white canvas umbrellas. A perfect morning spot, it specializes in juices and smoothies, from kelp to papaya. The energetic staff serves omelets and whole-wheat pancakes for breakfast, and burgers, purified salads, soups, and Mexican specialties for lunch. There are plenty of vegetarian dishes such as soy burgers. The veggie and white-chicken sandwiches served on whole-wheat rolls are fabulous.

Bugambilia 100. (℃) 669/916-5815. Main courses $2.50–$6.60 (£1.25–£3.30). No credit cards. Daily 8am–10pm. From Pastelería Panamá on Sábalo, turn right on Las Garzas, then left 1 block down onto Laguna; the cafe is on your right.

DOWNTOWN & PLAYA NORTE
Moderate

Copa de Leche *(Moments)* MEXICAN   This shaded sidewalk cafe on the waterfront at Playa Olas Altas feels the way Mazatlán must have in the 1930s, and the food is consistently as good as the ocean view. The menu includes *pechugas en nogada* (chicken breast in pecan-and-pomegranate sauce); shrimp in tamarind sauce; traditional *alambre* barbecue (beef cooked with onion, peppers, mushrooms, ham, and bacon); wonderful seafood soup loaded with squid, shrimp, and chunks of fish; and great shrimp with chipotle sauce. Inside, the decor is updated Mexican, the bar is an old wooden boat, and the dining tables are covered with linen cloths. They also have live music on Friday and Saturday nights.

Av. Olas Altas 1220 A Sur. (℃) 669/982-5753. Breakfast $6–$8 (£3–£4); main courses $5.80–$18 (£2.90–£9). MC, V. Daily 7am–11pm. From El Shrimp Bucket (at Mariano Escobedo and Olas Altas), turn south and walk half a block down Olas Altas; the cafe is on your left.

El Shrimp Bucket *(Moments)* MEXICAN/SEAFOOD   El Shrimp Bucket is among the most popular restaurants in town. The specialty is Mazatlán's famous shrimp, in the air-conditioned dining room or under umbrellas in the center courtyard. For wining, dining, and dancing, this is a great place for a rousing time.

In the Hotel La Siesta, Av. Olas Altas 111 (at Mariano Escobedo). (℃) 669/981-6350 or 982-8019. Mexican plates $5–$11 (£2.50–£5.25); seafood and steak $9–$22 (£4.50–£11). AE, MC, V. Daily 6:30am–11pm.

SHOPPING

Mazatlán shopping runs the gamut from precious stones to seashells—with plenty of T-shirts in between. Most stores are open Monday through Saturday from 9 or 10am to 6 or 8pm. Very few close for lunch, and many stores are open on Sunday afternoon.

La Zona Dorada is the best area for shopping. For a huge selection of handicrafts from all over Mexico, visit the **Mazatlán Arts and Crafts Center,** Calle Gaviotas and

Avenida Rodolfo T. Loaiza. It accepts cash only. Nearby **Sea Shell City,** Av. Playa Gaviotas 407 ((© **669/913-1301)** is exactly what the name implies—more shell-cov ered decorative items than you ever dreamed could exist, from the tacky to the sublime. It's open daily 9am to 8pm. **Gallery Michael,** Av. Las Garzas 18, off Avenida Camarón Sábalo (© **669/916-7816** or -5511; www.michaelgallerymexico.com), has an excellent selection of Tlaquepaque crafts and fine silver jewelry. It is near the Dairy Queen and does not accept credit cards.

For fine jewelry, seek out **Rubio Jewellers,** in the Costa de Oro Hotel, Av. Camarón Sábalo 710 (© **669/914-3167;** www.rubiojewellers.com). Shops throughout the Zona Dorada carry a good selection of clothing, fabrics, silver jewelry, leather, art, and crafts. They also carry Sergio Bustamante's jewelry and sculptures.

The **Centro Mercado** in Old Mazatlán is another kind of shopping experience. Here you'll find women selling fresh shrimp under colorful umbrellas; open-air food stalls; and indoor shops stacked with pottery, clothing, and crafts (mostly of lesser quality). Small galleries and shops are beginning to appear in Old Mazatlán; one of the nicest is **NidArt Galería,** Av. Libertad 45 and Carnaval (© **669/981-0002,** or 985-5991 for after-hours appointments; www.nidart.com), next to the Angela Peralta Theater. It features changing exhibits of contemporary art. Open Monday through Saturday from 10am to 2pm or after hours by appointment.

La Gran Plaza is a large shopping mall 3 blocks from the waterfront on Avenida de los Deportes. The plaza has a large supermarket, department stores, and specialty shops. A good place for buying basic items, it's open daily from 10am to 9pm.

MAZATLAN AFTER DARK

Mazatlán is known for its vibrant Mexican fiestas and equally colorful local bar scene, where dancing on bars, atop tables, and inside cages can be a nightly event. Traditional mariachi groups, *tambora* bands, and live romantic music create a festive mood in many restaurants and hotel bars.

Happy hour specials abound in value-oriented Mazatlán. One particular favorite is **El Adobe,** in the Costa de Oro hotel (© **669/913-5344,** ext. 1166, or 913-5043). This three-level restaurant and bar has views to the Pacific, overlooking the cascading waterfalls and hotel gardens. From 7am to 10pm, El Adobe serves two-for-one tropical drinks in oversize brandy snifters.

A free **fireworks** show takes place every Sunday at 8pm on the beach fronting the Hotel Playa Mazatlán, Av. Rodolfo T. Loaiza 202, in the Zona Dorada (© **669/913-5320** or 989-0555). The display is visible from the beach and from the hotel's Terraza Playa restaurant (see "Where to Dine," above).

The same hotel presents Mazatlán's most popular **Fiesta Mexicana,** complete with buffet, open bar, folkloric dancing, and live music. Fiestas begin at 7pm Tuesday, Thursday, and Saturday year-round; try to arrive by 6pm to get a good table. Tickets are $35 (£18).

CLUBS & BARS

Joe's Oyster Bar   Beer, burgers, fresh oysters, and high-volume dance music are the house specialties at this casual, *palapa*-topped, open-air club. It's open daily from 11am to 2:30am. On the beachfront at Los Sábalos Hotel, Av. Rodolfo T. Loaiza 100. © **669/983-5333.**

Valentino's & the Fiestaland Complex   If you're going out at night, chances are, you'll be headed here, because the popularity of the **Valentino's** club has resulted in its expansion to an entire array of nocturnal options. The centerpiece remains Valentino's, dramatically perched on a rocky outcropping overlooking the sea, in an all-white, Moorish-looking building, and featuring a good high-tech light show complete with green laser beams. For a break from the pulsating dance floor, there are pool tables in another room, and some (relatively) quiet areas for talking. Foam parties are the feature every Thursday night. Part of the complex is the **Bora Bora,** a pub-style bar complete with volleyball court and surfing simulator, the **Mikonos** piano bar, and **Canta Bar,** which features karaoke. Looking for televised sports? **Bali Hai** is your spot, while **Pepe's and Joe** offers a brew and pub ambience. Open daily from 9pm to 4am. Punta Camarón, near the Camarón Sábalo traffic circle. ℭ 669/989-1600. Cover $6–$15 (£3–£7.50).

ROAD TRIPS FROM MAZATLAN
TEACAPAN: ABUNDANT WILDLIFE & A RUSTIC VILLAGE

Just 2 hours (131km/81 miles) south of Mazatlán is the fishing village of Teacapán, at the tip of an isolated peninsula that extends 29km (18 miles) down a coastline of pristine beaches. Mangrove lagoons and canals border its other side. Palm and mango groves, cattle ranches, and an occasional cluster of houses dot the peninsula, which ends at the Boca de Teacapán, a natural marina separating the states of Sinaloa and Nayarit. Shrimping boats line the beach at the edge of the marina, which backs up to the worn houses and dirt streets of town. A rugged place, it is recommended for those interested in birding.

Birders hire local fishermen to take them out around the lagoons, where they can see herons, flamingos, Canadian ducks, and countless other species. Inland, the sparsely populated land is a haven for deer, ocelot, and wild boars. There's talk of making the entire peninsula into an ecological preserve, and thus far, residents have resisted attempts by developers to turn the area into a large-scale resort. For now, visitors to Teacapán find the ultimate peaceful refuge.

GETTING THERE   By Car   Drive south from Mazatlán on the highway to Escuinapa. The right turn for the road to Teacapán is unsigned; ask for directions in Escuinapa. If you're arriving from the south, turn left at the Bancomer building.

By Bus   Autotransportes Escuinapa runs several second-class buses daily to Escuinapa; the fare is about $5.50 (£2.25). From there you can transfer to Teacapán (about $3.50/£1.75). The second-class bus station is behind the first-class station, across the lot where the buses park.

Where to Stay

Villas Maria Fernanda   This small resort offers a selection of villas and one larger casa that sleeps up to 10 people. All are spacious, with simple, traditional furnishings in a colorful Mexican style, plus full kitchen facilities. Boat tours, bird-watching tours, and horseback riding are available. The hotel is adjacent to a small restaurant, which serves all meals. It's at the entrance to the estuary, making it ideal for bird-watchers who want to explore the area.

Domicilio Conocido, Teacapán, Sin. ℭ 695/954-5393. Fax 695/953-1343. www.villasmariafernanda.com. 6 units. Villas $65 (£33) double; houses $160 (£80). AE. Free parking. **Amenities:** Restaurant; outdoor pool; Jacuzzi; water slide; children's playground. *In room:* A/C, TV, kitchen.

COPALA: AN OLD SILVER TOWN

Popular tours from Mazatlán stop here for lunch only, but Copala is well worth an overnight stay. The town was founded in 1565, and from the late 1880s to the early 1900s it was the center of the region's silver-mining boom. When the mines closed, the town was nearly deserted. Today, it's a National Historic Landmark with 600 full-time residents and a part-time community of retired Canadian and U.S. citizens devoted to Copala's picturesque solitude.

Every building in town is painted white, and most have red-tile roofs splashed with bougainvillea. Cobblestone streets wind from the entrance to town up slight hills to the main plaza and the 1610 Cathedral of San José. The town kicks into high gear (relatively speaking) around noon, when tour buses arrive and visitors stroll the streets, surrounded by small boys selling geodes extracted from the local hills. By 3pm, most of the outsiders have left. You can wander the streets in peace and visit the century-old cemetery, the ruins of haciendas, and the neighborhoods of white villas.

GETTING THERE   **Tours** go to Copala and Concordia (see "Organized Tours," earlier in this chapter). Copala is an easy 2-hour **drive** from Mazatlán; drive south for about 25 minutes until you get to the detour for Durango, then turn west and drive to Concordia. From there, follow the signs for Copala; it's about 22km (14 miles). The Autotransportes Concordia **bus** service runs four buses daily from the second-class bus station, behind the first-class bus station. The fare is $4 (£2); check the schedule carefully before departing so you don't get stranded in Copala.

3 Costa Alegre: Puerto Vallarta to Barra de Navidad ★★★

Costa Alegre is one of Mexico's most spectacular coastal areas, a 232km (144-mile) stretch that connects tropical forests with a series of dramatic cliff-lined coves. Tiny outpost towns line the coast, while dirt roads trail down to a succession of magical coves with pristine beaches, most of them steeped in privileged exclusivity. Considered one of Mexico's greatest undiscovered treasures, this area is becoming a favored hideaway for publicity-fatigued celebrities and those in search of natural seclusion.

The area is referred to as **Costa Alegre (Happy Coast)**—the marketer's term—and **Costa Careyes (Turtle Coast),** after the many sea turtles that nest here. It is home to an eclectic array of the most captivating and exclusive places to stay in Mexico, with a selective roster of activities that includes championship golf and polo. Along the line, however, you will encounter the funky beach towns that were the original lure for travelers who discovered the area.

Stops along Highway 200, as it meanders between Puerto Vallarta to the north and Manzanillo to the south, can be an enjoyable day trip, but travelers usually make the drive en route to a destination along the coast.

EXPLORING COSTA ALEGRE   Costa Alegre is more an ultimate destination than a place to rent a car and take a drive. Most of the beaches are tucked into coves accessible by dirt roads that can extend for kilometers inland. If you do drive along this coast, Highway 200 is safe, but it's not lit and it curves through the mountains, so travel only during the day. A few buses travel this route, but they stop only at the towns that line the highway; many of them are several kilometers inland from the resorts along the coast.

ALONG COSTA ALEGRE (NORTH TO SOUTH)
CRUZ DE LORETO'S LUXURY ECO-RETREAT
Hotelito Desconocido ★★★ *Moments*   The fact that the Hotelito Desconocido ("little unknown hotel") is ecologically minded is a bonus, but it's not the principal appeal. A cross between *Out of Africa* and *Blue Lagoon*, it is among my favorite places

in Mexico. Think camping out with luxury linens, romantic candles everywhere, and a symphony performed by cicadas, birds, and frogs.

The rustic, open-air rooms, called *palafitos,* are in cottages perched on stilts over a lagoon. A grouping of suites is on the ample sand bar that separates the tranquil estuary from the Pacific Ocean. However, these are the least desirable units, and are often damp from the ocean air. Also here is a saltwater pool—the ocean is too aggressive for even seasoned swimmers.

Ceiling fans cool the air, and water is solar-heated. It's easy to disconnect here. In fact, it's mandatory: There's no electricity, no phones, no neighboring restaurants, nightclubs, or shopping—only delicious tranquillity. What the service lacks in polish it makes up for in enthusiasm. Rates do not include meals or drinks; a meal plan is mandatory, because there are no other options nearby (making the entire package somewhat pricey)—but it's a unique experience.

Playón de Mismaloya s/n, Cruz de Loreto, 48360 Tomatlán, Jal. ℭ 800/851-1143 in the U.S. and Canada (reservations: ℭ 01-800/013-1313 in Mexico, or 322/281-4010 or 322/222-2546). Fax 322/281-4130. www.hotelito.com. 24 units. High season $410–$485 (£220–£243) double, $540–$815 (£270–£408) suite; low season $350 (£175) double, $516–$625 (£258–£313) suite. Mandatory daily meal plan $90 (£45) per person. Children are discouraged. AE, MC, V. Take Hwy. 200 south for 1 hr., turn off at exit for Cruz de Loreto, and continue on clearly marked route on unpaved road for about 25 min. All activities are subject to an extra charge. Free parking. **Amenities:** 2 restaurant/ bars; primitive-luxury spa; whirlpool; sauna; sailboards; kayaks; mountain bikes; massage; birding tours; hiking trails; horseback riding; billiards; beach volleyball. *In room:* No phone.

LAS ALAMANDAS: AN EXCLUSIVE LUXURY RESORT

Las Alamandas ⚜⚜⚜   Almost equidistant between Manzanillo (1½ hr.) and Puerto Vallarta (1¾ hr.) lies Mexico's original ultra-exclusive resort. A dirt road winds for about a mile through a tiny village to the guardhouse of Las Alamandas, on 28 hectares (69 acres) set against low hills that are part of a 600-hectare (1,500-acre) estate. The resort consists of villas and *palapas* spread among four beaches, gardens, lakes, lagoons, and a bird sanctuary. It's designed for privacy—guests rarely catch a glimpse of one another. The resort has air-conditioning, telephones, and a beachside massage *palapa,* yet manages to keep the experience as natural as possible. The resort accommodates only 30 guests.

The six spacious villas have brightly colored decor and tiled verandas with ocean views. They have several bedrooms (each with its own bathroom) and can be rented separately; guests who rent entire villas have preference for reservations. Some villas are on the beach, others across a cobblestone plaza. TVs with VCRs are available on request, but there's no outside reception. When you reserve your room, you can arrange for van transportation to and from Manzanillo ($293/£147 one-way) and Puerto Vallarta ($289/£145 one-way), as well as air transport from Puerto Vallarta.

Hwy. 200, Km 83 48850 Manzanillo–Puerto Vallarta, Jal. Mailing address: Domicilio Conocido Costa Alegre QUE-MARO Jalisco, Apdo. Postal 201, 48980 San Patricio Melaque, Jal. ℭ 888/882-9616 in the U.S. and Canada, or 322/285-5500. Fax 322/285-5027. www.alamandas.com. 14 units. High season $480–$990 (£240–£495) double, $2,070–$2,490 (£1,035–£1,245) villa; low season $370–$720 (£185–£360) double, $1,040–$2,070 (£520–£1,035) villa. Meal plans available. AE, MC, V. Free parking. **Amenities:** Restaurant; 18m (59-ft.) outdoor pool; lighted tennis court; weight room; boogie boards; mountain bikes; concierge; tour desk; room service; birding boat tours; hiking trails; horseback riding; book and video library; landing strip (make advance arrangements). *In room:* A/C, minibar.

CAREYES

The Careyes Hotel ⚜⚜   The Careyes is a gem of a resort on a small, pristine cove between dramatic cliffs adorned by the exclusive villas of Careyes. (This area has practically defined the architectural style that defines Mexico beach chic—with bold washes

Costa Alegre & Central Pacific Coast

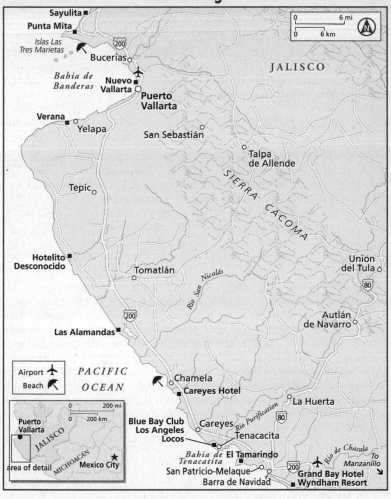

of vibrant colors, open spaces, and tropical gardens.) Stylishly simple, if dated accommodations all face the ocean. Guests come for isolation, but you can enjoy many services, including a full European spa and polo. It's rustic and sophisticated; room facades are awash in scrubbed pastels and form a U around the center lawn and freeform pool. Some rooms have balconies; all have ocean views. Twenty rooms have private pools, and villas are available for rent. Roughly 150km (93 miles) south of Puerto Vallarta, the Careyes is about a 2-hour drive north of Manzanillo on Highway 200, and about a 1-hour drive from the Manzanillo airport. Taxis from the Manzanillo airport charge around $100 (£50) one-way. Manzanillo and Puerto Vallarta airports have car-rental counters. A car would be useful only for exploring the coast—Barra de Navidad and other resorts, for example—and the hotel can make touring arrangements.

Hwy. 200 Km 53.5, 48970 Careyes, Jal. CP. Mailing address: Apdo. Postal 24, 48970 Cihuatlán, Jal. ⓒ 800/525-4800 in the U.S. and Canada, 315/351-0000 or -0606. Fax 315/351-0100. www.elcareyesresort.com. 51 units. High season $399–$425 (£200–£213) double, $555–$625 (£278–£313) suite; low season $345–$379 (£173–£190) double, $499–$565 (£250–£283) suite. AE, MC, V. Free parking. **Amenities:** Restaurant; bar; deli; large beachside pool; privileges at exclusive El Tamarindo resort (40km/25 miles south), w/18-hole mountaintop golf course; 2 tennis courts; paddle court; weight equipment; state-of-the-art spa; steam room; hot and cold plunge pools; sauna; sailboards; kayaks; Aquafins; children's programs (during Christmas and Easter vacations only); 24-hr. business center with wireless Internet access; room service; massage; laundry service; book and video library. *In room:* A/C, TV/DVD, CD player, minibar, minifridge, hair dryer.

TENACATITA BAY

Located an hour (53km/33 miles) north of the Manzanillo airport, this jewel of a bay is accessible by an 8km (5-mile) dirt road that passes through a small village set among banana plants and coconut palms. Sandy, serene beaches dot coves around the bay (frolicking dolphins are a common sight), and exotic birds fill a coastal lagoon. Swimming and snorkeling are good, and the bay is a popular stop for luxury yachts. Just south of the entrance to Tenacatita is a sign for the all-inclusive **Sun Resorts Los Angeles Locos,** as well as the exclusive **El Tamarindo** resort and golf club. There is no commercial or shopping area, and dining options outside hotels are limited to a restaurant or two that may emerge during the winter months (high season). Relax— that's what you're here for.

Blue Bay Club Los Angeles Locos 🏖 On a 5km (3-mile) stretch of sandy beach, Los Angeles Locos offers an abundance of activities programs, entertainment, and dining options, which offer guests excellent value. It's a good choice for families and groups of friends. All rooms have ocean views, with either balconies or terraces. The three-story hotel is basic in decor and amenities, but comfortable. The attraction here is the wide array of on-site activities, plus a "Mangrove" cruise excursion (included in the room rate). **La Lagarta Disco** is a little on the dark and smoky side but can really rock, depending on the crowd—it's basically the only option on the bay.

Carretera Federal 200 Km 20, Tenacatita 48989, Municipio de la Huerta, Jal. ⓒ 800/483-7986 in the U.S., 800/713-3020 in Mexico; 315/351-5020 or -5100. Fax 315/351-5412. www.losangeleslocos.com. 204 units. High season $140 (£70) double; low season $110 (£55) double. Children 5–12 $35 (£18) year-round. Rates are all-inclusive. Ask about family specials. AE, MC, V. Free parking. **Amenities:** 2 restaurants and snack bar (w/buffets and a la carte dining); 3 bars; dance club; adult outdoor pool; kids' outdoor pool adjacent to the beach; 3 tennis courts; exercise room; sailboards; kayaks; Hobie cats; horseback riding; basketball court; pool tables; kids' club; massage; babysitting; laundry service. *In room:* A/C, TV.

El Tamarindo (Yellowstone Club World) 🏖🏖🏖 *(Finds* A personal favorite, El Tamarindo is a gem amid stunning jungle surroundings, with exquisite facilities, gracious service, and absolute tranquillity. Each exclusive thatched-roof villa has a splash pool and whirlpool, hammock, plus lounging and dining areas that overlook a private lawn and complement the stunning bedrooms. Service throughout the resort is exceptional. The bedrooms—with dark hardwood floors and furnishings—can be closed off for air-conditioned comfort, but the remaining areas are open to the sea breezes and heady tropical air. Beachfront bungalows are on a calm cove. The nonbeachside bungalows have more privacy and similar decor and amenities. El Tamarindo has a championship 18-hole golf course designed by David Fleming, with 7 oceanside holes and dramatic views. Equally exceptional are their spa services, with most massages and treatments provided in beachfront *cabañas,* or the resort's Spa Hut. The resort restaurant is the only dining option, but the menu changes daily and won't disappoint.

Anyone squeamish about creepy-crawlies may be uncomfortable in the beginning, but listening to the life around you is sensational. On 800 hectares (1,976 acres) of tropical rainforest bordering the Pacific Ocean, you'll feel as if you've found your own personal bit of heaven here.

Carretera Barra de Navidad–Puerto Vallarta Km 7.5, 48970 Cihuatlán, Jal. © 866/717-4316 in the US; 315/351-5032. Fax 315/351-5070. www.ycwtamarindo.com. 29 bungalows. High season $495–$1,190 (£248–£595) villas; low season $415–$839 (£208–£420) villas. AE, MC, V. From Puerto Vallarta (3 hr.) or the Manzanillo airport (40 min.), take Hwy. 200, then turn west at the clearly marked exit for El Tamarindo; follow signs for about 25 min. Free valet parking. **Amenities:** Restaurant; bar; large beachside pool w/whirlpool; 2 clay tennis courts; yoga classes; spa services; *temazcal* (pre-Hispanic sweat lodge); sailboards; kayaks; Aquafin sailboats; mountain bikes; estuary bird-watching tours; hiking trails; horseback riding; room service; *In room:* A/C, TV, CD player, Wi-Fi, hair dryer, safe.

BARRA DE NAVIDAD & MELAQUE

This pair of rustic beach villages (only 5km/3 miles apart) has been attracting travelers for decades. Only 30 minutes north of Manzanillo's airport and about 100km (62 miles) north of downtown Manzanillo, Barra has a few brick or cobblestone streets, good budget hotels and restaurants, and funky beach charm. All of this lies incongruously next to the superluxurious Grand Bay Hotel, which sits on a bluff across the inlet from Barra.

In the 17th century, Barra de Navidad was a harbor for the Spanish fleet; from here, galleons first set off in 1564 to find China. Located on a crescent-shaped bay with curious rock outcroppings, Barra de Navidad and neighboring Melaque are connected by a continuous beach on the same wide bay. It's safe to say that the only time Barra and Melaque hotels are full is during Easter and Christmas weeks. **Barra de Navidad** has more charm, more tree-shaded streets, better restaurants, more stores, and more conviviality between locals and tourists. Barra is very laid-back; faithful returnees adore its lack of flash. Other than the Grand Bay Hotel, on the cliff across the waterway in what is called Isla Navidad (although it's not an island), nothing is new or modern. But there's a bright edge to Barra, with more good restaurants and limited—but existent—nightlife.

Melaque, on the other hand, is larger, sun-baked, treeless, and lacking in attractions. It does, however, have plenty of cheap hotels available for longer stays, and a few restaurants. Although the beach between the two is continuous, Melaque's beach, with deep sand, is more beautiful than Barra's. Both villages appeal to those looking for a quaint, quiet, inexpensive retreat rather than a modern, sophisticated destination.

Isla Navidad Resort has a manicured 27-hole golf course and the superluxurious Grand Bay Hotel, but the area's pace hasn't quickened as fast as expected. The golf is challenging and delightfully uncrowded, with another exceptional course at nearby El Tamarindo. It's a serious golfer's dream.

ESSENTIALS

GETTING THERE & DEPARTING **Buses** from Manzanillo frequently run up the coast along Highway 200 on their way to Puerto Vallarta and Guadalajara. The fare is about $4 (£2). Most stop in the central villages of Barra de Navidad and Melaque. From the Manzanillo airport, it's only around 30 minutes to Barra, and **taxis** are available. The fare from Manzanillo to Barra is around $45 (£23); from Barra to Manzanillo, $35 (£18). From Manzanillo, the highway twists through some of the Pacific Coast's most beautiful mountains. Puerto Vallarta is 3 hours by **car** and 5 hours by bus, north on Highway 200 from Barra.

VISITOR INFORMATION   The **tourism office** for both villages is at Jalisco 67 (between Veracruz and Mazatlán), Barra (©/fax **315/355-5100;** www.barradenavidad. com); it's open Monday through Friday from 9am to 5pm.

ORIENTATION   In Barra, hotels and restaurants line the main beachside street, **Legazpi.** From the bus station, beachside hotels are 2 blocks straight ahead, across the central plaza. Two blocks behind the bus station and to the right is the lagoon side. More hotels and restaurants are on its main street, **Morelos/Veracruz.** Few streets are marked, but 10 minutes of wandering will acquaint you with the village's entire layout. There's a taxi stand at the intersection of Legazpi and Sinaloa streets. Legazpi, Jalisco, Sinaloa, and Veracruz streets border Barra's **central plaza.**

ACTIVITIES ON & OFF THE BEACH

Swimming and enjoying the attractive beach and views of the bay take up most tourists' time. You can hire a small boat for a coastal ride or fishing in two ways. Go toward the *malecón* on Calle Veracruz until you reach the tiny boatmen's cooperative, with fixed prices posted on the wall, or walk two buildings farther to the water taxi ramp. The water taxi is the best option for going to Colimilla (5 min.; $2.50/£1.25) or across the inlet (3 min.; $1/50p) to the Grand Bay Hotel. Water taxis make the rounds regularly, so if you're at Colimilla, wait, and one will be along shortly. At the cooperative, a 30-minute **lagoon tour** costs $20 (£10), and a **sea tour** costs $25 (£13). **Sportfishing** is $80 (£40) for up to four people for a half-day in a small *panga* (open fiberglass boat, like the ones used for water taxis).

Surfing along Costa Alegre is gaining ground, thanks in large part to Germaine Badke and his **South Swell Mex Surf Shop** (© 315/100-4332; www.southswell mex.com). The shop offers boogie board and surfboard rentals, surfboard and surf supply sales, and will also create a custom-designed board. Surf lessons are also available. They're in Suite 17 of the Hotel Alondra.

Isla Navidad Country Club (© 314/337-9024; www.islanavidad.com) has a beautiful and challenging 27-hole, 7,053-yard, par-72 **golf course** that is open to the public. Grand Bay Hotel guests pay greens fees of $175 (£88) for 18 holes, $192 (£96) for 27 holes; nonguests pay $207 and $230 (£104 and £115), respectively. Prices include a motorized cart. Caddies are available, as are rental clubs.

Beer Bob's Books, Avenida Tampico #8, between Sinaloa and Guanajuato, is a book-lover's institution in Barra and a sort of community service that the rather grouchy Bob does for fun. His policy of "leave a book if you take one" allows vacationers to select from hundreds of neatly shelved paperbacks, as long as they leave a book in exchange. It's open Monday through Friday from noon to 3pm and occasionally in the evenings. "Beer Bob" got his name because in earlier days, when beer was cheap, he kept a cooler stocked, and book browsers could sip and read. (When beer prices went up, Bob put the cooler away.)

WHERE TO STAY

Low season in Barra is any time except Christmas and Easter weeks. Except for those 2 weeks, it doesn't hurt to ask for a discount at the inexpensive hotels. To arrange **real estate rentals,** contact **The Crazy Cactus,** Veracruz 165, a half-block inland from the town church on Legazpi (©/fax **315/355-6099;** crazycactusmx@yahoo.com). The store may be closed May through October.

Barra de Navidad Bay Area

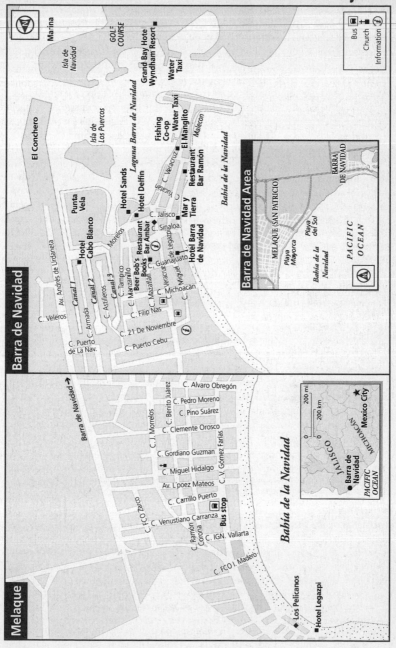

Barra de Navidad

- Marina
- Isla de Navidad
- GOLF COURSE
- El Conchero
- Isla de Los Puercos
- Laguna Barra de Navidad
- Grand Bay Hotel Wyndham Resort
- Water Taxi
- Fishing Co-op
- Water Taxi
- El Manglito
- Malecon
- Restaurant Bar Ramón
- C. Veracruz
- C. Yucatan
- Bahia de la Navidad
- Hotel Sands
- Hotel Delfin
- Punta Vela
- C. Jalisco
- Mar y Tierra
- C. Sinaloa
- Hotel Cabo Blanco
- Morelos
- Restaurant Bar Ambar
- Beer Bob's Books
- Hotel Barra de Navidad
- C. Guanajuato
- C. Manzanillo
- C. Tampico
- C. Veracruz
- C. Mazatlán
- C. Legazpi
- C. Miguel
- C. Michoacán
- Canal 1
- Canal 2
- Canal 3
- C. Armada
- C. Astilleros
- Av. Andrés de Urdaneta
- C. Filip Nas
- C. Veleros
- C. 21 De Noviembre
- C. Puerto de La Nav.
- C. Puerto Cebu

Barra de Navidad Area

- BARRA DE NAVIDAD
- MELAQUE (SAN PATRICIO)
- Playa Mayorca
- Playa del Sol
- Bahia de la Navidad
- PACIFIC OCEAN

Melaque

- Barra de Navidad →
- C. Alvaro Obregón
- C. Pedro Moreno
- C. Pino Suárez
- C. Benito Juárez
- C. Clemente Orosco
- C.J. Morelos
- C. Gordiano Guzman
- C. Miguel Hidalgo
- Av. L'poez Mateos
- C.V. Gómez Farías
- C. Carrillo Puerto
- Bus stop
- C. FCO Zarco
- C. Venustiano Carranza
- C. Ramón Corona
- C. IGN. Vallarta
- C. FCO I. Madero
- Bahia de la Navidad
- Los Pelicanos
- Hotel Legazpi

Bus
Church
Information

Inset (Mexico)

- 200 mi
- 200 km
- JALISCO
- MICHOACÁN
- Mexico City
- Barra de Navidad
- PACIFIC OCEAN

Very Expensive

Grand Bay Hotel Isla Navidad Resort *(R) Overrated*   Across the yacht channel from Barra de Navidad, this luxurious hotel opened in 1997 on 480 hectares (1,186 acres) next to its 27-hole golf course. Now operated by Wyndham Resorts, it overlooks the village, bay, Pacific Ocean, and Navidad lagoon. The hotel's beach is narrow and on the lagoon. A better beach is opposite the hotel on the bay in Barra de Navidad. The spacious rooms are sumptuously outfitted with marble floors, large bathrooms, and hand-carved wood furnishings. Prices vary according to view and size of room, but even the modest rooms are large, and all have cable TV. Each comes with a king-size or two double beds, ceiling fans plus air-conditioning, and a balcony. All suites have a steam sauna and telephones in the bathroom as well as a sound system. The hotel is a short water-taxi ride across the inlet from Barra de Navidad; it is also on a paved road from Highway 200. Although the hotel bills itself as being on the Island of Navidad at Port Navidad, the port is the marina, and the hotel is on a peninsula.

Circuito de los Marinos s/n, 28830 Isla Navidad, Col. (C) **877/999-3223** in US; 01-800/849-2373 in Mexico, or 314/331-0500. Fax 314/331-0570. www.islanavidad.com. 199 units. High season $499 (£250) double, $580–$892 (£290–£446) suite; low season $429 (£215) double, $507–$805 (£254–£403) suite. AE, DC, DISC, MC, V. Free parking. **Amenities:** 2 restaurants; 2 bars; golf club w/food and bar service; outdoor swimming pool w/water slides and swim-up bar; 27-hole, par-72 golf course; golf club w/pro shop and driving range; 3 lighted grass tennis courts; small workout room; marina w/private yacht club; fishing, boat tours, and other excursions can be arranged; kids' club w/activity program; concierge; business center; salon; room service; babysitting; laundry service; dry cleaning. *In room:* A/C, TV, minibar, hair dryer, iron, safe.

Moderate

Hotel Cabo Blanco *(R)(R)*   Located on the point where you cross over to Isla Navidad, the Cabo Blanco is an outstanding option for family vacations or longer-term stays. Rooms are pleasantly rustic, with tile floors, large tile tubs, separate dressing areas, and stucco walls. The hotel overlooks the bay, but it's a 5-minute walk to the beach. The beamed-ceiling lobby is in its own building; rooms are in hacienda-style buildings surrounded by gardens. The atmosphere is generally tranquil, except during weekends and Mexican holidays, when this hotel tends to fill up. Because the Cabo Blanco doesn't front the beach, it has an affiliated beach club and restaurant, Mar y Tierra (see "Where to Dine," below).

Armada y Bahía de la Navidad s/n, 48987 Barra de Navidad, Jal. (C) **800/710-5690** in Mexico; 315/355-6495 or -6496. Fax 315/355-6494. www.hotelcaboblanco.com. 101 units. $100 (£50) double; $256 (£128) suite with kitchenette. All-inclusive plans also available. AE, MC, V. Limited street parking. **Amenities:** 2 restaurants; 4 outdoor pools (2 adults only); 2 tennis courts; concierge; tour desk; car-rental desk; laundry service. *In room:* A/C, TV.

Inexpensive

Hotel Barra de Navidad *(R)*   At the northern end of Legazpi, this popular, comfortable beachside hotel is among the nicest in the town. It has friendly management, and some rooms with balconies overlooking the beach and bay. Other, less-expensive rooms afford only a street view. Only the oceanview rooms have air-conditioning. A nice swimming pool is on the street level to the right of the lobby.

Legazpi 250, 48987 Barra de Navidad, Jal. (C) 315/355-5122. Fax 315/355-5303. www.hotelbarradenavidad.com. 60 units. $72–$82 (£36–£41) double. MC, V. Free parking. **Amenities:** Outdoor pool. *In room:* A/C (in some rooms).

Hotel Delfín   One of Barra's better-maintained hotels, the four-story (no elevator) Delfín is on the landward side of the lagoon. It offers pleasant, basic, well-maintained, and well-lit rooms. Each has red-tile floors and a double, two double, or two single beds. The tiny courtyard, with a small pool and lounge chairs, sits in the shade of an enormous rubber tree. From the fourth floor, there's a view of the lagoon. A breakfast buffet is served from 8:30 to 10:30am (see "Where to Dine," below).

Morelos 23, 48987 Barra de Navidad, Jal. (℄ 315/355-5068. Fax 315/355-6020. www.hoteldelfinmx.com. 24 units. $49 (£25) double; ask about low-season discounts. MC, V. Free parking. **Amenities:** Restaurant; heated outdoor pool; gym.

Hotel Sands   The colonial-style Sands, across from the Hotel Delfín (see above) on the lagoon side at Jalisco, offers small but homey rooms with red-tile floors and windows with both screens and glass. The remodeled bathrooms have new tiles and fixtures. Lower rooms look onto a public walkway and wide courtyard filled with greenery and singing birds; upstairs rooms are brighter. Twelve rooms (suites or bungalows) have air-conditioning and kitchenette facilities. The hotel is known for its warm hospitality and high-season happy hour (2–6pm) at the pool terrace bar beside the lagoon. On weekends from 9pm to 4am, an adjacent patio "disco" plays recorded music for dancing. Breakfast is served from 7:30am to noon. Fishing trips can be arranged, and tours to nearby beaches are available.

Morelos 24, 48987 Barra de Navidad, Jal. (℄/fax **315/355-5018.** 42 units. High season $80 (£40) double; low season $54 (£27) double. Rates include breakfast. Room-only rates $10 (£5) less. Discounts for stays of 1 week or more. MC, V (6% surcharge). **Amenities:** Restaurant; bar; outdoor pool w/whirlpool overlooking lagoon beach; children's play area; tour desk. *In room:* A/C (in some rooms), kitchenette (in some rooms).

WHERE TO DINE

El Manglito ⚔ SEAFOOD/MEXICAN   On the placid lagoon, with a view of the palatial Grand Bay Hotel, El Manglito serves home-style Mexican food to a growing number of repeat diners. The whole fried fish accompanied by drawn garlic butter, boiled vegetables, rice, and french fries, is a crowd-pleaser. Other enticements include boiled shrimp, chicken in orange sauce, and shrimp salad.

Veracruz 17, near the boatmen's cooperative. No phone. Main courses $5.50–$12 (£2.25–£6). No credit cards. Daily 9am–11pm.

Hotel Delfín BREAKFAST   The second-story terrace of this small hotel is a pleasant place to begin the day. The self-serve buffet offers an assortment of fresh fruit, juice, granola, yogurt, milk, pastries, and unlimited coffee. The price includes made-to-order eggs and delicious banana pancakes—for which the restaurant is known.

Morelos 23. (℄ **315/355-5068.** www.hoteldelfinmx.com. Breakfast buffet $3 (£1.50). No credit cards. Daily 8:30am–noon.

Mar y Tierra INTERNATIONAL   Hotel Cabo Blanco's beach club is also a popular restaurant and bar and a great place to spend a day at the beach. On the beach, there are shade *palapas* and beach chairs, and a game of volleyball seems constantly in progress. The colorful restaurant is decorated with murals of mermaids. Perfectly seasoned shrimp fajitas come in plentiful portions.

Legazpi s/n (at Jalisco). (℄ **315/355-5028.** Main courses $12–$19 (£6–£9.50). MC, V. Wed–Mon 10am–6pm.

Restaurant Bar Ambar CREPES/ITALIAN/FRENCH   This cozy, thatched-roof, upstairs restaurant is open to the breezes. The crepes are named after towns in France; the delicious *crêpe Paris,* for example, is filled with chicken, potatoes, spinach, and green sauce. International main dishes include imported (from the U.S.) rib-eye steak in Dijon mustard sauce, mixed brochettes, quiche, and Caesar salad. Ambar serves Spanish-style tapas from noon until 6pm, and adds French specialties during dinner. Pastas and pizzas are also served.

López de Legazpi 160, across from the church. © 315/355-8169. Crepes $9.50–$14 (£4.75–£7); main courses $16–$27 (£8–£14). No credit cards. Daily 6pm–midnight.

Restaurant Bar Ramón ✪ (Value SEAFOOD/MEXICAN   It seems that everybody eats at Ramón's, where the chips and fresh salsa arrive unbidden, and service is prompt and friendly. The food is especially good—however, most options are fried. Try fresh fried shrimp with french fries or any daily special that features vegetable soup or chicken-fried steak. Great value.

Legazpi 260. © 315/355-6435. Main courses $7–$13 (£3.50–£6.50). No credit cards. Daily 7am–11pm.

BARRA DE NAVIDAD AFTER DARK

When dusk arrives, visitors and locals alike find a cool spot to sit outside, sip cocktails, and chat. Many outdoor restaurants and stores in Barra accommodate this relaxing way to end the day, adding extra tables and chairs for drop-ins.

During high season, the **Hotel Sands** poolside and lagoon-side bar has happy hour from 2 to 6pm. The colorful **Sunset Bar and Restaurant,** facing the bay at the corner of Legazpi and Jalisco, is a favorite for sunset watching and a game of oceanside pool or dancing to live or taped music. It's most popular with travelers ages 20 to 30. In the same vein, **Chips Restaurant,** on the second floor, facing the ocean at the corner of Yucatán and Legazpi, near the southern end of the *malecón,* has an excellent sunset vista. Live music follows the last rays of light, and patrons stay for hours. **Piper Lover Bar & Grill,** Legazpi 154 A (© **315/355-6747;** www.piperlover.com) is done in the style of the Carlos Anderson's chain—but it's not one of them. Still, it is lively, with pool tables and occasional live music.

At the **Disco El Galeón,** in the Hotel Sands on Calle Morelos, cushioned benches and cement tables encircle the round dance floor. It's all open air, and about as stylish as you'll find in Barra. It serves drinks only. Admission is $6.50 (£3.25), and it's open Friday and Saturday from 9pm to 4am.

A VISIT TO MELAQUE (SAN PATRICIO)

For a change of scenery, you may want to wander over to Melaque (aka San Patricio), 5km (3 miles) from Barra on the same bay. You can walk on the beach from Barra or take one of the frequent local buses from the bus station near the main square in Barra. The bus is marked MELAQUE. To return to Barra, take the bus marked CIHUATLAN.

Melaque's pace is even more laid-back than Barra's, and though it's a larger village, it seems smaller. It has fewer restaurants and less to do. Although there are more hotels, or "bungalows," as they are usually called, few manage the charm of those in Barra; if Barra hotels are full on a holiday weekend, Melaque would be a second choice. The paved road ends where the town begins. A few yachts bob in the harbor, and the palm-lined beach is gorgeous.

If you come by bus from Barra, you can exit anywhere in town or stay on until the last stop, which is the bus station in the middle of town a block from the beach. Restaurants and hotels line the beach. Coming into town from the main road, you'll be on the town's main street, **Avenida López Mateos.** You'll pass the main square on the way to the waterfront, where there's a trailer park. The street going left (southeast) along the bay is **Avenida Gómez Farías;** the one going right (northwest) is **Avenida Miguel Ochoa López.**

WHERE TO DINE   At the north end of Melaque beach is **Los Pelícanos** (no phone). It serves the usual seafood specialties; the tender fried squid is delectable. In addition, you can find burritos, nachos, and hamburgers. Many Barra guests come here to stake a place on the beach and use the restaurant as headquarters for sipping and nipping. Open daily from 8am to 10pm, it's a peaceful place to watch the pelicans bobbing. The restaurant is at the far end of the bay before the **Hotel Legazpi** (✆ **315/355-5397**), a pleasant place to stay. It has 20 rooms, charges $40 (£20) for a double, and doesn't accept credit cards.

In addition to the Los Pelícanos, there are many rustic *palapa* **restaurants** on the beach and farther along the bay at the end of the beach.

4 Manzanillo ⋆

256km (159 miles) SE of Puerto Vallarta; 267km (166 miles) SW of Guadalajara; 64km (40 miles) SE of Barra de Navidad

Manzanillo has long been known as a resort town with wide, curving beaches, legendary sportfishing, and a highly praised diversity of dive sites. Golf is also an attraction here, with two popular courses in the area.

One reason for its popularity could be Manzanillo's enticing tropical geography—vast groves of tall palms, abundant mango trees, and successive coves graced with smooth sand beaches. To the north, mountains blanketed with palms rise alongside the shoreline. And over it all lies the veneer of perfect weather, with balmy temperatures and year-round sea breezes. Even the approach by plane into Manzanillo showcases the promise—you fly in over the beach and golf course. Once on the ground, you exit the airport through a palm grove.

Manzanillo is a dichotomous place—it is both Mexico's busiest commercial seaport and a tranquil, traditional town of multicolor houses cascading down the hillsides to meet the central commercial area of simple seafood restaurants, shell shops, and a few salsa clubs. The activity in Manzanillo divides neatly into two zones: the downtown commercial port and the luxury Santiago Peninsula resort zone to the north. The busy harbor and rail connections to Mexico's interior dominate the downtown zone. A visit to the town's waterfront *zócalo* provides a glimpse into local life. The exclusive Santiago Peninsula, home to the resorts and golf course, separates Manzanillo's two golden sand bays.

ESSENTIALS
GETTING THERE & DEPARTING   By Plane   Alaska Airlines (✆ **800/252-7522** in the U.S., or 314/334-2211) offers service from Los Angeles; **US Airways** (**America West;** ✆ **800/428-4322** in the U.S.) flies from Phoenix. Ask a travel agent about the numerous **charters** from the States in the winter.

The **Playa de Oro International Airport** is 40km (25 miles) northwest of town. *Colectivo* (minivan) airport service is available from the airport; hotels arrange returns. Make reservations for return trips 1 day in advance. The *colectivo* fare is based on zones and runs $11 to $15 (£5.50–£7.50) for most hotels. Private taxi service between the airport and downtown area is around $35 (£18). **Budget** (✆ **800/472-3325** in the U.S., or 314/333-1445), **Hertz** (✆ **314/333-3191**), and **Alamo** (✆ **314/334-0124**) have counters in the airport open during flight arrivals; they will also deliver a car to your hotel. Daily rates run $60 to $80 (£30–£40). You need a car only if you plan to explore surrounding cities and the Costa Alegre beaches.

By Car   Coastal Highway 200 leads from Acapulco (south) and Puerto Vallarta (north). From Guadalajara, take **Highway 54** through Colima into Manzanillo. Outside Colima you can switch to a toll road, which is faster but less scenic.

By Bus   Buses run to Barra de Navidad (1½ hr. north), Puerto Vallarta (5 hr. north), Colima (1½ hr. east), and Guadalajara (4½ hr. north), with deluxe service and numerous daily departures. Manzanillo's **Central Camionera** (bus station) © 314/332-0123, is about 12 long blocks east of town. If you follow Hidalgo east, the station will be on your right.

VISITOR INFORMATION   The **tourism office** (© 314/333-3838; fax 314/333-2080; www.manzanillo.com.mx) is on the Costera Miguel de la Madrid 875-A, Km 8.5. It's open Monday through Friday from 9am to 7pm, and Saturday from 9am to 2pm.

CITY LAYOUT   The town lies at one end of an 11km-long (7-mile) beach facing Manzanillo Bay and its commercial harbor. The beach has four sections—**Playa Las Brisas, Playa Azul, Playa Salahua,** and **Playa Las Hadas.** At the other end of the beaches is the high, rocky **Santiago Peninsula.** Santiago is 11km (7 miles) from downtown; it's the site of many beautiful homes and the best hotel in the area, Las Hadas, as well as the hotel's Mantarraya Golf Course. The peninsula juts into the bay, separating Manzanillo Bay from Santiago Bay. Playa Las Hadas is on the south side of the peninsula, facing Manzanillo Bay, and **Playa Audiencia** is on the north side, facing Santiago Bay. The inland town of **Santiago** is opposite the turnoff to Las Hadas.

Activity in downtown Manzanillo centers on the *zócalo,* officially known as the Jardín Alvaro Obregón. A railroad, shipyards, and a basketball court with constant pickup games separate it from the waterfront. The plaza has flowering trees, a fountain, twin kiosks, and a view of the bay. It is a staple of local life, where people congregate on park benches to swap gossip and throw handfuls of rice to the ever-present *palomas* (doves—really just pigeons). Large ships dock at the pier nearby. **Avenida México,** the street leading out from the plaza's central gazebo, is the town's principal commercial thoroughfare. This area is currently undergoing a government-funded renaissance, so look for new improvements.

Once you leave downtown, the **Costera Miguel de la Madrid** highway (or just Costera Madrid) runs through the neighborhoods of Las Brisas, Salahua, and Santiago to the **hotel zones** on the Santiago Peninsula and at Miramar. Shell shops, minimalls, and several restaurants are along the way.

There are two main lagoons. **Laguna de Cuyutlán,** almost behind the city, stretches south for miles, paralleling the coast. **Laguna de San Pedrito,** north of the city, parallels the Costera Miguel de la Madrid; it's behind Playa Las Brisas beach. Both are good birding sites. There are also two bays. **Manzanillo Bay** encompasses the harbor, town, and beaches. The Santiago Peninsula separates it from the second bay, **Santiago.** Between downtown and the Santiago Peninsula is **Las Brisas,** a flat peninsula with a long stretch of sandy golden beach, a lineup of inexpensive but run-down hotels, and a few good restaurants.

GETTING AROUND   By Taxi   Taxis in Manzanillo are plentiful. Fares are fixed by zones; rates for trips in town and to more distant points should be posted at your hotel. Daily rates can be negotiated for longer drives outside the Manzanillo area.

By Bus   The *camionetas* (local buses) make a circuit from downtown in front of the train station, along the Bay of Manzanillo, to the Santiago Peninsula and the Bay of Santiago to the north; the fare is 10¢ (5p). The ones marked LAS BRISAS go to the Las Brisas crossroads, to the Las Brisas Peninsula, and back to town; MIRAMAR, SANTIAGO, and SALAHUA buses go to outlying settlements along the bays and to most restaurants

Manzanillo Area

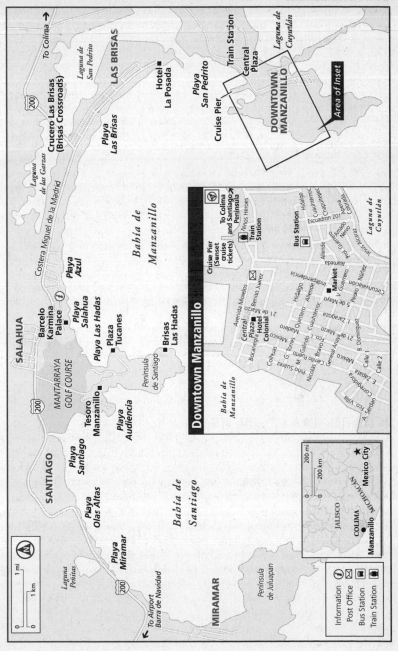

To Colima →

Laguna de Cuyutlán

LAS BRISAS

Laguna de San Pedrito

200

Crucero Las Brisas
(Brisas Crossroads)

Laguna de las Garzas

Hotel
La Posada

Playa
Las Brisas

Playa
San Pedrito

Train Station

Central
Plaza

**DOWNTOWN
MANZANILLO**

Cruise Pier

Area of Inset

Costera Miguel de la Madrid

Laguna de la Madrid

Playa
Azul

SALAHUA

Barcelo
Karmina
Palace ⓘ

Playa
Salahua

Plaza
Tucanes

Playa Las Hadas

Brisas
Las Hadas

*Bahía de
Manzanillo*

MANTARRAYA
GOLF COURSE

Tesoro
Manzanillo

Playa
Audiencia

Península
de Santiago

SANTIAGO

Playa
Santiago

Playa
Olas Altas

*Bahía de
Santiago*

Playa
Miramar

Laguna
Peñitas

200

**To Airport
Barra de Navidad ↙**

Península
de Juluapan

MIRAMAR

⊕ 1 mi

1 km

Downtown Manzanillo

⊛

Cruise Pier
(Sunset
cruise
tickets)

**To Colima
and Santiago ↗
Peninsula**

Niños Héroes

Train
Station

Hidalgo

Cuauhtémoc
Chapultepec

Escuadron 201

V. de Arendo
Nuevo

Prol. Guerrero

Cuauhtémoc
Cordoba

Jesus Alcaraz

Avenida Morelos

⊠

21 de Marzo

Benito Juárez

Allende

Alameda

Independencia

Hidalgo

Allende

Bus Station

⬛

Circunvalación

Laguna de
Cuyutlán

**Central
Plaza**
Bocanegra

**Hotel
Colonial**

Avenida
México

México

Madero

Quintero

Cuauhtémoc

Market

V. Guerrero

Pedro Núñez

5 de Mayo

I. Zaragoza

Colimas

G. Torres

M. Galindo

Bravo

Fco. I.
Madero

21 de
Marzo

México

Colimas

Pino Suárez

Nicolás Bravo

Carrillo Puerto

General Anaya

E. Zapata

A. Serdán

Corregidora

Fco. Villa

E. Zapata

Calle 1

Calle 2

*Bahía de
Manzanillo*

200 mi

200 km

0   0

Mexico City ★

JALISCO

MICHOACÁN

COLIMA

Manzanillo ●

Information ⓘ
Post Office ⊠
Bus Station ⬛
Train Station ⬛

371

mentioned below. Buses marked LAS HADAS go to the Santiago Peninsula and pass the Las Hadas resort and the Tesoro Manzanillo and Plaza Las Glorias hotels. This is an inexpensive way to see the coast as far as Santiago and to tour the Santiago Peninsula.

FAST FACTS: Manzanillo

American Express American Express has no local office in Manzanillo, but we highly recommend **Bahías Gemelas Travel Agency,** Blvd. Costero Miguel de la Madrid 1556, Las Gaviotas (✆ **314/333-1000**; fax 314/333-0649). It's open Monday through Friday from 9am to 2pm and 4 to 7pm, Saturday from 9am to 2pm.

Area Code The telephone area code is **314.**

Bank Banamex, just off the plaza on Avenida Juárez, downtown (✆ **314/332-0115**), is open Monday through Friday from 9am to 4pm, Saturday 10am to 2pm.

Hospital Contact the **Cruz Roja (Red Cross)** (✆ **314/336-5770**) or the **General Hospital** (✆ **314/332-1903** or -0089).

Internet Access **Digital Center,** Bulevar Miguel de la Madrid 964-B (✆ **314/333-9191;** www.digitalcenter.manzanillo.com), is located in the hotel zone, near the Hotel Marbella and Fiesta Americana hotels. It charges $2 (£1) per hour, and also has printers. It's open Monday through Friday from 9am to 8pm, Saturday from 9am to 2pm. They also have computer repair services available.

Police Both the general police and Tourism Police are available by calling ✆ **314/332-1004** or -1002.

Post Office The *correo,* Dr. Miguel Galindo 30, opposite Farmacia de Guadalajara, downtown (✆ **314/332-0022**), is open Monday through Friday from 8:30am to 4pm, Saturday from 9am to 1pm.

ACTIVITIES ON & OFF THE BEACH

Activities in Manzanillo revolve around its golden sand beaches, which frequently accumulate a film of black mineral residue from nearby rivers. Most of the resort hotels are completely self-contained. Manzanillo's public beaches provide an opportunity to see more local color and scenery. They are the daytime playground for those staying at places off the beach or without pools.

BEACHES **Playa Audiencia,** on the Santiago Peninsula, offers the best swimming as well as snorkeling, but **Playa San Pedrito,** shallow for a long way out, is the most popular beach for its proximity to downtown. **Playa Las Brisas,** located south of Santiago Peninsula as you're heading to downtown Manzanillo, offers an optimal combination of location and good swimming. **Playa Miramar,** on the Bahía de Santiago past the Santiago Peninsula, is popular with bodysurfers, windsurfers, and boogie boarders. It's accessible by local bus from town. The major part of **Playa Azul,** also south of the Santiago Peninsula, drops off sharply but is noted for its wide stretch of golden sand.

BIRDING Birding is good in several lagoons along the coast. As you go from Manzanillo past Las Brisas to Santiago, you'll pass **Laguna de Las Garzas (Lagoon of the Herons),** also known as Laguna de San Pedrito, where many white pelicans and huge herons fish in the water. They nest here in December and January. Directly behind downtown is the **Laguna de Cuyutlán** (follow the signs to Cuyutlán), where you'll usually find birds in abundance; species vary between summer and winter.

DIVING   **Underworld Scuba** 𝒜𝒜 (☏/fax **314/333-3678;** cell 314/358-0327; www.gomanzanillo.com), owned by longtime resident and local diving expert Susan Dearing, conducts highly professional diving expeditions and classes. Susan's warm enthusiasm and intimate knowledge of the area make this one of my top recommendations for dive outfitters in Mexico. Many locations are so close to shore that there's no need for a boat. Close-in dives include the jetty, with coral growing on the rocks at 14m (46 ft.), and a nearby sunken frigate downed in 1959 at 8m (26 ft.). Divers can see abundant sea life, including coral reefs, seahorses, giant puffer fish, and moray eels. A dive requiring a boat costs $60 (£30) per person for one tank (with a three-person minimum) or $80 (£40) for two tanks ($10/£5 discount if you have your own equipment). You can also rent weights and a tank for beach dives for $10 (£5). A three-stop snorkel trip costs $45 (£23). All guides are certified divemasters, and the shop offers certification classes (PADI, YMCA, and CMAS) in very intensive courses of various durations. The owner offers a 10% discount on your certification when you mention Frommer's. MasterCard and Visa are accepted.

ESCORTED TOURS   Because Manzanillo is so spread out, you might consider a city tour. Reputable local tour companies include **HECtours** (☏ **314/333-1707;** www.hectours.com) and **Bahías Gemelas Travel Agency** (☏ **314/333-1000;** fax 314/333-0649). Schedules are flexible; a half-day city tour costs around $25 (£13). Other tours include the daylong Colima Colonial Tour ($69/£35), which stops at Colima's Archaeological Museum and principal colonial buildings, and passes the active volcano. Offerings change regularly, so ask about new tours.

FISHING   Manzanillo is famous for its fishing, particularly sailfish. Marlin and sailfish are abundant year-round. Winter is best for dolphin fish and dorado (mahimahi); in summer, wahoo and rooster fish are in greater supply. The international sailfish competition is held around the November 20 Revolution Day holiday, and the national sailfish competition is in February. You can arrange fishing through travel agencies or directly at the fishermen's cooperative (☏ **314/332-1031**), located downtown where the fishing boats moor. Call from 6am to 2pm or 5 to 8pm. A fishing boat is approximately $45 (£23) for eight people to $55 (£28) for 12 people per hour, with most trips lasting about 5 hours.

GOLF   The 18-hole **La Mantarraya Golf Course** (☏ **314/331-0101**) is open to nonguests as well as guests of Las Hadas. At one time, La Mantarraya was among the top 100 courses in the world, but newer entries have surpassed it. Still, the compact, challenging 18-hole course designed by Roy and Pete Dye is a beauty, with banana trees, blooming bougainvillea, and coconut palms at every turn. A lush and verdant place (12 of the 18 holes are played over water), it remains a favorite.

When the course was under construction, workers dug up pre-Hispanic ceramic figurines, idols, and beads where the 14th hole now lies. It is believed to have been an important ancient burial site. The course culminates with its signature 18th hole, with a drive to the island green off El Tesoro (the treasure) beach, directly in front of the Karminda Palace Resort. Local lore says this beach still may hold buried treasure from Spanish galleons, whose crews were the first to recognize the perfection of this natural harbor, and who used it during the 16th century as their starting point for voyages to the Pacific Rim. Greens fees are $160 (£80) for 18 holes, $95 (£48) for 9 holes; cart rental costs $55 (£28) for 18 holes and $35 (£18) for 9 holes.

The fabulous Isla Navidad Country Club 27-hole golf course associated with the **Grand Bay Hotel** (© 314/337-9024) in Barra de Navidad, an easy distance from Manzanillo, is also open to the public. The Robert von Hagge design is long and lovely, with each hole amid rolling, tropical landscapes. It is wide open, with big fairways and big greens, and features plenty of water (2 lagoon holes, 13 lakeside holes, and 8 holes along the Pacific). The greens fees, including a motorized cart, are $180 (£90) for 18 holes, $200 (£100) for 27 holes. Barra is about a 1- to 1½-hour drive north of Manzanillo on Highway 200.

A MUSEUM   The **Museum of Archaeology and History** (© 314/332-2256) is a small but impressive structure that houses exhibits depicting the region's history, plus rotating displays of contemporary Mexican art. It's on Avenida Niños Héroes at Avenida Teniente Azueta, on the road leading between the downtown and Las Brisas areas. Every Friday evening, the museum hosts free cultural events, which might be a trio playing romantic ballads or a chamber music ensemble. Performances begin at 8pm. Hours are Tuesday through Saturday from 10am to 2pm and 5 to 8pm, Sunday from 10am to 1pm.

SHOPPING   Manzanillo has numerous shops that carry Mexican crafts and clothing, mainly from Guadalajara. Almost all are downtown on the streets near the central plaza. Shopping downtown is an experience—for example, you won't want to miss the shop bordering the plaza that sells a combination of shells, religious items (including shell-framed Virgin of Guadalupe nightlights), and orthopedic supplies. The Plaza Manzanillo is an American-style mall on the road to Santiago, and a traditional *tianguis* (outdoor) market in front of the entrance to Club Maeva sells touristy items from around Mexico. Most resort hotels also have boutiques or shopping arcades.

SUNSET CRUISES   To participate in this popular activity, buy tickets from a travel agent or your hotel tour desk. Most cost around $30 (£15). The trips vary in their combinations of drinks, music, and entertainment and last 1½ to 2 hours. Departing from Las Hadas are **El Explorer** and **Antares.**

WHERE TO STAY

Manzanillo's strip of coastline consists of three areas: **downtown,** with its shops, markets, and commercial activity; **Las Brisas,** the hotel-lined beach area immediately north of the city; and **Santiago,** the town and peninsula, now virtually a suburb, to the north at the end of Playa Azul. Transportation by bus or taxi makes all three areas fairly convenient to each other. Reservations are recommended during the Easter, Christmas, and New Year's holidays.

DOWNTOWN

Hotel Colonial 𝕲   An old favorite, this three-story colonial-style hotel is in the central downtown district. Popular for its consistent quality, ambience, and service, it has beautiful blue-and-yellow tile and colonial-style carved doors and windows in the lobby and restaurant. Rooms provide basic comforts, with minimal furniture and red-tile floors. The hotel is 1 block inland from the main plaza at Juárez and Galindo.

Av. México 100 and González Bocanegra, 28200 Manzanillo, Col. © 314/332-1080, -0668, or -1230. 42 units. $48 (£24) double. MC, V. Limited street parking. **Amenities:** Restaurant; bar. *In room:* A/C, cable TV.

LAS BRISAS

Some parts of the Las Brisas area look run-down; however, it still lays claim to one of the best beaches in the area and is known for its constant gentle sea breezes—a pleasure in the summer.

Hotel La Posada ⏉ This small inn has a bright-pink stucco facade with a large arch that leads to a broad tiled patio right on the beach. The rooms have exposed brick walls and simple furnishings with Mexican decorative accents. It remains popular with longtime travelers to Manzanillo. The atmosphere is casual and informal—help yourself to beer and soft drinks; at the end of your stay, owners Juan and Lisa Martinez will count the bottle caps you deposited in a bowl labeled with your room number. The restaurant, which is open to nonguests, is open daily during high season from 8 to 11am and 1:30 to 8pm. A meal costs around $7 (£3.50). During low season, the restaurant is open from 8am to 3pm. Stop by for a drink at sunset; the bar's open until 9pm all year. The hotel is at the end of Las Brisas Peninsula, closest to downtown, and is on the local Las Brisas bus route.

Av. Lázaro Cárdenas 201, Las Brisas (Apdo. Postal 135), 28200 Manzanillo, Col. ⏉/fax **314/333-1899.** www.hotel-la-posada.info. 23 units. High season $78 (£39) double; low season $58 (£29) double. Rates include full breakfast. MC, V. Free parking. **Amenities:** Restaurant; bar; Internet cafe; laundry service; currency exchange; safe.

SANTIAGO

Five kilometers (3 miles) north of Las Brisas is the wide Santiago Peninsula. The settlement of Salahua is on the highway where you enter the peninsula to reach the hotels Las Hadas, Plaza Las Glorias, and Tesoro Manzanillo, as well as the Mantarraya Golf Course. Buses from town marked LAS HADAS pass by these hotels every 20 minutes. Past the Salahua turnoff, at the end of the settlement of Santiago, an obscure road on the left is marked ZONA DE PLAYAS and leads to the hotels on the other side of the peninsula and Playa de Santiago.

Barceló Karmina Palace ⏉⏉⏉ *Kids* The quality of rooms and services at this all-inclusive resort makes the newest of Manzanillo's hotels one of the area's best values. It's the best choice for families visiting Manzanillo. The buildings resemble Maya pyramids, and even though the architecture at first might seem a little overdone, somehow it works. Rooms are all very large suites, with rich wood accents, comfortable recessed seating areas with pull-out couches, and two 27-inch TVs in each room. The extra-large bathrooms have marble floors, twin black marble sinks, separate tubs, and glassed-in showers. Most rooms have terraces or balconies with views of the ocean, overlooking the tropical gardens and swimming pools. Master suites have spacious sun terraces with private splash pools, plus a full wet bar, full refrigerator, and a large living room area with 42-inch TV. Two full-size bedrooms close off from the living/dining area. The kids' club offers a host of activities—all included in the price. The gym and European-style spa are exceptionally well equipped.

Av. Vista Hermosa 13, Fracc. Península de Santiago, 28200 Manzanillo, Col. **888/234-6222** in the U.S. and Canada, or 314/334-1300, 331-1313, or 01-800/507-4930 in Mexico. Fax 314/334-1108. www.barcelokarminapalace.com. 324 units. $278–$338 (£139–£169) double; $908 (£454) 2-bedroom suites for 4. Rates are all-inclusive. Special packages and Web specials available; ask about seasonal specials. 2 children younger than 8 stay free in parent's room. AE, MC, V. Free parking. **Amenities:** 2 restaurants; snack bar; 5 bars; 8 connected swimming pools; tennis courts; health club w/treadmills and Cybex equipment; full spa facilities; men's and women's sauna and steam rooms; sailboards; beach volleyball; kids' activity program; concierge; car rental; room service; currency exchange; safe. *In room:* A/C, TV, minibar, hair dryer, iron, safe ($2/£1).

Brisas Las Hadas Golf Resort & Marina 𝒦𝒦   For me, Las Hadas is synonymous with a visit to Manzanillo. This elegant beachside resort is built in Moorish style into the side of the rocky peninsula. Rooms are spread over landscaped grounds and over-look the bay; cobbled lanes lined with colorful flowers and palms connect them. The resort is large but maintains an air of seclusion. (Motorized carts are on call for trans-portation within the property.)

Views, room size, and amenities differentiate the six types of accommodations, which can vary greatly. If you're not satisfied with your room, ask to be moved—a few of the rooms are significantly less attractive than others. Understated and spacious, the better units have white-marble floors, sitting areas, and large, comfortably furnished balconies. Nine suites have private pools. The lobby is a popular place for curling up in one of the overstuffed seating areas or, at night, for enjoying a drink and live music. Pete and Roy Dye designed La Mantarraya, the hotel's 18-hole, par-71 golf course.

If you are visiting on a cruise ship or staying at another hotel, you can enjoy Las Hadas beach for a day by purchasing a day pass from the hotel's gate guard.

Av. de los Riscos s/n, Santiago Peninsula, 28200 Manzanillo, Col. ⓒ **888/559-4329** in the U.S. and Canada, or 314/ 331-0101. www.brisas.com.mx. 234 units. High season $206–$327 (£103–£164) double, $386–$626 (£193–£313) Fantasy Suite; low season $175–$379 (£88–£190) double, $386–$626 (£193–£313) Fantasy Suite. AE, DC, MC, V. Free guarded parking. **Amenities:** 3 restaurants, including the elegant Legazpi (see "Where to Dine," below); 3 lounges and bars; 2 outdoor pools; small workout room; marina for 70 vessels; scuba diving; snorkeling; water-skiing; sailing and trimaran cruises; concierge; tour desk; travel agency; car rental; shopping arcade; room service; in-room massage; babysitting; laundry service; dry cleaning. *In room:* A/C, TV, minibar, hair dryer, safe.

Plaza Tucanes 𝒦   The sunset-colored walls of this pueblolike hotel ramble over a hillside on the Santiago Peninsula. The restaurant on top and most rooms afford a broad vista of other red-tiled rooftops and either the palm-filled golf course or the bay. It's one of Manzanillo's undiscovered resorts, known more to wealthy Mexicans than to Americans. Originally conceived as private condominiums, the accommodations were designed for living; each spacious unit is stylishly furnished, and very comfort-able. Each has a huge living room; a small kitchen/bar; one, two, or three large bed-rooms with tile or brick floors; large bathrooms with Mexican tiles; huge closets; and large furnished private patios with views. Some units contain whirlpool tubs, and a few rooms can be partitioned off and rented by the bedroom only. Rooms can be a long walk from the main entrance, through a succession of stairways and paths. If stair climbing bothers you, try to get a room by the restaurant and pool—you'll have a great view, and a hillside rail elevator goes straight from top to bottom.

Av. de Tesoro s/n, Santiago Peninsula, 28200 Manzanillo, Col. ⓒ **314/334-1625.** Fax 314/334-0090. www.plaza tucanes.com.mx. 112 units. $146 (£73) double; $250 (£125) double all inclusive. Packages available. AE, MC, V. Free parking. **Amenities:** 2 restaurants, including Argentine steakhouse; outdoor pool; mini golf; recreational park; kids' club; game area; room service; babysitting (w/advance notice); beach club on Las Brisas beach, w/pool and small restaurant; transportation to and from beach club (once daily in each direction). *In room:* A/C, TV, safe.

Tesoro Manzanillo Resort 𝒦 *Kids*   Formerly the Gran Costa Real and Sierra, this 21-floor hotel, overlooking La Audiencia beach, offers all-inclusive package options and a full program of activities, dining, and entertainment. Its excellent kids' program makes it a top choice for families. In 2007, it opened the onsite Corsarlos Water Park, complete with waterslides, pools, and activities. Architecturally, it mimics the white Moorish style of Las Hadas that has become so popular in Manzanillo. Inside, it's pala-tial in scale and awash in pale-gray marble. Room decor picks up the pale-gray theme with armoires that conceal the TV and minibar. Most standard rooms have two double beds or a king-size bed, plus a small table, chairs, and desk. Several rooms at the end of most floors are small, with one double bed, small porthole-size windows, no balcony, and no view. Most rooms, however, have balconies and ocean or hillside views. The 10 honeymoon suites have king-size beds and chaises. Junior suites have sitting areas with couches and large bathrooms. Scuba-diving lessons take place in the pool, and excellent scuba-diving sites are within swimming distance of the shore.

Av. La Audiencia 1, Los Riscos, 28200 Manzanillo, Col. © 866/998-3637 in the U.S., or 314/333-2000. Fax 314/333-2611 www.tesororesorts.com. 332 units. High season $230–$340 (£115–£170) double, $240–$370 (£120–£185) suite; low season $200 (£100) double, $220 (£110) suite. Rates are all-inclusive. AE, MC, V. Free parking. **Amenities:** 3 restaurants; 4 bars; grand pool on the beach; children's pool; 4 lighted tennis courts; health club w/exercise equipment, aerobics, and hot tub; men's and women's sauna and steam rooms; travel agency; spa; room service; laundry service; currency exchange. *In room:* A/C, TV, minibar, hair dryer.

WHERE TO DINE
DOWNTOWN
Roca del Mar MEXICAN/INTERNATIONAL Join the locals at this informal cafe facing the plaza. The large menu includes club sandwiches, hamburgers, *carne asada a la tampiqueña* (thin grilled steak served with rice, poblano pepper, an enchilada, and refried beans), fajitas, fish, shrimp, and vegetable salads. A specialty is its paella (served on Sun and Tues), and the economical *pibil* tacos are outstanding. This cafe, remodeled in 2007, is very clean and offers sidewalk dining.

Blvd. Costero. © 314/336-9097. Main courses $5–$14 (£2.50–£7). No credit cards. Daily 7:30am–11pm.

LAS BRISAS
The Hotel La Posada (see "Where to Stay," above) offers breakfast to nonguests at its beachside restaurant; it's also a great place to mingle with other tourists and enjoy the sunset and cocktails.

La Toscana ★★★ *(Finds* SEAFOOD/INTERNATIONAL You're in for a treat at La Toscana, one of Manzanillo's most popular restaurants, located on the beach in Las Brisas. It's homey, casual, and small, so reservations are highly recommended. The exquisite cuisine belies the atmosphere, with starters that include escargot and salmon carpaccio. Among the grilled specialties are shrimp imperial wrapped in bacon, red snapper tarragon, dorado basil, sea bass with mango and ginger, and tender fresh lobsters (four to a serving). Live music frequently sets the scene.

Bulevar Miguel de la Madrid 3177. © 314/333-2515. Reservations highly recommended. Main courses $8–$25 (£4–£13). MC, V. Daily 6:30pm–2am. 100m (328 ft.) from Hotel Fiesta Mexicana.

SANTIAGO ROAD
The restaurants below are on the Costera Madrid between downtown and the Santiago Peninsula, including the Salahua area.

Benedetti's Pizza PIZZA There are several branches in town, so you'll probably find a Benedetti's not far from where you are staying. The variety is extensive; add some *chimichurri* sauce to your sesame-crust pizza to enhance the flavor. Benedetti's specializes in seafood pizza, such as smoked oyster and anchovy. You can also select from pasta, sandwiches, burgers, fajitas, salads, Mexican soups, cheesecake, and pie.

Bulevar Miguel de la Madrid, near the Las Brisas Glorietta on the ocean side (west). © 314/333-1592 or 334-0141. Pizza $9–$12 (£4.50–£6); main courses $2–$5.50 (£1–£2.75). AE, MC, V. Daily 10am–11:30pm.

Bigotes II *(Finds* SEAFOOD   Locals flock to this large, breezy restaurant (the name translates as "Mustaches") by the water for the good food and festive atmosphere. Strolling singers serenade diners as they dig into large portions of grilled seafood, or their signature "Mustache Shrimp."

Puesta del Sol 3. ℭ **314/333-1236.** Main courses $10–$23 (£5–£12). MC, V. Daily noon–10pm. From downtown, follow the Costera Madrid past the Las Brisas turnoff; the restaurant is behind the Penas Coloradas Social Club, across from the beach.

El Fogón *(Finds* MEXICAN   Locals consider this to be the best Mexican restaurant in town. The menu features a selection of unique and traditional Mexican dishes. *Molcajetes* (meat, seafood, and vegetables grilled in a stone dish) are the house specialty; varieties include shrimp, beef, and quail.

Bulevar Miguel de la Madrid across from Pacifico Azul. ℭ **314/333-3094.** Main courses $7–$13 (£3.50–£6.50). MC, V. Daily 1pm–midnight. From downtown, follow the Costera Madrid; the restaurant is located just before the Soriana grocery store.

SANTIAGO PENINSULA

Legazpi ✹✹ INTERNATIONAL   This is a top choice in Manzanillo for sheer elegance, gracious service, and outstanding food. The candlelit tables are set with silver and flowers. Enormous bell-shaped windows on two sides show off the sparkling bay below. The sophisticated menu includes prosciutto with melon marinated in port wine, crayfish bisque, broiled salmon, roast duck, lobster, veal, and flaming desserts.

In the Brisas Las Hadas hotel, Santiago Peninsula. ℭ **314/331-0101.** Main courses $8.50–$16 (£4.25–£8). AE, MC, V. High season daily 7–11:30pm; closed low season.

MANZANILLO AFTER DARK

Nightlife in Manzanillo is much more exuberant than you might expect, but then Manzanillo is not only a resort town—it's a thriving commercial center. Clubs and bars change from year to year, so check with your concierge for current hot spots. Some area clubs have a dress code prohibiting shorts or sandals, principally applying to men.

El Bar de Félix, between Salahua and Las Brisas by the Avis rental-car office (ℭ **314/333-1875**), is open Tuesday through Sunday from 2pm to midnight, and has an $8 (£4) minimum consumption charge. Music ranges from salsa and ranchero to rock and house—it's the most consistently lively place in town, with pool tables and TVs broadcasting sports events. The adjacent (and related) **Vog Disco** (ℭ **314/333-1875**), Bulevar Costera Miguel de la Madrid Km 9.2, features alternative music in a cavernous setting, with a midnight light show; it's Manzanillo's current late-night hot spot, open until 5am, but only on Friday and Saturday. The cover charge for women is $10 (£5), for men $15 (£7.50). Also very popular—with a built-in crowd—is the nightclub at the **Club Maeva Hotel & Resort** (ℭ **01-800/849-1987** in Mexico), on the inland side of the main highway, north of the Santiago Peninsula. It's open Tuesday, Thursday, and Saturday from 11pm to 2am. Couples are given preferential entrance. Nonguests are welcome but must pay an entrance fee, typically $20 to $30 (£10–£15), after which all drinks are included. Note that when Club Maeva is fully booked, entrance to nonguests may be difficult to impossible—ask your hotel front desk if they can secure a pass for you. The fee varies depending on the night of the week and the time of year.

11

Acapulco & the Southern Pacific Coast

by Juan Cristiano

It was this region's exotic tropical beaches and rich jungle scenery that first lured travelers to Mexico. Although the southern Pacific geography may be uniform, the resorts along this coast couldn't be more varied, ranging from high-energy seaside cities to pristine, primitive coves.

Spanish conquistadors came to this coast for its numerous sheltered coves and protected bays, from which they set sail to the Far East. Centuries later, Mexico's first tourists came for the same natural features, but with a different type of escape in mind.

Over the years, the area developed a diverse selection of resorts. Each is distinct, and there's one for almost any type of traveler. The region encompasses the country's oldest resort, **Acapulco;** its newest, the **Bahías de Huatulco;** and a

side-by-side pair of opposites—modern **Ixtapa** and the charming fishing village of **Zihuatanejo.** Between Acapulco and Huatulco lies **Puerto Escondido,** a laid-back beach town on a picturesque bay with world-class waves.

This chapter covers coastal towns in two Mexican states, Guerrero and Oaxaca. Stunning coastline and tropical mountains grace the entire region, but outside the urban centers, few roads are paved, and these two states remain among Mexico's poorest, despite decades of incoming tourist dollars (and many other currencies). Tourism in both states has suffered recently from reports of drug-related crime and some social unrest, but these problems have generally not affected the key tourist areas.

EXPLORING THE SOUTHERN PACIFIC COAST

Time at the beach used to be the top priority for most travelers to this part of Mexico. Today, ecotourism, adventure tourism, and more culturally oriented travel are gaining ground. Each of the beach towns in this chapter is capable of satisfying your sand and surf needs. You could also combine several coastal resorts into a single trip or mix the coastal with the colonial—say, Puerto Escondido and Oaxaca (see chapter 12), or Acapulco and Taxco (see chapter 6).

The resorts have distinct personalities, but you get the beach wherever you go, whether you choose a city that offers virtually every luxury imaginable or a rustic town providing little more than seaside relaxation.

The largest and most decadent of Mexican resort destinations, **Acapulco** leapt into the international spotlight in the late 1930s when movie stars made it their playground. Today, though increasingly challenged by other seaside destinations, Acapulco still lures visitors with its glitzy nightlife and sultry beaches (even if the Hollywood celebrities who made it a household name have long since moved on). Of all the resorts in this chapter, Acapulco has the best airline connections, the broadest range of late-night entertainment, the most savory dining, and the widest range of accommodations. The beaches are generally wide and clean, and although the bay itself remains suspect, it's cleaner than in past years.

The resort of **Ixtapa** and its neighboring seaside village, **Zihuatanejo,** offer beachbound tourist attractions on a smaller, less hectic scale than Acapulco. They attract travelers with their complementary contrasts—sophisticated high-rise hotels in one, local color and leisurely pace in the other. Their excellent beaches front clean ocean waters. To get there, many people fly into Acapulco, then make the 4- to 5-hour trip north by rental car or bus.

Puerto Escondido, noted for its celebrated surf break, laid-back village ambience, attractive and inexpensive inns, and nearby nature excursions, is a worthy destination and an exceptional value. It's 6 hours south of Acapulco on coastal Highway 200. Most people fly from Mexico City or drive up from Huatulco.

The **Bahías de Huatulco** encompass a total of nine bays—each lovelier than the last—on a pristine portion of Oaxaca's coast. Development of the area has been gradual and well planned, with great ecological sensitivity. The town of **Huatulco,** 130km (80 miles) south of Puerto Escondido, is emerging as Mexico's most authentic adventure tourism haven. In addition to an 18-hole golf course, cruise-ship pier, and a handful of resort hotels, it offers a growing array of soft adventures that range from bay tours to diving, river rafting, and rappelling. Dining and nightlife remain limited, but the setting is beautiful and relaxing.

1 Acapulco ★★

366km (227 miles) S of Mexico City; 272km (169 miles) SW of Taxco; 979km (607 miles) SE of Guadalajara; 253km (157 miles) SE of Ixtapa/Zihuatanejo; 752km (466 miles) NW of Huatulco

I like to think of Acapulco as a diva—a little past her prime, perhaps overly made up, but still capable of captivating an audience. It's tempting to dismiss Acapulco as a passé resort: Drug-related violence, underinvestment, and poverty in some parts of this huge city have led many tourists to head for glitzier Mexican resorts such as Cancún and Cabo San Lucas. But Acapulco surprisingly retains its appeal, and its temptations are hard to resist. This is a place where beautiful bodies pack the sun-soaked beaches, daring men dive from cliffs into the sea, romantic couples dine alongside unforgettable views of the bay, and uninhibited revelers dance the rest of the night away. Acapulco has world-class resorts, yet they're often much less expensive than comparable hotels elsewhere. Though most beach resorts are made for relaxing, Acapulco offers nonstop, 24-hours-a-day energy. Its perfectly sculpted bay is an adult playground filled with water-skiers in sexy *tanga* swimsuits and darkly tanned, mirrorshaded guys on jet skis. Visitors play golf and tennis with intensity, but the real sport is the nightlife, which has made this city famous for decades. Back in the days when there was a jet set, they came to Acapulco—filmed it, sang about it, wrote about it, and lived it.

It's not hard to understand why: The view of Acapulco Bay, framed by mountains and beaches, is breathtaking day or night. Playa Diamante (Diamond Beach), just south of the bay, is by far the best beach within driving distance of Mexico City. At night, a trendy set of upper-class Mexicans and international visitors fills the top restaurants, bars, and nightclubs, which are some of the hottest in the country.

> **Tips Car & Bus Travel Warning Eases**
>
> Car robberies and bus hijackings on Highway 200, south of Acapulco on the way to Puerto Escondido and Huatulco, used to be common, and you may have heard warnings about the road. The trouble has all but disappeared, thanks to military patrols and greater police protection. However, as in most of Mexico, it's advisable to travel the highways during daylight hours only—not so much because of carjackings, but because highways are unlit, and animals can wander onto them.

Acapulco tries hard to hold on to its image as the ultimate extravagant party town, and remains a top weekend and vacation destination for affluent residents of Mexico City, in particular. It's still the top choice for those who want to have dinner at midnight, dance until dawn, and sleep all day on a sun-soaked beach.

ESSENTIALS
GETTING THERE & DEPARTING

BY PLANE   See chapter 3 for information on flying from the United States or Canada to Acapulco. Local numbers for major airlines with nonstop or direct service to Acapulco are **AeroMéxico** (✆ 744/485-1600 inside Mexico), **American** (✆ 744/481-0161,** or 01-800/904-6000 inside Mexico for reservations), **Continental** (✆ 744/466-9063), **Mexicana** (✆ 744/466-9138 or 486-7585), and **US Airways** (✆ 744/466-9257).

AeroMéxico flies from Guadalajara, Mexico City, Tijuana, and Monterrey; **Aviacsa** (✆ 01800/711-6733) flies from Mexico City; **InterJet** (✆ 01800/01-12345) is a low-cost carrier that flies from Toluca, about an hour from Mexico City; **Mexicana** flies from Mexico City. Check with a travel agent about **charter** flights.

The airport (airport code: ACA) is 22km (14 miles) southeast of town, over the hills east of the bay. Private **taxis** are the fastest way to get downtown; they cost $30 to $50 (£15–£25). The major **rental-car** agencies all have booths at the airport. **Transportes Terrestres** has desks at the front of the airport where you can buy tickets for minivan *colectivo* transportation into town ($20/£10). You must reserve return service to the airport through your hotel.

BY CAR   From Mexico City, take either the curvy toll-free **Highway 95D** south (6 hr.) or scenic **Highway 95,** the four- to six-lane toll highway (3½ hr.), which costs around $50 (£25) one-way. The free *"libre"* road from Taxco is in good condition; you'll save around $40 (£20) in tolls from there through Chilpancingo to Acapulco. From points north or south along the coast, the only choice is **Highway 200,** where you should always try (as on all Mexican highways) to travel by day.

BY BUS   The **Estrella de Oro** terminal is at Av. Cuauhtémoc 1490, and the **Estrella Blanca** terminal (also called Central de Autobuses) is at Av. Cuauhtémoc 1605. **Turistar, Estrella de Oro,** and **Estrella Blanca** have almost hourly service for the 5- to 7-hour trip to Mexico City ($30–$50/£15–£25), and daily service to Zihuatanejo ($14/£7). Buses also serve other points in Mexico, including Chilpancingo, Cuernavaca, Iguala, Manzanillo, Puerto Vallarta, and Taxco.

Acapulco Bay Area

To Pie de la Cuesta
Ixtapa - Zihuatanejo

Guerrero

Av. Constituyentes

Mendoza

Av. Cuauhtémoc

Escudero Serdán

Vasco Nuñez

Río Camarón

PARQUE PAPAGAYO

La Quebrada **6**

5

Market

Playa Hornos

Playa Hornitos

Zócalo

commercial wharfs

Playa
La Angosta

"Downtown (Old) Acapulco" See Inset

Costera M. Alemán

Playa Larga

La Pinzona

Av. de la Aguada

Gran Vía Tropical

Av. López Mateos

4 Peninsula de las Playas

3

2

1

Playa Caletilla

Playa Caleta

Bahía de Acapulco

Isla de la
Roqueta

**Playa
Roqueta**

UNITED STATES

MEXICO

*Gulf of
Mexico*

PACIFIC
OCEAN

**Mexico
City**★

Acapulco

0   500 mi

0   500 km

Punta
Bruja

Acapulco Region

Río Coyuca

200

95

200

*Laguna de
Coyuca*

ACAPULCO

*Laguna de
Tres Palos*

Pie de la Cuesta

*Bahía de
Acapulco*

Barra Vieja

Estrella de Oro Bus ⬛

To México City ↑

0   1/2 mi
0   0.5 km

Beach 🏖
Bus Station ⬛

Masseu
Naveganて
Reyes
Católicos
Cosa
Pizarro
Playa Paraíso
Pinzón
Universidad
Playa Condesa
Morro
Herradura
Costera M. Alemán
Picuda
Del Mar
Sola
Farallon Island
El Morro
Deportes
Golf Club
Las Palmas
Victoria
Trinidad
Cristóbal Colón
Santa María
Yucatán
Bravo
Playa Icacos

Playa Guitarron
⬛ Icacos Naval Base

ACCOMMODATIONS ⬛
Calinda Beach Acapulco **9**
Camino Real Acapulco Diamante **14**
Casa Yal'ma Ka'an **15**
Fairmont Acapulco Princess **15**
Fairmont Pierre Marques **15**
Fiesta Americana Villas **8**
Hotel Costa Linda **2**
Hotel Elcano **10**
Hotel El Mirador Acapulco **5**
Hotel Los Flamingos **1**
Hotel Misión **16**
Hotel Sands **7**
Hyatt Regency Acapulco **12**
Las Brisas **13**
Quinta Real **15**

ATTRACTIONS ●
Cathedral **17**
Centro Acapulco (Convention Center) **11**
Fuerte de San Diego/Museo Histórico de Acapulco **19**
La Quebrada/Cliff Divers **6**
Mágico Mundo Marino **3**
Plaza de Toros **4**
Zócalo/Plaza Álvarez **18**

Downtown (Old) Acapulco

Vicente Guerrero
Nicolás
A. Serdán
Cuauhtémoc
Flecha Roja Bus Stop ⬛
Nación
Progreso
Escudero
V. de León
Galeana
Cuauhtémoc
5 de Mayu
Lerdo Tejada
La Quebrada
Iglesias
Valle
Galeana
Hornitos
17
Hidalgo
Carranza
La Paz
Morelos
Fort San Diego
16
18
B. Juárez
Costera Miguel Alemán
19
La Pinzona
Arteaga
A. Breton
To Playa Hornos →
commercial wharfs
Bahía de Acapulco
Carretera
Playa Caleta ↓
Escénica
To Bahía de Puerto Marqués & Airport ↓

383

ORIENTATION

VISITOR INFORMATION   The **State of Guerrero Tourism Office** operates the **Procuraduría del Turista** (©/fax **744/484-4416**), on the street level of the **Convention Center**, set back from the main Costera Alemán, down a lengthy walkway with fountains. The office offers maps and information about the city and state, as well as police assistance for tourists; it's open daily from 8am to 11pm.

CITY LAYOUT   Acapulco stretches more than 6km (4 miles) around the huge bay, so trying to take it all in by foot is impractical. The tourist areas are roughly divided into three sections. On the western end of the bay is **Acapulco Viejo (Old Acapulco)**, the original town that attracted the jet-setters of the 1950s and 1960s—and today it looks as if it's still locked in that era, though a renaissance is slowly getting under way.

The second section, in the center of the bay, is the **Zona Hotelera (Hotel Zone);** it follows the main boulevard, **Costera Miguel Alemán** (or just "the Costera"), as it runs east along the bay from downtown. Towering hotels, restaurants, shopping centers, and strips of open-air beach bars line the street. At the far eastern end of the Costera lie the golf course and the International Center (a convention center). **Avenida Cuauhtémoc** is the major artery inland, running roughly parallel to the Costera.

The third major area begins just beyond the Hyatt Regency Hotel, where the name of the Costera changes to **Carretera Escénica (Scenic Hwy.),** which continues all the way to the airport. The hotels along this section of the road are lavish, and extravagant private villas, gourmet restaurants, and flashy nightclubs built into the hillside offer dazzling views. The area fronting the beach here is **Acapulco Diamante**, Acapulco's most desirable address.

Street names and numbers in Acapulco can be confusing and hard to find. Many streets are not well marked or change names unexpectedly. Street numbers on the Costera are illogical, so don't assume that similar numbers will be close together.

GETTING AROUND   **By Taxi**   Taxis are more plentiful than tacos in Acapulco—and practically as inexpensive, if you're traveling in the downtown area only. Just remember that you should always establish the price with the driver before starting out. Hotel taxis may charge three times the rate of a taxi hailed on the street, and nighttime taxi rides cost extra, too. Taxis are also more expensive if you're staying in the Diamante section or south. The minimum fare is $2.50 (£1.25) per ride for a roving VW Bug–style taxi in town; the fare from Puerto Marqués to the hotel zone is $10 (£5), or $12 (£6) into downtown. *Sitio* taxis are nicer cars, but more expensive, with a minimum fare of $4 (£2).

The fashion among Acapulco taxis is flashy, with Las Vegas–style lights—the more colorful and pulsating, the better.

By Bus   Even though the city has a confusing street layout, using city buses is amazingly easy and inexpensive. Two kinds of buses run along the Costera: pastel color-coded buses and regular "school buses." The difference is the price: New air-conditioned tourist buses (Aca Tur Bus) are $1 (50p); old buses are 50¢ (25p). Covered bus stops are all along the Costera, with handy maps on the walls showing routes to major sights and hotels.

The best place near the *zócalo* to catch a bus is next to Sanborn's, 2 blocks east. CALETA DIRECTO or BASE-CALETA buses will take you to the Hornos, Caleta, and Caletilla beaches along the Costera. Some buses return along the same route; others go around the peninsula and return to the Costera.

For expeditions to more distant destinations, there are buses to **Puerto Marqués** to the east (marked PUERTO MARQUES–BASE) and **Pie de la Cuesta** to the west (marked ZOCALO–PIE DE LA CUESTA). Be sure to verify the time and place of the last bus back if you hop on one of these.

By Car   Rental cars are available at the airport and at hotel desks along the Costera. Unless you plan on exploring outlying areas, trust me, you're better off taking taxis or using the easy and inexpensive public buses.

FAST FACTS: Acapulco

American Express   The main office is in the Gran Plaza shopping center, Costera Alemán 1628 (© **744/435-2200**). It's open Monday through Friday from 9am to 6pm and Saturday 9am to 1pm.

Area Code   The telephone area code is **744.**

Climate   Acapulco boasts sunshine 360 days a year, with average daytime temperatures of 80°F (27°C). Humidity varies, with approximately 59 inches of rain per year. June through October is the rainy season, though July and August are relatively dry. Tropical showers are brief and usually occur at night.

Consular Agents   The **United States** has an agent at the Hotel Acapulco Continental, Costera Alemán 121, Loc. 14 (© **744/469-0556**); the office is open Monday through Friday from 10am to 2pm. The **Canadian** office is at the Centro Comercial Marbella, Loc. 23 (© **744/484-1305**). The toll-free emergency number inside Mexico is © **01-800/706-2900**. The office is open Monday through Friday from 9am to 5pm.

Currency Exchange   Numerous banks along the Costera are open Monday through Friday from 9am to 6pm, Saturday from 10am to 2pm. Banks and their ATMs generally have the best rates. *Casas de cambio* (currency-exchange booths) along the street may have better rates than hotels.

Drugstores   One of the largest drugstores in town is **Farmacia Daisy,** Francia 49, across the traffic circle from the convention center (© **744/48126350**). Sam's Club and Wal-Mart, both on the Costera, have pharmacy services and lower prices on medicine.

Hospital   **Hospital Magallanes,** Av. Wilfrido Massieu 2, Fracc. Magallanes (© **744/469-0270**), has an English-speaking staff and doctors. For local emergencies, call the **Cruz Roja (Red Cross),** Av. Ruiz Cortines s/n (© **065** or 744/445-5912).

Internet Access   **@canet,** Costera Alemán 1632 Int., La Gran Plaza, Loc. D-1, lower floor (©/fax **744/486-9186** or -8182), is open weekdays from 10am to 9pm and weekends from 11:30am to 9pm. Internet access costs $2.50 (£1.25) per hour. This is a computer shop that also offers Internet access and has a very helpful staff. Also along the Costera strip is the **Santa Clara Cafe,** Costera Alemán 136, serving coffee, pastries, and ice cream, along with Internet service for $1 (50p) for 20 minutes. It's open 9am to 11pm.

Parking   It is illegal to park on the Costera at any time. Try parking along side streets or in one of the few covered parking lots, such as in Plaza Bahía and in Plaza Mirabella.

Post Office The *correo* is next door to Sears, close to the Fideicomiso office. It's open Monday through Friday from 9am to 5pm, Saturday from 9am to 2pm. Other branches are in the Estrella de Oro bus station on Cuauhtémoc, inland from the Acapulco Qualton Hotel, and on the Costera near Caleta Beach.

Safety Riptides claim a few lives every year, so pay close attention to warning flags posted on Acapulco beaches. Red or black flags warn swimmers to stay out of the water, yellow flags signify caution, and white or green flags mean it's safe to swim. As is the case anywhere, tourists are vulnerable to thieves. This is especially true when shopping in a market, lying on the beach, wearing jewelry, or visibly carrying a camera, purse, or bulging wallet.

Telephone Acapulco phone numbers seem to change frequently. The most reliable source for telephone numbers is the **Procuraduría del Turista,** on the Costera in front of the convention center (© **744/484-4416**), which has an exceptionally friendly staff.

Tourist Police Policemen in white and light-blue uniforms belong to the Tourist Police (© **066** for emergencies, or 744/485-0490), a special corps of English-speaking police established to assist tourists.

ACTIVITIES ON & OFF THE BEACH

Acapulco is known for its great beaches and watersports, and few visitors bother to explore its traditional downtown area. But the shaded *zócalo* (also called Plaza Alvarez) is worth a trip, to experience a glimpse of local life and color. Inexpensive cafes and shops border the plaza. At its far north end is the **cathedral Nuestra Señora de la Soledad,** with blue, onion-shaped domes and Byzantine towers. Though reminiscent of a Russian Orthodox church, it was originally (and perhaps appropriately) built as a movie set, then later adapted into a house of worship. From the church, turn east along the side street going off at a right angle (Calle Carranza, which doesn't have a marker) to find an arcade with newsstands and more shops. The hill behind the cathedral provides an unparalleled view of Acapulco. Take a taxi to the top of the hill from the main plaza, and follow signs to **El Mirador (lookout point).**

Local travel agencies book city tours, day trips to Taxco, cruises, and other excursions and activities. Taxco is about a 3-hour drive inland from Acapulco (see chapter 6 for more information).

THE BEACHES   Here's a rundown on the beaches, going from west to east around the bay. **Playa la Angosta** is a small, sheltered, often-deserted cove just around the bend from **La Quebrada** (where the cliff divers perform).

South of downtown on the Peninsula de las Playas lie the beaches **Caleta** and **Caletilla.** Separating them is a small outcropping of land that contains the aquarium and water park **Mágico Mundo Marino,** which is open daily from 9am to 6pm (© **744/483-1215**) and costs $5 (£2.50) to enter. You'll find thatched-roofed restaurants, watersports equipment for rent, and brightly painted boats that ferry passengers to **Roqueta Island.** You can rent beach chairs and umbrellas for the day. Mexican families favor these beaches because they're close to several good value hotels. In the late afternoon, fishermen pull their colorful boats up on the sand; you can buy the fresh catch of the day and, occasionally, oysters on the half shell.

Pleasure boats dock at **Playa Manzanillo,** south of the *zócalo.* Charter fishing trips sail from here. In the old days, the downtown beaches—Manzanillo, Honda, Caleta, and Caletilla—were the focal point of Acapulco. Today, beaches and resort developments stretch along the 6.5km (4-mile) length of the shore.

East of the *zócalo,* the major beaches are **Hornos** (near Papagayo Park), **Hornitos, Paraíso, Condesa,** and **Icacos,** followed by the naval base (La Base) and **Punta del Guitarrón.** After Punta del Guitarrón, the road climbs to the legendary Las Brisas hotel. Past Las Brisas, the road continues to the small, clean bay of **Puerto Marqués,** followed by **Punta Diamante,** about 20km (12 miles) from the *zócalo.* The fabulous Acapulco Princess, the Quinta Real, and the Pierre Marqués hotels dominate the landscape, which fronts the open Pacific.

Playa Puerto Marqués, in the bay of Puerto Marqués, is an attractive area for swimming. The water is calm and the bay sheltered. Water-skiing can also be arranged. Past the bay lies **Revolcadero Beach,** a magnificent wide stretch of beach on the open ocean, where many of Acapulco's grandest resorts are found.

Other beaches lie farther north and are best reached by car, though buses also make the trip. **Pie de la Cuesta** is 13km (8 miles) west of town. Buses along the Costera leave every 5 or 10 minutes; a taxi costs about $20 (£10). The water is too rough for swimming, but it's a great spot for checking out big waves and the spectacular sunset, especially over *coco locos* (drinks served in fresh coconuts with the tops whacked off) at a rustic beachside restaurant. The area is known for excellent birding and surrounding coconut plantations.

If you're driving, continue west along the peninsula, passing **Coyuca Lagoon** on your right, until almost to the small air base at the tip. Along the way, various private entrepreneurs, mostly young boys, will invite you to park near different sections of beach. You'll also find *colectivo* boat tours of the lagoon offered for about $10 (£5).

BAY CRUISES & ROQUETA ISLAND   Acapulco has virtually every kind of boat to choose from—yachts, catamarans, and trimarans (single- and double-deckers). Cruises run morning, afternoon, and evening. Some offer buffets, open bars, and live music; others just snacks, drinks, and taped music. Prices range from $24 to $40 (£12–£20). Cruise operators come and go, and their phone numbers change so frequently from year to year that it's pointless to list them here; to find out what cruises are currently operating, contact any Acapulco travel agency or your hotel's tour desk, and ask for brochures or recommendations.

Boats from Caletilla Beach to **Roqueta Island**—a good place to snorkel, sunbathe, hike to a lighthouse, visit a small zoo, or have lunch—leave every 15 minutes from 7am until the last one returns at 7pm. There are also primitive-style glass-bottom

---

Tips **To Swim or Not to Swim in the Bay?**

In the past decade, the city has gone to great lengths (and great expense) to clean up the waters off Acapulco. Nevertheless, this is an industrial port that was once heavily polluted, so many choose to stick to their hotel pool. You may notice the fleet of power-sweeper boats that skim the top of the bay each morning to remove debris and oil. The bay beaches that remain most popular are **Caleta** and **Caletilla beaches,** as well as **Playa Puerto Marqués.**

> **Tips   Tide Warning**
>
> Each year, at least one or two unwary swimmers drown in Acapulco because of deadly riptides and undertow (see "Safety" in "Fast Facts," above). Swim only in Acapulco Bay or Puerto Marqués Bay—and be careful of the undertow no matter where you go. If you find yourself caught in the undertow, head back to shore at an angle instead of trying to swim straight back.

---

boats that circle the bay as you look down at a few fish and watch a diver swim down to the underwater sanctuary of the Virgin of Guadalupe, patron saint of Mexico. The statue of the Virgin—created by sculptor Armando Quesado—was placed there in 1958, in memory of a group of divers who lost their lives at the spot. You can purchase tickets ($5/£2.50) directly from any boat that's loading.

WATERSPORTS & BOAT RENTALS   An hour of **water-skiing** at Coyuca Lagoon can cost as little as $35 (£18) or as much as $70 (£35).

Scuba diving costs about $80 (£40) for 4 hours of instruction, when you book through a hotel or travel agency. Dive trips start at around $90 (£45) per person for one or two tank dives. One reputable shop, near Club de Esquís, is **Divers de México** (© 744/482-1398). We also recommend **Fish-R-Us,** 3 Cerrada del Blvd. de las Naciones (© 744/482-8282; www.fish-r-us.com). They offer shore and boat dives, usually to Roqueta Island. Sunken ships, sea mountains, and cave rock formations are all on display around the area. **Boat rentals** are cheapest on Caletilla Beach, where you can usually find inner tubes, small boats, canoes, paddleboats, and chairs for rent.

For **deep-sea fishing** excursions, go to the boat cooperative's pink building opposite the *zócalo,* or book a day in advance (© 744/482-1099). Charter trips run $250 to $450 (£125–£225) for 6 to 7 hours, tackle and bait included, with an extra charge for ice, drinks, and lunch. Credit cards are accepted, but you're likely to get a better deal by paying cash. Boats leave at 7am and return at 2pm. If you book through a travel agent or hotel, prices start at around $250 (£125) for four people. Also recommendable is **Fish-R-Us,** 3 Cerrada del Blvd. de las Naciones (© 744/482-8282). In addition to traditional fishing charters, they also offer private yacht charters, scuba diving, and a 3-hour Night of Delight cruise, with dinner served on board. Prices vary per the service requested and number of people; call for details.

Parasailing, though not free from risk (the occasional thrill-seeker has collided with a palm tree or even a building), can be brilliant. Floating high over the bay hanging from a parachute towed by a motorboat costs about $35 (£18). Most of these rides operate on Condesa Beach, but they also can be found independently operating on the beach in front of most hotels along the Costera.

GOLF & TENNIS   Both the **Acapulco Princess** (© 744/469-1000) and **Pierre Marqués** (© 744/466-1000) hotels share top-notch golf courses. The Princess's course is a rather narrow, level, Ted Robinson design. The Marques course, redesigned by Robert Trent Jones in 1972 for the World Cup Golf Tournament, is longer and more challenging. A morning round of 18 holes at either course costs $125 (£63) for guests and $135 (£68) for nonguests (discounted rates for afternoon rounds); American Express, Visa, and MasterCard are accepted, and the cart is included in the fee. Tee times begin at 7:30am, and reservations should be made a day in advance. Club rental is available for an extra $40 (£20). The **Mayan Palace Golf Club,** Geranios 22

(© 744/469-6043 or 466-2260), designed by Latin American golf great Pedro Guericia, lies farther east. Greens fees are $135 (£68) for visitors, and caddies are available for an additional $18 (£9). At the **Club de Golf Acapulco,** off the Costera next to the convention center (© 744/484-0781), you can play 9 holes for $35 (£18) and 18 holes for $60 (£30), with equipment renting for $10 (£5).

The Robert von Hagge–designed course at the exclusive **Tres Vidas Golf Club,** Carretera a Barra Vieja Km 7 (© 744/444-5126), is spectacular. The par-72, 18-hole course, right on the edge of the ocean, is landscaped with nine lakes, dotted with palms, and home to a flock of ducks and other birds. The club is open only to members, guests of members, and guests at Tres Vidas. Greens fees are $200 (£100), including cart; a caddy is $20 (£10). Also here is a clubhouse with a restaurant (daily 7am–10pm), as well as a pool and beach club. American Express, Visa, and MasterCard are accepted.

The **Club de Tenis Hyatt,** Costera Alemán 1 (© 744/484-1225), is open daily from 7am to 11pm. Outdoor courts cost $10 (£5) per hour during the day, $15 (£7.50) per hour at night; Rackets rent for $3 (£1.50) and a set of balls costs $2 (£1). Many of the hotels along the Costera have tennis facilities for guests; the best are at the Fairmont Princess, Mayan Palace, and Las Brisas hotels. The **Fairmont Princess** (© 744/469-1000) also allows nonguests to play for $20 (£10) per hour.

RIDING & BULLFIGHTS   You can go **horseback riding** along the beach. Independent operators stroll the Hotel Zone beachfront offering rides for about $25 to $45 (£13–£23) for 1 to 2 hours. Horses are also commonly found on the beach in front of the Acapulco Princess Hotel. There is no phone; you go directly to the beach to make arrangements.

Traditionally called Fiesta Brava, **bullfights** are held during Acapulco's winter season at a ring (called Plaza de Toros) up the hill from Caletilla Beach. Tickets purchased through travel agencies cost around $17 to $40 (£8.50–£20) and usually include transportation to and from your hotel. You can also buy a general admission ticket at the stadium for $4.50 (£2.25). Be forewarned that this is a true bullfight—meaning

---

Moments **Death-Defying Divers**

High divers perform at La Quebrada each day at 12:45, 7:30, 8:30, 9:30, and 10:30pm. Admission is $3.50 (£1.75) for adults, $1 (50p) for kids under 11. From a spotlit ledge on the cliffs, divers (holding torches for the final performance) plunge into the roaring surf of an inlet that's just 7m (23 ft.) wide, 4m (13 ft.) deep, and 40m (131 ft.) below—after wisely praying at a small shrine nearby. To the applause of the crowd, divers climb up the rocks and accept congratulations and gifts of money from onlookers. This is the quintessential Acapulco experience. No visit is complete (even for jaded travelers) without watching the cliff divers. To get there from downtown, take the street called La Quebrada from behind the cathedral for 4 blocks.

The public areas have great views, but arrive early, because performances quickly fill up. Another option is to watch from the lobby bar and restaurant terraces of the **Hotel Plaza Las Glorias/El Mirador.** The bar imposes a $20 (£10) cover charge, which includes two drinks. You can get around the cover by having dinner at the hotel's **La Perla restaurant.** Reservations (© 744/483-1221, ext. 802) are recommended during high season.

A House of Art

Of all the exclusive villas and homes in Acapulco, one stands far apart from the others. Though not as elegantly impressive as the villas of Las Brisas, the **home of Dolores Olmedo** in Acapulco's traditional downtown area is a work of art. In 1956, the renowned Mexican artist Diego Rivera covered its outside wall with a mural of colorful mosaic tiles, shells, and stones. The work is unique and one of the last he created. The Olmedo mural, which took him 18 months to complete, features Aztec deities such as Quetzalcoatl and Tepezcuincle, the Aztec dog. Rivera and Olmedo were lifelong friends, and Rivera lived in this house for the last 2 years of his life, during which time he also covered the interior with murals. The home isn't a museum, so you have to settle for a look at the exterior masterpiece. The house is a few blocks behind the Casablanca Hotel, a short cab ride from the central plaza, at Calle Cerro de la Pinzona 6. Have the driver wait while you look around.

---

things generally do not fare well for the bull. The festivities begin at 5:30pm each Sunday from January to March.

A MUSEUM & A WATER PARK   The original **Fuerte de San Diego,** Costera Alemán, east of the *zócalo* (☏ **744/482-3828**), was built in 1616 to protect the town from pirate attacks. At that time, the port reaped considerable income from trade with the Philippine Islands (which, like Mexico, were part of the Spanish Empire). The fort you see today was rebuilt after considerable earthquake damage in 1776, and most recently underwent renovation in 2000. The structure houses the **Museo Histórico de Acapulco (Acapulco Historical Museum)** 🕉🕉, with exhibits that tell the story of Acapulco from its role as a port in the conquest of the Americas to a center for local Catholic conversion campaigns and for exotic trade with the Orient. Other exhibits chronicle Acapulco's pre-Hispanic past, the coming of the conquistadors (complete with Spanish armor), and Spanish imperial activity. Temporary exhibits are also on display. Admission to the museum is $3.90 (£1.95), free on Sunday. It's open Tuesday through Sunday from 9am to 6pm. To reach the fort, follow Costera Alemán past Old Acapulco and the *zócalo;* the fort is on a hill on the right.

The **Parque Acuático el CICI** 🕉, Costera Alemán at Colón (☏ **744/484-8033**), is a sea-life and water park east of the convention center. It offers guests swimming pools with waves, water slides, and water toboggans, and has a cafeteria and restrooms. The park is open daily from 10am to 6pm. General admission is $10 (£5) and free for children younger than 2. There are **dolphin shows** (in Spanish) weekdays at 2pm and weekends at 2 and 4pm. There's also a dolphin swim program, which includes 30 minutes of introduction and 30 minutes to 1 hour of swim time. The cost for this option is $90 (£45) for the half-hour swim, $130 (£65) for the hour; both options include total access to the water park, and are available by reservation only. Shows are at 10:30am, 12:30, and 4:30pm. Reservations are required; there is a 10-person maximum per show for the dolphin swim option. The minimum age is 4 years.

SHOPPING

Acapulco is not among the best places to buy Mexican crafts, but it does have a few interesting shops, and the Costera is lined with places to buy tourist souvenirs, including silver jewelry, Mexico knickknacks, and the ubiquitous T-shirt.

The shopkeepers aren't pushy, but they'll test your bargaining mettle. The starting price will be steep, and dragging it down may take some time. Before buying silver, examine it carefully and look for ".925" stamped on the back. This supposedly signifies that the silver is 92.5% pure, but the less expensive silver metal called "alpaca" may also bear this stamp. (Alpaca is generally stamped MEXICO or MEX, often in letters so tiny that they are hard to read and look similar to the three-digit ".925").

P&P Jewelers, located at the Quebrada where the cliff divers perform (✆ 744/482-3428; www.plazataxco.com.mx), is a large store selling silver and gold pieces, including quality silver from Taxco. It's open daily from 10am to 10pm.

Sanborn's, a good department store and drugstore chain, offers an array of staples, including cosmetics, music, clothing, books, and magazines. It has a number of locations in Acapulco, including downtown at Costera Miguel Alemán 209, across from the boat docks (✆ 744/482-6167); Costera Miguel Alemán 1226 at the Condo Estrella Tower, close to the convention center (✆ 744/484-2035), and on Costera Miguel Alemán 163, at the Hotel Calinda (✆ 744/481-2426).

Acapulco also has a Sam's Club and a Wal-Mart on the inland side of the main highway just prior to its ascent to Las Brisas.

Boutiques selling resort wear crowd the Costera Alemán. These stores carry attractive summer clothing at prices lower than you generally pay in the United States. If there's a sale, you can find incredible bargains. One of the nicest air-conditioned shopping centers on the Costera is **Plaza Bahía,** Costera Alemán 125 (✆ 744/485-6939 or -6992), which has four stories of shops, movie theaters, a bowling alley, and small fast-food restaurants. The center is just west of the Costa Club Hotel. The bowling alley, **Aca Bol in Plaza Bahía** (✆ 744/485-0970 or -7464), is open daily from noon to 1am. Another popular shopping strip is the **Plaza Condesa,** adjacent to the Fiesta Americana Condesa; shops include Guess, Izod, and Bronce Swimwear. **Olvido Plaza,** near the restaurant of the same name, has Tommy Hilfiger and Aca Joe.

Acapulco has a few notable fine-art galleries. My favorite, **Galería Espacio Pal Kepenyes** ★★, Costera Guitarrón 140, on the road to the Radisson (✆ 744/484-3738), carries the work of Pal Kepenyes, whose stunning bronzes are among Acapulco's most notable public sculptures. The gallery shows smaller versions, as well as signature pieces of jewelry in brass, copper, and silver, by appointment only.

WHERE TO STAY

The listings below begin with the most expensive resorts south of town in Diamante and continue along Costera Alemán to the less expensive, more traditional hotels north of town, in the downtown or "Old Acapulco" part of the city. Hotel prices have tended to fall or stay the same in Acapulco in recent years. Especially in the Expensive category, inquire about promotional rates or check with the airlines for air-hotel packages. During Christmas and Easter weeks, considered the highest season here, some hotels double their normal rates. Low season lasts September through November and April through June; the rest of the year is mid-season. The rates below do not include the 17% tax. Private **villas** are available for rent all over the hills south of town; staying in one of these palatial homes is an unforgettable experience. **Se Renta** (www.acapulcoluxuryvillas.com) handles some of the most exclusive villas.

SOUTH OF TOWN

Acapulco's most exclusive and renowned hotels, restaurants, and villas nestle in the steep forested hillsides here, between the naval base and Puerto Marqués. This area is several kilometers from the heart of Acapulco; you'll pay about $20 (£10) round-trip taxi fare every time you venture off the property into town.

Very Expensive

Quinta Real 🌟🌟🌟 This exquisite hotel offers the most exclusive accommodations in Acapulco, with just 74 suites perched on a small cliff with uninterrupted views of the Pacific Ocean and Diamante Beach. Part of Mexico's top hotel line, the Quinta Real is defined by understated elegance and attention to detail, designed for relaxing and getting away from it all. (This is not the right place for those looking for entertainment or family-friendly services; for that, I suggest the Fairmont Acapulco Princess.) The suites come in different sizes, with California-style furnishings, still-life paintings, extensive use of marble, and light neutral colors. The larger Governor suites have high ceilings, separate living and dining rooms, and terraces with private plunge pools. The inviting hotel pool lies just steps from the beach, where there's also a casual seafood restaurant and beach club. Next to the lobby, the hotel's gourmet restaurant serves delectable Mexican and international cuisine. Service throughout the Quinta Real is impeccable.

Paseo de la Quina 6, Desarrollo Inmobiliario Real Diamante, 39907 Acapulco, Gro. ✆ **744/469-1500.** Fax 744/469-1516. www.quintareal.com. 74 units. $370 (£185) and up suite. AE, MC, V. **Amenities:** 2 restaurants; lobby bar; 2 outdoor pools (1 for children); spa treatments; massage; fitness center; beach club; concierge; room service; babysitting; laundry service. *In room:* A/C, TV, minibar, hair dryer, iron, safe.

Expensive

Camino Real Acapulco Diamante 🌟🌟 *(Kids)* Tucked in a secluded location on 32 hectares (79 acres), this relaxing, self-contained resort is an ideal choice for families, or for those who already know Acapulco and don't care to explore much. I consider it one of Acapulco's finest places in terms of contemporary decor, services, and amenities. I like its location on the Playa Puerto Marqués, which is safe for swimming, but you do miss out on compelling views of Acapulco Bay, and you'll need to drive at least 15 minutes from here to any attractions or entertainment. From Carretera Escénica, a handsome brick road winds down to the hotel, overlooking Puerto Marqués Bay. The lobby has an inviting terrace facing the water. The spacious rooms have balconies or terraces, small sitting areas, marble floors, ceiling fans (in addition to air-conditioning), and contemporary Mexican furnishings.

Carretera Escénica Km 14, Baja Catita s/n, Pichilingue, 39867 Acapulco, Gro. ✆ **744/435-1010.** Fax 744/435-1020. www.caminoreal.com/acapulco. 157 units. High season $256 (£128) and up double. Rates include buffet breakfast. Ask about low-season and midweek discounts. AE, MC, V. Parking $6 (£3). **Amenities:** 2 restaurants; lobby bar; 3 outdoor pools (1 for children); tennis court; health club w/aerobics, spa treatments, massage, and complete workout equipment (extra charge); watersports equipment rentals; children's activities; concierge; tour desk; car-rental desk; salon; room service; babysitting; laundry service. *In room:* A/C, TV, minibar, hair dryer, iron, safe.

Casa Yal'ma Ka'an 🌟🌟 *(Finds)* A romantic hideaway 20 minutes south of Diamante, Casa Yal'ma Ka'an is a small ecological retreat with its own ocean beach. Stone paths with little bridges meander past several lookout towers and over lily ponds with

---

⟨Fun Fact⟩ Acapulco, Queen of the Silver Screen

Besides hosting legendary stars of the silver screen, Acapulco has played a few starring roles as well. More than 250 films were shot here, including *Rambo II* (1985), which used the Pie de la Cuesta lagoon as its backdrop.

palms and flowers, and the beautiful pool lies just steps from the Pacific. In addition to featuring its own beach club, Casa Yal'ma Ka'an offers a *temazcal*, a Mayan rustic steam bath that will be prepared for you with candles and aromatherapy amenities. Seven individual thatched-roof cottages have king beds, rustic wood furnishings, stone bathrooms, and private sitting decks. Gourmet breakfasts are served under a giant *palapa* overlooking the pool and beach, and private romantic dinners can be arranged on the beach. Service throughout this exclusive hotel is outstanding; children younger than 17 are not allowed.

Carretera hacia Barra Vieja Km 29 L189, 39867 Acapulco, Gro. © 744/444-6389 or -6390. www.casayalmakaan.com. 7 units. High season $280 (£140) double; low season $250 (£125) double. Rates include American breakfast. MC, V. Free parking. **Amenities:** Restaurant; pool bar; outdoor pool; beach club; spa treatments. *In room:* A/C, TV, safe.

Fairmont Acapulco Princess ⊛⊛⊛   The famous Princess hotel has been fully renovated and once again reigns as Acapulco's leading resort. Sitting on 480 beachfront acres of tropical gardens, pools, and golf courses, it's as wonderful for families as for couples seeking romance. Guest rooms are housed in three 15-story buildings shaped like Aztec pyramids, with modern Mexican decor and terraces with views of the ocean, gardens, or golf course. Five beautiful free-form pools, including a saltwater lagoon dotted with waterfalls, are surrounded by gardens with 750 plant species and swans, flamingos, and other tropical birds. The wide beach offers many watersports activities, including parasailing, deep-sea fishing, scuba diving, water-skiing, and sailing. The kids' club focuses on beach and pool activities and is one of the best you'll find. The resort also offers world-class tennis, golf, and spa facilities, and enough dining and entertainment options to obviate your need to leave the facility. A free shuttle runs between the Princess and quieter Pierre Marqués next door.

Playa Revolcadero s/n, Colonia Granjas del Marques, 39907 Acapulco, Gro. © 800/441-1414 in the U.S. or 744/469-1000. Fax 744/469-1016. www.fairmont.com/acapulco. 1,017 units. $249 (£125) and up double. AE, MC, V. Free parking. **Amenities:** 5 restaurants; deli; 5 bars; 5 outdoor pools; Willow Stream spa; fitness center; championship golf course; 8 outdoor lighted tennis courts and 2 indoor tennis courts; water sports activities; kids' club; concierge; shopping arcade; room service; laundry service. *In room:* A/C, TV w/pay movies, safe.

Fairmont Pierre Marqués ⊛⊛   The refined Fairmont Pierre Marqués is both more exclusive and relaxed than the famous Fairmont Princess next door, to which guests also have access. It once served as a private home for J. Paul Getty and is today one of Acapulco's most prestigious hotels. Together, the Pierre Marqués and the Princess offer more activities than you are likely to have time for, with three pools alone at the Pierre Marqués, a beautiful Pacific beach with watersports activities, championship golf, tennis, and a state-of-the-art spa and fitness center. Luxurious guest rooms include villas, bungalows, and low-rise pavilions overlooking the pools, tropical gardens, or beach. Fine dining is available here or at the Princess, with a shuttle regularly connecting the two hotels. Service throughout the hotel is outstanding. The Fairmont lies in Diamante, about a 20-minute drive from the center of Acapulco.

Playa Revolcadero s/n, Colonia Granjas del Marques, 39907 Acapulco, Gro. © 800/441-1414 in the U.S. or 744/435-2600. Fax 744/466-1046. www.fairmont.com/pierremarques. 335 units. $259 (£130) and up double. AE, MC, V. Free parking. **Amenities:** Restaurant; cafe; 2 bars; 3 outdoor pools; health club and spa; championship golf course; 5 outdoor lighted tennis courts (10 additional courts at Fairmont Princess, including 2 indoor courts); concierge; gift shop; deli; room service; laundry service. *In room:* A/C, TV w/pay movies, Wi-Fi, iron, hair dryer, safe.

Las Brisas ⊛⊛⊛ *(Moments)*   This is a local landmark dating from 1957, often considered Acapulco's signature hotel. On a hillside with the best bay views of any hotel in Acapulco, Las Brisas is known for its tiered pink stucco facade, private pools, and 50 pink Jeeps rented exclusively to guests. The retro guest rooms are like separate villas sculpted from a terraced hillside, with panoramic views of Acapulco Bay from a balcony or terrace, as well as a private or semiprivate pool. They have been upgraded and retain the beloved "Las Brisas" style with pink and stone walls, whitewashed wood furnishings, flatscreen TVs and DVD players, and marble bathrooms. Early each morning, continental breakfast arrives in a cubbyhole. The spacious Regency Club rooms, at the apex of the property, offer the best views. In case you tire of your own pool, Las Brisas runs a beach club less than a kilometer (a half-mile) away, on Acapulco Bay; continuous shuttle service departs from the lobby. Mandatory service charges cover the shuttle service and all tips.

Apdo. Carretera Escénica 5255, Las Brisas, 39868 Acapulco, Gro. © 888/559-4329 in the U.S., or 744/469-6900. Fax 744/446-5332. www.brisas.com.mx. 263 units. High season $350 (£175) shared pool, $445 (£223) private pool, $550 (£275) Royal Beach Club; low season $250 (£125) shared pool, $334 (£167) private pool, $410 (£205) Royal Beach Club. $20 (£10) per day service charge. Rates include continental breakfast. AE, MC, V. Free parking. **Amenities:** 2 restaurants; deli; private beach club w/fresh- and saltwater pools; 4 lighted tennis courts; gym; concierge; guest-only tours and activity program; tour desk; Jeep rental for $81 (£41) per day; shopping arcade; salon; room service; in-room massage; babysitting; laundry service; dry cleaning. *In room:* A/C, TV, DVD, minibar, hair dryer, safe.

COSTERA HOTEL ZONE
Moderate

Calinda Beach   You'll see this tall cylindrical tower rising at the eastern edge of Condesa Beach. Each room has a view, usually of the bay. Guest rooms have a simple beach feel, with white tile floors, blue and yellow fish-themed bedspreads, and small bathrooms. It affords the most reasonably priced lodgings along the strip of hotels facing popular Condesa Beach. Package prices are available, and the hotel frequently offers promotions, such as rates that include breakfast. The hotel features a narrow pool next to the beach.

Costera Alemán 1260, 39300 Acapulco, Gro. © 744/435-0600. Fax 744/484-4676. www.hotelcalindabeach.com. 357 units. High season $180 (£90) double; low season $140 (£70) double. Ask about promotional specials. AE, DC, MC, V. Parking $5 (£2.50). **Amenities:** 2 restaurants; poolside snacks; lobby bar w/live music; 2 outdoor pools; small gym; travel agency; salon; room service; babysitting; laundry service; pharmacy. *In room:* A/C, TV, safe.

Fiesta Americana Villas Acapulco 🏖   The Fiesta Americana is a long-standing favorite deluxe hotel in the heart of the beach-bar action. The 19-story structure towers above Condesa Beach, just east and up the hill from the Glorieta Diana traffic circle. The studios, suites, and villas have marble floors, and can be loud if you're overlooking the pool area. Each has a private terrace or balcony with ocean view. The more expensive rooms feature the best bay views, and all have purified tap water. The hilltop swimming pool affords one of the city's finest views. The location is great for accessing Acapulco's numerous beach activities, shopping, and more casual nightlife.

Costera Alemán 97, 39690 Acapulco, Gro. © 800/343-7821 in the U.S., or 744/435-1600. Fax 744/435-1645. www. fiestamericana.com. 324 units. High season $210 (£105) double, $280 (£140) suite; low season $100–$130 (£50–£65) double, $200 (£100) suite. AE, DC, MC, V. Free parking. **Amenities:** 3 restaurants; deli; lobby bar; 2 outdoor pools; spa with massage service; room service; laundry service. *In room:* A/C, TV, iron, hair dryer, safe.

Hotel Elcano 🏖🏖 *Finds*   An Acapulco classic, the Elcano is another personal favorite. It offers exceptional service and a prime location—on a broad stretch of beach (on the bay) in the heart of the hotel zone. The retro-style, turquoise-and-white lobby, and beachside pool area are the closest you can get to a South Beach, Miami, atmosphere in Acapulco, and its popular open-air restaurant adds to the lively waterfront scene. On the whole, the Elcano reminds me of a set from a classic Elvis-in-Acapulco movie.

Rooms are continually upgraded, bright, and very comfortable. They feature classic navy-and-white tile accents, white wicker furniture, and tub/shower combinations. The large junior suites, all on corners, have two queen-size beds and huge closets. Studios are small but adequate, with king-size beds and small sinks outside the bathroom area. In the studios, a small portion of the TV armoire serves as a closet, and there are no balconies, only large sliding windows. All rooms have purified tap water. Avoid the noisy rooms near the ice machines.

Costera Alemán 75, 39690 Acapulco, Gro. Ⓒ **744/435-1500.** Fax 744/484-2230. www.hotel-elcano.com. 180 units. High season $125 (£63) studio, $145 (£73) standard double, $155 (£78) junior suite, $195 (£98) penthouse suite; rates higher during holiday periods. Ask about promotional discounts. AE, MC, V. Free parking. **Amenities:** Restaurant; beachside pool; small workout room; shopping arcade; salon; room service; massage; babysitting; laundry service. *In room:* A/C, TV, minibar, hair dryer, safe.

Hyatt Regency Acapulco *Ⓐ*   A sprawling oasis, the Hyatt is one of the largest of Acapulco's hotels, although no longer as modern as many other resorts. The buzzing lobby encloses a sitting area and bar where there's live music every evening. A free-form pool fronts a broad stretch of beach with calm waters, one of the most inviting in Acapulco. The guest rooms are beginning to show their age, but they also have balconies with spectacular views of Acapulco Bay. Some contain kitchenettes. Regency Club guests receive continental breakfast, afternoon canapés, and other upgraded amenities. This hotel caters to a large Jewish clientele and has a full-service kosher restaurant, synagogue, and Sabbath elevator. Cruise passengers docking in Acapulco often stay here as well. The Alory Spa offers a broad menu of spa services and massage treatments.

Costera Alemán 1, 39869 Acapulco, Gro. Ⓒ **800/233-1234** in the U.S. and Canada, 01-800/005-0000 in Mexico, or 744/469-1234. Fax 744/484-3087. www.acapulco.regency.hyatt.com. 640 units. High season $200–$260 (£100–£130) double, $290 (£145) Regency Club; low season $100 (£50) and up double, $130 (£65) and up Regency Club. AE, DC, MC, V. Valet parking $5 (£2.50). **Amenities:** 3 restaurants; cantina; lobby bar; 2 large, shaded free-form outdoor pools; small gym; spa; children's programs; concierge; tour desk; car-rental desk; business center; shopping arcade; salon; room service; in-room massage; babysitting; laundry service; dry cleaning; safe. *In room:* A/C, TV, minibar, hair dryer, iron, safe.

Inexpensive

Sand's Acapulco *Ⓚids Ⓥalue*   A good option for budget-minded families, this unpretentious 1960s-style motel nestles on the inland side, opposite the giant resort hotels and away from the Costera traffic. Guest rooms have basic furnishings with colorful linens, wall-to-wall carpeting, and tile bathrooms with showers only. The bungalows are smaller and less expensive, but more enticing than the motel rooms because they are surrounded by a small garden. Some units have kitchenettes, and all have a terrace or balcony. The family-friendly motel exudes great energy, with a kids' pool and a special play area for youngsters, including mini-golf. The rates are reasonable, the accommodations satisfactory, and the location excellent.

Costera Alemán 178, 39670 Acapulco, Gro. Ⓒ **744/484-2260.** Fax 744/484-1053. www.sands.com.mx. 93 units. High season $150 (£75) standard double, $100 (£50) bungalow; low season $70 (£35) standard double, $50 (£25) bungalow. AE, MC, V. Limited free parking. **Amenities:** Outdoor pool; children's pool; squash court; children's playground; concierge; babysitting; laundry service. *In room:* A/C, TV, minibar.

DOWNTOWN (ON LA QUEBRADA) & OLD ACAPULCO BEACHES

Numerous budget hotels dot the streets fanning out from the *zócalo*. They're among the best values in town, but be sure to check your room first to see that it meets your needs. Several hotels in this area are close to Caleta and Caletilla beaches, or on the back of the hilly peninsula, at Playa la Angosta.

Moderate

Hotel Mirador Acapulco ℛ   An Old Acapulco landmark dating from 1934, El Mirador Hotel enjoys an unforgettable view of the famous cove where the cliff divers perform. It has been renovated with tropical landscaping and extensive Mexican tile. The hotel's guest rooms are staggered along the edge of a cliff with double or queen-size beds and traditional furnishings, small kitchenette areas with minifridge and coffeemaker, and large bathrooms with marble counters. Most have a separate living room, some have a whirlpool tub, and all are accented with colorful Saltillo tile and other Mexican decorative touches. Ask for a room with a balcony or ocean view. Many guests gravitate to the large, breezy lobby bar as day fades into night on the beautiful cove. A set-price, three course dinner without wine ($39/£20) at La Perla restaurant affords stunning views of the cliff-diving show. Nearby is a protected cove with good snorkeling.

Quebrada 74, 39300 Acapulco, Gro. ℂ **744/483-1221** for reservations. Fax 744/482-4564. www.miradoracapulco. com. 133 units, including 9 junior suites with whirlpools. High season $185 (£93) double, $231 (£116) junior suite; low season $85 (£43) double, $150 (£75) junior suite. Add $13 (£6.50) for kitchenette. AE, MC, V. **Amenities:** 2 restaurants; lobby bar; 3 outdoor pools, including 1 rather rundown saltwater pool; massage service; room service; laundry service. *In room:* A/C, TV, minibar.

Inexpensive

Hotel Costa Linda *(Value*   Budget-minded Mexican and American families and couples are drawn to the sunny, well-kept rooms of the Costa Linda, one of the best values in the area. All rooms have individually controlled air-conditioning and a minifridge, and some have a small kitchenette (there's a $10/£5 charge for using the kitchenette). Closets and bathrooms are ample in size, and mattresses are firm. Cozy as the Costa Linda is, it is adjacent to one of the busier streets in Old Acapulco, so traffic noise can be bothersome. It's just a 1-block walk down to lively Caleta beach, and guests also have free beach access at the nearby Acamar hotel.

Costera Alemán 1008, 39390 Acapulco, Gro. ℂ **744/482-5277** or -2549. 44 units. High season $100 (£50) double; low season $50 (£25) double. Children younger than 8 stay free in parent's room. AE, MC, V. Free parking. **Amenities:** Small outdoor pool. *In room:* A/C, TV.

Hotel Los Flamingos ℛ *(Finds*   An Acapulco landmark, Los Flamingos, perched on a cliff 150m (492 ft.) above Acapulco Bay, once entertained John Wayne, Cary Grant, Johnny Weissmuller, Fred McMurray, Errol Flynn, Red Skelton, Roy Rogers, and others. In fact, the stars liked it so much that at one point they bought it and converted it into a private club. The place is a real find in a kitschy campy sort of way—although the aged rooms are simple and lack modern luxuries, much of the hotel retains the charm of a grand era. Photographs of the old movie stars line the hotel walls, and outdoor passages wind their way along the cliff overlooking the ocean. Most rooms feature dramatic sea views and a large balcony or terrace, although few have air-conditioning and bathrooms are bare-bones. Thursdays at Los Flamingos are especially popular, with a *pozole* party and live music by a Mexican band that was probably around in the era of Wayne and Weissmuller. Even if you don't stay here, plan to at least come for a margarita or "coco loco" cocktail (invented here) at sunset, and walk along the dramatic lookout point.

López Mateos s/n, Fracc. Las Playas, 39300 Acapulco, Gro. ℂ **744/482-0690.** Fax 744/483-9806. 36 units. High season $76 (£38) double, $99 (£50) superior double with A/C, $117 (£59) junior suite; low season $70 (£35) double, $80 (£40) superior double, $91 (£46) junior suite. AE, MC, V. **Amenities:** Restaurant; bar; outdoor pool; tour desk; gift shop; room service; laundry service. *In room:* A/C (in some), TV, no phone.

Hotel Misión   Enter this hotel's plant-filled brick courtyard, shaded by two enormous mango trees, and you'll retreat into an earlier, more peaceful Acapulco. This tranquil 19th-century hotel lies 2 blocks inland from the Costera and the *zócalo*. The original L-shaped building is at least a century old. The rooms have colonial touches, such as colorful tile and wrought iron, and come simply furnished, with a fan and one or two beds with good mattresses. Breakfast is served on the patio.

Felipe Valle 12, 39300 Acapulco, Gro. © 744/482-3643. Fax 744/482-2076. 27 units. High season $50 (£25) double; low season $40 (£20) double. No credit cards.

WHERE TO DINE

Diners in Acapulco enjoy stunning views and fresh seafood. The quintessential setting is a candlelit table with the glittering bay spread out before you. If you're looking for a romantic spot, Acapulco brims with such inviting places; most sit along the southern coast, with views of the bay. If you're looking for simple food or an authentic local dining experience, you're best off in Old Acapulco. Cheap, fresh seafood can also be found at any of the simple restaurants in the local "Barra Vieja" neighborhood near Diamante. *Note:* A deluxe establishment in Acapulco may not cost much more than a mass-market restaurant. The proliferation of U.S. franchises has increased competition, and even the more expensive places have reduced prices. Trust me—the locally owned restaurants offer the best food and the best value.

SOUTH OF TOWN: LAS BRISAS AREA
Very Expensive

Baikal ⊙ FUSION/FRENCH/ASIAN   The exquisite Baikal is the best place in Acapulco for an over-the-top dining experience, although you will be paying top dollar for the view. You enter from the street, then descend a spiral staircase into the stunning bar and restaurant, awash in muted tan and cream colors of luxurious fabrics and natural accents of stone, wood, and water. The restaurant itself is constructed into the cliff, providing sweeping views of Acapulco Bay's glittering lights. The large dining room, with a two-story ceiling, has comfortable seating, including sofas that border the room. The creative menu combines fusion fare, and then adds a dash of Mexican flare. Start with the scallops in chipotle vinaigrette or the oriental-style salad. Notable entrees include steamed red snapper with *huitlachoche*, baby back ribs with foie gras, or medallions of New Zealand lamb in a sweet garlic sauce. There's also an extensive selection of wines. Baikal has a private VIP dining room, wine cellar, and elegant bar, ideal for enjoying a sunset cocktail or after-dinner drink. It's east of town on the scenic highway just before the entrance to the Las Brisas hotel.

Carretera Escénica 16 and 22. © 744/446-6845 or -6867. www.baikal.com.mx. Reservations required (reservaciones@baikal.com.mx). Main courses: $21–$99 (£11–£50). AE, MC, V. Sun–Thurs 7pm–1am; Fri–Sat 7pm–2am. Closed Mon during summer.

Becco ⊙⊙ ITALIAN/SEAFOOD   Currently the hottest table in Acapulco, Becco features floor-to-ceiling windows that stretch three floors overlooking the bay. A spiral staircase leads down from the entrance past the cocktail lounge and into the minimalist dining room, which has contemporary cement floors, large white pillars, and refined wood tables and chairs. The multilevel room buzzes with the chatter of Mexico's elite, many on vacation from the capital. The menu involves a rich selection of *antipasti,* including carpaccios, brochettes, and prosciutto with mozzarella; my favorite starter is seared tuna over a bed of spinach served with fries. The top pastas

---

(*Moments* **Dining with a View**

Restaurants with unparalleled views of Acapulco include **Baikal, Becco, Zibu,** and **Casa Nova** in the Las Brisas area, **El Olvido** along the Costera, **Su Casa** on a hill above the convention center, and the appropriately named **Bella Vista Restaurant** at the Las Brisas hotel.

---

are homemade taglioli with lobster, spaghetti *allo scoglio* loaded with shrimp, calamari, clams, and crayfish, and seafood risotto. The chefs will prepare the fresh catches anyway you like. Becco has an extensive wine and champagne selection—all visible through the glass-enclosed cellar.

Carretera Escénica 14. (✆) 744/446-7402. www.beccoalmare.com. Reservations required. Main courses $20–$38 (£10–£19). AE, MC, V. Sun–Thurs 7pm–midnight; Fri–Sat 7pm–1am.

Casa Nova ✖ GOURMET ITALIAN Enjoy an excellent though very expensive meal and a fabulous view of glittering Acapulco Bay at this spot east of town. The cliff-side restaurant offers several refined dining rooms, awash in marble and stone accents, and outdoor terrace dining with a stunning view. If you arrive before your table is ready, have a drink in the comfortable lounge. This is a long-standing favorite of Mexico City's elite; dress tends toward fashionable, tropical attire. The best dishes include veal scaloppini and homemade pastas, such as linguine with Portobello mushrooms. A changing tourist menu offers a sampling of the best selections for a fixed price. There's also an ample selection of reasonably priced national and imported wines. And there's live music nightly.

Carretera Escénica 5256. (✆) 744/446-6237. Reservations required. Main courses $19–$52 (£9.50–£26). AE, MC, V. Mon–Sat 7–11:30pm.

Zibu ✖✖✖ SEAFOOD/THAI With a gorgeous view over the sea, Zibu blends Mexican and Thai architectural and culinary styles to create a breathtaking dining experience. The open-air venue is furnished with rattan tables and chairs surrounded by warm lighting of candles, tiki torches, and lamps; a semicircular pool serves as a moat between the ultrachic restaurant and *palapa*-topped lounge. Consider starting with the sea scallop carpaccio or sea bass tartare, and continue with the shrimp medallions with ginger and mango or grilled fish filet with almonds and soy (there are also meat dishes). Although it's not on the menu (just ask for it), the Thai salad with shrimp tempura, mint, cilantro, lettuce, mango, red and green peppers, and soy is out of this world. Finish with a tropical fruit plate and variety of sorbets. The beautiful glass-enclosed wine cellar houses a well-balanced though expensive collection, including a thoughtful selection of French wines. Service is gracious and attentive, and Asian lounge and Thai music plays in the background.

Av. Escénica s/n, Fracc. Glomar. (✆) 744/433-3058 or -3069. Reservations recommended. Main courses $16–$54 (£8–£27). AE, MC, V. Sun–Thurs 7pm–midnight; Fri–Sat 7pm–1am.

COSTERA HOTEL ZONE
Very Expensive
El Olvido ✖✖ FRENCH/MEXICAN El Olvido gives you all the glittering bayview ambience of the posh Las Brisas restaurants, without the taxi ride. The menu is one of the most sophisticated in the city. It's expensive, but each dish is delightful in

presentation and taste. Start with 1 of the 12 house specialty drinks, such as Olvido, made with tequila, rum, Cointreau, tomato juice, and lime juice. Soups include delicious cold avocado, and thick black bean and chorizo. Among the innovative entrees are quail with honey and *pasilla* chiles, thick sea bass with a mild sauce of cilantro and avocado, and lamb chops with chipotle. For dessert, I recommend chocolate fondue or *guanábana* (a tropical fruit) mousse in a rich *zapote negro* (black tropical fruit) sauce. El Olvido sits at the back of the Plaza Marbella shopping center fronting Diana Circle. Although the bay view is lovely, a drawback is that the dance clubs down the shoreline can often be heard after 10pm.

Glorieta Diana traffic circle, Plaza Marbella. ① **744/481-0203**, -0256, or -0214. www.elolvido.com.mx. Reservations recommended. Main courses $15–$40 (£7.50–£20). AE, MC, V. Daily 6pm–midnight.

Su Casa/Angel and Shelly's *☆☆* INTERNATIONAL   Relaxed elegance and terrific food at reasonable prices are what you get at Su Casa. Owners Shelly and Angel Herrera created this pleasant, breezy, open-air restaurant on the patio of their hillside home overlooking the city ("Angel and Shelly's"—previously called La Margarita—is the indoor restaurant below Su Casa that's open during the rainy season). Both Shelly and Angel are experts in the kitchen and are on hand nightly to greet guests on the patio. The menu changes often. Some items are standard, such as shrimp *a la patrona* in herbs and spices, grilled fish, steak, and chicken. The *pasta el padrino*, with fresh shrimp and creme *chipotle*, is a delicious new addition to the menu. Many entrees come with garnishes of cooked banana or pineapple. The margaritas are big and delicious. The banana split or any of the flambées make desert hard to resist.

V. Anahuac 110. ① **744/484-4350** or -1261. Fax 744/484-0803. www.sucasa-acapulco.com. Reservations recommended. Main courses $17–$35 (£8.50–£18). MC, V. Daily 6pm–midnight.

Moderate

El Cabrito *☆☆* NORTHERN MEXICAN   With its hacienda-inspired entrance, waitresses in white dresses and *charro*-style neckties, and location in the heart of the Costera, this typical Mexican restaurant targets tourists. But its authentic and delicious food attracts Mexicans in the know—a comforting stamp of approval. Among its specialties are *cabrito al pastor* (roasted goat), *charro* beans, Oaxaca-style *mole*, and *burritos de machaca* (made with shredded beef). A whole *cabrito* is usually being slowly roasted inside the glass-enclosed *parilla*. Bottles of beer are brought to your table in buckets of ice and then poured in frosty cold mugs. El Cabrito lies on the ocean side of the Costera, south of the convention center.

Costera Alemán 1480. ① **744/484-7711**. Main courses $6–$18 (£3–£9). AE, MC, V. Daily 2pm–midnight.

Inexpensive

100% Natural *☆ (Kids* MEXICAN/HEALTH FOOD   Healthy, delicious, and inexpensive Mexican food is the specialty at this tropical plant–filled restaurant, on the second level of the shopping center across from the Acapulco Plaza Hotel. (This chain has five other branches in Acapulco, including another one farther east on the Costera.) If you've over-indulged the night before, get yourself back on track here with one of the outstanding breakfast selections, such as whole-wheat pancakes with apple and cinnamon, a vegetarian omelet, or any one of nine fresh-fruit plates. Yogurt shakes, steamed vegetables, and cheese enchiladas are alternatives to the yummy sandwiches served on whole-grain breads. Don't miss one of the fruit *licuados*, blended fresh fruit with your choice of yogurt or milk. The 16-page menu offers almost too many choices.

Costera Miguel Alemán 200, across from the Costa Club Hotel. ℂ **744/485-3982.** Breakfasts $3.50–$5; (£1.75–£2.50); sandwiches $5–$7.50 (£2.50–£3.75); other food items $5–$10 (£2.50–£5). AE, MC, V. Open 24 hr.

El Zorrito 𝑅𝑅 MEXICAN/TACOS If you're looking for excellent, no-nonsense Mexican food, El Zorrito is your place. Plastic tables and chairs, a dozen spinning ceiling fans, and photos of famous diners fill the open-air dining space. Waiters with their names printed on the back of their shirts traverse the restaurant with a smile, making sure customers are well fed and attended to. You can watch as homemade tortillas are prepared hot off the *comal* (the cast iron plate used to make tortillas) and an expert team of cooks work harmoniously in the open kitchen. The food here is spicy and delicious, and the tacos are among the best you'll find.

Costera Miguel Alemán 212, across from the Costa Club Hotel. ℂ **744/485-3735.** Breakfasts $3–$5 (£1.50–£2.50); tacos $6.50–$8 (£3.75–£4); other dishes $6.50–$15 (£3.75–£7.50). AE, MC, V. Open 24 hr.

Ika Tako 𝑅𝑅 *Finds* SEAFOOD/TACOS These fresh fish, shrimp, and seafood tacos (many served in combinations that include grilled pineapple, fresh spinach, grated cheese, garlic, and bacon) are so tasty that they're addicting. An unusual selection of nine sweet and spicy salsas accompanies them, and there are also excellent burritos, meat and chicken dishes, and vegetarian selections. Unlike most inexpensive places to eat, the setting is also lovely, with a handful of tables overlooking tropical trees and the bay below. The lighting may be bright, the atmosphere occasionally hectic, and the service dependably slow, but the tacos are delectable. Consider the *takabrían,* which comes with shrimp, octopus, calamari, pepper, onion, and cheese. You can also order beer, wine, soft drinks, and dessert here. This restaurant is along the Costera, next to Beto's lobster restaurant. There's another branch across from the Hyatt Regency hotel.

Costera Alemán 99. ℂ **744/484-9521.** Main courses $5–$16 (£2.50–£8). AE, MC, V. Daily 5pm–3am.

DOWNTOWN: THE *ZOCALO* AREA

The old downtown abounds with simple, inexpensive restaurants serving tasty eats. It's easy to pay more elsewhere for food that's not as consistently good as in this part of town. To explore, start at the *zócalo* and stroll west along Juárez. After about 3 blocks, you'll come to Azueta, lined with small seafood cafes and streetside stands.

Inexpensive

El Amigo Miguel 𝑅 *Finds* MEXICAN/SEAFOOD Locals know that El Amigo Miguel is a standout among downtown seafood restaurants—you can easily pay more elsewhere but not eat better. Impeccably fresh seafood reigns; the large, open-air dining room, 3 blocks west of the *zócalo,* is usually brimming with seafood lovers. When it overflows, head to a branch across the street, with the same menu. Try delicious *camarones borrachos* (drunken shrimp), in a sauce made with beer, ketchup, and bits of fresh bacon—it tastes nothing like the individual ingredients. *Filete Miguel* is a fresh fish filet (often red snapper or sea bass) stuffed with seafood and covered in a wonderful chipotle pepper sauce. Grilled shrimp with garlic and *mojo de ajo* (whole red snapper) are served at their classic best. Meat dishes are available, as well.

Juárez 31, at Azueta (second location across the street at Juárez 16). ℂ **744/483-6981.** Main courses $6–$15 (£3–£7.50). AE, MC, V. Daily 9:30am–8:30pm.

Mariscos Pipo 𝑅 SEAFOOD Check out the photographs of Old Acapulco on the walls while relaxing in this airy dining room decorated with hanging nets, fish, glass

---

Moments   If There's *Pozole,* It Must Be Thursday

If you're visiting Acapulco on a Thursday, indulge in the local custom of eating *pozole,* a bowl of white hominy and meat in broth, garnished with sliced radishes, shredded lettuce, onions, oregano, and lime, served with crispy tostadas. The traditional version includes pork, but a newer chicken version has also become a standard. You can also find green *pozole,* which is made by adding a paste of roasted pumpkin seeds to the traditional *pozole* base. Green *pozole* is also traditionally served with a side of sardines. For a singular Acapulco experience, enjoy your Thursday *pozole* at the cliff-side restaurant of the Hotel Los Flamingos (see above).

---

buoys, and shell lanterns. The English-language menu lists a wide array of seafood, including ceviche, lobster, octopus, crayfish, clams, baby-shark quesadillas, and fish prepared anyway you want. This local favorite is 2 blocks west of the *zócalo* on Breton, just off the Costera. Another bustling branch, open daily from 1 to 9:30pm, is at Costera Alemán and Canadá (© **744/484-0165**).

Almirante Breton 3. © **744/482-2237**. Main courses $9–$45 (£4.50–£23). AE, MC, V. Daily 1–9:30pm.

ACAPULCO AFTER DARK

SPECIAL ATTRACTIONS   Many major hotels schedule Mexican fiestas and other theme nights that include dinner and entertainment, including Las Brisas (© **744/469-6900**) and the Mayan Palace (© **744/469-6000**). Local travel agencies will have information.

NIGHTCLUBS & DANCE CLUBS   Acapulco is even more famous for its nightclubs than for its beaches. Because clubs frequently change ownership—and often, names—it's difficult to give specific and accurate recommendations. But some general tips will help. Cover charges vary but are almost always higher for men. Drinks can cost anywhere from $5 to $15 (£2.50–£7.50). Don't even think about going out to one of the hillside dance clubs before 11pm, and don't expect much action until after midnight. But it will keep going until 4 or 5am, and possibly later.

Many dance clubs periodically waive their cover charge or offer some other promotion to attract customers. Look for promotional materials in hotel reception areas, at travel desks or concierge booths, in local publications, and on the beach.

The high-rise hotels have their own bars and sometimes dance clubs. Informal lobby or poolside cocktail bars often offer free live entertainment.

THE BEACH BAR ZONE   Prefer a little fresh air with your nightlife? The young, hip crowd favors the growing number of open-air oceanfront dance clubs along Costera Alemán, most of which feature techno or alternative rock. There's a concentration of them between the Fiesta Americana and Continental Plaza hotels. An earlier and more casual option to the glitzy dance clubs, these places include the jamming **Disco Beach** (© **744/484-8230**), **El Sombrero** (you'll know it when you see it), **Tabú,** and the pirate-themed **Barbaroja.** These mainly charge a cover (around $10/£5) and offer an open bar. Women frequently drink free or with a lesser charge (men may pay more, but then, this is where the beach babes are). Disco Beach is the most popular of the bunch and occasionally—such as during spring break—has live bands on the beachfront stage. Their Friday night foam parties are especially popular. Most of the smaller establishments do not accept credit cards; when they do, Master-Card and Visa are more widely accepted than American Express.

If you are brave enough—or inebriated enough—there's a **bungee jump** in the midst of the beach bar zone at Costera Alemán 101 (© **744/484-7529**). For $60 (£30) you get one jump, plus a T-shirt, diploma, and membership. Additional jumps are $30 (£15), and your fourth jump is free. For $90 (£45), you can jump as many times as you like from 11am to 1am.

Alebrijes Stadium seating, booths, and round tables surround the vast dance floor (the 1,200-capacity club doubles as a venue for concerts and live performances by Mexico's most notable singers). Music includes pop, hip-hop, rock, and electronic music. The dress code forbids shorts, T-shirts, tennis shoes, flip-flops, and jeans. The average age is late teens to early 20s. Open daily from 11pm to 5am. Costera Alemán 3308, across from the Hyatt Regency Acapulco. © **744/484-5902**. Cover (including open bar with national drinks) $30 (£15) for women, $40 (£20) for men.

Baby-O ℱℱℱ This longtime Acapulco hot spot is a throwback to the town's heady disco days, although the music is exceptionally contemporary. The mid- to late-20s crowd dances to everything from house to hip-hop and techno to dance. Across from the Days Inn and Hooters, Baby-O has a dance floor surrounded by several tiers of tables and sculpted, cavelike walls, serviced by three bars. Drinks cost $5 to $7 (£2.50–£3.50). Three-dimensional laser shows and vapor effects keep the dancing going strong. Service is excellent. This is a high-class dance club attracting a beautiful clientele. It opens at 10:30pm, and you'd be wise to make a reservation. Costera Alemán 22. © **744/484-7474** or 481-1035. www.babyo.com.mx. Cover $20 (£10) for women, $60 (£30) for men.

Carlos 'n' Charlie's For fun, danceable music and good food, you can't go wrong with this branch of the Carlos Anderson chain. It's always packed. Come early and get a seat on the terrace overlooking the Costera. This is a great place to go for late dinner and a few drinks before moving on to a club. It's east of the Glorieta Diana traffic circle, across the street from the Fiesta Americana Condesa. It's open daily from 1pm to 1am. Costera Alemán 999. © **744/484-1285** or -0039. www.carlosandcharlies.com/acapulco/index.htm.

Classico ℱℱ One of the newest and hottest clubs in town, Classico is a raging party into the wee hours. A winding mirrored glass entrance leads into this small but trendy *antro* (disco). Digital screens and candlelit tables surround the illuminated dance floor, where music includes house, hip-hop, and reggaeton mixed by top DJs and blasted over a high-tech sound system. The glittery disco and outdoor deck sits just in front of Palladium and attracts a young, trendy crowd—many in slinky outfits. The club is open Friday and Saturday from 11pm to 6am. Carretera Escénica, in front of Palladium. © **744/446-6455**. www.classicodelmar.com. Cover $30 (£15) for men, free for women.

Mambo Café ℱℱ Part of a national chain, the vibrant Mambo Café hosts groups from the Dominican Republic, Cuba, Mexico, Venezuela, and Colombia. Sexy dancers swing their hips to salsa, merengue, cumbia, and pop. The tropical club attracts locals as well as tourists, and is considered the best Latin dance spot in town. Tables surround the dance floor, and patrons can order drinks by the glass or the bottle. Open Wednesday to Saturday from 10pm to 5am; live music starts at midnight. Costera Alemán 1632. © **744/485-9688**. www.gpofreedom.com.mx. Cover $10 (£5).

Mandara *(Moments* Venture into this minimalist chrome-and-neon extravaganza perched on the side of the mountain for a true Acapulco nightlife experience. The plush, dim club has a sunken dance floor and panoramic view of the lights of Acapulco Bay. The club also has an intimate piano bar, Siboney, upstairs overlooking the dance floor; it has a special champagne menu and draws a more mature and moneyed crowd. The after-hours lounge Privado, also in the same building, opens its doors at 4:30am. Downstairs, there's pumped-in mood smoke, alternating with fresh oxygen to keep you dancing. Tight and slinky is the norm for women; no shorts for men. The club opens nightly at 10:30pm; fireworks rock the usually full house at 3am, which is when a stylized dance performance takes place on weekends, in the style of Euro clubs. Call to find out if you need reservations; this club tends to be busiest on Friday nights. Carretera Escénica, between Los Rancheros Restaurant and La Vista Shopping Center. © 744/446-5711 or -5712. www.acapulcomandara.com. Cover $30 (£15) for women, $40 (£20) for men, includes open bar; or pay $10 (£5) for entrance to Siboney, and purchase drinks separately.

Palladium *(* This cliffside club currently reigns as the top spot in town, and is found just down the road from Mandara. Generally, it welcomes a younger, rowdier crowd that enjoys the fabulous views and the dancing platforms set in the 50m-wide (164-ft.) glass windows overlooking the bay. Around 3:30am, Silver Man—complete with an Aztec headdress—performs, followed by a spray of fireworks outside the windows. Palladium has welcomed the world's finest DJs as special guests, and the music seems to rock the earth below. The layout of the club is more open, which makes it easier than most places for meeting people. Carretera Escénica. © 744/481-0330 or 446-5483. www.palladium.com.mx. Cover $30 (£15) for women, $40 (£20) for men, includes open bar.

Salon Q This place bills itself as "the cathedral of salsa," and it's a fairly accurate claim—Salon Q is *the* place to get down and enjoy the Latin rhythms. Frequently, management raises the cover and features impersonators of top Latin American musical acts. Open daily from 10pm to 5am. Costera Alemán 3117. © 744/481-0114. Cover $13–$25 (£6.50–£13), includes open bar.

2 Northward to Zihuatanejo & Ixtapa *(*

576km (357 miles) SW of Mexico City; 565km (350 miles) SE of Manzanillo; 253km (157 miles) NW of Acapulco

Side-by-side beach resorts, Ixtapa and Zihuatanejo share geography, but they couldn't be more different in character. Ixtapa is a model of modern infrastructure, services, and luxury hotels, while Zihuatanejo—"Zihua" to the locals—is the quintessential Mexican beach village. For travelers, this offers the intriguing possibility of visiting two distinct destinations in one vacation. Those looking for luxury should opt for Ixtapa (eex-*tah*-pah). You can easily make the quick 6.5km (4-mile) trip into Zihuatanejo for a sampling of the simple life in a *pueblo* by the sea. Those who prefer a more rustic retreat with real personality should settle in Zihuatanejo (see-wah-tah-*neh*-hoh). It's known for its long-standing community of Swiss and Italian immigrants, and its legendary beach playboys.

The area, with a backdrop of the Sierra Madre and a foreground of Pacific Ocean waters, provides a full range of activities and diversions. Scuba diving, deep-sea fishing, bay cruises to remote beaches, and golf are among the favorites. Nightlife in both towns borders on subdued; Ixtapa is the livelier.

This dual destination is the choice for the traveler looking for a little of everything, from resort-style indulgence to unpretentious simplicity. These two resorts are more

> ### *Tips* Motorist Advisory
>
> Motorists planning to follow Highway 200 northwest up the coast from Ixtapa or Zihuatanejo toward Lázaro Cárdenas and Manzanillo should be aware of reports of car and bus hijackings on that route, especially around Playa Azul, with bus holdups more common than car holdups. Before heading in that direction, ask locals and the tourism office about the status of the route. Don't drive at night. Police and military patrols of the highway have increased, and the number of incidents has dropped dramatically.

welcoming to couples and adults than families, with a number of places that are off-limits to children younger than 16—something of a rarity in Mexico.

ESSENTIALS
GETTING THERE & DEPARTING

BY PLANE   These destinations tend to be even more seasonal than most resorts in Mexico. Flights are available year-round from U.S. gateways, but they operate less frequently in the summer. See chapter 3, "Planning Your Trip to Mexico," for information on flying to Ixtapa/Zihuatanejo from the United States and Canada. **AeroMéxico** and **Click Mexicana** fly daily from Mexico City; **InterJet** flies daily from neighboring Toluca (about an hour from Mexico City). Here are the local numbers of some carriers: **AeroMéxico** (© 755/554-2018 or -2019), **Alaska Airlines** (© 755/554-8457), **Continental** (© 755/554-4219), **Click Mexicana** (© 01-800/112-5425 toll-free in Mexico), **InterJet** (© 01-800/011-2345 toll-free in Mexico), and **US Airways** (© 755/554-8634). Ask your travel agent about **charter flights** and packages.

The **Ixtapa/Zihuatanejo airport** (© **755/554-2070**) is about 11km (7 miles) and 15 minutes south of Zihuatanejo. Taxi fares to the Ixtapa hotel zone are $32 (£16) and to Zihuatanejo $28 (£14). **Transportes Terrestres** (© **755/554-3298**) *colectivos* (minivans) transport travelers to hotels in Ixtapa and Zihuatanejo for about $12 (£6) and can be purchased just outside the baggage-claim area. Car-rental agencies with booths in the airport include **Hertz** (© **800/654-3131** in the U.S., or 755/554-2952) and **Budget** (© **800/527-0700** in the U.S., or 755/553-0397).

BY CAR   From Mexico City (about 8–9 hrs.), you can take **Highway 15** to Toluca, then **Highway 130/134** the rest of the way. On the latter road, highway gas stations are few. Another route is the four-lane **Highway 95D** to Iguala, then **Highway 51** west to **Highway 134**. A new toll road, **Highway 37** from Morelia to Ixtapa, cuts about an hour off the total trip time.

From Acapulco (2½–3 hr.) or Manzanillo (11 hr.), the only choice is the coastal **Highway 200**. The ocean views along the winding, mountain-edged drive from Manzanillo can be spectacular, although there are many speed bumps along the way that make for slow going.

BY BUS   Zihuatanejo has two bus terminals: the **Central de Autobuses Estrella Blanca** (© **755/554-3477**), Paseo Zihuatanejo at Paseo la Boquita, opposite the Pemex station and IMSS Hospital, from which most lines operate, and the **Estrella de Oro** station (© **755/554-2175**), a block away. At the Central de Autobuses, several companies offer daily service to and from Acapulco, Puerto Escondido, Huatulco,

ACCOMMODATIONS

Amuleto **8**
Barceló Ixtapa **2**
Brisas del Mar **5**
Bungalows Ley **4**
Casa Kau-Kan **11**
La Casa Que Canta **6**
Las Brisas Ixtapa **3**
NH Krystal Ixtapa **1**
The Tides **9**
Villa Guadalupe **10**
Villas San Sebastián **7**

To Acapulco

Paseo La Roqueta

Bus Terminal

Bus to Ixtapa

Paseo Cocotal

ZIHUATANEJO CENTRO

Guerrero
Galeana
Ascencio
Pescador
Ejido
González
N. Bravo
Alvarez
Altamirano

Paseo Zihuatanejo

Cuauhtémoc
5 de Mayo

Pier Playa Principal

Playa Madera

Zihuatanejo Bay

Playa La Ropa

Playa Las Gatas

Punta San Esteban

Playa Majahua

See "Downtown Zihuatanejo" map

IXTAPA'S COMMERCIAL ZONE

Ruben's

Golden Cookie Shop

Villa de la Selva Restaurant

Playa Vista Hermosa

Playa Palmar

Punta Carrizo

PACIFIC OCEAN

Los Morros

Marina Ixtapa

Beccofino

Playa San Juan

Playa Casa Blanca

Punta Ixtapa

Playa Cuata

Playa Quieta

Playa Linda

Isla Ixtapa

2 mi
2 km

Airport
Bus

VERACRUZ
Mexico City
JALISCO
MICHOACÁN
GUERRERO
OAXACA
Zihuatanejo & Ixtapa

200 mi
200 km

Manzanillo, Puerto Vallarta, and other cities. At the other station, first-class Estrella de Oro buses run daily to Acapulco.

The trip from Mexico City to Zihuatanejo (bypassing Acapulco) takes 9 hours; from Acapulco, it's 4 to 5 hours. From Zihuatanejo, it's 6 or 7 hours to Manzanillo, and it's an additional 6 hours to Puerto Vallarta.

ORIENTATION

VISITOR INFORMATION   The **State Tourism Office** (②/fax **755/544-8361**) is in the center of Zihuatanejo on Galo 1, next to Plaza Kyoto; it's open Monday through Friday from 8am to 6pm and Saturday from 9am to 1pm. The **Zihuatanejo Tourism Office** (② **755/554-2001;** www.ixtapa-zihuatanejo.gob.mx) is on the main square at Av. Zihuatanejo Poniente 21; it's open Monday through Friday from 8am to 6pm and serves basic tourist-information purposes. The **Convention and Visitor's Bureau** is another source of information, it's in Ixtapa at Paseo de Las Gaviotas 12 (② **755/553-1270;** www.ixtapa-zihuatanejo.org) and open Monday through Friday from 9am to 2pm and 4pm to 7pm.

CITY LAYOUT   The fishing village and resort of **Zihuatanejo** spreads out around the beautiful Bay of Zihuatanejo, framed by downtown to the north and a beautiful long beach and the Sierra foothills to the east. The heart of Zihuatanejo is the waterfront walkway **Paseo del Pescador** (also called the *malecón*), bordering the Municipal Beach. Rather than a plaza, as in most Mexican villages, the town centerpiece is a **basketball court,** which fronts the beach. It's a point of reference for directions. The main thoroughfare for cars is **Juan Alvarez,** a block behind the *malecón*. Sections of several of the main streets are designated *zona peatonal* (pedestrian zone).

A cement-and-sand walkway runs from the *malecón* in downtown Zihuatanejo along the water to **Playa Madera.** The walkway is lit at night. Access to Playa La Ropa (Clothing Beach) is by the main road, **Camino a Playa La Ropa.** Playa La Ropa and Playa Las Gatas (Cats Beach) are connected only by boat.

A good highway connects Zihua to **Ixtapa,** 6km (4 miles) northwest. The 18-hole **Ixtapa Golf Club** marks the beginning of the inland side of Ixtapa. Tall hotels line Ixtapa's wide beach, **Playa Palmar,** against a backdrop of lush palm groves and mountains. Access is by the main street, **Bulevar Ixtapa.** On the opposite side of the main boulevard lies a large expanse of small shopping plazas (many with air-conditioned shops) and restaurants. At the far end of Bulevar Ixtapa, **Marina Ixtapa** has excellent restaurants, private yacht slips, and an 18-hole golf course. Condominiums and private homes surround the marina and golf course, and additional exclusive residential areas are rising in the hillsides past the marina on the road to Playa Quieta and Playa Linda. Ixtapa also has a paved bicycle track that begins at the marina and continues around the golf course and on toward Playa Linda.

GETTING AROUND   Taxi fares are reasonable, but from midnight to 5am, rates increase by 50%. The average fare between Ixtapa and Zihuatanejo is $5.50 (£2.25). Within Zihua, the fare runs about $3 (£1.50); within Ixtapa it averages $3 to $5 (£1.50–£2.50). Radio cabs are available by calling ② **755/554-3680** or -3311, however taxis are available from most hotels. A **shuttle bus** (80¢/20p) runs between Zihuatanejo and Ixtapa every 15 or 20 minutes from 5am to 11pm daily, but is almost always very crowded with commuting workers. In Zihuatanejo, it stops near the corner of Morelos/Paseo Zihuatanejo and Juárez, about 3 blocks north of the market. In Ixtapa, it makes numerous stops along Bulevar Ixtapa.

Note: The road from Zihuatanejo to Ixtapa is a broad, four-lane highway, which makes driving between the towns easier and faster than ever. Street signs are becoming more common in Zihuatanejo, and good signs lead in and out of both towns. However, both locations have an area called the Zona Hotelera (Hotel Zone), so if you're trying to reach Ixtapa's Hotel Zone, signs in Zihuatanejo pointing to that village's Hotel Zone may be confusing.

FAST FACTS: Zihuatanejo & Ixtapa

American Express The main office is in Av. Colegio Heróico Militar 38 in Plaza San Rafael, Loc. 7, Centro (© 755/544-6242; fax 755/544-6244). It's open Monday through Friday from 9am to 2pm and 4pm to 6pm.

Area Code The telephone area code is 755.

Banks Ixtapa's banks include Bancomer, in the La Puerta Centro shopping center. The most centrally located of Zihuatanejo's banks is Banamex, Calle Ejido at Vicente Guerreo. Banks change money during business hours, which are generally Monday through Friday from 9am to 4pm, Saturday from 10am to 1pm. ATMs and currency exchange are available during these and other hours.

Climate Summer is hot and humid, though tempered by sea breezes and brief showers; September is the peak of the tropical rainy season, with showers concentrated in the late afternoons.

Drugstore There's a branch of Farmacías Coyuca (© 755/554-5390) in Zihuatanejo, open from 8am to 11pm.

Hospital Hospital de la Marina Ixtapa is at Bulevar Ixtapa s/n, in back of the artisans' market (© 755/553-0499). In Zihuatanejo, there's the Clinica Maciel (© 755/554-2380; La Palmas 12) or Hospital Hernández Montejano, Juan Alvarez s/n (© 755/554-5404). Dial © 065 from any phone for emergencies.

Internet Access Ixtapa hotels generally have Internet access. Access is cheaper in Zihuatanejo; the most popular is Zihuatanejo Bar Net, Agustín Ramírez 2, on the ground floor of the Hotel Zihuatanejo Centro (© 755/554-3661). High-speed access is $2 (£1) per hour; it's open 9am to 11pm daily.

Post Office The *correo* is in the SCT building, Edificio SCT, behind El Cacahuate in Zihuatanejo (© 755/554-2192). It's open Monday through Friday from 8am to 6pm, Saturday from 9am to 1pm.

ACTIVITIES ON & OFF THE BEACH

The **Museo de Arqueología de la Costa Grande** (© 755/554-7552) traces the history of the area from Acapulco to Ixtapa/Zihuatanejo (the Costa Grande) from pre-Hispanic times, when it was known as Cihuatlán ("the Land of Women" in the Nahuatl language), through the Colonial Era. Most of the museum's pottery and stone artifacts give evidence of extensive trade with far-off cultures and regions, including the Toltec and Teotihuacán near Mexico City, the Olmec on the Pacific and Gulf coasts, and areas known today as the states of Nayarit, Michoacán, and San Luis Potosí. Local indigenous groups gave the Aztec tribute items, including cotton *tilmas* (capes) and *cacao* (chocolate), representations of which can be seen here. This museum, in Zihuatanejo near Vicente Guerrero at the east end of Paseo del Pescador, easily merits the half-hour or less it takes to stroll through; signs are in Spanish and English, and an accompanying brochure is available in English. Admission is $1 (50p), and it's open Tuesday through Sunday from 10am to 6pm.

THE BEACHES   In Zihuatanejo   At Zihuatanejo's town beach, **Playa Municipal,** the local fishermen pull their colorful boats up onto the sand, making for a fine photo op. The small shops and restaurants lining the waterfront are great for people-watching and absorbing the flavor of daily village life. **Playa Madera (Wood Beach),** just east of Playa Municipal, is open to the surf but generally peaceful. A number of attractive budget lodgings overlook this area.

All beaches in Zihuatanejo are safe for swimming. Undertow is rarely a problem, and the municipal beach is protected from the main surge of the Pacific. Beaches in Ixtapa are more dangerous for swimming, with frequent undertow problems.

South of Playa Madera is Zihuatanejo's largest and most beautiful beach, **Playa La Ropa** *(★★,* a long sweep of sand with a great view of the sunset. Some lovely small hotels and restaurants nestle in the hills; palm groves edge the shoreline. Although it's also open to the Pacific, waves are usually gentle. There are a number of beachside restaurants, as well as beach operators renting kayaks, Hobie Cat sailboats, and snorkeling equipment. A taxi from town costs $3.50 (£1.75). The name Playa La Ropa (Clothing Beach) comes from an old tale of the sinking of a *galeón* during a storm. The silk clothing that it was carrying back from the Philippines washed ashore on this beach—hence the name.

The nicest beach for swimming, and the best for children, is the secluded **Playa Las Gatas (Cats Beach),** across the bay from Playa La Ropa and Zihuatanejo. The small coral reef just offshore is a nice spot for snorkeling and diving, and a little dive shop on the beach rents gear. The waters at Las Gatas are exceptionally clear, without undertow or big waves. Open-air seafood restaurants on the beach make it an appealing lunch spot. The PADI-certified **Carlo Scuba** (© **755/554-6003;** www.carloscuba.com), arranges **scuba-diving** and snorkeling trips from here. Kayaks are also available for rent. Small *pangas* or *lanchas* (boats) with shade run to Las Gatas from the Zihuatanejo town pier, a 10-minute trip; the captains will take you across whenever you wish between 9am and 5pm for $3.50 (£1.75) round-trip. Usually the last boat back leaves Las Gatas at 6:30pm (5:30pm in low season), but check to be sure.

Playa Larga is a beautiful, uncrowded beach between Zihuatanejo and the airport, with several small *palapa* restaurants, hammocks, and wading pools.

In Ixtapa   Ixtapa's main beach, **Playa Palmar,** is a lovely white-sand arc on the edge of the Hotel Zone, with dramatic rock formations silhouetted in the sea. The surf can be rough; use caution, and don't swim when a red flag is posted. Several of the nicest beaches in the area are essentially closed to the public. Although by law all Mexican beaches are open to the public, it is common practice for hotels to create artificial barriers (such as rocks or dunes).

Club Med and Qualton Club have largely claimed **Playa Quieta,** on the mainland across from Isla Ixtapa. The remaining piece of beach was once the launching point for boats to Isla Ixtapa, but it is gradually being taken over by a private development. Isla Ixtapa–bound boats now leave from the jetty on **Playa Linda,** about 13km (8 miles) north of Ixtapa. Inexpensive water taxis ferry passengers to Isla Ixtapa. Playa Linda is the primary out-of-town beach, with watersports equipment and horse rentals available. **Playa las Cuatas,** a pretty beach and cove a few miles north of

Ixtapa, and **Playa Majahua,** an isolated beach just west of Zihuatanejo, are both being transformed into resort complexes. Lovely **Playa Vista Hermosa** is framed by striking rock formations and bordered by the Las Brisas hotel high on the hill. All of these are very attractive beaches for sunbathing or a stroll but have heavy surf and strong undertow. Use caution if you swim here.

WATERSPORTS & BOAT TRIPS   Probably the most popular boat trip is to **Isla Ixtapa** for snorkeling and lunch at the El Marlin restaurant, one of several on the island. You can book this outing as a tour through local travel agencies, or go on your own from Zihuatanejo by following the directions to Playa Linda above and taking a boat from there. Boats leave for Isla Ixtapa every 10 minutes between 9am and 5pm, so you can depart and return as you like. The round-trip boat ride is $3 (£1.50). Along the way, you'll pass dramatic rock formations and see in the distance **Los Morros de Los Pericos islands,** where a great variety of birds nest on the rocky points jutting out into the blue Pacific. On Isla Ixtapa, you'll find good snorkeling, diving, and other watersports. Gear is available for rent on the island. Be sure to catch the last water taxi back at 5pm, and double-check that time upon arrival on the island.

Local travel agencies can usually arrange day trips to Los Morros de Los Pericos islands for **birding,** though it's less expensive to rent a boat with a guide at Playa Linda. The islands are offshore from Ixtapa's main beach.

Sunset cruises on the sailboat *Picante,* arranged through **Yates del Sol** (✆ 755/554-2694 or -8270; www.picantecruises.com), depart from the Zihuatanejo town marina at Puerto Mío. The evening cruises last 2 hours, cost $54 (£26) per person, and include an open bar and hors d'oeuvres. There's also a "Sail and Snorkel Adventure" day trip to **Playa Manzanillo** on the very comfortable, rarely crowded sailboat. The 4-hour trip begins at 10am, costs $74 (£37) per person, and includes an open bar and lunch (snorkeling gear $7/£3.50 extra). Another option is the *Dancer Cruise* (✆ 755/544-8302; www.dancercruise.com), which also offers sunset and snorkeling trips departing from Zihuatanejo Bay for roughly the same prices. Schedules and special trips vary, so check the website for current information.

You can arrange **fishing trips** with the **boat cooperative** (✆ 755/554-2056) at the Zihuatanejo town pier. They cost $180 to $450 (£90–£225), depending on boat size, number of people, trip length, and so on. Most trips last about 7 hours. The cooperative only accepts cash; no credit cards. The price includes soft drinks, beer, bait, and fishing gear, but not lunch. You'll pay more for a trip arranged through a local travel agency. The least expensive trips are on small launches called *pangas;* most have shade. Both small-game and deep-sea fishing are offered. The fishing is adequate, though not on par with that of Mazatlán or Baja. Other trips combine fishing with a visit to the near-deserted ocean beaches that extend for miles along the coast. Sam Lushinsky at **Ixtapa Sport-fishing Charters,** 19 Depue Lane, Stroudsburg, PA 18360 (✆ 570/688-9466; fax 570/688-9554; www.ixtapasportfishing.com), is a noted outfitter. Prices range from $210 to $445 (£105–£223) per day, for 8 to 13m (25–42 ft.) custom cruisers, fully equipped. They accept MasterCard and Visa.

Boating and fishing expeditions from the new **Marina Ixtapa,** a bit north of the Ixtapa Hotel Zone, can also be arranged. As a rule, everything available in or through the marina is more expensive and more Americanized.

Sailboats, sailboards, and other **watersports equipment** rentals are usually available at stands on Playa La Ropa, Playa las Gatas, Isla Ixtapa, and at the main beach, Playa Palmar, in Ixtapa. There's **parasailing** at La Ropa and Palmar. **Kayaks** are available for rent at hotels in Ixtapa and some watersports operations on Playa La Ropa. **The Tides** has a beach club in front of the hotel on La Ropa with sailboat, sailboard, and kayak rentals open to the public.

The PADI-certified **Carlo Scuba,** on Playa Las Gatas (© **755/554-6003;** www. carloscuba.com), arranges **scuba-diving trips.** Fees start at $60 (£30) for a one-tank dive, or $80 (£40) for two dives, including all equipment and a drink. This shop has been around since 1962, and is very knowledgeable about the area, which has nearly 30 different dive sites, including walls and caves. Diving takes place year-round, though the water is clearest July to August and November to February, when visibility is 30m (100 ft.) or better. The nearest decompression chamber is in Ixtapa Marina. Advance reservations for dives are advised during Christmas and Easter.

Surfing is particularly good at **Petacalco Beach** north of Ixtapa. **Swimming with dolphins** is possible at **Delfiniti Ixtapa** (www.delfiniti.com), arranged through any of the hotels or travel agents in town.

GOLF, TENNIS & HORSEBACK RIDING   In **Ixtapa,** the **Club de Golf Ixtapa Palma Real** (© **755/553-1062** or -1163), in front of the Barceló Hotel, has an 18-hole course designed by Robert Trent Jones, Jr. The greens fee is $85 (£44); caddies cost $25 (£13) for 18 holes, $20 (£10) for 9 holes; electric carts are $35 (£18); and clubs are $30 (£15). Tee times begin at 7am. The **Marina Ixtapa Golf Course** (© **755/553-1410;** fax 755/553-0825), designed by Robert von Hagge, has 18 challenging holes. The greens fee is $90 (£45); carts cost $35 (£18); caddies cost $20 (£10); and club rental is $35 (£18). Discounted rates are available after 1:30pm. The first tee time is 7am. Call for reservations 24 hours in advance. Both courses accept American Express, MasterCard, and Visa.

In Ixtapa, the **Club de Golf Ixtapa** (© **755/553-1062** or -1163) has lighted **public tennis courts.** Fees are $85 (£43) an hour during the day, $14 (£7) at night. Call for reservations. In Zihuatanejo, the **Tides** (© **755/555-5500**) has lit tennis courts open to $30 (£15) an hour; private lessons cost $70 (£35) an hour.

For **horseback riding,** the largest local stable is on **Playa Linda** (no phone), offering guided trail rides from the Playa Linda beach (about 13km/8 miles north of Ixtapa). It's just next to the pier where the water taxis debark to Isla Ixtapa. Groups of three or more riders can arrange their own tour, which is especially nice around sunset (though you'll need mosquito repellent). Riders can choose to trace the beach to the mouth of the river and back through coconut plantations, or hug the beach for the entire ride (which usually lasts 1–1½ hr.). The fee is around $40 (£20), cash only. Travel agencies in either town can arrange your trip but will charge a bit more for transportation. Reservations are suggested in high season. Another good place to ride is in Playa Larga. There is a ranch on the first exit coming from Zihuatanejo (no phone, but you can't miss it—it is the first corral to the right as you drive toward the beach). The horses are in excellent shape. The fee is about $40 (£20) for 1½ hours, and includes transportation to and from your hotel as well as a drink. To arrange riding in advance, call co-owner Ignacio Mendiola on his cellphone at © **755/559-8884.**

SHOPPING
ZIHUATANEJO
Zihuatanejo has its quota of T-shirt and souvenir shops, but it has also become a better place to buy crafts, folk art, and jewelry. Shops are generally open Monday through Saturday from 10am to 2pm and 4 to 8pm. Many better shops close Sunday, but some smaller souvenir stands stay open, and hours vary.

Downtown Zihuatanejo

ACCOMMODATIONS ■
Amuleto **15**
Brisas del Mar **8**
Bungalows Ley **7**
La Casa Que Canta **10**
Posada Citlali **4**
The Tides **13**
Villa Guadalupe **9**
Villas San Sebastián **12**

DINING ◆
Coconuts **3**
Kau-Kan **11**
La Casa Vieja **6**
La Perla **14**
La Sirena Gorda **2**
Nueva Zelanda **1**

ATTRACTIONS ●
Museo de Arqueologia **5**

To Ixtapa

Main Bus Terminal

Avenida Morelos

Tres Estrellas Bus Terminal

Paseo Zihuatanejo

Paseo del Palmar

I. Altamirano

Cuauhtémoc

Avenida Nava

Vicente Guerrero

Benito Juárez

C. González

Municipal Market

Kioto   Plaza

5 de Mayo

Galeana

Ejido

Paseo de la Boquita

Canal

Calle Adelita

Artisan's Market

N. Bravo
Pedro Ascencio

Avenida Ramírez

Calle Mateos

Las Salinas

J.N. Alvarez del Pescador

Paseo

Playa Madera

Playa Municipal

Muelle Pier

Camino a playa la Ropa

Bahía de Zihuatanejo

Playa La Ropa

Punta Godomia

Bus 🚌
Post Office ✉

Playa Las Gatas

0   330 feet
0   100 meters

The **artisans' market** on Calle Cinco de Mayo is a good place to start shopping before moving on to specialty shops. It's open daily from 8am to 9pm. The **municipal market** on Avenida Benito Juárez sprawls over several blocks (about 5 blocks inland from the waterfront), but most vendors hawk the same things—*huaraches,* hammocks, and baskets. On the sand next to the pier, there's a daily fish market, and just behind it on Paseo del Pescador there's a small seashell market. Spreading inland from the waterfront some 3 or 4 blocks are numerous small shops well worth exploring.

Besides the places listed below, check out **Alberto's,** Cuauhtémoc 12 and 15 (no phone), for jewelry. Also on Cuauhtémoc, 2 blocks down from the Nueva Zelanda Coffee Shop, is a small shop that looks like a market stand and sells beautiful tablecloths, napkins, and other linens; all are handmade in Aguascalientes.

Casa Marina   This small complex extends from the waterfront to Alvarez near Cinco de Mayo and houses five shops, each specializing in handcrafted wares from all over Mexico. Items include handsome rugs, textiles, masks, colorful woodcarvings, and silver jewelry. Café Marina, the small coffee shop in the complex, sells shelves and shelves of used paperback books in several languages. Open daily from 9am to 9pm during the high season, Monday through Saturday 9am to 2pm and 5 to 9pm the rest of the year. Paseo del Pescador 9. © 755/554-2373.

El Jumil   With small fishing boats pulled up on the sand just in front, this exotic beachside store sells coconut shell masks, exotic figurines, indigenous masks (including those used for ceremonial dances), Oaxacan pottery, and other regional art and crafts. Casa Marina, Paseo del Pescador 9. © 755/554-6191.

Fruity Keiko   Next to Coconuts restaurant (p. 417), this impressive little shop sells gorgeous gifts from across Mexico. Fruity Keiko carries carefully selected crafts and folk art, including some made by Mexico's best present-day artists. There's also a small selection of regional jewelry, handmade dresses, and Talavera pottery. Prices are higher here than if you were in the towns where these goods are actually made. Open Monday through Saturday from 10am to 9pm and Sunday from noon to 8pm. Vicente Guerrero 5 at Alvarez, opposite the Hotel Citali. © 755/554-6578.

IXTAPA

Shopping in Ixtapa is not especially memorable, with T-shirts and Mexican crafts the usual wares. **Ferrioni, Bye-Bye, Aca Joe,** and **Navale** sell brand-name sportswear. All of these shops are in the same area on Bulevar Ixtapa, across from the beachside hotels, and most are open daily from 9am to 2pm and 4 to 9pm.

Decoré Ixtapa   This small boutique shop at the entrance to the Ixtapa Marina sells fine Mexican furniture and decorations. Among the selections are wood and glass furnishings, onyx lamps, beautiful vases, handbags, and other luxury items. Bulevar Ixtapa. © 755/553-3550. www.decoreixtapa.com.

La Fuente   This terrific shop carries gorgeous Talavera pottery, jaguar-shaped wicker tables, hand-blown glassware, masks, tin mirrors and frames, hand-embroidered clothing from Chiapas, and wood furniture. Open daily from 9am to 10pm during high season, daily from 10am to 9pm in low season. Los Patios Center, Bulevar Ixtapa. © 755/553-0812.

WHERE TO STAY

Larger high-rise hotels and all-inclusive resorts, dominate accommodations in Ixtapa and on Playa Madera. Package deals for these are readily available on line. There are only a few choices in the budget range. If you're looking for lower-priced rooms, Zihuatanejo offers more selection and better values, although it also has some very expensive (and wonderful) boutique hotels. Lodgings in both towns offer free parking. High season here generally runs from November 15 to April 30, and low season from May 1 to November 14. The rates quoted below do not include the 17% tax.

ZIHUATANEJO

Some of the hotels in Zihuatanejo and its nearby beach communities are more economical than those in Ixtapa, while others are far more expensive and exclusive. The term "bungalow" is used loosely—it may mean an individual unit with a kitchen and bedroom, or just a bedroom. It may also be like a hotel, in a two-story building with multiple units, some of which have kitchens. It may be cozy or rustic, with or without a patio or balcony. Accommodations in town are generally very basic, though clean and comfortable.

Playa Madera and Playa La Ropa, separated by a craggy shoreline, are both accessible by road. Prices tend to be higher here than in town, but the value is much better, and people tend to find that the beautiful, tranquil setting is worth the extra cost. The town is 5 minutes away by taxi and 20 minutes by foot.

In Town
Inexpensive
Posada Citlali   In this cheerful, three-story hotel, small rooms with fans surround a shaded, plant-filled courtyard that holds comfortable rockers and chairs. It's centrally located and a good value for the price, but very basic. Bottled water is in help-yourself containers on the patio. The stairway to the top two floors is narrow and steep.

Vicente Guerrero 3 (near Alvarez), 40880 Zihuatanejo, Gro. ☏ 755/554-2043. 19 units. $35–$50 (£17–£25) double. No credit cards. *In room:* TV, fan, no phone.

Playa Madera
Madera Beach is a 15-minute walk along the street, a 10-minute walk along the beach pathway, or a cheap taxi ride from Zihuatanejo. Most of the accommodations are on Calle Eva S. de López Mateos, the road overlooking the beach. Many hotels are set against the hill and have steep stairways.

Moderate
Brisas del Mar   This simple but enchanted beach hotel has just 30 cheerful suites, all with private terraces overlooking Zihuatanejo Bay. The larger and more expensive units offer separate sitting areas, Jacuzzi tubs, and kitchenettes. Located above Playa Madera, the family-run establishment is known for its friendly service, and maid service includes an artistic presentation of flower petals on the bed. There's direct beach access, a pool, and spa services, including in-room massages upon request. The restaurant and lounge terrace boast a wonderful view of the sea.

Calle Eva S. de López Mateos s/n, Playa Madera, 40880 Zihuatanejo, Gro. ☏ 755/554-2142. www.hotelbrisas delmar.com. 30 units. High season $149–$211 (£75–£106) double; low season $102–$161 (£51–£81) double. MC, V. **Amenities:** Restaurant; bar; outdoor pool, gift shop, massage, laundry service. *In room:* TV.

Inexpensive
Bungalows Ley   No two suites are the same at this small complex, one of the nicest on Playa Madera. If you're traveling with a group, you may want to book the most expensive suite (Club Madera); it has a rooftop terrace, outdoor bar and grill, and spectacular view. All the units are immaculate; the simplest are studios with one king bed and a kitchen in the same room. Rooms have terraces or balconies just above the beach, and all are decorated in pastel colors. Bathrooms, however, tend to be small and dark, with showers only. The hotel has no pool but leads right to the beach.

Calle Eva S. de López Mateos s/n, Playa Madera (Apdo. Postal 466), 40880 Zihuatanejo, Gro. ☏ 755/554-4087. www.zihua.net/bungalosley. 8 units. $90 (£45) double with A/C; $170 (£85) 2-bedroom suite with kitchen (up to 4 persons). Low-season discounts available after 6 nights stay. MC, V. Follow Mateos to the right, up a slight hill; it's on your left. *In room:* A/C, TV, safe.

Playa La Ropa
Playa La Ropa is a 20- to 25-minute walk south of town on the east side of the bay, or it's a $4 (£2) taxi ride.

Expensive

Amuleto ⭐⭐   Perched on a hill high above the bay, this intimate boutique hotel was designed for people who want to relax in luxury and exclusivity. Amuleto, which has only six units, boasts stunning panoramic views of Zihuatanejo Bay that make it seem like you're on top of the world. The *palapa*-covered restaurant serves innovative international food and overlooks a small infinity pool framed by the bay. Each of the bungalow-like units is individually decorated with Mexican and Asian designs using organic textures and earth colors. The *palapa* suite, for example, features meticulous stone, tile, and woodwork, a bed with 1,000-thread-count Egyptian cotton sheets, a separate sitting area with onyx lamps and bamboo chairs, a rooftop terrace with its own hammock surrounded by bougainvillea, and a private plunge pool. The eco-friendly hotel offers gourmet breakfasts and customizes dishes upon request.

Calle Escénica 9, Playa La Ropa, 40880 Zihuatanejo, Gro. Ⓒ 213/280-1037 in the U.S., or 755/544-6222. Fax 310/496-0286 in the U.S. www.amuleto.net. 6 units. High season $400–$700 (£200–£350) double; low season $250–$550 (£125–£275) double. $100 (£50) extra person. AE, MC, V. **Amenities:** Restaurant; outdoor pool, gym, massage. *In room:* A/C, free Wi-Fi, minibar, safe.

La Casa Que Canta ⭐⭐⭐   "The House that Sings" opened in 1992, an exclusive boutique hotel that sits on a mountainside overlooking Zihuatanejo Bay. It's one of the most romantic accommodations in the world. The striking molded-adobe architecture typifies the rustic-chic style known as Mexican Pacific, with gentle music that plays across the different walkways. Individually decorated rooms have handsome natural-tile floors, unusual painted Michoacán furniture, antiques, and stretched-leather *equipale*-style chairs and tables with hand-loomed fabrics throughout. All of the exquisite rooms offer large, beautifully furnished terraces with bay views. Hammocks hang under the thatched-roof terraces. Most of the spacious units are suites, and 10 of them have private pools. Rooms meander up and down the hillside, and while no staircase is terribly long, there are no elevators. An adjacent private villa, El Murmello, has four suites, all with private plunge pools. A "well-being" center offers massage, spa services, and yoga. La Casa Que Canta sits off the road leading to Playa La Ropa, but not on any beach (Playa La Ropa is down a steep hill). The hotel's service is remarkably gracious, and you'll find La Casa Que Canta pretty close to heaven.

Camino Escénico a Playa La Ropa, 40880 Zihuatanejo, Gro. Ⓒ 888/523-5050 in the U.S., or 755/555-7000, -7026, or -7030. Fax 755/554-7900. www.lacasaquecanta.com. 21 units. $465–$840 (£233–£420) double; 5-night minimum stay required Jan–Apr. AE, MC, V. Children younger than 16 not accepted. **Amenities:** Restaurant (open to outside guests with reservation only); bar; freshwater outdoor pool on main terrace; saltwater outdoor pool on bottom level; spa; fitness center; yoga and stretching; cooking classes; boutique shop; room service; laundry service. *In room:* A/C, minibar.

The Tides ⭐⭐   Under changed management at what was previously Villa del Sol, The Tides sits on one of Mexico's most beautiful beaches. Suites feature one or two bedrooms, living areas, large terraces, and private plunge pools. Rooms are decorated with modern Mexican touches and include comfy lounges, excellent reading lights, CD players, and hammocks that beckon at siesta time. There are 11 beachside suites and one presidential suite. Those units that don't overlook the beach surround a fountain-filled lagoon and tropical gardens with enchanted lighting at night. Service remains first-rate, though perhaps not as personalized as when this was Villa del Sol. The Tides allows children only in two-bedroom suites and generally has a quiet feel. The meal plan (breakfast and dinner) is mandatory in December and includes an excellent variety of cuisine. In addition to the exquisite beach area, pools, restaurants, and bars, the Tides offers a full-service spa, tennis courts, and beach club. You can even request a massage on the sand.

Playa la Ropa (Apdo. Postal 84), 40880 Zihuatanejo, Gro. © **866/905-9560** in the U.S., or 755/555-5500. Fax 755/554-2758. www.tideszihuatanejo.com. 70 units. High season $500–$550 (£250–£275) double, $875–$1,700 suite (£438–£850); low season $330–$360 (£165–£180) double, $570–$1,150 suite (£285–£575) double. Meal plan $75 (£38) per person in Dec (mandatory). AE, MC, V. **Amenities:** 2 open-air beachside restaurants; 3 bars; 4 outdoor pools (including 18m/59-ft. lap pool); 2 lighted tennis courts; full-service spa; tour desk; car rental; salon; room service. In room: A/C, TV, free Wi-Fi, minibar, hair dryer, safe.

Moderate

Villa Guadalupe 🏖🏖 *(Finds* A long wood staircase descends through jungle-like surroundings alongside the tiered villas of Villas Guadalupe, toward the sea. The adobe wall and *palapa*-roof villas seem to blend into the landscape, and carefully chosen pieces of Mexican art add to the magical ambience. Each of the individually decorated rooms at this boutique hotel has beach white furnishings and a private terrace with a spectacular view of Zihuatanejo Bay; the largest suite has its own plunge pool. Service is personalized and friendly, and the hotel has a very relaxed, intimate feel. Continental breakfast is served by the small infinity pool, and a beautiful restaurant looks over the water at the sister Tentaciones Hotel, just up the hill. This is the most luxurious accommodation you will find in Zihuatanejo at this price.

Camino Escénico a Playa La Ropa, 40880 Zihuatanejo, Gro. © **755/554-3443.** Fax 755/554-6185. www.zihuatanejo.net/villa-guadalupe. 8 units. High season $170–$400 (£85–£200) double; low season $115–$300 (£58–£150) double. AE, MC, V. Follow the road leading south out of town toward Playa La Ropa, take the 1st right after the traffic circle, and go left on Adelita. **Amenities:** Breakfast terrace; outdoor pool. In room: TV, minibar, safe.

Villas San Sebastián On the mountainside above Playa La Ropa, this nine-villa complex offers great views of Zihuatanejo's bay. The one- and two-bedroom villas surround tropical vegetation and a central swimming pool. Each has a kitchenette and a spacious private terrace. The personalized service is one reason these villas come so highly recommended; owner Luis Valle, whose family has lived in this community for decades, is usually available to help guests with any questions or needs.

Bulevar Escénico Playa La Ropa (across from the Dolphins Fountain). © **755/554-4154.** Fax 755/554-3220. 11 units. High season $145 (£73) 1-bedroom villa, $255 (£128) 2-bedroom villa; low season $98 (£49) 1-bedroom villa, $165 (£83) 2-bedroom villa. No credit cards. **Amenities:** Outdoor pool. In room: TV, A/C; free Wi-Fi, kitchenette.

Playa Zihuatanejo
Moderate

Casa Kau-Kan 🏖🏖 Casa Kau-Kan is an upscale bohemian oasis on the long, secluded beach of Playa Larga. It's located about 20-minutes south of Zihuatanejo on the open Pacific Ocean. The spacious bungalow-like accommodations surrounded by palm trees feature private sitting areas, canopied beds, and bamboo furnishings; four have private terrace pools. Owned by Ricardo Rodriguez who also runs Kau-Kan restaurant (p. 417), the hotel serves delicious fresh seafood. There's not much to do in the immediate surroundings except tan, swim, eat, read, and enjoy the quiet lazy days, although horseback riding and kite-surfing are also offered on the beach immediately in front. You should be an experienced swimmer to go in the ocean here, which typically has waves perfect for body-surfing. Hotel service is friendly and extremely attentive(whether it's a coconut or a cocktail you desire, it'll be right up.

Playa Larga s/n, 40880 Zihuatanejo, Gro. © **755/554-8446.** Fax 755/554-5731. www.casakaukan.com. 10 units. High season $120–$235 (£60–£118) double; low season $90–$200 (£45–£100) double. AE, MC, V. Children younger than 15 not accepted. **Amenities:** Restaurant; pool. In room: A/C, minibar, safe.

IXTAPA
Expensive
Barceló Ixtapa *(Kids) (Value)* An excellent value and a great choice for families, this grand 12-story all-inclusive resort hotel (formerly the Sheraton) has large, handsomely furnished public areas facing the beach. It's an inviting place to sip a drink and people-watch. Most rooms have balconies with ocean or mountain views. Nonsmoking rooms are available. Gardens surround the large pool, with a swim-up bar and separate section for children. They host a Mexican fiesta night on Wednesdays.

Bulevar Ixtapa, 40880 Ixtapa, Gro. (C) 755/555-2000. Fax 755/553-2438. www.barcelo.com. 340 units. High season $380 (£190) double all-inclusive; low season $270 (£135) double all-inclusive. AE, DC, MC, V. **Amenities:** 4 restaurants; lobby bar; nightclub; beachside pool; fitness room; concierge; travel agency; car rental; salon; room service; laundry service; rooms for those w/limited mobility. *In room:* A/C, TV, minibar, free Wi-Fi, safe.

Las Brisas Ixtapa *(Kids)(Kids)* Set above the high-rise hotels of Ixtapa on a rocky promontory, Las Brisas is the best of Ixtapa's resorts. Notable for its private beach cove and striking stepped architecture, designed by renowned architect Ricardo Legorreta, Las Brisas features large stone and stucco public areas, recently renovated guest rooms with upscale beach decor and oceanview terraces with hammocks, and multitier swimming pools with waterfalls. All rooms face the hotel's gorgeous private beach, which can be accessed by an elevator; although enticing, the water is sometimes rough and can be dangerous for swimming. The six master suites come with private pools, and three floors are reserved for nonsmokers. Beach Club rooms offer upgraded amenities, complimentary cocktails, and continental breakfast. Internet specials are usually available, and guests receive discounts at a nearby golf course.

Bulevar Ixtapa s/n at Playa Vista Hermosa, 40880 Ixtapa, Gro. (C) 888/559-4329 in the U.S., or 755/553-2121. Fax 755/553-1091. www.brisas.com.mx. 423 units. High season $285 (£143) deluxe double, $490 (£245) Royal Beach Club; low season $196 (£98) deluxe double, $230 (£115) Royal Beach Club. AE, MC, V. **Amenities:** 5 restaurants; 3 bars (including lobby bar w/piano music at sunset); 4 outdoor pools (1 for children); 4 lighted tennis courts w/pro on request; fitness center; travel agency; car rental; shopping arcade; salon; room service; massage; babysitting; salon; laundry service; rooms for those w/limited mobility; executive rooms; elevator to secluded beach. *In room:* A/C, TV, minibar, hair dryer, safe.

NH Krystal Ixtapa *(Kids)(Kids)* Krystal hotels are known in Mexico for quality rooms and service, and this was the original hotel in the chain. It upholds its reputation for attentive service and is particularly welcoming toward families. Many staff members have been with the NH Krystal for its more than 20 years of operation and are on hand to greet return guests. This large, V-shaped hotel has ample grounds and a terrific pool area. Most of the spacious guest rooms feature oceanview balconies and tile bathrooms, while master suites have larger balconies that double as living areas. Some rates include breakfast buffet. The center of Ixtapa nightlife is here, at the hotel's **Christine** dance club.

Bulevar Ixtapa s/n, 40880 Ixtapa, Gro. (C) 888/726-0528 in the U.S., or 755/555-0510. Fax 755/553-0226. www. nh-hotels.com. 255 units. High season $250 (£125) and up double, $350 (£175) suite; low season $100 (£50) and up double, $350 (£175) suite. 2 children younger than 12 stay free in parent's room. Ask about special packages. AE, DC, MC, V. **Amenities:** 4 restaurants; lobby bar; nightclub; outdoor pool and kids pool; gym; kids' club; travel agency; car rental; salon; room service; laundry service. *In room:* A/C, TV, minibar, safe.

WHERE TO DINE
ZIHUATANEJO
Zihuatanejo's **central market,** on Avenida Benito Juárez about 5 blocks inland from the waterfront, will whet your appetite for cheap and tasty food. It's best at breakfast

and lunch, before the market activity winds down in the afternoon. Look for what's hot and fresh. The market area is one of the coast's best places to shop and people-watch.

Moderate

Coconuts 𝒦𝒦 INTERNATIONAL/SEAFOOD   Not only is the food innovative and delicious, but the restaurant is also in a historic building—the oldest in Zihuatanejo. This popular restaurant in a tropical garden was the weigh-in station for Zihua's coconut industry in the late 1800s. "Fresh" is the operative word on this creative, seafood-heavy menu. Chef David Dawson checks what's fresh at the market, then uses only top-quality ingredients in dishes such as grilled red snapper or other fish prepared anyway you like, such as with fresh fruit salsa. The bananas flambé (for two) has earned a loyal following, with good reason. Expect friendly, efficient service here. Live music happens Sunday nights.

Augustín Ramírez 1 (at Vicente Guerrero). ⓒ 755/554-2518 or -7980. Reservations recommended. Main courses $12–$28 (£6–£14). AE, MC, V. High season daily 6–11pm. Closed July–Sept (rainy season).

Inexpensive

La Sirena Gorda MEXICAN   For one of the most popular breakfasts in town, head to La Sirena Gorda. "The Fat Mermaid," as it translates into English, serves a variety of eggs and omelets, hotcakes or French toast, and fruit with granola and yogurt. The house specialty is seafood tacos—fish in a variety of sauces, plus lobster—but I consider them overpriced, at $6 and $23 (£3 and £12) respectively. A taco is a taco is a . . . you know. I'd recommend something from the short list of daily specials, such as blackened red snapper, tuna, or steak. The food is excellent, and patrons enjoy the casual sidewalk-cafe atmosphere. Illustrations of colorful fat mermaids decorate the walls, and miniature wood boats hang from the ceiling.

Paseo del Pescador. ⓒ 755/554-2687. Breakfast $3–$5.50 (£1.50–£2.75); main courses $6–$15 (£3–£7.50). No credit cards. Thurs–Tues 8:30am–10:30pm. From the basketball court, face the water and walk to the right; La Sirena Gorda is on your right just before the town pier.

Nueva Zelanda MEXICAN   This open-air snack shop serves rich cappuccino sprinkled with cinnamon, fresh-fruit *licuados* (smoothies mixed with water or milk), and pancakes with real maple syrup. The mainstays are *tortas* and enchiladas, and service is friendly and efficient. There's a second location in Ixtapa, in the back section of the Los Patios shopping center (ⓒ 755/553-0838), next to Señor Frog's.

Cuauhtémoc 23 (at Ejido). ⓒ 755/554-2340. Tortas $3 (£1.50); enchiladas $6 (£3); *licuados* $2.50 (£1.75); cappuccino $2.50 (£1.25). No credit cards. Daily 7am–10pm. From the waterfront, walk 3 blocks inland on Cuauhtémoc; the restaurant is on your right.

PLAYA MADERA & PLAYA LA ROPA
Expensive

Kau-Kan 𝒦𝒦𝒦 MEDITERRANEAN/SEAFOOD   Candlelit tables and lamps dot this romantic open-air restaurant with an unforgettable view of Zihuatanejo Bay. There are just a handful of tables, but both the food and service are superb. Head Chef Ricardo Rodriguez supervises every detail, and the fresh dishes are prepared with care and meticulously presented. Among my favorite appetizers are crab and olive tarts and the mahimahi carpaccio. For a main dish, consider the baked potato stuffed with lobster, or the shrimp prepared in a basil and garlic sauce. To top off your meal, go for a pecan and chocolate cake served with dark-chocolate sauce, accompanied by one of the aromatic Central American coffees. If you're looking for a romantic dinner outside your hotel, reserve a candlelit table at Kau-Kan and try to arrive in time for the sunset.

Camino a Playa La Ropa. ⊘ 755/554-8446. Reservations recommended. Main courses $14–$34 (£7–£17). AE, MC, V. Daily 5–10:30pm. From downtown on the road to La Ropa, Kau-Kan is on the right side of the road past the 1st curve.

Moderate

La Casa Vieja ⊘ MEXICAN   A casual yet intimate Mexican restaurant at the entrance to Playa Madera, "The Old House" serves delicious fish and traditional dishes, such as filet *a la tampiqueña* (tenderloin steak) and *cochinita pibil* (slow-roasted pork). Among the fresh fish selections prepared anyway you like are tuna, red snapper, and mahimahi. Tiny white lights, twig lamps, and plants decorate the open-air dining room. Service is friendly and relaxed, and soft music plays in the background. The number of Mexicans dining here testifies to the restaurant's quality. Delicious *pozole* is served on Thursdays.

Josefa Ortíz de Domínguez 7. ⊘ 755/554-9770. Main courses $11–$17 (£5.50–£8.50). MC, V. Mon–Sat noon–11pm; Sun 9am–11pm. Restaurant is at the entrance of road leading into Playa Madera.

Inexpensive

La Perla SEAFOOD   Among the many *palapa*-style restaurants on Playa La Ropa, La Perla, with tables under the trees and thatched roof, is the most popular. Somehow, the combination of a long stretch of pale sand and plastic chairs under *palapas* and simple beach food served slowly make La Perla a local tradition. The menu is a mix of Mexican and "gringo" selections, including a 1-kilo (2.2-lb.) grilled or broiled lobster for $40 (£20). Cold beer and cocktails are available whether or not you eat.

Playa La Ropa. ⊘ 755/554-2700. Breakfast $3–$7.50 (£1.50–£3.75); main courses $9.50–$22 (£4.75–£11). AE, MC, V. Daily 11am–10pm; breakfast served 10am–noon. Near the southern end of La Ropa Beach, take the right fork in the road; there's a sign in the parking lot.

IXTAPA
Expensive

Beccofino ⊘⊘⊘ NORTHERN ITALIAN   This restaurant is a standout in Mexico. Owner Angelo Rolly Pavia serves the flavorful northern Italian specialties he grew up knowing and loving. I strongly recommend one of the homemade seafood pastas, which may include calamari, shrimp, clams, mussels, and crayfish. Ravioli, a house specialty, comes stuffed with beef or seafood. The garlic bread is terrific, and there's an extensive wine list. A popular place in a breezy marina location, the restaurant tends to be loud when it's crowded. It's also a popular breakfast spot.

Marina Ixtapa. ⊘ 755/553-1770. Breakfast $7–$18 (£3.50–£9); main courses $18–$28 (£9–£14). AE, MC, V. Daily 9:30am–11:30pm.

Villa de la Selva ⊘⊘ MEXICAN/MEDITERRANEAN   Clinging to the edge of a cliff, this elegant restaurant enjoys the most spectacular sea and sunset view in Ixtapa. Beautiful wood terraces surrounded by a palm and mango tree–filled jungle look directly over the bay, just steps below. Try to come early to get one of the best vistas, especially on the lower terrace. Hidden speakers create music that seems to come from the sea. The cuisine is artfully presented and classically rich. To start, I recommend the coconut shrimp in a mango and chile sauce or the tuna carpaccio. For a main course, a wonderful dish is *Filet Villa de la Selva,* red snapper topped with shrimp and hollandaise sauce. Finish with chocolate mousse or bananas Singapore, and come here with someone looking for romance.

Paseo de la Roca. ℭ **755/553-0362**. www.villadelaselva.com. Reservations recommended during high season. Main courses $19–$32 (£9.50–£26). AE, MC, V. Daily 6–11pm. Closed Sept.

Inexpensive

Casa Morelos ☞ MEXICAN   This is a great place for tasty, cheap Mexican seafood. You can order fresh fish anyway you like, such as with lemon and olive oil, mustard, orange, mango, garlic, or chile. You might have the delicious seafood fajitas, or perhaps shrimp enchiladas. The fish tacos *al pastor* are the best in the area. The *mar y tierra* is a succulent shrimp and steak dish, while *mar y mar* is shrimp and lobster. Service is friendly at this casual eatery, which offers indoor and outdoor seating.

Centro Comercial La Puerta. ℭ **755/553-0578**. Main dishes $13–$29 (£6.50–£15). MC, V. Daily 8am–midnight. Located next to Señor Frog's.

Golden Cookie Shop ☞ PASTRIES/DELI   This German bakery and deli's freshly baked goods beg for a detour, and the coffee menu is the most extensive in town. Come for one of the creative breakfast pancake plates, or for a healthy triple-decker sandwich. Nutritional cookies, breads, pastries, and cakes are available, as well as vegetarian and low-carb selections. Large sandwiches on fresh soft bread come with a choice of sliced meats.

Los Patios Center. ℭ **755/553-0310**. www.goldencookieshop.com.mx. Breakfast $4–$8 (£2–£4); sandwiches $7.50–$8.50 (£3.75–£4.25); main courses $8.50–$13 (£4.25–£6.50). MC, V. Daily 8am–3pm. Go to the second floor of "Los Patios" commercial center.

ZIHUATANEJO & IXTAPA AFTER DARK

With an exception or two, Zihuatanejo nightlife dies down around 11pm or midnight. For a good selection of clubs, dance spots, hotel fiestas, special events, and fun watering holes with live music and dancing, head for Ixtapa. Just keep in mind that the shuttle bus stops at 11pm, and a taxi to Zihuatanejo after midnight costs 50% more than the regular price. During the off season (after Easter and before Christmas), hours vary: Some places open only on weekends, while others close completely. In Zihuatanejo, a lively bar showing satellite TV sports, is **Bandido's,** at the corner of Cinco de Mayo and Pedro Ascencio in Zihuatanejo Centro, across from the Artisans' Market (ℭ **755/553-8072**). It features live music Wednesday through Saturday, and is open nightly until 2am. There's no cover, and people often come to salsa dance.

THE CLUB & MUSIC SCENE

Many dance clubs stay open until the last customers leave, so closing hours depend upon revelers. Most dance clubs have a ladies' night at least once a week—admission and drinks are free for women.

Carlos 'n' Charlie's   Knee-deep in bric-a-brac, silly sayings, and photos from the Mexican Revolution, this somewhat cheesy restaurant/nightclub offers party ambience and good food. The eclectic menu includes iguana in season (with Alka-Seltzer and aspirin on the house). Out back by the beach is a partly shaded open-air section with a raised wooden platform for "pier" dancing at night. The recorded rock 'n' roll mixes with sounds of the ocean surf. The restaurant is open daily from 10am to midnight; pier dancing is nightly from 9pm to 3am. A pool and bar are open here during the day. Bulevar Ixtapa, just north of the Best Western Posada Real, Ixtapa. ℭ **755/553-0085**. Cover (including 2 drink tokens) after 10pm $10 (£5). No cover Sun–Fri during off-season.

Christine   This longstanding dance club is best known for its midnight light show, which features classical music played on a mega sound system. A semicircle of tables in tiers overlooks the dance floor. The crowd tends to be in their 20s and 30s. No sneakers, flip-flops, or shorts are allowed, and reservations are recommended during high season. Open Thursday to Saturday at 10:30pm. Off-season hours vary. In the NH Krystal, Bulevar Ixtapa, Ixtapa. © 755/555-0510. Cover free–$20 (£10).

Señor Frog's   A companion restaurant to Carlos 'n' Charlie's, Señor Frog's has several dining sections and a warehouselike bar with raised dance floors. Large speakers play electronic, rock, and Latin music, sometimes even prompting dinner patrons to shimmy by their tables between courses. The restaurant is open daily from 6 to 11:30pm; the bar stays open until 4am. In the La Puerta Center, Bulevar Ixtapa, Ixtapa. © 755/553-2282. Friday cover (including 2 drinks) $10 (£5).

Zihablue   One of Zihuatanejo's few nightlife options, Zihuablue opened in late 2007 across from Kau-Kan restaurant. The chic Mediterranean lounge is an open-air oasis with a candlelit bar, small dance floor, canapé beds and sofas, and sand floor. Ambient music fills the air of this small, exclusive retreat, open from 8pm to 2am November through May. Above the lounge is a fine seafood restaurant. Carretera Escenica La Ropa s/n, next to Kau-Kan restaurant. © 755/554-4844. No cover.

HOTEL FIESTAS & THEME NIGHTS

A number of hotels hold Mexican fiestas and other special events that include dinner, drinks, live music, and entertainment for a fixed price (generally $44/£22). The **Barceló Ixtapa** (© 755/555-2000) stages a popular Wednesday night fiesta; the **Dorado Pacífico** (© 755/553-2025) in Ixtapa hosts a Tuesday night fiesta. Only the Barceló Ixtapa offers them in the off season. Call for reservations or visit a travel agency for tickets, and be sure you understand what the price covers, as drinks, tax, and tip are not always included.

3 Puerto Escondido ★★★

368km (228 miles) SE of Acapulco; 240km (149 miles) NW of Salina Cruz; 80km (50 miles) NW of Puerto Angel

Puerto Escondido seems disconnected from the rest of the world, an idyllic beach town stuck in time. I'd call it the best overall beach value in Mexico, and it retains the same casual beach feel that has drawn people here for decades. Although it has long been known as one of the world's top surf sites, today its appeal is broadening. Think alternative therapies, great vegetarian restaurants, hip nightlife, inexpensive hotel and dining options, and some of Mexico's best coffee shops. It's for those whose priorities include the dimensions of the surf break (big), the temperature of the beer (cold), the strength of the coffee (espresso), and the optimal tanning angle. The young and very aware crowd that comes here measures time by the tides, and the pace is relaxed.

The location of "Puerto," as the locals call it, makes it an ideal jumping-off point for ecological explorations of neighboring jungle and estuary sanctuaries, as well as indigenous mountain settlements. Increasingly, it attracts those seeking both spiritual and physical renewal, with abundant massage and bodywork services, yoga classes, and exceptional and varied healthful dining options.

People come from the United States, Canada, and Europe to stay for weeks and even months—easily and inexpensively. Expats have migrated here from Los Cabos, Acapulco, and Puerto Vallarta seeking what originally attracted them to their former homes—stellar beaches, friendly locals, and low prices. Added pleasures include an absence of beach vendors and time-share sales, an abundance of English speakers, and terrific, inexpensive dining and nightlife.

ACCOMMODATIONS

Best Western Posada Real **1**
Bungalows & Cabañas Acuario **8**
Hotel Arco Iris **7**
Hotel Casa Blanca **4**
Hotel Castillo de Reyes **2**
Hotel Flor de María **5**
Hotel Santa Fe **6**
Paraíso Escondido **3**
Rockaway **9**

Map not to scale

To Oaxaca ←

Av. 8 Norte
Av. 7 Norte
Av. 6 Norte
Av. 5 Norte
Av. 4 Norte
Av. 3 Norte
Av. 2 Norte
Av. 1 Norte
Av. Hidalgo

Av. 3 Oriente
Av. 2 Oriente
Av. 1 Oriente
Av. Oaxaca
Av. 1 Poniente
Av. 2 Poniente
Av. 3 Poniente
Av. 5 Poniente

Av. Benito Juárez

Carretera Costera

Av. Juárez

← To Acapulco

Playa Bacocho

Playa Carrizalillo

Camino a Puerto Angelito

Playa Puerto Angelito

Av. Unión

Av. Pérez Gazga

Av. Soledad
Av. Libertad
Av. Revolución
Av. Maris

Laguna Agua Dulce

Playa Principal

Playa Marineros

Playa Zicatela

Carretera Costera

Av. del Morro

To Puerto Ángel, Huatulco & Tehuantepec ↘

Faro (lighthouse)

PACIFIC OCEAN

Airport ✈
Church ✝
Information ℹ
Post Office ⊠

Gulf of Mexico

VERACRUZ
OAXACA
Puerto Escondido •
GUERRERO
MICHOACÁN
Mexico City ★
PACIFIC OCEAN

200 mi
200 km

This is a real place, not a produced resort. A significant number of visitors are European travelers, and it's common to hear a variety of languages on the beach and in the bars. Puerto Escondido is also a favorite among Mexican college students. Solo travelers will probably make new friends within an hour of arriving. There are still surfers here, lured by the best break in Mexico, but espresso cafes and live music are becoming just as ubiquitous.

The city has been dismissed as a colony of former hippies and settled backpackers, but it's so much more. I have a theory that those who favor Puerto are just trying to keep the place true to its name (*escondido* means "hidden") and undiscovered by tourists. Don't let them trick you—visit, and soon, before it, too, changes.

ESSENTIALS
GETTING THERE & DEPARTING
BY PLANE   Aero Tucán (✆ 954/582-3461), and **Aerovega** (✆ 954/582-0151) operate daily morning flights to and from Puerto Escondido on small planes; the fare is about $100 (£50) each way to Oaxaca. **Click Mexicana** (✆ 01-800/112-5425 toll-free in Mexico; www.click.com.mx) flies jets to and from Mexico City daily. The price is about $150 (£75) each way.

If flights to Puerto Escondido are booked, you have the (possibly less expensive) option of flying into **Huatulco** on a scheduled or charter flight. This is especially viable if your destination is Puerto Angel, which lies between Puerto Escondido and Huatulco. An airport taxi costs about $80 (£40) to Puerto Angel, and approximately $130 (£725) to Puerto Escondido. If you can find a local taxi, rather than a government-chartered cab, you can reduce these fares by about 50%, including the payment of a $5 (£2.50) mandatory airport exit tax. There is frequent bus service between the three destinations. **Budget** (✆ 958/581-9000 or 800/527-0700 in U.S) at the Huatulco airport, has cars available for one-way travel to Puerto Escondido, with an added drop charge of about $50 (£25). In Puerto Escondido, Budget is at the entrance to Bacocho (✆ 954/582-0312).

Arriving: The Puerto Escondido **airport** (airport code: PXM) is about 4km (2½ miles) north of the center of town, near Playa Bacocho. The *colectivo* **(minibus)** to hotels costs $3.50 (£1.75) per person. **Aerotransportes de Pasajeros Turistas de Oaxaca** sells *colectivo* tickets to the airport via **Turismo Dimar Travel Agency** (✆/fax 954/582-0737 or -2305) on Avenida Pérez Gasga (the pedestrian-only zone) next to Hotel Casa Blanca. A minibus picks you up at your hotel.

BY CAR   From Oaxaca, **Highway 175** via Pochutla is the least bumpy road. The 240km (149-mile) trip takes 5 to 6 hours. **Highway 200** from Acapulco is also a good road and should take about 6 hours to travel. However, this stretch of road has been the site of numerous car and bus hijackings and robberies at night in recent years—travel only during the day.

From Salina Cruz to Puerto Escondido is a 5-hour drive, past the Bahías de Huatulco and the turnoff for Puerto Angel. The road is paved but can be rutty during the rainy season. The trip from Huatulco to Puerto Escondido takes just under 2 hours; you can easily hire a taxi for a fixed rate of about $50 (£25) an hour.

BY BUS   Buses run frequently to and from Acapulco and Oaxaca, and south along the coast to and from Huatulco and Pochutla, the transit hub for Puerto Angel. The main bus station for **Estrella Blanca, Oaxaca Pacífico,** and **Estrella del Valle** is the

Central Camionera, just north of the city center. First-class buses run to Huatulco, Oaxaca, and Mexico City. Several buses also leave daily for Pochutla, Salina Cruz (5 hr.), and Oaxaca (7 hr. via second-class bus). **Cristóbal Colón** buses (© **954/582-1073**) serve Salina Cruz, Tuxtla Gutiérrez, San Cristóbal de las Casas, and Oaxaca.

Arriving: Minibuses from Pochutla or Huatulco will let you off anywhere, including the spot where Pérez Gasga leads down to the pedestrians-only zone.

ORIENTATION

VISITOR INFORMATION   The **State Tourist Office, SEDETUR** (© **954/582-0175**), which has a very helpful staff, is less than 1km (a half mile) from the airport at the corner of Carretera Costera and Bulevar Benito Juárez. It's open Monday through Friday from 8am to 5pm. A tourist kiosk at the west end of the Adoquín (in the town center) is open Monday through Saturday from 9am to 2pm and 4pm to 6pm.

CITY LAYOUT   Looking out on the Bahía Principal and its beach, to your left you'll see the eastern end of the bay, consisting of a small beach, **Playa Marineros,** followed by rocks jutting into the sea. Beyond this is **Playa Zicatela,** unmistakably the main surfing beach. Zicatela Beach has come into its own as the most popular area for visitors, with restaurants, bungalows, surf shops, and hotels, well back from the shoreline. The west side of the bay, to your right, is about 1.5km long (1 mile), with a lighthouse and a long stretch of fine sand. Beaches on this end are not quite as accessible by land, but hotels are overcoming this difficulty by constructing beach clubs reached by steep private roads and jeep shuttles.

The town of Puerto Escondido has roughly an east-west orientation, with the long Zicatela Beach turning sharply southeast. Residential areas behind Zicatela Beach tend to have unpaved streets; the older town, with paved streets, is north of the Carretera Costera (Hwy. 200). The streets are numbered; Avenida Oaxaca divides east *(oriente)* from west *(poniente),* and Avenida Hidalgo divides north *(norte)* from south *(sur).*

South of this is the original **tourist zone,** through which Avenida Pérez Gasga makes a loop. Part of this loop is a paved pedestrians-only zone, known locally as the Adoquín, after the hexagonal bricks used in its paving. Hotels, shops, restaurants, bars, travel agencies, and other services are all here. In the morning, taxis, delivery trucks, and private vehicles may drive here, but at noon it closes to all but foot traffic.

Avenida Pérez Gasga angles down from the highway at the east end; on the west, where the Adoquín terminates, it climbs in a wide northward curve to cross the highway, after which it becomes Avenida Oaxaca.

The beaches—Playa Principal in the center of town and Marineros and Zicatela, southeast of the town center—are connected. It's easy to walk from one to the other, crossing behind the separating rocks. Puerto Angelito, Carrizalillo, and Bacocho beaches are west of town and accessible by road or water. Playa Bacocho is where you'll find the few more expensive hotels.

GETTING AROUND   Almost everything is within walking distance of the Adoquín. **Taxis** around town are inexpensive; call © **954/582-0990** or -0955 for service. It's also easy to hire a boat and possible to walk beside the sea from the Playa Principal to the tiny beach of Puerto Angelito, though it's a bit of a hike.

FAST FACTS: Puerto Escondido

Area Code   The telephone area code is **954**.

Currency Exchange   Banamex, Bancomer, Banorte, and HSBC all have branches in town, and all will change money during business hours; hours vary, but you can generally find one of the above open Monday through Saturday from 9am to 3pm. ATMs are also available, as are currency-exchange offices.

Drugstore   **Farmacía de Más Ahorro,** Avenida 1 Norte at Avenida 2 Poniente (© **954/582-1911**), is open from 7am to 3am.

Hospital   **Unidad Médico–Quirúrgica del Sur,** Av. Oaxaca 113 (© **954/582-1288**), offers 24-hour emergency services and has English-speaking staff and doctor.

Internet Access   On Zicatela Beach, **Internet Acuario** is a small, extremely busy Internet service at the entrance to the Bungalows & Cabañas Acuario, Calle de Morro s/n (© **954/582-1026**). It's open daily from 8am to 10pm and charges just $1.50 (75p) per hour.

Post Office   The *correo,* on Avenida Oaxaca at the corner of Avenida 7 Norte (© **954/582-0959**), is open Monday through Friday from 8am to 3pm.

Safety   Depending on whom you talk to, you need to be wary of potential beach muggings, primarily at night. Lighting at Playa Principal and Playa Zicatela has caused the crime rate to drop considerably. Local residents say most incidents happen after tourists overindulge and then go for a midnight stroll along the beach. Puerto is so casual that it's an easy place to let your guard down. Don't carry valuables, and use common sense and normal precautions. Also, respect the power of the magnificent waves here. Drownings occur all too often.

Seasons   Season designations are somewhat arbitrary, but most consider high season to be from mid-December to January, around and during Easter week, July and August, and other school and business vacations.

Telephones   Numerous businesses offer long-distance telephone service. Many are along the Adoquín; several accept credit cards. The best bet remains a pre-paid Ladatel phone card.

WHAT TO SEE & DO IN PUERTO ESCONDIDO

BEACHES   Playa Principal, where small boats are available for fishing and tour services, and **Playa Marineros,** adjacent to the town center on a deep bay, are the best swimming beaches. Beach chairs and sun shades rent for about $5 (£2.50), which may be waived if you order food or drinks from the restaurants that offer them. **Playa Zicatela,** which has lifeguards and is known as the "Mexican Pipeline," adjoins Playa Marineros and extends southeast for several kilometers. The surfing part of Zicatela, with large curling waves, is about 4km (2½ miles) from the town center. Due to the size and strength of the waves (particularly in summer), it's not a swimming beach, and only experienced surfers should attempt to ride Zicatela's powerful waves. Stadium-style lighting has been installed in both of these areas, in an attempt to crack down on nighttime beach muggings. It has diminished the appeal of the Playa Principal restaurants—patrons now look into the bright lights rather than at the sea. Lifeguard service has recently been added to Playa Zicatela, although the lifeguards are known to go on strike. The best beach for learning how to surf is called **La Punta.**

Barter with one of the fishermen on the main beach for a ride to **Playa Manzanillo** and **Puerto Angelito,** two beaches separated by a rocky outcropping. Here, and at other small coves just west of town, swimming is safe and the overall pace is calmer than in town. You'll also find *palapas,* hammock rentals, and snorkeling equipment. The clear blue water is perfect for snorkeling. Local entrepreneurs cook fresh fish, tamales, and other Mexican dishes right at the beach. Puerto Angelito is also accessible by a road that's a short distance from town, so it tends to be busier. You can also take a cab to the cliff above **Playa Carrizalillo,** and descend one hundred odd stone stairs to a calm and secluded swimming beach. **Playa Bacocho** is on a shallow cove (dangerous for swimming) farther northwest and is best reached by taxi or boat rather than on foot. It's also the location of the Villa Sol Beach Club. A charge of $10 (£5) gives you access to pools, food and beverage service, and facilities.

SURFING   Zicatela Beach, 2.5km (1½ miles) southeast of Puerto Escondido's town center, is a world-class surf spot. A surfing competition in August and Fiesta Puerto Escondido, held for at least 3 days each November, celebrate Puerto Escondido's renowned waves. There is also a surfing exhibition and competition in February, for Carnaval. The tourism office can supply dates and details. Beginning surfers often start at Playa Marineros, before graduating to Zicatela's awesome waves, although you will see intermediate surfers out at **La Punta,** at the southernmost end of Playa Zicatela. The waves and strong currents make Zicatela dangerous for swimming.

NESTING RIDLEY TURTLES   The beaches around Puerto Escondido and Puerto Angel are nesting grounds for the endangered Ridley turtle. During the summer, tourists, on lucky occasions, can see the turtles laying eggs or observe the hatchlings trekking to the sea.

Escobilla Beach near Puerto Escondido seems to be the favored nesting grounds of the Ridley turtle. In 1991, the Mexican government established the Centro Mexicano la Tortuga, known locally as the **Turtle Museum.** On view are examples of all species of marine turtles living in Mexico, plus six species of freshwater turtles and two species of land turtles. The center ((*C*) **958/584-3376**) lies on **Mazunte Beach** ⊛, near the town of the same name about an hour and a half from Puerto Escondido. Hours are Wednesday through Sunday from 9:30am to 5pm; suggested donation is $2 (£1). If you come between July and September, ask to join an overnight expedition to Escobilla Beach to see mother turtles scuttle to the beach to lay their eggs. The museum is near a unique shop that sells excellent naturally produced soaps, shampoos, bath oils, and other personal-care products. All are packaged by the local community as part of a project to replace lost income from turtle poaching. Buses go to Mazunte from Puerto Angel about every half-hour, and a taxi ride is around $5.50 (£2.75). You can fit this in with a trip to Zipolite Beach (see "A Trip to Puerto Angel: Backpacking Beach Haven," later in this chapter). Buses from Puerto Escondido don't stop in Mazunte; you can cover the 65km (40 miles) in a taxi or rental car.

The tourism cooperative at **Ventanilla** provides another chance to get up close to the turtles. The villagers here have created their own ecological reserve that encompasses a nearby lagoon, inhabited by crocodiles and dozens of species of birds, and a beach where sea turtles lay their eggs. A boat ride to see the crocs costs $4 (£2) and

Ecotours & Other Adventurous Explorations

An excellent provider of ecologically oriented tour services is **Rutas de Aventura** (★, Hotel Santa Fe (© 954/582-0170; www.rutasdeaventura.com.mx). Gustavo Boltjes speaks fluent English and offers kayak adventures, hiking excursions, and mountain-bike tours. He also leads waterfall hikes, camping trips, and overnight agrotourism adventures to learn about local farming and organic coffee production, including trips to a local coffee plantation.

Turismo Dimar Travel Agency, on the landward side just inside the Adoquín (© 954/582-0737 or -2305; fax 954/582-1551; vww.viajesdimar.com; daily 8am–9pm), is another excellent source of information and can arrange all types of tours and travel. Manager Gaudencio Díaz Martinez speaks English and can arrange individualized tours or more organized ones, such as **Michael Malone's Hidden Voyages Ecotours.** Malone, a Canadian ornithologist, leads dawn and sunset trips in high season (winter) to **Manialtepec Lagoon,** a bird-filled mangrove lagoon about 20km (12 miles) northwest of Puerto Escondido. The tour ($40/£20) includes a stop on a secluded beach for a swim.

One of the most popular all-day tours offered by both companies is to **Chacahua Lagoon National Park,** about 65km (40 miles) west. It costs $45 (£23) with Dimar, $52 (£26) with Michael Malone. These are true ecotours— small groups treading lightly. You visit a beautiful sandy spit of beach and the lagoon, which has incredible bird life and flowers, including black orchids. Crocodiles are sometimes spotted here, too. Locals provide fresh barbecued fish on the beach. If you know Spanish and get information from the tourism office, it's possible to stay overnight under a small *palapa*, but bring insect repellent.

An interesting and slightly out-of-the-ordinary excursion is **Aventura Submarina,** Av. Pérez Gasga 601A, in front of the tourism office (© 954/582-2353). Jorge, who speaks fluent English and is a certified scuba instructor, guides individuals and small groups of qualified divers along the Coco trench just offshore. The price is $60 (£30) for a two-tank dive. This outfit offers a refresher scuba course at no extra charge. Jorge also arranges deep-sea fishing, surfing, and trips to lesser-known yet nearby swimming beaches. **Omar** (© 954/559-4406) runs dolphin watching tours in high season (winter).

Fishermen keep their colorful *pangas* (small boats) on the beach beside the Adoquín. A **fisherman's tour** around the coastline in a *panga* costs about $35 (£18), but a ride to Puerto Angelito beaches is only $5 (£2.50). Most hotels offer or will gladly arrange tours to meet your needs. The waters here are filled with marlin, tuna, and swordfish.

nothing on the menu at the restaurant is over $7 (£3.50). Turtles lay their eggs here year round, although summer is the prime season, so there's always a possibility that a nest is about to hatch. Helping the locals release the eggs is free. Ventanilla is a $2 (£1) taxi ride from Mazunte or the nearby beaches, but if you're planning to stay past sunset, ask your driver to wait; it's a long walk in the dark to the main highway.

GUIDED WALKING TOURS   For local information and guided walking tours, visit the **Oaxaca Tourist Bureau** booth (© **954/582-1186;** ginainpuerto@yahoo. com). It's just west of the pedestrian street. Ask for Gina, who speaks excellent English and is incredibly helpful. She provides information with a smile, and many say she knows more about Puerto Escondido than any other person. On her days off, Gina offers walking tours to the market and to little-known nearby ruins. Filled with history and information on native vegetation, a day with Gina promises fun, adventure, and insight into local culture.

A Mixtec ceremonial center was discovered in early 2000, just east of Puerto Escondido, and since is considered a major discovery. The site covers many acres with about 10 pyramids and a ball court, with the pyramids appearing as hills covered in vegetation. A number of large carved stones have been found. Situated on a hilltop, it commands a spectacular view of Puerto Escondido and the Pacific coast. The large archaeological site spans several privately owned plots of land and is not open to the public, although Gina has been known to offer a guided walking tour to it.

SHOPPING

During high season, businesses and shops are generally open all day. During low season, many close between 2 and 4pm.

The Adoquín holds a row of tourist shops selling straw hats, postcards, and T-shirts, plus a few excellent shops featuring Guatemalan, Oaxacan, and Balinese clothing and art. You can also get a tattoo or rent surfboards and boogie boards. Interspersed among the shops, hotels, restaurants, and bars are pharmacies and minimarkets. The largest of these is **Oh! Mar,** Av. Pérez Gasga 502. It sells anything you'd need for a day at the beach, plus phone (Ladatel) cards and Cuban cigars.

Also of interest is **Bazar Santa Fe** 𝕮𝕮, Hotel Santa Fe lobby, Calle del Morro s/n, Zicatela Beach (© **954/582-0170**), a small shop that sells antiques, vintage Oaxacan embroidered clothing, jewelry, religious artifacts, and gourmet organic coffee. At **Bikini Brazil,** Playa Zicatela, Calle del Morro s/n (© **954/582-2555**), you'll find the hottest bikinis under the sun imported from Brazil, land of the *tanga* (string bikini). The sexy competition is **Amazonia do Brazil,** Playa Zicatela, Calle del Morro s/n (© **954/100-1315**). Another cool beach shop on Playa Zicatela, Calle del Moro s/n, is **Trapoy y Harapos** (© **954/582-0759**), which sells bathing suits, sandals, and surfboards. The first surf shop in Puerto Escondido, **Central Surf** (© **954/582-2285;** www.centralsurfshop.com), on Zicatela Beach, Calle del Morro s/n, rents and sells surfboards, offers surf lessons, and sells related gear, including custom-made surf trunks. Another reputable surf shop is **Colorada,** Zicatela Beach, Calle del Morro s/n (© **954/582-4458**). Board rentals usually go for about $10 to $20 (£5–£10) per day, with lessons available for $60 (£30) for 2 hours. In front of the Rockaway Resort on Zicatela Beach, there's a 24-hour **minisuper** (no phone) that sells the necessities: beer, suntan lotion, and basic food.

WHERE TO STAY

The rates posted below do not include the 18% tax.

MODERATE

Best Western Posada Real *Kids*   On a clifftop overlooking the beach, the expanse of manicured lawn that backs this all-inclusive hotel is one of the most popular places in town for a sunset cocktail. The smallish standard rooms are less enticing than the hotel grounds (six "extra large" rooms are available, and preferable for families). A big plus here is Coco's Beach Club, with a 1km (half-mile) stretch of soft-sand beach, large swimming pool, playground, and bar with occasional live music. A shuttle ride (or a lengthy walk down a set of stairs) will take you there. This is a great place for families, and it's open to the public (nonguests pay $2.50/£1.25 to enter). The hotel lies 5 minutes from the airport and about the same from Puerto Escondido's tourist zone, but you'll need a taxi to get to town. Rates include breakfast, lunch, dinner, and unlimited domestic drinks, tips, and taxes.

Av. Benito Juárez S/N, Fracc. Bacocho, 71980 Puerto Escondido, Oax. © 800/528-1234 in the U.S., or 954/582-0237. Fax 954/582-0192. www.posadareal.com.mx. 100 units. High season $130 (£75) double; low season $105 (£63) double. AE, MC, V. Free parking. **Amenities:** 2 restaurants; lobby bar; sunset bar; beach club w/food service; 2 outdoor pools; wading pool; putting green; tennis court; travel agency; car rental; laundry service. *In room:* A/C, TV, hair dryer, safe, free Wi-Fi.

Caracol Plaza   This new hotel sits on a small hill overlooking the bay. Guest rooms feature high ceilings, arched French windows, lovely wood furnishings, and small bathrooms. Ask for a room with a bay view. The large white hotel has an adult and children's pool, Mexican restaurant, and *palapa* bar with a great view of the sea. The friendly staff will help you with your travel plans. The hotel's one drawback is that it's away from the beach, to which you'll need to drive.

7a. Oriente s/n y 1a. Sur, Col. Marinero, 71980 Puerto Escondido, Oax. © **954/582-3814.** www.oaxaca-mio.com/ caracolplaza.htm. 152 units. High season $140 (£70) double; low season $70 (£35) double. AE, MC, V. Free parking. **Amenities:** Restaurant; bar; outdoor pool; kids pool. *In room:* A/C, TV, minibar, dataport, safe.

Hotel Santa Fe *(★★★ (Finds*   If Puerto Escondido is the best beach value in Mexico, then the Santa Fe is, without a doubt, one of the best hotel values in Mexico. It boasts a wonderful combination of unique Spanish-colonial style, a welcoming staff, and attractive if somewhat basic rooms. The hotel has grown up with the surfers who came to Puerto in the 1960s and 1970s and nostalgically return today. It's about 1km (a half mile) southeast of the town center, off Highway 200, at the curve in the road where Marineros and Zicatela beaches join—a prime sunset-watching spot. The three-story hacienda-style buildings have clay-tiled stairs, archways, and blooming bougainvillea. They surround two courtyard swimming pools. The ample but simply styled rooms feature large tile bathrooms, colonial furnishings, hand-woven fabrics, and both air-conditioning and ceiling fans. Most have a balcony or terrace, and the master and presidential suites enjoy ocean views. Bungalows are next to the hotel; each has a living room, kitchen, and bedroom with two double beds. The restaurant (see "Where to Dine," below), one of the best on the southern Pacific coast, is supplied by its own farm. At night, candles and lamps throughout the beachside hotel create a magical atmosphere.

Calle del Morro (Apdo. Postal 96), 71980 Puerto Escondido, Oax. © 954/582-0170 or -0266. Fax 954/582-0260. www.hotelsantafe.com.mx. 61 units, 8 bungalows. High season $173 (£87) double, $189 (£95) junior suite, $273 (£137) suite, $183 (£92) bungalow; low season $126 (£63) double, $162 (£81) junior suite, $263 (£132) suite, $136 (£68) bungalow. AE, MC, V. Free parking. **Amenities:** Restaurant; bar; 3 outdoor pools; tour service; car rental; Internet kiosk; massage; babysitting; laundry. *In room:* A/C, TV, safe.

Paraíso Escondido *(★★ (Finds*   This eclectic inn is hidden away on a shady street a couple of short blocks from the Adoquín and Playa Principal. It's very popular with families, and has a small, intimate feel. A curious collection of Mexican folk art, masks, religious art, and paintings make this an exercise in Mexican magic realism. An inviting pool—surrounded by gardens, Adirondack chairs, and a fountain—affords a

commanding view of the bay. The colonial-style rooms each have one double and one twin bed, a built-in desk, tile floors, a small bathroom, and a cozy balcony or terrace with French doors. The suites have much plusher decor than the rooms, with recessed lighting, desks set into bay windows, living areas, and large private balconies overlooking the bay. The penthouse suite has a kitchenette, a tile chessboard inlaid in the floor, and murals adorning the walls—it is the owners' former apartment.

Calle Unión 10, 71980 Puerto Escondido, Oax. ☎ 954/582-0444. Fax 954/582-2767. www.hotelparaisoescondido. net. 25 units. $65 (£33) double; $120 (£60) suite; $150 (£75) penthouse suite. MC, V. Free parking. **Amenities:** Restaurant; bar; outdoor pool; wading pool. *In room:* A/C, TV.

INEXPENSIVE

Bungalows & Cabañas Acuario ⏏ Facing Zicatela Beach, this surfer's sanctuary offers cheap accommodations plus an on-site gym, surf shop, and Internet cafe. The two-story hotel and bungalows surround a pool shaded by great palms. Rooms are small and basic; bungalows offer basic kitchen facilities but don't have air-conditioning. The cabañas are more open and have hammocks. The adjoining retail area has public telephones, money exchange, a pharmacy, and a vegetarian restaurant. If you're traveling during low season, you can probably negotiate a better deal than the rates listed below once you're there.

Calle del Morro s/n, 71980 Puerto Escondido, Oax. ☎ **954/582-0357.** Fax 954/582-1027. 40 units. High season $57 (£29) double, $65 (£33) double with A/C, $110 (£65) bungalow; 20% less in low season. No credit cards. Free parking. **Amenities:** Restaurant; Internet cafe; well-equipped gym; outdoor pool; Jacuzzi; tour desk. *In room:* No phone except in suite and 2 bungalows.

Hotel Arco Iris ⏏ *Value* Rooms at the Arco Iris occupy a three-story colonial-style house that faces Zicatela Beach. Each is simple yet comfortable, with a spacious terrace or balcony with hangers for hammocks to rent—all have great views, but the upstairs ones are better (12 units include kitchenettes). Beds come with mosquito nets, and bedspreads made using beautifully worked Oaxacan textiles. The restaurant/bar runs one of the most popular happy hours in town, daily from 5:30 to 7:30pm, with live music during high season. Deep Blue Dive shop is connected to the lobby and offers day and night dives, scuba courses, and dolphin- and whale-watching trips.

Calle del Morro s/n, Playa Zicatela, 71980 Puerto Escondido, Oax. ☎/fax **954/582-2344.** 35 units. $63–$70 (£32–£35) double, $90 (£45) double with kitchen. Extra person $4 (£2). Rates 10%–20% higher at Easter and Christmas. MC, V. Ample free parking for cars and campers. **Amenities:** Restaurant; bar; outdoor pool; wading pool; TV/game room w/foreign channels; tour desk. *In room:* No phone.

Hotel Casa Blanca ⏏ *Value* If you want to be in the heart of the Adoquín, this is your best bet for excellent value and ample accommodations. The courtyard pool and adjacent *palapa* make great places to hide away and enjoy a margarita or a book from the hotel's exchange rack. The bright, simply furnished rooms offer a choice of bed combinations, but all have at least two beds and a fan. Some rooms have both air-conditioning and a minifridge. The best rooms have a balcony overlooking the action in the street below, but light sleepers should consider a room in the back. Some rooms accommodate up to five. This is an excellent and economical choice for families.

Av. Pérez Gasga 905, 71980 Puerto Escondido, Oax. ☎ **954/582-0168.** www.ptohcasablanca.com. 25 units. High season $52 (£26) double, $95 (£48) double with A/C; low season $38 (£19) double, $85 (£43) double with A/C. MC, V. Limited street parking. **Amenities:** Outdoor pool; safe; money exchange. *In room:* TV, A/C (in some rooms), minifridge (in some rooms), fan, no phone.

Hotel Flor de María   Though not right on the beach, the Flor de María offers a welcoming place to stay. This cheery, three-story hotel faces the ocean, which you can see from the rooftop. Built around a garden courtyard, each room is colorfully decorated with beautiful *trompe l'oeil* still lifes and landscapes. Rooms have double beds with orthopedic mattresses, and views that vary between the ocean, courtyard, and exterior. On the roof are a small pool, a shaded hammock terrace, and an open-air bar (noon–8pm during high season) with cable TV. It's a great sunset spot. The hotel lies about .5km (⅓ mile) from the Adoquín, 60m (197 ft.) up a cobblestone road from Marineros Beach on Calle Marinero at the eastern end of the beach.

Playa Marineros, 71980 Puerto Escondido, Oax. © 954/582-0536. Fax 954/582-2617. 24 units. $45–$65 (£23–£33) double. Ask about off-season long-term discounts. AE, MC, V. Limited parking. **Amenities:** Restaurant; bar; small outdoor pool; Internet kiosk; small gym.

Rockaway   Facing Playa Zicatela, this surfer's sanctuary offers very clean, cheap accommodations geared for surfers, including newer hotel-style rooms and older cabañas. Every unit is equipped with a private bathroom, as well as ceiling fan and mosquito net. The good-size swimming pool and *palapa* bar form a popular gathering spot. The cabañas in the older section do not have hot water; those in the newer section feature A/C, hot water, and cable TV.

Calle del Morro s/n, 71980 Puerto Escondido, Oax. © 954/582-0668. Fax: 954-582-2420. 14 units. High season $60 (£30) double room, $40 (£20) cabaña; low season $40 (£20) double room, $20 (£10) cabaña. No credit cards. Free parking. **Amenities:** Bar; outdoor pool. *In room:* A/C (in some), TV (in some), ceiling fans, mosquito nets, no phone.

WHERE TO DINE

In addition to the places listed below, a Puerto Escondido tradition is the *palapa* restaurants on Zicatela Beach, for early-morning surfer breakfasts or casual dining and drinking at night. One of the most popular is **Los Tíos**, offering very reasonable prices and surfer-size portions. After dinner, enjoy homemade Italian ice cream from **Gelateria Giardino**. It has two locations, on Calle del Morro at Zicatela Beach, and Pérez Gasga 609, on the Adoquín (© **954/582-2243**).

EXPENSIVE

Pascal 👯👯 *(Finds* FRENCH   With an enchanted location on the edge of the bay, Pascal features a beautiful beachside terrace with views of the bobbing boats in front. Opened in 2006, it has quickly become one of the city's top restaurants. All of the French-inspired dishes are prepared by chef-owner Pascal on the outdoor grill using only fresh ingredients, and some of the specials include Chateaubriand, rack of lamb, fondue bourguignon, fish and seafood brochettes, and grilled lobster served in the shape of a tower. The bouillabaisse tastes heavenly. Open only for dinner, Pascal offers candlelit tables amidst towering palm trees, a centerpiece fountain, and live music weekends. Service is refined though sometimes slow, and the cuisine matches the quality you would expect from a fine French restaurant. There's an enticing selection of French and international wines, as well.

Playa Principal s/n (off the Adoquín). © **954/103-0668**. Reservations recommended. Main courses $6–$25 (£3–£13). No credit cards. Daily 6pm–midnight.

MODERATE

Cabo Blanco   INTERNATIONAL   People come to this beachside "rock and blues" bar and grill for a good time and simple beach food, which includes grilled fish, shrimp, steaks, and ribs topped with a variety of flavorful sauces. Favorites are dill-Dijon mustard, wine-fennel, and Thai curry. A bonus is that Cabo Blanco turns into a rowdy Zicatela Beach bar, with special Monday night parties featuring an all-you-can-eat buffet plus dancing, and a Friday night reggae dance. The top-notch team of bartenders keeps the crowd well-served, if not always well-behaved.

Calle del Morro s/n. © 954/582-0337. www.geocities.com/oaxiki/cabo_blanco_pe.html. Main courses $7–$15 (£3.50–£7.50). V. Dec–Apr daily 6pm–2am.

Restaurant Santa Fe ★★★ *(Finds)* INTERNATIONAL   The Hotel Santa Fe's beachside restaurant sits under a welcoming *palapa*, with the gentle waves crashing just in front. The excellent fish and seafood selections include crayfish, red snapper, tuna, octopus, and giant shrimp prepared any way you like. More traditional dishes, such as Oaxacan-style enchiladas with homemade tortillas and *mole*, are also available. The restaurant offers numerous vegetarian and vegan selections, including chiles rellenos with cheese, rice, and beans, and breaded tofu with salad and rice. The food is served on beautiful hand-painted ceramic place settings, and the organic coffee is grown at the hotel's own farm. Even if you don't plan to dine, this is an ideal spot to come for a sunset cocktail and perhaps an hors d'oeuvre.

In the Hotel Santa Fe, Calle del Morro s/n. © 954/582-0170. Breakfast $4–$7 (£2–£3.50); main courses $5.50–$25 (£2.75–£13). AE, MC, V. Daily 7am–10:30pm.

INEXPENSIVE

Cafecito ★ *(Value)* FRENCH PASTRY/MEXICAN   Carmen started with a small bakery in Puerto, and when she opened this cafe years ago on Zicatela Beach, with the motto "Big waves, strong coffee!," it quickly eclipsed the bake shop, and now is her main business. But not to worry—it still features all the attractions of her early *patisserie*, with the added attraction of serving full meals all day long. This cafe/restaurant sits under a big *palapa* facing the beach. Giant shrimp dinners cost less than $10 (£5), and creative daily specials are always a sure bet. An oversize mug of cappuccino is $2.20 (£1.10), and a mango éclair—worth any price—is a steal at $1.20 (60p). Smoothies, natural juices, and a variety of coffee selections are available.

Calle del Morro s/n, Playa Zicatela. © 954/582-0516. Pastries $1–$2 (50p–£1); breakfast $3–$4.50 (£1.50–£2.25); main courses $3–$9 (£1.50–£4.50). No credit cards. Daily 6am–10pm.

El Jardín ★★ *(Value)* ITALIAN   This wonderful restaurant facing Zicatela Beach is generally packed. It's known for its generous use of fresh, healthy ingredients, including lots of olive oil, tomatoes, and Italian vinaigrette. Among the choices are delicious New York–style pizza, vegetarian sandwiches, crepes, pastas, and large creative salads such as the *Rey de Reyes* with spinach, tomato, avocado, pickled eggplant, brown rice, and tofu. There's also a wide selection of fresh fish and seafood. Under a *palapa* roof, El Jardín's extensive menu includes fruit smoothies, Italian and Mexican coffees, herbal teas, and a complete juice bar. The restaurant makes its own tempeh, tofu, pastas, and whole-grain breads. The rich tiramisu is to die for.

Calle del Morro s/n, Playa Zicatela. © 954/582-2315. Main courses $3–$10 (£1.50–£5). No credit cards. Daily 8am–11pm.

Flor de María INTERNATIONAL   This first-floor, open-air hotel dining room near the beach is particularly popular with locals. The menu changes daily but always includes fresh fish, grilled meats, and pastas. The restaurant sits in the Hotel Flor de María, just steps from the center of town and up a cobblestone road from Playa Marinero at the eastern end of the beach.

In Hotel Flor de María, Playa Marinero. © 954/582-0536. Breakfast $2–$3.50 (£1–£1.75); main courses $5–$14 (£2.50–£7). No credit cards. Daily 8–11am and 6–9pm. Closed May–June and Sept–Oct.

La Galería (★ ITALIAN   At the east end of the Adoquín, La Galería offers a satisfying range of eats in a cool, creative setting. Dark-wood beams tower above, contemporary works by local artists grace the walls, and jazz music plays. Specialties include homemade pasta and brick-oven pizza (the five-cheese pizza is especially delicious), but burgers and steaks are also available. Cappuccino and espresso, plus desserts such as apple empanadas with vanilla ice cream, finish the meal. Continental and American breakfasts are available in the morning.

Av. Pérez Gasga s/n. © 954/582-2039. Breakfast $3–$5 (£1.50–£2.50); main courses $5–$10 (£2.50–£5). No credit cards. Daily 8am–11pm.

Las Margaritas (★ *Value* MEXICAN   One of the tastiest Mexican restaurants in town, Las Margaritas lies off a busy street, a short drive from the Adoquín. The casual, open-air terrace offers wood tables and chairs as well as an open kitchen, bar, and tortilla stand where you can watch authentic dishes being made. This is Mexican food prepared as though you were in a family's home, featuring such dishes as *empanadas,* quesadillas, fish and seafood brochettes, steaks, and *mole* that explodes with flavor.

8 norte s/n (1 block from the market). © 954/582-0212. Breakfasts $3–$4.50 (£1.50–£2.25); main courses $4–$12 (£2–£6). MC, V. Daily 8am–6pm.

PUERTO ESCONDIDO AFTER DARK

Sunset watching is a ritual to plan your days around, and good lookout points abound. At Zicatela you can watch sun descend behind the surfers, and at **La Galería,** located on the third floor of the Arco Iris hotel, you can catch up on local gossip while enjoying a sundowner. It has a nightly happy hour (with live music during high season) from 5:30 to 7:30pm. Other great sunset spots are the **Hotel Santa Fe,** at the junction of Zicatela and Marineros beaches, and the rooftop bar of **Hotel Flor de María.** For a more tranquil, romantic setting, take a cab or walk a half-hour or so west to the cliff-top lawn of the **Hotel Posada Real.**

Puerto's nightlife will satisfy anyone dedicated to late nights and good music. Most nightspots are open until 3am or until customers leave; none of them have phones. The Adoquín offers an ample selection of clubs. Favorites include **Wipeout,** a multilevel club that packs in the crowds until 4am, and **Blue Station,** open from 9pm to 1am.

On Zicatela Beach, **Bar Fly** sits upstairs overlooking the beach and features a DJ spinning Latin, retro, and electronic hits. It's open nightly from 9pm to 3am on Calle de Moro s/n. Don't miss **Cabo Blanco's** (see "Where to Dine," above) Monday night dine-and-dance party (all you can eat), or its Friday reggae night. An added draw is the complimentary snacks with drink purchase, in the style of Mexico's cantina tradition. **Casa Babylon,** a few doors down, is a bohemian beach bar with a book exchange and table games. It's open nightly from 7pm until late, and has a hip surfer vibe. At the end of Zicatela Beach, **La Piedra de la Iguana** plays electronic, trance, and house music and has its own iguana nursery. This is a late night venue, opening at 2am and staying open to 8am in high season.

There's a movie theater on Playa Zicatela called **Cinemar.** It's a pretty simple setup consisting of a small bookstore, large screen, and some beach chairs. It serves up popcorn and movies nightly, and also rents surfboards during the day.

> **(Warning Important Travel Note**
>
> Although car and bus hijackings along Highway 200 north to Acapulco have greatly decreased (thanks to improved security measures and police patrols), you're still wise to travel this road only during the day.

A TRIP TO PUERTO ANGEL: BACKPACKING BEACH HAVEN

Seventy-four kilometers (46 miles) southeast of Puerto Escondido and 50km (30 miles) northwest of the Bays of Huatulco lies the tiny fishing port of **Puerto Angel** (*pwer*-toh *ahn*-hehl). With its beautiful beaches, unpaved streets, and budget hotels, Puerto Angel is popular with the international backpacking set and those seeking an inexpensive and restful vacation. Repeated hurricane damage and the 1999 earthquake took its toll on the village, driving the best accommodations out of business, but Puerto Angel continues to attract visitors. Its small bay and several inlets offer peaceful swimming and good snorkeling. The village's way of life is slow and simple: Fishermen leave very early in the morning and return with their catch before noon. Taxis make up most of the traffic, and the bus from Pochutla passes every half-hour or so.

ESSENTIALS

GETTING THERE & DEPARTING By Car   North or south from **Highway 200,** take coastal **Highway 175** inland to Puerto Angel. The road is well marked with signs to Puerto Angel. From Huatulco or Puerto Escondido, the trip should take about an hour.

By Taxi   Taxis are readily available to take you to Puerto Angel or Zipolite Beach for a reasonable price (about $3/£1.50 to or from either destination), or to the Huatulco airport or Puerto Escondido (about $50/£25).

By Bus   There are no direct buses from Puerto Escondido or Huatulco to Puerto Angel; however, numerous buses leave Puerto Escondido and Huatulco for Pochutla, 11km (7 miles) north of Puerto Angel. Take the bus to Pochutla, and then switch to a bus going to Puerto Angel. If you arrive in Pochutla from Huatulco or Puerto Escondido, you may be dropped at one of several bus stations that line the main street; walk 1 or 2 blocks toward the large sign reading POSADA DON JOSE. The buses to Puerto Angel are in the lot just before the sign.

ORIENTATION   The town center is only about 4 blocks long, oriented more or less east-west. There are few signs in the village, and, off the main street, much of Puerto Angel is a narrow sand-and-dirt path. The navy base is toward the west end of town, just before the creek crossing toward Playa Panteón (Cemetery Beach).

Puerto Angel has several public (Ladatel) telephones that use widely available prepaid phone cards. The closest bank is **Bancomer** in Pochutla, which changes money Monday through Friday from 9am to 6pm, Saturday from 9am to 1pm. The *correo* **(post office),** open Monday through Friday from 9am to 3:30pm, is on the curve as you enter town.

BEACHES, WATERSPORTS & BOAT TRIPS

The golden sands and peaceful village life of Puerto Angel and the nearby towns are all the reasons you'll need to visit. Playa Principal, the main beach, lies between the

Mexican navy base and the pier that's home to the local fishing fleet. Near the pier, fishermen pull their colorful boats onto the beach and unload their catch in the late morning while trucks wait to haul it off to processing plants in Veracruz. The rest of the beach seems light years from the world of work and commitments. Except on Mexican holidays, it's relatively deserted. It's important to note that Pacific coast currents deposit trash on Puerto Angel beaches. The locals do a fairly good job of keeping it picked up, but the currents are constant.

Playa Panteón is the main swimming and snorkeling beach. Cemetery Beach, ominous as that sounds, is about a 15-minute walk from the center, straight through town on the main street that skirts the beach. The *panteón* (cemetery), on the right, is worth a visit, with its brightly colored tombstones and bougainvillea.

In Playa Panteón, some of the *palapa* restaurants and a few of the hotels rent snorkeling and scuba gear and can arrange boat trips, but they tend to be expensive. Check the quality and condition of gear—particularly scuba gear—that you're renting.

Playa Zipolite (see-poh-*lee*-teh) and its village are 6km (4 miles) down a paved road from Puerto Angel and about an hour and a half from Puerto Escondido. Taxis charge about $3 (£1.50) from Puerto Angel. You can catch a *colectivo* on the main street in the town center and share the cost.

Zipolite is well known as a good surf break and as a nude beach, although there's more nudity these days at nearby Chambala beach. Although public nudity (including topless sunbathing) is technically illegal, it's allowed here—this is one of only a handful of beaches in Mexico that permits it. This sort of open-mindedness has attracted an increasing number of young European travelers. Most sunbathers concentrate beyond a large rock outcropping at the far end of the beach. Police will occasionally patrol the area, but they are much more intent on drug users than on sunbathers. The ocean and currents are strong (that's why the surf is so good), and a number of drownings have occurred over the years—so know your limits. There are places to tie up a hammock and a few *palapa* restaurants for a lunch and a cold beer.

Hotels in Playa Zipolite are basic and rustic; most have rugged walls and *palapa* roofs. Prices range from $10 to $50 (£5–£25) a night.

Traveling north on Highway 175, you'll come to another hot surf break and a beach of spectacular beauty: **Playa San Agustinillo.** If you want to stay in San Agustinillo, there are no formal accommodations, but you'll see numerous signs for local guesthouses, which rent rooms for an average of $10 to $20 (£5–£10) a night, often with a home-cooked meal included. One of the pleasures of a stay in Puerto Angel is discovering the many hidden beaches nearby and spending the day. Local boatmen and hotels can give details and quote rates for this service.

You can stay in Puerto Angel near Playa Principal in the tiny town, or at Playa Panteón. Most accommodations are basic, older, cement-block style hotels, not meriting a full-blown description. Between Playa Panteón and town are several bungalow and guesthouse setups with budget accommodations.

4 Bahías de Huatulco

64km (40 miles) SE of Puerto Angel; 680km (422 miles) SE of Acapulco

Huatulco has the same unspoiled nature and laid-back attitude as its neighbors to the north, Puerto Angel and Puerto Escondido, but with a difference. Amid the natural splendor, you'll also encounter indulgent hotels and modern roads and facilities.

Pristine beaches and jungle landscapes can make for an idyllic retreat from the stress of daily life—and when viewed from a luxury hotel balcony, even better. Huatulco is for those who want to enjoy the beauty of nature during the day, and then retreat to well-appointed comfort by night.

Undeveloped stretches of pure white sand and isolated coves await the promised growth of Huatulco, which lags far behind Cancún, the previous resort planned by FONATUR, Mexico's Tourism Development arm. FONATUR development of the Bahías de Huatulco is an ambitious project that aims to cover 21,000 hectares (51,870 acres) of land, with over 16,000 hectares (39,520 acres) to remain ecological preserves. The small local communities have been transplanted from the coast into Crucecita. The area consists of three sections: **Santa Cruz, Crucecita,** and **Tangolunda Bay** (see "City Layout," below).

Though Huatulco has increasingly become known for its ecotourism attractions— including river rafting, rappelling, and hiking jungle trails—it has yet to develop a true personality. There's little shopping, nightlife, or even dining outside of the hotels, and what is available is expensive for the quality. However, the service in the area is generally very good.

A cruise ship dock in Santa Cruz Bay has given the sleepy resort an important business boost. The dock handles up to two 3,000-passenger cruise ships at a time (passengers are currently ferried to shore aboard tenders). Still being refined is the relatively new 20,000-hectare (49,400-acre) "eco-archaeological" park, **El Botazoo,** at Punta Celeste, where there is a recently discovered archeological site. Hiking, rappelling, and bird-watching are popular activities there. This new development is all being handled with ecological sensitivity in mind.

If you're drawn to snorkeling, diving, boat cruises, and simple relaxation, Huatulco nicely fits the bill. Nine bays encompass 36 beaches and countless inlets and coves. Huatulco's main problem has been securing enough incoming flights. It relies heavily on charter service from the United States and Canada.

ESSENTIALS
GETTING THERE & DEPARTING
BY PLANE   Click Mexicana flights (© **01-800/112-5425** toll-free in Mexico; www.click.com.mx) connect Huatulco with Mexico City. Prices start at about $150 (£75) each way. **Aero Tucán** (© **954/582-3461**) operates daily flights to and from Oaxaca on small planes for about $100 (£50) each way.

From Huatulco's international airport (airport code: HUX; © **958/581-9007** or -9008), about 20km (12 miles) northwest of the Bahías de Huatulco, private **taxis** charge $44 (£22) to Crucecita, $46 (£23) to Santa Cruz, and $51 (£26) to Tangolunda. **Transportes Terrestres** (© **958/581-9014** or -9024) *colectivos* fares are about $10 (£5) per person. When returning, make sure to ask for a taxi, unless you have a lot of luggage. Taxis to the airport run $42 (£21), but unless specifically requested, you'll get a Suburban, which costs $56 (£28).

Budget (© **800/527-0700** in the U.S., or 958/581-9000) has an office at the airport that is open for flight arrivals. **Dollar** (© **958/587-1381**) also has rental offices downtown and offers one-way drop service for about $50 (£25) additional if you're traveling to Puerto Escondido. Because Huatulco is spread out and has excellent roads, you may want to consider a rental car, at least for 1 or 2 days, to explore the area.

BY CAR   Coastal Highway 200 leads to Huatulco (via Pochutla) from the north and is generally in good condition. The drive from Puerto Escondido takes just under

2 hours. The road is well maintained, but it's windy and doesn't have lights, so avoid travel after sunset. Allow at least 6 hours for the trip from Oaxaca City on mountainous **Highway 175.**

BY BUS   There are three bus stations in Crucecita, all within a few blocks, but none in Santa Cruz or Tangolunda. The **Gacela** and **Estrella Blanca** station, at the corner of Gardenia and Palma Real, handles service to Acapulco, Mexico City, Puerto Escondido, and Pochutla. The **Cristóbal Colón** station (© **958/587-0261**) is at Av. Riscalillo, Sector T. It serves destinations throughout Mexico, including Oaxaca, Puerto Escondido, and Pochutla. The **Estrella del Valle** station, on Jasmin between Sabali and Carrizal, serves Oaxaca.

ORIENTATION
VISITOR INFORMATION   The **State Tourism Office,** or Oficina del Turismo (© **958/581-0176;** www.baysofhuatulco.com.mx), has an information booth in Tangolunda Bay, near the Grand Pacific hotel. It's open Monday to Friday from 8am to 5pm.

CITY LAYOUT   The overall resort area is called **Bahías de Huatulco** and includes nine bays. The town of Santa María de Huatulco, the original settlement in this area, is 27km (17 miles) inland. **Santa Cruz Huatulco,** usually called Santa Cruz, was the first developed area on the coast. It has a central plaza with a bandstand kiosk, which has been converted into a cafe that serves regionally grown coffee. It also has an artisans' market on the edge of the plaza that borders the main road, a few hotels and restaurants, and a marina where bay tours and fishing trips set sail. **Juárez** is Santa Cruz's 4-block-long main street, anchored at one end by the Hotel Castillo Huatulco and at the other by the Meigas Binniguenda hotel. Opposite the Hotel Castillo is the marina, and beyond it are restaurants in new colonial-style buildings facing the beach. The area's banks are on Juárez. It's impossible to get lost and you can take in almost everything at a glance. This bay is the site of Huatulco's cruise-ship dock.

About 3km (2 miles) inland from Santa Cruz is **Crucecita,** a planned city that sprang up in 1985. It centers on a lovely grassy plaza. This is the residential area for the resorts, with neighborhoods of new stucco homes mixed with small apartment complexes. Crucecita has evolved into a lovely, traditional town where you'll find the area's best, and most reasonably priced, restaurants, plus some shopping and several less-expensive hotels.

Until other bays are developed, **Tangolunda Bay,** 5km (3 miles) east, is the focal point of development. Over time, half the bays will have resorts. For now, Tangolunda has an 18-hole golf course, as well as the Las Brisas, Quinta Real, Barceló Huatulco, Royal, Casa del Mar, and Camino Real Zaashila hotels, among others. Small strip centers with a few restaurants occupy each end of Tangolunda Bay. **Chahué Bay,** between Tangolunda and Santa Cruz, is a small bay with a beach club and other facilities under construction along with houses and a few small hotels.

GETTING AROUND   Crucecita, Santa Cruz, and Tangolunda are too far apart to walk, but **taxis** are inexpensive and readily available. Crucecita has taxi stands opposite the Hotel Grifer and on the Plaza Principal. Taxis are readily available through hotels in Santa Cruz and Tangolunda. The fare between Santa Cruz and Tangolunda is roughly $2.50 (£1.25); between Santa Cruz and Crucecita, $2; between Crucecita and Tangolunda, $2.50 (£1.25). To explore the area, you can hire a taxi by the hour (about $15/£7.50 per hour) or for the day.

There is **minibus service** between towns; the fare is 50¢ (25p). In Santa Cruz, catch the bus across the street from Castillo Huatulco; in Tangolunda, in front of the Grand Pacific; and in Crucecita, cater-cornered from the Hotel Grifer.

FAST FACTS: Bahías de Huatulco

Area Code The area code is **958.**

Banks All three areas have banks with ATMs, including the main Mexican banks, Banamex and Bancomer, and HSBC. They change money during business hours, Monday through Friday from 9am to 4pm. Banks line Calle Juárez in Santa Cruz, and surround the central plaza in Crucecita.

Drugstores **Farmacía del Carmen,** just off the central plaza in Crucecita (© **958/587-0878**), is one of the largest drugstores in town. It's open Monday through Saturday from 8am to 10pm and Sunday from 8am to noon. **Farmacía La Clínica** (© **958/587-0591**), Sabalí 1602, Crucecita, offers 24-hour service and delivery.

Emergencies **Police emergency** (© **060**); **federal police** (© **958/587-0815**); **transit police** (© **958/587-0186**); and **Cruz Roja (Red Cross),** Bulevar Chahué 110 (© **958/587-1188**).

Information **Oficina del Turismo,** the State Tourism Office (© **958/581-0176** or -0177; sedetur6@oaxaca.gob.mx) has an information module in Tangolunda Bay, near the Campo de Golf. It's open weekdays, 8am to 5pm.

Internet Access Several Internet cafes are in Crucecita. One is at the cafe in the Misión de los Arcos, Av. Gardenia 902 (© **958/587-0165**), which, in addition to paid service, is also a free wireless hot spot; another is on the ground-floor level of the **Hotel Plaza Conejo,** Av. Guamúchil 208, across from the main plaza (© **958/587-0054**, -0009; conejo3@mexico.com). It's about $1 (50p) per hour.

Medical Care **Clínica Médico Quirúrgica,** Jabali 403 (© **958/587-0687** or -0600) is a medical clinic with emergency care run by Dr. Ricardo Carrillo, who speaks English.

Post Office The *correo,* at Bulevar Chahué 100, Sector R, Crucecita (© **958/587-0551**), is open Monday through Saturday from 8am to 4pm.

BEACHES, WATERSPORTS & OTHER THINGS TO DO

Attractions around Huatulco concentrate on the nine bays and their watersports. The number of ecotours and interesting side trips into the surrounding mountains is growing. Though it isn't a traditional Mexican town, the community of Crucecita is worth visiting. Just off the central plaza is the **Iglesia de Guadalupe,** with a large mural of Mexico's patron saint gracing the entire ceiling of the chapel. The image of the Virgin is set against a deep blue night sky, and includes 52 stars—a modern interpretation of Juan Diego's cloak.

You can dine in Crucecita for a fraction of the price in Tangolunda Bay, with the added benefit of some local color. Considering that shopping in Huatulco is generally poor, you'll find the best choices here, in the shops around the central plaza. They tend to stay open late, and offer a good selection of regional goods and typical tourist take-homes, including *artesanía,* silver jewelry, Cuban cigars, and tequila. A small, free trolley train takes visitors on a short tour of the town.

BEACHES A section of the beach at Santa Cruz (away from the small boats) is an inviting sunning spot. Beach clubs for guests at nonoceanfront hotels are here. In addition, several restaurants are on the beach, and *palapa* umbrellas run down to the water's edge. For about $15 (£7.50) one-way, *pangas* from the marina in Santa Cruz will ferry you to **La Entrega Beach,** also in Santa Cruz Bay. There you'll find a row of *palapa* restaurants, all with beach chairs out front. Find an empty one, and use that restaurant for your refreshment needs. A snorkel equipment rental booth is about midway down the beach, and there's some fairly good snorkeling on the end away from where the boats arrive.

Between Santa Cruz and Tangolunda bays is **Chahué Bay.** The beach club has *palapas,* beach volleyball, and refreshments for an entrance fee of about $3 (£1.50). However, a strong undertow makes this a dangerous place for swimming.

Tangolunda Bay beach, fronting the best hotels, is wide and beautiful. Theoretically, all beaches in Mexico are public; however, nonguests at Tangolunda hotels may have difficulty entering the hotels to get to the beach.

BAY CRUISES & TOURS Huatulco's major attraction is its coastline—a magnificent stretch of pristine bays bordered by an odd blend of cactus and jungle vegetation right at the water's edge. The only way to really grasp its beauty is to take a cruise of the bays, stopping at **Organo** or **Maguey Bay** for a dip in the crystal-clear water and a fish lunch at a *palapa* restaurant on the beach.

One way to arrange a bay tour is to go to the **boat-owners' cooperative** (© 958/ 587-0081), located in the red-and-yellow tin shack at the entrance to the marina. Prices are posted, and you can buy tickets for sightseeing, snorkeling, or fishing. Beaches other than La Entrega, including Maguey and San Agustín, are noted for offshore snorkeling. They also have *palapa* restaurants and other facilities. Several of these beaches, however, are completely undeveloped, so you will need to bring your own provisions. Boatmen at the cooperative will arrange return pickup at an appointed time. Prices run about $25 (£13) for 1 to 10 persons to La Entrega, and $50 (£25) for a trip to Maguey and Organo bays. The farthest bay is San Agustín; that all-day trip will run $100 (£50) in a private *panga.*

Another option is to join an organized daylong bay cruise. Any travel agency can easily make arrangements. Cruises are $30 (£15) per person, plus $5 (£2.50) for snorkeling-equipment rental and lunch. One excursion is on the *Tequila,* complete with guide, drinks, and onboard entertainment. Another, more romantic option is the *Luna Azul,* a 13m (43-ft.) sailboat that runs bay tours and sunset sails.

Ecotours are growing in popularity and number throughout the Bays of Huatulco. The mountain areas surrounding the Copalita River are also home to other natural treasures worth exploring, including the **Copalitilla Cascades.** Thirty kilometers (19 miles) north of Tangolunda at 395m (1,296 ft.) above sea level, this group of waterfalls—averaging 20 to 25m (66–82 ft.) in height—form natural whirlpools and clear pools for swimming. The area is also popular for horseback riding and rappelling.

An all-day **shopping tour** takes you around the area, including a small village called La Crucecita, to peruse quality hand-made arts and crafts and experience authentic Oaxacan cuisine. Contact **Paraíso Tours** (www.paraisohuatulco.com) for reservations.

Guided **horseback riding** through the jungles and to Conejos and Magueyito beach makes for a wonderful way to see the natural beauty of the area. The ride lasts

3 hours, with departures at 9:45am and 1:45pm, and costs $35 to $45 (£18–£23). Contact **Caballo del Mar Ranch** (© **958/589-9387**).

Another recommended guide for both **hiking** and **bird-watching** is Laura Gonzalez, of **Nature Tours Huatulco** (© **958/583-4047** or 589-0636; lauriycky@hotmail. com). Choices include a hike around Punta Celeste with views of the river, open sea, and forest, for sightings of terrestrial and aquatic birds. The 3½-hour tour can be made in the early morning or late afternoon, and costs $45 (£23). An 8-hour excursion to the Ventanilla Lagoons takes you by boat through a mangrove to view birds, iguanas, and crocodiles. The cost is $80 (£40), including lunch. Tours include transportation, binoculars, specialized bird guide, and beverages.

GOLF & TENNIS   The 18-hole, par-72 **Tangolunda Golf Course** (© **958/581-0037**) is adjacent to Tangolunda Bay. It has tennis courts as well for $11 (£5.50) per hour. The greens fee is $80 (£40) for 18 holes and $64 (£32) for 9 holes; carts cost $34 (£17). Tennis courts are also available at the **Barceló** hotel (© **958/581-0055**) for $10 (£5) per person per hour.

SHOPPING   Shopping in the area is limited and unmemorable. It concentrates in the **Santa Cruz Market,** by the marina in Santa Cruz, and in the **Crucecita Market,** on Guamúchil, a half-block from the plaza. Both are open daily from 10am to 8pm (no phones). Among the prototypical souvenirs, you may want to search out regional specialties, which include Oaxacan embroidered blouses and dresses, and *barro negro,* pottery made from dark clay exclusively found in the Oaxaca region. Also in Crucecita is the Plaza Oaxaca, adjacent to the central plaza. Its clothing shops include **Poco Loco Club/Coconut's Boutique** (© **958/587-0279**), for casual sportswear; and **Mic Mac** (© **958/587-0565**), for beachwear and souvenirs. **Coconuts** (© **958/587-0057**) has English-language magazines, books, and music.

WHERE TO STAY

Moderate- and budget-priced hotels in Santa Cruz and Crucecita are generally more expensive than similar hotels in other Mexican beach resorts. The luxury hotels have comparable rates, especially when they're part of a package that includes airfare. The trend here is toward all-inclusive resorts, which in Huatulco are an especially good option, given the lack of memorable dining and nightlife options. Hotels that are not oceanfront generally have an arrangement with a beach club at Santa Cruz or Chahué Bay, and offer shuttle service. Low-season rates apply August through November only. Parking is free at these hotels; the 18% tax is not included in the rack rates listed below.

EXPENSIVE

Camino Real Zaashila 🍴🍴 *(Kids*   One of the original hotels in Tangolunda Bay, the Camino Real Zaashila sits on a wide stretch of sandy beach secluded from other beaches by small rock outcroppings. It has been renovated with a newly designed palapa bar with sit-down check-in. The calm water, perfect for swimming and snorkeling, makes it ideal for families. The white stucco building is Mediterranean in style and washed in colors on the ocean side. The boldly decorated rooms are large and have an oceanview balcony or terrace and a large bathroom with an Italian marble tub/shower combination. Each of the 41 club rooms on the lower levels has its own private plunge pool and includes buffet breakfast and evening cocktails. The main pool is a free-form design that spans 500 feet of beach, with chaises built into the shallow edges. Well-manicured tropical gardens surround it and the guest rooms.

Bulevar Benito Juárez 5, Bahía de Tangolunda, 70989 Huatulco, Oax. ℂ 800/722-6466 in the U.S., or 958/581-0460. Fax 958/581-0468. www.camino-zaashila.com. 120 units. High season $220 (£110) double, $250 (£125) club room; low season $130 (£65) double, $250 (£125) club room. AE, DC, MC, V. **Amenities:** 3 restaurants (1 Oaxacan); lobby bar w/live music; 2 large outdoor pools; outdoor whirlpool; lighted tennis court; beachside watersports center; kids' club; tour and travel agency services; room service; laundry service. *In room:* A/C, TV, free Wi-Fi, minibar, safe.

Quinta Real 🏵🏵🏵   Double Moorish domes mark this romantic, relaxed hotel, known for its richly appointed cream-and-white decor and complete attention to detail. From the welcoming reception area to the luxurious beach club below, the staff emphasizes excellence in service. The small groupings of suites are built into the sloping hill to Tangolunda Bay and offer spectacular views of the ocean and golf course. Suites on the eastern edge of the resort sit above the highway, which generates some traffic noise. Interiors are elegant and comfortable, with stylish Mexican furniture, original art, wood-beamed ceilings, and marble tub/shower combinations with whirlpool tubs. Balconies have overstuffed seating areas and stone-inlay floors. Eight Grand Class Suites and the Presidential Suite have private pools. The most luxurious hotel in Huatulco, the Quinta Real is perfect for weddings, honeymoons, or small corporate retreats.

Bulevar Benito Juárez Lt. 2, Bahía de Tangolunda, 70989 Huatulco, Oax. ℂ 888/561-2817 in the U.S, or 958/581-0428, -0430. Fax 958/581-0429. www.quintareal.com. 28 units. High season $390 (£195) Master Suite, $440 (£220) Grand Class Suite, $490 (£245) suite with private pool; low season $295 (£148) Master Suite, $345 (£173) Grand Class Suite, $395 (£198) suite with private pool. AE, MC, V. **Amenities:** Restaurant (breakfast, dinner); poolside restaurant (lunch); bar w/stunning view; beach club w/2 outdoor pools (1 for children); tennis court; concierge; tour desk; room service; in-room massage; laundry service; dry cleaning. *In room:* A/C, TV, minibar, hair dryer, safe.

MODERATE

Gala Resort 🏵 *Kids*   With all meals, drinks, entertainment, tips, and a slew of activities included in the price, the all-inclusive Gala is a value-packed experience. It caters to adults of all ages (married and single) who enjoy both activity and relaxation. An excellent—but often overcrowded—kids' activity program makes it a great option for families. There are pool activities for adults as well as children, and evening entertainment too. Rooms have tile floors and Oaxacan wood trim, large tub/shower combinations, and ample balconies. Royal Club rooms offer upgraded amenities and views of Tangolunda Bay.

Bulevar Benito Juárez s/n, Bahía de Tangolunda, 70989 Huatulco, Oax. ℂ 958/581-0000. Fax 958/581-0220. www.gala-resort-huatulco.com. 290 units. High season $258–$320 (£129–£160) double, $402 (£201) junior suite, for children 12–17 $78 (£39), children 8–11 $54 (£27); low season $150–$258 (£75–£129) double, $299 (£150) junior suite, children 12–17 $90 (£45), children 8–11 $60 (£30). Children younger than 8 stay free in parent's room. Ask about special promotions. AE, MC, V. **Amenities:** 4 restaurants (buffet, a la carte); 3 bars; 5 outdoor pools, including a large free-form pool; 3 lighted tennis courts; full gym; complete beachside watersports center. *In room:* A/C, TV, Wi-Fi (fee), minibar, hair dryer, safe.

Hotel Meigas Binniguenda 🏵   Huatulco's first hotel retains the charm and comfort that originally made it memorable. Rooms have Mexican-tile floors, foot-loomed bedspreads, and colonial-style furniture; French doors open onto tiny wrought-iron balconies overlooking Juárez or the pool and gardens. There's a section with newer rooms that have modern teak furnishings. A nice shady area surrounds the small pool in back of the lobby. The hotel is away from the marina at the far end of Juárez, only a few blocks from the water. It offers free transportation every hour to the beach club at Chahué.

Bulevar Santa Cruz 201, 70989 Santa Cruz de Huatulco, Oax. ℂ 958/587-0078. Fax 958/587-0129. www.meicerhotels. com. 165 units. Year-round $100–$150 (£50–£75) double. Children younger than 7 stay free in parent's room. MC, V. **Amenities:** Large, *palapa*-topped restaurant and bar; small outdoor pool; shuttle to beach. *In room:* A/C, TV, safe.

INEXPENSIVE

Hotel Las Palmas The central location and accommodating staff add to the appeal of the bright, basic rooms at Las Palmas. Located a half-block from the main plaza, it's connected to the popular El Sabor de Oaxaca restaurant (see "Where to Dine," below), which offers room service to guests. Rooms have tile floors, cotton textured bedspreads, tile showers, and cable TV. This hotel is partnered with two other inexpensive and reliable options in Huatulco, in case this one sells out.

Av. Guamúchil 206, 70989 Bahías de Huatulco, Oax. ☎ 958/587-0060. Fax 958/587-0057. 10 units. High season $60 (£30) double; low season $40 (£20) double. AE, MC, V. **Amenities:** Currency exchange; safe. *In room:* A/C, TV.

Misión de los Arcos *ʀʀ Finds* This exceptional hotel, just a block from the central plaza, is similar in style to the elegant Quinta Real—but at a fraction of the cost. The hotel is mostly white, accented with abundant greenery, giving it a fresh, inviting feel. Simple rooms continue the theme, washed in white, with cream and beige bed coverings and upholstery. Built-in desks, French windows, and minimal but interesting decorative accents give this budget hotel a real sense of style. At the entrance level, an excellent cafe offers high-speed Internet access, Huatulco's regionally grown coffee, tea, pastries, and ice cream. It's open from 7:30am to 11:30pm. The adjacent Terra-Cotta restaurant (see below) serves breakfast, lunch, and dinner, and is equally stylish and budget-friendly. Although there's no pool, for $2.50 (£1.25) guests can use the Castillo Beach Club, at Chahué bay, open daily from 9am to 7pm. The hotel lies next door to La Crucecita's central plaza, close to all the shops and restaurants.

Gardenia 902, La Crucecita, 70989 Huatulco, Oax. ☎ 958/587-0165. Fax 958/587-1903. www.misiondelosarcos. com. 13 units. High season $75 (£38) double, $80–$100 (£40–£50) suite; low season $45 (£23) double, $55–$75 (£28–£38) suite. Rates increase over Christmas and Easter holiday periods. AE, MC, V. Street parking. **Amenities:** Restaurant; nearby beach club; laundry service. *In room:* A/C, TV, free Wi-Fi.

WHERE TO DINE

El Sabor de Oaxaca *ʀʀʀ* OAXACAN This is the best place in the area to enjoy authentic, richly flavorful Oaxacan food, among the best of traditional Mexican cuisine. This colorful restaurant is a local favorite that also meets the quality standards of tourists. Among the most popular items are mixed grill for two, with a Oaxacan beef filet, tender pork tenderloin, chorizo (zesty Mexican sausage), and pork ribs; and the Oaxacan special for two, a generous sampling of the best of the menu, with tamales, Oaxacan cheese, chiles rellenos, pork *mole,* and more. If you're feeling adventurous, try the salty grilled *chapulines* (grasshoppers, a Oaxacan specialty). Generous breakfasts include eggs, bacon, ham, beans, toast, and fresh orange juice.

Av. Guamúchil 206, Crucecita. ☎ 958/587-0060. Fax 958/587-0057. Breakfast $4–$6 (£2–£3); main courses $6–$15 (£3–£7.50). AE, MC, V. Daily 7am–11pm.

Noches Oaxaqueñas/Don Porfirio *ʀ* SEAFOOD/OAXACAN This dinner show presents the colorful, traditional folkloric dances of Oaxaca in an open-air courtyard reminiscent of an old hacienda (but in a modern strip mall). The dancers perform traditional ballet under the direction of owner Celicia Flores Ramírez, wife of Don Willo Porfirio. The menu includes the *plato oaxaqueño,* a generous, flavorful sampling of traditional Oaxacan fare, with a tamal, a *sope* (a thick tortilla), Oaxacan cheese, grilled filet, pork enchilada, and a chile relleno. Other house specialties include grilled lobster, shrimp with mescal flambéed at the table, and spaghetti marinara with seafood. Meat lovers can enjoy American-style cuts or a juicy *arrachera* (skirt steak).

The show takes place nightly at 8pm during high season, and Tuesday, Thursday, and Saturday nights at 8pm in low season.

Bulevar Benito Juárez s/n (across from Royal Maeva), Tangolunda Bay. ℂ **958/581-0001.** Main courses $10–$20 (£5–£10). AE, MC, V. Daily noon–11pm. Shows ($12/£6) extra.

Restaurante Bar Doña Celia ✿✿ SEAFOOD   Doña Celia, an original Huatulco resident, remains in business in the same area where she started her little thatch-roofed restaurant years ago. With outdoor tables fronting Santa Cruz, it offers fabulous seafood in picturesque surroundings. Among her specialties are *filete empapelado* (foil-wrapped fish baked with tomato, onion, and cilantro) and *filete almendrado* (fish filet covered with hotcake batter, beer, and almonds). Or you might opt for a whole grilled fish with just lemon and garlic. The *ceviche* is terrific—one order is plenty for two— as is *platillo a la huatulqueño* (shrimp and young octopus fried in olive oil with chile and onion, served over white rice). There are also mouth-watering lobster selections, including lobster tacos. The restaurant is basic, but the food and setting are reason enough for its popularity.

Santa Cruz Bay. ℂ **958/587-0128.** Breakfast $3.50–$7 (£1.75–£3.50); seafood $8–$30 (£4–£15). MC, V. Daily 8:30am–11pm.

Terra-Cotta ✿ *Finds* INTERNATIONAL/MEXICAN   Located inside the Hotel Misión de los Arcos, this stylish yet casual restaurant is best known for breakfast, and it's just as tasty at lunch and dinner. Start the day in this white-washed, Mediterranean setting with gourmet coffee, fruit salad, and an array of morning favorites, including specials such as French toast stuffed with cream cheese and orange marmalade. Lunch and dinner share the same menu, which offers fajitas, baby back ribs, gourmet tacos, and 25 different sandwich options. Scrumptious desserts such as caramelized pineapple with coconut ice cream offer a sweet finish.

Gardenia 902, at the Hotel Misión de los Arcos, in front of La Crucecita's central plaza. ℂ **958/587-0165.** Breakfast $1.50–$6 (75p–£3); lunch and dinner main courses $4–$14 (£2–£7). AE, MC, V. Daily 7:30am–11:30pm.

HUATULCO AFTER DARK

There's a very limited selection of dance clubs around Huatulco—meaning that's where everyone goes. Huatulco seems to have the least consistent nightlife of any resort in Mexico, and clubs seem to change ownership—and names—almost annually. Check with your hotel concierge to see if any new places have opened; none of the places listed below have phones. The current hot spot is **Bar La Crema,** in Crucecita (about 4 blocks south of the *zócalo,* at the corner of Bugambilia and La Ceiba), with a lounge atmosphere and a mix of tunes. Nearby is **Café Dublin,** Carrizal 504 (1 block east and a half-block south from the *zócalo*), an Irish pub with a book exchange. Both bars open in the evening during high season and stay open as long as the management sees fit; hours are sporadic in low season. On the east side of the *zócalo* lies **Bar La Iguana,** playing rock music and featuring televised sports. The bar is typically open daily from noon to 4am during high season, with limited hours in low season.

La **Papaya,** on Bulevar Chahué, is a popular dance club, open Thursday through Saturday into the wee hours. Each Wednesday, the Barceló Resort hosts its **Fiesta Mexicana** from 7 to 11pm, featuring folkloric dances, mariachi music, and a buffet of Mexican food and drinks.

12

The Southernmost States: Oaxaca & Chiapas

by David Baird

Oaxaca and Chiapas have larger Indian populations than the other states in Mexico. These Indians don't just keep to their own little villages; you see them everywhere. Over the centuries, their practices, beliefs, and customs have shaped the local culture, making these two states fascinating places to visit.

In **Oaxaca,** there is a large population of Zapotec and Mixtec Indians in the central highlands surrounding Oaxaca City. It's a land of mountains and valleys checkered with cornfields, at its prettiest during the rainy season (Jun–Oct), when the corn is green. The villages here are famous for their crafts and attract visitors from all over the world. Many families now earn more by selling handicrafts than they do by growing corn. But growing corn carries much more weight in their ordering of things—it's part of their identity, it's part of what makes them Indians.

Their ancestors established agriculture and civilization in these valleys centuries ago. They were the ones who built and rebuilt the magnificent ceremonial center of **Monte Albán** high upon a mountaintop above Oaxaca City. Up there, you'll find an intriguing collection of buildings, ball courts, and plazas with designs distinctive from those of the Maya to the east and the many cultures of central Mexico to the northwest.

But my favorite part of a trip here is visiting the **city of Oaxaca,** a colonial city of stone buildings, plazas, and courtyards. With the pleasures of elegant surroundings, good food, and warm, welcoming people, I find myself very much at home here.

Chiapas, too, has a central highland area that produces beautiful handicrafts. Its center is the town of **San Cristóbal de las Casas,** which is higher, cooler, and wetter than Oaxaca. It's best to come here during the relatively dry season (late Oct–May). San Cristóbal is much smaller, with a more provincial version of colonial architecture—narrow cobblestone streets, tile roofs, old adobe walls, and wooden balconies. It looks less monumental and more Indian.

Besides the beauty of the mountains and the many handicrafts, what brings people here are the villages of the highland Maya, a people who cling so tenaciously to their beliefs and traditions that for a long time the area attracted more anthropologists than tourists. These communities have a high degree of autonomy in religious and social practices; a visit to the church in **San Juan Chamula** will bring this home in a way no description can.

North and east of San Cristóbal are the lowlands, where you can visit the famous ruins of **Palenque,** a Maya city of the Classic age. Thanks to the deciphering work of epigraphers, we know much about the history of Palenque and its kings. One was King Pacal, who lay buried for centuries inside his pyramid until an archaeological team discovered him in the 1950s.

EXPLORING OAXACA & CHIAPAS

Airline service to Oaxaca has improved in the past few years. The same cannot be said of Chiapas, where the most common port of entry for Palenque as well as the highlands is still the airport at Villahermosa, Tabasco. There are fewer flights into Tuxtla Gutiérrez (near San Cristóbal) and hardly any to San Cristóbal.

Most travelers should choose between visiting Oaxaca or Chiapas and not try to do both in the same trip unless they have a lot of time. First, the connections between these states are not good. So your choices will probably be to fly via Mexico City or take an overnight bus. Another thing to consider is that both Oaxaca and Chiapas offer so much to do that each place can easily absorb a week or 2-week vacation. And, if choosing Oaxaca, keep in mind that Oaxaca's coastal resorts—including Puerto Escondido and Puerto Angel—are not far away. See chapter 11 for more information.

1 Oaxaca City ✲✲✲

520km (322 miles) SE of Mexico City; 230km (143 miles) SE of Tehuacán; 269km (167 miles) NE of Puerto Escondido

What you see today when you walk through the historic district of Oaxaca (wah-*hah*-kah) is largely the product of 3 centuries of colonial society. The city is famous for its green building stone and for its own particular style of colonial architecture—an adaptation to the frequent earthquakes that plagued the city in colonial times and still occasionally shake things up. Building walls and facades are thick and broad with heavy buttressing, colonnades are low and spaced closely, and bell towers are squat with wide bases. The impression is one of great mass and solidity.

Before the arrival of the Spanish, the central valley of Oaxaca was an important and populous region. Olmec influence reached the area around 1200 B.C.; by 800 B.C. the Zapotec (the original builders of Monte Albán) occupied the valley. Their civilization flourished about the same time as Teotihuacán in central Mexico. Trade between the two areas intensified and remained important until the Conquest. There was also trade with the Maya to the east. In early post-Classic times, the Mixtec first appeared in the region and slowly, through war and conquest, gained ascendancy over much of the Zapotec homeland before both peoples were humbled by the Aztec and later the Spaniards. To this day, the two principal ethnic groups in Oaxaca remain the Zapotec and Mixtec, whose tonal languages are closely related to each other but far different from the Aztec language Náhuatl.

The city of Oaxaca, originally called Antequera, was founded just a few years after the Spanish vanquished the Aztec. Most of Oaxaca's central valley was granted to Hernán Cortez for his services to the crown. Three centuries of colonial rule followed, during which the region remained calm.

In the years following independence, there was more or less continuous upheaval. From the 1830s to the 1860s, the Liberals and Conservatives fought for control of Mexico's destiny, with the French eventually intervening on the side of the Conservatives. One man, a Zapotec Indian from Oaxaca, led the resistance against the French and played the key role in shaping Mexico's future. He was Benito Juárez, and his handiwork is known to history as *La Reforma.*

Born in the village of Guelatao, north of Oaxaca City, Juárez was adopted by a wealthy Oaxacan family who clothed and educated him in return for his services as a houseboy. He fell in love with the daughter of his benefactor and promised he would become rich and famous and return to marry her. He did all three and became president of the republic in 1861. Juárez is revered throughout Mexico.

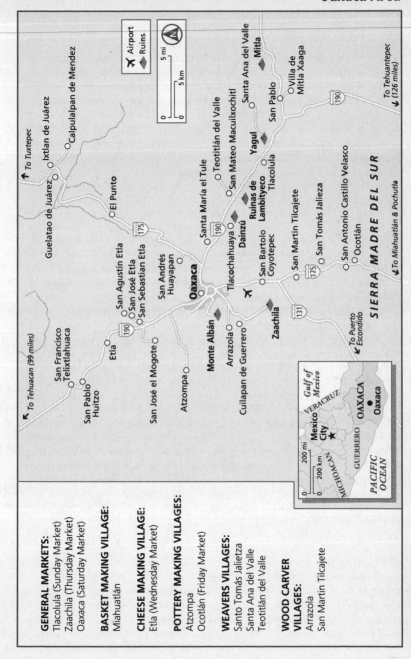

Oaxaca Area

GENERAL MARKETS:
Tlacolula (Sunday Market)
Zaachila (Thursday Market)
Oaxaca (Saturday Market)

BASKET MAKING VILLAGE:
Miahuatlán

CHEESE MAKING VILLAGE:
Etla (Wednesday Market)

POTTERY MAKING VILLAGES:
Atzompa
Ocotlán (Friday Market)

WEAVERS VILLAGES:
Santo Tomás Jalietza
Santa Ana del Valle
Teotitlán del Valle

WOOD CARVER VILLAGES:
Arrazola
San Martín Tilcajete

✈ Airport
◈ Ruins

0 5 mi
0 5 km

To Tuxtepec ↑
Ixtlan de Juárez
Calpulalpan de Mendez
Guelatao de Juárez ↑
El Punto
175
Santa María el Tule
Teotitlán del Valle
San Mateo Macuilxochitl
Santa Ana del Valle
Mitla
Villa de Mitla Xaaga
San Pablo
190
To Tehuantepec ↓ (126 miles)
Yagul
Ruinas de Lambityeco
Dainzú
Tlacolula
San Martín Tilcajete
San Tomás Jalieza
San Antonio Castillo Velasco
Ocotlán
190
Santa María el Tule
Tlacochahuaya
San Bartolo Coyotepec
131
175
To Miahuatlán & Pochutla ↓
San Andrés Huayapan
San Sebastián Etla
San José Etla
San Agustín Etla
Etla
190
San José el Mogote
Atzompa
Oaxaca
Monte Albán
Arrazola
Cuilapan de Guerrero
Zaachila
To Puerto Escondido ↙
San Francisco Telixtlahuaca
San Pablo Huitzo
To Tehuacan (99 miles) ↙

SIERRA MADRE DEL SUR

Gulf of Mexico
VERACRUZ
MICHOACÁN
Mexico City ★
GUERRERO
OAXACA
Oaxaca ●
PACIFIC OCEAN
0 200 mi
0 200 km

Peace & Poverty in Oaxaca

After the political upheaval of 2006 and early 2007, Oaxacan society has gradually returned to what it was, only poorer. The local economy is so dependent on tourism and the sale of artisan goods that the absence of visitors resulted in the almost universal impoverishment of the city and the surrounding valleys. The mood is darker, too. All parties in the crisis—from the demonstrators, to the local authorities, to the shopkeeper classes, to the average man on the street—feel that the national government abandoned Oaxaca. And there is widespread disgust with the present governor, Ulises Ruíz, for his actions and lack of accountability.

Many look back wistfully to the days when one political party, the PRI, controlled national politics. In the face of unrest, the first thing the political bosses used to do would be to yank the governor, under the general rule that any politician who let the situation get so out of hand was inept and deserved to be sacked. But in a country now practicing pluralistic democracy, this isn't so easy. Everything is under negotiation, and Oaxaca is not the first item on the agenda of any of the national parties. The heads of the PRI in Mexico City are backing Gov. Ruíz because they feel they have to keep their party together, not because they like him, and President Calderón needs the support of the PRI to get his agenda passed through the legislature.

But as time passes, the natural gumption of Oaxacans is making a comeback, along with their "We'll get by somehow" attitude. Between the governor and the political movement demanding change, there is an uneasy truce. Most people are probably content to wait out the governor's term of office. Meanwhile, the tourists are returning, both domestic and international. I had a pleasant time on my last trip and found Oaxaca to be much like it was before the troubles.

So, if you're considering a trip to Oaxaca, go ahead. You can check international news sources before you commit, but my guess is that things will remain calm. There are no elections or other events in the near future that might incite social unrest besides the annual teachers' demonstrations in May/June (avoid these months). In any case, exercise caution. In my experience in Latin America, it's not uncommon to see a surge in petty crime and lawlessness after a period of political protests.

ESSENTIALS
GETTING THERE & DEPARTING

BY PLANE   Continental ExpressJet (© 800/231-0856 in the U.S., or 01-800/900-5000 in Mexico; www.continental.com) has nonstop service to/from Houston. Mexicana (© 800/531-7921 in the U.S., or 951/516-8414; www.mexicana.com) and AeroMéxico (© 800/237-6639 in the U.S., or 951/516-1066; www.aeromexico.com.mx) have flights daily to and from Mexico City. Click, a Mexicana affiliate (© 01/800-122-5425 in Mexico; www.clickmx.com), has service to/from Mexico City. Aviacsa (© 01-800/006-2200 in Mexico, or 951/514-5187; www.aviacsa.com) connects Oaxaca to Mexico City and Acapulco. Aerovega (© 951/516-4982) flies a

Downtown Oaxaca

ATTRACTIONS ●

Basílica de la Soledad **11**
Casa de Juárez **3**
Catedral de Oaxaca **16**
Iglesia de San Felipe Neri **13**
Iglesia de Santo Domingo **5**
Mercado de Artesanía **18**
Museo de Arte Contemporaneo (MACO) **15**
Museo Regional de Oaxaca **4**
Rufino Tamayo Museo de Arte Prehispánico **12**
San Juan de Dios **19**
Teatro Macedonio de Alcalá **17**

ACCOMMODATIONS ■

Casa Cid de León **14**
Casa Colonial B&B **10**
Casa Cué **20**
Casa Vértiz **8**
Hotel Aitana **7**
Hotel Camino Real **9**
Hotel Casa Arnel **2**
Hotel Maela **8**
Hotel Victoria **1**
Las Golondrinas **6**

Bus 🚌
Information ⓘ
Post Office ✉
Closed to Traffic ----

**Map labels:**
Pan American Hwy.
Avenida Niños Héroes de Chapultepec
To Tule, Mitla → & Tehuantepec
Bus Station 🚌

UNITED STATES
Gulf of Mexico
MEXICO
Mexico ★City
PACIFIC OCEAN
Oaxaca

0   200 yds
0   200 m

To Mexico City
Olivera
Gómez Farías
JUÁREZ PARK
Rufino Tamayo
Panoramic View
Humboldt
García Vigil
Alcalá
Zarate
Berriozábal
CERRO DEL FORTÍN
Carranza
Santo Domingo Plaza
Avenida Juárez
Constitución
Allende
Gurrión
Porfirio Díaz
N. Bravo
L. Abasolo
Pino Suárez
Matamoros
Murguía
Reforma
5 de Mayo
Av. Morelos
Crespo
Tinoco y Palacios
Avenida Independencia
Catedral
Alameda de León
Avenida Hidalgo
Zócalo
Galeana
Mier y Terán
Trujano
Vicente Guerrero
M. Fiallo
J.P. García
Las Casas
Colón
Markets
20 de Noviembre
Aldama
Rayón
Bus
G. Díaz Ordaz
Mina
Arteaga
Information
Post Office
Zaragoza
Closed to Traffic
Arista
Burgoa
M. Cabrera
C.M. Bustamente
Armienta
y López
M. Fiallo
Nuño del Mercado
Xóchitl
Moctezuma
Vega
Arroyo River
To Monte Albán
Porfirio Díaz Bridge
To Zaachila
To Airport & Coyotepec

six-passenger twin-engine Aero-Commander to and from Puerto Escondido and Bahías de Huatulco once daily (twice if there are enough passengers). Make arrangements for Aerovega at the Monte Albán Hotel facing the Alameda (next to the *zócalo*, or town square). The cost is roughly $100/£50 each way.

BY CAR   It's a 5-hour drive from Mexico City on the toll road, **Highway 135D,** which begins at Cuacnoapalan, about 80km (50 miles) east-southeast of Puebla, and runs south, terminating in Oaxaca; the one-way toll is $30 (£15).

BY BUS   First-class and deluxe buses to and from Mexico City use the *autopista* (superhighway toll road), which takes 6 hours. A few make a short stop in Nochistlán, which isn't much of a delay. Most buses leave from Mexico City's **TAPO (east) bus station.** There is infrequent service to and from Mexico City's Central del Norte (north), and the Central del Sur (south, also called Taxqueña). No service runs from the Mexico City airport. The **main bus station** in Oaxaca is on Calzada Niños Héroes. In was enlarged and remodeled in 2007, which has vastly improved bus travel to Oaxaca.

ADO (Autobuses del Oriente) and its affiliates handle most of the first-class and deluxe bus service. Your options are: *primera clase* (ADO), with almost hourly departures and a one-way fare of $35 (£18); *de lujo* (ADO GL) with five or more departures per day for $41 (£21) one-way; and *servicio ejecutivo* (UNO), with four departures per day for $58 (£29) one-way. *De lujo* has the same seats as first class, but more legroom, free soda and bottled water, and separate bathrooms for men and women. *Servicio ejecutivo* has all this plus super-wide seats that recline far back. During holidays, you need to reserve a seat. Native Oaxaqueños living outside the state fill the buses for the Days of the Dead, Holy Week, and Christmas. It's possible to reserve seats over the Internet for the higher levels of service, and to check departure times and prices at **www.adogl.com.mx** and **www.uno.com.mx**.

Buses serve Tuxtla Gutiérrez and San Cristóbal de las Casas (two overnight buses); Puebla (10 a day); Tehuacán (four a day); Veracruz (four a day); Villahermosa (two a day); and Huatulco, and Puerto Escondido on the coast (two a day). These last buses take 10 hours to reach Puerto Escondido because they go by way of Huatulco; for a faster trip, see below.

You can buy your tickets ahead of time at one of the downtown offices of **Ticket Bus.** There's one on 20 de Noviembre 103-D, near the corner of Hidalgo, 1 block from the *zócalo* (© **951/514-6655**). Office hours are Monday through Saturday from 9am to 10pm, Sunday from 9am to 4pm.

The **Viajes Atlántida** agency, La Noria 101, near Armenta y López (© **951/514-7077**), offers daily service to Pochutla in Suburbans. It's much faster than the bus. There are nine runs daily (4 hr.; $14/£7). From Pochutla you can catch a *colectivo* (Volkswagen van) to **Puerto Escondido, Huatulco,** or **Puerto Angel** (which run 1–1½ hr.). You should buy your tickets in advance. The agency is open daily from 5:30am to 11:30pm.

The speediest buses to Puerto Escondido—6 hours away over a tortuous road— leave from the *terminal de segunda clase* (second-class terminal) Armenta y López 721, across from the Red Cross. Two lines serve the route: Pacífico Oaxaca and Estrella del Valle. Many people who go to Puerto Escondido on these buses say that if they had it to do over, they'd fly. Motion sickness is the main reason; there are hundreds of curves through the mountains.

ORIENTATION

ARRIVING BY PLANE   The airport is south of town; it's about a 20-minute cab ride. Buy a ticket at the window on your left as you exit the airport. A private cab is $12 (£6); a *colectivo* is $3 (£1.50) per person for downtown locations, more for outlying areas.

The same company provides service from the town to the airport. Go to **Transportes Aeropuerto Oaxaca** (© 951/514-4350), on the Alameda, in the building facing the cathedral. It doesn't accept phone reservations, so drop by Monday through Saturday from 9am to 2pm or 5 to 8pm to buy your ticket and arrange hotel pickup. The cost is $3.50 (£1.75) from downtown hotels, $7 (£3.50) and up from outlying hotels, and more if you have extra luggage.

ARRIVING BY BUS   The ADO first-class bus station is a short distance north of the center of town. A taxi ride to downtown is $3 (£1.50). If you're coming from the Pacific coast, you may arrive at the Central Camionera de Segunda Clase (second-class bus terminal) next to the Abastos Market. It's 10 long blocks southwest of the *zócalo*.

VISITOR INFORMATION   The **State Tourist Office** (©/fax 951/516-0123) is at Murguía 206, between Reforma and 5 de Mayo. There you will find an information desk open every day from 8am to 8pm. Tourism also has an information office at Calle Independencia 607, corner of García Vigil, in front of the Alameda. It shares the building with a museum, Museo de los Pintores, and shares the same hours: Tuesday to Sunday from 10am to 8pm.

CITY LAYOUT   Oaxaca's east–west axis is **Independencia.** When streets cross Independencia and the north–south axis, **Alcalá/Bustamante,** their names change. The city's center is the *zócalo,* a large square surrounded by stone archways, and the **Alameda,** a smaller plaza attached to the northwest part of the *zócalo.* Oaxaca's cathedral faces the Alameda; its Palacio del Gobierno faces the *zócalo.* A few blocks to the north is the **Plaza de Santo Domingo.** The area between these two open spaces holds most of the historic district's shops, hotels, and restaurants. Two of the streets that run from Santo Domingo toward the *zócalo*—**Alcalá** and **Cinco de Mayo**—are partly closed to traffic.

GETTING AROUND   By Car   If you want to rent a car, try **Arrendadora Express,** 20 de Noviembre 103-B (© 951/516-6776). Rental cars in Oaxaca are expensive, and the process is not exactly streamlined.

By Taxi   If you want to reach some of the outlying villages, I recommend hiring a taxi or signing up for a tour. Most taxi drivers have set hourly rates for touring the Oaxacan valleys. A trustworthy and careful taxi driver who speaks English is **Tomás Ramírez.** You can reach him at home (© 951/511-5061; tomasramirez@prodigy.net.mx).

By Bus   Buses to the outlying villages of Guelatao, Teotitlán del Valle, Tlacolula, and Mitla leave from the second-class station just north of the Abastos Market. *Colectivos* leave for nearby villages from Calle Mercaderes, on the south side of the Abastos Market.

FAST FACTS: Oaxaca

American Express   The office, in **Viajes Micsa,** is at Valdivieso and Hidalgo, at the northeast corner of the *zócalo* (© 951/516-2700; fax 951/516-7475). American

Express office hours are Monday through Friday from 9am to 2pm and 4 to 6pm, Saturday from 9am to 1pm. The travel agency stays open later and doesn't close for lunch.

Area Code   The telephone area code is **951.**

Books, Newspapers & Magazines   **Amate Books,** Alcalá 307-2, a few steps from Santo Domingo (*(*) **951/516-6960**), has perhaps the best selection anywhere of books in English about Mexico. It stocks English-language magazines as well as a number of books about Oaxacan handicrafts. Hours are Monday through Saturday from 10:30am to 2:30pm and 3:30 to 7:30pm. A couple of monthly freebies, the English-language *Oaxaca Times* and the trilingual (English, Spanish, and French) *OAXACA,* circulate through the city and have information for tourists.

Consulates   The **Canadian consulate,** Pino Suárez 700-11B (*(*) **951/513-3777**), is open daily from 11am to 2pm. The **U.S. Consular Agency** is at Alcalá 407, Int. 20 (*(*)/fax **951/514-3054**). Hours are Monday through Friday from 10am to 3pm.

Currency Exchange   *Casas de cambio* cluster on the streets at the northeast corner of the *zócalo,* at Alcalá and Valdivieso. These places post their rates, have short lines, and keep better hours than banks. Several exchange Canadian dollars.

Doctor   Dr. Carlos Arnaud Carreño is a reputable internist at Calle Reforma 905 (*(*) **951/515-4053**). Hours are Monday through Friday noon to 2pm and 4 to 8pm.

Emergencies   The phone number for emergencies is *(*) **060.**

Internet Access   In the downtown area, there are more than 20 Internet access services and cybercafes. Most are along Alcalá and around the *zócalo* and the Plaza Santo Domingo.

Population   Oaxaca has 510,000 residents.

Post Office   The *correo* is at the corner of Independencia and Alameda Park. It is open Monday through Friday from 8am to 5pm, Saturday from 9am to 1pm.

Seasons   April and May are the hottest, driest months. (Also in May, rural teachers invade the *zócalo* and create havoc in the downtown area while they demonstrate for higher wages.) The rains come in June and improve things considerably. June through March, the city is most enjoyable. High seasons for tourists, when you can expect higher hotel rates, are late July and August (especially around the Guelaguetza), early November (around the Days of the Dead), the entire month of December, and during Easter.

Shipping   The cheapest way to transport your goods is to have them packed securely so that you can check them as extra baggage on your flight home. Another way is to ship them. Many stores will pack and ship their own merchandise, but not other stores' goods.

SPECIAL EVENTS & FESTIVALS

Oaxaca is famous for its exuberant traditional festivals. The most important ones are **Holy Week,** the **Guelaguetza** in July, **Días de los Muertos** in November, and the **Night of the Radishes** and **Christmas** in December. Make hotel reservations at least 2 months in advance if you plan to visit during these times.

At festival time in Oaxaca, sidewalk stands near the cathedral sell *buñuelos,* a thin, crisp, sweet snack food. It is customary to serve *buñuelos* in cracked or otherwise flawed dishes; after you've finished eating, you smash the crockery on the sidewalk for good luck. Don't be timid! You can wash down the *buñuelos* with hot *ponche* (a steaming fruit punch) or *atole.*

HOLY WEEK During Holy Week, figurines made of palm leaves are sold on the streets. On Palm Sunday, the Sunday before Easter, there are colorful parades. On the following Thursday, Oaxaca residents follow the Procession of the Seven Churches. Hundreds of the pious walk from church to church, praying at each one. The next day, Good Friday, many of the *barrios* (neighborhoods) have *encuentros:* Groups depart separately from the church, carrying religious figures through the neighborhoods, then "encounter" each other back at the church. Throughout the week, each church sponsors concerts, fireworks, fairs, and other entertainment.

FIESTA GUELAGUETZA On the last two Mondays in July, Oaxaca holds the Fiesta Guelaguetza. In the villages of central Oaxaca, a *guelaguetza* (literally, a gift) is a celebration by a family in need of assistance to hold a wedding or some other community celebration. Guests bring gifts, which the family repays when they attend other *guelaguetzas.* The Fiesta Guelaguetza, begun in 1974, brings dancers from all the state's various ethnic groups to Oaxaca. For many communities, participation has become a matter of intense civic pride, and an opportunity to show people in the state capital and those from other ethnic groups the beauty of their traditional clothing and dance. Some 350 different *huipiles* (women's overblouses) and dresses can be seen during the performances. In the afternoon, there is an interpretive dance of the legend of Princess Donají.

The performances take place in the stadium that crowns the Cerro del Fortín each Monday from 10am to 1pm. Admission ranges from free (Section C) to $50 to $70 (£25–£35; Section A). Reserve tickets in advance—no later than May—through the State Tourism Office. A travel agency may be able to help you. I recommend Sections 5 and 6 in Palco (gallery) A for the best seating. The ticket color matches the color of your seat. You will be sitting in strong sunlight, so wear a hat and long sleeves.

Even if you don't attend the dances, you can enjoy the festival atmosphere that engulfs the city. There are fairs, exhibits, and a lot of gaiety. On the Sunday nights before the Guelaguetza, university students present an excellent program in the Plaza de la Danza at the Soledad church. The production, the *Bani Stui Gulal,* is an abbreviated history of the Oaxaca valley. The program begins at 9pm; arrive early, because the event is free and seating is limited.

DIAS DE LOS MUERTOS The Mexican Days of the Dead festival (Nov 1–2) has garnered worldwide attention. It is celebrated across Oaxaca with more enthusiasm than in the rest of Mexico, which says quite a lot. Markets brim with marigolds—the flower of the underworld—and every household fills an altar with them and the favorite dishes, drinks, and cigarettes of the deceased. People visit relatives and friends, and anyone who visits is offered food. This is also the time to pay one's respects at the graveyard. Try to take one of the nocturnal cemetery tours offered around this time. **Hotel Casa Arnel** (© **951/515-2856**) runs one. Another common form of celebrating is for young men to dress up in macabre outfits and frolic in the streets in Carnaval-like fashion.

DECEMBER FESTIVALS The December Festivals begin on the 12th with the **Fiesta de la Virgen de Guadalupe (Festival of the Virgin of Guadalupe)** and continue on the 16th with a *calenda,* or procession, to many of the older churches in the *barrios,* all accompanied by dancing and costumes. Festivities continue on the 18th with the **Fiesta de la Soledad** in honor of the Virgen de la Soledad, patroness of Oaxaca State. A large fireworks construction known as a *castillo* is erected in Plaza de la Soledad. When it is ignited, look out. December 23 is **La Noche de Rábanos** (the Night of the Radishes), when Oaxaqueños build fantastic sculptures out of enormous radishes, flowers, and cornhusks. Displays on three sides of the *zócalo* are set up from 3pm on. By 6pm, when the show officially opens, lines to see the figures are 4 blocks long. It's well organized and overseen by a heavy police presence. On December 24, around 8:30pm, each Oaxacan church organizes a procession with music, floats, enormous papier-mâché dancing figures, and crowds bearing candles, all of which converge on the *zócalo.*

EXPLORING OAXACA

There is so much sightseeing to do inside and outside Oaxaca that you have to be sure to allow for some idle time in the *zócalo.* In the traffic-free square, you can relax while getting a feel for the town and Oaxacan society. I recommend going in the late afternoon and taking a seat at the outdoor cafe with the best view of the cathedral. You can get a beer or order a bowl of the traditional drink of Oaxaca: chocolate. The afternoon light filters through the shiny green leaves of the laurel trees, heightening the color of the cathedral's green stone. As dusk comes, a small drill corps enters stage left and performs a flag-lowering ceremony with much pomp and circumstance. Then the *marimba* or the municipal band usually strikes up in the central bandstand.

The city contains museums worth visiting, some interesting churches, and colorful markets. Outside town are the famous ruins of Monte Albán and Mitla and area villages known for their arts and crafts.

MUSEUMS

Museo de Arte Contemporáneo de Oaxaca   The MACO, 2½ blocks north of the *zócalo,* exhibits the work of contemporary artists, primarily from Oaxaca state (which has produced some of Mexico's most famous painters). It also books traveling exhibitions. A small bookstore is to your right as you enter. The 18th-century building merits a visit for its own sake. It's called the Casa de Cortés, and many locals say that it was built by order of Hernán Cortez after he received the title of Marqués of the Valley of Oaxaca. In fact, the record shows that it was build a century later.
Alcalá 202, between Murguía and Morelos. ⓒ 951/514-2228. Admission $2 (£1). Wed–Mon 10:30am–8pm.

Museo Regional de Oaxaca ⭐⭐⭐   Next to the Santo Domingo Church (6 blocks north of the *zócalo*) is the most impressive museum in the city, housed in a former Dominican convent—one of the greatest of colonial Mexico. Construction was largely completed by the early 1600s. The government has spent millions to renovate the former convent, and it shows. The stairs, the arches, the cupolas—everywhere you look, there are lovely details in stone or in the remnants of Colonial-Era murals. The museum is an ambitious project that displays the course of human development in the Oaxaca valley from earliest times to the 20th century.

The most treasured possessions are the artifacts from Monte Albán's Tomb 7, which were discovered in 1932. The tomb contained 12 to 14 corpses and some 500 pieces of jewelry and art, making use of almost 3.6kg (8 pounds) of gold and turquoise, conch shell, amber, and obsidian. This is part of a larger collection of artifacts from Monte Albán, which you would do well to see before going up to the ruins. In the many ceramics and carvings you can see definite Olmec and Teotihuacán influences, yet they display a style distinctly different from either culture. Other rooms are dedicated to the present-day ethnographic makeup of Oaxaca and a brief history of the efforts of the Dominican order in the region. Attached to the convent is the Santo Domingo Church (see "Churches," below). From some points on the north side of the convent you can look down over the recently opened botanical garden. Admission to the garden is free but by guided tour only (at 1 and 6pm). Sign up at the front desk of the museum the same day of the tour. There are two tours a week in English; ask for info at the front desk.

Gurrión at Alcalá. (✆) **951/516-2991.** Admission $4.50 (£2.25). $3.50 (£1.75) for use of video camera. Tues–Sun 10am–6:15pm.

Rufino Tamayo Museo de Arte Prehispánico de México ⟨★★★⟩   The artifacts displayed in this museum were chosen "solely for the aesthetic rank of the works, their beauty, power, and originality." The result is a striking collection of pre-Hispanic art. The famed Oaxacan artist Rufino Tamayo amassed the collection over a 20-year period. The artifacts range from the pre-Classic period up to the Aztec, from far northwest Nayarit to southeastern Chiapas: terra-cotta figurines, scenes of daily life, lots of female fertility figures, Olmec and Totonac sculpture from the Gulf Coast, and Zapotec long-nosed figures. The well-displayed works reveal the great variety of styles of pre-Columbian art in Mexico.

Av. Morelos 503, north of the zócalo between Tinoco y Palacios and Porfirio Díaz. (✆) **951/516-4750.** Admission $3.50 (£1.75). Mon and Wed–Sat 10am–2pm and 4–7pm; Sun 10am–3pm. Closed holidays.

CHURCHES

Basílica de la Soledad ⟨★★⟩   The Basílica is the religious center of Oaxaca, and its Virgin is the patroness of the entire state. Adjoining the church is a former convent with a small but charming museum in back. A huge celebration on and around December 18 honors the Virgin, attracting penitents from all over Oaxaca. She is famous for her vestments, which are encrusted with pearls. (Until a few years ago, she had a crown of silver and jewels, which was stolen.) As with most Virgins, there is a story behind her. The short version is that her figure (actually just her hands and face) was found in a box on the back of a burro that didn't belong to anyone. The burro sat down on an outcropping of rock and refused to get up. This was the spot where the Virgin revealed herself and, consequently, where the basilica (completed in 1690) was constructed. You can still see the outcropping of rock, surrounded by a cage of iron bars, immediately to your right along the wall as you enter the church.

The concave facade of the church projecting forward from the building is unique in Mexico's religious architecture. The way the top is rounded and the tiers are divided suggests an imitation in stone of the baroque wooden *retablos* (altarpieces) common in Mexican churches. The interior is most impressive, too, but what I really like is the museum, which contains a curious blend of pieces—some museum quality, others mere trinkets that might as well have come from my grandmother's attic.

The Basílica's upper plaza is an outdoor patio and theater (Plaza de la Danza) with stone steps that serve as seats. Here, spectators view the famous Bani Stui Gulal (see "Fiesta Guelaguetza" under "Special Events & Festivals," above). When visiting the Basílica, it is traditional to eat ice cream; there are vendors in the lower plaza in front of the church.

Independencia at Galeana. No phone. Museum: Admission whatever you wish to donate. Mon–Sat 10am–2pm and 4–6pm; Sun 11am–2pm. Basílica: Daily 7am–2pm and 4–9pm.

Catedral de Oaxaca 𝒦𝒦   The cathedral was built in 1553 and reconstructed in 1773. Its elaborate 18th-century baroque facade is an excellent example of the Oaxacan style. The central panel above the door depicts the assumption of the Virgin. Note the heavy, elaborate frame around the picture and the highly stylized wavelike clouds next to the cherubs—these elements, repeated in other churches in the region, are telltale signs of Oaxacan baroque. An uncommon and quite lovely detail is how the Virgin's cape and its folds are depicted in angular lines and facets. The cathedral's interior is not as interesting as its exterior because it was plundered during the Wars of Reform.

Fronting the Parque Alameda. No phone. Free admission. Daily 7am–9pm.

Iglesia de San Felipe Neri   This church, 2½ blocks northeast of the *zócalo,* was built in 1636 and displays all the architectural opulence of that period: The altar and nave are covered with ornately carved, gilded wood, and the walls are frescoed. In the west transept and chapel is a small figure of St. Martha and the dragon; the faithful have bedecked her with ribbons in hopes of obtaining her assistance.

Tinoco y Palacios at Independencia. No phone. Free admission. Daily 8am–11pm.

Iglesia de Santo Domingo 𝒦𝒦𝒦 *(Moments*   There are 27 churches in Oaxaca, but none can equal the splendor of this one's interior. The church was started in the 1550s by Dominican friars and finished a century later; it contains the work of all the best artists of that period. Ornate plaster statues and flowers cover the extravagantly gilded walls and ceiling. When the sun shines through the yellow stained-glass window, it casts a golden glow over the whole interior and looks like a baroque vision of heaven. Just as you enter, look up at the ceiling formed by the choir loft to examine the elaborate genealogical tree of the Dominican order, which starts with don Domingo de Guzmán, Saint Dominic himself.

Corner of Gurrión and Alcalá. No phone. Free admission. Daily 7am–2pm and 4–11pm.

San Juan de Dios   This is the oldest church in Oaxaca, originally built in 1521 or 1522 of adobe and thatch. Construction of the present structure started during the mid-1600s and included a convent and hospital (where the 20 de Noviembre Market is now). The exterior is sweetly simple; the interior has an ornate altar and Urbano Olivera paintings on the ceiling. Oaxaqueños especially revere the glass shrine to the Virgin near the entrance, as well as one dedicated to Christ (off to the right). Because it's by the market, 1 block west and 2 blocks south of the *zócalo,* many of the people who visit the church are villagers who have come to Oaxaca to buy and sell.

20 de Noviembre s/n (corner of Aldama and Arteaga). No phone. Free admission. Daily 6am–11pm.

MORE ATTRACTIONS

Besides visiting the places mentioned below, try to get to the **Casa de Cortés,** which houses the Museo de Arte Contemporáneo (see above), and the former convent of **Santa Catalina,** home of the Hotel Camino Real (see below).

Casa de Juárez   This modest museum occupies the house where Benito Juárez first lived when he came to the city as a servant boy. It doesn't have any of his personal effects or any furniture belonging to the house, but it shows how a typical 19th-century household would have looked.

García Vigil 609. ℭ **951/516-1860.** Admission $3.50 (£1.75). Tues–Sat 10am–7pm; Sun 10am–5pm.

Cerro del Fortín To capture Oaxaca in a glance, take a cab to the top of this hill on the west side of town for a panoramic view. It's especially pretty just before sunset. Atop the hill are the statue of Benito Juárez and a stadium built to hold 15,000 spectators. The annual Fiesta Guelaguetza is held here. You can walk to the hill: Head up Díaz Ordaz/Crespo and look for the Escaleras del Fortín (Stairway to the Fortress) shortly after you cross Calle Delmonte; the 218 steps (interrupted by risers) are a challenge, but the view is worth it.

Díaz Ordaz at Calle Delmonte. No phone.

Teatro Macedonio de Alcalá This beautiful 1903 Belle Epoque theater, 2 blocks east of the *zócalo,* holds 1,300 people and is still used for concerts and performances in the evening. Peek through the doors to see the marble stairway and Louis XV vestibule. Sometimes a list of events is posted on the doors.

Independencia at Armenta y López. No phone. Open only for events.

SHOPPING

Oaxaca and the surrounding villages are wonderful hunting grounds for handcrafted pottery, woodcarvings, and weavings. The hunt itself may be the best part. Specialties include the shiny **black pottery** for which Oaxaca is famous, **woolen textiles** with the deep reds and purples produced using the natural dye *cochineal,* and highly imaginative *alebrijes* **(wood carvings).**

SHOPS & GALLERIES

Most of the shops, galleries, and boutiques are in the area between **Santo Domingo** and the *zócalo,* comprising the streets of **Alcalá, 5 de Mayo,** and **García Vigil** and the **cross streets.** Customary store hours are from 10am to 2pm and 4 to 7pm Monday through Saturday.

Artesanías e Industrias Populares del Estado de Oaxaca ARIPO is a government store with a broader range of goods than most shops, including masks, baskets, clothing, furniture, and cutlery. The staff speaks English and will ship your purchases anywhere. Open Monday through Friday from 9am to 8pm, Saturday from 10am to 6pm, and Sunday from 11am to 4pm. It is 2 blocks above the Benito Juárez house. García Vigil 809 (at Cosijopi). © 951/514-4030.

Galería Arte de Oaxaca This gallery represents some of the state's leading contemporary artists. It's 2 blocks north and 1 block east of the *zócalo.* Murguía 105. © 951/514-0910 or -1532.

Galería Quetzalli A modest-looking art gallery behind the Church of Santo Domingo, Galería Quetzalli represents some of the big names in Mexican art—Francisco Toledo and José Villalobos—and some up-and-coming artists. Quetzalli also has a gallery at Murguía 400. Constitución 104. © 951/514-0030.

Indigo Beautiful and uncommon (and expensive) objects can be found here. The store can really test your resolution not to buy more artwork; go in and take a peek. Allende 104. © 951/514-8338.

La Mano Mágica Come here to see some of the best rug weaving in Oaxaca (by Arnulfo Mendoza) before you head to Teotitlán to see the work of other weavers. In the back rooms you can find well-chosen pieces of regional folk art. Shipping is available. The store is opposite the Museo de Arte Contemporáneo. Alcalá 203 (between Morelos and Matamoros). © 951/516-4275.

MARO   This is the store of Mujeres Artesanas de la Región de Oaxaca, a cooperative of women artisans. You'll find all the handicrafts of the state represented. Things are well priced and the quality of the goods is high. Open daily 9am to 8pm. 5 de Mayo 204 (between Murguía and Morelos). ℂ 951/516-0670.

MARKETS

There are two market areas: one just south of the *zócalo*, and the newer Abastos Market, about 10 blocks west. Both areas bustle with people and are surrounded by small shops selling anything from hardware to leather goods to fabrics.

A few shops specialize in chocolate (not for eating, but for making hot chocolate) and *mole* paste. The neighboring state of Tabasco grows most of the cacao beans used for the chocolate. They are ground with almonds and cinnamon and pressed into bars or tablets. To prepare the drink, you dissolve the chocolate in hot milk or water (the more traditional drink) and beat until frothy. *Mole* paste, which contains chocolate, is used to make the classic Oaxacan dishes *mole negro* and *mole rojo*. A good place to hunt for chocolate and *mole* paste is along Mina street, on the south side of the 20 de Noviembre Market (see listing below). Here you'll find **Chocolate Mayordomo** and **Chocolate La Soledad**. Both offer a variety of preparations to fit American and European tastes, but I like the traditional Mexican best.

Note: Markets are generally open daily from 8am to 5pm.

Benito Juárez Market   One block south of the *zócalo*, this covered market is big and busy; stalls sell vegetables, flowers, medicinal preparation, meats, cheeses, and even clothing. Between calles Las Casas, Cabrera, Aldama, and 20 de Noviembre.

Mercado Abastos   The Abastos Market is open daily but is most active on Saturday, when Indians from the villages come to town to sell and shop. You'll see dried chiles, herbs, vegetables, crafts, bread, and even burros for sale at this bustling market. Ten blocks west of *zócalo*, between Calle Mercaderes and the *periférico*.

Mercado de Artesanía   Located 1 block south and 1 block west of the 20 de Noviembre Market, this market sells mostly textiles and articles of clothing at cheap prices. J. P. García and Zaragoza.

20 de Noviembre Market   This market is just south of the Benito Juárez Market, across Aldama. There are a lot of food stalls, but also some arts and crafts. On the south side, along Mina, are stores selling chocolate and *mole* paste. Between calles Aldama, Cabrera, Mina, and 20 de Noviembre.

OTHER THINGS TO DO

COOKING CLASSES   Susana Trilling (ℂ 951/518-7726; www.seasonsofmy heart.com), author of the cookbook *Seasons of My Heart*, operates a cooking school of the same name just outside Oaxaca. In downtown Oaxaca, Señora Pilar Cabrera, owner of La Olla restaurant, gives cooking classes at Libres 205. She can be reached at ℂ **951/516-5704** or at bugambilias2@yahoo.com.mx.

SPANISH CLASSES   Oaxaca has about a half-dozen language schools. With prior notice, most can arrange homestays with a Mexican family for students looking for total immersion. With little notice, most can arrange a week of classes for visitors to brush up their language skills. The **Instituto Cultural Oaxaca**, Av. Juárez 909 (Apdo. Postal 340, 68000 Oaxaca, Oax.; ℂ **951/515-3404**; www.instculturaloax.com.mx), has the biggest name and perhaps the least flexibility. Besides language skill, classes focus on Oaxaca's history and archaeology. The **Instituto de Comunicación y Cultura,** Alcalá 307–312

(68000 Oaxaca, Oax.; ©/fax **951/516-3443;** www.iccoax.com), provides group and private instruction and uses music, art, and handicrafts to get students into the swing of things. Classes are small. **Becari Language School,** M. Bravo 210 (68000 Oaxaca, Oax.; © **951/514-6076;** www.becari.com.mx), was founded in 1994, and I'm hearing more and more good things from students—lots of flexibility and small classes.

HIKING & BIKING   Northwest of the city of Oaxaca is a mountain range known as the Sierra Norte that is cooler and wetter than the valley. The native communities offer guides and simple lodging for active sorts who are interested in seeing yet another side of Mexico. Several ecotourism outfits work with these communities. For information, ask at the State Tourism Office. **Zona Bici,** García Vigil 406 (© **951/516-0953;** www.oaxacawebs.org/zonabici), does bike tours on back roads for about $40 (£20) for a 4-hour tour.

WHERE TO STAY

High season includes Easter, July, August, early November, and most of December. You should have no difficulty finding a room the rest of the time, and promotional rates are usually available. The prices listed below include the 18% tax. Most evenings are cool enough that you don't need air-conditioning, but for about 60 days a year, mostly from April to June, it comes in handy, and not every hotel has it.

VERY EXPENSIVE

Camino Real Oaxaca ����   A magnificent hotel in a 16th-century landmark convent, this is the place to cloister yourself when in Oaxaca. Several beautiful courtyards with age-old walls bring to mind the original purpose of the building. The rooms, however, do not. All are comfortable and have the conveniences you would expect in a hotel of this caliber (no small feat given the constraints imposed by the infrastructure). Exterior rooms are equipped with noise-reducing windows. Interior rooms with views of the courtyards are more expensive. The main difference between "deluxe" and "club" is the size of the room. Service is good. The location—between the *zócalo* and Santo Domingo on a pedestrian-only street—is ideal.

5 de Mayo 300, 68000 Oaxaca, Oax. © **800/722-6466** in the U.S. and Canada, or 951/501-6100. Fax 951/516-0732. www.caminoreal.com/oaxaca. 91 units. $354–$414 (£177–£207) deluxe; $396–$426 (£198–£213) club; $500 (£250) junior suite. Discounts and promotions available in low season. AE, MC, V. Valet parking $16 (£8). **Amenities:** Restaurant; 2 bars; large outdoor swimming pool; free membership for guests at local health club; children's activities in high season; tour desk; car-rental desk; room service; babysitting; laundry service; dry cleaning; nonsmoking rooms. *In room:* A/C, TV, minibar, hair dryer, safe.

Casa Cid de León ��   Casa Cid de León has easily the largest suites in downtown Oaxaca. Each is extravagantly decorated in colonial style, with a few modern touches and fresh-cut flowers. The one that garners the most attention (La Bella Epoca) has three balconies facing the street and a large sitting room. The two-story, two-bathroom suite (El Mío Cid) would be perfect for a family. One of the downstairs suites, La Dominica, is my favorite for its space and comfort. Guests have access to a rooftop terrace. The location, 2 blocks north of the *zócalo,* is excellent, and Señora Cid de León is a most accommodating hotel owner. The hotel offers custom tours of the city and surrounding valley.

Av. Morelos 602, 68000 Oaxaca, Oax. © **951/514-1893.** Fax 951/514-7013. www.casaciddeleon.com. 4 units. $222–$270 (£111–£135) suite. Rates include juice, coffee, airport transfer, and tour of city. AE, MC, V. Valet parking $10 (£5). **Amenities:** Tour and limo service; business services; in-room salon services; room service; in-room massage; babysitting; laundry service. *In room:* A/C, TV, hair dryer.

EXPENSIVE

Hotel Victoria ★★ *Finds* High above the downtown area, the Hotel Victoria offers that rare combination of proximity and the feeling of distance. It is ideal for those who want a little more peace than staying downtown can offer. And you're only a couple of minutes away on the hotel's shuttle bus. The Victoria also has a lovely view. You can enjoy it from a room or suite in one of the main buildings (three stories, no elevator), or you can stay in one of the villas distributed about the grounds, each with its own terrace. Rooms are large and carpeted and have modern furnishings.

Lomas del Fortín 1, 68070 Oaxaca, Oax. © 951/515-2633. Fax 951/515-2411. www.hotelvictoriaoax.com.mx. 149 units. $182 (£91) standard double; $236 (£118) villa; $304 (£157) junior suite. AE, MC, V. Free parking. **Amenities:** Restaurant; bar; large outdoor swimming pool; tennis court; complimentary shuttle to downtown; babysitting; laundry service; dry cleaning; nonsmoking rooms. *In room:* A/C, TV, minibar, hair dryer, safe.

MODERATE

Casa Colonial Bed and Breakfast ★ The casual and comfortable setting created by attentive hosts Jane and Thornton Robison promptly sets guests at ease. This is an especially attractive place for first-timers to Oaxaca, who can tap into the owners' knowledge of the area and perhaps even tour some villages with them. The good-size rooms open to a large garden with tall jacaranda trees; they are simply but comfortably furnished. Breakfast is substantial: fresh fruit, yogurt, hot cereal, eggs, bacon, juice, and coffee. The hotel is farther from downtown than most of the others listed here. Rooms are not available for the Day of the Dead season or Christmas. Occasionally there is live music on Sunday afternoons.

Negrete 105 (Apdo. Postal 640), 68000 Oaxaca, Oax. © 800/758-1697 in the U.S., or ©/fax 951/516-5280. www.casa-colonial.com. 15 units. $95 (£48) double. Rates include full breakfast. MC, V. Free parking. Pass La Soledad church on Av. Morelos, and angle right for a couple of blocks; the green house with purple trim (there's no sign) will be on your left. *In room:* No phone.

Casa Vértiz ★ *Value* Small courtyard hotel in good location. Rooms are medium size and come with either one or two queen-size beds. They are nicely done, with tile floor, beamed ceiling, stucco walls, and a few artsy decorations. There's good luggage space. Bathrooms are a little on the small side but attractive. A few come with tub/shower combinations.

Reforma 404, 68000 Oaxaca, Oax. © 951/516-1700. www.hotelvertiz.com.mx. 14 units. $100–$115 (£50–£58) double. MC, V. Free secured parking nearby. **Amenities:** Restaurant; bar; tours; room service; laundry service; dry cleaning; nonsmoking rooms. *In room:* A/C (in 12 units), TV, Wi-Fi, coffeemaker, hair dryer, safe.

Hotel Aitana ★ *Finds* This stylish hotel is only 8 blocks from the *zócalo* and 6 blocks from Santo Domingo, but it's about 30m (98 ft.) uphill on a noisy street. All the rooms are away from the street, though, past a courtyard restaurant. They are well lit and beautifully decorated. Most hold two twin beds; a few have either two doubles or a king. Bathrooms are attractive and spacious, with tub/shower combinations.

Crespo 313, 68000 Oaxaca, Oax. © 951/514-3788 or -3839. Fax 951/516-9856. www.hotelaitanaoaxaca.com.mx. 23 units. High season $100–$120 (£50–£60) double, $140 (£70) junior suite; low season $50–$60 (£25–£30), $80 (£40) junior suite. Rates include full breakfast, and often the 3rd night is free. MC, V. Secure parking $5 (£2.50). **Amenities:** Restaurant; bar; tour info; room service; laundry service; dry cleaning. *In room:* TV, coffeemaker, hair dryer.

INEXPENSIVE

Hotel Casa Arnel *Value* *Kids* Not far from the bus station, this budget hotel is less than a kilometer (about a half-mile) from the *zócalo* but still within walking distance of most sights. It's a great choice for those traveling with kids: The Cruz family lives here with a couple of their children, and parrots hang out in the shady garden. From the rooftop terrace, you can admire the view and soak up some sun. Most rooms are plain but comfortable; some share bathrooms. Across the street in the new wing are three additional rooms with double beds and private bathrooms, plus four furnished, full-service apartments with fully equipped kitchens. Breakfast, at extra cost, is served on the patio. At Christmas, the family involves guests in the traditional Mexican celebrations, or *posadas,* which are held during the 12 nights before Christmas.

Aldama 404, Col. Jalatlaco, 68080 Oaxaca, Oax. ℂ/fax 951/515-2856. www.casaarnel.com.mx. 40 units. $24–$28 (£12–£14) double w/shared bathroom; $40–$45 (£20–£23) with private bathroom; $70–$80 (£35–£40) suite; $450 (£225) apt monthly. Rates rise 30% for Easter, Guelaguetza, Días de los Muertos, and Christmas. No credit cards. Self-parking $3. **Amenities:** Tours; Internet access; laundry service. *In room:* No phone.

Hotel Casa Cué *Value* A modern hotel 2 blocks from the *zócalo,* Casa Cué has good air-conditioning, good service, and bathrooms with instantly hot water. The lovely terrace on top of the three-story building (there's no elevator) has patio furniture and a fine view of the mountains. The midsize standard rooms are attractively furnished and well lit; most contain two twin beds. Junior suites are large and come with a sofa, coffee table, and writing table; most hold two double beds (some have one king and one double). The suites are still larger, and the second bedroom makes them perfect for a family. The hotel is well managed. It's across the street from the market, which can be a little noisy, but the double-glazed windows do a good job of blocking out the noise.

Aldama 103, 68000 Oaxaca, Oax. ℂ/fax 951/516-1336. www.mexonline.com/casacue.htm. 23 units. $60–$72 (£30–£40) double; $79–$92 (£43–£51) junior suite; $96–$130 (£53–£72) suite. AE, MC, V. Free covered, secure parking. **Amenities:** Tour info; car-rental desk; laundry service. *In room:* A/C, TV.

Hotel Maela This is a family hotel that the owners keep improving. The upkeep is good, the prices are good, and the location is a block behind Santo Domingo. Rooms are medium to small. Most have one double, two doubles, or one queen-size bed. The staff is very helpful.

Constitución 206, 68000 Oaxaca, Oax. ℂ/fax 951/516-6022. www.mexonline.com/maela.htm. 26 units. High season $60 (£30) double; low season $54 (£28). No credit cards. Free guarded parking. *In room:* TV, safe.

Las Golondrinas *ℱ* This charming one-story hotel sits amid rambling patios with roses, Fuchsia, bougainvillea, and mature banana trees. Owned and managed by Guillermina and Jorge Velasco, Las Golondrinas (The Swallows) is very popular, so make reservations in advance. The simply furnished rooms, with windows and doors opening onto courtyards, all have tile floors and a small desk and chairs. Each holds either one full or two twin beds. A few rooms have a king-size bed and go for a higher price. Breakfast is served between 8 and 10am in a small tile-covered cafe in a garden setting ($3–$7/£1.50–£3.50); nonguests are welcome. The hotel is 6½ blocks north of the *zócalo.*

Tinoco y Palacios 411 (between Allende and Bravo), 68000 Oaxaca, Oax. ℂ 951/514-3298 or ℂ/fax 951/514-2126. www.hotellasgolondrinas.com.mx. 26 units. $50–$60 (£25–£30) double. No credit cards. No parking. **Amenities:** Laundry service. *In room:* No phone.

WHERE TO DINE

Oaxacan cooking has a great reputation in Mexico. It makes use of more ingredients from the lowlands than central Mexican cooking. It's known for its *moles,* and for a wide variety of chiles, many of which you don't find in other parts of the country. Oaxaca is also known for its *mezcal,* a distillate of the *agave* or maguey plant (a different variety from the blue *agave* from which tequila is made). This drink has a rougher

Finds Oaxacan Street Food

Unless it's during a festival, don't be surprised to find many restaurants empty. Oaxaqueños do not frequent restaurants but do like eating in market and street stalls. They favor foods such as tacos, tamales, *tlayudas* (12-in. tortillas, slightly dried, with a number of toppings), and *empanadas* (in Oaxaca, large tortillas heated on the *comal*—a flat, earthenware pan—or among the coals, with several types of fillings). For adventurous diners, here are my picks for enjoying the people's food.

Empanadas are a morning food, and the best place to eat them is in **La Merced** market (on Murguía, about 10 blocks east of Alcalá), where you'll find a number of food stalls. Everyone has a favorite (mine comes with *huitlacoche*); try **La Güerita** or **La Florecita.**

The following places open only at night: A little *taquería* (taco stand) called **Tacos Sierra** (on corner of Morelos and Alcalá) is a Oaxacan institution. They make simple tacos with pork filling and a spicy salsa, but I can never order enough. It closes when the pork runs out, usually by 10pm. Don't expect these tacos to come cheap. Another *taquería* is **El Mesón,** which is across from the northeast corner of the *zócalo* at Hidalgo 805. It serves *tacos de la parrilla* (grill) and *de cazuela* (clay pot).

For *tlayudas,* seek out **El Chepil,** a hole-in-the-wall on Constitución around the corner from Calzada de la Revolución. They come with a number of toppings, and with *tasajo* (dried beef) or *cecina* (pork rubbed with red chile) on the side. If you don't like lard, tell them that you want yours *sin asiento.* This is also a good place for getting *tostadas.* For tamales, find the woman who sets up her little stand on Avenida Hidalgo and 20 de Noviembre, in front of the pharmacy. She often doesn't get there until 7:30pm, but when she does, she quickly draws a crowd that buys tamales to go. They sell six flavors, and my favorite is always the last one I've eaten. Given that you're in Oaxaca, though, you might want to ask for a tamal made with *mole negro, mole amarillo,* or *chepil* (an herb).

taste than tequila, and it's commonly drunk with lime and *sal de gusano* (salt with powdered *chile* and ground-up maguey worms—the same that show up in some bottles of *mezcal*). Any cantina worth its salt will offer *sal de gusano* to its customers.

Something else bears mentioning. Restaurateurs here seem bent on providing travelers with something more cosmopolitan than the local cuisine. I'm not sure why. Perhaps it's the product of a certain neocolonialist bias, or perhaps it's just the need to get fancy, but a number of fine dining places are trying hard and, in my opinion, are overrated. **Casa Oaxaca,** the restaurant (Constitución 104; ② **951/516-8889**), gets the best press. If you're tired of *moles,* then you might want to try this place once; don't go twice. **Los Danzantes** (Macedonio Alcalá 403; ② **951/501-1184**) brings Mexico City chic to Oaxaca. I like what the owners have done with the place but not with the food. Go for drinks. **La Biznaga** (García Vigil 512; ② **915/516-1800**) usually has the most interesting menu—try it sometime when you feel completely at leisure, because the service is absurdly slow.

Good coffee and espresso are easier to find these days, but you still have to make a point of seeking it out. **Café Brújula** ((✆ 951/526-0056) at 409 D García Vigil serves excellent coffee and light food to go with it. Another option is **Café Nuevo Mundo** ((✆ 951/501-2122) at M. Bravo 206.

EXPENSIVE

El Ché ✿ STEAKS   If you need a break from Mexican food, you can have a steak and salad in comfortable surroundings, and wash it all down with a glass of hearty red. The restaurant offers both American and Argentine cuts of beef; the rib-eye and the *churrasco* are the most popular. (To tell them how you'd like it cooked, see our dining guide.) The margaritas are good.

5 de Mayo 413. (✆ 951/514-2122. Reservations recommended during special festivals. Steaks $16–$24 (£8–£12). MC, V. Mon–Sat 1–11pm, Sun 1–9pm.

MODERATE

El Asador Vasco INTERNATIONAL/MEXICAN   Of the restaurants circling the *zócalo,* this is the best bet. It certainly offers the most pleasant dining area: Tables overlook the *zócalo* from a second-floor stone archway. Take your pick of purely Mexican specialties (chiles rellenos, *moles, carne asada*) or dishes with a European twist (snapper filet cooked in olive oil and *guajillo* chile).

Portal de Flores 11. (✆ 951/514-4755. Main courses $8–$16 (£4–£8). MC, V. Daily 1–11:30pm.

El Naranjo OAXACAN/MEXICAN   The new owner, Andrew Peterson, brought in cookbook author David Hoyer to create new dishes for the restaurant. The menu has an obvious American touch and includes things Mexicans wouldn't dream of—vegetables served as a side to *mole,* a *sope* buried under melted cheese, a *caldo tlalpeño* without garbanzos). Putting that aside, it's apparent that they're investing a lot of effort in the food and service. The vegetables were tender and cooked well, and the salads were fresh, but I still felt nostalgia for the former chef's *mole negro,* those little *taquitos de Santa Clara,* and more than a couple of her chiles rellenos.

Trujano 203. (✆ 951/514-1878. Reservations accepted. Main courses $9–$22 (£4.50–£11). AE, MC, V. Mon–Sat 1–10pm.

Marco Polo ✿ SEAFOOD   If the weather's nice, you can enjoy dining outdoors in Marco Polo's shaded patio. The ceviche tostadas or the seafood cocktails are great starters (if you like your cocktail less tomato-y, tell the waiter you want it *a la marinera*). The specialty is the oven-baked fish (whole or filet), prepared several ways—I like their basic method, with just a *chile guajillo* marinade. For dessert, try the baked bananas. Marco Polo is just north of the central downtown area; it fronts the park known as Paseo Juárez.

Pino Suárez 806. (✆ 951/513-4308. Breakfast $3 (£1.50); main courses $9–$15 (£4.50–£7.50). AE, MC, V. Wed–Mon 8am–6pm.

Los Pacos OAXACAN   This restaurant specializes in *moles.* They even serve a small sampler *(mole combinado),* or you can try *mole* in another form, as *enmoladas,* or with *chilaquiles.* I especially like the *negro* and the *rojo moles.* The table sauces are good, too. Besides that, you can try a couple of other local dishes, such as the *filete al mezcal*), but I would avoid the *botana oaxaqueña* (not just here, but in any local restaurant). There's a medium-size dining room as you enter, a couple of tables on the way to the kitchen, and a rooftop terrace that works well for dining in the evening.

Abasolo 121. (✆ 951/516-1704. Reservations accepted. Main courses $8–$16 (£4–£8). MC, V. Mon–Sat 12:30–9:45pm.

Yu Ne Nisa ☞ REGIONAL   In the hot lowlands of eastern Oaxaca, an area called the isthmus, you find a different cooking tradition known as *cocina istmeña*. You can sample some of the region's specialties at this restaurant, located in a residential part of the Colonia Reforma. Start off with some *garnachas* for appetizers—little corn patties covered in sauce—and then try one of the regional specialties such as shrimp *mole* or another kind of *mole* called *gucheguiña*. It just depends on what the owner has cooked up that day. Seafood plays a big part in *cocina istmeña*. Usually the chef can offer guests seafood cocktails and soups.

Amapolas 1425, Col. Reforma. ℭ 951/515-6982. Main courses $7–$12 (£3.50–£6). No credit cards. Daily 1–8pm.

INEXPENSIVE

Doña Elpidia ✦*Finds* OAXACAN   The phrase "home-style cooking" is bandied about a lot, but in this case it really means something. For the traveler, it means a meal just like one you'd get in a Mexican home. The house is 5½ blocks south of the *zócalo*, in the untouristy working-class part of the city. Look for a small sign saying only RESTAURANT. Upon entering, you will find some tables in a garden patio. There is also a dining room. The *comida corrida* includes bread, an appetizer, vegetable or pasta soup, rice, a main course (often a *mole*), and dessert. Beer and other beverages are extra. In high season, they often open for breakfast.

Miguel Cabrera 413 (between Arista and Nuño del Mercado). ℭ 951/516-4292. Fixed-price lunch $4.50 (£2.75). No credit cards. Daily 1–6pm.

Itanoni ☞ *Finds* MEXICAN/REGIONAL   This business began as a tortilla shop. The owner then decided to branch out into making other things besides tortillas. He is dedicated to preserving different forms of native corn and makes use of their varying characteristics in the cooking. The dishes are simple and safe, and include traditional *antojitos* such as tacos, *quesadillas, memelitas,* and a couple I had never heard of: *tetelas,* and his own *"de ese."* I like these last two a lot. You can get them with a variety of fillings, including bean, cheese, mushrooms, *huitlacoche,* and others. This place is well worth the short cab ride from downtown.

Belisario Domínguez 513, Col. Reforma. ℭ 951/513-9223. Antojitos $1–$2 (50p–£1). MC, V. Mon–Sat 8am–4pm; Sun 8am–2pm.

OAXACA AFTER DARK

If you are interested in seeing the region's traditional dances, you can check out the small-scale **Guelaguetza** performed by professional dancers at the Hotel Camino Real on Friday from 7 to 10pm. The cost ($30/£15) includes a buffet. **La Casa de Cantera,** Murguía 102 (ℭ **951/514-7585**), offers something similar. The $12 (£6) cover is for the show only, which runs every night from 8:30 to 10:15pm. Drinks and supper cost extra. Call for reservations.

Concerts and dance programs take place all year at the **Teatro Macedonio de Alcalá,** Independencia and Armenta y López. Schedules are often posted by the front doors of the theater. In the early evening, the *zócalo* is a happening place, with all sorts of people out and about. The municipal brass band and marimba players perform free concerts on alternating nights. As the night wears on, you'll usually find some mariachis hanging about.

For salsa, go to **La Candela,** Murguía 413 (ℭ **951/514-2010**), with live music Thursday through Saturday from 10:30pm to 2am. The cover is usually $4 (£2).

ROAD TRIPS FROM OAXACA

The countryside around Oaxaca is dotted with small archaeological sites and villages, and the most important are easy to reach. The landmark ruins in the region are **Monte Albán** (30 min.) and **Mitla** (1 hr.). If you're heading toward Mitla, you can make some interesting stops (see "The Road to Mitla: Ruins & Rug Weavers," below). A number of interesting villages in other directions make good day trips from Oaxaca. The State Tourism Office will give you a map that shows nearby villages where beautiful handicrafts are made. The visits are fun excursions by car or bus. If you would like a guided tour of archeological ruins or crafts villages, contact **Juan Montes Lara.** He is the thinking-person's guide to this area, as well as to most of southern Mexico. He speaks English and conducts tours for small groups throughout Oaxaca and Chiapas. He stays pretty busy, so contact him well in advance—the best way is by e-mail (© **951/515-7731;** jmonteslara@yahoo.com).

Many villages have, in the past several years, developed fine small municipal museums. **San José El Mogote,** site of one of the earliest pre-Hispanic village-dweller groups, has a display of carvings and statues found in and around the town, and a display model of an old hacienda. **Teotitlán del Valle** also has a municipal museum; it features displays on the weaving process. Ask at the State Tourism Office for more information.

MONTE ALBAN: RUINS WITH A VIEW

Had I been the priest-king of a large Indian nation in search of the perfect site on which to build a ceremonial center, this would have been it. **Monte Albán** sits on a mountain that rises from the middle of the valley floor—or, rather, divides two valleys. From here you can see all that lies between you and the distant mountains.

Starting around 2000 B.C., village-dwelling peoples of unknown origin inhabited the Oaxaca valleys. Between 800 and 500 B.C., a new ceramic style appeared, indicating an influx of new peoples, now called Zapotec. Around 500 B.C., these peoples began the monumental exercise of leveling the top of a mountain, where they would build Monte Albán (*mohn*-teh ahl-*bahn*).

Very little of the original structures remain; they've either been obscured beneath newer construction or had their stones reused for other buildings. The **Danzantes friezes** (see below) date from this period.

A center of Zapotec culture, Monte Albán was also influenced by contemporary cultures outside the valley of Mexico. You can see Olmec influence in the early sculptures; more recent masks and sculptures reflect contact with the Maya. When Monte Albán was at its zenith in A.D. 300, it borrowed architectural ideas from Teotihuacán. By around A.D. 800, the significance of Monte Albán in Zapotec society began to wane. Although most likely never completely abandoned, it became a shadow of its former grandeur. At the beginning of the 13th century, the Mixtec appropriated Monte Albán. The Mixtec, who had long coexisted in the area with the Zapotec, began expanding their territory. At Monte Albán, they added little to the existing architecture; however, they seem to have considered it an appropriate burial ground for their royalty. They left many tombs, including **Tomb 7,** with its famous treasure.

Monte Albán centers on the **Great Plaza,** a man-made area created by flattening the mountaintop. From this plaza, aligned north to south, you can survey the Oaxacan valley. The excavations at Monte Albán have revealed more than 170 tombs, numerous ceremonial altars, stelae, pyramids, and palaces.

Begin your tour of the ruins on the eastern side of the Great Plaza at the I-shaped **ball court.** This ball court differs slightly from Maya and Toltec ball courts in that there are no goal rings, and the sides of the court slope. Also on the east side of the plaza are several **altars** and **pyramids** that were once covered with stucco. Note the sloping walls, wide stairs, and ramps; all are typical of Zapotec architecture and reminiscent of the architecture of Teotihuacán. The building, slightly out of line with the plaza (not on the north–south axis), is thought by some to have been an observatory; it was probably aligned with the heavenly bodies rather than with the points of the compass.

The south side of the plaza has a large **platform** that bore several stelae, most of which are now in the National Museum of Anthropology in Mexico City. There's a good view of the surrounding area from the top of this platform.

The west side has more ceremonial platforms and pyramids. Atop the pyramid substructure are four columns that likely supported the roof of the temple at one time.

The famous building of **Los Danzantes (the dancers)** on the west side of the plaza is the earliest known structure at Monte Albán. This building is covered with large stone slabs that have distorted naked figures carved into them (the ones you see are copies; the originals are protected in the site museum). There is speculation about who carved these figures and what they represent, although there is a distinct resemblance to the Olmec baby faces at La Venta, in Tabasco State. The distorted bodies and pained expressions might connote disease. Clear examples of figures representing childbirth, dwarfism, and infantilism are visible. Because of the fluid movement represented in the figures, they became known as Los Danzantes—merely a modern label for these ancient and mysterious carvings.

The **Northern Platform** is a maze of temples and palaces interwoven with subterranean tunnels and sanctuaries. Take time to wander here, for there are numerous reliefs, glyphs, paintings, and friezes along the lintels and jambs as well as the walls. In this section of the ruins, you are likely to see vendors discreetly selling "original" artifacts found at the site. These guys come from the nearby town of Arrazola, where the fabrication of "antiquities" is a long-standing cottage industry. I like to buy a piece from them occasionally and pretend I'm getting the real thing just to get an opportunity to talk with them.

Leaving the Great Plaza, head north to the **cemetery** and **tombs.** If you have a day to spend at Monte Albán, be sure to visit some of the tombs, which contain magnificent glyphs, paintings, and stone carvings of gods, goddesses, birds, and serpents. Lately, the tombs have been closed to the public, but check anyway. Of the excavated tombs, the most famous is **Tomb 7,** next to the parking lot. It yielded some 500 pieces of gold, amber, and turquoise jewelry, as well as silver, alabaster, and bone art objects. This amazing collection is on display at the Museo Regional de Oaxaca (p. 452).

As you enter the site, you'll see a museum, a shop with guidebooks to the ruins, a cafe, and a craft shop. Video camera permits cost $5 (£2.50). The site is open daily from 8am to 6pm. Admission to the ruins is $4 (£2). Licensed guides charge $15 (£7.50) per person for a walking tour.

To get to Monte Albán, take a bus from the Hotel Rivera del Angel, at the corner of Mier y Terán and Díaz Ordáz. **Autobuses Turísticos (© 951/516-5327)** makes seven runs daily, at 8:30, 9:30, 10:30, and 11:30am and 12:30, 1:30, and 3:30pm. Return service leaves the ruins at 11am, noon, 1, 2, 3, 4, and 5pm. The round-trip fare is $4 (£2). The ride takes a half-hour, and your scheduled return time is 2 hours after arrival. It's possible to take a later return for an additional $2 (£1), though you won't be guaranteed a seat; be sure to inform the driver of your intent. During high season, additional buses usually run. If you're driving from Oaxaca, take Calle Trujano out of town. It becomes the road to Monte Albán, about 10km (6¼ miles) away.

THE ROAD TO MITLA: RUINS & RUG WEAVERS

East of Oaxaca, the Pan American Highway (Hwy. 190) leads to Mitla and passes several important archaeological sites, markets, and craft villages. You can visit the famous El Tule tree, an enormous, ancient cypress; the church at Tlacochahuaya, a lovely example of a 17th-century village church; the ruins at Dainzú, Lambityeco, and Yagul; the weaver's village of Teotitlán del Valle; and the village of Tlacolula, with its famous Dominican chapel.

Many little stops dot this route, and some are a bit off the highway, so I recommend hiring a taxi, renting a car, or signing up with a small tour rather than using local bus transportation. If you take a tour, ask which sites it includes. To get to the highway, go north from downtown to Calzada Niños Héroes and turn right. This feeds directly on to the highway. All the sites are listed in order, from west (Oaxaca) to east (Mitla).

SANTA MARIA DEL TULE'S 2,000-YEAR-OLD TREE   Santa María del Tule is a small town 8km (5 miles) outside Oaxaca. It's famous for the immense **El Tule Tree,**

an *ahuehuete* (Montezuma cypress, akin to the bald cypress) standing in a churchyard just off the main road. Now over 2,000 years old, it looks every bit its age, the way large cypresses do. However, this one is the most impressive tree I've ever seen for the sheer width of its trunk and canopy. It is said to have the broadest trunk of any tree in the world. When the tree was younger, the entire region around Santa María del Tule was marshland; in fact, the word *tule* means "reed." Now, the water table has dropped, so to protect the tree, a private foundation waters and takes care of it. The 25¢ (13p) admission fee goes toward these efforts.

The **Iglesia de San Jerónimo Tlacochahuaya,** 6km (4 miles) farther along, is the next stop. You'll see a sign pointing right; go less than another kilometer (about a half-mile) into town. Inside the church are an elaborately carved altar and a crucifix fashioned out of a ground paste made from the corn plant. The murals decorating the walls were the work of local artists of the 18th century and are a sweet mix of Spanish and Indian aesthetics. Make a point of seeing the beautifully painted baroque organ in the choir loft. The church is usually open daily from 10am to 2pm and 4 to 8pm.

DAINZU'S ZAPOTEC RUINS Three kilometers (2 miles) farther, visible from the highway (26km/16 miles from Oaxaca), you'll see a sign pointing to the right. It's less than a kilometer (under a half-mile) to the ruins, which were first excavated in the 1960s. Dainzú is a pre-Classic site that dates from between 700 and 600 B.C. Increasingly sophisticated building continued until about A.D. 300. The site occupies the western face of a hill, presumably for defense. The main building is a platform structure whose walls were decorated with carvings resembling Monte Albán's Danzantes. These carvings are now in a protective shed; a caretaker will unlock it for interested parties. These figures show Olmec influence but differ from the Danzantes because they wear the trappings of the "ball game," which make them, in all likelihood, the earliest representations of the ball game in Mexico. And, in fact, a partially reconstructed ball court sits below the main structure. The site provides an outstanding view of the valley. Admission is $3 (£1.50).

TEOTITLAN DEL VALLE'S BEAUTIFUL RUGS The next major turnoff you come to is 2km (1½ miles) farther along, 3km (2 miles) from the highway. This is Teotitlán, famous for weaving, and now an obviously prosperous town, to judge by all the current development. This is where you'll want to go for rugs, and you'll find no shortage of weavers and stores. Most weavers sell out of their homes and give demonstrations. The prices are considerably lower than in Oaxaca.

The church in town is well worth a visit. The early friars used pre-Hispanic construction stones to build the church and then covered them with adobe. When the townspeople renovated the church, they rediscovered these stones with carved figures, and now proudly display them. You'll see them in odd places in the walls of the church and sacristy. Teotitlán also has a small community museum, opposite the artisans' market and adjacent to the church. The museum has an interesting exhibit on natural dye-making, using herbs, plants, and cochineal (a red dye derived from insects).

For a bite to eat, consider the **Restaurant Tlamanalli,** Av. Juárez 39 (© **951/524-4006**), run by three Zapotec sisters who serve Oaxacan cuisine. Its reputation attracts lots of foreigners. It's on the right on the main street as you approach the main part of town, in a red brick building with black wrought iron window covers. It's open Monday through Friday from 1 to 4pm. A bit farther on, there's another nice restaurant on the left where the main street intersects with the town center.

LAMBITYECO'S RAIN GOD   Getting back to the highway and continuing eastward, in 3km (2 miles) you'll see a turnoff on the right for the small archaeological site of Lambityeco. Of particular interest are the two beautifully executed and preserved **stucco masks** of the rain god Cocijo. At Lambityeco, a major product was salt, distilled from saline groundwater nearby. Admission is $3 (£1.50).

TLACOLULA'S FINE MARKET & UNIQUE CHAPEL   Located about 30km (18 miles) from Oaxaca (1.5km/1 mile past Lambityeco), Tlacolula is in *mezcal* country, and along the road from here to Mitla, you'll see a couple of small distilleries and distillery outlets advertising their product. Feel free to stop by any one of them to taste their wares. *Mezcal* is distilled from a species of agave different from that of tequila. Most *mezcal* has a very strong smell and may or may not come with a worm in the bottle. Many of these small distilleries flavor their *mezcal* in much the same way that Russians flavor vodka.

Sunday is market day in Tlacolula, with rows of textiles fluttering in the breeze and aisle after aisle of pottery and baskets. If you don't go on market day, you won't have to compete with crowds. The **Capilla del Mártir** of the parochial church is a stunning display of virtuosity in wrought iron. The doorway, choir screen, and pulpit, with their baroque convolutions, have no equals in Mexico's religious architecture. Also eye-catching (to say the least) are the graphic, almost life-size sculptures of the 12 apostles in their various manners of martyrdom. A few years ago, a secret passage was found in the church, leading to a room that contained valuable silver religious pieces. The silver was hidden during the Revolution of 1916; the articles are now back in the church.

YAGUL'S ZAPOTEC FORTRESS   Yagul, a fortress city on a hill overlooking the valley, is a couple of kilometers (about 1½ miles) farther on down the highway. You'll see the turnoff to the left; it's less than a kilometer (about a half-mile) off the road. The setting is spectacular, and because the ruins are not as fully reconstructed as those at Monte Albán, you're likely to have the place to yourself. It's a good place for a picnic lunch.

The city was divided into two sections: the fortress at the top of the hill and the palaces lower down. The center of the palace complex is the plaza, surrounded by four temples. In the center is a ceremonial platform, under which is the **Triple Tomb.** The door of the tomb is a large stone slab decorated on both sides with beautiful hieroglyphs. The tomb may be open for viewing; if there are two guards, one can leave the entrance to escort visitors.

Look for the beautifully restored, typically Zapotec **ball court.** North of the plaza is the **palace** structure built for the chiefs of the city. It's a maze of rooms and patios decorated with painted stucco and stone mosaics. Visible here and there are ceremonial mounds and tombs decorated in the same geometric patterns found in Mitla. The panoramic view of the valley from the fortress is worth the rather exhausting climb.

Admission is $4 (£2). Still cameras are free, but use of a video camera costs $5 (£2.50). The site is open daily from 8am to 5:30pm.

It's just a few kilometers farther southeast to Mitla. The turnoff comes at a very obvious fork in the road.

MITLA'S LARGE ZAPOTEC & MIXTEC SITE   Mitla is 4km (2¾ miles) from the highway; the turnoff terminates at the **ruins** by the church. If you've come here by bus, it's less than a kilometer (about half a mile) up the road from the dusty town square to the ruins; if you want to hire a cab, there are some in the square.

The Zapotec settled Mitla around 600 B.C., and it became a Mixtec bastion in the late 10th century. This city was still flourishing at the time of the Spanish Conquest, and many of the buildings were used through the 16th century.

Tour groups often bypass the **town of Mitla** (pop. 7,000), but it is worth a visit. The University of the Americas maintains the **Museum of Zapotec Art** (previously known as the Frissell collection) in town. It contains some outstanding Zapotec and Mixtec relics. Admission is $3 (£1.50). Be sure to look at the Leigh collection, which contains some real treasures. The museum is in a beautiful old hacienda.

You can easily see the most important buildings in an hour. Mixtec architecture is based on a quadrangle surrounded on three or four sides by patios and chambers, usually rectangular. The chambers are under a low roof, which is excellent for defense but makes the rooms dark and close. The stone buildings are inlaid with small cut stones to form geometric patterns.

There are five groups of buildings, divided by the Mitla River. The most important buildings are on the east side of the ravine. The **Group of the Columns** consists of two quadrangles, connected at the corners with palaces. The building to the north has a long chamber with six columns and many rooms decorated with geometric designs. The most common motif is the zigzag pattern, the same one seen repeatedly on Mitla blankets. Human and animal images are rare in Mixtec art. In fact, only one **frieze** has been found (in the Group of the Church, on the north patio). Here, you'll see a series of figures painted with their name glyphs.

Admission to the site is $4 (£2). Use of a video camera costs $5 (£2.50). Entrance to the museum is included in the price. It's open daily from 8am to 5pm.

Outside the ruins, vendors will hound you. The moment you step out of a car, every able-bodied woman and child for miles around will come charging over with shrill cries and a basket full of bargains—heavily embroidered belts, small pieces of pottery, fake archaeological relics, and cheap earrings. Offer to pay half the price the vendors ask. There's a modern handicrafts market near the ruins, but prices are lower in town.

SOUTH OF MONTE ALBAN: ARRAZOLA, CUILAPAN & ZAACHILA

ARRAZOLA: WOODCARVING CAPITAL   Arrazola lies in the foothills of Monte Albán, about 24km (15 miles) southwest of Oaxaca. The tiny town's most famous resident is **Manuel Jiménez,** the septuagenarian grandfather of the resurgence in woodcarving as folk art. Jiménez's polar bears, anteaters, and rabbits carved from copal wood are shown in galleries throughout the world; his home is a magnet for folk-art collectors. Now the town is full of other carvers, all making fanciful creatures painted in bright, festive colors. Little boys will greet you at the outskirts offering to guide you to individual homes for a small tip. Following them is a good way to get to know the town, and after a bit you can take your leave of them.

If you're driving to Arrazola, take the road out of Oaxaca City that goes to Monte Albán, then take the left fork after crossing the Atoyac River and follow the signs for Zaachila. Turn right after the town of Xoxo and you will soon reach Arrazola. You can also take a bus from the second-class station near the Abastos Market.

CUILAPAN'S DOMINICAN MONASTERY   Cuilapan (kwi-*lah*-pan) is about 15km (9⅓ miles) southwest of Oaxaca. The Dominican friars inaugurated their second **monastery** here in 1550. Parts of the convent and church were never completed due to political complications in the late 16th century. The roof of the monastery has fallen in, but the cloister and the church remain. The church, which is still in use, is being restored. There are three naves with lofty arches, large stone columns, and many frescoes. It is open daily from 10am to 6pm; entry is $3 (£1.50), and $4 (£2) for a video camera. The monastery is visible on the right a short distance from the main road to Zaachila, and there's a sign as well. The bus from the second-class station stops within a few hundred feet of the church.

ZAACHILA: MARKET TOWN WITH MIXTEC TOMBS   Farther on from Cuilapan, 24km (15 miles) southwest of Oaxaca, Zaachila (sah-*chee*-lah) has a **Thursday market;** baskets and pottery are sold for local household use, and the produce market is always full. Also take note of the interesting livestock section and a **mercado de madera (wood market)** just as you enter town.

Behind the church is the entrance to a small **archaeological site** containing several mounds and platforms and two interesting tombs. The artifacts found here now reside in the National Museum of Anthropology in Mexico City, but **Tomb 1** contains carvings that are worth checking out.

At the time of the Spanish Conquest, Zaachila was the last surviving city of the Zapotec rulers. When Cortez marched on the city, the Zapotec offered no resistance, and he formed an alliance with them. This outraged the Mixtec, who invaded Zaachila shortly afterward. The site and tombs are open daily from 9am till 4pm, and the entrance fee is $3 (£1.50).

To return to Oaxaca, your best option is to line up with locals to take one of the *colectivos* on the main street across from the market. If you're driving, see the directions for Arrazola, above.

SOUTH ALONG HIGHWAY 175

SAN BARTOLO COYOTEPEC'S POTTERY   San Bartolo is the home of the famous **black pottery** sold all over Oaxaca. It's also one of several little villages named Coyotepec in the area. Buses frequently operate between Oaxaca and this village, about 15km (10 miles) south on Highway 175. In 1953, a native woman named Doña Rosa invented the technique of smoking the pottery during firing to make it black and rubbing the fired pieces with a piece of quartz to produce a sheen. Doña Rosa died in 1979, and her son, **Valente Nieto Real,** carries on the tradition. Watching Valente change a lump of coarse clay into a work of art with only two crude plates (used as a potter's wheel) is an almost magical experience. The family's home and factory is a few blocks off the main road; you'll see the sign as you enter town. It's open daily from 9am to 5:30pm.

You can buy black pottery at many shops on the little plaza or in the artists' homes. Villagers who make pottery often place a piece of their work near their front door, by the gate, or on the street. It's their way of inviting prospective buyers to come in.

SAN MARTIN TILCAJETE: WOODCARVING VILLAGE   San Martín Tilcajete, about 15km (10 miles) past San Bartolo, is home to **woodcarvers** who produce *alebrijes*—fantastical, brightly painted animals and imaginary beasts—much like those produced in Arrazola. You can wander from house to house viewing the amazing collections of hot-pink rabbits; 1m (4-ft.), bright-blue twisting snakes; and two-headed Dalmatians.

SANTO TOMAS JALIETZA   About 2km (1½ mile) beyond San Martín, you'll see a sign on the left for this village of **weavers** who use backstrap looms. The village cooperative runs a market in the middle of town. Prices are fixed; you'll find the greatest variety of goods on Friday.

OCOTLAN Twenty minutes farther on Highway 175 brings you to this fairly large market town. This city is notable for a few reasons: One is the **Aguilar sisters** (Josefina, Guillermina, Irene, and Concepción) and their families, who produce red clay pottery figures that are colorful, sometimes humorous, and prized by collectors. You'll see their row of home-workshops on the right as you enter. There are pottery figures on the fence and roof. (Don't go around town asking for the Aguilar family. Most of the town's inhabitants are named Aguilar.)

Ocotlán is also the home of **Rodolfo Morales,** a painter who, upon becoming rich and famous, took an active role in aiding his hometown with renovation projects. Two projects worth visiting are the parish church and former convent. Inside the convent, you can see some of the original decorations of the Dominicans. The noticeable sheen of the stucco walls is produced using the viscous innards of the nopal cactus. The convent is now a community museum.

Friday is market day in Ocotlán, and the town fills with people and goods. It's a very good market where you can find a variety of things at reasonable prices.

NORTH OF OAXACA
GUELATAO: BIRTHPLACE OF BENITO JUAREZ
High in the mountains north of Oaxaca, this lovely town has become a living monument to its favorite son, Benito Juárez. Although usually peaceful, the town comes to life on **Juárez's birthday** (Mar 21). The museum, statues, and plaza all attest to the town's obvious devotion to the patriot.

A second-class bus departs from Oaxaca's first-class station six times daily. There are also several departures from the second-class station. The trip takes at least 2 hours, through gorgeous mountain scenery. Buses return to Oaxaca every 2 hours until 8pm.

2 Villahermosa

142km (88 miles) NW of Palenque; 160km (100 miles) N of San Cristóbal de las Casas

Villahermosa (pop. 295,000) is the capital and the largest city in the state of Tabasco. It lies in a shallow depression about an hour's drive from the Gulf coast, at the confluence of two rivers: the Grijalva and the Carrizal. The land is marshy, with shallow lakes scattered here and there. For most of the year it's hot and humid. Why bother coming here? Because it has the giant Olmec heads set outside in something that's half-museum and half-park. Also, because it has the closest international airport to the ruins of Palenque and the highlands of Chiapas.

Recent Flooding: In October and November 2007, there was tremendous flooding in the area, which forced many thousands from their homes in Tabasco and lowland Chiapas—particularly in Villahermosa, making for a humanitarian disaster on a par with New Orleans. It will be some time before life returns to normal for the city. At press time, several hotels and a few of the museums were still closed. Transportation infrastructure, however, is quickly returning to normal.

Oil has brought money to this town and raised prices. Villahermosa is one of the most expensive cities in the country and contrasts sharply with inexpensive Chiapas. The money is being sucked into the modern western sections surrounding a development called Tabasco 2000. This area, especially the neighborhoods around the **Parque–Museo La Venta,** is the most attractive part of town, surrounded, as it is, by small lakes. The historic center has been left to decay. It's gritty, crowded, and unpleasant. The only real reason to stay downtown is for the cheap hotels.

ESSENTIALS

GETTING THERE & DEPARTING

BY PLANE   Continental ExpressJet (© **800/525-0280** in the U.S., or 01-800/ 900-5000 in Mexico; www.continental.com) has direct service to/from Houston on a regional jet. **Mexicana** (© **800/531-7921** in the U.S., 01-800/502-2000; www. mexicana.com) and **AeroMéxico** (© **800/237-6639** in the U.S., or 01-800/021-4000; www.aeromexico.com) both have flights to and from Mexico City. **Aviación de Chiapas (Aviacsa;** © **993/316-5700** or 01-800/006-2200; www.aviacsa.com) flies to and from Mexico City and Mérida. The regional airline **Aerolitoral,** a subsidiary of AeroMéxico (© **800/237-6639** in the U.S., or 993/312-6991), goes through Mexico City with a connection to Veracruz, Tampico, Monterrey, and Houston. **Click** (© **01-800/122-5425** in Mexico; www.clickmx.com), a Mexican budget airline, provides nonstop service to and from Mexico City.

BY CAR   Highway 180 connects Villahermosa to Campeche (6 hr.). **Highway 186,** which passes by the airport, joins **Highway 199** to Palenque and San Cristóbal de las Casas. The road to Palenque is a good one, and the drive takes 2 hours. Between Palenque and San Cristóbal the road enters the mountains and takes 4 to 5 hours. On any of the mountainous roads, road conditions are apt to get worse during the rainy season from May to October.

BY BUS   The bus station is at Mina and Merino (© 993/312-8900), 3 blocks off Highway 180. There are eight nonstop buses per day to/from Palenque (2½ hr.). There are eight nonstop buses per day to Mexico City (10 hr.), six deluxe service on **ADO-GL,** and two super deluxe on **UNO.**

ORIENTATION

ARRIVING   Villahermosa's **airport** is 10km (6¼ miles) east of town. Driving in, you'll cross a bridge over the Río Grijalva; turn left to reach downtown. Taxis to the downtown area cost $15 (£7.50).

Parking downtown can be difficult; it's best to find a parking lot. Use one that's guarded around the clock.

VISITOR INFORMATION   The **State Tourism Office** (© 993/316-5122, ext. 229) has two information booths. The one at the **airport** is staffed daily from 10am to 5pm; the one at **Parque–Museo La Venta** (next to the ticket counter for the park) is staffed Tuesday to Sunday from 10am to 5pm.

CITY LAYOUT   The downtown area, including the pedestrian-only **Zona Luz,** is on the west bank of the Grijalva River. About 1.5km (1 mile) upstream (south) is **CICOM,** with the large archaeology museum named for the poet Carlos Pellicer Cámara. The **airport** is on the east side of the river. Highway 180 passes the airport and crosses the river just north of downtown, becoming **Bulevar Ruiz Cortines.** To get to the downtown area, turn left onto **Madero** or **Pino Suárez.** By staying on Ruiz Cortines you can reach the city's biggest attraction, the Parque–Museo la Venta. It's well marked. Just beyond that is the intersection with **Paseo Tabasco,** the heart of the modern hotel and shopping district.

GETTING AROUND   Taxis are your best way to get around town. Villahermosa is rare for being a Mexican city without meaningful public transportation.

FAST FACTS   American Express is represented by Turismo Creativo, Av. Paseo Tabasco 1404, Col. Tabasco 2000 (© **993/310-9900**). The telephone **area code** is **993.** There aren't a lot of *casas de cambio,* but you can exchange money at the airport, the hotels, and downtown banks on calles Juárez and Madero. ATMs are plentiful.

EXPLORING VILLAHERMOSA

Major sights include the **Parque–Museo La Venta** and the **Museo Regional de Antropología Carlos Pellicer Cámara.**

Museo Regional de Antropología Carlos Pellicer Cámara ☞☞   This museum on the west bank of the river, about 1.5km (1 mile) south of the town center, will probably remain closed until 2009, due to the 2007 floods. It normally has a well-organized collection of pre-Hispanic artifacts, not only from the local region (Totonac, Zapotec, and Olmec), but from other parts of Mexico and Central America, as well.

The second floor is devoted to the Olmec. The third floor features artifacts from central Mexico, including the Tlatilco and Teotihuacán cultures; the Huasteca culture of Veracruz, San Luis Potosí, and Tampico states; and the cultures of Nayarit State, on the west coast. Photographs and diagrams provide vivid images, but the explanatory signs are mostly in Spanish. Look especially for the figurines that were found in this area and for the colorful Codex (an early book of pictographs).

CICOM Center, Av. Carlos Pellicer Cámara 511. © **993/312-6344.** Admission $3 (£1.50). Tues–Sun 9am–5pm.

Parque–Museo La Venta ☞☞   The Olmec created the first civilization in Mexico and developed several cultural traits that later spread to all subsequent civilizations throughout Mesoamerica. In addition to their monumental works, they carved small, exquisite figurines in jade and serpentine, which can be seen in the Museo Regional de Antropología (see above). Once inside the park and museum, a trail leads you from one sculpture to the next. Most of the pieces are massive heads or altars. These can be as tall as 2m (6 ft.) and weigh as much as 40 tons. The faces seem to be half adult, half infant. They have highly stylized mouths with thick fleshy lips that turn down. Known as the "jaguar mouth," this is a principal characteristic of Olmec art. At least 17 heads have been found: 4 at La Venta, 10 at San Lorenzo, and 3 at Tres Zapotes— all Olmec cities on Mexico's east coast. The pieces in this park were taken from La Venta, a major city during the pre-Classic period (2000 B.C.–A.D. 300). Most were sculpted around 1000 B.C. without the use of metal chisels. The basalt rock used for these heads and altars was transported to La Venta from more than 113km (70 miles) away. It is thought that the rock was brought most of the way by raft. Most of these pieces were first discovered in 1938. Now all that remains at La Venta are some grass-covered mounds that were once earthen pyramids. An exhibition area at the entrance to the park does a good job of illustrating how La Venta was laid out and what archaeologists think the Olmec were like.

As you stroll along, you will see labels identifying many species of local trees, including a grand ceiba tree of special significance to the Olmec and, later, the Maya. A few varieties of local critters scurry about, seemingly unconcerned with the presence of humans or with escaping from the park. Allow at least 2 hours for wandering through the junglelike sanctuary and examining the 3,000-year-old sculpture. *Note:* Don't forget the mosquito repellent.

Bulevar Ruiz Cortines s/n. © **993/314-1652.** Admission $4 (£2). Tues–Sun 8am–4pm.

WHERE TO STAY & DINE

You pay a little extra for rooms in Villahermosa, but you'll probably only spend 1 or 2 nights here. My favorites in descending order of price are the following: **Hyatt Regency Villahermosa** Hotel (© **800/233-1234** in the U.S., or 993/310-1234; www. villahermosa.regency.hyatt.com); **Best Western Hotel Maya Tabasco** (© **800/528-1234** in the U.S. and Canada, or 993/358-1111, ext. 822; www.hotelmaya.com.mx); **Hotel Plaza Independencia** (© **993/312-1299** or -7541; www.hotelesplaza.com. mx); and **Hotel Provincia Express** (© **993/314-5376**).

Like other Mexican cities, Villahermosa has seen the arrival of U.S. franchise restaurants, but as these things go, I prefer the Mexican variety: **Sanborn's,** Av. Ruiz Cortines 1310, near Parque–Museo La Venta (© **993/316-8722**), and **VIPS,** Av. Fco. I. Madero 402, downtown (© **993/312-3237**). Both usually do a good job with traditional dishes such as enchiladas or *antojitos* (supper dishes). But if you're looking for something beyond the standard fare, take a taxi to **Jangada** (© **993/317-6050**), an all-you-can-east seafood restaurant, with a wonderful variety of seafood cocktails, ceviche, grilled fish, and soups. It's on the west side of town in the La Choca neighborhood on Paseo de la Choca 126. The only problem is that it closes at 7pm. If you want to eat later, there's a sister restaurant next door that's a Brazilian-style steakhouse called Rodizio. It stays open until 9pm. It is quite good as well.

3 Palenque (★(★

142km (88 miles) SE of Villahermosa; 229km (142 miles) NE of San Cristóbal de las Casas

The ruins of Palenque look out over the jungle from a tall ridge that juts out from the base of steep, thickly forested mountains. It is a dramatic sight colored by the mysterious feel of the ruins themselves. The temples here are in the Classic style, with high-pitched roofs crowned with elaborate combs. Inside many are representations in stone and plaster of the rulers and their gods, which give evidence of a cosmology that is—and perhaps will remain—impenetrable to our understanding. This is one of the grand archaeological sites of Mexico.

Eight kilometers (5 miles) from the ruins is the town of Palenque. There you can find lodging and food, as well as make travel arrangements. Transportation between the town and ruins is cheap and convenient.

ESSENTIALS
GETTING THERE & DEPARTING
BY PLANE   There is no regular commercial air service to Palenque.

BY CAR   The 230km (143-mile) trip from San Cristóbal to Palenque takes 5 hours and passes through lush jungle and mountain scenery. Take it easy, though, and watch out for potholes and other hindrances. **Highway 186** from Villahermosa should take about 2 hours. You may encounter military roadblocks that involve a cursory inspection of your travel credentials and perhaps your vehicle.

BY BUS   The two first-class bus stations are 2 blocks apart. Both are on Palenque's main street between the main square and the turnoff for the ruins. The smaller company, **Transportes Rodolfo Figueroa** (© **916/345-1322**), offers first-class service four times a day to and from San Cristóbal (5 hr.) and Tuxtla (6½ hr.). **ADO/ Cristóbal Colón** (© **916/345-1344**) runs to those destinations and Campeche (six per day, 5 hr.), Villahermosa (nine per day, 2 hr.), and Mérida (two per day, 9 hr.).

ORIENTATION

VISITOR INFORMATION   The downtown tourism office is a block from the main square at the corner of Avenida Juárez and Abasolo. It's open Monday to Saturday from 9am to 9pm, Sunday from 9am to 1pm. There's no phone at the downtown office. To get info over the phone, call the tourism office's business office (© **916/345-0356**).

CITY LAYOUT   **Avenida Juárez** is Palenque's main street. At one end is the **main plaza;** at the other is the oversized sculpture of the famous Maya head that was discovered here. To the right of the statue is the entrance to the Cañada; to the left is the road to the ruins, and straight ahead past the statue are the airport and the highway to Villahermosa. The distance between the town's main square and the monument is about 1.5km (1 mile).

La Cañada is a restaurant and hotel zone tucked away in the forest. Aside from the main plaza area, this is the best location for travelers without cars, because the town is within a few blocks, and the buses that run to the ruins pass right by.

GETTING AROUND   The cheapest way to get back and forth from the ruins is on the white **VW buses** *(colectivos)* that run down Juárez every 10 minutes from 6am to 6pm. The buses pass La Cañada and hotels along the road to the ruins and can be flagged down at any point, but they may not stop if they're full. The cost is $1 (50p) per person.

FAST FACTS   The telephone area code is **916.** As for the **climate,** Palenque's high humidity is downright oppressive in the summer, especially after rain showers. During the winter, the damp air can occasionally be chilly in the evening. Rain gear is handy at any time of year. **Internet service** and **ATMs** are easily available.

EXPLORING PALENQUE

The reason to come here is the ruins; although you can tour them in a morning, many people savor Palenque for days. There are no must-see sights in town.

PARQUE NACIONAL PALENQUE ✸✸✸

A **museum and visitor center** sits not far from the entrance to the ruins. Though it's not large, the museum is worth the time it takes to see; it's open Tuesday to Sunday from 10am to 5pm and is included in the price of admission. It contains well-chosen and artistically displayed exhibits, including jade from recently excavated tombs. Explanatory text in Spanish and English explains the life and times of this magnificent city. New pieces are sometimes added as they are uncovered in ongoing excavations.

The **main entrance,** about 1km (½ mile) beyond the museum, is at the end of the paved highway. There you'll find a large parking lot, a refreshment stand, a ticket booth, and several shops. Among the vendors selling souvenirs are often some Lacandón Indians wearing white tunics and hawking bows and arrows.

Admission to the ruins is $7 (£3.50). The fee for using a video camera is $5 (£2.50). Parking at the main entrance and at the visitor center is free. The site and visitor center shops are open daily from 8am to 4:45pm.

TOURING THE RUINS   Pottery shards found during the excavations show that people lived in this area as early as 300 B.C. By the Classic period (A.D. 300–900), Palenque was an important ceremonial center. It peaked around A.D. 600 to 700.

When John Stephens visited the site in the 1840s, the ruins that you see today were buried under centuries of accumulated earth and a thick canopy of jungle. The dense jungle surrounding the cleared portion still covers unexcavated temples, which are easily discernible in the forest even to the untrained eye. But be careful not to drift too far from the main path—there have been a few incidents where tourists venturing alone into the rainforest were assaulted.

Of all Mexico's ruins, this is the most haunting, because of its majesty; its history, recovered by epigraphers; and its mysterious setting. Scholars have identified the rulers and constructed their family histories, putting visitors on a first-name basis with these ancient people etched in stone. You can read about it in *A Forest of Kings,* by Linda Schele and David Freidel.

As you enter the ruins, the building on your right is the **Temple of the Inscriptions,** named for the great stone hieroglyphic panels found inside. (Most of the panels, which portray the family tree of King Pacal, are in the National Anthropological Museum in Mexico City.) This temple is famous for the crypt of King Pacal deep inside the pyramid, but the crypt is closed to the public. The archaeologist Alberto Ruz Lhuller discovered the tomb in the depths of the temple in 1952—an accomplishment many scholars consider one of the great discoveries of the Maya world. In exploratory excavations, Ruz Lhuller found a stairway leading from the temple floor deep into the base of the pyramid. The original builders had carefully concealed the entrance by filling the stairway with stone. After several months of excavation, Ruz Lhuillier finally reached King Pacal's crypt, which contained several fascinating objects, including a magnificent carved stone sarcophagus. Ruz Lhuller's own gravesite is opposite the Temple of the Inscriptions, on the left as you enter the park.

Just to your right as you face the Temple of the Inscriptions is **Temple 13,** which is receiving considerable attention from archaeologists. They recently discovered the burial of another richly adorned personage, accompanied in death by an adult female and an adolescent. Some of the artifacts found there are on display in the museum.

Back on the main pathway, the building directly in front of you is the **Palace,** with its unique tower. The explorer John Stephens camped in the Palace when it was completely covered in vegetation, spending sleepless nights fighting off mosquitoes. A pathway between the Palace and the Temple of the Inscriptions leads to the **Temple of the Sun,** the **Temple of the Foliated Cross,** the **Temple of the Cross,** and **Temple 14.** This group of temples, now cleared and in various stages of reconstruction, was built by Pacal's son, Chan-Bahlum, who is usually shown on inscriptions with six toes. Chan-Bahlum's plaster mask was found in Temple 14 next to the Temple of the Sun. Archaeologists have begun probing the Temple of the Sun for Chan-Bahlum's tomb. Little remains of this temple's exterior carving. Inside, however, behind a fence, a carving of Chan-Bahlum shows him ascending the throne in A.D. 690. The panels depict Chan-Bahlum's version of his historic link to the throne.

To the left of the Palace is the North Group, also undergoing restoration. Included in this area are the **Ball Court** and the **Temple of the Count.** At least three tombs, complete with offerings for the underworld journey, have been found here, and the lineage of at least 12 kings has been deciphered from inscriptions left at this site.

Just past the North Group is a small building (once a museum) now used for storing the artifacts found during restorations. It is closed to the public. To the right of the building, a stone bridge crosses the river, leading to a pathway down the hillside to the new museum. The rock-lined path descends along a cascading stream on the banks of which grow giant ceiba trees. Benches are placed along the way as rest areas, and some small temples have been reconstructed near the base of the trail. In the early morning and evening, you may hear monkeys crashing through the thick foliage by the path; if you keep noise to a minimum, you may spot wild parrots as well. Walking downhill (by far the best way to go), it will take you about 20 minutes to reach the main highway. The path ends at the paved road across from the museum. The *colectivos* (minibuses) going back to the village will stop here if you wave them down.

WHERE TO STAY

English is spoken in all the more expensive hotels and about half of the inexpensive ones. The quoted rates include the 17% tax. High season in Palenque is Easter week, July to August, and December.

EXPENSIVE

Chan-Kah Resort Village ⍟   This hotel is a grouping of comfortable, roomy bungalows that offer privacy and quiet in the surroundings of a tropical forest. The hotel is on the road between the ruins and the town, but because the town of Palenque isn't particularly worth exploring, you won't miss much by staying here. The grounds are beautifully tended, and there is an inviting pool that resembles a lagoon. A broad stream runs through the property. Some of the bungalows can have a musty smell. Christmas prices will be higher than those quoted here, and you may be quoted a higher price if you reserve a room in advance from outside the country. The outdoor restaurant and bar serves only passable Mexican food. Room service is pricey.

Where to Stay & Dine in Palenque

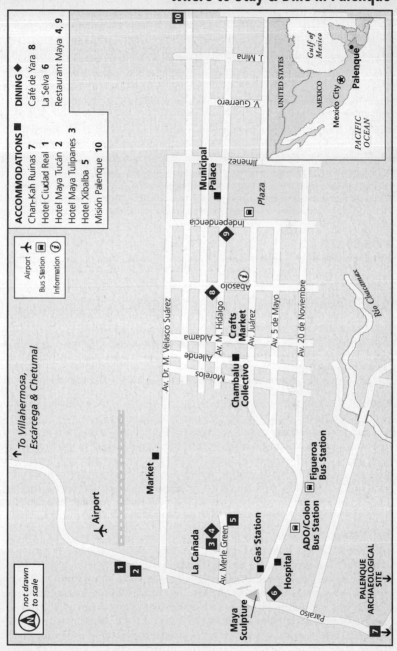

ACCOMMODATIONS ■
Chan-Kah Ruinas **7**
Hotel Ciudad Real **1**
Hotel Maya Tucán **2**
Hotel Maya Tulipanes **3**
Hotel Xibalba **5**
Misión Palenque **10**

DINING ◆
Café de Yara **8**
La Selva **6**
Restaurant Maya **4, 9**

Airport ✈
Bus Station ▣
Information ⓘ

Ⓝ not drawn to scale

To Villahermosa, Escárcega & Chetumal

Airport

Market

Av. Dr. M. Velasco Suárez

Av. M. Velasco Suárez

Abasolo ⓘ

Av. M. Hidalgo

Av. Aldama

Av. Allende

Av. Morelos

Crafts Market

Chambalu Collectivo ■

Av. Juárez

Av. 5 de Mayo

Av. 20 de Noviembre

Independencia

Plaza

Jiménez

Municipal Palace

V. Guerrero

J. Mina

Río Chacamax

La Cañada

Av. Merle Green

Gas Station

Hospital

ADO/Colon Bus Station

Figueroa Bus Station

Maya Sculpture

Paraíso

PALENQUE ARCHAEOLOGICAL SITE →

UNITED STATES
MEXICO
Mexico City ✪
Palenque ●
Gulf of Mexico
PACIFIC OCEAN

477

Carretera Las Ruinas Km 3, 29960 Palenque, Chi. ℂ 916/345-1100. Fax 916/345-0820. www.chan-kah.com.mx. 73 units. $150 (£75) double. MC, V. Free guarded parking. **Amenities:** Restaurant; bar; 3 outdoor pools (1 large w/natural spring); game room; room service; laundry service. *In room:* A/C, hair dryer.

Misión Palenque 🌟🌟   This hotel has returned to being among the most comfortable in the city after a total remodeling that includes new air-conditioning and other amenities. Rooms are medium-size and attractively furnished with light, modern furniture. Bathrooms are spacious with ample counters. The hotel has extensive grounds, and is very quiet. In one corner of the property, a natural spring flows through an attractive bit of jungle, where the hotel has installed the spa. Part of the spa is a *temazcal* or Native American steam bath. There's also a mud bath along with the more common elements. The hotel is a few blocks east of the town's main square.

Periférico Oriente d/c, 29960 Palenque, Chi. ℂ 916/345-0241, or 01/800-900-3800 in Mexico. Fax 916/345-0300. www.hotelesmision.com.mx. 156 units. $140 (£70) double. AE, MC, V. Free guarded parking that includes vehicle checkup. **Amenities:** Restaurant; bar; 2 outdoor pools; 2 tennis courts; fitness room; spa; Jacuzzi; tour service; carrental desk; courtesy trips to ruins; room service; in-room massage; babysitting; laundry service. *In room:* A/C, TV, hair dryer (on request), safe.

MODERATE

Hotel Ciudad Real   Though not really fancy, this hotel does the important things right—the rooms are ample, quiet, and well lit. They are comfortably, if plainly, furnished. Suites have a sitting room with sleeping sofa. Most units hold two double beds; some king-size beds are available. All rooms have a small balcony, which in the best case overlooks an attractive garden. When making a reservation, specify the hotel in Palenque. It's at the edge of town in the direction of the airport.

Carretera a Pakal-Na Km 1.5, 29960 Palenque, Chi. ℂ 916/345-1343 (reservations: ℂ 967/678-4400). www.ciudad real.com.mx. 72 units. High season $110 (£55) double, $130 (£65) suite; low season $100 (£50) double, $120 (£60) suite. AE, MC, V. Free secured parking. **Amenities:** Restaurant; bar; outdoor pool; baby pool; game room; travel agency; car-rental desk; room service; laundry service; nonsmoking rooms. *In room:* A/C, TV, hair dryer.

Hotel Maya Tucán   Book a room in back, and you will have a view of the hotel's natural pond. The cheerfully decorated rooms are adequate in size; they have double beds and large bathrooms. Suites are larger and have king-size beds. The grounds are well tended and lush; scarlet macaws kept by the hotel fly about the parking lot. The Maya Tucán is on the highway to the airport. Bathrooms are larger and better lit but done with less polish than at Ciudad Real. Beds have rubber mattress covers.

Carretera-Palenque Km 0.5, 29960 Palenque, Chi. ℂ 916/345-0443. Fax 916/345-0337. mayatucan@palenque. com.mx. 56 units. $110 (£55) double, $140 (£70) suit. MC, V. Free secured parking. **Amenities:** Restaurant; bar; outdoor pool; room service; laundry service. *In room:* A/C, TV, hair dryer, no phone.

Hotel Maya Tulipanes   This is an attractive hotel tucked away in the Cañada. I like it for its location, and the close attention paid by the management. Service and upkeep are both good. Rooms are medium to large and come with a queen-size, a king-size, or two double beds. Tropical vegetation adorns the grounds along with some reproductions of famous Mayan architecture. The Maya Tulipanes has an arrangement with a sister hotel at the ruins of Tikal, in Guatemala. The travel agency operates daily tours to Bonampak and other attractions.

Calle Cañada 6, 29960 Palenque, Chi. ℂ 916/345-0201 or -0258. Fax 916/345-1004. www.mayatulipanes.com.mx. 73 units. High season $120 (£60) standard; low season $70 (£35) standard. Internet packages available. AE, MC, V. Free secured parking. **Amenities:** Restaurant; bar; outdoor pool; travel agency; ground transportation to/from Villahermosa airport; room service; laundry service; nonsmoking rooms. *In room:* A/C, TV, Wi-Fi, hair dryer, no phone.

INEXPENSIVE

Hotel Xibalba   This modern small two-story hotel is inspired by Maya architecture. The medium-to-small rooms are clean and cheerful. The upstairs units are a little smaller than the downstairs. Most of the beds have firm mattresses. You can arrange a trip to Bonampak or Misol Ha with the hotel management, which owns a travel agency, Viajes Shivalva (pronounced like Xibalba: "shee-*bahl*-bah").

Calle Merle Green 9, Col. La Cañada, 29960 Palenque, Chi. © 916/345-0392. Fax 916/345-0411. www.palenquemx. com/shivalva. 15 units. $50–$60 (£25–£30) double. MC, V. No parking. **Amenities:** Restaurant; bar; laundry service; travel agency. *In room:* A/C, TV, no phone.

WHERE TO DINE

Palenque and, for that matter, the rest of backwater Chiapas, is not for gourmets. Who'd a thunk? I had an easy time eliminating a number of restaurants that didn't even seem to be keeping up the appearance of serving food. But the situation has been improving, and you can at least get some decent Mexican food.

MODERATE

La Selva ✹ MEXICAN/INTERNATIONAL   At La Selva (the jungle), you dine under a large, attractive thatched roof beside well-tended gardens. The menu includes seafood, freshwater fish, steaks, and Mexican specialties. The most expensive thing on the menu is *pigua*, freshwater lobster caught in the large rivers of southeast Mexico. These can get quite large—the size of small saltwater lobsters. This and the finer cuts of meat have been frozen, but you wouldn't want otherwise in Palenque. I liked the fish stuffed with shrimp, and the *mole* enchiladas. La Selva is on the highway to the ruins, near the statue of the Maya head.

Carretera Palenque Ruinas Km 0.5. © 916/345-0363. Main courses $8–$17 (£4–£8.50). MC, V. Daily 11:30am– 11:30pm.

INEXPENSIVE

Café de Yara MEXICAN   A small, modern cafe and restaurant with a comforting, not overly ambitious menu. The cafe's strong suit is healthy salads (with disinfected greens), and home-style Mexican entrees, such as the beef or chicken *milanesa* or chicken cooked in a *chile pasilla* sauce.

Av. Hidalgo 66 (at Abasolo). © 916/345-0269. Main courses $4–$7 (£2–£3.50). MC, V. Daily 7am–11pm.

Restaurant Maya and Maya Cañada ✹ MEXICAN   These two are the most consistently good restaurants in Palenque. One faces the main plaza from the corner of Independencia and Hidalgo, the other is in the Cañada (© **916/345-0216**). Menus are somewhat different, but much is the same. Both do a good job with the basics—good strong, locally grown coffee and soft, pliant tortillas. The menu offers a nice combination of Mexican standards and regional specialties. If you're in an exploratory mood, try one of the regional specialties such as the *mole chiapaneco* (dark red, like *mole poblano*, but less sweet) or any of the dishes based on *chaya* or *chipilin* (mild-flavored local greens), such as the soup with *chipilin* and *bolitas de masa* (corn dumplings). If you want something more comforting, go for the chicken and rice vegetable soup, or the *sopa azteca*. The plantains stuffed with cheese and fried Mexican-style are wonderful. Waiters sometimes offer specials not on the menu, and these are often the thing to get. You can also try *tascalate,* a pre-Hispanic drink made of water, *masa*, chocolate, and *achiote*, and served room temperature or cold.

Av. Independencia s/n. ⒸⓉ **916/345-0042**. Breakfast $4–$5 (£2–£2.50); main courses $6–$12 (£3–£6). AE, MC, V. Daily 7am–11pm.

ROAD TRIPS FROM PALENQUE

BONAMPAK & YAXCHILAN: MURALS IN THE JUNGLE

Intrepid travelers may want to consider the day trip to the Maya ruins of Bonampak and Yaxchilán. The **ruins of Bonampak,** southeast of Palenque on the Guatemalan border, were discovered in 1946. The site is important for the vivid **murals** of the Maya on the interior walls of one temple. Particularly striking is an impressive battle scene, perhaps the most important painting of pre-Hispanic Mexico. Reproductions of these murals are on view in the Regional Archaeology Museum in Villahermosa.

Several tour companies offer a day trip. The drive to Bonampak is 3 hours. From there you continue by boat to the **ruins of Yaxchilán,** famous for its highly ornamented buildings. Bring rain gear, boots, a flashlight, and bug repellent. All tours include meals and cost about $60 (£30). No matter what agency you sign up with, the hours of departure and return are the same because the vans of the different agencies caravan down and back for safety. You leave at 6am and return at 7pm.

Try **Viajes Na Chan Kan** (ⒸⓉ **916/345-2154**), at the corner of avenidas Hidalgo and Jiménez, across from the main square, or **Viajes Shivalva,** Calle Merle Green 1 (ⒸⓉ **916/ 345-0411;** fax 916/345-0392). A branch of Viajes Shivalva (ⒸⓉ **916/345-0822**) is a block from the *zócalo* (main plaza) at the corner of Juárez and Abasolo, across the hall from the State Tourism Office. It's open Monday to Saturday from 9am to 9pm.

WATERFALLS AT MISOL HA & AGUA AZUL

A popular excursion from Palenque is a day trip to the Misol Ha waterfall and Agua Azul. **Misol Ha** is 20km (12 miles) from Palenque, in the direction of Ocosingo. It takes about 30 minutes to get there, depending on the traffic. The turn-off is clearly marked; you'll turn right and drive another 1½ km (1 mile). The place is absolutely beautiful. Water pours from a rocky cliff into a broad pool of green water bordered by thick tropical vegetation. There's a small restaurant and some rustic cabins for rent for $30 to $40 (£15–£20) per night, depending on the size of the cabin. The place is run by the *ejido* cooperative that owns the site, and it does a good job of maintaining the place. To inquire about the cabins, call ⒸⓉ **916/345-1506.** Admission for the day is $1 (50p).

Approximately 44km (27 miles) beyond Misol Ha are the **Agua Azul waterfalls**— 270m (886 ft.) of tumbling falls with lots of water. There are cabins for rent here, too, but I would rather stay at Misol Ha. You can swim either above or below the falls, but make sure you don't get pulled by the current. You can see both places in the same day or stop to see them on your way to Ocosingo and San Cristóbal. Agua Azul is prettiest after 3 or 4 consecutive dry days; heavy rains can make the water murky. Check with guides or other travelers about the water quality before you decide to go. The cost to enter is $2 (£1) per person. Trips to both of these places can be arranged through just about any hotel.

OCOSINGO & THE RUINS OF TONINA

By the time you get to Agua Azul, you're half way to Ocosingo, which lies halfway between Palenque and San Cristóbal. So, instead of returning for the night to Palenque, you can go on to Ocosingo. It's higher up and more comfortable than Palenque. It's a nice little town, not touristy, not a lot to do other than see the ruins of Toniná. But it is a nice place to spend the night so that you can see the ruins early before moving on to San Cristóbal. There are about a half dozen small hotels in town;

the largest is not the most desirable. I would stay at the **Hospedaje Esmeralda** (© **919/673-0014**) or the **Hotel Central** (© **919/673-0024**) on the main square. Both of these are small and simple, but welcoming.

Ruins of Toniná 𝄂

The ruins of Toniná (the name translates as "house of rocks") are 14km (9 miles) east of Ocosingo. You can take a cab there and catch a *colectivo* to return. The city dates from the Classic period and covered a large area, but the excavated and restored part is all on one hillside that faces out towards a broad valley. This site is not really set up for lots of tourists. There's a lot of up and down, and some of it is a little precarious. It's not a good place to take kids. Admission is $3.50 (£1.75).

This complex of courtyards, rooms, and stairways is built on multiple levels that are irregular and asymmetrical. The overall effect is that of a ceremonial area with multiple foci instead of a clearly discernable center.

As early as A.D. 350, Toniná emerged as a dynastic center. In the 7th and 8th centuries it was locked in a struggle with rival Palenque and, to a lesser degree, with far-away Calakmul. This has led some scholars to see Toniná as more militaristic than its neighbors—a sort of Sparta of the classic Maya. Toniná's greatest victory came in 711, when, under the rule of Kan B'alam, it attacked Palenque and captured its king, K'an Joy Chitam, depicted on a stone frieze twisted, his arms bound with rope.

But the single most important artifact yet found at Toniná, is up around the fifth level of the acropolis—a large stucco frieze divided into panels by a feathered framework adorned with the heads of sacrificial victims (displayed upside down) and some rather horrid creatures. The largest figure is a skeletal image holding a decapitated head—very vivid and very puzzling. There is actually a stylistic parallel with some murals of the Teotihuacán culture of central Mexico. The other special thing about Toniná is that it holds the distinction of having the last ever date recorded in the long count (A.D. 909), which marks the end of the Classic period.

4 San Cristóbal de las Casas 𝄂𝄂𝄂

229km (142 miles) SW of Palenque; 80km (50 miles) E of Tuxtla Gutiérrez; 74km (46 miles) NW of Comitán; 166km (103 miles) NW of Cuauhtémoc; 451km (280 miles) E of Oaxaca

San Cristóbal is a colonial town of white stucco walls and red-tile roofs, of cobblestone streets and narrow sidewalks, of graceful arcades and open plazas. It lies in a green valley 2,120m (6,954 ft.) high. The city owes part of its name to the 16th-century cleric Fray Bartolomé de las Casas, who was the town's first bishop and spent the rest of his life waging a political campaign to protect the indigenous peoples of the Americas.

Surrounding the city are many villages of Mayan-speaking Indians who display great variety in their language, dress, and customs, making this area one of the most fascinating in Mexico. San Cristóbal is the principal market town for these Indians, and their point of contact with the outside world. Most of them trek down from the surrounding mountains to sell goods and run errands.

Several Indian villages lie within reach of San Cristóbal by road: **Chamula,** with its weavers and unorthodox church; **Zinacantán,** whose residents practice their own syncretic religion; **Tenejapa, San Andrés,** and **Magdalena,** known for brocaded textiles; **Amatenango del Valle,** a town of potters; and **Aguacatenango,** known for embroidery. Most of these "villages" consist of little more than a church and the municipal government building, with homes scattered for miles around and a general gathering only for church and market days (usually Sun).

Many Indians now live on the outskirts of town because they've been expelled from their villages over religious differences. They are known as *los expulsados*. No longer involved in farming, they make their living in commerce and handicrafts. Most still wear traditional dress, but they've adopted Protestant religious beliefs that prevent them from partaking in many of their community's civic and religious celebrations.

The influx of outsiders hasn't created in most Indians a desire to adopt mainstream customs and dress. It's interesting to note that the communities closest to San Cristóbal are the most resistant to change. The greatest threat to the cultures in this area comes not from tourism but from the action of large market forces, population pressures, environmental damage, and poverty. The Indians aren't interested in acting or looking like the foreigners they see. They may steal glances or even stare at tourists, but mainly they pay little attention to outsiders, except as potential buyers for handicrafts.

You may see or hear the word *Jovel*, San Cristóbal's Indian name, incorporated often in the names of businesses. You'll hear the word *coleto*, used in reference to someone or something from San Cristóbal. You'll see signs for *tamales coletos, pan coleto,* and *desayuno coleto* (Cristóbal breakfast).

ESSENTIALS
GETTING THERE & DEPARTING
BY PLANE   Flights from Mexico City have been canceled. The closest airport is in Tuxtla Gutiérrez.

BY CAR   From Tuxtla Gutiérrez, the 1½-hour trip winds through beautiful mountain country. From Palenque, the road is just as beautiful (if longer—5 hr.), and it provides jungle scenery, but portions of it may be heavily potholed or obstructed during rainy season. Check with the local state tourism office before driving.

BY TAXI   Taxis from Tuxtla Gutiérrez to San Cristóbal cost around $50 (£25). Another way to travel to and from Tuxtla is by *combi*. The Volkswagen vans, which can get extremely crowded, make the run every 15 to 30 minutes. They can be found just off the highway by the bus station. You'll have to ask someone to point them out to you because there isn't a sign.

BY BUS   The two bus stations in town are directly across the Pan American Highway from each other. The smaller one belongs to **Transportes Rodolfo Figueroa,** which provides first-class service to and from Tuxtla (every 40 min.) and Palenque (four buses per day, with a stop in Ocosingo—cheaper than the competition). For other destinations, go to the large station run by **ADO** and its affiliates, Altos, Cristóbal Colón, and Maya de Oro. This company offers service to and from Tuxtla (12 buses per day), Palenque (almost every hour), and several other destinations: Mérida (two buses per day), Villahermosa (two buses per day), Oaxaca (two buses per day), and Puerto Escondido (two buses per day). To buy a bus ticket without going down to the station, go to the **Ticket Bus** agency, Real de Guadalupe 5 (© **967/678-8503**). Hours are Monday to Saturday from 7am to 11pm, Sunday from 9am to 5pm.

ORIENTATION
ARRIVING   To get to the main plaza from the highway, turn on to **Avenida Insurgentes** (at the traffic light). From the bus station, the main plaza is 9 blocks north up Avenida Insurgentes (a 10-min. walk, slightly uphill). Cabs are cheap and plentiful.

VISITOR INFORMATION   The **State Tourism Office** is better than the municipal office. It's just half a block south of the main plaza, at Av. Hidalgo 1-B (© **967/**

San Cristóbal de las Casas

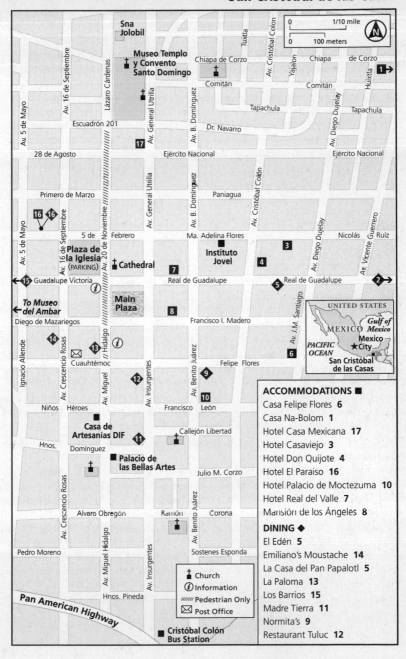

ACCOMMODATIONS ■
Casa Felipe Flores **6**
Casa Na-Bolom **1**
Hotel Casa Mexicana **17**
Hotel Casaviejo **3**
Hotel Don Quijote **4**
Hotel El Paraíso **16**
Hotel Palacio de Moctezuma **10**
Hotel Real del Valle **7**
Mansión de los Ángeles **8**

DINING ◆
El Edén **5**
Emiliano's Moustache **14**
La Casa del Pan Papalotl **5**
La Paloma **13**
Los Barrios **15**
Madre Tierra **11**
Normita's **9**
Restaurant Tuluc **12**

The Zapatista Movement & Chiapas

In January 1994, Indians from this area rebelled against the Mexican government over health care, education, land distribution, and representative government. Their organization, the **Zapatista Liberation Army,** known as EZLN (Ejército Zapatista de Liberación Nacional), and its leader, Subcomandante Marcos, have become emblematic of the problems Mexico has with social justice. In the last couple of years, the rhetoric of armed revolt has ended, and the Zapatistas are talking about building a broad leftist coalition—but not a political party. What this means for Mexican politics is not clear, but for travelers it means not having to worry about political unrest.

678-6570); it's open Monday to Friday from 8am to 8pm, Saturday from 9am to 8pm, and Sunday from 9am to 2pm. The **Municipal Tourism Office** (℗/fax **967/678-0665**) is in the town hall, west of the main square. Hours are Monday to Saturday from 9am to 8pm. Check the bulletin board here for apartments, shared rides, cultural events, and local tours. Both offices are helpful, but the state office is open an hour later and is better staffed.

CITY LAYOUT   San Cristóbal is laid out on a grid; the main north-south axis is **Insurgentes/Utrilla,** and the east–west axis is **Mazariegos/Madero.** All streets change names when they cross either of these streets. The *zócalo* (main plaza) lies where they intersect. An important street to know is **Real de Guadalupe,** which runs from the plaza eastward to the church of Guadalupe; located on it are many hotels and restaurants. The market is 7 blocks north of the *zócalo* along Utrilla.

Take note that this town has at least three streets named Domínguez and two streets named Flores. There's Hermanos Domínguez, Belisario Domínguez, and Pantaleón Domínguez, and María Adelina Flores and Dr. Felipe Flores.

GETTING AROUND   Most of the sights and shopping in San Cristóbal are within walking distance of the plaza.

Urbano **buses** (minibuses) take passengers between town and the residential neighborhoods. All buses pass by the market and central plaza on their way through town. Utrilla and Avenida 16 de Septiembre are the two main arteries; all buses use the market area as the last stop. Any bus on Utrilla will take you to the market.

Colectivos to outlying villages depart from the public market at Avenida Utrilla. Buses late in the day are usually very crowded. Always check to see when the last or next-to-last bus returns from wherever you're going, and then take the one before that—those last buses sometimes don't materialize, and you might be stranded. I speak from experience!

Rental cars come in handy for trips to the outlying villages and may be worth the expense when shared by a group, but keep in mind that insurance is invalid on unpaved roads. Try **Optima Car Rental,** Av. Mazariegos 39 (℗ **967/674-5409**). Office hours are daily from 9am to 1pm and 5 to 8pm. You'll save money by arranging the rental from your home country; otherwise, a day's rental with insurance will cost around $60 (£30) for a VW Beetle with manual transmission, the cheapest car available.

Scooters can be rented from Darren and Natasha, two easygoing Australians who tell me that they've found the best way to enjoy the city and surrounding countryside. Look for **Croozy Scooters** (© 967/631-4329) at Belisario Domínguez 7-A.

Bikes are another option for getting around the city; a day's rental is about $10 (£5). **Los Pingüinos,** Av. Ecuador 4-B (© 967/678-0202; pinguinosmex@yahoo. com), offers bike tours to a few out-of-town locations. Tours in the valley around San Cristóbal last 4 to 6 hours and cost $25 to $30 (£13–£15). It's open daily from 10am to 2:30pm and 4 to 7pm.

FAST FACTS: San Cristóbal de las Casas

Area Code The telephone area code is **967.**

Books The People of the Bat: Mayan Tales and Dreams from Zinacantán, by Robert M. Laughlin, is a priceless collection of beliefs from that village near San Cristóbal. Another good book with a completely different view of today's Maya is *The Heart of the Sky,* by Peter Canby, who traveled among the Maya to chronicle their struggles (and wrote his book before the Zapatista uprising).

Bookstore For the best selection of new and used books and reading material in English, go to **La Pared,** Av. Hidalgo 2 (© **967/678-6367**). The owner, Dana Gay Burton, keeps a great collection of books on the Maya, and Mexico in general, both fiction and nonfiction.

Bulletin Boards San Cristóbal is a cultural crossroads for travelers, and several places maintain bulletin boards with information on Spanish classes, local specialty tours, rooms or houses to rent, rides needed, and so on. These include boards at the **Tourism Office, Café El Puente, Madre Tierra,** and **Casa Na-Bolom.**

Climate San Cristóbal can be chilly when the sun isn't out, especially during the winter. It's 2,120m (6,954 ft.) above sea level. Most hotels are not heated, although some have fireplaces. There is always a possibility of rain, but I would avoid going to San Cristóbal from late August to late October, during the height of the rainy season.

Currency Exchange There are at least five *casas de cambio* on Real de Guadalupe, near the main square, and a couple under the colonnade facing the square. Most are open until 8pm, and some are open Sunday. There are also a number of ATMs.

Doctor Try **Dr. Roberto Lobato,** Av. Belisario Domínguez 17, at Calle Flavio A. Paniagua (© **967/678-7777**). Don't be unsettled by the fact that his office is next door to Funerales Canober.

Internet Access There are Internet cafes everywhere.

Parking If your hotel does not have parking, use the *estacionamiento* (underground public lot) in front of the cathedral, just off the main square on 16 de Septiembre. Entry is from Calle 5 de Febrero.

Post Office The *correo* is at Crescencio Rosas and Cuauhtémoc, a block south and west of the main square. It's open Monday to Friday from 8am to 7pm, Saturday from 9am to 1pm.

Spanish Classes The **Instituto Jovel,** María Adelina Flores 21 (Apdo. Postal 62), 29250 San Cristóbal de las Casas, Chi. (⊘/fax **967/678-4069**), gets higher marks for its Spanish courses than the competition. It also offers classes in weaving and cooking. The **Centro Bilingüe,** at the Centro Cultural El Puente, Real de Guadalupe 55, 29250 San Cristóbal de las Casas, Chi. (⊘ **800/303-4983** in the U.S., or ⊘/fax 967/678-3723), offers classes in Spanish. Both schools can arrange home stays for their students.

Telephone The best price for long-distance telephone calls and faxing is at **La Pared** bookstore (see "Bookstore," above) at Av. Hidalgo 2, across the street from the State Tourism Office.

EXPLORING SAN CRISTOBAL

San Cristóbal is a lovely town in a lovely region. A lot of people come for the beauty, but the main thing that draws most visitors here is the highland Maya. They can be seen anywhere in San Cristóbal, but most travelers take at least one trip to the outlying villages to get a close-up of Maya life.

ATTRACTIONS IN TOWN

Casa Na-Bolom 🐾🐾   If you're interested in the anthropology of the region, you'll want to visit this house museum. Stay here, if you can. The house, built as a seminary in 1891, became the headquarters of anthropologists Frans and Trudy Blom in 1951, and the gathering place of outsiders interested in studying the region. Frans Blom led many early archaeological studies in Mexico, and Trudy was noted for her photographs of the Lacandón Indians and her efforts to save them and their forest homeland. A room at Na-Bolom contains a selection of her Lacandón photographs, and postcards of the photographs are on sale in the gift shop (daily 9am–2pm and 4–7pm). A tour of the home covers the displays of pre-Hispanic artifacts collected by Frans Blom; the cozy library, with its numerous volumes about the region and the Maya (weekdays 10am–2pm); and the gardens Trudy Blom started for the ongoing reforestation of the Lacandón jungle. The tour ends with a showing of *La Reina de la Selva,* an excellent 50-minute film on the Bloms, the Lacandón, and Na-Bolom. Trudy Blom died in 1993, but Na-Bolom continues to operate as a nonprofit public trust.

The 12 guest rooms, named for surrounding villages, are decorated with local objects and textiles. All rooms have fireplaces and private bathrooms. Prices (including breakfast and admission to the museum) are $70 (£35) single, $90 (£45) double.

Even if you're not a guest here, you can come for a meal, usually an assortment of vegetarian and other dishes. Just be sure to make a reservation at least 2½ hours in advance, and be on time. The colorful dining room has one large table, and the eclectic mix of travelers sometimes makes for interesting conversation. Breakfast costs $5 to $7 (£2.50–£3.50); lunch and dinner cost $15 (£7.50) each. Dinner is served at 7pm. Following breakfast (8–10am), a guide not affiliated with the house offers tours to San Juan Chamula and Zinacantán (see "The Nearby Maya Villages & Countryside," below).

Av. Vicente Guerrero 3, 29200 San Cristóbal de las Casas, Chi. ⊘ **967/678-1418.** Fax 967/678-5586. Group tour and film $5 (£2.50). Tours daily 11:30am (Spanish only) and 4:30pm. Leave the square on Real de Guadalupe, walk 4 blocks to Av. Vicente Guerrero, and turn left; Na-Bolom is 5½ blocks up Guerrero.

Catedral San Cristóbal's main cathedral was built in the 1500s. It has little of interest inside besides a lovely, uncommon beam ceiling and a carved wooden pulpit.

Calle 20 de Noviembre at Guadalupe Victoria. No phone. Free admission. Daily 7am–6pm.

El Mercado Once you've visited Santo Domingo (see listing below), meander through the San Cristóbal town market and the surrounding area. Every time I do, I see something different to elicit my curiosity.

By Santo Domingo church. No phone. Mon–Sat 8am–7pm.

Museo del Ambar ⚓ If you've been in this town any time at all, you know what a big deal amber is here. Chiapas is the third-largest producer of amber in the world, and many experts prefer its amber for its colors and clarity. A couple of stores tried calling themselves museums, but they didn't fool anybody. Now a real museum moves methodically through all the issues surrounding amber—mining, shaping, and identifying it, as well as the different varieties found in other parts of the world. It's interesting, it's cheap, and you get to see the restored area of the old convent it occupies. There are a couple of beautiful pieces of worked amber that are on permanent loan—make sure you see them. In mid-August, the museum holds a contest for local artisans who work amber. Check it out.

Exconvento de la Merced, Diego de Mazariegos s/n. ℂ **967/678-9716.** Admission $2 (£1). Tues–Sun 10am–2pm and 4–7pm.

Museo Templo y Convento Santo Domingo Inside the front door of the carved-stone plateresque facade, there's a beautiful gilded wooden altarpiece built in 1560, walls with saints, and gilt-framed paintings. Attached to the church is the former Convent of Santo Domingo, which houses a small museum about San Cristóbal and Chiapas. The museum has changing exhibits and often shows cultural films. It's 5 blocks north of the *zócalo*, in the market area.

Av. 20 de Noviembre. ℂ **967/678-1609.** Free admission to church; museum $2 (£1). Museum Tues–Sun 10am–5pm; church daily 10am–2pm and 5–8pm.

Palacio de las Bellas Artes Don't miss this building if you are interested in the arts. It periodically hosts dance events, art shows, and other performances. The schedule of events is usually posted on the door if the Bellas Artes is not open. There's a public library next door. Around the corner, the Centro Cultural holds concerts and other performances; check the posters on the door to see what's scheduled.

Av. Hidalgo, 4 blocks south of the plaza. No phone.

Templo de San Cristóbal For the best view of San Cristóbal, climb the seemingly endless steps to this church and *mirador* (lookout point). A visit here requires stamina. There are 22 more churches in town, some of which also demand strenuous climbs.

At the very end of Calle Hermanos Domínguez.

HORSEBACK RIDING

The **Casa de Huéspedes Margarita,** Real de Guadalupe 34, and **Hotel Real del Valle** (see "Where to Stay," below) can arrange horseback rides for around $15 (£7.50) for a day, including a guide. Reserve your steed at least a day in advance. A horseback-riding excursion might go to San Juan Chamula, to nearby caves, or up into the hills.

THE NEARBY MAYA VILLAGES & COUNTRYSIDE

The Indian communities around San Cristóbal are fascinating worlds unto themselves. If you are unfamiliar with these indigenous cultures, you will understand and appreciate more of what you see by visiting them with a guide, at least for your first foray out into the villages. Guides are acquainted with members of the communities and are viewed with less suspicion than newcomers. These communities have their own laws and customs—and visitors' ignorance is no excuse. Entering these communities is tantamount to leaving Mexico, and if something happens, the state and federal authorities will not intervene except in case of a serious crime.

The best guided trips are the locally grown ones. Three operators go to the neighboring villages in small groups. They all charge the same price ($12/£6 per person), use minivans for transportation, and speak English; however, they do have their own interpretations and focus.

Pepe leaves from **Casa Na-Bolom** (see "Attractions in Town," above) for daily trips to San Juan Chamula and Zinacantán at 10am, returning to San Cristóbal between 2 and 3pm. Pepe looks at cultural continuities, community relationships, and religion.

Alex and Raúl can be found in front of the cathedral between 9:15 and 9:30am. They are quite personable and get along well with the Indians in the communities. They focus on cultural values and their expression in social behavior, which provides a glimpse of the details and the texture of life in these communities (and, of course, they talk about religion). Their tour is very good. They can be reached at © 967/678-3741 or chamul@hotmail.com.

For excursions farther afield, see "Road Trips from San Cristóbal," later in this chapter. Also, Alex and Raúl can be contracted for trips to other communities besides Chamula and Zinacantán; talk to them.

CHAMULA & ZINACANTAN   A side trip to the village of San Juan Chamula will get you into the spirit of life around San Cristóbal. Sunday, when the market is in full swing, is the best day to go for shopping; other days, when you'll be less impeded by eager children selling their crafts, are better for seeing the village and church.

The village, 8km (5 miles) northeast of San Cristóbal, has a large church, a plaza, and a municipal building. Each year, a new group of citizens is chosen to live in the municipal center as caretakers of the saints, settlers of disputes, and enforcers of village rules. As in other nearby villages, on Sunday local leaders wear their leadership costumes, including beautifully woven straw hats loaded with colorful ribbons befitting their high position. They solemnly sit together in a long line somewhere around the central square. Chamula is typical of other villages in that men are often away working in the "hot lands," harvesting coffee or cacao, while women stay home to tend the sheep, the children, the cornfields, and the fires.

Don't leave Chamula without seeing the **church interior**. As you step from bright sunlight into the candlelit interior, you feel as if you've been transported to another country. Pine needles scattered amid a sea of lighted candles cover the tile floor. Saints line the walls, and before them people are often kneeling and praying aloud while passing around bottles of Pepsi-Cola. Shamans are often on hand, passing eggs over sick people or using live or dead chickens in a curing ritual. The statues of saints are similar to those you might see in any Mexican Catholic church, but beyond sharing the same name, they mean something completely different to the Chamulas. Visitors can walk carefully through the church to see the saints or stand quietly in the background.

In Zinacantán, a wealthier village than Chamula, you must sign a strict form promising *not to take any photographs* before you see the two side-by-side **sanctuaries.** Once permission is granted and you have paid a small fee, an escort will usually show you the church, or you may be allowed to see it on your own. Floors may be covered in pine needles here, too, and the rooms are brightly sunlit. The experience is an altogether different one from that of Chamula.

AMATENANGO DEL VALLE   About an hour's ride south of San Cristóbal is Amatenango, a town known mostly for its **women potters.** You'll see their work in San Cristóbal—small animals, jars, and large water jugs—but in the village, you can visit the potters in their homes. Just walk down the dirt streets. Villagers will lean over the walls of family compounds and invite you in to select from their inventory. You may even see them firing the pieces under piles of wood in the open courtyard or painting them with color derived from rusty iron water. The women wear beautiful red-and-yellow *huipiles,* but if you want to take a photograph, you'll have to pay. To get here, take a *colectivo* from the market in San Cristóbal. Before it lets you off, be sure to ask about the return-trip schedule.

AGUACATENANGO   This village, 16km (10 miles) south of Amatenango is known for its **embroidery.** If you've visited San Cristóbal's shops, you'll recognize the white-on-white and black-on-black floral patterns on dresses and blouses for sale. The locals' own regional blouses, however, are quite different.

TENEJAPA   The **weavers** of Tenejapa, 28km (17 miles) from San Cristóbal, make some of the most beautiful and expensive work you'll see in the region. The best time to visit is on market day (Sun and Thurs, though Sun is better). The weavers of Tenejapa taught the weavers of San Andrés and Magdalena—which accounts for the similarity in their designs and colors. To get to Tenejapa, try to find a *colectivo* in the very last row by the market, or hire a taxi. On Tenejapa's main street, several stores sell locally woven regional clothing, and you can bargain for the price.

THE HUITEPEC CLOUD FOREST   **Pronatura,** Av. Benito Juárez 11-B (© **967/ 678-5000**), a private, nonprofit, ecological organization, offers environmentally sensitive tours of the cloud forest. The forest is a haven for **migratory birds,** and more than 100 bird species and 600 plant species have been discovered here. Guided tours run from 9am to noon Tuesday to Sunday. They cost $25 (£13) per group of up to eight people. Make reservations a day in advance. To reach the reserve on your own, drive on the road to Chamula; the turnoff is at Km 3.5. The reserve is open Tuesday to Sunday from 9am to 4pm.

SHOPPING

Many Indian villages near San Cristóbal are noted for **weaving, embroidery, brocade work, leather,** and **pottery,** making the area one of the best in the country for shopping. You'll see beautiful woolen shawls, indigo-dyed skirts, colorful native shirts, and magnificently woven *huipiles,* all of which often come in vivid geometric patterns. A good place to find textiles as well as other handicrafts, besides what's mentioned below, is in and around Santo Domingo and the market. There are a lot of stalls and small shops in that neighborhood that make for interesting shopping. Working in leather, the craftspeople are artisans of the highest caliber. Tie-dyed *jaspe* from Guatemala comes in bolts and is made into clothing. The town is also known for **amber,** sold in several shops, one of the best of which is mentioned below.

CRAFTS

Casa de Artesanías Amanecer   The showroom has examples of every craft practiced in the state. It is run by the government in support of Indian crafts. You should take a look, if only to survey what crafts the region practices. It's open Monday to Friday from 9am to 9pm, Saturday 10am to 9pm, and Sunday 10am to 3pm. Niños Héroes at Hidalgo. © 967/678-1180.

El Encuentro   Noted for having reasonable prices, this shop carries many ritual items, such as new and used men's ceremonial hats, false saints, and iron rooftop adornments, plus many *huipiles* and other textiles. It's open Monday to Saturday from 9am to 8pm. Calle Real de Guadalupe 63-A (between Diego Dujelay and Vicente Guerrero). © 967/678-3698.

La Galería   This art gallery beneath a cafe shows the work of well-known national and international painters. Also for sale are paintings and greeting cards by Kiki, the owner, a German artist who has found her niche in San Cristóbal. There are some Oaxacan rugs and pottery, plus unusual silver jewelry. It's open daily from 10am to 9pm. Hidalgo 3. © 967/678-1547.

Lágrimas de la Selva   "Tears of the Jungle" deals in amber and jewelry, and no other amber shop in town that I know of has the variety, quality, or artistic flair of this one. It's not a bargain hunter's turf, but a great place for the curious to go. Often you can watch the jewelers in action. Open daily from 10am to 8pm. Hidalgo 1-C (half block south of the main square). © 967/674-6348.

TEXTILES

Plaza de Santo Domingo   The plazas around this church and the nearby Templo de Caridad fill with women in native garb selling their wares. Here you'll find women from Chamula weaving belts or embroidering, surrounded by piles of loomed woolen textiles from their village. Their inventory includes Guatemalan shawls, belts, and bags. There are also some excellent buys on Chiapanecan-made wool vests, jackets, rugs, and shawls, similar to those at Sna Jolobil (described below), if you take the time to look and bargain. Vendors arrive between 9 and 10am and begin to leave around 3pm. Av. Utrilla. No phone.

Sna Jolobil   Meaning "weaver's house" in Mayan, this place is in the former convent (monastery) of Santo Domingo, next to the Templo de Santo Domingo. Groups of Tzotzil and Tzeltal craftspeople operate the cooperative store, which has about 3,000 members who contribute products, help run the store, and share in the moderate profits. Their works are simply beautiful; prices are high, as is the quality. It's open Monday to Saturday from 9am to 2pm and 4 to 6pm; credit cards are accepted. Calzada Lázaro Cárdenas 42 (Plaza Santo Domingo, between Navarro and Nicaragua). © 967/678-2646.

Unión Regional de Artesanías de los Altos   Also known as J'pas Joloviletic, this cooperative of weavers is smaller than Sna Jolobil (described above) and not as sophisticated in its approach to potential shoppers. It sells blouses, textiles, pillow covers, vests, sashes, napkins, baskets, and purses. It's near the market and worth looking around. Open Monday to Saturday from 9am to 2pm and 4 to 7pm, Sunday from 9am to 1pm. Av. Utrilla 43. © 967/678-2848.

WHERE TO STAY

Among the most interesting places to stay in town is the seminary-turned-hotel-museum **Casa Na-Bolom;** see "Attractions in Town," earlier in this chapter.

Hotels in San Cristóbal are inexpensive. You can do pretty well for $40 to $60 (£20–£30) per night per double. Rates listed here include taxes. High season is Easter week, July, August, and December.

MODERATE

Casa Felipe Flores 𝒢𝒢   This beautifully restored colonial house is the perfect setting for getting a feel for San Cristóbal. The patios and common rooms are relaxing and comfortable, and their architectural details are so very *coleto*. The guest rooms are nicely furnished and full of character. And they are warm in winter. The owners, Nancy and David Orr, are gracious people who enjoy sharing their appreciation and knowledge of Chiapas and the Maya. Their cook serves up righteous breakfasts.

Calle Dr. Felipe Flores 36, 29230 San Cristóbal de las Casas, Chi. ©/fax 967/678-3996. www.felipeflores.com. 5 units. $90–$110 (£45–£50) double. Rates include full breakfast. 10% service charge. No credit cards. Limited street parking. **Amenities:** Tour info; laundry service; library. *In room:* No phone.

Hotel Casa Mexicana 𝒢𝒢   Created from a large mansion, this beautiful hotel with a colonial-style courtyard offers comfortable lodging. Rooms, courtyards, the restaurant, and the lobby are decorated in modern-traditional Mexican style, with warm tones of yellow and red. The rooms are carpeted and come with two double beds or one king-size. They have good lighting, electric heaters, and spacious bathrooms. Guests are welcome to use the sauna, and inexpensive massages can be arranged. The hotel handles a lot of large tour groups; it can be quiet and peaceful one day, full and bustling the next. There is a new addition to the hotel across the street, but I like the doubles in the original section better. This hotel is 3 blocks north of the main plaza.

28 de Agosto 1 (at Utrilla), 29200 San Cristóbal de las Casas, Chi. © 967/678-1348 or -0698. Fax 967/678-2627. www.hotelcasamexicana.com. 55 units. High season $100 (£50) double, $160 (£80) junior suite, $180 (£90) suite; low season $85 (£43) double, $140 (£70) junior suite, $170 (£85) suite. AE, MC, V. Free secure parking 1½ blocks away. **Amenities:** Restaurant; bar; sauna; tour info; room service; massage; babysitting; laundry service. *In room:* TV, hair dryer (on request).

Hotel Casavieja   The Casavieja is aptly named: It has a charming old feel that is San Cristóbal to a tee. Originally built in 1740, it has undergone restoration and new construction faithful to the original design in essentials such as wood-beam ceilings. One nod toward modernity is carpeted floors, a welcome feature on cold mornings. The rooms also come with electric heaters. Bathrooms vary, depending on what section of the hotel you're in, but all are adequate. The hotel's restaurant, Doña Rita, faces the interior courtyard, with tables on the patio and inside, and offers good food at reasonable prices. The hotel is 3½ blocks northeast of the plaza.

María Adelina Flores 27 (between Cristóbal Colón and Diego Dujelay), 29200 San Cristóbal de las Casas, Chi. ©/fax 967/678-6868 or -0385. www.casavieja.com.mx. 39 units. $66–$82 (£33–£41) double. AE, MC, V. Free parking. **Amenities:** Restaurant; bar; room service; laundry service. *In room:* TV.

Hotel El Paraíso   For the independent traveler, this is a safe haven from the busloads of tour groups that can disrupt the atmosphere and service at other hotels. Rooms are small but beautifully decorated. They have comfortable beds and good reading lights; some even have a ladder to a loft holding a second bed. Bathrooms are small, too, but the plumbing is good. The entire hotel is decorated in terra cotta and blue, with beautiful wooden columns and beams supporting the roof. The hotel's restaurant, El Edén (see "Where to Dine," below) may be the best in town.

Av. 5 de Febrero 19, 29200 San Cristóbal de las Casas, Chi. © 967/678-0085 or -5382. Fax 967/678-5168. www.hotelposadaparaiso.com. 14 units. $60–$72 (£30–£36) double. AE, MC, V. No parking. **Amenities:** Restaurant; bar; tour info; room service; laundry service. *In room:* TV.

Mansión de los Angeles   This hotel with a good location offers good service and tidy rooms and public areas. Guest rooms are medium size and come with either a single and a double bed or two double beds. The rooms are warmer and better lit than at most hotels in this town. They are also quiet. Some of the bathrooms are a little small. Most rooms have windows that open onto a pretty courtyard with a fountain. The rooftop sun deck is a great siesta spot.

Calle Francisco Madero 17, 29200 San Cristóbal de las Casas, Chi. ℂ 967/678-1173 or -4371. hotelangeles@ prodigy.com.mx. 20 units. $60–$72 (£30–£36) double. MC, V. Limited street parking. In room: TV.

INEXPENSIVE

Hotel Don Quijote   Rooms in this three-story hotel (no elevator) are small but quiet, carpeted, and well lit, but a little worn. All have two double beds with reading lamps over them, tiled bathrooms, and plenty of hot water. There's complimentary coffee in the mornings. It's 2½ blocks east of the plaza.

Cristóbal Colón 7 (near Real de Guadalupe), 29200 San Cristóbal de las Casas, Chi. ℂ 967/678-0920. Fax 967/678-0346. 24 units. $28–$40 (£14–£20) double. MC, V. Limited street parking. In room: TV.

Hotel Palacio de Moctezuma   This three-story hotel has open courtyards and more greenery than others in this price range. Fresh-cut flowers tucked around tile fountains are its hallmark. The rooms have carpeting and tiled bathrooms with showers; many are quite large but, alas, can be cold in winter. The restaurant looks out on the interior courtyard. On the third floor is a solarium with comfortable tables and chairs and great city views. The hotel is 3½ blocks southeast of the main plaza.

Juárez 16 (at León), 29200 San Cristóbal de las Casas, Chi. ℂ 967/678-0352 or -1142. Fax 967/678-1536. 42 units. $38–$44 (£19–£22) double. MC, V. Free limited parking. **Amenities:** Restaurant. In room: TV, no phone.

Hotel Real del Valle *Value*   This hotel has great location just off the main plaza. The rooms in the back three-story section have new bathrooms, big closets, and tile floors. The beds are comfortable, and the water is hot—all for a good price. In winter the rooms are a little cold. Amenities include a rooftop solarium.

Real de Guadalupe 14, 29200 San Cristóbal de las Casas, Chi. ℂ 967/678-0680. Fax 967/678-3955. hrvalle@mundo maya.com.mx. 36 units. $28–$38 (£14–£19) double. No credit cards. Free parking. **Amenities:** Solarium; laundry service. In room: TV, no phone.

WHERE TO DINE

San Cristóbal is not known for its cuisine, but you can eat well at several restaurants. For baked goods, try the **Panadería La Hojaldra,** Insurgentes 14 (ℂ **967/678-4286**). It's open daily from 8am to 9:30pm. In addition to the restaurants listed below, consider making reservations for dinner at Casa Na-Bolom (see "Attractions in Town," earlier in this chapter).

MODERATE

El Edén *Value* INTERNATIONAL   This is a small, quiet restaurant where it is obvious that somebody who enjoys the taste of good food prepares the meals; just about anything except Swiss rarebit is good. The meats are especially tender, and the margaritas are especially dangerous (one is all it takes). Specialties include Swiss cheese fondue for two, Edén salad, and brochette. This is where locals go for a splurge. It's 2 blocks from the main plaza.

In the Hotel El Paraíso, Av. 5 de Febrero 19. ℂ 967/678-5382. Breakfast $5 (£2.50); main courses $6–$12 (£3–£6). AE, MC, V. Daily 8am–9pm.

La Paloma INTERNATIONAL/MEXICAN   La Paloma I particularly like in the evening because the lighting is so well done. Both the Mexican and the other dishes are much more mainstream than what you get at Los Barrios—fewer surprises. For starters, I enjoyed the *quesadillas* cooked Mexico City style (small fried packets of *masa* stuffed with a variety of fillings). Don't make my mistake of trying to share them with your dinner companion; it will only lead to trouble. Mexican classics include *albóndigas en chipotle* (meatballs in a thick chipotle sauce), Oaxacan black *mole*, and a variety of chiles rellenos. Avoid the *profiteroles*.

Hidalgo 3. ℂ **967/678-1547.** Main courses $7–$15 (£3.50–£7.50). MC, V. Daily 9am–midnight.

Los Barrios CONTEMPORARY MEXICAN   For Mexican food in San Cristóbal, I can't think of a better place than this. The tortilla soup was the best I've had here (called *sopa de la abuela*). For something different, there's a mushroom–and–cactus paddle soup. The main courses, while kept to a manageable number, offer enough variety to please several tastes. There are a couple of novel chile relleno combinations and a chicken breast *adobado* with plantain stuffing. The restaurant is in a patio with an interesting rough-wood enclosure. It's quiet and inviting.

Guadalupe Victoria 25 (between 3 de Mayo and Matamoros). ℂ **967/678-1910.** Main courses $6–$10 (£3–£5). MC, V. Mon–Sat 1–10pm; Sun buffet 1:30–6pm.

Pierre ⊛ FRENCH   Who would have thought that you could get good French food in San Cristóbal? And yet, Frenchman Pierre Niviere offers an appealing selection of traditional French dishes, simplified and tweaked for the tropical surroundings. I showed up on a Sunday, enjoyed the fixed menu, and left well satisfied.

Real de Guadalupe 73. ℂ **967/678-7211.** Main courses $6–$16 (£3–£8); Sunday fixed menu $10 (£5). No credit cards. Daily 1:30–11pm.

INEXPENSIVE

Emiliano's Moustache ⟨Finds⟩ MEXICAN/TACOS   Like any right-thinking traveler, I initially avoided this place on account of its unpromising name and some cartoonlike figures by the door. But a conversation with some local folk overcame my prejudice and tickled my sense of irony. Sure enough, the place was crowded with *coletos* enjoying the restaurant's highly popular *comida corrida* and delicious tacos, and there wasn't a foreigner in sight. The daily menu is posted by the door; if that doesn't appeal, you can choose from a menu of taco plates (a mixture of fillings cooked together and served with tortillas and a variety of hot sauces).

Crescencio Rosas 7. ℂ **967/678-7246.** Main courses $4–$8 (£2–£4); *comida corrida* $4 (£2). No credit cards. Daily 8am–midnight.

La Casa del Pan Papalotl VEGETARIAN   This place is best known for its vegetarian lunch buffet with salad bar. The vegetables and most of the grains are organic. Kippy, the owner, has a home garden and a field near town where she grows vegetables. She buys high-altitude, locally grown, organic red wheat with which she bakes her breads. These are all sourdough breads, which she likes because she feels they are easily digested and have good texture and taste. The pizzas are a popular item. The restaurant shares space with other activities in the cultural center El Puente, which has gallery space, a language school, and cinema.

Real de Guadalupe 55 (between Diego Dujelay and Cristóbal Colón). ℂ **967/678-7215.** Main courses $5–$10 (£2.50–£5); lunch buffet $5–$6 (£2.50–£3). No credit cards. Mon–Sat 9am–10pm, lunch buffet 2–4pm.

Madre Tierra INTERNATIONAL/VEGETARIAN   A lot of vegetarians live in this town, and they have many options. This one is almost an institution in San Cristóbal. The restaurant is known for its baked goods, pastas, pizza, and quiche. They also offer fresh salads and international main courses that are safe and dependable. Good for breakfast, too. Madre Tierra is 3½ blocks south of the plaza.

Av. Insurgentes 19. ℂ 967/678-4297. Main courses $4–$8 (£2–£4); *comida corrida* (served after noon) $6 (£3). No credit cards. Restaurant daily 8am–9:45pm. Bakery Mon–Sat 9am–8pm; Sun 9am–2pm.

Normita's MEXICAN   Normita's is famous for its *pozole,* a hearty chicken and hominy soup to which you add a variety of things. It also offers cheap, dependable, short-order Mexican mainstays. Normita's is an informal "people's" restaurant; the open kitchen takes up one corner of the room, and tables sit in front of a large mural of a fall forest scene from some faraway place. It's 2 blocks southeast of the plaza.

Av. Juárez 6 (at Dr. José Flores). No phone. Breakfast $2–$3 (£1–£1.50); *pozole* $3 (£1.50); tacos $2.50 (£1.25). No credit cards. Daily 7am–11pm.

Restaurant Tuluc *Value* MEXICAN/INTERNATIONAL   A real bargain here is the popular *comida corrida*—it's delicious and filling. Other favorites are sandwiches and enchiladas. The house specialty is *filete Tuluc,* a beef filet wrapped around spinach and cheese served with fried potatoes and green beans; while not the best cut of meat, it's certainly priced right. The Chiapaneco breakfast is a filling quartet of juice, toast, two Chiapanecan tamales, and coffee. Tuluc also has that rarest of rarities in Mexico, a nonsmoking section. The restaurant is 1½ blocks south of the plaza.

Av. Insurgentes 5 (between Cuauhtémoc and Francisco León). ℂ 967/678-2090. Breakfast $2–$3 (£1–£1.50); main courses $4–$5 (£2–£2.50); *comida corrida* (served 2–4pm) $4 (£2). No credit cards. Daily 7am–10pm.

COFFEEHOUSES

Because Chiapas-grown coffee is highly regarded, it's not surprising that coffeehouses proliferate here. Most are concealed in the nooks and crannies of San Cristóbal's side streets. Try **Café La Selva,** Crescencio Rosas 9 (ℂ **967/678-7244**), for coffee served in all its varieties and brewed from organic beans; it is open daily from 9am to 11pm. A more traditional-style cafe, where locals meet to talk over the day's news, is **Café San Cristóbal,** Cuauhtémoc 1 (ℂ **967/678-3861**). It's open Monday to Saturday from 9am to 10pm, Sunday from 9am to 9pm. There is also a coffee museum with a cafe inside with the confusing name **Café Museo Café.** It's at María Adelina Flores 10 (ℂ **967/678-7876**).

SAN CRISTOBAL AFTER DARK

San Cristóbal is blessed with a variety of nightlife, both resident and migratory. There is a lot of live music, surprisingly good and varied. The bars and restaurants are cheap. And they are easy to get to: You can hit all the places mentioned here without setting foot in a cab. Weekends are best, but on any night you'll find something going on.

Almost all the clubs in San Cristóbal host Latin music of one genre or another. **El Cocodrilo** (ℂ **967/678-1140**), on the main plaza in the Hotel Santa Clara, has acoustic performers playing Latin folk music *(trova, andina).* Relax at a table in what usually is a not-too-crowded environment. After that your choices are varied. For Latin dance music there's a place just a block away on the corner of Madero and Juárez called **Latino's** (ℂ **967/678-9972**)—good bands playing a mix of salsa, merengue, and cumbia. On weekends it gets crowded, but it has a good-size dance floor. Another club, **Blue** (© 967/678-2000), is in the opposite direction on the other side of the main square. It has live music on weekends playing salsa, reggae, and some electronic music. The place is dark and has just a bit of the urban edge to it. From there you can walk down the pedestrian-only 20 de Noviembre to visit a couple of popular bars— **Revolución** and **El Circo.**

ROAD TRIPS FROM SAN CRISTOBAL

For excursions to nearby villages, see "The Nearby Maya Villages & Countryside," earlier in this chapter; for destinations farther away, there are several local travel agencies. But first you should try **Alex and Raúl** (p. 488). You can also try **ATC Travel and Tours,** Calle 5 de Febrero 15, at the corner of 16 de Septiembre (© 967/678-2550; fax 967/678-3145), across from El Fogón restaurant. The agency has bilingual guides and reliable vehicles. ATC regional tours focus on birds and orchids, textiles, hiking, and camping.

Strangely, the cost of the trips includes a driver but not necessarily a bilingual guide or guided information of any kind. You pay extra for those services, so when checking prices, be sure to flesh out the details.

PALENQUE, BONAMPAK & YAXCHILAN

For information on these destinations, see the section on Palenque, earlier in this chapter.

CHINCULTIC RUINS, COMITAN & MONTEBELLO NATIONAL PARK

Almost 160km (100 miles) southeast of San Cristóbal, near the border with Guatemala, is the **Chincultic** archaeological site and Montebello National Park, with **16 multicolored lakes** and exuberant pine-forest vegetation. Seventy-four kilometers (46 miles) from San Cristóbal is **Comitán,** a pretty hillside town of 40,000 inhabitants, known for its flower cultivation and a sugar cane–based liquor called *comitecho.* It's also the last big town along the Pan-American Highway before the Guatemalan border.

The Chincultic ruins, a late Classic site, have barely been excavated, but the main **acropolis,** high up against a cliff, is magnificent to see from below and is worth the walk up for the view. After passing through the gate, you'll see the trail ahead; it passes ruins on both sides. More unexcavated tree-covered ruins flank steep stairs leading up the mountain to the acropolis. From there, you can gaze upon distant Montebello lakes and miles of cornfields and forest. The paved road to the lakes passes six lakes, all different colors and sizes, ringed by cool pine forests; most have parking lots and lookouts. The paved road ends at a small restaurant. The lakes are best seen on a sunny day, when their famous brilliant colors are optimal.

Most travel agencies in San Cristóbal offer a daylong trip that includes the lakes, the ruins, lunch in Comitán, and a stop in the pottery-making village of Amatenango del Valle. If you're driving, follow Highway 190 south from San Cristóbal through the pretty village of Teopisca and then through Comitán; turn left at La Trinitaria, where there's a sign to the lakes. After the Trinitaria turnoff and before you reach the lakes, there's a sign pointing left down a narrow dirt road to the Chincultic ruins.

13

Eastward from Mexico City: Puebla & Veracruz

by David Baird

El *Oriente* is what the Mexicans call this region, by which they mean all the land stretching from the central valley of Mexico east to the Gulf. (So when you see signs advertising *"tacos orientales,"* don't think of egg rolls.) El Oriente encompasses the states of Puebla, Tlaxcala, and Veracruz, and has much to recommend it. For adventure travelers, it affords excellent white-water rafting, challenging climbs that include Mexico's highest mountain—a dormant volcano called the Pico de Orizaba—and scuba diving along Veracruz's coastal reefs. For the culture crowd, the region has three fascinating ruins, some excellent museums and historical sites, and great food.

Puebla and Cholula have the ideal highland climate, beautiful colonial architecture, incredible food, and a strong culture. The ruins in the area feature the startlingly vivid pre-Columbian murals of Cacaxtla, the great ceremonial center of El Tajín, and the New World's largest man-made structure, the great pyramid of Cholula. The port of **Veracruz** is a fun town for music and food, and for soaking up the easy-going rhythms of the Tropics.

1 Puebla & Cholula ✶✶✶

128km (79 miles) E of Mexico City; 285km (177 miles) W of Veracruz

Puebla and Cholula sit in a broad valley that lies between mountain ranges and snow-capped volcanoes. The valley is 2,150m (7,050 ft.) above sea level and has a mild climate and fertile soils. While Puebla was founded by the Spanish in early colonial times, Cholula's origins date back to the earliest civilizations of Mexico. Until the Spanish arrived, it had displayed a remarkable continuity for an ancient city in central Mexico. It seems never to have been sacked and abandoned in the manner of Teotihuacán or Tula or many other cities. And, although it was a large city, it was never the capital of an empire. Rather, it seems to have played the role of religious center. The Spanish chroniclers noted that it had 365 temples, one for each day of the year. But none of this remains today as the city was sacked and destroyed during the Spanish Conquest. Only the Great pyramid still stands.

Though these two cities—one Indian, one Spanish—have recently grown together into one metropolitan area, they still remain worlds apart. This is readily apparent to the visitor. Puebla has a large historic center with magnificent architecture, including so many convents, churches, and public palaces that it has been named a UNESCO World Heritage Site. Its architecture differs from that of the rest of Mexico in the extensive use of painted tiles, gold leaf, and molded plaster. Facades and exterior walls

Puebla

Church ✝
Information ⓘ
Pedestrian Only ⁓⁓

0   1/4 mi
0   0.25 km

Gulf of Mexico

VERACRUZ

Mexico City ★ ●PUEBLA Puebla

GUERRERO   OAXACA

10 Poniente ← ②   ③   ④   10 Oriente   To Veracruz ↗

9 Norte   7 Norte   5 Norte   3 Norte   5 de Mayo   2 Norte   4 Norte   6 Norte

8 Poniente →   **NORTE**   8 Oriente

Mercado La Victoria

6 Poniente ←   6 Oriente

✝ ⑤

4 Poniente →   4 Oriente   ⑥

①   2 Poniente ←   ⑧   2 Oriente   ⑦

PONIENTE   **ORIENTE**

La Reforma →   ⑪ ⑩ ⑨   Palafox y Mendoza

Plaza de la Constitutión (Zócalo)   ⑮

3 Poniente ←   ⑫   ⑬   3 Oriente

⑭   ✝ ⑰   ⑯

PASEO BRAVO

5 Poniente →   5 Oriente

⑳   ⓘ ⑲⑱   ㉖

7 Poniente ←   ㉕   7 Oriente

㉑

13 Sur   11 Sur   9 Sur   7 Sur   5 Sur   3 Sur   16 de Septiembre   2 Sur   4 Sur   6 Sur   Blvd. Héroes del 5 de Mayo

㉒ ↓㉓   ㉔

9 Poniente →   **SUR**   9 Oriente

ACCOMMODATIONS ■
Crowne Plaza Hotel **1**
Hotel Camino Real Puebla **21**
Hotel Colonial **15**
Hotel Posada San Pedro **8**
Hotel Puebla Plaza **20**
Hotel Royalty **11**
Mesón Sacristia de la Compañia **16**
Mesón Sacristia de las Capuchinas **22**
NH Puebla **12**

DINING ◆
Ekos **9**
Fonda de Santa Clara **14**
La Conjura **24**
La Guadalupana **26**

ATTRACTIONS ●
Biblioteca Palafoxiana **18**
Callejón de los Sapos **25**
Casa de la Cultura **19**
Casa de los Muñecos **10**
Casa del Alfeñique **6**
Cathedral **17**
Exconvento de Santa Mónica **4**
Exconvento de Santa Rosa **3**
Iglesia de Santo Domingo **5**
Mercado de Artesanías (El Parián) **7**
Museo Ampara **23**
Museo Bello y González **13**
Museo Nacional del Ferrocarril **2**

are commonly surfaced with clay and Talavera tiles to hide or lend color to the dark gray-black building stone. Cholula, on the other hand, has an architecture that reflects humility and simplicity and has nothing of the grandiose about it. The building materials are of the simplest sort, and the churches, houses, and plazas are unassuming in size and design, with an inherent Indian quality in their most expressive designs.

There are several reasons to visit this part of the world: to eat the food for which Puebla is famous, to enjoy the colonial surroundings, to gaze upon the volcanoes, to see the Grand Pyramid, and to visit the Talavera workshops. Depending on how much you want to do, you could stay here anywhere between 3 days and a week.

ESSENTIALS

GETTING THERE & DEPARTING   By Plane   Puebla has an international airport, but most air travelers still fly into Mexico City because it has more flights. From the Mexico City airport you can take an express bus directly to Puebla. Look for area E-2 and find the upstairs concourse that spans the passenger pickup area. You'll find ticket counters at the end of the concourse. Buses for Puebla leave every half-hour and cost $17 (£8.50). They will arrive at either the main bus station (CAPU) or the small downtown bus station. **Continental ExpressJet** (© **800/231-0856** in the U.S., or 01-800/900-5000 in Mexico; www.continental.com) has a direct flight connecting Puebla and Houston.

By Car   There are two roads to Puebla from the capital: **Highway 150,** an old, winding two-lane road where traffic is often slow; and **Highway 150D,** a four-lane modern toll road that's much faster. From Veracruz, take Highway 150D west. From Xalapa, take **Highway 140** west to the intersection with 150D. Tolls from Mexico City run $14 (£7); from Veracruz, $30 (£15).

By Bus   The ride from **Veracruz** to Puebla takes 3½ hours and costs around $22 (£11). From **Mexico City,** it takes 2 hours and costs $12 (£6). Several bus lines have regular departures from Mexico City's **TAPO bus station,** as frequently as every 15 minutes. You can also catch a bus to Puebla directly from the **Mexico City airport** (see "By Plane," above).

You'll probably arrive at a large **bus station,** known by its acronym, CAPU. To get to downtown Puebla, look for one of several booths marked TAXI AUTORIZADO. Many buses to and from the Mexico City airport use the small downtown **Estrella Roja station** at 4 Poniente 2110.

VISITOR INFORMATION   The **State Tourism Office** (© **222/246-2044**) is at Calle 5 Oriente 3, across the street from the south side of the cathedral. The office is open Monday through Saturday from 8am to 8pm, Sunday from 9am to 2pm. The city's tourism office is under the archway that runs along Palafox y Mendoza in front of the *zócalo* (Portal Hidalgo 14; © **222/404-5047**). It's open Monday to Friday 9am to 8pm, with shorter hours on the weekends.

CITY LAYOUT   Puebla's streets are laid out on a Cartesian quadrant, the two main avenues serve as x- and y-axes. Instead of positive and negative numbers, you have even and odd. Streets north of the **horizontal axis** (Reforma/Palafox y Mendoza) are numbered 2, 4, 6, and so on. Streets to the south are 3, 5, 7, and so on. The **north–south axis** (5 de Mayo/16 de Septiembre) does the same thing. East of it are even-numbered streets, and west are odd-numbered. Street names also include a direction—*norte, sur, oriente, poniente* (north, south, east, west). So if someone tells you that a church is on Calle 7 Oriente, then you know what part of town it's in: "Oriente" tells you that it's the eastern portion of an east–west street, and the odd number indicates that it's south of Palafox y Mendoza.

Don't count on taxi drivers to know where certain restaurants, hotels, or attractions are located; keep addresses handy.

FAST FACTS: Puebla

American Express The office is at Plaza Dorado 2, Loc. 21, Col. Ansures (© **222/ 229-1500**). Hours are Monday through Friday from 9am to 6pm, Saturday 9am to 1pm.

Area Code The telephone area code is **222**.

Drugstores Pharmacies are almost as common as churches. They usually close around 9pm but take turns staying open late *(de turno)*. Should you need something overnight, **Farmatodo** (© **222/237-7133**) delivers around the clock.

Emergency The emergency number is © **066**.

Hospital **Beneficiencia Española** is at 19 Norte 1001 (© **222/232-0500**).

Internet Access There are several Internet access businesses downtown. Ask around; preferably ask young people.

Population Puebla has 1.8 million residents; the metro area has over 2 million.

Post Office The *correo* is around the corner from the State Tourism office, on Av. 16 de Septiembre. Hours are Monday through Friday from 9am to 6pm, and Saturday mornings.

EXPLORING PUEBLA

Puebla is a city full of stories and anecdotes that color the colonial houses and convents of the historic district. For historical tours of the city or a tour of surrounding area, you might want a guide. One I can recommend is **Carlos Rivero Tours** (© **222/ 304-2855;** www.riveros.com.mx). He speaks English, knows his city, and is very capable. For a quick sightseeing tour of the city, you can hop on one of the buses that park on the street between the *zócalo* and the cathedral (Calle 3 Oriente). Tours are in Spanish, depart every half-hour, and cost $5 (£2.50). Or you can climb on to one of the new **Turibus** (www.turibus.com.mx) open-air double-decker buses, with narrative in several languages. The circuit of both buses includes a quick view of the site where the Battle of Cinco de Mayo was fought. Your ticket ($10/£5) is valid for the entire day and allows you to get off at any location and board the next bus that comes along.

CHURCHES

If you were to stop to examine every church you pass in Puebla, you would be in for a long stay. Still, it is something I enjoy doing, even with the smaller churches. Many have simple, austere interiors that express a sweetness and humility that I like. Three churches in the Puebla's historic district require special mention.

The **cathedral** 🔒🔒🔒, completed in 1649, has the tallest bell towers in Mexico. Its dark-stone exterior and severe *Herrerian* (Spanish Renaissance) design lend it a lugubrious appearance that may befit a cathedral but takes a little while to warm up

Cinco de Mayo & the Battle of Puebla

In the United States, the Mexican holiday Cinco de Mayo is often compared to the Fourth of July, but it's not Mexican Independence Day. The date commemorates the Battle of Puebla, on May 5, 1862, which resulted in a memorable victory against foreign invaders.

At the time, Napoleon III of France was scheming to occupy Mexico. A well-trained and handsomely uniformed army of 6,000, under the command of General Laurencez, landed in Veracruz with the objective of occupying Mexico City. In its path were 4,000 ill-equipped Mexicans under General Ignacio Zaragoza. Despite the odds, the Mexicans won a resounding victory. The French were humiliated and suffered their first defeat in nearly a half-century at the hands of the penniless, war-torn republic of Mexico.

For Mexico, it marked the nation's first victory against foreign attack, and the battle remains a matter of national pride. Never mind that by the following year the French were in possession of both Puebla and Mexico City. Today, the Cinco de Mayo holiday is an enduring symbol of Mexico's sense of patriotism.

On a trip to Puebla, you can visit the forts of Guadalupe and Loreto, where the battle took place, just north of the old part of the city.

to. The inside is worth a peek. Near the front doors, you can usually find guides (or they'll find you) who offer a short tour.

The **Iglesia de Santo Domingo** ⊛⊛⊛, on the corner of 5 de Mayo and 4 Poniente, was originally part of a Dominican monastery completed in 1611. Lining the walls of the nave are some exquisite baroque altars. In the left transept you'll find the **Capilla del Rosario,** built in 1690. It is a masterpiece of gold leaf and plaster convolutes dedicated to the Virgin of the Rosary. Some point to it as the epitome of Mexican baroque architecture. Note, too, the intricate Talavera wainscoting.

The massive **church of La Compañía,** built by the Jesuits, is where La China Poblana worshipped and was briefly entombed. Look to the right of the church doorway and you'll see a curious bit of text in Talavera. It marks the date of the execution of a con man, who arrived in Mexico on a boat from Spain carrying papers identifying him as a *visitador* (papal emissary and inspector). He was wined and dined by the bishops in the capital and in Puebla, and lived the good life for several weeks before being found out. As the text notes, he was executed, and his head was hung above the doorway. The message, I guess: It's not nice to fool the mother church.

Near Cholula are two other intriguing churches: Santa María Tonantzintla and San Francisco Acatepec. See more about them later in this chapter.

MUSEUMS

In addition to the museums listed below, there are a couple of smaller attractions worth visiting: The **Biblioteca Palafoxiana** ⊛ is an impressive colonial library, the collection of the famous 17th-century bishop who went on to become viceroy, Juan Palafox y Mendoza. The library is on the second floor of the Casa de Cultura, next to the state tourism office. The **Casa de Alfeñique** is a colonial mansion and a landmark known for its exterior plaster decoration, reminiscent of cake icing; the museum collection, a hodgepodge of things Poblano, is fun if you have time. It's at the intersection of calles 4 Oriente and 6 Norte. The **Casa de los Muñecos,** Calle 2 Norte 4, is more important for its exterior than for the museum collection inside. The large grotesques that adorn the late-18th-century façade are said to be caricatures of the town council, though this story is apocryphal.

Exconvento de Santa Mónica   After independence, a long political struggle ensued between the national government and the Church. It climaxed in the Reform Wars of the 1850s, when the liberal government instituted several anticlerical measures, including appropriation of the convents. The nuns at Santa Mónica discreetly walled up their doors and kept functioning as a religious community with the aid of their neighbors and the blind eye of local officials. They survived with a little assistance from the outside as, over the years, the convent slowly crumbled around them. Then, in 1934 (during another political feud between church and state), a local official "discovered" them. This history makes for an interesting visit: displays include the contents of this and two other clandestine convents confiscated at the same time. These nuns weren't sitting on great treasures—most of the paintings are poor representatives of their era—but you will find a rare set of paintings on velvet predating Elvis or poker-playing dogs. Don't miss the crypt, the chapel, and the upper and lower *coros* (choirs). In the church next door, the much-revered image of *Nuestro Señor de las Maravillas* appears alongside the back of the nave, to the left as you enter.

Calle 18 Poniente 103. (C) 222/232-0178. Admission $3 (£1.50). Tues–Sun 9am–6pm.

Exconvento de Santa Rosa   Unlike its neighbor, this former convent was unable to postpone confiscation and served variously as barracks, hospital, and public housing. It's now the home of the **Museo de Arte Popular.** You can see the kitchen where *mole* was invented, and afterward the museum guide will take you upstairs to see displays of the crafts practiced in the state. If you enjoy handicrafts, don't miss this place; it has some rare and lovely examples of artisanship. Tours take 1 hour and usually start on the hour.

Calle 3 Norte 1203. (C) 222/232-9240. Admission $2 (£1). Tues–Sun 10am–4pm.

Fun Fact La China Poblana: Princess, Slave, Mystic, Icon.

In Puebla you'll notice the iconic figure of "La China Poblana" virtually everywhere. She was an historical figure whose life would make for a great opera. She was a young princess from India (not China) who was captured by Portuguese pirates, sold into slavery, and shipped to Mexico on a Philippine galleon in the 17th century. Eventually she was sold to a rich family of Puebla. This family, impressed with the woman's simplicity and spirituality, eventually adopted her. Thus freed from domestic chores, she delved into a life of religious devotions, mixing elements of her native beliefs with Catholicism. She gradually gained fame as a mystic who led an austere life of prayer, and became revered by the population of the city. At her death, she was interred in the church of the Compañía, but church authorities later moved her remains when a cult began to form around them. Her form of dress has become the standard folkloric outfit of the city.

Museo Amparo 🎨🎨🎨 The finest museum in the city, the Museo Amparo (named for the deceased wife of the founder) has a stunning collection of pre-Columbian pieces from across Mexico, beautifully displayed and intelligently organized. Its collections of colonial and modern art are quite good, and the museum gets important traveling exhibitions, which usually don't require an additional admission charge. The collection of *arte virreinal* (colonial art) is on the second floor and includes decorative objects and furniture. It is exhibited in the restored living quarters of the original mansion. The interiors are from the Porfiriato (1870s), with the elaborate decoration that the period is known for. Audio tours of the pre-Columbian collection are available. Or you can hire an English-speaking guide for the entire museum ($20/£10). Signs are in Spanish and English; cameras are prohibited.

Calle 2 Sur 708. No phone. Admission $3.50 (£1.75) adults; $2 (£1) children 3–12 and students; free Mon. Wed–Mon 10am–6pm.

Museo Bello y González 🎨🎨 Located near the corner of Calle 3 Sur and Calle 3 Poniente, a block west of the *zócalo,* this museum houses a fine collection of 17th-, 18th-, and 19th-century art, furniture, and antiques from all over the world. Many of the Oriental objects in the museum were brought over in colonial times on the Philippine galleon. Viewing the house is another reason for seeing the place. At present, only the first floor is open to the public. My favorite room is almost completely covered in Talavera, and the display cabinets are filled with Talavera from several centuries. The museum is named for José Luis Bello y González, the father of Mariano Bello, the man who gathered this collection. A guided tour (in English or Spanish) is included in the price of admission.

Calle 3 Poniente 302. ✆ 222/232-9475. Admission $1.50 (75p). Tues–Sun 10am–5pm.

Museo Nacional del Ferrocarril This museum is a treat for railroad buffs. It consists of a large open area with several train engines (both steam and diesel), baggage cars, passenger cars, a presidential car, a dining car, Pullman coaches, and a caboose. You can board and inspect the cars. Even those not interested in railroads might enjoy seeing the design and details of some of these—they're a microcosm of a bygone era. A small gallery exhibits railway landscapes.

Calle 11 Norte and Calle 12 Poniente. ✆ 222/232-4988. Free admission. Tues–Sun 10am–5pm.

SHOPPING

Puebla is the home of **Talavera** 🎨🎨🎨—a type of brightly colored, intensively decorated majolica earthenware. The Moors developed the technique for making it, and later started making it in Spain, in a town called Talavera. After the discovery of the New World, artisans brought the method to Puebla. And now, ironically, the making of Talavera has all but died out in Spain, but here it is practiced with great pride and fervor. There is even an association of Talavera makers in Puebla and Cholula that establishes standards and certifies manufacturers. To be officially certified, a workshop must use only the traditional methods and ingredients (no commercial ceramic mix or glazes); practically everything must be done by hand. There's no restriction on artistic taste, just the methods for making Talavera. So there's a good bit of variety from one workshop to another. The genuine article is not cheap, so you should look around in the showrooms until you learn how to discern the cheap knock-offs from the real stuff and find a piece you prefer over other styles.

If you're interested in watching people make Talavera, consider a workshop tour; several workshops offer one. **Uriarte Talavera,** Calle 4 Poniente 911 (© 222/232-1598), charges $2 (£1) for its tour, but other places are free. The factory showroom has an impressive facade made completely of Talavera. And inside you'll see some great pieces displayed. There are nine or ten other certified manufacturers. Some use more modern patterns; some are more traditional. A couple of makers are in Cholula. One workshop has a small restaurant in downtown Puebla that serves meals on its own Talavera. It's a pretty little place called **Talavera Celia** at Calle 5 Oriente 608 (© 222/242-3663). There's one workshop in the Parián area—**Talavera Armando,** at Calle 6 Norte 408 (© 222/232-6468). If enough people are around, they'll get a free tour. **Talavera de la Luz** specializes in large maps and panoramic views rendered in Talavera tiles. It has shown some of its largest pieces in museums in the United States.

The **Mercado de Artesanías (El Parián)** is a pedestrian-only, open-air shopping area just east of Calle 6 Norte between calles 2 and 6 Oriente. You'll see rows of neat brick shops selling inexpensive crafts and souvenirs. The shops are open daily from 10am to 8pm. Bargain to get a good price. While you're in this area, you can take a look at the **Teatro Principal.**

For antiques browsing, go to **Callejón de los Sapos (Alley of the Frogs),** about 3 blocks southeast of the *zócalo* near Calle 4 Sur and Calle 7 Oriente. Wander in and out; there's good stuff, large and small. Shops are generally open daily from 10am to 2pm and 4 to 6pm. On Saturday mornings, there's a flea market in the little square. If you're there between 12:30 and 5:30pm, stop by **La Pasita,** across Calle 5 from the Plaza de los Sapos, to taste homemade cordials and browse through the owner's humorous collection of Mexicana. Start with a *pasita,* then work your way up to a China Poblana—a layered cordial of red, white, and green liqueurs.

If you're out walking around Puebla, you might amble over to a short stretch of Calle 6 Oriente between 4 Norte and 5 de Mayo. It has a few picturesque sweet shops selling candies for which Puebla is known, including *camotes* (sweets made from yams in various flavors), which are very popular with Mexicans but are not to my taste. There's also one of those Victorian-Era shopping malls made of wrought iron, which has been fixed up nicely: Ex-Mercado La Victoria, which is behind Santo Domingo.

WHERE TO STAY

Except for two small properties in Cholula, all these establishments are in Puebla's city center. Staying in Cholula is a bit more relaxing because it still feels like a small town. From late March through May the area can experience heat waves. Consider getting a room with air-conditioning for those months. Prices quoted include the 17% tax.

VERY EXPENSIVE

Hotel Camino Real Puebla ☆☆☆ This hotel, in the 16th-century former convent of the Immaculate Conception, is a nicely restored colonial gem. Courtyards spill into more courtyards, and remnants of poly-chromed Colonial-Era frescos are everywhere, even in the rooms. Rooms are decorated in handsome blue-and-yellow schemes inspired by Talavera colors. All have tile floors and original paintings, and some contain antiques. The hotel is 2½ blocks south of the *zócalo.*

Calle 7 Poniente 105 (between Calle 3 Sur and Av. 16 de Septiembre), Centro Histórico, 72000 Puebla, Pue. © 800/722-6466 in the U.S., or 222/229-0909 or -0910. Fax 222/232-9251. www.caminoreal.com/puebla. 84 units. $190–$250 (£95–£125) deluxe; $250–$330 (£125–£165) superior deluxe; $280–$500 (£140–£250) suite. Promotional rates sometimes available. AE, DC, MC, V. Valet parking $5 (£2.50). **Amenities:** 2 restaurants; bar; whirlpool; salon;

tour desk; car rental; business center; room service; babysitting; laundry service; dry cleaning, nonsmoking rooms. *In room:* A/C, TV, minibar, coffeemaker, hair dryer, iron, safe.

Hotel La Quinta Luna 🏵🏵🏵   This small hotel in Cholula is simple and elegant. The owners rescued this single-story colonial house from ruins and must have spent a fortune on it. The six rooms are all off a large courtyard. The rooms are spacious, comfortable, and some of the detailing is simply perfect. The windows are double glazed for quiet. The bathrooms are modern and each is finished differently, but they are all large and functional. Some come with tubs, others just showers. The service is personal, and the food at the little restaurant is quite good.

Calle 3 Sur 702, 72760 Cholula, Pue. ⓒ 800/728-9098 in the U.S. and Canada, or 222/247-8915. Fax 222/247-8916. www.laquintaluna.com. 7 units. $193 (£97) double; $222 (£111) junior suite; $270 (£135) and up master suite. AE, MC, V. Free secured parking. **Amenities:** Restaurant; bar; library; spa; concierge; tour guide; free airport pickup; room service; in-room massage; laundry service; dry cleaning, nonsmoking rooms. *In room:* TV w/DVD, Wi-Fi, minibar, coffeemaker, hair dryer, safe.

EXPENSIVE

Estrella de Belem 🏵🏵🏵   Another small hotel in Cholula, this one occupies a smaller house than Quinta Luna, but its location is great, a block from the entrance to the pyramid. The service is friendly and personal. A young Mexican couple, fluent in English, own and manage the house, and they are quite amiable. Rooms are an attractive mix of old and modern, except for one master suite decorated exclusively with 1890s furnishings and details. All rooms have heated floors and large bathrooms; master suites come with two-person Jacuzzi tubs and king-size beds. Junior suites come with a queen size bed. The rooftop pool with terrace is a big plus, as are the elaborate breakfasts. This property is completely nonsmoking.

Av. 2 Oriente 410, 72760 Cholula, Pue. ⓒ 222/26101925. Fax 222/261-1725. www.estrelladebelem.com.mx. 6 units. $170 (£85) junior suite; $220 (£110) master suite. Rates include full breakfast. AE, MC, V. Free secured parking. No children. **Amenities:** Bar; pool; spa; tours; in-room massage; laundry service; dry cleaning, nonsmoking rooms. *In room:* A/C, TV, Wi-Fi or high-speed Internet access, hair dryer, iron, safe.

Mesones Sacristía 🏵🏵🏵   These two hotels share an owner, but each provides a unique way to delve into Puebla's colonial past. If you're looking for modern convenience rather than atmosphere, stay at the Holiday Inn or the Crowne Plaza. If you want colonial flavor seasoned with contemporary sophistication or gaiety, try one of these unique hotels. Both are elegant adaptations of colonial houses in excellent locations, but otherwise they're very different. The **Mesón Sacristía Capuchinas** has quiet rooms with lots of privacy and a smart blend of colonial and modern architecture. The small restaurant has won praise for its modern international cooking. The sister hotel, **Mesón Sacristía de la Compañía,** is less quiet and more fun. It lets guests experience the old city in all its antiquity and even quirkiness. The doors haven't been resized, for instance, and you receive a massive colonial skeleton key to your room. Despite basic modern amenities such as plumbing, electricity, and (as of 2007) air conditioning, the interiors still feel like a step back in time. In the courtyard, a great restaurant and popular nightspot serves Poblano specialties. A guitarist performs romantic songs and ballads until about 11pm. Sometimes the entertainment is a guitar trio or members of a *tuna* (traditional Spanish music sung to the accompaniment of string instruments). It's not a place for someone who likes to retire early. The hotels offer packages for guests interested in cooking lessons or Talavera.

Calle 6 Sur 304, Callejón de los Sapos, 72000 Puebla, Pue. ⓒ/fax 222/232-4513 or 242-3554. www.mesones-sacristia. com. 7 units at Mesón Sacristía Capuchinas; 8 units at Mesón de la Sacristía de la Compañía. $170 (£85) junior suite;

$200 (£100) suite. Rates include full breakfast. AE, MC, V. Free secure parking. **Amenities:** Restaurant; bar; access to local health club; tour and activities desk; car rental; room service; in-room massage; laundry service; dry cleaning. *In room:* A/C, TV, coffeemaker, hair dryer.

MODERATE

Hotel Posada San Pedro 💰 *Kids*   This convenient and comfortable downtown hotel is a better bargain than others in the neighborhood, and the quality of amenities is equally high, especially for families. Spacious rooms come with plain wooden furniture, carpeting, and midsize bathrooms. One section of the hotel has air-conditioning. There is a well-manicured courtyard with a small pool, surrounded by four stories of rooms. It's a family hotel, with afternoon videos for the kids and child care, provided arrangements are made for it.

Calle 2 Oriente 202, 72000 Puebla, Pue. ✆ 222/891-5700 or 01-800/712-2808 in Mexico. Fax 222/246-5376. www.hotelposadasanpedro.com.mx. 80 units. $80–$100 (£40–£50) double; $100–$120 (£50–£60). Internet specials available. AE, MC, V. Free covered parking. **Amenities:** Restaurant; bar; outdoor heated pool; tour info; car rental; business center; room service; babysitting; laundry service; dry cleaning, nonsmoking rooms. *In room:* AC (in one section), TV, Wi-Fi or high-speed Internet access, hair dryer.

NH Puebla 💰💰   This new property is unabashedly modern, spare, attractive, and calming. The common areas all have soft diffuse lighting, the surfaces and colors are muted, and the guests seem to respond by relaxing and talking in mellow tones. The rooms have lots of modern design elements. Good space, good lighting, comfortable furniture (as opposed to some other modern hotels), and nicely styled functional bathrooms. The location is right downtown.

Calle 5 Sur 105, 72000 Puebla, Pue. ✆ 888/726-0528 in the U.S., or 222/309-1919. www.nh-hotels.com. 128 units. $100–$170 (£50–£85) double; $150–$220 (£75–£110) junior suite. AE, MC, V. Valet parking $3 (£1.50). **Amenities:** Restaurant; bar; small heated outdoor pool; fitness room; room service; babysitting; laundry service; dry cleaning; nonsmoking rooms. *In room:* A/C, TV, Wi-Fi, coffeemaker, hair dryer, iron, safe.

INEXPENSIVE

Hotel Colonial   This four-story hotel (with elevator) has a great location. The rooms are ample and attractive, but avoid units along Calle 3, which are noisy from traffic below. The furnishings are simple; standard rooms usually contain twin beds with thin pillows. Bathrooms are basic but sufficient. The hotel's restaurant is good. The Colonial is 1 block east of the *zócalo*, on a pedestrian walkway.

Calle 4 Sur 105 (between Palafox y Mendoza and 3 Oriente), 72000 Puebla, Pue. ✆ 222/246-4199. Fax 222/246-0818. www.colonial.com.mx. 67 units. $72 (£34) double. AE, MC, V. No parking. **Amenities:** Restaurant; tour info; business center; room service; laundry service; dry cleaning. *In room:* TV, safe.

Hotel Puebla Plaza   The Puebla Plaza is almost in the shadow of the cathedral. Rooms are small to midsize, with small bathrooms equipped with showers. Reserve a room in back to avoid the commotion in the front courtyard and at the restaurant next door. The lower prices apply to rooms with one double bed.

Calle 5 Poniente 111, 72000 Puebla, Pue. ✆ 222/246-3175 or 01-800/926-2703 in Mexico. Fax 222/242-5792. www.hotelpueblaplaza.com.mx. 48 units. $55–$60 (£23–£30) double. AE, MC, V. Secure parking $4 (£2). **Amenities:** Restaurant; tour info. *In room:* TV, Wi-Fi.

Hotel Royalty   This hotel on Puebla's main square is a sweet deal. You get the central location, yet the rooms are pretty quiet. They are small to medium in size (there's a good bit of variation), and they have either two double or two twin beds. Most of the junior suites have balconies or at least windows that look out over the square. Some of these have larger beds yet don't cost that much more.

Portal Hidalgo 8, 72000 Puebla, Pue. © 222/242-4740, or 01-800/638-9999 in Mexico. www.hotelr.com. 45 units. $60 (£30) double; $74 (£36) junior suite. Rates include full breakfast. AE, MC, V. No parking. **Amenities:** Restaurant; tour info; room service; laundry service; dry cleaning. *In room:* TV, Wi-Fi, safe.

WHERE TO DINE

Puebla is known throughout Mexico for *mole poblano,* a spicy sauce with more than 20 ingredients, including chocolate. Another regional specialty, *pipián,* is somewhat like *mole* but based on ground, toasted pumpkin seeds. From July to September, it's the season for *chiles en nogada,* and the city goes crazy for them. You'll see them as daily specials on all the menus. This is a dish of contrasts involving a poblano chile; a spicy-sweet filling made of pork, chicken, and sweetmeats; and a walnut cream sauce.

Besides the restaurants listed below, try those in the **Mesones Sacristía** (see above). I've enjoyed the *mole* at the **Compañía** hotel restaurant. Also, I've eaten well in the museum restaurant at **La Casa de los Muñecos.** It has a good reputation and a menu that features several local foods. For a steak, try **Chimichurri** (© **222/249-1534**) at the corner of Av. Juárez and 27 Sur, in the restaurant district (take a cab).

VERY EXPENSIVE

La Conjura &&& SPANISH   It seems strange to eat Spanish food in this city known for its Mexican cuisine, but this restaurant is special. It plays with combinations of Old- and New-World ingredients, such as tapas of *chistorra* (Spanish sausage) cooked with a small amount of *guajillo* peppers, or a shrimp dish with locally made goat cheese and passion fruit sauce. The ambitious menu changes daily, with offerings of seafood, lamb, and beef. On my last visit, I was especially impressed by the *arroz negro con calamares* (rice with squid cooked in the squid's ink), the *huachinango en alberino* (snapper in a scented wine sauce topped with mussels, clams, and shrimp), and a cream soup of sweet peppers and clams. The small, attractive dining room with its low, vaulted ceiling was formerly a bodega.

Calle 9 Oriente 201. © 222/232-9693. Reservations recommended. Tapas $5–$10 (£2.50–£5); main courses $20–$40 (£10–£20). AE, DC, MC, V. Sun–Mon 2–6pm; Tues–Sat 2–11pm.

EXPENSIVE

Ekos && NUEVA COCINA   This restaurant covers all the bases: good food, attentive service, comfortable furniture, and attractive surroundings. The menu has some dishes you just can't miss, such as a seafood chile relleno in a bean-and-*huitlacoche* sauce or a nicely seared sea bass on a bed of sautéed artichoke hearts. Dishes come and go depending on the season, but some standards will always be present, such as a well-prepared tortilla soup and a delicious bean soup. The restaurant occupies the small covered courtyard of a small luxury hotel called Casona de la China Poblana, which is across the street from the church of La Compañía.

Calle 4 Norte 2. © 222/242-5621, ext. 115. Reservations accepted. Main courses $15–$22 (£7.50–£11). MC, V. Sun–Tues 8am–6pm; Wed–Sat 8am–midnight.

MODERATE

Fonda de Santa Clara *Overrated* REGIONAL   This is one of those restaurants invariably associated with a particular city. For many people, it is the automatic choice in Puebla. Unfortunately, this has resulted in a decline in quality. Still, many visitors love it. The *mole* is worth trying. It's 1½ blocks west of the *zócalo.*

Calle 3 Poniente 307. © 222/242-2659. Main courses lunch $7–$12 (£3.50–£12), dinner $9–$14 (£4.50–£7). AE, DC, MC, V. Daily 9am–10pm.

La Guadalupana REGIONAL/MEXICAN This restaurant off the Callejón de Los Sapos serves regional specialties and new favorites, such as fajitas served in a steaming hot stone *molcajete.* The restaurant has two dining areas—the central front courtyard of a colonial house and the narrow patio of a former working-class *vecindad* (an enclosed grouping of simple apartments that share kitchen and bathroom areas).

Calle 5 Oriente 605. (C) 222/482-5136. Reservations accepted. Main courses $7–$12 (£3.50–£6). AE, MC, V. Daily 8am–9pm.

Mi Ciudad MEXICAN For an excellent *mole* or *pipián,* take a cab to this restaurant, in the middle of Puebla's restaurant and club district along Avenida Juárez. The dining room is large, with lots of references to Puebla in the decoration. The menu is large as well. Two cream soups, *chile atole* and *sopa poblana,* are excellent choices. By special request, they will prepare half-portions of either *mole* and *pipián* or *pipián rojo* and *pipián verde;* they're not on the menu, but you can ask for them anyway. The menu is large and varied, and the service is attentive.

Av. Juárez 2507. (C) 222/231-5326. Reservations recommended. Main courses $7–$14 (£3.50–£7). AE, DC, MC, V. Tues–Sat 1:30pm–midnight; Sun 1:30–6:30pm.

PUEBLA AFTER DARK

Mariachis play daily, beginning at 6pm, on **Plaza de Santa Inés,** Calle 11 Poniente and Calle 3 Sur. They stroll through the crowds that gather at the sidewalk cafes. Another square where you can hear live music is **Plaza de los Sapos,** Calle 7 Oriente near Calle 6 Sur. To get there, walk 2 blocks south from the *zócalo* and take a left onto Calle 7 Oriente, toward the river. The plaza will be on your left, spreading out between Calle 7 and Calle 5 Oriente just past Calle 4 Sur. If you take Calle 5 Oriente from the cathedral to reach the Plaza de los Sapos, you'll pass several local hangouts where students and artists gather for conversation, coffee, drinks, snacks, and live music.

Another place to hear live music is down the block from los Sapos at **Mesón Sacristía de la Compañía,** Calle 6 Sur 304. A singer-guitarist entertains with popular ballads from 9pm to midnight. The moderately priced restaurant serves a complete selection of Puebla specialties.

Teorema, Reforma 540, near Calle 7 Norte (© 222/242-1014), is a good coffee shop and bookstore that features guitarists and folksingers every evening. It's open daily from 9:30am to 2:30pm and 4:30pm to midnight.

EXPLORING CHOLULA
VOLCANOES & PYRAMIDS

On the eastern outskirts of Puebla is the small town of **Cholula,** which offers a good vantage point for viewing the volcanoes, Popocatépetl and Ixaccihuatl. These volcanoes separate the Valley of Mexico from the Valley of Puebla. The best time for viewing them in on a clear morning in the winter or early spring when the snow caps would be at their largest.

In pre-Columbian times, Cholula was a large city—the religious capital of highland Mexico. The Spanish razed the hundreds of temples that stood here, and we know little about them. But the **Great Pyramid** still exists, the largest pyramid in the New World. At first glimpse, it looks more like a hill crowned by a church (Nuestra Señora de los Remedios). All the surfacing of the pyramid was removed in earlier times, but you can readily make out the geometry of the stepped platform, which rises from the ground in four levels. One face of the pyramid has been partially reconstructed. Tunnels dug by archaeologists give you an idea of how the thing was built. From atop the neighboring platform (if the guards allow you to climb it), you can get a view of the volcano with the church in the foreground. The entrance fee for the Cholula pyramid is $3.70 (£1.85); the site is open Tuesday through Sunday from 9am to 5:45pm. Tour guides charge $10 (£5) per person and can be located at the entrance to the main tunnel.

While you're in Cholula, you might want to walk around the town's center. A restaurant under the stone archway bordering the *zócalo* offers a decent, inexpensive meal. It's called **Los Tulipanes.**

TONANTZINTLA & SAN FRANCISCO ACATEPEC

A perfect complement to this trip is a visit to the church of **Tonantzintla** ✶✶✶, just to the south. Leave the town on Bulevar Miguel Alemán, which becomes the road to Tonantzintla. Less than 1.5km (1 mile) ahead, the church is within plain sight of the road. It's justly famous for its jewel-box interior, executed in an endearing style that people have come to call Indian baroque. It has mesmerized many visitors, including R. Gordon Wasson, who saw in its manifold imagery allusions to a secret mushroom cult. If this visit hasn't quenched your appetite for visiting churches, proceed a bit farther down the road, and you will imperceptibly cross into the neighboring community of **San Francisco Acatepec** ✶✶. Its church is also along the road and stands out for its stunning tile facade.

2 Tlaxcala ✶

120km (75 miles) E of Mexico City; 40km (25 miles) N of Puebla

Tlaxcala is the capital of Mexico's smallest state (also named Tlaxcala) and a Colonial-Era city that is much slower paced than Puebla. It's close enough to be visited in a day trip from Puebla, but I enjoy spending the night and getting to know the city at leisure. To understand Tlaxcala and its inhabitants, one must go back 500 years, to before the Conquest, when the Tlaxcalan federation of city-states was the bitter rival of the Aztec empire, and both were locked in a mortal struggle that the Tlaxcalans were losing. Along come the conquistadors. And Cortez, crafty Spaniard that he was, plays on this enmity to enlist the Tlaxcalan warriors in his siege of the Aztec capital, Tenochtitlán, now Mexico City. As a reward for being the first and foremost allies of the Spanish, the Tlaxcalan rulers received special rights and privileges and a certain level of independence that no other cities enjoyed.

Over the centuries, while the power and wealth of Mexico was concentrated in the capital city, Tlaxcala became something of a backwater. But to this day (and I'm not exaggerating), locals conceive of Tlaxcala as the polar opposite and rival of Mexico City. The other notion that surfaces when you spend anytime chatting with the locals is a latent sheepishness for having befriended the invading forces, thus betraying the New World. As expiation for this, there is much made of the martyrdom of Xicoténcatl, a Tlaxcalan prince who rebelled against the Spanish and who now is symbol of cultural resistance in much the same way as Aztec prince Cuauhtémoc is for most Mexicans. And, after Mexico City acquired a holy patroness in the person of La Virgen de Guadalupe, another virgin made her appearance in Tlaxcala—**La Virgen de Ocotlán.**

This fascinating history and the relaxing pace of life here make for pleasant exploration. Tlaxcala attracts few tourists and retains its small-town atmosphere and overall low prices. Two blocks from the main plaza is a classic old bull ring, still in use, and across from it is the old **Templo de San Francisco,** supposedly the site where the Tlaxcalan chiefs were baptized. The church is noted for the elaborately inlaid Moorish ceiling below the choir loft. A painting inside the Chapel of the Third Order shows the baptism of the chiefs. To the right of the Templo is the **Exconvento,** now a museum containing early paintings and artifacts from nearby archaeological sites.

The **Government Palace** ★★, on the handsome, tree-shaped central *zócalo,* contains vivid murals by a local artist, Desiderio Hernández Xochitiotzin, who died in 2007. The murals illustrate the city's history. The expanded **Museo de Artesanías,** on Sanchez Piedras between Lardizábal and Primera de Mayo, showcases the state's wideranging crafts and customs. Here, local artisans give visitors demonstrations in such crafts as embroidery, weaving, and *pulque*-making (juice of fermented *agaves*). Don't plan to breeze through; tours are mandatory and rather structured, and they take an hour or more—but are interesting. The museum is open Tuesday through Sunday from 10am to 6pm; admission (including tour) is $1 (50p).

Less than 1km (just over half a mile) from the town center is the famed **Ocotlán Sanctuary** ★★, constructed after Juan Diego Bernardino claimed to have seen an apparition of the Virgin Mary on that site in 1541. Baroque inside and out, it has elaborate interior decorations of carved figures and curling gilded wood that date from the 1700s. The carvings are attributed to Francisco Miguel Tlayotehuanitzin, an Indian sculptor who labored for more than 20 years to create them.

Tlaxcala's **tourist information office** is at the intersection of avenidas Juárez and Lardizábal (© **246/465-0961,** or 01-800/509-6557 in Mexico). Office hours are Monday through Friday from 9am to 7pm, Saturday and Sunday from 10am to 2pm. It sponsors a Saturday tour of the city (in Spanish) and used to have a Sunday tour of the Cacaxtla site. **Cacaxtla** ✸✸✸ (pronounced "kah-*kahsh*-tlah") is perhaps Tlaxcala's main attraction. It's a pre-Hispanic hilltop site 19km (12 miles) southwest of the city with some of the most vivid murals in Mexico. But heavy rains in 2007 (and a lack of precaution by the caretakers) caused one of the murals to collapse. The site was closed on my last visit, and there was no word as to when it would reopen. Get more info at the tourist information office.

WHERE TO STAY & DINE IN TLAXCALA

Tlaxcala has several restaurants beneath the stone arches *(portales)* on the east side of the *zócalo.* One of them, Los Portales, has handmade corn tortillas all day and makes good breakfasts.

Hotel Alifer   The Alifer's rooms are carpeted and have midsize tile bathrooms with showers. The rooms are a little worn (you can see it in the carpeting), but they aren't dirty or uncomfortable. The poor lighting is the only other thing that I can complain about, which is saying quite a lot for a hotel in this price range with this kind of location. The price varies by number and size of beds.

Morelos 11, 90000 Tlaxcala, Tlax. © 246/462-5678. www.hotelalifer.com. 40 units. $38–$60 (£19–£30) double. MC, V. Free parking. **Amenities:** Restaurant. *In room:* TV.

Hotel Posada San Francisco   This occupies a 19th-century mansion on the town's main square known as the Casa de Piedra (House of Stone). Rooms are in the back of the property and most face the pool and patio. They're comfortable, simply furnished rooms with medium soft mattresses. Five rooms in the *zona rústica* have more character but are a little smaller. They are grouped around a small stone courtyard.

Plaza de la Constitución 17, 90000 Tlaxcala, Tlax. © 246/462-6022. Fax 246/462-6818. www.posadasanfrancisco.com. 68 units. $110 (£55) double; $170 (£85) suite. AE, MC, V. Free sheltered parking. **Amenities:** Restaurant; bar; outdoor pool; tennis court; game room; room service; massage; laundry service; dry cleaning. *In room:* TV, Wi-Fi, hair dryer.

EXPLORING THE CACAXTLA ARCHAEOLOGICAL SITE

Make sure the site is open before you travel to see the ruins (see above). This site was uncovered in 1975. What the archeologists found—vivid murals in red, blue, black, yellow, and white, showing Maya warriors (from the Yucatán)—revolutionized our understanding of settlement patterns in central highland Mexico. Since then, more murals, history, and at least eight construction phases have been uncovered.

Scholars attribute the influence of the site to a little-known tri-ethnic group (Náhuatl, Mixtec, and Chocho-popoloca) known as Olmec-Xicalanca, from Mexico's Gulf Coast. Among the translations of its name, "merchant's trade pack" seems most revealing. Like Casas Grandes, north of Chihuahua City and Xochicalco between Cuernavaca and Taxco, Cacaxtla appears to have been an important crossroads for merchants, astronomers, and others in the Mesoamerican world. Its apogee, between A.D. 650 and 900, corresponds with the abandonment of Teotihuacán, the decline of the Classic Maya civilization, and the emergence of the Toltec culture at Tula.

How—or even if—those events affected Cacaxtla isn't known. The principal **mural** apparently is a vividly detailed victory scene, with triumphant dark-skinned warriors wearing jaguar skins, and the vanquished dressed in feathers and having their intestines extracted. Numerous symbols of Venus (a half-star with five points) found painted at the site have led archaeoastronomy scholar John Carlson to link historical events such as wars, captive taking, and ritual sacrifice with the appearance of Venus; all of this was likely undertaken in hope of assuring the continued fertility of crops.

The latest mural discoveries show a wall of corn plants from which human heads sprout, next to a merchant whose pack is laden with goods. The murals flank a grand **acropolis** with unusual architectural motifs. A giant steel roof protects the grand plaza and murals.

Xochitécatl is a small ceremonial center on a hilltop overlooking Cacaxtla, about 1km (a half mile) to the east and in plain sight of Cacaxtla. It was probably inhabited, at least in the classical period, by the same people living in Cacaxtla. A curious **circular pyramid** stands atop this hill, 180km (590 ft.) above the surrounding countryside. Beside it are two other **pyramids** and three massive **boulders** (one about 3m/10 ft. in diameter), which were hollowed out for some reason. Hollowed boulders appear to have been restricted to the Puebla-Tlaxcala valley. Excavation of the Edificio de la Espiral (circular pyramid), dated between 1000 and 800 B.C. (middle formative period), encountered no stairways. Access is thought to have been by its spiral walkway. Rounded boulders from the nearby Zahuapan and Atoyac rivers were used in its construction. Rounded pyramids in this part of Mexico are thought to have been dedicated to Ehecatl, god of the wind. The base diameter exceeds 55m (180 ft.); it rises to a height of 15m (50 ft.).

The stepped and terraced **Pyramid of the Flowers,** made of rounded boulders, was started during the middle formative period. Modifications continued into colonial times, as exemplified by faced-stone and stucco-covered adobe. Of the 30 bodies found during excavations, all but one were children. Little is known about the people who built Xochitécatl. Evidence suggests that the area was dedicated to Xochitl, goddess of flowers and fertility. The small **museum** contains pottery and small sculpture, and a **garden** holds larger sculpture.

Admission is $4 (£2; a single ticket is good for both sites), plus $6 (£3) for a video or still camera. Both sites are open Tuesday through Sunday 10am to 5pm.

3 Xalapa ⓕ

102km (63 miles) NW of Veracruz; 203km (126 miles) NE of Puebla

Xalapa (pronounced "hah-*lah*-pa" and sometimes spelled "Jalapa") is a highland city in the middle of Mexico's prime coffee-growing area and the capital of the state of Veracruz. Less than 2 hours from the port of Veracruz, it offers an easy escape from the high temperatures there. It's a hilly city, crisscrossed by narrow, winding streets and alleys. A fine, misty rain known as *chipi chipi* often floats in the air, cloaking the views in a vaporous shroud.

Tasty Fun Fact

Xalapa, or "Jalapa," lent its name to the famed jalapeño pepper.

When the sky is clear, you can sometimes make out in the distance the snow-capped peak of Pico de Orizaba (also known as Citlaltépetl), an extinct volcano that is Mexico's tallest peak at 5,747m (18,850 ft.).

Xalapa is a university town and has the best music school in the country, which is part of the University of Veracruz. Xalapa is also known for its symphony orchestra. If your interests are more archaeological, you've come to the right place; Xalapa's anthropology museum is second only to Mexico City's monster of a museum. And for active sorts, there's excellent white-water rafting nearby.

ESSENTIALS

GETTING THERE   Veracruz, 1½ hours away, has the closest major airport, although some charter flights use the small Xalapa airport. If you're **driving** from Veracruz, take Highway 180 to Cardel, and then go west on Highway 140. From Papantla, you can avoid the mountains by taking Highway 180 south to Cardel. From Mexico City and Puebla, there's a turn-off for Highway 140 on the toll highway to Veracruz (150D). Fog is common and dangerous between Perote and Xalapa. The trip by bus to or from Papantla takes 4 hours.

The **bus station** (CAXA) is 2.5km (1½ miles) east of the town center just off Calle 20 de Noviembre. Taxis are downstairs, and prices are controlled. Tickets to downtown cost around $3.50 (£1.75). Buses run to Veracruz every 20 to 30 minutes and to Puebla 15 times a day. You can buy tickets downtown at the **Ticket Bus** agency, Allende 110 (© **01-800/702-8000**). The office is open Monday through Saturday from 9am to 8:30pm. Several travel agencies sell bus tickets as well.

VISITOR INFORMATION   Go to the **tourist information booth** at the Ayuntamiento (city hall), across from the Plaza Juárez. Hours are Monday through Friday from 9am to 3pm and 4 to 7pm.

CITY LAYOUT   Xalapa is a hilly town with streets that defy order. In the center of town is the large **Plaza Juárez,** where on a clear day the Pico de Orizaba is visible to the southwest. Across the street (north) from the plaza is the Ayuntamiento (city hall); just east is the Palacio del Gobierno (state capitol). The cathedral is across (north) from this.

GETTING AROUND   Most of the recommended hotels and restaurants (see "Where to Stay" and "Where to Dine," below) are within easy walking distance of the central Plaza Juárez. Taxis in Xalapa are inexpensive, as are city buses. Because streets in the center of town are busy and narrow, cabs aren't allowed to stop just anywhere. Sometimes you have to look for a TAXI sign.

FAST FACTS   The telephone **area code** is © **228.** The city is 1,430m (4,690 ft.) above sea level. The **climate** is humid and cool for the most part. It can be warm from March to early May. The light *chipi chipi* rain comes and goes at any time of year. The rainy season is May through July and can bring strong downpours. The **American Express** office is in Viajes Xalapa, Clavijero 311 (© **228/817-4114**). Hours for traveler services are weekdays from 9am to 2pm and 4 to 7:30pm.

EXPLORING XALAPA

For information on cultural events, go to **El Agora,** a cultural center with a coffee shop beneath the Plaza Juárez (reached by steps on the south side of the plaza). Look for posters announcing upcoming concerts. There's usually something going on. Also, look in the local paper, *Diario de Xalapa* or in the "Cartelera," a monthly publication of the Instituto Veracruzano de Cultura.

Hacienda El Lencero   Occasionally called the Museo de Muebles (Furniture Museum), this country estate 14km (8⅔ miles) southeast of the town center was, for 14 years (1842–56), the home of Antonio López de Santa Anna, the 11-time president of Mexico. Here, he retreated from the world, though on occasion he opened his doors to receive notable visitors. Furniture from Mexico, Europe, and Asia fills the rooms, illustrating the cosmopolitan tastes of Mexico's upper classes during the 19th century. Among the notable pieces is the leader's bed, embellished with the national emblem (an eagle holding a serpent in its beak). The grounds are lovely and shaded by ancient trees. The grand house overlooks a spring-fed pond.

Carretera Xalapa-Veracruz Km 10. No phone. Admission $2.50 (£1.25); free guided tours (in Spanish only) on request. Tues–Sun 10am–5pm. Bus: Banderilla–P. Crystal–Lencero from Av. Lázaro Cárdenas to village of Lencero or nearby spot along the highway. Drive or take a taxi ($11/£5.50) about 10km (6 miles) south of town on Hwy. 140 toward Veracruz, past the country club; watch for the signs on the right.

Museo Antropología de Xalapa ★★★ This museum exhibits excellent examples of the megalithic heads and other monumental sculptures made by the Olmec—better than those in Mexico City or at the museum in Villahermosa. The collection of Totonac pieces, from the highly stylized smiling faces to the unadorned, realistic sculptures of faces and heads, is the best anywhere. The museum is laid out in order from earliest to latest cultures, from the Olmec—the mother culture of Mesoamerican civilization—to the post-Classic civilizations of Veracruz. Explanatory text is in Spanish. Bilingual guides are available. A taxi runs about $2 (£1).

Av. Xalapa s/n. ☎ 228/815-0910 or -0708. Admission $4 (£2); free for children younger than 12. Tues–Sat 9am–5pm.

RIVER RAFTING

Close by Xalapa are three popular rivers for rafting and a number of rafting companies that can accommodate you. No experience is necessary. If you're planning ahead, contact **Far Flung Adventures** at www.farflung.com. Another outfit that I can recommend is **México Verde** (© **01-800/362-8800** in Mexico, or 228/812-0134). Either company can do day trips from Xalapa (about $70/£35).

WHERE TO STAY

Mesón del Alférez 🏃🏃 In most other parts of Mexico, rooms such as these, in a beautiful colonial house, would go for much more money. The owners have thoroughly renovated the old house and retained its residential feel. Rooms are spacious and beautifully decorated. Standard rooms and junior suites come with one double bed, suites with a choice of two doubles or one king. Rooms are colonial in style, accented by bright colors and stone. In some, a loft creates extra space. There are two smaller rooms in front that get noise from the street. Additional rooms are around the corner in a modern house, Balcones del Alférez. They are comfortable, modern, and a little quieter. The hotel faces the back of the Palacio del Gobierno. Suites have two double beds.

Sebastián Camacho 2, corner of Zaragoza, 91000 Xalapa, Ver. ©/fax **228/818-0113.** www.pradodelrio.com. 28 units. $64 (£32) standard; $73 (£37) junior suite; $89 (£45) suite. Rates include continental breakfast. AE, MC, V. Free secure parking 2 blocks away. **Amenities:** Restaurant; tour desk; car rental; room service; laundry service. *In room:* TV, coffeemaker, hair dryer.

Posada del Cafeto (Value) This colorful, comfortable hotel has three stories of rooms surrounding a tidy garden. Furnishings and decor are simple and attractive, with handsome wood furniture and cheerful colors. Each room is slightly different. Some are small, but all have ample bathrooms. Bed choices include one double, two twins, a twin and a double, or two doubles for a higher rate.

Canovas 8 and 12, 91000 Xalapa, Ver. © **228/817-0023.** www.pradodelrio.com. 32 units. $46–$52 (£23–£26) double; $85 (£43) suite. Rates include continental breakfast. AE, MC, V. No parking. From Plaza Juárez, walk 4 blocks east on Zaragoza, then 1 block south where it bends; Canovas is the first street on the right; the *posada* is farther down on the right. Limited street parking. **Amenities:** Cafe (breakfast, supper); tour info; room service; laundry service. *In room:* TV, coffeemaker, hair dryer.

WHERE TO DINE

Because Xalapa is a student town, you can eat well for little money. **Callejón del Diamante** is an alley near the cathedral, with a half-dozen inexpensive restaurants that cater to office workers and students. One, **La Sopa,** offers a daily blue-plate special for $4 (£2). Most of these restaurants are open Monday through Saturday from 8am to 10pm. To find them, turn your back to the cathedral and walk left on Enríquez across Lucio 1 block; the Callejón will be on the left.

Churrería del Recuerdo MEXICAN This is a very popular place for supper, and I've eaten well here, but on my last visit I was a little disappointed—effort was lacking. Perhaps it will be fixed by the time you get there. The traditional supper fare is *antojitos*—enchiladas, *gorditas,* and tamales, which you can wash down with *tepache* (fermented pineapple drink). You might want to try the *churros,* best described as the Spanish equivalent of doughnuts, but crispy and usually eaten with hot chocolate. The restaurant is across from the Hotel Xalapa; take a cab ($3/£1.50 from downtown).

Victoria 158. © **228/841-4961.** Antojitos $4–$6 (£2–£3). No credit cards. Daily 6pm–midnight.

La Casona del Beaterio MEXICAN This restaurant occupies a colonial house near the main square. You can dine in a small patio by a fountain or in one of the large dining rooms under high, beamed ceilings. The menu offers variety—in addition to

Mexican standards, you'll find pastas, crepes, and burgers. The soups I tried, *sopa azteca* (tortilla soup) and *sopa de frijol* (bean soup), were good. Among the main courses is a platter of traditional dishes called *cazuelitas mexicanas*, which allows you to try a bit of several things. La Casona is 2 blocks east of Parque Juárez on the south side of the street. Live music begins at 9pm from Thursday to Sunday.

Zaragoza 20. ℭ **228/818-2119**. Breakfast $4–$6 (£2–£3); *comida corrida* Mon–Sat $6 (£3); main courses $6–$12 (£3–£6). AE, MC, V. Tues–Sun 9am–midnight; Mon 9am–11pm.

4 Veracruz City ✦

402km (250 miles) E of Mexico City; 279km (173 miles) E of Puebla; 102km (63 miles) SE of Xalapa

Veracruz has a reputation as a town with a rich history but little to show for it. True enough, because much of that rich history involved sackings by pirates; heavy bombardment by three different foreign powers (including during the wonderfully named French Pastry War); and epidemics of malaria, yellow fever, and cholera. One might not necessarily want to preserve such a history, even when those same events didn't destroy artifacts. For this reason, and for the character of the natives, Veracruz (unlike Puebla) is better suited to cafe-goers than museum-goers. With the exception of the old fort of San Juan de Ulúa and perhaps the aquarium, the museums can be missed. You come here for the feel of the tropics, the balmy air, and the carefree attitude of the locals.

Veracruz brings to mind other Gulf and Caribbean port cities—part New Orleans, part Maracaibo. Things such as schedules are managed rather loosely, even to a greater extent than in other parts of Mexico. If you expect punctuality and order, you'll just be banging your head against a wall. Here, you relax: You get your coffee in the morning at the Café de la Parroquia, you stroll down the *malecón* (boardwalk) in the evening, you take in the party scene at the *zócalo* (town square) at night. The city attracts a lot of Mexicans, who come to take a break from the social constraints of their hometowns. In many parts of Mexico, for instance, a woman walking into a bar by herself would be frowned upon; not here.

Music is important to Veracruz. Specific to the port city are *marimba, danzonera,* and *comparsa* (carnavalesque) music. Just south of the city begins the Jarocha region of the state, whose music is rhythmic, with sexually suggestive lyrics that depend on double meanings. This is the home of "La Bamba," popularized by Ritchie Valens. In the northern part of the state is the Huasteca region. Its music, the *huapango huasteco,* involves a violin, a couple of strumming guitars, and harmonized singing. Xalapa, the state's highland capital, is home to the largest and best music school in the country.

Cortez first landed a bit north of where the port is now, and his name for the place gives you an idea of what was on his mind: Villa Rica de la Vera Cruz ("Rich town of the true cross"). In colonial times, the Spanish galleons sailed for Spain from here, loaded with silver and gold. Pirates repeatedly attacked, and on occasion captured, the city. The citizens defended themselves, eventually constructing a high wall around the old town and a massive fort, San Juan de Ulúa. The walls surrounding the city are gone now, but the fort remains.

ESSENTIALS

GETTING THERE & DEPARTING **By Plane** **Continental** (ℭ **800/231-0856** in the U.S., or 01-800/900-5000 in Mexico; www.continental.com) has nonstop service

Downtown Veracruz

to and from Houston. **AeroMéxico** (℡ **800/237-6639** in the U.S., or 01-800/021-4000, or 229/935-0283 or 934-1534; www.aeromexico.com.mx) and **Mexicana** (℡ **800/531-7921** in the U.S., or 229/932-2242 or 938-0008; www.mexicana.com) and their affiliates offer service to and from Mexico City and other destinations within the country.

The **airport** is 11km (7 miles) from the town center. Getting there by **taxi** costs about $15 (£7.50). Major car-rental agencies with counters at the airport and locations in downtown hotels include **Avis** (℡ **800/331-1212** in the U.S., or 229/931-1580; www.avis.com), **Dollar** (℡ **800/800-4000** in the U.S., or 229/935-5231; www.dollar.com), and **National** (℡ **800/328-4567** in the U.S., or 229/931-7556; www.national.com).

By Car   From Mexico City (6 hr.) and Puebla (3½ hr.), take the *autopista* (**toll Hwy. 150D**) into Veracruz. From Xalapa (1½ hr.), take **Highway 140** to coastal toll **Highway 180** south.

By Bus   The **ADO** first-class bus station is 20 blocks south of the town center on Díaz Mirón between calles Orizaba and Molina. There is frequent service to Mexico City, Puebla, Xalapa, and other cities. Taxis wait in front of the terminal; the trip to the center costs around $2.50 (£1.25). You can buy a bus ticket downtown at the

Ticket Bus agency (℗ **01-800/702-8000** in Mexico) at the corner of Allende and Zamora. It's open Monday through Saturday from 10am to 7pm.

VISITOR INFORMATION   The **tourism office** (℗/fax **229/989-8817** or -8800, ext. 158), is downtown by the *zócalo,* on the ground floor of the Palacio Municipal (City Hall). It is open Monday through Friday from 8am to 8pm, Sunday from 10am to 6pm.

CITY LAYOUT   Downtown Veracruz is a jumble of streets. The social center of town is the *zócalo,* or town square (formally Plaza de Armas), where you'll find the tourism office. Two short blocks away is another landmark, *el malecón,* a long promenade fronting the harbor. Starting at the *malecón* and running south along the coast is **Bulevar Avila Camacho,** known as *el bulevar.* It connects downtown to Veracruz's hotel and restaurant zone, which stretches along the coast all the way to the onetime village of **Boca del Río.**

GETTING AROUND   Taxis are plentiful and inexpensive. Getting from the downtown area to the restaurant and hotel district to the south takes 5 to 10 minutes.

FAST FACTS: Veracruz

American Express **Viajes Reptur** represents American Express. The main office is at Serdán 690-B (℗ **229/931-0838**). Office hours for American Express–related business are Monday through Friday from 9am to 1:30pm and 4 to 6pm (but you can reach the staff during the lunch hour), and Saturday from 9am to 1pm.

Area Code The telephone area code is **229.**

Climate Veracruz is hot and humid most of the year, but the hottest months are May and June. In the winter, strong winds, known as *nortes,* occasionally bring cool, even chilly, weather.

Consulate The American consulate is closed, and there is no Canadian consulate. The **British Consulate** is at Independencia 1394 (℗/fax **229/931-6694**). It's open Monday through Friday from 9am to 1pm.

Drugstore **Farmacía Las Torres,** Av. Díaz Mirón 295, between Abasolo and Paso y Toncoso (℗ **229/932-2885**), is open daily 24 hours.

Emergencies Dial ℗ **060.**

High Season The peak tourist times are Carnaval, Easter, July and August, and December. Veracruz is more popular with Mexicans than with foreigners.

Hospital The **Hospital de María** is at Alacio Pérez 1004, between Carmen Serdán and 20 de Noviembre (℗ **229/931-3626** or -3619).

Police For non-emergencies, you can reach the police in Veracruz at ℗ **229/ 938-0664;** in Boca del Río, ℗ **229/986-1997.**

Post Office The *correo,* on Avenida de la República near the Maritime Customs House, is open Monday through Saturday from 8am to 4pm.

EXPLORING VERACRUZ

The *zócalo* ★★★ is the social hub, where locals hang out in the cafes chatting with friends while the *marimbas, Jarocha* bands, and mariachis make a lively scene, playing well into the night. Bordering the *zócalo* are the **cathedral** and the **Palacio Municipal (City Hall).** There always seems to be some kind of performance on the square: exhibitions of *danzón* (see "Music, Dance & Carnaval," below), clown acts, band concerts, and comedy sketches.

One block east is the **Plaza de la República,** a long plaza where you'll find the **post office,** the old **Customs house,** and the civil registry, all built around the turn of the 19th century. On the north side is the old train station, **Estación de Ferrocarriles,** with its remarkable yellow-and-blue tile facade. From the east side of this plaza, you can board a bus to Veracruz's most famous tourist attraction, the fortress of **San Juan de Ulúa.** Around the corner from the south side of the plaza is the *malecón* (boardwalk), where you can take a boat ride or have coffee at the city's most popular gathering spot, **El Café de la Parroquia.**

A national company called **Turibus** (www.turibus.com.mx) has started to run sightseeing buses around the downtown area and then south along the shore past the hotel zone all the way to the township of Boca del Rio. Explanations are given in several languages including English. You buy a ticket on board the bus ($10/£5), which entitles you to get off at any of the 20 stops and catch any later bus that same day. Schedules and hours of operation vary depending on the season. You can get details from the tourism office (see above).

MUSIC, DANCE & CARNAVAL

Hang out in the *zócalo* and you'll be serenaded with *danzonera, marimba, Jarocha,* mariachi, and *norteño* music playing to a large crowd of Veracruzanos who've stopped to drink some coffee or beer and chat with friends. On Tuesday, Thursday, and Saturday a band plays in front of the Palacio Municipal for couples dancing the *danzón.* It's a stately affair: They alternate between dancing perfectly erect in a slow rumbalike fashion and promenading arm in arm while the women wave their fans. The *danzón* came to Veracruz from Cuba in the 1890s; today you won't often see it elsewhere. On Wednesday you can see more *danzón* at 8pm at the **Plaza de la Campaña** for free.

If you would like to see more styles of traditional dance, inquire at the tourist office in the *zócalo* (see above) about performances by the **Ballet Tradiciones de México.** Several times throughout the year, the company appears at the **Teatro Clavijero** (© **229/931-0574,** or 932-6693 for reservations). Tickets cost $5 to $8 (£2.50–£4). The shows are fun and colorful.

In the week before Ash Wednesday, Veracruz explodes with **Carnaval,** one of the best in Mexico. By local tradition, Carnaval begins with the ritual burning of "ill humor" and ends with the funeral of "Juan Carnaval." Visitors flood in from all over the country, packing the streets and hotels.

Carros alegóricos (floats) are made with true Mexican flair—bright colors, papier-mâché figures, flowers, and live entertainment. Groups from neighboring villages dance in peacock- and pheasant-feathered headdresses. Draculas, drag queens, and women in sparkling dresses fill the streets. The parades follow Bulevar Avila Camacho; most of the other activities center in the *zócalo* and begin around noon, lasting well into the night.

On the Sunday before Ash Wednesday, the longest and most lavish of the Carnaval parades takes place on the *malecón.* Parades on Monday and Tuesday are scaled-down versions of the Sunday parade (ask at the tourist office about these routes); by Wednesday, it's all over.

THE TOP ATTRACTIONS

El Acuario ✯ (Kids) For most Mexican visitors, the aquarium is one of the city's major attractions. The largest aquarium in Latin America, with nine freshwater and 15 saltwater tanks, it's an impressive sight that can hold its own with American public aquariums. The doughnut-shaped tank gives the illusion of being surrounded by the ocean and its inhabitants. The large shark tank also impresses. To reach it, take a cab.

Plaza Acuario Veracruzano, Bulevar M. Avila Camacho. ℂ 229/931-1020. Admission $6 (£3) adults, $3 (£1.50) children 2–12. Daily 10am–7pm.

Fort of San Juan de Ulúa ✯✯✯ Built to ward off pirates and foreign invasions, the fortress was enlarged throughout the colonial period until it became the massive work you see today. After independence, the fort served as a prison noted for its harsh conditions and for the famous people incarcerated there, among them Benito Juárez. It's a formidable example of colonial military architecture, with crenellated walls projecting straight up some 11m (36 ft.) from the water's edge, and bastions at each corner. Inside is a large courtyard, with wide ramps along the inside walls, storehouses, barracks, and old prison cells. English-speaking guides are available at the entrance. A narrow stretch of landfill connects the onetime island to the mainland.

ℂ 229/938-5151. Admission $4 (£2). Tues–Sun 9am–4:30pm. Taxis charge $5 (£2.50). Cross the bridge that heads north between Av. de la República and Av. Morelos, then turn right past the container storage and piers.

MORE ATTRACTIONS

Baluarte Santiago Built in 1635, this bastion is all that remains of the wall and fortifications that encircled the city. It was one of the nine original bastions protecting the wall. A small collection of pre-Hispanic gold jewelry, recovered several years ago by a fisherman along the coast just north of Veracruz, is on permanent display here.

Calle Canal, between Gómez Farías and 16 de Septiembre. ℂ 229/931-1059. Admission $3 (£1.50). Tues–Sun 10am–4:30pm.

Museo de la Ciudad This small city museum is on the ground floor of a 19th-century building. The exhibits concern the history of the city and its social evolution from colonial times to the present. Text and audio are in Spanish; most of the exhibits are photos or dioramas.

Zaragoza 397. ℂ 229/989-8872. Admission $3 (£1.50). Tues–Sun 10am–6pm. From the Palacio Municipal, walk 5 blocks south on Zaragoza; it's on the right.

Museo Histórico Naval This museum occupies the building that once housed Mexico's naval academy. Exhibits concern the history of navigation, including nautical paraphernalia, the history of the naval academy, and Mexico's struggles with other countries. In the courtyard, the foundations of the old wall that used to encircle the city are visible. As you enter, look for uniformed guides, who will show you around free.

Calle Arista between Landero y Coss and Gómez Farías. ℂ 229/931-4078. Free admission. Tues–Sun 10am–5pm.

OTHER THINGS TO SEE & DO

BEACHES Veracruz has beaches, but they mostly have brown sand, and the Gulf water is a dull green. The nearest true beach is at the **Villa del Mar,** a little ways down *el bulevar,* followed by **Costa de Oro** and then **Mocambo** beach.

BOAT TRIPS   Boats tour the harbor (most narration is in Spanish only), around the tankers and ships docked in the port and San Juan de Ulúa fortress, and out to the Isle of Sacrifices. Departures are sporadic (depending on the weather and demand) from the *malecón* in front of the Hotel Emporio. The cost is $8 (£4) for adults and $4 (£2) for children ages 2 to 8.

EXCURSIONS   Popular day-trip destinations include **La Antigua;** the Totonac ruins at **Zempoala; Xalapa,** the state capital and home of an excellent anthropology museum; and the archaeological site at **El Tajín.** For prices and reservations, contact **VIP Tours** (© **229/922-3315** or -1918) or **Centro de Reservaciones de Veracruz** (© **229/935-6422**).

For the actively inclined, **river rafting, mountain climbing,** and **diving** are all options. River rafting centers outside Xalapa (see "Xalapa: Museums & White Water," below). **Divers** can explore series of reefs and shipwrecks south of town toward Boca del Río. Contact **Dorado Divers** (© **229/931-4305**) for details.

SHOPPING   Veracruz excels in one category of shopping and no other. It has sublimely **tacky souvenirs,** which make perfect payback for co-workers who have burdened you with white elephants. On the *malecón* across from Café de la Parroquia, you'll find a long row of small souvenir shops that constitute Veracruz's version of San Francisco's Fisherman's Wharf. Another place of interest (not so much for buying as for looking) is the **city market** at the corner of Madero and Cortez.

WHERE TO STAY

Most hotels have high- and low-season rates. High-season rates apply during Carnaval, Easter, July and August, December, and long weekends. Low season is the rest of the year. Prices quoted include the 17% tax.

VERY EXPENSIVE

Fiesta Americana Veracruz 🏖🏖 *Kids*   Veracruz's most resortlike hotel is six stories high and very long, stretching out across a wide beachfront. Spacious and decorated in muted colors, most rooms have either terraces or balconies, and all have ocean views. Each contains two full beds or one king. It's on the Playa Costa de Oro, one of Veracruz's nicest beaches, but there is also a large and inviting pool area, with an ample shaded section.

Bulevar Avila Camacho s/n, 94299 Boca del Río, Ver. © 800/343-7821 in the U.S. and Canada, or 229/989-8989. Fax 229/989-8909. www.fiestaamericana.com. 233 units. $210–$240 (£105–£120) double; $270–$310 (£135–£155) junior suite. AE, DC, MC, V. Free secure parking. **Amenities:** 3 restaurants; poolside snack bar; bar; 2 large pools (1 indoor); lighted tennis court; health club; spa; 2 whirlpools; watersports equipment rental; children's activities; concierge; tour desk; car rental; business center; salon; room service; babysitting; laundry service; dry cleaning; non-smoking rooms; executive-level rooms. *In room:* A/C, TV, minibar, coffeemaker, hair dryer, iron, safe.

EXPENSIVE

Gran Hotel Diligencias 🏖🏖🏖   This new hotel, in a completely refurbished building facing the *zócalo,* is now the place to stay downtown. The location is excellent and the rooms are better than anything else downtown. I had a large standard with a window looking out over the square, and yet the room was quiet. Bathrooms are large and attractive and the mattresses are comfortable. Plans are in the works to open a beach club so that guests can have a place to enjoy the water.

Independencia 1115, 91700 Veracruz, Ver. © 229/923-0280, or 01-800/505-5595 in Mexico. www.granhoteldiligencias. com. 120 units. High season $190 (£95) double; low season $150 (£75) double. AE, MC, V. Free valet parking. **Amenities:** Restaurant; bar; outdoor pool; fitness center; Jacuzzi; concierge; tour desk; car rental; business center; salon;

room service; in-room massage; babysitting; laundry service; dry cleaning; nonsmoking rooms. *In room:* A/C, TV, high-speed Internet access, coffeemaker, hair dryer, safe.

Hotel Emporio ☆ Across from the *malecón* by the old lighthouse, the Emporio occupies an excellent location. Most of the rooms in the nine-story building have a view of the harbor. Some have balconies, others simply a large window. In 2007 and 2008, the hotel was closed and completely gutted in order to perform a top-to-bottom renovation. Check the webpage to see if it has reopened yet.

Paseo del Malecón s/n, 91700 Veracruz, Ver. ☎ 229/932-0020, or 01-/800-295-3000 in Mexico. Fax 229/931-2261. www.hotelesemporio.com. 203 units. High season $200 (£100) double, $220 (£110) junior suite; low season $150 (£75) double, $180 (£90) junior suite. AE, MC, V. Free guarded parking. **Amenities:** 2 restaurants; bar; 2 large outdoor pools; heated indoor pool; health club; game room; tour desk; car rental; business center; executive services; room service until midnight; babysitting; laundry service; nonsmoking rooms. *In room:* A/C, TV, high-speed Internet access, coffeemaker, hair dryer, safe.

Hotel Lois ☆ Good location, good service, and a wide variety of amenities for the price are the biggest reasons for staying here. The Lois is located on the coast between downtown and the hotel-and-restaurant zone. It's in a modern 10-story building. Newly remodeled rooms are competitively priced and comfortable. They are midsize, with two double beds or one king. Bathrooms are medium size. The lighting, though not great, is better than other hotels in this price range. The suites are larger, with larger bathrooms, and some contain Jacuzzi tubs. The large pool area on the third floor affords a good view of the coastline. The hotel bar has live music 2 nights a week.

Calzada Ruiz Cortines 10, 94294 Boca del Río, Ver. ☎ 229/937-8290, or 01-800/712-9136 in Mexico. www.hotel lois.com.mx. 116 units. High season $150 (£75) double, $180 (£90) suite; low season $124 (£62) double, $150 (£75) suite. AE, MC, V. Free secure parking. **Amenities:** Restaurant; 2 bars; large outdoor pool; squash courts; health club w/sauna, Jacuzzi; game rooms; tour desk; car rental; business center; salon; massage; babysitting; room service until 11:30pm; laundry service; dry cleaning. *In room:* A/C, TV, high-speed Internet access, hair dryer, safe.

Hotel Mocambo ☆☆ *Kids* The Mocambo, built in 1932, was the city's first resort hotel, host to presidents and movie stars during the 1940s and '50s. It's on the beach in the hotel zone south of downtown. In contrast to the bunched rooms and boxy corridors of modern hotels, its low buildings make luxurious use of space, with wide, breezy walkways and terraces that overlook the ocean, the gardens, and the coconut palms. The grounds and a small play area are fenced in so kids can't escape, and there's a water slide at the pool. The architecture is simple and of the period. The hotel may show its age, but it echoes Mexico's Belle Epoque with stylish touches such as the Art Deco indoor pool. Most of the simply furnished rooms are large, with sea views and tile floors. My favorite rooms are those on the upper floors, which have balconies.

Boca del Río (Apdo. Postal 263), 91700 Veracruz, Ver. ☎ 229/922-0205. Fax 229/922-0212. www.hotelmocambo. com.mx. 103 units. High season $145–$165 (£73–£83) junior suite; low season $92–$120 (£46–£60) junior suite. AE, MC, V. Free guarded parking. **Amenities:** 2 restaurants; 2 bars; 3 pools (1 indoor); lighted tennis court; gym w/sauna and steam room; spa; whirlpool; children's activities (high season only); tour desk; car rental; room service; babysitting; laundry service; dry cleaning; nonsmoking rooms. *In room:* A/C, TV.

MODERATE
Hotel Colonial Two hotels sit next door to each other on the *zócalo:* the Hotel Colonial (which isn't so colonial), and the Hotel Imperial (which isn't so imperial). In terms of rooms, services, and price, they are much the same—comfortable, but not fancy. The location is great: you can enjoy the music and party atmosphere in the *zócalo* and then retire to your room (preferably an interior one). The Colonial has two sections. Rooms in the new section are larger and brighter, with better A/C. Rooms

in the old section are darker and worn. The Imperial's lobby is more impressive, but the pool emits a smell of chlorine to parts of the hotel, and the Colonial seems to be better managed. Still, I think of these hotels as interchangeable. If you can't get a room at the Colonial, try the Imperial (② **229/932-1204**). Lower rates are for the old section.

Miguel Lerdo 117, 91700 Veracruz, Ver. ②/fax **229/932-0193**. 174 units. High season $62–$82 (£31–£41) double, $90 (£45) balcony room; low season $50–$58 (£25–£29) double, $70 (£40) balcony room. AE, MC, V. Covered guarded parking $3 (£1.50). **Amenities:** Sidewalk cafe and bar; indoor pool; room service; laundry service; nonsmoking rooms. *In room:* A/C, TV.

WHERE TO DINE

If you want to have seafood with the locals, go to the city fish market on Landero y Coss around the corner from the *malecón*. Facing the street are several small restaurants. Find the one called **La Cría**.

VERY EXPENSIVE

Restaurant El Cacharrito 🍴🍴 STEAKS   Midway between downtown and Mocambo beach is this family-run steakhouse. The steaks are expertly cooked and served Argentine style. They should be eaten Argentine style, too, meaning you should wash them down with ample amounts of wine. You'll find a large wine list for the purpose. The *bife de chorizo* (rib-eye) is the most popular cut. Also, you might want to try the Argentine *empanadas* or the *jugo de carne,* a rich and satisfying essence of beef. El Cacharrito is around the corner from the Hotel Lois.

Bulevar Ruiz Cortines 15. ② **229/937-7027**. Reservations recommended during Carnaval. Steaks $20–$40 (£10–£20). MC, V. Daily 2–11pm.

MODERATE

Gran Café del Portal *(Value* MEXICAN   In the *portales* that face the front door of the cathedral is this dependable restaurant with good prices and local color. In the evenings a parade of strolling troubadours, harpists, marimba players, and shoeshine men passes by. For the midafternoon meal, the *comida corrida* provides lots of food at a reasonable price. Avoid the overcooked pasta and most beef dishes, which are tough. The exception is the tenderized *milanesa,* which is good. For seafood, ask the waiter what's freshest. The enchiladas and the soups are good, and the *flan napolitano* could feed a family of four.

Independencia at Zamora. ② **229/931-2759**. Main courses $6–$14 (£3–£7); *comida corrida* Mon–Sat $6–$8 (£3–£4), Sun $8–$10 (£4–£5). No credit cards. Daily 7am–midnight.

Mariscos Villa Rica Mocambo 🍴🍴🍴 SEAFOOD   This establishment prides itself on cooking Veracruz style. The menu includes all the seafood standards, plus a few dishes that are harder to come by in Mexico, let alone north of the border. Everything I tried, I enjoyed enormously. For starters, try a classic seafood cocktail. Veracruzano specialties include *pampano al acuyo* (pompano cooked in a sauce of green herbs), conch filet *al ajillo* (with toasted strips of *guajillo* peppers), and *steak de camarón a la naranja* (shrimp pressed together and cooked in orange sauce). Service is excellent. Look for an open-air thatched structure below the Mocambo hotel.

Calzada Mocambo 527. ② **229/922-2113**. Main courses $10–$20 (£5–£10). AE, MC, V. Daily noon–10pm.

INEXPENSIVE

Gran Café de la Parroquia 🍴🍴 *(Moments* MEXICAN/COFFEE   More than a coffeehouse, La Parroquia is an institution. Making the scene here for morning or afternoon coffee is mandatory on any trip to Veracruz. The action takes place in a large, bustling dining area facing the *malecón*. There's nothing fancy about it; the furniture is simple but comfortable and there's a minimum of decoration. The thing to order is *café lechero*. You'll get two fingers of dark coffee in a glass. Add sugar, if desired, and stir, clinking your spoon against the glass. This will attract the attention of the waiter who circulates with the kettle of steaming milk. Don't be shy. The sound of clinking glass rings throughout the dining room. The cafe also offers pastries and decent breakfasts, but some of the main courses disappoint.

Av. Gómez Farías 34. (℗ **229/932-2584.** Breakfast $2–$5(£1–£2.50); coffee $1–$2 (50p–£1); main courses $4–$10 (£2–£5). No credit cards. Daily 6am–1am.

Samborcito *Finds* REGIONAL No need to say the name twice to any cab driver in town; everybody knows this place. Samborcito is simple eating at its best for either breakfast or lunch. The name pokes fun at Sanborn's, the oldest, best-known chain of restaurants in Mexico (never mind the difference in spelling). Classic dishes include *picadas* (*masa* pancake with cheese and sauce—a Veracruz tradition), and puffy *gordita* (puffy soft tortilla with black-bean paste and flavored with the toasted leaf of the aguacatillo—not spicy), and the *empanada de picadillo*. Tamales are available on weekends. It all happens under a long thatched roof, and there's live music on weekends. Samborcito is near downtown; a cab will run about $2 (£1).

16 de Septiembre 727. (℗ **229/931-4388.** Breakfast $3–$5 (£1.50–£2.50); *antojitos* $2–$5 (£1–£2.50); main courses $7–$16 (£3.50–£8). MC, V. Daily 7am–6pm.

VERACRUZ AFTER DARK

The first thing that always comes to mind with Veracruz is the scene on the *zócalo*, which on a weekend can go on until the wee hours of the morning. The evening shows presented by the municipal government can be quite good. I've seen some great dance troupes perform *Jarocho*.

There's a small bar downtown with a real local feel, where on weekends you can hear live groups play *son montuno*, an old-style Latin tropical music. The bar's name is **Rincón de la Trova** (no phone) and it's at Plazuela de la Lagunilla 59. Live music is Thursday to Saturday. Friday and Saturday there's a $3 (£1.50) cover.

There are several dance clubs to choose from. Most play Latin music and are in or near the hotel zone. One that signs good acts is **La Casona de la Condesa** (℗ **229/933-5451**) at Bulevar Avila Camacho 2014, Fracc. Costa de Oro. There are several clubs for dancing to salsa and such. Two are in the vicinity of the Hotel Lois. **Carioca** (℗ **229/937-8290**), at Calz. A Ruiz Cortines 10, and **Kachimba** (℗ **229/927-1981**), at Bulevar Avila Camacho s/n. Any taxi driver would know where these places are.

5 El Tajín & the Town of Papantla

THE RUINS OF ZEMPOALA

Headed north on Highway 180 towards Papantla, you'll pass by the village of **Antigua** 22km (14 miles), north of the port of Veracruz. It's not very well known today, but for 75 years beginning in 1525, it was the main port used by the Spanish. The village is known locally for its seafood restaurants and is especially popular on weekends.

Continuing north you come to the ruins of **Zempoala**, 40km (25 miles) north of Veracruz. The ruins are surrounded by lush foliage. Though not as large as the site of El Tajín, they're still noteworthy. Zempoala was the principal city of the Totonac at the time of the Spanish Conquest. The name means "place of the 20 waters," for the several creeks that meander near the site.

Zempoala is a late post-classic city. Most of the buildings date from the 14th century. The Great Temple is constructed in the Aztec style. The Temple of Quetzalcoatl, the feathered serpent god, is a square platform, and the Temple of Ehecatl, god of the wind, is (as usual) round. On weekends and during vacation months, you're likely to find a group of the famous *voladores* (flyers) from Papantla performing their acrobatic ritual (see the "The Ruins of El Tajín" on p. 525).

Admission to the archaeological site is $4 (£2); it's open daily from 9am to 6pm. A video camera permit costs $4 (£2).

EL TAJÍN & THE CITY OF PAPANTLA

El Tajín (ehl tah-*heen*) is among the most important archaeological sites in Mexico. It has a large ceremonial center with several pyramids, platforms, and ball courts, some in the architectural styles of other cultures (Olmec, Teotihuacán, Maya) and some in the city's own unique style. It was probably built and inhabited (at least in its last stages) by the Totonac Indians who still live in this region. The Totonac culture is most famous for the "dance" of the *voladores,* a pre-Columbian religious ritual in which four men are suspended from the top of a tall pole while another beats a drum and plays a flute while balancing himself at the top.

The major stopover for seeing these ruins is **Papantla,** a hilly city of 165,000 in the coastal lowlands 225km (140 miles) north of Veracruz. In many respects, it's a typical Mexican town with lots of clay tile roofs, a jumble of small shops, and a lively street scene. It's best known for producing vanilla beans. Vanilla is native to Mexico and was used principally to flavor chocolate, also indigenous to Mexico.

ESSENTIALS

GETTING THERE   By Car If you're driving from the south, follow the coastal road, **Highway 180,** from Veracruz. From Xalapa, it's best to do the same: drive down to the coast and then north.

By Bus The quaint **ADO station** (© 784/842-0218) is at the corner of Venustiano Carranza and Benito Juárez, 4 blocks below the main square. Almost all buses are *de paso* (originating elsewhere), so departure times can be a little earlier or later than the schedule says. Taxis pass in front of the station frequently.

CITY LAYOUT Easily visible from many parts of town, the parish church and the Hotel El Tajín are at the top of a hill. This is where you'll find the *zócalo.*

GETTING AROUND Taxis are available around the central plaza, and **city buses** go to the ruins of El Tajín (see below). Almost everything worth seeing is within easy walking distance of the central plaza.

FAST FACTS The telephone **area code** is **784.** The **climate** is steamy for most of the year except for a few occasions in winter when a north wind blows.

SPECIAL EVENTS The **Feast of Corpus Christi,** the ninth Sunday after Easter, is part of a very special week in Papantla. Well-known Mexican entertainers perform, and the native *voladores* make special appearances. Lodging is scarce during this week, so be sure to book ahead.

EXPLORING PAPANTLA & EL TAJÍN

In Papantla, the shady *zócalo* built of ceramic tile is where couples and families come in the evenings to sit or stroll. The large wall below the church facing the *zócalo* is covered with the image of El Tajín and a modern depiction of Totonac carved reliefs.

THE RUINS OF EL TAJIN   The city lies among some low hills clothed in thick tropical forest. The views are lovely, but climbing on the pyramids is forbidden; your best view is from a high terrace that supports the Tajín Chico buildings towards the back. The city is divided into **Tajín Viejo** and **Tajín Chico**—the old and new sections. Of the 150 buildings identified at the site, 20 have been excavated and conserved, resurrecting their forms from what were grass-covered mounds. At least 12 ball courts have been found, of which 6 have been excavated. The most impressive structure, in the old section, is the **Pyramid of the Niches,** which is a unique stone-and-adobe pyramid with 365 recesses extending to all four sides of the building. The pyramid was formerly covered in red-painted stucco, and the niches were painted black. Try to imagine how that must have looked. Near the Pyramid of the Niches is a restored **ball court** with beautiful carved reliefs depicting gods and kings.

The most important building in the Tajín Chico section is the **Temple of the Columns.** A stairway divides the columns, three on either side, each decorated with reliefs of priests and warriors and hieroglyphic dates. Many mounds remain unexcavated, but with the reconstruction that has been done so far, it's increasingly easier to visualize the ruins as a city.

In a clearing near the museum, a group of local Totonac Indians called *voladores* **(flyers)** performs their acrobatic and symbolic ritual. This is a traditional, solemn ceremony that dates back centuries. The Totonac perform the unusual ritual in honor of the four directions of the earth. There's no set schedule for performances; the sound of a slow-beating drum and flute signals that the *voladores* are preparing to perform. Five flyers, dressed in brightly colored ceremonial garments and cone-shaped hats with ribbons and small round mirrors, climb to a square revolving platform at the top of a 25m (82-ft.) pole. Four of the five flyers perch on the sides of the platform and attach themselves by the waist to a rope, while the fifth stands atop the pole and plays an instrument called a *chirimía,* used in rituals by the Toltec and Olmec. The instrument is a small bamboo flute with a deerskin drum attached. The performer plays the three-holed flute with his left hand and beats the drum with his right hand. When the time is right, the four flyers fall backward, suspended by the rope, and descend as they revolve around the post.

The small but impressive **museum** is worth seeing as well. A small snack and gift shop and small restaurant are across from the museum. Admission to the site and museum is $5 (£2.50). The fee to use a personal video camera is $3.50 (£1.75). If you look like a professional photographer, the authorities will ask you to get a permit from the **Instituto Nacional de Antropología e Historia** in Mexico City. If you watch a performance of the *voladores,* one of them will collect an additional $2 (£1) from each spectator. The site is open daily from 9am to 5pm.

To El Tajín from Papantla, taxis charge about $20 (£10), but it's easy to take a local bus. Look for buses marked CHOTE/TAJIN, which run beside the town church (on the uphill side) every 15 minutes beginning at 7am. Buses marked CHOTE pass more frequently and leave you at the Chote crossroads; from there, take a taxi for around $5 (£2.50). From Veracruz, take Highway 180 to Papantla, then Route 127, a back road to Poza Rica that runs through El Tajín.

SHOPPING   There are two markets in Papantla, both near the central plaza. **Mercado Juárez** is opposite the front door of the church. **Mercado Hidalgo** is 1 block downhill on the same street. The former has more food stalls, where you can order a bowl of *zacahuil*, a typical dish of the region. The latter has locally made baskets; vanilla extract; *Xanath*, a locally produced vanilla liqueur; and whole vanilla beans.

WHERE TO STAY

Hotel Provincia Express   Opened in 1990, this hotel is a good choice in a place with meager selections. Rooms are nicely furnished, with tile floors, and hold a king-size or two double beds. The medium-to-small bathrooms have showers. On occasion it takes a while for water to heat up, but it will. Nos. 1 to 6 have small balconies overlooking the *zócalo*. Others, toward the back, are windowless and quiet, and are reached through a tunnel-like hallway.

Enríquez 103, 93400 Papantla, Ver. ℂ 784/842-1645. Fax 784/842-4213. provinciaexpress_papantla@hotmail.com. 20 units. $48–$60 (£24–£30) double. MC, V. Free secure parking half a block away. **Amenities:** Cafe; room service; laundry service. *In room:* A/C, Wi-Fi in some, TV.

Hotel Tajín   At the top of the hill toward the back of the church sits this large, easily visible hotel. Rooms are medium sized, and several have a view. Bed choices include one or two doubles or one king.

Núñez 104, 93400 Papantla, Ver. ℂ 784/842-0121 or -1623. Fax 784/842-1062. hoteltajin@hotmail.com. 73 units. $40–$50 (£20–£25) double. MC, V. Free secure parking a half-block away. **Amenities:** Restaurant; pool; tennis court; tours; laundry service. *In room:* A/C, TV.

WHERE TO DINE

In the morning, numerous stands at the Mercado Juárez offer the local specialty, *zacahuil* (a huge tamal cooked in a banana leaf). In Papantla, the *zacahuil* is cooked in enough liquid to be served in a bowl. Look around until you see a cook with a line of patrons—that's where you'll get the best *zacahuil*.

Plaza Pardo MEXICAN   This upstairs restaurant facing the main plaza serves Mexican standards and a couple of regional dishes. A few tables are on a balcony looking out over the *zócalo*, church, and giant statue of the *volador*. Specialties include *bocales* (small *gorditas* with different fillings), enchiladas, and *mole*.

Enríquez 105-altos. ℂ 784/842-0059. Breakfast $2–$4 (£1–£2); sandwiches $2–$3 (£1–£1.50); main courses $4–$7 (£2–£3.50). No credit cards. Daily 7:30am–11pm.

14

Cancún

by Juan Cristiano

It may be commercialized and more American than Mexican in spirit, but Cancún is still one of the finest beach destinations in the world—with enough pleasure-pursuits to make even the most unrelenting hedonists blush.

Due to its ideal mix of elements—its transparent turquoise sea, powdery white beaches, and immense potential for growth—a group of Mexican government computer analysts targeted the town for tourism development in 1974, transforming it from a deserted beach to a five-star resort in little more than 3 decades. Since then, Cancún sustained the devastations of Hurricane Wilma and other powerful tropical storms, only to emerge stronger and more irresistible. In the wake of Hurricane Wilma, which tore through the Yucatán peninsula in 2005, wreckage rapidly gave way to exacting renovations, luxurious upgrades, and brand-new destinations.

The secret of Cancún's allure hasn't changed much over the decades—it's still all about the Caribbean beach. The city limits of Cancún (which means "golden snake" in Maya), stretch from the old city east to a 24km (15-mile) sliver of land that runs southwest, rimmed by white-sand beaches, connected to the mainland by two bridges. The land creates a ring around the expansive Nichupté lagoon, a lush reminder of Cancún's jungle past between the old and the new.

In addition to its spectacular coastline, Cancún also affords visitors the highest quality accommodations; easy access by air; an unrivaled range of shopping, world-class dining and nightlife; and endless outdoor activities. And it's a gateway to the nearby ruins of Tulum, Chichén Itzá, and Cobá.

Cancún embodies Caribbean splendor and the exotic joys of Mexico, but even a traveler feeling apprehensive about visiting foreign soil will feel completely at ease here. English is spoken and dollars accepted; roads are well-paved and lawns manicured. Some travelers are surprised to find that Cancún is more like a U.S. beach resort than a part of Mexico. Indeed, signs of Americanism are rampant. U.S. college students continue to descend in droves during Spring Break—which, depending on your perspective, may be reason to rush headlong into the party or stay far, far away during this season. One astonishing statistic suggests that more Americans travel to Cancún than to any other foreign destination in the world. Indeed, almost three million people visit annually—most of them on their first trip to Mexico.

Yet Cancún is a convenient distance from the more traditional Mexican resorts of Isla Mujeres and the coastal zone now known as the Riviera Maya—extending down from Cancún, through Playa del Carmen, to the Maya ruins at Tulum, Cozumel, Chichén Itzá, and Cobá. All make for an easy day trip.

You will likely run out of vacation days, however, before you run out of things to do in Cancún proper. Snorkeling, dolphin swims, jungle tours, and visits to ancient Maya ruins and modern ecological theme parks are among the most popular diversions. A dozen malls sell name-brand and duty-free merchandise (with European goods for less than in the U.S.). With tens of thousands of hotel rooms and more than 350 restaurants and nightclubs, there's something for every taste and budget.

A day here might begin with a jet-ski tour of the nearby jungles or a visit to Maya ruins, followed by an afternoon of watersports or lounging poolside. After soaking up the sun, you could browse through a Mexican *mercado* (market) in search of bargains or visit upscale stores for duty-free deals. Then dine at one of several five-diamond-rated restaurants before heading out to a rocking bar or dance club filled with others who cannot bear to go to bed until dawn.

Cancún's luxury hotels have pools so spectacular that you may find it tempting to remain poolside—but don't. Set aside some time to simply gaze into the ocean and wriggle your toes in the fine, brilliant white sand. It is, after all, what put Cancún on the map—and no tempest of nature has been able to sweep it away.

1 Orientation

GETTING THERE

BY PLANE   If this is not your first trip to Cancún, you'll notice that the airport's facilities and services continue to expand. **Aeromexico** (© 800/237-6639 in the U.S., or 01/800-021-4000 in Mexico; www.aeromexico.com) operates connecting service to Cancún through Mexico City. **Mexicana** (© 800/531-7921 in the U.S., 01/800-366-5400 in Mexico, or 998/881-9090; www.mexicana.com.mx) runs connecting flights to Cancún through Miami or Mexico City. In addition to these carriers, many **charter** companies—such as Apple Vacations and Funjet—travel to Cancún; these package tours make up as much as 60% of arrivals by U.S. visitors (see "Packages for the Independent Traveler," in chapter 3).

Regional carrier **Click Mexicana,** a Mexicana affiliate (© 01-800/112-5425 toll-free in Mexico; www.click.com.mx), flies from Cozumel, Havana, Mexico City, Mérida, Chetumal, and other points within Mexico. You'll want to confirm departure times for flights to the U.S. **Aviacsa** (© 01-800/711-6733 toll-free in Mexico; www. aviacsa.com), **Interjet** (© 01-800/01-12345 toll-free in Mexico; www.interjet.com. mx), and **Volaris** (© 01-800/7865-2747; www.volaris.com.mx) are three other regional carriers that fly to Cancún from Mexico City.

Here are the U.S. numbers of major international carriers serving Cancún: **Alaska** (© 800/426-0333; www.alaskaair.com), **American** (© 800/433-7300; www.aa.com), **Continental** (© 800/231-0856; www.continental.com), **Delta** (© 800/221-1212; www.delta.com), **Frontier** (© 800/432-1359; www.frontierairlines.com), **Northwest** (© 800/225-2525; www.nwa.com), **United** (© 800/241-6522; www.ual.com), and **US Airways** (© 800/428-4322; www.usairways.com).

Most major car-rental firms have outlets at the airport, so if you're renting a car, consider picking it up and dropping it off at the airport to save on airport-transportation costs. Another way to save money is to arrange for the rental before you leave home. If you wait until you arrive, the daily cost will be around $50 to $75 (£25–£38) for a compact vehicle. Major agencies include **Alamo** (© 800/462-5266; www.alamo. com), **Avis** (© 800/331-1212 in the U.S., or 998/886-0221; www.avis.com), **Budget**

Downtown Cancún

Area of detail

Cancún City

Isla Cancún (Zona Hotelera)

(i) Information
⊠ Post office
SM Supermanzana (Superblock)

SM 1 ↑ To Punta Sam & Puerto Juárez

Avenida Chichén Itzá
Avenida García de la Torre
Avenida Bonampak
Avenida J.C. Nader
Avenida Tulum
Avenida Uxmal Laurel
Avenida Yaxchilán
Avenida Tankah
Avenida Xkha
Avenida Cobá
Avenida Xcaret
Av. Yaxchilán
Avenida Sayil
Av. Copán
Avenida Bonampak
Boulevard Kukulcán →

SM 23
Chaca
SM 2
SM 2-A
Bus Station
SM 24
Allen
Rosas
Rosas
Margaritas
Margaritas
Pino
Azucenas
Azucenas
Avenida Uxmal
Valpich
Soliman
Nicchehabi
Conoco
Yoquen
Tauch
Av. Yaxchilán
Jazmines
Jazmines
SM 22
Tulipanes
Tulipanes
Claveles
Claveles
Crisantemas
SM 28
Mercado 28
Av. Sunyaxchen
Sarnullo
Marañon
Gladiolas
Gladiolas
Parque Palapas
Orquideas
Orquideas
Grosella
Grosella
Nancen
Chiabal
Coco
Chiabal
Piña
Caimito
SM 25
Guaya
Guaya
Ciruela
Anona
Guanabana
Guanabana
Caimite
SM 35
SM 52
SM 20
Venado
Venado
Reno
Reno
Jaleb
Jaleb
Tejon
Tejon
Pecari
Pecari
Liebre
Liebre
Jabali
Alce
Alce
Antilope
Antilope
Labná
Gacela
Gacela
SM 18
SM 15
SM 15-A
Lluvia
Lluvia
Agua
Agua
Viento
Viento
Mar
Mar
Fuego
Rubia
Rubia
Mero
Mero
Huachinango
Huachinango
Mojarra
Lima
Tizoni
Barracuda
Barracuda
Cazon
Cazon
Pargo
Pargo
Cherna
Cherna
Robalo
Juriel
Robalo
Sierra
Sierra
Brisa
Nube
Nube
Cielo
Cielo
Tierra
Tierra
Fuego
SM 5
SM 3
SM 4
SM 4-A
SM 7
PUERTO CANCÚN

To Hotel Zone (Cancún Island)

To Plaza Las Americas ↓

Bullfight ring

0   200 yds
0   200 m
N

ACCOMMODATIONS ■
Hotel Hacienda **10**
Radisson Hacienda Cancun **2**
Rey del Caribe Hotel **3**
Xbalamque **7**

DINING ◆
La Habichuela **6**
Labná **5**
100% Natural **9**
Périco's **8**
Pizza Rolandi **1**
Roots **4**

Tips **The Best Websites for Cancún**

- **All About Cancún: www.cancunmx.com** This site is a good place to start planning. Their database, called "The Online Experts," answers many of the most common questions. It's slow but current, with input from lots of recent travelers to the region.
- **Cancún Convention & Visitors Bureau: www.cancun.travel** The official site of the Cancún Convention & Visitors Bureau lists excellent information on events and attractions. Its hotel guide is one of the most complete available, and it has an active message board of recent visitors to Cancún.
- **Cancún Online: www.cancun.com** This comprehensive guide has lots of information about things to do and see in Cancún, though most details come from paying advertisers. The site lets you reserve package trips, accommodations, and tee times, or even plan a wedding online.
- **Cancún Travel Guide: www.go2cancun.com** These online information specialists are also an excellent resource for Cancún rentals, hotels, and attractions. Note that this site also lists only paying advertisers, which means you'll find most of the major players here.

(© 800/527-0700 in the U.S., or 998/886-0417; fax 998/884-4812; www.budget. com), **Dollar** (© 800/800-3665 in the U.S., or 998/886-2300; www.dollar.com), **National** (© 800/227-7368 in the U.S., or 998/886-0153; www.nationalcar.com), **Hertz** (© 800/654-3131 in the U.S. and Canada, or 998/884-1326; www.hertz. com), and **Thrifty** (© 800/847-4389; www.thrifty.com). If you're looking for an exotic car rental (such as a Porsche or Mercedes convertible) and don't mind paying a small fortune for it, try **Platinum** (© 998/883-5555; www.platinumcarrental.com), with an office inside the JW Marriott hotel. The Zona Hotelera (Hotel Zone) lies 10km (6¼ miles)—a 20-minute drive—from the airport along wide, well-paved roads.

The rate for a **private taxi** from the airport is $53 (£27) to Ciudad Cancún (downtown) or the Hotel Zone. The return trip with an airport taxi is discounted by 50%. *Colectivos* (vans) run from the airport into town. Buy tickets, which cost about $12 (£6), from the booth to the far right as you exit the airport terminal. There's **bus** transportation ($3.50/£1.75) from the airport to Ciudad Cancún. From there, you can take another bus for less than a dollar to Puerto Juárez, where passenger ferries leave to Isla Mujeres regularly. There is no *colectivo* service returning to the airport from Ciudad Cancún or the Hotel Zone, so you'll have to take a taxi, but the rate will be much less than for the trip from the airport. (Only federally chartered taxis may take fares *from* the airport, but any taxi may bring passengers *to* the airport.) Ask at your hotel what the fare should be, but expect to pay about half what you paid from the airport to your hotel.

BY CAR From Mérida or Campeche, take **Highway 180** east to Cancún. This is mostly a winding, two-lane road that branches off into the express **toll road 180D** between Izamal and Nuevo Xcan. Nuevo Xcan is approximately 40km (25 miles) from Cancún. Mérida is about 320km (199 miles) away.

BY BUS   Cancún's **ADO bus terminal** (© **998/884-4352** or 01800/702-8000) is in downtown Ciudad Cancún at the intersection of avenidas Tulum and Uxmal. All out-of-town buses arrive here. Buses run to Playa del Carmen, Tulum, Chichén Itzá, other nearby beach and archaeological zones, and other points within Mexico.

VISITOR INFORMATION

The **State Tourism Office (SEDETUR)**, Av. Yaxchilan Lote 6 SM 17, downtown across from Costco (© **998/881-9000;** www.qroo.gob.mx), is open Monday to Friday from 9am to 8pm. The **Cancún Municipal Tourism Office** is downtown at the Palacio Municipal (City Hall) on Avenida Tulum between Avenidas Uxmal and Coba (© **998/887-3379**). It's open Monday through Friday from 9am to 7pm. Each office lists hotels and their rates, as well as ferry schedules. For information prior to your arrival in Cancún, visit the Convention Bureau's website, **www.cancun.travel**.

Pick up copies of the free monthly booklet, *Cancún Tips* (www.cancuntips.com.mx), and a seasonal tabloid of the same name.

CITY LAYOUT

There are really two Cancúns: **Ciudad Cancún (Cancún City)** and **Isla Cancún (Cancún Island)**. The former, on the mainland, has restaurants, shops, and less expensive hotels, as well as pharmacies, dentists, automotive shops, banks, travel and airline agencies, and car-rental firms—all within an area about 9 square blocks. The city's main thoroughfare is **Avenida Tulum**. Heading south, Avenida Tulum becomes the highway to the airport and to Tulum and Chetumal; heading north, it intersects the highway to Mérida and the road to Puerto Juárez and the Isla Mujeres ferries.

The latter is a sandy strip 22km (14 miles) long, shaped like a "7." It's home to the famed **Zona Hotelera**, or Hotel Zone (also called the Zona Turística, or Tourist Zone), which stretches out along Isla Cancún, connected to the mainland by the Playa Linda Bridge at the north end and the Punta Nizuc Bridge at the southern end. Between the two areas lies Laguna Nichupté. Avenida Cobá from Cancún City becomes Bulevar Kukulkán, the island's main traffic artery. Cancún's international airport is just inland from the south end of the island.

FINDING AN ADDRESS   Cancún's street-numbering system is a holdover from its early days. Addresses are still given by the number of the building lot and by the *manzana* (block) or *supermanzana* (group of blocks). The city is relatively compact, and the downtown commercial section is easy to cover on foot.

On the island, addresses are given by kilometer number on Bulevar Kukulkán or by reference to some well-known location. In Cancún, streets are named after famous Maya cities. Boulevards are named for nearby archaeological sites, Chichén Itzá, Tulum, and Uxmal.

GETTING AROUND

BY TAXI   Taxi prices in Cancún are clearly set by zone, although keeping track of what's in which zone can take some doing. The minimum fare within the Hotel Zone is $6 (£3) per ride, making it one of the most expensive taxi areas in Mexico. In addition, taxis operating in the Hotel Zone feel perfectly justified in having a discriminatory pricing structure: Local residents pay about half of what tourists pay, and prices for guests at higher-priced hotels are about double those for budget hotel guests—these are all established by the taxi union. Rates should be posted outside your hotel;

if there's a question, all drivers are required to have an official rate card in their taxis, though it's generally in Spanish.

Within the downtown area, the cost is about $2 (£1) per cab ride (not per person); within any other zone, it's $6 (£3). Traveling between two zones will also cost $6 (£3), and if you cross two zones, it's $8 (£4). Settle on a price in advance, or check at your hotel. Trips to the airport from most zones cost $15 (£7.50). Taxis can also be rented for $20 (£10) per hour for travel around the city and Hotel Zone, but this rate can generally be negotiated down to about $15 (£7.50). If you want to hire a taxi to take you to Chichén Itzá or along the Riviera Maya, expect to pay about $30 (£15) per hour—many taxi drivers feel that they are also providing guide services.

BY BUS   Bus travel within Cancún continues to improve and is increasingly popular. In town, almost everything lies within walking distance. **Ruta 1** and **Ruta 2** (HOTELES) city buses travel frequently from the mainland to the beaches along Avenida Tulum (the main street) and all the way to Punta Nizuc at the far end of the Hotel Zone on Isla Cancún. **Ruta 8** buses go to Puerto Juárez/Punta Sam for ferries to Isla Mujeres. They stop on the east side of Avenida Tulum. All these city buses run between 6am and 10pm daily. Beware of private buses along the same route; they charge far more than the public ones. Public buses have the fare painted on the front; at press time, the fare was 60¢ (30p).

BY MOPED   Mopeds are a convenient but dangerous way to cruise through the very congested traffic. Rentals start at about $35 (£18) for a day, and a credit card voucher is required as security. You should receive a crash helmet (it's the law) and instructions on how to lock the wheels when you park. Read the fine print on the back of the rental agreement regarding liability for repairs or replacement in case of accident, theft, or vandalism.

FAST FACTS: Cancún

American Express The local office is at La Isla Shopping Center in the hotel zone (📞 998/883-3918; www.americanexpress.com/mexico), and there's another branch inside the airport. It's open Monday through Friday from 9am to 6pm, Saturday from 9am to 1pm.

Area Code The telephone area code is **998**.

Climate It's hot but not overwhelmingly humid. The rainy season is May through October. August through October is hurricane season, which brings erratic weather. November through February is generally sunny but can also be cloudy, windy, somewhat rainy, and even cool.

Consulates The **U.S. Consular Agent** is in the Plaza Caracol 2, Bulevar Kukulkán Km 8.5, 3rd level, 320–323 (📞 998/883-0272). The office is open Monday through Friday from 9am to 2pm. The **Canadian Consulate** is in the Plaza Caracol, 3rd level, Loc. 330 (📞 998/883-3360). The office is open Monday through Friday from 9am to 3:30pm. The **United Kingdom** has a consular office at the Royal Sands Hotel in Cancún (📞 998/881-0100, ext. 65898; fax 998/848-8662; information@britishconsulateCancun.com). The office is open Monday through

Friday from 9am to 5pm. Irish, Australian, and New Zealand citizens should contact their embassies in Mexico City.

Crime Car break-ins are just about the only frequent crime here. They happen frequently, especially around the shoppIng centers in the Hotel Zone. Rapes have also been reported in Cancún. Most have taken place at night or in the early morning.

Currency Exchange Most banks sit downtown along Avenida Tulum and are usually open Monday through Friday from 9am to 2pm, although some are open later and even half the day on Saturday. Many have automated teller machines for after-hours cash withdrawals. In the Hotel Zone, you'll find banks in the Kukulcán Plaza and next to the convention center. There are also many *casas de cambio* (exchange houses). Downtown merchants are eager to change cash dollars, but island stores don't offer very good exchange rates. Avoid changing money at the airport as you arrive, especially at the first exchange booth you see—its rates are less favorable than those of any in town or others farther inside the airport concourse. Dollars are widely accepted throughout Cancún.

Drugstores Across the street from Señor Frog's in the Hotel Zone, at Bulevar Kukulkán Km 9.5, **Farmacías del Ahorro** (© **998/892-7291**) offers 24-hour service and free delivery. Plenty of drugstores are in the major shopping malls in the Hotel Zone, and are open until 10pm. In downtown Cancún, **Farmacía Cancún** is located at Av. Tulum 17 (© **998/884-1283**). It's open Monday to Saturday from 9am to 10pm and Sunday from 10am to 10pm. You can stock up on over-the-counter and many prescription drugs without a prescription.

Emergencies To report an emergency, dial © **060,** which is supposed to be similar to 911 emergency service in the United States. For first aid, the **Cruz Roja,** or Red Cross (© **065** or 998/884-1616; fax 998/883-9218), is open 24 hours on Av. Yaxchilán between avenidas Xcaret and Labná, next to the Telmex building. **Galenia Hospital** is one of the city's most modern, offering full emergency and other services with excellent care, at Av. Tulum, SM 12, at Nizuc (© **998/891-5200;** www.hospitalgalenia.com). **AMAT,** Av, Nader 13, SM 2, at Av. Uxmal (© **998/887-4422**), is a small emergency hospital with some English-speaking doctors. It's open 24 hours. Desk staff may have limited command of English. **Air Ambulance** (Global Ambulance) service is available by calling © **01-800/305-9400** in Mexico. It is usually easier and less expensive to arrange medical air evacuation services through a U.S. rather than Mexican company.

Internet Access **Häagan-Dazs** on the bottom floor of Kukulcán Plaza, Bulevar Kukulkán Km 13, has a free hotspot for wireless Internet access. Most hotels now have Internet access, and five star hotels have business centers.

Luggage Storage & Lockers Hotels will generally tag and store luggage while you travel elsewhere.

Newspapers & Magazines Most hotel gift shops and newsstands carry English-language magazines and English-language Mexican newspapers, such as the *Miami Herald.*

Police Cancún has a fleet of English-speaking tourist police to help travelers. Dial © **998/885-2277.** The **Procuraduría Federal del Consumidor (consumer**

protection agency), Av. Cobá 9–11 (© **998/884-2634**), is opposite the Social Security Hospital and upstairs from the Fenix drugstore. It's open Monday through Friday from 9am to 3pm.

Post Office The main *correo* lies at the intersection of avenidas Sunyaxchen and Xel-Ha (© **998/884-1418**). It's open Monday through Friday from 9am to 4pm, and Saturday from 9am to noon for the purchase of stamps only.

Safety Besides car break-ins, Cancún sustains very little crime. People are generally safe late at night in tourist areas; just use ordinary common sense. Some rapes have been reported, and most have taken place late at night or early morning. As at any other beach resort, don't take money or valuables to the beach. See "Crime," above.

Swimming on the Caribbean side presents a danger because of the undertow. See the information on beaches in "Beaches, Watersports & Boat Tours," later in this chapter, for information about flag warnings

Seasons Technically, high season runs from December 15 to April; low season extends from May to December 15, when prices drop 10% to 30%. Some hotels are starting to charge high-season rates during June and July, when Mexican, European, and school-holiday visitors often travel, although rates may still be lower than in winter months.

2 Where to Stay

Island hotels—almost all of them offering modern facilities and English-speaking staffs—line the beach like concrete dominoes. Extravagance is the byword in the newer hotels. Some hotels, while exclusive, affect a more relaxed attitude. The water on the upper end of the island facing Bahía de Mujeres is placid, while beaches lining the long side of the island facing the Caribbean are subject to choppier water and crashing waves on windy days. (For more information on swimming safety, see "Beaches, Watersports & Boat Tours," later in this chapter.) Be aware that the farther south you go on the island, the longer it takes (20–30 min. in traffic) to get back to the "action spots," which are primarily between the Plaza Flamingo and Punta Cancún on the island and along Avenida Tulum on the mainland.

Following Hurricane Wilma's devastation, the news item that received the most coverage was the destruction of Cancún's famed white-sand beaches. Immediately following the storm, literally all of the sand was washed away from the northern border of Isla Cancún, and from Punta Cancún. However, thanks to Mother Nature and a $20-million effort by Mexico's government to pump the dislocated sand back to the beach, this is no longer an issue. The southern beaches of Isla Cancún actually benefited from the storm, and now they have especially wide beachfronts.

Almost all major hotel chains have real estate on Cancún Island. The reality is that Cancún is so popular as a package destination from the U.S. that prices and special deals are often the deciding factor for consumers rather than loyalty to any one hotel brand (see "Packages for the Independent Traveler," in chapter 3). Ciudad Cancún offers independently owned, smaller, less-expensive lodging, all a 5- to 10-minute cab ride from the beach; prices are lower here off season (May to early Dec). For condo, home, and villa rentals, check with **Cancún Hideaways** (© **817/522-4466;** fax

Isla Cancún (Zona Hotelera)

To Puerto Juárez & Punta Sam

Av. Tulum
Av. Bonarrpak
Av. Cobá
Paseo Kukulkán
CANCÚN CITY
Bullfight ring
Av. Nichupte
Paseo Mujeres
307
To Tulum & Chetumal

Playa Las Perlas
Playa Juventud
Blue Bay Getaway Cancún
Km 3
Km 3.5
Playa Linda
Km 4
Paseo Kukulkán

Ferry to Isla Mujeres
El Embarcadero Park
Playa Lagosta
Km 5
Playa Tortugas

See "Downtown Cancún" Map

Canal Nichupté

Laguna del Amor

Laguna de Nichupté

Beach
Golf
Ruins

0 — 2 mi
0 — 2 km
N

Laguna Inglé

To Airport

Bahía de Mujeres

Oasis Viva Beach Cancún
Presidente Inter-Continental
Km 7.5
Km 7
Km 8
Pok-Ta-Pok Golf Course
Laguna Bojórquez
Señor Frog's
Lorenzillo's
Plaza Flamingo

Dreams Cancún, Hacienda El Mortero, & R. Paloma Bonita
Fiesta Americana Coral Beach
Riu Palace Las Américas
Punta Cancún
Plaza Caracol
Km 8.5
Cancún Center
Km 9
Km 9.5
Dady'O/Dady Rock Bar & Grill Km 10
The City
Casa Rolandi
Carlos N'Charlies/ Forum by the Sea/ Coco Bongo
Playa Chacmool
Playa Gaviota
Flamingo Cancún

Royal
Km 11.5
Km 12
ME
Casa de las Margaritas
La Madonna
Thai
Plaza Kukulkán
La Destilería

La Isla Shopping Village

Puerto Madero
Km 14
Laguna Grill
Ritz Carlton & R. Club Grill
Le Méridien Cancún & Aioli
JW Marriott & Gustlno
Marriott Casamagna

Playa Delfines
Caribbean Sea

Ruinas del Rey
Canal Nizuc
Km 16
Hilton Cancún Golf & Spa Resort

Km 20
Westin Resort & Spa
Punta Nizuc

ACCOMMODATIONS

Blue Bay Getaway Cancún **Km 3.5**
Dreams Cancún Resort & Spa **Km 9.5**
Fiesta Americana Grand Coral Beach **Km 9.5**
Flamingo Cancún **Km 11.5**
Hilton Cancún Golf & Spa Resort **Km 17**
JW Marriott **Km 14.5**
Le Méridien Cancún Resort & Spa **Km 14**
Marriott Casa Magna **Km 14.5**

ME **Km 12**
Oasis Viva Beach Cancún **Km 8.5**
Presidente Inter-Continental Cancún **Km 7.5**
Ritz-Carlton **Km 13.5**
Riu Palace Las Americas **Km 8.5**
Royal **Km 11.5**
Westin Resort & Spa **Km 20**

DINING

Aioli **Km 14**
Casa de Las Margaritas **Km 12.5**
Casa Rolandi **Km 8.5**
Club Grill **Km 13.5**
Gustino **Km 14.5**
Hacienda El Mortero **Km 9.5**
La Destilería **Km 12.6**
La Madonna **Km 12.5**
Laguna Grill **Km 15**
Lorenzillo's **Km 10.5**
Paloma Bonia (at Punta Cancún) **Km 9.5**
Puerto Madero **Km 8.5**
Thai **Km 12.5**

535

817/557-3483; www.cancun-hideaways.com), a company specializing in luxury properties, downtown apartments, and condos—many at prices much lower than comparable hotel stays. Owner Maggie Rodriguez, a former resident of Cancún, has made this niche market her specialty.

The hotel listings in this chapter begin on Cancún Island and finish in Cancún City (the real downtown), where bargain lodgings are available. Unless otherwise indicated, parking is free at Cancún's hotels.

CANCUN ISLAND
VERY EXPENSIVE

Fiesta Americana Grand Coral Beach 🏿🏿 *(Kids)*   This spectacular resort sits on one of the best locations in Cancún, with 300m (984 ft.) of prime beachfront and proximity to the main shopping and entertainment centers. The all-suites hotel includes junior suites with sunken sitting areas, whitewashed furniture, marble bathrooms, and soothing California colors, although some could use an upgrade. Guests staying in Grand Club suites have access to a private rooftop lounge, exclusive check-in, continental breakfast, hors d'oeuvres, and beverages. Service throughout this five-diamond property is gracious and attentive, and the expansive lobby is embellished with elegant dark-green granite and fresh flowers. The hotel's idyllic Punta Cancún location has the advantage of facing the beach to the north where the surf is calm and perfect for swimming, although you may feel tempted not to leave the magnificent pool area. Families will appreciate the *Fiesta Kids Activities*, which include nonstop games, contests, and shows for the little ones. There are daylong sports and social activities planned for adults as well. The resort's international clientele includes many European, Japanese, Mexican, and American visitors.

Bulevar Kukulkán Km 9.5, 77500 Cancún, Q. Roo. © 800/343-7821 in the U.S., or 998/881-3200. Fax 998/881-3288. www.fiestamericana.com. 602 units. High season $514 (£257) and up double, $671 (£336) and up club-floor double; low season $339 (£170) and up double, $459 (£230) and up club-floor double. Parking $10 (£5). AE, MC, V. **Amenities:** 5 restaurants; 4 bars; outdoor pool w/swim-up bars; 3 indoor tennis courts; boutique spa; fitness center; sauna; watersports equipment/rentals; Kids' Club; multilingual concierge staff; travel agency; car-rental desk; business center; salon; room service; massage; babysitting; laundry service; concierge floor. *In room:* A/C, TV, Wi-Fi, minibar, hair dryer, coffeemaker, iron, safe, CD player.

Hilton Cancún Golf & Spa Resort 🏿🏿 *(Kids)*   Full of energy, this is a grand resort in every sense of the word. The Hilton Cancún sits on 100 hectares (247 acres) of prime beachside property, which means every room has a sea view (some have both sea and lagoon views). There's an 18-hole par-72 golf course across the street. Guest rooms are spacious and decorated in minimalist style. The Beach Club villas are the largest and best-located rooms, and come with continental breakfast and an evening cocktail hour. This Hilton is a kid-friendly hotel, with one of the island's best children's activity programs, children's pool, and babysitting. The spectacular multisection swimming pool stretches out to the gorgeous beach. The Hilton is especially appealing to golfers because it's one of only two in Cancún with an on-site course (the other is the Meliá). Greens fees for guests during high season are $99 (£50) for 9 holes, $149 (£75) for 18 holes (low season discounts offered), and comes with use of a cart. The Wellness Spa includes oceanfront massage *cabañas*, yoga, and aromatherapy. This Hilton has a friendly vibe and service is excellent.

Bulevar Kukulkán Km 17, Retorno Lacandones, 77500 Cancún, Q. Roo. © 800/228-3000 in the U.S., or 998/881-8000. Fax 998/881-8080. www.hiltoncancun.com. 426 units. High season $249 (£125) and up double, $309 (£155) and up villa room, $409 (£205) and up suite; low season $159 (£80) and up double, $199 (£100) and up villa room,

(*Tips*) **Deciphering Hotel Prices**

In all price categories, Cancún's hotels generally set their rates in dollars, so they are immune to variations in the peso. Travel agents and wholesalers always have air/hotel packages available, and Sunday papers often advertise inventory-clearing packages at prices much lower than the rates listed here. Cancún also has numerous all-inclusive properties, which allow you to take a fixed-cost vacation. Note that the price quoted when you call a hotel's reservation number from the United States may not include Cancún's 12% tax (a 10% federal tax and 2% state lodging tax). Prices can vary considerably throughout the year, so it pays to consult a travel agent or shop around.

$279 (£140) and up suite. AE, DC, MC, V. **Amenities:** 4 restaurants; 2 bars; 7 interconnected outdoor pools w/swim-up bar; golf course across the street; golf clinic; 2 lighted tennis courts; Wellness Spa w/spa services and fully equipped gym; 2 whirlpools; watersports center; Kids' Club; concierge; tour desk; car-rental desk; salon; room service; babysitting; laundry service. *In room:* A/C, TV, Wi-Fi, minibar, coffeemaker, hair dryer, iron, safe, bathrobes.

JW Marriott ☆☆☆ One of Cancún's most upscale and appealing properties, the JW Marriott offers elegance without pretense. From the expansive marble and flower-filled lobby to the luxurious oceanview guest rooms, the hotel combines classic and Caribbean styling with warm Mexican service. Guest rooms feature beautiful marble bathrooms with separate tub and shower, private balconies, flatscreen TVs, bathrobes and slippers, and twice-daily maid service. The inviting free-form infinity pool extends to the white-sand beach, and families feel as comfortable here as romance-seeking couples. A spectacular 3,252-sq.-m (35,000-sq.-ft.) spa includes an indoor pool and Jacuzzi, high-tech fitness center, and full range of massages, body scrubs and polishes, facials, and healing water treatments. Gustino is an outstanding Italian restaurant seated off the lobby (see "Where to Dine" later in this chapter), and after-noon tea with a musical trio is offered in the lobby lounge. Guests here also enjoy access to the adjacent Marriott Casa Magna.

Bulevar Kukulkán Km 14.5, 77500 Cancún, Q. Roo. (© 800/223-6388 in the U.S., or 998/848-9600. Fax 998/848-9601. www.jwmarriottcancun.com. 448 units. High season $449 (£225) and up double; low season $300 (£150) and up double. AE, DC, MC, V. Small pets allowed with prior reservation. **Amenities:** 3 restaurants; deli; lobby bar and pool bar; expansive outdoor pool; indoor pool; full-service spa; 3 whirlpools; sauna; steam room; access to Kids' Club at Marriott Casa Magna; concierge; travel agency; car rental; business center; shopping arcade; gift shop; salon; room service; medical services; laundry service; club floor w/special amenities and complimentary cocktails. *In room:* A/C, flatscreen TV, Wi-Fi, minibar, hair dryer, iron, safe.

Le Méridien Cancún Resort & Spa ☆☆ Le Méridien is among Cancún's most inviting luxury options, with a refined yet welcoming sense of personal service. From the intimate lobby and reception area to the best concierge service in Cancún, guests feel immediately pampered. The relatively small establishment is more of an elegant boutique hotel than an immense resort—a welcome relief. The decor throughout the rooms and common areas is classy and comforting, not overdone. Rooms are generous in size with small balconies overlooking the pool; due to the hotel's design, rooms do not have ocean views. Each has a large marble bathroom with a separate tub and glassed-in shower. The hotel attracts many Europeans as well as younger, sophisticated travelers, and it is ideal for a second honeymoon.

A highlight of—or even a reason for—staying here is the **Spa del Mar,** one of Mexico's most complete European spa facilities, with more than 4,570 sq. m (49,190 sq. ft.) of services dedicated to your body and soul. A complete fitness center with extensive cardio and weight machines sits on the upper level. The spa consists of a health snack bar, a full-service salon, and 14 treatment rooms, as well as men's and women's steam rooms, saunas, whirlpools, cold plunge pool, inhalation rooms, tranquillity rooms, lockers, and changing areas. **Aioli** is a splendid fine-dining restaurant (see "Where to Dine," later in this chapter).

Retorno del Rey Km 14, Zona Hotelera, 77500, Cancún, Q. Roo. ⓒ 800/543-4300 in the U.S., or 998/881-2200. Fax 998/881-2201. www.meridiencancun.com.mx. 213 units. High season $593 (£297) double, $680 (£340) suite; low season $430 (£215) double, $519 (£260) suite. Ask about special spa packages. AE, DC, MC, V. Small dogs accepted with prior reservation. **Amenities:** 2 restaurants; lobby bar; 3 cascading outdoor pools; 2 lighted championship tennis courts; whirlpool; watersports equipment/rentals; supervised children's program w/clubhouse, play equipment, wading pool; concierge; tour desk; car rental; business center; small shopping arcade; room service; massage *palapa* on the beach; babysitting; laundry service. *In room:* A/C, TV, Wi-Fi, minibar, hair dryer, iron, safe, CD player.

Ritz-Carlton Cancún ✸✸✸ *(Kids)*

The exclusive Ritz-Carlton fronts a 366m (1,200-ft.) white-sand beach, and all guest rooms overlook the ocean and pools. Rooms and public areas have the low-key elegance that's a hallmark of the Ritz chain—think plush carpets, chandeliers, fresh flowers, and rooms with marble baths, fluffy featherbeds, and 400-count bed linens. Several new features will enhance your stay, including a culinary center that schedules daily Mexican and Maya cooking classes, as well as wine and tequila tastings. A group of specially designed "Itzy Bitzy Ritz Kids" guest rooms offer baby-friendly amenities and conveniences. In addition to the daytime Kids Camp, the Ritz offers a "Kids' Night Out" program that allows parents to steal away for the evening. The beachfront Kayantá Spa bases many of its treatments on traditional Maya rituals and therapies. The resort's oceanfront restaurant, **Casitas,** is the only beachside dining spot in Cancún, where you can dine on steakhouse fare in one of 16 candlelit *cabañas.* The hotel's primary restaurant, **Club Grill,** is reviewed in the "Where to Dine" section, later. The resort itself as well as Club Grill and Fantino, another Ritz-Carlton restaurant, have received AAA five diamonds.

Retorno del Rey 36, off Bulevar Kukulkán Km 13.5, 77500 Cancún, Q. Roo. ⓒ 800/241-3333 in the U.S. and Canada, or 998/881-0808. Fax 998/881-0815. www.ritzcarlton.com. 365 units. May 1–Dec 19 $309–$409 (£154–£205) double, $509–$4,000 (£255–£2,000) club floor and suites; Dec 21–Jan 6 $869–$1,099 (£435–£550) double, $1,679–$5,500 (£840–£2,750) club floor and suites; Jan 7–Apr 30 $579–$679 (£290–£340) double, $799–$4,000 (£400–£2,000) club floor and suites. Ask about golf, spa, and weekend packages. AE, MC, V. **Amenities:** 6 restaurants; lounge w/ceviche bar; 2 outdoor pools (heated in winter); 3 lighted tennis courts; fully equipped fitness center; Kayantá Spa; culinary center; Kids Camp program; concierge; travel agency; business center; shopping arcade; salon; room service; babysitting; laundry service; dry cleaning; club floors. *In room:* A/C, TV, Wi-Fi, minibar, hair dryer, iron, safe, CD player.

Riu Palace Las Américas ✸

The all-inclusive Riu Palace is part of a family of Riu resorts in Cancún known for their grand, opulent style. This one is the smallest of the three, and the most over-the-top, steeped in pearl-white Greco style. The location is prime—near the central shopping, dining, and nightlife centers, and just a 5-minute walk to the Convention Center. All rooms are spacious junior suites with ocean or lagoon views, a separate seating area with sofa or sofa bed, and a balcony or terrace. Eight also feature a Jacuzzi. Two beautiful central pools overlook the ocean and a wide stretch of beach; one is heated during winter months. The hotel offers guests virtually 24 hours of all-inclusive snacks, meals, and beverages. Activities include water sports, daytime entertainment for adults and kids, live music and shows at night, and access to other Riu hotels in Cancún. The hotel's European opulence stands in contrast to the mostly informal North American guests.

Bulevar Kukulkán Km 8.5, Lote 4, 77500 Cancún, Q. Roo. © 888/666-8816 in the U.S., or 998/891-4300. www.riu. com. 372 units. High season $412 (£206) and up double; low season $322 (£161) and up double. Rates are all-inclusive, and 2-night stay may be required. AE, MC, V. **Amenities:** 5 restaurants; 5 bars including disco; 2 outdoor pools; access to golf and tennis; fitness center; spa (extra charges apply); solarium; room service; sports program; nonmotorized water sports including windsurfing, canoeing, snorkeling, and introductory scuba lessons. *In room:* A/C, TV, hair dryer, iron, safe.

Royal ☞☞ Opened in early 2007, this adults-only luxury hotel sits at the pinnacle of Cancún's all-inclusive establishments, offering a level of services and amenities unmatched almost anywhere. From the stunning infinity pools and gorgeous beach to the gourmet restaurants and sophisticated spa, the owners have spared no expense making this Cancún's Bellagio. The elegant marble lobby looks out one side to the Caribbean and the other to the lagoon. All of the innovative suites feature flatscreen TVs with CD/DVD players, marble bathrooms with rain showers, two-person Jacuzzis, and oceanview balconies with hammocks. Swim-up master suites have private plunge pools facing the resort's pool and beach; guests in the top-category suites have access to BMW Mini Coopers. The Maya-inspired oceanview spa includes a massage room, Jacuzzi, sauna, traditional *temazcal* steam bath, massage waterfall, and state-of-the-art fitness center. Actually, the range of services is almost hard to believe, except that you will be paying top dollar for it. The all-inclusive package includes gourmet meals, premium drinks, and evening entertainment.

Bulevar Kukulkán Km 11.5, 77500 Cancún, Q. Roo. © 800/760-0944 in the U.S., or 998/881-7340. www.realresorts. com.mx. 285 units. $444–$804 (£222–£402) double suite. AE, DC, MC, V. No children younger than 16. **Amenities:** 6 restaurants; 8 bars; expansive outdoor pool; tennis court; well-equipped fitness center; full-service-spa; sauna; steam room; concierge; travel agency; car rental; business center; salon; room service; laundry service; club floor w/special amenities and complimentary cocktails. *In room:* A/C, flatscreen TV, Wi-Fi, minibar, hair dryer, iron, safe.

EXPENSIVE

Dreams Cancún Resort & Spa ☞ *Kids* Formerly the Camino Real Cancún, the all-inclusive Dreams Resort has one of the island's most idyllic locations—29 hectares (71 acres) at the tip of Punta Cancún. The setting is casual, and the hotel welcomes children. The architecture of Dreams is contemporary and sleek, with bright colors and strategic angles. Rooms in the newer 17-story club section afford ocean views and extra services and amenities. Lower-priced rooms have lagoon views. The all-inclusive concept includes gourmet meals, 24-hour room service, premium brand drinks, and the use of all resort amenities, nonmotorized watersports, theme-night entertainment, and tips. The use of spa services is extra. Unfortunately, service at the resort is inconsistent, perhaps owing to the all-inclusive concept.

Bulevar Kukulkán, 77500 Punta Cancún (Apdo. Postal 14), Cancún, Q. Roo. © 866/237-3267 in the U.S., or 998/848-7000. Fax 998/848-7001. www.dreamscancun.com. 379 units. High season $500 (£250) double, $560 (£280) club double; low season $370 (£185) double, $430 (£215) club double. AE, DC, MC, V. **Amenities:** 4 restaurants; nightclub; 2 outdoor pools; private saltwater lagoon w/dolphins and tropical fish; lighted tennis court; fitness center w/steam bath; watersports; kayaks; paddleboats; Catamarans; beach volleyball; biking; archery; yoga; dance lessons; Kids' Club; travel agency; car rental; business center; salon; room service; massage; babysitting (w/advance notice). *In room:* A/C, TV/DVD player, minibar, hair dryer, iron, safe.

Marriott Casa Magna ☞☞ *Kids* This sprawling Marriott resort is one of the most enticing family destinations in Cancún. Entering through a half-circle of Roman columns, you pass through a domed foyer to a wide, lavishly marbled lobby filled with plants and shallow pools. It looks out to the sparkling pool and Jacuzzi at the edge of the beach. Guest rooms are decorated with Mexican-Caribbean furnishings and tiled floors; most have oceanview balconies. The hotel caters to family travelers with specially priced packages (up to two children stay free with parent) and the Kids' Club Amigos supervised children's program. Among the many places to dine here, the *tepanyaki*-style (cook-at-your-table) Mikado Japanese restaurant is the best.

Bulevar Kukulkán Km 14.5, 77500 Cancún, Q. Roo Ⓒ 800/228-9290 in the U.S., or 998/881-2000. Fax 998/881-2085. www.marriott.com. 452 units. $249–$309 (£125–£155) double; $454 (£227) and up suite. Ask about packages. AE, MC, V. **Amenities:** 4 restaurants; lobby bar w/live music; outdoor pool and whirlpool; 2 lighted tennis courts; spa; health club w/saunas, aerobics, and juice bar; concierge; business center; travel agency; car rental; spa; salon w/massage and facials; room service; babysitting; laundry service. *In room:* A/C, TV, minibar, coffeemaker, hair dryer, iron, safe.

ME ⓡ   The Spanish ME hotel by Meliá brings to Cancún a new level of minimalist chic with an atmosphere befitting a trendy nightclub more so than a beach resort. Bathed in hues of beige and mauve, with polished marble, onyx lamps, and modern artwork, the hotel creates its own fashion statement—and the hip clientele reflects it. The modern lobby feels a bit like an urban cocktail lounge, with designer bars, sensual artwork, and chill-out music filling the space. Guest rooms have distinctive contemporary furnishings, plasma TVs, CD players, and marble bathrooms with rain showers and Aveda bath products; half look to the Caribbean Sea and the other half to the lagoon. The super-stylish Yhi Spa overlooks the ocean and offers body glows and exfoliations, aromatherapy massages, body masks, and wraps. This is a place to indulge yourself until you're entirely rejuvenated.

Bulevar Kukulkán Km 12, 77500 Cancún, Q. Roo. Ⓒ 866/436-3542 in the U.S., or 998/881-2500. Fax 998/881-2501. www.mecancun.travel. 448 units. $239 (£120) and up double. AE, MC, V. **Amenities:** 3 restaurants; Internet cafe; 2 bars; 3 outdoor pools; beach club; fitness center; full-service luxury spa; whirlpool; salon; concierge; boutique; art gallery; concierge floor. *In room:* A/C, plasma TV, Wi-Fi, minibar, hair dryer, safe.

MODERATE

Flamingo Cancún ⓚⓘ𝒹𝓈   The all-inclusive Flamingo seems to have been inspired by the dramatic, slope-sided architecture of the Dreams Cancún, but the Flamingo is considerably smaller and less expensive (guests can opt out of the all-inclusive package, which includes three meals and domestic drinks). With two pools and a casual vibe, it's also a friendly, accommodating choice for families. The brightly colored blue and yellow guest rooms—all with balconies—border a courtyard facing the interior swimming pool and *palapa* pool-bar. The Flamingo lies in the heart of the island hotel district, opposite the Flamingo Shopping Center and close to other hotels, shopping centers, and restaurants.

Bulevar Kukulkán Km 11.5, 77500 Cancún, Q. Roo. Ⓒ 998/848-8870. Fax 998/883-1029. www.flamingocancun. com. 260 units. High season $199 (£100) double, low season $126 (£113) double; all-inclusive plan high season $400 (£200) double, low season $210 (£105) double. AE, MC, V. **Amenities:** 2 restaurants; 2 bars; 2 pools; fitness center; kids' club, travel agency; car rental; room service; safe. *In room:* A/C, TV, hair dryer, minibar.

Oasis Viva Beach Cancún   From the street, this all-inclusive hotel may not be much to look at, but on the ocean side, you'll find a small but pretty patio garden and Cancún's best beach for safe swimming. The location is ideal, close to all the shops and restaurants near Punta Cancún and the Cancún Center. Rooms overlook the lagoon or the ocean, and all were remodeled post–Hurricane Wilma. They are large, with simple decor, marble floors, and either two double beds or a king-size bed. Several studios have kitchenettes. There is wheelchair access within the hotel's public areas.

Bulevar Kukulkán Km 8.5, 77500 Cancún, Q. Roo. © **998/883-0800.** Fax 998/883-2087. www.oasishotels.com. 216 units. High season $232 (£116) and up double; low season $152 (£76) and up double. Rates are all-inclusive. Discounted rate for children. AE, MC, V. **Amenities:** 4 restaurants; 5 bars; 2 outdoor pools (1 for adults, 1 for children); marina. *In room:* A/C, TV.

Temptation Resort Spa ✚   This adults-only (21 and over) getaway is a spirited, sexy all-inclusive resort favored by people looking for significant social interaction. By day, pool time is all about flirting, seducing, and getting a little wacky with adult games (the main pools are top-optional). Come night, theme dinners, shows, and other live entertainment keep the party going. Note that tops are also optional on the beaches of Blue Bay, which has calm waters for swimming. The comfortable, modern rooms are housed in two sections with garden or ocean views. Surrounded by acres of tropical gardens, this moderate hotel is ideally located at the northern end of the Hotel Zone, close to the major shopping plazas, restaurants, and nightlife.

Bulevar Kukulkán Km 3.5, 77500 Cancún, Q. Roo. © **877/485-8367** in the U.S., or 998/848-7900. Fax 998/848-7994. www.temptationresorts.com/. 384 units. High season $179 (£89.50) per person per night double occupancy; low season $139 (£69.50) per person per night double occupancy. Rates include food, beverages, and activities. AE, MC, V. Guests must be at least 21 years old. **Amenities:** 6 restaurants; 5 bars; 3 outdoor pools; 7 whirlpools; spa with services for fee; exercise room w/daily classes; nonmotorized watersports equipment; snorkeling and scuba lessons; marina; game room w/pool and Ping-Pong tables; kids' club; limited room service; laundry. *In room:* A/C, TV, hair dryer.

CANCUN CITY
MODERATE
Radisson Hacienda Cancún ✚ *(Value)*   This is downtown Cancún's top hotel, and one of the best values in the area. The Radisson offers all the expected comforts of a chain in an atmosphere of Mexican hospitality. Resembling a hacienda, the business-friendly hotel has rooms surrounding a large rotunda-style lobby with a cool onyx bar, lush gardens, and an inviting pool area. All have brightly colored fabric accents; views of the garden, the pool, or the street; and a small sitting area and balcony. The hotel is within walking distance of downtown Cancún dining and shopping.

Av. Nader 1, SM2, Centro, 77500 Cancún, Q. Roo. © **800/333-3333** in the U.S., or 998/881-6500. Fax 998/884-7954. www.radissoncancun.com. 248 units. $100 (£50) and up double; $120 (£60) and up junior suite. AE, MC, V. **Amenities:** 2 restaurants; lively lobby bar; outdoor pool w/adjoining bar and separate wading area for children; lighted tennis courts; small gym; sauna; business center; travel agency; car rental; salon; limited room service (until 1am); free Wi-Fi in lobby. *In room:* A/C, TV, coffeemaker, hair dryer, iron, safe.

Rey del Caribe Hotel ✚✚ *(Finds)*   This ecological hotel is a unique oasis where every detail works toward establishing harmony with the environment. You might easily forget you're in the midst of downtown Cancún in the tropical garden setting, with blooming orchids and other flowering plants. The lovely grounds include statues of Maya deities, hammocks, and a tiled swimming pool. There's a regularly changing schedule of yoga, Tai Chi, and meditation sessions, as well as special classes on astrology, tarot, and other subjects. The on-site spa offers facial and body treatments. Rooms are large and sunny, with a kitchenette and your choice of one king-size or two full-size beds; some have a terrace. The extent of ecological sensitivity is impressive—ranging from the use of collected rainwater to waste composting. Recycling is encouraged, and solar power is used wherever possible.

Av. Uxmal SM 2A (corner of Nader), 77500 Cancún, Q. Roo. © **998/884-2028.** Fax 988/884-9857. www.reycaribe. com. 31 units. High season $92 (£46) double; low season $65 (£33) double. Rates include breakfast. MC, V. **Amenities:** Outdoor pool; spa; massages; classes. *In room:* A/C, TV, kitchenette.

INEXPENSIVE

Hotel Hacienda *Value*   This simple little hotel is a great value. The facade has been remodeled to look like a hacienda. At press time, it was being expanded to include a restaurant and larger lobby with an Internet kiosk. Guest rooms are very basic; all have dark wood furnishings, whitewashed walls, small tiled bathrooms, and two double beds—but no views. There's a nice small pool and cafe under a shaded *palapa* in the back. You can easily walk to any point downtown from here.

Sunyaxchen 39–40, 77500 Cancún, Q. Roo. © **998/884-3672.** Fax 998/884-1208. www.berny.com.mx. 36 units. High season $60 (£30) double; low season $55 (£28) double. Street parking. From Av. Yaxchilán, turn west on Sunyaxchen; it's on the right next to the Hotel Caribe International, opposite 100% Natural. **Amenities:** Outdoor pool. *In room:* A/C, TV, fan.

Xbalamqué   Creatively designed to resemble a Maya temple, this downtown hotel features a full-service spa, lovely pool and waterfall, and an authentic Mexican cantina. Live music plays evenings in the bookstore/cafe adjacent to the lobby. Guest rooms and 10 junior suites have rustic furnishings with regional touches, colorful tile-work, and small bathrooms with showers. Ask for a room overlooking the ivy-filled courtyard. A tour desk is available to help you plan your vacation activities, and the spa offers some of the best rates of any hotel in Cancún. A small *tamaleria* serving delicious regional tamales has opened adjacent to the lobby.

Av. Yaxchilán 31, Sm. 22, Mza. 18, 77500 Cancún, Q. Roo. © **998/884-9690.** Fax 998/884-9690. www.xbalamque. com. 99 units. High season $95 (£48) double; low season $75 (£38) double. AE, MC, V. **Amenities:** Restaurant; cafe; Internet cafe; cantina; lobby bar; outdoor pool; spa; travel agency. *In room:* A/C, TV.

3 Where to Dine

More than 300 restaurants spanning North American, European, and Asian cuisines have opened across Cancún. They have come to supplement the many U.S.-based franchise chains that have long dominated the Cancún restaurant scene. These include Hard Rock Cafe, Rainforest Cafe, Tony Roma's, T.G.I. Friday's, Ruth's Chris Steak House, and the gamut of fast-food burger places. The establishments listed here are typically locally owned, one-of-a-kind restaurants or exceptional selections at area hotels. Many schedule live music. Unless otherwise indicated, parking is free.

One unique way to combine dinner with sightseeing is aboard the **Lobster Dinner Cruise** (© **998/849-4748;** www.thelobsterdinner.com). Cruising around the tranquil, turquoise waters of the lagoon, passengers feast on lobster dinners accompanied by wine. Cost is $74 (£37) per person. There are two daily departures from the Aquatours Marina (Bulevar Kukulkán 6.5). A sunset cruise leaves at 5pm during the winter and 5:30pm during the summer; a moonlight cruise leaves at 8pm winter, 8:30pm summer. Another—albeit livelier—lobster dinner option is the **Captain Hook Lobster Dinner Cruise** (© **998/849-4451**), which is similar, but with the added attraction of a pirate show, making this the choice for families. It costs $86 (£43) per person, departs at 7pm from El Embarcadero, and returns at 10:30pm.

CANCUN ISLAND
VERY EXPENSIVE

Aioli ☆☆ FRENCH   The quality and originality of the cuisine and excellence of service make this a top choice for fine-dining in Cancún. The Provençal—but definitely not provincial—Aioli offers exquisite French and Mediterranean gourmet specialties in a warm and cozy country French setting. Though it serves perhaps the best breakfast buffet in Cancún (for $24/£12), most diners from outside the hotel come here in the evening, when low lighting and superb service promise a romantic experience. Delectable starters include foie gras and risotto with wild mushrooms; among the best main courses are pan-seared jumbo shrimp in lobster sauce, roasted lamb with a tarragon crust, and breast of duck. Desserts are decadent, especially the signature "Fifth Element," rich with chocolate.

In Le Méridien Cancún Resort & Spa, Retorno del Rey Km 14. ⓒ 998/881-2200. Reservations recommended. No sandals or tennis shoes; men must wear long pants. Main courses $26–$37 (£13–£19). AE, MC, V. Daily 6:30am–11pm.

Club Grill 𝓡𝓡𝓡 INTERNATIONAL   The five-diamond Club Grill is the place for that special night out. Cancún's most acclaimed dining room is also among its most delicious. Even rival restaurateurs give it an envious thumbs-up. The gracious service starts as you enter the anteroom, with its elegant seating and superb selection of cocktails and wines. It continues in the candlelit dining room with shimmering silver and crystal. Sophisticated plates of peppered scallops, truffles, and potatoes in tequila sauce; grilled lamb; or mixed grill arrive at a leisurely pace. The restaurant is exclusively nonsmoking, and service is impeccable. A band plays romantic music for dancing from 7:30pm on.

In the Ritz-Carlton Cancún, Retorno del Rey, 36 Bulevar Kukulkán Km 13.5. ⓒ 998/881-0808. Reservations required. No sandals or tennis shoes; men must wear long pants and collared shirt. Main courses $39–$59 (£20–£30). AE, DC, MC, V. Tues–Sun 7–11pm.

Lorenzillo's 𝓡𝓡 *Kids* SEAFOOD   This longtime Cancún favorite hasn't changed much over the years. Lobster remains the top pick, and part of the appeal is selecting your dinner from the giant lobster tank set in the lagoon (Lorenzillo's sits right on the lagoon under a giant *palapa* roof). A dock leads down to the main dining area, and when that's packed (which is often), a wharf-side bar handles the overflow. To start, I recommend *El Botin*, which consists of two soft-shell crabs breaded and fried to perfection. Good bets for the entree include lobster (which comes prepared in any of 20 different ways), shrimp stuffed with cheese and wrapped in bacon, the *Pescador* (Caribbean grouper prepared to taste), and seafood-stuffed calamari. Desserts include the tempting "Martinique": warm apples, raisins, and walnuts caramelized with rum and wrapped in a pastry with vanilla ice cream. Lorenzillo's is as popular with families as it is with couples looking for lagoon-side romance.

Bulevar Kukulkán Km 10.5. ⓒ 998/883-1254. www.lorenzillos.com.mx. Reservations recommended. Main courses $19–$44 (£20–£22). AE, MC, V. Daily 1pm–midnight.

EXPENSIVE
Casa de las Margaritas 𝓡 MEXICAN   La Casa de las Margaritas is a celebration of the flavors and *¡fiesta!* spirit of Mexico. With a decor as vibrant as a *piñata*, waiters dressed in regional costumes, and a soundtrack of background music that ranges from mariachi to *marimba,* the experience here is a crash course in the buoyant spirit of this colorful country. On the menu, best bets include the Margarita shrimp, flambéed in brandy, white wine, and chipotle chili sauce; chicken breast served with homemade *mole;* or traditional chicken enchiladas topped with tomato-and-sun-dried-pepper sauce with lettuce, avocado slices, and white cheese from Oaxaca. Inside La Isla shopping center, Casa de las Margaritas also serves a spectacular Sunday brunch buffet. Live music is offered nightly from 8 to 9pm.

Paseo Kukulkán Km 12.5, La Isla Shopping Mall, Loc. E-17. ℭ **998/883-3222** or -3054. www.lacasadelasmargaritas. com. Reservations recommended. Main courses $13–$45 (£6.50–£23), Sun brunch $17 (£8.50). AE, MC, V. Mon–Sat 1–9:30pm; Sun brunch noon–5pm.

Casa Rolandi 𝕽𝕽𝕽 SWISS/ITALIAN   Like its sister location in Isla Mujeres, Casa Rolandi blends sophisticated Swiss-Italian cuisine with fresh Caribbean fish and Mexican produce. Famous personalities, from international actors to American presidents, have dined here. The casually elegant restaurant offers white linen tables with roses and candles at night, yet welcomes informal dress. Among the sophisticated selections are homemade ravioli stuffed with wild mushrooms over a creamy Alba truffle sauce; tagliolini with sautéed shrimp and ginger doused with sparkling wine; fresh fish (usually snapper or sea bass) baked in salt and accompanied by fresh vegetables and seasoned mashed potatoes; and grilled 18-ounce rib-eye served sizzling. Finish with the sublime tiramisu served with chocolate and rum cream. Service is personalized and friendly.

Bulevar Kukulkán Km 8.5, in Plaza Caracol. ℭ **998/883-2557.** www.rolandi.com. Reservations recommended. Main courses $17–$38 (£8.50–£19). AE, MC, V. Sun–Thurs 1–11:30pm; Fri–Sat 1pm–2am.

Gustino 𝕽𝕽 ITALIAN   JW Marriott's signature restaurant Gustino offers romantic Italian dining unsurpassed in Cancún. The refined dining room includes a gorgeous centerpiece candle display, floor-to-ceiling windows looking out to a lazy man-made lagoon and the beach beyond, and live saxophone. Among the rich selection of *antipastis,* the black shell mussels, minestrone, and *Festival dei Frutti de Mare* for two are the best. For a main course, consider homemade pasta, the veal scaloppini, or filet of beef tenderloin in a red-wine sauce served with fresh vegetables. There's also a wide selection of fresh fish and seafood. Gustino boasts an open kitchen and wine cellar with an excellent variety of international grapes. Service is outstanding.

In the JW Marriott, Bulevar Kukulkán Km 14.5. ℭ **998/848-9600.** Reservations required. Main courses $14–$27 (£7–£14). AE, DC, MC, V. Daily 6–11pm.

Hacienda El Mortero 𝕽 *Kids* MEXICAN   There's no escaping the fact that this traditional Mexican restaurant, which replicates an early 17th-century hacienda in the northern state of Durango, looks out of place next to a row of dance clubs in history-free Cancún. But if you're spending your entire trip in town, this may be your first opportunity to see what a Spanish colonial hacienda is supposed to look like. Popular with families and large groups, this festive restaurant serves authentic Mexican cuisine representing several regions. One popular option is the mixed *parillada* for two, which combines meat, seafood, and chicken with enough calories to feed a small village. I recommend the flavorful fish tacos, shrimp *pastor* with grilled pineapple, or filet mignon prepared with four chilies. A number of fish and meat dishes are prepared tableside, and the tortillas are homemade. Vegetarian tacos with a cilantro sauce are also available. The restaurant offers 100 types of tequila and mariachi music nightly.

At entrance to Punta Cancún, Bulevar Kukulkán Km 9.5. ℭ **998/848-9800.** www.elmorterocancun.com. Reservations recommended. Main courses $18–$50 (£9–£25). AE, MC, V. Daily 6–11pm.

Laguna Grill 𝕽𝕽 FUSION   Laguna Grill offers diners a contemporary culinary experience in a picturesque setting overlooking the lagoon. A tropical garden welcomes you at the entrance, while a small creek traverses the restaurant set with tables made from the trunks of tropical trees. As magical as the decor is, the real star here is the kitchen, with its selection of Pacific Rim cuisine fused with regional flavors.

Starters include martini *gyoza* (steamed dumplings), filled with shrimp and vegetables, or seafood ceviche in sesame oil and curry. Fish and seafood dominate the menu, in preparations that combine Asian and Mexican flavors such as ginger, cilantro, garlic, and hoisin sauce. Grilled shrimp are marinated in rum, mint, and lime; surf-and-turf fusion dishes may include grilled lobster, beef, and shrimp skewers. For beef-lovers, the rib-eye served with mashed potatoes and black olives is excellent. For dessert, I recommend the crème brûlée served with a touch of Bailey's. If you're an early diner, request a table on the outside deck for a spectacular sunset view. An impressive selection of wines is available.

Bulevar Kukulkán Km 16.5. ℂ 998/885-0267. www.lagunagrill.com.mx. Reservations recommended. Main courses $16–$47 (£8–£24). AE, MC, V. Daily 4pm–midnight.

Paloma Bonita *✦* *Kids* REGIONAL/MEXICAN/NOUVELLE MEXICAN In a stylish setting over the water, with mariachis serenading diners, Paloma Bonita captures the essence of Mexico through its music and food. Because Paloma Bonita is in a hotel (Dreams Cancún), prices are higher than at traditional Mexican restaurants in Ciudad Cancún, but this is a good choice for the Hotel Zone. There are three sections: La Cantina Jalisco, with an open kitchen and tequila bar; the Salón Michoacán, which features that state's cuisine; and the Patio Oaxaca. The menu encompasses the best of Mexico's other cuisines, with a few international dishes. A traditional starter is the *nopalitos* (cactus) salad with a vinaigrette dressing. For a main course, I recommend the stuffed chili La Doña—a mildly hot poblano pepper filled with lobster and *huitlacoche* (a type of mushroom that grows on corn) in a cream sauce.

In the Hotel Dreams, Punta Cancún (enter from the street). ℂ 998/848-7082. Reservations recommended. Main courses $11–$52 (£5.50–£26). AE, DC, MC, V. Daily 6–11:30pm.

Puerto Madero *✦✦* ARGENTINE/STEAKS/SEAFOOD As a tribute to the famed Puerto Madero of Buenos Aires, this trendy restaurant has quickly earned a reputation for its authentic Argentine cuisine and buzzing atmosphere. Overlooking the Nichupté Lagoon, the decor re-creates a 20th-century dock warehouse, with elegant touches of modern architecture. Puerto Madero offers an extensive selection of prime quality beef cuts, pastas, grilled fish (my favorite here is swordfish), and shellfish, meticulously prepared with Buenos Aires gusto. In addition to the classic *carpaccio,* the tuna tartar and halibut steak are favorites, but the real standouts here are the tender grilled steaks (particularly the rib-eye), served in ample portions. Enjoy a cocktail or glass of wine from the extensive selection, while viewing the sunset from the lagoon-side deck. Service is excellent.

Marina Barracuda, Bulevar Kukulkán Km 14. ℂ 998/885-2829 or -2830. www.puertomaderocancun.com. Reservations recommended. Main courses $14–$52 (£7–£26). AE, MC, V. Daily 1pm–1am.

MODERATE
La Destilería MEXICAN La Destilería is more than a tequila-inspired restaurant overlooking a lagoon; it's a minimuseum honoring the "spirit" of Mexico. It serves over 150 brands of tequila, including some treasures that never find their way north across the border. No surprise, the margaritas are among the island's best. When you decide to order food with your tequila, you'll find an authentic Mexican menu, with everything from quesadillas with squash blossom flowers to fresh tuna with jalapenos or *arrachera* beef fajitas. The breaded fish tacos served with guacamole are amazing.

Bulevar Kukulkán Km 12.65, across from Kukulcán Plaza. ℂ 998/885-1086 or -1087. www.cmr.ws. Main courses $12–$28 (£6–£14). AE, MC, V. Daily 1pm–midnight.

Thai ★★★ *(Moments* THAI   This sensual restaurant and lounge feels like it belongs in Southeast Asia rather than the edge of a Mexican shopping plaza. The stunning outdoor setting includes thick foliage and plenty of bamboo, with individual *palapas* (each with its own table and sofa) constructed like tiny islands over the expansive lagoon. Unobtrusive service, soft red and blue lighting, and Asian chill and lounge music contribute to the ambience. Classic Thai specialties such as spicy chicken soup, Thai salad, chicken satay, and chicken and shrimp curries are served alongside exotic cocktails to the beautiful crowd. A DJ works the stylish lounge on weekends. Thai opens at sunset.

La Isla Shopping Center, Loc. B-4. © 998/144-0364. Reservations recommended during high season. Main courses $13–$31 (£6.50–£16). AE, MC, V. Daily 6pm–1am.

CANCUN CITY
EXPENSIVE

La Habichuela ★★★ *(Moments* GOURMET SEAFOOD   In a musically accented garden setting with flowering white-lit hibiscus trees, this downtown Caribbean seafood restaurant is ideal for a romantic evening. For an all-out culinary adventure, try *habichuela* (string bean) soup; shrimp in any number of sauces, including Jamaican tamarind, tequila, or ginger and mushroom; and Maya coffee with *xtabentun* (a strong, sweet, anise-based liqueur). Grilled seafood and steaks are excellent, and the menu includes luscious ceviche, Caribbean lobsters, an inventive seafood "parade," and shish kabob flambé. For something divine, try *cocobichuela,* lobster and shrimp in curry served in a coconut shell and topped with fruit. Top it off with one of the boozy butterscotch crepes. Service here is fabulous.

Margaritas 25. © 998/884-3158. www.lahabichuela.com. Reservations recommended in high season. Main courses $15–$46 (£7.50–£23). AE, MC, V. Daily noon–midnight.

Périco's ★★ *(Finds* MEXICAN/SEAFOOD/STEAKS   Périco's is a joyous parade of performance, play, and brightly colored tourist hilarity. The unique restaurant features entertaining waiters dressed in a variety of festive costumes, murals that seem to dance off the walls, a bar area with saddles for barstools, and leather tables and chairs. Its extensive menu offers well-prepared steak, seafood, and traditional Mexican dishes for reasonable rates (except for lobster and surf and turf). This is a place not only to eat and drink, but also to let loose and join in the fun, so don't be surprised if diners drop their forks and don sombreros to shimmy and shake in a conga line around the dining room. The entertainment kicks off at 7:30pm.

Yaxchilán 61. © 998/884-3152. www.pericos.com.mx. Reservations recommended. Main courses $14–$41 (£7–£21). AE, MC, V. Daily noon–1am.

MODERATE

Labná ★★ YUCATECAN   To steep yourself in Yucatecan cuisine and music, head directly to this showcase of Maya moods and regional foods. Specialties served here include a sublime lime soup, *poc chuc* (marinated, barbecue-style pork), chicken or pork *pibil* (sweet and spicy barbecue sauce served over shredded meat wrapped in banana leaves), and appetizers such as *papadzules* (tortillas stuffed with boiled eggs in a pumpkin seed sauce). The Labná Special is a sampler of four typically Yucatecan main courses, including *poc chuc,* while another specialty of the house is baked suckling pig, served with guacamole. The refreshing Yucatecan beverage, *agua de chaya*— sweetened water and the leaf of the *chaya* plant, abundant in the area, to which sweet

Xtabentun liquor (a type of anise) can be added for an extra kick—is also served here. The vaulted ceiling dining room is decorated with black-and-white photographs of the region from the 1900s. A local trio plays weekend afternoons.

Margaritas 29, next to City Hall and the Habichuela restaurant. ℂ 998/892-3056. Main courses $7–$20 (£3.50–£10). AE, MC, V. Daily noon–10pm.

INEXPENSIVE
100% Natural *VEGETARIAN/MEXICAN   If you want a healthy reprieve from an overindulgent night—or just like your meals as fresh and natural as possible—this is your oasis. No matter what your dining preference, you owe it to yourself to try a Mexican tradition, the fresh-fruit *licuado*. These smoothie-like drinks combine fresh fruit, ice, and water or milk. More creative combinations may mix in yogurt, granola, or other goodies. 100% Natural serves more than just meal-quality drinks—there's a bountiful selection of simple Mexican fare and terrific sandwiches served on wholegrain bread, with options for vegetarians. Breakfast is delightful, and there's an attached bakery featuring all-natural baked goods such as chocolate croissants and apple cinnamon muffins. There are several 100% Natural locations in town, including branches at Playa Chac-Mool, in front of Señor Frog's, and downtown.

Av. Sunyaxchen 63. ℂ 998/884-0102. www.100natural.com.mx. Reservations not accepted. Main courses $5–$16 (£2.50–£8). AE, MC, V. Daily 7am–11pm.

Pizza Rolandi *Kids ITALIAN   At this shaded patio restaurant known for dependably tasty Italian delights, you can choose from an enticing selection of spaghetti, calzones, and Italian-style chicken and beef, as well as from almost two dozen delicious, if greasy, wood-oven pizzas (individual size). Why not try the deliciously spicy "Fiesta Mexicana" pizza with tomato, cheese, Mexican pepperoni, and jalapenos? A Cancún institution, Pizza Rolandi has a duplicate branch on Isla Mujeres (see chapter 15). It's as popular with locals as with tourists.

Cobá 12. ℂ 998/884-4047. Fax 998/884-4047. www.rolandi.com. Pasta $9–$12 (£4.50–£6); pizza and main courses $7–$14 (£3.50–£7). AE, MC, V. Daily 12:30pm–12:30am.

Roots INTERNATIONAL   This popular hangout for local residents is also a fun spot for visitors to Cancún. Located in the heart of downtown, this dimly-lit restaurant and jazz club offers a smooth cosmopolitan ambience. The Caribbean-themed menu offers a range of casual dining choices, including salads, pastas, and fresh fish and steaks grilled on the *parilla*. It's accompanied by live music, including flamenco, jazz, and fusion. Decking the walls are original works of art by local painters. The music starts at 10:30pm, and Roots seldom fills up before 9:30pm.

Tulipanes 26, SM 22. ℂ 998/884-2437. Main courses $6–$17 (£3–£8.50). MC, V. Tues–Sat 6pm–1am.

4 Beaches, Watersports & Boat Tours

THE BEACHES   Big hotels dominate the best stretches of beach. All of Mexico's beaches are public property, so you can use the beach of any hotel by walking through the lobby or directly onto the sand. Be especially careful on beaches fronting the open Caribbean, where the undertow can be quite strong. By contrast, the waters of **Bahía de Mujeres** (Mujeres Bay), at the north end of the island, are usually calm and ideal for swimming. Get to know Cancún's water-safety pennant system, and make sure to check the flag at any beach or hotel before entering the water. Here's how it goes:

White	Excellent
Green	Normal conditions (safe)
Yellow	Changeable, uncertain (use caution)
Black or red	Unsafe—use the swimming pool instead!

In the Caribbean, storms can arrive and conditions can change from safe to unsafe in a matter of minutes, so be alert: If you see dark clouds heading your way, make for the shore and wait until the storm passes.

Playa Tortuga (Turtle Beach), Playa Langosta (Lobster Beach), Playa Linda (Pretty Beach), and Playa Las Perlas (Beach of the Pearls) are some of the public beaches. At most beaches, you can rent a sailboard and take lessons, ride a parasail, or partake in a variety of watersports. There's a small but beautiful portion of public beach on **Playa Caracol,** by the Xcaret Terminal. It faces the calm waters of Bahía de Mujeres and, for that reason, is preferable to those facing the Caribbean.

WATERSPORTS   Many beachside hotels offer watersports concessions that rent rubber rafts, kayaks, and snorkeling equipment. On the calm Nichupté lagoon are outlets for renting **sailboats, jet skis, sailboards,** and **water skis.** Prices vary and are often negotiable, so check around.

DEEP-SEA FISHING   You can arrange a shared or private deep-sea fishing charter at one of the numerous piers or travel agencies, and prices fluctuate widely depending on the length of the excursion (there's usually a 4-hour minimum), number of people, and quality of the boat. Marinas will sometimes assist in putting together a group. Charters include a captain, a first mate, bait, gear, and beverages. Rates are lower if you depart from Isla Mujeres or from Cozumel—and frankly, the fishing is better closer to those departure points.

SCUBA & SNORKELING   Known for its shallow reefs, dazzling color, and diversity of life, Cancún is one of the best places in the world for beginning scuba diving. Punta Nizuc is the northern tip of the **Gran Arrecife Maya (Great Mesoamerican Reef),** the largest reef in the Western Hemisphere and one of the largest in the world. In addition to the sea life along this reef system, several sunken boats add a variety of dive options. Inland, a series of caverns and cenotes (wellsprings) are fascinating venues for the more experienced diver. Drift diving is the norm here, with popular dives going to the reefs at **El Garrafón** and the **Cave of the Sleeping Sharks**—although be aware that the famed "sleeping sharks" have departed, driven off by too many people watching them snooze.

A variety of hotels offer resort courses that teach the basics of diving—enough to make shallow dives and slowly ease your way into this underwater world of unimaginable beauty. One preferred dive operator is **Scuba Cancún,** Bulevar Kukulkán Km 5 (© **998/849-4736;** www.scubacancun.com.mx), on the lagoon side. Full open water PADI certification takes 3 days and costs $410 (£205). A half-day resort course for beginners with theory, pool practice, and a one-tank dive at a reef costs $88 (£44). Scuba Cancún is open daily from 7am to 8pm. For certified divers, Scuba Cancún also offers PADI specialty courses and diving trips in good weather to 18 nearby reefs, as well as to Cenotes Caverns (9m/30 ft.) and Cozumel. The average dive is around 11m (36 ft.), while advanced divers descend farther (up to 18m/60 ft). Two-tank dives to reefs around Cancún cost $68 (£34); those to farther destinations cost $140 (£70). Discounts apply if you bring your own gear. Dives usually start around 9:30am and return by 1:30pm. Snorkeling trips cost $29 (£15) and leave daily at 1:30pm and 4pm for shallow reefs about a 20-minute boat ride away.

The largest dive operator is **Aquaworld,** across from the Meliá Cancún at Bulevar Kukulkán Km 15.2 (© **998/848-8327;** www.aquaworld.com.mx). It offers resort courses and diving at a reef barrier, as well as snorkeling, parasailing, jet-ski "jungle tours," fishing, day trips to Isla Mujeres and Cozumel, and other watersports activities. Single tank dives cost $60 (£30); two-tank dives $65 (£33). Aquaworld has the **Sub See Explorer,** a boat with picture windows that hang beneath the surface. The boat doesn't submerge—it's an updated version of a glass-bottom boat—but it does provide nondivers with a worthwhile peek at life beneath the sea.

Besides snorkeling at **El Garrafón Natural Park** (see "Boating Excursions," below), travel agencies offer an all-day excursion to the natural wildlife habitat of **Isla Contoy,** which usually includes time for snorkeling. The island, 90 minutes past Isla Mujeres, is a major nesting area for birds and a treat for nature lovers. You can call any travel agent or see any hotel tour desk to get a selection of boat tours to Isla Contoy. Prices range from $45 to $75 (£23–£38), depending on the length of the trip, and generally include drinks and snorkeling equipment.

The Great Mesoamerican Reef also offers exceptional snorkeling opportunities. In Puerto Morelos, 37km (23 miles) south of Cancún, the reef hugs the coastline for 15km (9⅓ miles). The reef is so close to the shore (about 460m/1,509 ft.) that it forms a natural barrier for the village and keeps the waters calm on the inside of the reef. The water here is shallow, from 1.5 to 9m (5–30 ft.), resulting in ideal conditions for snorkeling. Stringent environmental regulations implemented by the local community have kept the reef here unspoiled. Only a select few companies are allowed to offer snorkel trips, and they must adhere to guidelines that will ensure the reef's preservation. **Cancún Mermaid** (© **998/843-6517;** www.cancunmermaid.com) is considered the best—it's a family-run ecotour company that has operated in the area since the 1970s. It's known for highly personalized service. The tour typically takes snorkelers to two sections of the reef, spending about an hour in each area. When conditions allow, the boat drops off snorkelers and then follows them along with the current—an activity known as "drift snorkeling," which enables snorkelers to see as much of the reef as possible. The trip costs $50 (£25) for adults, $35 (£18) for children, and includes boat, snorkeling gear, life jackets, a light lunch, bottled water, sodas, and beer, plus round-trip transportation to and from Puerto Morelos from Cancún hotels. Departures are Monday through Saturday at 9am. For snorkelers who just can't get enough, a combo tour for $30 (£15) more adds a bicycle tour to additional snorkeling destinations. Reservations are required at least 1 day in advance; MasterCard and Visa are accepted.

JET-SKI/FAST BOAT TOURS   Several companies offer the thrilling **Jungle Cruise,** in which you drive your own small speed boat (called a *lancha*) or WaveRunner rapidly through Cancún's lagoon and mangrove estuaries out into the Caribbean Sea and a shallow reef. The excursion lasts about 2½ hours and costs $55 to $60 (£28–£30), including snorkeling equipment. Many people prefer the companies offering two-person boats rather than WaveRunners, since they can sit side by side rather than one behind the other.

Jungle cruise operators and names offering excursions change often. To find out what's available, check with a local travel agent or hotel tour desk. The popular **Aquaworld,** Bulevar Kukulkán Km 15.2 (© **998/848-8327**), calls its trip the Jungle Tour and charges $60 (£30) for the 2½-hour excursion, which includes 45 minutes of snorkeling time. It even gives you a free snorkel, but has the less desirable one-behind-the-other seating configuration. Departures are daily at 9am, noon, and 2:30pm. If you'd prefer a side-by-side boat, try **Blue Ray,** Bulevar Kukulkán Km 13.5, next to Mambo Café (© **998/885-1108**), which charges $55 (£28) with departures every hour between 9am and 3pm. Expect to get wet, and wear plenty of sunscreen.

BOATING EXCURSIONS

ISLA MUJERES   The island of **Isla Mujeres,** just 13km (8 miles) offshore, is one of the most pleasant day trips from Cancún. At one end is **El Garrafón Natural Park,** which is good for snorkeling. At the other end is a captivating village with small shops, restaurants, and hotels, and **Playa Norte,** the island's best beach. If you're looking for relaxation and can spare the time, it's worth several days. For complete information about the island, see chapter 15.

There are four ways to get there: **public ferry** from Puerto Juárez, which takes between 15 and 20 minutes; **shuttle boat** from Playa Linda or Playa Tortuga—an hour-long ride, with irregular service; **water taxi** (more expensive, but faster), next to the Xcaret Terminal; and daylong **pleasure-boat trips,** most of which leave from the Playa Linda pier.

The inexpensive but fast Puerto Juárez **public ferries** ✔ lie just a few kilometers from downtown Cancún. From Cancún City, take the Ruta 8 bus on Avenida Tulum to Puerto Juárez. The air-conditioned *Caribbean Express* and *Ultramar* boats (15–20 min.) cost $4 (£2) per person. Departures are every half-hour from 6 to 8:30am and then every 15 minutes until 8:30pm. The slower *Caribbean Savage* (45–60 min.) costs about $3.50 (£1.75). It departs every 2 hours, or less frequently depending on demand. Upon arrival, the ferry docks in downtown Isla Mujeres near all the shops, restaurants, hotels, and Norte beach. You'll need a taxi to get to El Garrafón park at the other end of the island. You can stay as long as you like on the island and return by ferry, but be sure to confirm the time of the last returning ferry.

Pleasure-boat cruises to Isla Mujeres are a favorite pastime. Modern motor yachts, catamarans, trimarans, and even old-time sloops—more than 25 boats a day—take swimmers, sun lovers, snorkelers, and shoppers out on the translucent waters. Some tours include a snorkeling stop at El Garrafón, lunch on the beach, and a short time for shopping in downtown Isla Mujeres. Most leave at 9:30 or 10am, last about 5 or 6 hours, and include continental breakfast, lunch, and rental of snorkel gear. Others, particularly sunset and night cruises, go to beaches away from town for pseudo-pirate shows and include a lobster dinner or Mexican buffet (p. 542). If you want to actually see Isla Mujeres, go on a morning cruise, or travel on your own using the public ferry from Puerto Juárez. Prices for the day cruises run around $56 (£28) per person. Reservations aren't necessary.

An all-inclusive entrance fee of $65 (£33), $49 (£25) for children to **Garrafón Natural Reef Park** ✔✔ (© **998/849-4748;** www.garrafon.com) includes transportation from Cancún, meals, open bar with domestic drinks, access to the reef, as well as use of snorkel gear, kayaks, inner tubes, life vests, the pool, hammocks, and public facilities and showers (but not towels, so bring your own). There are also nature trails and several on-site restaurants.

Other excursions go to the **reefs** in glass-bottom boats, so you can have a near-scuba-diving experience and see many colorful fish. However, the reefs are some

---

Tips **An All-Terrain Tour**

Cancún Mermaid (© 998/843-6517; www.cancunmermaid.com) offers all-terrain-vehicle (ATV) jungle tours for $49 (£25) per person if riding double or $66 (£33) if riding single. The ATV tours travel through the jungles of Cancún and emerge on the beaches of the Riviera Maya. The 5-hour tour (including transportation time from your hotel to the destination) includes gear, instruction, the services of a tour guide, lunch, and bottled water; it departs Monday through Saturday at 8am and 1:30pm. Reservations are required.

---

distance from the shore and are impossible to reach on windy days with choppy seas. They've also suffered from over-visitation, and their conditions are far from pristine. Nautibus's **Atlantis Submarine** (© 987/872-5671; www.atlantisadventures.com) takes you close to the aquatic action. Departures vary, depending on weather conditions. Prices are $79 (£40) for adults, $45 (£23) for children ages 4 to 12. The submarine descends to a depth of 30m (98 ft.). Atlantis Submarine departs daily at 9am, 11am, and noon; the tour lasts about 40 minutes. The submarine departs from Cozumel, so you either need to take a ferry to get there or purchase a package that includes round-trip transportation from your hotel in Cancún ($103/£52 adults, $76/£38 children 4–12). Reservations are recommended.

5 Outdoor Activities & Attractions

OUTDOOR ACTIVITIES

DOLPHIN SWIMS   On Isla Mujeres, you can swim with dolphins at **Dolphin Discovery** ★★ (© 998/877-0207 or 849-4757; www.dolphindiscovery.com). Groups of eight people swim with two dolphins and one trainer. Swimmers view an educational video and spend time in the water with the trainer and the dolphins before enjoying 15 minutes of free swimming time with them. Reservations are recommended (you can book online), and you must arrive an hour before your assigned swimming time, at 10:30am, noon, 2pm, or 3:30pm. The cost is $139 (£70) per person for the Dolphin Royal Swim. There are less expensive programs that allow you to learn about, touch, and hold the dolphins (but not swim with them) starting at $79 (£40). Ferry transfers from Playa Langosta in Cancún are available.

La Isla Shopping Center, Bulevar Kukulkán Km 12.5, has an impressive **Interactive Aquarium** (© 998/883-0411, -0436, or -0413; www.aquariumcancun.com.mx), with dolphin swims and shows and the chance to feed a shark while immersed in the water in an acrylic cage. Guides inside the main tank use underwater microphones to point out the sea life, and even answer your questions. Open exhibition tanks enable visitors to touch a variety of marine life, including sea stars and manta rays. The educational dolphin program costs $65 (£33), while the dolphin swim is $135 (£68) and the shark-feeding experience runs $65 (£33). The entrance fee to the aquarium is $13 (£6.50) for adults, $9 (£4.50) for children under 11, and it's open daily from 9am to 6pm.

GOLF & TENNIS   The 18-hole **Pok-Ta-Pok Club,** or Club de Golf Cancún (© 998/ 883-0871), is a Robert Trent Jones, Sr., design on the northern leg of the island. Greens fees run $135 (£68) for 18 holes including breakfast or lunch and golf cart (discounted twilight fees), with clubs renting for $40 (£20). A caddy costs $25 (£13). The club is open daily from 6:30am to 5pm and accepts American Express, Master-Card, and Visa.

The **Hilton Cancún Golf & Spa Resort** (© 998-881-8016) has a championship 18-hole, par-72 course around the Ruinas Del Rey. Greens fees during high season for the public are typically $199 (£100) for 18 holes and $149 (£75) for 9 holes; Hilton Cancún guests pay discounted rates of $149 (£75) for 18 holes, or $99 (£50) for 9 holes, which includes a golf cart. Low season and twilight discounts are available. Golf clubs and shoes are available for rent. The club is open daily from 6am to 6pm and takes American Express, MasterCard, and Visa. The **Gran Meliá Cancún** (© 998/881-1100) has a 9-hole executive course; the fee is $30 (£15). The club is open daily from 7am to 3pm and accepts American Express, MasterCard, and Visa.

The first Jack Nicklaus Signature Golf Course in the Cancún area has opened at the **Moon Palace Spa & Golf Club** (© 998-881-6000; www.palaceresorts.com), along the Riviera Maya. The $260 (£130) greens fee includes cart, snacks, and drinks.

HORSEBACK RIDING Cancún Mermaid (© 998/843-6517; www.cancun mermaid.com), about 30 minutes south of town at the Rancho Loma Bonita, is a popular option for horseback riding. Five-hour packages include 2 hours of riding through the mangrove swamp to the beach, where you have time to swim and relax. The tour costs $66 (£33) for adults and $60 (£30) for children under 13. The ranch also offers a four-wheel ATV ride on the same route as the horseback tour. It costs $66 (£33) if you want to ride on your own, and $49 (£25) per person if you double up. Prices for both tours include transportation to the ranch, riding, soft drinks, lunch, a guide, and insurance. Only cash or traveler's checks are accepted.

ATTRACTIONS

BULLFIGHTS Cancún has a small bullring, **Plaza de Toros** (© 998/884-8372), near the northern (town) end of Bulevar Kukulkán at Av. Bonampak and Sayil. Bull-fights take place every Wednesday at 3:30pm during the winter tourist season. A sport introduced to Mexico by the Spanish viceroys, bullfighting is now as much a part of Mexican culture as tequila. The bullfights usually include four bulls, and the specta-cle begins with a folkloric dance exhibition, followed by a performance by the *charros* (Mexico's sombrero-wearing cowboys). You're not likely to see Mexico's best bullfights in Cancún—the real stars are in Mexico City. Keep in mind that if you go to a bull-fight, *you're going to see a bullfight,* so stay away if you're an animal lover or you can't bear the sight of blood. Buy tickets, which cost $40 (£20) for adults and are free for children under 6, at the Plaza ticket counter the day of the event or in advance from a travel agent; seating is by general admission. American Express, MasterCard, and Visa are accepted.

6 Shopping

Despite the surrounding natural splendor, shopping has become a favorite activity. Can-cún is known throughout Mexico for its diverse shops and festive malls catering to inter-national tourists. Visitors from the United States may find apparel more expensive in Cancún, but the selection is much broader than at other Mexican resorts. Numerous duty-free shops offer excellent value on European goods. The largest is **UltraFemme,** Avenida Tulum, Supermanzana 25 (© 998/884-1402), specializing in imported cosmetics, perfumes, and fine jewelry and watches. The downtown Cancún location offers slightly lower prices than branches in Plaza Caracol, La Isla, and Kukulcán Plaza. It's open Monday to Saturday from 9:30am to 9pm and Sunday from 2 to 9pm.

Handicrafts are more limited and more expensive in Cancún than in other regions of Mexico because they are not produced here. They are available, though; several **open-air crafts markets** are on Avenida Tulum in Cancún City and near the convention center in the Hotel Zone. One of the biggest is **Coral Negro,** Bulevar Kukulkán Km 9.5, next to Plaza Dady'O, open daily from 7am to 11pm. **Plaza La Fiesta,** next to the Cancún Center (© **998/883-4519**), is a large Mexican outlet store selling handicrafts, jewelry, tequila, leather, and accessories. It's open daily from 7am to midnight.

Cancún's main venues are the **malls**—not quite as grand as their U.S. counterparts, but close. All are air-conditioned, sleek, and sophisticated. Most are on Bulevar Kukulkán between Km 7 and Km 12. They offer everything from fine crystal and silver to designer clothing and decorative objects, along with numerous restaurants and clubs. Stores are generally open daily from 10am to 10pm.

The **Kukulcán Plaza** (© **998/885-2200;** www.kukulcanplaza.com) houses more than 300 shops, restaurants, and entertainment. There's a bank; a bowling alley; several crafts stores; a Play City with gambling machines; a liquor and tobacco store; several bathing-suit specialty stores; music stores; a leather goods shop (including shoes and sandals); and a store specializing in silver from Taxco. U.S. franchise eateries include Häagen-Dazs and Ruth's Chris Steak House. The adjacent Luxury Avenue complex features designer labels such as Cartier, Louis Vuitton, Pineda Covalín, Salvatore Ferragamo, and Ultrafemme. The mall is open daily from 10am to 10pm, until 11pm during high season. Assistance for those with disabilities is available upon request, and wheelchairs, strollers, and lockers are available at the information desk.

The long-standing **Plaza Caracol** (© **998/883-1038;** www.caracolplaza.com) was being renovated at press time and holds, among other things, Cartier jewelry, Señor Frog's clothing, Samsonite luggage, and La Fisheria and Casa Rolandi restaurants. It's just before you reach the convention center as you come from downtown Cancún.

The entertainment-oriented **Forum by the Sea,** Bulevar Kukulkán Km 9 (© **998/ 883-4425;** www.forumbythesea.com.mx), received a complete face-lift after Hurricane Wilma. Most people come here for the food and fun, choosing from Hard Rock Cafe, Carlos 'n' Charlie's, Rainforest Cafe, and CoCo Bongo, plus an extensive food court. Shops include Diesel, Harley Davidson, Señor Frog's, Sunglass Island, and Zingara Beachwear and Swimwear. The mall is open daily from 10am to midnight (bars remain open later).

One of Mexico's most appealing malls is the **La Isla Shopping Village,** Bulevar Kukulkán Km 12.5 (© **998/883-5025;** www.laislacancun.com.mx), a wonderful open-air complex that borders the lagoon. Walkways lined with quality shops and restaurants cross little canals (boat rides are even offered through the canals), and there's a boardwalk along the lagoon and an interactive aquarium and dolphin swim facility (p. 551). Shops include Bulgari, Diesel, DKNY, Guess, Nautica, Nine West, Tommy Hilfiger, UltraFemme, and Zara, as well a large Mexican handicrafts store called Casa Bonita. Dining choices include the romantic Thai restaurant (p. 546). You will also find a movie theater and several bars, including La Madonna (p. 555).

7 Cancún After Dark

One of Cancún's main draws is its active nightlife. While the partying often begins by day at the beach, the cool crowd heads at happy hour to the many bars located along the Hotel Zone, which often serve two-for-one drinks at sunset. Hotels play in the happy hour scene, with special drink prices to entice visitors and guests from other resorts. Come night, the hottest centers of action are also along Kukulcán and include **Plaza Dady'O, Forum by the Sea,** and **La Isla Shopping Village.** These places transform into spring break madness for most of March and April.

THE CLUB & MUSIC SCENE

Clubbing in Cancún is a favorite part of the vacation experience and can go on each night until the sun rises over that incredibly blue sea. Several big hotels have nightclubs or schedule live music in their lobby bars. At the clubs, expect to stand in long lines on weekends, pay a cover charge of about $40 (£20) with open bar, or $15 to $25 (£7.50–£13) without open bar and then pay $8 to $10 (£4–£5) for a drink. Some of the higher-priced clubs include live entertainment. The places listed in this section are air-conditioned and accept American Express, MasterCard, and Visa.

A great idea to get you started is the **Bar Hopper Tour** ⭐⭐ with tickets available at Señor Frog's, most hotels, or various travel agencies around town. For $65 (£33), it takes you by bus to the Congo Bar, Señor Frog's, and CoCo Bongo, where you bypass any lines and spend about an hour at each establishment. The price includes entry to the bars, one welcome drink at each, and transportation by air-conditioned bus, allowing you to get a great sampling of the best of Cancún's nightlife. The tour runs from 8pm into the wee hours, with the meeting point at the Congo Bar.

Numerous restaurants, such as **Carlos 'n' Charlie's, Hard Rock Cafe, Señor Frog's,** and **T.G.I. Friday's,** double as nighttime party spots, offering wildish fun at a fraction of the price of more costly clubs.

Bling ⭐⭐⭐ This is one of the coolest nightspots in Cancún, featuring a chic outdoor terrace overlooking the lagoon. A fashionable 30-something crowd congregates amid sofas under the stars, a killer sound system, and flowing cocktails. A sushi and sashimi bar and some Mediterranean dishes are also offered. This upscale lounge is considerably more sophisticated than Cancún's typical frat-style bars, and it's open daily from 6pm to 4am. Bulevar Kukulkán, Km 13.5. © **998/840-6014.**

The City ⭐⭐ One of Cancún's hottest and largest nightclubs, The City features progressive electronic music spun by some of the world's top DJs (the DJ station looks like an airport control tower). This is where Paris Hilton parties when she comes to town. With visiting DJs from New York, L.A., and Mexico City, the music is sizzling. You actually need never leave, as The City is a day-and-night club. The City Beach Club opens at 10am and features a pool with a wave machine for surfing and boogie-boarding, a tower-high waterslide, food and bar service, plus beach *cabañas.* The Terrace Bar, overlooking the action on Bulevar Kukulkán, serves food and drinks all day long. For a relaxing evening vibe, the Lounge features comfy couches, chill music, and an extensive menu of martinis, snacks, and desserts. Open at 10:30pm, the 2,500-sq.-m (26,910-sq.-ft.) nightclub features nine bars, stunning light shows, and several VIP areas. Bulevar Kukulkán, Km 9.5. © **998/848-8380.** www.thecitycancun.com. Cover $25 (£13); $45 (£23) with open bar.

CoCo Bongo ✦✦✦ Continuing its reputation as the hottest party venue in town, CoCo Bongo's appeal is that it combines an enormous dance club with extravagant theme shows. It has no formal dance floor, so you can dance anywhere; and that includes on the tables, on the bar, or even on the stage with the occasional live band. This place can, and regularly does, pack in as many as 3,000 people. You have to experience it to believe it. Despite its capacity, lines are long on weekends and in high season. The music alternates between Caribbean, salsa, house, hip-hop, techno, and classics from the 1970s, '80s, and '90s. Open from 10:30pm to 3:30am, CoCo Bongo draws a hip young crowd. Forum by the Sea, Bulevar Kukulkán Km 9.5. ℂ 998/883-5061. www. cocobongo.com.mx. Cover $45 (£23) with open bar.

Dady'O This is a popular rave among the young and brave with frequent long lines. MTV, Playboy, Fashion TV, and E! Entertainment have all hosted events here. It opens nightly at 10pm and has a giant dance floor and awesome light system. Bulevar Kukulkán Km 9.5. ℂ 998/883-3333. www.dadyo.com.mx. Cover $20 (£10); $45 (£23) with open bar.

Dady Rock Bar and Club The offspring of Dady'O, it opens at 8pm and goes as long as any other nightspot, offering a combination of live rock bands and DJs spinning grooves, along with an open bar, full meals, a buffet, and dancing. Bulevar Kukulkán Km 9.5. ℂ 998/883-1626. Cover $16 (£8); $35 (£18) with open bar.

La Madonna This architecturally dazzling martini bar and restaurant emerges unexpectedly from La Isla shopping center like an Italian Renaissance showroom along the canal. With more than 180 creative martini selections accompanied by relaxing lounge music, La Madonna also offers authentic Italian and Swiss cuisine. Enjoy your red mandarin, lychee, or vanilla peach martini alongside Cancún's beautiful people on the expansive outdoor patio or upstairs terrace. Inside, the expansive dining room resembles one of the mystical Buddha Bars, with an enormous replica of the Mona Lisa looking over the dazzled clientele. It's open daily from 1pm to 1am. La Isla Shopping Village, Bulevar Kukulkán Km 12.5. ℂ 998/883-2222.

The Lobby Lounge ✦ The most refined of Cancún's nightly gathering spots, with a terrace overlooking the lagoon, a special martini collection, and a list of more than 80 premium tequilas for tasting or sipping. There's also a sushi and seafood bar, as well as a humidor collection of Cuban cigars. It's open daily from 5pm to 1am, with live music Thursday through Sunday. Ritz-Carlton Cancún, Retorno del Rey 36, off Bulevar Kukulkán Km 13.5. ℂ 998/881-0808.

Mambo Cafe ✦✦ If you're looking for a hot Latin night out, Mambo Café is your place. The tropical rhythm club features a live Cuban band nightly, starting at 11:30pm, when sexy salsa dancers hit the floor with fervor. Every night has a drinking theme, whether it's two-for-one Tuesday, $3 (£1.50) Wednesday, or ladies-drink-free Thursday. Mambo Café is open nightly from 10pm to 4am, and salsa dance classes are Thursday at 9:30pm. Bulevar Kukulkán, Km 13.5. ℂ 998/840-6498. www.mambo cafe.com.mx. Cover $10 (£5); $30 (£15) with open bar.

THE PERFORMING ARTS

Several hotels host **Mexican fiesta nights,** including a buffet dinner and a folkloric dance show; admission, including dinner, ranges from $35 to $50 (£18–£25), unless you're at an all-inclusive resort that includes this as part of the package. Check out the **Fiesta Americana Coral Beach's** (ℂ 998/881-3200) a la carte dining show four times a week.

15

Isla Mujeres & Cozumel

by David Baird

Mexico's two main Caribbean islands are idyllic escapes from the hustle and bustle of Cancún and the Riviera Maya. Neither Isla Mujeres nor Cozumel is particularly large, and they have that island feel—with small roads that don't go very far, lots of mopeds, few if any trucks, and a sense of remoteness from the rest of the world. Yet they're just a short ferry ride from the mainland. Both offer a variety of lodging options, ample outdoor activities, and a laid-back atmosphere that contrasts with much of the mainland experience.

Isla Mujeres is a fish-shaped island 13km (8 miles) northeast of Cancún, which makes it a quick boat ride away. One of the most popular excursions from Cancún is a day trip to Isla Mujeres on a party boat. But if you want to do more than wander the streets, shop, or lie on the beach, it's best to stay overnight. Hotels range from rustic to regal.

Passenger ferries travel to Isla Mujeres from Puerto Juárez, and car ferries leave from Punta Sam, both near Cancún. More expensive passenger ferries, with fewer departures, leave from the Playa Linda pier on Cancún Island.

Larger than Isla Mujeres and farther from the mainland (19km/12 miles off the coast from Playa del Carmen), **Cozumel** has its own international airport. Life here revolves around two major activities: scuba diving and cruise ships making a port of call. (Cozumel is far and away the most popular destination along this coast for both activities.)

Despite the cruise-ship traffic and all the stores spawned by it, however, life on the island moves at a relaxed pace. There is just one town, San Miguel de Cozumel. North and south of town are resorts. The rest of the shore is deserted and predominantly rocky, with a scattering of small sandy coves that you can have practically all to yourself.

1 Isla Mujeres ★★★

13km (8 miles) N of Cancún

Isla Mujeres (Island of Women) is a casual, laid-back refuge from the heady tempo of Cancún. It lies not far off the coast and is visible from the resort. As Caribbean islands go, Isla is a bargain and a good fit for anyone who prefers simplicity and ease over variety and action. The island's only town is right next to North Beach, the best beach on the island. With beach towel in hand, you can leisurely stroll there from any hotel in town; there's no need for transportation. Don't think that Isla is an escape from commercialism—it isn't, though commercialism is writ small here, which is characteristic of the place. The island is small, the town is small, the hotels (with a couple of exceptions) are small, the restaurants, the bars, the excursion boats—small,

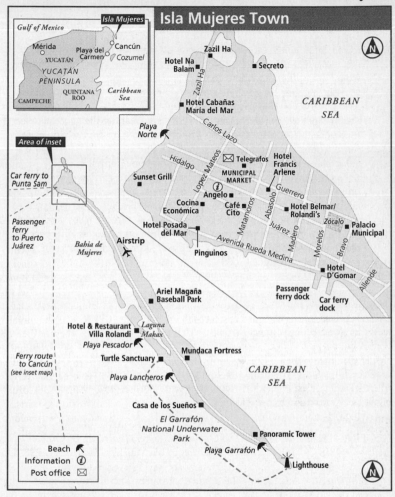

Isla Mujeres Town

Gulf of Mexico
Mérida
YUCATÁN
YUCATÁN
PENINSULA
CAMPECHE
QUINTANA
ROO
Playa del
Carmen
Cancún
Cozumel
Caribbean
Sea
Isla Mujeres

Area of inset

Car ferry to
Punta Sam

Passenger
ferry
to Puerto
Juárez

Bahía de
Mujeres

Ferry route
to Cancún
(see inset map)

Zazil Ha
Hotel Na
Balam
Secreto
Hotel Cabañas
María del Mar
CARIBBEAN
SEA
Carlos Lazo
Playa
Norte
Hidalgo
Sunset Grill
Lopez Mateos
Telegrafos
MUNICIPAL
MARKET
Hotel
Francis
Arlene
Guerrero
Angelo
Cocina
Económica
Café
Cito
Matamoros
Abasolo
Juárez
Hotel Belmar/
Rolandi's
Zócalo
Palacio
Municipal
Hotel Posada
del Mar
Madero
Morelos
Bravo
Airstrip
Avenida Rueda Medina
Pinguinos
Passenger
ferry dock
Hotel
D'Gomar
Allende
Ariel Magaña
Baseball Park
Car ferry
dock
Hotel & Restaurant
Villa Rolandi
Laguna
Makax
Playa Pescador
Turtle Sanctuary
Mundaca Fortress
Playa Lancheros
CARIBBEAN
SEA
Casa de los Sueños
El Garrafón
National Underwater
Park
Panoramic Tower
Playa Garrafón
Lighthouse

Beach
Information
Post office

small, small. There are several inexpensive hotels, mostly in town, and a smattering of luxury boutique hotels spread out to other parts of the island.

The small scale of the island heightens the contrast between high season and low season, making the crowds and bustle much more noticeable at peak travel times. At midday, suntanned visitors from the Cancún tour boats hang out in open-air cafes and stroll the pedestrian streets lined with zealous souvenir vendors calling attention to their wares. The scene takes on a carnivalesque hue during the hours when the tour-boat traffic is at its peak. Then, later in the afternoon, things settle down.

Trips to the Isla Contoy bird sanctuary are popular, as are the diving, snorkeling, and fishing jaunts. In 1998, the island's coral coast became part of Mexico's Marine National Park system. The reef suffered substantial hurricane damage in 2005, but it's rebounding. The water clarity illuminates the wonderful array of coral and tropical

> ## ⌒Tips   The Best Websites for Isla Mujeres & Cozumel
>
> - **Isla Mujeres Tourist Information: www.isla-mujeres.net** The official site of the Isla Mujeres Tourism Board provides complete information on Isla, from getting there to where to stay.
> - **My Isla Mujeres: www.myislamujeres.com** Get a local's view of the island; the active chat room and message boards are especially good.
> - **Cozumel.net: www.cozumel.net** This site is a cut above the typical dining/ lodging/activities sites. Click on "About Cozumel" to find schedules for ferries and island-hop flights, and to check the latest news. There's also a comprehensive listing of B&Bs and vacation-home rentals.
> - **Cozumel Travel Planner: www.go2cozumel.com** This is a well-done guide to area businesses and attractions, by an online Mexico specialist.
> - **Cozumel Hotel Association: www.islacozumel.com.mx** Operated by the tourism-promotion arm of the hotel association, this site gives more than just listings of the member hotels. There's info on packages and specials, plus brief descriptions of most of the island's attractions, restaurants, and recreational activities.

fish living here. The underwater life you are likely to see includes French angelfish, longspine squirrelfish, trumpet fish, four-eye butterfly fish, green angelfish, stoplight parrotfish, southern stingrays, sharp-nose puffer fish, blue tang, and great barracuda.

The island and several of its hotels attract regular gatherings of yoga practitioners. In the evening, most people find the slow, casual pace one of the island's biggest draws. The cool night breeze is a perfect accompaniment to casual open-air dining and drinking in small street-side restaurants.

ESSENTIALS

GETTING THERE & DEPARTING   Puerto Juárez, just north of Cancún, is the **dock** (© 998/877-0382) for passenger ferries to Isla Mujeres. *Ultramar* (© 998/843-2011; www.granpuerto.com.mx) has fast boats leaving every half-hour from "Gran Puerto" in Puerto Juárez, making the trip in 15 minutes. There is storage space for luggage and the fare is about $4 (£2) each way. These boats operate daily, starting at 6am and usually ending at 10:30pm (check beforehand for latest schedules). They might leave early if they're full, so arrive ahead of schedule. Pay at the ticket office—or, if the ferry is about to leave, aboard.

Note: Upon arrival by taxi or bus in Puerto Juárez, be wary of pirate "guides" who tell you either that the ferry is canceled or that it's several hours until the next ferry. They'll offer the services of a private *lancha* (small boat) for about $40 (£20)—and it's nothing but a scam. Small boats are available and, on a co-op basis, charge $15 to $25 (£18–£13) one-way, based on the number of passengers. They take about 50 minutes and are not recommended on days with rough seas. Check with the ticket office—the only accurate source for information.

Taxi fares are posted by the street where the taxis park, so be sure to check the rate before agreeing to a taxi for the ride back to Cancún. Rates generally run $12 to $15 (£6–£7.50), depending upon your destination. Moped and bicycle rentals are also readily available as you depart the ferry. This small complex also has public bathrooms, luggage storage, a snack bar, and souvenir shops.

Isla Mujeres is so small that a vehicle isn't necessary, but if you're taking one, you'll use the **Punta Sam** port a little beyond Puerto Juárez. The 40-minute car ferry (© 998/877-0065) runs five or six times daily between 8am and 8pm, year-round except in bad weather. Times are generally as follows: Cancún to Isla 8 and 11am and 2:45, 5:30, and 8:15pm; Isla to Cancún 6:30 and 9:30am and 12:45, 4:15, and 7:15pm. Always check with the tourist office in Cancún to verify this schedule. Cars should arrive an hour before the ferry departure to register for a place in line and pay the posted fee, which varies depending on the weight and type of vehicle. A gas pump is at Avenida Rueda Medina and Calle Abasolo, northwest of the ferry docks.

Ferries to Isla Mujeres also depart from **Playa Linda,** known as the Embarcadero pier in Cancún, but they're less frequent and more expensive than those from Puerto Juárez. There are four to six scheduled departures per day to Isla Mujeres, depending upon the season. Adult fares are $15 (£7.50) round trip; kids ages 3 to 12 pay $7.50 (£3.75); children younger than 3 ride free. A **Water Taxi** (© 998/886-4270 or -4847; asterix@cablered.net.mx) to Isla Mujeres operates from **Playa Caracol,** between the Fiesta Americana Coral Beach Hotel and the Xcaret terminal on the island; prices are about the same as those from Playa Linda.

To get to Puerto Juárez or Punta Sam from **Cancún,** take any Ruta 8 city bus from Avenida Tulum. From the Cancún airport, take the shuttle bus to the pier ($16/£8).

Arriving   Passenger ferries arrive at the docks in the center of town. The main road that passes in front is Avenida Rueda Medina. Most hotels are close by. Tricycle taxis are the least expensive and most fun way to get to your hotel; you and your luggage pile in the open carriage compartment, and the driver pedals through the streets. Regular taxis are always lined up in a parking lot to the right of the pier, with their rates posted. If someone on the ferry offers to arrange a taxi for you, politely decline, unless you'd like some help with your luggage down the short pier—it just means an extra, unnecessary tip for your helper.

VISITOR INFORMATION   The **City Tourist Office** (©/fax 998/877-0767 or -0307) is at Av. Rueda Medina 130, just across the street from the pier. It's open Monday through Friday from 9am to 4pm, closed on Saturdays and Sundays. *Islander* is a free publication with local information, advertisements, and event listings.

ISLAND LAYOUT   Isla Mujeres is about 8km (5 miles) long and 4km (2½ miles) wide, with the town at the northern tip. "Downtown" is a compact 4 blocks by 6 blocks, so it's very easy to get around. The **passenger ferry docks** are at the center of town, within walking distance of most hotels, restaurants, and shops. The street running along the waterfront is **Avenida Rueda Medina,** commonly called the *malecón* **(boardwalk).** The **Mercado Municipal (town market)** is by the post office on **Calle Guerrero,** an inland street at the north edge of town, which, like most streets in the town, is unmarked.

GETTING AROUND   A popular form of transportation on Isla Mujeres is the electric **golf cart,** available for rent at many hotels or rental shops for $15 (£7.50) per hour or $45 (£23) per day. Prices are set the same at all rental locations. **El Sol Golf Cart Rental,** Av. Benito Juárez Mza 3 #20 (corner of Matamoros; © 998/877-0791) is one good option in the town center. The golf carts don't go more than 30kmph (20 mph), but they're fun. Anyway, you aren't on Isla Mujeres to hurry. Many people enjoy touring the island by *moto* (**motorized bike or scooter**). Fully automatic versions are available for around $35 (£18) per day or $8 (£4) per hour. They come with helmets and seats for two people. There's only one main road with a couple of offshoots, so you won't get lost. Be aware that the rental price does not include insurance, and any injury to yourself or the vehicle will come out of your pocket. **Bicycles** are also available for rent at some hotels for $4 (£2) per hour or $10 (£5) per day, usually including a basket and a lock.

If you prefer to use a taxi, rates are about $2.50 (£1.25) for trips within the downtown area, or $5 (£2.50) for a trip to the southern end of Isla. You can also hire them for about $10 (£5) per hour. The number to call for taxis is ⓒ **998/877-0066.**

FAST FACTS: Isla Mujeres

Area Code The telephone area code is **998.**

Consumer Protection You can reach the local branch of **Profeco** consumer protection agency at ⓒ **998/887-3960.**

Currency Exchange Isla Mujeres has numerous *casas de cambio,* or currency exchanges, along the main streets. Most of the hotels listed here change money for their guests, although often at less favorable rates than the commercial enterprises. There is only one bank in Isla, **HSBC Bank** (ⓒ **998/877-0005**), across from the ferry docks. It's open Monday through Friday from 8:30am to 6pm, and Saturdays from 9am to 2pm. It has ATM machines.

Drugstore **Isla Mujeres Farmacía** (ⓒ **998/877-0178**) has the best selection of prescription and over-the-counter medicines.

Emergencies To report an emergency, dial ⓒ **065** anywhere in Mexico.

Hospital The **Hospital de la Armada** is on Avenida Rueda Medina at Ojón P. Blanco (ⓒ **998/877-0001**). It's less than a kilometer (a half-mile) south of the town center. It will only treat you in an emergency. Otherwise, you're referred to the **Centro de Salud** on Avenida Guerrero, a block before the beginning of the *malecón* (ⓒ **998/877-0117**).

Internet Access Owned by a lifelong resident of Isla, **Cyber Isla Mujeres.com,** Av. Francisco y Madero 17, between Hidalgo and Juárez streets (ⓒ **998/877-0272**), offers Internet access for $1.50 (75p) per hour, daily 7am to 10pm, and serves complimentary Veracruzano coffee all day.

Post Office The *correo* is at Calle Guerrero 12 (ⓒ **998/877-0085**), at the corner of López Mateos, near the market. It's open Monday through Friday from 9am to 4pm.

Taxis To call for a taxi, dial ⓒ **998/877-0066.**

Telephone Ladatel phones accepting coins and prepaid phone cards are at the plaza and throughout town.

Tourist Seasons Isla Mujeres's tourist season (when hotel rates are higher) is a bit different from that of other places in Mexico. High season runs December through May, a month longer than in Cancún. Some hotels raise their rates in August, and some raise their rates beginning in mid-November. Low season is from June to mid-November.

BEACHES & OUTDOOR ACTIVITIES

THE BEACHES   The most popular beach in town is **Playa Norte** ★. The long stretch of beach extends around the northern tip of the island. This is perhaps the world's best municipal beach—a wide swath of fine white sand and calm, translucent, turquoise-blue water. The beach is easily reached on foot from the ferry and from all downtown hotels. Watersports equipment, beach umbrellas, and lounge chairs are available for rent. Areas in front of restaurants usually cost nothing if you use the restaurant as your headquarters for drinks and food, and the best of them have hammocks and swings from which to sip your piña coladas.

   Garrafón Natural Reef Park ★★ (see "Snorkeling," below) is best known as a snorkeling area, but there is a nice stretch of beach on either side of the park. **Playa Lancheros** is on the Caribbean side of Laguna Makax. Local buses go to Lancheros, and then turn inland and return downtown. The beach at Playa Lancheros is nice, with a variety of casual restaurants.

SWIMMING   Playa Norte is the best swimming beach, with Playa Lancheros second. There are no lifeguards on duty on Isla Mujeres, which does not use the system of water-safety flags employed in Cancún and Cozumel. The bay between Cancun and Isla Mujeres is calm, with warm, transparent waters ideal for swimming, snorkeling, and diving. The east side of the island facing the open Caribbean Sea is typically rougher with much stronger currents.

SNORKELING   One of the most popular places to snorkel is **Garrafón Natural Reef Park** ★★ (see below). **Manchones Reef,** off the southeastern coast, is also good. It's just offshore and accessible by boat. Around *el faro* (the lighthouse) in the **Bahía de Mujeres** at the southern tip of the island, you can snorkel some. The water is about 2m (6½ ft.) deep. Boatmen will take you for around $25 (£13) per person if you have your own snorkeling equipment or $30 (£15) if you use theirs.

DIVING   Most of the dive shops on the island offer the same trips for the same prices: one-tank dives cost about $50 (£25), two-tank dives about $70 (£35). **Bahía Dive Shop,** Rueda Medina 166, across from the car-ferry dock (© 998/877-0340), is a full-service shop that offers dive equipment for sale or rent. The shop is open daily from 10am to 7pm, and accepts MasterCard and Visa. Another respected dive shop is **Coral Scuba Center,** at Matamoros 13A and Rueda Medina (© 998/877-0061 or -0763). It's open daily from 8am to 12:30pm and 4 to 10pm. Both offer 2-hour snorkeling trips for about $20 (£11).

   Cuevas de los Tiburones (Caves of the Sleeping Sharks) is Isla's most renowned dive site—but the name is slightly misleading, as shark sightings are rare these days. Two sites where you could traditionally see the sleeping shark are the Cuevas de Tiburones and **La Punta,** but the sharks have mostly been driven off, and a storm collapsed the arch featured in a Jacques Cousteau film showing them, but the caves survive. Other dive sites include a **wreck** 15km (9⅓ miles) offshore; **Banderas** reef, between Isla Mujeres and Cancún, where there's always a strong current; **Tabos** reef on the eastern shore; and **Manchones** reef, 1km (a half-mile) off the southeastern tip of the island, where the water is 4.5 to 11m (15–36 ft.) deep. **The Cross of the Bay** is close to Manchones reef. A bronze cross, weighing 1 ton and standing 12m (40 ft.) high, was placed in the water between Manchones and Isla in 1994, as a memorial to those who have lost their lives at sea.

FISHING   To arrange a day of fishing, ask at the **Sociedad Cooperativa Turística** (the boatmen's cooperative), on Avenida Rueda Medina (© **998/877-1363**), next to Mexico Divers and Las Brisas restaurant, or the travel agency mentioned in "A Visit to Isla Contoy," below. Four to six others can share the cost, which includes lunch and drinks. Captain Tony Martínez (© **998/877-0274**) also arranges fishing trips aboard the *Marinonis,* with advanced reservations recommended. Year-round you'll find bonito, mackerel, kingfish, and amberjack. Sailfish and sharks (hammerhead, bull, nurse, lemon, and tiger) are in good supply in April and May. In winter, larger grouper and jewfish are prevalent. Four hours of fishing close to shore costs around $120 (£60); 8 hours farther out goes for $250 (£125). The cooperative is open Monday through Saturday from 8am to 1pm and 5 to 8pm, and Sunday from 7:30 to 10am and 6 to 8pm.

YOGA   Increasingly, Isla is becoming popular among yoga enthusiasts. The trend began at **Hotel Na Balam** ⊛⊛ (© **998/877-0279** or -0058; www.nabalam.com), which offers yoga classes under its large poolside *palapa,* complete with yoga mats and props. The hotel also offers yoga instruction vacations featuring respected teachers and a more extensive practice schedule; the current schedule of yoga retreats is posted on their website. Another Yoga center springing up and drawing together its community is **Elements of the Island** (www.elementsoftheisland.com). It's located at Juárez 64, between López Mateos and Matamoros. And there's **Casa de los Sueños Resort and Zenter** (© **998/877-0651;** www.casadelossuenosresort.com), which regularly holds yoga classes, as well as chi gong and Pilates.

MORE ATTRACTIONS

DOLPHIN DISCOVERY ⊛⊛   You can swim with dolphins (© **998/849-4748** or 849-4757; fax 998/849-4751; www.dolphindiscovery.com) in an enclosure at Treasure Island, on the side of Isla Mujeres that faces Cancún. Groups of eight people swim with two dolphins and one trainer. Swimmers view an educational video and spend time in the water with the trainer and the dolphins before enjoying 15 minutes of free swimming time with them. Reservations are necessary, and you must arrive an hour before your assigned swimming time, at 10:30am, noon, 2 or 3:30pm. The cost is $139 (£70) per person for the Dolphin Royal Swim. There are less-expensive programs that allow you to learn about, touch, and hold the dolphins (but not swim with them) starting at $79 (£40).

TURTLE SANCTUARY ⊛⊛   Years ago, fishermen converged on the island nightly from May to September to capture turtles when they would come ashore to lay eggs. Then a concerned fisherman, Gonzalo Chale Maldonado, began convincing others to spare at least the eggs, which he protected. It was a start. Following his lead, the fishing ministry founded the **Centro de Investigaciones Pesqueras** to find ways to protect the species and increase the turtle populations. Although the local government provides some assistance, most of the funding comes from private-sector donations. Since the center opened, tens of thousands of young turtles have been released, and local schoolchildren have participated, helping to educate a new generation of islanders for the cause. Releases are scheduled from May to October, and visitors are invited to take part. Inquire at the center.

   Three species of sea turtles nest on Isla Mujeres. An adult green turtle, the most abundant species, is 1 to 1.5m (3¼–5 ft.) long and can weigh 450 pounds. At the center, visitors walk through the indoor and outdoor turtle pool areas, where the creatures paddle around. Turtles are separated by age, from newly hatched up to 1 year. People who come here usually end up staying at least an hour, especially if they opt for the guided tour, which I recommend. They also have a small gift shop and snack bar. The sanctuary is on a spit of land jutting out from the island's west coast. The address is Carr. Sac Bajo #5; you'll need a taxi to get there. Admission is $2 (£1.50); the shelter is open daily from 9am to 5pm. For more information, call © **998/877-0595.**

GARRAFON NATIONAL PARK AND PUNTA SUR ☞☞   El Garrafón (© **998/ 849-4748;** www.garrafon.com) is at the southern end of the island. The pricy but well-equipped park has two restaurant/bars, beach chairs, a swimming pool, kayaks, changing rooms, rental lockers, showers, a gift shop, and snack bars. Once a public national underwater park, Garrafón is now operated by Dolphin Discovery. Public facilities have vastly improved, with the addition of new attractions and facilities each year. Activities include snorkeling and Snuba (a tankless version of scuba diving, when you descend while breathing through a long air tube); "Sea Trek," which allows you to explore the Caribbean seabed wearing a helmet with compressed air; crystal-clear canoes for viewing underwater life; and a zip-line that takes you over the water. On land, there are tanning decks, shaded hammocks, a 12m (40-ft.) climbing tower, and—of course—a souvenir superstore. A new panoramic tower had yet to open as of my last trip. At 50m (164-ft.) high, it will afford visitors a bird's-eye view of the entire island. Several restaurants and snack bars are available. Basic admission is $36 (£18); the all-inclusive package is $50 (£25; American Express, MasterCard, and Visa are accepted). More expensive packages include transportation and/or swims with dolphins at Dolphin Discovery. The park is open daily in high season from 9am to 5pm. In low season it closes for 2 or 3 days per week.

Next to the panoramic tower you'll find **Sculptured Spaces,** an impressive and extensive garden of large sculptures donated to Isla Mujeres by internationally renowned sculptors as part of the 2001 First International Sculpture Exhibition. Among Mexican sculptors represented by works are José Luis Cuevas and Vladimir Cora.

Nearby is the **Caribbean Village,** with narrow lanes of colorful clapboard buildings that house cafes and shops displaying folkloric art. Plan to have lunch or a snack here at the kiosk and stroll around, before heading on to the lighthouse and Maya ruins.

Also at this southern point of the island, and part of the ruins, is **Cliff of the Dawn,** the southeasternmost point of Mexico. Services are available from 9am to 5pm, but you can enter at any time; if you make it there early enough to see the sunrise, you can claim you were the first person in Mexico that day to be touched by the sun!

A MAYA RUIN ☞☞   Just beyond the lighthouse, at the southern end of the island, are the remains of a small Maya temple. Archaeologists believe it was dedicated to the moon and fertility goddess Ixchel. The location, on a lofty bluff overlooking the sea, is worth seeing and makes a great place for photos. It is believed that Maya women traveled here on annual pilgrimages to seek Ixchel's blessings of fertility.

A PIRATE'S FORTRESS   Almost in the middle of the island is large building purported to have been a pirate fortress. A slave trader who arrived here in the early 19th century, claimed to have been the pirate Mundaca Marecheaga. He set up a business selling slaves to Cuba and Belize and prospered here. According to island lore, a charming local girl captivated him, only to spurn him in favor of a local. Admission is $2 (£1); the fortress is open daily from 10am to 6pm.

A VISIT TO ISLA CONTOY Try to visit this pristine uninhabited island, 30km (20 miles) by boat from Isla Mujeres. It became a national wildlife reserve in 1981. Lush vegetation covers the oddly shaped island, which is 6km (3¾ miles) long and harbors 70 species of birds as well as a host of marine and animal life. Bird species that nest on the island include pelicans, brown boobies, frigates, egrets, terns, and cormorants. Flocks of flamingos arrive in April. Most excursions troll for fish (which will be your lunch), anchor en route for a snorkeling expedition, skirt the island at a leisurely pace for close viewing of the birds without disturbing the habitat, and then pull ashore. While the captain prepares lunch, visitors can swim, sun, follow the nature trails, and visit the fine nature museum, which has bathroom facilities. The trip from Isla Mujeres takes about 45 minutes each way and can be longer if the waves are choppy. Because of the tight-knit boatmen's cooperative, prices for this excursion are the same everywhere: $40 (£22). You can buy a ticket at the **Sociedad Cooperativa** on Avenida Rueda Medina, next to Mexico Divers and Las Brisas restaurant (© **998/ 877-1363**). Isla Contoy trips leave at 9am and return around 4:30pm. The price (cash only) is $55 (£28) for adults, $28 (£14) for children. Boat captains should respect the cooperative's regulations regarding ecological sensitivity and boat safety, including the availability of life jackets for everyone on board. If you're not given a life jacket, ask for one. Snorkeling equipment is usually included in the price, but double-check before heading out.

SHOPPING

Shopping is a casual activity here. Several shops, especially concentrated on Avenida Hidalgo, sell Saltillo rugs, onyx, silver, Guatemalan clothing, blown glassware, masks, folk art, beach paraphernalia, and T-shirts in abundance. Prices are lower than in Cancún or Cozumel.

WHERE TO STAY

You'll find plenty of hotels in all price ranges on Isla Mujeres. Rates peak during high season, which is the most expensive and most crowded time to go. Elizabeth Wenger of **Yucatán Peninsula Travel** in Montello, Wisconsin (© **800/552-4550** in the U.S.), specializes in Mexico travel and books a lot of hotels in Isla Mujeres. Her service is invaluable in the high season. Those interested in private home rentals or longer-term stays can contact **Mundaca Travel and Real Estate** in Isla Mujeres (© **998/877-0025;** fax 998/877-0076; www.mundaca.com.mx), or book online with **Isla Beckons** property rental service (www.islabeckons.com).

VERY EXPENSIVE

Casa de los Sueños Resort & Spa Zenter Originally built as a private residence and later converted into an adults-only boutique hotel in 1998, this property has nine guest rooms loaded with plush amenities and thoughtful comforts, and each comes with a balcony or terrace overlooking the water. There's an open breezeway, tropical gardens, a sunken living area (with Wi-Fi access), and an infinity pool that melts into the cool Caribbean waters. One master suite has an extra-large bathroom area with whirlpool and steam room/shower. The Zenter has an extensive menu of massages and holistic spa treatments, and yoga classes, held either outdoors or in a serene indoor space. The property is on the west side of the southern end of the island.

Carretera Garrafón Lote 9, Fracc. Mar Turquesa, 77400 Isla Mujeres, Q. Roo. © **998/877-0651** or -0369. Fax 998/877-0708. www.casadelossuenosresort.com. 9 units. High season $386–$496 (£193–£248) double; low season $330–$440 (£165–£220) double. Rates include continental breakfast and taxes. AE, MC, V. No one younger than 21.

Amenities: Restaurant; bar; infinity pool; tour desk; watersports equipment; spa; open-air massage area; room service; yoga center; nonsmoking rooms. *In room:* A/C, minibar, hair dryer, safe.

Hotel Villa Rolandi Gourmet & Beach Club ★★★ *(Moments)*   Villa Rolandi is a romantic escape on a little sheltered cove with a pristine white-sand beach. Each of the luxurious suites holds a separate sitting area and large terrace or balcony with private whirlpool overlooking the sea. All rooms feature in-room sound systems, subtle lighting, and marble surfaces. The bathrooms have Bulgari products and enticing showers with multiple showerheads that convert into steam baths. In-room breakfast is delivered through a small portal. The hotel spa also offers an outdoor Thalasso therapy whirlpool and beachside massages. The owner is a Swiss-born restaurateur who made a name for himself with his restaurants on Isla Mujeres and in Cancún. This intimate hideaway is ideal for honeymooners.

Fracc. Lagunamar, SM 7, Mza. 75, Locs. 15 and 16, 77400 Isla Mujeres, Q. Roo. (C) **998/877-0700.** Fax 998/877-0100. www.villarolandi.com. 28 units. High season $504 (£252) double, $560 (£280) junior suite; low season $358–$426 (£179–£213) double, $426–$492 (£213–£246) junior suite. Rates include continental breakfast, and a la carte lunch or dinner in the on-site restaurant. AE, MC, V. **Amenities:** Restaurant (see "Where to Dine," below); infinity pool w/waterfall; small fitness room; spa; airport transfer via van and catamaran; concierge; tour desk; room service; nonsmoking rooms. *In room:* TV, minibar, hair dryer, safe.

EXPENSIVE

Hotel Na Balam ★★ *(Finds)*   This popular, two-story hotel on Playa Norte has simple, comfortable rooms and well-tended beach grounds. Rooms are in three sections; some face the beach, and others are across the street in a garden setting with a swimming pool. The large rooms contain a king-size or two double beds, a seating area, folk-art decorations, and a terrace or balcony with hammocks. Master suites have additional amenities, including small pools with hydromassage. The older section is well kept and surrounds a peaceful, palm-filled, sandy inner yard and Playa Norte. The hotel gets a lot of Yoga practitioners and offers classes on a regular basis. The restaurant, **Zazil Ha,** is one of the island's most popular (see "Where to Dine," below). A beachside bar serves a selection of natural juices and is one of the most popular spots for sunset watching.

Zazil Ha 118, 77400 Isla Mujeres, Q. Roo. (C) **998/877-0279.** Fax 998/877-0446. www.nabalam.com. 33 units. High season $264–$496 (£132–£248) suite; low season $198–$416 (£99–£213) suite. Ask about weekly and monthly rates. AE, MC, V. **Amenities:** Restaurant; snack bar; bar; outdoor swimming pool; yoga classes; spa; mopeds, golf carts for rent; game room w/TV; diving and snorkeling trips available; salon; in-room massage; babysitting; laundry service; Wi-Fi. *In room:* A/C, minibar, hair dryer, safe, no phone.

Secreto ★★ *(Finds)*   This boutique hotel has a chic Mediterranean feel. It has nine suites that overlook an infinity-edge pool and the open sea beyond. Located on the northern end of the island, Secreto lies within walking distance of town, yet feels removed enough to make for an idyllic retreat. Tropical gardens surround the pool area, and an outdoor living area offers comfy couches and places to dine. Guest rooms are contemporary, featuring clean, white spaces and several extras. Each includes a veranda with private *cabaña* ideal for ocean-gazing beyond Halfmoon Beach. Three suites include king-size beds draped in mosquito netting, while the remaining six have two double beds. Secreto is distinguished by its style and service.

Sección Rocas, Lote 1, 77400 Isla Mujeres, Q. Roo. (C) **998/877-1039.** Fax 998/877-1048. www.hotelsecreto.com. 9 units. $252–$280 (£126–£140) double. Extra person $25 (£13). 1 child younger than 5 stays free in parent's room. Rates include continental breakfast. AE, MC, V. **Amenities:** Bar; coffee service; outdoor pool; tours, diving, and snorkeling available; dinner delivery from Rolandi's restaurant available; nonsmoking rooms. *In room:* A/C, TV/DVD, minibar, fridge, hairdryer, iron, safe, CD player.

MODERATE

Hotel Cabañas María del Mar ☞ A good choice for simple beach accommodations, the Cabañas María del Mar is on the popular Playa Norte. The older two-story section behind the reception area and beyond the garden offers nicely outfitted rooms facing the beach. All have two single or double beds, refrigerators, and oceanview balconies strung with hammocks. Eleven single-story *cabañas* closer to the reception area are decorated in a rustic Mexican style. The third section, **El Castillo,** is located across the street, over and beside Buho's restaurant. All rooms are "deluxe," though some are larger than others. The five rooms on the ground floor have large patios. Upstairs rooms have small balconies. Most have ocean views. The central courtyard contains a small pool.

Av. Arq. Carlos Lazo 1 (on Playa Norte, one-half block from the Hotel Na Balam), 77400 Isla Mujeres, Q. Roo. © 800/223-5695 in the U.S. and Canada, or 998/877-0179. Fax 998/877-0213. www.cabanasdelmar.com. 73 units. High season $134–$146 (£67–£73) double; low season $82–$108 (£41–£54) double. MC, V. **Amenities:** Pool; golf cart and *moto* rentals; nonsmoking rooms. *In room:* A/C, fridge (in some), safe.

INEXPENSIVE

Hotel Belmar ☞☞ In the center of Isla's entertainment district, this charming three-story hotel (no elevator) sits above Rolandi's restaurant. The simple, attractive rooms come with tile floors, nicely finished bathrooms, and either a king bed or two twins or two doubles. The rooms are well maintained and have good, quiet air conditioning. It's one of the few island hotels that offer televisions with U.S. channels. One large suite with a sitting area, large patio, and whirlpool goes for close to $100 (£50). The rooms have double-glazed windows. Though I had no trouble with noise from the restaurant in my third-floor room, light sleepers might want to look elsewhere.

Av. Hidalgo 110 (between Madero and Abasolo, 3½ blocks from the passenger-ferry pier), 77400 Isla Mujeres, Q. Roo. © 998/877-0430. Fax 998/877-0429. www.rolandi.com. 11 units. High season $56 (£28) double; low season $35–$45 (£18–£23) double. AE, MC, V. **Amenities:** Restaurant/bar (see "Where to Dine," below); room service; laundry service. *In room:* A/C, TV, fan.

Hotel D'Gomar *Value* This hotel is at the bottom of the inexpensive range while still being comfortable. The basic accommodations are regularly updated. Rooms have two double beds and a wall of windows affording breezes and views. The higher prices are for air-conditioned rooms. The hotel is four stories with no elevator, but it's conveniently located cater-cornered from the ferry pier (look right). The name of the hotel is the most visible sign on the skyline.

Rueda Medina 150, 77400 Isla Mujeres, Q. Roo. ©/fax 998/877-0541. www.hoteldgomar.com. 20 units. High season $60–$66 (£30–£33) double; low season $40–$56 (£20–£28) double. MC, V. *In room:* A/C (in some), fan, no phone.

Hotel Francis Arlene ☞ The Magaña family operates this neat little two-story inn built around a shady courtyard. It's bright, cheerful, well managed, and has attractive common spaces. For these reasons, it gets a lot of return guests; it's especially popular with families and seniors. Some rooms have ocean views, and all are remodeled or updated each year. They are comfortable, with tile floors, tiled bathrooms, and a very homey feel. Each downstairs room has a coffeemaker, refrigerator, and stove; each upstairs room comes with a refrigerator and toaster. Some have either a balcony or a patio. Higher prices are for the 14 rooms with air-conditioning; other units have fans. Rates are substantially better if quoted in pesos.

Guerrero 7 (5½ blocks inland from the ferry pier, between Abasolo and Matamoros), 77400 Isla Mujeres, Q. Roo. ℭ/fax **998/877-0310** or -0861. www.francisarlene.com. 24 units. High season $60–$90 (£30–£45) double; low season $45–$70 (£23–£35) double. MC, V. **Amenities:** Safe; currency exchange. *In room:* A/C (in some), kitchenettes (in some), fridge, no phone.

Hotel Posada del Mar *(Kids)*

Simply furnished, quiet, and comfortable, this long-established hotel faces the water 3 blocks north of the ferry pier. This is probably the best choice in Isla for families. For the spaciousness of the rooms (half of which have ocean views) and the location, it's also among the island's best values. A wide, appealing but seldom-used stretch of Playa Norte lies across the street, where watersports equipment is available for rent. A casual *palapa* bar and a lovely pool are on the back lawn along with hammocks, and the restaurant **Pinguinos** (see "Where to Dine," below) is by the sidewalk at the front of the property and also provides room service to hotel guests.

Av. Rueda Medina 15 A, 77400 Isla Mujeres, Q. Roo. ℭ **800/544-3005** in the U.S. and Canada, or 998/877-0044. Fax 998/877-0266. www.posadadelmar.com. 52 units. High season $110 (£55) double; low season $66 (£33) double. Children younger than 12 stay free in parent's room. AE, MC, V. **Amenities:** Restaurant/bar; outdoor pool. *In room:* A/C, TV, fan.

WHERE TO DINE

At the **Municipal Market,** next to the telegraph office and post office on Avenida Guerrero, obliging, hardworking women operate several little food stands. At the **Panadería La Reyna** (no phone), at Madero and Juárez, you can pick up inexpensive sweet bread, muffins, cookies, and yogurt. It's open Monday through Saturday from 7am to 9:30pm. For a frozen treat, check out **Cool** ice cream store (ℭ **998/167-6351**), on Av. Madero between Hidalgo and Juárez. It serves some wonderful flavors. The German and Peruvian owners might be opening another store on north Juárez.

EXPENSIVE

Casa Rolandi *(★★)* ITALIAN/SEAFOOD A gourmet restaurant that's outside town in the Villa Rolandi hotel, this place offers a beautiful setting with windows facing out over the western shore of the island and an open-air terrace. The menu here is more sophisticated than Rolandi's downtown, including some original creations not offered by the other locale. But there are several dishes common to both, including one of the signature dishes, *pescado a la sal* (fish baked in a cocoon of salt and egg whites). Both restaurants make good use of wood-burning stoves to produce some great baked fish dishes. And take care with the wood-oven-baked bread; it arrives looking like a puffer fish, and it's so divine you're apt to fill up on it. This is a great place to enjoy the sunset. They stock a selection of fine international wines and more than 80 premium tequilas. Service is personalized and attentive.

On the pier of Villa Rolandi, Lagunamar SM 7. ℭ **998/877-0700.** Reservations necessary. Main courses $8–$35 (£4–£18). AE, MC, V. Daily 7–10:30pm.

Sunset Grill *(★★)* SEAFOOD/STEAKS

This outdoor venue approaches the ideal for a beach restaurant, with its comfortable tables and chairs by the water, under a shady *palapa.* When the sun goes down, the restaurant sets up tables on the beach, and, weather permitting, there's no better ambience. The breakfasts are good, lunch includes a variety of sandwiches and burgers, and for dinner they serve such specialties as fish seared in a light *achiote* sauce, fish and chips, and a variety of steaks. To get to this restaurant, you have to walk through the parking lot of the Nautibeach Condominiums, which you access via a sand road that is the continuation of Rueda Medina.

Nautibeach Condominiums, North Beach. © 998/877-0785. Reservations recommended. Main courses $14–$24 (£7–£12); sandwiches and breakfasts $6–$9 (£3–£4.50). AE, MC, V. Daily 8am–9pm.

MODERATE

Angelo 𝒢 ITALIAN   An Italian restaurant in the town center, Angelo offers an enticing selection of antipasti, pasta, grilled seafood, and wood oven-baked pizzas. The Sardinian-born owner instills his menu with the flavors of his homeland, including a rich tomato sauce. Consider starting with a bowl of seafood soup or black mussels *au gratin* and continuing with the grilled shrimp kabobs or seafood pasta in an olive oil and white-wine sauce. The open-air restaurant includes an inviting sidewalk terrace and lies across the street from a casual Cuban restaurant also owned by Angelo.

Av. Hidalgo 14 (between Lopez Mateos and Matamoros). © 998/877-1273. Main courses $8–$12 (£4–£6). MC, V. Daily 4pm–midnight.

Pinguinos MEXICAN/SEAFOOD   Seafood grilled Mexican style is the specialty of this open-air restaurant and bar facing the ocean. Late in the evening, it's sometimes a place to party. Dishes include fresh lobster—you'll get a large, beautifully presented lobster tail with a choice of butter, garlic, and secret sauces. The grilled seafood platter, seafood casserole, and fajitas are also standouts. Breakfasts include fresh fruit, yogurt, and granola, or sizable platters of eggs, served with homemade wheat bread.

In front of the Hotel Posada del Mar (3 blocks west of the ferry pier), Av. Rueda Medina 15-A. © 998/877-0044, ext. 157. Breakfast $4–$8 (£2–£4); main courses $5–$12 (£2.50–£6); lobster $15–$40 (£7.50–£20). AE, MC, V. Daily 7am–11pm; bar closes at midnight.

Rolandi's 𝒢 ITALIAN/SEAFOOD   This restaurant is an Isla institution. The plate-size pizzas and calzones feature exotic ingredients—including lobster, black mushrooms, pineapple, and Roquefort cheese—as well as more traditional tomatoes, olives, basil, and salami. A wood-burning oven imparts the signature flavor of the pizzas, as well as baked chicken, roast beef, and mixed seafood casserole with lobster. The extensive menu offers a selection of salads and appetizers, plus an ample array of homemade pasta dishes, steaks, fish, and desserts. The setting is the open courtyard of the Hotel Belmar, with a porch overlooking the action on Avenida Hidalgo.

Av. Hidalgo 10 (3½ blocks inland from the pier, between Madero and Abasolo). © 998/877-0430, ext. 18. Main courses $8–$16 (£4–£8). AE, MC, V. Daily 11am–11pm.

Zazil Ha 𝒢𝒢 CARIBBEAN/INTERNATIONAL   Here you can enjoy some of the island's best food while sitting at tables on the sand among palms and gardens. Come night, candlelit tables sparkle underneath the open-air *palapa*. Specialties include Mayan chicken stuffed with corn mushroom and goat cheese, black pasta with calamari and pesto sauce, and fish of the day with *achiote* sauce draped in a banana leaf. A selection of fresh juices complements the vegetarian options, and there's even a special menu for those participating in yoga retreats. The delicious breads are baked in house. Between the set meal times, you can order all sorts of enticing food, such as tacos and sandwiches, ceviche, terrific nachos, and vegetable and fruit drinks.

At the Hotel Na Balam (at the end of Playa Norte, almost at the end of Calle Zazil Ha). © 998/877-0279. Fax 998/877-0446. Breakfast $4–$10 (£2–£5); main courses $8–$22 (£4–£11). AE, MC, V. Daily 7:30am–10:30pm.

INEXPENSIVE

Café Cito CREPES/SANDWICHES/COFFEE/FRUIT DRINKS   Brisa and Luis Rivera own this adorable, Caribbean-blue corner restaurant where you can begin the day with flavorful coffee and a croissant and cream cheese (this is the only place in town where you can have breakfast until 2pm). Terrific crepes come with yogurt, ice cream, fresh fruit, or *dulce de leche* (caramel sauce made from goat's milk), as well as ham and cheese.

Calle Matamoros 42, at Juárez. ℂ 998/877-1470. Crepes $3–$6 (£1.50–£3); breakfast $4–$6 (£1.95–£3); sandwiches $3.50–$4.50 (£1.95–£2.50). No credit cards. Daily 7am–2pm.

ISLA MUJERES AFTER DARK

Those in a party mood by day's end may want to start out at the beach bar of the **Na Balam** hotel on Playa Norte, which usually hosts a crowd until around midnight. On Saturday and Sunday, live music plays between 4 and 7pm. **Jax Bar & Grill** on Avenida Ruedo Medina, close to Hotel Posada del Mar, is a Texas-style sports bar offering live music nightly. **Las Palapas Chimbo's** restaurant on the beach becomes a jammin' dance joint with a live band from 9pm until whenever. Farther along the same stretch of beach, **Buho's**, the restaurant/beach bar of the Cabañas María del Mar, has its moments as a popular, low-key hangout, complete with swinging seats over the sand! **Pinguinos** in the Hotel Posada del Mar offers a convivial late-night hangout, where a band plays nightly during high season from 9pm to midnight. If you want to sample one of nearly 100 tequila brands on a relaxing sidewalk terrace, stop by **La Adelita,** located at Av. Hidalgo 12 and open nightly from 5:30pm to 2:30am. Near Matamoros and Hidalgo, **KoKo Nuts** caters to a younger crowd, with international music for late-night dancing. **Om Bar and Chill Lounge,** on Calle Matamoros, serves cocktails in an atmosphere that includes jazzy Latino music, open from 6pm to 2am. For a late-night dance club, **Club Nitrox,** on Avenida Guererro, is open Wednesday to Sunday from 9pm to 3am. In general, the crowds hitting these bars are in their 20s.

2 Cozumel ✭✭✭

70km (43 miles) S of Cancún; 19km (12 miles) SE of Playa del Carmen

Cozumel has ranked for years among the top five dive destinations in the world. Tall reefs line the southwest coast, creating towering walls that offer divers a fairy-tale landscape to explore. For nondivers, it has the beautiful water of the Caribbean with all the accompanying watersports and seaside activities. The island gets a lot more visitors from North America than Europe for reasons that probably have to do with the limited flights. It is in many ways more cozy and mellow than the mainland—no big highways, no big construction projects. It's dependable. And one of my favorite things about this island is that the water on the protected side (western shore) is as calm as an aquarium, unless a front is blowing through. The island is 45km (28 miles) long and 18km (11 miles) wide, and lies 19km (12 miles) from the mainland. Most of the terrain is flat and clothed in a low tropical forest.

The only town on the island is San Miguel, which, despite the growth of the last 20 years, can't be called anything more than a small town. It's not a stunningly beautiful town, but it and its inhabitants are agreeable—life moves along at a slow pace, and every Sunday evening, residents congregate around the plaza to enjoy live music and see their friends. Staying in town can be fun and convenient. You get a choice of a number of restaurants and nightspots.

Because Cozumel enjoys such popularity with the cruise ships, the waterfront section of town holds wall-to-wall jewelry stores, duty-free, and souvenir shops. This and the area around the town's main square are about as far as most cruise-ship passengers venture into town.

Should you come down with a case of island fever, **Playa del Carmen** and the mainland are a 40-minute ferry ride away. Some travel agencies on the island can set you up with a tour of the major ruins on the mainland, such as **Tulum** or **Chichén Itzá,** or a visit to a nature park such as **Xel-Ha** or **Xcaret** (see "Trips to the Mainland," later in this chapter).

The island has its own ruins, but they cannot compare with the major sites of the mainland. During pre-Hispanic times, Maya women would cross over to the island to make offerings to the goddess of fertility, Ixchel. More than 40 sites containing shrines remain around the island, and archaeologists still uncover the small dolls that were customarily part of those offerings.

ESSENTIALS
GETTING THERE & DEPARTING

BY PLANE   During high season, there are several more international commercial flights in and out of Cozumel's airport (CZM) than in low season, including a few flights from northern U.S. cities. You might also inquire about buying a ticket on one of the charter flights. Some packagers, such as **FunJet** (www.funjet.com), will sell you just a ticket. But look into packages, too. Several of the island's independent hotels work with packagers.

BY FERRY   Passenger ferries run to and from Playa del Carmen. **Barcos México** (© 987/872-1508 or -1588) and **Ultramar** (© 987/869-2775) offer departures almost every hour in the morning and about every 2 hours in the afternoon. The schedules change according to seasons. The trip takes 30 to 45 minutes, depending on conditions, and costs $11 (£5.50) one-way. The boats are air-conditioned. In Playa del Carmen, the ferry dock is 1½ blocks from the main square. In Cozumel, the ferries use Muelle Fiscal, the town pier, a block from the main square. Luggage storage at the Cozumel dock costs $2 (£1) per day.

The car ferry that used to operate from Puerto Morelos now uses the Calica pier just south of Playa del Carmen. The fare for a standard car is $80 (£40). **Marítima Chancanaab** (© 987/872-7671 or -7504) has four departures daily from Calica at 4am, 8am, 1:30pm, and 6pm. Arrive 1 hour before departure. The schedule is subject to change, so double-check it. The ferry docks in Cozumel at the **Muelle Internacional** (the **International Pier,** which is south of town near La Ceiba Hotel).

BY BUS   If you plan to travel on the mainland by bus, there is a ticket office for **ADO buses** called **Ticket Bus** where you can purchase tickets in advance. One is located on the municipal pier and is open while the ferries are running. Another is on Calle 2 Norte and Avenida 10 (© 987/872-1706). Hours are from 8am to 9pm daily.

ORIENTATION

ARRIVING   Cozumel's **airport** is inland from downtown. **Transportes Terrestres** provides hotel transportation in air-conditioned Suburbans. Buy your ticket as you

---

Tips **Be Streetwise**

North–south streets—the *avenidas*—have the right of way, and traffic doesn't slow down or stop.

Cozumel

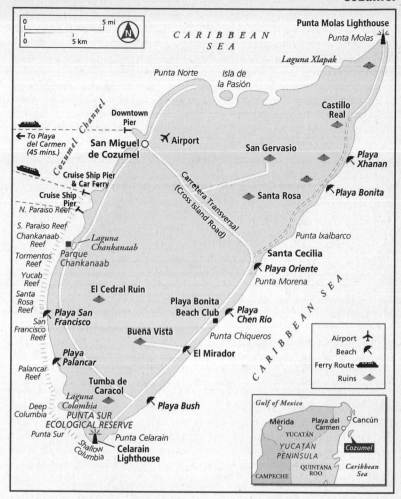

exit the terminal. To hotels downtown, the fare is $7 (£3.50) per person; to hotels along the north shore, $10 (£5), and to hotels along the south shore, $11 to $15 (£5.50–£7.50). Passenger ferries arrive at the Muelle Fiscal, the municipal pier, by the town's main square. Cruise ships dock at the **Punta Langosta** pier, several blocks south of the Muelle Fiscal, and at the **International Pier,** which is at Km 4 of the southern coastal road. A third cruise ship pier, the **Puerta Maya,** suffered the most damage from Hurricane Wilma and will be nonoperational for at least another year. The International Pier was also damaged, but one side was working when I was last on the island, and the other side was scheduled to open sometime in 2008. On days when several cruise ships arrive, some of the boats will anchor offshore, and tender boats will ferry passengers and crew to land. It seems to be working smoothly—I heard no complaints from passengers.

An All-Inclusive Vacation in Cozumel

Booking a room at an all-inclusive should be done through a vacation packager. Booking lodging directly through the hotel usually doesn't make sense, even with frequent-flier mileage to burn, because the discounts offered by most packagers are so deep. I include websites for you to find out more info about the properties, but don't expect to find clear info on rates. The game of setting rates with these hotels is complicated and always in flux. All these beach properties made significant upgrades to the rooms when they made repairs after the hurricane, so expect such things as new mattresses and extra amenities.

Two all-inclusives are north of town: **El Cozumeleño** (www.elcozumeleno. com) and the **Meliá Cozumel** (www.meliacozumel.com). Both occupy multi-story modern buildings. Both have attractive rooms. El Cozumeleño is the larger of the two resorts and has the nicest hotel pool on the island. It's best suited for active types. The Meliá is quieter and offers golf discounts for the nearby golf course. The Cozumeleño has a small beach that was lost with Wilma, but the hotel brought in sand to replace what was lost and is back to normal. The Meliá's beach is long and narrow and pretty, but occasionally seaweed washes up, which doesn't happen on the rest of the island's coast. The advantages of staying in these two are the proximity to town, with its restaurants, clubs, movie theaters, and so on, and the fact that most rooms at these hotels come with views of the ocean.

A recent addition to the all-inclusives is the **Cozumel Palace** (www.palace resorts.com). It's right on the water on the southern fringes of town, occupying the property that used to be Plaza las Glorias. It's right on the water,

VISITOR INFORMATION   The **Municipal Tourism Office** (©/fax **987/869-0212**) has an information booth at the municipal ferry pier, on the main square. It's open 8am to 8pm Monday to Saturday. There are other information booths at each of the ferry piers and at the airport.

CITY LAYOUT   San Miguel's main waterfront street is **Avenida Rafael Melgar.** Running parallel to Rafael Melgar are other *avenidas* numbered in multiples of five—5, 10, 15. **Avenida Juárez** runs perpendicular to these, heading inland from the ferry dock. Avenida Juárez divides the town into northern and southern halves. The *calles* (streets) that parallel Juárez to the north have even numbers. The ones to the south have odd numbers, except for Calle Rosado Salas, which runs between calles 1 and 3.

ISLAND LAYOUT   One road runs along the western coast of the island, which faces the Yucatán mainland. It has different names. North of town it's **Santa Pilar** or **San Juan;** in the city it is **Avenida Rafael Melgar;** south of town it's **Costera Sur.** Hotels stretch along this road north and south of town. The road runs to the southern tip of the island (Punta Sur), passing **Chankanaab National Park. Avenida Juárez** (and its extension, the **Carretera Transversal**) runs east from the town across the island. It passes the airport and the turnoff to the ruins of San Gervasio before but without a beach. But that's not so bad. The water is usually so calm on Cozumel's west shore that swimming here is like swimming in the pool, and you can snorkel right out of the hotel.

Of the all-inclusives to the south, my favorites are the two **Occidental** properties (**Allegro Cozumel** and **Grand Cozumel;** www.occidentalhotels.com) and the **Iberostar Cozumel** (www.iberostar.com). These are village-style resorts with two- and three-story buildings, often with thatched roofs, spread over a large area at the center of which is the pool and activities area. The Allegro is older than the other two and has the plainest rooms, but these were completely remodeled after the hurricane. The Grand Cozumel, next door to the Allegro, is the newest property. Its rooms are larger and more attractive than the Allegro, and staying here gives you access to both Occidental resorts. Like the Occidental chain, Iberostar has several properties in the Mexican Caribbean. This one is the smallest. I like its food and service and the beauty of the grounds. The rooms are attractive and well maintained. The added sand from Wilma improved the resort a lot. The advantage to staying in these places is that you're close to a lot of dive sites; the disadvantage is that you're somewhat isolated from town, and you don't have the views that the taller buildings in the north give you.

Of the other all-inclusives, I've heard several complaints about the service at the **Reef Club** (unless you stay in the VIP section), and I think the rooms are too closely set together. The **Costa Club** is on the inland side of the road in a crowded section of the island.

reaching the undeveloped ocean side of the island. It then turns south and follows the coast to the southern tip, where it meets the Costera Sur.

GETTING AROUND   You can walk to most destinations in town. Getting to out-lying hotels and beaches requires a taxi, rental car, or moped.

Car rentals are roughly the same price as on the mainland, depending on demand. **Avis** (© 987/872-0099) and **Executive** (© 987/872-1308) have counters in the air-port. Other major rental companies have offices in town. Rentals are easy to arrange through your hotel or at any of the many local rental offices.

Moped rentals are readily available and cost $20 to $40 (£15–£20) for 24 hours, depending upon the season. If you rent a moped, be careful. Riding a moped made a lot more sense when Cozumel had less traffic; now it involves a certain amount of risk as taxi drivers and other motorists have become more numerous and pushier. Moped accidents easily rank as the greatest cause of injury in Cozumel. Before renting one, inspect it carefully to see that all the gizmos—horn, light, starter, seat, mirror—are in good shape. I've been offered mopeds with unbalanced wheels, which made them unsteady at higher speeds, but the renter quickly exchanged them upon my request. You are required to stay on paved roads. It's illegal to ride a moped without a helmet outside of town (subject to a $25/£13 fine).

Cozumel has lots of **taxis** and a strong drivers' union. Fares have been standardized—there's no bargaining. Here are a few sample fares for two people (there is an additional charge for extra passengers to most destinations): island tour, $50 (£25); town to southern hotel zone, $6 to $18 (£3–£9); town to northern hotels, $5 to $7 (£2.50–£3.50); town to Chankanaab, $10 (£5) for up to four people; in and around town, $3 to $4 (£1.50–£2).

FAST FACTS: Cozumel

Area Code The telephone area code is **987.**

Climate From October to December there can be strong winds all over the Yucatán, as well as some rain. June through October is the rainy season.

Clinics **Médica San Miguel** (✆ **987/872-0103**) works for most things and includes intensive-care facilities. It's on Calle 6 Norte between Av. 5 and 10. **Centro Médico Cozumel** (✆ **987/872-3545**) is an alternative. It's at the intersection of Calle 1 Sur and Av. 50.

Currency Exchange The island has several banks and *casas de cambio,* as well as ATMs. Most places accept dollars, but you usually get a better deal paying in pesos.

Diving Bring proof of your diver's certification and your log. Underwater currents can be strong, and many of the reef drops are quite steep, so dive operators want to make sure divers are experienced.

Emergencies To report an emergency, dial ✆ **065,** which is similar to 911 emergency service in the United States.

Internet Access Several cybercafes are in and about the main square. If you go just a bit off Avenida Rafael Melgar and the main square, prices drop. **Modutel,** Av. Juárez 15 (at Av. 10), offers good rates. Hours are Monday through Saturday from 10am to 8pm.

Post Office The *correo* is on Avenida Rafael Melgar at Calle 7 Sur (✆ **987/872-0106**), at the southern edge of town. It's open Monday through Friday from 9am to 3pm, Saturday from 9am to noon.

Recompression Chamber There are four *cámaras de recompresión.* The best are **Buceo Médico Mexicano,** staffed 24 hours, at Calle 5 Sur 21-B, between Avenida Rafael Melgar and Avenida 5 Sur (✆ **987/872-2387** or -1430); and the **Hyperbaric Center of Cozumel** (✆ **987/872-3070**) at Calle 6 Norte, between avenidas 5 and 10.

Seasons High season is August and from Christmas to Easter.

EXPLORING THE ISLAND

For **diving** and **snorkeling,** there are plenty of dive shops to choose from, including those recommended below. For **island tours, ruins tours** on and off the island, **evening cruises,** and other activities, go to a travel agency, such as **InterMar Cozumel Viajes,** Calle 2 Norte 101-B, between avenidas 5 and 10 (✆ **987/872-1535** or -2022;

San Miguel de Cozumel

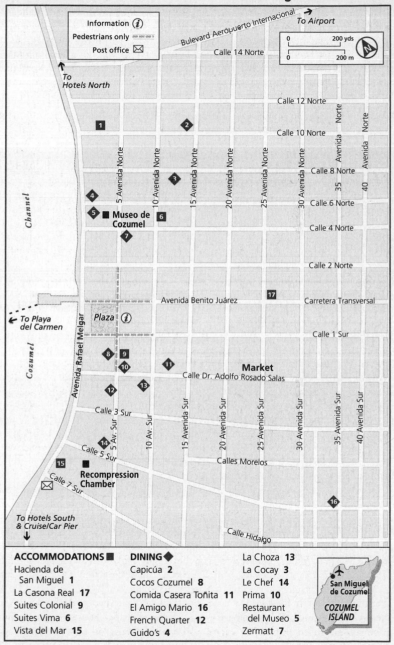

Information (i)
Pedestrians only
Post office ✉

To Airport

Bulevard Aeropuerto Internacional

Calle 14 Norte

0   200 yds
0   200 m

To
Hotels North

To Playa
del Carmen

To Hotels South
& Cruise/Car Pier

Channel

Cozumel

Avenida Rafael Melgar

5 Avenida Norte
10 Avenida Norte
15 Avenida Norte
20 Avenida Norte
25 Avenida Norte
30 Avenida Norte
35 Avenida Norte
40 Avenida Norte

Calle 12 Norte
Calle 10 Norte
Calle 8 Norte
Calle 6 Norte
Calle 4 Norte
Calle 2 Norte

Museo de
Cozumel

Avenida Benito Juárez

Carretera Transversal

Plaza (i)

Calle 1 Sur

Market
Calle Dr. Adolfo Rosado Salas

5 Av. Sur
10 Av. Sur
15 Avenida Sur
20 Avenida Sur
25 Avenida Sur
30 Avenida Sur
35 Avenida Sur
40 Avenida Sur

Calle 3 Sur
Calle 5 Sur
Calles Morelos
Calle 7 Sur

Recompression
Chamber

Calle Hidalgo

ACCOMMODATIONS ■
Hacienda de
  San Miguel 1
La Casona Real 17
Suites Colonial 9
Suites Vima 6
Vista del Mar 15

DINING ◆
Capicúa 2
Cocos Cozumel 8
Comida Casera Toñita 11
El Amigo Mario 16
French Quarter 12
Guido's 4

La Choza 13
La Cocay 3
Le Chef 14
Prima 10
Restaurant
  del Museo 5
Zermatt 7

San Miguel
de Cozumel

COZUMEL
ISLAND

Carnaval

Carnaval (similar to Mardi Gras) is Cozumel's most colorful fiesta. It begins the Thursday before Ash Wednesday, with daytime street dancing and nighttime parades on Thursday, Saturday, and Monday (the best).

fax 987/872-0895; cozumel@travel2mexico.com). Office hours are Monday through Saturday from 8am to 8pm, Sunday from 9am to 5pm.

WATERSPORTS

SCUBA DIVING   Cozumel is the number-one dive destination in the Western Hemisphere. Don't forget your dive card and dive log. Dive shops will rent you scuba gear, but won't take you out on a boat until you show some documentation. If you have a medical condition, bring a letter signed by a doctor stating that you've been cleared to dive. A two-tank morning dive costs from $60 to $85 (£30–£43); some shops offer an additional afternoon one-tank dive for $30 (£15) for those who took the morning dives. A lot of divers save some money by buying a dive package with a hotel. These usually include two dives a day.

Diving in Cozumel is drift diving, which can be a little disconcerting for novices. The current that sweeps along Cozumel's reefs, pulling nutrients into them and making them as large as they are, also dictates how you dive here. The problem is that it pulls at different speeds at different depths and in different places. When it's pulling strong, it can quickly scatter a dive group. The role of the dive master becomes more important, especially with choosing the dive location. Cozumel has a lot of dive locations. To mention but a few: the famous **Palancar Reef,** with its caves and canyons, plentiful fish, and sea coral; the monstrous **Santa Rosa Wall,** famous for its depth, sea life, coral, and sponges; the **San Francisco Reef,** with a shallower drop-off wall and fascinating sea life; and the **Yucab Reef,** with its beautiful coral.

I've seen a number of news reports about reef damage caused by hurricane Wilma. Almost all of it occurred in the shallower parts, above 15m (50 ft.). In deeper areas, the currents produced by Wilma actually improved matters by clearing sand away from parts of the reef, and in some cases exposing new caverns. Wildlife is plentiful. In the shallow parts fan coral and such are gradually growing back.

Finding a dive shop in town is even easier than finding a jewelry store. Cozumel has more than 50 dive operators. I know and can recommend Bill Horn's **Aqua Safari,** which has a location on Avenida Rafael Melgar at Calle 5 (© **987/872-0101;** fax 987/872-0661; www.aquasafari.com). I also know Roberto Castillo at **Liquid Blue Divers** (© **987/869-2812;** www.liquidbluedivers.com), on Avenida 5 between Rosado Salas and Calle 3 Sur. He does a good tour, has a fast boat, and keeps the number of divers to 12 or fewer. His wife, Michelle, handles the Internet inquiries and reservations and is quick to respond to questions.

A popular activity in the Yucatán is cenote diving. The peninsula's underground **cenotes** (seh-*noh*-tehs)—sinkholes or wellsprings—lead to a vast system of underground caverns. The gently flowing water is so clear that divers seem to float on air through caves complete with stalactites and stalagmites. If you want to try this but didn't plan a trip to the mainland, contact **Yucatech Expeditions,** Avenida 5, on the corner of Calle 3 Sur (©/fax **987/872-5659;** www.yucatech.net), which offers a trip five times a week. Cenotes are 30 to 45 minutes from Playa del Carmen, and a dive in each cenote lasts around 45 minutes. Dives are within the daylight zone, about 40m (131 ft.) into the caverns, and no more than 18m (59 ft.) deep. Company owner Germán Yañez Mendoza inspects diving credentials carefully, and divers must meet his list of requirements before cave diving is permitted. For information and prices, call or drop by the office.

SNORKELING   Anyone who can swim can snorkel. When contracting for a snorkel tour, stay away from the companies that cater to the cruise ships. Those tours are crowded and not very fun. For a good snorkeling tour, contact **Victor Casanova** (© 987/872-1028; wildcatcozumel@hotmail.com). He speaks English, owns a couple of boats, and does a good 5-hour tour. He takes his time and doesn't rush through the trip. You can also try the **Kuzamil Snorkeling Center,** 50 Av. bis 565 Int. 1, between 5 Sur and Hidalgo, Colonia Adolfo López Mateos (© 987/872-4637 or -0539). Even though you won't see a lot of the more delicate structures, such as fan coral, you will still see plenty of sea creatures and enjoy the clear, calm water of Cozumel's protected west side.

BOAT TRIPS   Travel agencies and hotels can arrange boat trips, a popular pastime on Cozumel. There are evening cruises, cocktail cruises, glass-bottom boat cruises, and other options. One novel boat ride is offered by **Atlantis Submarines** (© 987/872-5671). The sub can hold 48 people. It operates almost 3km (2 miles) south of town in front of the Casa del Mar hotel and costs $81 (£41) per adult, $46 (£23) for kids ages 4 to 12. This is a superior experience to the **Sub See Explorer** offered by **Aqua World,** which is really just a glorified glass-bottom boat.

FISHING   The best months for fishing are March through June, when the catch includes blue and white marlin, sailfish, tarpon, and swordfish. The least expensive option would be to contact a boat owner directly. Try Victor Casanova, listed above under "Snorkeling." Or try an agency such as **Aquarius Travel Fishing,** Calle 3 Sur 2 between Avenida Rafael Melgar and Avenida 5 (© 987/872-1092; gabdiaz@yahoo.com).

CHANKANAAB NATIONAL PARK & PUNTA SUR ECOLOGICAL RESERVE

Chankanaab National Park ❀ is the pride of many islanders. In Mayan, Chankanaab means "little sea," which refers to a beautiful land-locked pool connected to the sea through an underwater tunnel—a sort of miniature ocean. Snorkeling in this natural aquarium is not permitted, but the park has a beach for sunbathing and snorkeling. Arrive before 9am to stake out a chair and *palapa* before the cruise-ship crowd arrives. The snorkeling is also best before noon. There are bathrooms, lockers, a gift shop, several snack huts, a restaurant, and a *palapa* for renting snorkeling gear.

You can also swim with dolphins. **Dolphin Discovery** (© 800/293-9698; www.dolphindiscovery.com) has several programs for experiencing these sea creatures. These are popular, so plan ahead—you should make reservations well in advance. The surest way is through the website—make sure to pick the Cozumel location, as there are a couple of others on this coast. There are three different programs for swimming with dolphins. The one of longest duration costs $139 (£70) and features close interaction with the beautiful swimmers. There are also swim and snorkel programs for $75 and $100 (£38–£50) that get you in the water with these creatures.

Surrounding the land-locked pool is a botanical garden that did suffer greatly from the hurricane and will take some time to come back. Admission to the park is expensive, costing $17 (£8.50) for adults, $8 (£4) for children 9 to 12. I think the authorities are trying to recoup some of the money spent restoring the park, and it is being marketed to the cruise-ship crowd. The park is open daily from 8am to 5pm. It's south of town, just past the Fiesta Americana Hotel. Taxis run constantly between the park, the hotels, and town ($10/£5 from town for up to four people).

Punta Sur Ecological Reserve (admission $10/£5) is a large area that encompasses the southern tip of the island, including the Columbia Lagoon. The only practical way of going there is to rent a car or scooter; there is no taxi stand, and, usually, few people. This is an ecological reserve, not a park, so don't expect much infrastructure. The reserve has an information center, several observation towers, and a snack bar. The observation towers were destroyed in the hurricane and were still not reconstructed on my last visit. The information center was struck hard, too. And many of the trees on this side of the island came down, while others completely lost their leaves. These will make a comeback, but before you go all the way out to the park and pay admission, ask around about the condition of the vegetation—it adds a good bit to a visit here. Punta Sur has some interesting snorkeling (bring your own gear), and lovely beaches that are kept as natural as possible. Regular hours are daily 9am to 5pm.

THE BEACHES

Along both the west and east sides of the island you'll see signs advertising beach clubs. A "beach club" in Cozumel can mean just a *palapa* hut that's open to the public and serves soft drinks, beer, and fried fish. It can also mean a recreational beach with the full gamut of offerings from banana boats to parasailing. They also usually have locker rooms, a pool, and food. The two biggest of these are **Mr. Sancho's** (© 987/879-0021; www.mrsanchos.com) and **Playa Mía** (© 987/872-9030; www.playamia.com). They get a lot of business from the cruise ships. Mr. Sancho's is free, while Playa Mía charges between $12 (£6) for simple admission to $42 (£21) for the full all-inclusive package. Quieter versions of beach clubs are **Playa San Francisco** (no phone), **Paradise Beach** (no phone, next to Playa San Francisco), and **Playa Palancar** (no phone). All of these beaches are south of Chankanaab Park and easily visible from the road. Several have swimming pools with beach furniture, a restaurant, and snorkel rental. Most of these beaches cost around $5 (£2.50).

Once you get to the end of the island, the beach clubs become simple places where you can eat, drink, and lay out on the beach for free. **Paradise Cafe** is on the southern tip of the island across from Punta Sur Nature Park, and as you go up the eastern side of the island you pass **Playa Bonita, Chen Río,** and **Punta Morena** (not yet back in business on my last visit). Except on Sunday, when the locals head for the beaches, these places are practically deserted. Most of the east coast is unsafe for swimming because of the surf. The beaches tend to be small and occupy gaps in the rocky coast.

TOURS OF THE ISLAND

Travel agencies can arrange a variety of tours, including horseback, Jeep, and ATV tours. Taxi drivers charge $50 (£25) for a 4-hour tour of the island, which most people would consider only mildly amusing, depending on the driver's personality. The best horseback tours are offered at **Rancho Palmitas** (no phone) on the Costera Sur highway, across from the Occidental Cozumel resort. Unless you're staying in a resort on the south end, talk to the owners of Cocos Cozumel restaurant to arrange a tour (see the listing later in this chapter, making sure to note the limited hours). Rides can be from 1 to 2½ hours long and cost $20 to $30 (£10–£15).

OTHER ATTRACTIONS

MAYA RUINS   One of the most popular island excursions is to **San Gervasio** (100 B.C.–A.D. 1600). Follow the paved transversal road. You'll see the well-marked turnoff about halfway between town and the eastern coast. About 3km (2 miles) farther, pay the $6 (£3) fee to enter; still and video camera permits cost $5 (£2.50) each. A small tourist center at the entrance sells cold drinks and snacks. The ruins are open from 7am to 4pm.

When it comes to Cozumel's Maya ruins, getting there is most of the fun—do it for the mystique and for the trip, not for the size or scale of the ruins. The buildings, though preserved, are crudely made and would not be much of a tourist attraction if they were not the island's principal ruins. More significant than beautiful, this site was once an important ceremonial center where the Maya gathered, coming even from the mainland. The important deity was Ixchel, the goddess of weaving, women, childbirth, pilgrims, the moon, and medicine. Although you won't see any representations of Ixchel at San Gervasio today, Bruce Hunter, in his *Guide to Ancient Maya Ruins,* writes that priests hid behind a large pottery statue of her and became the voice of the goddess, speaking to pilgrims and answering their petitions. Ixchel was the wife of Itzamná, the sun god.

Guides charge $20 (£10) for a tour for one to six people. A better option is to find a copy of the green booklet *San Gervasio,* sold at local checkout counters and bookstores, and tour the site on your own. Seeing it takes 30 minutes. Taxi drivers offer a tour for about $30 (£15); the driver will wait for you outside the ruins.

A HISTORY MUSEUM   The **Museo de la Isla de Cozumel** ⚓, Avenida Rafael Melgar between calles 4 and 6 Norte (© **987/872-1475**), is more than just a nice place to spend a rainy hour. On the first floor an exhibit illustrates endangered species, the origin of the island, and its present-day topography and plant and animal life, including an explanation of coral formation. The second-floor galleries feature the history of the town, artifacts from the island's pre-Hispanic sites, and Colonial-Era cannons, swords, and ship paraphernalia. It's open daily from 9am to 5pm (but closes at 4pm on Sundays). Admission is $3 (£1.50). A rooftop restaurant serves breakfast and lunch (and you don't need to pay admission to eat there).

GOLF   Cozumel has a new 18-hole course designed by Jack Nicklaus. It's at the **Cozumel Country Club** (© **987/872-9570**), north of San Miguel. Greens fees are $169 (£85) for a morning tee time, including cart rental and tax. Afternoon tee times cost $105 (£53). Tee times can be reserved 3 days in advance. A few hotels have special memberships with discounts for guests and advance tee times; guests at Playa Azul Golf and Beach Club pay no greens fees, but the cart costs $25 (£13).

TRIPS TO THE MAINLAND

PLAYA DEL CARMEN & XCARET   Going on your own to the nearby seaside village of **Playa del Carmen** and the **Xcaret** nature park is as easy as a quick ferry ride from Cozumel (for ferry information, see "Getting There & Departing," earlier in this chapter). For information on Playa and Xcaret, see chapter 16. Cozumel travel agencies offer an Xcaret tour that includes the ferry ride, transportation to the park, and the admission fee. The price is $100 (£55) for adults, $55 (£30) for kids. The tour is available Monday through Saturday.

CHICHEN ITZA, TULUM & COBA Travel agencies can arrange day trips to the ruins of **Chichén Itzá** 🗝🗝🗝 by air or bus. The ruins of **Tulum** 🗝, overlooking the Caribbean, and **Cobá** 🗝, in a dense jungle setting, are closer and cost less to visit. These latter two cities are quite a contrast to Chichén Itzá. Cobá is a large, mostly unrestored city beside a lake in a remote jungle setting, while Tulum is smaller, more compact, and right on the beach. It's more intact than Cobá. A trip to both Cobá and Tulum begins at 8am and returns around 6pm. A shorter, more relaxing excursion goes to Tulum and the nearby nature park of Xel-Ha.

SHOPPING

If you're looking for silver jewelry or souvenirs, go no farther than the town's coastal avenue, Rafael Melgar. Along this road you find one store after another—jewelry, souvenirs, and duty-free merchandise. But, if you're looking for something original, seek out a gallery and store called **Inspiración** (© 987/869-8293) on Avenida 5 between Rosado Salas and Calle 3. Owner Dianne Hartwig displays the creations of some of the best-known folk artists in the Yucatan—objects that are very hard to come by if you don't actually go the villages where many of these artists live. She also represents some talented contemporary local artists. Stores carrying Mexican handicrafts include **Los Cinco Soles** (© 987/872-2040), **Indigo** (© 987/872-1076), and **Viva México** (© 987/872-5466). All of these are on Avenida Rafael Melgar. There are also some import/export stores in the Punta Langosta Shopping Center in the southern part of town in front of the cruise ship pier. Prices for serapes, T-shirts, and the like are lower on the side streets off Avenida Melgar.

WHERE TO STAY

I've grouped Cozumel's hotels by location—**north** of town, **in town,** and **south** of town—and I describe them in that order. The prices I've quoted are rack rates and include the 12% tax. High season is from December to Easter. Expect rates from Christmas to New Year's to be still higher than the regular high-season rates quoted here. Low season is the rest of the year, though a few hotels raise their rates in August when Mexican families go on vacations.

All of the beach hotels in Cozumel, even the small ones, have deals with vacation packagers. Keep in mind that some packagers will offer last-minute deals to Cozumel with hefty discounts; if you're the flexible sort, keep an eye open for these.

Most hotels have an arrangement with a dive shop and offer dive packages. These can be good deals, but if you don't buy a dive package, it's quite okay to stay at one hotel and dive with a third-party operator—any dive boat can pull up to any hotel pier to pick up customers. Most dive shops won't pick up from the hotels north of town.

All the beach hotels suffered damage from the two hurricanes that passed through here. All were closed. Most took advantage of the closure to make upgrades to amenities and rooms. This is good news for those who come now. Some of the hotels in town are also remodeling, but nothing major.

As an alternative to a hotel, you can try **Cozumel Vacation Villas and Condos,** Av. Rafael Melgar 685 (between calles 3 and 5 Sur; © 800/224-5551 in the U.S., or 987/872-0729; www.cvvmexico.com), which offers accommodations by the week.

NORTH OF TOWN

Carretera Santa Pilar, or San Juan, is the name of Avenida Rafael Melgar's northern extension. All the hotels lie close to each other on the beach side of the road a short distance from town and the airport.

Very Expensive

Playa Azul Golf-Scuba-Spa ⓡⓡⓡ   This quiet hotel is perhaps the most relaxing of the island's properties. It's smaller than the others, and service is personal. It's an excellent choice for golfers; guests pay no greens fees, only cart rental. The hotel's small, sandy beach with shade *palapas* has a quiet little beach bar. Almost all the rooms have balconies and ocean views. The units in the original section are all suites—very large, with oversize bathrooms with showers. The new wing has mostly standard rooms that are comfortable and large. The corner rooms are master suites and have large balconies with Jacuzzis overlooking the sea. If you prefer lots of space over having a Jacuzzi, opt for a suite in the original building. Rooms contain a king-size bed or two double beds; some suites offer two convertible single sofas in the separate living room. The hotel also offers deep-sea- and fly-fishing trips.

Carretera San Juan Km 4, 77600 Cozumel, Q. Roo. ⓒ **987/869-5160** or -5165. Fax 987/869-5173. www.playa-azul. com. 50 units. High season $263 (£132) double, $314–$364 (£157–£182) suite; low season $196–$202 (£98–£101) double, $246–$342 (£123–£171) suite. Rates include unlimited golf and full breakfast. Internet specials available. AE, MC, V. Free guarded parking. **Amenities:** Restaurant; 2 bars; medium-size outdoor pool; unlimited golf privileges at Cozumel Country Club; spa; dive shop; watersports gear rental; game room; tour info; room service; in-room massage; babysitting; laundry service, nonsmoking rooms. *In room:* A/C, TV, fridge, coffeemaker, hair dryer, safe.

Expensive

Condumel Condobeach Apartments   If you want some distance from the crowds, consider lodging here. It's not a full-service hotel, but in some ways it's more convenient. The one-bedroom apartments are designed and furnished in practical fashion—airy, with sliding glass doors that face the sea and allow for good cross-ventilation (especially in the upper units). They also have ceiling fans, air-conditioning, and two twin beds or one king-size. Each apartment has a separate living room and a full kitchen with a partially stocked fridge, so you don't have to run to the store on the first day. There's a small, well-tended beach area (with shade *palapas* and a grill for guests' use) that leads to a low, rocky fall-off into the sea.

Carretera Hotelera Norte s/n, 77600 Cozumel, Q. Roo. ⓒ **987/872-0892**. Fax 987/872-0661. www.condumel.com. 10 units. High season $160 (£80) double; low season $134 (£67) double. No credit cards. *In room:* A/C, kitchen, no phone.

IN TOWN

Staying in town is not like staying in Playa del Carmen, where you can walk to the beach. The oceanfront in town is too busy for swimming, and there's no beach, only the *malecón*. Prices are considerably lower, but you'll have to drive or take a cab to the beach; it's pretty easy. English is spoken in almost all of the hotels.

Moderate

Hacienda San Miguel ⓡ *Value*   This is a peaceful hotel built in Mexican colonial style around a large garden courtyard. The property is well maintained and the service is good. It's located a half-block from the shoreline on the town's north side. Rooms are large and attractive and come with equipped kitchens, including full-size refrigerators. Most of the studios have a queen-size bed or two doubles. The junior suites have more living area and come with a queen-size and a twin bed. The two-bedroom suite comes with four double beds.

Calle 10 Norte 500 (between Rafael Melgar and Av. 5), 77600 Cozumel, Q. Roo. ⓒ **866/712-6387** in the U.S., or 987/872-1986. Fax 987/872-7036. www.haciendasanmiguel.com. 11 units. High season $105 (£53) studio, $120 (£60) junior suite, $165 (£83) 2-bedroom suite; low season $90 (£45) studio, $105 (£53) junior suite, $136 (£68) 2-bedroom suite. Rates include continental breakfast and free entrance to Mr. Sancho's beach club. MC, V. Guarded parking on street. **Amenities:** Tour Info; car rental. *In room:* A/C, TV, kitchen, hair dryer, safe, no phone.

Vista del Mar ⓡ   This hotel is located on the town's shoreline boulevard. All the rooms in front have ocean views. The balconies are large enough to be enjoyable and are furnished with a couple of chairs. Rooms are a little larger than your standard room, with better lighting than you find in most of the hotels in town. They are simply furnished and decorated, but come with several amenities. Bathrooms are medium-size or a little smaller and have showers. The rooms in back go for $10 (£5.50) less than the oceanview rooms and look out over a small pool and large Jacuzzi.

Av. Rafael Melgar 45 (between Calles 5 and 7 Sur), 77600 Cozumel, Q. Roo. ⓒ 888/309-9988 in the U.S., or 987/872-0545. Fax 987/872-7036. www.hotelvistadelmar.com. 20 units. High season $90–$100 (£45–£50) double; low season $80–$90 (£40–£45). Discounts sometimes available. AE, MC, V. Limited street parking. **Amenities:** Bar; outdoor pool; Jacuzzi; tour info; car rental; in-room massage; laundry service. *In room:* A/C, TV, fridge, hair dryer, safe.

Inexpensive

La Casona Real ⓥalue   Five blocks from the waterfront, this two-story hotel is a bargain for those wanting a hotel with a pool. The rooms are small to medium in size but modern and attractive and come with good air conditioning. The hotel underwent a complete remodeling after the hurricanes. Management changed, too. Rooms are attractive and come with two double beds or one king-size (costing $10/£5 less). The beds are comfortable. Bathrooms are medium in size. A courtyard with an oval pool is on the west side of the building. This is not the quietest of properties. Next door is a club that opens on weekends with drag queen shows from Acapulco (see "Cozumel After Dark," below). On the other side of the hotel is a fairly busy street.

Av. Juárez 501, 77600 Cozumel, Q. Roo. ⓒ 987/872-5471. 14 units. $45–$55 (£23–£28) double. Discounts sometimes available in low season. No credit cards. Limited street parking. **Amenities:** Medium-size outdoor pool. *In room:* A/C, TV, no phone.

Suites Vima ⓥalue   This three-story hotel is 4 blocks from the main square. It offers large, plainly furnished rooms for a good price. The lighting is okay, the showers are good, and every room comes with it's own fridge, which for island visitors can be a handy feature. The rooms are fairly quiet. Choose between two doubles or one king bed. There is no restaurant, but there is a pool and lounge area. As is the case with other small hotels on the island, the staff at the front desk doesn't speak English. Reservations through e-mail can be made in English. This is one of the few hotels in town that doesn't use high season/low season rates.

Av. 10 Norte between Calles 4 and 6, 77600 Cozumel, Q. Roo. ⓒ 987/872-5118. suitesvima@hotmail.com. 12 units. $55 (£28) double. No credit cards. Limited street parking. **Amenities:** Pool. *In room:* A/C, fridge.

SOUTH OF TOWN

The hotels in this area tend to be more spread out and farther from town than hotels to the north. Some are on the inland side of the road; some are on the beach side, which means a difference in price. Those farthest from town are all-inclusive properties. The beaches tend to be slightly better than those to the north, but all the hotels have swimming pools and piers from which you can snorkel, and all of them accommodate divers. Head south on Avenida Rafael Melgar, which becomes the coastal road **Costera Sur** (also called Carretera a Chankanaab).

Very Expensive

Presidente InterContinental Cozumel ⓡⓡⓡ   Palatial in scale and modern in style, the Presidente spreads out across a long stretch of coast with only distant hotels for neighbors. The rooms have all been redesigned top to bottom, and the smallest rooms were eliminated. Another pool has been added with a larger pool area. Rooms come in three categories depending mostly on location—pool view, ocean view, and beach front. All come with such offerings as a pillow menu. A terrace or a balcony offers the indoor/outdoor mix that's so enjoyable in a beach hotel. Downstairs rooms are beachfront, ocean suites, and reef rooms (larger and practically right up to the water), upstairs are ocean view. Rooms are oversize and have large, beautifully finished bathrooms. A long stretch of sandy beach, dotted with *palapas* and palm trees, fronts the entire hotel. This property is now a member of Leading Hotels of the World.

Costera Sur Km 6.5, 77600 Cozumel, Q. Roo. © 800/327-0200 in the U.S., or 987/872-9500. Fax 987/872-9528. www.intercontinentalcozumel.com. 220 units. High season $318 (£159) pool view, $382 (£191) ocean view, $503 (£252) and up for beach fronts and suites; low season $254–$301 (£127–£156) pool view, $299–$346 (£150–£173) ocean view, $322–$466 (£161–£233) and up for beach fronts and suites. Internet specials sometimes available. AE, MC, V. Free valet parking. Amenities: 3 restaurants; 4 bars; 2 outdoor pools; wading pool; access to golf club; 2 lighted tennis courts; fully equipped fitness center; spa; dive shop; watersports equipment rental; children's club; concierge; tour desk; car rental; business center; shopping arcade; room service; 24-hr. butler service in reef section; in-room massage; babysitting; laundry service; dry cleaning; nonsmoking rooms. *In room:* A/C, TV w/pay movies, Wi-Fi, minibar, coffeemaker, hair dryer, safe.

Expensive

El Cantil Condominiums 𝒦𝒦   A condo property on the south side of town that rents out 30 (of the 45 total) units by the night or the week. This place is worth consideration because it's an attractive property with large rooms and convenient location. The shore here is rocky, but there's a sandy area for guests and a beautiful seaside pool and Jacuzzi, as well as a boat dock and easy entry into the sea. Extras include free long-distance calls to the U.S.

Av. Rafael Melgar, between calles 13 and 15. 77600 Cozumel, Q. Roo. © 954/323-8491 in the U.S., or 987/869-1517. Fax 987/869-2053. www.elcantilcondos.com. 30 units. $170–$200 (£85–£100) studio, $260–$310 (£130–£155) 1-bedroom, $320–$370 (£160–£185) 2-bedroom. AE, DISC, MC, V. Free sheltered parking. Amenities: Restaurant (see "Where to Dine," below); bar; heated outdoor pool; saltwater Jacuzzi; watersports equipment rental; concierge; tour desk; car rental, business center; room service; laundry service and coin-op laundry; nonsmoking rooms. *In room:* A/C, TV, Wi-Fi or high-speed Internet access, kitchens in all but studio units, hair dryer, safe.

WHERE TO DINE

The island offers a number of good restaurants. Taxi drivers will often steer you toward restaurants that pay them commissions; don't heed their advice.

Zermatt (© 987/872-1384), a nice little bakery, is on Avenida 5 at Calle 4 Norte. **Le Chef** (© 987/876-3437), at Avenida 5 and Calle 5 Sur, is a deli/gourmet food store. It has a daily menu of salads, pizzas, and prepared foods, as well as cold meats, cheeses, baguettes, and other makings for a picnic. For inexpensive local fare during the day, I like **Comida Casera Toñita** (© 987/872-0401), at Calle Rosado Salas 265 between avenidas 10 and 15. It closes at 6pm. For morning tacos de *cochinita pibil* (traditionally a breakfast item), go to **El Amigo Mario** (© 987/872-0742) on Calle 5 Sur, between Francisco Mújica and Avenida 35. The doors close at half past noon.

Finally, there's a new restaurant in town called **The Wynston** (© 987/869-1517). It's on the top floor of El Cantil condos and has great views of the ocean. The owner also owns Prima. It had opened when I was last in Cozumel, but I didn't get a chance to try it. The menu is mostly steaks and seafood; main courses run from $18 to $40 (£9–£20). Definitely make reservations in high season.

VERY EXPENSIVE

Cabaña del Pescador (Lobster House) 𝒦𝒦 LOBSTER   Lobster is the main attraction here. You select a lobster tail, and brothers Fernando or Enrique will weigh it, boil it with a hint of spices, and serve it with melted butter, accompanied by sides of rice, vegetables, and bread. Does lobster require anything more? This is the only thing on the menu on Fernando's side of the restaurant, but Enrique will cook up steaks, shrimp, or fish if you don't feel like lobster. The setting is quite tropical—a pair of thatched bungalows bordering a pond with lily pads and reeds, traversed by a small footbridge. The rooms are softly lit with the glow of candles and furnished with rustic tables and chairs. A year later, you could still see some of the marks left by Hurricane Wilma, but the Cabaña del Pescador has lost none of its charm. The restaurant rambles around quite a bit, so explore until you find the spot most to your taste.

Carretera Santa Pilar Km 4 (across from Playa Azul Hotel). No phone. Reservations not accepted. Lobster (by weight) $25–$40 (£13–£20). No credit cards. Daily 6–10:30pm.

EXPENSIVE

French Quarter ★★ SOUTHERN   You can dine very well here in a comfortable upstairs open-air setting. The owners are from Louisiana and care a great deal about food. You can order Southern and Creole classics, such as jambalaya and étouffée, or you can order the daily catch stuffed or blackened, or choose a steak of imported Black Angus beef. I tried a filet mignon with red-onion marmalade, which was delicious. The downstairs bar is a popular hangout for many of the locals.

Av. 5 Sur 18. ⓒ **987/872-6321.** Reservations recommended during Carnaval. Main courses $10–$30 (£5–£15). AE, MC, V. Wed–Mon 5–11pm.

Guido's ★★ MEDITERRANEAN   The inviting interior, with director's chairs and rustic wood tables, makes this a restful place in daytime and a romantic spot at night. The specialty is oven-baked pizzas. Also keep an eye out for the daily specials, which may include an appetizer of sea bass carpaccio, a couple of meat dishes, and usually a fish dish, depending on what the daily catch is. The other thing that people love here is the *pan de ajo*—a house creation of bread made with olive oil, garlic, and rosemary. There's a good wine list.

Av. Rafael Melgar, between calles 6 and 8 Norte. ⓒ **987/872-0946.** Reservations accepted. Main courses $13–$21 (£7.15–£12); pizzas $12–$13 (£6.60–£7.15). AE, MC, V. Mon–Sat 11am–11pm.

La Cocay ★★★ SEAFOOD/MEDITERRANEAN   This kitchen serves the most original cooking on the island. The dining room and outdoor courtyard, modern in style and softly lit, make for a comfortable ambience. I tried a few tapas for appetizers, and they were beautifully seasoned concoctions of garbanzos, chorizo, bell peppers, panela cheese, and sun-dried tomatoes on small slices of bread. For a main course, try the subtle and tender grilled fish in lavender sauce. The choice of meat dishes is usually good. And give special consideration to the daily specials and the wonderful chocolate torte. It takes a little extra time to prepare, so order it early.

Calle 8 Norte 208 (between avs. 10 and 15). ⓒ **987/872-5533.** Reservations recommended. Main courses $9–$30 (£4.50–£15). AE, MC, V. Mon–Sat 1:30–11pm.

Prima ★★★ ITALIAN/INTERNATIONAL   Everything at this ever-popular hangout is fresh—pastas, vegetables, and seafood. The menu changes daily and concentrates on seafood. It might include shrimp scampi, fettuccine with pesto, and lobster and crab ravioli with cream sauce. The fettuccine Alfredo is wonderful, the salads crisp, and the steaks are Black Angus beef. Pizzas are cooked in a wood-burning oven. Desserts include Key lime pie and tiramisu. The food and the service are consistently good here. Dining is upstairs on an open-air terrace.

Calle Rosado Salas 109A (corner of Av. 5) ℂ **987/872-4242**. Reservations recommended during high season. Pizzas and pastas $6–$14 (£3–£7); seafood $12–$20 (£6–£10); steaks $15–$20 (£7.50–£10). AE, MC, V. Daily 4:30–10pm.

MODERATE

Capicúa TAPAS/SEAFOOD   A new restaurant for the island, Capicúa looks to attract customers bored with the usual run of the island's restaurants with some original cooking. The selection of *tapas* varies, but usually includes such things as smoked duck or abalone. And for those wanting something closer to comfort food there are barbecued chicken wings or shrimp *al ajillo* (with garlic and strips of toasted *guajillo chile*). I enjoyed the mahimahi encrusted with white and black sesame seeds, which was cooked just right. Salads can be had, too. There is an okay selection of wines and a full bar. The house in which the restaurant is located is decorated with a sense of humor; choose between a dining room with one of those beautiful, old tile floors and an old patio sheltered by a large tamarind tree.

Calle 10 Norte 299 (corner of Av. 15). ℂ **987/869-8265**. Reservations accepted. Tapas $4–$10 (£2–£5); main courses $10–$15 (£5–£7.50). MC, V. Tues–Sun 5pm–midnight.

El Moro ⊛ *(Value* REGIONAL   El Moro is an out-of-the-way place that has been around for a long time and has always been popular with the locals, who come for the food, the service, and the prices—but not the decor, which is orange, orange, orange, and Formica. Get there by taxi, which will cost a couple of bucks. Portions are generous. Any of the shrimp dishes use the real jumbo variety when available. For something different, try the *pollo Ticuleño*, a specialty from the town of Ticul, a layered dish of tomato sauce, mashed potatoes, crispy baked corn tortillas, and fried chicken breast, topped with shredded cheese and green peas. Other specialties include enchiladas and seafood prepared many ways, plus grilled steaks and sandwiches.

75 bis Norte 124 (between calles 2 and 4 Norte). ℂ **987/872-3029**. Reservations not accepted. Main courses $5–$15 (£2.50–£7.50). MC, V. Fri–Wed 1–11pm.

La Choza ⊛ YUCATECAN/MEXICAN   For Mexican food, I like this place, and so do a lot of locals. Platters of poblano chiles stuffed with shrimp, grilled *brochetas* (kebobs), and *pollo en relleno negro* (chicken in a sauce of blackened chiles) are among the specialties. The table sauces and guacamole are great, and the daily specials can be good, too. This is an open-air restaurant with well-spaced tables under a tall thatched roof. Breakfasts are good as well.

Rosado Salas 198 (at Av. 10 Sur). ℂ **987/872-0958**. Reservations accepted for groups of 6 or more. Breakfast $4 (£2); main courses $10–$16 (£5–£8). AE, MC, V. Daily 7am–10pm.

INEXPENSIVE

Cocos Cozumel MEXICAN/AMERICAN   Cocos offers the largest breakfast menu on the island, including all the American and Mexican classics, from *huevos divorciados* (fried eggs on corn tortillas) to ham and eggs. Indulge in such stateside favorites as hash browns, corn flakes and bananas, gigantic blueberry muffins, cinnamon rolls, and bagels, or go for something with tropical ingredients, such as a blended fruit drink. The service and the food are excellent. The American and Mexican owners, Terri and Daniel Ocejo, are good folk and can set you up with a horseback ride or fishing or snorkeling trips.

Av. 5 Sur 180 (1 block south of the main plaza). ℂ **987/872-0241**. Breakfast $4–$6 (£2–£3). No credit cards. Tues–Sun 6am–noon. Closed Sept–Oct.

Restaurant del Museo BREAKFAST/MEXICAN   The most pleasant place in San Miguel for breakfast or lunch (weather permitting) is at this rooftop cafe above the island's museum. It offers a serene view of the water, removed from the traffic noise below and sheltered from the sun above. Choices are limited to American and Mexican breakfast staples, and lunch dishes such as sandwiches and enchiladas.

Av. Rafael Melgar (corner of Calle 6 Norte). ℰ **987/872-0838.** Reservations not accepted. Breakfast $4–$5 (£2–£2.50); lunch main courses $5–$10 (£2.50–£5). No credit cards. Daily 7am–2pm.

COZUMEL AFTER DARK

Most of the music and dance venues are along Avenida Rafael Melgar. **Carlos 'n' Charlie's** (ℰ **987/869-1648** or -1646), which is in the Punta Langosta shopping center, practically next to **Señor Frog's** (ℰ **987/869-1650**). Punta Langosta is just south of Calle 7 Sur. The **Hard Rock Cafe** (ℰ **987/872-5271**) is also on Avenida Rafael Melgar, at #2, just north of the municipal pier.

In town, there are a few Latin music clubs. These open and close with every high season. They do well when people have cash in their pockets, but then they have to close down when the flow of tourism stops bringing in money. There's a sports bar at the corner of Avenida 5 and Calle 2 Norte called **All Sports Bar** (ℰ **987/869-2246**), which operates as a salsa club Thursday to Saturday from 10pm to 3am. So go for sports, stay for salsa. Also, there's a working-class night club on Avenida Juárez, between avenidas 25 and 30, called **Los Delfines** (no phone), which puts on drag shows from Thursday to Sunday. These start around 11pm.

On Sunday evenings, the place to be is the main square, which usually has a free concert and lots of people strolling about and visiting with friends.

The town of San Miguel has three **movie theaters.** Your best option is **Cinépolis,** the modern multicinema in the Chedraui Plaza Shopping Center at the south end of town. It mainly shows Hollywood movies. Most of these are in English with Spanish subtitles *(película subtitulada);* before buying your tickets, make sure the movie hasn't been dubbed *(doblada).*

16

The Caribbean Coast: The Riviera Maya, Including Playa del Carmen & the Costa Maya

by David Baird

Famously distinguished by its soft white sand and turquoise water, the Yucatán's Caribbean coast stretches 380km (236 miles) from Cancún all the way to Chetumal, at the border with Belize.

The world's second-longest reef system protects most of the shoreline. Where the reef breaks, you find good beaches in the gaps, such as Playa del Carmen, Xpu-Ha, and Tulum. Surf action cleans away silt and sea grass and erodes rocks here, leaving the bottom sandy.

Where the reef is prominent, you get good snorkeling and diving, with lots of fish and other sea creatures. Here mangrove often lines the shore, and beaches are usually sandy up to the water's edge but shallow, with a silty or rocky floor.

The northern half of the coast is now known as the "Riviera Maya"; the southern half, the "Costa Maya." In between is the large Sian Ka'an Biosphere Reserve. Inland you'll find jungle, caverns, cenotes (limestone wells that lead to an underwater river), and the better known ruins of the Maya.

Activities abound, as do lodging options. On this coast you can stay in a variety of communities or distance yourself from all of them. Just about every type of accommodations you can think of is a possibility: rustic cabins, secluded spa resorts, boutique hotels, B&Bs, or all-inclusive megaresorts. With so many options, you'll need to make some tough calls. I hope that what follows will help you decide.

EXPLORING MEXICO'S CARIBBEAN COAST

A single road, Highway 307, runs down the coast from Cancún to Chetumal. The section between Cancún's airport and Playa del Carmen (51km/32 miles) is a four-lane divided highway with speed limits up to 110kmph (68 mph). There are a couple of traffic lights and several reduced-speed zones around the major turnoffs. From Playa to Tulum (80km/50 miles) expect road construction, as the government is widening the highway to four lanes. The project is complete as far south as Paamul, and as of the time of this writing, construction is ongoing around Akumal. It still takes about 1½ hours to drive from the Cancún airport to Tulum.

From Tulum, the highway turns inland to skirt the edges of Sian Ka'an. The roadway is narrower, without shoulders, and in some areas the forest crowds in on both sides. The speed limit is mostly 80kmph (50 mph), but you'll need to slow down where the road passes through villages and keep an eye out for *topes* (speed bumps).

After the town of Limones, new road construction has widened and smoothed the highway. To drive from Tulum to Chetumal takes 3 hours.

COASTAL STOPS NORTH TO SOUTH

PUERTO MORELOS This town between Cancún and Playa remains a little village affectionately known by the locals as "Muerto Morelos" (*muerto* means "dead"), for its phenomenally quiet low season. It has a few small hotels and rental houses, and nearby are a few secluded spa resorts. The coast is sandy and well protected by an off-shore reef, which means good snorkeling and diving nearby, but the lack of surf means sea grass and shallow water. If you're looking for good swimming, head farther down the coast. If you're looking for a relaxing seaside retreat with a clean beach in an easy-going community, this will work for you.

PLAYA DEL CARMEN Playa, as it is called, is the most happening place on the coast—a delightful beach (especially when the wind and currents are flowing in the right direction), hotels for every budget, a good choice of restaurants, and an active nightlife, most of which is on or around Quinta Avenida (Fifth Avenue), Playa's well-known promenade. In the last few years, the town has grown quickly, and local residents and the tourism board are working to keep it from becoming a smaller version of Cancún.

PUERTO AVENTURAS The first major town south of Playa is a modern condo-marina development with a 9-hole golf course, several restaurants, and a few hotels. I don't think it's a fun place to stay, but you might come here to go deep-sea fishing or swim with dolphins.

AKUMAL A bit farther south are Akumal and Half Moon Bay. The community is relatively old for this shore, which means that it's already built up and doesn't have the boomtown feel of Playa and Tulum. Akumal has a strong ecological orientation and is a prominent scuba and snorkeling center. The locals are a mix of Americans and Mexicans who enjoy the unhurried lifestyle of the tropics, making this a good place to relax and work on your hammock technique. There are a few hotels; most of the lodging is rental houses and condos. Consequently, the town is a favorite with families who enjoy the calmness of the place and can save money by buying groceries and cooking for themselves.

TULUM The town of Tulum (near the ruins of the same name) has a hotel district of about 30 *palapa* (palm-leaf roofed) hotels, which stretch down the coast of the Punta Allen peninsula. A few years ago, it was mainly a destination for backpacker types, but with some of the most beautiful beaches on this coast and many improvements in hotel amenities, it now attracts people with big budgets. Here you can enjoy the beach in relative solitude and quiet (unless your hotel is busy building additional rooms). The downside of this is that Tulum doesn't have the variety of restaurants that Playa and Cancún do, but you can still eat well.

COSTA MAYA South of Tulum lies the large Sian Ka'an Biosphere Reserve and, beyond that, what is known as the Costa Maya, which designates the rest of the coast all the way down to Belize. The Costa Maya is a relaxing getaway. Most of the coast is along the Majahual Peninsula, which has a lot of sandy beaches with silt bottoms. It's attractive to scuba divers, snorkelers, fly fishermen, and people who want to get away from the crowds. Farther south is Lake Bacalar, a large, clear freshwater lake. Inland from here are the impressive Maya ruins of the Río Bec area.

THINGS TO DO ALONG THE RIVIERA MAYA

If you need a break from lounging on the beach, you can find plenty of activities up and down this coast. The following is a brief list to help you consider your options.

DAY SPA To relax after all that exertion, try **Spa Itzá.** It's in downtown Playa between calles 12 and 14 in a retail area called Calle Corazón. The phone number is (C) **984/803-2588.**

DEEP-SEA FISHING The largest marina on the coast is at **Puerto Aventuras,** not far south of Playa. Here's where you'll find most of your options for boating and fishing. See p. 606.

GOLF & TENNIS The Playacar Golf Club ((C) **984/873-4990;** www.palace-resorts.com/playacar-golf-club) has an 18-hole **golf course** designed by Robert von Hagge. It's run by the Palace Resorts hotel chain, which offers golf packages. Greens fees are $180 (£90) in the morning (including tax and cart) and $120 (£60) after 2pm; club rental costs $30 (£15). The club also has two **tennis** courts, which cost $10 (£5) per hour. If you stay at one of the Mayakoba resort hotels, you'll have access to a course designed by Greg Norman, which hosts a PGA tour event. See **www.mayakoba.com.**

HORSEBACK RIDING A few places along the highway offer horseback rides. The best of these, **Rancho Punta Venado,** is just south of Playa, past the Calica Pier. This ranch is less touristy than the others, and the owner takes good care of his horses. It has a nice stretch of coast with a sheltered bay and offers kayaking and snorkeling outings. It's best to make arrangements in advance and tell them you're a Frommer's reader, so that they can schedule you on a day when they have fewer customers. E-mail (ptavenado@yahoo.com) is the best way to reach them; sometimes they don't answer their office number (C) **984/803-5224.** Another option is to call the ranch's cellphone from Mexico ((C) **044-984/116-3213);** there is a charge for the call. Talk to Gabriela or Francisco; both speak English. Or try dropping by. The turn-off for the ranch is 2km (1¼ miles) south of the Calica overpass near Km 279.

SCUBA & SNORKELING In Playa, **Tank-Ha Dive Center** ((C) **984/873-0302;** www.tankha.com) arranges reef and cavern diving. Snorkeling trips cost around $40 (£20) per person. Two-tank dive trips are $70 (£35); resort courses with SSI and PADI instructors cost $110 (£55). The area around Akumal has a number of underwater caverns and cenote that are popular scuba and snorkeling destinations. The **Akumal Dive Shop** specializes in cavern diving and offers a variety of dives. But the easiest way to try cavern diving or snorkeling is through **Hidden Worlds Cenotes,** which is right on the highway, 15km (9 miles) south of Akumal. They provide everything, including wet suit. See "South of Playa del Carmen," later in this chapter.

SWIMMING WITH DOLPHINS In the two nature parks south of Playa, Xcaret and Xel-Ha, you can interact with these intelligent creatures. Also, there's an outfit in Puerto Aventuras called **Dolphin Discovery** that is quite good. See "South of Playa del Carmen," later in this chapter, and "Swimming with Dolphins," p. 551.

TOURS From Playa and the rest of the coast there are tours to all of the below-mentioned ruins. The tour buses usually stop at a few places along the way for refreshments and souvenirs, which is why I prefer the small tours. Some combine the ruins of Tulum with a visit to a nature park. There is a tour agency in Playa called **Alltournative** ((C) **800/507-1902** in the U.S. and Canada, or 984/803-9999; www.alltournative. com), which offers small tours that combine a little of everything: culture (visit a contemporary Maya village), adventure (kayaking, rappelling, snorkeling, cenote diving), natural history, and ruins. It offers these tours daily using vans for transportation. The tours are fun. You can call the agency directly or arrange a tour through your hotel; they pick up at most of the large resorts along the coast. **Selvática** (© **866/552-8825** in the U.S. or 998/898-4312; www.selvatica.com.mx), operating out of offices in Cancún, offers guests a little adventure tourism in the jungle, with 2.5km (1½ miles) of zip lines strung up in the forest canopy. The tour also includes biking and swimming in cenotes. In high season you should make your reservation a month before your trip. The $70 to $80 (£35–£40) cost includes transportation, activities, a light lunch, locker, and all equipment. Another interesting option is an ecological tour of the **Sian Ka'an Biosphere Reserve.** To do this, however, you have to get to Tulum. See the Tulum section, later in this chapter.

VISITING THE RUINED CITIES OF THE MAYA   Four cities are within easy reach of Playa and most of the coast. The easiest to access is **Tulum** (see "Tulum, Punta Allen & Sian Ka'an," later). A half-hour inland from Tulum on a pock-marked road is **Cobá** (see "Cobá Ruins," later), rising up from a jungle setting. This city has not been reconstructed to the same degree as the other three and doesn't have the rich imagery or clearly delineated architecture. The other two cites, **Chichén Itzá** and **Ek Balam,** are 2½ hours distant in the interior of the peninsula. My favorite way to see them is to rent a car and drive to Chichén in the afternoon, check into a hotel (perhaps one with a pool), see the sound-and-light show that evening, and then tour the ruins in the cool of the morning before the big bus tours arrive. Then drive back via Valladolid and Ek Balam. See chapter 17 for a description of these places.

XCARET & XEL-HA NATURE PARKS   These parks make full-day excursions, offering opportunities for swimming, snorkeling, and other seaside activities, and educational tours about the region's natural history and local Maya culture and entertainment. They are completely self-contained and offer food, drink, watersports equipment, and various kinds of merchandise. Xcaret is just south of Playa, while Xel-Ha is farther south, almost to Tulum. (See section 3, later in this chapter.)

Cozumel is a half-hour away by ferry from Playa, but it makes for a poor day trip unless you simply want to shop. You'll see exactly what the cruise-ship passengers see—lots of duty-free, souvenir, and jewelry stores. To enjoy Cozumel best, you have to spend at least a couple of nights there to explore the island. See chapter 15.

1 Puerto Morelos & Vicinity

BETWEEN CANCUN & PLAYA DEL CARMEN

The coast directly south of the Cancún airport has several roadside attractions, all-inclusive hotels, small *cabaña* hotels, and some spa resorts. Much of the latest development is targeting the well-heeled traveler—small luxury hotels with or without a marina and with or without a golf course. This stretch of coast between the airport and Playa del Carmen is only 51km (32 miles) long. Midway is Puerto Morelos.

ROADSIDE ATTRACTIONS   Near the Puerto Morelos turnoff is **Rancho Loma Bonita,** which has all the markings of a tourist trap and offers horseback riding and ATV tours. For this sort of activity, I prefer Rancho Punto Venado, just south of Playa (see "Things to Do Along the Riviera Maya," earlier in this chapter). You'll also come across **Jardín Botánico Dr. Alfredo Barrera** (no phone). Opened in 1990 and named after a biologist who studied tropical forests, the botanical garden is open Monday to

The Yucatán's Upper Caribbean Coast

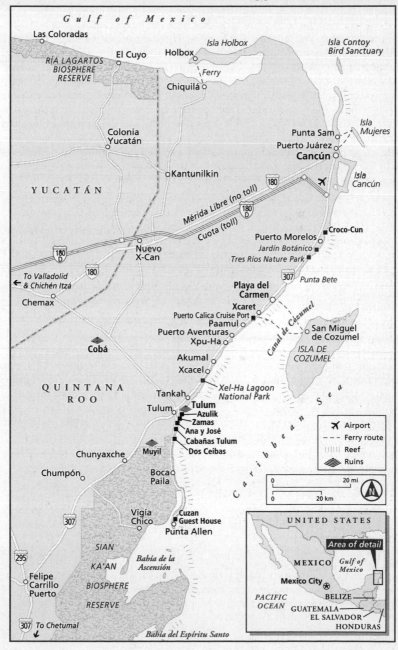

Gulf of Mexico

Las Coloradas

El Cuyo

Holbox

Isla Holbox

Isla Contoy
Bird Sanctuary

RÍA LAGARTOS
BIOSPHERE
RESERVE

Ferry

Chiquilá

Colonia
Yucatán

Punta Sam

Isla
Mujeres

Puerto Juárez

Cancún

Kantunilkin

YUCATÁN

180

Isla
Cancún

Mérida Libre (no toll)

180

Cuota (toll)

180
D

Nuevo
X-Can

Puerto Morelos

Croco-Cun

Jardín Botánico

Tres Ríos Nature Park

To Valladolid
& Chichén Itzá

180

307

Punta Bete

Chemax

Playa del
Carmen

Xcaret

Puerto Calica Cruise Port

Paamul

San Miguel
de Cozumel

Puerto Aventuras

Cobá

Xpu-Ha

ISLA DE
COZUMEL

Akumal

Xcacel

QUINTANA
ROO

Tankah

Tulum

Xel-Ha Lagoon
National Park

Tulum

Azulik

Zamas

Ana y José

Cabañas Tulum

Chunyaxche

Muyil

Dos Ceibas

Chumpón

Boca
Paila

Vigía
Chico

Cuzan
Guest House

Punta Allen

SIAN

307

KA'AN

Bahía de la
Ascensión

295

BIOSPHERE

Felipe
Carrillo
Puerto

RESERVE

307 To Chetumal

Bahía del Espíritu Santo

Caribbean Sea

✈ Airport

– – – Ferry route

||||| Reef

◆◆◆ Ruins

0   20 mi

0   20 km

N

UNITED STATES

Area of detail

MEXICO

Gulf of
Mexico

Mexico City

BELIZE

PACIFIC
OCEAN

GUATEMALA

EL SALVADOR

HONDURAS

Saturday from 9am to 5pm. Admission is $7 (£3.50). This place is disappointing because it's not maintained well. It will be of most interest to gardeners and plant enthusiasts, but it will probably bore children. They are much more likely to enjoy the interactive zoo, **CrocoCun** (© **998/850-3719**), a zoological park a mile north of Puerto Morelos. It raises crocodiles from eggs and keeps several species of animals native to the Yucatán Peninsula. A visit to the reptile house is fascinating, though it may make you wary of venturing into the jungle. The rattlesnakes and boa constrictors are particularly intimidating, and the tarantulas are downright enormous. The guided tour lasts 1½ hours. The guides have great enthusiasm, and the spider monkeys and wild pigs entrance kids. Wear plenty of bug repellent. The onsite restaurant, CrocoCun, is open daily from 8:30am to 5:30pm. Entrance fees are high: $18 (£9) adults, $12 (£6) children 6 to 12, free for children younger than 6.

NEW GOLF RESORT

Competition for the luxury tourism market has heated up with the arrival of **Mayakoba.** They started with a golf course designed by Greg Norman. Then they organized a PGA tour event here in 2007—the first PGA tournament ever in Mexico. And they've lined up a dazzling collection of resort properties: Fairmount, Viceroy, Rosewood, and Banyan Tree. When I visited, only the Fairmount was open, but the rest were going to be in operation by 2008. The resorts are designed to be a kind of connected endeavor—guests of one resort can sample the amenities of the other three, including restaurants and spas. For more information, check out **www.mayakoba.com**.

SPA RESORTS 𝕲𝕲𝕲

In the area around Puerto Morelos, four spa resorts provide variations on the hedonistic resort experience. Only 20 to 30 minutes from the Cancún airport, they are well situated for a quick weekend escape from the daily grind. You can jet down to Cancún, get whisked away by the hotel car, and be on the beach with a cocktail in hand before you can figure out whether you crossed a time zone. All four resorts pride themselves on their service, amenities, and spa and salon treatments. Being in the Yucatán, they add the healing practices of the Maya, especially the use of *temazcal,* the native steam bath. Rates quoted below include taxes but not the 5% to 10% service charge.

Ceiba del Mar   This resort consists of seven three-story buildings set on a landscape of ponds and pools. Two years ago, the rooftop sections were converted to penthouses, and the other rooms were remodeled. Rooms are large with a terrace or balcony. Bathrooms are large, with showers, tubs, and stone counters. Service remains the same—attentive and unobtrusive—exemplified by the morning coffee and juice delivery, accomplished without disturbing the guests through the use of a blind pass-through. The spa area is ample, quite attractive, and well designed.

Av. Niños Héroes s/n, 77580 Puerto Morelos, Q. Roo. © **877/545-6221** in the U.S., or 998/872-8060. Fax 998/872-8061. www.ceibadelmar.com. 88 units. High season $460–$515 (£230–£258) deluxe and junior suite, from $884 (£442) suite; low season $436–$492 (£218–£246) deluxe and junior suite, from $822 (£411) suite. Rates include continental breakfast. Spa packages available. AE, MC, V. Free parking. **Amenities:** 2 restaurants; 2 bars; 2 outdoor pools (1 heated); lighted tennis court; complete state-of-the-art gym w/sauna, steam room, whirlpool, and Swiss showers; spa offering a wide variety of treatments; dive shop w/watersports equipment; bikes; concierge; tour info; car rental; salon; room service; babysitting; laundry service; nonsmoking rooms. *In room:* A/C, TV/VCR, Wi-Fi, minibar, hair dryer, safe, CD player.

Maroma   This resort has been around the longest, owns a large parcel of land inland that it protects from development, and has a gorgeous beach and beautifully manicured grounds. Two- and three-story buildings house the large guest rooms; most have king-size beds. The grounds are lovely, and the beach is fine white sand. The hotel has also spent a lot of effort and money on upgrades to the rooms. Nine new suites are outrageous examples of extravagance. There is a new beach bar that makes for an enjoyable place to pass the evening hours; it's a little more glitzy than the old one but still comfy. As at the Tides Riviera Maya (see below), but to a lesser degree, the smaller size makes for more personal service and a deeper sense of escape.

Carretera 307 Km 51, 77710 Q. Roo. ℂ 866/454-9351 in the U.S., or 998/872-8200. Fax 998/872-8220. www.maromahotel.com. 65 units. $570(£285) gardenview double; $684 (£342) premium double; $930 (£465) oceanfront double; from $1,276 (£638) suite. Rates include ground transfer, full breakfast, and snorkeling tour. AE, MC, V. Free valet parking. No children younger than 16 allowed. **Amenities:** Restaurant; 3 bars; 3 outdoor spring-fed pools; fitness center; spa; Jacuzzi; steam bath; watersports equipment rental; game room; concierge; tours; car rental; salon; room service; in-room massage; laundry service; dry cleaning. *In room:* A/C, hair dryer.

Paraíso de la Bonita   This resort has the most elaborate spa of all. I'm not a spa-goer and cannot discuss the relative merits of different treatments, but my work takes me to plenty of spas, and this one, which operates under the French system of thalas-sotherapy, is beyond anything I've seen. It uses seawater, sea salts, and sea algae in its treatments. The beach is open. The pool area and the common areas of the spa are uncommonly attractive. The rooms occupy some unremarkable three-story buildings. They are, in decor and furnishings, more impressive than the rooms of the three other resorts reviewed in this section. The ground-floor rooms have a plunge pool; upstairs rooms come with a balcony.

Carretera Cancún–Chetumal Km 328, Bahía Petempich, 77710 Q. Roo. ℂ 866/751-9175 in the U.S., or 998/872-8300. Fax 998/872-8301. www.paraisodelabonita.com. 90 units. High season from $1,008 (£504) suite; low season from $800 (£400) suite. Rates include ground transfer. AE, MC, V. Free valet parking. No children younger than 12 allowed. **Amenities:** 2 restaurants; 2 bars; 4 outdoor pools; lighted tennis court; spa; 2 Jacuzzis; watersports equipment rental; concierge; tour info; rental cars; salon; room service; in-room massage; laundry service; dry cleaning; nonsmoking rooms. *In room:* A/C, TV/DVD, minibar, hair dryer, safe.

The Tides Riviera Maya (formerly Ikal del Mar)   The smallest of the four resorts in this section, this property is all about privacy and tranquillity. Thirty well-separated bungalows—each with its own piece of jungle, a little pool, and an outdoor shower—are connected by lit pathways meandering through the vegetation. The bungalows are large, filled with amenities, and decorated in a modern, spare style. The bathrooms have only a shower. Service here is the most personal of the four—you never have to leave your bungalow. The bar and restaurant, overlooking an inviting pool, make for an attractive common area. And of course, there's the spa. The beach was narrow and rocky, but the hurricane widened it considerably. The new owners have made numerous improvements in the rooms and the spa as run by Ikal del Mar.

Playa Xcalacoco, Carretera Cancún–Tulum, 77710 Q. Roo. ℂ 800/578-0281 in the U.S. and Canada, or 984/877-3000. Fax 713/528-3697. www.tidesrivieramaya.com. 30 units. High season from $784 (£392) villa; low season from $655 (£328) double. Rates include full breakfast. AE, MC, V. Free secure parking. Children younger than 18 not accepted. **Amenities:** Restaurant; 2 bars; large outdoor pool; spa; 2 Jacuzzis; steam bath; watersports equipment; concierge; tour info; car rental; courtesy shuttle to Playa; salon; room service; in-room massage; laundry service. *In room:* A/C, TV/DVD, fridge, hair dryer, safe.

PUERTO MORELOS

Puerto Morelos remains a quiet place—perfect for lying on the white-sand beach and reading, with the occasional foray into watersports, especially snorkeling, diving, kitesurfing, windsurfing, and kayaking. A prominent reef offshore was declared a national park for its protection. It's shallow and easy to snorkel, and it protects the coast from storm surges. The beaches are great, maintained by the local government. The water is shallow, calm, and clear, with sea grass growing on the bottom. The town is small, and the inhabitants are laid-back. There is a large English-language bookstore that sells new and used titles. The car ferry that used to depart from here for Cozumel has moved down the coast to the Calica pier just south of Playa del Carmen.

ESSENTIALS
GETTING THERE   **By Car**   At Km 31 there's a traffic light at the intersection, and a large sign pointing to Puerto Morelos.

By Bus   Buses from Cancún to Tulum and Playa del Carmen usually stop here, but be sure to ask in Cancún if your bus makes the Puerto Morelos stop.

EXPLORING IN & AROUND PUERTO MORELOS
Puerto Morelos attracts visitors who seek seaside relaxation without crowds and high prices. The town has a few hotels and a few restaurants. For outdoor recreation, there are two dive shops and plenty of recreational boats for fishing or snorkeling. Try **Dive In Puerto Morelos** (www.diveinpuertomorelos.com) at Av. Rojo Gómez 14. On the main square, **Alma Libre** (© **998/871-0713;** www.almalibrebooks.com) sells more English-language books than any other in the Yucatán. The owners, a couple of Canadians named Joanne and Rob Birce, stock everything from volumes on Maya culture to English classics to maps of the region. The store is open October through the first week in June, Tuesday to Sunday from 10am to 3pm and 6 to 9pm.

The reef directly offshore is very shallow and protected by law. Snorkelers are required to wear life vests to prevent them from diving down to the reef. I'm unaccustomed to snorkeling in a vest and found it bothersome, but it didn't prevent me from getting a close look at the reef, which is quite shallow—3m (10 ft.) at its deepest, rising to within a foot of the surface. In a short time, I spotted four different eels and sea snakes, lots of fish, and a ray.

WHERE TO STAY
Rates include the 12% hotel tax. For condo rentals check out the website of Alma Libre books (see above).

Amar Inn   Simple rooms on the beach, in a home-style setting, make this small inn a good place for those wanting a quiet seaside retreat. The cordial hostess, Ana Luisa Aguilar, is the daughter of Luis Aguilar, a Mexican singer and movie star of the 1940s and 1950s. She keeps busy promoting environmental and equitable-development causes. She can line up snorkeling and fishing trips and jungle tours for guests with local operators. There are three *cabañas* in back, opposite the main house, and six upstairs rooms with views of the beach. The most expensive rooms are the third-story "penthouse" rooms with a great view of the ocean. The *cabañas* get less of a cross-breeze than the rooms in the main house. Bedding choices include one or two doubles, one king-size, or five twin beds. A full Mexican breakfast is served in the garden.

Av. Javier Rojo Gómez (at Lázaro Cárdenas), 77580 Puerto Morelos, Q. Roo. © **998/871-0026.** amar_inn@hotmail. com. 10 units. High season $55–$85 (£28–£43) double; low season $40–$75 (£20–£38) double. Rates include full breakfast. No credit cards. Limited free parking. **Amenities:** Tour and rental info. *In room:* Fan, fridge, no phone.

Hacienda Morelos   This hotel on the water has pleasant rooms and good prices. The simple rooms are spacious and comfortable and all have ocean views. Most come

Beach Cabañas

Five kilometers (3 miles) north of Playa are some economical lodgings on a mostly rocky beach. A sign that says PUNTA BETE marks the access road to Xcalacoco; in a short time you reach the water. Before you do, the road forks off in a few places, and you'll see signs for different *cabañas*. The word may conjure up visions of idyllic dwellings with thatched roofs, but on the Yucatecan coast, it usually means simple lodging. This is mostly the case here; rates run $70 to $85 (£35–£43) a night for two people. Of the four groupings of *cabañas* in Xcalacoco, the best is **Coco's Cabañas** (www.travel-center.com). It's a handful of rooms with electricity and ceiling fans; a good little budget restaurant; and a small pool. Two of the rooms have air-conditioning. Next door is the spa resort Tides Riviera Maya (see "Spa Resorts," above).

with two double beds, and some have a king-size bed. There's a small pool and a restaurant on the premises. It's close to the main square, so you don't need a car.

Av. Rafael Melgar 2 Lote 5, 77580 Puerto Morelos, Q. Roo. (©) 998/871-0448. www.haciendamorelos.com. 31 units. $89 (£45) double. Promotional rates sometimes available. MC, V. Limited free parking. **Amenities:** Restaurant; bar; outdoor pool. *In room:* A/C, TV, safe, no phone.

WHERE TO DINE

Most of Puerto Morelos's restaurants are on or around the main square. These include **Los Pelícanos** for seafood, **Bodo's** (in the hotel Hacienda Morelos) for good lunch specials and a few German dishes, **David Lau's** for Asian food, **El Pirata** if you have kids (for it's large menu), and **Le Café d'Amancia** for coffee and pastries. The most expensive is **John Grey's,** a couple blocks north of the plaza and 3 blocks inland. It's open for dinner except on Sundays. The owner is a former chef for the Ritz-Carlton.

SOUTH OF PUERTO MORELOS

Petit Lafitte Hotel 🌟🌟 One kilometer (a half-mile) south of the original Posada Lafitte, this new property has the same easy-going attitude that characterized the old property. In relative isolation, you still get all the amenities of a relaxing vacation. The three-story building has 30 units, and plans are in place to build a dozen or more freestanding bungalows. Rooms are comfortable and contemporary. The staff is the same from the old property, so service is still personal and attentive.

Carretera Cancún–Tulum Km 63 (Xcalacoco), 77710 Playa del Carmen, Q. Roo. (©) 800/538-6802 in the U.S. and Canada. www.mexicoholiday.com. 30 units. High season $250–$275 (£125–£138) double, $270–$350 (£135–£175) bungalow; low season $180–$200 (£90–£100) double, $200–$270 (£100–£135) double. Minimum 2–4 nights. Rates include breakfast and dinner. MC, V. Free guarded parking. **Amenities:** Restaurant; bar; outdoor pool; ground transfer; activities desk; laundry service. *In room:* A/C, Wi-Fi, minibar, safe.

2 Playa del Carmen 🌟🌟🌟

32km (20 miles) S of Puerto Morelos; 70km (43 miles) S of Cancún; 10km (6½ miles) N of Xcaret; 13km (8 miles) N of Puerto Calica

Though it no longer has the feel of a village, Playa still provides that rare combination of simplicity (at its core, still primarily a beach town) and variety (many unique hotels, restaurants, and stores). There is a comfortable feel to the town. The local architecture has adopted elements of native building—rustic clapboard walls; stucco; thatched roofs; rough-hewn wood; and a ramshackle, unplanned look to many structures. Cheap-looking commercial architecture has intruded, with chain restaurants and stores, detracting from Playa's individuality, but Playa still retains the feel of a cosmopolitan getaway with a counterculture ethos.

A strong European influence has made topless sunbathing (nominally against the law in Mexico) a nonchalantly accepted practice anywhere there's a beach. The beach grows and shrinks, from broad and sandy to narrower with rocks, depending on the currents and wind. When this happens, head to the beaches in north Playa.

From Playa, it's easy to shoot out to Cozumel on the ferry, drive south to the nature parks and the ruins at Tulum and Cobá, or drive north to Cancún. Directly south of town is the Playacar development, which has a golf course, several large all-inclusive resorts, and a residential development.

ESSENTIALS
GETTING THERE & DEPARTING
BY AIR   You can fly into Cancún and take a bus directly from the airport (see "By Bus," below), or fly into Cozumel and take the passenger ferry.

BY CAR   Highway 307 is the only highway that passes through Playa. As you approach Playa from Cancún, the highway divides. Keep to the inside lanes to permit turning left at any of the traffic lights. The two main arteries into Playa are Avenida Constituyentes, which works well for destinations in northern Playa, and Avenida Juárez, which leads to the town's main square. If you stay in the outside lanes, you will need to continue past Playa until you get to the turnaround, and then double back, staying to your right.

BY FERRY   Air-conditioned passenger ferries to Cozumel leave from the town's pier 1 block from the main square. There is also a car ferry to Cozumel from the Calica pier just south of the Playacar development. The schedule for the passenger ferries has been in flux. Lately, ferries have been departing every hour in the mornings, and every

---

(Tips Driving the Riviera Maya

Driving along this coast isn't difficult. There's only one highway, so you can't get lost. Speed limits are clearly posted, but lots of cars ignore them, *except around Playa*, where police are known to ticket drivers. Watch your speed when you're passing through town. Maximum speed for the center lanes is 60kmph (40 mph) and, for the outside lanes, it's 40kmph (25 mph).

South of Playa, the highway is four lanes as far as Akumal. South of there it's still undivided. You're not allowed to stop on the highway to make a left turn. You're supposed to pull over to the right and wait for traffic in both directions to clear before crossing the road. Another tip: Drivers here customarily pretend that there's a center passing lane. Oncoming traffic moves to the right to make room for the passing vehicle. You should do the same, but look out for cyclists and cars on the shoulder. This is why I recommend not driving at night. There are several more gas stations in the Riviera Maya now, so you shouldn't have a problem getting gas. But make sure the attendant gives you back the right amount of money—I've had people try to short-change me.

Playa del Carmen

ACCOMMODATIONS ■
Acanto Hotel and Suites **1**
Deseo Hotel + Lounge **3**
Jardín de Murieta **8**
Jungle Caribe **7**
Hotel Lab Nah **10**
Hotel Lunata **6**
Playa Maya **11**

DINING ◆
Casa Mediterranea **9**
Estas Son Las Mañanitas **12**
La Casa del Agua **13**
La Parrilla **5**
Media Luna **2**
La Tarraya Restaurant/Bar **14**
Yaxché **4**

2 hours in the afternoons. For more information about both ferries, see "Getting There & Departing" in the Cozumel section of chapter 15.

BY TAXI Taxi fares from the Cancún airport are about $60 to $70 (£30–£35) one-way.

BY BUS **Autobuses Riviera** offers service from the Cancún airport about 12 times a day. Cost is $8 (£4) one-way. You'll see a ticket counter in the corridor leading out of the airport. From the Cancún bus station there are frequent departures—almost every 30 minutes.

ORIENTATION

ARRIVING Playa has two **bus** stations. Buses coming from Cancún and places along the coast, such as Tulum, arrive at the Riviera bus station, at the corner of Juárez and Quinta Avenida, by the town square. Buses coming from destinations in the interior of the peninsula arrive at the new ADO station, on Avenida 20 between calles 12 and 14.

A word of caution: Approach any timeshare salesperson as you would a wounded rhino. And remember that whatever free trinket is offered for simply viewing apartments, it either won't materialize or won't be worth the time you invest in your dealings with these people. You have been warned.

CITY LAYOUT   The main street, **Avenida Juárez,** leads to the town square from Highway 307. As it does so, it crosses several numbered avenues that run parallel to the beach, all of which are multiples of 5. **Quinta Avenida (Fifth Avenue)** is closest to the beach; it's closed to traffic from the *zócalo* to Calle 6 (and some blocks beyond, in the evening). On this avenue are many hotels, restaurants, and shops. Almost the entire town is north and west of the square. To the south is "Playacar" a golf-course development of private residences and a dozen resort hotels.

FAST FACTS: Playa del Carmen

Area Code The telephone area code is **984.**

Currency Exchange Playa has several banks and ATMs. Many currency-exchange houses are close to the pier or along Quinta Avenida at Calle 8.

Doctor For serious medical attention, go to **Hospitén** in Cancún (© **998/881-3700**). In Playa, **Dr. G. Ambriz** speaks English and was trained in the U.S. and Europe. His office is at the corner of Avenida 30 and Calle 14 (© **984/109-1245**).

Drugstore The **Farmacía del Carmen,** Avenida Juárez between avenidas 5 and 10 (© **984/873-2330**), is open 24 hours.

Internet Access Internet cafes are all over town; most have fast connections.

Parking Most parking in Playa is on the street. Spots can be hard to come by. The most accessible parking lot is the Estacionamiento México, at avenidas Juárez and 10 (where the entrance is located). It's open daily 24 hours and charges $1.25 (65p) per hour, $10 (£5.50) per day. There's also a 24-hour lot a block from the pier, where you can leave your car while you visit Cozumel.

Post Office The *correo,* on Avenida Juárez, 3 blocks from the plaza, is on the right past the Hotel Playa del Carmen and the launderette.

Seasons The main high season is from mid-December to Easter. There is a mini high season in August. Low season is all other months.

WHERE TO STAY

Playa has a lot of small hotels with affordable prices that give you a better feel for the town than staying in one of the resorts in Playacar. Don't hesitate to book a place that's not on the beach. Town life here is much of the fun, and staying on the beach in Playa has its disadvantages—in particular, the noise from a couple of beach bars. Beaches are public property in Mexico, and you can lay out your towel anywhere you like. There are some beach clubs in north Playa where, for a small sum, you can have the use of lounge chairs, towels, and food and drink.

High season is mid-December to Easter. August is also high season for some hotels but not others. At other times of the year, you can come to Playa and score walk-in offers. The rates listed below include the 12% hotel tax. I don't include the rates for Christmas to New Year's, which are still higher than the standard high-season rates.

VERY EXPENSIVE

Acanto Hotel & Suites ★★ *(Finds*   In my view, this property is (dare I say it) the most romantic in Playa. There is intimacy and drama and an even a sense of isolation.

Seven stylish suites, endowed with color and texture, encircle a pool and softly lit courtyard. Figures of Buddha and Asian decoration add an exotic feel and draw a division between this small enclave and the larger world outside the hotel's door. The suites come with kitchens so you can, should you choose, limit your comings and goings. The rooms are large and comfortable and come with a queen bed and small sitting area. The location is great, just around the corner from Quinta Avenida, on a secluded street. There are plans to build more units next door with the same concept.

Calle 16 Bis (between avs. 5th and 1st) 77710 Playa del Carmen, Q. Roo. ℭ 631/882-1986 in the U.S. or 984/873-1252. www.acantohotels.com. 7 units. $170–$215 (£85–£158) suite. 3-night minimum stay for holidays. AE, MC, V. Street parking. **Amenities:** Small outdoor pool; tour info; in-room massage; laundry service; nonsmoking rooms. *In room:* A/C, TV, coffeemaker, hair dryer, safe, CD player, no phone.

Deseo Hotel + Lounge ✶✶✶   This hotel is designed to foster social interaction. The lounge plays the central role, appropriating the functions of lobby, restaurant, bar, and pool area at once. It's a raised open-air platform with bar, pool, self-serve kitchen, and daybeds for sunning or sipping an evening drink when the bar is in full swing. The clientele is predominantly 25- to 45-year-olds.

The guest rooms are comfortable, original, and striking but don't tempt one to stay indoors—no TV, no cushy armchair. Their simplicity gives them an almost Asian feel, heightened by nice touches such as sliding doors of wood and frosted glass. All rooms have king-size beds with deep mattresses. From the bottom of each bed, a little drawer slides out with a night kit containing incense, earplugs, and condoms.

And in case Deseo doesn't work for you, the owners have opened another archly styled hotel 2 blocks down called **Hotel Básico** (ℭ **984/879-4448;** www.hotel basico.com). It's a fun mix of industrial and '50s styles, built with materials that have found a lot of favor with architects these days: concrete, plywood, and plastics. Along with all this you get a cushy bed and a forceful shower. As with Deseo, the common areas are not wasted space.

Av. 5 (at Calle 12), 77710 Playa del Carmen, Q. Roo. ℭ **984/879-3620.** Fax 984/879-3621. www.hoteldeseo.com. 15 units. $199 (£100) lounge view; $222 (£111) balcony; $274 (£137) suite. Rates include continental breakfast. AE, MC, V. No parking. Children younger than 18 not accepted. **Amenities:** Bar; small rooftop pool; Jacuzzi; tour info; room service; in-room massage; laundry service. *In room:* A/C, minibar, hair dryer (on request), safe.

EXPENSIVE

Hotel Lunata ✶✶   In the middle of Playa, there isn't a more comfortable or more attractive place to stay than this small hotel on Quinta Avenida. The rooms offer character, good looks, and polish. There are a few standard rooms, which are midsize and come with a queen-size or a double bed. Deluxe rooms are large and come with a king-size bed and small fridge. Junior suites come with two doubles. Bathrooms are well designed and have good showers. Light sleepers should opt for a room facing the garden. On my last stay, I took a room facing the street with double-glazed glass doors that opened to a balcony. I enjoyed looking out over Quinta Avenida, and, with the doors shut, the noise was not bothersome.

Av. 5 (between calles 6 and 8), 77710 Playa del Carmen, Q. Roo. ℭ **984/873-0884.** Fax 984/873-1240. www.lunata. com. 10 units. High season $129 (£65) standard, $169–$179 (£85–£90) deluxe and junior suite; low season $115 (£58) standard, $135–$159 (£68–£80) deluxe and junior suite. Rates include continental breakfast. Promotional rates available. AE, MC, V. Secure parking $5 (£2.50). No children younger than 13 allowed. **Amenities:** Free use of bike and watersports equipment; tour desk; in-room massage; laundry service; nonsmoking rooms. *In room:* A/C, TV, fridge (in some), hair dryer (on request), safe, no phone.

Los Itzaes 🎉 This small hotel in the middle of Playa accommodates business people, making it something of a refuge from tourists. The rooms are attractive and comfortable, with good A/C and double glazed windows. The mattresses are comfortable. Rates include membership at one of the local beach clubs. Rooms with a king bed cost a little less than rooms with two doubles. Junior suites have two doubles and a sofa bed. There is no pool, but there is an enjoyable rooftop whirlpool tub.

Av. 10 between calles 6 and 8, 77710 Playa del Carmen, Q. Roo. ℂ 984/873-2397 or -2398. www.itzaes.com. 16 units. $150–$175 (£75–£88) standard; $220–$250 (£110–£125) suites. Rates include full breakfast and beach club membership. 5-night minimum stay during holidays. AE, MC, V. Secured parking $13. Small pets accepted. **Amenities:** Restaurant; bar; small outdoor Jacuzzi; tour info; ground transfer; in-room massage; laundry service, nonsmoking rooms. *In room:* A/C, TV, Wi-Fi, minibar, hair dryer, safe.

Playa Maya 🎉 *Value* This is the best beach hotels in downtown Playa. There are many reasons to like it (good location, good price, comfortable rooms, and helpful management), but one thing that strikes my fancy is that you enter the hotel from the beach. This little detail isn't good reason to choose a hotel, but it establishes the mood of the overall place and gives it a remove from the busy street scene. What's more, the design and location make it a quiet hotel; it's a couple of blocks from the nearest live-music venue and sheltered by the neighboring hotels. The pool and sunning terrace are attractive and nicely set apart. Rooms are large with midsize bathrooms; a couple of them have private garden terraces with Jacuzzis, while others have balconies that face the beach.

Zona FMT (between calles 6 and 8 Norte), 77710 Playa del Carmen, Q. Roo. ℂ 984/803-2022. www.playa-maya.com. 20 units. High season $150–$196 (£75–£98) double; low season $112–$168 (£56–£84) double. Rates include continental breakfast. MC, V. Limited street parking. **Amenities:** Restaurant; bar; outdoor pool; Jacuzzi; tour info; room service; massage; laundry service. *In room:* A/C, TV, Wi-Fi, fridge, hair dryer, safe.

INEXPENSIVE

Hotel Lab Nah *Value* Good rooms in a central location for a good price are the main attraction at this economy hotel in the heart of Playa. The cheapest rooms have windows facing Quinta Avenida. There was some noise—mostly late-night bar hoppers. It didn't bother me too much. Nevertheless, I think it's worth the money to get one of the partial oceanview standards with balcony on the third floor because they are quieter and larger. The gardenview rooms are directly below the oceanview, are just as large and quiet, but not quite as fixed up. And the difference in price is little. A rooftop *palapa* is the largest room available, good for more than couple.

Calle 6 (and Av. 5), 77710 Playa del Carmen, Q. Roo. ℂ 984/873-2099 www.labnah.com. 33 units. High season $50–$80 (£25–£40) double, $105 (£53) rooftop *palapa;* low season $45–$60 (£23–£30) double, $80 (£40) rooftop *palapa.* Rates include continental breakfast. MC, V. Limited street parking. **Amenities:** Small outdoor pool; tour info; laundry service. *In room:* A/C, hair dryers in some, no phone.

Jardín de Murieta *Value Finds* Besides the economical rates, I like this place for its central, yet half-hidden location in a small interior property without any street frontage on la Quinta. Rooms vary a good bit, but most are large, bright, and cheerful. And the location is quiet. Four rooms have kitchenettes, which can work for some simple meals. Most of the rooms encircle a tree-shaded patio with a few shops and a restaurant. The place has a pleasant, quirky feel.

Av. 5 Norte 173 (between calles 6 and 8), 77710 Playa del Carmen, Q. Roo. ℂ 984/873-0224. www.jardindemurieta.com. 10 units. High season $56–$96 (£28–£48) double; low season $46–$72 (£23–£36) double. No credit cards. Limited street parking. **Amenities:** Restaurant; tour info. *In room:* A/C, TV, Wi-Fi, kitchenette (in 4), fridge, no phone.

WHERE TO DINE

Aside from the restaurants listed below, I would point you in the direction of a few that don't need a full review. For a delicious Veracruz-style breakfast in pleasant, breezy surroundings, try the upstairs terrace restaurant of the **Hotel Básico,** at Quinta Avenida and Calle 10 Norte. For fish tacos and inexpensive seafood, try **El Oasis,** on Calle 12, between avenidas 5 and 10 (no phone). For *arrachera* (fajita) tacos, the place to go is **Super Carnes H C de Monterrey** (© **984/803-0488**) on Calle 1 Sur between avenidas 20 and 25.

EXPENSIVE

La Casa del Agua 𝄢𝄢 EUROPEAN/MEXICAN   Excellent food in inviting surroundings. Instead of obtrusive background music, you hear the sound of falling water. The German owners work at presenting what they like best about the Old and New worlds. They do a good job with seafood—try the grilled seafood for two. For a mild dish, try chicken in a scented sauce of fine herbs accompanied by fettuccine; for something heartier, there's the tortilla soup listed as "Mexican soup." The restaurant offers a number of cool and light dishes that would be appetizing for lunch or an afternoon meal, for example, an avocado stuffed with shrimp and flavored with a subtle horseradish sauce on a bed of alfalfa sprouts and julienne carrots—a good mix of tastes and textures. For dessert, try the chocolate mousse. This is an upstairs restaurant under a large and airy *palapa* roof.

Av. 5 (at Calle 2). © **984/803-0232.** Reservations recommended in high season. Main courses $16–$26 (£8–£13). MC, V. Daily 10am–midnight.

La Parrilla MEXICAN/GRILL   Still a fun place, but it's having problems handling its success. Prices have gone up, and service is slower. But the fajitas remain good as well as many of the Mexican standards such as tortilla soup, enchiladas, and quesadillas. Mariachis show up around 8pm; plan accordingly.

Av. 5 (at Calle 8). © **984/873-0687.** Reservations recommended in high season. Main courses $10–$25 (£5–£13). AE, MC, V. Daily noon–1am.

Yaxché 𝄢𝄢𝄢 YUCATECAN   The menu here makes use of many native foods and spices to present a more elaborate regional cooking than the usual offerings at Yucatecan restaurants—and it was about time for someone to show a little creativity with such an interesting palette of tastes. Excellent examples are a cream of *chaya* (a native leafy vegetable), and an *xcatic* chile stuffed with *cochinita pibil.* I also like the classic Mexican-style fruit salad with lime juice and dried powdered chile. There are several seafood dishes; the ones I had were fresh and well prepared.

Calle 8 (between avs. 5 and 10). © **984/873-2502.** Reservations recommended in high season. Main courses $10–$26 (£5–£13). AE, MC, V. Daily noon–midnight.

MODERATE

Casa Mediterránea 𝄢𝄢𝄢 ITALIAN   Tucked away on a quiet little patio off Quinta Avenida, this small, homey restaurant serves excellent food. Maurizio Gabrielli and Mary Michelon are usually there to greet customers and make recommendations. Maurizio came to Mexico to enjoy the simple life, and this inclination shows in the restaurant's welcoming, unhurried atmosphere. The menu is mostly northern Italian, with several dishes from other parts of Italy. There are daily specials, too. Pastas (except penne and spaghetti) are made in-house, and none is precooked. Try fish and shrimp ravioli or penne alla Veneta. The lobster is prepared beautifully. There are several

Choosing an All-Inclusive in the Riviera Maya

More than 40 all-inclusive resorts line this coast. Most people are familiar with the concept—large hotels that work with economies of scale to offer lodging, food, and drink all for a single, low rate. All-inclusives offer convenience and economy, especially for families with many mouths to feed. Because they are enclosed areas, they make it easy for parents to watch their children.

A certain sameness pervades these hotels so that a lot can be said that applies to all. They're usually built around a large pool with activities and an activities organizer. There is often a quiet pool, too. One large buffet restaurant and a snack bar serve the needs of most guests, but there will be a couple of specialty restaurants at no extra charge but for which the guest has to make reservations. Colored bracelets serve to identify guests. In the evenings a show is presented at the hotel's theater.

These resorts work best for those who are looking for a relaxing beach vacation and to get away from the cold weather. They don't work for those who aim to get away from crowds—these hotels are large and operate with a high occupancy rate. Yes, staying at these all-inclusives is convenient and hassle-free. They make everything easy, including taking tours and day trips—all the organizing is done for you. On the downside, you don't often get the spontaneity or the sense of adventure that comes with other styles of travel. The question you have to ask yourself is "what kind of vacation am I looking for?"

The best way to get a room at an all-inclusive is through a vacation packager or one of its travel agents. You get a better deal than by contacting the

wines, mostly Italian, to choose from. The salads are good and carefully prepared—dig in without hesitation.

Av. 5 (between calles 6 and 8; look for a sign for Hotel Marieta). © **984/876-3926.** Reservations recommended in high season. Main courses $12–$22 (£6–£11). No credit cards. Wed–Mon 2–11pm.

El Asador de Manolo 𝕲𝕲 STEAKS/ARGENTINE   If I want a steak in Playa, this is where I go. (Well, actually, I would try the address listed below in hopes that the restaurant pulled off the move as planned, but this being Mexico, I would be prepared to find it back at it's old location on Avenida 10 between 24 and 26.) The owner is an Argentine who has been living in Mexico so long, he's gone Mexican. But the food is faithful to his native land: steaks, good *empanadas,* and southern-style pastas, and you can't go wrong with any of the soups. When ordering a steak, see p. 769, "Appendix B," for the proper terminology. For dessert there are crepes and flan.

Calle 28 (at Av. 10). © **984/803-0632.** Reservations recommended in high season. Main courses $7–$20 (£3.50–£10); steaks $14–$30 (£7–£15). MC, V. Mon–Fri 1–11pm; Sat–Sun 4pm–midnight.

La Cueva del Chango 𝕲 MEXICAN   Good food in original surroundings with a relaxed "mañana" attitude. True to its name ("The Monkey's Cave"), the place suggests a cave and has little waterways meandering through it, and there are two spider hotel directly. Even if you have frequent-flier miles to burn, you will still find it difficult to match the rates of a full package offered by one of the biggies like Funjet.

Of the many all-inclusives in the Riviera Maya, there are a few that are my favorites and might bear looking into.

Of the several all-inclusives that are in Playa del Carmen/Playacar, I like **Iberostar Quetzal** or **Tucán** (two names for different halves of the same hotel; www.iberostar.com). The food is better than at most, and the central part of the hotel is made of raised walkways and terraces over the natural mangrove habitat. Other resorts in Playacar that bear investigation are the **Sandos Playacar** and any of the hotels in the southern half. Those in the northern half are losing beach.

The **Hotel Copacabana** in Xpu-Ha (www.hotelcopacabana.com) has raised walkways, preserving much of the flora and making it visually interesting. And Xpu-Ha is blessed with a stunning beach.

Aventura Spa Palace (www.palaceresorts.com) is another hotel in the Palace chain—this one is just for grownups. It has a large spa and gym and attractive common areas and guest rooms. There is a large pool but no beach; guests can take a shuttle to the Xpu-Ha property if they want.

Freedom Paradise (www.freedomparadise.com) is billed as the first size-friendly vacation resort. The management has worked hard to create an environment that large people will find comfortable. I like it because it doesn't have all the froufrou of so many other resorts—it's friendly and unpretentious.

monkeys that hang about in the back of the place. But take away the water and the monkeys, and, oddly enough, it brings to mind the Flintstones. You'll enjoy great juices, blended fruit drinks, salads, soups, Mexican specialties with a natural twist, and handmade tortillas. The fish is fresh and delicious. Mosquitoes can sometimes be a problem at night, but the management has bug spray for the guests.

Calle 38 (between Av. 5 and the beach, near the Shangri-la Caribe). ℂ **984/116-3179.** Main courses $8 $14 (£4 £7). No credit cards. Mon–Sat 8am–11pm; Sun 8am–2pm.

La Vagabunda ITALIAN/MEXICAN   This place is old-style Playa in its simple charm. A large *palapa* shelters several simple wood tables sitting on a gravel floor. It's low-key and quiet—a good place for breakfast, with many options, including delicious blended fruit drinks, waffles, and omelets. The specials are a good value. In the afternoon and evening, they serve light fare such as panini, pastas, and ceviche.

Av. 5 (between calles 24 and 26). ℂ **984/873-3753.** Breakfast $4–$6 (£2–£3); main courses $7–$12 (£3.50–£6). MC, V. High season daily 7am–11:30pm; low season daily 7am–3:30pm.

Media Luna 𝕽𝕽 FUSION   This restaurant has an inventive menu that favors grilled seafood, sautés, and pasta dishes. Everything is fresh and prepared beautifully. Try the very tasty pan-fried fish cakes with mango and honeyed hoisin sauce. Another choice is the black pepper–crusted fish. Be sure to eye the daily specials. For lunch you can get sandwiches and salads, as well as black-bean quesadillas and crepes. The decor is primitive-tropical chic.

Av. 5 (between calles 12 and 14). (🕾 **984/873-0526.** Breakfast $4–$6 (£2–£3); sandwich with salad $5–$7 (£2.50–£3.50); main courses $8–$15 (£4–£7.50). No credit cards. Daily 8am–11:30pm.

INEXPENSIVE

La Tarraya Restaurant/Bar *Value* SEAFOOD/YUCATECAN THE RESTAURANT THAT WAS BORN WITH THE TOWN, proclaims the sign. It's right on the beach, where the water practically laps at the foundation. Because the owners are fishermen, the fish is so fresh it's still practically wiggling. The wood hut doesn't look like much, but they also have tables right on the beach. You can have your fish prepared in several ways. If you haven't tried the Yucatecan specialty *tik-n-xic*—fish with *achiote* and bitter-orange sauce, cooked in a banana leaf—this is a good place to do so. I can also recommend the ceviche and the beer.

Calle 2 Norte. (🕾 **984/873-2040.** Main courses $5–$10 (£2.50–£5); whole fish $9 (£4.50) per kilogram (2.2 lbs.). No credit cards. Daily noon–9pm.

PLAYA DEL CARMEN AFTER DARK

It seems as if everyone in town is out strolling along "la Quinta" until midnight; there's pleasant browsing, dining, and drinking available at the many establishments on the street. Here's a quick rundown of the bars that you won't find on Quinta Avenida. The beach bar that is an institution in Playa is the **Blue Parrot** (🕾 **984/873-0083**). It gets live acts, mostly rock, and attracts a mixed crowd. It's between calles 12 and 14. Just to the south is **Om** (no phone), which gets a younger crowd with louder musical acts.

Alux (🕾 **984/110-5050**) is a one-of-a-kind club occupying a large cave with two dramatically lit chambers and several nooks and sitting areas. It's worth going to, if only for the novelty. The local conservancy group approved all the work, and great care was taken not to contaminate the water, which is part of a larger underground river system. The club books a variety of music acts, usually with no cover. Often there's belly dancing, which is quite in keeping with the surroundings, and I couldn't help but think that I had stepped into a scene from a James Bond film. The bar is cash only and is open Tuesday to Sunday from 7pm to 2am. Take Avenida Juárez across to the other side of the highway—2 blocks down on your left.

For movie going, **Cine Hollywood,** Avenida 10 and Calle 8, in the Plaza Pelícanos shopping center, shows a lot of films in English with Spanish subtitles. Before you buy your ticket, make sure the film is subtitled *(subtitulada)* and not dubbed *(doblada)*.

3 South of Playa del Carmen

South of Playa del Carmen you'll find a succession of small communities and resorts and two nature parks. From north to south, this section covers them in the following order: Xcaret, Paamul, Puerto Aventuras, Xpu-Ha, Akumal, Xel-Ha, Punta Solimán, and Tankah. This section spans about 56km (35 miles).

HEADING SOUTH FROM PLAYA DEL CARMEN Renting a car is the best way to move around down here. Southbound buses depart regularly from Playa, but the best they might do is get you close to your destination. And from the highway it can be a hot walk to the coast. Another option is to hire a car and driver.

Beyond Paamul, you'll see signs for this or that *cenote* or cave. There are thousands of cenotes in the Yucatán, and each is slightly different. These turnoffs are less visited than the major attractions and can make for a pleasant visit. Two major attractions bear specific mention: **Hidden Worlds,** offering remarkable snorkeling and diving tours of a couple of cenotes, and **Aktun Chen** cavern with a small nature park. Both are south of Akumal and described later in this chapter.

XCARET: A PARK CELEBRATING THE YUCATAN

A billboard in the airport of faraway Guadalajara reads in Spanish "And when visiting Xcaret, don't forget to enjoy the pleasures of the Riviera Maya, too." An exaggeration, but its point is well taken: Xcaret (pronounced "eesh-ca-*ret*") is the biggest attraction in these parts and is practically a destination unto itself. It even has its own resort. If you're coming to these shores to avoid crowds, avoid this place. If you're here for entertainment and activities, you should consider visiting Xcaret. What Xcaret does, it does very well, and that is to present in one package a little bit of everything that the Yucatán (and the rest of Mexico for that matter) has to offer.

Think of the activities that people come to the Yucatán for: hanging out on the beach, scuba and snorkeling, cavern diving, visiting ruins, taking a siesta in a hammock under a grove of palm trees, hiking through tropical forest, meeting native Maya peoples—Xcaret has all that plus handicraft exhibitions; a bat cave; a butterfly pavilion; mushroom and orchid nurseries; and lots of wildlife on display, including native jaguars, manatees, sea turtles, monkeys, macaws, flamingos, and a petting aquarium. Children love it. What probably receives most of the comments is the underground river (a natural feature of the park and common in much of the Yucatán) that's been opened in places to allow snorkelers to paddle along with the current. What else? A number of tours and shows, including *charros* (Mexican cowboys), from the state of Jalisco, and the Totonac Indian *voladores* ("flyers" who do a daring pole dance high above the ground), from the state of Veracruz.

The park is famous for its evening spectacle that is a celebration of the Mexican nation. I've seen it and have to say that it is some show, with a large cast and lots of props. It starts with the Maya and an interpretation of how they may have played the pre-Hispanic ball game/ritual known as *pok-ta-pok,* and then to another version of a ball game still practiced in the western state of Michoacán. From there it moves on to the arrival of the Spanish and eventually to the forging of the new nation, its customs, its dress, and its music and dance.

Xcaret is 10km (6½ miles) south of Playa del Carmen (you'll know when you get to the turnoff). It's open daily from 8:30am to 9pm. Admission prices are $59 (£30) for adults, $41 (£21) for children 5 to 12. Some activities cost extra: horseback ride $30 (£15), snuba/sea trek/snorkel tour $45 (£23), scuba $50 to $75 (£25–£38), swimming with dolphins $115 (£108). Other costs: lockers $2 (£1) per day, snorkel equipment $10 (£5) per day, food and drink variable. The park is an all-day affair; it's best to arrive early and register for tours and activities right away. For more info, call C 998/883-3143 or visit www.xcaret.net.

Four kilometers (2½ miles) south of the entrance to Xcaret is the turnoff for **Puerto Calica,** the cruise-ship pier. Passengers disembark here for tours of Playa, Xcaret, the ruins, and other attractions on the coast.

PAAMUL: SEASIDE GETAWAY

About 15km (10 miles) beyond Xcaret and 25km (15 miles) from Playa del Carmen is Paamul, which in Mayan means "a destroyed ruin." The exit is clearly marked. At Paamul (also written Pamul), you can enjoy the Caribbean with relative quiet; the water at the out-of-the-way beach is wonderful, but the shoreline is rocky. There are four rooms for rent, a restaurant, and many trailer and RV lots with hookups.

There's also a dive shop. **Scuba-Mex** (C 984/875-1066; fax 984/874-1729; www. scubamex.com) is a fully equipped PADI- and SSI-certified dive shop next to the *cabañas.* Using two boats, the staff takes guests on dives 8km (5 miles) in either direction. If it's too choppy, the reefs in front of the hotel are also good. The cost for a two-tank dive is $50 (£25), plus $25 (£13) to rent gear. Snorkeling is also excellent in this protected bay and the one next to it. The shop offers a great 3-hour snorkeling trip ($25/£13).

WHERE TO STAY & DINE

Cabañas Paamul 𝕽 Mostly Paamul works with the trailer crowd renting spaces by the day or month. But there are also 12 modern units called "junior suites" on or near the water's edge that are comfortable and spacious. These units are large and come with a kitchenette and two queen beds. Slightly cheaper, but more limited in size and amenities are the "eco-cabañas." Trailer guests have access to 12 showers and separate bathrooms for men and women. Laundry service is available nearby. The large, breezy *palapa* restaurant is a Brazilian-style grill under the management of Kalú da Silva, a retired Brazilian soccer player, who closed his restaurant in León, Guanajuato, to live on the coast. Restaurant customers are welcome to use the beach, which is rocky along this stretch of the coast. Prices very according to season.

Carretera Cancún–Tulum Km 85. (C 984/875-1053. paamulmx@yahoo.com. 22 units; 190 trailer spaces (all with full hookups). $100–$150 (£50–£75) junior suite; $80–$120 (£40–£60) *cabaña.* RV space with hookups $30 (£15) per day, $600 (£300) per month. No credit cards. Ask about discounts for stays longer than 1 week. Free parking. **Amenities:** Restaurant; bar; dive shop. *In room:* A/C, TV, kitchenette.

PUERTO AVENTURAS: A RESORT COMMUNITY

Five kilometers (3 miles) south of Paamul and 104km (65 miles) from Cancún is the glitzy development of Puerto Aventuras, on Chakalal Bay. It's a condo/marina community with a 9-hole golf course. At the center of the development is a collection of restaurants bordering a dolphin pool. They offer a variety of food—Mexican, Italian, steaks, even a popular pub. The major attraction is the dolphins. To swim with them in a highly interactive program, you must make reservations by contacting **Dolphin Discovery** (C 998/849-4757; www.dolphindiscovery.com). Make reservations well in advance—the surest way is through the website. A 1-hour session costs $125 (£63). There are shorter programs that cost less.

This is also the place to come for boating and deep-sea fishing. I recommend **Capt. Rick's Sportfishing Center** (C 984/873-5195 or -5387; www.fishyucatan.com). The best fishing on this coast is from March to August. The captain will be happy to combine a fishing trip with some snorkeling, which makes for a leisurely day.

Tips **In Case of Emergency**

The Riviera Maya, south of Puerto Aventuras, is susceptible to power failures that can last for hours. Gas pumps and cash machines shut down when this happens, and once the power returns, they attract long lines. It's a good idea to keep a reserve of gas and cash.

I don't find Puerto Aventuras to be an interesting place for lodging and prefer to stay elsewhere on the coast. It's like a mini Cancún, but lacking Cancún's vibrancy. There are a couple of fancy hotels. The main one is the **Omni Puerto Aventuras** (© 800/843-6664 in the U.S., or 984/873-5101). It looks larger than its 30 rooms would indicate and was probably intended to be bigger but didn't get the expected traffic.

XPU-HA: BEAUTIFUL BEACH

Three kilometers (2 miles) beyond Puerto Aventuras is **Xpu-Ha** (eesh-poo-*hah*) ⭐⭐⭐, a wide bay lined by a broad, beautiful sandy beach. Much of the bay is taken up by private houses and condos. There are a few all-inclusive resorts. One is **Xpu-Ha Palace** and another is the **Copacabana.** These suffered a lot of damage with Hurricane Emily but are open and back in business. Only a part of Xpu-Ha Palace is open as the other half awaits repair. The beach is big enough to accommodate the hotel guests, residents, and day-trippers without feeling crowded.

Besides the establishments reviewed here, a few hotels offer basic lodging—a couple of beds, cement floors, small private bathrooms, and minimal decoration. These rent on a first-come, first-served basis. Rates vary from $50 to $80 (£25–£40) a night, depending upon how busy they are. Lodging options are better in nearby Akumal, and, if you're renting a car, you can come for the day to enjoy the beach.

Al Cielo ⭐ *Moments*   This is a good choice if you want a small hotel on the beach where you can go native. The four rooms (two upstairs, two down) occupy a large thatched building right on the beach. The restaurant is very popular, but the rooms are rustic and simple, which sometimes works to draw guests into the beach experience as an escape from the modern world. If you're looking for more amenities, this won't be for you.

Carretera Cancún-Tulum Km. 118, 77710 Xpu-Ha, Q. Roo. No phone. www.alcielohotel.com. 4 units. $212–$258 (£106–£129) double. MC, V. No children accepted. Rates include full breakfast. Free secure parking. **Amenities:** Restaurant; bar; Hobie cat; tour info; room service. *In room:* Fan, Wi-Fi, hair dryer, safe, no phone.

Esencia ⭐⭐⭐   There's not a property on this entire coast that epitomizes leisure and escape more than this one. Lots of space, lots of beauty, lots of privacy, and an air of serenity pervades the entire complex. And, of course, the beach is magnificent. Service is personal and understated (a service fee is added to the room rate). If the spa were any more relaxing, it would lead to an out-of-body experience.

Predio Rústico Xpu-Ha, Fracc. 16 y 18, L. 18, 19 (exit Xpu-Ha-2), 77710 Xpu-Ha, Q. Roo. © 877/528-3490 in the U.S. or Canada, or © 984/873-4830. www.hotelesencia.com. 29 units. High season $582 (£291) and up for room or suite; low season $494 (£247) and up for room or suite. AE, MC, V. Free valet parking. **Amenities:** Restaurant; 2 bars; 2 pools; spa; Jacuzzi; concierge; tour desk; room service; in-room massage; babysitting; laundry; nonsmoking rooms. *In room:* A/C, TV/DVD, high-speed Internet access, minibar, hair dryer, safe.

AL: BEAUTIFUL BAYS & CAVERN DIVING

inuing south on Highway 307 for 2km (1¼ miles), you'll come to the turnoff for mal, marked by a traffic light. This is a small, ecologically oriented community built on the shores of two beautiful bays. Akumal has been around long enough that it feels more relaxed than booming places such as Playa and Tulum, and hotel rooms tend to go for less here. Akumal draws a lot of families, who can save money by renting a condo with a kitchen to fix meals. Less than 1km (a half-mile) down the road is a white arch. Just before it are a couple of grocery stores (the one named Super Chomak has an ATM) and a laundry service. Just after it (to the right) is the Hotel Akumal Caribe. If you follow the road to the left and keep to the left, you'll reach Half Moon Bay, lined with two- and three-story condos, and eventually Yal-ku Lagoon, which is a snorkeling park. For renting a condo, contact **Info-Akumal** (© **800/381-7048** in the U.S.; www.info-akumal.com), **Akumal Vacations** (© **800/448-7137** in the U.S.; www.akumalvacations.com), or **Loco Gringo** (www.locogringo.com).

Both bays have sandy beaches with rocky or silt bottoms. This is a popular diving spot. There are three dive shops in town and at least 30 dive sites offshore. The **Akumal Dive Shop** (© **984/875-9032;** www.akumal.com), one of the oldest and best dive shops on the coast, offers courses in technical diving and cavern diving trips. It and **Akumal Dive Adventures** (© **984/875-9157**), at the Vista del Mar hotel on Half Moon Bay, offer resort courses as well as complete certification.

Yal-ku Lagoon snorkeling park is like a miniature and more primitive Xel-Ha. It's open daily from 8am to 5:30pm. Admission is $7 (£3.50) for adults, $4 (£2) for children 3 to 14. The lagoon is about 700m (2,296 ft.) long and about 200m (656 ft.) at its widest. You can paddle around comfortably in sheltered water with little current and see fish and a few other creatures. It makes for a relaxing outing, but for sheer variety, I prefer snorkeling along the reefs.

WHERE TO STAY

The rates below are for two people and include taxes. Most hotels and condo rentals charge higher rates than those listed here for the holidays.

Hotel Akumal Caribe ★★ (Kids)　The hotel rooms and garden bungalows of this hotel sit along Akumal Bay. Both are large and comfortable, with tile floors and good-size bathrooms. The 40 **bungalows** are furnished simply and comfortably, with kitchenettes. The 21 rooms in the three-story beachside **hotel** are more elaborately furnished, with refrigerators. They have a king-size bed or two queen-size beds, tile floors, and Mexican accents. There is a large pool on the grounds. Other rooms belonging to the hotel are condos and the lovely **Villas Flamingo** on Half Moon Bay. The villas have two or three bedrooms and large living, dining, and kitchen areas, as well as lovely furnished patios just steps from the beach. The four villas share a pool.

Carretera Cancún–Tulum (Hwy. 307) Km 104. © 984/206-3500. www.hotelakumalcaribe.com. (Reservations: P.O. Box 13326, El Paso, TX 79913; © 800/351-1622 in the U.S., 800/343-1440 in Canada, or 915/584-3552.) 70 units. High season $123 (£62) bungalow, $156 (£78) hotel room, $190–$360 (£95–£180) villa or condo; low season $100 (£50) bungalow, $122 (£61) hotel room, $130–$212 (£65–£106) villa or condo. Reservations with prepayment by check only. AE, MC, V. Free parking. Low-season packages available. **Amenities:** 2 restaurants; bar; large outdoor pool; dive shop; tour desk; children's activities (seasonal); in-room massage; babysitting. *In room:* A/C, kitchenette (in some), fridge, coffeemaker, no phone.

Vista del Mar Hotel and Condos ★ (Value)　This beachside property is a great place to stay for several reasons. It offers hotel rooms at good prices, and large, fully equipped condos that you don't have to rent by the week. The lovely, well-tended beach in front of the hotel has chairs and umbrellas. There's an on-site dive shop, which eliminates the hassle of organizing dive trips. Hotel rooms are small and contain either a queen-size bed or a double and a twin bed. They consist of a well-equipped kitchen, a living area, two or three bedrooms, and one to three bathrooms. All have balconies or terraces facing the sea and are furnished with hammocks. Several rooms come with whirlpool tubs.

Half Moon Bay, 77760 Akumal, Q Roo. (C) 877/425-8625 in the U.S. Fax 505/988-3882. www.akumalinfo.com. 27 units. High season $102 (£51) double, $207–$325 (£104–£163) condo; low season $84 (£42) double, $124–$196 (£62–£98) condo. MC, V. Limited free parking. **Amenities:** Restaurant; bar; small outdoor pool; watersports equipment rental; dive shop. *In room:* A/C, TV, kitchenette, fridge, coffeemaker, CD player, no phone.

WHERE TO DINE

There are about 10 places to eat in Akumal, and there's a convenient grocery store, **Super Chomak,** by the archway. The **Turtle Bay Café and Bakery** is good (not open for supper in low season), as is **La Buena Vida,** on Half Moon Bay.

XEL-HA: SNORKELING & SWIMMING 𝒢𝒢

Before you get to Xel-Ha (shell-*hah*) nature park, you'll pass the turnoff for **Aktun Chen** 𝒢 cavern (a bit beyond Akumal). Of the several caverns that I've toured in the Yucatán, this is one of the best—it has lots of geological features, good lighting, several underground pools, and large chambers, all carefully preserved. The tour takes about an hour and requires a good amount of walking, but the footing is good. You exit not far from where you enter. There is also a zoo with specimens of the local fauna. Some of the critters are allowed to run about freely. In my opinion, the cost of admission is high—$17 (£8.50) for adults, $9 (£4.50) for children—but this is true of several attractions on this coast. The cavern is open 9am to 5pm daily. The turnoff is to the right, and the cave is about 4km (2½ miles) from the road.

Thirteen kilometers (8 miles) south of Akumal is **Xel-Ha** ((C) 998/884-9422 in Cancún, 984/873-3588 in Playa, or 984/875-6000 at the park; www.xelha.com.mx). The centerpiece of Xel-Ha is a large, beautiful lagoon, where freshwater and saltwater meet. You can swim, float, and snorkel in beautifully clear water surrounded by jungle. A small train takes guests upriver to a drop-off point. There, you can store all your clothes and gear in a locked sack that is taken down to the locker rooms in the main part of the building. The water moves calmly toward the sea, and you can float along with it. Snorkeling here is more comfortable than on the open sea—there are no waves and currents to pull you about, but there are several species of fish, including rays.

Inside the park, you can rent snorkeling equipment and an underwater camera. Platforms allow nonsnorkelers to view the fish. Another way to view fish is to use the park's snuba gear—a contraption that allows you to breathe air through 6m (20-ft.) tubes connected to scuba tanks floating on the surface. It frees you of the cumbersome tank while allowing you to stay down without having to hold your breath. Rental costs $50 (£25) for about an hour. Like snuba but more involved is sea-trek, a device consisting of an elaborate plastic helmet with air hoses. It allows you to walk around on the bottom breathing normally and perhaps participate in feeding the stingrays.

The park has completely remodeled and enlarged the dolphin area. This has improved the experience of swimming with these intelligent, powerful creatures. A 1-hour swim costs $125 (£63) plus park admission. You can also participate in a program that includes transportation from most hotels in the Riviera Maya and takes you to the dolphin area. It includes locker and equipment, too, all for $139 (£76). Make reservations ((C) 998/887-6840) at least 24 hours in advance.

Other attractions include a plant nursery; an apiary for the local, stingerless Maya bees; and a lovely path through the tropical forest bordering the lagoon. Xel-Ha is open daily from 8:30am to 5pm. Parking is free. Admission is $40 (£20) adults, and $30 (£15) children ages 5 to 11; children younger than 5 enter free. Admission includes use of inner tubes, life vest, and shuttle train to the river, and the use of changing rooms and showers. (Though not listed on the website, the park often has discount admission during the weekend.) An all-inclusive option includes snorkeling equipment rental, locker rental, towels, food, and beverages: Adults cost $75 (£38), children cost $50 (£25). These prices are not discounted on the weekend. The park has five restaurants, two ice-cream shops, and a store. It accepts American Express, MasterCard, and Visa, and it has an ATM.

Signs clearly mark the turnoff to Xel-Ha, close to the ruins of Tulum. A popular day tour from Cancún or Playa combines the two. If you're traveling on your own, the best time to enjoy Xel-Ha without the crowds is during the weekend from 9am to 2pm.

About 2km (1 mile) south of Xel-Ha are the **Hidden Worlds Cenotes** (✪✪✪ (✆ 984/877-8535; www.hiddenworlds.com.mx), which offers an excellent opportunity to snorkel or dive in a couple of nearby caverns. The caverns are part of a vast network that makes up a single underground river system. The water is crystalline (and cold), and the rock formations impressive. These caverns were filmed for the IMAX production *Journey into Amazing Caves.* The people running the show are resourceful. The snorkel tour costs $40 (£20) and takes you to two different caverns (a half-tour costs $25/£13). The main form of transportation is "jungle mobile," with a guide who throws in information and lore about the jungle plant life that you see. You'll be walking some, so take shoes or sandals. I've toured several caverns, but floating through one gave me an entirely different perspective. For divers, a one-tank dive is $50 (£25), a two-tank experience is $90 (£45). The owners have also installed a 180m (590-ft.) zip line on the property. I haven't tried it, but it looks fast.

PUNTA SOLIMAN & TANKAH BAYS

The next couple of turnoffs lead to Punta Solimán and Tankah bays. On Punta Solimán Bay is a beach restaurant called **Oscar y Lalo's.** Here you can rent kayaks and snorkel equipment and paddle out to the reefs for some snorkeling. Three kilometers (2 miles) farther is the turnoff for Tankah Bay, which has a handful of lodgings and some rental houses. The most interesting hotel is **Casa Cenote** (✆ 998/874-5170; www.casacenote.com). It has an underground river that surfaces at a cenote in the back of the property then goes underground and bubbles up into the sea just a few feet offshore. Casa Cenote has seven rooms, all on the beach. The double rate runs from $150 to $200 (£75–£100) depending upon the season, including breakfast. The American owner provides kayaks and snorkeling gear and can arrange dives, fishing trips, and sailing charters.

A beach road connects the two bays. I found the snorkeling in Tankah better than in Punta Solimán. Snorkeling in the latter was both interesting and frustrating. I've never before experienced so many thermoclines, which are produced by freshwater seeping from the floors of the bay and coming in contact with the warmer saltwater. Light passing through the water is refracted in funny ways. At first I found the effect interesting—it lent an ethereal shininess to everything I was seeing—but then it just got annoying as it cut down sharply on visibility. At one point I was floating through some of the worst of it, trying not to stir up the water, when a giant silvery barracuda came ghostlike through the shimmering water and crossed my field of vision about

2m (6 ft.) away. As he passed slowly by me, I was astonished at how beautiful and luminescent he looked. Still, I will take clear water over shimmering water every time.

4 Tulum (★(★(★, Punta Allen & Sian Ka'an

Tulum *pueblo* (130km/80 miles from Cancún) is a small town on Highway 307 where it intersects the road to Cobá. Nearby is an incredible beach, which has become the Tulum hotel zone—a collection of about 30 *palapa* hotels stretching from the Tulum ruins southward, along the Punta Allen Peninsula, all the way to the entrance to the Sian Ka'an Biosphere Reserve. The Tulum ruins are a walled Maya city of the post-Classic age perched on a rocky cliff overlooking the Caribbean. Tulum beach used to be a destination for backpackers, but the *palapa* hotels have gone upscale, and the beach now attracts a well-heeled crowd that seeks to get away from the bustle of the big hotels and resorts. The town of Tulum has several modest hotels, more than a dozen restaurants, several stores and pharmacies, three cybercafes, a few dive shops, a bank, two ATMs, and a new bus station.

For those who really want to leave the modern world behind, there's the Punta Allen Peninsula. Getting to the end of the peninsula from Tulum can take 1½ to 3 hours, depending on the condition of the road, which can be downright ugly. It's a quiet, out-of-the-way place; the generator (if there is one) shuts down at 10pm. For most people, Tulum will be far enough away from the crowds. But in Punta Allen, you'll find great fishing and snorkeling, the natural riches of the Sian Ka'an Biosphere Reserve, and a chance to rest up at what truly feels like the end of the road. A few beach *cabañas* offer reliable power, telephones, and hot showers.

ORIENTATION   To visit the Tulum area, get a rental car; it will make everything much easier. From the north you'll pass the entrance to the ruins before the town. After the ruins, you'll come to a highway intersection with a traffic light. To the right is the highway leading to the ruins of Cobá (see "Cobá Ruins," below); to the left is the Tulum hotel zone, which begins about 2km (1½ miles) away. The road sign reads BOCA PAILA, which is a place halfway down the **Punta Allen Peninsula.** This road eventually goes all the way to the tip of the peninsula and the town of Punta Allen, a lobstering and fishing village. It is a rough road that is slow going for most of the way. A few kilometers down the road is the entrance to the **Biosphere Reserve.**

The town of Tulum is growing quickly. It now extends for 3 or 4 blocks in either direction from the highway. The highway widens here and is called Avenida Tulum. It is lined with stores, restaurants, and what seems like a drug store on every corner. One

---

Tips Getting to the Beach

If you're staying elsewhere but want some beach time in Tulum, the easiest thing to do is drive to El Paraíso Beach Club. It's about 1km (a half-mile) south of the ruins (take a left at the "T" junction). This is a great place—there's a long, broad beach that is pure sand, and access is free. The owners make money by selling food and drink, so they ask you not to bring your own. If you want isolation, drive down the dirt road towards Punta Allen. After you pass the last of the beach hotels there are a couple of places where the beach comes into view. You can pull over and spread out your beach towel.

place that I find handy is a travel agency/communications/package center called **Savana** (© 984/871-2081) on the east side of Avenida Tulum between calles Orion and Beta. Most of the staff speaks English and can answer questions about tours and calling home. There's also a good bicycle rental store: **Iguana Bike** (© 984/871-2357; hugo_bike@hotmail.com) on Calle Satélite Sur near the corner of Calle Andrómeda. The owner, Hugo Herrera, maintains his bikes well and organizes tours.

EXPLORING THE TULUM ARCHEOLOGICAL SITE

Thirteen kilometers (8 miles) south of Xel-Ha are the ruins of Tulum, a Maya fortress-city on a cliff above the sea. The ruins are open to visitors daily from 7am to 5pm in the winter, 8am to 6pm in the summer. It's always best to go early, before the crowds start showing up (around 9:30am). The entrance to the ruins is about a 5-minute walk from the archaeological site. There are artisans' stands, a bookstore, a museum, a restaurant, several large bathrooms, and a ticket booth. Admission fee to the ruins is $5 (£2.50). If you want to ride the shuttle from the visitor center to the ruins, it's another $1.50 (75p). Parking is $3 (£1.50). A video camera permit costs $4 (£2). Licensed guides have a stand next to the path to the ruins and charge $20 (£10) for a 45-minute tour in English, French, or Spanish for up to four persons. In some ways, they are like performers and will tailor their presentation to the responses they receive from you. Some will try to draw connections between the Maya and Western theology, and they will point out architectural details that you might otherwise miss.

By A.D. 900, the end of the Classic period, Maya civilization had begun its decline, and the large cities to the south were abandoned. Tulum is one of the small city-states that rose to fill the void. It came to prominence in the 13th century as a seaport, controlling maritime commerce along this section of the coast, and remained inhabited well after the arrival of the Spanish. The primary god here was the diving god, depicted on several buildings as an upside-down figure above doorways. Seen at the Palace at Sayil and Cobá, this curious, almost comical figure is also known as the bee god.

The most imposing building in Tulum is a large stone structure above the cliff called the **Castillo** (castle). Actually a temple as well as a fortress, it was once covered with stucco and painted. In front of the Castillo are several unrestored palacelike buildings partially covered with stucco. On the **beach** below, where the Maya once came ashore, tourists swim and sunbathe, combining a visit to the ruins with a dip in the Caribbean.

The **Temple of the Frescoes,** directly in front of the Castillo, contains interesting 13th-century wall paintings, though entrance is no longer permitted. Distinctly Maya, they represent the rain god Chaac and Ixchel, the goddess of weaving, women, the moon, and medicine. On the cornice of this temple is a relief of the head of the rain god. If you pause a slight distance from the building, you'll see the eyes, nose, mouth, and chin. Notice the remains of the red-painted stucco—at one time all the buildings at Tulum were painted bright red.

Much of what we know of Tulum at the time of the Spanish Conquest comes from the writings of Diego de Landa, third bishop of the Yucatán. He wrote that Tulum was a small city, inhabited by about 600 people who lived in platform dwellings along a street and supervised the trade traffic from Honduras to the Yucatán. Though it was a walled city, most of the inhabitants probably lived outside the walls, leaving the interior for the residences of governors and priests and ceremonial structures. Tulum survived about 70 years after the conquest, when it was finally abandoned. Because of the great number of visitors this site receives, it is no longer possible to climb all of the ruins. In many cases, visitors are asked to remain behind roped-off areas to view them.

WHERE TO STAY

If you can afford staying at one of the small beach hotels in Tulum, do so. The experience is enjoyable and relaxing. But most are on the expensive side. Demand is high, supply is limited, and the hotels have to generate their own electricity (bring a flashlight). Most of the inexpensive hotels are not that comfortable. If you're on a budget, you will be more comfortable staying in Akumal or in one of the modest hotels in town and be a day-tripper to the beach.

Take the Boca Paila road from Highway 307. Three kilometers (2 miles) ahead, you come to a T-junction. To the south are most of the *palapa* hotels; to the north are several, too. The rates listed below don't include the week of Christmas and New Year, when prices go above regular high-season rates.

Very Expensive

Ana y José 🏵🏵   This *palapa* hotel has gone "boutique" with a spa, suites, and serious remodeling of rooms. It's a far cry now from what it used to be—a simple collection of cabins and a restaurant on the beach. Now there are marble countertops and marble tile floors. Rooms are large and comfortable. There's A/C in all the lower rooms that don't catch the sea breeze. The beach here is excellent. Ana y José is 6.5km (4 miles) south of the Tulum ruins.

Carretera Punta Allen Km 7 (Apdo. Postal 15), 77780 Tulum, Q. Roo. ℂ 998/880-5629. Fax 998/880-6021. www. anayjose.com. 22 units. $232–$256 (£116–£128) garden and pool view; $304–$370 (£152–£185) beachfront and ocean view. AE, MC, V. Free parking. **Amenities:** Restaurant; outdoor pool; spa; tour info; car rental. *In room:* A/C in some rooms, safe, no phone.

Azulik 🏵🏵   Azulik is all about slowing down, leaving civilization behind (except for such niceties as indoor plumbing and room service), and enjoying the simple life (with or without clothes). I enjoyed the simple life during a brief stay here, and appreciated the design and positioning of the individual *cabañas*. Most sit on a stone ledge above the sea. The ledge is just high enough to provide privacy while you sit out on the semi-shaded wood deck in front of your *cabaña* enjoying either the sun or the stars. For that purpose, they come with chairs, hammocks, and a wooden tub for soaking. (There is a larger wooden tub indoors for bathing.) Each *cabaña* is constructed entirely of wood and glass and thatch. There is no electricity, only candles. Each has a king-size bed with mosquito netting and a queen-size bed, suspended on ropes, for lounging during the day.

Carretera Boca Paila Km 5.5, 77780 Tulum, Q. Roo. ℂ 877/532-6737 in the U.S. and Canada. www.azulik.com. 15 units. High season $325–$350 (£163–£175) double; low season $255–$285 (£128–£143) double. MC, V. Limited free parking. Children younger than 18 not accepted. **Amenities:** Restaurant; bar; spa; room service. *In room:* Safe, no phone.

Moderate

Posada Dos Ceibas 🏵   Of all the places along this coast, this one reminds me the most of the way hotels in Tulum used to be: simple, quiet, and ecological without being pretentious. This is a good choice for a no-fuss beach vacation. The one- and two-story cottages are spread out through the vegetation. Rooms are simply furnished and come with ceiling fans, and almost all have private patios or porches. Price varies according to the size of the rooms. The grounds are well tended. The electricity is solar generated and comes on at 6pm. There is a pure sand beach.

Carretera Tulum-Boca Paila Km 10, 77780 Tulum, Q. Roo. Ⓒ **984/877-6024.** www.dosceibas.com. 8 units. High season $130–$250 (£65–£125) double; low season $90–$160 (£45–£80). MC, V. **Amenities:** Restaurant; massage; yoga classes. *In room:* No phone.

Zamas 𝒢𝒢 A couple from San Francisco has made this rustic getaway most enjoyable by concentrating on the essentials: comfort, privacy, and good food. The *cabañas* are simple, attractive, well situated for catching the breeze. Most rooms are in individual structures; the suites and oversize rooms are in modest two-story buildings. For the money, I like the garden *palapas,* which are attractive, spacious, and comfortable, and come with a queen-size bed and a twin or a king- and queen-size bed. Two small beachfront *cabañas* with one queen-size bed go for a little less. The most expensive rooms are the upstairs oceanview units, which enjoy a large terrace and lots of sea breezes. They come with a king-size and a queen-size bed or two queen-size beds. The restaurant serves the freshest seafood—I've seen the owner flag down passing fishermen to buy their catch. A white-sand beach stretches between rocky areas.

Carretera Punta Allen Km 5, 77780 Tulum, Q. Roo. Ⓒ **415/387-9806** in the U.S. www.zamas.com. 20 units. High season $120–$160 (£60–£80) beachfront double, $130–$160 (£65–£80) garden double, $200 (£100) oceanview double; low season $90–$125 (£45–£63) beachfront double, $95–$125 (£48–£63) garden double, $145 (£73) oceanview double. No credit cards. Limited free parking. **Amenities:** Restaurant. *In room:* No phone.

Inexpensive

Cabañas Tulum Next to Ana y José is a row of cinderblock bungalows facing the same beautiful ocean and beach. Rooms are simple and poorly lit, with basic bathrooms. All rooms have two double beds (most with new mattresses), screens on the windows, a table, one electric light, and a porch facing the beach. Electricity is available from 7 to 11am and 5 to 11pm.

Carretera Punta Allen Km 7 (Apdo. Postal 63), 77780 Tulum, Q. Roo. Ⓒ **984/115-9912.** Fax 984/802-5326. www.hotels tulum.com. 32 units. $70–$100 (£35–£50) double. No credit cards. Limited free parking. **Amenities:** Restaurant; game room. *In room:* No phone.

WHERE TO DINE

There are several restaurants in the town of Tulum. They are reasonably priced and do an okay job. On the main street are **Charlie's** (Ⓒ **984/871-2136**), my favorite for Mexican food, and **Don Cafeto's** (Ⓒ **984/871-2207**). **La Nave** (Ⓒ **984/871-2592**) is a good Italian restaurant. At **Azafrán** (Ⓒ **984/129-6130**), you can get surprisingly sophisticated cooking served in a small, rustic dining room. Also in town are a couple of roadside places that grill chicken and serve it with rice and beans. And there's a local people's restaurant at the southern end of town called **Doña Tina.** Meals on the coast are going to be more expensive but more varied. Many of the hotels have restaurants—I've eaten well at **Copal,** north of the T-junction, and **Zamas,** which is south.

EXPLORING THE PUNTA ALLEN PENINSULA

If you've been captured by an adventurous spirit and have an excessively sanguine opinion of your rental car's off-road capabilities, you might want to take a trip down the Punta Allen Peninsula, especially if your interests lie in fly-fishing, birding, or simply exploring new country. The far end of the peninsula is only 50km (30 miles) away, but it can be a very slow and bouncy trip (up to 3 hr., depending on the condition of the road). Not far from the last *cabaña* hotel is the entrance to the 500,000-hectare (1.3-million-acre) **Sian Ka'an Biosphere Reserve** (see below).

The Sian Ka'an Biosphere Reserve

Down the peninsula a few miles south of the Tulum ruins, you'll pass the guardhouse of the Sian Ka'an Biosphere Reserve. The reserve is a tract of 500,000 hectares (1.3 million acres) set aside in 1986 to preserve tropical forests, savannas, mangroves, coastal and marine habitats, and 110km (70 miles) of coastal reefs. The area is home to jaguars; pumas; ocelots; margays; jaguarundis; spider and howler monkeys; tapirs; white-lipped and collared peccaries; manatees; brocket and white-tailed deer; crocodiles; and green, loggerhead, hawksbill, and leatherback sea turtles. It also protects 366 species of birds—you might glimpse of an ocellated turkey, a great curassow, a brilliantly colored parrot, a toucan or trogon, a white ibis, a roseate spoonbill, a jabiru (or wood stork), a flamingo, or one of 15 species of herons, egrets, and bitterns.

The park has three parts: a "core zone" restricted to research; a "buffer zone," to which visitors and families already living there have restricted use; and a "cooperation zone," which is outside the reserve but vital to its preservation. There are two principal entrances to the biosphere reserve: one is from the community of Muyil, which is off Highway 307, south of Tulum (you take a boat down canals built by the Maya that connect to the Boca Paila lagoon); the other is from the community of Punta Allen (by Jeep down the peninsula, which separates the Boca Paila Lagoon from the sea).

Visitors can arrange day trips in Tulum from **Centro Ecológico de Sian Ka'an** (© **984/871-2499;** www.cesiak.org). It's office is at Av. Tulum 68. This is a nonprofit for the support of Sian Ka'an.

Halfway down the peninsula, at a small bridge, is the **Boca Paila Fishing Lodge** (www.bocapaila.com). Not for the general traveler, it specializes in hosting fly-fishers, with weeklong all-inclusive fishing packages. At this point, the peninsula is quite narrow. You can see the Boca Paila lagoon on one side and the sea on the other. Another 25km (15 miles) gets you to the village of Punta Allen. Before the town is a little hotel called **Rancho Sol Caribe.** It has only four rooms and a lovely beach all to itself. Punta Allen is a lobstering and fishing village on a palm-studded beach. Isolated and rustic, it's very much the laid-back end of the line. It has a lobster cooperative, a few streets with modest homes, and a lighthouse. The **Cuzan Guesthouse** (www.fly fishmx.com) is a collection of 12 cabins and one restaurant on a nice sandy beach. Its main clientele is fly-fishers, and it offers all-inclusive fishing packages. But co-owner Sonia Litvak, a Californian, will rent to anyone curious enough to want to go down there. She also offers snorkeling trips and boat tours.

5 Cobá Ruins

168km (104 miles) SW of Cancún

Older than most of Chichén Itzá and much larger than Tulum, Cobá was the dominant city of the eastern Yucatán before A.D. 1000. The site is large and spread out, with thick forest growing between the temple groups. Rising high above the forest canopy are tall and steep pyramids of the Classic Maya style. Of the major sites, this one is the least reconstructed and so disappoints those who expect another Chichén Itzá. The stone sculpture here has worn off and has become impossible to make out. But the structures themselves and the surrounding jungle and twin lakes make the experience enjoyable. This is not a cenote area, and the water has nowhere to go but stay on the surface. The forest canopy is also higher than in the northern part of the peninsula.

ESSENTIALS

GETTING THERE & DEPARTING   By Car   The road to Cobá begins in Tulum and continues for 65km (40 miles). Watch out for both *topes* (speed bumps) and potholes. The road is going to be repaved and widened this year. Close to the village of Cobá you will come to a triangle offering you three choices: Nuevo Xcan, Valladolid, and Cobá. Make sure not to get on the other two roads. The entrance to the ruins is a short distance down the road past some small restaurants and the large lake.

By Bus   Several buses a day leave Tulum and Playa del Carmen for Cobá. Several companies offer bus tours.

EXPLORING THE COBA RUINS

The Maya built many intriguing cities in the Yucatán, but few grander than Cobá ("water stirred by wind"). Much of the 67-sq.-km (26-sq.-mile) site remains unexcavated. A 100km (62-mile) *sacbé* (a pre-Hispanic raised road) through the jungle linked Cobá to Yaxuná, once an important Maya center 50km (30 miles) south of Chichén Itzá. It's the Maya's longest known *sacbé*, and at least 50 shorter ones lead from here. An important city-state, Cobá flourished from A.D. 632 (the oldest carved date found here) until after the rise of Chichén Itzá, around 800. Then Cobá faded in importance and population until it was finally abandoned. Scholars believe Cobá was an important trade link between the Yucatán Caribbean coast and inland cities.

Once at the site, keep your bearings—you can get turned around in the maze of dirt roads in the jungle. And bring bug spray. As spread out as this city is, renting a bike (which you can do at the entrance for $3/£1.50) is a good option. Branching off from every labeled path, you'll notice unofficial narrow paths into the jungle, used by locals as shortcuts through the ruins. These are good for birding, but be careful to remember the way back.

The **Grupo Cobá** holds an impressive pyramid, **La Iglesia (the Temple of the Church)**. Take the path bearing right after the entrance. The urge to climb the temple is great, but the view is better from El Castillo in the Nohoch Mul group farther back.

From here, return to the main path and turn right. You'll pass a sign pointing right to the ruined *juego de pelota* **(ball court)**, but the path is obscure.

Continuing straight ahead on this path for 5 to 10 minutes, you'll come to a fork in the road. To the left and right you'll notice jungle-covered, unexcavated pyramids, and at one point, you'll see a raised portion crossing the pathway—this is the visible remains of the *sacbé* to Yaxuná. Throughout the area, carved stelae stand by pathways or lie forlornly in the jungle underbrush. Although protected by crude thatched roofs, most are weatherworn enough that they're indiscernible.

The left fork leads to the **Nohoch Mul Group,** which contains **El Castillo.** With the exception of Structure 2 in Calakmul, this is the tallest pyramid in the Yucatán (even higher than El Castillo at Chichén Itzá and the Pyramid of the Magician at

Uxmal). Visitors can climb to the top. From this lofty perch, you can see unexcavated jungle-covered pyramidal structures poking up through the forest canopy all around.

The right fork (more or less straight on) goes to the **Conjunto Las Pinturas.** Here, the main attraction is the **Pyramid of the Painted Lintel,** a small structure with traces of its original bright colors above the door. You can climb up for a close look. Though maps of Cobá show ruins around two lakes, there are really only two excavated groups.

Admission is $4 (£2), free for children younger than age 12. Parking is $1 (50p). A video camera permit costs $4 (£2). The site is open daily from 8am to 5pm, sometimes longer. *Note:* Visit Cobá in the morning or after the heat of the day has passed. Mosquito repellent, drinking water, and comfortable shoes are imperative.

WHERE TO STAY & DINE

If nightfall catches you in Cobá, you have limited lodging choices. There is one tourist hotel called **Villas Arqueológicas Cobá,** which fronts the lake. Though smaller than its sister hotels in Uxmal and Chichén Itzá, it's the same in style—modern rooms that are attractive and functional, so long as you're not too tall. It has a restaurant that serves all three meals and a swimming pool. The hotel could be empty or full given that most of its business comes from bus tours. This hotel and the other Villas Arqueológicas were sold in late 2007 by Club Med to the Islander Collection, a Mexican hotel group. To make reservations, call © **987/872-9300, ext. 8101.** There's also a cheap hotel in town called **El Bocadito** (no phone), with simple rooms for $25 (£13) per night. It has a small restaurant; there are a couple more eateries in the town as well.

EN ROUTE TO THE LOWER CARIBBEAN COAST: FELIPE CARRILLO PUERTO

Mexico's lower Caribbean coast is officially called the Costa Maya. This area attracts fishermen, divers, archeology enthusiasts, birders, and travelers looking to get away from the crowds. For divers there is some great diving along the coastal reefs and at the Chinchorro Reef, which lies about 30km (20 miles) offshore (see below). You'll find sandy beaches good for sunbathing, but not for swimming because of the prominent coastal reef. But if you want to snorkel or dive among less-visited reefs, kayak in calm turquoise water, or perhaps do fly-fishing away from the crowds, this area is a great option. And there's fine swimming in Lake Bacalar.

You also might enjoy the astounding Maya ruins in the Río Bec area, west of Bacalar. Here, too, you'll find a richer ecosystem than the northern part of the peninsula. The forest canopy is higher, and the wildlife is more abundant. If you're interested in exploring this territory, see "Side Trips to Maya Ruins from Chetumal," later in this chapter.

Continue south on Highway 307 from Tulum. The road narrows, the speed limit drops, and you begin to see *topes.* Down the road some 25km (15 miles), a sign points to the small but interesting ruins of **Muyil.** Take bug spray. The principal ruins are a small group of buildings and a plaza dominated by the Castillo, a pyramid of medium height but unusual construction. From here, a canal dug by the Maya enters what is now the Sian Ka'an Biosphere Reserve and empties into a lake, with other canals going from there to the saltwater estuary of Boca Paila. The local community offers a boat ride through these canals and lakes. The 3½-hour tour includes snorkeling the canal and letting the current carry you along. Soft drinks are also included. This is much the same Sian Ka'an tour offered by travel agencies in Tulum, but without some of the infrastructure. The agencies charge more but provide transportation, better interpretation, and lunches.

Felipe Carrillo Puerto (pop. 60,000) is the first large town you pass on the road to Ciudad Chetumal. It has two gas stations, a market, a bus terminal, and a few modest hotels and restaurants. Next to the gas station in the center of town is a bank with an ATM. Highway 184 goes from here into the interior of the peninsula, leading eventually to Mérida, which makes Carrillo Puerto a turning point for those making the "short circuit" of the Yucatán Peninsula.

The town is of interest for having been a rebel stronghold during the War of the Castes and the center of the intriguing millenarian cult of the "Talking Cross." The town is still home to a strong community of believers in the cult who practice their own brand of religion and are respected by the entire town. Every month, a synod of sorts is held here for the church leaders of 12 neighboring towns.

6 Majahual, Xcalak & the Chinchorro Reef

South of Felipe Carrillo Puerto, the speed bumps begin in earnest. In 45 minutes you reach the turnoff for Majahual and Xcalak, which is after the town of Limones. From here, the highway has been widened and repaved. The roadwork was done to facilitate bus tours from the cruise-ship pier in **Majahual** (mah-hah-*wahl*) to some of the Maya ruins close by. Many passengers elect to enjoy some beach time in Majahual instead. The best option is to keep your distance from the pier and stay either in the lower Majahual area or at the bottom of the peninsula near Xcalak. You'll come to the turnoff for Xcalak before you get to Majahual. Xcalak has a decent dive shop. From Majahual to Xcalak takes a little less than an hour.

Xcalak (eesh-kah-*lahk*) is a depopulated, weather-beaten fishing village with a few comfortable places to stay and a couple of restaurants. It once had a population as large as 1,200 before the 1958 hurricane washed most of the town away; now it has only 300 permanent residents. It's charming in a run-down way, and you'll certainly feel miles away from the crush of the crowds. From here you work your way back up the coast to get to one of the several small inns just beyond the town.

ORIENTATION

ARRIVING   By Car   Driving south from Felipe Carrillo Puerto, you'll come to the clearly marked turnoff onto Highway 10, 2.5km (1½ miles) after Limones, at a place called Cafetal (before the turnoff, there's a gas station). From there it's a 50km (30-mile) drive to the coast, and Majahual. The pier is north of the road; Hotel Balamkú, which I like, is to the south. If you're going to Xcalak, the turn-off will be 2km (1¼ miles) before Majahual, at a military checkpoint. The road is paved, but usually with some potholes. It's 55km (34 miles) long.

DIVING THE CHINCHORRO REEF

The **Chinchorro Reef Underwater National Park** is 38km (24 miles) long and 13km (8 miles) wide. The oval reef is as shallow as 1m (3¼ ft.) on its interior and as deep as 900m (2,952 ft.) on its exterior. It lies some 30km (19 miles) offshore. Locals claim it's the last virgin reef system in the Caribbean. It's invisible from the ocean side; hence, one of its diving attractions is the **shipwrecks**—at least 30—that decorate the underwater landscape. One is on top of the reef. Divers have counted 40 cannons at one wreck site. On the west side are walls and coral gardens.

The Yucatán's Lower Caribbean Coast

Aventuras XTC (© 983/839-8865; www.xtcdivecenter.com) is a fully equipped dive shop in Xcalak (technical diving, Nitrox, snorkel and fishing trips). You can arrange dives to the local reefs, San Pedro in Belize, and to the Chinchorro Reef.

WHERE TO STAY & DINE

Balamkú Inn on the Beach 🐟🐟
This is a comfortable and friendly place to stay in south Majahual. Rooms are in one- and two-story thatched bungalows distributed across 110m (360 ft.) of beautiful white beach. They are large and breezy with large attractive bathrooms and comfortable mattresses. All have terraces facing the beach. This hotel is very ecological. All the energy is produced by wind and sun. To run this kind of operation takes a rare combination of skill and talent, which these owners have in ample supply.

Carretera Costera Km 5.7, Majahual, Q. Roo. © 983/839-5332. www.balamku.com. 10 units. $75–$85 (£38–£43) double. Rates include full breakfast. AE, MC, V for deposits only; no credit cards at hotel. Free guarded parking. **Amenities:** Watersports equipment; activities arranged; airport transportation arranged; in-room massage; non-smoking rooms. *In room:* Wi-Fi, no phone.

Costa de Cocos Dive & Fly-Fishing Resort 🐟🐟
Several freestanding *cabañas* sit around a large, attractive sandy beach graced with coconut palms. The *cabañas* are comfortable and have a lot of cross-ventilation, ceiling fans, hot water, and comfortable beds.

They also come with 24-hour electricity using wind and solar power and purified tap water. One is a two-bedroom unit with two bathrooms. Activities include kayaking, snorkeling, scuba diving, and fly-fishing. The resort has experienced English-speaking fishing guides and a dive instructor. It has a large dive boat capable of taking divers to the Chinchorro Reef. The casual restaurant/bar offers good home-style cooking.

Carretera Majahual–Xcalak Km 52, Q. Roo. No phone. www.costadecocos.com. 16 *cabañas*. High season $85 (£43) double; low season $79 (£40) double. Dive and fly-fishing packages available by e-mail request. Rates include breakfast buffet. AE, MC, V. Free parking. **Amenities:** Restaurant; bar; watersports equipment; dive shop. *In room:* No phone.

Hotel Tierra Maya ⟨★⟩ This is a comfortable, modern-style hotel on the beach. Rooms in the two-story building are spacious and designed to have good cross ventilation. They come with ceiling fans. Each has a private balcony or terrace that looks out to the sea, hammocks, and bottled purified water. Solar generators provide electricity. Bathrooms are large, and beds are either twins or queen-size beds. The owners arrange diving, fishing, and snorkeling trips for guests. Guests have Internet access and the use of kayaks and bikes.

Carretera Majahual–Xcalak Km 54, Q. Roo. No phone. www.tierramaya.net. 7 units. High season $90–$110 (£50– £61) double; low season $70–$90 (£39–£50) double. Rates include continental breakfast. MC, V for advance payments. Limited free parking. **Amenities:** Restaurant; bar; kayaks; bikes; Internet access. *In room:* No phone.

7 Lago Bacalar ★★★

104km (65 miles) SW of Felipe Carrillo Puerto; 37km (23 miles) NW of Chetumal

Bacalar Lake is an elaborate trick played upon the senses. I remember once standing on a pier on the lake and gazing down into perfectly clear water. As I lifted my eyes I could see the blue tint of the Caribbean. Beyond lay a dense tropical forest. A breeze blowing in from the sea smelled of the salt air, and though I knew it to be untrue, I couldn't help but believe that the water I was gazing on was, in fact, an inlet of the sea and not a lake at all—perhaps a well-sheltered lagoon like Xel-Ha. Lakes in tropical lowlands, especially those surrounded by tropical jungle, are turbid and muddy. How could this one be so clear? It's because Bacalar is not fed by surface runoff, but by several cenote that lie beneath its surface. Only in the Yucatán is such a thing possible.

This is the perfect spot for being bone idle. But there's plenty to do, too. You can explore the jungle, visit some particularly elegant Maya ruins in the nearby Río Bec area, or take in a wonderful museum about the Maya in Chetumal. The town of Bacalar is quiet and quaint. There are a few stores and a couple of restaurants. An 18th-century fort with a moat and stout bastions is by the lake. Inside the fort is a small museum (admission is 50¢/25p) that has several artifacts on display. All text is in Spanish.

ORIENTATION Driving south on Highway 307, the town of Bacalar is 1½ hours beyond Felipe Carrillo Puerto, clearly marked by signs. If you're driving north from Chetumal, it takes about a half-hour. Buses going south from Cancún and Playa del Carmen stop here, and there are frequent buses from Chetumal. There are now a couple of gas stations on the highway here.

WHERE TO STAY

Hotel Laguna The Laguna overlooks the lake from a lovely vantage point. All the rooms share the view and have little terraces that make enjoyable sitting areas. The midsize rooms have ceiling fans, and most come with two double beds. The mattresses in the bungalows aren't good. The bathrooms are simple but have no problem delivering hot water. A restaurant that shares the same view is open from 7am to 9pm. The bar makes a credible margarita. The highest occupancy rates are from July to August and December to January, when you should make a reservation. The hotel is hard to spot from the road; look for the sign about 1km (half a mile) after you pass through the town of Bacalar.

Bulevar Costera de Bacalar 479, 77010 Lago Bacalar, Q. Roo. ℂ 983/834-2206. Fax 983/834-2205. 34 units. $55 (£28) double; $93–$116 (£48–£58) bungalow for 5–8 persons. MC, V. Free parking. **Amenities:** Restaurant; bar; small outdoor pool, boat rides on the lake. *In room:* No phone.

Rancho Encantado Cottage Resort 🌟🌟 This serene lakeside retreat consists of 13 white-stucco cottages scattered over a shady lawn beside the smooth Lago Bacalar. Each is large and has louvered windows, a red-tile floor, a dining table and chairs, a living room or sitting area, a porch with chairs, and hammocks strung between trees. Some rooms have cedar ceilings and red-tiled roofs, and others have thatched roofs. Four cottages are waterfront (nos. 9–12). Beds come in different combinations of doubles and twins. The "laguna suite" is a one-bedroom townhouse with study, air-conditioning, and private dock; it rents by the week. Orange, lime, mango, sapote, Ceiba, banana, palm, and oak trees; wild orchids; and bromeliads on the grounds make great bird shelters, attracting flocks of chattering parrots, turquoise-browed motmots, toucans, and many more species. The hotel offers almost a dozen excursions.

Carretera Bacalar–Felipe Carrillo Puerto Km 3, 77930 Chetumal, Q. Roo. ℂ/fax **983/101-3358.** www.encantado. com. (Reservations: P.O. Box 1256, Taos, NM 87571. ℂ **800/505-6292** in the U.S., or ℂ/fax 505/894-7074.) 13 units. High season $160–$190 (£80–£95) double; low season $110–$150 (£55–£75) double. Rates include continental breakfast and dinner. MC, V. Free parking. **Amenities:** Restaurant; bar; large outdoor whirlpool; spa; watersports equipment; tour desk; massage. *In room:* Fridge, coffeemaker.

WHERE TO DINE

Besides the restaurants at the hotels discussed above, you may enjoy the **Restaurante Cenote Azul** (ℂ **983/834-2460;** www.cenoteazul.com.mx), a comfortable open-air thatched-roof restaurant on the edge of the beautiful Cenote Azul. Main courses cost $5 to $16 (£2.50–£8). To get to Restaurant Cenote Azul, follow the highway to the south edge of town and turn left at the restaurant's sign; follow the road around to the restaurant. At the restaurant, you can take a dip in placid Cenote Azul as long as you don't have creams or lotions on your skin.

8 Chetumal

251km (156 miles) S of Tulum; 37km (23 miles) S of Lago Bacalar

Capital of the state, and the second-largest city (after Cancún), Chetumal (pop. 210,000) is not a tourist destination. The old part of town, down by the river (Río Hondo), has a Caribbean feel, but the rest is unremarkable. Chetumal is the gateway to Belize, Tikal, and the Río Bec ruins. If you're going to spend the night here, visit the **Museo de la Cultura Maya** (ℂ **983/832-6838**), especially if you plan to follow the Río Bec ruin route (see "Side Trips to Maya Ruins from Chetumal," below).

ESSENTIALS
GETTING THERE & DEPARTING
BY PLANE Aviacsa (ℂ **983/872-7698**) and **Click** (ℂ **983/832-6675**) have a direct flight to and from Mexico City. The airport is west of town, just north of the entrance from the highway.

BY CAR   It's a little more than 3 hours from Tulum. If you're heading to Belize, you won't be able to take your rental car because the rental companies won't allow it. To get to the ruins of Tikal in Guatemala, you must go through Belize to the border crossing at Ciudad Melchor de Mencos. To drive into Chetumal, there's a flyover now where the road splits off for Belize.

BY BUS   The main bus station (© 983/832-5110) is 20 blocks from the town center on Insurgentes at Niños Héroes. Buses go to Cancún, Tulum, Playa del Carmen, Puerto Morelos, Mérida, Campeche, Villahermosa, and Tikal, Guatemala.

To Belize: Buses depart from the Lázaro Cárdenas market (most often called *el mercado nuevo*). Ask for **Autobuses Novelo.** The company has local service every 45 minutes ($12/£6) and four express buses per day ($16/£8).

VISITOR INFORMATION
The **State Tourism Office** (© 983/835-0860, ext. 1811) is at Calzada del Centenario 622, between Comonfort and Ciricote. It's open Monday to Friday from 9am to 6pm.

ORIENTATION
The telephone **area code** is **983.**

Traffic enters the city from the west and feeds onto Avenida Obregón into town. Stay on Obregón and don't take the exit for Av. Insurgentes. Eventually you'll cross Avenida Héroes, which is the main north–south street.

A MUSEUM NOT TO MISS
Museo de la Cultura Maya 👁👁👁   This modern museum unlocks the complex world of the Maya through interactive exhibits and genuine artifacts. Push a button, and an illustrated description appears, explaining the medicinal and domestic uses of plants with their Mayan and scientific names; another exhibit describes the social classes of the Maya by their manners of dress. One of the most fascinating exhibits describes the Maya's ideal of personal beauty and the subsequent need to deform craniums, scar the face and body, and induce cross-eyed vision. An enormous screen flashes images taken from an airplane flying over more than a dozen Maya sites from Mexico to Honduras. Another large television shows the architectural variety of Maya pyramids and how they were probably built. Then a walk on a glass floor takes you over representative ruins in the Maya world. In the center of the museum is the three-story, stylized, sacred Ceiba tree, which the Maya believed connected Xibalba (the underworld), Earth, and the heavens. If you can arrange it, see the museum before you tour the Río Bec ruins.

Av. Héroes s/n. © 983/832-6838. Admission $6 (£3.30). Tues–Thurs 9am–7pm; Fri–Sat 9am–8pm. Between Colón and Gandhi, 8 blocks from Av. Obregón, just past the Holiday Inn.

WHERE TO STAY
Hotel Holiday Inn Puerta Maya   This modern hotel (formerly the Hotel Continental) has the best air-conditioning in town and is only a block from the Museo de la Cultura Maya. Most rooms are midsize and come with two double beds or one king-size bed. Bathrooms are roomy and well lit.

Av. Héroes 171, 77000 Chetumal, Q. Roo. © 800/465-4329 in the U.S., or 983/835-0400. Fax 983/832-1676. 85 units. $125 (£69) double. AE, MC, V. Free secure parking. From Av. Obregón, turn left on Av. Héroes, go 6 blocks, and look for the hotel on the right. **Amenities:** Restaurant; bar; midsize outdoor pool; fitness room; room service; laundry service. *In room:* A/C, TV, Wi-Fi.

Hotel Nachancán   One block from *el mercado nuevo* (the new market), this hotel offers plain rooms, with one or two double beds. Bathrooms are small, with no counter space, but they offer plenty of hot water.

Calzada Veracruz 379, 77000 Chetumal, Q. Roo. (C) **983/832-3232**. 20 units. $31 (£16) double; $50 (£25) suite. No credit cards. Drive the length of Av. Obregón to where it stops at Calzada Veracruz, turn left, and drive 2km (1¼ miles); the hotel will be on the right. Off-street parking. **Amenities:** Restaurant; bar. *In room:* A/C, TV, no phone.

WHERE TO DINE

For an economical meal with some local atmosphere, try **Restaurante Pantoja,** on the corner of calles Ghandi and 16 de Septiembre ((C) **983/832-3957**), 2 blocks east of the Museum of Maya Culture. It offers a cheap daily special, good green enchiladas, and such local specialties as *poc chuc* (grilled marinated pork). It's open Monday to Saturday from 7am to 7pm. To sample excellent *antojitos*, the local supper food, go to **El Buen Gusto,** on Calzada Veracruz across from the market (no phone). A Chetumal institution, it serves excellent *salbutes* and *panuchos* (both dishes are similar to *gorditas*), tacos, and sandwiches. It's open in the morning until 2pm and then opens again around 7pm and closes at midnight. If for some reason it's closed, go next door **La Ideal,** which many locals hold to be the better of the two supper joints. It has delicious *tacos de pierna* (soft tacos with thinly sliced pork shoulder) and *agua de horchata* (water flavored with rice, vanilla, and toasted pumpkin seed).

ONWARD FROM CHETUMAL

From Chetumal you have several choices. The Maya ruins of Lamanai, in Belize, are an easy day trip if you have transportation (not a rental car). You can explore the Río Bec ruin route directly west of the city (see below) by taking Highway 186. If you want a guided tour of any of the ruins, contact Luis Téllez ((C) **983/832-3496;** www.mayaruinsandbirds.com). He lives in Chetumal, knows the region, stays up to date with the archeological excavations, and knows the wildlife of the region. He speaks English and is a good driver.

9 Side Trips to Maya Ruins from Chetumal

West of Bacalar and Chetumal is the **Río Bec** area, where you can visit several Maya cities. These are picturesque and display a style of architecture that's very different from the northern Yucatán sites. From Highway 307, take Highway 186 west. The road, a clearly marked federal highway, heads into the state of Campeche. Along the way are several ruins, some very close to the road, others a bit of a drive. You could fit visits to several of the ruins into a day trip, or you could spend the night in the area. There are a few jungle hotels in the area. Here they are in order of most expensive to least expensive: The **Explorean** ((C) **888/679-3748** in the U.S.; www.theexplorean.com) is an ecolodge for adventure travelers who like their comfort. It sits all alone on the crest of a small hill not far from the ruins of Kohunlich. The **Chicanná Eco Village** ((C) **983/816-2233** in Campeche for reservations), is just beyond the town of Xpujil. **Puerta Calakmul Hotel** (www.puertacalakmul.com.mx), at the turnoff for the ruins of Calakmul, was recently purchased by the owners of Chicanná Eco Village. **Río Bec Dreams** ((C) **983/871-6057;** www.riobecdreams.com) is a good choice because the owners live on the premises and keep maintenance and service sharp. It's 11km (7 miles) west of Xpujil. **Restaurant y Hotel Calakmul** ((C) **983/871-6029**) is in the town of Xpujil.

The following section lists sites in the order in which you would see them driving from Bacalar or Chetumal. For a map of this area, consult the Yucatán Peninsula map (in the color insert in the front of this book). Entry to each site costs $2 to $4 (£1.10–£2.20). Informational signs at each building within the sites are in Mayan, Spanish, and English. Keep the mosquito repellent handy.

Opening Hours
The archaeological sites along the Río Bec are open daily, 8am to 5pm.

Dzibanché (tzee-bahn-*cheh*) means "place where they write on wood." Two large adjoining plazas have been cleared. Despite centuries of an unforgiving wet climate, a wood lintel in good condition with a date carving (indicating A.D. 733) still supports a partially preserved corbelled arch on top of this building. Inside the Temple of the Owl, the tomb of a queen was discovered.

Kohunlich (koh-*hoon*-leek), 42km (26 miles) from the turnoff for Highway 186, dates from around A.D. 400. The turnoff is well marked on the left. The ruins are only 8km (5 miles) from the highway. You'll find a large, shady ceremonial area flanked by four large pyramids. Continue walking, and just beyond this grouping you'll come to Kohunlich's famous Pyramid of the Masks under a thatched covering.

Xpujil (eesh-poo-*heel*), **Becán** (beh-*kahn*), and **Chicanná** (chee-kah-*nah*) are close to the highway just past the border that separates Quintana Roo from Campeche. Here you'll find the elegant high-pitched roofs and decorative staircases that are a principal feature of the sites in this region. Becán has an impressive arrangement of plazas with several tall pyramids. A temple on top of Structure 1 had a ritual doorway, in the form of the Earth Monster's mouth, which could be reached by a secret stairway. Some large chambers beneath another structure were closed on my last visit due to hurricane damage. Beside the ball court is a richly decorated figure of a Maya nobleman with an elaborate headdress. Chicanná was a large walled city; several of its buildings are restored. This area is about 150km (100 miles) from Chetumal.

Calakmul is another walled city. The site is quite large and beautiful, but it's also 90 minutes from the highway on a one-lane paved road. Its grand pyramid is the tallest pyramid in the Yucatán, at 54m (177 ft.). It has several elegant structures and many stelae, most of which are thoroughly weathered and unreadable.

Balamkú, close to the highway not far beyond the turnoff for Calakmul, has some buildings in beautiful condition. In one you'll find a chamber with three large sculpted figures descending into the underworld in the gaping mouths of animals.

17

Mérida, Chichén Itzá & the Maya Interior

by David Baird

Ask most people about the Yucatán, and they think of Cancún, the Caribbean coast, and Chichén Itzá. With a little exploring, though, you'll find a world beyond the region's tourist magnets. You might spend a morning scrambling over Maya ruins and in the afternoon take a dip in the cool, clear water of a cenote (a limestone well that leads to an underground river). The next day may find you strolling along a lonely beach or riding in a skiff through mangroves to visit a colony of pink flamingos. By the evening, you might be dancing in the central plaza of the Yucatán capital, **Mérida.** This chapter covers the interior of the Yucatán peninsula, including the famous Maya ruins at **Chichén Itzá** and **Uxmal,** the flamingo sanctuaries at **Celestún** and **Río Lagartos,** as well as many other spots that might find special favor with you.

EXPLORING THE YUCATAN'S MAYA HEARTLAND

The best way to see the Yucatán is by car. The terrain is flat, there is little traffic once you get away from the cities, and the main highways are in good shape. If you drive at all around this area, you will add at least one new word to your Spanish vocabulary—*topes* (*toh*-pehs), meaning speed bumps. And along with *topes* you might learn a few new curse words. *Topes* come in varying shapes and sizes and with varying degrees of warning. Don't let them surprise you.

Off the main highways, the roads are narrow and rough, but hey—you'll be driving a rental car. Rentals are, in fact, a little pricey compared with those in the U.S. (due perhaps to wear and tear?), but some promotional deals are available, especially in low season. For more on renting a car, see "By Car," in "Mérida: Gateway to the Maya Heartland," below.

Plenty of buses ply the roads between the major towns and ruins. And plenty of tour buses circulate, too. But buses to the smaller towns and ruins and the haciendas are infrequent. One bus company, Autobuses del Oriente (ADO), controls most of the first-class bus service and does a good job with the major destinations. Second-class buses go to some out-of-the-way places, but they can be slow, stop a lot, and usually aren't air-conditioned. I will take them to cover short distances. If you don't want to rent a car, a few tour operators transport small groups to more remote attractions such as ruins, cenotes, and villages.

The Yucatán is *tierra caliente* (the hot lands). Don't travel in this region without a hat, sun block, mosquito repellent, and water. The coolest weather is from November to February; the hottest is from April to June. From July to October, thundershowers

Tips **The Best Websites for Mérida, Chichén Itzá & the Maya Interior**

- **Maya: Portraits of a People: www.nationalgeographic.com/explorer/ maya/more.html** A fascinating collection of articles from *National Geographic* and other sources.
- **Yucatán Travel Guide: www.mayayucatan.com** Yucatán's Ministry of Tourism maintains this site. It has an update section and good general info on different destinations in the state.
- **Mexico's Yucatán Directory: www.mexonline.com/yucatan.htm** A nice roundup of vacation rentals, tour operators, and information on the Maya sites. For more information on Mexico's indigenous history, see the links on the pre-Columbian page (www.mexonline.com/precolum.htm).

moderate temperatures. More tourists come to the interior during the winter months, but not to the same extent as on the Caribbean coast. The high-season/low-season distinction is less pronounced here.

Should you decide to travel into this part of the world, don't miss **Mérida.** It is, and has been for centuries, the cultural and commercial center of the Yucatán. You won't find a more vibrant tropical city anywhere. Every time I visit, there is some festival or celebration to attend, on top of the nightly performances that the city offers its citizens and visitors. It's also the Yucatán's shopping center, where you can buy the area's specialty items, such as hammocks, Panama hats, and the embroidered native blouses known as *huipiles.* Aside from Mérida, here are some other places to consider.

CHICHEN ITZA & VALLADOLID These destinations are almost midway between Mérida and Cancún. From Mérida, it's 2½ hours by car to Chichén on the new *autopista* (toll road). You can spend a day at the ruins and then stay at one of the nearby hotels—or drive 40km (25 miles) to Valladolid, a quiet, charming colonial town with a pleasant central square. Valladolid features two eerie cenotes. The spectacular ruins at Ek Balam are only 40km (25 miles) to the north. Also in the area is the Río Lagartos Nature Reserve, teeming with flamingos and other native birds.

CELESTUN NATIONAL WILDLIFE REFUGE These flamingo-sanctuary wetlands along the Gulf coast contain a unique shallow-water estuary where freshwater from cenotes mixes with saltwater, creating the perfect feeding ground for flamingos. Touring this area by launch is relaxing and rewarding. Only 1½ hours from Mérida, Celestún makes for an easy day trip.

DZIBILCHALTUN This Maya site, now a national park, is 14km (8⅔ miles) north of Mérida along the road to Progreso. Here you'll find pre-Hispanic ruins, nature trails, a cenote, and the Museum of the Maya. You can make this the first stop in a day trip to Progreso and other attractions north of Mérida.

PROGRESO A modern city and Gulf Coast beach escape 34km (21 miles) north of Mérida, Progreso has a wide beach and oceanfront drive that's popular on the weekends and during the summer. The recent arrival of cruise ships might make Progreso even more popular, but with so much beach, you'll easily have a place to yourself.

From Progreso, you can drive down the coast to **Uaymitún** to see some flamingos and visit the recently excavated ruins of **Xcambó.**

UXMAL   Smaller than Chichén, but architecturally more striking and mysterious, Uxmal is about 80km (50 miles) south of Mérida. You can see it in a day, though it's a good idea to extend that somewhat to see the sound-and-light show and spend the night at one of the hotels by the ruins. Several other nearby sites make up the Puuc route and can be explored the following day. It's also possible, though a bit rushed, to see Uxmal and the other ruins on a 1-day trip by special excursion bus from Mérida.

CAMPECHE   This beautiful, walled colonial city has been so meticulously restored that it's a delight just to stroll down the streets. Campeche is about 3 hours southwest of Mérida in the direction of Palenque. A full day should give you enough time to see its highlights and museums, but there is something about Campeche that makes you want to linger.

1 Mérida: Gateway to the Maya Heartland /★/★

1,440km (893 miles) E of Mexico City; 320km (198 miles) W of Cancún

Mérida is the capital of the state of Yucatán and has been the dominant city in the region since the Spanish Conquest. It is a busy city and suffers from the same problems that plague other colonial cities in Mexico—traffic and noise. Still, it is a fun city and has many admirers. I get comments from people all the time about how much they enjoyed Mérida. People there know how to have a good time, and they seem driven to organize concerts, theater productions, art exhibitions, and such. In recent years the city has been in the midst of a cultural explosion.

ESSENTIALS
GETTING THERE & DEPARTING
BY PLANE   AeroMéxico (© **01-800/021-4000** in Mexico, or 999/927-9277; www.aeromexico.com) flies nonstop to/from Miami and Mexico City. **Mexicana** (© **01-800/502-2000** in Mexico, or 999/924-6633; www.mexicana.com.mx) has nonstop service to and from Mexico City. **Continental** (© **999/946-1888** or -1900; www.continental.com) has nonstop service to and from Houston. **Click** (© **01-800/ 122-5425** in Mexico), a Mexican budget airline, provides nonstop service to and from Mexico City and Veracruz. **Aviacsa** (© **01-800/006-2000** in Mexico) provides nonstop service to and from Villahermosa and Mexico City.

BY CAR   Highway 180 is the old *carretera federal* (federal highway) between Mérida and Cancún. The trip takes 6 hours, and the road is in good shape; you will pass through many Maya villages. A four-lane divided *cuota,* or *autopista* (toll road) parallels Highway 180 and begins at the town of Kantunil, 56km (35 miles) east of Mérida. By avoiding the tiny villages and their not-so-tiny speed bumps, the *autopista* cuts 2 hours from the journey between Mérida and Cancún; one-way tolls cost $32 (£16). Coming from the direction of Cancún, Highway 180 enters Mérida by feeding into Calle 65, which passes 1 block south of the main square.

Coming from the south (Campeche or Uxmal), you will enter the city on Avenida Itzáes. To get to the town center, turn right on Calle 59 (the first street after the zoo).

A *periférico* (loop road) encircles Mérida, making it possible to skirt the city. Directional signs into the city are generally good, but going around the city on the loop requires vigilance.

BY BUS   There are five bus stations in Mérida, two of which offer first-class buses; the other three provide local service to nearby destinations. The larger of the first-class stations, **CAME,** is on Calle 70, between calles 69 and 71 (see "City Layout," below). The ADO bus line and its affiliates operate the station. When you get there, you'll see a row of ticket windows; all but the last couple to the right sell first-class tickets. The last two windows sell tickets for ADO's deluxe services, ADO-GL and UNO. The former is only slightly better than first class; the latter has super-wide roomy seats. Unless it's a long trip, I generally choose the bus that has the most convenient departure time. Tickets can be purchased in advance; just ask the ticket agent for the different options and departure times for the route you need.

The other first-class station is the small **Maya K'iin** used by the bus company **Elite.** It's at Calle 65 no. 548, between calles 68 and 70.

To and from Cancún: You can pick up a bus at the CAME (almost every hour) or through Elite (five per day). Both bus lines also pick up passengers at the Fiesta Americana Hotel, across from the Hyatt (12 per day). You can buy a ticket in the hotel's shopping arcade at the **Ticket Bus** agency or at the Elite ticket agency. Cancún is 4 hours away; a few buses stop in **Valladolid.** If you're downtown, you can purchase tickets from the agency in Pasaje Picheta, on the main square a couple of doors down from the Palacio de Gobierno.

To and from Chichén Itzá: Three buses per day (2½-hr. trip) depart from the CAME. Also, check out tours operating from the hotels in Mérida if you want to visit for the day.

To and from Playa del Carmen, Tulum, and Chetumal: From the CAME, there are 10 departures per day for Playa del Carmen (5-hr. trip), six for Tulum (6-hr. trip), and eight for Chetumal (7-hr. trip). From Maya K'iin there are three per day to Playa, which stop at the Fiesta Americana.

To and from Campeche: From the CAME station, there are 36 departures per day. Elite has four departures per day. It's a 2½-hour trip.

To and from Palenque and San Cristóbal de las Casas: There is service to San Cristóbal twice daily from the CAME, and once daily on Elite. To Palenque there are three and one, respectively. There have been reports of minor theft on buses to Palenque. You should do three things: Don't take second-class buses to this destination; check your luggage so that it's stowed in the cargo bay; and put your carry-on in the overhead rack, not on the floor.

The main **second-class bus station** is around the corner from the CAME on Calle 69, between calles 68 and 70.

To and from Uxmal: There are four buses per day. (You can also hook up with a tour to Uxmal through most hotels or any travel agent or tour operator in town.) One bus per day combines Uxmal with the other sites to the south (Kabah, Sayil, Labná, and Xlapak—known as the Puuc route) and does the whole round-trip in a day. It stops for 2 hours at Uxmal and 30 minutes at each of the other sites.

To and from Progreso and Dzibilchaltún: Transportes AutoProgreso offers service to/from its station at Calle 62 no. 524, between calles 65 and 67. The trip to Progreso takes an hour by second-class bus.

To and from Celestún: The Celestún station is at Calle 50 between calles 65 and 67. The trip takes 1½ to 2 hours, depending on how often the bus stops. There are 10 buses per day.

To and from Izamal: The bus station is at the corner of Calle 65 and Calle 48. Departures are every half-hour. The trip takes 1½ hours.

ORIENTATION

ARRIVING BY PLANE   Mérida's airport is 13km (8 miles) from the city center on the southwestern outskirts of town, near the entrance to Highway 180. The airport has desks for rental cars, hotel reservations, and tourist information. Taxi tickets to town ($16/£8) are sold outside the airport doors, under the covered walkway.

VISITOR INFORMATION   There are city tourism offices and state tourism offices, which have different resources; if you can't get the information you're looking for at one, go to the other. I have better luck with the city's **visitor information office** (© 999/942-0000, ext. 80119), which is on the ground floor of the Ayuntamiento building facing the main square on Calle 62. Look for a glass door under the arcade. Hours are Monday to Saturday from 8am to 8pm and Sunday from 8am to 2pm. Monday through Saturday, at 9:30am, the staff offers visitors a free tour of the area around the main square. The state operates two downtown tourism offices: One is in the **Teatro Peón Contreras,** facing Parque de la Madre (© 999/924-9290); and the other is on the main plaza, in the **Palacio de Gobierno,** immediately to the left as you enter. These offices are open daily from 8am to 9pm. There are also information booths at the airport and the CAME bus station.

Also keep your eye out for the free monthly magazine *Yucatán Today;* it's a good source of information for Mérida and the rest of the region.

CITY LAYOUT   Downtown Mérida has the standard layout of towns in the Yucatán: Streets running north–south are even numbers; those running east–west are odd numbers. The numbering begins on the north and the east sides of town, so if you're walking on an odd-numbered street and the even numbers of the cross streets are increasing, then you are heading west; likewise, if you are on an even-numbered street and the odd numbers of the cross streets are increasing, you are going south.

Address numbers don't tell you anything about what cross street to look for. This is why addresses almost always list cross streets, usually like this: "Calle 60 no. 549 × 71 y 73." The "×" is a multiplication sign—shorthand for the word *por* (meaning "by")—and *y* means "and." So this place would be on Calle 60 between calles 71 and 73. Outside of the downtown area, the numbering of streets gets a little crazy, so it's important to know the name of the neighborhood *(colonia)* where you're going. This is the first thing taxi drivers will ask you.

The town's main square is the busy **Plaza Mayor,** known as **El Centro.** It's bordered by calles 60, 62, 61, and 63. Calle 60, which runs in front of the cathedral, is an important street to remember; it connects the main square with several smaller plazas, some theaters and churches, and the University of Yucatán, just to the north. Here you'll find a concentration of handicraft shops, restaurants, and hotels. Around Plaza Mayor are the cathedral, the Palacio de Gobierno (state government building), the Ayuntamiento (town hall), and the Palacio Montejo. The plaza always has a crowd, and it's full on Sunday, when it holds a large street fair. (See "Daily Festivals & Special Events in Mérida," below.) Within a few blocks are several smaller plazas and the bustling market district.

Mérida's most fashionable district is the broad, tree-lined boulevard **Paseo de Montejo** and its surrounding neighborhood. The Paseo de Montejo parallels Calle 60 and begins 7 blocks north and a little east of the main square. There are a number of

Moments Daily Festivals & Special Events in Mérida

Many Mexican cities offer weekend concerts in the park and such, but Mérida surpasses them all by offering performances every day of the week. Unless otherwise indicated, admission to the following is free.

Sunday   Each Sunday from 9am to 9pm, there's a fair called *Mérida en Domingo* (Mérida on Sunday). The main plaza and a section of Calle 60 from El Centro to Parque Santa Lucía close to traffic. Parents come with their children to stroll around and take in the scene. There are booths selling food and drink, along with a lively little flea market and used-book fair, children's art classes, and educational booths. At 11am in front of the Palacio del Gobierno, musicians play everything from jazz to classical and folk music. Also at 11am, the police orchestra performs Yucatecan tunes at the Santa Lucía park. At 11:30am, you'll find bawdy comedy acts at the Parque Hidalgo, on Calle 60 at Calle 59. There's a lull in the midafternoon, and then the plaza fills up again as people walk around and visit with friends. Around 7pm in front of the Ayuntamiento, a large band starts playing mambos, rumbas, and cha-chas with great enthusiasm; you may see 1,000 people dancing in the street. Afterward, folk ballet dancers reenact a typical Yucatecan wedding inside.

Monday   Every Monday at 9pm in front of the *Palacio Municipal* performers play *Vaquería regional,* traditional music and dancing to celebrate the Vaquerías feast, which was associated originally with the branding of cattle on Yucatecan haciendas. Among the featured performers are dancers with trays of bottles or filled glasses balanced on their heads—a sight to see.

Tuesday   At 9pm in Parque Santiago, Calle 59 at Calle 72, the Municipal Orchestra plays Latin and American big-band music from the 1940s.

Wednesday   At 9pm in the Teatro Peón Contreras, Calle 60 at Calle 57, the University of Yucatán Ballet Folklórico presents "Yucatán and Its Roots." Admission is $5 (£2.75).

Thursday   Yucatecan *trova* music (boleros, baladas) and dance are presented at the Serenata in Parque Santa Lucía at 9pm.

Friday   At 9pm in the courtyard of the University of Yucatán, Calle 60 at Calle 57, the University of Yucatán Ballet Folklórico performs typical regional dances from the Yucatán.

Saturday   Noche Mexicana at the park at the beginning of Paseo de Montejo begins at 9pm. It features several performances of traditional Mexican music and dance. Some of the performers are amateurs who acquit themselves reasonably well; others are professional musicians and dancers who thoroughly know their craft. Food stands sell very good *antojitos* (finger foods), as well as drinks and ice cream.

trendy restaurants, modern hotels, offices of various banks and airlines, and a few clubs here, but the boulevard is mostly known for its stately mansions built during the boom times of the henequén industry. Near where the Paseo intersects Avenida Colón, you'll find the two fanciest hotels in town: the Hyatt and the Fiesta Americana.

GETTING AROUND   By Car   In general, reserve your car in advance from the U.S. to get the best weekly rates during high season (Nov–Feb); in low season, I usually do better renting a car once I get to Mérida. The local rental companies are competitive and have promotional deals that you can get only if you are there. When comparing, make sure that it's apples to apples; ask if the price quote includes the IVA tax and insurance coverage. Practically everybody offers free mileage. For tips on saving money on car rentals, see "Getting Around," in chapter 3. Rental cars are generally a little more expensive (unless you find a promotional rate) than in the U.S. By renting for only a day or two, you can avoid the high cost of parking lots in Mérida. These *estacionamentos* charge one price for the night and double that if you leave your car for the following day. Many hotels offer free parking, but make sure they include daytime parking in the price.

By Taxi   Taxis are easy to come by and much cheaper than in Cancún.

By Bus   City buses are a little tricky to figure out but aren't needed very often because almost everything of interest is within walking distance of the main plaza. Still, it's a bit of a walk from the plaza to the Paseo de Montejo, and you can save yourself some work by taking a bus, minibus, or *colectivo* (Volkswagen minivan) that is heading north on Calle 60. Most of these will take you within a couple of blocks of the Paseo de Montejo. The *colectivos* or *combis* (usually painted white) run out in several directions from the main plaza along simple routes. They usually line up along the side streets next to the plaza.

FAST FACTS: Mérida

American Express   The office is at Paseo de Montejo 492 (© **999/942-8200**). It's open for travelers' services weekdays from 9am to 2pm and 4 to 6pm.

Area Code   The telephone area code is **999**.

Bookstore   The English-language bookstore **Amate Books** (© **999/924-2222**) is at Calle 60 453-A, by Calle 51. It stocks a large selection of books on many subjects and is open Tuesday through Sunday from 10:30am to 8:30pm. The **Librería Dante,** Calle 59 between calles 60 and 62 (© **999/928-3674**), has a small selection of English-language cultural-history books on Mexico.

Business Hours   Generally, businesses are open Monday to Saturday from 10am to 2pm and 4 to 8pm.

Climate   From November to February, the weather can be pleasantly cool and windy. In other months, it's just hot, especially during the day. Rain can occur any time of year, especially during the rainy season (July–Oct), and usually comes in the form of afternoon tropical showers.

Consulates   The **American Consulate** has moved. It's now at Calle 60 no. 338-K, 1 block north of the Hyatt hotel (Col. Alcalá Martín). The phone number is © **999/942-5700**. Office hours are Monday to Friday from 9am to 1pm.

Currency Exchange I prefer *casas de cambio* (currency exchange offices) over banks. There are many of these; one called **Cambios Portales,** Calle 61 no. 500 (© **999/923-8709**), is on the north side of the main plaza in the middle of the block. It's open daily from 8:30am to 8:30pm. There are also many ATMs; one is on the south side of the same plaza.

Drugstore **Farmacía Yza,** Calle 63 no. 502, between calles 60 and 62 (© **999/ 924-9510**), on the south side of the plaza, is open 24 hours.

Hospitals The best hospital is **Centro Médico de las Américas,** Calle 54 no. 365 between 33-A and Avenida Pérez Ponce. The main phone number is © **999/ 926-2619**; for emergencies, call © **999/927-3199.** You can also call the **Cruz Roja (Red Cross)** at © **999/924-9813.**

Internet Access There are so many Internet access providers in town that you hardly have to walk more than a couple of blocks to find one.

Police Mérida has a special body of police to assist tourists. They patrol the downtown area and the Paseo de Montejo. They wear white shirts bearing the words POLICIA TURISTICA. Their phone number is © **999/925-2555.**

Post Office The *correo* moved recently. It's now on calle 53 between calles 52 and 54. It's open Monday to Friday from 8am to 4:30pm, Saturday from 9am to 1pm.

Seasons There are two high seasons for tourism, but they aren't as pronounced as on the coast. One is in July and August, when Mexicans take their vacations, and the other is between November 15 and Easter Sunday, when Canadians and Americans flock to the Yucatán to escape winter weather.

Spanish Classes Maya scholars, Spanish teachers, and archaeologists from the United States are among the students at the **Centro de Idiomas del Sureste,** Calle 14 no. 106 at Calle 25, Col. México, 97000 Mérida, Yuc. (© **999/926-1155**; fax 999/926-9020). The school has two locations: in the Colonia México, a northern residential district, and on Calle 66 at Calle 57, downtown. Students live with local families or in hotels; sessions running 2 weeks or longer are available for all levels of proficiency and areas of interest. For brochures and applications, contact the director, Chloe Conaway de Pacheco.

Telephones There are long-distance phone service centers at the airport and the bus station. In the downtown area is **TelWorld,** Calle 59 no. 495-4 between calles 56 and 58. To use the public phones, buy a **Ladatel** card from just about any newsstand or store. The cards come in a variety of denominations and work for long distance within Mexico and even abroad.

EXPLORING MERIDA

Most of Mérida's attractions are within walking distance from the downtown area. To see a larger area of the city, take a popular **bus tour** by **Transportadora Carnaval.** The owner bought a few buses, painted them bright colors, pulled out the windows, raised the roof several inches, and installed wooden benches; the overall effect will remind you of the folksy buses of coastal Latin America, known as *chivas* in Colombia and Venezuela or as *guaguas* in other places. You can find these buses on the corner of calles 60 and 55 (next to the church of Santa Lucía) at 10am and 1, 4, and 7pm. The tour costs $7 (£3.50) per person and lasts 2 hours. A national company, called Turibus, operates another city tour in large, modern, bright-red, double-decker buses. You can pick them up in front of the cathedral every half-hour. The tour costs $8 (£4). Another option for seeing the city is a **horse-drawn carriage**. A 45-minute ride around central Mérida costs $25 (£13). You can usually find the carriages beside the cathedral on Calle 61.

EXPLORING PLAZA MAYOR   Downtown Mérida is a great example of a lowland colonial city. The town has a casual, relaxed feel. Buildings lack the severe baroque and neoclassical features that characterize central Mexico; most are finished in stucco and painted light colors. Mérida's gardens add to this relaxed, tropical atmosphere. Gardeners don't strive for control over nature. Here, natural exuberance is the ideal; plants grow in a wild profusion that disguises human intervention. Mérida's plazas are a slightly different version of this aesthetic: Unlike the highland plazas, with their carefully sculpted trees, Mérida's squares are typically built around large trees that are left to grow as tall as possible. Hurricane Isidore blew down several of these in 2002 and has changed the appearance of these plazas as well as the Paseo de Montejo.

Plaza Mayor has been relandscaped after the hurricane and is now the exception to the rule. It still remains a comfortable and informal place to meet up with friends. Even when there's no orchestrated event in progress, the park is full of people sitting on the benches, talking, or taking a casual stroll. A plaza like this is a great advantage for a big city such as Mérida, giving it a personal feel and a sense of community. Notice the beautiful scale and composition of the major buildings surrounding it. The most prominent of these is the cathedral.

The oldest **cathedral** on the continent, it was built between 1561 and 1598. Much of the stone in the cathedral's walls came from the ruined buildings of Tihó, the former Maya city. The original finish was stucco, and you can see some remnants still clinging to the bare rock. However, people like the way the unfinished walls show the cathedral's age. Notice how the two top levels of the bell towers are built off-center from their bases, marking them as later additions. Inside, decoration is sparse, with altars draped in fabric colorfully embroidered like a Maya woman's shift. The most notable item is a picture of Ah Kukum Tutul Xiú, chief of the Xiú people, visiting the Montejo camp to make peace; it's hanging over the side door on the right.

To the left of the main altar is a small shrine with a curious figure of Christ that is a replica of one recovered from a burned-out church in the town of Ichmul. In the 1500s a local artist carved the original figure from a miraculous tree that was hit by lightning and burst into flames—but did not char. The statue later became blistered in the church fire at Ichmul, but it survived. In 1645 it was moved to the cathedral in Mérida, where the locals attached great powers to the figure, naming it *Cristo de las Ampollas* (Christ of the Blisters). It did not, however, survive the sacking of the cathedral in 1915 by revolutionary forces, so another figure, modeled after the original, was made. Take a look in the side chapel (daily 8–11am and 4:30–7pm), which contains a life-size diorama of the Last Supper. The Mexican Jesus is covered with prayer crosses brought by supplicants asking for intercession.

Next door to the cathedral is the old bishop's palace, now converted into the city's contemporary art museum, **Museo de Arte Contemporáneo Ateneo de Yucatán** (© **999/928-3236**). The palace was confiscated and rebuilt during the Mexican Revolution in 1915. The museum's entrance faces the cathedral from the recently constructed walkway between the two buildings called the Pasaje de la Revolución. The 17 exhibition rooms display work by contemporary artists, mostly from the Yucatán. (The best known are Fernando García Ponce and Fernando Castro Pacheco, whose works also hang in the government palace described below.) Nine of the rooms hold the museum's permanent collection; the rest are for temporary exhibits. It's open Wednesday to Monday from 10am to 6pm. Admission is free.

As you move clockwise around the plaza, the **Palacio Montejo** is on the south side. Its facade, with heavy decoration around the doorway and windows, is a good example of the Spanish architectural style known as plateresque. But the content of the decoration is very much a New World creation. Conquering the Yucatán was the Montejo family business, begun by the original Francisco Montejo and continued by his son and nephew, both named Francisco Montejo. Construction of the house started in 1542 under the son, Francisco Montejo El Mozo ("The Younger"). Bordering the entrance are politically incorrect figures of conquistadors standing on the heads of vanquished Indians—borrowed, perhaps, from the pre-Hispanic custom of portraying victorious Maya kings treading on their defeated foes. The posture of the conquistadors and their facial expression of wide-eyed dismay make them less imposing than the Montejos might have wished. A bank now occupies the building, but you can enter the courtyard, view the garden, and see for yourself what a charming residence it must have been for the descendants of the Montejos, who lived here as recently as the 1970s. (Curiously enough, Mérida society keeps track of who is descended from the Montejos, as well as who is descended from the last Maya king, Tutul Xiú.)

In stark contrast to the severity of the cathedral and Casa Montejo is the light, unimposing **Ayuntamiento** or **Palacio Municipal (town hall).** The exterior dates from the mid–19th century, an era when a tropical aesthetic tinged with romanticism began asserting itself across coastal Latin America. On the second floor, you can see the meeting hall of the city council and enjoy a view of the plaza from the balcony. Next door to the Ayuntamiento is a recently completed building called **El Nuevo Olimpo (The New Olympus).** It took the place of the old Olimpo, which a misguided town council demolished in the 1970s, to the regret of many older Meridanos. The new building tries to incorporate elements of the original while presenting something new. It holds concert and gallery space, a bookstore, and a lovely courtyard. There is a comfortable cafe under the arches, and a bulletin board at the entrance to the courtyard with postings of upcoming performances.

Cater-cornered from the Nuevo Olimpo is the old **Casa del Alguacil (Magistrate's House).** Under its arcades is something of an institution in Mérida: the **Dulcería y Sorbetería Colón,** an ice-cream and sweet shop that will appeal to those who prefer less-rich ice creams. A spectacular side doorway on Calle 62 bears viewing, and across the street is the **Cine Mérida,** with two movie screens showing art films and one stage for live performances. Returning to the main plaza, down a bit from the ice-cream store, is a **shopping center** of boutiques and convenience food vendors called **Pasaje Picheta.** At the end of the arcade is the **Palacio de Gobierno (state government building),** dating from 1892. Large murals by the Yucatecan artist Fernando Castro Pacheco, completed between 1971 and 1973, decorate the walls of the courtyard. Scenes from Maya and Mexican history abound, and the painting over the stairway depicts the Maya spirit with ears of sacred corn, the "sunbeams of the gods." Nearby is a painting of mustachioed Lázaro Cárdenas, who as president, in 1938, expropriated 17 foreign oil companies and was hailed as a Mexican liberator. Upstairs is a long, wide gallery with more of Pacheco's paintings, which achieve their effect by localizing color and imitating the photographic technique of double exposure. The palace is open Monday to Saturday from 8am to 8pm, Sunday from 9am to 5pm. There is a small tourism office to the left as you enter.

Farther down Calle 61 is the **Museo de la Ciudad (City Museum).** It faces the side of the cathedral and occupies the former church of San Juan de Dios. An exhibit outlining the history of Mérida will be of interest to those curious about the city; there is explanatory text in English. Hours are Monday to Friday from 10am to 2pm and 4 to 8pm, Saturday and Sunday from 10am to 2pm. Admission is free.

EXPLORING CALLE 60   Heading north from Plaza Mayor up Calle 60, you'll see many of Mérida's old churches and squares. Several stores along Calle 60 sell gold-filigree jewelry, pottery, clothing, and folk art. A stroll along this street leads to the Parque Santa Ana and continues to the fashionable boulevard Paseo de Montejo and its **Museo Regional de Antropología (Anthropology Museum).**

The first place of interest is the **Teatro Daniel de Ayala,** only because it sometimes schedules interesting performances. On the right side of Calle 60 will be a small park called **Parque Cepeda Peraza** (or Parque Hidalgo). Named for 19th-century General Manuel Cepeda Peraza, the *parque* was part of Montejo's original city plan. Small outdoor restaurants front hotels on the park, making it a popular stopping place at any time of day. Across Calle 59 is the **Iglesia de Jesús,** or El Tercer Orden (the Third Order). Built by the Jesuit order in 1618, it has the richest interior of any church in Mérida, making it a favorite spot for weddings. The entire block on which the church stands belonged to the Jesuits, who are known as great educators. The school they left behind after their expulsion became the Universidad de Yucatán.

On the other side of the church is the **Parque de la Madre.** The park contains a modern statue of the Madonna and Child, a copy of the work by Renoir. Beyond the Parque de la Madre and across the pedestrian-only street is the **Teatro Peón Contreras,** an opulent theater designed by Italian architect Enrico Deserti a century ago. The theater is noted for its Carrara marble staircase and frescoed dome. Try to peek inside, and check the schedule to see if any performances will take place during your stay. National and international performers appear here often. In the southwest corner of the theater, facing the Parque de la Madre, is a **tourist information office.** Across Calle 60 is the main building of the **Universidad de Yucatán.** Inside is a flagstone courtyard where the *ballet folklórico* performs on Friday nights.

A block farther north is **Parque Santa Lucía.** Bordered by an arcade on the north and west sides, this park was where visitors first alighted from the stagecoach. On Sunday, Parque Santa Lucía holds a used-book market, and several evenings a week it hosts popular entertainment. On Thursday nights, performers present Yucatecan songs and poems. Facing the park is the **Iglesia de Santa Lucía** (1575).

Four blocks farther up Calle 60 is **Parque Santa Ana;** if you turn right, you'll come to the beginning of the Paseo de Montejo in 2 blocks.

EXPLORING THE PASEO DE MONTEJO   The Paseo de Montejo is a broad, tree-lined boulevard that runs north-south starting at Calle 47, 7 blocks north and 2 blocks east of the main square. In the late 19th century, stalwarts of Mérida's upper crust (mostly plantation owners) decided that the city needed something grander than its traditional narrow streets lined by wall-to-wall town houses. They built this monumentally proportioned boulevard and lined it with mansions. Things went sour when the henequén industry went bust, but several mansions survive—some in private hands, others as offices, restaurants, or consulates. Today, this is the fashionable part of town, with many restaurants, trendy dance clubs, and expensive hotels.

Of the mansions that survived, the most notable is the Palacio Cantón, which houses the **Museo Regional de Antropología (Anthropology Museum)** ★★ (© 999/ 923-0557). Designed and built by Enrico Deserti, the architect of the Teatro Peón Contreras, it was constructed between 1909 and 1911, during the last years of the Porfiriato. It was the residence of General Francisco Cantón Rosado, who enjoyed his palace for only 6 years before dying in 1917. For a time the mansion served as the official residence of the state's governor. Viewing the museum affords you an opportunity to see some of the surviving interior architecture.

The museum's main focus is the pre-Columbian cultures of the peninsula, especially the Maya. Topics include cosmology, history, and culture. Starting with fossil mastodon teeth, the exhibits take you through the Yucatán's history, paying special attention to the daily life of its inhabitants.

Exhibits illustrate such strange Maya customs as tying boards to babies' heads to create the oblong shape that they considered beautiful and filing teeth or perforating them to inset jewels. Enlarged photos of several archaeological sites and drawings illustrate the various styles of Maya dwellings. Captions for the permanent displays are mostly in Spanish, but even if you barely know Spanish, this is a worthwhile stop, providing background for explorations of Maya sites. The museum is open Tuesday to Saturday from 8am to 8pm, Sunday from 8am to 2pm. Admission is $4 (£2).

SHOPPING

Mérida is known for hammocks, *guayaberas* (lightweight men's shirts worn untucked), and Panama hats. Baskets and pottery made in the Yucatán are for sale in the **central market.** Mérida is also the place to pick up prepared *adobo,* a pastelike mixture of ground *achiote* seeds (annatto), oregano, garlic, and other spices used as a marinade for making dishes such as *cochinita pibil* (pit-baked pork). Simply mix the paste with sour orange to a soupy consistency before applying to the meat. Try it on chicken for *pollo pibil.* It can be purchased in a bottle, too.

EXPLORING THE MARKET   Mérida's bustling **market district** is a few blocks southeast of the Plaza Mayor. The market and surrounding few blocks make up the commercial center of the city. Hordes of people come here to shop and work. It is by far the most crowded part of town, and the city government is refurbishing the whole area to relieve the traffic congestion. Behind the post office (at calles 65 and 56) is the oldest part of the market, the **Portal de Granos (Grains Arcade),** a row of maroon arches where the grain merchants used to sell their goods. Just east, between calles 56 and 54, is the market building, Mercado Lucas de Gálvez. The city has built a new municipal market building on the south side of this building, but it was having difficulty persuading the market venders to move. When this happens the city's plan is to tear down the Lucas de Gálvez and replace it with a plaza. Inside, chaos seems to reign, but after a short while a certain order emerges. Here you can find anything from fresh fish to flowers to leather goods. In and around the market, you can find more locally manufactured goods; a secondary market is on Calle 56, labeled **Bazaar de Artesanías (crafts market)** in big letters. Another crafts market, **Bazaar García Rejón,** lies a block west of the market on Calle 65 between calles 58 and 60.

CRAFTS

Casa de las Artesanías ★   This store occupies the front rooms of a restored monastery. Here you can find a wide selection of crafts, 90% of which come from the Yucatán. For the most part, the quality of work is higher than elsewhere, but so are the prices. The monastery's back courtyard is used as a gallery, with rotating exhibits on folk and fine arts. It's open Monday to Saturday from 9am to 8pm, Sunday from 9am to 1pm. Calle 63 no. 513 (between calles 64 and 66). © 999/928-6676.

Miniaturas   This fun little store is packed to the rafters with miniatures, a traditional Mexican folk art form that has been evolving in a number of directions, including social and political satire, pop art, and bawdy humor. Alicia Rivero, the owner, collects them from several parts of Mexico and offers plenty of variety, from traditional miniatures, such as dollhouse furniture, to popular cartoon characters and celebrities. The store also sells other forms of folk art such as masks, games, and traditional crafts. Hours are Monday to Saturday from 10am to 8pm. Calle 59 no. 507A-4 (between calles 60 and 62). © 999/928-6503.

GUAYABERAS

Business suits are hot and uncomfortable in Mérida's tropical climate, so businessmen, bankers, and bus drivers alike wear the *guayabera,* a loose-fitting shirt decorated with narrow tucks, pockets, and sometimes embroidery, worn over the pants rather than tucked in. Mérida is famous as the best place to buy *guayaberas,* which can go for less than $15 (£7.50) at the market or for more than $50 (£25) custom-made. A *guayabera* made of linen can cost about $80 (£40). Most are made of cotton, although other materials are available. The traditional color is white.

Most shops display ready-to-wear shirts in several price ranges. *Guayabera* makers pride themselves on being innovators. I have yet to enter a shirt-maker's shop in Mérida that did not present its own version of the *guayabera.* When looking at *guayaberas,* here are a few things to keep in mind: When Yucatecans say *seda,* they mean polyester; *lino* is linen or a linen/polyester combination. Take a close look at the stitching and such details as the way the tucks line up over the pockets; with *guayaberas,* the details are everything.

Guayaberas Jack   The craftsmanship here is good, the place has a reputation to maintain, and some of the salespeople speak English. Prices are as marked. This will give you a good basis of comparison if you want to hunt for a bargain elsewhere. If the staff does not have the style and color of shirt you want, they will make it for you in about 3 hours. This shop also sells regular shirts and women's blouses. Hours are Monday to Saturday from 10am to 8pm, Sunday from 10am to 2pm. Calle 59 no. 507A (between calles 60 and 62). © 999/928-6002.

HAMMOCKS

Natives across tropical America used hammocks long before the Europeans arrived in the New World. The word comes from the Spanish *hamaca,* which is a borrowing from Taino, a Caribbean Indian language. Hammocks are still in use throughout Latin America and come in a wide variety of forms, but none is so comfortable as the Yucatecan hammock, which is woven with cotton string in a fine mesh. For most of us, of course, the hammock is lawn furniture, something to relax in for an hour or so on a lazy afternoon. But for the vast majority of Yucatecans, hammocks are the equivalent of beds, and they greatly prefer hammocks to mattresses. I know a hotel owner who has 150 beds in his establishment but won't sleep on any of them. When he does, he complains of waking up unrested and sore. Many well-to-do Meridanos keep a bed just for show. In hotels that cater to Yucatecans, you will always find hammock hooks in the walls because many Yucatecans travel with their own hammock.

My advice to the hammock buyer: The woven part should be cotton, it should be made with fine string, and the strings should be so numerous that when you get in it and stretch out diagonally (the way you're supposed to sleep in these hammocks), the gaps between the strings remain small. Don't pay attention to the words used to describe the size of a hammock; they have become practically meaningless. Good hammocks don't cost a lot of money ($20–$35/£10–£18). If you want a superior hammock, ask for one made with fine crochet thread, *hilo de crochet* (the word *crochet* is also over used, but you can readily see the difference). This could run as high as $120 (£60).

Nothing beats a tryout; the shops mentioned here will gladly hang a hammock for you to test-drive. When it's up, look to see that there are no untied strings. You can also see what street vendors are offering, but you have to know what to look for, or they are likely to take advantage of you.

Hamacas El Aguacate El Aguacate sells hammocks wholesale and retail. It has the greatest variety and is the place to go for a really fancy or extra-large hammock. A good hammock is the no. 6 in cotton; it runs around $32 (£16). The store is open Monday to Friday from 8:30am to 7:30pm, Saturday from 8am to 5pm. It's 6 blocks south of the main square. Calle 58 no. 604 (at Calle 73). © **999/928-6429.**

Tejidos y Cordeles Nacionales This place near the municipal market sells only cotton hammocks, priced by weight—a pretty good practice because hammock lengths are fairly standardized. The prices are better than at El Aguacate, but quality control isn't as good. My idea of a good hammock is one that weighs about 1½ kilograms (3½ lb.) and runs about $25 (£13). Calle 56 no. 516-B (between calles 63 and 65). © **999/928-5561.**

PANAMA HATS

Another useful and popular item is this soft, pliable hat made from the fibers of the jipijapa palm in several towns south of Mérida along Highway 180, especially Becal, in the neighboring state of Campeche. The hat makers in these towns work inside caves so that the moist air keeps the palm fibers pliant.

Jipi hats come in various grades determined by the quality (pliability, softness, and fineness) of the fibers and closeness of the weave. The difference in weave is easy to see, as a fine weave improves the shape of a hat. It has more body and retains its shape better. You'll find Panama hats for sale in several places, but often without much selection. One of the market buildings has a hat store: Walk south down Calle 56 past the post office; right before the street ends in the market place, turn left into a passage with hardware stores at the entrance. The fourth or fifth shop is **Casa de los Jipis.**

WHERE TO STAY

Mérida is easier on the budget than the resort cities. The stream of visitors is steadier than on the coast, so most hotels no longer use a high-season/low-season rate structure. Still, you are more likely to find promotional rates during low season. Mérida has a convention center, which attracts large trade shows that can fill the city's hotels, so it's a good idea to make reservations. The rates quoted here include the 17% tax. When inquiring about prices, always ask if the price quoted includes tax. Most hotels in Mérida offer at least a few air-conditioned rooms, and some also have pools. But many inexpensive hotels haven't figured out how to provide a comfortable bed. Either the mattresses are poor quality, or the bottom sheet is too small to tuck in properly. Some hotels here would offer a really good deal if only they would improve their beds. One last thing to note: Without exception, every hotel in Mérida that doesn't have its

Where to Stay & Dine in Mérida

UNITED STATES

MEXICO

Gulf of
Mexico

Mexico
City ★

Mérida ●

0   500 mi
0   500 km

✝ Church
ⓘ Information
⚋⚋⚋ Pedestrian Only
✉ Post Office

Map not
to scale Ⓝ

Av. Colon
Av. Perez
Reforma
Calle 35
Calle 37
Calle 39
Paseo de Montejo
Calle 41
Calle 43
Calle 45
Calle 47
✝ Parque
Santa Ana
Calle 49
Calle 51
Calle 53
Parque
Santa Lucía
Calle 55
Calle 57
Parque
Santiago
Calle 72
Calle 70
Calle 68
Calle 66
Calle 64
Calle 62
Calle 59
ⓘ
✝ Parque de la Madre
Parque
Hidalgo
Calle 61
Calle 60
ⓘ
Plaza
Mayor
✝ Catedral de
San Ildefonso
Calle 58
Calle 56
Calle 54
Calle 63
ⓘ
Calle 65
Portal de
Granos
✉ Mercado
Lucas de Gálvez
Calle 67
Bazaar de
Artesanías
Bus
Station
Parque
San Juan
Calle 69
Calle 69

ACCOMMODATIONS ■
Casa Mexilio Guest House **6**
Casa San Juan **20**
Fiesta Americana Mérida **1**
Hotel Caribe **18**
Hotel Dolores Alba **19**
Hotel Maison Lafitte **12**
Hotel Marionetas **4**

Hotel MedioMundo **5**
Hotel Mucuy **14**
Hyatt Regency Mérida **2**

DINING ◆
Alberto's Continental **9**
Amaro **11**
Café Alameda **13**

Casa de Frida **8**
Eladio's **16**
El Templo **17**
La Flor de Santiago **7**
Restaurante Kantún **3**
Restaurant Los
Almendros **15**
Vito Corleone **10**

own parking has an arrangement with a nearby parking garage, where, for a fee, you can park your car. Or you can park on the street, where for the most part cars are safe from vandalism. In Mérida, free parking is a relative concept—for many hotels, free parking means only at night; during the day there may be a charge.

VERY EXPENSIVE
Fiesta Americana Mérida *★★* This six-story hotel on the Paseo de Montejo is built in the grand *fin-de-siècle* style of the old mansions along the Paseo. Guest rooms are off the cavernous lobby, so all face outward and have views of one or another of the avenues. The rooms are comfortable and large, with furnishings and decorations striving for, and achieving, innocuousness in light, tropical colors. The floors are tile and the bathrooms large and well equipped. Service is very attentive, better than at the Hyatt. There is a shopping center on the ground floor, below the lobby.

Av. Colón 451, corner of Paseo Montejo, 92127 Mérida, Yuc. **©** **800/343-7821** in the U.S. and Canada, or 999/942-1111. Fax 999/942-1112. www.fiestaamericana.com.mx. 350 units. $220 (£110) double; $260 (£130) executive level; $280 (£140) junior suite. AE, DC, MC, V. Free secure parking. **Amenities:** 2 restaurants; bar; midsize outdoor pool; tennis court; health club w/saunas, men's steam room, unisex whirlpool; children's programs; concierge; tour desk; small business center; shopping arcade; room service; massage; babysitting; laundry service; dry cleaning; executive-level rooms. *In room:* A/C, TV w/pay movies, high-speed Internet access, minibar, coffeemaker, hair dryer, safe.

Hyatt Regency Mérida *★★* This Hyatt is much like Hyatts elsewhere, wherein lies this hotel's chief asset. The rooms are dependably comfortable and quiet, the quietest in a noisy city. They're carpeted and well furnished, with great bathrooms. In decoration and comfort, I find them superior to those of the Fiesta Americana, but they certainly don't have any local flavor. The Hyatt's facilities, especially its tennis courts and health club, also rank above the Fiesta Americana's. The pool is more attractive and larger, but its location keeps it in the shade for most of the day, and the water never gets a chance to heat up. Rising 17 stories, the Hyatt is not hard to find in Mérida's skyline; it's near the Paseo de Montejo and across Avenida Colón from the Fiesta Americana.

Calle 60 no. 344 (at Av. Colón), 97000 Mérida, Yuc. **©** **800/223-1234** in the U.S. and Canada, or 999/942-1234. Fax 999/925-7002. www.merida.regency.hyatt.com. 299 units. $200 (£100) standard double; $220 (£110) Regency Club double. Ask about promotional rates. AE, DC, MC, V. Free guarded parking. **Amenities:** 2 restaurants; 2 bars (1 swim-up, open seasonally); large outdoor pool; 2 lighted tennis courts; state-of-the-art health club w/men's and women's whirlpool, sauna, and steam rooms; children's activities (seasonal); concierge; tour desk; car rental; business center; shopping arcade; room service; massage; babysitting; laundry service; dry cleaning; nonsmoking rooms; executive-level rooms. *In room:* A/C, TV, minibar, hair dryer.

MODERATE
Casa Mexilio Guest House *★* *(Moments)* This bed-and-breakfast is unlike any other I know. The owners are geniuses at playing with space in an unexpected and delightful manner. Rooms are at different levels, creating private spaces joined to each other and to rooftop terraces by stairs and catwalks. Most are spacious and airy, furnished and decorated in an engaging mix of new and old, polished and primitive. Five come with air-conditioning. A small pool with a whirlpool and profuse tropical vegetation take up most of the central patio. Breakfasts are great. It's 4 blocks west of the plaza. A small bar serves drinks during happy hour, and, weather permitting, you can have your cocktail on one of the rooftop terraces.

Calle 68 no. 495 (between calles 57 and 59), 97000 Mérida, Yuc. **©** **877/639-4546** in the U.S. and Canada, or 999/928-2505. www.casamexilio.com. 9 units. $50–$85 (£25–£43) double; $120 (£60) penthouse. Rates include full breakfast. MC, V. Limited street parking. **Amenities:** Bar; small outdoor pool; whirlpool; nonsmoking rooms. *In room:* A/C (in some), no phone.

Hotel Caribe   This three-story colonial-style hotel (no elevator) is great for a couple of reasons: Its location at the back of Plaza Hidalgo is both central and quiet, and it has a nice little pool and sun deck on the rooftop with a view of the cathedral. The rooms are moderately comfortable, though they aren't well lit and have only small windows facing the central courtyard. Thirteen *clase económica* rooms don't have air-conditioning, but standard rooms do; and superior rooms (on the top floor) have been remodeled and have safes, hair dryers, larger windows, and quieter air-conditioning. Avoid the rooms on the ground floor. The hotel offers a lot of variety in bedding arrangements, mostly combinations of twins and doubles. Mattresses are often softer than standard. Nearby parking is free at night but costs extra during the day beginning at 7am. The restaurant serves good Mexican food.

Calle 59 no. 500 (at Calle 60), 97000 Mérida, Yuc. (© 888/822-6431 in the U.S. and Canada, or 999/924-9022. Fax 999/924-8733. www.hotelcaribe.com.mx. 53 units. $50 (£25) *clase económica* double; $66–$78 (£33–£39) standard or superior double. AE, MC, V. Free nearby night parking. **Amenities:** Restaurant; bar; small outdoor pool; tour desk; room service; laundry service. *In room:* A/C (in some), TV, hair dryer (in some), safe (in some).

Hotel Maison Lafitte 🟊   This three-story hotel has modern, attractive rooms with good air-conditioning, and tropical touches such as wooden louvers over the windows and light furniture with caned backs and seats. Rooms are medium to large, with mid-size bathrooms that have great showers and good lighting. Most rooms come with either two doubles or a king-size bed. Rooms are quiet and overlook a pretty little garden with a fountain. A few rooms don't have windows. The location is excellent.

Calle 60 no. 472 (between calles 53 and 55), 97000 Mérida, Yuc. (© 800/538-6802 in the U.S. and Canada, or 999/928-1243. Fax 999/923-9159. www.maisonlafitte.com.mx. 30 units. $82 (£41) double. Rates include full breakfast. AE, MC, V. Free limited secure parking for compact cars. **Amenities:** Restaurant; bar; small outdoor pool; tour desk; car rental; room service; in-room massage; laundry service; dry cleaning. *In room:* A/C, TV, Wi-Fi, minibar, hair dryer, safe.

Hotel Marionetas 🟊   This quiet and attractive B&B, 6 blocks north of the main square, has a comforting feel to it. Even though I've heard the story, I'm still not clear on how the hosts, Sofi (Macedonian) and Daniel (Argentinean), ended up in Mérida. But they are engaging, interesting people and attentive innkeepers. They have created a lovely space with common areas in front, rooms in back, and a lush garden/pool area in between. It's the kind of place that tempts you to lounge about.

Calle 49 no. 516 (between calles 62 and 64), 97000 Mérida, Yuc. (© 999/928-3377. www.hotelmarionetas.com. 8 units. $80–$95 (£40–£48) double. Rates include full breakfast. 2-night minimum stay. MC, V. Free secure parking for compact cars. Children under 12 not accepted. **Amenities:** Small outdoor pool; tour desk; in-room massage; laundry service; nonsmoking rooms. *In room:* A/C, Wi-Fi, fridge, hair dryer, safe.

Hotel MedioMundo 🟊 *(Finds*   This is a quiet courtyard hotel with beautiful rooms and a good location 3 blocks north of the main plaza. The English-speaking owners, Nicole and Nelson, have been in the hotel business for years and have invested their money in the right places, going for high-quality mattresses, good lighting, quiet air-conditioning, lots of space, and good bathrooms with strong showers. What they didn't invest in were TVs, which adds to the serenity. Higher prices are for the eight rooms with air-conditioning, but all units have windows with good screens and get ample ventilation. Breakfast is served in one of the two attractive courtyards.

Calle 55 no. 533 (between calles 64 and 66), 97000 Mérida, Yuc. (©/fax 999/924-5472. www.hotelmediomundo. com. 12 units. $60–$90 (£30–£45) double. MC, V. Limited street parking. **Amenities:** Small outdoor pool; tour info; in-room massage; laundry service; nonsmoking rooms. *In room:* A/C (in some), no phone.

Of Haciendas & Hotels

Haciendas in the Yucatán have had a bumpy history. During the colonial period they were isolated, self-sufficient fiefdoms–not terribly efficient, but they didn't have to be. Mostly they produced foodstuffs—enough for the needs of the owners and peasants plus a little extra that the owners could sell for a small sum in the city. The owners, though politically powerful, especially within the confines of their large estates, were never rich.

This changed in the 19th century, when the expanding world market created high demand for henequén, the natural fiber of the sisal plant, which was used to bale hay. In a few years, all of the haciendas shifted to mass production of this commodity. Prices and profits kept climbing through the end of the century and into the 20th. Hacienda owners now had lots of cash to spend on their estates and on heavy machinery to process the henequén fiber more efficiently. Then came the bust. Throughout the 1920s, prices and demand fell, and no other commodity could replace sisal. The haciendas entered a long decline, but by then, the cultivation and processing of sisal had become part of local culture.

To see and understand what things were like during the golden age, you can visit a couple of haciendas. One, by the name of **Sotuta de Peón,** has recently been refurbished and runs much like in the old days—a living museum involving an entire community (see "Side Trips from Mérida," later in this chapter). At the other one, **Yaxcopoil** (see "En Route to Uxmal," later in this chapter), you can wander the shell of a once-bustling estate and look for remnants of splendor.

Now another boom of sorts has brought haciendas back; this time as retreats, country residences, and hotels. The hotels convey an air of the past—elegant gateways, thick walls, open arches, and high ceilings—you get the feel of an era gone by. Indeed, there are a few features that make a guest feel like lord and master, especially the extravagant suites and personal service. But what strikes me the most when I visit these haciendas is the contrast between them and the world outside. They are like little islands of order and tranquillity in the sea of chaos that is the Yucatán.

There are five luxury hacienda hotels. The most opulent of these is **La Hacienda Xcanatún** (© **888/883-3633** in the U.S.; www.xcanatun.com). It's

INEXPENSIVE

Casa San Juan *Value*   This B&B, in a colonial house, is loaded with character and provides a good glimpse of the old Mérida that lies behind the colonial facades in the historic district. Guest rooms are beautifully decorated, large, and comfortable. Those in the original house have been modernized but maintain a colonial feel, with 7m (23-ft.) ceilings and 45cm-thick (18-inch) walls. The modern rooms in back look out over the rear patio. The lower rate is for the rooms without air-conditioning (they have ceiling and floor fans). Choice of beds includes one queen-size, one double, or two twins, on the outskirts of Mérida, off the highway to Progreso. The suites are large and have extravagant bathrooms. The decor is in muted colors with rich materials and modern pieces that evoke the simplicity of an earlier age. It has the best restaurant in the Mérida area and a complete spa. The owners personally manage their hotel and keep the service sharp.

The other four luxury hotels are all owned by Roberto Hernández, one of the richest men in Mexico. The hospitality and reservation system are handled by **Starwood Hotels** (© 800/325-3589 in the U.S. and Canada; www.luxurycollection.com). The owner has taken great pains to restore all four haciendas to original condition, and all are beautiful. **Temozón,** off the highway to Uxmal, is the most magnificent. **Uayamón,** located between the ruins of Edzná and the colonial city of Campeche, is perhaps the most romantic. **Hacienda San José Cholul,** located east of Mérida towards Izamal, is my personal favorite, and picturesque **Santa Rosa** lies southwest of Mérida, near the town of Maxcanú. Packages are available for staying at two or more of these haciendas. All offer personal service, activities, and spas.

Two haciendas offer economical lodging. On the western outskirts of Mérida by the highway to Chichén Itzá and Cancún is **Hacienda San Pedro Nohpat** (© 999/988-0542; www.haciendaholidays.com). It retains only the land that immediately surrounds the residence, but it offers a great bargain in lodging—large, comfortable rooms and an attractive garden area and pool. The other is **Hacienda Blanca Flor** (© 999/925-8042; www.mexonline.com/blancaflor.htm), which lies between Mérida and Campeche just off the highway. It's the only hacienda hotel that actually operates like one, producing most of the food served there. The owners work with bus tours but also welcome couples and individuals. Rooms are in a modern building and are large and simply furnished.

Two other haciendas can be leased by small groups for retreats and group vacations: **Hacienda Petac** (© 800/225-4255 in the U.S.; www.haciendapetac.com) and **Hacienda San Antonio** (© 999/910-6144; www.haciendasanantonio.com.mx). Both have beautiful rooms, common areas, and grounds.

all with good mattresses and sheets. Breakfast includes fruit or juice, coffee, bread, and homemade preserves. Casa San Juan is 4 blocks south of the main square.

Calle 62 no. 545a (between calles 69 and 71), 97000 Mérida, Yuc. ©/fax 999/986-2937. www.casasanjuan.com. 8 units (7 with private bathroom). $30–$60 (£15–£30) double. Rates include continental breakfast. No credit cards. Parking nearby $2 (£1). *In room:* A/C (in some), no phone.

Hotel Dolores Alba *Value*   The Dolores Alba offers attractive, comfortable rooms, an inviting swimming pool, good A/C, and free parking, all for a great price. The three-story section (with elevator) surrounding the back courtyard offers large rooms with good-size bathrooms. Beds (either two doubles or one double and one twin) have supportive foam-core mattresses, usually in a combination of one medium-firm and one medium-soft. All rooms have windows or balconies looking out over the pool. An old mango tree shades the front courtyard. The older rooms in this section are decorated with local crafts and have small bathrooms. The family that owns the Hotel Dolores Alba outside Chichén Itzá manages this hotel; you can make reservations at one hotel for the other. This hotel is 3½ blocks from the main square.

Calle 63 no. 464 (between calles 52 and 54), 97000 Mérida, Yuc. (℃ **999/928-5650**. Fax 999/928-3163. www.dolores alba.com. 100 units. $45 (£23) double. MC, V (with 8% surcharge). Internet specials available. Free guarded parking. **Amenities:** Restaurant; outdoor pool; tour desk; room service; laundry service; Laundromat. *In room:* A/C, TV, safe.

Hotel Mucuy *(Value*   The Mucuy is a simple, quiet, pleasant hotel in a great location. The gracious owners strive to make guests feel welcome, with conveniences such as a communal refrigerator in the lobby and, for a small extra charge, the use of a washer and dryer. Guest rooms are basic; most contain two twin beds or a queen (with comfortable mattresses) and some simple furniture. A neat garden patio with comfortable chairs is the perfect place for sitting and reading. The Mucuy is named for a small dove said to bring good luck to places where it alights. The hotel has a few rooms with A/C, which cost $5 (£2.50) more. English is spoken.

Calle 57 no. 481 (between calles 56 and 58), 97000 Mérida, Yuc. (℃ **999/928-5193**. Fax 999/923-7801. www.mucuy. com or cofelia@yahoo.com.mx. 21 units. $22 (£11) double. No credit cards. Limited street parking. **Amenities:** Small outdoor pool; tour info; self-serve laundry. *In room:* A/C (in some), no phone.

WHERE TO DINE

The people of Mérida have strong ideas and traditions about food. Certain dishes are always associated with a particular day of the week. In households across the city, Sunday would feel incomplete without *puchero* (a kind of stew). On Monday, at any restaurant that caters to locals, you are sure to find *frijol con puerco* (pork and beans). Likewise, you'll find *potaje* (potage) on Thursday; fish, of course, on Friday; and *chocolomo* (a beef dish) on Saturday. These dishes are heavy and slow to digest; they are for the midday meal, and not suitable for supper. What's more, Meridanos don't believe that seafood is a healthy supper food. All seafood restaurants in Mérida close by 6pm unless they cater to tourists. The preferred supper food is turkey (which, by the way, is said to be high in tryptophan, a soporific), and it's best served in the traditional *antojitos—salbutes* (small thin rounds of *masa* fried and topped with turkey, pork, or chicken, and onions, tomatoes, and lettuce) and *panuchos* (sliced open and lightly stuffed with bean paste, before having toppings added)—and turkey soup.

Another thing you may notice about Mérida is the surprising number of Middle Eastern restaurants. The city received a large influx of Lebanese immigrants around 1900. This population has had a strong influence on local society, to the point where Meridanos think of kibbe the way Americans think of pizza. Speaking of pizza, if you want to get some to take back to your hotel room, try **Vito Corleone,** on Calle 59 between calles 60 and 62. Its pizzas have a thin crust with a slightly smoky taste from the wood-burning oven.

It's becoming more difficult to recommend good restaurants for fine dining in the downtown area. Most of the best places are in the outlying districts, near the upper-class neighborhoods and shopping plazas. They are a little difficult to get to. If you want something special, I would recommend dining at the Hacienda Xcanatún on the outskirts of town, off the Progreso road. (See "Of Haciendas & Hotels," above.)

EXPENSIVE

Alberto's Continental LEBANESE/YUCATECAN   There's nothing quite like dining here at night in a softly lit room or on the wonderful old patio framed in Moorish arches. Nothing glitzy—just elegant *mudejar*-patterned tile floors, simple furniture, decoration that's just so, and the gurgling of a fountain creating a romantic mood. I find the prices on the expensive side. For supper, you can choose a sampler plate of four Lebanese favorites, or traditional Yucatecan specialties, such as *pollo pibil* or fish Celestún (bass stuffed with shrimp). You can finish with Turkish coffee.

Calle 64 no. 482 (at Calle 57). ℂ **999/928-5367**. Reservations recommended. Main courses $8–$22 (£4–£11). AE, MC, V. Daily 1–11pm.

Casa de Frida ⍟⍟ MEXICAN   If you're longing for some classic Mexican food from the central highlands, try this place. It serves some of the dishes Mexico is best known for, such as *mole poblano* and *sopa azteca*. The *mole* was good when I was last there, as was an interesting *flan de berenjena* (a kind of eggplant timbale). This is a comfortable no-nonsense sort of place decorated a la Mexicana. The menu has enough breadth to satisfy any appetite.

Calle 61 no. 526 (at Calle 66). ℂ **999/928-2311**. Reservations recommended. Main courses $10–$13 (£5–£6.50). No credit cards. Mon–Sat 6–10pm.

MODERATE

Amaro REGIONAL/VEGETARIAN   The menu at this courtyard restaurant lists some interesting vegetarian dishes, such as *crema de calabacitas* (cream of squash soup), apple salad, and avocado pizza. There is also a limited menu of fish and chicken dishes; you might want to try the Yucatecan chicken. The *agua de chaya* (chaya is a leafy vegetable prominent in the Maya diet) is refreshing on a hot afternoon. All desserts are made in-house. The restaurant is a little north of Plaza Mayor.

Calle 59 no. 507 Interior 6 (between calles 60 and 62). ℂ **999/928-2451**. Main courses $5–$9 (£2.50–£4.50). MC, V. Mon–Sat 11am–2am.

El Príncipe Tutul Xiú ⍟⍟ *Finds* REGIONAL   Yucatecan specialties from a limited menu. The original is in the town of Maní—the owner opened this restaurant because he got tired of hearing Meridanos asking him why he didn't open one in the capital. It's a short taxi ride from downtown, and to return you can pick up a local bus that passes by the restaurant. This is a great place to try the famous *sopa de lima,* and one of the six typical main courses, served with great handmade tortillas. And you can order, with confidence, one of the flavored waters such as an *horchata* or *tamarindo.*

Calle 123 no. 216 (between calles 46 and 46b), Colonia Serapio Rendón. ℂ **999/929-7721**. Reservations not accepted. Main courses $6 (£3). MC, V. Daily 11am–6pm.

El Templo ⍟ MEXICAN NUEVA COCINA   The odd layout of the place and the decor, which plays loosely with Mexican popular culture and iconography, are amusing. And the triptych menu, divided into Yucatecan, Mexican, and original, holds a lot of uncommon choices, plus a couple of daily specials. Sample dishes include the Cornish game hen in a guava-lime glaze and a salmon in a tamarind and black sesame sauce. I get the feeling that chef hasn't settled down into a groove yet, but there is no denying his enthusiasm. I just hope the locals enjoy this place as much as I did.

Calle 59 no. 438 (between calles 50 and 52). ℂ **999/930-9303**. Reservations accepted. Main courses $7–$10 (£3.50–£5). MC, V. Mon–Sat 6–1pm.

Restaurante Kantún ☆☆ *Value* SEAFOOD   This modest restaurant serves up the freshest seafood for incredibly low prices. The owner-chef is always on the premises taking care of details. The menu includes excellent ceviche and seafood cocktails and fish cooked in a number of ways. I had the *especial Kantún,* which was lightly battered and stuffed with lobster, crab, and shrimp. The dining room is air-conditioned, the furniture comfortable, and the service attentive.

Calle 45 no. 525-G (between calles 64 and 66). ℂ 999/923-4493. Reservations recommended. Main courses $6–$12 (£3–£6). MC, V. Daily noon–8pm (occasionally closes Mon).

Restaurant Los Almendros *Overrated* YUCATECAN   Ask where to eat Yucatecan food, and locals will inevitably suggest this place, mostly because it was the first place to offer tourists such Yucatecan specialties as *salbutes, panuchos* and *papadzules, cochinita pibil,* and *poc chuc.* The menu even comes with color photographs to facilitate acquaintance with these strange-sounding dishes. The food is okay and not much of a risk, but you can find better elsewhere. The service is slow. Still, it's a safe place to try Yucatecan food for the first time, and it's such a fixture that the idea of a guidebook that doesn't mention this restaurant is unthinkable. It's 5 blocks east of Calle 60, facing the Parque de la Mejorada.

Calle 50A no. 493. ℂ 999/928-5459. Main courses $6–$10 (£3–£5). AE, MC, V. Daily 10am–11pm.

INEXPENSIVE

Café Alameda MIDDLE EASTERN/VEGETARIAN   The trappings here are simple and informal (metal tables, plastic chairs), and it's a good place for catching a light meal. The trick is figuring out the Spanish names for popular Middle Eastern dishes. Kibbe is *quebbe bola* (not *quebbe cruda*), hummus is *garbanza,* and shish kabob is *alambre.* I leave it to you to figure out what a spinach pie is called (and it's excellent). Café Alameda is a treat for vegetarians, and the umbrella-shaded tables on the patio are perfect for morning coffee and *mamules* (walnut-filled pastries).

Calle 58 no. 474 (between calles 55 and 57). ℂ 999/928-3635. Main courses $2–$5 (£1–£2.50). No credit cards. Daily 8am–5pm.

Eladio's ☆ YUCATECAN   This is where locals come to relax in their off hours, drink very cold beer, and snack on Yucatecan specialties. There are four or five of these restaurants scattered about the city; this is the closest to the center of downtown. You have two choices: order a beer and enjoy *una botana* (a small portion that accompanies a drink, in this case usually a Yucatecan dish), or order from the menu. *Cochinita, poc chuc,* and *relleno negro* (turkey flavored with burnt chiles) are all good. Or try the *panuchos* or *salbutes.* Often there is live music in this open-air restaurant, which is 3 blocks east of Parque de la Mejorada.

Calle 59 (at Calle 44). ℂ 999/923-1087. Main courses $4–$8 (£2–£4). AE, MC, V. Daily noon–9pm.

La Flor de Santiago REGIONAL   This is a curious place with classic ambience and classically slow service. I like it best in the morning for breakfast. The dining area is very typical of Mérida, with its high ceiling, plain furniture, and local clientele. A wood-fired stove produces baked goods, and there's a sampling of Yuctecan specialties on the menu. Often it can be annoying because the cooks run out of food.

Calle 70 no. 478 (between calles 57 and 59). ℂ 999/928-5591. *Comida corrida* $4 (£2); main courses $5–$6 (£2.50–£3). No credit cards. Daily 7am–11pm.

MERIDA AFTER DARK

For nighttime entertainment, see the box, "Daily Festivals & Special Events in Mérida," earlier in this chapter, or check out the theaters noted here.

Teatro Peón Contreras, Calle 60 at Calle 57, and **Teatro Ayala,** Calle 60 at Calle 61, feature a wide range of performing artists from Mexico and around the world. **El Nuevo Olimpo,** on the main square, schedules frequent concerts; and **Cine Mérida,** a half-block north of the Nuevo Olimpo, has two screens for showing classic and art films, and one live stage.

Mérida's club scene offers everything from ubiquitous rock/dance to some one-of-a-kind spots that are nothing like what you find back home. Most of the dance clubs are in the big hotels or on Paseo de Montejo. For dancing, a small cluster of clubs on Calle 60, around the corner from Santa Lucía, offer live rock and Latin music. For salsa, go to **Mambo Café** in the Plaza las Américas shopping center.

ECOTOURS & ADVENTURE TRIPS

The Yucatán Peninsula has seen a recent explosion of companies that organize nature and adventure tours. One well-established outfit with a great track record is **Ecoturismo Yucatán,** Calle 3 no. 235, Col. Pensiones, 97219 Mérida (© **999/920-2772;** fax 999/925-9047; www.ecoyuc.com). Alfonso and Roberta Escobedo create itineraries to meet just about any special or general interest you may have for going to the Yucatán or southern Mexico. Alfonso has been creating adventure and nature tours for more than a dozen years. Specialties include archaeology, birding, natural history, and kayaking. The company also offers day trips that explore contemporary Maya culture and life in villages in the Yucatán. Package and customized tours are available.

SIDE TRIPS FROM MERIDA
SOTUTA DE PEON

What started out as one man's hobby—to restore an old hacienda for a weekend getaway and perhaps see what it takes to plant a couple of acres of henequén—spiraled out of control until it grew into one of the best living-museums you'll see anywhere; it has engrossed the imagination of an entire rural community. Presto! You have a completely functional *hacienda henequenera.*

You can arrange transportation from any of Mérida's hotels by calling **Hacienda Sotuta de Peón** at © 999/941-8639. Call to make a reservation even if you have your own car, and be sure to bring your bathing suit; there's a cenote on the property. The best days to visit are when the giant fiber-extracting machine is in operation—Tuesday, Thursday, or Saturday. The tour starts with a visit to the henequén fields via mule-drawn carts, the same as are used to transport the leaves of the plant to the hacienda's headquarters. You get to see it being harvested, and later, processed at the *casa de máquinas,* and even used in the manufacturing of twine and such. Along the way you get a glimpse into the local culture surrounding henequén production. You visit a house of one of the workers, as well as the house of the *hacendado* (the owner). You can also try some of the regional cooking—a restaurant on the premises turns out some good food. Admission costs $25 (£13) per adult, $15 (£7.50) per child. Transportation is extra. For more information, see www.haciendatour.com.

IZAMAL

Izamal is a sleepy town some 80km (50 miles) east of Mérida, an easy day trip by car. You can visit the famous Franciscan convent of San Antonio de Padua and the ruins of four large pyramids that overlook the center of town. One pyramid is partially reconstructed. Life in Izamal is easygoing in the extreme, as evidenced by the *victorias,* the horse-drawn buggies that serve as taxis here. Even if you come by car, you should make a point of touring the town in one of these. There is also a sound and light show in the old convent. The half-hour show costs $4.50 (£2.25) and is held on Tuesday, Thursday, Friday, and Saturday at 8:30pm. It's in Spanish, but you can rent headphones in other languages for $2.50 (£1.25).

CELESTUN NATIONAL WILDLIFE REFUGE: FLAMINGOS & OTHER WATERFOWL

On the coast, west of Mérida, is a large wetlands area that has been declared a biopreserve. It is a long, shallow estuary where freshwater mixes with Gulf saltwater, creating a habitat perfect for flamingos and many other species of waterfowl. This *ría* (estuary), unlike others that are fed by rivers or streams, receives fresh water through about 80 cenotes, most of which are underwater. It is very shallow (.3–1m/1–4 ft. deep) and thickly grown with mangrove, with an open channel .5km (a quarter-mile) wide and 50km (31 miles) long, sheltered from the open sea by a narrow strip of land. Along this corridor, you can take a launch to see flamingos as they dredge the bottom of the shallows for a species of small crustacean and a particular insect that make up the bulk of their diet.

You can get here by car or bus; it's an easy 90-minute drive. (For information on buses, see "Getting There & Departing: By Bus," earlier in this chapter.) To drive, leave downtown Mérida on Calle 57. Shortly after Santiago Church, Calle 57 ends and there's a dogleg onto Calle 59-A. This crosses Avenida Itzáes, and its name changes to Jacinto Canek; continue until you see signs for Celestún Highway 178. This will take you through Hunucmá, where the road joins Highway 281, which takes you to Celestún. You'll know you have arrived when you get to the bridge.

In the last few years, the state agency CULTUR has come into Celestún and established order where once there was chaos. Immediately to your left after the bridge, you'll find modern facilities with a snack bar, clean bathrooms, and a ticket window. Prices for tours are fixed. A 75-minute tour costs about $50 (£25) and can accommodate up to six people. You can join others or hire a boat by yourself. On the tour you'll definitely see some flamingos; you'll also get to see some mangrove close up, and one of the many underwater springs. Please do not urge the boatmen to get any closer to the flamingos than they are allowed to; if pestered too much, the birds will abandon the area for another, less fitting habitat. The ride is quite pleasant—the water is calm, and CULTUR has supplied the boatmen with wide, flat-bottom skiffs that have canopies for shade.

In addition to flamingos, you will see frigate birds, pelicans, spoonbills, egrets, sandpipers, and other waterfowl feeding on shallow sandbars at any time of year. At least 15 duck species have been counted, and there are several species of birds of prey. Of the 175 bird species that are here, some 99 are permanent residents. Nonbreeding flamingos remain here year-round; the larger group of breeding flamingos takes off around April to nest on the upper Yucatán Peninsula east of Río Lagartos, returning to Celestún in October.

Hotel Eco Paraíso Xixim 🌟🌟 Eco Paraíso is meant to be a refuge from the modern world. It sits on a deserted 4km (2½-mile) stretch of beach that was once part of a coconut plantation. It attracts much the same clientele as the former-haciendas-turned-luxury-hotels, but in some ways it has more going for it (like the beach). Some guests come here for a week of idleness; others use this as a base of operations for visiting the biopreserve and making trips to the Maya ruins in the interior. The hotel offers its own tours to various places. Rooms are quite private; each is a separate bungalow with *palapa* roof. Each comes with two comfortable queen-size beds, a sitting area, ceiling fans, and a private porch with hammocks. On my last visit, the food was very good, and the service was great. The hotel composts waste and treats and uses wastewater.

Antigua Carretera a Sisal Km 10, 97367 Celestún, Yuc. (*C*) **988/916-2100.** Fax 988/916-2111. www.ecoparaiso.com. 15 units. High season $220 (£110) double; low season $184 (£92) double. Rates include 2 meals per person. AE, MC, V. Free parking. **Amenities:** Restaurant; bar; midsize outdoor pool; tour desk. *In room:* Coffeemaker, hair dryer, safe.

DZIBILCHALTUN: MAYA RUINS & MUSEUM

This destination makes for a quick morning trip that will get you back to Mérida in time for a siesta, or it could be part of a longer trip to Progreso, Uaymitún, and Xcambó. It's located 14km (8⅔ miles) north of Mérida along the Progreso road and 4km (2½ miles) east of the highway. To get there, take Calle 60 all the way out of town and follow signs for Progreso and Highway 261. Look for the sign for Dzibilchaltún, which also reads UNIVERSIDAD DEL MAYAB; it will point you right. After a few miles, you'll see a sign for the entrance to the ruins and the museum. If you don't want to drive, take one of the *colectivos* that line up along Parque San Juan.

Dzibilchaltún was founded about 500 B.C., flourished around A.D. 750, and was in decline long before the coming of the conquistadors. Since the ruins were discovered in 1941, more than 8,000 buildings have been mapped. The site covers an area of almost 15 sq. km (6 sq. miles) with a central core of almost 25 hectares (62 acres), but the area of prime interest is limited to the buildings surrounding two plazas next to the cenote, and another building, the Temple of the Seven Dolls, connected to these by a *sacbé* (causeway). Dzibilchaltún means "place of the stone writing," and at least 25 stelae have been found.

Start at the **Museo del Pueblo Maya,** which is worth seeing. It's open Tuesday to Sunday from 8am to 4pm. Admission is $6 (£3). The museum's collection includes artifacts from various sites in the Yucatán. Explanations are printed in bilingual format and are fairly thorough. Objects include a beautiful example of a plumed serpent from Chichén Itzá and a finely designed incense vessel from Palenque. From this general view of the Maya civilization, the museum moves on to exhibit specific artifacts found at the site of Dzibilchaltún, including the rather curious dolls that have given one structure its name. Then there's an exhibit on Maya culture in historical and present times, including a collection of *huipiles,* the woven blouses that Indian women wear. From here a door leads out to the site.

The first thing you come to is the *sacbé* that connects the two areas of interest. To the left is the **Temple of the Seven Dolls.** The temple's doorways and the *sacbé* line up with the rising sun at the spring and autumnal equinoxes. To the right are the buildings grouped around the Cenote Xlacah, the sacred well, and a complex of buildings around **Structure 38,** the **Central Group** of temples. The Yucatán State Department of Ecology has added nature trails and published a booklet (in Spanish) of birds and plants seen along the mapped trail.

PROGRESO, UAYMITUN & XCAMBO: GULF COAST CITY, FLAMINGO LOOKOUT & MORE MAYA RUINS

For a beach escape, go to the port of Progreso, Mérida's weekend beach resort. This is where Meridanos have their vacation houses and where they come in large numbers in July and August. It is also the part-time home of some Americans and Canadians escaping northern winters. Except for July and August, it is a quiet place where you can enjoy the Gulf waters in peace. Along the *malecón*, the wide oceanfront drive that extends the length of a sandy beach, you can pull over and enjoy a swim anywhere you like. The water here isn't the blue of the Caribbean, but it's clean. A long pier extends several kilometers into the gulf to load and unload large ships. Cruise ships dock here twice a week. Along or near the *malecón* are several hotels and a number of restaurants where you can get good fresh seafood.

From Mérida, buses to **Progreso** leave from the bus station at Calle 62 no. 524, between calles 65 and 67, every 15 minutes, starting at 5am. The trip takes almost an hour and costs $3 (£1.50).

If you have a car, you might want to drive down the coastal road east toward Telchac Puerto. After about 20 minutes, on the right you'll see a large, solid-looking wooden observation tower for viewing flamingos. A sign reads UAYMITUN. The state agency CULTUR constructed the tower, operates it, and provides binoculars free of charge. A few years ago, flamingos from Celestún migrated here and established a colony. Your chances of spotting them are good, and you don't have to pay for a boat.

Twenty minutes farther down this road, there's a turnoff for the road to Dzemul. On my last trip I didn't see any flamingos at Uaymitún, but just after turning here, I found a flock of 500, only 30m (98 ft.) from the highway. After a few minutes, you'll see a sign for **Xcambó** that points to the right. This Maya city is thought to have prospered as a production center for salt. Archaeologists have reconstructed the small ceremonial center, which has several platforms and temples. Admission is free. After viewing these ruins, you can continue on the same road through the small towns of Dzemul and Baca. At Baca, take Highway 176 back to Mérida.

EN ROUTE TO UXMAL

Two routes go to Uxmal, about 80km (50 miles) south of Mérida. The most direct is Highway 261 via Umán and Muna. On the way, you can stop to see Hacienda Yaxcopoil, which is 30km (20 miles) from Mérida. If you have the time and want a more scenic route, try the meandering State Highway 18. It's sometimes called the Convent Route, but all tourism hype aside, it makes for a pleasant drive with several interesting stops. One thing you might do is make your trip to Uxmal into a loop by going one way and coming back the other with an overnight stay at Uxmal. You could plan on arriving in Uxmal in the late afternoon, attend the sound-and-light show in the evening, and see the ruins the next morning while it is cool and uncrowded.

While traveling in this area you'll pass through small villages without directional signs, so get used to poking your head out the window and saying *"Buenos días. ¿Dónde está el camino para . . . ?"* This translates as "Good day. Where is the road to . . . ?" I end up asking more than one person. The streets in these villages are full of children, bicycles, and livestock, so drive carefully and, as always, keep an eye out for unmarked *topes*. The attractions on these routes all have the same hours: Churches are open daily from 10am to 1pm and 4 to 6pm; ruins are open daily from 8am to 5pm.

HIGHWAY 261: YAXCOPOIL & MUNA From downtown, take Calle 65 or 69 to Avenida Itzáes and turn left; this feeds onto the highway. You can save some time by looping around the busy market town of Umán. To do so, take the exit for Highway 180 Cancún and Campeche, and then follow signs towards Campeche. You'll be on 180 headed south; take it for a few miles to where it intersects with Highway 261;

take the exit labeled uxmal. Very shortly you'll come to the town and **Hacienda Yax-copoil** (yash-koh-*poyl;* © 999/900-1193; www.yaxcopoil.com), a ruined hacienda in plain sight on the right side of the road. In the front courtyard—now a parking lot—is a giant Indian laurel tree. You can take a half-hour tour of the place, including the manor, and the henequén factory. It's open from Monday to Saturday from 8am to 5pm and Sunday 9am to 1pm. Admission is $5 (£2.50). It's a little overpriced because the owners have not put much effort into making it a special attraction, but the grounds are attractive, and there are some things of interest.

After Yaxcopoil comes the little market town of **Muna** (65km/40 miles from Mérida). Here you can find excellent **reproductions of Maya ceramics.** An artisan named Rodrigo Martín Morales has worked 25 years perfecting the style and methods of the ancient Maya. He and his family have two workshops in town. They do painstaking work and sell a lot of their production to archeologists and museum stores. The first store is on the right at the junction of a bypass for Muna. Look for a typical Maya dwelling and a small store. The main store is 3km (2 miles) farther on, just as you enter Muna. Keep an eye out for two large Ceiba trees growing on the right-hand side of the road. Under the trees, a small plaza with stalls sells handicrafts or food. Make a right turn and go down 45m (150 ft.). On your left will be a store. It's not well marked, but it will be obvious. The name of the place is **Taller de Arte-sanía Los Ceibos** (© 997/971-0036). The family will be working in the back. Only Spanish is spoken. The store is open from 9am to 6pm daily. In addition to ceramics, Rodrigo works in stone, wood, and jade. Uxmal is 15km (9⅓ miles) beyond Muna.

HIGHWAY 18 (THE CONVENT ROUTE): KANASIN, ACANCEH, MAYAPAN & TICUL   From downtown take Calle 63 east to Circuito Colonias and turn right; look for a traffic circle with a small fountain and turn left. This feeds onto Highway 18 to Kanasín (kah-nah-*seen*) and then Acanceh (ah-kahn-*keh*). In **Kanasín,** the highway divides into two roads, and a sign will tell you that you can't go straight; instead, you go to the right, which will curve around and flow into the next parallel street. Go past the market, church, and the main square on your left, and then stay to the right when you get to a fork.

Shortly after Kanasín, the highway has been upgraded and now bypasses a lot of villages. After a few of these turnoffs you'll see a sign pointing left to Acanceh. Across the street from and overlooking Acanceh's church is a restored pyramid. On top of this pyramid, under a makeshift roof, are some large stucco figures of Maya deities. The caretaker, Mario Uicab, will guide you up to see the figures and give you a little explanation (in Spanish). Admission is $2.50 (£1.25). There are some other ruins a couple of blocks away called **El Palacio de los Estucos.** In 1908, a stucco mural was found here in mint condition. It was left exposed and has deteriorated somewhat. Now it is sheltered, and you can still easily distinguish the painted figures in their original colors. To leave Acanceh, head back to the highway on the street that passes between church and the plaza.

The next turnoff will be for **Tecoh** on the right side. Tecoh's parish church sits on a massive pre-Columbian raised platform—the remains of a ceremonial complex that was sacrificed to build the church. With its rough stone and simple twin towers that are crumbling around the edges, the church looks ancient. Inside are three carved *retablos* (altarpieces) covered in gold leaf and unmistakably Indian in style. In 1998, they were refurbished and are well worth seeing.

Also in Tecoh are some caverns, shown by a local. The bad news is that the owner doesn't have a very good flashlight, and I found myself groping around in the dark. You'll find them as you leave town heading back to the highway. Then it's on to the ruins of Mayapán.

MAYAPAN ⊙★

Founded, according to Maya lore, by the man-god Kukulkán (Quetzalcoatl in central Mexico) in about A.D. 1007, Mayapán quickly established itself as the most important city in northern Yucatán. For almost 2 centuries, it was the capital of a Maya confederation of city-states that included Chichén Itzá and Uxmal. But before 1200, the rulers of Mayapán ended the confederation by attacking and subjugating the other two cities. Eventually, a successful revolt by the other cities brought down Mayapán, which was abandoned during the mid-1400s.

The city extended out at least 4 sq. km (1½ sq. miles), but the ceremonial center is quite compact. In the last few years, archaeologists have been busy excavating and rebuilding it, and work continues. Several buildings bordering the principal plaza have been reconstructed, including one that is similar to El Castillo in Chichén Itzá. The excavations have uncovered murals and stucco figures that provide more grist for the mill of conjecture: atlantes (columns in the form of a human figure supporting something heavy, in the way Atlas supported the sky in Greek myth), skeletal soldiers, macaws, entwined snakes, and a stucco jaguar. This place is definitely worth a stop.

The site is open daily from 8am to 5pm. Admission is $3.50 (£1.75). Use of a personal video camera is $4 (£2).

FROM MAYAPAN TO TICUL   About 20km (12 miles) after Mayapán, you'll see the highway for **Mama** on your right. This will put you on a narrow road that quickly enters the town. For some reason I really like this village; some parts of it are quite pretty. It's often called Mamita by the locals, using the affectionate diminutive suffix. The main attraction is the church and former convent. Inside are several fascinating *retablos* sculpted in a native form of baroque. During the restoration of these buildings, colonial-age murals and designs were uncovered and restored. Be sure to get a peek at them in the sacristy. From Mama, continue on for about 20km (12 miles) to Ticul, a large (for this area) market town with a couple of simple hotels.

TICUL

Best known for the cottage industry of *huipil* (native blouse) embroidery and for the manufacture of women's dress shoes, Ticul isn't the most exciting stop on the Puuc route, but it's a convenient place to wash up and spend the night. It's also a center for large commercially produced pottery; most of the widely sold sienna-colored pottery painted with Maya designs comes from here. If it's a cloudy, humid day, the potters may not be working (part of the process requires sun drying), but they still welcome visitors to purchase finished pieces.

Ticul is only 20km (12 miles) northeast of Uxmal, so thrifty tourists stay either here or in Santa Elena instead of the more expensive hotels at the ruins. On the main square is the **Hotel Plaza,** Calle 23 no. 202, near the intersection with Calle 26 (© **997/972-0484**). It's a modest but comfortable hotel. A double room with air-conditioning costs $35 (£18); without air-conditioning, $25 (£13). In both cases, there's a 5% charge if you want to pay with a credit card (MasterCard and Visa accepted). Get an interior room if you're looking for quiet, because Ticul has quite a lively plaza. From Ticul, you can do one of two things: head straight for Uxmal via Santa Elena, or loop around the Puuc Route, the long way to Santa Elena. For information on the Puuc route, see "The Puuc Maya Route & Village of Oxkutzcab," below.

FROM TICUL TO UXMAL Follow the main street (Calle 23) west through town. Turn left on Calle 34. It's 15km (9⅓ miles) to Santa Elena; and from there another 15km (9⅓ miles) to Uxmal. In Santa Elena, by the side of Highway 261, is a clean restaurant with good food, **El Chaac Mool,** and on the opposite side of the road is the **Flycatcher Inn B&B** (see listing, below).

2 The Ruins of Uxmal ⟨★⟨★⟨★

80km (50 miles) SW of Mérida; 19km (12 miles) W of Ticul; 19km (12 miles) S of Muna

The ceremonial complex of Uxmal (pronounced "oosh-*mahl*") is one of the masterworks of Maya civilization. It is strikingly different from all other cities of the Maya for its expansive and intricate facades of carved stone. Unlike other sites in northern Yucatán, such as Chichén Itzá and Mayapán, Uxmal isn't built on a flat plane. The builders worked into the composition of the ceremonial center an interplay of elevations that adds complexity. And then, there is the strange and beautiful oval-shaped Pyramid of the Magician, which is unique among the Maya. The great building period took place between A.D. 700 and 1000, when the population probably reached 25,000. After 1000, Uxmal fell under the sway of the Xiú princes (who may have come from central Mexico). In the 1440s, the Xiú conquered Mayapán, and not long afterward the age of the Maya ended with the arrival of the Spanish conquistadors.

Close to Uxmal, four smaller sites—**Sayil, Kabah, Xlapak,** and **Labná**—can be visited in quick succession. With Uxmal, these ruins are collectively known as the **Puuc route.** See "Seeing Puuc Maya Sites," below, if you want to explore these sites.

ESSENTIALS

GETTING THERE & DEPARTING   By Car   Two routes to Uxmal from Mérida, Highway 261 and State Highway 18, are described in "En Route to Uxmal," above. *Note:* There's no gasoline at Uxmal.

By Bus   See "Getting There & Departing," in "Mérida: Gateway to the Maya Heartland," earlier in this chapter, for information about bus service between Mérida and Uxmal. To return, wait for the bus on the highway at the entrance to the ruins. To see the sound-and-light show, don't bother with regular buses; sign up with a tour operator in Mérida.

ORIENTATION   Entrance to the ruins is through the visitor center where you buy your tickets (two per person, hold on to both). It has a restaurant; toilets; a first-aid station; shops selling soft drinks, ice cream, film, batteries, and books; a state-run Casa de Artesanía (crafts house); and a small museum, which isn't very informative. The site is open daily from 8am to 5pm. Admission to the archaeological site is around $11 (£5.50), which includes admission to the nightly sound-and-light show. Bringing in a video camera costs $4 (£2). Parking costs $1 (50p). If you're staying the night in Uxmal, it is possible (and I think preferable) to get to the site late in the day and buy a ticket that allows you to see the sound-and-light show that evening and lets you enter the ruins the next morning to explore them before it gets hot. Just make sure that the ticket vendor knows what you intend to do and keep the ticket.

Guides at the entrance of Uxmal give tours in a variety of languages and charge $40 (£20) for a single person or a group. The guides frown on unrelated individuals joining a group. They'd rather charge you as a solo visitor, but you can ask other English speakers if they'd like to join you in a tour and split the cost. As at other sites, the guides vary in quality but will point out areas and architectural details that you might otherwise miss. You should think of these guided tours as performances—the guides try to be as entertaining as possible and adjust their presentations according to the interests of the visitors.

Included in the price of admission is a 45-minute **sound-and-light show,** each evening at 7pm. It's in Spanish, but headsets are available for rent ($2.50/£1.25) for listening to the program in several languages. The narrative is part Hollywood, part high school, but the lighting of the buildings is worth making the effort to see it. After the show, the chant *"Chaaac, Chaaac"* will echo in your mind for weeks.

A TOUR OF THE RUINS
THE PYRAMID OF THE MAGICIAN   As you enter the ruins, note a *chultún,* or cistern, where Uxmal stored its water. Unlike most of the major Maya sites, Uxmal has no cenote to supply fresh water. The city's inhabitants were much more dependent on rainwater, and consequently venerated the rain god Chaac with unusual devotion.

Rising in front of you is the Pirámide del Adivino. The name comes from a myth told to John Lloyd Stephens on his visit in the 19th century. It tells the story of a magician-dwarf who reached adulthood in a single day after being hatched from an egg and built this pyramid in one night. Beneath it are five earlier structures. The pyramid has an oval base and rounded sides. You are looking at the east side. The main face is on the west side. Walk around the left or south side to see the front. The pyramid was designed so that the east side rises less steeply than the west side, which shifts the crowning temples to the west of the central axis of the building, causing them to loom above the plaza below. The temple doorway is heavily ornamented, characteristic of the Chenes style, with 12 stylized masks representing Chaac.

THE NUNNERY QUADRANGLE   From the plaza you're standing in, you want to go to the large Nunnery Quadrangle. Walk out the way you walked into the plaza, turn right, and follow the wall of this long stone building until you get to the building's main door—a corbelled arch that leads into the quadrangle. You'll find yourself in a plaza bordered on each side by stone buildings with elaborate facades. The 16th-century Spanish historian Fray Diego López de Cogullado gave the quadrangle its name when he decided that its layout resembled a Spanish convent.

The quadrangle does have a lot of small rooms, about the size of a nun's cell. You might poke your head into one to see the shape and size of it, but don't bother trying to explore them all. These rooms were long ago abandoned to the swallows that fly above the city. No interior murals or stucco work have been found here—at least, not yet. No, the richness of Uxmal lies in the stonework on its exterior walls.

The Nunnery is a great example of this. The first building your eye latches onto when you enter the plaza is the north building in front of you. It is the tallest, and the view from the top includes all the major buildings of the city, making it useful for the sound-and-light show. The central stairway is bordered by a common element in Puuc architecture, doorways supported by rounded columns. The remnants of the facade on the second level show elements used in the other three buildings and elsewhere throughout the city. There's a crosshatch pattern and a pattern of square curlicues, called a step-and-fret design, and the long-nosed god mask repeated vertically, used often to decorate the corners of buildings—what I call a Chaac stack. Though the facades of these buildings share these common elements and others, their composition varies. On the west building you'll see long feathered serpents intertwined at head and tail. A human head stares out from a serpent's open mouth. I've heard and read a number of interpretations of this motif, repeated elsewhere in Maya art, but they all leave me somewhat in doubt. And that's the trouble with symbols: They are usually the condensed expression of multiple meanings, so any one interpretation could be true, but only partially true.

THE BALL COURT Leaving the Nunnery by the same way you entered, you will see straight ahead a ball court. What would a Maya city be without a ball court? And this one is a particularly good representative of the hundreds found elsewhere in the Maya world. Someone has even installed a replica of one of the stone rings that were the targets for the players, who would make use of their knees, hips, and maybe their arms to strike a solid rubber ball (yes, the Maya knew about natural rubber and extracted latex from a couple of species of rubber trees). The inclined planes on both sides of the court were in play and obviously not an area for spectators, who are thought to have observed the game from atop the two structures.

THE GOVERNOR'S PALACE Continuing in the same direction (south), you come to the large raised plaza on top of which sits the Governor's Palace, running in a north-south direction. The surface area of the raised plaza measures 140m × 170m (459 ft. × 558 ft.), and it is raised about 10m (33 ft.) above the ground—quite a bit of earth-moving. Most of this surface is used as a ceremonial space facing the front (east side) of the palace. In the center is a double-headed jaguar throne, which is seen elsewhere in the Maya world. From here, you get the best view of the building's remarkable facade. Like the rest of the palaces here, the first level is smooth, and the second is ornate. Moving diagonally across a crosshatch pattern is a series of Chaac masks. Crowning the building is an elegant cornice projecting slightly outward from above a double border, which could be an architectural reference to the original crested thatched roofs of the Maya. Human figures adorned the main doors, though only the headdress survives of the central figure.

THE GREAT PYRAMID Behind the palace, the platform descends in terraces to another plaza with a large pyramid on its south side. This is known as the Great Pyramid. On top is the Temple of the Macaws, for the repeated representation of macaws on the face of the temple, and the ruins of three other temples. The view from the top is wonderful.

THE DOVECOTE This building is remarkable in that roof combs weren't a common feature of temples in the Puuc hills, although you'll see one (of a very different style) on El Mirador at Sayil.

WHERE TO STAY

Flycatcher Inn B&B *Value* This pleasant little bed-and-breakfast is in the village of Santa Elena, just off Highway 261. The rooms are quiet, attractive, and spacious, and come with comfortable beds and decorative ironwork made by one of the owners, Santiago Domínguez. The other owner is Kristine Ellingson, an American from the Northwest who has lived in Santa Elena for years and is happy to aid her guests in their travels. Last year they replaced the mattresses in all the rooms, added a cottage, and made various improvements to the hotel's large grounds.

Carretera Uxmal–Kabah, 97840 Santa Elena, Yuc. No phone. www.flycatcherinn.com. 7 units. $45–$65 (£23–£33) double ($10/£5 extra for A/C). Rates include breakfast. No credit cards. Free secure parking. *In room:* A/C in 6 units.

Hacienda Uxmal and The Lodge at Uxmal ✿✿✿ The Hacienda is the oldest hotel in Uxmal. Located just up the road from the ruins, it was built for the archaeology staff. Rooms are large and airy, exuding a feel of days gone by, with patterned tile floors, heavy furniture, and louvered windows. Room nos. 202 through 214 and 302 through 305 are the nicest of the superiors. Corner rooms are labeled A through F and are even larger and come with Jacuzzi tubs. A handsome garden courtyard with towering royal palms, a bar, and a pool adds to the air of tranquillity. A guitar trio usually plays on the open patio in the evenings.

The Lodge is right at the entrance to the ruins. It's made up of several two-story thatched buildings ("bungalows") situated around two pools and surrounded by landscaped grounds. Each building has a large, open breezeway with ceiling fans and rocking chairs. Rooms are extra large and attractively finished with details such as carved headboards. Bathrooms are large and come with stone countertops and either a bathtub or a Jacuzzi tub. Upstairs rooms have thatched roofs.

High season is from November through April; low season May to October.

Carretera Mérida–Uxmal Km 80, 97844 Uxmal, Yuc. ✆ **997/976-2011.** www.mayaland.com. (Reservations: Mayaland Resorts, Robalo 30 SM3, 77500 Cancún, Q. Roo; ✆ 800/235-4079 in the U.S., or 998/887-2450; fax 998/887-4510.) 113 units. Hacienda: High season rooms from $172 (£86), suites from $404 (£202); low season rooms from $103 (£52), suites from $298 (£149). Lodge: High season bungalows from $266 (£133); low season bungalows from $184 (£92). AE, MC, V. Free guarded parking. **Amenities:** 2 restaurants; bar; 4 outdoor pools; tour info; laundry service; nonsmoking rooms. *In room:* A/C, TV, minibar, coffeemaker, hair dryer (upon request).

Villas Arqueológicas Uxmal ✿ This hotel and its sister properties were recently sold to a Mexican resort group called Islander Collection, but it's still business as usual, much as it was when the place was part of ClubMed. A two-story layout surrounds a garden patio and a pool. At guests' disposal are a tennis court, a library, and an audiovisual show on the ruins in English, French, and Spanish. Each of the modern, medium-size rooms has a double and a twin bed that fit into spaces that are walled on three sides. Very tall people should stay elsewhere. You can also ask for rates that include half- or full board.

Ruinas Uxmal, 97844 Uxmal, Yuc. ✆ **987/872-9300,** ext. 8101. www.islandercollection.com. 48 units. $130 (£65) double. Rates include continental breakfast. Half-board (breakfast plus lunch or dinner) $20 (£10) per person; full board (3 meals) $40 (£20) per person. AE, MC, V. Free guarded parking. **Amenities:** Restaurant; bar; outdoor pool; tennis court, laundry service. *In room:* A/C, hair dryer.

WHERE TO DINE

I've eaten well at the hotel restaurant of the Lodge at Uxmal, ordering the Yucatecan specialties, which were fresh and well prepared. I've also eaten well at the hotel restaurant at the Villas Arqueológicas, but again, keeping it simple. There are some *palapa* restaurants by the highway as you approach the ruins from Mérida. I've had good and bad experiences at these. They do a lot of business with bus tours, so the best time to try them is early afternoon.

THE PUUC MAYA ROUTE & VILLAGE OF OXKUTZCAB

South and east of Uxmal are several other Maya cities worth visiting. Though smaller in scale than Uxmal or Chichén Itzá, each contains gems of Maya architecture. The Palace of Masks at **Kabah,** the palace at **Sayil,** and the fantastic caverns of **Loltún** are well worth viewing.

Kabah is 28km (17 miles) southeast of Uxmal via Highway 261 through Santa Elena. From there it's only a couple kilometers to Sayil. Xlapak is almost walking

---

Tips **Seeing Puuc Maya Sites**

All of these sites are currently undergoing excavation and reconstruction, and some buildings may be roped off when you visit. The sites are open daily from 8am to 5pm. Admission is $2 to $3 (£1–£1.50) for each site, and $5 (£2.50) for Loltún. Loltún has specific hours for tours—9:30 and 11am, and 12:30, 2, 3, and 4pm. Even if you're the only person at the cave at one of these times, the guide must give you a tour, and he can't try to charge you more money as if you were contracting his services for an individual tour. Sometimes the guides try to do this. Use of a video camera at any time costs $4 (£2); if you're visiting Uxmal in the same day, you pay only once for video permission and present your receipt as proof at each ruin.

---

distance (through the jungle) from Sayil, and Labná is just a bit farther east. A short drive beyond Labná brings you to the caves of Loltún. Oxkutzcab is at the road's intersection with Highway 184, which you can follow west to Ticul or east all the way to Felipe Carrillo Puerto. If you aren't driving, a daily bus from Mérida goes to all these sites, with the exception of Loltún. (See "By Bus" in "Getting There & Departing," earlier in this chapter.)

PUUC MAYA SITES

KABAH *&*   To reach Kabah from Uxmal, head southwest on Highway 261 to Santa Elena (1km/½ mile), and then south to Kabah (13km/8 miles). The ancient city lies along both sides of the highway. Turn right into the parking lot.

The most outstanding building at Kabah is the **Palace of Masks,** or Codz Poop ("rolled-up mat"), named for its decorative motif. You'll notice it to the right as you enter. Its outstanding feature is the Chenes-style facade, completely covered in a repeated pattern of 250 masks of Chaac, each one with curling remnants of Chaac's elephant-trunk-like nose. There's nothing else like this facade in all of Maya architecture. For years, parts of this building lay lined up in the weeds like pieces of a puzzle awaiting the master puzzle-solver to put them into place. Sculptures from this building are in the anthropology museums in Mérida and Mexico City.

Just behind and to the left of the Codz Poop is the **Palace Group** (also called the East Group), with a fine Puuc-style colonnaded facade. Originally it had 32 rooms. On the front are seven doors, two divided by columns, a common feature of Puuc architecture. Across the highway is what was once the **Great Temple.** Past it is a **great arch,** which was much wider at one time and may have been a monumental gate into the city. A *sacbé* linked this arch to a point at Uxmal. Compare this corbelled arch to the one at Labná (see below), which is in much better shape.

SAYIL   About 4km (2½ miles) south of Kabah is the turnoff (left, or east) to Sayil, Xlapak, Labná, Loltún, and Oxkutzcab. The ruins of **Sayil** ("place of the ants") are 4km (2½ miles) along this road.

Sayil is famous for **El Palacio** *&&*. This palace of more than 90 rooms is impressive for its size alone. At present it is roped off. Climbing is not permitted. But this is unimportant because what makes it a masterpiece of Maya architecture is the facade, which is best appreciated from the ground. It stretches across three terraced levels, and its rows of columns give it a Minoan appearance. On the second level, notice the upside-down stone figure known to archaeologists as the Diving God, or Descending God, over the doorway; the same motif was used at Tulum a couple of centuries later. The large circular basin on the ground below the palace is an artificial catch basin for a *chultún* (cistern); this region has no natural cenotes (wells) to use to irrigate crops.

In the jungle beyond El Palacio is **El Mirador,** a small temple with an oddly slotted roof comb. Beyond El Mirador, a crude stele (tall, carved stone) has a phallic idol carved on it in exaggerated proportions. Another building group, the Southern Group, is a short distance down a trail that branches off from the one heading to El Mirador.

XLAPAK   Xlapak (*shla*-pahk) is a small site with one building; it's 5.5 km (3½ miles) down the road from Sayil. The Palace at Xlapak bears the masks of the rain god Chaac. You won't miss much if you skip this place.

LABNA   Labná, which dates from between A.D. 600 and 900, is 30km (19 miles) from Uxmal and only 3km (2 miles) past Xlapak. Descriptive placards fronting the main buildings are in Spanish, English, and German. The first thing you see on the left as you enter is **El Palacio,** a magnificent Puuc-style building much like the one at Sayil, but in poorer condition. Over a doorway is a large, well-conserved mask of Chaac with eyes, a huge snout nose, and jagged teeth around a small mouth that seems on the verge of speaking. Jutting out on one corner is a highly stylized serpent's mouth from which pops a human head with an unexpectedly serene expression. From the front, you can gaze out to the enormous grassy interior grounds flanked by vestiges of unrestored buildings and jungle.

From El Palacio, you can walk across the interior grounds on a reconstructed *sacbé* leading to Labná's **corbelled arch.** At one time, there were probably several such arches spread through the region. This one has been extensively restored, although only remnants of the roof comb can be seen. It was once part of a more elaborate structure that is completely gone. Chaac's face is on the corners of one facade, and stylized Maya huts are fashioned in stone above the two small doorways.

You pass through the arch to **El Mirador,** or El Castillo. Towering above a large pile of rubble is a singular room crowned with a roof comb etched against the sky.

There's a snack stand with toilets at the entrance.

LOLTUN   The caverns of Loltún are 31km (19 miles) past Labná on the way to Oxkutzcab, on the left side of the road. These fascinating caves, home of ancient Maya, were also used as a refuge during the War of the Castes (1847–1901). Inside are statuary, wall carvings and paintings, *chultunes* (cisterns), and other signs of Maya habitation. Guides will explain much of what you see. When I was there, the guide spoke English but was a little difficult to understand.

The admission price includes a 90-minute **tour;** tours begin daily at 9:30 and 11am, and 12:30, 2, 3, and 4pm. The floor of the cavern can be slippery in places; if you have a flashlight, take it with you. Admission is $5 (£2.50). What you see is quite interesting. I've heard reports of guides canceling the regularly scheduled tour so that they can charge for a private tour. Don't agree to such a thing.

To return to Mérida from Loltún, drive the 7km (4½ miles) to Oxkutzcab. From there, you have a couple of options for returning to Mérida: The slow route is through Maní and Teabo, which will allow you to see some convents and return by Highway 18, known as the "Convent Route" (see "En Route to Uxmal," earlier in this chapter). Alternately, you can head towards Muna to hook up with Highway 261 (also described earlier).

OXKUTZCAB

Oxkutzcab (ohsh-kootz-*kahb*), 11km (7 miles) from Loltún, is the center of the Yucatán's fruit-growing region. Oranges abound. The tidy village of 21,000 centers on a beautiful 16th-century church and the market. **Su Cabaña Suiza** (no phone) is a dependable restaurant in town. The last week of October and first week of November is the **Orange Festival,** when the village turns exuberant, with a carnival and orange displays in and around the central plaza.

EN ROUTE TO CAMPECHE

From Oxkutzcab, head back 43km (27 miles) to Sayil, and then drive south on Highway 261 to Campeche (126km/78 miles). After crossing the state line, you'll pass through the towns of Bolonchén and Hopelchén. The drive is pleasant, and there's little traffic. Both towns have gas stations. When going through the towns, watch carefully for directional traffic signs so that you stay on the highway. From Hopelchén, Highway 261 heads west. After 42km (26 miles), you'll find yourself at Cayal and the well-marked turnoff for the ruins of the city of Edzná, 18km (11 miles) farther south.

EDZNA ✦ This city is interesting for several reasons. The area was populated as early as 600 B.C., with urban formation by 300 B.C. From that point on, Edzná grew impressively in a way that evinces considerable urban-planning skills. An ambitious and elaborate canal system was dug, which must have taken decades to complete, but would have allowed for a great expansion in agricultural production and, hence, concentration of population. This made Edzná the preeminent city for a wide territory.

Another boom in construction began around A.D. 500, amid the Classic period. This was when the city's most prominent feature, the **Great Acropolis,** was started.

Sitting on top of this raised platform are five main pyramids, the largest being the much-photographed **Pyramid of Five Stories.** It combines the features of temple platform and palace. In Maya architecture, you have palace buildings with many vaulted chambers and you have solid pyramidal platforms with a couple of interior temples or burial passages. These are two mutually exclusive categories—but not here. Such a mix is found only in the Puuc and Río Bec areas and only in a few examples, and none similar to this, which makes this pyramid a bold architectural statement. The four lesser pyramids on the Acropolis are each constructed in a different style, and each is a pure example of that style. It's as if the rulers of this city were flaunting their cosmopolitanism, showing that they could build in any style they chose but preferred creating their own, superior architecture.

West of the Acropolis, across a large open plaza, is a long, raised building whose purpose isn't quite clear. But its size, as well as that of the plaza, makes you wonder just how many people this city actually held to necessitate such a large public space.

The site takes an hour to see and is open daily from 8am to 5pm. Admission is $4 (£2), plus it's around $4 (£2) to use your video camera.

3 Campeche ✦✦

251km (156 miles) SW of Mérida; 376km (233 miles) NE of Villahermosa

Campeche, the capital of the state of the same name, is a beautifully restored colonial city. The facades of all the houses in the historic center of town have been repaired and painted, all electrical and telephone cables have been routed underground, and the streets have been paved to look cobbled. Several Mexican movie companies have taken advantage of the restoration to shoot period films here.

Despite its beauty, not many tourists come to Campeche. Those who do, tend to be either on their way to the ruins at Palenque (see chapter 12) or the Río Bec region (see chapter 16) or the kind of travelers who are accidental wanderers. A couple of things do need to be said: Campeche is not geared to foreign tourism the way Mérida is, so expect less in the way of English translations and such at museums and other sights. Also, expect less in the way of nightlife, except on weekend nights when they block off the main square for a street party.

If you're interested in seeing the ruins along the Río Bec route, see the section "Side Trips to Maya Ruins from Chetumal," in chapter 16. Calakmul ☆☆☆ is a large and important site, with the tallest pyramid in the Yucatán peninsula, and if you're going that far, you should stop at Balamkú and perhaps a few other ruins in the area. From the Campeche side you can get information and contract a tour with one of several tour operators. You can also rent a car. Calakmul is too far away for a day trip. There are a few small hotels in the area. Hotel Del Mar in Campeche has two: **Chicanná Eco-village** and **Puerta Calakmul.**

From the Calakmul area, it's easy to cross over the peninsula to Yucatán's southern Caribbean coast. Then you can head up the coast and complete a loop of the peninsula.

Campeche has an interesting history. The conquistadors arrived in 1517, when Francisco de Córdoba landed here while exploring the coast and stayed just long enough to celebrate Mass. Attempts to settle here were unsuccessful because of native resistance until Montejo The Younger was able to secure a settlement in 1540.

In the 17th and 18th centuries, pirates repeatedly harassed the city. The list of Campeche's attackers reads like a who's who of pirating. On one occasion, several outfits banded together under the famous Dutch pirate Peg Leg (who most likely was the inspiration for the many fictional one-legged sailors) and managed to capture the city. The Campechanos grew tired of hosting pirate parties and erected walls around the city, showing as much industry then as they now show in renovating their historic district. The walls had a number of *baluartes* (bastions) at critical locations. For added security, they constructed two forts, complete with moats and drawbridges, on the hills flanking the city. There were four gates to the city, and the two main ones are still intact: the Puerta de Mar (Sea Gate) and the Puerta de Tierra (Land Gate). The pirates never cared to return, but, in Mexico's stormy political history, the city did withstand a couple of sieges by different armies. Eventually, in the early 1900s, the wall around the city was razed, but the bastions and main gates were left intact, as were the two hilltop fortresses. Most of the bastions and both forts now house museums.

ESSENTIALS

GETTING THERE & DEPARTING   By Plane   AeroMéxico (© 981/816-6656; www.aeromexico.com.mx) flies once daily to and from Mexico City. The **airport** is several kilometers northeast of the town center, and you'll have to take a taxi into town (about $5/£2.50).

By Car   Highway 180 goes south from Mérida, passing near the basket-making village of Halacho and near Becal, known for its Panama-hat weavers. The trip takes 2½ hours. At Tenabo, take the shortcut (right, Highway 24) to Campeche rather than going farther to the crossroads near Chencoyí. The longer way from Mérida is along Highway 261 past Uxmal.

When returning to Mérida via Highway 180, go north on Avenida Ruiz Cortines, bearing left to follow the water (this becomes Avenida Pedro Sainz de Baranda, but there's no sign). Follow the road as it turns inland to Highway 180, where you turn left (there's a gas station at the intersection).

If you're leaving Campeche for Edzná and Uxmal, go north on either Ruiz Cortines or Gobernadores and turn right on Madero, which feeds onto **Highway 281.** To go south to Villahermosa, take Ruiz Cortines south.

By Bus ADO (© 981/816-2802) offers a first-class *de paso* (passing through) bus to Palenque (6 hr.; $16/£8) four times a day and buses to Mérida (2½ hr.; $8/£4) every hour from 5:30am to midnight. The ADO **bus station** is on Avenida Patricio Trueba, a kilometer (a half-mile) from the Puerta de Tierra.

INFORMATION The **State of Campeche Office of Tourism** (©/fax 981/816-6767; www.campechetravel.com) is in Plaza Moch-Couoh, Avenida Ruiz Cortines s/n, 24000 Campeche. This is in one of the state buildings between the historic center and the shore. There are also information offices in the bastions of Santa Rosa, San Carlos, and Santiago. It's open Monday to Friday from 9am to 2pm and 4 to 7pm.

CITY LAYOUT The most interesting part of the city is the restored old part, most of which once lay within the walls. Originally, the seaward wall was at the water's edge, but now land has been gained from the sea between the old walls and the coastline. This is where you'll find most of the state government buildings, which were built in a glaringly modernist style around **Plaza Moch-Couoh:** buildings such as the office tower **Edificio de los Poderes (Judicial Building)** or **Palacio de Gobierno (headquarters for the state of Campeche),** and the futuristic **Cámara de Diputados (Chamber of Deputies),** which looks like a cubist clam.

Campeche's system of street numbering is much like that of other cities in the Yucatán, except that the numbers of the north–south streets increase as you go east instead of the reverse. (See "City Layout" in "Mérida: Gateway to the Maya Heartland," earlier in this chapter.)

GETTING AROUND Most of the recommended sights, restaurants, and hotels are within walking distance of the old city, except for the two fort-museums. Campeche isn't easy to negotiate by bus, so take taxis for anything beyond walking distance—they are inexpensive.

FAST FACTS: Campeche

American Express Local offices are at Calle 59 no. 4 and 5 (© 981/811-1010), in the Edificio Del Mar, a half-block toward town from the Hotel Del Mar. Open Monday to Friday from 9am to 2pm and 5 to 7pm, and Saturday from 9am to 1pm. This office does not cash traveler's checks.

Area Code The telephone area code is 981.

ATMs There are more than 10 cash machines around the downtown area.

Emergencies To report an emergency, dial © 060, which is supposed to be similar to 911 emergency service in the United States.

Internet Access There are plenty of places to check e-mail, too—just look for signs with the words INTERNET or CYBERCAFE.

Post Office The *correo* is in the Edificio Federal, at Avenida 16 de Septiembre and Calle 53 (© **981/816-2134**), near the Baluarte de Santiago; it's open Monday to Saturday from 7:30am to 8pm. The telegraph office is also here.

EXPLORING CAMPECHE

With beautiful surroundings, friendly people, and an easy pace of life, Campeche is worthy of at least a day on your itinerary. It has some interesting museums, one outstanding restaurant, and plenty to do.

INSIDE THE CITY WALLS

A good place to begin is the pretty *zócalo,* or **Parque Principal,** bounded by calles 55 and 57 running east and west and calles 8 and 10 running north and south. On Saturday nights and Sundays, the city closes the main square to traffic and contracts bands to play. People set up tables in the streets and the entire scene becomes a fun kind of block party. Construction of the church on the north side of the square began in 1650 and was finally completed 150 years later. A pleasant way to see the city is to take the *tranvía* (trolley) tour that leaves three or four times a day from the main plaza; check with one of the tourist information offices for the schedule. The cost is $7 (£3.50) for a 45-minute tour.

Baluarte de la Soledad   This bastion next to the sea gate houses Maya stelae recovered from around the state. Many are badly worn, but the line drawings beside the stones allow you to appreciate their former design.

Calle 57 and Calle 8, opposite Plaza Principal. No phone. Admission $2.50 (£1.25). Tues–Sat 9am–8pm; Sun 9am–1pm.

Baluarte de San Carlos/Museo de la Ciudad   The city museum deals primarily with the design and construction of the fortifications. A model of the city shows how it looked in its glory days and provides a good overview for touring within the city walls. There are several excellent ship models as well. All text is in Spanish.

Circuito Baluartes and Av. Justo Sierra. No phone. Admission $2.50 (£1.25). Tues–Sat 9am–8pm; Sun 9am–1pm.

Baluarte de Santiago   The Jardín Botánico Xmuch'haltun is a jumble of exotic and common plants within the stone walls of this bastion. More than 250 species of plants and trees share a small courtyard.

Av. 16 de Septiembre and Calle 49. No phone. Free admission. Mon–Fri 9am–8pm; Sat–Sun 9am–1pm.

Casa no. 6 Centro Cultural   In this remodeled colonial house, you'll see some rooms decorated with period furniture and accessories. The patio of mixtilinear arches supported by simple Doric columns is striking. Exhibited in the patio are photos of the city's fine colonial architecture. Several of the photographed buildings have recently been renovated. There is also a small bookstore in back, as well as temporary exhibition space.

Calle 57 no. 6. No phone. Free admission. Daily 9am–9pm.

Puerta de Tierra   At the Land Gate is a small museum displaying portraits of pirates and the city founders. The 1732 French 5-ton cannon in the entryway was found in 1990. On Tuesday, Friday, and Saturday at 8pm, there's a light-and-sound show, as long as 15 or more people have bought tickets. Some shows are in English and some are in Spanish; it depends on the audience. The show is amusing.

Calle 59 at Circuito Baluartes/Av. Gobernadores. No phone. Free admission to museum; show $3 (£1.50) adults, $1 (50p) children younger than 11. Daily 9am–9pm.

OUTSIDE THE WALLS: SCENIC VISTAS

Fuerte–Museo San José el Alto   This fort is higher and has a more sweeping view of Campeche and the coast than Fuerte San Miguel, but it houses only a small exhibit of 16th- and 17th-century weapons and scale miniatures of sailing vessels. It's a nice place for a picnic. Take a cab. En route, you will pass an impressive statue of Juárez.

Av. Morazán s/n. No phone. Admission $2.50 (£1.25). Tues–Sun 8am–8pm.

Fuerte–Museo San Miguel ★★   For a good view of the city and a great little museum, take a cab up to Fuerte–Museo San Miguel. San Miguel is a small fort with a moat and a drawbridge. Built in 1771, it was the most important of the city's defenses. General Santa Anna captured it when he attacked the city in 1842. The museum of the Maya world was renovated in 2000 and now is well worth seeing. It groups the artifacts around central issues in Maya culture. In a room devoted to Maya concepts of the afterlife, there's a great burial scene with jade masks and jewelry from Maya tombs at Calakmul. Another room explains Maya cosmology, another depicts war, and another explains the gods. There are also exhibits on the history of the fort.

Ruta Escénica s/n. No phone. Admission $2.50 (£1.25). Tues–Sat 9am–8pm; Sun 8am–noon.

SHOPPING

Casa de Artesanías Tukulná   This store, run by DIF (a government family-assistance agency), occupies a restored mansion. There is an elaborate display of regional arts and crafts in the back. The wares in the showrooms represent everything that is produced in the state. There are quality textiles, clothing, and locally made furniture. Open Monday to Saturday from 9am to 8pm. Calle 10 no. 333 (between calles 59 and 61). © 981/816-9088.

WHERE TO STAY

Rates quoted include the 17% tax.

VERY EXPENSIVE

Hacienda Puerta Campeche ★★★   This hotel was created from several adjoining colonial houses. It's a beautiful and original property just inside the Puerta de Tierra in Campeche's colonial center. There is a tropical garden in the center and a pool that runs through the ruined walls of one of the houses. It's quite picturesque. Rooms are colonial with flare—large with old tile floors, distinctive colors, and beamed ceilings. "Hacienda" is in the name to make it apparent that this is one of the properties connected to the four haciendas managed by Starwood hotels. (See "Of Haciendas & Hotels" in the Mérida section, earlier in this chapter.)

Calle 59 71, 24000 Campeche, Camp. © 800/325-3589 in the U.S. or Canada, or 981/816-7508. www.luxurycollection. com. 15 units. $400 (£200) superior; $500 (£250) and up for suite. AE, MC, V. Free guarded parking. **Amenities:** Restaurants; 2 bars; outdoor pool; spa services; concierge; tours; car-rental desk; airport transportation; room service; babysitting; laundry service. *In room:* A/C, TV, high-speed Internet access, minibar, fridge, coffeemaker, hair dryer, iron.

EXPENSIVE

Hotel Del Mar ★   Rooms in this four-story hotel are large, bright, and comfortably furnished. All have balconies that face the Gulf of Mexico. The beds (two doubles or one king-size) are comfortable. The Del Mar is on the main oceanfront boulevard, between the coast and the city walls. It offers more services than the Baluartes and is a little more expensive. You can make a reservation here to stay in the Río Bec area, or you can buy a package that includes guide and transportation. The hotel also offers a tour to Edzná.

Av. Ruiz Cortines 51, 24000 Campeche, Camp. © 981/811-9192 or -9193. Fax 981/811-1618. www.delmarhotel. com.mx. 146 units. $126 (£63) double; $140 (£70) executive-level double. AE, MC, V. Free parking. **Amenities:** 2 restaurants; bar; large outdoor pool; gym w/sauna; travel agency; car-rental desk; business center; room service; babysitting; laundry service; nonsmoking rooms; executive level. *In room:* A/C, TV, safe.

MODERATE
Hotel Baluartes ✦ Between the Sea Gate and the Gulf of Mexico, this was the city's original luxury hotel. All the rooms have been completely refurbished with new tile floors, new furniture, and new mattresses—one king-size bed or two doubles. They are cheerful and have good lighting, but the bathrooms are small.

Av. 16 de Septiembre no. 128, 24000 Campeche, Camp. © 981/816-3911. Fax 981/816-2410. www.baluartes.com.mx. 128 units. $108 (£54) double; $158 (£79) suite. Rates include breakfast buffet. AE, MC, V. Free guarded parking. **Amenities:** 2 restaurants; bar; large outdoor pool; travel agency; car rental; room service; laundry service; nonsmoking rooms. *In room:* A/C, TV, hair dryer, safe.

Hotel Francis Drake ✦ *Value* A three-story hotel in the *centro histórico* (historical district) with comfortable, attractive rooms at good prices. Rooms are midsize and come with tile floors and one king-size bed, two doubles, or two twins. The bathrooms are modern with large showers. Suites are larger and better furnished. The location is excellent.

Calle 12 no. 207 (between calles 63 and 65), 24000 Campeche, Camp. © 981/811-5626 or -5627. www.hotelfrancis drake.com. 24 units. $76 (£38) double; $86 (£43) junior suite; $99 (£50) suite. AE, MC, V. Limited free parking. **Amenities:** Restaurant; tour info; car-rental desk; room service; laundry service. *In room:* A/C, TV, minibar, hair dryer.

INEXPENSIVE
Hotel Colonial *Moments* What, you ask, in a cheap hotel could possibly qualify for a Frommer's Mexican Moment? Well, first of all, the hotel hasn't changed in 50 years; it exudes an air of the past long since disappeared with the coming of globalization. The rooms have the original tiles—once made in Mérida, but alas, no longer—beautiful things with lovely colors in swirls and geometrics; each room has a different pattern. And then there's the plumbing, which, in my room was so bodacious in design and execution that to hide it within the walls would have been pure Philistinism. Remarkable, too, are the bathroom fixtures, the four-color paint job, and the '40s-style furniture. Sure, you have to make sacrifices for such character—the rooms and bathrooms are small, and the mattresses aren't the best—but even character aside, this hotel is cleaner and more cheerful than any in its class.

Calle 14 no. 122, 24000 Campeche, Camp. © 981/816-2222. 30 units. $24 (£12) double; $34 (£17) double with A/C. No credit cards. *In room:* A/C (some units), no phone.

WHERE TO EAT
Campeche is a fishing town, so seafood predominates. The outstanding restaurant is **La Pigua.** For breakfast, you have your hotel restaurant or one of the traditional eateries such as **La Parroquia.** For a light supper, either get some *antojitos* (small dishes) in the old *barrio* of San Francisco, or have supper above the main plaza at **La Casa Vieja.** If you want a steak, your best bet is **Cactus.**

MODERATE

Cactus STEAKS/MEXICAN   If seafood isn't to your taste, try this steakhouse; it's a favorite with the locals. The rib-eyes are good, as is everything but the *arrachera*, which is the same cut of meat used for fajitas and is very tough.

Av. Malecón Justo Sierra. ℭ 981/811-1453. Main courses $10–$20 (£5–£10). No credit cards. Daily 7am–2am.

Casa Vieja MEXICAN/INTERNATIONAL   I'm afraid that Casa Vieja has gotten a little old. There's been a drop in effort here, but it still has the prettiest dining space in the city—an upstairs arcade overlooking the main square. Your best option is to order something simple. If you're lucky, they'll be on the upswing in that mysterious cycle of quality through which so many restaurants operate.

Calle 10 no. 319. ℭ 981/811-1311. Reservations not accepted. Main courses $6–$16 (£3–£8). No credit cards. Tues–Sun 9am–2am; Mon 5:30pm–2am.

La Pigua ᏝᏝᏝ SEAFOOD   The dining area is an air-conditioned version of a traditional Yucatecan cabin, but with walls of glass looking out on green vegetation. The owner has recently remodeled and enlarged his restaurant so that there's less trouble getting a table these days. He also is now opening in the evenings to accommodate tourists. Spanish nautical terms pepper the large menu as the headings for different courses. Sure to be on the menu is fish stuffed with shellfish, which I wholeheartedly recommend. If you're lucky, you might find pompano in a green-herb sauce seasoned with a peppery herb known as *hierba santa*. Other dishes that are sure to please are coconut-battered shrimp with applesauce and *chiles rellenos* with shark. Service is excellent, and the accommodating owner can have your favorite seafood prepared in any style you want.

Av. Miguel Alemán no. 179A. ℭ 981/811-3365. Reservations recommended. Main courses $10–$20 (£5–£10). AE, MC, V. Daily noon–8pm. From Plaza Principal, walk north on Calle 8 for 3 blocks; cross Av. Circuito by the botanical garden where Calle 8 becomes Miguel Alemán; the restaurant is 1½ blocks farther up, on the right side of the street.

INEXPENSIVE

Cenaduría Portales Ꮭ ANTOJITOS   This is the most traditional of supper places for Campechanos. It's a small restaurant under the stone arches that face the Plaza San Francisco in the *barrio* (neighborhood) of San Francisco. This is the oldest part of town, but it lies outside the walls just to the north. Don't leave without ordering the *horchata* (a sweet milky-white drink made of a variety of things, in this case coconut). For food, try the turkey soup, which is wonderful, and the *sincronizadas* (tostadas) and *panuchos*.

Calle 10 no. 86, Portales San Francisco. ℭ 981/811-1491. Antojitos 40¢–$1.50 (22p–75p). No credit cards. Daily 6pm–midnight.

La Parroquia MEXICAN   This local hangout offers good, inexpensive fare. It's best for breakfasts and the afternoon *comida corrida*. Selections on the *comida corrida* might include pot roast, meatballs, pork, or fish, with rice or squash, beans, tortillas, and fresh-fruit-flavored water.

Calle 55 no. 9. ℭ 981/816-8086. Breakfast $4 (£2); main courses $4–$12 (£2–£6); *comida corrida* (served noon–3pm) $4–$5 (£2–£2.50). MC, V. Daily 24 hr.

4 The Ruins of Chichén Itzá ᏝᏝᏝ

179km (111 miles) W of Cancún; 120km (74 miles) E of Mérida; 138km (86 miles) NW of Tulum

The fabled ruins of Chichén Itzá (no, it doesn't rhyme with "chicken pizza"; the accents are on the last syllables: chee-*chen* eet-*zah*) are the Yucatán's best-known ancient monuments. They are plenty hyped, but the ruins live up to it. Walking among these stone platforms, pyramids, and ball courts gives you an appreciation for this ancient civilization that books cannot convey. The city is built on a scale that evokes a sense of wonder: To fill the plazas during one of the mass rituals that occurred here a millennium ago would have required an enormous number of celebrants. Even today, with the massive flow of tourists through these plazas, the ruins feel empty.

When visiting the ruins, keep in mind that much of what is said about the Maya (especially by tour guides, who speak in tones of utter certainty) is merely educated guessing. This much we do know: The area was settled by farmers as far back as the 4th century A.D. The first signs of an urban society appear in the 7th century in the construction of stone temples and palaces in the traditional Puuc Maya style. These buildings can be found in the "Old Chichén" section of the city. Construction continued for a couple hundred years. In the 10th century (the post-Classic Era), the city came under the rule of the Itzáes, who arrived from central Mexico by way of the Gulf Coast. They may have been a mix of highland Toltec Indians (the people who built the city of Tula in central Mexico) and lowland Putún Maya, who were a commercial people thriving on trade between the different regions of the area. In the following centuries, the city saw its greatest growth. Most of the grand architecture was built during this age in a style that is clearly Toltec influenced. The new rulers may have been refugees from Tula. There is a myth told in pre-Columbian central Mexico about a fight that occurred between the gods Quetzalcoatl and Tezcatlipoca, which resulted in Quetzalcoatl being forced to leave his homeland and venture east. This may be a shorthand account of a civil war in Tula, different religious factions, with the losers fleeing to the Yucatán, where they were welcomed by the local Maya. Over time, the Itzáes adopted more and more the ways of the Maya. Sometime at the end of the 12th century, the city was captured by its rival, Mayapán.

Though it's possible to make a day trip from Cancún or Mérida, it's preferable to overnight here or in nearby Valladolid. It makes for a more relaxing trip. You can see the light show in the evening and return to see the ruins early the next morning when it is cool and before the tour buses arrive.

ESSENTIALS

GETTING THERE & DEPARTING   By Plane   Travel agents in the United States, Cancún, and Cozumel can arrange day trips from Cancún and Cozumel.

By Car   Chichén Itzá is on old Highway 180 between Mérida and Cancún. The fastest way to get there from either city is to take the *autopista* (or *cuota*). The toll is $8 (£4) from Mérida, $22 (£11) from Cancún. Once you have exited the *autopista*, you will turn onto the road leading to the village of Pisté. Once in the village, you'll reach a T junction at Highway 180 and turn left to get to the ruins. The entrance to the ruins is well marked. If you stay on the highway for a few kilometers more you'll come to the exit for the hotel zone at Km 121 (before you reach the turn-off, you'll pass the eastern entrance to the ruins, which is usually closed). Chichén is 1½ hours from Mérida and 2½ hours from Cancún. From Tulum, take the highway that leads to Cobá and Chemax. It connects to Hwy. 180 a bit east of Valladolid.

By Bus   From Mérida, there are three first-class ADO buses per day. There are also a couple of first-class buses to Cancún and Playa. Otherwise, you can buy a second-class bus ticket to Valladolid and a first-class from there. If you want to take a day trip from Mérida or Cancún, go with a tour company.

AREA LAYOUT   The village of **Pisté,** where most of the economical hotels and restaurants are located, is about 2.5km (1½ miles) to the west of the ruins. Public buses can drop you off here. And located on the old highway 2.5km (1½ miles) east from the ruins is another economical hotel, the Hotel Dolores Alba (see "Where to Stay," below). Situated at the ruins of Chichén Itzá are three luxury hotels.

EXPLORING THE RUINS

The site occupies 6.5 sq. km (2½ sq. miles), and it takes most of a day to see all the ruins, which are open daily from 8am to 5pm. Service areas are open from 8am to 10pm. Admission is $10 (£5), free for children younger than age 12. A video camera permit costs $4 (£2). Parking is extra. *You can use your ticket to reenter on the same day.* The cost of admission includes the **sound-and-light show,** which is worth seeing since you're being charged for it anyway. The show, held at 7 or 8pm depending on the season, is in Spanish, but headsets are available for rent in several languages. The narrative is okay, but the real reason for seeing the show is the lights, which show off the beautiful geometry of the city.

The large, modern visitor center, at the main entrance where you pay admission, is beside the parking lot. It consists of a museum, an auditorium, a restaurant, a bookstore, and bathrooms. You can see the site on your own or with a licensed guide who speaks English or Spanish. Guides usually wait at the entrance and charge around $45 (£23) for one to six people. Although the guides frown on it, there's nothing wrong with approaching a group of people who speak the same language and asking if they want to share a guide. These guides can point out architectural details you might miss on your own. Chichén Itzá has two parts: the central (new) zone, which shows distinct Toltec influence, and the southern (old) zone, with mostly Puuc architecture.

EL CASTILLO   As you enter from the tourist center, the magnificent 25m (82-ft.) El Castillo pyramid (also called the Pyramid of Kukulkán) will be straight ahead across a large open area. It was built with the Maya calendar in mind. The four stairways leading up to the central platform each have 91 steps, making a total of 364, which when you add the central platform equals the 365 days of the solar year. On either side of each stairway are nine terraces, which total 18 on each face of the pyramid, equaling the number of months in the Maya religious calendar. On the facing of these terraces are 52 panels (we don't know how they were decorated), which represent the 52-year cycle when both the solar and religious calendars would become realigned. The pyramid's alignment is such that on the **spring** or **fall equinox** (Mar 21 or Sept 21) a curious event occurs. The setting sun casts the shadow of the terraces onto the ramp of the northern stairway. A diamond pattern is formed, suggestive of the geometric designs on snakes. Slowly it descends into the earth. The effect is more conceptual than visual, and to view it requires being with a large crowd. It's much better to see the ruins on other days when it's less crowded.

El Castillo was built over an earlier structure. A narrow stairway at the western edge of the north staircase leads inside that structure, where there is a sacrificial altar-throne—a red jaguar encrusted with jade. The stairway is open from 11am to 3pm and is cramped, usually crowded, humid, and uncomfortable. A visit early in the day is best. Photos of the jaguar figure are not allowed.

JUEGO DE PELOTA (MAIN BALL COURT)   Northwest of El Castillo is Chichén's main ball court, the largest and best preserved anywhere, and only one of nine ball courts built in this city. Carved on both walls of the ball court are scenes showing

Maya figures dressed as ball players and decked out in heavy protective padding. The carved scene also shows a headless player kneeling with blood shooting from his neck; another player holding the head looks on.

Players on two teams tried to knock a hard rubber ball through one of the two stone rings placed high on either wall, using only their elbows, knees, and hips. According to legend, the losing players paid for defeat with their lives. However, some experts say the victors were the only appropriate sacrifices for the gods. One can only guess what the incentive for winning might be in that case. Either way, the game must have been riveting, heightened by the wonderful acoustics of the ball court.

THE NORTH TEMPLE   Temples are at both ends of the ball court. The North Temple has sculptured pillars and more sculptures inside, as well as badly ruined murals. The acoustics of the ball court are so good that from the North Temple, a person speaking can be heard clearly at the opposite end, about 135m (443 ft.) away.

TEMPLE OF JAGUARS   Near the southeastern corner of the main ball court is a small temple with serpent columns and carved panels showing warriors and jaguars. Up the steps and inside the temple, a mural chronicles a battle in a Maya village.

TZOMPANTLI (TEMPLE OF THE SKULLS)   To the right of the ball court is the Temple of the Skulls, an obvious borrowing from the post-Classic cities of central Mexico. Notice the rows of skulls carved into the stone platform. When a sacrificial victim's head was cut off, it was impaled on a pole and displayed in a tidy row with others. Also carved into the stone are pictures of eagles tearing hearts from human victims. The word *Tzompantli* is not Mayan but comes from central Mexico. Reconstruction using scattered fragments may add a level to this platform and change the look of this structure by the time you visit.

PLATFORM OF THE EAGLES   Next to the Tzompantli, this small platform has reliefs showing eagles and jaguars clutching human hearts in their talons and claws, as well as a human head emerging from the mouth of a serpent.

PLATFORM OF VENUS   East of the Tzompantli and north of El Castillo, near the road to the Sacred Cenote, is the Platform of Venus. In Maya and Toltec lore, a feathered monster or a feathered serpent with a human head in its mouth represented Venus. This is also called the tomb of Chaac-Mool because a Chaac-Mool figure was discovered "buried" within the structure.

SACRED CENOTE   Follow the dirt road (actually an ancient *sacbé,* or causeway) that heads north from the Platform of Venus; after 5 minutes you'll come to the great natural well that may have given Chichén Itzá (the Well of the Itzáes) its name. This well was used for ceremonial purposes. Sacrificial victims were thrown in. Anatomical research done early in the 20th century by Ernest A. Hooten showed that bones of both children and adults were found in the well.

Edward Thompson, who was the American consul in Mérida and a Harvard professor, purchased the ruins of Chichén early in the 20th century and explored the cenote with dredges and divers. His explorations exposed a fortune in gold and jade. Most of the riches wound up in Harvard's Peabody Museum of Archaeology and Ethnology—a matter that continues to disconcert Mexican classicists today. Excavations in the 1960s unearthed more treasure, and studies of the recovered objects detail offerings from throughout the Yucatán and even farther away.

TEMPLO DE LOS GUERREROS (TEMPLE OF THE WARRIORS)   Due east of El Castillo is one of the most impressive structures at Chichén: the Temple of the Warriors, named for the carvings of warriors marching along its walls. It's also called the Group of the Thousand Columns for the rows of broken pillars that flank it. During the recent restoration, hundreds more of the columns were rescued from the rubble and put in place, setting off the temple more magnificently than ever. A figure of Chaac-Mool sits at the top of the temple, surrounded by impressive columns carved in relief to look like enormous feathered serpents. South of the temple was a square building that archaeologists call **El Mercado (The Market);** a colonnade surrounds its central court. Beyond the temple and the market in the jungle are mounds of rubble, parts of which are being reconstructed.

The main Mérida-Cancún highway once ran straight through the ruins of Chichén, and though it has been diverted, you can still see the great swath it cut. South and west of the old highway's path are more impressive ruined buildings.

TUMBA DEL GRAN SACERDOTE (TOMB OF THE HIGH PRIEST)   Past the refreshment stand to the right of the path is the Tomb of the High Priest, which stood atop a natural limestone cave in which skeletons and offerings were found, giving the temple its name.

CASA DE LOS METATES (TEMPLE OF THE GRINDING STONES)   This building, the next one on your right, is named after the concave corn-grinding stones the Maya used.

TEMPLO DEL VENADO (TEMPLE OF THE DEER)   Past Casa de los Metates is this fairly tall though ruined building. The relief of a stag that gave the temple its name is long gone.

CHICHANCHOB (LITTLE HOLES)   This next temple has a roof comb with little holes, three masks of the rain god Chaac, three rooms, and a good view of the surrounding structures. It's one of the oldest buildings at Chichén, built in the Puuc style during the late Classic period.

EL CARACOL (OBSERVATORY)   Construction of the Observatory, a complex building with a circular tower, was carried out over centuries; the additions and modifications reflected the Maya's careful observation of celestial movements and their need for increasingly exact measurements. Through slits in the tower's walls, astronomers could observe the cardinal directions and the approach of the all-important spring and autumn equinoxes, as well as the summer solstice. The temple's name, which means "snail," comes from a spiral staircase within the structure.

On the east side of El Caracol, a path leads north into the bush to the **Cenote Xtoloc,** a natural limestone well that provided the city's daily water supply. If you see lizards sunning there, they may well be *xtoloc,* the species for which this cenote is named.

TEMPLO DE LOS TABLEROS (TEMPLE OF PANELS)   Just south of El Caracol are the ruins of a *temazcalli* (a steam bath) and the Temple of Panels, named for the carved panels on top. This temple was once covered by a much larger structure, only traces of which remain.

EDIFICIO DE LAS MONJAS (EDIFICE OF THE NUNS)   If you've visited the Puuc sites of Kabah, Sayil, Labná, or Xlapak, the enormous nunnery here will remind you of the palaces at those sites. Built in the late Classic period, the new edifice was constructed over an older one. Suspecting that this was so, Le Plongeon, an archaeologist working early in the 20th century, put dynamite between the two and blew away part of the exterior, revealing the older structures within. You can still see the results of Le Plongeon's indelicate exploratory methods.

On the east side of the Edifice of the Nuns is **Anexo Este (annex)** constructed in highly ornate Chenes style with Chaac masks and serpents.

LA IGLESIA (THE CHURCH)   Next to the annex is one of the oldest buildings at Chichén, the Church. Masks of Chaac decorate two upper stories. Look closely, and you'll see other pagan symbols among the crowd of Chaacs: an armadillo, a crab, a snail, and a tortoise. These represent the Maya gods, called *bacah,* whose job it was to hold up the sky.

AKAB DZIB (TEMPLE OF OBSCURE WRITING)   Beloved of travel writers, this temple lies east of the Edifice of the Nuns. Above a door in one of the rooms are some Mayan glyphs, which gave the temple its name because the writings are hard to make out. In other rooms, traces of red handprints are still visible. Reconstructed and expanded over the centuries, Akab Dzib may be the oldest building at Chichén.

CHICHEN VIEJO (OLD CHICHEN)   For a look at more of Chichén's oldest buildings, constructed well before the time of Toltec influence, follow signs from the Edifice of the Nuns southwest into the bush to Old Chichén, about 1km (a half-mile) away. Be prepared for this trek with long trousers, insect repellent, and a local guide. The attractions here are the **Templo de los Inscripciones Iniciales (Temple of the First Inscriptions),** with the oldest inscriptions discovered at Chichén, and the restored **Templo de los Dinteles (Temple of the Lintels),** a fine Puuc building. Some of these buildings have recently undergone restoration.

WHERE TO STAY

The expensive hotels in Chichén all occupy beautiful grounds, are close to the ruins, and serve decent food. All have toll-free reservations numbers. These hotels do a lot of business with tour operators—they can be empty one day and full the next. From these hotels you can easily walk to the back entrance of the ruins, next to the Hotel Mayaland. There are several inexpensive hotels in the village of Pisté, just to the west of the ruins. There is no advantage to staying in Pisté other than the proximity to Chichén Itzá. It is an unattractive village with little to recommend it. Another option is to stay in the colonial town of Valladolid, 40 minutes away.

EXPENSIVE

Hacienda Chichén Resort *&&*   This is the smallest and most private of the hotels at the ruins, also the quietest. This former hacienda served as the headquarters for the Carnegie Institute's excavations in 1923. Several bungalows scattered about the property were built to house the institute's staff. Each one houses one or two units. Rooms come with a dehumidifier, a ceiling fan, and good air-conditioning. The floors are ceramic tile, the ceilings are stucco with wood beams, and the walls are decorated with carved stone trim. Trees and tropical plants fill the manicured gardens. You can enjoy these from your room's porch or from the terrace restaurant, which occupies part of the original main house. Standard rooms come with a queen-size, two twin, or two double beds. Suites come with king-size beds.

Zona Arqueológica, 97751 Chichén Itzá, Yuc. ⓒ/fax 985/851-0045. www.haciendachichen.com. (Reservations office in Mérida: 877/631-4005 in the U.S., or 999/920-8407.) 28 units. High season $188 (£94) double, $199–$264

(£100–£132) suite; low season $140 (£70) double, $152–$193 (£76–£97) suite. AE, MC, V. Free guarded parking. **Amenities:** Restaurant; 2 bars; large outdoor pool; spa; nonsmoking rooms. *In room:* A/C, minibar, hair dryer, no phone.

Hotel & Bungalows Mayaland, The Lodge at Chichén Itzá ⭐⭐⭐ The main doorway frames El Caracol (the Observatory) in a stunning view—that's how close these hotels are to the ruins. There is an entrance right by the hotel. The long main building is three stories high. The rooms are large, with comfortable beds and large tiled bathrooms. Bungalows, scattered about the rest of the grounds, are built native style, with thatched roofs and stucco walls; they're a good deal larger than the rooms. The grounds are gorgeous, with huge trees and lush foliage—the hotel has had 75 years to get them in shape. The suites are on the top floor of the main building and come with terraces and two-person Jacuzzis. The Lodge consists of two groupings of larger bungalows in the back of the property surrounded by a lovely garden and pool area. High season is November through April (higher still for the March equinox); low season is May through October.

Zona Arqueológica, 97751 Chichén Itzá, Yuc. © **985/851-0100.** www.mayaland.com. (Reservations: Mayaland Resorts, Robalo 30 SM3, 77500 Cancún, Q. Roo; © 800/235-4079 in the U.S., or 998/887-2495; fax 998/887-4510.) 97 units. Hotel: High season rooms from $172 (£86), suites and bungalows from $254 (£127); low season rooms from $103 (£52), suites and bungalows from $168 (£84). Lodge: High season bungalows from $285 (£143); low season bungalows from $192 (£96). AE, MC, V. Free guarded parking. **Amenities:** 2 restaurants; bar; 3 outdoor pools; tour desk; room service; babysitting; laundry service. *In room:* A/C, TV, minibar, coffeemaker.

MODERATE

Villas Arqueológicas Chichén Itzá ⭐ This hotel is built around a courtyard and pool. Two massive royal Poinciana trees tower above the grounds, and bougainvillea drapes the walls. This chain has similar hotels at Cobá and Uxmal, and is no longer part of ClubMed. The rooms are modern and comfortable, unless you're 1.9m (6 ft., 2 in.) or taller—each bed is in a niche, with walls at the head and foot. Most rooms have one double bed and a twin bed. You can book a half- or full-board plan or just the room.

Zona Arqueológica, 97751 Chichén Itzá, Yuc. © **987/872-9300, ext. 8101** or 985/851-0034 or 985/856-2830. www.islandercollection.com. 40 units. $120 (£60) double. Rates include continental breakfast. Half-board (breakfast plus lunch or dinner) $20 (£10) per person; full board (3 meals) $38 (£19) per person. AE, MC, V. Free parking. **Amenities:** Restaurant; bar; large outdoor pool; tennis court; tour desk. *In room:* A/C, hair dryer.

INEXPENSIVE

Hotel Dolores Alba *(Value* This place is of the motel variety, perfect if you come by car. It is a bargain for what you get: two pools (one really special), *palapas* and hammocks around the place, and large, comfortable rooms. The restaurant serves good meals at moderate prices. There is free transportation to the ruins and the Caves of Balankanché during visiting hours, though you will have to take a taxi back. The hotel is on the highway 2.5km (1½ miles) east of the ruins (toward Valladolid). Rooms come with two double beds.

Carretera Mérida–Valladolid Km 122, Yuc. © **985/858-1555.** www.doloresalba.com. (Reservations: Hotel Dolores Alba, Calle 63 no. 464, 97000 Mérida, Yuc.; © 999/928-5650; fax 999/928-3163.) 40 units. $45 (£23) double. MC, V (8% service charge). Free parking. **Amenities:** Restaurant; bar; 2 outdoor pools; room service. *In room:* A/C, TV, no phone.

WHERE TO DINE

Although there's no great food in this area, there is plenty of decent food. The best idea is to stick to simple choices. The restaurant at the visitor center at the ruins serves decent snack food. The hotel restaurants mostly do a fair job, and, if you're in the village of Pisté, you can try one of the restaurants along the highway there that cater to the bus tours, such as **Fiesta** (© 985/851-0111). The best time to go is early lunch or regular supper hours, when the buses are gone.

OTHER ATTRACTIONS IN THE AREA

Ik-Kil is a large cenote on the highway just across from the Hotel Dolores Alba, 2.5km (1½ miles) east of the main entrance to the ruins. And it's deep, with lots of steps leading down to the water's edge. Unlike Dzitnup, these steps are easy to manage. The view from both the top and the bottom is dramatic, with lots of tropical vegetation and curtains of hanging tree roots stretching all the way to the water's surface. Take your swimsuit and enjoy the cold water. The best swimming is before 11:30am, at which time bus tours start arriving from the coast. These bus tours are the main business of Ik-Kil, which also has a restaurant and souvenir shops. Ik-Kil is open from 8am to 5pm daily. Admission is $6 (£3) per adult, $3 (£1.50) per child 7 to 12 years old.

The **Cave of Balankanché** is 5.5km (3½ miles) from Chichén Itzá on the road to Valladolid and Cancún. Taxis will make the trip and wait. The entire excursion takes about a half-hour, but the walk inside is hot and humid. Of the cave tours in the Yucatán, this is the tamest; it has good footing and requires the least amount of walking and climbing. It includes a cheesy and uninformative recorded tour. The highlight is a round chamber with a central column that gives the impression of being a large tree. You exit the same way you enter. The cave became a hideout during the War of the Castes. You can still see traces of carving and incense burning, as well as an underground stream that supplied water to the refugees. Outside, take time to meander through the botanical gardens, where most of the plants and trees are labeled with their common and botanical names.

Admission is $5 (£2.50), free for children 6 to 12. Children younger than age 6 are not admitted. Use of a video camera costs $4 (£2) or it's free if you've already bought a video permit in Chichén the same day. Tours in English are at 11am and 1 and 3pm, and, in Spanish, at 9am, noon, and 2 and 4pm. Double-check these hours at the main entrance to the Chichén ruins.

5 Valladolid

40km (25 miles) E of Chichén Itzá; 160km (100 miles) SW of Cancún; 98km (61 miles) NW of Tulum

Valladolid (pronounced "bah-yah-doh-*leed*") is a small, pleasant colonial city halfway between Mérida and Cancún. The people are friendly and informal, and, except for the heat, life is easy. The city's economy is based on commerce and small-scale manufacturing. There is a large cenote in the center of town and a couple more 4km (2½ miles) down the road to Chichén. Not far away are the intriguing ruins of Ek Balam, the flamingo-infested waters of Rio Lagartos, and the sandy beaches of Holbox (see "Side Trips from Valladolid," below).

ESSENTIALS

GETTING THERE & DEPARTING By Car From Mérida or Cancún, you have two choices: the *cuota* (toll road) or Highway 180. The toll from Cancún is $20 (£10), from Mérida $10 (£5). The *cuota* passes 2km (1¼ miles) north of the city; the exit is at the crossing of Highway 295 to Tizimín. **Highway 180** takes significantly longer because it passes through a number of villages (with their requisite speed bumps). Both 180 and 295 lead directly to downtown. Leaving is just as easy: From the main square, Calle 41 turns into 180 East to Cancún; Calle 39 heads to 180 West to Chichén Itzá and Mérida. To take the *cuota* to Mérida or Cancún, take Calle 40 (see "City Layout," below).

By Bus   There are several direct buses to Mérida (13 per day) or Cancún (five per day). Each runs $11 (£5.50). You can also get direct buses for Playa (five per day) and Tulum (four per day). Buses to Playa take the toll road and cost $14 (£7); buses to Tulum take the shortcut via Chemax and cost $6 (£3). To get to Chichén Itzá, take a second-class bus, which leaves every hour and sometimes on the half-hour. The recently remodeled bus station is at the corner of calles 39 and 46.

VISITOR INFORMATION   The small **tourism office** is in the Palacio Municipal. It's open Monday to Friday from 8am to 9pm, Saturday and Sunday from 9am to 9pm.

CITY LAYOUT   Valladolid has the standard layout for towns in the Yucatán: Streets running north-south are even numbers; those running east-west are odd numbers. The main plaza is bordered by Calle 39 on the north, 41 on the south, 40 on the east, and 42 on the west. The plaza is named Parque Francisco Cantón Rosado, but everyone calls it **El Centro.** Taxis are easy to come by.

EXPLORING VALLADOLID

Before it became Valladolid, the city was a Maya settlement called Zací (zah-*kee*), which means "white hawk." There is one cenote in town: **Cenote Zací,** at the intersection of calles 39 and 36, in a small park. A trail leads down close to the water. Caves, stalactites, and hanging vines contribute to a wild, prehistoric feel. The park has a large *palapa* restaurant. Admission is $1.50 (75p).

Ten blocks to the southwest of the main square is the Franciscan monastery of **San Bernardino de Siena** (1552). Most of the compound was built in the early 1600s; a large underground river is believed to pass under the convent and surrounding neighborhood, which is called Barrio Sisal. "Sisal," in this case, is a corruption of the Mayan phrase *sis-ha,* meaning "cold water." The *barrio* underwent extensive restoration and is now a delight to behold.

Valladolid's main square is the social center of town and a thriving market for Yucatecan dresses. On its south side is the principal church, **La Parroquia de San Servacio.** Vallesoletanos, as the locals are known, believe that almost all cathedrals in Mexico point east, and they cherish a local legend to explain why theirs points north—but don't believe a word of it. On the east side of the plaza is the municipal building, **El Ayuntamiento.** Get a look at the dramatic paintings outlining the peninsula's history. My favorite depicts a horrified Maya priest foreseeing the arrival of Spanish galleons. On Sunday nights, beneath the stone arches of the Ayuntamiento, the municipal band plays *jaranas* and other traditional music of the region.

SHOPPING

The **Mercado de Artesanías de Valladolid (crafts market),** at the corner of calles 39 and 44, gives you a good idea of the local merchandise. Perhaps the main handicraft of the town is embroidered Maya dresses, which can be purchased here or from women around the main square. The area around Valladolid is cattle country; locally made leather goods such as *huaraches* (sandals) and bags are inexpensive and plentiful. On the main plaza is a small shop above the municipal bazaar. A good sandal maker has a shop called **Elios,** Calle 37 no. 202, between calles 42 and 44 (no phone). An Indian named **Juan Mac** makes *alpargatas,* the traditional sandals of the Maya, in his shop on Calle 39, near the intersection with Calle 38, 1 block from the main plaza.

It's almost on the corner, across from the Bar La Joya. There's no sign, but the door jamb is painted yellow. Juan Mac can be found there most mornings. Most of his output is for locals, but he's happy to knock out a pair for visitors. He also makes a dress *alpargata,* but I like the standard ones better.

WHERE TO STAY

Aside from the hotels listed below, you can stay in town at **Hotel Zací,** Calle 44 between calles 37 and 39 ((C) **985/856-2167**), for about $40/night. Or María de la Luz on the main square for about $45. The Zací has nicer beds.

For something a bit different, you can stay in a small ecohotel in the nearby village of Ek Balam, close to the ruins: **Genesis Retreat Ek Balam** ((C) **985/858-9375;** www.genesisretreat.com). It is owned and operated by a Canadian woman, Lee Christie. She takes guests on tours of the village showing what daily life is like among the contemporary Maya. There are other activities, too. She rents some simple *cabañas* (with shared or private bathrooms) that surround a lovely pool and a restaurant.

El Mesón del Marqués ⟨✦⟩   This was originally a small colonial hotel that has grown large and modern. The first courtyard surrounds a fountain and abounds with hanging plants and bougainvillea. This was the original house, now occupied mostly by the restaurant (see "Where to Dine," below). In back are the new construction and the pool. Rooms are medium to large and are attractive. Most come with two double beds. The hotel is on the north side of El Centro, opposite the church.

Calle 39 no. 203, 97780 Valladolid, Yuc. (C) **985/856-3042** or -2073. Fax 985/856-2280. www.mesondelmarques.com. 90 units. $58 (£29) double; $72 (£36) superior; $110 (£55) junior suite. AE. Free secure parking. **Amenities:** Restaurant; bar; outdoor pool; room service; laundry service. *In room:* A/C, TV.

Casa Quetzal ⟨✦⟩   The landlady, Judith Fernández, is a gracious Mexican woman who moved to Valladolid to slow down. She has created an airy and attractive lodging space in the refurbished Barrio Sisal, which is within easy walking distance of the main square. Emphasis is on comfort and service—good linens and mattresses, quiet A/C, and a large and inviting central courtyard. There is a full line of spa treatments and therapies. English is spoken, and Sra. Fernández has lined up a good guide you can contract to take you to outlying areas.

Calle 51 no. 218, Barrio Sisal, 97780 Valladolid, Yuc. (C)/fax **985/856-4796.** www.casa-quetzal.com. 7 units. $70 (£35) double. Rates include full breakfast. 2-night minimum stay. No credit cards. Free secure parking. **Amenities:** Small outdoor pool; spa; tour info; room service; babysitting; laundry. *In room:* A/C, TV, Wi-Fi, no phone.

WHERE TO DINE

Valladolid is not a center for haute cuisine, but you can try some of the regional specialties. Some of the best food I had was at **El Mesón del Marqués** right on the main square. There is another restaurant on the main square called **Las Campanas,** which is okay. Locals like to eat at one of the stalls in the **Bazar Municipal,** next door to the Mesón del Marqués. They also frequent the **taco stands** that set up around the square. I did a quick sampling of *cochinita pibil, bistec,* and *lechón asado* at the three most popular stands. I enjoyed it all and wasn't the worse for it. These stands serve customers only until around noon.

SIDE TRIPS FROM VALLADOLID
CENOTES DZITNUP & SAMMULA

The **Cenote Dzitnup** ⟨✦⟩ (also known as Cenote Xkekén) is 4km (2½ miles) west of Valladolid off Highway 180 in the direction of Chichén Itzá. It is worth a side trip, especially if you have time for a dip. You can take the bike trail there. Antonio Aguilar, who owns a sporting goods store at Calle 41 no. 225, between calles 48 and 50, rents bikes. Once you get there, you descend a short flight of rather perilous stone steps, and at the bottom, inside a beautiful cavern, is a natural pool of water so clear and blue that it seems plucked from a dream. If you decide to swim, be sure that you don't have creams or other chemicals on your skin—they damage the habitat of the small fish and other organisms living there. Also, no alcohol, food, or smoking is allowed in the cavern. Admission is $2.50 (£1.25). The cenote is open daily from 7am to 7pm. If it's crowded, about 90m (295 ft.) down the road on the opposite side is another recently discovered cenote, **Sammulá,** where you can swim.

EK BALAM: DARK JAGUAR ☆☆☆

About 18km (11 miles) north of Valladolid, off the highway to Río Lagartos, are the spectacular ruins of **Ek Balam,** which, owing to a certain ambiguity in Mayan, means either "dark jaguar" or "star jaguar." Relatively unvisited by tourists, the Ek Balam ruins are about to hit it big. A new road now runs from the highway to the ruins.

Take Calle 40 north out of Valladolid to Highway 295; go 20km (12 miles) to a large marked turnoff. Ek Balam is 13km (8 miles) from the highway; admission is $3 (£1.50); $4 (£2) for each video camera. The site is open daily from 8am to 5pm.

In the last few years, a team of archeologists have been doing extensive excavation and renovation. What they have found has the world of Mayan scholars all aquiver. Built between 100 B.C. and A.D. 1200, the smaller buildings are architecturally unique—especially the large, perfectly restored **Caracol.** Flanked by two smaller pyramids, the imposing central pyramid is about 160m (525 ft.) long and 60m (197 ft.) wide. At more than 30m (100 ft.) high, it is easily taller than the highest pyramid in Chichén Itzá. On the left side of the main stairway, archaeologists have uncovered a large ceremonial doorway of perfectly preserved stucco work. It is an astonishingly elaborate representation of the gaping mouth of the underworld god. Around it are several beautifully detailed human figures. Excavation inside revealed a long chamber filled with Mayan hieroglyphic writing. From the style, it appears that the scribes probably came from Guatemala. So far this chamber is closed to the public. From this script, an epigrapher, Alfonso Lacadena, has found the name of one of the principal kings of the city—Ukit Kan Le'k Tok'. If you climb to the top of the pyramid, in the middle distance you can see untouched ruins looming to the north. To the southeast, you can spot the tallest structures at **Cobá,** 50km (31 miles) away.

Also visible are the **raised causeways** of the Maya—the *sacbé* appear as raised lines in the forest. More than any of the better-known sites, Ek Balam inspires a sense of mystery and awe at the scale of Maya civilization and the utter ruin to which it fell.

RIO LAGARTOS NATURE RESERVE ☆

Some 80km (50 miles) north of Valladolid (40km/25 miles north of Tizimín) on Highway 295 is Río Lagartos, a 50,000-hectare (123,500-acre) refuge established in 1979 to protect the largest nesting population of flamingos in North America. The nesting area is off limits, but you can see plenty of flamingos as well as many other species of fowl and take an enjoyable boat ride around the estuary here.

To get to Río Lagartos, you pass through Tizimín, which is about 30 minutes away. If you need to spend the night there, try **Hotel 49,** Calle 49 373-A (© **986/863-2136**), by the main square. There is not much to do in Tizimín unless you are there during the first 2 weeks of January, when it holds the largest fair in the Yucatán. The prime fiesta day is January 6.

SEEING THE RIO LAGARTOS REFUGE   Río Lagartos is a small fishing village of around 3,000 people who make their living from the sea and from the occasional tourist who shows up to see the flamingos. Colorfully painted houses face the *malecón* (the oceanfront street), and brightly painted boats dock here and there.

When you drive into town, keep going straight until you get to the shore. Look for where Calle 10 intersects with the *malecón;* it's near a modern church. There, in a little kiosk, is where the guides can be found (no phone). The sign reads PARADOR TURISTICO NAHOCHIN. There you can make arrangements for a 2-hour tour, which will cost $50 to $60 (£25–£30) for two to three people. The best time to go is in the early morning, so it's best to overnight here at one of the cheap hotels along the *malecón.* I looked at a few and liked **Posada Lucy** (no phone; $25/£13 for two).

I had a pleasant ride the next morning and saw several species of ducks, hawks, cranes, cormorants, an osprey, and lots of flamingos. The guide also wanted to show me how easy it was to float in some evaporation pools used by the local salt producer at Las Coloradas (a good source of employment for the locals until it was mechanized) and a place where fresh water bubbles out from below the saltwater estuary.

ISLA HOLBOX ⚓

A sandy strip of an island off the northeastern corner of the Yucatán Peninsula, Holbox (pronounced "hohl-*bosh*") was a remote corner of the world with only a half-deserted fishing village, until tourists started showing up for the beach. Now it's a semiprosperous little community that gets its livelihood from tourist services, employment at the beach hotels, and tours. It's most popular with visitors from May to September, when over a hundred **whale sharks** congregate in nearby waters (why precisely they come here is not known). These gentle giants swim slowly along the surface of the water and don't seem to mind the boat tours and snorkelers that come to experience what it's like to be in the wild with these creatures. Whale sharks don't fit the common picture of a shark; they are much larger, attaining a length of up to 18m (59 ft.), and they are filter feeders for the most part, dining on plankton and other small organisms. That said, they can do some mischief if you annoy them.

The beach here is broad and sandy (with fine-textured sand). It is also shallow. Instead of the amazing blue color of the Caribbean, it's more of a dull green. There are several beach hotels just beyond town. These experienced lots of damage from Hurricane Emily in the summer of 2005, but they've since come back: **Villas Flamingos** (© **800/538-6802** in the U.S. and Canada) and **Villas Delfines,** which has an office in Cancún (© **998/884-8606** or 984/875-2197; www.holbox.com). The latter is a personal favorite. Rates run between $100 and $150 (£55–£83) for a large freestanding beach bungalow with a large porch, a thatched roof, mosquito netting, and plenty of cross-ventilation. This is very much an ecohotel, with composting toilets and solar water heaters. There is a pool, a good restaurant, and lovely grounds. If you want A/C, try **Casa Sandra** (© **984/875-2171**).

From Valladolid, take Highway 180 east for about 90km (56 miles) toward Cancún; turn north after Nuevo Xcan at the tiny crossroads of El Ideal. Drive nearly 100km (62 miles) north on a state highway to the tiny port of Chiquilá, where you can park your car in a secure parking lot; walk 180m (590 ft.) to the pier, and catch the ferry to the island. It runs 10 times per day. When you get off in the village, you can contract with one of the golf cart taxis for a ride to your hotel.

The Copper Canyon

by David Baird

18

If you are interested in viewing a rugged and beautiful land, if you're interested in taking one of the most remarkable train trips in the world, if you're interested in hiking or riding horseback through remote areas to see an astonishing variety of plants and animals, or if you're curious about a land still populated by indigenous people living pretty much the way they have for centuries, the Copper Canyon is the place to go.

The first time I went, I had a vision of the Grand Canyon, because I had read many remarks comparing the two. The comparison is misleading, however, and does neither place justice. The canyons are not alike; they have different topography, geology, climate, flora, and fauna, and different local cultures, too.

When people say **Copper Canyon,** they are referring to a section of the Sierra Madre of northwestern Mexico known as the **Sierra Tarahumara** (after the Indians

who live there). The area was formed through violent volcanic uplifting followed by the gradual process of erosion that carved a vast network of canyons into the soft volcanic stone. In geological terms, it's much newer than the Grand Canyon.

Crossing the Sierra Tarahumara is the famed **Chihuahua al Pacífico (Chihuahua to the Pacific)** railway. Acclaimed as an engineering marvel, the 624km (387-mile) railroad has 39 bridges—the highest is more than 300m (984 ft.) above the Chinipas River, and the longest is about .5km (⅓ mile) long—and 86 tunnels, including one that stretches more than 1.5km (1 mile) long. It climbs from **Los Mochis,** at sea level, up nearly 2,425m (7,954 ft.) through some of Mexico's most magnificent scenery— thick pine forests, jagged peaks, and shadowy canyons—before descending to the city of **Chihuahua.**

EXPLORING THE COPPER CANYON

The principal airports for the region are Los Mochis and Chihuahua, the two terminal points of the railroad. This chapter covers these cities and how to get there.

It's easier now than ever before to get to the region, thanks to improved connecting flights out of Chihuahua and Los Mochis. But moving through the canyon still requires planning. Train tickets and hotel rooms are limited, and in high season (Mar–Apr and Oct–Nov) tour companies buy up large blocks of both. If going in high season, you should work your trip around an itinerary and have train tickets and hotel reservations *in hand* when you arrive in the region. You can make arrangements on your own or go through a travel agent or tour operator. (For tips, see "Choosing a Package or Tour Operator," below.) During the rest of the year it's possible to buy train tickets as you need them and make last-minute reservations or no reservations at all. There is a small risk that you might run into a large group that has taken all the hotel rooms, but in most locations now, somebody usually has an inexpensive cabin for rent. The most plentiful lodging is to be found in Creel, which makes it a good base of operations for a minimally planned trip.

WHEN TO GO There are two high seasons for the Sierra: from mid-October to mid-November and March through April. These months are the most popular because of the likelihood of moderate temperatures—but even in these months, temperatures in the bottom of the canyon will be warm. Most canyon visitors stay up in the rim country. To avoid the crowds and get cheaper prices, I suggest **going in August or September** (the rainy season). During that time, barring drought, you'll find occasional afternoon thundershowers (very pretty in the canyon land), green vegetation, flowing water, and comfortable temperatures up along the rim. If you plan to do some serious hikes into the canyon, consider going in the winter, when temperatures at the bottom will be the least tropical. **Avoid the Sierra from late April through June.** This is the driest part of the year, with chronic water shortages in many of the towns and hotels; the vegetation is brown, and the canyons can be hazy.

1 The Copper Canyon Train & Stops Along the Way

TRAIN ESSENTIALS

First-class service between Chihuahua and Los Mochis operates daily in both directions. Departure times are listed below. Second-class trains also run daily. They stop more frequently than the first-class trains and are slower. First-class service has undergone major improvements. The passenger cars have been revamped, with clean bathrooms that work and improved seating and windows. (They already were air-conditioned in summer and heated in winter.) The train now hauls both a dining car and a club car. In addition, it makes fewer stops than before. The new owner, **Ferromex** (www.ferromex.com.mx), invested heavily in improving the tracks, making delays due to landslides less frequent. It has also spruced up some of the local stations.

The train makes 12 stops; the five of principal interest to travelers are described in detail below. The schedule is a word problem that would gratify any high school algebra teacher: Two trains depart from opposite ends of the line (Chihuahua and Los Mochis) at the same time (6am) to meet at point x. So that you don't have to solve for y, I've included the "official" schedule below.

Train Departure Times

From Los Mochis		From Chihuahua	
Los Mochis	6am	Chihuahua	6am
El Fuerte	9am	Creel	11:35am
Bahuichivo/Cerocahui	1:10pm	El Divisadero	1:30pm
Barrancas	2:25pm	Barrancas	2pm
El Divisadero	2:35pm	Bahuichivo/Cerocahui	3:15pm
Creel	4:50pm	El Fuerte	7:20pm
Chihuahua (arrives)	10:25pm	Los Mochis (arrives)	10:25pm

Actual times vary. The local people at each stop are well attuned to train times, so it's good to ask them. The stops are short except at **El Divisadero,** where you have 20 minutes to get out and walk down the steps to the overlook for a spectacular panorama of the canyon, and perhaps time to buy a trinket or a taco from one of the many vendors.

The Copper Canyon

DELAYS Travelers may have to contend with delays because of landslides, minor derailments, or maintenance projects. Traveling in this region requires some flexibility and patience. In case of a major service interruption, you can travel on a highway that parallels the railway from Chihuahua as far as Cerocahui, but the final stretch from Cerocahui to El Fuerte is not much of an option because it requires four-wheel-drive.

Tips Which Direction Should I Travel?

For sightseeing, **Los Mochis,** the western terminus, is the better starting place: The most scenic part of the 15- to 16-hour journey comes between **El Fuerte** and **Bahuichivo/Cerocahui,** which you are guaranteed to see in daylight if you come from Los Mochis. The train that starts in Chihuahua often gets to this area in darkness. This chapter lists the stops in order from Los Mochis to Chihuahua.

BUYING A TICKET   The train offers no rail pass; you must buy a ticket for a particular day, point of departure, and destination. This is not usually a problem during the off season. You can buy a ticket for the first leg of your trip when you get to Los Mochis or Chihuahua, and then buy the rest each time you board the train. You're not going to have a guaranteed seat, but there's usually abundant seating during this part of the year. If you have an itinerary, you'll have guaranteed seating throughout the trip. You may not get to choose which seat, but that's a minor issue. Should you deviate from your itinerary, you can buy a new ticket at the local station or aboard the train. The cost of a ticket for the entire trip one-way is $130 (£65).

To reserve tickets ahead of time, call the railway directly (© **888/484-1623** in the U.S. or Canada, or 614/439-7212). A few days before your trip, you will need to call again to reconfirm your reservations. Then you can buy the tickets at the station the morning of your departure with cash or credit card (MasterCard or Visa). For more information, see **www.chepe.com.mx**. If you actually want to purchase tickets ahead of time, you can do so from a local travel agency in Chihuahua or Los Mochis. To start out in Chihuahua, contact **Turismo al Mar** (© 614/410-9232 or 416-5950; www.copper-canyon.net); from Los Mochis, contact **Viajes Araceli** (© 668/815-5780; fax 668/815-8787; ventasaracely@viajearacely.com) or **Viajes Flamingo** (© 668/812-1613; fax 668/812-0046; www.mexicoscoppercanyon.com). Travel agencies outside of Mexico sell tickets only as part of a package that includes transportation to the region and hotel accommodations. A wide variety of packages and custom trips are available. Look into these carefully before you book (see "Choosing a Package or Tour Operator," below).

LODGING   If you spend a night at any spot en route, you'll have roughly 24 hours to explore, unless you're heading back in the direction from which you came. Drivers from all canyon hotels pick up guests from the train station; if you don't have a reservation, ask a driver about room availability. Standard accommodations in the canyon are getting more expensive, especially in El Divisadero and Cerocahui. In high season, I wouldn't arrive at either place without reservations. Rates for hotels in both of these towns usually include meals. The number of rooms is limited, and with groups of 40 or 50 people going through the Sierra, a hotel can be empty one day and full the next. When hotels are full, you'll notice a decline in service in the dining room, or you'll have to wait in line at the buffet even if you're not part of the group. Overbooking rooms also seems to be a problem with some of the large hotels, though it's not common enough that you should worry about it. In Creel, you find the greatest variety of accommodations and restaurants. This is where most of the economical hotels are.

CLIMATE   Los Mochis and El Fuerte are warm year-round. Chihuahua can be warm in summer, windy at almost any time, and freezing in winter. The canyon rim may experience freezes from November through March; the bottom of the canyon may get cool enough for a sweater. In the other half of the year, it's hot below and cool above.

Tips Going Solo on Foot: Not a Good Idea

If you're planning to hike in the Copper Canyon, it's a good idea to have company, especially someone who knows the area. Guides tell me that they come across lost hikers all the time. Also, ankles can get sprained, knees can give out— it helps to have someone who knows where to get the nearest horse and such.

Tips   Choosing a Package or Tour Operator

A number of tour operators and packagers offer trips to the Copper Canyon. You can purchase your package through a travel agency; those that do frequent business with Copper Canyon trips have better knowledge of what's out there. Keep in mind that the travel agent may try to steer you toward one package over another because it pays a higher commission.

The industry breaks down into the following categories:

BUS TOURS   Some outfits run buses from El Paso to Chihuahua or Tucson to Los Mochis, and then put their customers on the train. The usual length of stay in the Sierra is 2 nights before returning by bus to the U.S. These tours involve a lot of sitting on a bus or train, but they are the least expensive.

TRAIN TOURS   Sierra Madre Express, P.O. Box 26381, Tucson, AZ 85726 (© 800/666-0346 in the U.S.), runs its own deluxe trains, complete with dining and Pullman cars, through the canyon. The trip takes a week, with 2 nights in the canyon. **Tauck Tours** (© 800/468-2825 in the U.S.) uses this train.

STANDARD PACKAGES   This option merely bundles airfare, train tickets, and lodging. Hotels in the canyon send drivers to meet the train, so getting to your hotel is not hard once you're in the canyon. With these tours, you can have more time in the canyon, but once you're there, it's up to you to line up activities.

CUSTOM TOUR OPERATORS   These outfits sell fixed package tours through travel agents only because it simplifies the agent's job. If you eliminate the middle person and call any of the outfits directly, you might be able to arrange a custom trip. Travel through these companies generally allows you more time in the canyon and a better experience. Some assemble small groups with a guide; some allow you to travel by yourself and supply you with contacts in different locations. As the number of people visiting the Sierra increases, these companies are taking people deeper into the mountains to get away from the effects of mass tourism. The best of the bunch is **Canyon Travel** (formerly Columbus), 900 Ridge Creek Lane, Bulverde, TX 78163-2872 (© 800/843-1060 in the U.S. and Canada, or 830/885-2000; www.canyontravel.com). Canyon Travel is pretty much in a class by itself. It has lined up some beautiful small lodges in the canyons and in El Fuerte and staffed them with talented local guides. It also offers a lot of flexibility, and it responds quickly to problems.

Other operators that provide good service are **The California Native,** 6701 W. 87th Place, Los Angeles, CA 90045 (© 800/926-1140 in the U.S.; www.calnative.com), and **Native Trails,** 613 Querétaro, El Paso, TX 79912-2210 (© 800/884-3107 in the U.S.; www.nativetrails.com).

STOP 1: EL FUERTE 🐟

El Fuerte is on the coastal plain before the foothills of the Sierra Madre. It has charming cobblestone streets and handsome colonial mansions and is the prettiest town along the train route. At only 80m (262 ft.) above sea level, it is most comfortable in

---

Tips **Money Changing: Be Prepared**

Be sure to start the journey with adequate funds, because exchanging money outside of Creel is almost impossible; even credit cards are good only at the expensive hotels. (I won't use a credit card at some of the hotels listed in this chapter because they use radio communication to the main office to confirm a card—hardly a secure system.)

---

winter. The town owes its origin to silver mining, and its existence in recent times to booming agriculture. From the late 18th century onward, the town has been under the control of a few families, and to this day, much of the real estate in and about the center of town remains in their hands. The town's plaza is quaint and handsome, with a 19th-century bandstand surrounded by graceful palms. One way to see the town is to take a taxi from Los Mochis and pick up the train the next day. An added advantage to this plan is that it allows you an extra hour in bed. The train station is a few kilometers from town.

EXPLORING THE TOWN   Possible activities include visiting nearby villages, birding, fishing for black bass and trout, and hunting for duck and dove. Hotels can arrange guides and all equipment if they're notified in advance.

WHERE TO STAY & DINE

Besides the restaurants at the hotels mentioned here, there are inexpensive restaurants on and near the central plaza.

Hotel El Fuerte ⍟   This is a charming inn loaded with character. Rooms have double or king-size beds, tiled bathrooms, and colonial furnishings. The courtyard and common areas are shady and cool. During high season, this hotel usually books up with tour groups, but it's a good option for the rest of the year.

Montesclaro 37, 81820 El Fuerte, Sin. ℂ 698/893-0226. Fax 698/893-1246. www.hotelelfuerte.com.mx. 49 units. $80–$120 (£40–£60) double. MC, V. Free parking. **Amenities:** Restaurant; bar; Jacuzzi; tour info; room service, laundry service, nonsmoking room. *In room:* A/C, TV, hair dryer, no phone.

Hotel La Choza   Two stories of rooms are arranged around a modern courtyard/parking lot. The upstairs rooms are nicer, as they come with a *bóveda* ceiling, but all are comfortable and colorfully decorated and have nice, midsize bathrooms. Most have two double beds.

Cinco de Mayo 101, 81820 El Fuerte, Sin. ℂ 698/893-1274. www.hotellachoza.com. 36 units. $80 (£40) double. MC, V. Free secure parking. **Amenities:** Restaurant; bar/dance club; outdoor pool; room service. *In room:* A/C, TV, no phone.

Hotel Posada del Hidalgo ⍟⍟   This handsome hotel is one of the Balderrama properties and can be booked through the central reservations office in Los Mochis. It, too, fills up fast with several tour groups. The mansion section, with open arcades around a central patio, belonged to silver barons in the 18th century; there's even a steep carriage ramp from its days as a stagecoach stop. There are three courtyards, each in a different style, with bougainvillea and tall palm trees. The guest rooms are nicely finished with lovely tile or hardwood floors, attractive furniture, and good bathrooms. All have two double beds.

Hidalgo 101, 81820 El Fuerte, Sin. ℂ 800/896-8196 in the U.S. (to the Hotel Santa Anita in Los Mochis) or 698/893-1194 in El Fuerte. Fax 698/893-1194. www.hotelposadadelhidalgo.com. 68 units. $140 (£70) double. AE, MC, V. Free parking. **Amenities:** Restaurant; bar; outdoor pool; spa; Jacuzzi. *In room:* A/C, hair dryer, no phone.

Río Vista Lodge *(finds)*   Free-spirited owner Chal Gámez has done it his way in this small hotel on a hill atop the town. The common areas and rooms hold fanciful murals, artifacts of Yaqui and Maya Indians, decorations from northern Mexico, and a few things reminiscent of the Old West. The outdoor dining area is a lovely place to gaze out over the river or watch the swarms of hummingbirds that feast at Chal's feeders. These birds seem little bothered by the proximity of humans—you can even put your hand under the feeder and be fanned by their wings. Meals are simple but good.

Cerro de la Pilas s/n, 81820 El Fuerte, Sin. ⓒ/fax 698/893-0413. hotelriovista@hotmail.com. 18 units. $58 (£29) double. MC, V. Free parking. **Amenities:** Restaurant. *In room:* A/C, hair dryer, no phone.

STOP 2: BAHUICHIVO & CEROCAHUI 👁👁👁

This is the first train stop in canyon country. **Bahuichivo** is merely the train depot and didn't exist before the railroad's construction. The village of **Cerocahui** (elevation 1,670m/5,478 ft.) dates from before the Colonial Era. It's home to 600 people and is in a valley about 10km (6¼ miles) from the train stop. The road is unpaved, so the trip takes about 30 minutes. The most dramatic part of the train ride is the section between El Fuerte and Bahuichivo.

EXPLORING CEROCAHUI   Built around a sweet-looking mission church, Cerocahui consists of little more than rambling unpaved streets and 100 or so houses. It enjoys a wonderful view of the mountains, but you have to take an excursion to get real canyon vistas. All hotels can arrange horseback rides to nearby waterfalls and other scenic spots, as well as trips to **Cerro Gallego,** a famous lookout point with a beautiful vista of Urique Canyon. It's possible to see the waterfall on arrival, schedule the Gallego trip for the next morning, have lunch, and still make the train. I like the quiet of Cerocahui, however, and recommend staying here as long as you can, provided you like hiking or horseback riding. There are a number of secluded places, both near and far, to visit. One possible trip is a hike down to the mining town of **Urique** at the bottom of the Urique Canyon (one of several canyons that make up the Copper Canyon), and then a car ride back up. There are a few simple but comfortable hotels where you can stay for between $30 and $40 (£15–£20) a night. The nicest is **Hotel Barrancas Urique** (ⓒ 635/456-6076). It can provide you with a guide if you feel like doing some more hiking. The rooms come with fans, but the hotel might install air-conditioning units in a couple of the rooms.

WHERE TO STAY & DINE

Rates for doubles in the two hotels listed below include all meals for two people and transportation to and from the train station. The Paraíso del Oso is less than a kilometer (about a mile) short of the village. The mission is in Cerocahui proper. In the town, you can find simple lodging for a fraction of the cost of the other places. There are also some cabins for rent up above town. They go for $60 (£30) for two people and include transportation from the train station. You can reserve a cabin through Río Vista Lodge (see above) or by calling ⓒ 635/456-5257 and saying you want a cabin in Cerocahui (the staff speaks English).

Hotel Misión Cerocahui 👁   Established years ago, the Hotel Misión is right on the town's little plaza. Guest rooms have hot water and electricity. The lobby and restaurant area surrounds a large rock fireplace, where a local guitarist and singer sometimes entertain in the evenings. The food is usually good, and the ranch-style rooms (with tile floors, wood-burning stoves, and kerosene lanterns) are comfortable. The hotel offers several tours, including rides to Cerro Gallego, Urique, and the local waterfalls. There are also hiking, mountain biking, and horseback riding trips.

Domicilio Conocido, Cerocahui. www.hotelmision.com. (Reservations: Hotel Santa Anita, Apdo. Postal 159, 81200 Los Mochis, Sin. © 800/896-8196 in the U.S.) 38 units. $226 (£113) double. Rates include meals. AE, MC, V. Free parking. **Amenities:** Restaurant.

Paraíso del Oso ⊕ *(Moments* Opened in 1990, Paraíso del Oso sits in a sheltered hollow with a backdrop of impressive stone palisades less than a kilometer (about a half-mile) from the town. Owner Doug Rhodes is an avid horseman and takes guests for rides that can last anywhere from 3 hours to more than a week. Rooms come with two double beds and ranch furniture. They are comfortable, with wood-burning stoves and plenty of hot water. Solar-generated electricity fuels such vital services as refrigeration, while lanterns provide light. This and the utter solitude of the area are charming traits that make you feel more in touch with the Sierra than you would at the big canyon hotels along the railroad tracks. There is a cash bar, a small but good library, wireless Internet, and topographical maps of the area.

Cerocahui. © 800/884-3107 or 915/833-3107 in the U.S., or 614/421-3372. Fax 614/421-3372. www.mexicohorse.com. (Reservations: Paraíso del Oso, P.O. Box 31089, El Paso, TX 79931.) 21 units. $185 (£93) double. Rates include meals. MC, V. Free parking. **Amenities:** Bar. *In room:* No phone.

STOPS 3 & 4: BARRANCAS/EL DIVISADERO ⊕⊕
Between Bahuichivo and here, the train stops at San Rafael to change crews. By the time it arrives in this area, it is at the highest part of its journey. Many packages include at least a night here for soaking up the great views of the canyons. Two nights would be better if you want to do some hiking or horseback riding.

Barrancas and El Divisadero are less than 3km (2 miles) apart. Coming from Los Mochis, you'll arrive at Barrancas first. At this stop, drivers from the **Hotel Mirador,** the **Hotel Rancho,** and the **Mansion Tarahumara** meet passengers. Then the train takes you to El Divisadero (elevation 2,240m/7,347 ft.), where you'll find the **Hotel Divisadero-Barrancas,** taco stands (at train time), and the most **spectacular view of the canyon** that you'll get if you are making no overnight stops. The train stops for 20 minutes—time enough to walk down the steps to the lookout to enjoy the view and purchase one or two mementos from the Tarahumara Indians, who sell sweet-smelling pine-needle baskets, homemade violins, and wood and cloth dolls. Hotels arrange various excursions, including a visit to a cave-dwelling Tarahumara family, hiking, and horseback riding. All hotels listed below offer free secure parking.

WHERE TO STAY & DINE
Hotel Divisadero-Barrancas ⊕⊕ This location, on the edge of the canyon overlook, provides the most spectacular view of any hotel in the canyon. The restaurant has a large picture window, perfect for hours of sitting and gazing at the canyon. The rooms are in four sections. The newest section (nos. 35–48) is a two-story building perched on the edge of the canyon. These rooms have sliding glass doors that open on to balconies with a view. The bathrooms are midsize and modern. The new rooms are probably the quietest, but I also like the original section (rooms 1 through 10). These are made of logs and stones and are more rustic, which for me is a good part of their appeal.

El Divisadero. © 800/232-4219 in the U.S. and Canada, or 635/578-3060. www.hoteldivisadero.com. (Reservations: Av. Mirador 4516, Apdo. Postal 661, Col. Residencial Campestre, 31238 Chihuahua, Chih.; © 614/415-1199; fax 614/415-6575.) 52 units. High season $220 (£110) double; low season $160 (£80) double. Rates include meals and 2 tours. AE, MC, V. **Amenities:** Restaurant; bar; tours. *In room:* Coffeemaker.

Hotel Mirador ⟨★★⟩ *(Moments)*   The Mirador sits on the edge of the canyon 5 minutes up the mountain from its sister hotel, the Hotel Rancho (see below). Every room has a dramatic balcony that seems to hang right over the cliff's edge. The views are beautiful. Rooms have attractive decorations and furniture, with bold Mexican color combinations; most hold two double beds. Each room has its own heater. The common areas are also comfortable and attractive.

El Divisadero. ⟨© 635/578-3020. (Reservations: Hotel Santa Anita, Apdo. Postal 159, 81200 Los Mochis, Sin.; © 800/896-8196 in the U.S.) Fax 668/812-0046. www.mexicoscoppercanyon.com/mirador. 65 units. $260 (£130) double. Rates include meals. AE, MC, V. **Amenities:** Restaurant; bar; tour info; transportation to and from train station. *In room:* Hair dryer, no phone.

Hotel Rancho   The train stops right in front of this inn. Rooms are comfortable, with two double beds and a wood-burning iron stove. As in other lodges, meals are a communal affair in the cozy living and restaurant area, and the food is good. You can rent horses or hike to the Tarahumara caves and to the rim of the canyon, where a more expensive sister hotel, the Hotel Mirador (see above), has a beautiful restaurant and bar with a magnificent view. This hotel sometimes accommodates overbooking at its sister hotel.

El Divisadero. © 635/578-3020. (Reservations: Hotel Santa Anita, Apdo. Postal 159, 81200 Los Mochis, Sin.; © 800/896-8196 in the U.S.) Fax 668/812-0046. www.mexicoscoppercanyon.com/rancho. 25 units. $226 (£113) double. Rates include meals. AE, MC, V. **Amenities:** Restaurant; bar; transportation to and from train station. *In room:* Hair dryer, no phone.

Mansion Tarahumara ⟨★⟩   The Mansion Tarahumara spreads across a mountainside above the train stop at Posada Barrancas. The setting is lovely. The cabin rooms offer more privacy and space than the hotel rooms, but not direct views of the canyon. Made of stone and wood, each room has a big fireplace, a wall heater, and two double beds. The castlelike structure, which is the first thing that catches the guest's eye, houses the restaurant and bar. It offers lovely views from its big windows and good food from its kitchen.

El Divisadero. © 635/578-3030. (Reservations: Mansion Tarahumara, Calle Juárez 1602-A, Col. Centro, 31000 Chihuahua, Chih.; © 614/415-4721; fax 614/416-5444.) www.mansiontarahumara.com.mx. 60 units. $172 (£86) double. Rates include meals. MC, V. **Amenities:** Restaurant; bar; heated outdoor pool; Jacuzzi; tours; transportation to and from train station. *In room:* No phone.

STOP 5: CREEL ⟨★⟩

This rustic logging town with a handful of paved streets offers the most economical lodgings in the canyon. Creel (rhymes with "feel") is also the starting point for some of the best side trips, especially hiking and overnight camping.

ESSENTIALS

GETTING THERE & DEPARTING   By Train   See the chart on p. 678 for "official" arrival and departure times.

By Car   From Chihuahua, follow the signs to La Junta until you see signs for Hermosillo. Follow those signs until you see signs to Creel (left). The trip takes about 4 hours on a paved road.

By Bus   Estrella Blanca (© 635/456-0073), next to the Hotel Korachi, has six trips to Chihuahua per day. The trip takes 4 hours and costs $18 (£9). This is a lot cheaper and faster than the train.

ORIENTATION   The train station, around the corner from the Mission Store and the main plaza, is in the heart of the village and within walking distance of all lodgings except the Copper Canyon Sierra Lodge. Look for your hotel's van waiting at the station (unless you're staying at the Casa de Huéspedes Margarita, which is only 2 blocks away). There's one main street, **López Mateos,** and almost everything is within a couple of blocks.

FAST FACTS   The telephone **area code** is **635.** Electricity is available 24 hours daily in all Creel hotels. (In other parts of the canyon, electricity is sporadic or not available.) Creel has one ATM, one bank, and one *casa de cambio.* The best sources of **information** are the Mission Store and the hotels. Several businesses and many of the hotels offer long-distance **telephone** service; look for LARGA DISTANCIA signs or ask at your hotel. Creel sits at an **elevation** of 2,210m (7,248 ft.) and has a **population** of around 6,000. It's the largest town in the canyon area.

EXPLORING CREEL

You'll occasionally see the Tarahumara as you walk around town, but mostly, you'll see rugged logging types and tourists from around the world.

Several stores around Creel sell Tarahumara arts and crafts. The best is **Artesanías Misión (Mission Crafts),** which sells quality merchandise at reasonable prices; all profits go to the Mission Hospital run by Father Verplancken, a Jesuit, and benefit the Tarahumara. Here you'll find dolls, pottery, woven purses and belts, drums, violins (an instrument borrowed from the Spanish), bamboo flutes, bead necklaces, bows and arrows, cassettes of Tarahumara music, woodcarvings, baskets, and heavy wool rugs, as well as an excellent supply of books and maps relating to the Tarahumara and the region. It's open daily from 9:30am to 1pm, and Monday through Saturday from 3 to 6pm. It's beside the railroad tracks on the main plaza.

WHERE TO STAY

Though a small town, Creel has several places to stay, all with free parking. A lot of these hotels cater to backpackers. It's advisable to make reservations during high season.

Expensive

Copper Canyon Sierra Lodge ★★ *Finds*   About 20 minutes (22km/14 miles) southwest of Creel, the Sierra Lodge has everything you hope for in a mountain lodge—rock walls, beamed ceilings, lantern lights, and wood-burning stoves; in other words, rustic charm and no electricity. Its out-of-town location is a great starting point for self-guided hikes and walks in the mountains to the Cusárare Waterfalls. This hotel has a sister lodge in Batopilas, which is beautiful and runs about the same per room.

Apdo. Postal 3, 33200 Creel, Chih. (℃ 800/776-3942 in the U.S. Fax 635/456-0036 (in Creel). www.coppercanyon lodges.com. 22 units. $160 (£80) double. Rates include meals. No credit cards. *In room:* No phone.

The Lodge at Creel   Each of this Best Western hotel's cheerfully decorated cabins holds four units, built completely of pine, including the furniture. Most have two double beds, and some have their own porches. Their construction, decor, and layout remind me of old-style motels that you find next to U.S. national parks. The lobby, next to the dining area, has a phone for guests' use and a small gift shop. The hotel offers 3-night backpacking trips to the bottom of the canyon, among other tours, for 4 to 10 people. The on-site restaurant serves all three meals. The van meets all trains.

Av. López Mateos 61, 33200 Creel, Chih. (℃ 877/844-0409 in the U.S., or 635/456-0071. Fax 635/456-0082. www. thelodgeatcreel.com. 38 units. $120 (£60) double. AE, MC, V. **Amenities:** Restaurant; bar; fitness room; Jacuzzi; sauna; tours; room service; nonsmoking rooms. *In room:* TV, high-speed Internet, coffeemaker, hair dryer, safe, no phone.

Moderate

Hotel Parador de la Montaña   This is the largest hotel in town, located 4 blocks west of the plaza. The comfortable rooms have two double beds, high wood-beamed ceilings, central heating, tiled bathrooms, and thin walls. Guests congregate in the restaurant, bar, and lobby, which has a roaring fireplace. The hotel caters to groups and offers some 10 overland tours, priced from $20 to $70 (£10–£35).

Av. López Mateos s/n, 33200 Creel, Chih. ✆ **635/456-0023.** Fax 635/456-0085. (Reservations: Calle Allende 1414, 31300 Chihuahua, Chih.; ✆ 614/415-5408.) www.hotelparadorcreel.com. 50 units. $92 (£46) double. AE, MC, V. **Amenities:** Restaurant; bar; tours. *In room:* TV, no phone.

Inexpensive

Hotel Nuevo   The Nuevo has two sections: the older one, across the tracks from the train station and next to the restaurant and variety store, and newer log *cabañas* in back. Rooms are small to midsize and not as attractive as the higher-priced (and carpeted) *cabañas*. Half the rooms have TVs. The nice hotel restaurant is open from 8:30am to 8pm, and the small general store carries local crafts as well as basic supplies. Ask at the store about rooms.

Francisco Villa 121, 33200 Creel, Chih. ✆ **635/456-0022.** Fax 635/456-0043. 27 units. $40–$80 (£20–£40) double. MC, V. **Amenities:** Restaurant; general store. *In room:* TV (in some), no phone.

WHERE TO DINE

There are several places to eat in Creel, but no standouts. Aside from the restaurants at the hotels, you might want to try one of the establishments on López Mateos, such as the **Caballo Bayo, Tío Molcas,** or **Verónica's.**

NEARBY EXCURSIONS

Close by are several canyons, waterfalls, a lake, hot springs, Tarahumara villages and cave dwellings, and an old Jesuit mission. Ten kilometers (6 miles) north of town is an ecotourism complex, **San Ignacio de Arareko** (✆ **635/456-0126**). It has a lake, hiking and biking trails, horses, cabins, and a crafts shop, all run by indigenous peoples of the *ejido* (cooperative)—a change from the *mestizo* population's almost total control of tourism in Mexico. **Batopilas,** an 18th-century silver-mining town at the bottom of the canyon, requires an overnight excursion. You can ask for information about these and other things to do at your hotel, or go by the office of **The 3 Amigos** (✆ **635/456-0179;** www.amigos3.com) at Av. López Mateos 46 in downtown Creel. These guys rent pickups with crew cabs or mountain bikes and can give you maps and advice on where to go, depending on your interests.

From Creel, you can drive to **El Divisadero** (see "Stops 3 & 4: Barrancas/El Divisadero," above, for details) on a recently paved road. The trip takes about an hour.

ORGANIZED TOURS   Hotels offer 2- to 10-hour organized tours that cost $20 to $90 (£10–£45) per person (4-person minimum). All tour availability depends on whether a group can be assembled; your best chance is at the **Hotel Parador de la Montaña.**

Tips **Caution: Don't Be a Dope**

It's no secret that marijuana farmers use clandestine farmlands in the Copper Canyon, and that rumors link prominent names in the state to their activities. This has never affected any of my trips to the region. If you are hiking the backwoods and happen upon a field of marijuana, simply leave the area.

Basaseachic Falls

This is an exhausting day tour to what is billed as the tallest single cascade in North America. The best time to go is during the rainy season, from July to September. The tour costs around $60 (£30) per person and takes about 11 hours. Driving time is 4 hours one-way, and the strenuous hike to the bottom and back up takes 3 hours—not a lot of time to be by the falls. Another option is to stay in one of the simple accommodations that have opened near the falls, if you can get transportation back the next day. Ask around Creel.

Batopilas

You can make an overnight side trip from Creel to the old silver-mining town of Batopilas, founded in 1708. It's 7 to 9 hours from Creel by town bus, 5 hours by sport utility vehicle, along a narrow, winding dirt road through some of the most spectacular scenery in the Copper Canyon. In Batopilas, which lies beside a river at the bottom of a deep canyon, the weather is tropical, though it can get cool in the evenings. You can visit a beautiful little church and do several walks, including one to **Misión Satevó,** a ruined mission church that dates from the early 18th century. The place has many colorful little details: The dry-goods store has the original shelving and cash register, cobblestone streets twist past whitewashed homes, miners and ranchers come and go on horseback, and the Tarahumara frequently visit. A considerable number of pigs, dogs, and flocks of goats roam at will—this is, after all, Chihuahua's goat-raising capital.

Getting There   From Creel, take the **bus** from the Restaurant Herradero, López Mateos s/n, three doors past the turnoff to Hotel Plaza Mexicana. It goes to Batopilas on Tuesday, Thursday, and Saturday, leaving Creel at 7am and arriving midafternoon. Tickets are sold at the restaurant. Several Suburban-type **vans** offer transportation. One leaves on Monday, Wednesday, and Friday at 10:30am and arrives midafternoon. Both bus and van return the following day. There are no bathrooms, restaurants, or other conveniences of civilization along the way, but the bus may stop to allow passengers to stretch and find a bush.

Where to Stay & Dine   Batopilas has a few little restaurants and inns. There are no telephones, though, so don't expect to make reservations. One night probably isn't enough for a stay here, since you arrive midafternoon and must leave at 7am or 10:30am the next day.

The staff at the Hotel Parador de la Montaña in Creel provides information about vacancies at the basic, comfortable, 10-room **Hotel Mary** (formerly Parador Batopilas). All rooms have private bathrooms and cost around $22 (£11) double per night. There are also the rustic **Hotel Batopilas** and **Hotel Las Palmeras,** with five or six rooms each; if all else fails, you can probably find a family willing to let you stay in an extra room.

Restaurants in Batopilas are informal, so bring along some snacks and bottled water to tide you over; snacks are available at the general store. The place to eat in Batopilas is **Doña Mica's,** facing a little plaza tucked behind the main square. Ask anyone for directions (everyone knows her). She serves meals on her front porch surrounded by plants, but it's best to let her know in advance when to expect you. On short notice, she can probably rustle up some scrambled eggs.

2 Los Mochis: The Western Terminus

202km (121 miles) SW of Alamos; 80km (50 miles) SW of El Fuerte; 309km (192 miles) SE of Guaymas; 416km (258 miles) NW of Mazatlán

Los Mochis, in Sinaloa State, is a coastal city of 350,000 founded in 1893 by Benjamin Johnson of Pennsylvania. It is a wealthy city in a fertile agricultural area, but holds little of interest for the visitor. The most important aspects of the city are that it is a boarding point for the train, it has an airport, and it is connected to La Paz, Baja California, by ferry, and to the U.S. border by highway.

ESSENTIALS

GETTING THERE & DEPARTING   By Plane   AeroMéxico/Aerolitoral (© 800/ 237-6639 in the U.S., or 668/815-2570 for reservations; www.aeromexico.com.mx) has direct service from Phoenix, Chihuahua, Hermosillo, Mazatlán, and La Paz. The airport is 21km (13 miles) north of town; transportation is by *combi* (collective mini-van) or airport taxi ($10/£5).

By Train   The first-class **Chihuahua al Pacífico (Copper Canyon train)** runs between Los Mochis and Chihuahua once daily, departing at 6am. First-class fare is $130 (£65).

By Car   Coastal Highway 15 is well maintained in both directions leading into Los Mochis.

By Ferry   A ferry plies the waters between La Paz and Topolobampo, the port for Los Mochis carrying passengers, vehicles, and cargo. The company, **Baja Ferries** (© 668/ 817-3752 or -3864; www.bajaferries.com), uses a larger and more dependable ship than the company that used to operate this ferry route.

By Bus   Buses serve Los Mochis, however marginally. Most are *de paso*—passing through. All bus stations are downtown, within walking distance of the hotels. The **first-class station** is near Juárez at Degollado 200. From here, Elite buses go to and from Tijuana, Monterrey, Nogales, and Ciudad Juárez. Auto-transportes Transpacífi-cos, in the same station, serves Nogales, Tijuana, Mazatlán, Guadalajara, Querétaro, and Mexico City. A lot of travelers who arrive in Los Mochis prefer to go directly to El Fuerte, spend the night there, and then catch the train. There are two places to catch the bus to El Fuerte (1½–2 hr.). The first is at the **Mercado Independencia;** the bus stops at the corner of Independencia and Degollado. The other is at the **corner of Cuauhtémoc and Prieto,** near the Hotel América. Ask hotel desk clerks or the tourism office for a schedule. These are second-class buses, which stop frequently, pro-longing the trip well beyond the normal 1-hour travel time.

CITY LAYOUT   Los Mochis contains no central plaza, and streets run northwest to southeast and southwest to northeast.

FAST FACTS   The local **American Express** representative is **Viajes Araceli,** Av. Alvaro Obregón 471-A Poniente (© 668/815-5780; fax 668/815-8787). *Note:* Changing money outside of Los Mochis is difficult, so stock up on pesos before board-ing the train. Most places in the canyons do not accept credit cards. The telephone **area code** for Los Mochis is **668.**

EXPLORING LOS MOCHIS

For most travelers, Los Mochis is a stopover en route to somewhere else. There isn't much here, but the town is pleasant, and you can enjoy some excellent seafood. The **Viajes Flamingo** travel agency, on the ground floor of the Hotel Santa Anita (① **668/ 812-1613** or -1929), arranges a city tour, hunting and fishing trips, and a harbor tour around **Topolobampo Bay.** The harbor tour is fun. The agency is open Monday through Saturday from 8:30am to 1pm and 3 to 6:30pm. The boat ride is really just a spin in the bay and not especially noteworthy, although the bay is pretty and dolphins often show up.

WHERE TO STAY

Hotel Corintios   Behind a campy entrance with Greek columns and mirrored glass are two stories of rooms with ample light, carpeted floors, and adequate space for two comfortable double beds and luggage. The bathrooms are midsize and have marble tub/showers but poor lighting. The junior suites come with a king-size bed.

Obregón 580 Poniente, 81200 Los Mochis, Sin. ① **668/818-2300** or 01-800/690-3000 in Mexico. Fax 668/818-2277. www.hotelcorintios.com. 59 units. $78 (£39) double, $86 (£43) junior suite. AE, MC, V. Rates include continental breakfast. Free parking. **Amenities:** Restaurant; Jacuzzi; room service; laundry service, nonsmoking rooms. *In room:* A/C, TV, Wi-Fi.

Hotel Las Fuentes   Among the inexpensive hotels in town, I like this one best. The rooms are cheerful and clean and the staff is helpful. Rooms come with one or two double beds, and the cost varies accordingly. Bathrooms are midsize with a shower. The hotel is 5 minutes from downtown on one of the main arteries.

Bulevar Adolfo López Mateos 1251-A Norte, 81220 Los Mochis, Sin. ① **668/818-8871** or -8172. Fax 668/812-5983. www.hotellasfuentes.com. 38 units. $50 (£25) double. AE, MC, V. Free secure parking. **Amenities:** Restaurant; bar; room service; laundry service. *In room:* A/C, TV, Wi-Fi.

Hotel Santa Anita   The Santa Anita is the choice of most travelers going to the canyon; not only is it a comfortable, quiet hotel, but it offers reliable transportation to and from the train station. The rooms are modern and well furnished but vary a good deal in size. All are carpeted and have comfortable beds, color TVs with U.S. channels, and tap water purified for drinking. The hotel's popular restaurant is just off the lobby. There are two bars, one with live music at least 1 day a week.

Leyva, at the corner of Hidalgo (Apdo. Postal 159), 81200 Los Mochis, Sin. ① **800/896-8196** in the U.S., or 668/818-7046. Fax 668/812-0046. 116 units. $140 (£70) double. AE, MC, V. Free parking. **Amenities:** Restaurant; bar; transportation to and from the train station; business center; room service; laundry service; nonsmoking rooms. *In room:* A/C, TV, hair dryer.

WHERE TO DINE

El Farallón ⟨⟨ SEAFOOD   If you like seafood, there's no reason to eat anywhere else in Los Mochis. Don't be put off by the menu, which is confusing—to put it simply, you can order seafood cooked any way you want. Try a Mexican style such as *al ajillo,* with toasted *guajillo* chiles. If you're hungry, I recommend the *mariscada* for two or more, which comes with a cold and a hot platter of a variety of fish and shellfish. Try *calamares* (squid), the cheapest thing on the platter. Forget about those rubbery rings fried up in other restaurants; because the squid get to be giant-size in this region's waters, the meat comes in big, tender chunks. One of my favorites is *machaca,* made with either shrimp or smoked marlin (cooked in a reduced fish stock, which is mild and satisfying). The atmosphere is casual, the air-conditioning functions with gusto, and the white-tiled dining area is simply furnished.

Obregón, at Angel Flores. (✆ **668/812-1428.** Main courses $8–$20 (£4–£10). AE, MC, V. Daily 8am–11pm. From the Hotel Santa Anita, turn right on Leyva and right again for 1 block on Obregón; it's on your left.

El Taquito *Value* MEXICAN   Any time of the day or night, El Taquito serves standard Mexican fare at a good price. With orange booths and Formica tables, the cafe looks like an American fast-food place. Tortilla soup comes in a large bowl, and both breakfast and main-course portions are quite generous.

Leyva at Barrera. (✆ **668/812-8119.** Breakfast $3–$6 (£1.50–£3); main courses $4–$8 (£2–£4). AE, DC, MC, V. Daily 24 hr. From the Hotel Santa Anita, turn left on Leyva, cross Hidalgo and go 1 block; it's on your right.

Restaurante España STEAK/SEAFOOD   This Spanish-style restaurant is a favorite among downtown professionals, who feast on large plates of paella (available Thurs and Sun after 1pm; at other times it's made to order, which takes 45 min.). The decor is upscale for Los Mochis, with a splashing fountain in the dining room and heavy, carved-wood tables and chairs.

Obregón 525 Pte. (✆ **668/812-2221.** Breakfast $4–$6 (£2–£3); main courses $9–$13 (£4.50–£6.50). AE, MC, V. Daily 7am–11pm. From the Hotel Santa Anita, turn right out the front door to Obregón, and then right on Obregón for 1½ blocks; it's on your right.

---

3 Chihuahua: The Eastern Terminus ✦

341km (211 miles) S of El Paso; 440km (273 miles) NW of Torreón

Chihuahua, a city of wide boulevards and handsome buildings, is the capital of the state of Chihuahua, the largest and richest in Mexico. The wealth comes from mining, timber, cattle raising, *maquiladoras* (assembly plants for export goods), and tourism. The city has grown a lot in the last 30 years, thanks mainly to an increase in manufacturing plants, and has lost its frontier feeling. But the historic center of Chihuahua retains much of its character and holds a few museums and buildings worth visiting, including the house where Pancho Villa once lived.

ESSENTIALS

GETTING THERE & DEPARTING   By Plane   Continental (✆ **800/525-0280** in the U.S., or 01-800/900-5000 in Mexico; www.continental.com) has nonstop service to and from Houston on a 50-seat jet. **AeroMéxico/Aerolitoral** (✆ **800/237-6639** in the U.S., or 614/415-6303; www.aeromexico.com.mx) flies direct from El Paso, Phoenix, Guadalajara, Hermosillo, Mexico City, Monterrey, Torreón, Tijuana, Culiacán, La Paz, and Los Mochis, with connecting flights from Los Angeles and San Antonio. **Transportes Terrestre** (✆ **614/420-3366**) controls minivan service from the airport ($7/£3.85 per person, $10/£5.50 if it's an early flight). Taxis from town charge $15 (£8.25) for up to four people.

By Train   The **Chihuahua al Pacífico** (✆ **614/439-7212;** fax 614/439-7208) leaves Chihuahua daily for Los Mochis by way of the Copper Canyon country. The complete train schedule and the train route appear in "The Copper Canyon Train & Stops Along the Way," earlier in this chapter. In that section you'll find information on purchasing tickets. It is easier to go through a travel agency than to deal directly with the company. The train is scheduled to leave at 6am daily. To get to the station in time, it's best to arrange transportation through one of the travel agencies recommended under

"Canyon Arrangements," in "Fast Facts: Chihuahua," below. They pick up clients taking the train each morning.

By Car **Highway 45** leads south from Ciudad Juárez; **Highway 16** south from Ojinaga; and **Highway 49** north from Torreón. For the drive to Creel, see "Getting There & Departing" under "Stop 5: Creel," earlier in this chapter.

By Bus The Central Camionera **Terminal de Autobuses (bus station)** is on Avenida Juan Pablo II, 8km (5 miles) northeast of town en route to the airport. Buses leave hourly for major points inland and north and south on the coast. Transportes Chihuahuenses, the big local line, offers first-class service to Ciudad Juárez every half-hour; the trip takes 4 hours. Transportes del Norte and Autobuses Estrella Blanca also run buses hourly from the border through Chihuahua to points south. Omnibus de México has *servicio ejecutivo* (deluxe service) from Juárez, Mexico City, and Monterrey. Futura/Turistar also has deluxe service to Monterrey and Durango.

For travel to Creel, look for the Estrella Blanca line. Buses leave every 2 hours from 6am to 6pm. Direct buses make the trip in 4 hours.

VISITOR INFORMATION For basic info, visit the **tourist information center** (© 614/410-1077 or 429-3596), Calle Aldama at Carranza in the Government Palace, just left of the altar and murals dedicated to Father Hidalgo. It's open Monday through Friday from 9am to 6pm, Saturday and Sunday from 10am to 5pm.

CITY LAYOUT The town center is laid out around the **Plaza Principal,** bounded by avenidas Libertad and Victoria (which run northeast-southwest) and Avenida Independencia and Calle 4 (which run northwest-southeast). The **cathedral** is at the southwest end of the plaza, and the city offices are on the northeast end. If you're standing on Independencia with the cathedral on your left, odd-numbered streets and blocks will be to your right, and even-numbered streets and blocks to your left.

GETTING AROUND Local buses run along main arteries beginning at the central plaza. Taxis are readily available. If you want to see the sights and have only 1 day, take a tour (see "Exploring Chihuahua," below).

FAST FACTS: Chihuahua

American Express The local representative is **Viajes Rojo y Casavantes,** with one agent in the Hotel San Francisco and a full office at Vicente Guerrero 1207 (© 614/415-4636; fax 614/415-5384).

Area Code The telephone area code is **614.**

Canyon Arrangements If you have waited to purchase train tickets and make canyon hotel reservations, contact **Turismo al Mar,** Calle Berna 2202, Colonia Mirador, 31270 Chihuahua, Chih. (© **614/410-9232** or 416-5950; fax 614/416-6589).

Elevation Chihuahua sits at 1,425m (4,374 ft.).

Emergencies Call © **060.**

Hospital **Clínica del Parque** is at Pedro Leal del Rosal and de la Llave (© 614/ 415-7411). For medical emergencies, call © **614/411-8141.**

Population Chihuahua has some 670,000 residents.

Safety See "Border Unrest Heads South", below.

Chihuahua

Escudero

Holiday Inn
Hotel & Suites

To Ciudad Juárez

J.D. Palomino

Bus

J.E. Múñoz

G. Conde

IMSS

Reforma

De Marzo

Progreso

Revolución

Calle 10

Bus

Julian Carrillo

Calle 6

Calle 4

Calle 2

Calle 3

Hotel Parador
Chihuahua

Av. Universidad

Niños Héroes

Posada Tierra
Blanca

Calle 5

Calle 7

Calle 9

Calle 13

Trias

Av. Ocampo

Av. Independencia

Doblado

Juárez

Libertad

Hidalgo's
Dungeon

Hotel
San Francisco

Catedral
Plaza Principal

Palacio del
Gobierno

Victoria

Aldama

Escorza

Guerrero

Av. V. Carranza

Calle 10

Morelos

Allende

G. Farias

Coronado

Lallave

Centro Cultural
Quinta Gameros

Calle 7

Paseo Bolívar

Irigoyen

PARQUE
LERDO

To Chihuahua al
Pacifico Railway

To Museo de la Revolución

Mina

UNITED STATES

Chihuahua

MEXICO

Mexico
City

0   500 mi

0   500 km

330 feet

100 meters

Bus

EXPLORING CHIHUAHUA

To see Chihuahua's sights in 1 day, consider taking a 3-hour city tour; English-speaking guides are available. Three recommended agencies are **Torre del Sol,** Independencia 116-2 (© **614/415-7380**), in the Hotel Palacio del Sol; **Turismo al Mar** (see "Canyon Arrangements," in "Fast Facts," above); and **Viajes Rojo y Casavantes** (see "American Express," in "Fast Facts," above). Any of these will pick you up at your hotel. A half-day city tour includes visits to the museums, the churches, the colonial aqueduct, the state capital building, the state penitentiary, and more. A 7-hour trip to the Mennonite village near Cuauhtémoc costs about $35 (£18) per person, with a minimum of four people. Unless you have a particular interest in cheese making or the Mennonites, it's not worth your time.

SIGHTS IN TOWN

Hidalgo's Dungeon   Father Miguel Hidalgo y Costilla was a priest in Dolores, Guanajuato, when he started the War of Independence on September 15, 1810. Six months later, he was captured by the Spanish, brought to Chihuahua, and thrown in a dungeon for 98 days. He was then shot along with his lieutenants, Allende, Aldama, and Jiménez. The four were beheaded, and their heads hung in iron cages for 9½ years on the four corners of the Alhóndiga granary in Guanajuato (see chapter 7) as examples of the fate revolutionaries would meet. In this cell, Hidalgo lived on bread and water before his execution. The night before his death, he wrote a few words on the wall with a piece of charcoal to thank his guard and the warden for the good treatment they gave him. A bronze plaque commemorates his final message.

In the Palacio Federal, Av. Juárez at Guerrero. No phone. Admission $1 (50p). Tues–Sun 10am–6pm. From Plaza Principal, walk on pedestrian-only Calle Libertad for 3 long blocks to Guerrero, turn left, and walk to corner of Juárez; turn right and go a half-block; museum entrance is on the right, below the post office.

Museo de la Revolución 𝕶𝕶 *Finds*   The Revolution Museum is Pancho Villa's house, where Luz Corral de Villa, Pancho Villa's widow, lived until her death in 1981. Exhibits include Villa's weapons, some personal effects, lots of period photos, and the 1922 Dodge in which he was shot in 1923 (you'll see the bullet holes). I found it interesting and recommend seeing the place with a guide, who can add lots of biographical details about this larger-than-life character. Be sure to ask about Villa's opinions on marriage and about the total number of his offspring and grandchildren.

Calle 10 no. 3014 (at Méndez). © **614/416-2958**. Admission $2 (£1). Tues–Sat 9am–1pm and 3–7pm. Bus: Colonia Dale (runs west on Juárez, then south on Ocampo); exit at corner of Ocampo and Méndez.

Palacio del Gobierno   The Palacio del Gobierno is a magnificent, ornate structure dating in part from 1890; the original building, the Jesuit College, was built in 1718. A colorful, expressive mural encompasses the first floor of the large central courtyard and tells the history of the area around Chihuahua from the time of the first European visitation through the Revolution. In the far right corner, note the scene depicting Benito Juárez flanked by Abraham Lincoln and Simón Bolívar, liberator of South America. In the far left rear courtyard are a plaque and altar commemorating the execution in 1811 of Miguel Hidalgo, the father of Mexican independence; the plaque marks the spot where the hero was executed in the old building, and the mural portrays the scene.

Av. Aldama (between Guerrero and Carranza). © **614/410-6324**. Free admission. Daily 8am–10pm. With the cathedral on your right, walk along Independencia 1 block, turn left on Aldama, continue 2 long blocks, and cross Guerrero; entrance is on the left.

Quinta Gameros ✸✸ Quinta Gameros is a neoclassical, French Second Empire–style mansion with a beautiful Art Nouveau interior. Built in 1910 for Manuel Gameros, the mansion became a museum in 1961. Pancho Villa used it briefly as a headquarters. The interior walls, floors, and ceilings are lavishly decorated, which inspired the transfer of a beautiful collection of fine Mexican Art Nouveau furnishings from Mexico City to this museum. If you like design and beautiful antiques, especially Art Nouveau, don't miss this place.

Quinta Gameros, Paseo Bolívar 401. ✆ **614/416-6684.** Admission $2 (£1). Tues–Sun 11am–2pm and 4–7pm. Heading away from the Plaza Principal with the cathedral on your right, walk 7 blocks on Independencia to Bolívar, turn right, and walk 1 block; museum is on the right.

WHERE TO STAY
EXPENSIVE
Holiday Inn Hotel and Suites ✸ This Holiday Inn offers the most comfortable rooms in the downtown area. All units are suites, with kitchenettes that include stove, refrigerator, and coffeemaker. There's a sitting area, large writing table, and a choice of one king-size bed or two doubles. Guests have the use of a video library. The hotel staff is helpful and efficient. They can provide a continental breakfast for people heading off on the train, as well as a box lunch. The hotel is a 5-minute walk from downtown.

Calle Escudero 702 (between Av. Universidad and Av. de Montes), 31240 Chihuahua, Chih. ✆ **800/465-4329** in the U.S., or 614/439-0000. Fax 614/414-3313. 74 units. $160 (£80) double. Rates include breakfast buffet. AE, MC, V. Free secure parking. **Amenities:** Restaurant; bar; 2 pools (1 indoor); fitness room; Jacuzzi; steam room; game room; business center; room service; babysitting; laundry service; coin-op laundry; nonsmoking rooms. *In room:* A/C, TV, high-speed Internet access, kitchenette, fridge, coffeemaker, hair dryer, iron, safe.

Quality Inn Chihuahua San Francisco The good location and comfortable mid-size rooms are the main attractions here. Rooms are well furnished. The bathrooms are well equipped and have ample counter space. Bed choices include two doubles, a queen, or a king. Mattresses are firm. Don't worry about getting a view; ask for something quiet. This used to be called the Hotel San Francisco.

Victoria 409, 31000 Chihuahua, Chih. ✆ **800/847-2546** in the U.S., or 614/439-9000. Fax 614/415-3538. www.qualityinnchihuahua.com. 131 units. $110 (£55) double. AE, MC, V. Free covered parking and continental breakfast. From the cathedral, walk to Victoria and turn right; the hotel is 1½ blocks down on your right, before Av. Ocampo. **Amenities:** Restaurant (see review for Degá, below); bar; fitness room; travel agency; car rental; business center; room service; laundry service. *In room:* A/C, TV, coffeemaker, hair dryer, iron, safe.

MODERATE
Hotel Posada Tierra Blanca This downtown hotel has an attractive large pool area shaded by trees. Rooms are in two- and three-story buildings. They are large and

---

⚠ *Warning* Border Unrest Heads South

The U.S. Department of State Travel Advisory notes that drug-related violence along the U.S.–Mexico border continues to escalate. Clashes between heavily armed cartel members and Mexico's police have taken place as far south as Ciudad Chihuahua. These incidents are rare, given the affluence of the town and its distance from the border, but travelers should remain aware of their surroundings and take special precautions at night.

quiet (none have windows facing the street). Bathrooms are midsize with good counter space and better lighting than in most of the hotels in Chihuahua.

Niños Héroes 102, 31000 Chihuahua, Chih. (℃) **614/415-0000.** www.posadatierrablanca.com.mx. 94 units. $72 (£36) double. AE, MC, V. Free secure parking. **Amenities:** Restaurant; bar; large outdoor pool; fitness room; room service; laundry service. *In room:* A/C, TV, Wi-Fi.

INEXPENSIVE

Hotel Parador Chihuahua I like this motel for the price, the downtown location, and the well-maintained rooms. It occupies the interior of a small city block, with the rooms built around the pool and the garden area. The midsize rooms are carpeted and furnished rather plainly. You'll have a choice of one king-size bed or two doubles. Bathrooms are midsize.

Calle 3, no. 304 (between Julian Carrillo and Niños Héroes), 31000 Chihuahua, Chih. (℃) **614/415-0827.** www. paradorchihuahua.com. 34 units. $52 (£26) double. AE, MC, V. Free secure parking. **Amenities:** Restaurant; bar; small outdoor pool; room service; laundry service. *In room:* A/C, TV.

WHERE TO DINE

As a large city, Chihuahua has plenty of international restaurants, but we recommend sticking with steakhouses and Mexican cuisine.

Degá MEXICAN/INTERNATIONAL This restaurant bar at the Quality Inn Chihuahua San Francisco hotel draws both downtown workers and travelers. The breakfast buffet features made-to-order omelets. The steaks and Mexican dishes are well priced; try the *plato mexicano*, a popular dish that comes with a tamal, *chile relleno*, beans, chips, and guacamole.

In the Quality Inn Chihuahua San Francisco, Calle Victoria 409. (℃) **614/416-7550.** Breakfast $4–$7 (£2–£3.50); breakfast buffet $8 (£4); main courses $5–$17 (£2.50–£8.50); Sun buffet $10 (£5). AE, MC, V. Daily 7am–11pm.

La Calesa STEAKS/MEXICAN The dining room, with its heavy furniture, wood paneling, and bound menus, gets the message across that this is Chihuahua's establishment restaurant. Some of the steaks go by different names here, but the waiters are familiar with all the cuts. A pianist entertains diners from 2:30 to 5pm and 9pm to midnight.

Av. Colón 3300, corner of Av. Juárez. (℃) **614/410-1038.** Steaks $12–$22 (£6–£11); Mexican dishes $7–$10 (£3.50–£5). AE, MC, V. Daily 12:30pm–midnight.

Restaurante Todo de Maíz ★ *Finds* MEXICAN To eat cheaply and well in Chihuahua is a bit of a trick—unless you dine at this place. When I'm in Chihuahua, I never miss it. Señora María Matilde Salazar is a great cook and an unabashed leftist. She keeps quality and freshness up by keeping the menu simple. Between 1 and 2:30pm she offers a *comida corrida* that's a bargain. The rest of the time she makes tacos, quesadillas, tostadas, and *peneques* (a local form of *antojito* that's like a *gordita*) all made with corn *masa*, as the restaurant's name suggests. This place is down the street from the Holiday Inn.

Calle Escudero 2103 (between calles 21 and 23). (℃) **614/4145778.** Comida corrida $4 (£2); antojitos $2–$3 (£1–£1.50). No credit cards. Mon–Fri 9am–5pm; Sat 11am–5pm.

Rincón Mexicano ★ MEXICAN The Rincón serves great Mexican food and offers a substantial number of choices. Good appetizers include *quesadillas de huitlacoche* (corn empanadas with cheese and corn fungus) for the adventurous, and *chile con asadero* (melted spicy cheese). For a main dish that gives you a little of everything, try *enchiladas tres moles.* As you would expect of a restaurant in Chihuahua, the emphasis is on beef, prepared in very Mexican ways such as *puntas en chile pasado* (beef tips cooked in a dried chili sauce) or *molcajete de res* (fajitas cooked and served in a steaming stone vessel accompanied by tortillas). The interior is easy on the eyes, with muted tones of yellow and orange, good lighting, and tablecloths. A guitar trio occasionally performs soft music in the evenings. The restaurant is a short taxi ride from downtown. Av. Cuauhtémoc 2224. ℭ 614/411-1510 or -1427. Main courses $8–$16 (£4–£8). AE, MC, V. Daily noon–midnight.

CHIHUAHUA AFTER DARK
Most nighttime action takes place in hotel lobby bars (see "Where to Stay," above). At the **Quality Inn Chihuahua San Francisco,** there's live music Monday through Saturday, with happy hour from 5 to 8pm. The lobby bar at the **Hotel Palacio del Sol** schedules live entertainment nightly.

Los Cabos & Baja California

by Joy Hepp

Baja California is rife with complimentary contrasts: hot desert and cool ocean, manicured golf greens and craggy mountains, glistening resorts and frontier land, under the influence of the U.S. as well as Mexico. The amalgam of Mexican and American cultures here is striking and peculiar; it's a particular blend that doesn't exist elsewhere, even in Americanized resorts such as Cancún.

The hybridization is due, in no small part, to the fact that the Baja Peninsula is and is not part of Mexico. Attached mostly to the United States and separated from all but a sliver of Mexico by the Sea of Cortez (Gulf of California), the peninsula consists of one long granite ridge extending about 1,500km (930 miles)—longer than Italy—from Mexico's northernmost city of **Tijuana** to **Cabo San Lucas** at its southern tip. Desert terrain rises from both coasts; forests of *cardón* cactus, spiky elephant trees, and spindly ocotillo bushes populate the raw landscape. Long stretches of open highway crisscrossed by roadrunners and tumbleweed are interrupted by the occasional dusty pueblo and jaw-dropping coastline. Baja is part Wild West, part country club, part seafaring paradise, part adventure wonderland, and there's room enough for all of its visitors to blaze their own trails. For more detailed coverage of this region, consult *Frommer's Los Cabos & Baja*.

EXPLORING THE REGION

The weather in this land of extremes can be sizzling hot in summer, and cold and windy in winter. Winter is often warm enough for watersports, but bring a wetsuit if you're a serious diver or snorkeler, as well as warmer clothes for chilly temperatures. Although Baja's climate varies greatly by season, it is predictable—an important quality for the increasing number of golfers looking for sunny skies. Rainy days are few and far between, with most showers concentrated in September.

THE TWO CABOS Nearly two million visitors—a number that is steadily growing—are lured to Los Cabos (the capes), the twin towns at the peninsula's southernmost tip, each year. **Cabo San Lucas** holds court on the Western cape, and **San José del Cabo**

Tips The Best Websites for Los Cabos & Baja

- All About Cabo: www.allaboutcabo.com
- Baja Quest: www.bajaquest.com
- Baja Insider: www.bajainsider.com
- Visit Los Cabos: www.visitloscabos.travel

The Baja Peninsula

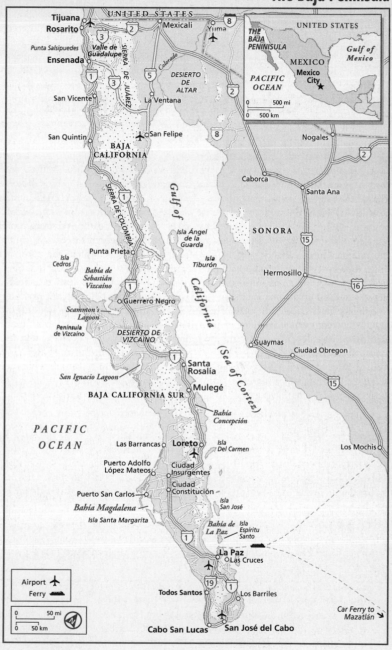

United States

Tijuana
Rosarito
Punta Salsipuedes
Ensenada
Valle de Guadalupe
SIERRA DE JUAREZ
Mexicali
Yuma
8
Colorado
DESIERTO DE ALTAR
5
2
San Vicente
La Ventana
San Quintin
San Felipe
8
BAJA CALIFORNIA
SIERRA DE COLOMBIA
Gulf of
Caborca
Santa Ana
Nogales
2
SONORA
15
Isla Cedros
Punta Prieta
Isla Ángel de la Guarda
Isla Tiburón
Hermosillo
16
Bahía de Sebastián Vizcaíno
California
Scammon's Lagoon
Guerrero Negro
Península de Vizcaíno
DESIERTO DE VIZCAÍNO
Guaymas
Ciudad Obregon
15
San Ignacio Lagoon
Santa Rosalía
(Sea of Cortez)
Mulegé
BAJA CALIFORNIA SUR
Bahía Concepción
PACIFIC OCEAN
Las Barrancas
Loreto
Isla Del Carmen
Los Mochis
Puerto Adolfo López Mateos
Ciudad Insurgentes
Ciudad Constitución
Puerto San Carlos
Isla San José
Bahía Magdalena
Isla Santa Margarita
Bahía de La Paz
Isla Espíritu Santo
La Paz
Las Cruces
Todos Santos
19
Los Barriles
Car Ferry to Mazatlán
Cabo San Lucas
San José del Cabo

Airport
Ferry

0   50 mi
0   50 km

THE BAJA PENINSULA
UNITED STATES
Gulf of Mexico
PACIFIC OCEAN
MEXICO
Mexico City
0   500 mi
0   500 km

rounds out the Eastern cape. Connected only by the **Tourist Corridor,** 33km (21 miles) of coastline studded with golf courses, luxury resorts, and master-planned communities, the two capes could not be more different.

Cabo San Lucas, also known as Land's End, is twofold. Most obviously, she's the rowdy younger sister who takes tequila shots from a holster while dancing on the table chanting, "What happens in Cabo stays in Cabo," and wraps up the night at a local American fast-food joint. The other side of San Lucas is a bling-flashing older brother who frequents swanky clubs, sips champagne in his oceanfront Jacuzzi, or cruises the bay in his luxury yacht. Somewhere in between are the fun-loving aunts and uncles who've come to fish for marlin and/or take a peep at Sammy Hagar.

On the other hand, San José del Cabo, on the eastern side of Baja's tip, is a decidedly more "Mexican" experience. Colorful 18th-century homes-turned-artisan shops, vibrant flowering trees, world-class waves, and exquisite restaurants draw well-tanned West Coast surfers; jolly snowbirds in search of sun and margaritas; celebrities and executives looking for respite from the rat race; and couples and families who wake up early to walk on the beach, go for a swim, take a tour, and spend the afternoon relaxing before enjoying a nice dinner on the town. The tree-lined streets of the downtown area are particularly enchanting, and the melodies of Ranchero or Banda music float from century-old homes still inhabited after generations.

Baja can seem like one of the least crowded corners of Mexico. **Todos Santos,** an artistic community on the Pacific side of the coastal curve (1 hour north of the tip), and Baja's **East Cape** both draw travelers who find that Los Cabos has outgrown them. **La Paz,** capital of Baja Sur, remains an easygoing maritime port skirted by white-sand beaches and a smattering of islands worth exploring.

MID BAJA   Among the highlights of the mid-Baja region are the east-coast towns of **Loreto, Bahía Magdalena, Mulegé,** and **Santa Rosalía.** These towns have a much richer cultural heritage than those in Baja Sur. Although Loreto is experiencing growth—driven by a real estate project just outside of town—the remaining east coast towns have all but escaped the tourism boom experienced by the two Cabos.

These mid-Baja towns were the center of the 18th-century Jesuit mission movement. Today, they attract travelers who are drawn to Baja's wild natural beauty but find the popularity of Los Cabos a bit overwhelming. This area's natural attractions have made it a center for sea kayaking, sportfishing, diving, and hiking—including excursions to view indigenous cave paintings.

Whale-watching is also excellent. Many tour companies operate out of Loreto and the smaller neighboring towns (see "Whale-watching in Baja," later in this chapter).

BAJA NORTE   **Tijuana** has the dubious distinction of being the most visited and perhaps most misunderstood town in all of Mexico. New cultural and sporting attractions, extensive shopping, and strong business growth—of the reputable kind—are brightening Tijuana's image.

Tranquil **Rosarito Beach** has reemerged as a resort town; it got a boost after the movies *Titanic* and *Master and Commander* were filmed there, and Fox Studios converted the former set into a film-themed amusement park. Farther south on the Pacific Coast, the lovely port town of **Ensenada** is known for surfing and sportfishing. Tours of nearby inland vineyards (Mexico's wine country) are growing in popularity.

1 Los Cabos: Resorts, Watersports & Golf ★★★

The two towns at the southern tip of the rugged Baja Peninsula are grouped together as Los Cabos, although they couldn't be more different. San José del Cabo and Cabo San Lucas are separated not just by 33km (21 miles), but also by distinct attitudes and ways of life. Where Cabo San Lucas mirrors a spirited version of the Los Angeles lifestyle, San José del Cabo remains a traditional, tranquil Mexican small town, although recent gentrification is turning it into the more sophisticated of the two resorts. Because each Cabos has its own character and attractions, we treat them separately; but it's common to stay in one—or in the Corridor between—and make day trips to the other.

The golden days of Los Cabos began when silver-screen greats such as Bing Crosby, John Wayne, and Ava Gardner ventured south in the 1950s. Sportfishing was the first draw, but the transfixing landscape, rich waters, and nearly flawless climate quickly gained the favor of other explorers. The only way to get to the soon-to-be "marlin capital of the world" was by boat or private airplane. As such, Los Cabos was born of exclusivity and extravagance. Fishing remains a lure today, although golf may have overtaken it as the principal attraction. By the early 1980s, the Mexican government realized Los Cabos' growth potential and invested in new highways, airport facilities, golf courses, and marine facilities. Increased air access and the opening of Transpeninsular Highway 1 (in 1973) paved the way for booming growth.

Today, Los Cabos is not just about marlin and the links. It has become a hub for surfing, hiking, diving, whale-watching, sea kayaking, and spas. And there's always an isolated, wild beach on which to picnic, camp, or simply watch the tide come in.

The road from Cabo San Lucas to San José del Cabo is the centerpiece of resort growth. Known as the "Tourist Corridor," or simply "the Corridor," this four-lane stretch offers cliff-top vistas and an easy ride between the towns, but still has no night-time lighting and bears too many roadside memorials to count—fair warning that cautious driving is imperative, especially at night. Deluxe resorts and renowned golf courses are here, along with dramatic beaches and coves. The view is especially outstanding in January and February, when gray whales often spout close to shore.

The Los Cabos area is more expensive than other Mexican resorts because luxury is the norm among local hotels, and real estate prices make the San Diego market seem tame. However, a new boom in all-inclusive resorts and off-season travel deals is making Los Cabos vacations more affordable.

You should consider renting a car, even if only for a day or two, because there's too much to see to spend an hour waiting at the bus stop or hundreds of dollars on expensive taxis. For those who like the freedom to explore on their own terms, a rental car is essential, not to mention economical. And to best understand Los Cabos, both capes need your attention.

San José del Cabo, with its pastel cottages and narrow streets lined with flowering trees, retains the air of a provincial Mexican town. The main square, adorned with a wrought iron bandstand and shaded benches, faces the cathedral, which was built on the site of an early mission. San José is becoming increasingly sophisticated, with a collection of noteworthy cafes, art galleries, interesting shops, and intriguing inns adding a newly refined flavor to the downtown area. This is the best choice for those who want to enjoy the paradoxical landscape but still be aware that they're in Mexico.

ESSENTIALS

Getting There & Departing

By Plane   **AeroMéxico** (© 800/237-6639 in the U.S., 01-800/021-4010 in Mexico, or 624/146-5098 or -5097; www.aeromexico.com) flies nonstop from San Diego and Ontario and has connecting flights from other cities; **American Airlines** (© 800/223-5436 in the U.S., or 624/146-5300 or -5309; www.aa.com) flies from Dallas/Ft. Worth, Los Angeles, Chicago, and New York; **US Airways/America West** (© 800/235-9292 in the U.S., or 624/146-5380; www.usairways.com) operates nonstop flights from Phoenix, Las Vegas, Oakland, and San Diego; **Alaska Airlines** (© 800/252-7522 in the U.S., or 624/146-5100 or -5101; www.alaskaair.com) flies from Los Angeles, Portland, San Diego, Seattle, and San Francisco; **Continental** (© 800/537-9222 in the U.S., or 624/146-5080; www.continental.com) flies nonstop from Houston and Newark; **Delta** (© 800/241-4141 in the U.S. or 624/146-5005; www.delta.com) has flights from Atlanta, Cincinnati, New York, and Salt Lake City; **Frontier** (© 800/432-1359 in the U.S. or 624/146-5421; www.frontierairlines.com) has nonstop service from Denver, and connecting flights through Kansas City, Los Angeles, Sacramento, and San José; **Mexicana** (© 800/531-7921 in the U.S., or 624/146-5002; www.mexicana.com) has direct or connecting flights from Guadalajara, Las Vegas, Los Angeles, Sacramento, and Mexico City; **United Airlines** (© 800/538-2929 in the U.S., or 624/146-5433; www.united.com) flies nonstop from Chicago, San Francisco, and Denver; **Aereo Calafia** (© 624/143-4302; www.Aereocalafia.com) offers regular flights within Baja as well as from Mazatlán and Puerto Vallarta.

By Car   From San Diego, drive south on Highway 1. Night driving is inadvisable, so the drive takes about 2½ days. From La Paz, take Highway 1 south; the drive takes 3 to 4 hours. Or take Highway 1 south just past the village of San Pedro, and then take Highway 19 south (a less winding road) through Todos Santos to Cabo San Lucas, where you pick up Highway 1 east to San José del Cabo. From Cabo San Lucas, it's a half-hour drive to San José.

By Bus   The **Terminal de Autobuses (bus station),** on Valerio Gonzalez, a block east of Highway 1 (© 624/143-7880), is open daily from 5:30am to 8pm.

Orientation

ARRIVING   Los Cabos International **Airport** (© 624/146-5111) serves both Cabos and the Corridor in between. San José is 13km (8 miles) from the airport and Cabo San Lucas is a 48km (30 miles) drive. As Los Cabos grows in popularity, the number of flights coming into the destination has increased steadily each year (in 2007, there were 2,901,200 passengers—up 6.6% from 2006), justifying continuous construction and two separate terminals. Be sure to request the correct terminal when you head home. Upon arriving, pass customs and baggage claim, and turn right once you exit the sliding doors. Ask for the shuttle desk while breezing past the timeshare booths that hawk free amenities in exchange for attending their sales pitch presentation. You'll have plenty of encounters with timeshare salespeople—especially in Cabo San Lucas—so feel free to head straight for a taxi or shuttle if you want to get to the beach in a hurry. At about $10 to $17 (£5–£8.50) per person, depending on the location of your hotel, shuttles are the most economic transportation option. **Josefinos** (© 624/146-5354) is located in the airport. A private van for up to five passengers is $70 (£35) and may be able to whisk away your large group more quickly than a

San José del Cabo

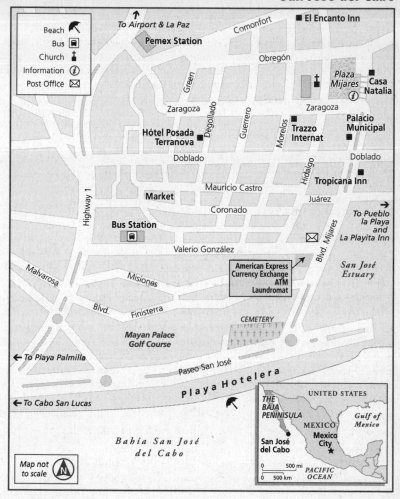

regular shuttle. Taxis charge about $20 to San José and upwards of $35 (£18) to San Lucas.

For those who like their freedom, it's helpful to have a car in Los Cabos, and rental is very affordable when booked online in advance. However, the major car-rental agencies all have counters at the airport, open during flight arrivals for last-minute booking. **Avis** (© **800/331-1212** in the U.S., or 624/146-0201; www.avis.com) is open daily 7am to 9pm; **Budget** (© **800/527-0700** in the U.S., 624/146-5333 at the airport, or 624/143-4190 in Cabo San Lucas; www.budget.com) is open daily 8am to 10pm; **Hertz** (© **800/654-3131** in the U.S., 624/146-1803 in San José del Cabo, or 624/105-1428 in Cabo San Lucas; www.hertz.com) is open daily 8am to 8pm; and

National (© **800/328-4567** in the U.S., 624/146-5022 at the airport, or 624/142-2424 in San José del Cabo; www.nationalcar.com) is open daily 8am to 8pm.

VISITOR INFORMATION San José's city tourist information office (©/fax **624/142-3310** or -9628) is in the old post office building on Zaragoza at Mijares. It offers maps, free local publications, and other basic information about the area. It's open Monday through Friday from 8:30am to 3pm. Prior to arrival, contact the **Los Cabos Tourism Board** (© **866/567-2226** in the U.S., or 624/143-4777; www.visitlos cabos.org).

CITY LAYOUT San José del Cabo sprawls from the airport halfway to San Lucas, but two main areas are most enticing to visitors: **downtown,** or *el centro,* has restaurants, shopping, sophisticated inns, and traditional budget hotels, while the **hotel zone** is lined with all-inclusive resorts along the beach. **Zaragoza** is the main street leading from the highway into town; **Paseo San José** runs parallel to the beach and is the principal boulevard of the hotel zone. The 1.6km-long (1 mile) **Bulevar Mijares** connects the two areas and is the center of most tourist activity in San José.

GETTING AROUND There is no local bus service between downtown and the beach, but it's about a 30-minute walk from the center of downtown to the sand, and **taxis** (© **624/142-0580**) connect the two for about $5 (£2.50) each way. For day trips to **Cabo San Lucas,** ask your concierge if your hotel has a daily shuttle or just catch a **bus** (see "Getting There & Departing," above) or a cab.

FAST FACTS: San José del Cabo

Area Code The local telephone area code is **624.**

Banks Banks exchange currency during business hours, which are generally Monday through Friday from 8:30am to 6pm, and Saturday from 10am to 2pm. There are several major banks with ATMs on Zaragoza between Morelos and Degollado and in the downtown.

Drugstores **Farmacía ISSSTE,** Carretera Transpeninsular Km 34, Plaza California, Loc. 7 (© **624/142-2645**), is open daily from 8am to 8pm.

Emergencies Dial © **066,** or the local police number at City Hall: © **624/142-0361.**

Hospital **Hospital General** is at Retorno Atunero s/n, Col. Chamizal (© **624/142-0013**).

Internet Access **Trazzo Internet,** on the corner of Zaragoza and Morelos, across from the cathedral downtown (© **624/142-0303;** fax 624/142-1220; www.trazzodigital.com) is open Monday through Friday 8am to 9pm, and Saturday from 9am to 7pm. They charge $2.50 (£1.25) for 30 minutes or less of high-speed Internet access. They also have printing, copy, and fax services available.

Post Office The *correo,* Bulevar Mijares 1924, at Valerio Gonzalez (© **624/142-0911**), is open Monday through Friday from 8am to 6pm, Saturday from 9am to noon. For more substantial mailings, Mail Boxes Etc., Plaza Las Palmas Km 31 (© **624/142-4355**), is open Monday through Friday from 8:30am to 5:30pm and Saturday from 9am to noon.

OUTDOOR ACTIVITIES: BEACHES, SPORTS & MORE

Although the water activities hub is on Cabo San Lucas's Medano Beach, San José is tops for outdoor adventure, and its relaxed pace also makes it an ideal place to unwind in the sand. From quiet coves to advanced surf breaks and untouched beaches to a living estuary, San José has relaxation and adventure by land and by sea.

ADVENTURE TOURS **Tío Sports** (© 624/143-3399; www.tiosports.com) arranges a variety of land- and water-based adventure and nature tours, including popular ATV tours to La Candelaria; parasailing; and kayak, catamaran, snorkeling, and diving trips. The website gives current prices. **Baja Wild** (© 624/172-6300; www.bajawild.com) is ideal for a wide range of adventure, as they offer every excursion imaginable in Los Cabos from rock climbing to kayaking, hiking to rappelling, and more. **Baja Outback** (© 624/142-9200; www.bajaoutback.com) provides single- and multiday adventure tours throughout Southern Baja. Armed with a naturalist guide and an expedition guide, who provide information and offer driving instruction over the two-way radios that connect each Hummer in the caravan, you take the wheel of your own H2 Hummer and discover mountain, desert, and sea.

BEACHES The best beach safe for swimming is **Palmilla Beach** ★★★, which fronts the glitzy One&Only Palmilla resort 8km (5 miles) west of San José. With its rocky coves, soft sand, and visible sea life, this beach has been home to fishermen for centuries and is the preeminent picnic destination for Mexican families on Sunday afternoons. Past the rock formations, the beach curves east and the culminating swim is well worth the pebble-strewn stroll. Locals agree there's just something about the water on the other side of the rocks. Perfect for swimming, the water in Palmilla Bay has a sort of magic unlike anywhere else and, when you emerge, you'll feel it for yourself. To reach Playa Palmilla, enter the lush Palmilla community at Km 27.5 on the highway, take the road toward the beach, and then take the fork to the left (without entering the hotel grounds) and park in the lot.

Estero San José, a natural freshwater estuary on which the ancient Pericúe Indians built their civilization centuries ago, has at least 270 species of birds and is on the east end of the hotel zone. The estuary is a protected ecological reserve and merits a sunset beach walk from the Hotel Presidente InterContinental to the river mouth where the spring-fed estuary meets the Sea of Cortez.

For a list of other beaches worth exploring if you have a rental car, see "Outdoor Activities: Fishing, Golf & More," under "Cabo San Lucas," later in this chapter.

FISHING The least expensive way to enjoy deep-sea fishing is to pair up with another angler and charter a *panga*, a 7m (23-ft.) skiff used by local fishermen, from

---

⌒Tips **Swimming Safety**

Although this area is ideal for watersports, occasional strong currents and undertows can make swimming dangerous at most **beaches in San José, the Tourist Corridor,** and **Cabo San Lucas.** Check conditions before entering the surf. Swimming is generally safe at **Palmilla Beach** (see "Beaches," above), though it, too, can be rough. The safest area beach for swimming is **Medano Beach** in Cabo San Lucas.

Pueblo la Playa, the beach near the new Puerto Los Cabos Marina. Several *panga* fleets offer 6-hour sportfishing trips, usually from 6am to noon, for $210 to $550 (£105—£225). Two or three people can split the cost. For information, visit the fishermen's cooperative in Pueblo la Playa (no phone) or contact **Gordo Banks Pangas** (© 624/142-1147; www.gordobanks.com). For larger charter boats, you'll depart from the marina in Cabo San Lucas (see "Outdoor Activities: Fishing, Golf & More," under "Cabo San Lucas," later in this chapter).

GOLF   Los Cabos has become Latin America's leading golf destination, with a collection of top signature courses and others under construction. The lowest greens fees in the area are at the 9-hole **Mayan Palace Golf Los Cabos,** Paseo Finisterra 1 (© 624/142-0900 or -0901), which is the first right turn east of the yellow Fonatur statue in the highway roundabout. See p. 722 for fees.

HORSEBACK RIDING   Horses can be rented near the Presidente InterContinental, Fiesta Inn, and in the Costa Azul Canyon for $20 to $25 (£10–£13) per hour. Most people choose to ride on the beach, but a trip up the arroyo also could prove scenic. For a more organized riding experience—English or Western—there's **Cuadra San Francisco Equestrian Center,** Km 19.5, along the Corridor, in front of the Casa del Mar resort (© 624/144-0160; www.loscaboshorses.com). Owned by master horseman Francisco Barrena, his more than 30 years of experience in training horses and operating equestrian schools will comfort any level rider, as will his expertise in selecting and fitting a horse to riders' skill levels. A 2-hour canyon ride in and around Arroyo San Carlos or Venado Blanco costs $85 (£43); a 1-hour ride to the beach or desert is $40 (£20). Private tours go for $55 (£28) per hour and equestrian aficionados may schedule a dressage class for $80 (£40).

SEA KAYAKING   Guided, ecology-minded **ocean kayak tours** are available through **Ramon's Ecotours** (© 624/122-3696; www.ramonsecotours.com), **Cabo Expeditions** (© 624/143-2700), and **Cabo Acuadeportes** (© 624/143-0117; www.allaboutcabo.com/cabosanlucaswatersports.htm). Most ocean kayaking tours depart from Cabo San Lucas, curve around the bay toward the Arch, and break for snorkeling at Lover's Beach.

SNORKELING & DIVING   **Manta** (© 624/144-3871; www.caboscuba.com) and **Amigos del Mar** in Cabo San Lucas (© 513/898-054 in the U.S., or 624/143-0505; www.amigosdelmar.com) are two of the most reputable dive operations in Los Cabos. Manta offers everything from advanced dive trips to PADI openwater diver certification. Prices start at $60 (£30) for a one-tank dive and at $170 (£85) for 2 days of diving. Night dives are $70 per person. The 4-day PADI certification course, which certifies you to scuba dive anywhere in the world, costs $450 (£225). Among the area's best dive sites are **Gordo Banks** and **Cabo Pulmo.** Gordo Banks is an advanced dive site where you can see whale sharks and hammerhead sharks. It's a deep dive—27 to 30m (90–98 ft.)—with limited visibility (9–12m/ 30–40 ft.). Most dives are drift dives, and wetsuits are highly recommended. Cabo Pulmo, a protected marine park 72km (45 miles) northeast of San José, has seven sites geared for divers of all experience levels, plus some of the most beautiful stretches of Baja beach, so it never feels crowded. **Cabo Pulmo Beach Resort** (© 562/141-0884 in the U.S., or 624/141-0884; www.cabopulmo.com) offers charming rental bungalows to call home in between dives or long walks on the beach.

SURFING 🏄🏄   Surfing is becoming one of the hottest trends in the entire destination, drawing land-locked Midwesterners and SoCal surf aficionados alike to the wide range of waves at Baja's tip. **Playa Costa Azul,** at Km 29, on Highway 1 just south of San José, has the most popular surfing beaches in the area. The **Costa Azul Surf Shop,** Km 28, Playa Costa Azul (© **624/142-2771;** www.costa-azul.com.mx), offers surfing lessons, surfboard and snorkeling equipment rentals, and specialized surf excursions to any of the 15 local breaks. Excursions include transportation and a DVD video of the day, and owner Alejandro Olea handcrafts all rental boards. Just $20 (£10) a day will get you a board, leash, shade umbrella, beach chair, and car rack. One-hour lessons are $55 (£28), and special packages are available. **Cabo Surf Hotel** (© **858/964-5117** in the U.S., or 624/142-2666; www.cabosurfhotel.com) offers surf lessons and daily board rentals for $37 (£19).

The surf switches sides with the seasons, so the waves break on the eastern side of the peninsula in the spring and summer (Mar–Oct) and the Pacific plays host to surfers in the fall and winter (Nov–Mar). The most popular summer breaks start at Acapulquito and extend up the East Cape, while the hot spot for winter waves is Los Cerritos Beach, south of Todos Santos. As every break has its secret—from rocks covered in sea urchins to territorial locals—your best bet is to hook up with a reputable surf shop or guide to take you to the break that's right for you.

TENNIS   Tennis is available at many resorts throughout Los Cabos, but if you're staying somewhere tennis isn't available, the two courts at the **Mayan Palace Resort Golf Los Cabos,** Paseo Finisterra 1 (© **624/142-0905**), rent for $14 (£7) an hour during the day, $22 (£11) an hour at night. Call the club to reserve. Club guests also can use the swimming pool.

WHALE-WATCHING   From January through March, migrating gray and humpback whales visit Los Cabos to breed and bear their calves, creating one of Baja's most impressive spectacles. Practically every local tour company advertises whale-watching tours that range from an hour to a half-day. Options include Zodiac-style rafts, sportfishing boats, glass-bottom boats, and cruise catamarans, all of which depart from the Cabo San Lucas Marina and cost $35 to $50 (£18–£25), depending on the type of boat and whether the trip includes snacks and beverages. The ultimate whale excursion is a trip to **Magdalena Bay. BookCabo.com** (© 624/142-9200; www. bookcabo.com) offers luxury bus tours from San José to San Carlos, where lobster dinners await in your 2-night stay at the quaint Alcatraz Hotel. The next morning entails cruising around the bay observing the whales and, hours later, lunching on Margarita Island. The cost is $289 per person (£145) based on double occupancy and $180 (£90) for kids 3 to 10 years old. Flying tours on Baja-based airline, **Aereo Calafia** (© 624/143-4302; www.Aereocalafia.com), fly from San Lucas—a 75-minute flight—to Magdalena, where you board a *panga* and spend 3 hours watching gray whales and humpbacks loll around the coastal lagoons before returning the same day. This tour is $420 (£210), including air transportation, the tour, and lunch. You also can spot whales from the shore in Los Cabos; good spots include the beach by the Westin Resort & Spa; at Esperanza Resort in the Punta Ballena community, and along the beaches and cliffs of the Corridor.

SHOPPING

San José is the capes' seat of artisan finery, design boutiques, and hip art galleries, clustered around **Bulevar Mijares** and **Zaragoza.** Start in the main plaza and head northwest toward the historic gallery district for a peek at the paintings and sculptures of Pez Gordo Gallery, the Fine Art Annex, Old Towne Gallery, and Galería de Ida Victoria. Head any other direction from the main plaza for crafts boutiques. The following businesses accept credit cards (American Express, MasterCard, and Visa).

Las Tiendas de Palmilla   The ultimate in luxury, style, and home design can be found in San José's opulent shopping center, located on the grounds of the One&Only Palmilla Resort. Among other shops, **Casa Vieja** sells fine linen dresses and Pineda Covalín silk scarves, **Cabana** sells chic women's clothing and resort wear, **Tiki Lounge** is the local Tommy Bahama outpost, **Q Boutique** houses Diamonds International's connoisseur collection, and the Guadalajara-headquartered **Antigua de México** sells furniture from the state of Jalisco. Store hours vary; most are open Monday to Friday 9am to 9pm. Km 27.5 Carretera Transpeninsular. www.lastiendasdepalmilla.com.

Mejicanissimo [em]This shop sells everything from locally made soaps and Damiana tea to embroidered linens and exquisite Emilia Castillo sterling-silver-embedded porcelain. The luminous owner, Magdalena del Río, supplies most of the area's luxury resorts with their fine Oaxacan embroidery, often used for tablecloths and throw pillows. Right across from the plaza, it can't be missed. Open Monday through Saturday from 10am to 9pm. Zaragoza, across from the cathedral. ✆ 624/142-3090.

Necri ✿   This shop sells the finest in Talavera ceramics and pewter accessories. Shipping is available. Open Monday through Saturday from 9am to 9pm. Zaragoza at Hidalgo, fronting the giant fig tree in the plaza. ✆ 624/142-2777.

SAX   For unusual and well-priced jewelry, visit this lovely shop where two local designers (who also happen to be sisters) create one-of-a-kind pieces using silver, coral, and semiprecious stones. They'll even create a special request design for you and have it ready in 24 hours. Open Monday through Saturday from 10am to 9pm, closed Sunday. On Mijares next to Casa Natalia. ✆ 624/142-6053; www.saxstyle.com.

WHERE TO STAY

There's more demand than supply in Baja Sur—especially during the idyllic winter months—so prices tend to be higher than those for equivalent accommodations in other parts of Mexico. It's best to call ahead for reservations. Properties in the beachside hotel zone often offer package deals that bring room rates down to the moderate range, especially during summer months. Check with your travel agent. High season generally denotes December through April and low season is from May through November. Rates listed below do not include tax, which is 15%, and most resorts in Los Cabos offer free parking—although that, too, is changing.

Expensive

Casa Natalia ✿✿✿ *(Finds)*   This acclaimed boutique hotel is exquisite. Owners Nathalie and Loic have transformed a former residence into a beautiful amalgam of palms, waterfalls, and flowers. The inn is a completely renovated historic home that combines modern architecture with traditional Mexican touches. All rooms have sliding glass doors that open onto small private terraces or balconies with hammocks and chairs, shaded by bougainvillea and bamboo. Rooms are equipped with CD and DVD players, along with a small collection of DVDs. The two spa suites each have a private terrace with a whirlpool and hammock. Tall California palms surround a small court-yard pool, and the terraces face onto it. Casa Natalia offers its guests privacy, style, and romance. It's in the heart of downtown San José, just off the central plaza. The excel-lent onsite restaurant, **Mi Cocina,** is reviewed in "Where to Dine," below.

Bulevar Mijares 4, 23400 San José del Cabo, B.C.S. © **888/277-3814** in the U.S., 866/826-1170 in Canada, or 624/142-5100. Fax 624/142-5110. www.casanatalia.com. 20 units. High season $320 (£160) double, $460 (£230) spa suite; low season $250 (£125) double, $395 (£198) spa suite. AE, MC, V. Children younger than 14 not accepted. Free parking. **Amenities:** Gourmet restaurant; bar; heated outdoor pool w/waterfall and swim-up bar; access and trans-portation to private beach club; concierge; room service; in-room spa services; laundry service. *In room:* A/C, TV/DVD, Wi-Fi, hair dryer, safe, fan.

Moderate

El Encanto Inn ⭑ *Value*   On a quiet street in the historic downtown district, this charming inn borders a grassy courtyard with a fountain and small pool. It's a relax-ing alternative to busy hotels and an excellent value. Rooms are decorated with rustic wood and contemporary iron furniture. Nice-size bathrooms have colorful tile accents. Rooms have two double beds, while suites have king-size beds and a sitting room. A pool area with a *palapa* bar and 14 impeccable poolside suites were recently added. These newer suites have minibars and other extras, while all rooms offer DirecTV satel-lite. The owners, Cliff and Blanca (a lifelong resident of San José), can arrange fishing packages and golf and diving outings. The inn is a half-block from the church.

Morelos 133 (between Obregón and Comonfort), 23400 San José del Cabo, B.C.S. © **210/858-6649** or 624/142-0388. www.elencantoinn.com. 26 units. $95 (£48) double; $114–$246 (£57–£123) suite. MC, V. Limited street parking available. **Amenities:** Restaurant, small outdoor pool; *palapa* bar; spa. *In room:* A/C, TV, coffeemaker, fan.

La Marina Inn   This impeccably clean and friendly courtyard hotel (formerly La Playita Hotel) is an ideal place for visitors looking for a little bit of "old" San Jose, as the new Puerto Los Cabos community and marina continue to grow and evolve around it. For now, it's the only hotel on the only beach in San José that's safe for swimming. Steps from the water and the lineup of fishing *pangas* on the new marina, the two stories of sunlit rooms frame a patio with a pool just large enough to allow you to swim laps. Each room is spacious, with high-quality basic furnishings, screened windows, a nicely tiled bathroom, and cable TV. Two large suites on the second floor have full kitchens. The inn's La Marina Café, open from 9am until 5pm, serves killer Bloody Marys for breakfast and their famous fish tacos all day.

Pueblo la Playa, Apdo. Postal 437, 23400 San José del Cabo, B.C.S. ©/fax **624/142-4166.** 27 units. $75 (£38) for a double and $145–$195 (£54–£87) suite. MC, V. Free parking. From Bulevar Mijares, follow sign pointing to Pueblo la Playa for about 3km (2 miles); hotel is on the left. **Amenities:** Restaurant; kayak rental, outdoor pool. *In room:* A/C, TV.

Tropicana Inn ⭑   This hacienda-style hotel, a longstanding favorite in San José, welcomes many repeat visitors. Just behind the Tropicana Bar and Grill, it frames a plant-filled courtyard with a graceful arcade bordering the rooms and inviting swimming pool. Each nicely furnished, medium-size room in the L-shaped building (which has a two- and a three-story wing) has tile floors, two double beds, a window looking out on the courtyard, and a brightly tiled bathroom with shower. Each morning, freshly brewed coffee, delicious sweet rolls, and fresh fruit are set out for hotel guests. There's room serv-ice until 10pm from the adjacent Tropicana Bar and Grill (owned by the hotel).

Bulevar Mijares 30 (1 block south of the town square), 23400 San José del Cabo, B.C.S. © **624/142-0907** or -1580. Fax 624/142-1590. 38 units. High season $90 (£45) double; low season 10% less. Rates include continental break-fast. AE, MC, V. Free limited parking. **Amenities:** Restaurant/bar; small outdoor pool; tour desk; room service; laundry service. *In room:* A/C, TV, minibar, coffeemaker.

Inexpensive

Hotel Posada Terranova   This small family-owned hotel is so famous for its traditional Mexican breakfasts and charming outdoor dining terrace that locals often forget it's even a hotel. While local Mexicans and expats love it for weekend brunch, the budget traveler will love it for its spare decor, clean rooms, soft sheets, ideal location in the center of downtown San José and, yes, for its huevos rancheros and fresh-squeezed OJ in the morning.

Degollado, between Doblado and Zaragoza, 23400 San José del Cabo, B.C.S. ℂ 624/142-0534. Fax 624/142-0902. www.hterranova.com.mx. 25 units. $70 (£35) single and double. Seasonal rates available. Rates include continental breakfast. MC, V. Free parking. **Amenities:** Restaurant, bar, room service. *In room:* A/C, satellite TV, fan, no phone.

WHERE TO DINE
Expensive

Baan Thai 👧👧 *Finds* PAN-ASIAN   Asian food is hard to come by in Los Cabos, and Baan Thai—set in one of San José's lovely historic buildings—does an impressive job of seasoning these flavors with a dash of Mexico. Move beyond traditional Asian starters, such as spring rolls or satay, to one of Baan Thai's more unique offerings, such as Thai pizza topped with curried lamb, or the coconut-crusted fish cakes. From there, move on to entrees such as wok-tossed lobster or freshwater crayfish brushed with a lime/soy marinade. An impressive wine list and full bar service are available to complement your meal. Dine outdoors on the exotic garden patio or take a seat in the air-conditioned indoor dining room.

Morelos s/n, 1 block behind the church and plaza. ℂ 624/142-3344. Reservations recommended. Main courses $10–$25 (£5–£13). MC, V. Mon–Sat noon–10:30pm.

Don Emiliano 👧👧👧 *Finds* MEXICAN   If years of queso dip and fried chimichangas have framed your vision of Mexican food, be prepared for your world to come crashing delightfully down. Sparkling seasonal menus, rooted in Mexican traditions such as Days of the Dead and Independence Day, include rare *mole* sauces and stuffed chiles drenched in walnut cream sauce and pomegranate seeds *(chile en nogada)*. On a regular basis, traditional staples such as flavored tamales and grilled farm cheese atop roasted tomatillo salsa grace the menu. The wine list is extensive, with both Mexican and imported wines, and fresh-mint mojitos are in ample supply, served by a warm staff. For nearly a decade, Chef Margarita C. de Salinas has been the official gala chef for the Mexican government, which means she travels the world preparing gourmet Mexican fare for heads of state, while her son, Angel, holds down the fort with such graciousness and culinary precision it must be a secret family recipe. Try the tasting menu or create your own, but whatever you do, don't miss the locally made *queso corazón* (a local cow's milk cheese) to start.

Bulevar Mijares 27, downtown San José. ℂ 624/142-0266. www.donemiliano.com.mx. Reservations recommended. Main courses $18–$25 (£9–£13). AE, MC, V. Daily 6–10pm.

Mi Cocina 👧👧👧 NOUVELLE MEXICAN/EURO   Widely appreciated as one of Los Cabos' finest restaurants, Mi Cocina doesn't rely solely on the romance of its setting—the food is superb, creative, and consistently flavorful. Notable starters include steamed baby clams topped with a creamy cilantro sauce and served with garlic croutons, or a healthy slice of Camembert cheese, fried and served with homemade toast and grapes. Among the favorite main courses are the baked baby rack of lamb served with grilled vegetables, and the Provençal-style shrimp served with risotto, roasted tomato, basil, and cilantro-fish consommé. Save room for dessert; choices include their famous chocolate-chocolate cake and a perfect crème brûlée. The full-service *palapa* bar offers an excellent selection of wines, premium tequilas, and single-malt scotches. Be adventurous and try one of their special martinis—like the Flor de México, an adaptation of the Cosmo, using Jamaica (hibiscus flower infusion) rather than cranberry juice.

In the Casa Natalia hotel, Bulevar Mijares. ℂ **624/142-5100**. www.casanatalia.com/dining.cfm. Reservations recommended. Main courses $18–$54 (£9–£27). AE, MC, V. Daily 6:30am–10pm (hotel guests only 6:30am–6pm).

Tequila Restaurant ⭑ MEDITERRANEAN/ASIAN   Contemporary fusion cuisine with a light and flavorful touch is the star attraction here, although the garden setting is lovely, with rustic *equipal* furniture and lanterns scattered among palms and mango trees. Organic produce and good greens are hard to find in these parts, so Tequila's homegrown produce, harvested from owner Enrique Silva's ranch, is a welcome dose of light-and-fresh fare, accompanying almost every entree. Try the shrimp risotto or beef tenderloin in rosemary-cabernet sauce. Other enjoyable options include perfectly seared tuna with cilantro and ginger and rack of lamb topped with tamarind sauce. The accompanying whole-grain bread arrives fresh and hot with a pesto-infused olive oil, and attentive service complements the fine meal. Cuban cigars and an excellent selection of tequilas are available, as is an extensive wine list emphasizing California vintages.

Manuel Doblado s/n, near Hidalgo. ℂ **624/142-1155** or -3753. www.tequilarestaurant.com. Reservations recommended. Main courses $10–$45 (£5–£23). AE. Daily 6–10:30pm.

Moderate

Zipper's ⭑⭑ MEXICAN/BEACHFRONT GRILL   If cheeseburgers in paradise is your mission, Zipper's is the real deal. Located along the Corridor near San José del Cabo, surfers downing icy Pacíficos and fresh shrimp ceviche merge with fishermen bolting Sauza and fried-fish tacos. However, the not-so-humble cheeseburger is the star of Zipper's gringo-fabulous menu. Service is slow, so pass the time watching pelicans swoop the swells, catching rays in board shorts and bikinis, and blissing out to the Jimmy Buffet–laced Radio Margaritaville, which is Zipper's 24/7 soundtrack. You won't find dance contests and Jet Ski vendors here; located beneath a beachfront *palapa* that faces a surf break of the same name, Zipper's is a stripped-down sensory experience that rivals even the swankiest Los Cabos restaurant—at a slightly lesser price tag.

Km 28.5 on Transpeninsular Highway, in Playa Costa Azul, just south of San José. ℂ **624/172-6162**. Cheeseburgers and sandwiches $8–$10 (£4–£5); main courses $13–$18 (£6.50–£9). No credit cards. Daily 11am–10:30pm.

Inexpensive

Las Guacamayas ⭑⭑⭑ *Finds* TACOS   This off-the-beaten-path dive is home to the most delectable tacos in all of Los Cabos. If you can get over the plastic chairs, occasional wandering roosters, and low-hanging fruit trees in the courtyard, which is packed nightly, you'll be mesmerized by this meticulously run hotspot for both gringos and Mexicans. Traditionalists wisely go for the *tacos al pastor*—shaved pork tacos with onion, cilantro, and pineapple in a corn or flour tortilla, but the *quesadillas chilangas*— crispy fried tortillas stuffed with an assortment of fillings—are a blissful indulgence.

Pace yourself. The addicting flavors and rock-bottom prices may inspire you to stay all night.

Driving east on Transpeninsular Hwy., turn left at the Pescador street sign. The street winds into the Chamizal neighborhood. Take your second left and look for the neon sign. Guacamayas is on the right-hand side. © 624/172-6162. Tacos, stuffed potatoes, and more $1.50–$7 (75p–£3.50). No credit cards. Weekdays 6pm–midnight; 'til 4am Fri–Sat. Closed on Tues.

SAN JOSE AFTER DARK

The nightlife in San José is a bit more understated than in San Lucas, but a new crop of swanky clubs, wine bars, and neighborhood hangouts is pumping electronic DJ music till 2 or 3am on the weekends, drawing locals and San José visitors alike. Those intent on bumping and grinding to American music will have better luck in San Lucas.

El Moro   In San José's gallery district in the old brick building formerly known as Rawhide, Pez Gordo Gallery owner, Dana Lieb, has opened this rustic bar for locals looking for a place to kick back and, well, drink. Obregón and Zaragoza. No phone.

El Spicy Coopers   The latest hip addition to the art district, with vintage posters of Maria Felix on the walls, this bohemian cantina serves spaghetti dinners and other Mediterranean-influenced dishes. The house band, Pulpos en su Tinta, plays everything from Rumba to Rock en Español. On Morelos across from Baan Thai, © 624/156-8717.

O2 Restaurant, Dance Club and Oxygen Bar   The one place to dance to American hip-hop in San José, this place is also the area's only public beach club. It's located right on the beach on the north side of the hotel zone. Take in some pure oxygen before heading home. On the beach in Plaza Los Soles, behind Mega supermarket. No phone.

Red ✪✪   A sleek martini bar facing the hotel zone, this San Lucas spin-off also offers light meals, awesome wood-fired pizza, and DJ music. Paseo San José, adjacent to the roundabout behind Mega supermarket. No phone.

Tommy's Barefoot Cantina   Next door to La Marina Inn, Tommy's offers a great mix of seafood and standard favorites, plus occasional live jazz or tropical music. It's open daily from noon to 11pm. On Pueblo La Playa, next door to La Marina Inn. No phone.

Tropicana   This bar features American sports events and live mariachi music nightly from 6 to 9pm, with live Mexican and Cuban dance music playing from 9:30pm until about 1am on weekends. Bulevar Mijares. © 624/142-1580.

THE CORRIDOR: BETWEEN THE TWO CABOS

The Corridor between the towns of San José del Cabo and Cabo San Lucas contains some of Mexico's most lavish resorts. Most growth at the tip of the peninsula is occurring along the Corridor, which already has become center stage for championship golf. The five major resort areas are **Palmilla, Querencia, Cabo Real, Cabo del Sol,** and **Punta Ballena** and each is an enclosed master-planned community sprinkled with multimillion-dollar homes (or the promise of them). All but Punta Ballena have championship golf and all but Querencia, which is a private residential community, have ultraluxury resorts within their gates. If you plan to explore the region while staying at a Corridor hotel, you'll need a rental car (available at the hotels) for at least 1 or 2 days. Even if you're not staying here, the beaches and dining options are worth investigating. All hotels listed here offer free parking and qualify as very expensive; quoted rates do not include tax, which is 12% in Baja, and some of the more luxurious resorts also add a 15% service charge to the tab to save guests from having to tip hotel staff. Most resorts offer golf and fishing packages.

WHERE TO STAY

Casa del Mar Beach Golf & Spa Resort ☆ *Finds*   A little-known treasure, this intimate resort is one of the best values along the Corridor and its 2006 renovation makes it even better. The hacienda-style building offers luxury accommodations in an intimate setting, as well as an on-site spa and nearby golf facilities. It's convenient to the 18-hole championship Cabo Real, a Robert Trent Jones, Jr., golf course. Guest rooms have a bright feel, with white marble floors, light wicker furnishings, a separate sitting area, and a large whirlpool tub plus separate shower. Balconies have oversize chairs with a view of the ocean beyond the pool. It's a romantic hotel for couples and honeymooners; it's known for welcoming, personalized service.

Km 19.5 on Hwy. 1, Cabo San Lucas, B.C.S. ℂ 888/227-9621 in the U.S., or 624/144-0030 or 145-7700. Fax 624/144-0034. www.casadelmarmexico.com. 56 units. High season $456 (£228) standard ocean view, $830 (£415) master ocean front suite; low season $377 (£189) standard ocean view, $736 (£368) ocean front suite. AE, MC, V. **Amenities:** Restaurant; lobby and pool bars; beach club (adults only) w/outdoor pool and hot tub; 6 other outdoor pools; privileges at Cabo Real golf club; 2 lighted tennis courts; small workout room; full-service spa; tour desk; room service; babysitting; laundry service; dry cleaning. *In room:* A/C, TV, minibar, hair dryer, safe, Jacuzzi.

Esperanza ☆☆☆   On a bluff overlooking two small, rocky coves, this new luxury resort along Cabo's Corridor amply compensates for the absence of a sandy beach with its pampering services and stylish details. Created by the famed Auberge Resorts group, the architecture of this hotel is dramatic, elegant, and comfortable. The casitas and villas spread across 7 hectares (17 acres), designed to resemble a Mexican village, and connect to the resort facilities by stone footpaths. The top-floor suites have handmade *palapa* ceilings and a private outdoor whirlpool spa. All rooms are exceptionally spacious, with woven wicker and tropical wood furnishings, original art, rugs and fabrics in muted colors with jewel-tone color accents. Frette linens grace the extra-comfortable feather beds. Terraces are large, extending the living area into the outdoors. All have hammocks and views of the Sea of Cortez. The oversize bathrooms have separate tubs and showers with dual showerheads.

Carretera Transpeninsular Km 7 on Hwy. 1, at Punta Ballena, Cabo San Lucas, B.C.S. ℂ 866/311-2226 in the U.S., or 624/145-6400. Fax 624/145-6499. www.esperanzaresort.com. 50 suites, 6 villas. High season $950–$1,525 (£475–£673) oceanview casita, $1,000–$1,875 (£500–£938) beachfront casita, $3,000–$7,000 (£1,500–£3,500) oceanfront suite; low season $400–$1,675 (£200–£838) oceanview casita, $475–$1,125 (£238–£563) beachfront casita, $2,500–$4,000 (£1,250–£2,000) oceanfront suite. AE, MC, V. **Amenities:** Oceanfront restaurant; sushi and ceviche bar; swimming pool; golf privileges; fitness center; full-service luxury spa; yoga studio with complimentary daily classes; art gallery; concierge; gourmet market; room service; babysitting; laundry service; dry cleaning; private beach w/club. *In room:* A/C, plasma TV w/DVD, Wi-Fi, hair dryer, safe, stereo, in-suite bar.

Las Ventanas al Paraíso ☆☆☆   Las Ventanas is known for its luxury accommodations and attention to detail. With adobe structures and rough-hewn wood accents, the architecture provides a soothing complement to the desert landscape. The only color comes from the dazzling *ventanas* (windows) of pebbled rainbow glass handmade by regional artisans. Richly furnished, Mediterranean-style rooms are large (starting at 300 sq. m/3,229 sq. ft.) and appointed with every conceivable amenity, from wood-burning fireplaces, iPods, and aromatherapy turn-down service to computerized

The Two Cabos & the Corridor

telescopes for star gazing or whale watching. Sizable whirlpool tubs overlook each room. Larger suites have extras such as rooftop terraces, sunken whirlpools on a private patio, or a personal pool. The surrounding condominiums are spacious with full kitchens, but the rooms and suites have better views. The spa is considered among the best in Mexico, with a focus on holistic healing and three new Spa Suites that cater to guests' individual goals, from beauty to weight loss. With a staff that outnumbers guests by four to one, this is the resort for those who can afford to be seriously spoiled. They even have rental Porsche Boxsters and special packages for pampered pets. The 15% service charge is not included in the prices below.

Km 19.5 on Hwy. 1, 23410 San José del Cabo, B.C.S. (C) **888/525-0483** or 888/767-3966 in the U.S., or 624/144-2800. Fax 624/144-2801. www.lasventanas.com. 61 suites. High season $725 (£363) garden-view double, $1,000 (£500) oceanview double, $1,150 (£575) split-level oceanview suite with rooftop terrace, $1,200 (£600) split-level oceanfront suite with rooftop terrace, $2,950–$5,900 (£1,475–£2,950) luxury suites (1–3 bedrooms); low season $500 (£250) gardenview double, $700 (£350) oceanview double, $875 (£438) split-level oceanview suite with rooftop terrace, $1000 (£500) split-level oceanfront suite with rooftop terrace, $2,100–$4400 (£1,050–£2,200) luxury suites. Spa Suites packages start at $6,220 (£3,110) for a 4-night program for 2. Spa and golf packages and inclusive meal plans available. AE, DC, MC, V. Free valet parking. **Amenities:** Infinity swimming pool; oceanview restaurant; terrace bar w/live music; seaside grill; fresh-juice bar; access to adjoining championship Cabo Real golf course; deluxe European spa w/complete treatment and exercise facilities; watersports; tour services; Porsche Boxster rental; shuttle services; room service; laundry service; sportfishing and luxury yachts; pet packages, including treats and massages. *In room:* A/C, TV/DVD, Wi-Fi, minibar, hair dryer, iron, safe, CD player.

One&Only Palmilla *(Overrated)*

The One&Only Palmilla is among the most spectacular resort hotels anywhere—certainly within Mexico. Decor features muted desert colors and luxury fabrics, with special extras such as flatscreen TVs with DVD/CD players, and Bose surround-sound systems. Guests receive twice-daily maid service, a personal butler, and an aromatherapy menu. Yet unless you're a Fortune 500 CEO or a Hollywood A-lister, staff mostly runs the gamut from indifferent to defiant. Nonetheless, Charlie Trotter's C restaurant offers impeccable 24-hour in-room dining. The guest-only spa and its 13 private treatment villas are reason enough to put up with the resort's too-cool attitude. The resort's own championship golf course, designed by Jack Nicklaus, is available for guests. The lush tropical resort also has two lighted tennis courts, a 600 sq. m (6,458-sq. ft.) fitness center, and a yoga garden.

Carretera Transpeninsular Km 7.5, 23400 San José del Cabo, B.C.S. (C) **866/829-2977** in the U.S., or 624/146-7000. Fax 624/146-7001. www.oneandonlypalmilla.com. 172 units. High season $650 (£325) double, $975–$2,600 (£488–£1,300) suite; low season $500 (£250) double, $775–$2,050 (£388–£1,025) suite. AE, MC, V. **Amenities:**

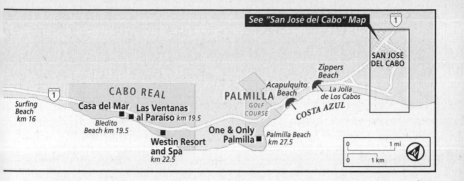

Map labels:

See "San José del Cabo" Map

SAN JOSÉ DEL CABO

Zippers Beach

Acapulquito Beach

PALMILLA
GOLF COURSE

La Jolla de Los Cabos

COSTA AZUL

CABO REAL

Casa del Mar   Las Ventanas al Paraíso km 19.5

Surfing Beach km 16

Bledito Beach km 19.5

One & Only Palmilla

Westin Resort and Spa km 22.5

Palmilla Beach km 27.5

0   1 mi
0   1 km

---

2 restaurants; 2 bars; pool bar; 2 infinity swimming pools; championship Palmilla golf course; deluxe European spa w/complete treatment and exercise facilities; watersports; tour services; car rental; room service; laundry service; dry cleaning; yoga garden; sportfishing. *In room:* A/C, TV/DVD, minibar, coffeemaker, hair dryer, iron, safe, CD player.

Westin Resort & Spa, Los Cabos *Kids*   The architecturally dramatic Westin sits at the end of a long paved road atop a seaside cliff. Vivid terra cotta yellow and pink walls rise against a landscape of sandstone, cacti, and palms, with fountains and gardens lining the long pathways from the lobby to the rooms. The rooms, all of which are ocean view, are sleek and spacious, with fluffy Heavenly Beds and walk-in showers separate from the bathtubs. The seaside 18-hole putting green, first-rate fitness facility, and freshly renovated La Cascada restaurant set this property apart from other Corridor resorts. Plus, it's one of the best options along the corridor for families; it is smoke-free and offers a wealth of activities for children—not to mention Heavenly Dog Beds for beloveds of the canine persuasion.

Hwy. 1 Km 22.5, San José del Cabo, B.C.S. © **800/228-3000** in the U.S., or 624/142-9000. Fax 624/142-9010. www. westin.com/loscabos. 243 units. High season $344 (£177) oceanview double; $750 (£375) suite; low season 25% discount. AE, DC, MC, V. **Amenities:** 6 restaurants; 2 bars; 3 outdoor pools; nearby Palmilla and Cabo Real golf courses; 18-hole putting course; 2 tennis courts; full fitness center and spa; children's activities; concierge; Xplora Adventours services; car rental; business services; salon; 24-hr. room service; babysitting; laundry service. *In room:* A/C, TV, high-speed Internet access, minibar, hair dryer, safe.

WHERE TO DINE

C *GOURMET*   Under the direction of renowned Chicago chef Charlie Trotter (this is his first restaurant outside the U.S.), a table for dinner at C is the most coveted reservation in Cabo. Baja's influence on Trotter's culinary innovation is obvious in the menu selections, which change daily but emphasize seafood and indigenous ingredients, although some meat and game are on the menu. To experience the best, order the signature *degustation* menu; each small dish is paired with an individual wine selection. The 110-seat dining room is L.A.-chic and gives no hint that you're in Mexico, despite the prevalent water theme and the series of blue cylindrical aquariums that separate the dining room from the exhibition kitchen. There are also two glass-enclosed wine rooms in the main dining area, and the overall atmosphere is bright and a bit loud. C also offers a 10-seat private dining room, and an invitation-only Chef's Kitchen Table, seating eight. Many consider a meal at C worth the trip to Cabo, and although the setting is visually stunning and the flavors superb, I found the service pretentious and the prices excessive—even for Cabo, which is saying a lot. Formal resort attire is requested, and reservations are an absolute must during high season.

One&Only Palmilla, Hwy. 1, Km 7.5. © 624/146-7000. www.oneandonlyresorts.com. Reservations required during high season. Main courses $45–$200 (£23–£100). AE, MC, V. Daily 5–11pm.

Nick-San ✹✹✹ JAPANESE/SUSHI   If you eat one meal out in Los Cabos, do it at Nick-San. No matter your fancy—raw, cooked, vegetarian, carnivorous, traditional, or out there—this dining experience is so superb, it may shift your world view. Owned by Masayuki Niikura, Angel Carbajal, and his sister, Carmen Carbajal, who started their sushi dynasty 12 years ago at the original Nick-San in downtown Cabo San Lucas, the newer and swankier outpost at Las Tiendas de Palmilla assures a taste of teppanyaki Nirvana on both ends of the Corridor. The fire of Mexico meets traditional Japanese ingredients in such delicacies as tuna tostada, locally caught sea bass sashimi, and lobster with curried cream sauce. The low-lit atmosphere suits an intimate occasion or a night out with friends, and the meticulous service is always warm and personal. Because the entire menu is too delectable to pick one thing, let someone else make the decision for you: Ask for the chef's tasting plate and, whatever you do, do not miss the lobster tempura roll or the salmon yuzu. Just be sure to let your server know when you've had enough or the plates will keep on coming. By the time the check rolls around, you'll be so enamored it won't even faze you.

Tiendas de Palmilla, Hwy. 1, Km 27.5 © 624/144-6262 or -6263. www.nicksan.com. Reservations required unless you care to sit at the bar. Sashimi, rolls, and main courses $15–$50 (£7.50–£25). AE, MC, V. Tues–Sun 12:30–10:30pm.

CABO SAN LUCAS

183km (114 miles) S of La Paz; 33km (21 miles) W of San José del Cabo; 1,792km (1,111 miles) SE of Tijuana

The hundreds of luxury hotel rooms along the Corridor north of Cabo San Lucas have transformed this formerly rustic and rowdy outpost. Although it retains boisterous nightlife, Cabo San Lucas is no longer the simple town Steinbeck wrote about. Once legendary for big-game fish, Cabo San Lucas now draws more people for its nearby world-class fairways and greens. This has become Mexico's most elite resort destination. Travelers enjoy a growing roster of adventure-oriented activities as well as sumptuous spa services, and the nightlife is as hot as the desert in July. A collection of popular restaurants and bars along Cabo's main street stay open and active until the morning's first fishing charters head out to sea. Despite the growth in diversions, Cabo remains more or less a one-stoplight town, with almost everything along the main strip.

ESSENTIALS

GETTING THERE & DEPARTING   By Plane   For information, see "Getting There & Departing," under San José del Cabo. Local airline numbers are: **Alaska Airlines** (© **624/146-5100** or -5101) and **Mexicana** (© **624/146-5002**).

By Car   From La Paz, the best route is **Highway 1** south past San Pedro, and then **Highway 19** south through Todos Santos to Cabo San Lucas, a 2-hour drive.

By Bus   The **bus terminal** (© **624/143-5020**) is on Héroes at Morelos; it is open daily from 7am to 10pm. Buses go to La Paz every 2 hours starting at 7:15am, with the last departure at 8:15pm. To and from San José, the more convenient and economical **Suburcabos** public bus service runs every 15 minutes and costs $2.50.

Arriving   At the airport, either buy a ticket for a *colectivo* (shuttle) from **Josefinos** (© **624/146-5354**), the authorized transportation booth inside the building (about

Cabo San Lucas

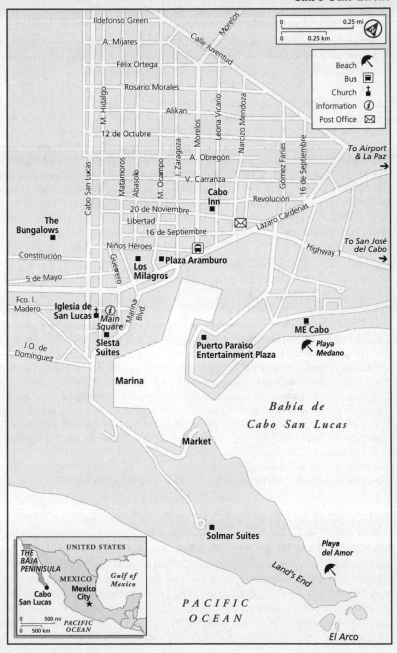

Ildefonso Green
A. Mijares
Félix Ortega
Rosario Morales
Alikan
12 de Octubre

Calle Juventud
Morelos

M. Hidalgo
Cabo San Lucas
Matamoros
Abasolo
M. Ocampo
I. Zaragoza
Morelos
Leona Vicario
Narciso Mendoza

A. Obregón
V. Carranza
Cabo
Inn
20 de Noviembre
Libertad
16 de Septiembre

Gómez Farías
16 de Septiembre
Revolución
Lázaro Cárdenas

To Airport
& La Paz →

To San José
del Cabo →

Highway 1

The
Bungalows
Constitución
5 de Mayo
Fco. I.
Madero
J.O. de
Domínguez

Guerrero
Niños Héroes
Los
Milagros
Plaza Aramburo

Iglesia de
San Lucas
Main
Square
Siesta
Suites

Marina
Blvd.

Puerto Paraiso
Entertainment Plaza

ME Cabo
Playa
Medano

Marina

Market

Bahía de
Cabo San Lucas

Solmar Suites

Playa
del Amor

Land's End

PACIFIC
OCEAN

El Arco

Beach
Bus
Church
Information
Post Office

0   0.25 mi
0   0.25 km

Inset map

THE
BAJA
PENINSULA
UNITED STATES
MEXICO
Cabo
San Lucas
Mexico
City
Gulf of
Mexico
PACIFIC
OCEAN
0   500 mi
0   500 km

> ## ⎛Tips⎞ Information, Please
>
> The many "visitor information" booths along the street in Cabo are actually timeshare sales booths, and their staffs will pitch a visit to their resort in exchange for discounted tours, rental cars, or other giveaways.

$13/£6.50), or arrange for a rental car, the most economical way to explore the area. Up to four people can share a private taxi, which costs about $60 (£30).

VISITOR INFORMATION   The **Los Cabos Tourism Office** (© **624/146-9628**) is in San José, in the Plaza San José, Locs. 3 and 4, and is open daily from 8am to 3pm. The English-language *Los Cabos Guide, Los Cabos News, Destino Los Cabos* and the irreverent and extremely entertaining *Gringo Gazette* are distributed free at most hotels and shops and have up-to-date information on new restaurants and clubs. If you fall so deeply in love with Los Cabos as to want to own a piece of it, the *Baja Real Estate Guide* is a great place to start (www.tregintl.com).

CITY LAYOUT   The small town spreads out north and west of the harbor of **Cabo San Lucas Bay,** edged by foothills and desert mountains to the west and south. The main street leading into town from the airport and San José del Cabo is **Lázaro Cárdenas;** as it nears the harbor, **Bulevar Marina** branches off from it and becomes the main artery that curves around the waterfront.

GETTING AROUND   Taxis are easy to find but expensive, in keeping with the high cost of everything else. Expect to pay about $15 to $25 (£7.50–£13) for a taxi between Cabo and the Corridor hotels.

For day trips to San José del Cabo, take the Suburcabos (see "Getting There & Departing," above) or a cab. You'll see car-rental specials advertised in town, but before signing on, be sure you understand the total price after insurance and taxes are added. Rates can run between $50 and $75 (£25–£38) per day, with insurance an extra $10 (£5) per day. One of the best and most economical agencies is **Advantage Rent-A-Car** (© **624/143-0909;** ©/fax 624/143-0466), on Lázaro Cárdenas between Leona Vicario and Morelos. VW sedans rent for $80 (£40) per day, and weekly renters receive 1 free day. A collision damage waiver will add $22 (£11) per day to the price. If you pick up the car downtown, you can return it to the airport at no extra charge.

FAST FACTS: Cabo San Lucas

Area Code   The telephone area code is **624.**

Beach Safety   Before swimming in the open water, *check if conditions are safe.* Undertows and large waves are common. **Medano Beach,** close to the marina and town, is the principal beach that's safe for swimming. The ME Cabo resort on Medano Beach has a roped-off swimming area to protect swimmers from personal watercraft and boats. Colored flags to signal swimming safety aren't generally found in Cabo, and neither are lifeguards, so be aware.

Currency Exchange   Banks exchange currency during normal business hours, generally Monday through Friday from 9am to 6pm, Saturday from 10am to

2pm. Currency-exchange booths, throughout Cabo's main tourist areas, aren't as competitive, but they're more convenient. ATMs are widely available and even more convenient, dispensing pesos—and, in some cases, dollars—at bank exchange rates.

Drugstore **Farmacía Aramburo,** in Plaza Aramburo, on Lázaro Cárdenas at Zaragoza (© **624/143-1489**) stocks a wide selection of toiletries and medicine. It's open daily from 8am to 10pm and accepts MasterCard and Visa.

Emergencies & Hospital In Cabo, **Amerimed** (© **624/143-9671**) is a 24-hour, American-standards clinic with bilingual physicians, emergency air evacuation services, and accepts major credit cards. Most of the larger hotels have a doctor on call.

Internet Access **Cabo Mail** (© **624/143-7796**), Plaza Aramburo on Lázaro Cárdenas, charges $1 (50p) for 1 to 10 minutes, and 10¢ (5p) for each additional minute. They also offer long-distance VOIP access, fax, copies, memory-stick photo downloads, color printing, and CD/DVD recording. It's open Monday through Friday from 9am to 9pm, Saturday from 9:30am to 6pm, and Sundays from noon to 6pm.

Post Office The *correo* is at Lázaro Cárdenas between Medano and Gomez Farías (© **624/143-0048**), on the highway to San José del Cabo, east of the bar El Squid Roe. It's open Monday through Friday from 9am to 5pm, Saturday from 9am to 3pm.

OUTDOOR ACTIVITIES: FISHING, GOLF & MORE

Although superb sportfishing put Cabo San Lucas on the map, there's more to do than drop your line and wait for the Big One. For most cruises and excursions, try to make fishing reservations at least a day in advance; keep in mind that some trips require a minimum number of people. Most sports and outings can be arranged through a travel agency; fishing can also be arranged directly at one of the fishing-fleet offices at the marina. The marina is on the south side of the harbor.

Besides fishing, there are kayak trips ($65/£33 for a sunset trip around the Arch rock formation; $40/£20 for morning trips) and boat trips to Los Arcos or uninhabited beaches. All-inclusive daytime or sunset cruises are available on a variety of boats, including a restored pirate ship. Many of these trips include snorkeling; and serious divers have great underwater venues to explore.

Between January and March, whale-watching is extremely popular. Guided ATV tours take you down dirt roads and canyons to an ancient Indian village. And then there's the challenge of world-class golf, a major attraction of Los Cabos.

For a complete rundown of what's available, look to **Book Cabo** (© **624/142-9200;** www.bookcabo.com). It offers tours from the best local companies and you can book ahead online. Most businesses in this section are open daily from 10am to 2pm and 4 to 7pm.

BEACHES   All along the curving sweep of sand known as Medano Beach, on the east side of the bay, you can rent snorkeling gear, boats, Wave Runners, kayaks, and sailboards. You can also take windsurfing lessons. This is the town's main beach and is a great place for safe swimming, happy-hour imbibing, and people-watching from one of the many outdoor restaurants along its shore.

Beach aficionados may want to rent a car (see "Getting Around," above) and explore the five more remote beaches and coves between the two Cabos: Playa Palmilla, Chileno, Santa María, Barco Varado, and Lover's Beach. Beaches other than Medano are not considered safe for swimming, although many people don't heed the warning. Experienced snorkelers may wish to check them out, but other visitors should go for the view only. Always check at a hotel or travel agency for directions and swimming conditions. Although a few travel agencies run snorkeling tours to some of these beaches, there's no public transportation: Your options for beach exploring are to rent a car or have a cab drop you off at the beach of your choice.

ATV TRIPS   Expeditions on ATVs to visit La Candelaria, an Indian pueblo in the mountains, are available through travel agencies. A 440-pound weight limit per two-person vehicle applies. Most guided tours cost around $45 (£23) per person on a single vehicle, or $60 (£30) for two riding on one ATV. The vehicles are also available for rent ($35/£18 for 3 hr.).

Tío Sports (© **624/143-3399;** www.tiosports.com) offers day trips to La Candelaria, an isolated Indian village in the mountains 40km (25 miles) north of Cabo San Lucas. Described in *National Geographic,* the old pueblo is known for the practice of white and black witchcraft, but the locals chuckle at the mention of *brujería.* Lush with palms, mango trees, and bamboo, the settlement gets its water from an underground river that emerges at the pueblo. The return trip of the tour travels down a steep canyon, along a beach (giving you time to swim), and through town. Departing at 9am, the 5-hour La Candelaria tour costs around $80 (£40) per person or $100 (£50) for two on the same ATV.

CRUISES   Glass-bottom boats leave from the town marina daily every 45 minutes between 9am and 4pm. They cost about $14 (£7) for a 1-hour tour, which passes sea lions and pelicans on its way to the famous **El Arco (the Arch)** at Land's End, where the Pacific and the Sea of Cortez meet. Boats drop you off at Playa de Amor; make sure you confirm with your driver which boat will pick you up—it's usually a smaller one run by the same company that ferries people back at regular intervals—and when. Check the timing to make sure you have the correct boat, or expect an additional $10 (£5) charge for boarding the boat of an eager competitor.

A number of **daylong** and **sunset cruises** come in a variety of boats and catamarans. They cost $30 to $50 (£15–£25) per person, depending on the boat, duration of cruise, and amenities. A sunset cruise on the 13m (43-ft.) catamaran *Pez Gato* (© **624/143-3797;** www.pezgatocabo.com) departs from the Tesoro Resort dock (Dock #4, 50m/164 ft. from the main dock) between 4:30 and 5:30pm, depending on the season. A 2-hour cruise costs $35 (£18) and includes an open bar and appetizers. The seasonal (winter) whale-watching tour leaves at 10:30am and returns at 1:30pm. It costs $35 (£18) and includes open bar and snacks. Similar boats leave from the marina and the Tesoro Resort. Check with travel agencies or hotel tour desks.

DRIVING TOURS   A uniquely "Cabo" experience is offered by **Baja Outback** (© **624/142-9215;** fax 624/142-3166; www.bajaoutback.com) via their caravan-style Hummer Adventures. You drive these luxury Hummer H2s, along a dusty trail paved by local ranchers to cruise desert and beachfront terrain in style, while learning about the surrounding area through expert guides. Communication links as many as 10 vehicles in the caravan, allowing you to listen to the narrations of the guide. There's a choice of four routes, which include treks to Todos Santos, the East Cape, Santiago and Cañón de la Zorra, and Rancho la Verdad. Tours depart at 9am and return at 3pm, with prices ranging from $165 to $220 (£83–£110), depending upon the route, and include lunch. Visa, MasterCard, and American Express are accepted, and you must have your valid driver's license. Special group rates are also available.

If this sounds too tame, **Wide Open Baja Racing Experience** (© 866/734-9651 in the U.S., or 624/143-4170; office in Plaza Nautica; www.wideopenbaja.com) gives you the chance to drive actual Chenowth Magnum racecars at Wide Open's 600-hectare (1,482-acre) racing ranch on the Pacific Coast. There's varied terrain to drive, with twists, turns, sand washes, and plenty of bumps for thrill seekers. Session times for the **Test Drive** are at 10am and 1:30pm. The price of $250 (£125) includes shuttle transportation from downtown Cabo to the ranch, driver orientation, and safety equipment. Private group rates are also available. Wide Open Baja also offers multiday tours driving race vehicles through Cabo, Ensenada, and the entire Baja peninsula.

GOLF Los Cabos has become the golf capital of Mexico, and although most courses are along the Corridor, people look to Cabo San Lucas for information about this sport in Baja Sur. The master plan for Los Cabos golf calls for a future total of 207 holes. Fees listed below are for 18 holes, including golf cart, water, club service, and tax. Summer rates are about 25% lower, and many hotels offer golf packages.

Specialty tour operators **Golf Adventures** (© 800/841-6570 in the U.S.; www.golfadventures.com) offers golf packages to Los Cabos, which includes accommodations, greens fees, and other amenities.

The 27-hole course at the **Palmilla Golf Club** (© 800/386-2465 in the U.S., or 624/144-5250; www.oneandonlyresorts.com; daily 7am–7pm) was Mexico's first Jack Nicklaus Signature layout, on 360 hectares (900 acres) of dramatic oceanfront desert. The course offers your choice of two back-9 options, with high-season greens fees of $265 (£133), lower after 1pm, and low-season greens fees running between $190 and $210 (£95–£105). Guests at some hotels pay discounted rates.

Just a few kilometers away is another Jack Nicklaus Signature course, the 18-hole Ocean Course at **Cabo del Sol,** the posh resort development in the Corridor (© 866/231-4677 in the U.S:, or 624/145-8200; www.cabodelsol.com). The 7,100-yard Ocean Course is known for its challenging 3 finishing holes, and greens fees start at $250 (£125) in the low season and range to $350 (£175) for the high season. Tom Weiskopf designed the new 18-hole Desert Course, for which greens fees are $220 (£110) in high season, $185 (£93) in low season. Desert Course twilight play ranges from $120 to $165 (£60–£83) in low and high seasons, respectively.

The 18-hole, 6,945-yard course at **Cabo Real,** by the Meliá Cabo Real Hotel in the Corridor (© 877/795-8727 in the U.S., or 624/144-1200; www.caboreal.com; daily 6:30am–6pm), was designed by Robert Trent Jones, Jr., and features holes that sit high on mesas overlooking the Sea of Cortez. Fees run $280 (£140) for 18 holes. After 3pm, rates drop to $140 (£70) in the low season and $180 (£90) in the high season. Kids 16 and younger than play for $92 (£46) year round.

An 18-hole course designed by Roy Dye is at the **Cabo San Lucas Country Club,** formerly the Raven Club (© 888/328-8501 in the U.S., or 624/143-4653; fax 624/143-5809). The entire Dye-design course overlooks the juncture of the Pacific Ocean and Sea of Cortez, including the famous rocks of Land's End. It includes a 607-yard, par-5 7th hole. High season greens fees are $186 (£93) for 18 holes, $149 (£75) for the noon rate, and $105 (£53) after 2:30pm. In summer, greens fees drop to $109 (£55) for 18 holes and $79 (£40) after 10:30am.

The lowest greens fees in the area are at the public 9-hole **Mayan Palace Golf Los Cabos** (© 624/142-0900 or -0901) in San José del Cabo (see earlier in this chapter). Greens fees are just $99 (£50) for 18 holes with equipment; rates drop to $69 (£35) for 18 holes after 3pm. All greens fees include the use of a cart.

HORSEBACK RIDING   You can rent **horses** through **Rancho Colín** (© 624/143-3652) for $30 (£14) per hour; the 2-hour desert-and-beach trail ride is $60 (£30); and the 3½-hour tour through the mountains is $80 (£40). If you're interested in a sunset ride with a view of the Sea of Cortez, be sure to call ahead to make sure you book the right time. The ranch is open daily from 8am to noon and 2 to 5pm and is across from the Hotel Club Las Cascadas. For information on the highly recommended **Cuadra San Francisco Equestrian Center,** see p. 706.

SNORKELING & DIVING   Several companies offer snorkeling; a 2-hour cruise to sites around El Arco is $30 (£15), and a 4-hour trip to Santa María is $55 (£30), including gear. Among the beaches visited on different trips are Playa de Amor, Santa María, Chileno, and Barco Varado. Snorkeling gear rents for $10 to $15 (£5–£8.50). Contact **Book Cabo** (© 624/142-9200; www.bookcabo.com). For scuba diving, contact **Manta Diving** (© 624/144-3871; www.caboscuba.com) and **Amigos del Mar** in Cabo San Lucas (© 800/344-3349 in the U.S., or 624/143-0505; www.amigosdelmar.com). Dives are along the wall of a canyon in San Lucas Bay, where you can see the cascading sand falls by Anegada Rock. There are also scuba trips to Santa María Beach and more distant places, including Gordo Banks and Cabo Pulmo. Prices start at $60 (£30) for a one-tank dive and from $170 (£85) for 2 days of diving. Night dives are $70 (£35) per person. Trips to the coral outcropping at Cabo Pulmo start at $130 (£65). You'll need a wet suit for winter dives. A 5-hour resort course is available for $115, and open-water certification is $4,500 (£2,250).

SPORTFISHING   To make your own arrangements, go to the marina on the south side of the harbor, where you'll find several fleet operators with offices near the docks. *Panga* fleets offer the best deals; 5 hours of fishing for two or three people costs $200 to $450 (£100–£225), plus a 20% tip. But stroll around the marina and talk with the captains—you might be able to negotiate a better deal. Try **Pisces Fleet,** located in the Cabo Maritime Center, behind Tesoro Resort and next to Captain Tony's on the marina (© 619/819-7983 from the U.S. or 624/143-1288; www.piscessportfishing. com; daily 10am–4pm; Visa and MasterCard accepted), or **Minerva's** (© 624/143-1282; www.minervas.com; daily 6am–8pm; American Express, MasterCard, and Visa accepted), on the corner of Bulevar Marina and Madero. A day on a fully equipped cruiser with captain and guide starts at around $800 (£400) for up to six people. For deluxe trips with everything included aboard a 12m (40-ft.) boat, you'll have to budget around $1,500 (£750) and up. If you're traveling in your own vessel, you'll need a fishing permit, which you can get at Minerva's Baja Tackle. Depending on the size of the boat, it will cost $36 to $109 (£18–£55) per month. Daily permits for individuals ($12/£6) and weekly and monthly permits are also available.

The fishing here lives up to its reputation: Bringing in a 100-pound marlin is routine, although decades of pressure on Sea of Cortez fisheries should inspire you to release your prized catch. Angling is good all year, though the catch varies with the season. Sailfish and wahoo are best from June through November; yellowfin tuna, May through December; yellowtail, January through April; black and blue marlin, July through December. Striped marlin and dorado, or mahimahi, are prevalent year-round.

SURFING   Stellar surfing can be found from November through April all along the Pacific beaches north and west of town, and the East Cape is the ultimate North American surfing destination from May through October. (Also see "Surfing" in "San José del Cabo," earlier in this chapter, for details on Costa Azul and East Cape breaks.)

Surf & Sleep

If you can't get enough of the surf, stay where wave-riding is the specialty and not just another activity. The Los Cabos area has two outposts that cater to surfers, one along Los Cabos Corridor and the other on the Pacific coast, near Todos Santos.

The **Cabo Surf Hotel** (© **858/964-5146** from the U.S., or 624/142-2666; www.cabosurfhotel.com) has 16 beachfront rooms in a secluded, gated boutique resort. It's 13km (8 miles) west of San José del Cabo, across from the Querencia golf course, on Playa Acapulquito, which is the most popular surfing beach in Los Cabos. Along with a choice of rooms and suites, it's equipped with an oceanfront terrace restaurant, surf shop, and the Mike Doyle Surf School, which offers day lessons and more intensive instruction. Rates range from $265 to $375 (£133–£188) for a double and $290 to $850 (£145–£425) for suites and villas. Promotional rates are available during summer months, which is optimum for surfers who seek the Sea of Cortez's summertime swells.

The **Pescadero Surf Camp** (© **612/130-3022** or 134-0480; www.pescadero surf.com) is a sparse Pacific getaway at Km 64 on Highway 1 toward Todos Santos. Eight poolfront casitas, each equipped with a minifridge, start at $30 (£15), and the two-story suite rents for $60 (£30) a night. Although it's a kilometer (half-mile) from the beach, this surf camp is a comfortable step up from the beach camping that's a way of life for most surf mongers and, in the winter, when the waves—and sometimes winds—are at their strongest, it's nice to have a roof overhead. The property's brand new pool has a BYOB swim-up bar that's ideal for cooling off between surf excursions, and a large outdoor kitchen provides a space to prepare your own meals. Owner Jaime Dobies also offers 1½-hour lessons for $50 (£25), board rental for $20 (£10) a day, boogie and skim board rental for $10 (£5) a day, and day-long guided surf safaris starting at $100 (£50) per person. He also repairs boards, should your baby get dinged in action.

Of course, if you're coming to Baja strictly for the surf, you may join the other hard-core wave-riders and camp along the sugary beaches of the East Cape in the summer and the Pacific in the winter. Most beaches—especially the ones fronting secluded surf breaks—are safe and accommodating for overnight stays.

The areas to the east and west of Los Cabos, known as the East Cape and the Pacific side, respectively, have yet to face the onslaught of development that's so rapidly changed the tip. An hour-long drive up the western coast to the little towns of Pescadero and Todos Santos can be a great surf journey, as can a summer trek up the Sea of Cortez coastline toward Cabo Pulmo. Your best bet is to visit **www.costa-azul. com.mx/area-maps.htm** for a detailed look at the different breaks, excursions, rental equipment, and lessons available.

Many beach breaks are ride-worthy at different times, depending on the wave conditions, but a vicious shore break and strong undertow characterize much of the beach around Todos Santos. The ocean's unruliness has helped keep industrial tourism at bay, but it also means you have to hunt a little harder to find playful waves.

WHALE-WATCHING   Whale-watching cruises are the best way to get up close and personal with nature's most majestic seafaring mammals. See "Whale-Watching in Baja," p. 748, for information on the excursions, which operate between January and March.

A BREAK FROM SPORTS: EXPLORING CABO SAN LUCAS

FESTIVALS & EVENTS   **October 12** is the festival of the patron saint of Todos Santos, a town about 105km (65 miles) north. **October 18** is the feast of the patron saint of Cabo San Lucas, celebrated with a fair, feasting, music, dancing, and other special events.

HISTORIC CABO SAN LUCAS   Watersports and outright partying are Cabo's main attractions, but there are also a few cultural and historical points of interest. The Spanish missionary Nicolás Tamaral established the **Iglesia de San Lucas (Church of San Lucas)** on Calle Cabo San Lucas, close to the main plaza, in 1730. A large bell in a stone archway commemorates the completion of the church in 1746. The Pericúe Indians, who resisted Tamaral's demands that, among other things, they practice monogamy, eventually killed him in a violent uprising. Buildings on the streets facing the main plaza are gradually being renovated to house restaurants and shops, and the picturesque block has the most Mexican ambience in town.

DAY TRIPS   Most local and hotel travel agencies book day trips to the city of **La Paz;** they cost around $60 (£30), including beverages and a tour of the countryside along the way. Usually there's a stop at the weaving shop of Fortunato Silva, who spins his own cotton and weaves it into wonderfully textured rugs and textiles. Day trips are also available to **Todos Santos** ($60/£30), with a guided walking tour of the mission, museum, Hotel California, and various artists' homes. (For more information, see "La Paz: Peaceful Port Town" and "Todos Santos: A Creative Oasis," later in this chapter.)

SHOPPING

San José has the better shopping of the two towns, when it comes to quality and uniqueness, but if you're after a beer-themed T-shirt, Cabo San Lucas can't be topped. Nevertheless, the **Puerto Paraíso Entertainment Plaza** (© **624/144-3000;** www. puertoparaiso.com) does have a selection of designer clothing stores, knickknack shops, and swimwear boutiques. Opened in 2002, this is now the focal point for locals' entertainment and tourists' exploration. It's a truly world-class mall, complete with free parking, movie theaters, a video arcade, a food court, and various restaurants, not the least of which is **Ruth's Chris Steak House,** adjacent to the marina (© **624/ 144-3232;** www.ruthschris.com.mx; daily 1–11:30pm). With more than 50,000 sq. m

(538,195 sq. ft.) of air-conditioned space on three levels, it's a shame so much of the mall is still empty. Rumor has it that developers are taking their time to rent the spaces, so don't expect the equivalent of a U.S. shopping mall experience for a few years. The plaza is located marina-side, between the Plaza Bonita Mall and Marina Fiesta Resort—you can't miss it if you try. Most other shops in Cabo are on or within a block or two of Boulevard Marina and the plaza.

In addition to the mall, I recommend the following specialty stores.

Baja Body Deli   This is a true gem of a spa boutique. Fragrant candles, Baja-grown loose teas and dried herbs, handmade cut-to-order soaps, luxury bathrobes, and other pampering products make this a stylish oasis in a sea of commercial shops. They specialize in custom-scented body lotion, hair care, massage oil, sprays, and scrubs. Open Monday through Saturday 10am to 7:30pm. Matamoros, near corner of Lázaro Cardenas. © 624/122-3272.

El Callejón   This has San Lucas's best selection of fine Mexican furniture and decor items, plus gifts, accessories, tableware, fabrics, and lamps. Open Monday through Friday 10am to 7pm and 10am to 5pm on Saturdays. Hidalgo, between Madero and Cardenas. © 624/143-3188.

J & J Habanos   J & J is Cabo's largest cigar shop, selling premium Cuban and fine Mexican cigars—it even has a walk-in humidor. They also sell fine tequila and espresso. Open Monday through Saturday 9am to 10pm, Sunday 9am to 9pm. Madero between Bulevar Marina and Guerrero. © 624/143-6160 or -3839.

Ultrafemme   Mexico's largest duty-free shop has an excellent selection of fine jewelry and watches, including Rolex, Cartier, Omega, TAG Heuer, Tiffany, and Tissot; perfumes, including Lancôme, Chanel, Armani, Carolina Herrera; and other gift items, all at duty-free prices. Open daily 10am to 9:30pm. Plaza UltraFemme, Bulevar Marina. © 624/145-6090.

WHERE TO STAY

High-season prices are in effect from December to Easter. Several hotels offer package deals that significantly lower the nightly rate; ask your travel agent for information. Budget accommodations are scarce, but the number of small inns and B&Bs is growing; several notable ones have opened in recent years. Because most of the larger hotels are well maintained and offer packages through travel agents, I will focus on smaller, unique accommodations.

Expensive

ME Cabo   If you've come to Cabo to party, this is your place. Formerly the Meliá San Lucas, the newly renovated ME Cabo is Sol Meliá's foray into hip, making it Cabo's hottest hotspot. Upgraded rooms, a new adult-focused floor called "The Level," and the addition of the swank Nikki Beach stake a glam claim on this beachfront property, which is geared toward those who'd rather party than relax. Its location on Medano Beach is central to any other action you may want to seek but, with Nikki Beach and Passion, you'll find plenty right here. Rooms are awash in fiery red and white, with a sleek, contemporary decor. All suites have ocean views and private terraces looking across to the famed El Arco. Master suites have a separate living room area. Guests gather by the beachfront pool, where oversized daybeds perfectly accommodate this lounge atmosphere. There are also VIP tepees, and the live-DJ music keeps the party here going day and night.

Playa El Medano s/n; 23410 Cabo San Lucas, B.C.S. ℂ **624/145-7800.** Fax 624/143-0420. www.mecabo.travel. 150 units. High season $356–$540 (£178–£270) double, $1,100 (£550) chic suite, $2,100 (£1,050 loft suite; low season $269–$441 (£135–£221) double, $756 (£378) chic suite, $1,100 (£550) loft suite. AE, MC, V. Free parking. **Amenities:** Restaurant; bar/dance club; 2 outdoor pools; beach club; Jacuzzi; concierge; boutique; tour desk; car rental; room service; laundry service; dry cleaning. *In room:* A/C, TV, Wi-Fi in some rooms, minibar, coffeemaker, hair dryer, safe, Nintendo.

Moderate

The Bungalows Hotel *Finds*
This is one of the most special places to stay in Los Cabos. Each "bungalow" is a charming retreat decorated with authentic Mexican furnishings. Terra-cotta tiles, hand-painted sinks, wooden chests, blown glass, and other creative touches make you feel as if you're a guest at a friend's home rather than a hotel. Each room has a kitchenette, purified water, VCR, and designer bedding. Rooms surround a lovely heated pool with cushioned lounges and tropical gardens. A brick-paved breakfast nook serves a gourmet breakfast with fresh-ground coffee and fresh juices. Under the owner's warm and welcoming management, this is Cabo's most spacious, comfortable, full-service inn. A 100% smoke-free environment, it is 5 blocks from downtown Cabo.

Miguel A. Herrera s/n, in front of Lienzo Charro, Cabo San Lucas, B.C.S. ℂ/fax **624/143-5035** or -0585. www. cabobungalows.com. 16 units. High season $135–$155 (£68–£88) suite; low season $105–$115 (£53–£58) suite. Extra person $20 (£10). Rates include full breakfast. AE, V. Street parking available. **Amenities:** Breakfast room; outdoor pool; concierge; tour desk. *In room:* A/C, TV/VCR, kitchenette, fridge, coffeemaker.

Los Milagros Hotel
The elegant whitewashed two-level buildings containing the 12 suites and rooms of Los Milagros (the Miracles) border either a grassy garden area or the small tile pool. Rooms contain contemporary iron beds with straw headboards, buff-colored tile floors, and artistic details. Some units have kitchenettes, the master suite has a sunken tub, and there's coffee service in the mornings on the patio. Evenings are romantic: Candles light the garden and classical music plays. Request a room in one of the back buildings, where pomegranate trees buffer others' conversations. It's just 1½ blocks from the Giggling Marlin and Cabo Wabo.

Matamoros 116, 23410 Cabo San Lucas, B.C.S. ℂ/fax **718/928-6647** in the U.S., or 624/143-4566. www.losmilagros. com.mx. 12 units. $95 (£48) double, $100 (£50) kitchenette suite, $125 (£63) master suite. Ask about summer discounts, group rates, long-term discounts. No credit cards, but payable through PayPal. Free secure parking. **Amenities:** Small outdoor pool; rooftop terrace; business services. *In room:* A/C, TV, Wi-Fi.

Inexpensive

Cabo Inn *Finds*
This three-story hotel on a quiet street is a real find, and it keeps getting better. It offers a rare combination of low rates, extra-friendly management, and great, funky style. Rooms are basic and very small, with either two twin beds or one queen; although this was a bordello in a prior incarnation, everything is kept new and updated, from the mattresses to the minifridges. Muted desert colors add a spark of personality. The rooms surround a courtyard where you can enjoy satellite TV, a barbecue grill, and free coffee. The third floor has a rooftop terrace with *palapa* and a small swimming pool. Also on this floor is a suite equipped with a king-size bed and Jacuzzi. It's a colorful, *palapa*-topped, open-air room with hanging *tapetes* (woven palm mats) for additional privacy. A large fish freezer is available, and most rooms have kitchenettes. The hotel is just 2 blocks from downtown and the marina. A lively restaurant next door will even deliver pitchers of margaritas and dinner to your room.

20 de Noviembre and Leona Vicario, 23410 Cabo San Lucas, B.C.S. ℂ/fax **619/819-2727** in the U.S., or 624/143-0819. www.caboinnhotel.com. 23 units. Year-round $39 (£20) single; $58 (£29) double; $79 (£40) triple; $120

(£60) up to 6 people; $120 (£60) suite with Jacuzzi. No credit cards. Street parking. **Amenities:** Small rooftop pool and sunning area; communal TV; barbecue. *In room:* A/C, fridge.

Siesta Suites   Reservations are a must at this immaculate, small inn that's popular with return visitors. (It's especially popular with fishermen.) The very basic rooms have white-tile floors and white walls, kitchenettes with seating areas, refrigerators, and sinks. The mattresses are firm, and the bathrooms are large and sparkling clean. Rooms on the fourth floor have two queen-size beds each. The accommodating proprietors offer free movies and VCRs, a barbecue pit and outdoor patio table on the second floor, and a comfortable lobby with a TV. They also arrange fishing trips. Weekly and monthly rates are available. The hotel is 1½ blocks from the marina, where parking is available.

Calle Emiliano Zapata between Guerrero and Hidalgo, 23410 Cabo San Lucas, B.C.S. ℂ **866/271-0952** in the U.S., or 624/143-2773. www.cabosiestasuites.com. 20 suites. $64–$76 (£32–£38) double. $400–$500 (£200–£250) weekly rates. AE, MC, V. Parking available at marina. **Amenities:** Outdoor pool; barbecue pit. *In room:* A/C, VCR, kitchenette (in some), fridge, fan.

WHERE TO DINE

It's not uncommon to pay a lot for mediocre food in Cabo, so try to get a couple of unbiased recommendations. If people are only drinking and not dining, take that as a clue—many seemingly popular places are long on party atmosphere but short on food. Prices may decrease the farther you walk inland. The absolute local favorite is **Gardenia's Tacos,** a bare-bones eatery on Paseo Pescadores (same street as McDonald's) that serves Cabo San Lucas's best tacos. Streets to explore for other good restaurants include Hidalgo and Lázaro Cárdenas, plus the marina at the Plaza Bonita. Note that many restaurants automatically add the tip (15%) to the bill; make sure you ask.

Very Expensive
Edith's Restaurante 𝓡𝓡𝓡 SEAFOOD/STEAKS/MEXICAN   Prices may seem over the top and reservations hard to come by, but once you sit down at one of Edith Jiménez's cheerful tables, you will see you're not only paying for an exquisite meal, but also for the time of your life. Lanterns light the open-air way for highly trained waiters, and bouquets of fresh lilies always perfume the entrance and washrooms. No detail is overlooked and, without exception, everyone in the house is in full celebration mode. You will be, too, after a celestial pitcher of margaritas or a bottle from Edith's carefully stocked cellar. While the lobster, shrimp, seafood, and steak combinations are worth every last peso, the grilled tuna is beyond compare when it comes to quality and value. And if Mexican food is what you crave, both the Tampiqueña and the Pancho Villa offer a magnanimous sampling of some of Mexico's most prized traditional dishes, which are abundant enough for two, especially when kicked off with the squash blossom quesadillas or a Caesar salad.

Camino a Playa Medano. ℂ 624/143-0801. www.edithscabo.com. Reservations strongly recommended. Main courses $20–$84 (£10–£42). MC, V. Daily 5–11pm.

Expensive
Nick-San 𝓡𝓡 JAPANESE/SUSHI   This is the original branch of exceptional Japanese cuisine and sushi in Los Cabos. Now joined by a second location in the Corridor near San José, Nick-San's innovative flavors have two splendid homes. See p. 716 for menu details.

Bulevar Marina, Plaza de la Danza, Loc. 2. ℂ 624/143-4372. www.nicksan.com Reservations recommended. Main courses $15–$50 (£7.50–£25). MC, V. Daily 11:30am–10:30pm.

Moderate

La Dolce ITALIAN   This restaurant is the offspring of Puerto Vallarta's La Dolce Vita, with authentic Italian thin-crust, brick-oven pizzas, fresh pasta dishes, and other specialties. Most of its business is from local customers, underscoring the attention to detail and reasonable prices. The simple menu also features sumptuous calzones and delightful starters, plus great salads. This is the best late-night dining option, and there's also an equally loved branch on the main square in San José del Cabo that's open from 2 to 11pm.

M. Hidalgo and Zapata s/n. ℂ 624/143-4122 or -9553. Main courses $7.50–$19 (£3.75–£9.50). MC, V. Tues–Sun 6–11pm.

Mi Casa Restaurant ✶ MEXICAN   The building's vivid cobalt-blue facade is your first clue that this place celebrates Mexico, and the menu confirms that impression. This is one of Cabo's most renowned Mexican restaurants. Traditional specialties such as *manchamanteles* (literally, "tablecloth stainers"), *cochinita pibil*, and *chiles en nogada* are menu staples. Fresh fish is prepared with delicious seasonings from throughout Mexico. Especially pleasant at night, the restaurant's tables, scattered around a large patio, are set with colorful cloths, traditional pottery, and glassware. It's across from the main plaza.

Calle Cabo San Lucas (at Madero). ℂ 624/143-1933. www.micasarestaurant.com. Reservations recommended. Main courses $13–$40 (£6.50–£20). MC, V. Mon–Sat noon–3pm, daily 5:30–10:30pm.

Inexpensive

Cafe Canela ✶ COFFEE/PASTRY/LIGHT MEALS   This cozy, tasty cafe and bistro is a welcome addition to the Cabo Marina boardwalk. Espresso drinks or fruit smoothies and muffins are good eye-openers for early risers. Enjoy a light meal or a tropical drink either inside or on the bustling waterfront terrace. The appealing menu also offers breakfast egg wraps, salads (for example, curried chicken salad with fresh fruit), sandwiches (such as blue-cheese quesadillas with smoked tuna and mango), and pastas—all reasonably priced. Full bar service is also available.

Marina boardwalk, below Tesoro Resort. ℂ 624/143-3435. Main courses $5–$35 (£2.50–£18); coffee $1.75–$4.20 (90p–£2.10). AE, MC, V. Daily 6am–7pm.

Mocambo's ✶ SEAFOOD   The location of this longstanding Cabo favorite is not inspiring—it's basically a large cement building—but the food obviously is. The place is always packed, generally with locals tired of high prices and small portions. Ocean-fresh seafood is the order of the day, and the specialty platter can easily serve four people. The restaurant is 1½ blocks inland from Lázaro Cárdenas.

Av. Leona Vicario and 20 de Noviembre. ℂ 624/143-6070. Main courses $5–$30 (£2.50–£15). MC, V. Daily noon–10pm.

CABO SAN LUCAS AFTER DARK

Cabo San Lucas is the nightlife capital of Baja. After-dark fun starts with the casual bars and restaurants on Bulevar Marina or facing the marina, and transforms into a tequila-fueled dance club scene after midnight. You can easily find a happy hour with live music and a place to dance or a Mexican fiesta with mariachis.

MEXICAN FIESTAS & THEME NIGHTS   Some larger hotels have weekly fiesta nights and other buffet-plus-entertainment theme nights that can be fun as well as a good buy. Check travel agencies and the following hotels: the **Solmar** (ℂ 624/143-3535) and the **Finisterra** (ℂ 624/143-3333). Prices range from $25 (£13), not including drinks, tax, and tips, to $50 (£25), which covers everything, including an open bar with national drinks. Otherwise, Mi Casa (© **624/143-1933;** see "Where to Dine" section) is a veritable Mexican theme night every night.

SUNSET WATCHING   Come twilight, check out Land's End, where the two seas meet. At **Whale Watcher's Bar,** in the Hotel Finisterra (© **624/143-3333**), not only will you get a world-class view of the sun sinking into the Pacific, but you'll get a taste of "old Cabo." Mariachis play on Friday from 6:30 to 9pm, and the bar is open daily from 10am to 11pm. Another good place to watch the sunset is at the Pueblo Bonito Sunset Beach hotel—where nothing obstructs the setting sun—on the Pacific side of San Lucas (© **624/142-9797**).

Happy Hours, Clubs & Hangouts

If you shop around, you can usually find an *hora feliz* (happy hour) somewhere in town between noon and 7pm. The most popular places to drink and carouse until all hours are longstanding favorites such as the Nowhere Bar, the Giggling Marlin, El Squid Roe, and the Cabo Wabo Cantina.

Two places to enjoy a more refined setting are the **Sancho Panza Wine Bistro and Jazz Club** (see below) and **Red** (© **624/143-5645**), a food, wine and martini bar, on Zaragoza around the corner from Squid Roe. While Sancho Panza offers live classic jazz, Red brings smooth electronica, both of which set the stage for rich conversation.

Cabo Wabo Cantina   Owned by Sammy Hagar (formerly of Van Halen) and his Mexican and American partners, this "cantina" packs in youthful crowds, especially when rumors (frequent, and frequently false, just to draw a crowd) fly that a surprise appearance by a vacationing musician is imminent. One of Cabo's few air-conditioned dance venues, it's especially popular in the summer months. House band, Cabo, plays hard-rock covers every night. Overstuffed furniture frames the dance floor. Beer goes for $4 (£2), margaritas for $6 (£3). For snacks, the Taco Wabo, just outside the club's entrance, stays up late, too. The cantina is open from 11am to 4am. Vicente Guerrero at Lázaro Cárdenas. © **624/143-1188.** www.cabowabo.com.

El Squid Roe *(Moments*   El Squid Roe is one of the late Carlos Anderson's inspirations, and it still attracts wild, fun-loving crowds of all ages with its two stories of nostalgic decor. The eclectic food is far better than you'd expect from such a party place and, as fashionable as blue jeans, you can't come to Cabo without a visit here. Skinto-win is the theme as the dancing on tables moves into high gear around 9pm. The scene is mostly tourists jerking to American hip-hop from early evening to around midnight, and at 1am, the local Mexican crowd—just getting their night started—flow in, and the hips don't stop shaking until first light. Open daily from noon to 4am. Bulevar Marina, opposite Plaza Bonita. © **624/143-0655.** www.elsquidroe.com.

Nikki Beach   This haven of the hip hails from South Beach, Miami, and brought its ultracool vibe to the beach of the ME Cabo resort in March 2005. White-draped lounge beds scatter the outdoor area, under a canopy of umbrellas, surrounding a pool, and overlooking Cabo's best swimming beach. A teak deck offers covered dining. The music is the latest in electronic, house, and chill, with visiting DJs often playing on weekend nights. Sundays feature the signature beach brunch. It's a great choice for catching rays during the day while sipping tropical drinks, but its real appeal is the nocturnal action. Open Sunday to Wednesday from 11am to 1am (food service stops at 11pm), and Thursday to Saturday from 11am to 3am (food service stops at 1am). On the beach at the ME Cabo resort, on Medano Beach. © **624/145-7800.** www.nikkibeach.com.

Passion ME Cabo's most recent contribution to Cabo's growing high-end nightlife scene is Passion, arguably the most aphrodisiacal club in San Lucas. Champagne cocktails, the house music of resident and guest DJs, and a low-lit atmosphere prime Los Cabos' jet set for dancing and partying as long as they want. Open Sunday to Wednesday from 10am to 2am and Thursday to Saturday from 10am to 4am. In the ME Cabo resort, on Medano Beach. ☎ 624/145-7800.

Sancho Panza Wine Bistro and Jazz Club Sancho Panza combines a gourmet food market with a wine bar that features live jazz music plus an intriguing menu of Nuevo Latino cuisine (Mediterranean food with Latin flair). The place has a cozy neighborhood feeling, with tourists and locals sampling the selection of more than 150 wines, plus espresso drinks. During high season, make reservations. It's open daily from 4pm to midnight. Plaza Tesoro boardwalk, next to the Lighthouse. ☎ 624/143-3212. www.sanchopanza.com.

2 Todos Santos: A Creative Oasis ★★★

68km (42 miles) N of Cabo San Lucas

Although Todos Santos is well past its off-the-beaten-path days, it's still a favorite among Bohemian types looking either for regional up-and-coming artists or simply a piece of art that makes them feel good—and it's a prime destination among those simply weary of the L.A.-ization of Cabo San Lucas.

The art and artistry created here—from the kitchen to the canvas—is of an evolved type that seems to care less about commercial appeal than quality. In doing so, it becomes more of a draw. Not to be overlooked are the arts of agriculture, masonry, and weaving created by some of the town's original residents. From superb meals at **Café Santa Fe** to an afternoon browsing at **El Tecolote Libros,** Todos Santos is intriguing to its core. In fact, the Mexican government dubbed it a "Pueblo Mágico" in 2006, bringing official recognition, not to mention various infrastructure updates, to the town.

Not only is the town a cultural oasis in Baja, it's an oasis in the true sense of the word—in this desert landscape, Todos Santos enjoys an almost continuous water supply from the peaks of the Sierra de la Laguna mountains. It's just over an hour's drive up the Pacific coast from Cabo San Lucas; you'll know you've arrived when the arid coastal scenery suddenly gives way to verdant groves of palms, mangos, avocados, and papayas.

During the Mission Period of Baja, this oasis valley was deemed the only area south and west of La Paz worth settling—it had the only reliable water supply. In 1723, an outpost mission was established, followed by the full-fledged Misión Santa Rosa de Las Palmas in 1733. At the time, the town was known as Santa Rosa de Todos Santos; eventually shortened to its current name, it translates as "All Saints."

Over the next 200 years, the town alternated between prosperity and difficulty. Its most recent boom lasted from the mid-19th century until the 1950s, when the town flourished as a sugar-cane production center and began to develop a strong cultural core. Many of the buildings now being restored and converted into galleries, studios, shops, and restaurants were built during this era. It wasn't until the 1980s that a paved road connected Todos Santos with La Paz, and tourism began to draw new attention to this tranquil town.

The demand for the town's older colonial-style structures by artists, entrepreneurs, and foreign residents has resulted in a real-estate boom, and new shops, galleries, and cafes crop up continuously. The coastal strip south of Todos Santos—once the exclusive hideaway of impassioned surfers—has plans for development, so visit soon, before this perfect stretch of beach and desert changes. For the casual visitor, Todos Santos is easy to explore in a day, but a few tranquil inns welcome guests who want to stay a little longer.

WHAT TO SEE & DO

During the **Festival Fundador** (Oct 10–14)— a celebration of the founding of the town in 1723—streets around the main plaza fill with food, games, and wandering troubadours. Many of the shops and the Café Santa Fe close from the end of September through the festival. A new **Arts Festival,** in February, seems to be gaining importance. It includes film festivals, dance and music performances, and more.

Todos Santos has at least half a dozen galleries, including the noted **Galería de Todos Santos,** corner of Topete and Legaspi (© 612/145-0500), which features a changing collection of works by regional artists. It's open daily from 11am to 4pm (closed Sun May–Nov) and doesn't accept credit cards. The new **La Galera,** on Obregón (© 612/145-0215), houses a striking collection of local and regional Mexican artists, plus some handicrafts and jewelry from mainland Mexico. Keep an eye out for the brooding paintings of local Sebastián Díaz Duarte, La Galera's featured artist. It's open Monday through Saturday from 10am to 5pm.

El Tecolote Libros ✿✿✿ (© 612/145-0295), though tiny, gets our vote for the best bookstore in Mexico. It carries an exceptional selection of Latin American literature, poetry, children's books, and reference books centering on Mexico. Both English and Spanish editions, new and used, are in stock, along with maps, magazines, cards, and art supplies. Information on upcoming writing workshops and local reading groups also is posted here. The shop is at the corner of Hidalgo and Juárez. It's open Monday through Saturday, from 9am to 5pm, and Sunday, from 10am to 3pm.

WHERE TO STAY & DINE

Consider the **Todos Santos Inn** ✿✿, Calle Legaspi 33, between Topete and Obregón (© 612/145-0040; www.todossantosinn.com). An elegant place to stay, it is in a historic house that has served as a general store, cantina, school, and private residence. Now under new ownership, it retains its air of casual elegance, with luxurious white bed linens, netting draped romantically over the beds, Talavera tile bathrooms, antique furniture, and high, wood-beamed ceilings. Two rooms and four suites border a lush courtyard terrace, pool, and garden. Rates run $125 to $325 (£63–£163) per night depending on the room and the season. The suites are air-conditioned, but have neither television nor telephone. The hotel's wine bar, **La Copa,** is open to the public, serves libations Tuesdays through Saturdays from 5 to 9pm, and has an excellent selection of California and other imported wines. The hotel now accepts both Visa and MasterCard.

Hotel California, Calle Juárez, corner of Morelos (© 612/145-0525 or -0522), has been the stuff of legends—and the verdict is still out as to whether it's the source of inspiration for the Eagles' song of the same name. A few years back, it was a dilapidated guesthouse; however, after an extensive renovation, it's now the hippest place to stay in the area. Think Philippe Stark in the desert—the decor here is a fusion of jewel-tone colors with eclectic Mexican and Moroccan accents. Each room features a different decor, but all of it is high style, with rich hues and captivating details. Most rooms also offer an outdoor terrace or seating area. Rates for the 11 rooms range from $140 to $275 (£70–£138) in high season and are 20% less in the low season. It's so stylishly accommodating that although you can check out anytime you want—you may not want to! On the ground floor, you'll find the lobby and the low-lit library—with deep blue walls, a profusion of candles, and tin stars—as well as a small outdoor pool with sun chairs. Also at ground level is the **Emporio** boutique, which is well worth a visit for its rugs, jewelry, and glass lanterns; the **La Coronela Restaurant and Bar** (open daily 7am–11pm) is the nocturnal hot spot with live guitar, jazz, and blues on Saturday evenings. The recently added **Tequila Bar** is a small, decadently decorated spot, with red and black settees, and an extensive selection of tequilas, including their own Hotel California label.

For myself—and I would suspect many others—a meal at the **Café Santa Fe** ✹, Calle Centenario 4 (© 612/145-0340), is reason enough to visit Todos Santos. Much of the attention the town has received in recent years can be directly attributed to this outstanding cafe, and it continues to live up to its lofty reputation. Owners Ezio and Paula Colombo refurbished a large stucco house across from the plaza, creating an exhibition kitchen, several dining rooms, and a lovely courtyard adjacent to a flowering garden. The excellent northern Italian cuisine emphasizes local produce and seafood; try ravioli stuffed with spinach and ricotta in a Gorgonzola sauce, or ravioli with lobster and shrimp, with an organic salad. In high season, the wait for a table at lunch can be long. Everything is prepared to order, and reservations are recommended. Main courses run $10 to $20 (£5–£10). It's open Wednesday through Monday from noon to 9pm, closed September and October, and accepts MasterCard and Visa.

If you prefer a gourmet Mexican experience, the margaritas and the sopa tarasca, a decadent puree of white beans, chipotle peppers, and cream, at **Los Adobes** (© 612/145-0203; www.losadobestodossantos.com) are alone enough to inspire a visit to the fine-dining restaurant on Hidalgo, just down from El Tecolote Libros.

A more casual option, and a magical place to start the day, is the garden setting of the **Café Todos Santos,** Centenario 33, down the street from the Todos Santos Inn (© 612/145-0300). Among the espresso drinks is the bowl-size *caffe latte,* accompanied by a freshly baked croissant or one of the signature cinnamon buns. Lunch or a light meal may include a *frittata* (an egg-based dish similar to quiche), a hearty sandwich on home-baked bread, or a fish filet wrapped in banana leaves with coconut milk. Main courses average $3 to $6 (£1.50–£3). The cafe is open Tuesday through Sunday from 7am to 9pm; credit cards are not accepted.

3 La Paz: Peaceful Port Town ✹✹

176km (109 miles) N of Cabo San Lucas; 195km (121 miles) NW of San José del Cabo; 1,544km (957 miles) SE of Tijuana

La Paz means "peace," and the feeling seems to float on the ocean breezes of this provincial town. Despite being an important port, home to almost 200,000 inhabitants, and the capital of the state of Baja California Sur, it remains slow-paced and relaxed. Beautiful deserted beaches just minutes away complement the lively beach and palm-fringed *malecón* (seaside boulevard) that front the town center. The easygoing city is the guardian of "old Baja" atmosphere, and it has an unmistakable air of outdoor adventure, thanks to the ubiquity of skilled anglers, competitive freedivers, Baja 1000 racers, recreational (as in, noncommercial) spear fishermen, a marina full of large yachts, and kayak rental agencies.

Adventurous travelers enjoy countless options, including hiking, rock climbing, diving, fishing, and sea kayaking. Islands and islets sit just offshore, once hiding places for looting pirates but now magnets for kayakers and beachcombers. You can even camp overnight, posh safari-style, at **Baja Camp** (www.bajacamp.com) on Espíritu Santo, or swim with sea lions on Los Islotes. The best time for camping is from June through September.

The University of Southern Baja California adds a unique cultural presence that includes museums and a theater and arts center. The surrounding tropical desert diversity and pandemic wildlife are also compelling reasons to visit. Despite its name, La Paz has historically been a place of conflict between explorers and indigenous populations. Beginning in 1535, Spanish conquistadors and Jesuit missionaries arrived and exerted their influence on the town's architecture and traditions. From the time conquistadors saw local Indians wearing pearl ornaments, mass pearl harvesting lasted through the late 1930s, when all the pearls eventually were wiped out. John Steinbeck immortalized a local legend in his novella *The Pearl.*

La Paz is ideal for anyone nostalgic for Los Cabos the way it used to be—and it has the breathtaking sunsets not always visible at Baja's tip. From accommodations to taxis, it's also one of Mexico's most outstanding beach vacation values and a great place for family travelers. However, as is the case throughout Mexico, development activity in the areas immediately surrounding La Paz may change this in the coming years, so plan a visit now to experience the pearl of La Paz in its natural state.

ESSENTIALS

GETTING THERE & DEPARTING By Plane Both **Alaska Airlines** (© 800/ 252-7522) and **Delta** (© 800/241-4141) have nonstop flights from Los Angeles. **AeroMéxico** (© 800/237-6639 in the U.S., or 612/122-0091, -0093, or -1636) connects through Tucson and Los Angeles in the United States and flies from Mexico City and other points within Mexico. The airport is 18km (11 miles) northwest of town along the highway to Ciudad Constitución and Tijuana. Airport *colectivos* (around $12/£6.60 per person) run only from the airport to town, not vice versa, and a group shuttle is a flat charge of $25 (£13). **Taxi** service (around $27/£14) is available as well. Most major rental car agencies have booths inside the airport. **Budget**'s local number is © 612/124-6433 or 122-7655; you can contact **Avis** at © 612/122-2651, or **Alamo** at 612/122-6262.

By Car From San José del Cabo, **Highway 1** north is the more scenic route, and it passes through a mountain town called San Bartolo, where heavenly homemade macaroons made of thick, fresh-cut coconut and pralines made from *cajeta* (goat's-milk caramel) are well worth the slightly longer drive; a faster route is heading east of Cabo San Lucas, and then north to **Highway 19** through Todos Santos. A little before San Pedro, Highway 19 rejoins Highway 1 and runs north into La Paz; both trips takes 2½ to 3 hours. From northern Baja, Highway 1 south is the only choice.

By Bus The **Central Camionera** (main bus station) is at Jalisco and Héroes de la Independencia, about 25 blocks southwest of the center of town; it's open daily from 6am to 10pm. Bus service operates from the south (Los Cabos, 2½–3½ hr.) and north (as far as Tijuana). It's best to buy your ticket in person the day before, though reservations can be made over the phone at the bus station in your point of origin. Taxis are available in front of the station.

All routes north and south, as well as buses to Pichilingue, the ferry pier, and close to outlying beaches, are available through the **Transportes Aguila** station, sometimes called the beach bus terminal, on the *malecón* at Alvaro Obregón and Cinco de Mayo (*©* 612/122-7898). The station is open daily from 6am to 10pm. Buses to Pichilingue depart seven times a day from 8am to 5pm and cost $2 (£$1) one-way. Local buses arrive at the **beach station**, along the *malecón*. Taxis line up out front of both.

By Ferry Baja Ferries serves La Paz from Topolobampo (the port for Los Mochis) daily at 11:30pm and the return trip to Topolobampo leaves La Paz at 3pm daily. Tickets are available at the Baja Ferries office in La Paz, on the corner of Allende and Marcelo Rubio (*©* 612/123-6600 or -1313), or at any Banamex banks throughout Mexico (make payable to Baja Ferries, SA de CV, account #7145468 sucursal 001.) The local office is open daily 8am to 6pm. To make reservations from the U.S., call **800/884-3107.**

The ferry departs for Topolobampo daily at 11:30pm and arrives in La Paz 6 hours later. The ferries can carry 1,000 passengers, as well as accommodate vehicles and trucks. Passengers pay one fee for themselves ($68/£34 for a seat, $34/£17 for children ages 3 to 11, or $144/£72 for a cabin with four beds and one bathroom) and another for their vehicles ($100/£50). The ferries offer restaurant and bar service, as well as a coffee shop and live music, and a hot meal is included in the cost of the ticket. Access for those with disabilities is offered as well. Passengers are requested to arrive 3 hours prior to departure time. Information and updated schedules are available at **www.bajaferries.com.** Taxis meet each ferry as well and cost about $8 (£4) to downtown La Paz.

VISITOR INFORMATION   The most accessible visitor information office is on the corner of Alvaro Obregón and Nicolas Bravo (*©* 612/122-5939 or 612/124-0100; turismo@gbcs.gob.mx or turismo@lapaz.cromwell.com.mx). It's open daily from 8am to 8pm. The extremely helpful staff speaks English and can supply information on La Paz, Los Cabos, and the rest of the region. The official website of the La Paz Tourism Board is **www.vivalapaz.com.**

CITY LAYOUT   Although La Paz sprawls well inland from the *malecón* (Paseo Alvaro Obregón), you'll probably spend most of your time in the older, more congenial downtown section within a few blocks of the waterfront. The main plaza, **Plaza Pública,** or Jardín Velasco, is bounded by Madero, Independencia, Revolución, and Cinco de Mayo.

GETTING AROUND   Because most of what you'll need in town is on the *malecón,* between the tourist information office and the Hotel Los Arcos, or a few blocks inland from the waterfront, it's easy to get around La Paz on foot. Public buses go to some of the beaches north of town (see "Beaches & Sports," below). To explore the many beaches within 80km (50 miles) of La Paz, your best bet is to rent a car or hire a taxi. There are several car-rental agencies on the *malecón.*

FESTIVALS & EVENTS   February features the biggest and best **Carnaval/Mardi Gras** in Baja, as well as a 4- to 5-week **Festival of the Gray Whale** (starting in late Jan or early Feb, sometimes extending through early Mar). On May 3, **a festival** celebrates the city's founding by Cortez in 1535 and features *artesanía* exhibitions from southern Baja. An annual **marlin-fishing tournament** is in August; **other fishing tournaments** occur in September and November. On November 1 and 2, the **Days of the Dead,** altars are on display at the Anthropology Museum.

FAST FACTS: La Paz

Area Code The telephone area code is **612.**

Banks Banks generally exchange currency during normal business hours: Monday through Friday from 9am to 6pm, Saturday from 10am to 2pm. ATMs are readily available and offer bank exchange rates on withdrawals.

Drugstore One of the largest pharmacies is **Farmacía Baja California,** corner of Independencia and Madero (© **612/122-0240** or 123-4408). Open 7am to 9:30pm Monday to Saturday and Sundays from 8am to 9:30pm.

Emergencies Dial © **066** for general emergency assistance, or © **060** for the police.

Hospitals The two hospitals in the area are **Hospital Especialidades Médicas,** at Km 4.5 on the highway toward the airport (© **612/124-0400**), and **Hospital Juan María de Salvatierra** (© **612/122-1497**), Nicolás Bravo 1010, Col. Centro. Both are open 24 hours, and the former offers access to emergency air evacuation.

Internet Access In the fleeting world of Internet cafes, your best bet is to scan the *malecón* or ask your hotel concierge for their recommendations. However, **Omni Services,** which doubles as an Internet center and a real estate agency, offers Internet access, Wi-Fi, faxing, and long-distance VOiP phone service to the U.S. and Canada for 30¢ (15p) per minute on the *malecón,* Alvaro Obregón 460-C, close to Burger King (© **612/123-4888;** www.osmx.com). It also offers hookups for laptops, color printers, and copiers.

Post Office The *correo,* 3 blocks inland at Constitución and Revolución de 1910 (© **612/122-0388**), is open Monday through Friday from 8am to 5pm, Saturday from 8am to 1pm.

Tourism Office The office is at Carretera al Norte Km 5.5, Edificio Fidepaz, Col. Fidepaz, La Paz, B.C.S. (© **612/124-0100**), open daily 8am to 3pm. The tourist information booth on the *malecón* is open daily 8am to 8pm.

BEACHES & SPORTS

La Paz combines the unselfconscious bustle of a small capital port city with the charm of resort Mexico and beautiful, isolated beaches not far from town. Well on its way to becoming the undisputed adventure-tourism capital of Baja, it's the starting point for whale-watching, diving, sea kayaking, climbing, and hiking tours throughout the peninsula. For those interested in day adventures, travel agencies in major hotels or along the *malecón* usually can arrange all of the above, plus beach tours, sunset cruises, and visits to the sea lion colony. Agencies in the United States that specialize in Baja's natural history also book excursions (see "Special-Interest Trips," in chapter 3).

BEACHES Within a 10- to 45-minute drive from La Paz lie some of the loveliest beaches in Baja. Many rival those of the Caribbean with their clear, turquoise water.

The beach bordering the *malecón* is the most convenient in town. Although the sand in the Bay of La Paz is soft and white and the water appears turquoise and gentle, locals don't generally swim there. Because of the commercial port, the water is not considered as clean as that at the very accessible outlying beaches. With colorful playgrounds dotting the central beachfront and numerous open-air restaurants that front the water, it's best for a casual afternoon of post-sightseeing lunch and play.

The best beach nearby is immediately north of town at **La Concha Beach Resort;** nonguests may use the hotel restaurant and bar and rent equipment for snorkeling, diving, skiing, and sailing. It's 10km (6 miles) north of town on the Pichilingue Highway at Km 5.5. The other beaches are all farther north of town, but midweek you may have these distant beaches to yourself.

For more information about beaches and maps, check at the tourist information office on the *malecón*. For an overview of the beaches before deciding where to spend your precious vacation days, **Viajes Lybs,** Independencia 2050, between Mina and Galeana (© **612/122-4680;** fax 612/125-9600), offers a 4-hour beach tour for $25 (£14) per person, with stops at Balandra and El Tecolote beaches.

CRUISES   A popular and very worthwhile cruise is to **Isla Espíritu Santo** and **Los Islotes.** You visit the largest sea lion colony in Baja, stunning rock formations, and remote beaches, with stops for snorkeling, swimming, and lunch. If conditions permit, you may even be able to snorkel beside the sea lions. (*Note:* Remember sea lions are wild animals. Blowing bubbles in your face is their sign of warning, not of play, so steer clear of the giant bulls—who can be quite protective of their females—and let the curious babies come to you.) Boat and bus tours are available to **Puerto Balandra,** where bold rock formations rising up like humpback whales frame pristine coves of crystal-blue water and ivory sand. **Viajes Lybs** (see above) and other travel agencies can arrange these all-day trips, weather permitting. Price is $80 (£40) per person.

ECOTOURS   A wide selection of ecotours and adventure activities are available through **Baja Quest** and **Grupo Fun Baja** (© 612/121-5884 or 125-2366; www.funbaja.com). In addition to diving excursions (the company's specialty) they also offer ATV tours and kite surfing. **DeSea Baja** (© **310/691-8040** from the U.S. or 612/121-5100; www.deseabaja.com) offers driving tours in rental vehicles equipped for off-road adventures.

SCUBA DIVING   Scuba diving trips are best June through September. Fernando Aguilar's **Club Cantamar,** Obregón 1665-2 (© **612/122-1826;** fax 612/122-3296; www.clubcantamar.com), arranges them. Rates start at $105 (£53) per person for a daylong two-tank dive or $125 (£63), including rental equipment. Another excellent dive operator is **Baja Quest** (© **612/123-5320;** www.bajaquest.com.mx), at Rangel 10, between Sonora and Sinaloa. Day boat trips run approximately $125 (£60) for two-to-three tanks depending on dive site. They also offer other outdoor adventures including kayaking and various wildlife watching, not to mention service in English, Spanish, and Japanese.

Also of note is **DeSea Baja** (© **612/121-5100;** www.deseabaja.com), a complete tour company with expertise in diving and sportfishing. Prices are $147 (£74) for two-tank dives, including equipment, or $175 (£88) for three. They also offer private boats with guides for underwater photo or video diving, and private divemasters or instructors for yachts or charters. DeSea also offers **freediving,** including instruction from internationally renowned freediving instructors, Aharon and Maria Teresa (MT) Solomon. Courses include yoga-based breathing exercises, mental control, and the physiology of breath hold. Beginning through advanced instruction is available, as are live-aboard charters and **spearfishing** excursions.

SEA KAYAKING   Kayaking in the many bays and coves near La Paz is a paddler's dream, and because some of the area's special sites for swimming and snorkeling are only accessible by kayak, daylong or multiday trips can't be beat. In the waters near La Paz, the water clarity gives the sensation of being suspended in the air. Bring your own equipment, or let the local companies take care of you. Several companies in the U.S. (see "Special-Interest Trips," in chapter 3) can book trips in advance. Locally, **Baja Quest** (see above; daytrips start at $90/£45, and multiday trips also are available) and **Mar y Aventuras (Sea and Adventures;** ✆ **612/123-0559;** fax 612/122-3559; www.kayakbaja.com) arrange extended kayak adventures.

SPORTFISHING   La Paz, justly famous for its sportfishing, attracts anglers from all over the world. Its waters are home to more than 850 species of fish. The most economical approach is to rent a *panga* boat with a captain and equipment. It costs $125 (£63) for 3 hours, but you don't go very far out. Super *pangas,* which have a shade cover and comfortable seats, start at around $180 (£90) for two persons. Larger cruisers with bathrooms start at $400 (£200). Local hotels and tour agencies arrange sportfishing trips.

You can arrange sportfishing trips locally through hotels and tour agencies. **La Paz Sportfishing** (✆ **612/141-6403;** www.lapazsportfishing.com) rates start at $220 (£110) a day for two people. David Jones, of **The Fishermen's Fleet** (✆ **408/884-3932** in the US or 612/122-1313; fax 612/125-7334; www.fishermensfleet.com), uses popular *panga* fishing boats. David is super-professional, speaks English, and truly understands area fishing. The average price is $260 (£130) for the boat, but double-check what the price includes—you may need to bring your own food and drinks.

WHALE-WATCHING   Between January and March, and sometimes as early as December, 3,000 to 5,000 gray whales migrate from the Bering Strait to the Pacific coast of Baja. The main whale-watching spots are **Laguna San Ignacio** (on the Pacific near San Ignacio), **Magdalena Bay** (on the Pacific near Puerto López Mateos—about a 2-hr. drive from La Paz), and **Scammon's Lagoon** (near Guerrero Negro).

Most tours originating in La Paz go to Magdalena Bay, where the whales give birth to their calves in calm waters. Several companies arrange whale-watching tours that originate in La Paz or other Baja towns or in the United States; 12-hour tours from La Paz start at around $120 (£60) per person, including breakfast, lunch, transportation, and an English-speaking guide. Make reservations at **Viajes Lybs** (see above).

A BREAK FROM THE BEACHES: EXPLORING LA PAZ

Most tour agencies offer city tours of all the major sights. Tours last 2 to 3 hours, include time for shopping, and cost around $15 (£7.50) per person.

HISTORIC LA PAZ

When Cortez landed here on May 3, 1535, he named it Bahía Santa Cruz. It didn't stick. In April 1683, Eusebio Kino, a Spanish Jesuit, arrived and dubbed the place Nuestra Señora de la Paz (Our Lady of Peace). It wasn't until November 1, 1720, however, that Jaime Bravo, another Jesuit, set up a permanent mission. He used the same name as his predecessor, calling it the Misión de Nuestra Señora de la Paz. The mission church stands on La Paz's main square, on Revolución between Cinco de Mayo and Independencia.

The Anthropology Museum   The museum features large, though faded, color photos of Baja's prehistoric cave paintings. There are also exhibits on various topics, including the geological history of the peninsula, fossils, missions, colonial history, and daily life. All information is in Spanish.

Altamirano and Cinco de Mayo. ⓒ/fax **612/122-0162** or 125-6424. Admission $3 (£1.50). Daily 9am–6pm.

El Teatro de la Ciudad   The city theater is the cultural center, with performances by visiting and local artists. Bookings include small ballet companies, experimental and popular theater, popular music, and an occasional classical concert or symphony.

Av. Navarro 700. ⓒ **612/125-0486.**

NATURAL MUSEUMS OF LA PAZ

Increasingly, La Paz is drawing numbers of travelers enchanted with the beauty of the area's diverse natural environment. Several new centers have emerged, combining entertainment with environmental education.

Aquarium   The newest of La Paz's natural museums opened in late 2003 and already is undergoing renovation to improve visitors' introduction to marine life in the Sea of Cortez. New attractions include a shark tank, a turtle exhibit, and an audiovisual center that will enable further education to students and groups. When the aquarium reopens (at press time no official date has been set), guided tours will be offered.

Pichilingue Km 5.5, next to the Hotel La Concha. ⓒ **612/121-5872.** Admission $5 (£2.50) adults. Tues–Sun 10am–6pm.

Cactus Sanctuary 🦅   This 50-hectare (124-acre) natural reserve features 1,000 meters (3,300 ft.) of marked pathways and self-guided tours with information about the plants and animals of La Paz's desert region. Fifty unique areas have been identified, which you can explore in consecutive order, or any other progression of your choosing. Route maps and guided tours are available, as well as descriptive signs for many of the plants. There's a surprising amount of wildlife to see here, from the myriad types of cacti, many of which are endemic to Baja California, to the numerous plants and animals that support this unique ecosystem. The sanctuary is in the Ejido El Rosario; go to the Ejido's main office (the *delegación*), and they will provide you with a key to enter the reserve.

Ejido El Rosario. ⓒ **612/124-0245** (Dr. Hector Nolasco). hnolasco@cibnor.mx. $2 (£1) donation to enter. No fixed hours. 45 min. south of La Paz; take Hwy. 1 toward the town of El Triunfo; drive 10 min. inland along a dirt road.

Serpentarium 🦅   This mostly open-air natural museum offers plenty of opportunities to observe various species of reptiles that inhabit the region's ecosystem, including snakes, turtles, iguanas, lizards, and crocodiles. It's on the corner of Calle Brecha California and Calle La Posada. To get there, go to the southernmost point of the *malecón* at Calle Abasolo, where the last streetlights are, and just before the beach you'll see an unpaved street—that's Brecha California. If you're going with a group, e-mail **cobra293@hotmail.com** to make a reservation.

Calles Brecha California and La Posada. ⓒ **612/123-5731.** $8 (£4) adults, $5 (£2.50) children. Daily 10am–4pm.

SHOPPING

La Paz has little in the way of folk art or other treasures from mainland Mexico. The dense cluster of streets behind the **Hotel Perla,** between 16 de Septiembre and Degollado, is full of small shops, some tacky, others quite upscale. In this area, there is also a very small but authentic **Chinatown,** dating from the time when Chinese laborers were brought to settle in Baja. Serdán from Degollado south is home to dozens of sellers of dried spices, piñatas, and candy. Stores carrying crafts, folk art, clothing, handmade furniture and accessories lie mostly along the *malecón* (Paseo Obregón) or within 1 or 2 blocks. The **municipal market,** at Revolución and Degollado, has little of interest to visitors. Something you're sure to notice if you explore around the central plaza is the abundance of stores selling electronic equipment, including stereos, cameras, and televisions. This is because La Paz is a principal port for electronic imports to Mexico from the Far East and therefore offers some of the best prices in Baja and mainland Mexico.

Antigua California   This shop manages to stay in business as others come and go. It carries a good selection of folk art from throughout Mexico. It's open Monday to Saturday from 9:30am to 8:30pm, Sunday from 10:30am to 2:30pm. Paseo Alvaro Obregón 220, at Arreola. © 612/125-5230.

Artesanías Cuauhtémoc (The Weaver)   If you like beautiful hand-woven tablecloths, place mats, rugs, and other textiles, it's worth the long walk or taxi ride to this unique shop. Fortunato Silva, an elderly gentleman, weaves wonderfully textured cotton textiles from yarn he spins and dyes himself. He charges far less than what you'd pay for equivalent artistry in the United States. Open Monday through Saturday from 10am to 3:30pm and 6pm to 7pm. On the corner of Abasolo and Oaxaca, between Jalisco and Nayarit. © 612/122-4575.

Dorian's   If you've forgotten essentials or want to stock up on duty-free perfume or cosmetics, head for Dorian's, La Paz's major department store. La Paz is a duty-free port city, so prices are excellent. Dorian's carries a wide selection of stylish clothing, shoes, lingerie, jewelry, and accessories as well. Open daily from 10am to 9pm. 16 de Septiembre, between Esquerro and 21 de Agosto. © 612/122-8014.

Ibarra's Pottery   Here, you not only shop for tableware, hand-painted tiles, and decorative pottery, you can watch it being made. Each piece is individually hand-painted or glazed, and then fired. Open Monday to Saturday from 9am to 3pm. You can call ahead to schedule a tour. Guillermo Prieto 625, between Torre Iglesias and República. © 612/122-0404.

WHERE TO STAY

Grand Plaza La Paz ✛   Among La Paz's newest options in places to stay, this all-suite hotel offers travelers a comfortable sense of U.S. standards and modern conveniences. It's considered the best option for business travelers to the area, one of the few in town with a full business center, Internet access, secretarial assistance, and meeting space. Vacationers will also enjoy the hotels' location on the marina, as well as its range of helpful tour services and pleasant pool area. The clean, modern, and well-equipped rooms on three floors offer either views to the bay or overlooking the courtyard pool, with a choice of king or two double beds. Five different kinds of suites have a private balcony, and all have ocean views. The hotel is at the northern end of town, 5.6km (3½ miles) from downtown, at the Marina Fidepaz.

Lote A Marina Fidepaz, P.O. Box 482, 23090 La Paz, B.C.S. © 866/357-9711 in the U.S., or 612/124-0830 or -0833. Fax 612/124-0837. www.grandplazalapaz.com. 54 suites. High season $150 (£75) double; $475 (£238) suite; 30% discount during low season. AE, DC, MC, V. Free guarded parking. **Amenities:** Restaurant; 2 bars; outdoor pool; fitness center; squash court; sauna; whirlpool; concierge; tour desk; business center; room service; babysitting; laundry service; Wi-Fi in lobby. *In room:* A/C, TV, coffeemaker, hair dryer, iron, safe.

Hotel Los Arcos   This three-story, neocolonial-style hotel at the west end of the *malecón* is the best place for downtown accommodations with a touch of tranquillity. Although the hotel is a bit dated, Los Arcos has functional furnishings and amenities and is filled with fountains, plants, rocking chairs, and even a Ping-Pong table. Most of the rooms and suites come with two double beds. Each has a balcony overlooking the pool in the inner courtyard or the waterfront, plus a whirlpool tub. I prefer the South Pacific-style bungalows with thatched roofs and fireplaces in the back part of the property. Satellite TVs carry U.S. channels.

Av. Alvaro Obregón 498, between Rosales and Allende (Apdo. Postal 112), 23000 La Paz, B.C.S. © 800/347-2252 in the U.S., or 612/122-2744. Fax 612/125-4313. www.losarcos.com. 130 units. 52 bungalows. $100 (£50) double; $115 (£63) suite; $80–$100 (£40–£50) bungalow. AE, MC, V. Free guarded parking. **Amenities:** Cafeteria; restaurant; bar w/live music; 2 outdoor pools (1 heated); sauna; travel agency; fishing information desk; room service; laundry service. *In room:* A/C, TV, minibar.

Hotel Mediterrane ✦   Simple yet stylish, this unique inn mixes Mediterranean with Mexican, creating a cozy place for couples or friends to share. All rooms, two of which were remodeled this year, face an interior courtyard and are decorated with white-tile floors and *equipal* furniture, with colorful Mexican serapes draped over the beds. Some rooms have minifridges. All have VCRs. Its location is great—just a block from the *malecón*. The adjacent La Pazta restaurant (see "Where to Dine," below) is one of La Paz's best. Rates include use of kayaks and bicycles for exploring the town. This is a gay-friendly hotel.

Allende 36, 23000 La Paz, B.C.S. ©/fax 612/125-1195. www.hotelmed.com. 9 units. $66 (£33) double, $85 (£43) suite, plus $10 (£5) for additional person. AE, MC, V. Weekly discounts available. Street parking. *In room:* A/C, TV/VCR, Wi-Fi, no phone.

La Concha Beach Club Resort ✦   Ten kilometers (6 miles) north of downtown La Paz, this resort's setting is perfect: on a curved beach ideal for swimming and watersports. All rooms face the water and have double beds, balconies or patios, and small tables and chairs. Condos with full kitchens and one or three bedrooms are available on a nightly basis in the high-rise complex next door. They're worth the extra price for a perfect family vacation stay, although no children younger than 14 are allowed in the condos. The hotel offers scuba, fishing, and whale-watching packages.

Carretera Pichilingue Km 5, 23010 La Paz, B.C.S. © 800/999-2252 in the U.S., or 612/121-6161. www.laconcha. com. 113 units. $95 (£48) double; $138 (£69) junior suite; $175–$338 (£88–£169) condo. AE, DC, MC, V. Free guarded parking. **Amenities:** Restaurant (w/theme nights); 2 bars; beachside pool; Jacuzzi; complete watersports center w/Wave Runners, kayaks, and paddleboats; tour desk; business center; free twice-daily shuttle to town; room service; laundry service; babysitting; beach club w/scuba program. *In room:* A/C, TV, Internet access, minibar.

Posada de Las Flores ✦   New owner Giuseppe Marceletti has continued the tradition of hospitality in this elegant B&B (formerly Posada Santa Fe), the best bet for travelers looking for a more refined place to stay in La Paz. Each room is individually decorated with high-quality Mexican furniture and antiques, hand-loomed fabrics, and exquisite artisan details. Bathrooms are especially welcoming, with marble tubs and thick towels. Breakfast is served from 8 to 11am daily, and complimentary wake-up coffee service is available on request. Telephone, fax, and Internet service are available through the office. It's at the northern end of the *malecón*.

Alvaro Obregón 440, 23000 La Paz, B.C.S. © 619/378-0103 in the U.S., or 612/125-5871. www.posadadelas flores.com. 8 units. High season $180 (£90) double, $290 (£145) suite; low season $150 (£75) double, $250 (£125) suite. Rates include full breakfast. No children younger than 12 accepted. MC, V. Street parking. **Amenities:** Small outdoor pool; Internet access; hospitality desk. *In room:* A/C, TV, minibar, hair dryer.

WHERE TO DINE

Although La Paz is not known for culinary grandeur, it has a growing assortment of small, pleasant restaurants that are good and reasonably priced. In addition to the usual seafood and Mexican dishes, you can find Italian, French, Spanish, Chinese, and vegetarian offerings. Restaurants along the *malecón* tend to be more expensive than those a few blocks inland.

MODERATE

Buffalo Bar-B-Q 𝕏𝕏 ARGENTINEAN/GRILLED HAMBURGERS   This is the ultimate send-off meal before a fishing, diving, or cruising trip, where dinner no doubt will be the daily catch. Indoor seating plays second fiddle to the outdoor courtyard, which fronts a fiery grill on which prime cuts are turned into delicacies. The hamburgers are big, flavorful, and come in so many delectable styles—from the special-sauced New Mexico burger to the standard cheeseburger—that a carnivore may just call this heaven. Otherwise, Buffalo Bar-B-Q's stellar steaks, ribs, and wine list are a worthy tribute to the chef's Argentinean roots.

Madero 1240 (corner of Cinco de Mayo and Constitución). ✆ **612/128-8755.** www.buffalo-bbq.com. Hamburgers and main courses $8–$25 (£4–£13). AE, MC, V. Wed–Mon 2pm–midnight.

La Pazta 𝕏 ITALIAN/SWISS   The trendiest restaurant in town, La Pazta gleams with black-lacquered tables and white tile; the aromas of garlic and espresso float in the air. The menu features local fresh seafood in items such as pasta with squid in wine-and-cream sauce, and crispy fried calamari. There's also homemade lasagna, baked in a wood-fired oven. La Pazta's daytime cafe is appealing for breakfast, too. The restaurant is in front of the Hotel Mediterrane, 1 block inland from the *malecón*.

Allende 36. ✆ **612/125-1195.** www.hotelmed.com. Breakfast $2–$4 (£1.10–£2.20); main courses $8–$15 (£4.40–£8.25). AE, MC, V. Cafe Thurs–Tues 7am–11pm, restaurant 3–11pm.

INEXPENSIVE

El Quinto Sol VEGETARIAN   Not only is this La Paz's principal health food market, it's a cheerful, excellent cafe for fresh fruit *licuados* (smoothies), *tortas,* daily vegetarian lunch specials, and ice creams made from in-season fruit. Tables sit beside oversize wood-framed windows with flowering planters in the sills. Sandwiches are served on whole-grain bread—also available for sale—and the potato tacos are an excellent way for vegetarians to indulge in a Mexican staple. Owner Marta Alonso also offers free nightly meditation classes to clients.

Av. Independencia and B. Domínguez. ✆ 612/122-1692. Main courses $1.50–$7 (75p–£3.50). No credit cards. Mon–Sat 8am–4pm; store hours 8am–9pm.

LA PAZ AFTER DARK

A night in La Paz logically begins at a bar or cafe along the *malecón* as the sun sinks into the sea. A favorite ringside seat at dusk is a table at **La Terraza,** next to the Hotel Perla (✆ **612/122-0777**). La Terraza makes good schooner-size margaritas. **Pelícanos Bar,** on the second story of the Hotel Los Arcos (✆ **612/122-2744**), has a good view of the waterfront and a clubby, cozy feel. **Carlos 'n' Charlie's La Paz-Lapa** (✆ **612/ 122-9290**) has live music on weekends; and on the second-floor terrace above is **Casa de Villa,** where current pop music commingles with young *Paceños,* or La Paz locals, till late. **La Cabaña** nightclub (✆ **612/122-0777**), in the Hotel Perla, features Latin rhythms. It opens at 9pm, and there's a cover on weekends that varies depending on the event. **Las Varitas,** Independencia and Domínguez ((✆ **612/125-2025**), is where you'll hear Latin rock, ranchero, and salsa. It's open from 9pm to 3 or 4am, with cover charges around $5.50 (£2.25). Note that covers may rise or fall depending on the crowd.

4 Mid Baja: Loreto, Mulegé & Santa Rosalía

Halfway between the resort sophistication of Los Cabos and the frontier exuberance of Tijuana lies Baja's midsection, an area rich in history and culture. The indigenous cave paintings here are a UNESCO World Heritage Site, and the area was home to numerous Jesuit missions in the 1700s. These days, Mid Baja is known for its sea kayaking, freediving, sportfishing, off-road racing, and hiking.

Overlooked by many travelers (except avid sportfishermen), **Loreto** is a rare gem that sparkles under the desert sky. The purple hues of the Giganta Mountains meet the indigo waters of the Sea of Cortez, providing a spectacular backdrop of natural contrasts for the historic town. **Mulegé** is, literally, an oasis in the Baja desert. The only freshwater river (Río Mulegé) in the peninsula flows through town. And the port town of **Santa Rosalía,** while a century or so past its prime, makes a worthy detour, with its pastel clapboard houses and unusual steel-and-stained-glass church, designed by Gustave Eiffel (of Eiffel Tower fame).

It's far enough from the polished tourism gem of Los Cabos that the people's smiles are more sincere, and you rarely hear the timeshare salesman's grating "Hola, amiga" as you walk the streets. But plans may be in the works to change that. Developers north of the border are snapping up spots in Ensenada Blanca Bay and Loreto Bay. Mid Baja is still a decade or more from being a hot spot for anyone besides adventurers, racing teams, and RV caravans, but the plans are there. If you want a glimpse of the Wild West, now is the time to visit Loreto, Mulegé, Santa Rosalía, and San Ignacio.

The region is also a popular launch for whale-watching. To find out when, where, and how to view the gentle giants, see p. 748, "Whale-Watching in Baja."

LORETO & THE OFFSHORE ISLANDS
389km (241 miles) NW of La Paz; 533km (330 miles) N of Cabo San Lucas; 1,125km (698 miles) SE of Tijuana

The center of the Spanish mission effort during colonial times, Loreto was the first capital of the Californias and the first European settlement in the peninsula. Founded on October 25, 1697, it was selected by Father Juan María Salvatierra as the site of the first mission in the Californias. (California, at the time, extended from Cabo San Lucas to the Oregon border.) He held Mass beneath a figure of the Virgin of Loreto, brought from a town in Italy bearing the same name. For 132 years, Loreto served as the state capital, until an 1829 hurricane destroyed most of the town. The capital moved to La Paz the following year.

During the late 1970s and early 1980s, the Mexican government saw in Loreto the possibility for another megadevelopment along the lines of Cancún, Ixtapa, or Los Cabos. It invested in a golf course and championship tennis facility, modernized the infrastructure, and built an international airport and marina facilities at Puerto Loreto, several kilometers south of town. The economics, however, didn't make sense, and few hotel investors and even fewer tourists came. In the past 2 years, however, this effort has been revitalized, and the area is seeing a welcome influx of flights, as well as the addition of its first new hotel in years, a sprawling Inn at Loreto Bay (formerly the Camino Real). The Loreto Bay residential development has been a major part of

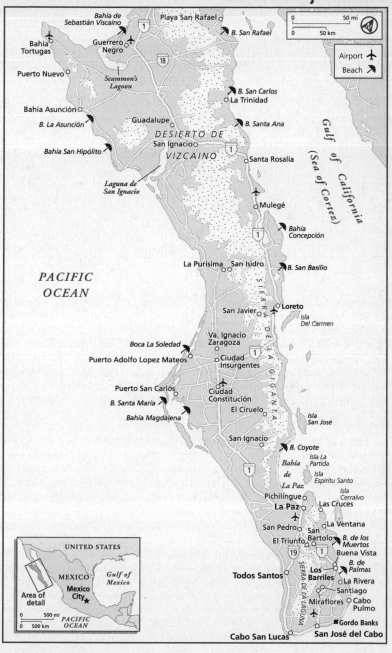

The Lower Baja Peninsula

Airport ✈
Beach ⏘

0   50 mi
0   50 km

Bahía de Sebastián Vizcaíno
Playa San Rafael
B. San Rafael
Bahía Tortugas
Guerrero Negro
Puerto Nuevo
Scammon's Lagoon
Bahía Asunción
B. La Asunción
Guadalupe
San Ignacio
B. San Carlos
La Trinidad
B. Santa Ana
DESIERTO DE VIZCAINO
Bahía San Hipólito
Laguna de San Ignacio
Santa Rosalía
Mulegé
Bahía Concepción
La Purisima
San Isidro
B. San Basílio
Loreto
Isla Del Carmen
San Javier
PACIFIC OCEAN
Gulf of California (Sea of Cortez)
Va. Ignacio Zaragoza
Boca La Soledad
Puerto Adolfo Lopez Mateos
Ciudad Insurgentes
Puerto San Carlos
B. Santa María
Ciudad Constitución
El Ciruelo
Bahía Magdalena
Isla San José
San Ignacio
B. Coyote
Isla La Partida
Bahía de La Paz
Isla Espíritu Santo
Isla Cerralvo
Pichilingue
La Paz
Las Cruces
San Pedro
La Ventana
El Triunfo
San Bartolo
B. de los Muertos
Buena Vista
B. de Palmas
Todos Santos
Los Barriles
La Rivera
Santiago
Miraflores
Cabo Pulmo
SIERRA DE LA LAGUNA
Gordo Banks
Cabo San Lucas
San José del Cabo
SIERRA DE LA GIGANTA

UNITED STATES
MEXICO
Gulf of Mexico
Mexico City
Area of detail
PACIFIC OCEAN
0   500 mi
0   500 km

renewed interest in the area, and it is bringing homes, condos, and other facilities to the area, with a rental program in place for vacation stays (© **877/865-6738** toll-free from the U.S., for rental information).

Soon, Loreto may become the next "new" place to go, but for now, downtown Loreto remains the heart rate–relaxing fishing village and gringo hideaway it's been for decades. The celebration of the town's 300th anniversary had the added benefit of updating the streets, plaza, and mission. Old Town Loreto is now a quaint showplace.

The *Loretanos,* Loreto-born Mexicans, are friendly and helpful; unlike the swarms of proprietary tourists that dominate the peninsula's northern and southern reaches, the mid-Baja region attracts a more unassuming set of visitors, and locals play the part of gracious hosts. Canadian and American expatriates who've settled in Loreto may be a bit more aloof with tourists, and who can blame them? They settled here when there was nothing, and they can't help but want it to stay that way for as long as possible.

The main reasons to come to Loreto center on the Sea of Cortez and the five islands just offshore, but the Sierra de La Giganta Mountains offer a wealth of opportunities for exploration as well. The reefs around Isla Coronado are home to schools of giant grouper, and beachgoers won't find a bay more beautiful than the one on Coronado's north side. Puerto Escondido shelters a growing yachting community; it's so lovely that most of the sailboats stay put year round. Kayakers launch here for trips to Isla del Carmen and Isla Danzante or down the remote mountain coast to La Paz; history buffs head for the mountains to visit some of the oldest Jesuit missions.

ESSENTIALS

The **Loreto International Airport** (© **613/135-0499** or -0498) is 6km (4 miles) southwest of town. **Taxis** (© **613/135-0047**) are readily available and charge about $20 (£10) for the 10-minute ride to Loreto. It is serviced by **AeroMéxico** (© **800/ 237-6639** in the U.S., or 613/135-1838), **Alaska Airlines** (© **800/252-7522;** www. alaskaair.com), and **Delta** (© **800/241-4141** in the U.S.), which all have nonstop flights from Los Angeles. **Continental** (© **800/523-3273** in the U.S.) also offers nonstop flights from Houston. Loreto's Terminal de Autobuses, or **bus station** (© **613/ 135-0767**), is on Salvatierra and Paseo Tamaral, a 10-minute walk from downtown. It's open 24 hours. The 5-hour trip from La Paz costs $25 (£13).

The city **tourist information office** (© **613/135-0411**) is in the southeast corner of the Palacio de Gobierno building, across from the town square. It offers maps, local free publications, and other basic information about the area. It's open Monday through Friday from 8am to 3pm. Information, which may be outdated, is also available at **www.gotoloreto.com** and **www.loreto.com.**

Salvatierra is the main street that runs northeast, merging into Paseo Hidalgo, which runs toward the beach. Calle de la Playa, also known as the Malecón, parallels the water; along this road you'll find many hotels, seafood restaurants, fishing charters, and the marina. Most of the town's social life revolves around the central square, the old mission, and the Malecón. The local telephone area code is **613.**

WHAT TO SEE & DO

The Sea of Cortez is the star in Loreto and the five islands just offshore make for some of the best kayaking, sailing–diving, and fishing in North America. Freediving, too, is becoming more popular. Loreto is the nearest major airport and city to **Bahía de Magdalena (Magdalena Bay),** the southernmost of the major gray whale–calving lagoons on the Pacific coast of Baja. For more information on popular whale-watching spots and tour operators, see "Whale-Watching in Baja," below.

Misión Nuestra Señora de Loreto was the first mission in the Californias, started in 1699. The original Virgen de Loreto, brought to shore by Padre Kino in 1697, is on display in the church's 18th-century gilded altar. The mission is on Salvatierra, across from the central square. Adjacent to the mission church and of equal or greater interest is the **Museo de las Misiones,** Salvatierra 16 (© **613/135-0441**). It has a small but complete collection of historical and anthropological exhibits from the Jesuit mission period. The museum is open Tuesday through Sunday from 9am to 1pm and 1:45pm to 6pm. Admission is $3 (£1.50).

WHERE TO STAY

In general, accommodations in Loreto are the kind you used to find all over Mexico: inexpensive and unique, with genuine, friendly owner-operators. And as Mid Baja is a mecca for RV explorers, **Rivera Del Mar RV Park & Camping** (© **613/135-0718;** www.riveradelmar.com) has deluxe hook-ups just 2 blocks from the beach. The rates quoted below do not include the 12% tax. Parking is free at all hotels in Mid Baja.

Inn at Loreto Bay *(Kids)*   One of Loreto's newest places to stay, the Inn at Loreto Bay (formerly the Camino Real) is on its own private cove a few kilometers outside of town, on a lovely beach, with calm waters perfect for swimming or kayaking. The hotel's brightly colored architecture complements sleek stone-floored guest rooms and warm-toned woven comforters. Master suites and presidential suites have large terraces and private Jacuzzis that overlook the bay. The ample space and recreational programs make this a great choice for families. Adjacent to Loreto's golf course, it's also ideal for anyone with a passion for the links. The upper-level Lobby Bar is a spectacular spot for a sunset cocktail, but the best place to take in the Sea of Cortez moonglow is from the terrace whirlpool tub.

Paseo de la Misión s/n, Nopoló, Loreto, B.C.S. © **866/850-0333** in the U.S., or 800/507-6979. reservations@loretobay. com. 156 units. High season $180–$305 (£90–£153); low season $155–$280 (£78–£140). Meal plans available. AE, MC, V. **Amenities:** 2 restaurants; 2 bars; outdoor pool; golf course; fitness center; concierge; tour desk; car rental; room service; child care; laundry service; Internet access. *In room:* A/C, satellite TV, minibar, hair dryer, safe, fan.

La Damiana Inn *(Finds)*   The location of the La Damiana Inn—in the heart of town on Calle Madero—is reason enough to book a reservation, but the warmth of color, style, and ownership make it the best accommodations value in Loreto. Debora Simmons lovingly operates this former family home, built in 1917. Today, its five rooms, all equipped with air conditioning and ceiling fans, offer a blend of twin, queen, and king beds that provide cozy resting places when you're not exploring the area. Wi-Fi throughout the hotel, laundry facilities, a shared living room, kitchen use, and free cuddles from two friendly house dogs are the perks that make La Damiana Inn seem like the home of a gracious friend. Pets welcome upon prior approval.

Madero, between Hidalgo and Jordan, Centro, 23880 Loreto, B.C.S. © **613/135-0356.** www.ladamianainn.com. 5 units. $53 (£27) double; $60 (£30) suite. No credit cards (American check accepted). **Amenities:** Wi-Fi; library; complimentary bikes; laundry service; TV; phone for local calls. *In room:* A/C, fan, no phone.

Posada de Las Flores *(★★★)*   The most luxurious place to stay in Loreto conveniently sits adjacent to the main square, in the heart of historic Loreto. Every room is beautifully decorated with fine Mexican arts and crafts, including heavy wood doors, Talavera pottery, painted tiles, candles, and Mexican scenic paintings. The colors and decor of the hotel are nouveau-colonial Mexico, with wood and tin accents. Large bathrooms have thick white towels and bamboo doors, with Frette bathrobes hanging in the closet. Every detail has been carefully selected, including the down comforters and numerous antiques tucked into corners. This hotel exudes class and refinement, from the general ambience to the warm polish of its employees. Italian-owned and operated, the sophisticated service has a European style to it. Only children older than 12 are welcome.

Salvatierra and Francisco I. Madera, Centro, 23880 Loreto, B.C.S. ℂ 619/378-0103 in the U.S., or 613/135-1162. Fax 613/135-1099. www.posadadelasflores.com. 15 units. High season $180 (£90) double, $290 (£145) suite; low season $150 (£75) double, $250 (£125) suite. Rates include continental breakfast. Children 11 or younger not permitted. MC, V. Street parking. **Amenities:** Breakfast restaurant; rooftop glass-bottom pool; hospitality desk. *In room:* A/C, TV, Wi-Fi, minibar, hair dryer.

An Ecoresort

Danzante Destination Resort 𝒜𝒜 *Finds*   This all-inclusive ecoresort offers guests everything that's wonderful about this area—sandy beaches, tranquillity, easy access to eco- and adventure activities—all in a lovely place to stay. It's 40km (25 miles) south of Loreto on serene Ensenada Blanca bay, home also to a tiny fishing village. The resort itself covers 4 hectares (10 acres) and is comprised of nine suites perched in a rocky hill facing the sea. Each king or queen room has a large Mexican-tile bathroom, beamed ceilings, handmade furnishings, large windows, and French doors that open onto a private thatched palm-covered terrace with hammocks. Lying in them and soaking in the view seems to be the favored activity of guests, yet there's much more you can do here—all activities are included in the room rate and include hiking, kayaking, snorkeling, and swimming at their secluded beach. Horseback riding is also available in the surrounding canyons, and diving, fishing, massage services, whale- and dolphin-watching, mission and cave painting tours, and "safari at sea" excursions can be arranged for an additional charge. For meals, included in the room rate, they serve a delicious selection of seafood, local fruits and vegetables, and organic produce from the on-site garden. The entire resort is solar powered and is owned by a couple who counts among their many accomplishments published books on Mexico travel and diving, underwater documentaries, explorations for sunken treasure, and guiding adventure tours worldwide. This may be their best achievement yet.

Highway 1 at Ligui, Ensenada Blanca, Loreto, B.C.S. ℂ 408/354-0042 in the U.S. www.danzante.com. info@danzante. com. 9 units. High season $199 per person (£50) queen suite; $225 per person (£113) king suite; low season $180 per person (£90) queen suite, $205 per person (£103) suite. All meals and activities included. MC, V. **Amenities:** Restaurant; bar; hilltop freshwater swimming pool; tour services; lending library; telescope for stargazing; cellphone at front desk, kayaks, horses, watersports, land and marine excursions. *In room:* Fan, hammock, no phone.

WHERE TO DINE

Dining in Loreto affords surprising variety, given the small size and laid-back nature of the town. However, don't expect anything fancy, even at the nicest restaurant. Big flavors come in humble packages in Loreto. In addition to the following hubs, the Wednesday two-for-one special at **Sushi Time** on the *malecón,* a vegetarian wood-fired pizza at **Pachamama** on Zapata, the grilled porterhouse at **El Nido** on Salvatierra, and the fried shrimp tacos at **Tacos el Rey** on Benito Juárez are all meals that will add flavor to your stay in Loreto.

Augie's Bar 𝒜 PIZZA/BAR   Located on the *malecón,* this is the preeminent happy-hour hotspot for the gringo community. Augie, who hales from the California video arcade business and does fun for a living, offers dancing lessons to patrons after they've had six drinks—and he keeps good on his promise. With TV sports of all kinds, ocean views, fabulous margaritas, tortilla pizzas that drive the town crazy, and an upstairs terrace that showcases Loreto's big-sky sunsets, this is the place to be after 4pm any day of the week.

On the corner of the Malecón and Zaragoza. No phone. Pizza $5–$8 (£2.50–£4). No credit cards. Daily 7am–11pm.

Café Olé LIGHT FARE   Although an espresso machine is hard to come by in this town, the breezy Café Olé is the best option for breakfast. Try eggs with *nopal* cactus, hotcakes, or a not-so-light lunch of a burger and fries. Tacos and some Mexican standards are also on the menu, as are fresh-fruit smoothies, or *licuados*.

Madero 14. ⏰ **613/135-0496.** Breakfast $2–$5 (£1–£2.50); sandwiches $2–$3.50 (£1–£1.75). No credit cards. Mon–Sat 7am–10pm; Sun 7am–2pm.

Del Borracho ⏰ BURGERS/SANDWICHES   If you're a *Three Amigos* fan from way back, Mike and Andrea Patterson's tribute to the obscure bar in the classic comedy will not disappoint. The movie often plays on loop in the background of this wooden saloon outside of town while chili dogs, milkshakes, sandwiches, and burgers make the rounds among a happy-bellied crowd who are chugging draft beer. The only place in town to serve Modelo Light and Modelo Negro on draft, Del Borracho's real claim to fame is the $3.50 (£1.75) bowl of blow-your-mind clam chowder that comes with a side of Andrea's homemade bread; of note for sports fans, Del Borracho has the NFL Sunday Ticket.

.5km (¼-mile) down the road to San Javier, 3.2km (2 miles) south of Loreto. ⏰ **613/137-0112.** Main courses $3–$5 (£1.50–£2.50). No credit cards. Daily sunrise–sunset.

LORETO AFTER DARK

Although selection is limited, Loreto after dark seems to offer a place for almost every nightlife preference. Happy hour starts in the late afternoon and ends shortly after sundown at bars like **Augie's Bar** (see above). Cocktails, music, and tapas flow into the wee hours at **Mike's Bar** on Paseo Hidalgo; and, if dancing is your game, the *malecón's* **Black&White** club gets going around 10pm Friday and Saturday nights. In addition, as is the tradition throughout Mexico, Loreto's central plaza offers a **free concert** when there's a cruise ship in port. However, Loretanos and their families are so hospitable that the best party may be the one to which you're unexpectedly invited. In Loreto, magic is bound to happen.

SANTA ROSALIA
61km (38 miles) N of Mulegé

Located in an *arroyo* (dry streambed) north of Mulegé, Santa Rosalía looks more like an old Colorado mining town than a Mexican port city. Founded by the French in 1855, the town has a European ambience combined with a distinctly Mexican culture. Pastel clapboard houses surrounded by picket fences line the streets, giving the town its nickname—*ciudad de madera* (city of wood). The large harbor and rusted ghost of a copper smelting facility dominate the central part of town bordering the waterfront. The town was a copper-mining center for years, and a French outfit operated here from 1885 until 1954, when the Mexicans regained the use of the land. Problems plagued the facility, which closed permanently in 1985.

Today, Santa Rosalía (pop. 14,000) is known for its man-made harbor—the recently constructed Marina Santa Rosalía, complete with concrete piers, floating

Moments **Whale-Watching in Baja**

Few sights inspire as much reverence as close contact with a whale in its natural habitat. The various protected bays and lagoons on Baja's Pacific coast are the preferred winter waters for migrating gray whales as they journey south to mate and give birth to their calves. These whales are known to be so friendly and curious that they frequently come up to the boats and stay close by, and sometimes even allow people to pet them.

The experience is particularly rewarding in the protected areas of the **El Vizcaíno Biosphere Reserve,** where you can easily see many whales. This area encompasses Guerrero Negro, Laguna San Ignacio, Bahía Magdalena, and the famous **Laguna Ojo de Liebre**—also known as **Scammon's Lagoon.**

Because these protected waters offer ideal conditions for gray whales during the winter, the neighboring towns have developed the infrastructure and services to accommodate whale watchers. Whale-watching season generally runs from January to March. But remember that the colder the water, the farther south the whales migrate, so check on water temperatures and whale sightings before you plan your expedition. The temperature on the boat can be cool, so bring a jacket.

Although you can fly from Los Cabos and La Paz, **Loreto** is the best place to launch a whale-watching journey, as it has a well-developed tourist infrastructure and a number of lovely resort hotels. Trips take you by road to Bahía Magdalena, where you board a skiff to get up close to the gentle giants. Locally based **Las Parras Tours** (© **613/135-0900;** www.mexonline.com/lasparras.htm) offers excellent tours. Prices for package trips from Loreto run around $90 to $100 (£45–£50) per person for a daylong trip. Among the many groups that run longer-term expeditions, which cost upwards of $1,500 (£750) per person for a multiday trip, is San Diego-based **Baja Expeditions** (© **800/843-6967** in the U.S., or 612/125-3828; www.bajaex.com).

docks, and full docking accommodations for up to a dozen ocean liners. Because this is the prime entry point of manufactured goods into Baja, the town abounds with auto parts and electronics stores, along with shops selling Nikes and sunglasses. The town has no real beach to speak of and few recreational attractions.

EXPLORING SANTA ROSALIA

The principal attraction in Santa Rosalía is the **Iglesia de Santa Bárbara,** a structure of galvanized steel designed by Gustave Eiffel (of Eiffel Tower fame) in 1884. It was created for the 1889 Paris World Expo, then transported here, section by section, and reassembled in 1897. Its somber gray exterior belies the beauty of the intricate stained-glass windows as viewed from inside.

The other sight to see is the former Fundación del Pacífico, or **Museo Histórico Minero de Santa Rosalía.** Located in a landmark wooden building, it houses a permanent display of artifacts from the days of Santa Rosalía's mining operations. It's open Monday through Friday from 8am to 2pm. Admission is free.

However, the city itself is the macro-attraction. Wooden saloons, wraparound verandas, and mountainous terrain make for a paradoxical contrast to the Mexicans milling in the streets. You can't get lost in this grid of one-way streets, so even if you're on your way some place else, a 15-minute drive through Santa Rosalía is a must. Here, in this thriving ghost town, you won't find hacienda-style architecture or red-tile roofs, but you will find the best bakery in Baja. **El Boleo,** at Avenida Obregón at Calle 4 (© **615/152-0310**), has been baking French baguettes since the late 1800s, but I recommend the pitahaya, a dense sweetbread stuffed with a kind of almond paste. It's 3 blocks west of the church and is open from 8am to 9pm Monday to Saturday, and Sunday 9am to 2pm.

WHERE TO STAY & DINE

Dining is limited in the small town of Santa Rosalía, but lunch at **El Muelle** restaurant, on Obregón, right across from the central plaza, is superb. The tacos, enchiladas in spicy fresh tomato sauce and breaded fish bathed in peppers and cheese are all good reasons to visit, but the main draw is the creamy chipotle smoked tuna dip that comes with chips before the meal. Follow it up with dessert bread from El Boleo.

Hotel Francés   Founded in 1886, the Hotel Francés once set the standard of hospitality in Baja Sur, welcoming European dignitaries and hosting the French administrators and businessmen of the mining operations. Today, it has a worn air of elegance but retains its position as the most welcoming accommodation in Santa Rosalía. Rooms are in the back, with wooden porches and balconies overlooking a small courtyard pool. Each room has individually controlled air-conditioning, plus windows that open for ventilation. Floors are wood-planked, and the small bathrooms are beautifully tiled. You have a choice of two double beds or one king. Telephone service is available in the lobby. The popular restaurant serves breakfast until noon.

Calle Jean Michel Cousteau s/n, 23920 Santa Rosalía B.C.S. ©/fax **615/152-2052.** 16 units. High season $71 (£36) double; low season $65 (£33) single or double. Rates include breakfast. No credit cards. Free parking. **Amenities:** Restaurant (7am–noon); small courtyard pool. *In room:* A/C, TV, Wi-Fi, no phone.

5 Tijuana & Rosarito Beach

Northern Baja California is not only Mexico's most infamous border crossing, but it also claims to be the birthplace of the original Caesar salad and the margarita. Long notorious as a hard-partying 10-block border town, **Tijuana** has cleaned up its act a bit on its way to becoming a full-scale city. A growing number of sports and cultural attractions now augment the legendary shopping experience and wild nightlife. **Rosarito Beach,** of *Titanic* fame, remains a more tranquil resort town; the decidedly laid-back atmosphere makes it easy to enjoy its miles of beachfront.

TIJUANA: BAWDY BORDER TOWN

In northern Baja, 26km (16 miles) south of San Diego, the first point of entry from the West Coast of the U.S. is infamous Tijuana—a town that continues to delude travelers into thinking that a visit there means they've been to Mexico. An important border town, Tijuana is renowned for its hustling, carnival-like atmosphere and easily accessible decadence.

Tijuana's "sin city" image is gradually morphing into that of a shopper's paradise and a nocturnal playground. Vineyards associated with the expanding wine industry

---

(Warning **Avoiding Danger**

Although Tijuana has the reputation for being a carefree party playground, now more than ever it's important to use common sense while visiting. In April 2008, the U.S. Department of State heightened its Travel Advisory after a series of shoot-outs between drug cartels and the federal police, sent in by President Felipe Calderón to eradicate the dealers, shook up this already rough-and-tumble city. While most of the people targeted in the attacks were involved in law enforcement or the drug trade, the violence has come close to innocent bystanders in some instances. One shootout caused a kindergarten to be shut down and another caused a high-speed chase that ended with a truck crashing into the airport before dawn. The Department of State reports that in 2007, dozens of U.S. citizens were kidnapped or killed in crimes apparently unrelated to drugs. Despite these shake-ups, however, life goes on in Tijuana as in any other large metropolitan city. (I was in town on a rainy day in February when dozens of families braved the cold weather to bring puffy jacket-wearing children to watch a Teletubbies-like live show at the **Central Cultural Tijuana**—in welcome contrast to recent reports of violence.) Locals are still very proud of their city's culture and welcome visitors with open arms. They also advise you, however, to say no to illegal drugs of any kind.

---

are nearby, and an increasing number of cultural offerings have joined the traditional sporting attractions of greyhound racing, jai alai, and bullfights.

You are less likely to find the Mexico you may be expecting here—no charming town squares and churches, no women in colorful embroidered skirts and blouses, no bougainvillea spilling out of every crevice. Tijuana has an urban culture, a profusion of U.S.-inspired goods and services, and relentless hawkers plying to the thousands of tourists who come for a taste of Mexico.

ESSENTIALS

A visit to Tijuana requires little in the way of formalities—people who stay less than 72 hours in the border zone do not need a tourist card. If you plan to stay longer, a tourist card is required and, beginning in January 2008, a passport will be required as well. If you're staying 7 days or less, tourist cards are free from the border crossing station or from any immigration office; they cost a small fee for more than 7 days.

From downtown San Diego, you also have the option of taking the **bright-red trolley** headed for San Ysidro and getting off at the last, or San Ysidro, stop (it's nicknamed the Tijuana Trolley for good reason). From here, follow the signs to walk across the border, or hop one of the buses ((℃ **664/685-1470**), which are located next to the trolley station. It's simple, quick, and inexpensive; the one-way fare is about $2 (£1). The last trolley leaving for San Ysidro departs downtown San Diego around midnight; the last returning trolley from San Ysidro is at 1am. On Saturday, the trolley runs 24 hours.

Once you're in Tijuana, it's easy to get around by taxi. Cab fares from the border to downtown average $5 (£2.50). You can also hire a taxi to Rosarito for about $20 (£10) one-way.

The Tijuana airport ((℃ **664/607-8201**) is about 8km (5 miles) east of the city. To drive to Tijuana from the U.S., take I-5 or 805 south to the Mexican border at San

Tijuana

SAN DIEGO

U.S.A.
MEXICO

■ San Ysidro (Blue Line) Station

U.S. Customs ■

■ Mexico Customs

Ave. Padre Kino

C. Coahuila

Ave. Internacional

Río Tijuana

(i)

Calle 1A

Calle 2A

(i)

Ave. Revolucion

Calle 3A

Calle 4A

Ave. Niños Heroes

Calle 5A

Calle 6A

ZONA
RÍO

Ave. Marquez de Leon

Ave. Paseo Tijuana

Ave. Independencia

Via Rapida Oriente

Via Rapida Poniente

Ave. Constitucion

Calle 7A

Ave. Ocampo

Ave. Negrete

Ave. Pio Pico

Ave. Cuauhtemoc

Ave. Paseo de los Heroes

2

(i)

CENTRO

Ave. Madero

Calle 10A

Calle 11A

3

✉

Ave. Sanchez Taboada

Blvd. Agua Caliente

Av. Diego Rivera

Av. J.M. Velasco

4

5

D.A. Siqueiros

6

C. Brasil

Blvd. Fundadores

Ave. Durango

Ave. Jalisco

C. 16 de Septiembre

Av. Rio Tijuana

Ave. Rodriguez

Blvd. Agua Caliente

Blvd. Salinas

C. España

Information *(i)*
Post Office ✉

| 0 | 1/2 mi |
| 0 | 0.5 km |

N

C. Hermosillo

7→

Tijuana

UNITED STATES

THE
BAJA
PENINSULA

MEXICO

Gulf of
Mexico

Mexico
City

PACIFIC
OCEAN

| 0 | 500 mi |
| 0 | 500 km |

Caliente Racetrack **7**
Hotel Lucerna **6**
L.A. Cetto Winery **3**
La Cantina de los Remidios **4**
Mundo Divertido La Mesa **5**
Pueblo Amigo Plaza **1**
Tijuana Cultural Center **2**

Ysidro. The drive from downtown San Diego takes about a half-hour, or you can leave your car in a San Ysidro parking lot and walk the 20 minutes to Avenida Revolución. For **tourist information,** visit the Centro Cultural Tijuana, Paseo de los Héroes and Mina (© **664/687-9600**). It's in the Zona Río, the principal shopping and dining district, adjacent to the Tijuana River. For information online, visit the Tijuana Tourism board's official website, **www.seetijuana.com**. Another recommendable site is **www.tijuanaonline.org**.

There are major banks with ATMs and *casas de cambio* (money-exchange houses) all over Tijuana, but you can easily come here—or to Rosarito and Ensenada, for that matter—without changing money, because dollars are accepted everywhere.

EXPLORING TIJUANA

For many visitors, Tijuana's main event is the bustling **Avenida Revolución,** which was constructed in 1889. Beginning in the 1920s, American college students, servicemen, and hedonistic tourists discovered this street as a center for illicit fun. Some of the original attractions—gambling, back-alley cockfights (now illegal), and girlie shows—have fallen by the wayside, with drinking and shopping the main order of business these days. You'll find the action between calles 1 and 9; the landmark Jai Alai Frontón Palace anchors the southern portion. If you don't want to navigate the area on your own, the **Tijuana Convention & Visitors' Bureau** (© **664/683-1405;** www.tijuanaonline.org) offers a 1-hour guided walking tour of the city, and **Eco Baja Tours** www.ecobajatours.com) offers a selection of tours, including visits to the Guadalupe Valley, La Bufadora, and Tecate.

If you're looking to see a different side of Tijuana, the best place to start is the **Centro Cultural Tijuana,** Paseo de los Héroes and Mina Zona Río (© **664/607-3097,** ext. 9650; www.cecut.gob.mx). You'll easily spot the ultramodern Tijuana Cultural Center complex, which houses an IMAX theater, the museum's permanent collection of Mexican artifacts, and a gallery of visiting exhibits. The center is open daily from 9am to 9pm. Admission to the permanent exhibits is free, there's a $2 (£1) charge for the special event gallery, and tickets for IMAX films are $4 (£2) for adults and $2.50 (£1.25) for children.

You'll find some classier shopping and a colorful local marketplace, plus go-karts and minigolf, at **Mundo Divertido La Mesa,** Vía Rápida Poniente 15035 (© **664/701-7133**). The park is open Monday through Friday from noon to 9pm and Saturdays and Sundays from 11am to 10pm. Admission is free, and several booths inside sell tickets for the various rides; most rides cost $1 to $11 (50p–£5.50).

The fertile valleys of northern Baja produce most of Mexico's finest wines and export many high-quality vintages to Europe. For an introduction to Mexican wines, stop into **Cava de Vinos L. A. Cetto (L. A. Cetto Winery),** Av. Cañón Johnson 2108, at Avenida Constitución Sur (© **664/685-3031,** ext. 128, or 638-1644; www.lacetto.com). Shaped like a wine barrel, this building's facade is made from old oak aging barrels—call it inspired recycling. Guided tours run Monday through Friday from 10am to 1:30pm and 4 to 6pm; it's open Saturdays from 10am to 4pm.

If your tastes run more toward *cerveza* than wines, plan to visit the **Tijuana Brewery,** 2951 Bulevar Fundadores, Col. Juárez (© **664/684-2406** or 638-8662; www.tjbeer.com). Here, guided tours (by prior appointment) demonstrate the beer-making process at the brewery. The family who owns the company has a long tradition of master brewers who worked in breweries in the Czech Republic, bringing their knowledge

> ## (Moments First Crush: The Annual Harvest Festival
>
> If you enjoyed a visit to L.A. Cetto, Tijuana's winery (or Ensenada's Bodegas de Santo Tomás, discussed later in this chapter), then you might want to come back for the Harvest Festival, held each year in late August or early September. Set among the endless vineyards of the fertile Guadalupe Valley, the day's events include the traditional blessing of the grapes, wine tastings, live music and dancing, riding exhibitions, and a country-style Mexican meal. L.A. Cetto offers a group excursion from Tijuana (about an hour's drive); San Diego's **Baja California Tours** ((C) **800/336-5454** in the U.S., or 858/454-7166) also organizes a daylong trip from San Diego.

back home to Tijuana. Cerveza Tijuana was founded in January 2000, and now has select distribution in the U.S. Its lager, dark, and light beers are all available to sample in the adjoining European-style pub, which features karaoke on Monday and Tuesday nights and live music Wednesday through Saturday. Appetizers and entrees are also available. Taberna TJ is open Monday to Saturday from 1pm to 2am.

Tijuana's biggest attraction is **shopping.** People come to take advantage of low prices on a variety of merchandise(terra cotta and colorfully glazed pottery, woven blankets and serapes, embroidered dresses and sequined sombreros, onyx chess sets, beaded necklaces and bracelets, silver jewelry, leather bags and *huarache* sandals, rain sticks, Cuban cigars, and Mexican liquors. You're permitted to bring $400 (£200) worth of purchases back across the border (sorry, no Cuban cigars allowed), including 1 liter (.26 gallons) of alcohol per person. Many Americans view Tijuana as a way to purchase inexpensive prescription drugs and bring them back across the border. Be aware—authorities have cracked down and are making surprise arrests of foreigners purchasing drugs without valid prescriptions from a Mexican doctor.

If a marketplace atmosphere and spirited bargaining are what you're looking for, head to **Mercado de Artesanías (crafts market),** Calle 2 and Avenida Negrete. Here, vendors of pottery, clayware, clothing, and other crafts fill an entire city block. Shopping malls are as common in Tijuana as in any big American city; you shouldn't expect to find typical souvenirs there, but shopping alongside residents and other intrepid visitors is often more fun than feeling like a sitting-duck tourist. One of the biggest, and most convenient, is **Plaza Río Tijuana,** Paseo de los Héroes 96 at Avenida Independencia, Zona Río ((C) **664/200-2828**), an outdoor plaza anchored by several department stores and featuring dozens of specialty shops and casual restaurants. **Plaza Agua Caliente** ((C) **664/681-7777**), at 4558 Bulevar Agua Caliente, Col. Aviación, is a more upscale shopping center, and in addition to fine shops and restaurants, is known for its emphasis on health and beauty, with day spas, gyms, and doctors offices found in abundance here. A comprehensive selection of shopping options is listed at **www.tijuanaonline.org/english/shopping/index.htm**.

OUTDOOR ACTIVITIES & SPECTATOR SPORTS
Tijuana is a spectator's (and gambler's) paradise.

BULLFIGHTING Whatever your opinion, bullfighting has a prominent place in Mexican heritage and is even considered an essential element of the culture. The skill and bravery of matadors is closely linked with cultural ideals regarding *machismo,* and some of the world's best perform at Tijuana's two stadiums. As in Spain, however, the bulls die. The season runs late spring to early fall (usually May to early Oct), with events held on Sunday at 4:30pm. Ticket prices range from $12 to $100 (£6–£50), the premium seats are on the shaded side of the arena, available at the bullring or in advance from San Diego's **Five Star Tours** (© **619/232-5049** or 664/622-2203). **Plaza de Toros Monumental,** also called Bullring-by-the-Sea (© **664/680-1808;** www. plazamonumental.com), is 10km (6 miles) west of downtown on Highway 1-D (before the first toll station); it's at the edge of both the ocean and the California border.

DOG RACING There's satellite wagering on U.S. horse races at the majestic **Caliente Racetrack,** off Bulevar Agua Caliente, 5km (3 miles) east of downtown (© **619/231-1910** or 664/682-3110; www.caliente.com.mx), but only greyhounds actually kick up dust at the track. Races are held daily at 7:45pm; at 1pm on Sunday, Monday, and Tuesday; and at 2pm on Saturday. Admission is free.

LUCHA LIBRE Although Jack Black made the flamboyant fighters popular with American filmgoers with his 2006 movie, *Nacho Libre,* Mexicans have always had a fondness for great masked fighters like El Santo and Rey Misterio. The matches—which feature up to five different bouts—are spectacular. The *luchadores* are equal parts athlete actor and boogeyman and audience members are never shy about joining in with jeers and taunts. **Auditorio Municipal** (© **664/681-6174**) at 12421 Blvd. Agua Caliente hosts fights just about every Friday night at 8:30pm. Ticket prices start at $5 (£2.50) and vary depending on the popularity of the fight.

A PLACE TO STAY

Hotel Lucerna Once the most chic hotel in Tijuana, Lucerna now feels slightly worn, though it still has personality. The flavor is Mexican Colonial—wrought-iron railings and chandeliers, rough-hewn heavy wood furniture, brocade wallpaper, and traditional tiles. The hotel is in the Zona Río, away from the noise and congestion of downtown, so a quiet night's sleep is easily attainable. All of the rooms in the five-story hotel have balconies or patios. Hotel rates in Tijuana are subject to a 12% tax.

Av. Paseo de los Héroes, 10902 Zona Río, Tijuana. © **664/633-3900.** 168 units. $190 (£95) double; $360 (£180) suite. AE, MC, V. Free parking. **Amenities:** Coffee shop; outdoor pool; room service. *In room:* A/C, satellite TV, coffeemaker, hair dryer, iron.

WHERE TO DINE

Cien Años MEXICAN This elegant and gracious Zona Río restaurant offers artfully blended Mexican flavors (tamarind, *poblano chile,* mango) in stylish presentations. If you're interested in haute cuisine for breakfast, lunch, or dinner, stop here; the buzz around Tijuana is all about this place.

José María Velazco 1407, Zona del Río. © **888/534-6088** or 619/819-5097 in the U.S.; 664/634-3039 or -3794. www.cien.info. Main courses $10–$20 (£5–£10). AE, MC, V. Mon–Thurs 8am–11pm; Fri–Sat 8am–midnight; Sun 8am–10pm.

La Cantina de los Remedios MEXICAN This is one of Tijuana's most festive atmospheres, wildly popular with Mexicans and Americans alike for it's typical Mexican cuisine and courtyard atmosphere. Another highlight is its all-inclusive menu option, which has made it a hit in seven other cities throughout Mexico. For one price, guests

Finds A Northern Baja Spa Sanctuary

One of Mexico's best-known spas is in northern Baja, just 58km (36 miles) south of San Diego. The **Rancho La Puerta** 🐾🐾 occupies 1,200 hectares (2,964 acres) of lush oasis surrounded by pristine countryside, which includes a 2.5-hectare (6-acre) organic garden and La Cocina Que Canta, a spa cuisine cooking school that opened in 2007. Cottages can accommodate up to 150 guests per week, and the ranch has a staff of almost 400. Each cottage has its own patio garden and is decorated with Mexican folk art. Inside the rooms are spacious living-room-sized seating areas, desks, CD players, hair dryers, robes, and safes, and most rooms have fireplaces.

Three swimming pools, four tennis courts, five hot tubs, saunas, steam rooms, and 11 gyms for aerobic and restorative classes, are only part of the facilities. Separate men and women's health centers offer the full range of spa services. Hiking trails surround the resort, and a labyrinth that is a full-size replica of the ancient labyrinth found in Chartres Cathedral allows for moving meditation.

There are also several lounges and shared spaces, including the library, with thousands of books to browse and read, an evening movie lounge, recreation room, and for those who can't conceive of totally disconnecting, the E-center, with 24-hour access to e-mail and Internet.

Rancho La Puerta runs weeklong programs—Saturday through Saturday—emphasizing a mind/body/spirit philosophy, and certain weeks throughout the year are geared specifically to one topic; Specialty Week themes range from couples to Pilates and dance to meditation. Prices begin at $2,795 (£1,380) for the week most of the year and $2,890 (£1,445) for the week from March through May. Included in the rates are all classes, meals, evening programs, and use of facilities. Personal spa services cost extra. You may be able to book shorter stays (3 nights or more); and rates may be prorated on a nightly basis.

For reservations or to request a brochure, visit **www.rancholapuerta. com**; call **800/443-7565** in the U.S., or fax 858/764-5560. American Express, MasterCard, and Visa are accepted.

can enjoy an appetizer, soup or salad, main course, dessert, and a cocktail. Here, the drink menu is extensive, inspiring the name *los remedios,* or the remedies.

Av. Diego Rivera 19 718, Zona del Río. © **664/634-3065**. All-inclusive meal $24–$39 (£12–£20). MC, V. Mon–Thurs 1pm–1am; Fri–Sat 1pm–2am; Sun 1–10pm.

TIJUANA AFTER DARK

Avenida Revolución is the city's nightlife center, often compared with Bourbon Street in New Orleans during Mardi Gras—though here the blowout is year-round.

Zona Río and Plaza Fiesta are more geared toward late-night dining and dance-clubbing than tequila swilling and barhopping. Although the nightlife scene changes regularly, perhaps the most popular dance club is **Baby Rock,** 1482 Diego Rivera

(© **664/634-2404**), Zona Río, near the Guadalajara Grill restaurant, a cousin to Acapulco's lively Baby O, which features everything from Latin rock to rap. It's open from 9pm to 3am, with a cover charge of $12 (£6) on Saturdays.

Also popular in Tijuana are sports bars, which feature wagering on events in the United States as well as races from Tijuana's Caliente track. The most popular cluster in the Pueblo Amigo and Vía Oriente areas and around Plaza Rio Tijuana in the Zona Río, a center designed to resemble a colonial Mexican village). Just beyond Zona Río you'll find **Tangaloo** (Av. Monterrey 3215; © **664/681-8091;** www.tangaloo.com; Thurs–Sun 9pm–4am), a hip club featuring DJs spinning electronic dance music, with a changing theme each Saturday night. Two of the town's hottest clubs, which are open until 4 or 5am on the weekends, **Rodeo Santa Fe** (© **664/682-4967;** cover $8/£4) and **Señor Frog's** (© **664/682-4964;** no cover), are in Pueblo Amigo Plaza, which is just off of Paseo Tijuana. Pueblo Amigo Plaza is less than 3km (2 miles) from the border, a short taxi ride or—during daylight hours—a pleasant walk.

ROSARITO BEACH: BAJA'S FIRST BEACH RESORT

Just 29km (18 miles) south of Tijuana and a complete departure in ambience, Rosarito Beach is a tranquil, friendly beach town. Hollywood has played a major part in Rosarito's recent renaissance—it was the location for the sound stage and filming of the Academy Award–winning *Titanic*. The former *Titanic* Museum—now called **Xploration**—continues to draw the fans of this film and moviegoers in general. The beaches between Tijuana and Rosarito are also known for excellent surf breaks.

GETTING THERE   Two roads run between Tijuana and Ensenada (the largest and third-largest cities in Baja)—the scenic, coast-hugging toll road (**Hwy. 1-D,** marked *cuota,* costs $2.40), and the free but slower public road (**Hwy. 1,** marked *libre*). Both roads pass through Rosarito Beach. If you're not driving, you can take a shuttle from the last trolley stop in San Ysidro. **Mexicoach** (© **619/428-9517** in the U.S., or 664/685-1470 locally; www.mexicoach.com) offers shuttle rides for about $10 (£5).

WHAT TO SEE & DO

A few kilometers south of Rosarito proper lies the **seaside production site** of 1997's megablockbuster *Titanic,* and more recently, *Master and Commander.* On 16 otherwise dry hectares (40 acres) along the Pacific Coast, the studio has several huge tanks that fill with water to reproduce seafaring conditions. Filled with *Titanic* memorabilia, it has now become the moviemaking theme park, **Xploration,** devoted to the art of moviemaking. The Cinemágico area has interactive displays about filmmaking and special effects, and guided tours are available in English and Spanish. There is also a play center for kids, plus a gift shop. Admission is $12 (£6) for adults, $9 (£4.50) for children 3 to 11. Xploration (© **866/369-2252** in the U.S., or 661/612-4294; www.xploration.com) is open Wednesday through Friday from 9am to 4:30pm, and Saturday and Sunday from 10am to 5:30pm. There's a food court with Dominos pizza, Subway, and even a Starbucks coffee.

If you have only a few hours to spend in Rosarito Beach, that's still enough time to have a swim or a horseback ride at the beach, shop for souvenirs, and dine on fish tacos or tamales from one of the family-run stands along **Bulevar Benito Juárez,** the town's main (and only) drag. The dozen or so blocks of Rosarito north of the Rosarito Beach Hotel are packed with stores typical of Mexican border towns: curio shops, cigar and *licores* (liquor) stores, and *farmacías* (where such drugs as Viagra, Retin-A, Prozac, and many more are available at low cost).

The Upper Baja Peninsula

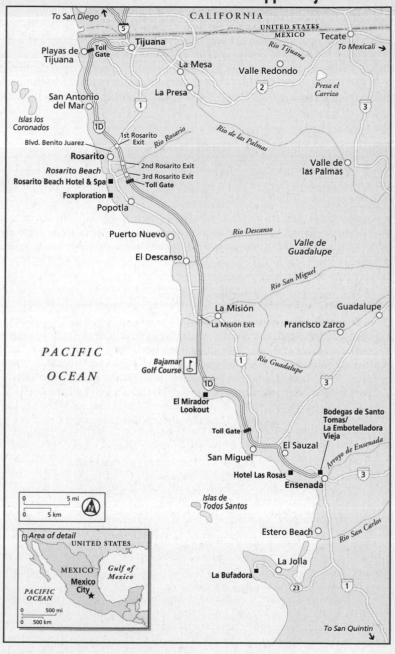

Because the legal drinking age in Baja is 18, the under-21 crowd from Southern California tends to flock across the border on Friday and Saturday nights. The most popular spot in town is **Papas & Beer** (© 661/612-0444; www.papasandbeer.com). It's a relaxed come-as-you-are-type club on the beach, just a block north of the hotel. Even for those young in spirit only, it's great fun, with outdoor tables and a bar surrounding a sand volleyball court. The **Salón Mexicano** (© 661/612-0144), in the Rosarito Beach Hotel, attracts a slightly more mature evening crowd, with live music and karaoke on Friday and Saturday.

WHERE TO STAY & DINE

Rosarito Beach Hotel & Spa   This family-owned resort had its glamorous heyday in the 1920s and is currently defined by glaring nighttime neon and party-mania. The Torres family is hoping to change the hotel's image yet again with the addition of a 17-story condo hotel scheduled to open in summer 2008. Despite the resort's ever-changing personality, its unique artistic construction and lavish decoration remain on the original property. It has a wide, family-friendly stretch of beach. The stately home of the original owners has been transformed into the full-service **Casa Playa Spa,** where massages and other treatments are only slightly less costly than in the U.S. You'll

---

Tips Surfing, Northern Baja Style

Surfers flock to the northern Baja coast for perpetual right-breaking waves, cheap digs and eats, and *Endless Summer*–type camaraderie.

Undoubtedly, the most famous surf spot in all of Mexico is **Killers,** at Todos Santos Island. This was the location of the winning wave in the 1997–98 K2 Challenge (a worldwide contest to ride the largest wave each winter—and be photographed doing it). Killers is a very makeable wave for confident, competent surfers. To get there you need a boat. You can get a lift from the local *panga* (skiff) fleet, for about $100 (£55) for the day. That's pretty much the going rate, and the tightly knit Ensenada *pangueros* aren't eager to undercut each other. It's about 15km (10 miles) out to the island; there you'll anchor and paddle into the lineup. You must bring everything you'll need—food, drink, sunscreen, and so on.

Other less radical and easier-to-reach spots include the rocky **Popotla** break, south of Rosarito, where you'll walk to the beach through the Popotla trailer park. **Calafia,** just a few kilometers south of Rosarito, has a reeling right point that can get very heavy. **San Miguel** is the point break just south of the final tollbooth on the highway into Ensenada. It's an excellent wave but generally crowded.

If you're a surfer looking to get your bearings or a beginner wanting to get your feet wet, stop by **Inner Reef** (© 661/613-2065; Km 34.5 on the free road, 9.7km/6 miles south of Rosarito). This tiny shack, painted green with blue flames, sells all the essentials: wax, leashes, patch kits, custom surfboards, rentals, and ding repairs. Owner Mitch Benson is there daily, 9am to 5pm in winter, and 8am to 6pm in summer. He also has a shop in front of Rosarito Beach Hotel.

pay more for a room with an ocean view, and more for the newer, air-conditioned units in the tower; the older rooms in the poolside building have only ceiling fans, but they prevail in the character department, with hand-painted trim and original tile. The mansion's dining room (Chabert's Restaurant) charges top dollar for Continental cuisine; Azteca is a casual Mexican restaurant in the main building.

Bulevar Benito Juárez, Zona Centro, 22710 Rosarito, B.C. ℭ 800/343-8582 in the U.S., or 661/612-0144. Fax 661/612-1125. www.rosaritobeachhotel.com. 278 units. $97–$167 (£49–£84) double; $125–$251 (£63–£126) suites. 2 children younger than 12 stay free in parent's room. Packages available. MC, V. Free parking. **Amenities:** 2 restaurants; bar; 2 outdoor pools; wading pool; spa; racquetball court; playground; room service; Wi-Fi in some areas of hotel. *In room:* A/C (in some), TV, fan (in some).

6 Ensenada: Port of Call

134km (83 miles) S of San Diego; 109km (68 miles) S of Tijuana

Ensenada is an attractive town on a lovely bay, surrounded by sheltering mountains. About 40 minutes from Rosarito, it's the kind of place that loves a celebration—be it for a bicycle race or a seafood festival.

GETTING THERE & INFORMATION   After passing through the final tollgate, **Highway 1-D** curves sharply toward downtown Ensenada.

The **Tourist and Convention Bureau booth** (ℭ 646/178-2411; www.enjoy ensenada.com) is at the western entrance to town, where the waterfront-hugging Bulevar Lázaro Cárdenas—aka Bulevar Costero—curves away to the right. It's open Tuesday through Sunday from 9am to 5pm. Taxis park along López Mateos.

EXPLORING ENSENADA

While Ensenada is technically a border town, one of its appeals is its multilayered vitality. The bustling port consumes the entire waterfront—beach access can be found only north or south of town—and the Pacific fishing trade and agriculture in the fertile valleys surrounding the city dominate the economy.

Even part-time oenophiles should visit the **Bodegas de Santo Tomás Winery** ⭐⭐, Av. Miramar 666, at Calle 7 (ℭ 646/178-3333; www.santo-tomas.com), the oldest winery in Mexico, and the largest in Baja. It uses old-fashioned methods of processing grapes, first cultivated from Spanish varietals in 1888, in the lush Santo Tomás Valley, where a Dominican mission of the same name was founded almost a century earlier. Tours in English run every hour from 9am to 5pm Monday through Saturday and from 10am to 4pm Sunday. The tour is free, and if you wish to follow it up with a tasting, $5 (£2.50) gets you a sampling of six young or low-priced wines, and the $10-option (£5) includes six older or high-priced wines and two reserves.

Ensenada's equivalent of Tijuana's Avenida Revolución is crowded **Avenida López Mateos,** roughly parallel to Bulevar Lázaro Cárdenas (Bulevar Costero); the highest concentration of shops and restaurants is between avenidas Ruiz and Castillo. Compared to Tijuana, there is more authentic Mexican art and craftwork in Ensenada. And Ensenada is home to a thriving adventure subculture: off-road racers, surfers, kayakers, and more flock to Ensenada in search of their adrenaline fix.

South of the city, 45 minutes by car along the rural Punta Banda peninsula, is one of Ensenada's major attractions: **La Bufadora,** a natural sea spout in the rocks. With each incoming wave, water is forced upward through the rock, creating a geyser whose loud grunt gave the phenomenon its name (it means "buffalo snort"). From downtown

Ensenada, take Avenida Reforma (Hwy. 1) south to Highway 23 west. La Bufadora is at the end of the road. Once parked (about $2/£1 per car in crude dirt lots), you must walk downhill to the viewing platform, at the end of a 270m (986-ft.) pathway lined with souvenir stands. Also, **Picacho del Diablo,** the 10,154-foot mountain located in the Sierra de San Pedro Mártir national park, draws hikers and backpackers eager to scale its two-pronged peak about 129km (80 miles) south of Ensenada.

WHERE TO STAY

Las Rosas Hotel & Spa   One of the most modern hotels in the area, Hotel Las Rosas still falls short of most definitions of luxurious, yet the pink oceanfront hotel 3km (2 miles) outside Ensenada is the favorite of many Baja aficionados. It offers most of the comforts of an upscale American hotel—which doesn't leave room for much Mexican personality, but surfers will appreciate the view of Todos Santos Island. The atrium lobby is awash in pale pink and sea foam green, a color scheme that pervades throughout—but the rooms received a welcome update in 2006. Some rooms have fireplaces, wireless Internet, and/or in-room whirlpools, and all have balconies overlooking the pool and ocean. One of the resort's main photo-ops is the swimming pool that overlooks the Pacific and features a vanishing edge that appears to merge with the ocean beyond. If you want to maintain the highest comfort level possible, this would be your hotel of choice.

Hwy. 1, 3km (2 miles) north of Ensenada. (C) 866/447-6727 in the U.S., or 646/174-4310. www.lasrosas.com. 48 units. $80–$142 (£40–£71) double; $105–$182 (£53–£91) suite. MC, V. Free parking. **Amenities:** Restaurant; cocktail lounge; outdoor pool; tennis court; small workout room; full-service spa; cliff-top hot tub; business center w/Internet; room service; laundry service. *In room:* TV, Wi-Fi in some, hair dryer, fan.

WHERE TO DINE

El Rey Sol ☞ FRENCH/SEAFOOD   If you've been to Ensenada without eating at El Rey Sol, you better not tell a local. *Ensenadenses* are as proud of this family-run French restaurant as they are of their festivals, and after one taste of the clams au gratin, Chateaubriand bouquetière, farm-fresh vegetables, or mango charlotte, you will understand why. El Rey Sol, which opened in 1947, also offers a selection of traditional Mexican plates for dinner as well as coffee and French pastries at the sidewalk cafe during the day.

Av. Lopez Mateos 1000. (C) 646/178-1733. Reservations recommended on weekends. Main courses $9–$19 (£4.95–£10). AE, MC, V. Daily 7:30am–10:30pm

ENSENADA AFTER DARK

Just like in *Casablanca,* where "everyone goes to Rick's," everyone's been going to **Hussong's Cantina,** Av. Ruiz 113, near Avenida López Mateos ((C) 646/178-3210), since the bar opened in 1892. Nothing much has changed—the place still sports Wild West–style swinging saloon doors, a long bar to slide beers along, and strolling mariachis bellowing above the din. Be aware that hygiene and privacy are low priorities in the restrooms. While the crowd (a pleasant mix of tourists and locals) at Hussong's can really whoop it up, they're amateurs compared to those who frequent **Papas & Beer,** Avenida Ruiz near Avenida López Mateos ((C) 646/174-0145; www.papasandbeer. com), across the street. A tiny entrance leads to the upstairs bar and dance club. The music is loud and the hip young crowd is definitely here to party. Papas & Beer has quite a reputation with the Southern California college crowd and has opened a branch in Rosarito Beach (see above).

Appendix A: Mexico Fast Facts

AREA CODES See "Staying Connected," p. 83.

ATM NETWORKS/CASHPOINTS See "Money & Costs," p. 63.

BUSINESS HOURS Most businesses in larger cities are open between 9am and 7pm; in smaller towns many close between 2 and 4pm. Most close on Sunday. In resort areas stores commonly open in the mornings on Sunday, and shops stay open late, until 8 or even 10pm. Bank hours are Monday through Friday from 9 or 9:30am to anywhere between 3 and 7pm. Banks open on Saturday for at least a half-day.

CAR RENTALS See p. 61 in chapter 3.

DRINKING LAWS The legal drinking age in Mexico is 18; however, asking for ID or denying purchase is extremely rare. Grocery stores sell everything from beer and wine to national and imported liquors. You can buy liquor 24 hours a day, but during major elections, dry laws often are enacted by as much as 72 hours in advance of the election—and they apply to tourists as well as local residents. Mexico does not have laws that apply to transporting liquor in cars, but authorities are beginning to target drunk drivers more aggressively. It's a good idea to drive defensively.

It's illegal to drink in the street but many tourists do. If you are getting drunk, you shouldn't drink in the street, because you are more likely to get stopped by the police.

DRIVING RULES See "Getting There & Getting Around," p. 57.

ELECTRICITY The electrical system in Mexico is 110 volts AC (60 cycles), as in the United States and Canada. In reality, however, it may cycle more slowly and overheat your appliances. To compensate, select a medium or low speed on hair dryers. Many older hotels still have electrical outlets for flat two-prong plugs; you'll need an adapter for any plug with an enlarged end on one prong or with three prongs. Many better hotels have three-hole outlets (*trifásicos* in Spanish). Those that don't may have loan adapters, but to be sure, it's always better to carry your own.

EMBASSIES & CONSULATES They provide valuable lists of doctors and lawyers, as well as regulations concerning marriages in Mexico. Contrary to popular belief, your embassy cannot get you out of jail, provide postal or banking services, or fly you home when you run out of money. Consular officers can provide advice on most matters and problems, however. Most countries have an embassy in Mexico City, and many have consular offices or representatives in the provinces.

The Embassy of the **United States** in Mexico City is at Paseo de la Reforma 305, next to the Hotel María Isabel Sheraton at the corner of Río Danubio (© **55/5080-2000**); hours are Monday through Friday from 8:30am to 5:30pm. Visit **http://mexico.us embassy.gov** for information related to U.S. Embassy services. There are U.S. Consulates at López Mateos 924-N, Ciudad Juárez (© 656/611-3000); Progreso 175, Guadalajara (© 333/268-2100); Av. Constitución 411 Pte., Monterrey (© 818/345-2120); Tapachula 96, Tijuana (© 664/622-7400); Monterrey 141, Hermosillo (© 662/289-3500); Primera 2002, Matamoros (© 868/812-4402); Calle 60 No. 338 K, Mérida (© 999/942-5700); Calle San Jose, Nogales, Sonora (© 631/311-8150); and Allende 3330, Col. Jardin, Nuevo Laredo (© 867/714-0512). In addition, there are consular agencies in Acapulco (© 744/469-0556); Cabo San Lucas (© 624/143-3566); Cancún (© 998/883-0272); Cozumel (© 987/872-4574); Ixtapa/Zihuatanejo (© 755/553-2100); Mazatlán (© 669/916-5889); Oaxaca (© 951/516-2853); Puerto Vallarta (© 322/222-0069); San Luis Potosí (© 444/811-7802); and San Miguel de Allende (© 415/152-2357).

The Embassy of **Australia** in Mexico City is at Rubén Darío 55, Col. Polanco (© 55/1101-2200; www.mexico.embassy.gov.au). It's open Monday through Thursday from 8:30am to 5:15pm.

The Embassy of **Canada** in Mexico City is at Schiller 529, Col. Polanco (© 55/5724-7900 or for emergencies 01-800/706-2900); it's open Monday through Friday from 9am to 1pm and 2 to 5pm. Visit www.dfait-maeci.gc.ca or www.canada.org.mx for addresses of consular agencies in Mexico. There are Canadian consulates in Acapulco (© 744/484-1305); Cancún (© 998/883-3360); Guadalajara (© 333/671-4740); Mazatlán (© 669/913-7320); Monterrey (© 818/344-2753); Oaxaca (© 951/513-3777); Puerto Vallarta (© 322/293-0098); San José del Cabo (© 624/142-4333); and Tijuana (© 664/684-0461).

The Embassy of **New Zealand** in Mexico City is at Jaime Balmes 8, 4th floor, Col. Los Morales, Polanco (© 55/5283-9460). It's open Monday through Thursday from 8:30am to 2pm and 3 to 5:30pm, and Friday from 8:30am to 2pm.

The Embassy of the **United Kingdom** in Mexico City is at Río Lerma 71, Col. Cuauhtémoc (© 55/5207-2089 or 5242-8500; www.embajadabritanica.com.mx). It's open Monday through Thursday from 8am to 4pm and Friday from 8am to 1:30pm.

The Embassy of **Ireland** in Mexico City is at Cda. Boulevard Manuel Avila Camacho 76, 3rd floor, Col. Lomas de Chapultepec (© 55/5520-5803). It's open Monday through Friday from 9am to 5pm.

The **South African** Embassy in Mexico City is at Andrés Bello 10, Edificio Fórum, 9th floor, Col. Polanco (© 55/5282-9260). It's open Monday through Friday from 8am to 4pm.

EMERGENCIES   In case of emergency, dial © 065 from any phone within Mexico. For police emergency numbers, turn to the "Fast Facts" sections in each of the individual chapters. The 24-hour **Tourist Help Line** in Mexico City is © 01-800/987-8224 or 55/5089-7500, or you can now simply dial © 078. The operators don't always speak English, but they are always willing to help.

GASOLINE (PETROL)   There's one government-owned brand of gas and one gasoline station name throughout the country—**Pemex** (Petroleras Mexicanas). There are two types of gas in Mexico: *magna,* 87-octane unleaded gas, and *premio,* which is 93-octane. In Mexico, fuel and oil are sold by the liter, which is slightly more than a quart (1 gal. equals about 3.8 liters). Many franchise Pemex stations have bathroom facilities and convenience stores—a great improvement over the old ones. Gas stations accept both credit and debit cards for gas purchases.

HOLIDAYS   For schedules, see "Calendar of Events," earlier in this chapter.

HOTLINES   There are several helpful numbers to know: **Tourist Help Line,** available 24 hours (© 01-800/987-8224 toll-free inside Mexico; or dial 078); **Mexico Hot Line** (© 800/446-3942); **U.S. Department of State Travel Advisory,** staffed 24 hours (© 202/647-5225); **National Passport Center** (© 877/487-2778); and the **U.S. Centers for Disease Control and Prevention International Traveler's Hot Line** (© 877/394-8747).

INSURANCE   Medical Insurance   Most U.S. health plans (including Medicare and Medicaid) don't cover travel to Mexico, and the ones that do often require you to pay for services upfront and reimburse you only after you return home.

As a safety net, you may want to buy travel medical insurance, particularly if you're traveling to a remote or high-risk area where emergency evacuation might be necessary. If you require additional medical insurance, try **MEDEX Assistance** (© 410/453-6300; www.medexassist.com) or **Travel Assistance International** (© 800/821-2828; www.travelassistance.com; for general information on services, call the company's **Worldwide Assistance Services, Inc.,** at © 800/777-8710).

Canadians should check with their provincial health plan offices or call **Health Canada** (© 866/225-0709; www.hc-sc.gc.ca) to learn the extent of their coverage and what documentation and receipts they must take home if they are treated overseas.

Travelers from the U.K. should carry their European Health Insurance Card (EHIC), which replaced the E111 form as proof of entitlement to free/reduced cost medical treatment abroad (© 0845 606 2030; www.ehic.org.uk). Note, however, that the EHIC covers only "necessary medical treatment." For repatriation costs, lost money, baggage, or cancellation, it's best to seek travel insurance from a reputable company (www.travelinsuranceweb.com).

Travel Insurance   The cost of travel insurance varies widely depending on the destination, the cost and length of your trip, your age and health, and the type of trip you're taking. Expect to pay between 5% and 8% of the vacation itself. You can get estimates from various providers through **InsureMyTrip.com.** Enter your trip cost and dates, your age, and other information, for prices from more than a dozen companies.

U.K. citizens and their families who make more than one trip abroad per year may find that an annual travel insurance policy is cheaper. Check **www.moneysuper market.com**, which compares prices across a wide range of providers for single- and multitrip policies.

Most big travel agencies offer their own insurance and will probably try to sell you their package when you book a holiday. Think before you sign. **Britain's Consumers' Association** recommends carefully reading the fine print before buying travel insurance. **The Association of British Insurers** (© 020/7600-3333; www.abi.org.uk) gives advice by phone and publishes *Holiday Insurance,* a free guide to policy provisions and prices. You might also shop around for better deals: Try **Columbus Direct** (© 0870/033-9988; www.columbusdirect.net).

Trip Cancellation Insurance   Trip-cancellation insurance will help retrieve your money if you have to back out of a trip or depart early, or if your travel supplier goes bankrupt. Trip cancellation traditionally covers contingencies such as sickness, natural disasters, and State Department advisories. The latest news in trip-cancellation insurance is the availability of **expanded hurricane coverage** and the **"any-reason"** cancellation coverage—which costs more but covers cancellations made for any reason. You won't get back 100% of your prepaid trip cost, but you'll be refunded a substantial portion. **TravelSafe** (© 888/885-7233; www.travelsafe.com) offers both types of coverage. Expedia also offers any-reason cancellation coverage for its air-hotel packages. For details, contact one of the following recommended insurers: **Access America** (© 866/807-3982; www.accessamerica.com); **Travel Guard International** (© 800/826-4919; www.travelguard.com); **Travel Insured International** (© 800/243-3174; www.travelinsured.com); and **Travelex Insurance Services** (© 888/457-4602; www.travelex-insurance.com).

LANGUAGE   Spanish is the official language in Mexico. English is spoken and understood to some degree in most tourist areas. Mexicans are very accommodating with foreigners who try to speak Spanish, even in broken sentences. See Appendix B for a glossary of simple phrases for expressing basic needs.

LEGAL AID   **International Legal Defense Counsel,** 405 Lexington Ave., 26th floor, New York, NY 10174 (✆ 212/907-6442), is a law firm specializing in legal difficulties of Americans abroad. See also "Embassies & Consulates" and "Emergencies," above.

LOST & FOUND   Be sure to tell all your credit card companies the minute you discover your wallet has been lost or stolen, and file a report at the nearest police precinct. Your credit card company or insurer will require a police report number or record of the loss in order to waive any fraudulent charges. Most credit card companies have an emergency toll-free number to call if your card is lost or stolen; they may be able to wire you a cash advance immediately or deliver an emergency credit card in a day or two. **Visa**'s Mexico emergency number is ✆ **001-800/847-2911.** American Express cardholders and traveler's check holders should call ✆ **001-800/001-3600.** Master-Card cardholders should call ✆ **001-800/307-7309.**

If you need emergency cash over the weekend, when all banks and American Express offices are closed, you can have money wired to you via **Western Union** (✆ **800/ 325-6000;** www.westernunion.com).

MAIL   Postage for a postcard or letter is 11 pesos ($1/50p); it may arrive anywhere from 1 to 6 weeks later. The price for registered letters and packages depends on the weight, and unreliable delivery time can take 2 to 6 weeks. The recommended way to send a package or important mail is through FedEx, DHL, UPS, or another reputable international mail service.

NEWSPAPERS & MAGAZINES   The English-language newspaper, the *Miami Herald,* is published in conjunction with *El Universal.* You can find it at most newsstands. *The News*—a new English-language daily with Mexico-specific news, published in Mexico City—launched in late 2007. Newspaper kiosks in larger cities also carry a selection of English-language magazines.

PASSPORTS   The websites listed provide downloadable passport applications as well as the current fees for processing applications. For an up-to-date, country-by-country listing of passport requirements around the world, go to the "International Travel" tab of the U.S. Department of State at **http://travel.state.gov**.

For Residents of Australia   You can pick up an application from your local post office or any branch of Passports Australia, but you must schedule an interview at the passport office to present your application materials. Call the **Australian Passport Information Service** at ✆ **131-232,** or visit the government website at **www.passports.gov.au**.

For Residents of Canada   Passport applications are available at travel agencies throughout Canada or from the central **Passport Office,** Department of Foreign Affairs and International Trade, Ottawa, ON K1A 0G3 (✆ **800/567-6868;** www.ppt.gc.ca). *Note:* Canadian children who travel must have their own passport. However, if you hold a valid Canadian passport issued before December 11, 2001, that bears the name of your child, the passport remains valid for you and your child until it expires.

For Residents of Ireland   You can apply for a 10-year passport at the **Passport Office,** Setanta Centre, Molesworth Street, Dublin 2 (✆ **01/671-1633;** www.irlgov.ie/ iveagh). Those under age 18 and over 65 must apply for a 3-year passport. You can also apply at 1A South Mall, Cork (✆ **21/494-4700)** or at most main post offices.

For Residents of New Zealand   You can pick up a passport application at any New Zealand Passports Office or download it from their website. Contact the **Passports Office** at ℂ **0800/225-050** in New Zealand or 04/474-8100, or log on to **www. passports.govt.nz.**

For Residents of the United Kingdom   To pick up an application for a standard 10-year passport (5-yr. passport for children under 16), visit your nearest passport office, major post office, or travel agency or contact the **United Kingdom Passport Service** at ℂ **0870/521-0410** or search its website at **www.ukpa.gov.uk.**

POLICE   In Mexico City, police are suspect as often as they are trustworthy; however, you'll find many who are quite honest and helpful. In the rest of the country, especially in the tourist areas, most are very protective of international visitors. Several cities, including Puerto Vallarta, Mazatlán, Cancún, and Acapulco, have a special corps of English-speaking Tourist Police to assist with directions, guidance, and more. In case of emergency, dial ℂ **065** from any phone within Mexico. For police emergency numbers, turn to "Fast Facts," in the individual chapters.

SMOKING   See p. 68 in chapter 3.

TAXES   The 15% IVA (value-added) tax applies on goods and services in most of Mexico, and it's supposed to be included in the posted price. This tax is 10% in Cancún, Cozumel, and Los Cabos. There is a 5% tax on food and drinks consumed in restaurants that sell alcoholic beverages with an alcohol content of more than 10%; this tax applies whether you drink alcohol or not. Tequila is subject to a 25% tax. Mexico imposes an exit tax of $24 (£12) on every foreigner leaving the country by plane.

TELEPHONES   See p. 83 in chapter 3, "Planning Your Trip to Mexico."

TIME   Central Time prevails throughout most of Mexico. The states of Sonora, Sinaloa, and parts of Nayarit are on Mountain Time. The state of Baja California Norte is on Pacific Time, but Baja California Sur is on Mountain Time. All of Mexico observes **daylight saving time.**

TIPPING   Most service employees in Mexico count on tips for the majority of their income, and this is especially true for bellboys and waiters. Bellboys should receive the equivalent of 50¢ (25p) to $1 (50p) per bag; waiters generally receive 10% to 15%, depending on the level of service. It is not customary to tip taxi drivers, unless they are hired by the hour or provide touring or other special services.

TOILETS   Public toilets are not common in Mexico, but an increasing number are available, especially at fast-food restaurants and Pemex gas stations. These facilities and restaurant and club restrooms commonly have attendants, who expect a small tip (about 50¢/25p).

USEFUL PHONE NUMBERS   **U.S. Department of State Travel Advisory** ℂ 202/ 647-5225 (manned 24 hrs.); **U.S. Passport Agency** ℂ 202/647-0518; **U.S. Centers for Disease Control International Traveler's Hotline** ℂ 404/332-4559.

VISAS   See p. 47 in chapter 3, "Planning Your Trip to Mexico."

WATER   Tap water in Mexico in generally not potable and it is safest to drink purified bottled water. Some hotels and restaurants purify their water, but you should ask rather than assume this is the case. Ice may also come from tap water and should be used with caution.

Appendix B:
Survival Spanish

Most Mexicans are very patient with foreigners who try to speak their language; it helps a lot to know a few basic phrases. I've included simple phrases for expressing basic needs, followed by some common menu items.

ENGLISH-SPANISH PHRASES

English	Spanish	Pronunciation
Good day	**Buen día**	Bwehn *dee*-ah
Good morning	**Buenos días**	*Bweh*-nohs *dee*-ahs
How are you?	**¿Cómo está?**	*Koh*-moh eh-*stah*
Very well	**Muy bien**	Mwee byehn
Thank you	**Gracias**	*Grah*-syahs
You're welcome	**De nada**	Deh *nah*-dah
Goodbye	**Adiós**	Ah-*dyohs*
Please	**Por favor**	Pohr fah-*bohr*
Yes	**Sí**	See
No	**No**	Noh
Excuse me	**Perdóneme**	Pehr-*doh*-neh-meh
Give me	**Déme**	*Deh*-meh
Where is . . . ?	**¿Dónde está . . . ?**	*Dohn*-deh eh-*stah*
the station	**la estación**	lah eh-stah-*syohn*
a hotel	**un hotel**	oon oh-*tehl*
a gas station	**una gasolinera**	*oo*-nah gah-soh-lee-*neh*-rah
a restaurant	**un restaurante**	oon res-tow-*rahn*-teh
the toilet	**el baño**	el *bah*-nyoh
a good doctor	**un buen médico**	oon bwehn *meh*-dee-coh
the road to . . .	**el camino a/hacia**	el cah-*mee*-noh ah/*ah*-syah
To the right	**A la derecha**	Ah lah deh-*reh*-chah
To the left	**A la izquierda**	Ah lah ees-*kyehr*-dah
Straight ahead	**Derecho**	Deh-*reh*-choh
I would like	**Quisiera**	Key-*syeh*-rah
I want	**Quiero**	*Kyeh*-roh
to eat	**comer**	koh-*mehr*
a room	**una habitación**	*oo*-nah ah-bee-tah-*syohn*

English	Spanish	Pronunciation
Do you have . . . ?	¿Tiene usted . . . ?	Tych-nch oo-*sted*
a book	un libro	oon *lee*-broh
a dictionary	un diccionario	oon deek-syoh-*nah*-ryoh
How much is it?	¿Cuánto cuesta?	*Kwahn*-toh *kweh*-stah
When?	¿Cuándo?	*Kwahn*-doh
What?	¿Qué?	Keh
There is	(¿)Hay (. . . ?)	Eye
(Is there . . . ?)		
What is there?	¿Qué hay?	Keh eye
Yesterday	Ayer	Ah-*yer*
Today	Hoy	Oy
Tomorrow	Mañana	Mah-*nyah*-nah
Good	Bueno	*Bweh*-noh
Bad	Malo	*Mah*-loh
Better (best)	(Lo) Mejor	(Loh) Meh-*hohr*
More	Más	Mahs
Less	Menos	*Meh*-nohs
No smoking	Se prohibe fumar	Seh proh-*ee*-beh foo-*mahr*
Postcard	Tarjeta postal	Tar-*heh*-tah poh-*stahl*
Insect repellent	Repelente contra	Reh-peh-*lehn*-teh *cohn*-trah
	insectos	een-*sehk*-tohs

MORE USEFUL PHRASES

English	Spanish	Pronunciation
Do you speak English?	¿Habla usted inglés?	*Ah*-blah oo-*sted* een-*glehs*
Is there anyone here	¿Hay alguien aquí	Eye *ahl*-gyehn ah-*kee*
who speaks English?	que hable inglés?	keh *ah*-bleh een-*glehs*
I speak a little Spanish.	Hablo un poco	*Ah*-bloh oon *poh*-koh
	de español.	deh eh-spah-*nyohl*
I don't understand	No (lo) entiendo	Noh (loh) ehn-*tyehn*-doh
Spanish very well.	muy bien el	mwee byehn el
	español.	eh-spah-*nyohl*
The meal is good.	Me gusta la comida.	Meh *goo*-stah lah koh-*mee*-dah
What time is it?	¿Qué hora es?	Keh *oh*-rah ehs
May I see your menu?	¿Puedo ver el menú	*Pweh*-doh vehr el meh-*noo*
	(la carta)?	(lah *car*-tah)
The check, please.	La cuenta, por favor.	Lah *kwehn*-tah pohr fa-*borh*
What do I owe you?	¿Cuánto le debo?	*Kwahn*-toh leh *deh*-boh
What did you say?	¿Mande? (formal)	*Mahn*-deh
	¿Cómo? (informal)	*Koh*-moh

English	Spanish	Pronunciation
I want (to see) . . .	Quiero (ver) . . .	*kyeh*-roh (vehr)
a room	un cuarto or	oon *kwar*-toh,
	una habitación	*oo*-nah ah-bee-tah-*syohn*
for two persons	para dos	*pah*-rah dohs
	personas	pehr-*soh*-nahs
with (without)	con (sin)	kohn (seen)
bathroom	baño	*bah*-nyoh
We are staying here	Nos quedamos aquí	Nohs keh-*dah*-mohs ah-*kee*
only . . .	solamente . . .	soh-lah-*mehn*-teh
one night.	una noche.	*oo*-nah *noh*-cheh
one week.	una semana.	*oo*-nah seh-*mah*-nah
We are leaving . . .	Partimos	Pahr-*tee*-mohs
	(Salimos) . . .	(sah-*lee*-mohs)
tomorrow.	mañana.	mah-*nya*-nah
Do you accept . . . ?	¿Acepta usted . . . ?	Ah-*sehp*-tah oo-*sted*
traveler's checks?	cheques de viajero?	*cheh*-kehs deh byah-*heh*-roh
Is there a	¿Hay una	Eye *oo*-nah
laundromat . . . ?	lavandería . . . ?	lah-*bahn*-deh-*ree*-ah
near here?	cerca de aquí?	*sehr*-kah deh ah-*kee*
Please send these	Hágame el favor de	Ah-gah-meh el fah-*bohr* deh
clothes to the	mandar esta ropa	mahn-*dahr* eh-stah *roh*-pah
laundry.	a la lavandería.	a lah lah-*bahn*-deh-*ree*-ah

NUMBERS

1	uno (*ooh*-noh)		17	diecisiete (dyeh-see-*syeh*-teh)
2	dos (dohs)		18	dieciocho (dyeh-*syoh*-choh)
3	tres (trehs)		19	diecinueve (dyeh-see-nweh-beh)
4	cuatro (*kwah*-troh)		20	veinte (*bayn*-teh)
5	cinco (*seen*-koh)		30	treinta (*trayn*-tah)
6	seis (sayes)		40	cuarenta (kwah-*ren*-tah)
7	siete (*syeh*-teh)		50	cincuenta (seen-*kwen*-tah)
8	ocho (*oh*-choh)		60	sesenta (seh-*sehn*-tah)
9	nueve (*nweh*-beh)		70	setenta (seh-*tehn*-tah)
10	diez (dyehs)		80	ochenta (oh-*chehn*-tah)
11	once (*ohn*-seh)		90	noventa (noh-*behn*-tah)
12	doce (*doh*-seh)		100	cien (syehn)
13	trece (*treh*-seh)		200	doscientos (do-*syehn*-tohs)
14	catorce (kah-*tohr*-seh)		500	quinientos (kee-*nyehn*-tohs)
15	quince (*keen*-seh)		1,000	mil (meel)
16	dieciséis (dyeh-see-*sayes*)			

TRANSPORTATION TERMS

English	Spanish	Pronunciation
Airport	**Aeropuerto**	Ah-eh-roh-*pwehr*-toh
Flight	**Vuelo**	*Bweh*-loh
Rental car	**Arrendadora de autos**	Ah-*rehn*-da-doh-rah deh *ow*-tohs
Bus	**Autobús**	Ow-toh-*boos*
Bus or truck	**Camión**	Ka-*myohn*
Lane	**Carril**	Kah-*reel*
Nonstop (bus)	**Directo**	Dee-*rehk*-toh
Baggage (claim area)	**Equipajes**	Eh-kee-*pah*-hehss
Intercity	**Foraneo**	Foh-rah-*neh*-oh
Luggage storage area	**Guarda equipaje**	*Gwar*-dah eh-kee-*pah*-heh
Arrival gates	**Llegadas**	Yeh-*gah*-dahss
Originates at this station	**Local**	Loh-*kahl*
Originates elsewhere	**De paso**	Deh *pah*-soh
Are seats available?	**¿Hay lugares disponibles?**	Eye loo-*gah*-rehs dis-pohn-*ee*-blehss
First class	**Primera**	Pree-*meh*-rah
Second class	**Segunda**	Seh-*goon*-dah
Nonstop (flight)	**Sin escala**	Seen ess-*kah*-lah
Baggage claim area	**Recibo de equipajes**	Reh-*see*-boh deh eh-kee-*pah*-hehss
Waiting room	**Sala de espera**	*Sah*-lah deh ehss-*peh*-rah
Toilets	**Sanitarios**	Sah-nee-*tah*-ryohss
Ticket window	**Taquilla**	Tah-*kee*-yah

DINING TERMINOLOGY
Meals
el desayuno   breakfast
la comida   main meal of the day, taken in the afternoon
la cena   supper

Courses
la botana   small serving of food that accompanies a beer or drink, and usually served free of charge
la entrada   appetizer
la sopa   soup course (This term does not necessarily mean soup; it can be a dish of rice or noodles, called *sopa seca* [dry soup].)
la ensalada   salad
el plato fuerte   main course
el postre   dessert
la comida corrida   inexpensive daily special, usually consisting of three courses
el menú del día   same as *comida corrida*

Degree of Doneness

rare *término un cuarto* (literally means one-fourth)
medium rare *término medio* (one-half)
medium *término tres cuartos* (three-fourths)
well done *bien cocido*
Note: Keep in mind, when ordering a steak, that *medio* does not mean medium.

Miscellaneous Restaurant Terminology

una cucharra a spoon
un cuchillo a knife
la cuenta the check
un plato a plate
un plato hondo a soup bowl
la propina the tip
una servilleta a napkin
un tenedor a fork
el vaso glass
IVA value-added tax
una fonda a food stall in the market or street; also used loosely or with nostalia to designate an informal restaurant

Index

Academia Falcón (Guanajuato), 210
Academia Hispano Americana (San Miguel), 197
Academic trips, 80–81
Acanceh, 651
Acapulco, 4, 379–403
  accommodations, 391–397
  American Express, 385
  beaches, 386–387
  boat excursions and cruises, 387–388
  climate, 385
  consular agents, 385
  currency exchange, 385
  getting around, 384–385
  hospitals, 385
  layout of, 384
  nightlife, 401–403
  outdoor activities, 388–389
  post office, 386
  restaurants, 397–401
  safety, 386
  shopping, 390–391
  tourist police, 386
  traveling to, 381
  visitor information, 384
Acapulco Historical Museum, 390
Accommodations
  best, 17–21
  boutique hotels, 80
  tips on, 85–86
Active vacations, best, 12–13
Acuario (Veracruz), 519
Acuario Mazatlán, 350
AeroMéxico Vacations, 78
Agua Azul waterfalls, 480
Aguacatenango, 481, 489
Aguilar sisters, 470
Airport security, 48
Airport taxes, 60
Air tours, Puerto Vallarta, 305
Air travel, 2, 57, 60
Akab Dzib (Chichén Itzá), 670
Aktun Chen cavern, 609

Akumal, 588, 608–609
Alameda Park (Mexico City), 145
Alaska Airlines Vacations, 78
Alebrijes (Acapulco), 402
Alfarería Tlaquepaque (Puerto Vallarta), 316
Alpargatas, 673–674
Altitude sickness, 66–67
Alux (Playa del Carmen), 604
Amatenango del Valle, 481, 489
Amatlán, 187
American Airlines Vacations, 78
American Express
  Acapulco, 385
  Campeche, 661
  Cancún, 532
  Chihuahua, 692
  Cuernavaca, 178
  Guadalajara, 276
  Ixtapa/Zihuatanejo, 407
  Los Mochis, 689
  Manzanillo, 372
  Mazatlán, 347
  Mérida, 631
  Mexico City, 110
  Morelia, 250
  Oaxaca City, 449
  Puebla, 499
  Puerto Vallarta, 300
  Querétaro, 224
  San Luis, 242
  San Miguel, 195
  Veracruz, 517
  Zacatecas, 234
AMTAVE (Asociación Mexicana de Turismo de Aventura y Ecoturismo, A.C.), 81
Angahuan, 271–272
Animal-rights issues, 77–78
Annual Witches Conference, 52
Año Nuevo, 51
Anthropology Museum (La Paz), 738
Anthropology Museum, Mérida, 636

Antigua, 523
Apple Vacations, 79
Aquarium, La Paz, 738
Aquarium, Veracruz, 519
Aqueduct, Morelia, 255
Aqueduct of Zacatecas, 236
Archaeological Conservancy, 80
Archaeological museums and exhibits. *See also entries starting with "Museo Arqueológico" and "Museum of Archaeology"*
  Chetumal, 622
  Guadalajara, 288
  Mexico City, 142
  Puerto Vallarta, 310
  San Cristóbal, 486
  Taxco, 166
Archaeological sites and ruins. *See also specific ruins and sites*
  Acanceh, 651
  best, 11–12
  Cacaxtla, 510–511
  Chichén Itzá, 665–670
  Chincultic, 495
  Cholula, 507–508
  Cobá, 615–618
  Cozumel, 570
  Cozumel area, 579–580
  Dainzú, 466
  Dzibilchaltún, 649
  Ek Balam, 675
  Isla Mujeres, 563
  Lambityeco, 467
  Mayapán, 652
  Mitla, 467–468
  Monte Albán, 463–465
  Palenque, 474–476
  Puuc Maya sites, 657–659
  Pyramids of Xochicalco (near Cuernavaca), 181
  Río Bec area, 623–624
  Riviera Maya, 590
  Teotihuacán, 154–158
  Tepozteco pyramid (Tepoztlán), 186
  Toniná, 481

Archaeological sites and ruins
    (cont.)
    Tulum, 612–613
    Tzintzuntzan, 268
    Uxmal, 654–655
    Xcambó, 650
    Yagul, 467
    Zaachila, 469
    Zempoala, 523–524
AREA Bar and Terrace at Hotel
    Habita (Mexico City), 152
Arrazola, 468
Art and architecture, 38–39
Artesanías e Industrias Popu-
    lares del Estado de Oaxaca
    (Oaxaca City), 455
Artesanías Vázquez (Guanaju-
    ato), 214
Art galleries. *See also* Handi-
    crafts and folk art
    Cozumel, 580
    Mexico City, 147–148
    Oaxaca City, 455
    Puerto Vallarta, 315–316
    Todos Santos, 731
Arts and crafts. *See also* Pot-
    tery and ceramics; Textiles
    Campeche, 663
    Cancún, 553
    Cozumel, 580
    Creel, 686
    Cuanajo, 269
    Guadalajara, 289–290
    Guanajuato, 215
    La Paz, 739
    Mérida, 636–637
    Morelia, 255
    Oaxaca City, 455–456
    Pátzcuaro, 263, 264–265
    Puerto Vallarta, 312, 316–317
        Huichol art, 313–314
    Querétaro, 225
    San Cristóbal, 489–490
    San Luis, 244–245
    San Miguel, 199
    Tepoztlán, 186
    Tijuana, 753
    Valladolid, 673–674
    Zacatecas, 235
Arvil. Galería de Arte y Libros
    de Arte (Mexico City), 147
Ash Wednesday, 52
Assumption of the Virgin
    Mary, 54
ATC Tours and Travel, 80–81
Atlantis Submarines
    Cancún, 551
    Cozumel, 577
ATMs (automated teller
    machines), 64–65

Atotonilco el Grande (near San
    Miguel), 199
ATV trips, Cabo San Lucas, 720
Auto insurance, 59
Avándaro, 172–175
Aventura Submarina (Puerto
    Escondido), 426
Avenue of the Dead (Teoti-
    huacán), 157
Ayuntamiento
    Mérida, 634
    Valladolid, 673
Aztec city of Tlatelolco (Mexico
    City), 144
Aztecs, 25–26
Azul 96 (Puerto Vallarta), 332

B aby-O (Acapulco), 402
Bahía de Magdalena, 744–745
Bahía de Mujeres (Cancún), 547
Bahías de Huatulco, 380,
    434–442
Bahuichivo, 683
Baja California, 5–6, 36, 698
    mid-Baja region, 700,
        742–749
Baja Expeditions, 81
Balamkú, 624
Ball court *(juego de pelota)*, 26
    Chichén Itzá, 667–668
    Cobá, 616
    Palenque, 476
    Uxmal, 655
Ballet Folklórico de México
    (Mexico City), 151
Ballet Tradiciones de México
    (Veracruz), 518
Balneario Ixtapan, 171
Baluarte de la Soledad
    (Campeche), 662
Baluarte de San Carlos/Museo
    de la Ciudad (Campeche),
    662
Baluarte de Santiago
    (Campeche), 662
Baluarte Santiago (Veracruz),
    519
Banderas Bay Trading Company
    (Puerto Vallarta), 316–317
Barceló La Jolla de Mismaloya
    (Puerto Vallarta), 302
Bar Constantini (Puerto
    Vallarta), 332
Bar Fly (Mexico City), 152
Bar Hopper Tour (Cancún), 554
Barra de Navidad, 363–368
Barrancas, 684
Basaseachic Falls, 688

Basilica, Pátzcuaro, 263
Basílica de la Soledad (Oaxaca
    City), 453–454
Basílica de la Virgen de
    Zapopan (Guadalajara),
    288–289
Basílica de Santa María de
    Guadalupe (Mexico City), 128
Batopilas, 687, 688
Bazar del Centro (Mexico City),
    148
Bazar del Sábado (Mexico
    City), 148
Bazar Hecht (Tlaquepaque),
    291
Beaches, 50. *See also entries
    starting with "Playa"; and
    specific beaches*
    Acapulco, 386–387
    Bahías de Huatulco, 438
    Barra de Navidad, 364
    best beach vacations, 7, 10
    Bucerías, 338
    Cabo San Lucas, 719–720
    Cancún, 547–548
    Cozumel, 578
    Holbox, 676
    Isla Mujeres, 561
    Ixtapa/Zihuatanejo, 407–409
    La Paz, 735–736
    Manzanillo, 372
    Mazatlán, 347–348
    Progreso, 649
    Puerto Angel, 433–434
    Puerto Escondido, 424–425
    Puerto Vallarta, 302–303
    San José del Cabo, 705
    Tulum, 611, 612
    Veracruz, 519
Becán, 624
Becari Language School
    (Oaxaca City), 457
Beer Bob's Books (Barra de
    Navidad), 364
Bengala (Mexico City), 152
Benito Juárez International Air-
    port (Mexico City), 96–97
Benito Juárez Market (Oaxaca
    City), 456
Biblioteca Palafoxiana (Puebla),
    500
Biking and mountain biking
    Isla Mujeres, 560
    Mazatlán, 350
    Oaxaca City, 457
Bird-watching
    Bahías de Huatulco, 439
    Celestún National Wildlife
        Refuge, 648

Huitepec Cloud Forest, 489
Ixtapa/Zihuatanejo area, 409
Manzanillo, 372–373
Mazatlán, 350
Rio Lagartos Nature Reserve, 675–676
Blessing of the Animals (San Miguel), 196
Bling (Cancún), 554
Boat excursions and cruises. *See also* Fishing; Whale-watching
Bahías de Huatulco, 438–439
Cabo San Lucas, 720
Cancún, 549–551
Cozumel, 577
Ixtapa/Zihuatanejo, 409
La Paz, 736
Mazatlán, 348
Puerto Vallarta, 299–300, 303–304
evening cruises, 331–332
Veracruz, 520
Boat rentals. *See also* Kayaking; Sailing
Acapulco, 388
Ixtapa/Zihuatanejo, 409–410
Boca de Tomatlán (Puerto Vallarta), 302
Bodegas de Santo Tomás Winery (Ensenada), 759
Bonampak, 480
Books, recommended, 40–41
Border violence, 69
Bribes and scams, 70–71
Brisas Hotels & Resorts, 85
Bucerías, 298, 337–339
Buddha Bar (Sayulita), 342
Bugs and bites, 67
Bullfights, 77
Acapulco, 389–390
Cancún, 552
Mazatlán, 349
Puerto Vallarta, 309
Tijuana, 754
Business hours, 761
Bustamante, Sergio, 291
Bus travel, 59, 62–63

Cabo Pulmo, 14–15
Cabo San Lucas, 698, 700, 702, 716–730
accommodations, 725–727
beaches, 719–720
beach safety, 718
festivals and special events, 724
getting around, 718
layout of, 718
nightlife, 728–730
outdoor activities, 719–724
restaurants, 727–728
shopping, 724–725
traveling to, 716, 718
visitor information, 718
Cabo Wabo Cantina (Cabo San Lucas), 729
Cacahuamilpa Caves or Grottoes (near Taxco), 187
Cacaxtla, 510–511
Cactus Sanctuary (La Paz), 738
Cafeina (Mexico City), 153
Café La Habana (Mexico City), 126
Calafia, 758
Calakmul, 624
Calderón, Felipe, 31
Calendar of events, 51–57
Caleta (Acapulco), 386
Caletas, 304
Caletilla (Acapulco), 386
The California Native, 81
Callejón de los Sapos (Puebla), 503
Campeche, 659–665
Cancún, 7, 527–555
accommodations, 534–542
American Express, 532
beaches and outdoor activities, 547–550
best websites for, 530
climate, 532
consulates, 532–533
crime, 533, 534
currency exchange, 533
drugstores, 533
emergencies, 533
getting around, 531–532
layout of, 531
nightlife, 554–555
outdoor activities and attractions, 551–552
police, 533–534
post office, 534
restaurants, 542–547
seasons, 534
shopping, 552–553
traveling to, 528, 530–531
visitor information, 531
what's new in, 4–5
Candlemas (Día de la Candelaria), 51
Canopy tours, Puerto Vallarta, 306–307
Canopy Tours de Los Veranos, 307
Cantinas, 220
Canyon Travel, 81–82
Capilla del Mártir (Tlacolula), 467
Capilla del Rosario (Puebla), 500
Cárdenas, Lázaro, 29
Caribbean coast, 587–624
Caribbean Village (Isla Mujeres), 563
Carlos 'n' Charlie's (Acapulco), 402
Carlos 'n' Charlie's, Ixtapa/Zihuatanejo, 419
Carlos O'Brian's (Puerto Vallarta), 332
Carnaval, 52
Mazatlán, 351
Veracruz, 518
Car rentals, 61–62
Car travel, 57–62
documents needed for, 58–59
highway safety, 70
Casa Borda (Casa de la Cultura de Taxco), 165
Casa de Alfeñique (Puebla), 500–501
Casa de Artesanías Amanecer (San Cristóbal), 490
Casa de Artesanías Tukulná (Campeche), 663
Casa de Capelo (Guanajuato), 214
Casa de Cortés (Oaxaca City), 454
Casa de Ecala (Querétaro), 225
Casa de Hidalgo (Dolores Hidalgo), 206
Casa de Juárez (Oaxaca City), 454
Casa de la Corregidora. (Querétaro), 225
Casa de la Cultura de Taxco (Casa Borda), 165
Casa de la Marquesa (Querétaro), 226
Casa del Artesano (San Luis), 245
Casa de la Salsa (Morelia), 260
Casa de las Artesanías
Guadalajara, 288
Mérida, 636–637
Morelia, 255
Casa de las Artesanías de Michoacán/Casa de los Once Patios (Pátzcuaro), 264
Casa de las Sirenas (Mexico City), 153

Casa de la Zacatecana (Querétaro), 226
Casa del Feng Shui (Puerto Vallarta), 316
Casa del Habano (Puerto Vallarta), 317
Casa de los Azulejos (Mexico City), 134
Casa de los Muñecos (Puebla), 501
Casa de los Once Patios (Pátzcuaro), 264
Casa del Tequila (Puerto Vallarta), 317
Casa Marina (Ixtapa/Zihuatanejo), 412
Casa Museo de Morelos (Morelia), 253
Casa Na-Bolom (San Cristóbal), 486
Casa no. 6 Centro Cultural (Campeche), 662
Casa Queretana de Artesanía (Querétaro), 225
Castillo (Tulum), 612
Castillo de Chapultepec/Museo Nacional de Historia (Mexico City), 137–138
Catedral (Cathedral)
    Cuernavaca, 179
    Guadalajara, 286–287
    Mazatlán (Cathedral of the Immaculate Conception), 352
    Mérida, 633
    Mexico City (Catedral Metropolitana), 136–137, 146
    Morelia, 252
    Oaxaca City, 454
    Puebla, 499–500
    San Cristóbal, 487
    San Luis, 244
    Veracruz, 518
    Zacatecas, 235
Cava de Vinos L. A. Cetto (Tijuana), 752
Cave of Balankanché, 672
Caves of the Sleeping Sharks (Isla Mujeres), 548, 561
Celestún National Wildlife Refuge, 626, 648
Cellphones, 84
Cenotes and cenote diving
    Chichén Itzá, 668
    Cozumel, 576–577
    Dzibilchaltún, 649
    Dzitnup, 674–675
    Ik-Kil, 672
    Lago Bacalar, 620

Valladolid, 673
Xel-Ha area, 610
Centers for Disease Control and Prevention, 66
Central Camionera (Morelia), 250
Centro Artesanal (Mercado de Curiosidades; Mexico City), 148
Centro Bilingüe (San Cristóbal), 486
Centro Comerical Galerias Vallarta, 312
Centro Cultural El Refugio (Guadalajara), 289
Centro Cultural Ignacio Ramírez (Bellas Artes/El Nigromante; San Miguel), 196
Centro Cultural Tijuana, 752
Centro de Idiomas (Mazatlán), 347
Centro Histórico and surrounding areas (Mexico City)
    restaurants, 124–125
    sights and attractions, 138–142
Centro Integral de Atención al Turista (CIAT; Mexico City), 101
Cerámica La Cruz (Guanajuato), 215
Ceramics and pottery. See also Talavera pottery
    Amatenango del Valle, 489
    Bahías de Huatulco, 439
    Dolores Hidalgo, 205–206
    Guadalajara, 287–289
    Guanajuato, 214, 215
    La Paz, 739
    Muna, 651
    Ocotlán, 470
    Puerto Vallarta, 316
    San Bartolo, 469
    Tepoztlán, 186
    Ticul, 652
    Tlaquepaque, 290–291
    Tonalá, 291–292
Cerocahui, 14, 683
Cerro de la Bufa (Zacatecas), 234, 236
Cerro de las Campanas (Querétaro), 227
Cerro del Fortín (Oaxaca City), 455
Cerro del Vigía (Mazatlán), 347
Cerro Gallego, 683
Chacahua Lagoon National Park, 426

Chahué Bay, 436, 438
Chamula, 481, 488
Chankanaab National Park, 577–578
Chapultepec Park (Mexico City), 102
    accommodations, 114–116
    historic buildings and monuments, 137–138
    restaurants near, 121–123
    sights and attractions, 139–140, 145
Charreadas. See Rodeos
Chetumal, 621–623
Chewing gum, 28
Chiapas, 4
    Zapatista movement and, 484
Chicanná, 624
Chichén Itzá, 5, 580, 626, 665–672
Chihuahua, 691–697
Chihuahua al Pacífico railway, 677–688
Chinchorro Reef Underwater National Park, 618–619
Chincua, 259
Chincultic, 495
Cholula, 496, 498, 500, 503, 504
    exploring, 507–508
Christine (Ixtapa), 419
Christine (Puerto Vallarta), 333
Christmas, 56
Christmas Posadas, 56
Churches. See under first significant word (e.g. Santo Domingo, Church of)
Cigars, Cabo San Lucas, 725
Cinco de Mayo, 28, 53, 500
Cine Bar (San Miguel), 205
The City (Cancún), 554
Classico (Acapulco), 402
Classic Vacations, 79
Cliff divers
    Acapulco, 389
    Mazatlán, 349
Cliff of the Dawn (Isla Mujeres), 563
Climate, 50
Cobá, 580, 615–618
Cocinar Mexicano (Tepoztlán), 186
CoCo Bongo (Cancún), 555
Collage Club (Puerto Vallarta), 333
College of San Nicolás de Hidalgo (Morelia), 254
Colonia Centro (Mexico City), 102

Coming About (Puerto Vallarta), 309
Comitán, 495
Compañía, Church of the (Guanajuato), 212
Compañía de Jesús, Iglesia de la (Morelia), 254
Conchas Chinas, 298
Condesa (Mexico City), cafes, 126
Condesa and Roma (Mexico City), 103
accommodations, 119–120
Conjunto Las Pinturas (Cobá), 617
Conservatorio de las Rosas (Morelia), 254
Constanzo (San Luis), 245
Constitution Day, 51–52
Continental Airlines Vacations, 78
Continental Vacations, 79
Convento de Guadalupe/Museo Virreinal de Guadalupe (Guadalupe), 238
Convent of San Bernardino de Siena (Mexico City), 137
Cooking classes
Oaxaca City, 456
Tepoztlán, 186
Copala, 352, 358–359
Copalitilla Cascades, 438
The Copper Canyon, 36, 306, 677–697
Copper Museum (Santa Clara del Cobre), 269
Corpus Christi, 53
The Corridor, 712–716
Corsica (Puerto Vallarta), 315
Cortez, Hernán, 26–27
Costa Alegre, 14, 359–369
Costa Careyes, 359
Costa de Oro (Veracruz), 519
Costa Maya, 587, 588
Coyoacán (Mexico City), 103
Coyuca Lagoon (Acapulco), 387
Cozumel, 556, 569–586, 590
accommodations, 580–583
all-inclusives, 572–573
beaches, 578
clinics, 574
exploring, 574–580
getting around, 573–574
layout of, 572–573
Maya ruins, 579
nightlife, 586
recompression chamber, 574

restaurants, 583–586
shopping, 580
tours, 578–579
traveling to, 570–571
visitor information, 572
Crafts. See also Pottery and ceramics; Textiles
Campeche, 663
Cancún, 553
Cozumel, 580
Creel, 686
Cuanajo, 269
Guadalajara, 289–290
Guanajuato, 215
La Paz, 739
Mérida, 636–637
Morelia, 255
Oaxaca City, 455–456
Pátzcuaro, 263, 264–265
Puerto Vallarta, 312, 316–317
Huichol art, 313–314
Querétaro, 225
San Cristóbal, 489–490
San Luis, 244–245
San Miguel, 199
Tepoztlán, 186
Tijuana, 753
Valladolid, 673–674
Zacatecas, 235
Creel, 685–687
Crime, 69–70
CrocoCun (near Puerto Morelos), 592
The Cross of the Bay (Isla Mujeres), 561
Crucecita, 436, 437–438
Cruise lines, 59
Cuanajo, 269
Cuernavaca, 175–185
accommodations, 182–183
activities and excursions, 181
exploring, 179–180
layout of, 176, 178
nightlife, 185
restaurants, 183–184
traveling to and from, 176
visitor information, 176
Cuevas de los Tiburones (Isla Mujeres), 561
Cuilapan, 468–469
Cuisine, 32–34
best, 21–22
cooking classes
Oaxaca City, 456
Tepoztlán, 186
trips, 83
Culinary Adventures, 83

Currency and currency exchange, 63–64
Customs regulations, 48–49

Dady'O (Cancún), 555
Dady Rock Bar and Club (Cancún), 555
Dainzú, 466
Day of the Dead
Janitzio, 268
Oaxaca City, 451
Pátzcuaro, 263
Deep-sea fishing. See Fishing
Delgado, Leandro, 205
Delta Vacations, 78, 79
De Santos (Puerto Vallarta), 333
Día de la Candelaria (Candlemas), 51
Día de la Constitución, 51–52
Día de la Marina, 53
Día de los Muertos
Janitzio, 268
Oaxaca City, 451
Pátzcuaro, 263
Día de los Reyes, 51
Día de San Pedro y San Pablo, 53
Díaz, Porfirio, 29
Diego Rivera Murals (Mexico City), 132
Dietary red flags, 66
Disabilities, travelers with, 71–72
Disco Club Paco Paco (Puerto Vallarta), 335
Diseño Artesano (Pátzcuaro), 264
Diving
Acapulco, 388
Akumal, 608
Cabo San Lucas, 722
Cancún, 548–549
Chinchorro Reef, 618–619
Cozumel, 574, 576–577
Isla Mujeres, 561
Ixtapa/Zihuatanejo, 410
La Paz, 736–737
Manzanillo, 373
Paamul, 606
Puerto Angel, 434
Puerto Morelos, 594
Puerto Vallarta, 306
Riviera Maya, 589
San José del Cabo, 706
Veracruz, 520
Xel-Ha area, 610
Zihuatanejo, 408

Dog racing, Tijuana, 754
Dolores Hidalgo, 205–206
Dolphins, swimming with, 78
    Acapulco, 390
    Cancún, 551
    Cozumel, 577–578
    Isla Mujeres, 562
    Ixtapa, 410
    Puerto Aventuras, 606
    Puerto Vallarta, 309
    Riviera Maya, 589
    Xel-Ha, 609
Dolphin shows, Acapulco, 390
Dominico de la Navidad,
    former convent, 187
The Dovecote (Uxmal), 655
Drinking laws, 761
Drinks, 34–35
Drugs, 31–32
    over-the-counter, 67
Dzibanché, 624
Dzibilchaltún, 626, 649
Dzitnup, Cenote, 674–675

Easter
    Pátzcuaro, 263
    Uruapan, 270
Ecotours. See also Sustainable
    tourism
    Bahías de Huatulco, 437, 438
    La Paz, 736
    Mérida, 647
    Puerto Escondido area, 426
    Puerto Vallarta, 306–307
Ek Balam, 675
El Acuario (Veracruz), 519
El Agora (Xalapa), 512
El Arco, 720
El Artesano (Querétaro), 227
El Bar de Félix (Manzanillo),
    378
El Bosque (Morelia), 255
El Botazoo (Punta Celeste), 435
El Carmen, church and former
    convent of (Morelia), 255
El Castillo
    Chichén Itzá, 667
    Cobá, 616–617
El Charro (Guadalajara), 290
El Divisadero, 678, 684–685,
    687
Electricity, 761
El Encuentro (San Cristóbal),
    490
El Estribo, 268
Elevation sickness, 66–67
El Faro (Mazatlán), 347

El Faro Lighthouse Bar (Puerto
    Vallarta), 333
El Fuerte, 681–683
El Garrafón Natural Park,
    548–550, 563
El Mercado (San Cristóbal), 487
El Mirador (Mazatlán), 349
El Mirador (San Miguel), 198
El Nuevo Olimpo (Mérida), 634
El Palacio de los Estucos
    (Acanceh), 651
El Pípila (Guanajuato), 210–211
El Rosario, 259
El Sagrario (San Luis), 244
El Santuario de Guadalupe
    (Morelia), 255
El Squid Roe (Cabo San Lucas),
    729
El Tajín, 524, 525
El Tecolote Libros (Todos
    Santos), 731
El Tigre golf course (Nuevo
    Vallarta), 308
El Tule tree (Santa María del
    Tule), 465–466
El Vizcaíno Biosphere Reserve,
    748
Embassies, Mexican, 46
Embassies and consulates,
    761–762
Emergencies, 762
Emigration to the U.S., 32
Encuentro Internacional del
    Mariachi (Guadalajara),
    284–285
Enrique Estrada Park
    (Zacatecas), 236
Ensenada, 700, 759–760
Escobilla Beach (near Puerto
    Escondido), 425
Escondido (near San Miguel),
    199
Escuinapa, 349
Estero San José (San José del
    Cabo), 705
Etc. Beach Club (Nuevo
    Vallarta), 336
Exconvento de Santa Mónica
    (Puebla), 501
Exconvento de Santa Rosa
    (Puebla), 501
Exposición Nacional de Arte
    Popular (FONART; Mexico
    City), 147

Fábrica La Aurora (San
    Miguel), 199
Fabrics. See Textiles

Fall Equinox, 54
Fall of Tenochtitlán (Mexico
    City), 54
Families with children, 73–74
Far Flung Adventures, 82
Feast of Corpus Christi
    (El Tajín), 524
Feast of San Antonio Abad, 51
Feast of San Isidro, 53
Feast of the Virgin of
    Guadalupe, 56, 130
Felipe Carrillo Puerto, 618
Female travelers, 74
Feria de Zacatecas, 234
Festival de México en el Centro
    Histórico (Mexico City),
    52–53, 110
Festival de Nuestra Señora de
    Santa Clara de Asis (Santa
    Clara del Cobre), 269
Festival Fundador (Todos
    Santos), 731
Festival Internacional Cervan-
    tino (Guanajuato), 210
Festival Internacional de Cine
    de Morelia, 252
Festival of San Cristóbal de las
    Casas, 56
Festival of the Holy Cross (San
    Miguel), 196
Fiesta Americana hotels, 85
Fiesta de los Locos (San
    Miguel), 196
Fiesta de los Rábanos
    (Oaxaca), 56
Fiesta Guelaguetza (Oaxaca
    City), 451
Fiesta Inn hotels, 85
Fiestas de la Vendimia, 54
Fiestas de Octubre (Guadala-
    jara), 54–55, 286
Fisherman's tours, Puerto
    Escondido, 426
Fishing
    Acapulco, 388
    Cabo San Lucas, 722–723
    Cancún, 548
    Cozumel, 577
    Isla Mujeres, 562
    Ixtapa/Zihuatanejo, 409
    La Paz, 737
    Manzanillo, 373
    Mazatlán, 348–349
    Puerto Aventuras, 606–607
    Puerto Vallarta, 307
    Punta Allen Peninsula, 615
    Riviera Maya, 589
    San José del Cabo, 705–706
Floating Gardens of Xochimilco
    (Mexico City), 145

FONART, San Luis, 244–245
Food and cuisine, 32–34
    best, 21–22
    cooking classes
        Oaxaca City, 456
        Tepoztlán, 186
    trips, 83
Foreign Student Study Center
    (Guadalajara), 276–277
Fort of San Juan de Ulúa
    (Veracruz), 519
Forum by the Sea (Cancún),
    553
Fox, Vicente, 30–31
Friday Pottery Market
    (Pátzcuaro), 264
Frommers.com, 77
Fuerte de San Diego
    (Acapulco), 390
Fuerte-Museo San José el Alto
    (Campeche), 663
Fuerte-Museo San Miguel
    (Campeche), 663
FunJet Vacations, 79

Galería AL (Arte Latinoameri-
    cano; Puerto Vallarta), 315
Galería Arte de Oaxaca, 455
Galería del Arcángel
    (Pátzcuaro), 264
Galería del Calzado (Guadala-
    jara), 290
Galería des Artistes (Puerto
    Vallarta), 315
Galería de Todos Santos, 731
Galería Espacio Pal Kepenyes
    (Acapulco), 391
Galería Iturbe (Pátzcuaro), 264
Galería Libertad (Querétaro),
    225
Galería Omar Alonso (Puerto
    Vallarta), 315
Galería Pacífico (Puerto
    Vallarta), 315–316
Galería Quetzalli (Oaxaca City),
    455
Galería Uno (Puerto Vallarta),
    316
Galleria Dante (Puerto
    Vallarta), 316
Garbo (Puerto Vallarta), 335
Garrafón Natural Park,
    548–550, 563
Gasoline, 60, 762
Gay and lesbian travelers,
    72–73
        International Gay Festival, 53
        Mazatlán, 348
        Puerto Vallarta, 335

Global Volunteers, 83
GOGO Worldwide Vacations, 79
Golf, 81
    Acapulco, 388–389
    Bahías de Huatulco, 439
    Barra de Navidad, 364
    Cabo San Lucas, 721–722
    Cancún, 551–552
    Cozumel, 579
    Cuernavaca, 181
    Ixtapa/Zihuatanejo, 410
    Los Cabos, 706
    Manzanillo, 373–374
    Mazatlán, 349–350
    Puerto Morelos, 592
    Puerto Vallarta, 307–308
    Riviera Maya, 589
The Gorky González Workshop
    (Guanajuato), 215
Government Palace (Tlaxcala),
    509
The Governor's Palace (Uxmal),
    655
Gran Arrecife Maya, 548
Gran Hotel Ciudad de México
    (Mexico City), 134
Great Mesoamerican Reef, 548
Great Pyramid (Cholula), 507
The Great Pyramid (Uxmal),
    655
Group of the Columns (Mitla),
    468
Grutas de Cacahuamilpa (near
    Taxco), 166, 187
Guadalajara, 3, 273–293
    accommodations, 277–281
    books, newspapers, and mag-
        azines, 276
    bus tours, 286
    climate and dress, 276
    consulates, 276
    currency exchange, 276
    emergencies, 276
    exploring in and near,
        284–292
    getting around, 275
    hospitals, 276
    language classes, 276–277
    layout of, 274
    neighborhoods in brief,
        274–275
    nightlife, 292
    police, 277
    post office, 277
    restaurants, 281–284
    safety, 277
    shopping, 289–292
    special events, 284–286
    traveling to, 274

Guadalupe, 238
Guadalupe, Iglesia de
    (Crucecita), 437
Guanajuato, 206–221
    accommodations, 215–218
    emergency and police, 209
    exploring, 210–214
    getting around, 209
    layout of, 209
    nightlife, 220–221
    orientation, 209
    restaurants, 218–220
    seasons, 210
    shopping, 214–215
    special events and festivals,
        210
    traveling to, 208–209
Guayaberas, Mérida, 637
Guelaguetza Dance Festival
    (Oaxaca), 53
Guelatao, 470
The Gulf Coast, 37

Habla Hispana (San Miguel),
    197
Hacienda El Lencero (Xalapa),
    512–513
Haciendas, in the Yucatán,
    642–643
Hammocks, Mérida, 637–638
Handicrafts and folk art. See
    also Pottery and ceramics;
    Textiles
    Campeche, 663
    Cancún, 553
    Cozumel, 580
    Creel, 686
    Cuanajo, 269
    Guadalajara, 289–290
    Guanajuato, 215
    La Paz, 739
    Mérida, 636–637
    Morelia, 255
    Oaxaca City, 455–456
    Pátzcuaro, 263, 264–265
    Puerto Vallarta, 312, 316–317
        Huichol art, 313–314
    Querétaro, 225
    San Cristóbal, 489–490
    San Luis, 244–245
    San Miguel, 199
    Tepoztlán, 186
    Tijuana, 753
    Valladolid, 673–674
    Zacatecas, 235
Harvest Festival (Tijuana), 753
Health concerns, 65–68

Health insurance, 763
Hemiciclo (Mexico City), 145
Hidalgo, Father Miguel, 27–28
Hidalgo's Dungeon (Chi-
    huahua), 694
Hidden Worlds Cenotes, 610
High-altitude hazards, 66–67
High divers
    Acapulco, 389
    Mazatlán, 349
High season, 49–50
Highway 18 (the Convent
    Route), 651
Highway 175, 469–470
Highway 200, motorist
    advisory, 381, 404
Highway 261, 650–651
Highway safety, 70
Hiking
    Bahías de Huatulco, 439
    Oaxaca City, 457
Hilo (Puerto Vallarta), 334
History of Mexico, 23–32
    books about, 40–41
Holbox, 676
Holy Week, 52
    Oaxaca City, 451
    Taxco, 165
Hornos Beach, 387
Horseback riding
    Acapulco, 389
    Bahías de Huatulco, 438–439
    Cabo San Lucas, 722
    Cancún, 552
    Ixtapa/Zihuatanejo, 410
    Mazatlán, 350
    Puerto Vallarta, 308–309
    Riviera Maya, 589
    San Cristóbal, 487
    San José del Cabo, 706
Hot Air Balloon Festival
    (León), 56
Hoteles Camino Real, 85–86
Hotlines, 762
Hot springs
House and Garden Tour (San
    Miguel), 198
House rentals and swaps, 86
Huatulco, 380
Huichol art, 313–315
Huichol Collection (Puerto
    Vallarta), 313
Huichol Indians, 235, 287, 289,
    296, 306, 340, 341
Huitepec Cloud Forest, 489
Humboldt House/Museo Vir-
    reinal de Taxco, 165
Hurricane season, 50

glesia . . . See under first sig-
    nificant word (e.g. Compañía
    de Jesús, Iglesia de la)
Ihuatzio, 268–270
Ik-Kil, 672
IMAC, 80
    Guadalajara, 277
Immaculate Conception, Cathe-
    dral of the (Mazatlán), 352
Independence Day, 54
Indigo (Oaxaca City), 455
Inner Reef, 758
Insects, 67
Inspiración (Cozumel), 580
Instituto Allende (San Miguel),
    197
Instituto Cultural Cabañas, 288
Instituto Cultural Oaxaca
    (Oaxaca City), 456
Instituto de Comunicación y
    Cultura (Oaxaca City),
    456–457
Instituto de la Artesanía Jali-
    sciense (Guadalajara),
    289–290
Instituto Jovel (San Cristóbal),
    486
Instituto Michoacano de Cul-
    tura (Morelia), 255
Insurance, 763
    auto, 59
    car-rental, 62
Interactive Aquarium (Cancún),
    551
International Association for
    Medical Assistance to Trav-
    ellers (IAMAT), 65–66
International Cervantes Festi-
    val (Guanajuato), 210
International Chamber Music
    Festival (San Miguel de
    Allende), 53–54
International Festival of Music
    (Morelia), 252
International Friendship Club
    (Puerto Vallarta), 306
International Guitar Festival
    (Morelia), 252
International Mariachi
    Festival, 54
International Organ Festival
    (Morelia), 252
Internet and e-mail access,
    84–85
Isla Contoy, 549, 564
Isla de la Piedra (Mazatlán),
    348

Isla de las Chivas (Mazatlán),
    348
Isla Espíritu Santo, 736
Isla Holbox, 676
Isla Ixtapa, 409
Isla Mujeres, 10, 550, 556–569
    accommodations, 564–567
    beaches and outdoor activi-
        ties, 561–562
    best websites for, 558
    currency exchange, 560
    emergencies, 560
    getting around, 559–560
    layout of, 559
    nightlife, 569
    restaurants, 567–569
    seasons, 560
    shopping, 564
    traveling to, 558–559
    visitor information, 559
Isla Navidad Resort, 363, 366
Itineraries, suggested, 87–93
Ixtaccihuatl, 175
Ixtapan de la Sal, 170–172
Ixtapa/Zihuatanejo, 7, 380,
    403–420
    accommodations, 412–416
    banks, 407
    beaches and outdoor activi-
        ties, 407–410
    getting around, 406–407
    hospitals, 407
    layout of, 406
    nightlife, 419
    post office, 407
    restaurants, 416–419
    shopping, 410–412
    traveling to, 404, 406
    visitor information, 406
Izamal, 647–648

J & B Salsa Club (Puerto
    Vallarta), 334
Janitzio, 262, 268
Jardín Borda (Cuernavaca),
    179–180
Jardín Botánico Dr. Alfredo Bar-
    rera (Puerto Morelos), 590,
    592
Jardín de la Reforma (Guanaju-
    ato), 212
Jardín Etnobotánico y Museo
    de Medicina Tradicional y
    Herbolaria (Cuernavaca), 180
Jardín Unión (Guanajuato), 220
Jardín Zenea (Querétaro), 224
Jesús, Iglesia de (Mérida), 635

Jiménez, Manuel, 468
Joe's Oyster Bar (Mazatlán), 357
Jornadas Alarconianas (Taxco), 165
Jorongo Bar (Mexico City), 152
Juárez, Benito, 28
Birthday of, 52
Guelatao, 470
Casa de Juárez (Oaxaca City), 454
Juárez Monument (Mexico City), 145
Juego de pelota (ball court), 26
Chichén Itzá, 667–668
Cobá, 616
Palenque, 476
Uxmal, 655
Jungle Tour (Mazatlán), 352

Kabah, 656–657
Kahlo, Frida, 143, 144
Museo (Mexico City), 130
Kanasín, 651
Karisma (Mexico City), 153
Kayaking, 82
Ixtapa/Zihuatanejo, 409–410
La Paz, 737
Mazatlán, 350
San José del Cabo, 706
Kidnappings, 69–70
Killers, 758
Kohunlich, 624
Kukulcán Plaza (Cancún), 553

La Alameda (San Luis), 244
Labná, 658
La Bodeguita del Medio (Guadalajara), 292
La Bodeguita del Medio (Puerto Vallarta), 332
Labor Day, 53
La Bufadora (near Ensenada), 759–760
La Calzada Fray Antonio de San Miguel (Morelia), 255
La Capilla de la Virgen del Patrocinio (Zacatecas), 236
La Casa . . . *See entries starting with "Casa"*
La Cava de la Princesa (San Miguel), 205
L. A. Cetto Winery (Tijuana), 752
La China Poblana, 501
La Clave Azul (Guanajuato), 221

La Compañía, church of (Puebla), 500
La Cruz de Huanaxcle, 298
La Dama de las Camelias (Guanajuato), 221
La Entrega Beach (Santa Cruz Bay), 438
La Galería (San Cristóbal), 490
Lago Bacalar, 14, 620–621
Lágrimas de la Selva (San Cristóbal), 490
La Gruta (near San Miguel), 199
Laguna de Cuyutlán (Manzanillo), 373
Laguna de Las Garzas (Manzanillo), 372–373
Laguna Ojo de Liebre, 748
Lagunilla Market (Mexico City), 149
La Huatápera (Uruapan), 270
La Iglesia
Chichén Itzá, 670
Cobá, 616
La Isla Shopping Village (Cancún), 553
La Madonna (Cancún), 555
La Mano Mágica (Oaxaca City), 455
Lambityeco, 467
La Mina Club (Zacatecas), 241
La Mina "El Edén" (Zacatecas), 236–237
Language, 764
Language classes, 80
Cuernavaca, 178
Guanajuato, 210
Mérida, 632
Oaxaca City, 456
San Cristóbal, 486
San Miguel, 197
Taxco, 164
LanguagePoint (San Miguel), 197
La Noche (Puerto Vallarta), 335
La Noche de Rábanos (Oaxaca City), 452
La Otra Cara de México (San Miguel), 198
La Parroquia (San Miguel), 196, 198
La Pasita (Puebla), 503
La Paz, 10, 700, 724, 732–742
accommodations, 739–740
beaches and sports, 735–737
exploring, 737–738
festivals and special events, 734–735
getting around, 734

layout of, 734
nightlife, 741–742
restaurants, 741
shopping, 738–739
traveling to, 733–734
visitor information, 734
Lapidaria de Querétaro, 227
Lapidaria Ramírez (Querétaro), 227
La Punta (Isla Mujeres), 561
La Punta (Puerto Escondido), 425
La Quebrada (Acapulco), 389
La Ruta Maya, suggested itinerary, 91–93
Las Animas Beach (Puerto Vallarta), 303
La Santa Cruz, church and convent of (Querétaro), 225
Las Estacas, 181
La Taboada (near San Miguel), 198
La Torre Latinoamericana (Mexico City), 146
Laura López Labra Designs (Puerto Vallarta), 314–315
La Valenciana (near Guanajuato), 213
Legal aid, 764
Liberty Travel, 79–80
Lienzo Charro de Jalisco (Guadalajara), 288
Living (Mexico City), 153
The Lobby Lounge (Cancún), 555
Loltún, 658
López Obrador, Andrés Manuel, 31
López Quiroga Gallery (Mexico City), 147
Loreto, 742–748
Loreto Chapel (San Luis), 244
Los Arcos, 303–304
Los Cabos, 5–6, 10, 698, 700, 701–730. *See also* Cabo San Lucas; San José del Cabo
traveling to, 702–704
Los Castillo (Taxco), 166–167
Los Danzantes (Monte Albán), 464
Los Flamingos Club de Golf (near Puerto Vallarta), 307–308
Los Islotes, 736
Los Mochis, 677, 679, 689–691
Los Morros de Los Pericos islands, 409
Los Pinos (Mazatlán), 348
Los Pinos (Mexico City), 145

Lost and found, 764
Low season, 50
Lucy's CuCu Cabaña (Puerto Vallarta), 317

Magdalena, 481
Magdalena Bay, 744–745
Mágico Mundo Marino (Acapulco), 386
Maguey Bay, 438
Mail, 764
Majahual, 618
Mama Mía (San Miguel), 205
Mambo Café
    Acapulco, 402
    Cancún, 555
Mandala (Puerto Vallarta), 334
Mandara (Acapulco), 403
Mantas Típicas (Pátzcuaro), 264
Manzanillo, 369–378
    accommodations, 374–377
    nightlife, 378
    restaurants, 377–378
    shopping, 374
Mar de Sueños (Puerto Vallarta), 315
Mariachi Loco (Puerto Vallarta), 333
Mariachis
    Guadalajara, 284–285, 292
    Mexico City, 151–152
    Puebla, 507
Marietas Islands, 303
Marina Ixtapa, 409
Marina Vallarta, 298, 303
    accommodations, 318–319
    restaurants, 323
    shopping, 312
Marina Vallarta Golf Club, 307
Market Plaza (Pátzcuaro), 265
Markets. *See also* Mercado Municipal
    Cuernavaca, 179
    Ixtapa/Zihuatanejo, 411
    La Paz, 739
    Mérida, 636
    Morelia, 253, 256
    Oaxaca City, 456
    Ocotlán, 470
    Papantla, 525–526
    Pátzcuaro, 263
    Puerto Vallarta, 310
    Tepoztlán, 186
    Zaachila, 469
MARO (Mujeres Artesanas de la Región de Oaxaca; Oaxaca City), 456
Marquez Sightseeing Tours, 186, 187

Mascota, 305
Maya civilization, 25
Mayapán, 652
Maya ruins. *See* Ruins and archaelogical sites
Mayólica Santa Rosa (Guanajuato), 215
Mazatlán, 343–359
    accommodations, 352–354
    American Express, 347
    exploring, 350–352
    getting around, 346
    layout of, 346
    nightlife, 357–358
    organized tours, 352
    outdoor activities, 347–350
    post office, 347
    restaurants, 355–357
    road trips from, 358–359
    Spanish-language classes, 347
    special events in nearby villages, 349
    spectator sports, 349
    traveling to, 343–344
    visitor information, 344, 346
Mazunte Beach, 425
Medical insurance, 763
MedjetAssist, 68
Melaque (San Patricio), 363, 368–369
Mercado Abastos (Oaxaca City), 456
Mercado de Artesanía (Oaxaca City), 456
Mercado de Artesanías de Valladolid, 673
Mercado de Artesanías (handicrafts market)
    Puebla (El Parián), 503
    San Miguel, 199
Mercado de Curiosidades (Centro Artesanal; Mexico City), 148
Mercado de Dulces (Morelia), 256
Mercado de la Ciudadela (Mexico City), 149
Mercado de la Merced (Mexico City), 149
Mercado González Ortega (Zacatecas), 235
Mercado Hidalgo
    Guanajuato, 214
    San Luis, 245
Mercado Insurgentes (Mexico City), 149
Mercado Jesús González Ortega (Zacatecas), 236
Mercado Libertad (Guadalajara), 288, 290

Mercado Municipal (municipal market)
    Isla Mujeres, 559
    Ixtapa/Zihuatanejo, 411
    Puerto Vallarta, 310, 312
    Taxco, 166
Mérida, 625–653
    accommodations, 638, 640–644
    American Express, 631
    bookstores, 631
    climate, 631
    consulates, 631
    currency exchange, 632
    ecotours and adventure trips, 647
    exploring, 632–636
    festivals and special events, 630
    getting around, 631
    hospitals, 632
    layout of, 629, 631
    nightlife, 647
    post office, 632
    restaurants, 644–646
    shopping, 636–637
    side trips from, 647–653
    Spanish classes, 632
    telephones, 632
    traveling to, 627–629
    visitor information, 629
Mesón Sacristía de la Compañía (Puebla), 507
Metropolitan Cathedral (Mexico City), 136–137, 146
Mexcaltitan, 306
Mexicana Vacations, 79
Mexican Revolution, 29
Mexico Art Tours, 80
Mexico City, 94–158. *See also* neighborhoods
    accommodations, 113–120
        Centro Histórico and surrounding areas, 118–119
        Chapultepec Park and Polanco, 114–116
        Condesa/Roma, 119–120
        near the airport, 120
    American Express, 110
    banks, 110
    bookstores, 110
    cafes, 126
    currency exchange, 111
    drugstores, 111
    emergencies, 111
    exploring, 126–146
    finding addresses in, 101
    getting around, 105–110

hospitals, 111
hot lines, 111
Internet access, 111
neighborhoods, 102–104
nightlife, 149–154
organized tours, 146
pollution, 111–112
post office, 112
restaurants, 120–126
restrooms, 112
safety and crime, 69, 112, 150, 151
shopping, 147–149
side trip to Teotihuacán, 154–158
specialized travel resources, 71–75
street maps, 102
taxes, 112–113
taxis, 69, 98–100, 105
telephones, 113
traveling to and from, 96–101
visitor information, 101
weather and clothing, 113
what's new in, 2
Mexico City Chamber of Commerce, 101
Mexico City Festival, 52–53
Mexico City Historical Center, 146
Mexico City Tourist Office, 101
Mexico Tourism Board, 45–46
Mexico Travel Link Ltd., 82
Mexico Travel Net, 79
Mezcal, 467
Michoacán, 248–272
Miniaturas (Mérida), 637
Misión Nuestra Señora de Loreto, 745
Misión Satevó, 688
Misol Ha waterfall, 480
Mitla, 463, 465, 467–468
Mocambo Beach (Veracruz), 519
Moctezuma II, 26–27
Monarch butterflies, 205, 259
Monte Albán, 463–465
Monumento a la Revolución (Mexico City), 138
Monumento a los Héroes de la Independencia (Mexico City), 138
Morelia, 249–260
accommodations, 256–257
exploring, 252–255
getting around, 250
nightlife, 260
orientation, 250
restaurants, 257–259

shopping, 255–256
special events & festivals, 252
traveling to, 249
Morelia Boys Choir, 254
Mosquitoes and gnats, 67
Mountain Travel Sobek, 82
Movies, Mexican, 41–43
Mr. Sancho's (Cozumel), 578
Mulegé, 742
Mummy Museum (Valenciana), 213
Muna, 651
Mundo Divertido La Mesa (Tijuana), 752
Museo Amparo (Puebla), 502
Museo Antropología de Xalapa, 513
Museo Arqueológico de Mazatlán, 350
Museo Arqueológico de Xochimilco (Mexico City), 142
Museo Arqueológico Guillermo Spratling (Taxco), 166
Museo Bello y González (Puebla), 502
Museo Casa de Allende (San Miguel), 198
Museo Casa Robert Brady (Cuernavaca), 180
Museo de Arqueología de la Costa Grande (Zihuatanejo), 407–408
Museo de Arqueología del Occidente de México (Guadalajara), 288
Museo de Arte (Querétaro), 226
Museo de Arte Carrillo Gil (MACG; Mexico City), 143
Museo de Arte Colonial (Morelia), 254–255
Museo de Arte Contemporáneo Ateneo de Yucatán (Mérida), 633–634
Museo de Arte Contemporáneo de Oaxaca (Oaxaca City), 452
Museo de Arte Moderno (Mexico City), 139
Museo de Arte Popular (Puebla), 501
Museo de Artesanías (Tlaxcala), 509
Museo de Artes Industrias Populares (Pátzcuaro), 263
Museo de Historia Natural de la Ciudad de Mexico (Mexico City), 139

Museo de la Ciudad (City Museum)
Campeche, 662
Guadalajara, 289
Mérida, 635
Veracruz, 519
Museo de la Ciudad de México (Mexico City), 140
Museo de la Cultura Maya (Chetumal), 621, 622
Museo de la Independencia (Dolores Hidalgo), 206
Museo de la Isla de Cozumel, 579
Museo del Ambar (San Cristóbal), 487
Museo de la Plateria (Taxco), 166
Museo de la Revolución (Chihuahua), 694
Museo de las Artes de la Universidad de Guadalajara, 289
Museo de las Misiones (Loreto), 745
Museo de la Toma de Zacatecas, 236
Museo del Cobre (Santa Clara del Cobre), 269
Museo del Estado (Morelia), 254
Museo de Los Momias (Valenciana), 213
Museo del Palacio de Bellas Artes (Mexico City), 134, 136
Museo del Pueblo de Guanajuato, 211
Museo del Pueblo Maya (Dzibilchaltún), 649
Museo del Templo Mayor (Mexico City), 132–134
Museo Diego Rivera (Guanajuato), 211
Museo Diego Rivera Anahuacalli (Mexico City), 142
Museo Dolores Olmedo Patiño (Mexico City), 143
Museo Estudio Diego Rivera (Mexico City), 143
Museo Exhacienda San Gabriel de Barrera (near Guanajuato), 214
Museo F. Goitia (Zacatecas), 237
Museo Franz Mayer (Mexico City), 140
Museo Frida Kahlo (Mexico City), 130
Museo Histórico de Acapulco, 390

Museo Histórico Minero de Santa Rosalía, 748–749
Museo Histórico Naval (Veracruz), 519
Museo Iconográfico del Quijote (Guanajuato), 211
Museo José Luis Cuevas (Mexico City), 140–141
Museo León Trotsky (Mexico City), 143–144
Museo Mural Diego Rivera (Mexico City), 141
Museo Nacional de Antropología (Mexico City), 110, 130–132
Museo Nacional de Arte (Munal; Mexico City), 141
Museo Nacional de Cerámica (Tonalá), 292
Museo Nacional de Historia (Mexico City), 137–138
Museo Nacional de la Estampa (Mexico City), 141
Museo Nacional de la Máscara (San Luis), 244
Museo Nacional de la Revolución (Mexico City), 138
Museo Nacional del Ferrocarril (Puebla), 502
Museo Nacional de San Carlos (Mexico City), 142
Museo Pantaleón Panduro (Guadalajara), 289
Museo Pedro Coronel (Zacatecas), 237
Museo Rafael Coronel (Zacatecas), 237
Museo Regional (Querétaro), 225
Museo Regional Cuauhnáhuac (Cuernavaca), 180
Museo Regional de Antropología (Mérida), 635, 636
Museo Regional de Antropología Carlos Pellicer Cámara (Villahermosa), 472
Museo Regional de Guadalajara, 287
Museo Regional de Oaxaca (Oaxaca City), 452–453
Museo Regional La Alhóndiga de Granaditas (Guanajuato), 211–212
Museo Regional Michoacano (Morelia), 253–254
Museo Río Cuale (Puerto Vallarta), 310
Museo Rufino Tamayo (Mexico City), 139

Museo Templo y Convento Santo Domingo (San Cristóbal), 487
Museo Virreinal de Guadalupe, 238
Museum of Archaeology and History (Manzanillo), 374
Museum of Zapotec Art (Mitla), 468
Music, 43–44
Veracruz, 515, 518

Nacional Monte de Piedad (Mexico City), 148
Nacional Monte de Piedad (National Pawn Shop; Mexico City), 149
National Auditorium (Mexico City), 151
National Ceramics Fair and Fiesta (Tlaquepaque), 53
National Copper Fair (Santa Clara del Cobre), 269
National Pawn Shop (Nacional Monte de Piedad; Mexico City), 148, 149
National Silver Fair (Taxco), 56
Natural Habitat Adventures, 82
NatureQuest, 82
Navy Day, 53
Newspapers and magazines, 764
New Year's Day, 51
New Year's Eve, 57
NH Hoteles, 86
Nieves del Correo (Morelia), 254
Nikki Beach
Cabo San Lucas, 729
Puerto Vallarta, 334
Nohoch Mul Group (Cobá), 616–617
No Name Bar&Grill (Puerto Vallarta), 335
Nuestra Señora de Guadalupe church (Puerto Vallarta), 310
Nuevo Vallarta, 298, 336–337
The Nunnery Quadrangle (Uxmal), 654–655

Oaxaca City, 444–470
accommodations, 457–459
consulates, 450
emergencies, 450
exploring, 452–455
getting around, 449
layout of, 449

nightlife, 462
road trips from, 463–470
shopping, 455–456
special events and festivals, 450–452
street food, 460
traveling to, 446, 448–449
visitor information, 449
Oaxaca state, 4, 37–38, 443
political and social conditions, 446
Ocosingo, 480–481
Ocotlán, 470
Ocotlán Sanctuary (Tlaxcala), 509
October Festivals (Guadalajara), 54–55
Ojo de Venado (Guanajuato), 215
Olinala (Puerto Vallarta), 317
Olmec civilization, 24–25
Olmedo, Dolores, home of (Acapulco), 390
O.M.R. Gallery (Mexico City), 147
Opals, Querétaro, 227
Open Air Expeditions, 304, 306
Organo Bay, 438
Orozco, 289
Orozco, José Clemente, 139, 142, 143
Our Lord of the Column (San Miguel), 196
Our Lord of the Conquest (San Miguel), 196
Outdoor activities, adventure and sports trips, 81–83
Oxkutzcab, 659

Paamul, 606
The Pacific Coast, 36–37
Package tours, 78–80
Palace of Masks (Kabah), 657
Palace of Quetzalpapalotl (Teotihuacán), 158
Palacio Clavijero (Morelia), 254
Palacio de Bellas Artes (Mexico City), 151
Palacio de Gobierno
Mérida, 634–635
San Luis, 242, 244
Zacatecas, 235
Palacio de Huitziméngari (Pátzcuaro), 263
Palacio de la Mala Noche (Zacatecas), 235
Palacio de las Bellas Artes (San Cristóbal), 487

Palacio del Gobierno
  Chihuahua, 694
  Guadalajara, 287
  Morelia, 252
Palacio de Minería (Mexico
  City), 136
Palacio Federal (Morelia), 255
Palacio Huitziméngari
  (Pátzcuaro), 265
Palacio Montejo (Mérida), 634
Palacio Municipal (City Hall)
  Mérida, 634
  San Luis, 244
  Veracruz, 518
Palacio Nacional (Mexico City),
  132
Palancar Reef, 576
Palenque, 473–481
Palladium (Acapulco), 403
Palmilla Beach (San José del
  Cabo), 705
Panama hats, 638
Panteón del Tepeyac (Mexico
  City), 128, 130
Papalote, Museo del Niño
  (Mexico City), 139–140
Papantla, 524–526
Papantla Flyers (Puerto
  Vallarta), 310
Papas & Beer
  Ensenada, 760
  Rosarito Beach, 758
Paradise Beach (Cozumel), 578
Paradise Cafe (Cozumel), 578
Parasailing
  Acapulco, 388
  Puerto Vallarta, 309
Paricutín volcano, 270,
  271–272
Parque Acuático el CICI
  (Acapulco), 390
Parque Agua Azul (Guadala-
  jara), 288
Parque Cepeda Peraza
  (Mérida), 635
Parque de la Madre (Mérida),
  635
Parque-Museo La Venta
  (Villahermosa), 472
Parque Nacional Eduardo Ruiz,
  271
Parque Nacional Palenque,
  474–476
Parque Principal (Campeche),
  662
Parque Santa Lucía (Mérida),
  635
Parra, Agustín, 291
Parroquia de San Servacio
  (Valladolid), 673

Partido Revolucionario Institucional (PRI), 29
Paseo de Montejo (Mérida),
  635–636
Passion (Cabo San Lucas), 730
Passports, 46–47, 764–765
Pátzcuaro, 260–270
  accommodations, 265–266
  climate, 262
  getting around, 262
  layout of, 262
  nightlife, 268
  restaurants, 267–268
  shopping, 264–265
  side trips from, 268–270
  special events, 262–263
  traveling to, 260, 262
  visitor information, 262
Petacalco Beach (near Ixtapa),
  410
Petrol, 762
Peyote People (Puerto
  Vallarta), 314
Pie de la Cuesta (Acapulco),
  387
Pineda Covalín (Mexico City),
  147–148
Planning your trip to Mexico,
  1–2, 45–86
  calendar of events, 51–57
  customs regulations, 48–49
  entry requirements, 46–48
  getting to and around, 57–63
  health concerns, 65–68
  money and costs, 63–65
  package tours, 78–80
  safety concerns, 68–71
  seasons, 49–50
  special-interest trips, 80–83
  sustainable tourism, 75–78
  telephones, 83–84
  visitor information, 45–46
Playa Anclote (Puerto Vallarta),
  303
Playa Audiencia (Manzanillo),
  372
Playa Azul (Manzanillo), 372
Playa Bacocho (Puerto
  Escondido), 425
Playa Caracol (Cancún),
  548, 559
Playa Carrizalillo (Puerto
  Escondido), 425
Playa del Carmen, 5, 10, 579,
  588, 595–604
Playa del Sol (Puerto Vallarta),
  302
Playa Destiladeras (Puerto
  Vallarta), 303

Playa la Angosta (Acapulco),
  386
Playa Lancheros (Isla Mujeres),
  561
Playa Larga (Zihuatanejo), 408
Playa La Ropa (Zihuatanejo),
  408
Playa Las Brisas (Manzanillo),
  372
Playa las Cuatas (near Ixtapa),
  408–409
Playa Las Gatas (Zihuatanejo),
  408
Playa Las Gaviotas (Mazatlán),
  348
Playa Linda (Cancún), 559
Playa Linda (Ixtapa), 408
Playa Los Muertos (Puerto
  Vallarta), 302
Playa Madera (Zihuatanejo),
  408
Playa Majahua (near
  Zihuatanejo), 409
Playa Manzanillo
  Acapulco, 387
  Puerto Escondido, 425
Playa Marineros (Puerto
  Escondido), 424
Playa Mía (Cozumel), 578
Playa Miramar (Manzanillo),
  372
Playa Mismaloya (Puerto Val-
  larta), 298–299, 302
Playa Municipal (Zihuatanejo),
  408
Playa Norte
  Cancún, 550
  Isla Mujeres, 561
  Mazatlán, 347
Playa Olas Altas
  Mazatlán, 347
  Puerto Vallarta, 302
Playa Palancar (Cozumel), 578
Playa Palmar (Ixtapa), 408
Playa Panteón (Puerto Angel),
  434
Playa Piedras Blancas (Puerto
  Vallarta), 303
Playa Principal (Puerto
  Escondido), 424
Playa Puerto Marqués
  (Acapulco), 387
Playa Quieta (Ixtapa), 408
Playa Sábalo (Mazatlán), 348
Playa San Agustinillo (near
  Puerto Angel), 434
Playa San Francisco (Cozumel),
  578
Playa San Pedrito (Manzanillo),
  372

Playa Vista Hermosa (Ixtapa), 409
Playa Zicatela (Puerto Escondido), 424–425
Playa Zipolite (Puerto Angel), 434
Plaza Caracol (Cancún), 553
Plaza Chica (Pátzcuaro), 263, 264
Plaza de Armas
  Guadalajara, 287
  San Luis, 242
  Zacatecas, 235
Plaza de Garibaldi (Mexico City), 152
Plaza de la República
  Mexico City, 138
  Veracruz, 518
Plaza de las Tres Culturas (Mexico City), 144
Plaza de los Fundadores (San Luis), 244
Plaza de los Sapos (Puebla), 507
Plaza de San Francisco (San Luis), 244
Plaza de Santa Inés (Puebla), 507
Plaza de Santo Domingo
  Mexico City, 144
  San Cristóbal, 490
Plaza de Toros (Cancún), 552
Plaza Grande, Pátzcuaro, 263, 264
Plaza Mayor (Mérida), 633–635
Plaza Peninsula (Puerto Vallarta), 312
Plaza Principal, Mazatlán, 351–352
Plaza San Fernando (Guanajuato), 212
Plaza San Roque (Guanajuato), 212
Plaza Tapatía (Guadalajara), 286
Plazuela del Baratillo (Guanajuato), 212
Plazuela del Carmen (San Luis), 244
Plazuela Machado (Mazatlán), 351
Pleasant Holidays, 79
Polanco (Mexico City), 102
  accommodations, 114–116
  historic buildings and monuments, 137–138
  restaurants, 121–123
  sights and attractions, 139–140
Police, 765

Popocatépetl, 175
Popotla, 758
Portal de Granos (Mérida), 636
Pottery and ceramics. *See also* Talavera pottery
  Amatenango del Valle, 489
  Bahías de Huatulco, 439
  Dolores Hidalgo, 205–206
  Guadalajara, 287–289
  Guanajuato, 214, 215
  La Paz, 739
  Muna, 651
  Ocotlán, 470
  Puerto Vallarta, 316
  San Bartolo, 469
  Tepoztlán, 186
  Ticul, 652
  Tlaquepaque, 290–291
  Tonalá, 291–292
Pozole, 401
Progreso, 626–627, 649–650
ProWorld Service Corps, 83
Puebla, 4, 496–508
  accommodations, 503–506
  American Express, 499
  Battle of, 500
  drugstores, 499
  exploring, 499–502
  layout of, 498–499
  nightlife, 507
  restaurants, 506–507
  shopping, 502–503
  traveling to, 498
  visitor information, 498
Puerco Azul (Puerto Vallarta), 317
Puerta de Tierra (Campeche), 662–663
Puerto Angel, 433–434
Puerto Angelito (Puerto Escondido), 425
Puerto Aventuras, 588, 606–607
Puerto Balandra, 736
Puerto Escondido, 7, 380, 420–434
  accommodations, 427–430
  getting around, 423
  guided walking tours, 427
  layout of, 423
  nightlife, 432–433
  post office, 424
  restaurants, 430–432
  safety, 424
  shopping, 427
  sights and activities, 424–427
  traveling to, 422–423
  visitor information, 423
Puerto Juárez, 558, 559
Puerto Marqués, 387

Puerto Morelos, 588, 590–595
Puerto Vallarta, 3–4, 7, 294–343
  accommodations, 317–323
  American Express, 300
  area layout, 298–299
  beaches, activities, and excursions, 302–306
  climate, 300
  consulates, 301
  consumer assistance, 300
  currency exchange, 300
  drugstores, 300–301
  emergencies, 301
  getting around, 299–300
  hospitals, 301
  Internet access, 301
  layout of, 298
  newspapers and magazines, 301
  nightlife, 331–335
  outdoor activities, 306–310
  post office, 301
  restaurants, 323–331
    jungle restaurants, 330
  safety, 301
  shopping, 310, 312
  side trips from, 335–343
  traveling to, 296–297
  walking tour, 310
Punta Allen Peninsula, 14, 611, 614–615
Punta Diamante, 387
Punta Mita, 14, 298, 303, 306, 339–340
Punta Mita Golf Club, 308
Punta Sam, 559
Punta Solimán Bay, 610–611
Punta Sur Ecological Reserve, 578
The Purépecha, 268–269
Puro Corazón (Mexico City), 148
The Puuc Maya Route, 653, 656–659
Pyramid of the Flowers (Cacaxtla), 511
Pyramid of the Magician (Uxmal), 654
Pyramid of the Moon (Teotihuacán), 157
Pyramid of the Niches (Tajín), 525
Pyramid of the Painted Lintel (Cobá), 617
Pyramid of the Sun (Teotihuacán), 157
Pyramids of Xochicalco (near Cuernavaca), 181

Querétaro, 3, 221–231
accommodations, 227–230
emergencies, 224
exploring, 224–227
layout of, 224
restaurants, 230–231
traveling to, 222
visitor information, 222
Querubines (Puerto Vallarta), 317
Quetzalcoatl Fountain (Guadalajara), 288
Quimixto Beach (Puerto Vallarta), 303
Quinta Gameros (Chihuahua), 695
Quinta Real Grand Class Hotels and Resorts, 86

Rafting
Veracruz, 520
Xalapa, 513–514
Ranch Disco Bar (Puerto Vallarta), 335
Rancho La Puerta, 755
Regional Ceramics Museum (Tlaquepaque), 290
Regions of Mexico, 36–38
Residencia de Gobernadores (Zacatecas), 235
Restaurants, types of, 35–36
Reto al Tepozteco, 54
Revolcadero Beach (Acapulco), 387
Rexo (Mexico City), 153
Ridley turtles, 425–426
Rincón Artesanal (Guanajuato), 215
Río Bec area, 623–624
Rio Lagartos Nature Reserve, 675–676
Rio Latino (Puerto Vallarta), 334
Rivera, Diego, 134, 136, 143, 180
Murals (Mexico City), 132
Museo Diego Rivera Anahua-calli (Mexico City), 142
Museo Diego Rivera (Guana-juato), 211
Museo Estudio Diego Rivera (Mexico City), 143
Museo Mural Diego Rivera (Mexico City), 141
River rafting
Veracruz, 520
Xalapa, 513–514

Riviera Maya, 5, 14, 587
all-inclusive resorts, 602–603
driving, 596
things to do along the, 589–590
Rodeos *(charreadas)*
Guadalajara, 288
Mazatlán, 349
Roqueta Island (Acapulco), 386, 387–388
Rosario, 349
Rosarito Beach, 700, 756–759
Rotonda de los Hombres Ilustres
Guadalajara, 287
Mexico City, 136
Route 66 (Puerto Vallarta), 333
Rufino Tamayo Museo de Arte Prehispánico de México (Oaxaca City), 453
Ruins and archaeological sites. *See also specific ruins and sites*
Acanceh, 651
best, 11–12
Cacaxtla, 510–511
Chichén Itzá, 665–670
Chincultic, 495
Cholula, 507–508
Cobá, 615–618
Cozumel, 570
Cozumel area, 579–580
Dainzú, 466
Dzibilchaltún, 649
Ek Balam, 675
Isla Mujeres, 563
Lambityeco, 467
Mayapán, 652
Mitla, 467–468
Monte Albán, 463–465
Palenque, 474–476
Puuc Maya sites, 657–659
Pyramids of Xochicalco (near Cuernavaca), 181
Río Bec area, 623–624
Riviera Maya, 590
Teotihuacán, 154–158
Tepozteco pyramid (Tepoztlán), 186
Toniná, 481
Tulum, 612–613
Tzintzuntzan, 268
Uxmal, 654–655
Xcambó, 650
Yagul, 467
Zaachila, 469
Zempoala, 523–524
Rutas de Aventura, 426

Safari Accents (Puerto Vallarta), 316
Safety concerns, 68–71
Sailing, Puerto Vallarta, 309
St. Peter and St. Paul Day, 53
Sala German Gedovius (San Luis), 244
Salon Q (Acapulco), 403
Salón Tenampa (Mexico City), 152
San Agustín, Church of
Guadalajara, 287
Zacatecas, 235
San Agustín, convent of (Querétaro), 226
San Andrés, 481
San Angel (Mexico City), 103
San Bartolo, 469
San Bernardino de Siena (Valladolid), 673
Sanborn's (Acapulco), 391
Sanborn's Mexico Insurance, 59
San Cayetano, church of (Valenciana), 213
Sancho Panza Wine Bistro and Jazz Club (Cabo San Lucas), 730
San Cristóbal de las Casas, 481–495
accommodations, 490–492
books, 485
climate, 485
coffeehouses, 494
currency exchange, 485
exploring, 486–489
getting around, 484–485
layout of, 484
nearby Maya villages, 488
nightlife, 494–495
post office, 485
restaurants, 492–494
road trips from, 495
shopping, 489–490
Spanish classes, 486
traveling to, 482
visitor information, 482, 484
San Diego, Church of
Guanajuato, 212
Morelia, 255
San Felipe Neri, Iglesia de (Oaxaca City), 454
San Francisco, church and con-vent of (Morelia), 253
San Francisco Acatepec, 508
San Francisco Church (Querétaro), 224
San Francisco Reef, 576
San Ignacio de Arareko, 687

San Jerónimo Tlacochahuaya, Iglesia de (Santa María del Tule), 466
San José del Cabo, 698, 700–712
  accommodations, 708–710
  layout of, 704
  nightlife, 712
  outdoor activities, 705–707
  restaurants, 710–712
  shopping, 708
  traveling to, 702–704
San José El Mogote, 463
San Juan Chamula, 488
San Juan de Dios (Oaxaca City), 454
San Juan de Ulúa (Veracruz), 518
San Juan Parangaricutiro, Church of (Angahuan), 272
San Juan Teotihuacán, 154–158
San Lucas, Iglesia de (Cabo San Lucas), 724
San Luis Potosí, 3, 241–247
  accommodations, 245–246
  climate, 242
  exploring, 242, 244
  layout of, 242
  nightlife, 247
  restaurants, 246–247
  shopping, 244–245
  traveling to, 241
  visitor information, 242
San Marcos National Fair (Aguascalientes), 53
San Martín Tilcajete, 469
San Miguel, 758
San Miguel de Allende, 2, 190–206
  accommodations, 200–203
  American Express, 195
  currency exchange, 195
  day-trip tours from, 205–206
  exploring, 196–199
  getting around, 194
  nightlife, 205
  parking, 195
  post office, 195
  restaurants, 203–205
  shopping, 199
  special events and festivals, 196
  traveling to, 193–194
San Nicolás de Hidalgo, College of (Morelia), 254
San Sebastián, 14, 342–343
Santa Anna, Antonio López de, 28
Santa Bárbara, Iglesia de (Santa Rosalía), 748

Santa Catalina (Oaxaca City), 454
Santa Clara, church and former Convent of (Querétaro), 226
Santa Clara del Cobre, 269
Santa Cruz, church and convent of (Querétaro), 225
Santa Cruz Huatulco, 436
Santa Fe (Mexico City), 103–104
Santa Lucía, Iglesia de (Mérida), 635
Santa María de Gracia, church of (Guadalajara), 287
Santa María del Tule, 465–466
Santa Mónica, Exconvento de (Puebla), 501
Santa Prisca y San Sebastián Church (Taxco), 166
Santa Rosa, Exconvento de (Puebla), 501
Santa Rosa de Viterbo, church and former convent of (Querétaro), 226–227
Santa Rosalía, 742, 747–749
Santa Rosa Wall, 576
Santiago, Church of (Mexico City), 144
Santiago de Querétaro, 3, 221–231
  accommodations, 227–230
  emergencies, 224
  exploring, 224–227
  layout of, 224
  restaurants, 230–231
  traveling to, 222
  visitor information, 222
Santo Domingo, Iglesia de
  Oaxaca City, 454
  Puebla, 500
  Zacatecas, 235
Santo Domingo, Museo Templo y Convento (San Cristóbal), 487
Santo Domingo Xocotitlán, 187
Santo Tomás Jalietza, 469–470
Sayil, 657–658
Sayulita, 340–342
Scammon's Lagoon, 748
Scams, 70–71
Scuba diving
  Acapulco, 388
  Akumal, 608
  Cabo San Lucas, 722
  Cancún, 548–549
  Chinchorro Reef, 618–619
  Cozumel, 574, 576–577
  Isla Mujeres, 561
  Ixtapa/Zihuatanejo, 410

  La Paz, 736–737
  Manzanillo, 373
  Paamul, 606
  Puerto Angel, 434
  Puerto Morelos, 594
  Puerto Vallarta, 306
  Riviera Maya, 589
  San José del Cabo, 706
  Veracruz, 520
  Xel-Ha area, 610
  Zihuatanejo, 408
Sculptured Spaces (Isla Mujeres), 563
Sea Kayak Adventures, 82
Seasons, 49–50
Sea Trek Ocean Kayaking Center, 82
Sea turtles
  Isla Mujeres, 562–563
  Ridley, 425–426
Secretaría de Educación Pública (Mexico City), 138–139
Semana Santa (Holy Week), 52
  Oaxaca City, 451
  Taxco, 165
Senior travelers, 73
Señor Frog's (Ixtapa), 420
Serafina (Puerto Vallarta), 317
Serpentarium (La Paz), 738
Shopping, best, 16–17
Sian Ka'an Biosphere Reserve, 611, 615
Silver Fair (Taxco), 165
Silver towns and cities, 190–192, 358–359
Siqueiros, David Alfaro, 139, 143, 196
Small Vallarta, 312
Smoking, 68
Sna Jolobil (San Cristóbal), 490
Snorkeling
  Akumal, 608
  Cabo San Lucas, 722
  Cancún, 548–549
  Cozumel, 574, 577
  Isla Mujeres, 561
  Puerto Angel, 434
  Puerto Morelos, 594
  Puerto Vallarta, 306
  Punta Solimán and Tankah bays, 610–611
  San José del Cabo, 706
  Xel-Ha, 609
Sotuta de Peón, 642, 647
Southern Pacific coast, 379–442
Spanish Institute, 80

Spanish-language classes, 80
  Cuernavaca, 178
  Guanajuato, 210
  Mérida, 632
  Oaxaca City, 456
  San Cristóbal, 486
  San Miguel, 197
  Taxco, 164
Sportfishing. See Fishing
Spratling Ranch Workshop
  (Taxco), 167
Spring Equinox, 52
Student travelers, 75
Studio Cathy Von Rohr (Puerto
  Vallarta), 316
Sun exposure, 66
SunTrips, 80
Suprema Corte de Justicia
  (Mexico City), 139
Surfing
  Barra de Navidad, 364
  Cabo San Lucas, 723–724
  Ixtapa/Zihuatanejo, 410
  Mazatlán, 348
  northern Baja coast, 758
  Puerto Angel, 434
  Puerto Escondido, 424–425
  San José del Cabo, 707
  Sayulita, 342
Sustainable tourism, 75–78.
  See also Ecotours
Swimming
  Isla Mujeres, 561
  Los Cabos, 705

Tajín Chico, 525
Tajín Viejo, 525
Talavera pottery
  Dolores Hidalgo, 206
  Guanajuato, 215
  Ixtapa, 412
  Mexico City, 140
  Puebla, 502
  San Miguel, 199
  Vallarta, 316, 317
Talpa de Allende, 305
Tane (Mexico City), 148
Tangolunda Bay, 436, 438
Tankah Bay, 610–611
Taxco, 159–170
  accommodations, 167–168
  exploring, 165–167
  layout of, 164
  nightlife, 170
  restaurants, 168–169
  traveling to and from,
    162, 164
  visitor information, 164

Taxes, 765
Taxis, 62
  Mexico City, 69
Teacapán, 358
Teatro Angela Peralta
  (Mazatlán), 351
Teatro Calderón (Zacatecas),
  236
Teatro Clavijero (Veracruz), 518
Teatro Daniel de Ayala
  (Mérida), 635
Teatro Degollado (Guadala-
  jara), 287
Teatro de la Ciudad (La Paz),
  738
Teatro de la Paz (San Luis), 244
Teatro Emperador Caltzontzin
  (Pátzcuaro), 263
Teatro Juárez (Guanajuato),
  212
Teatro Macedonio de Alcalá
  (Oaxaca City), 455, 462
Teatro Peón Contreras
  (Mérida), 635, 647
Tecoh, 651–652
Telephones, 83–84
Temple of the Columns (Tajín),
  525
Temple of the Count
  (Palenque), 476
Temple of the Frescoes (Tulum),
  612
Temple of the Inscriptions
  (Palenque), 475–476
Templo de Cata (near Guanaju-
  ato), 213–214
Templo de la Compañía de
  Jesús (Pátzcuaro), 264
Templo de las Capuchinas
  (Morelia), 253
Templo de las Monjas
  (Morelia), 255
Templo del Carmen (San Luis),
  244
Templo del Señor Santiago
  Tupátaro, 269
Templo de San Cristóbal (San
  Cristóbal), 487
Templo de San Francisco
  (Tlaxcala), 508–509
Templo de San José (San Luis),
  244
Templo Mayor (Mexico City),
  132–134
Tenacatita Bay, 362–363
Tenejapa, 481, 489
Tennis
  Bahías de Huatulco, 439
  Cancún, 551–552

Ixtapa/Zihuatanejo, 410
  Mazatlán, 349
  Puerto Vallarta, 310
  San José del Cabo, 707
Teorema (Puebla), 507
Teotihuacán, 25, 154–158
Teotitlán del Valle, 463, 466
Tepoznieves (Tepoztlán), 188
Tepozteco Challenge, 54
Tepozteco pyramid (Tepoztlán),
  186
Tepoztlán, 185–189
Tequila, 293
Tequila Express, 293
Tequilas, Puerto Vallarta, 317
Terminal Central de Autobuses
  del Norte (Mexico City), 100
Terminal Central de Autobuses
  del Sur (Mexico City), 100
Terminal de Autobuses de
  Pasajeros de Oriente
  (Mexico City), 100
Terminal Poniente de Auto-
  buses (Mexico City), 101
Teté Arte y Diseño (Tlaque-
  paque), 291
Textiles, 17
  Cuanajo, 269
  Ihuatzio, 270
  La Paz, 739
  Mexico City, 147, 148
  Pátzcuaro, 264
  San Cristóbal, 490
  Santo Tomás Jalietza,
    469–470
  Tenejapa, 489
  Teotitlán del Valle, 466
  Tepoztlán, 186
  Uruapan, 270
Thermal spas and hot springs
  Ixtapan, 171
  near San Miguel, 198–199
Three Kings' Day, 51
Ticul, 652–653
Tierra de Vinos (Mexico City),
  153–154
Tijuana, 700, 749–756
Tijuana Brewery, 752–753
Time zone, 765
Tío Lucas (San Miguel), 205
Tipping, 765
Tlacolula, 467
Tlaquepaque, 275, 290–291
Tlaxcala, 508–511
Todos Santos, 700, 724,
  730–732
Toilets, 765
Toll roads, 61
Toltec civilization, 25

Tonalá, 275, 291–292
Tonantzintla, church of, 508
Toniná, 481
Topolobampo Bay, 690
Tour Baja, 82
Town and Country, 80
Train travel
  Chihuahua al Pacífico railway,
    677–688
  Tequila Express, 293
Transportation Security Admin-
  istration (TSA), 48
Travel insurance, 763
Trek America, 82
Trip cancellation insurance, 763
Triple Tomb (Yagul), 467
Tropical illnesses, 67
Trotsky, León, Museo (Mexico
  City), 143–144
Tukari Servicios Turísticos,
  302, 304
Tulum, 5, 10, 580, 588,
  611–614
Tupátaro, 269
Turismo Dimar Travel Agency,
  426
Turtle Museum (near Puerto
  Escondido), 425
Turtles
  Isla Mujeres, 562–563
  Ridley, 425–426
Tzaráracua waterfall, 271
Tzintzuntzan, 262, 268

Unión Regional de Arte-
  sanías de los Altos (San
  Cristóbal), 490
United Vacations, 78
Universidad Nacional
  Autónoma de México
  (UNAM; Taxco), 164
University of Guadalajara
  School of Music, 287
Uriarte Talavera (Puebla), 503
Urique, 683
Uruapan, 270–272
US Airways Vacations, 78–79
Uxmal, 627, 653–659
  en route to, 650

Valentino's & the Fiestaland
  Complex (Mazatlán),
  357–358
Valladolid, 626, 672–676

Vallarta. See Puerto Vallarta
Vallarta Adventures, 302,
  304–307, 332, 342
Valle de Bravo, 172–175
20 de Noviembre Market
  (Oaxaca City), 456
Ventanilla, 425
Veracruz City, 4, 515–523
Veraventuras, 82–83
Villa, Pancho, 29
Villa del Mar (Veracruz), 519
Villahermosa, 470–473
Virgen de la Salud (Pátzcuaro),
  263
Virgen de Ocotlán (Tlaxcala),
  508
Visas, 47–48
Vista Vallarta Golf Club, 308
Vog Disco (Manzanillo), 378
Voice over Internet Protocol
  (VoIP), 84
Voladoresde Papantla (Puerto
  Vallarta), 310
Volunteer and working trips, 83

Warren Hardy Spanish (San
  Miguel), 197
Water, drinking, 66, 765
Watersports
  Cancún, 548
  Mazatlán, 349
Whale-watching
  Baja California, 748
  Cabo San Lucas, 724
  La Paz, 737
  Puerto Vallarta, 304
  San José del Cabo, 707
Whiskey Bar (Mexico City), 154
Wine Harvest Festival, 54
Women travelers, 74
Woodcarvings, 469
  Arrazola, 468
  Tzintzuntzan, 268

Xalapa, 511–515
Xcalak, 618
Xcambó, 650
Xcaret, 579, 590, 605–606
Xel-Ha, 590, 609–610
Xlapak, 658
Xochicalco, Pyramids of (near
  Cuernavaca), 181
Xochitécatl (Cacaxtla), 511
Xplora Adventours, 302

Xploration (Rosarito Beach),
  756
Xpu-Ha, 607
Xpujil, 624

Yagul, 467
Yal-ku Lagoon (Akumal), 608
Yaxchilán, 480
Yaxcopoil, 651
Yelapa, 322–323, 335–336
Yelapa Beach (Puerto Vallarta),
  303
Yoga, Isla Mujeres, 562
Yucab Reef, 576
Yucatán Peninsula, 37, 38,
  625–627

Zaachila, 469
Zacatecas, 231–241
  accommodations, 238–240
  climate, 234
  exploring, 234–238
  getting around, 232
  layout of, 232
  nightlife, 241
  restaurants, 240–241
  shopping, 235
  special events and festivals,
    234
  traveling to, 232
  visitor information, 232
Zapata, Emiliano, 29
Zapatista movement, 484
Zempoala, 523–524
Zicatela Beach (Puerto Escondido), 424–425
Zihablue (Zihuatanejo), 420
Zihuatanejo, 380. See also
  Ixtapa/Zihuatanejo
  accommodations, 412–415
  beaches, 408
  restaurants, 416–418
  shopping, 410–412
Zinacantán, 481, 489
Zinco (Mexico City), 153
Zócalo (Mexico City), 144–145
Zona Rosa (Mexico City),
  104, 147
  cafes, 126
  restaurants, 123–124
  sights and attractions, 138
Zoo (club; Puerto Vallarta),
  334–335
Z'Tai (Puerto Vallarta), 332–333

2 7 NOV. 2008